R. Gupta's®

Popular Master Guide

UPTET

Uttar Pradesh Teacher Eligibility Test

PRIMARY LEVEL

For Class 1 to 5

Conducted by

Uttar Pradesh Education Service Selection Commission (UPESSC)

by

RPH Editorial Board

2027
EDITION

RAMESH PUBLISHING HOUSE, NEW DELHI

Scheme of Exam

Primary Level (Class I-V)

S.No.	Subjects	No. of Questions	Marks
1.	Child Development and Pedagogy	30	30
2.	Language I (Hindi)	30	30
3.	Language II (English or Urdu or Sanskrit)	30	30
4.	Mathematics	30	30
5.	Environmental Education	30	30

- Duration of the Examination will be 150 minutes.
- There will be a total of 150 questions in the paper. All questions will be multiple choice type with four options.
- There will be no negative marking.
- Candidates who opt Sanskrit or Urdu in Language II other than English are advised to prepare the subject from their own resources.

Published by
O.P. Gupta *for* Ramesh Publishing House

Admin. Office
12-H, New Daryaganj Road, Opp. Officers' Mess,
New Delhi-110002 ✆ 23275224, 23245124

E-mail: info@rameshpublishinghouse.com
For Online Shopping: www.rameshpublishinghouse.com

Showroom
• Balaji Market, Nai Sarak, Delhi-6 ✆ 23282525 📱 9354373464
• 4457, Nai Sarak, Delhi-110006

Book Code: R-1480

ISBN: 978-93-87918-65-8

Price: ₹ 620

Printed at: Deepak Offset, Delhi

32. महावीर स्वामी का जन्म कहाँ हुआ था?

A. पावापुरी B. पारसौली

C. कुशीनगर D. वैशाली

33. स्वच्छंद में कौन-सी संधि है?

A. विसर्ग B. व्यंजन

C. गुण D. दीर्घ

34. महात्मा बुद्ध ने जब बुद्धत्व प्राप्त किया तब उनकी अवस्था कितनी थी?

A. 12 वर्ष B. 80 वर्ष

C. 45 वर्ष D. 35 वर्ष

35. ''श्रुति धर्म'' का क्या अर्थ है?

A. जैन धर्म B. वैदिक धर्म

C. मुस्लिम धर्म D. बौद्ध धर्म

36. 'ङ्' का उच्चारण स्थान होता है :

A. नासिक्य B. कंठ तलव्य

C. मूर्धन्य D. कंठोष्ठ्य

37. 'चार गज मलमल' में कौन-सा विशेषण है?

A. संख्यावाचक B. सार्वनामिक

C. परिमाणबोधक D. गुणवाचक

38. 'समास' का विलोम क्या है?

A. व्यास B. साहसिक

C. समस्या D. सामासिक

39. 'सुन्न' का तत्सम रूप क्या है?

A. सून B. शून्य

C. सूना D. सन्न

40. 'आँख की किरकिरी होने' का अर्थ है :

A. अप्रिय लगना B. बहुत प्रिय होना

C. कष्टदायक होना D. धोखा देना

41. निम्न में से किस शब्द की वर्तनी सही है?

A. अनुग्रहीत B. अनुग्रहित

C. अनग्रहीत D. अनुगृहीत

42. निम्नलिखित में शुद्ध शब्द है :

A. पैत्रिक B. पैत्रक

C. पैतरिक D. पैतृक

43. 'श' ध्वनि का उच्चारण स्थान क्या है?

A. दन्त B. दन्तालु

C. तालु D. मूर्धा

44. 'अत्यंत' शब्द में प्रयुक्त उपसर्ग है :

A. अत् B. अति

C. अत्य D. अ

45. 'उपत्यका' का अर्थ है :

A. सूर्य जिस पर्वत के पीछे से निकलता है

B. पर्वत के पास की भूमि

C. पर्वत का शिखर

D. प्राणियों के पेट का एक अंग

46. निम्नलिखित में मौखिक अभिव्यक्ति का रूप है :

A. शुद्ध वर्तनी B. आशु भाषण

C. श्रुतलेख D. सुलेख

47. हिन्दी भाषा की बोलियाँ हैं :

A. 15 B. 22

C. 18 D. 25

48. 'सामाजिक' शब्द में मूल शब्द और प्रत्यय है :

A. सामाज + इक B. समाज + इक

C. सा + माजिक D. सामा + जिक

49. 'तद्भव' पत्रिका के सम्पादक का नाम है :

A. लीलाधर जगूड़ी B. अखिलेश

C. हरे प्रकाश उपाध्याय D. विश्वनाथ प्रसाद तिवारी

50. 'बारह बरस लौ कूकर जीवै, अरु तेरह लौ जियै सियार–

यह पंकित किसकी है?

A. विद्यापति B. जगनिक

C. नरपति नाल्ह D. चन्दवरदाई

51. 'अकाल' का पर्यायवाची है :

A. दुर्भिक्ष B. अपरिहार्य

C. अँधियारा D. अक्षत

52. निम्नलिखित वाक्यों में कौन-सा मिश्र वाक्य है?

A. अध्यापकों के सम्मुख छात्र पढ़ते हैं।

B. क्या अध्यापकों के सम्मुख छात्र पढ़ते हैं।

C. अध्यापक देखते हैं कि छात्र पढ़ते हैं।

D. छात्र पढ़ते हैं और अध्यापक उन्हें देखते हैं।

53. 'जिसकी पूर्व से कोई आशा न हो' के लिए एक शब्द है :

A. प्रत्याशा B. अनाहूत

C. अपरिमेय D. अप्रत्याशित

54. 'मुझसे उठा नहीं गया' वाक्य में वाच्य है :

A. कर्तृवाच्य B. इनमें से कोई नहीं

C. भाववाच्य D. कर्मवाच्य

55. 'निष्कपट' शब्द का संधि-विच्छेद है :

A. निः + कपट B. निश् + कपट

C. नि + कपट D. निष् + कपट

56. इस देश में हिन्दी भाषा का प्रयोग लिखने एवं बोलने में किया जाता है :

A. ऑस्ट्रेलिया B. मारीशस

C. पाकिस्तान D. दक्षिण अमेरिका

57. 'सूर सागर' किस भाषा की रचना है?

A. अवधी
B. छत्तीसगढ़ी
C. ब्रज
D. बुन्देली

58. 'वीरों का कैसा हो वसंत' कविता किसकी लिखी है?

A. सुमित्रा कुमारी चौहान
B. रामधारी सिंह दिनकर
C. माखनलाल चतुर्वेदी
D. सुभद्रा कुमारी चौहान

59. 'क्षेत्रीय' में कौन-सा विशेषण है?

A. गुणवाचक
B. सार्वनामिक
C. परिमाण बोधक
D. संख्यावाचक

60. 'चौराहा' शब्द में समास है :

A. कर्मधारय समास
B. अव्ययीभाव समास
C. द्विगु समास
D. द्वंद्व समास

PART-III

LANGUAGE-II : ENGLISH

61. What kind of adjectives are used in the following sentence?

A live ass is better than a dead lion.

A. Descriptive
B. Quality
C. Indefinite
D. Quantity

62. Which of the following has been misspelt?

A. deciduous
B. entrance
C. governence
D. ambiguous

63. Pick out the correct synonym of the word:

attenuate

A. repent
B. make thin
C. divide
D. force

64. Pick the sentence with the correct conjunction:

A. No sooner had we reached the station but the train left.
B. No sooner had we reached the station and the train left.
C. No sooner had we reached the station when the train left.
D. No sooner had we reached the station than the train left.

65. Pick out the suitable antonym of the given word:

judicious

A. imprudent
B. careful
C. silly
D. sagacious

66. The meaning of the idiom "to put out" is:

A. To postpone
B. To go out
C. To extinguish
D. To wait

67. The sentence: "This is the house in which I was born", is:

A. A simple sentence
B. A compound-complex sentence
C. A complex sentence
D. A compound sentence

68. Fill in the blank:

'The objection was met out ____ the lawyer'.

A. with
B. from
C. by
D. to

69. Fill in the blank:

"______ of playing, the children went home".

A. Being tired
B. While tiring
C. Having tired
D. On tiring

70. Join the following sentence to make a simple sentence:

The coffee isn't too strong. It won't keep awake.

A. The coffee isn't too strong to keep us awake.
B. The coffee isn't too strong so as to keep us awake.
C. The coffee isn't too strong so it won't keep us awake.
D. The coffee isn't too strong and will not keep us awake.

71. Complete the following sentence with correct Conjunction:

______ he had not paid his bill, his electricity was cut off.

A. But
B. As
C. Unless
D. Either

72. Choose the correct figure of speech in the following sentence:

Death lays his icy hand on Kings.

A. Metaphor
B. Simile
C. Apostrophe
D. Personification

73. Choose the proper sequence to complete the following:

The guide said that
P. nowhere in the world
Q. a fairer building
R. you will find
S. than the Taj Mahal.

The proper sequence should be:

A. R Q P S
B. R Q S P
C. P S Q R
D. P R Q S

74. Give the meaning of the following proverb:

A bird in hand is worth two in a bush.

A. To catch two birds with your hands.
B. To trap birds in bushes.
C. It is better to be satisfied with what you have than to try to get what is not yours.
D. To be dissatisfied with what you have.

75. Choose the correct option to complete the sentence:

I ______ him since we met a year ago.

A. didn't see B. not saw
C. hadn't seen D. haven't seen

76. Who are the earliest known inhabitants of Antarctica?

A. American Scientists
B. It is has always been a desert
C. Dinosaurs
D. Indian Scientists

77. Which of the following words is a Adverb?

A. Apace B. Fury
C. Meek D. Face

78. Fill in the blank with suitable Pronoun:

My son and my daughter are very fond of ______.

A. herself B. himself
C. themselves D. each other

79. Which of the following is an example of Metaphor?

A. He is a big donkey.
B. My heart leaps up when I behold a rainbow in the sky.
C. The bitter-sweet memories of childhood are a source of great pleasure.
D. The face of the child is as soft as the petals of a rose.

80. Choose the correct option:

Study of population is known as:

A. Ecology B. Genealogy
C. Demography D. Astronomy

81. Transform the following into a Direct sentence:

'I asked Sheela if I might know her father'.

A. I said to Sheela, "May I know your father?"
B. I questioned Sheela, "Will I know your father?"
C. I asked Sheela, "Can I know your father?"
D. I told Sheela, "May I know your father?".

82. The idiom 'To ring one's own bell' means:

A. to think properly
B. to indulge in self praise
C. to commit a theft
D. to be one's publicity agent

Direction (Q.No. 83 to 90): *Read the passage below and answer the questions that follow by selecting the most appropriate option:*

The children of M.G. Vidyalaya, had a wonderful time yesterday. They were captivated by the speed, agility and showmanship of magician, Kim Rathod. The children watched him spell-bound for two hours. All that broke the silence was a gasp of astonishment or the sound of spontaneous applause, appreciating a trick. Out of his magic wand came flowers, ribbons and garlands of every possible colour and seemingly unending length. It came in such quick succession that everyone was left gasping. One or two young children came up to examine the thin stick wondering how it could hold so much. They were really frustrated. As if that was not magical enough he made a rabbit pop out of an empty wooden box. It went hopping around the stage. It was soon put back into the box and seconds later, he pulled out a rat, soft, white and squeaking. The little ones seemed a little frightened by this, while the others clapped and cheered loudly. This was the grand finale.

The children did not want it to end. They shouted 'encore', 'once more'. But Kim gave them a bright smile and vanished from the scene. The children were left searching here and there for him. Then they walked out excitedly recounting what they had seen and how wonderful it was. One of the boys Ravi declared loudly, it was the best magic show of the century.

83. What does 'encore' mean?

A. Never B. Now
C. Once more D. Try

84. What did Kim do in the end?

A. Performed the act once again
B. Sat down
C. Never performed the trick
D. Smiled and disappeared

85. What does 'Century' denote?

A. A period of one year
B. A period of hundred years
C. A period of fifty years
D. A period of ten years

86. What is the magician's name?

A. M.G. Vidyalaya B. Kiran Rathod
C. Kim Rathod D. Ravi

87. What is the meaning of 'captivated'?

A. Astonished B. Angered
C. Arrested D. Honoured

88. What is the meaning of 'spontaneous'?

A. Happening suddenly B. Continuous
C. Never D. Always

89. What is a 'Wand'?

A. Stick B. Box
C. Hat D. Cloth

90. What is the meaning of 'hopping'?

A. Running B. Singing
C. Standing D. Jumping

PART-IV

MATHEMATICS

91. If $\frac{a}{3}=\frac{b}{4}=\frac{c}{7}$, then value of $\frac{a+b+c}{c}$ is:

A. $\sqrt{2}$ B. $\frac{1}{\sqrt{7}}$

C. 2 D. 7

92. January 5, 1991 was a Saturday, what day of the week was on March 3, 1992?

A. Saturday B. Tuesday

C. Sunday D. Monday

93. Simplify: $\left[\left\{\left(\frac{1}{3}\right)^{-3}-\left(\frac{1}{4}\right)^{-2}\right\}\div\left(\frac{1}{4}\right)^{-3}\right]$.

A. $\frac{11}{64}$ B. $\frac{1}{16}$

C. $\frac{3}{64}$ D. $\frac{5}{24}$

94. To construct a triangle, the possible sides are:

A. 6 cm, 3 cm, 3 cm

B. 6.3 cm, 5.9 cm, 4.6 cm

C. 6.5 cm, 105 mm, 39 mm

D. 3.5 cm, 9.2 cm, 5.3 cm

95. Arrange $\sqrt{3}, \sqrt[3]{4}, \sqrt[4]{5}$ in ascending order.

A. $\sqrt{3}, \sqrt[3]{4}, \sqrt[4]{5}$ B. None of these

C. $\sqrt[4]{5}, \sqrt[3]{4}, \sqrt{3}$ D. $\sqrt[3]{4}, \sqrt{3}, \sqrt[4]{5}$

96. Which measures of central tendency get affected if the extreme observations on both the ends of a data arranged in descending order are removed?

A. Mean and Median

B. Mode and Median

C. Mean and Mode

D. Mean, Median and Mode

97. A cube of side 5 cm is painted on all its faces. If it is sliced into 1 cm³ cubes, how many cubes of 1 cm³ will have exactly one of their faces painted?

A. 142 B. 54

C. 42 D. 27

98. Find the sum of all the interior angles of a pentagon.

A. 450° B. 540°

C. 360° D. 180°

99. $\frac{4}{7}$ of a pole is in the mud. When $\frac{1}{3}$ of it is pulled out, an 8 meter long piece of the pole still remains in the mud. What is the total length of the pole?

A. 21 metre B. 12 metre

C. 30 metre D. 25 metre

100. A and B can do a piece of work in 12 days, B and C in 15 days, C and A in 20 days. How long would A take separately to do the same work?

A. 10 days B. 40 days

C. 30 days D. 20 days

101. H.C.F. of $\frac{14}{33}, \frac{42}{55}, \frac{21}{22}$ is:

A. $\frac{7}{330}$ B. $\frac{330}{17}$

C. $\frac{330}{7}$ D. $\frac{17}{330}$

102. Square root of $\left(7+2\sqrt{10}\right)$ is:

A. $\left(\sqrt{6}+1\right)$ B. $\left(2+\sqrt{5}\right)$

C. $\left(\sqrt{2}+\sqrt{5}\right)$ D. $\left(\sqrt{3}+2\right)$

103. A square and an equilateral triangle have a side in common. If side of triangle is 4/3 cm long, find the perimeter of the figure obtained.

A. $6\frac{2}{3}$ cm B. $5\frac{1}{3}$ cm

C. $\frac{16}{9}$ cm D. $\frac{16}{9}\left(\frac{\sqrt{3}}{4}+1\right)$ cm

104. Which of the following numbers is divisible by 99?

A. 114345 B. 3572406

C. 913462 D. 135792

105. What is π?

A. Rational number

B. Integer

C. Prime number

D. Irrational number

106. If $10^{3x} = 125$, then value of 10^{-2x} is:

A. $\frac{1}{5}$ B. $\frac{1}{25}$

C. $-\frac{1}{25}$ D. 25

107. 16075 is divided by a number to give quotient 167 and remainder 43, then divisor is:

A. 76 B. 86

C. 96 D. 56

108. The number of positive prime integers < 50 is:
A. 14 B. 25
C. 16 D. 15

109. Twice the larger of two numbers is three more than five times the smaller and the sum of four times the larger and three times the smaller is 71. What are the numbers?
A. 43, 8 B. 17, 1
C. 14, 5 D. 11, 9

110. A square with a side of 8 cm and a rectangle with length 16 cm have same area. What is the breadth of the rectangle?
A. 4 cm B. 12 cm
C. 6 cm D. 8 cm

111. If cost price of an article is $\frac{3}{2}$ of its selling price, then profit or loss per cent is:
A. $33\frac{1}{3}\%$ profit B. $33\frac{1}{8}\%$ profit
C. $33\frac{1}{8}\%$ loss D. $33\frac{1}{3}\%$ loss

112. When 121012 is divided by 12, the remainder is:
A. 0 B. 4
C. 3 D. 2

113. Digit of unit place in the product of (378 × 236 × 459 × 312) is:
A. 6 B. 4
C. 2 D. 8

114. What will be the median of the given data if the mean is 4.5?
5, 7, 7, 8, x, 5, 4, 3, 1, 2
A. 5.5 B. 4.5
C. 5 D. 6

115. Most important person, related with the method of 'Analysis of Variance' in Statistics:
A. R.A. Fisher B. Newton
C. Laplace D. Gauss

116. D, E, F are respectively the mid points of ΔABC. Which of the following statement is correct?

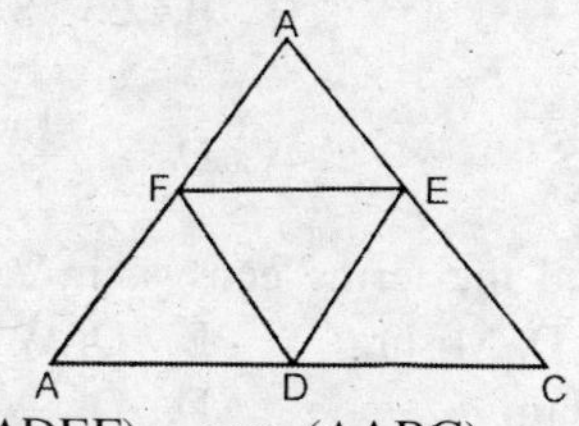

A. area (ΔDEF) = area (ΔABC)
B. area (ΔDEF) = $\frac{1}{4}$ area (ΔABC)
C. area (ΔDEF) = $\frac{1}{3}$ area (ΔABC)
D. area (ΔDEF) = $\frac{1}{2}$ area (ΔABC)

117. If Arithmetic mean of a given data is A, Geometric mean = G and Harmonic mean = H, then:
A. $A \leq G \geq H$ B. $A \geq H \geq G$
C. $A \geq G \geq H$ D. $A \leq G \leq H$

118. The difference and the product of two numbers are 5 and 36 respectively. Then the difference of their reciprocals is:
A. $\frac{5}{36}$ B. $\frac{9}{5}$
C. $\frac{5}{9}$ D. $\frac{31}{36}$

119. Who was the self taught Indian mathematical genius in 20th century?
A. Aryabhatta B. Harish Chandra
C. Srinivas Ramanujan D. Shridharacharya

120. The area of four walls of a room is 660 m^2 and the length is twice its width. If height of the room is 11 m, then area of its ceiling is:
A. 200 m^2 B. 75 m^2
C. 100 m^2 D. 150 m^2

PART-V

ENVIRONMENTAL STUDIES

121. Most Biodiversity is found in:
A. Flower's Valley
B. Dorang Valley
C. Silent Valley
D. Surma Valley

122. What is ***not*** true for LPG?
A. A clean fuel
B. Methane emitting
C. Burn with blue flame
D. High calorific value

123. The components of the ecosystem are:
A. Plants and animals
B. Producers, consumers and decomposers
C. Producers and consumers
D. Biotic and abiotic substance

124. Tropic of Capricorn is:

A. $23\frac{1}{2}^{\circ}$ B. 23° S

C. $23\frac{1}{2}^{\circ}$ S D. $23\frac{1}{2}^{\circ}$ N

125. Who coined the term "ecosystem"?

A. Dr. R. D. Mishra B. Dr. Wittaker

C. Dr. Odum D. Dr. A.G. Tansley

126. The problem of water pollution with Arsenic is maximum in:

A. Uttar Pradesh B. West Bengal

C. Bihar D. Madhya Pradesh

127. Deccan of the Western Ghats in India is drier because of:

A. low temperature effect

B. pressure effect

C. rain shadow effect

D. high altitude effect

128. The Wildlife Protection Act was passed in:

A. 1960 A.D. B. 1975 A.D.

C. 1972 A.D. D. 1962 A.D.

129. Solar radiation per unit area received at the outer limit of atmosphere is known as:

A. Insolation B. Heat budget

C. Solar constant D. Solar energy

130. Fundamental duties are adopted from which country's Constitution?

A. Germany B. USSR

C. USA D. United Kingdom

131. In a food chain of grassland ecosystem, the top consumers are:

A. Herbivorous

B. Either carnivorous and Herbivorous

C. Bacteria

D. Carnivorous

132. The main atmospheric layer near the surface of earth is:

A. Stratosphere B. Ionosphere

C. Mesosphere D. Troposphere

133. The Biodiversity Act was passed by the Indian Parliament.

A. 11th May, 1972 B. 11th December, 2002

C. 16th October, 1990 D. 10th December, 1980

134. Which one of the following agriculture practices is eco-friendly?

A. Shifting cultivation

B. Organic farming

C. Cultivation of high yielding varieties

D. Growing plants in glass house

135. Acid rain is concerned with presence of:

A. Hydrochloric acid B. Boric acid

C. Acetic acid D. Sulphuric acid

136. WWF stands for:

A. World Wide Fund B. World Watch Fund

C. World Wildlife Fund D. World War Fund

137. The valley of flowers is located in:

A. Jammu-Kashmir B. Uttarakhand

C. Sikkim D. Himachal Pradesh

138. Which of the following agencies is primarily concerned with the measurement of pollution in India?

A. Green Tribunal

B. Survey of India

C. Central Water Commission

D. Central Pollution Control Board

139. 'Cotopaxi' is an active volcano situated in:

A. Sicily B. Rockies

C. Andes D. Hawaii

140. Tsangpo river of Tibet in India is known as:

A. Ganga B. Indus

C. Brahmaputra D. Yamuna

141. The Pole star is:

A. North star B. West star

C. East star D. South star

142. 'Project Tiger' was started in India.

A. 1972 A.D. B. 1985 A.D.

C. 1981 A.D. D. 1973 A.D.

143. Kanha National Park is located in which Indian State?

A. West Bengal B. Gujarat

C. Tamil Nadu D. Madhya Pradesh

144. The Lucknow Pact of 1916 was made between:

A. The Congress and the Muslim League

B. The Moderates and Extremists

C. The British and the Indian

D. The Hindu and the Muslims

145. Where is the Wild Ass Sanctuary?

A. In Rajasthan B. In Bihar

C. In Madhya Pradesh D. In Gujarat

146. Carbon dating refes to:

A. Measurement of strength of rocks

B. All of these

C. Use of carbon for writing on white board

D. Measurement of age of bones or materials in ancient sites

147. The Constituent Assembly adopted National Anthem on:

A. 20 January, 1950 B. 13 November, 1949

C. 21 May, 1949 D. 24 January 1950

148. Biomagnification is:

A. increasing concentration of toxic substance in the tissues over time

B. all of these

C. to increase the size of picture using computer

D. increasing size of organism

149. Which of the following is ***not*** a abiotic component of biosphere?

A. Protein B. Phosphorus

C. Fungi D. Soil

150. The headquarter of Green Peace International is located in:

A. New York

B. Nagasaki

C. Amsterdam

D. Sydney

ANSWERS

1	2	3	4	5	6	7	8	9	10
B	D	C	D	D	A	D	C	A	D
11	**12**	**13**	**14**	**15**	**16**	**17**	**18**	**19**	**20**
D	C	C	A	B	A	D	A	C	D
21	**22**	**23**	**24**	**25**	**26**	**27**	**28**	**29**	**30**
A	D	C	B	C	D	A	D	D	D
31	**32**	**33**	**34**	**35**	**36**	**37**	**38**	**39**	**40**
A	D	B	D	B	A	C	A	B	A
41	**42**	**43**	**44**	**45**	**46**	**47**	**48**	**49**	**50**
D	D	C	B	B	B	C	B	B	B
51	**52**	**53**	**54**	**55**	**56**	**57**	**58**	**59**	**60**
A	C	D	C	A	B	C	D	A	C
61	**62**	**63**	**64**	**65**	**66**	**67**	**68**	**69**	**70**
B	C	B	D	A	C	C	C	A	A
71	**72**	**73**	**74**	**75**	**76**	**77**	**78**	**79**	**80**
B	D	D	C	D	B	A	D	A	C
81	**82**	**83**	**84**	**85**	**86**	**87**	**88**	**89**	**90**
A	D	C	D	B	C	A	A	A	D
91	**92**	**93**	**94**	**95**	**96**	**97**	**98**	**99**	**100**
C	B	A	B	C	C	B	B	A	C
101	**102**	**103**	**104**	**105**	**106**	**107**	**108**	**109**	**110**
A	C	A	A	D	B	C	D	C	A
111	**112**	**113**	**114**	**115**	**116**	**117**	**118**	**119**	**120**
D	B	B	B	A	B	C	A	C	A
121	**122**	**123**	**124**	**125**	**126**	**127**	**128**	**129**	**130**
C	B	D	C	D	B	C	C	C	B
131	**132**	**133**	**134**	**135**	**136**	**137**	**138**	**139**	**140**
D	D	B	B	D	C	B	D	C	C
141	**142**	**143**	**144**	**145**	**146**	**147**	**148**	**149**	**150**
A	D	D	A	D	D	D	A	C	C

EXPLANATORY ANSWERS

1. Kohler is associated with Gestalt theory of learning, which emphasizes insight rather than mere trial-and-error. His experiments showed that learning can occur suddenly when the individual perceives relationships between different elements of a problem. This highlighted the role of cognitive processes in learning.

2. McDougall proposed that human behavior is governed by a set of instincts, and in standard educational psychology references, these are taken as 14. Each instinct is associated with a specific emotion and drives behavior in a particular direction. This concept explains the biological basis of motivation.

3. Brainstorming model is designed to enhance creativity by encouraging free flow of ideas without criticism. It promotes divergent thinking where multiple solutions are explored. This method helps learners develop originality, flexibility and fluency in thinking.

4. Pavlov conducted experiments on dogs to explain classical conditioning. The dog learned to associate a neutral stimulus like a bell with food, eventually responding with salivation even in the absence of food. This demonstrated how learning can occur through association.

5. Originality, flexibility and fluency are core components of creativity. Originality refers to producing unique ideas, flexibility involves shifting perspectives, and fluency means generating many ideas. Together, they define creative thinking ability.

6. Combat is considered an instinct in McDougall's theory, representing the innate tendency to fight or defend. It is closely linked with the emotion of anger. Such instincts guide behavior in challenging or threatening situations.

7. Social development is mainly influenced by social environmental factors such as family, peers, school and cultural setting. These elements help children learn social norms, cooperation and adjustment. They play a major role in shaping behavior and personality.

8. The law of rapid growth states that physical development occurs quickly during certain stages like infancy and adolescence. During these periods, there is significant increase in height, weight and body structure. This law explains uneven growth patterns across life stages.

9. This theory is related to learning, not development, and was proposed by Pavlov. It explains behavior through stimulus-response association. Development theories focus on growth patterns, not conditioning mechanisms.

10. Hurlock stated that development leads to new characteristics and abilities, emphasizing qualitative changes. Development involves progressive changes in physical, mental and emotional aspects. It is a continuous and organized process.

11. Perception is the process of interpreting sensory information using past experience. While sensation only detects stimuli, perception gives it meaning. This helps individuals understand and respond to their environment effectively.

12. Edward Thorndike propounded the law of trial and error learning, also known as connectionism. He demonstrated through his puzzle box experiments that learning occurs gradually as responses that lead to success are strengthened. Errors are eliminated over repeated attempts, forming correct stimulus-response connections.

13. The I.Q. range of 90-109 is considered average intelligence. Individuals within this range show normal cognitive abilities and can perform everyday academic and social tasks effectively. This classification is widely accepted in standard intelligence testing scales.

14. Raymond Cattell proposed the Fluid and Crystallized Intelligence model. Fluid intelligence refers to problem-solving ability independent of experience, while crystallized intelligence is based on learned knowledge. This model explains different dimensions of intellectual functioning.

15. B.F. Skinner propounded the operant conditioning theory, which focuses on learning through consequences. Behavior is strengthened by reinforcement and weakened by punishment. This theory highlights the role of environment in shaping behavior.

16. A blueprint is an essential part of test construction. It provides a detailed plan about content areas, objectives, and weightage of questions. It ensures validity and balanced coverage of the syllabus.

17. Jean Piaget proposed the pre-operational stage as part of his theory of cognitive development. This stage occurs roughly between 2 to 7 years of age and is characterized by symbolic thinking and egocentrism. Children begin to use language but lack logical reasoning.

18. M.P.P.I. (Minnesota Multiphasic Personality Inventory) is used to measure personality traits. It assesses various psychological conditions and behavioral tendencies. It is widely used in clinical and counseling settings.

19. Learning depends on the learner's readiness, and readiness is mainly based on maturation. Motivation, guidance and interest help learning, but if the child has not reached the required stage of physical and mental maturity, proper learning cannot take place. Therefore, among the given options, maturation fits most accurately as the most essential condition for learning.

20. The period of infancyhood is generally considered from birth to 2 years. This stage includes very rapid physical growth, sensory development and early motor development. Hence, option D is more accurate than option C, which refers to a broader early childhood period.

21. Kohler's experiments aimed to show that learning occurs through insight, involving perception of the whole situation. He demonstrated that individuals can understand relationships and solve problems suddenly. This opposes trial-and-error learning.

22. Johann Friedrich Herbart proposed the Five Step System of lesson planning. These steps include preparation, presentation, association, generalization, and application. This system provides a structured approach to teaching.

23. Cannon described personality types based on glands and their hormonal influence. He emphasized how internal physiological processes affect behavior. His work contributed to understanding the biological basis of personality.

24. The statement "Creativity is a mental process to express the original outcomes" is associated with Crow and Crow. Creativity involves producing something original, useful or different through mental activity. Therefore, option B fits the given definition more accurately.

25. According to Skinner, language development occurs through imitation and reinforcement. Children learn words and structures by copying others and being rewarded. This reflects behaviorist principles of learning.

26. McDougall classified instincts into fourteen types. He linked each instinct with a specific emotion and behavior pattern. His theory explains the innate basis of human actions.

27. J.S. Dumvile defined attention as the concentration of consciousness upon one object rather than upon another. He explained that attention involves narrowing the field of consciousness so that one particular stimulus becomes clear and prominent. This definition highlights the selective and focused nature of mental activity in understanding any object or situation.

28. Francis Galton is known as the "Father of Eugenics". He studied heredity and believed that human qualities could be improved through selective breeding. His work laid the foundation for the concept of eugenics.

29. Dr. S. Jalota developed the General Mental Ability Test in Hindi for children aged 12 to 16 years. This test is used to measure overall mental capacity, including reasoning and intellectual abilities. It is widely used in educational and psychological assessment.

30. Charles Spearman proposed the Two Factor Theory of Intelligence. According to this theory, intelligence consists of a general factor (g) and specific factors (s). The general factor influences performance in all tasks, while specific factors are related to particular activities.

31. 'घुमक्कड़' शब्द 'घूमना' मूल धातु से बना है, जिसमें 'अक्कड़' प्रत्यय जुड़ता है। इस प्रकार 'घुम + अक्कड़' से 'घुमक्कड़' शब्द बनता है, जो ऐसे व्यक्ति को दर्शाता है जो निरंतर घूमता रहता है। यह प्रत्यय किसी आदत या प्रवृत्ति को प्रकट करने के लिए प्रयुक्त होता है।

32. गद्यांश में स्पष्ट रूप से बताया गया है कि महावीर स्वामी का जन्म वैशाली में हुआ था। उन्होंने जीवनभर भ्रमण किया और अंत में पावा में शरीर त्याग किया। इसलिए सही उत्तर वैशाली है।

33. 'स्वच्छंद' शब्द में व्यंज़न संधि होती है। यहाँ 'स्व' और 'छंद' के मेल से शब्द बना है, जिसमें व्यंजनों के मेल से परिवर्तन हुआ है। अतः यह व्यंजन संधि का उदाहरण है।

34. गद्यांश के अनुसार महात्मा बुद्ध ने 35 वर्ष की आयु में ज्ञान (बुद्धत्व) प्राप्त किया। इसके बाद वे 80 वर्ष की आयु तक लगातार भ्रमण करते रहे और धर्म का प्रचार करते रहे।

35. 'श्रुति धर्म' का अर्थ वैदिक धर्म है। श्रुति शब्द वेदों के लिए प्रयुक्त होता है, जिन्हें सुना गया ज्ञान माना जाता है। इसलिए श्रुति धर्म का संबंध वैदिक परंपरा से है।

36. 'ङ्' वर्ण का उच्चारण नासिका से होता है, इसलिए इसे नासिक्य ध्वनि कहा जाता है। यह क-वर्ग का अंतिम वर्ण है और इसके उच्चारण में वायु नासिका से निकलती है। इसलिए इसका स्थान नासिक्य माना जाता है।

37. 'चार गज मलमल' में 'चार गज' वस्तु की माप या परिमाण को दर्शाता है, न कि केवल गिनती को। यहाँ 'गज' एक माप की इकाई है, जिससे मलमल की लंबाई बताई जा रही है। इसलिए यह परिमाणबोधक विशेषण है, क्योंकि यह वस्तु की मात्रा/माप का बोध कराता है, केवल संख्या का नहीं।

38. 'समास' का विलोम 'व्यास' होता है। समास का अर्थ है संक्षेप में कहना, जबकि व्यास का अर्थ विस्तार से कहना होता है। इसलिए दोनों एक-दूसरे के विपरीत अर्थ देते हैं।

39. 'सुन्न' का तत्सम रूप 'शून्य' है। 'सुन्न' तद्भव शब्द है जो 'शून्य' से विकसित हुआ है। दोनों का अर्थ खाली या रिक्त होता है।

40. 'आँख की किरकिरी होना' मुहावरे का अर्थ है किसी को अप्रिय लगना या खटकना। यह उस स्थिति को दर्शाता है जब कोई व्यक्ति या वस्तु पसंद नहीं आती। इसलिए इसका अर्थ अप्रिय होना है।

41. 'अनुगृहीत' शब्द की वर्तनी सही है। इसमें 'गृ' धातु का प्रयोग होता है, जिसका अर्थ होता है कृपा करना या अनुग्रह करना। अन्य विकल्पों में वर्तनी की त्रुटि है।

42. 'पैतृक' शब्द शुद्ध रूप है, जिसका अर्थ होता है पिता से संबंधित या पूर्वजों से प्राप्त। यह 'पितृ' धातु से बना है, इसलिए इसका सही रूप 'पैतृक' होता है। अन्य विकल्पों में वर्तनी त्रुटिपूर्ण है।

43. 'श' ध्वनि का उच्चारण स्थान तालु होता है। यह तालव्य व्यंजन है और इसका उच्चारण जीभ को तालु से लगाकर किया जाता है। इसलिए इसे तालव्य वर्ग में रखा जाता है।

44. 'अत्यंत' शब्द में 'अति' उपसर्ग है। 'अति' का अर्थ होता है बहुत अधिक या अत्यधिक, और यह मूल शब्द 'अंत' के साथ मिलकर 'अत्यंत' बनाता है। यहाँ उपसर्ग के जुड़ने से अर्थ में तीव्रता आती है।

45. 'उपत्यका' का अर्थ पर्वत के पास या पर्वतों के बीच की भूमि होता है। यह वह क्षेत्र होता है जो घाटी के रूप में पाया जाता है। इसलिए यह पर्वतीय क्षेत्र के निकट स्थित भूमि को दर्शाता है।

46. आशु भाषण मौखिक अभिव्यक्ति का एक रूप है, जिसमें व्यक्ति तुरंत बोलकर अपने विचार व्यक्त करता है। यह बोलने की कला से संबंधित है, जबकि अन्य विकल्प लिखित अभिव्यक्ति से जुड़े हैं।

47. हिन्दी भाषा की प्रमुख बोलियाँ लगभग 18 मानी जाती हैं। ये विभिन्न क्षेत्रों में बोली जाती हैं और हिन्दी भाषा की विविधता को दर्शाती हैं। इन बोलियों का सांस्कृतिक और भाषाई महत्व है।

48. 'सामाजिक' शब्द 'समाज' मूल शब्द और 'इक' प्रत्यय से बना है। प्रत्यय जुड़ने से शब्द विशेषण बन जाता है, जिसका अर्थ समाज से संबंधित होता है। यह शब्द संरचना का सही विश्लेषण है।

49. 'तद्भव' पत्रिका के सम्पादक अखिलेश हैं। यह एक महत्वपूर्ण साहित्यिक पत्रिका है जो समकालीन हिन्दी लेखन को प्रस्तुत करती है। अखिलेश इसके प्रमुख संपादक के रूप में जाने जाते हैं।

50. "बारह बरस लौ कूकर जीवै..." यह पंक्ति कवि जगनिक की रचना है। यह वीर रस की परंपरा से संबंधित है और इसमें जीवन के साहस और वीरता का वर्णन मिलता है।

51. 'अकाल' का अर्थ होता है खाद्यान्न की कमी या भयंकर सूखा, जिसके कारण लोगों को भोजन नहीं मिल पाता। 'दुर्भिक्ष' भी इसी स्थिति को दर्शाता है जहाँ भुखमरी फैल जाती है। इसलिए 'अकाल' का सही पर्यायवाची 'दुर्भिक्ष' है।

52. यह मिश्र वाक्य है क्योंकि इसमें एक मुख्य वाक्य और एक आश्रित उपवाक्य होता है। 'कि छात्रा पढ़ते हैं' आश्रित उपवाक्य है जो मुख्य वाक्य पर निर्भर करता है। इसलिए यह मिश्र वाक्य की श्रेणी में आता है।

53. 'जिसकी पूर्व से कोई आशा न हो' का अर्थ होता है ऐसा जो पहले से अपेक्षित न हो। 'अप्रत्याशित' शब्द इसी अर्थ को व्यक्त करता है। यह शब्द अचानक या बिना उम्मीद के होने वाली घटना को दर्शाता है।

54. 'मुझसे उठा नहीं गया' वाक्य में कर्ता स्पष्ट रूप से क्रिया नहीं कर रहा बल्कि क्रिया के होने या न होने की स्थिति व्यक्त हो रही है। इसमें कार्य का भाव प्रमुख है, इसलिए यह भाववाच्य का उदाहरण है।

55. 'निष्कपट' का संधि-विच्छेद 'निः + कपट' है। यहाँ विसर्ग संधि के कारण 'निः' का 'निष्क' रूप बनता है। इस प्रकार यह शब्द बिना कपट या छल के अर्थ को व्यक्त करता है।

56. मारीशस एक ऐसा देश है जहाँ हिन्दी भाषा का प्रयोग बोलने और लिखने दोनों में किया जाता है। वहाँ भारतीय मूल के लोगों की संख्या अधिक है, जिससे हिन्दी का प्रचार-प्रसार हुआ है।

57. 'सूर सागर' प्रसिद्ध भक्त कवि सूरदास की रचना है, जो ब्रज भाषा में लिखी गई है। ब्रज भाषा में भक्ति साहित्य की समृद्ध परंपरा रही है। इसलिए इसका सही उत्तर ब्रज है।

58. 'वीरों का कैसा हो वसंत' कविता सुभद्रा कुमारी चौहान द्वारा लिखी गई है। यह कविता देशभक्ति और वीरता की भावना से प्रेरित है। इसमें राष्ट्रप्रेम और संघर्ष का भाव प्रकट होता है।

59. 'क्षेत्रीय' शब्द किसी क्षेत्र से संबंध या गुण को व्यक्त करता है, इसलिए यह गुणवाचक विशेषण है। यह संज्ञा के गुण या विशेषता को बताता है, जैसे क्षेत्रीय भाषा, क्षेत्रीय संस्कृति आदि। इसमें संख्या या परिमाण का बोध नहीं होता, बल्कि विशेषता का संकेत होता है।

60. 'चौराहा' (चौराहा) शब्द 'चार' और 'राहा/राह' से मिलकर बना है, जिसका अर्थ चार रास्तों का मिलन स्थान होता है। इसमें संख्या 'चार' के आधार पर समूह का बोध कराया जाता है, इसलिए यह द्विगु समास का उदाहरण है।

61. In the sentence "A live ass is better than a dead lion", the words 'live' and 'dead' describe the condition or quality of the nouns. Such adjectives express a characteristic or state, which falls under descriptive adjectives. They provide more information about the noun rather than quantity or number.

62. The correct spelling is "governance", not "governence". The other words-deciduous, entrance, and ambiguous-are correctly spelled. Therefore, option C contains the misspelt word.

63. The word "attenuate" means to reduce in force, effect, or thickness. It often refers to making something thinner or weaker. Hence, "make thin" is the correct synonym.

64. The correct correlative conjunction with "No sooner" is "than." This structure shows that one action happened immediately after another. Therefore, option D is grammatically correct.

65. "Judicious" means wise or showing good judgment. Its opposite is "imprudent", which means lacking wisdom or acting without proper judgment. Hence, option A is the correct antonym.

66. The idiom "to put out" means to extinguish, especially in reference to fire or light. It can also mean to stop something from burning. Therefore, option C is correct.

67. The sentence contains one main clause "This is the house" and one subordinate clause "in which I was born." The presence of a dependent clause makes it a complex sentence.

68. The correct phrase is "met out by", indicating that something is administered or delivered by someone. Here, the lawyer is the agent performing the action. Hence, "by" fits correctly.

69. "Being tired of playing" correctly expresses the reason why the children went home. It indicates their state or condition leading to the action. Other options are grammatically incorrect or awkward in usage.

70. 'too…to' structure is commonly used to convert two clauses into a single simple sentence by expressing result in a compact form. Here, "isn't too strong to keep us awake" combines both ideas without using conjunctions like 'and' or 'so'. This makes it a grammatically correct simple sentence with one main clause and an infinitive phrase.

71. The conjunction "As" is used to show cause or reason. The sentence indicates that because he had not paid his bill, the electricity was cut off. Therefore, "As" correctly connects the cause and effect.

72. In the sentence "Death lays his icy hand on Kings", death is given human qualities like having a hand. This attribution of human traits to a non-living concept is called personification. Hence, option D is correct.

73. The correct sequence forms the sentence: "The guide said that nowhere in the world you will find a fairer building than the Taj Mahal." This arrangement maintains logical and grammatical flow. Thus, option D is correct.

74. This proverb emphasizes the value of what one already possesses. It advises against risking a sure thing for uncertain gains. Hence, option C conveys the correct meaning.

75. The phrase "since we met a year ago" indicates present perfect tense. "Haven't seen" correctly expresses an action that has not occurred from the past up to now. Therefore, option D is correct.

76. Antarctica has no native human inhabitants and has always been a frozen desert. It is mainly inhabited temporarily by scientists. Thus, option B is the most appropriate.

77. "Apace" is an adverb meaning quickly or rapidly. The other options-fury (noun), meek (adjective), and face (noun/verb)-are not adverbs. Hence, option A is correct.

78. "My son and my daughter" refers to two people interacting mutually. "Each other" is the correct reciprocal pronoun used for two individuals. Therefore, option D fits appropriately.

79. This is a metaphor because it directly compares a person to a donkey without using "like" or "as". It implies foolishness or stubbornness. Hence, option A is the correct example of metaphor.

80. Demography means the study of population, including its size, growth, distribution, birth rate, death rate and related changes. Ecology studies organisms and environment, Genealogy studies family descent, and Astronomy studies celestial bodies. Therefore, the answer remains Demography.

81. The indirect sentence uses "asked" and "if", so the direct form must be a polite interrogative sentence. "Might" changes suitably into "may" in direct speech, and "her father" changes into "your father". Therefore, option A is the best direct form.

82. "To ring one's own bell" means to praise oneself or boast about one's own qualities and achievements. It is not related to theft or thinking properly. Therefore, the answer remains "to indulge in self praise".

83. In the passage, the children shouted "encore" and "once more" because they wanted the magic show to continue. "Encore" means a repeated or additional performance demanded by the audience. Therefore, option C is correct.

84. The passage clearly says that Kim gave the children a bright smile and vanished from the scene. He did not perform the act again, sit down, or refuse in an ordinary way. Therefore, option D is correct.

85. A century means a period of one hundred years. In the passage, Ravi uses the word to exaggerate how excellent the magic show was. Therefore, option B is correct.

86. The passage directly mentions the magician as Kim Rathod. M.G. Vidyalaya is the school, and Ravi is one of the boys. Therefore, option C is correct.

87. In the passage, "captivated" means deeply attracted, fascinated or held in attention by the magician's performance. Among the given options, "astonished" is the closest suitable meaning because the children were amazed by the tricks. Therefore, option A is the best answer.

88. "Spontaneous" means happening naturally, immediately or without being planned. In the passage, spontaneous applause means the children clapped instantly in appreciation of the trick. Therefore, option A is correct.

89. In the passage, the magician uses a "magic wand" from which flowers, ribbons and garlands appear. A wand is a thin stick used by magicians to perform tricks. Hence, the correct meaning is a stick.

90. The word "hopping" refers to moving by jumping, as described for the rabbit moving around the stage. It indicates small repeated jumps rather than running or standing. Therefore, the correct meaning is jumping.

91. Given, $\frac{a}{3} = \frac{b}{4} = \frac{c}{7} = k$ (say)

$\therefore \quad a = 3k, b = 4k, c = 7k$

$$\therefore \quad \frac{a+b+c}{c} = \frac{3k+4k+7k}{7k} = \frac{14k}{7k} = 2.$$

92. The year 1991 is an ordinary year.

So, it has 1 odd day.

5th day of the year was Saturday

$\therefore$ 5th day of the year 1992 will be 1 day beyond Saturday

Hence, 5th day of 1992 will be Sunday

Now, 5 January 1992 + 26 day January + 29 day February + 3 day March

$= \text{Sunday} + 58 \text{ day}$

$= \text{Sunday} + (7 \times 8 + 2) \text{ day}$

$= \text{Sunday} + 2 \text{ day} = \text{Tuesday}$

Hence, 3 March, 1992 will be Tuesday.

93. $\left[\left\{\left(\frac{1}{3}\right)^{-3} - \left(\frac{1}{4}\right)^{-2}\right\} \div \left(\frac{1}{4}\right)^{-3}\right]$

$= [\{(3)^3 - (4)^2\} \div (4)^3]$

$= [\{27 - 16\} \div 64]$

$= 11 \div 64 = \frac{11}{64}.$

94. For constructing a triangle, the sum of any two sides must be greater than the third side. In option B, 6.3 + 5.9 > 4.6, 5.9 + 4.6 > 6.3, and 6.3 + 4.6 > 5.9, so the triangle is possible. In the other options, at least one pair fails the triangle inequality.

95. $\sqrt{3}, \sqrt[3]{4}, \sqrt[4]{5}$

$\Rightarrow (3)^{\frac{1}{2}}, (4)^{\frac{1}{3}}, (5)^{\frac{1}{4}}$

$\Rightarrow (3)^{\frac{1}{2}\times 12}, (4)^{\frac{1}{3}\times 12}, (5)^{\frac{1}{4}\times 12}$

$\Rightarrow 3^6, 4^4, 5^3$

$\Rightarrow 729, 256, 125$

In ascending order:

$\therefore 125 < 256 < 729$

$\therefore \sqrt[4]{5} < \sqrt[3]{4} < \sqrt{3}.$

96. When extreme observations from both ends are removed, the mean is definitely affected because it depends on every value in the dataset, so removing any values changes the total sum and number of observations. The mode can also be affected if the extreme values happen to be repeated frequently and form the highest frequency. However, the median generally remains unchanged when equal values are removed from both ends because the central position of the data does not shift significantly.

97. $\because$ Exactly one of face painted in one side = 9

$\therefore$ Total number of cubes will have exactly one of their faces painted

$= 9 \times 6 = 54.$

98. Sum of interior angles of an n-sided polygon is $(n - 2) \times 180°$.

For a pentagon, $n = 5$, so the sum is

$(5 - 2) \times 180° = 3 \times 180° = 540°$

Therefore, the interior angles of a pentagon add up to 540°.

99. Let the total length of the pole is x metre

Then, $\frac{4}{7}x - \frac{1}{3}\left(\frac{4}{7}x\right) = 8$

$\Rightarrow \frac{4}{7}x\left(1 - \frac{1}{3}\right) = 8$

$\Rightarrow \frac{4}{7}x \times \frac{2}{3} = 8$

$\Rightarrow x = 8 \times \frac{21}{8}$

$\Rightarrow x = 21$ metre.

100. (A + B)'s 1 day's work $= \frac{1}{12}$

(B + C)'s 1 day's work $= \frac{1}{15}$

(C + A)'s 1 day's work $= \frac{1}{20}$

$\therefore$ 2(A + B + C)'s 1 day's work

$= \frac{1}{12} + \frac{1}{15} + \frac{1}{20}$

$= \frac{5+4+3}{60} = \frac{12}{60} = \frac{1}{5}$

$\Rightarrow$ (A + B + C)'s 1 day's work $= \frac{1}{5} \times \frac{1}{2} = \frac{1}{10}$

$\therefore$ A's 1 day's work = (A + B + C)'s 1 day's work – (B + C)'s 1 day's work

$= \frac{1}{10} - \frac{1}{15} = \frac{3-2}{30} = \frac{1}{30}$

Hence, A would take separately 30 days to do the same work.

101. H.C.F of $\frac{14}{33}, \frac{42}{55}, \frac{21}{22}$

$= \frac{\text{H.C.F. of 14, 42, 21}}{\text{L.C.M. of 33, 55, 22}} = \frac{7}{330}.$

102. $7 + 2\sqrt{10} = 5 + 2 + 2 \cdot \sqrt{5} \cdot \sqrt{2}$

$= \left(\sqrt{5}\right)^2 + \left(\sqrt{2}\right)^2 + 2 \cdot \sqrt{2} \cdot \sqrt{5}$

$= \left(\sqrt{2} + \sqrt{5}\right)^2$

$\Rightarrow 7 + 2\sqrt{10} = \left(\sqrt{2} + \sqrt{5}\right)^2$

Hence, Square root of $\left(7+2\sqrt{10}\right)$

$$= \sqrt{\left[\left(\sqrt{2}\right)+\left(\sqrt{5}\right)\right]^2}$$

$$= \left(\sqrt{2}+\sqrt{5}\right).$$

103. Given, Side of an equilateral triangle $= \frac{4}{3}$ cm

$\therefore$ The perimeter of the figure $= 5\times\frac{4}{3}$ cm

$$= \frac{20}{3} = 6\frac{2}{3} \text{ cm.}$$

104. $99 = 9 \times 11$

This number is also divisible by 9 and 11 also, and A number is divisible by 11 if the difference between the sum of its digits at old place and the sum of its digits at even places is either 0 or a number divisible by 11.

A. 114345

$\Rightarrow (5 + 3 + 1) - (4 + 4 + 1) = 9 - 9 = 0$

and sum of numbers

$= 1 + 1 + 4 + 3 + 4 + 5 = 18$

B. 3572406

$\Rightarrow (6 + 4 + 7 + 3) - (0 + 2 + 5) = 20 - 7 = 13$

and sum $= 3 + 5 + 7 + 2 + 4 + 0 + 6 = 27$

C. 913462

$\Rightarrow (2 + 4 + 1) - (6 + 3 + 9) = 7 - 18 = -11$

and sum $= 9 + 1 + 3 + 4 + 6 + 2 = 25$

D. 135792

$\Rightarrow (2 + 7 + 3) - (9 + 5 + 1) = 12 - 15 = -3$

and sum $= 1 + 3 + 5 + 7 + 9 + 2 = 27.$

Hence, (A) 114345 is divisible by 11 and 9 also. Hence, it is divisible by 99.

105. π (pi) is defined as the ratio of the circumference of a circle to its diameter, and its decimal expansion is non-terminating and non-repeating (3.14159...). Because it cannot be expressed as a ratio of two integers, it is not rational. It is also not an integer or a prime number, hence it is classified as an irrational number.

106. Given $10^{3x} = 125$

$\Rightarrow 10^{3x} = 5^3$

$\Rightarrow 10^x = (5^3)^{1/3}$

$\Rightarrow 10^x = 5$

Hence, $10^{-2x} = 5^{-2} = \frac{1}{25}$.

107. Given, dividend $= 16075$

quotient $= 167$

and remainder $= 43$

$\because$ dividend = divisor × quotient + remainder

$\therefore$ $16075 = \text{divisor} \times 167 + 43$

$\Rightarrow$ divisor $\times 167 = 16075 - 43 = 16032$

$\Rightarrow$ divisor $= \frac{16032}{167} = 96$

Hence, divisor = 96.

108. Positive prime integers less than 50 are 2, 3, 5, 7, 11, 13, 17, 19, 23, 29, 31, 37, 41, 43 and 47. Counting them gives 15 prime numbers. Hence, the number of positive prime integers below 50 is 15.

109. Let the two numbers are x and y

Then, $2x - 5y = 3$

$\Rightarrow 4x - 10y = 6$ ...(*i*)

and $4x + 3y = 71$ ...(*ii*)

Subtracting (*i*) from (*ii*), we get

$3y + 10y = 71 - 6$

$\Rightarrow 13y = 65$

$\Rightarrow y = 5$

Putting the value of y in (*ii*), we get

$4x + 3 \times 5 = 71$

$\Rightarrow 4x + 15 = 71$

$\Rightarrow 4x = 71 - 15$

$\Rightarrow 4x = 56$

$\Rightarrow x = 14$

Hence, the numbers are $x = 14$ and $y = 5$.

110. Given, Area of a square = Area of a rectangle

$\Rightarrow (\text{Side})^2 = \text{length} \times \text{breadth}$

$\Rightarrow (8)^2 = 16 \times \text{breadth}$

$\Rightarrow \text{breadth} = \frac{8^2}{16} = \frac{8\times8}{16} = \frac{8}{2} = 4$

Hence, the breadth of the rectangle = 4 cm.

111. Let the selling price of an article is ₹ x

Then, its the cost price = ₹ $\frac{3}{2}x$

$\therefore$ Loss = C.P. – S.P.

$= \frac{3}{2}x - x =$ ₹ $\frac{1}{2}x$

$\therefore$ $\text{loss\%} = \frac{\text{loss}\times100}{\text{C.P.}}$

$$= \frac{\frac{1}{2}x\times100}{\frac{3}{2}x} = \frac{100}{3} = 33\frac{1}{3}\%.$$

112. $121012 = 12 \times 10084 + 4$

When, 121012 is divided by 12, then remainder is 4.

113. Given, Product = 378 × 236 × 459 × 312
∵ unit digit in (378 × 236) = 8
and unit digit in (459 × 312) = 8
∴ unit digit in (8 × 8) = 4
Hence, unit digit in
(378 × 236 × 459 × 312) = 4.

114. Given,

$$\text{Mean} = \frac{5+7+7+8+x+5+4+3+1+2}{10}$$

$$\therefore \quad 4.5 = \frac{42+x}{10}$$

$$\Rightarrow \quad 42 + x = 45.0$$

$$\Rightarrow \quad x = 45.0 - 42 = 3$$

Hence, Given data:
5, 7, 7, 8, x, 5, 4, 3, 1, 2
⇒ 5, 7, 7, 8, 3, 5, 4, 3, 1, 2
Arranging in ascending order
∴ 1, 2, 3, 3, 4, 5, 5, 7, 7, 8
Here, number of data = n = 10 (even number)

$$\therefore \text{ Median} = \frac{1}{2}\left[\frac{n}{2}\text{th term} + \left(\frac{n}{2}+1\right)\text{th term}\right]$$

$$= \frac{1}{2}[\text{5th term} + \text{6th term}]$$

$$= \frac{1}{2}[4+5] = \frac{9}{2} = 4.5.$$

115. The method of Analysis of Variance, commonly called ANOVA, is most importantly associated with R.A. Fisher. He developed it as a statistical method to compare variation among groups. Therefore, Fisher is the key person related to ANOVA.

116. D, E, F are midpoints of the sides of triangle ABC, so joining them forms the medial triangle DEF.
Each side of ΔDEF is parallel to and half of the corresponding side of ΔABC.
Hence, ΔDEF is similar to ΔABC with scale factor

$$= \frac{1}{2}.$$

$$\text{Area ratio} = (\text{scale factor})^2$$

$$= \left(\frac{1}{2}\right)^2 = \frac{1}{4}$$

So, area(ΔDEF) $= \frac{1}{4}$ area(ΔABC).

117. For any set of positive numbers, there is a well-known inequality relation among means: Arithmetic Mean (A) ≥ Geometric Mean (G) ≥ Harmonic Mean (H).
This is called the AM ≥ GM ≥ HM inequality and holds true universally for positive data.
Hence, A ≥ G and G ≥ H, giving the correct relation as A ≥ G ≥ H.

118. Given, $x - y = 5$ ...(*i*)
and $xy = 36$

$$(x+y)^2 = (x-y)^2 + 4xy$$
$$= 5^2 + 4 \times 36$$
$$= 25 + 144 = 169$$
$$\Rightarrow \quad (x+y)^2 = (13)^2$$
$$\Rightarrow \quad x + y = 13 \quad ...(ii)$$

from adding (*i*) and (*ii*), we get
$$2x = 18 \Rightarrow x = 9$$
Putting the value of x in (*i*), we get
$$\therefore \quad 9 - y = 5$$
$$\Rightarrow \quad y = 9 - 5$$
$$\Rightarrow \quad y = 4$$
Hence, the difference of their reciprocals
$$= \frac{1}{y} - \frac{1}{x} = \frac{1}{4} - \frac{1}{9} = \frac{9-4}{36} = \frac{5}{36}.$$

119. Srinivas Ramanujan was the self-taught Indian mathematical genius of the 20th century. He made extraordinary contributions to number theory, infinite series, partitions and continued fractions. His work is famous because much of his mathematics developed without formal advanced training.

120. Given, $l = 2b$ and $h = 11$ m
and the area of 4 walls of a room = 660 m^2
$$2(lh + bh) = 660$$
$$\Rightarrow \quad 2h(l + b) = 660$$
$$\Rightarrow 2 \times 11(2b + b) = 660 \Rightarrow 22 \times 3b = 660$$
$$\Rightarrow 66b = 660$$
$$\Rightarrow \quad b = \frac{660}{66} = 10 \text{ m}$$
$$\therefore \quad l = 2b = 2 \times 10 = 20 \text{ m}$$
Hence, area of its ceiling = $l \times b$
$= 20 \times 10$ m^2 = 200 m^2.

121. Silent Valley in Kerala is known for its exceptionally rich biodiversity and dense tropical evergreen forests. It hosts a wide variety of flora and fauna, many of which are endemic and rare. Therefore, it is considered one of the most biodiversity-rich regions.

122. LPG (Liquefied Petroleum Gas) is mainly composed of propane and butane, not methane. It is a clean fuel, burns with a blue flame, and has a high calorific value. Hence, the statement that it is methane emitting is not true.

123. An ecosystem consists of both living (biotic) components like plants and animals and non-living (abiotic) components like air, water, and soil. These interact with each other to maintain ecological balance. Therefore, option D correctly represents all components.

124. The Tropic of Capricorn lies at 23½ degrees south of the Equator. It represents the southernmost latitude where the Sun can be directly overhead at noon (during the December solstice). Hence, the correct position is 23½° South.

125. The term "ecosystem" was coined by A.G. Tansley in 1935. He introduced it to describe the interaction between living organisms and their physical environment. This concept became fundamental in ecology.

126. Arsenic contamination in groundwater is most severe in West Bengal. The problem arises due to natural geological conditions and excessive groundwater extraction. It has affected large populations in the region.

127. The Deccan region lies on the leeward side of the Western Ghats. Moist winds from the Arabian Sea lose most of their moisture on the windward side, causing dryness on the other side. This is known as the rain shadow effect.

128. The Wildlife Protection Act in India was enacted in 1972. It provides legal protection to wild animals, birds and plants. It is a major step in conserving biodiversity.

129. Solar radiation received per unit area at the outer edge of Earth's atmosphere is called the solar constant. It is nearly constant and represents the total incoming solar energy. It is measured before atmospheric absorption.

130. Fundamental duties in the Indian Constitution were adopted from the USSR. They were added by the 42nd Amendment in 1976. These duties guide citizens toward responsible behavior.

131. In a grassland ecosystem, top consumers are carnivores. They feed on herbivores and occupy the highest trophic level. Examples include lions and wolves.

132. The troposphere is the lowest layer of the atmosphere, closest to Earth's surface. Most weather phenomena occur in this layer. It contains the majority of atmospheric gases.

133. The Biological Diversity Act was passed by the Indian Parliament on 11th December 2002. It aims to conserve biodiversity and ensure sustainable use. It also protects traditional knowledge.

134. Organic farming avoids chemical fertilizers and pesticides. It relies on natural methods, making it environmentally friendly. It helps maintain soil fertility and ecological balance.

135. Acid rain mainly results from sulphur dioxide and nitrogen oxides reacting with water to form acids. Sulphuric acid is a major component. It causes damage to vegetation, soil and structures.

136. WWF stands for World Wildlife Fund. It is an international organization working for conservation of nature and wildlife. It focuses on protecting endangered species and habitats.

137. Valley of Flowers is located in Uttarakhand in the Himalayan region. It is a UNESCO World Heritage Site known for its rich floral diversity and scenic beauty. The valley blooms with numerous endemic species during monsoon.

138. The Central Pollution Control Board (CPCB) is the main agency responsible for monitoring and measuring pollution levels in India. It sets standards and ensures implementation of environmental laws. It plays a key role in pollution control.

139. Cotopaxi is an active volcano located in the Andes Mountains in Ecuador. It is one of the highest active volcanoes in the world. Hence, it belongs to the Andes mountain range.

140. The Tsangpo river in Tibet enters India and is known as the Brahmaputra. It flows through Arunachal Pradesh and Assam. It is one of the major rivers of India.

141. The Pole Star, also known as Polaris, indicates the North direction. It appears almost stationary in the sky. Hence, it is called the North Star.

142. Project Tiger was launched in India in 1973. Its main objective was to conserve the declining population of tigers. It is one of the most important wildlife conservation programs.

143. Kanha National Park is located in Madhya Pradesh. It is famous for its rich wildlife including tigers and barasingha. It is one of the largest national parks in India.

144. The Lucknow Pact of 1916 was an agreement between the Indian National Congress and the Muslim League. It marked a moment of unity in the freedom struggle. Both agreed on constitutional reforms.

145. The Wild Ass Sanctuary is located in the Rann of Kutch in Gujarat. It is known for the Indian wild ass (khur). It is a protected area for this endangered species.

146. Carbon dating is a scientific method used to determine the age of ancient objects containing organic material. It measures the decay of carbon-14 isotopes. It is widely used in archaeology.

147. The Constituent Assembly adopted the National Anthem on 24 January 1950. "Jana Gana Mana" was formally accepted just before the Constitution came into effect. It represents national unity.

148. Biomagnification refers to the increase in concentration of toxic substances in organisms at successive trophic levels. It becomes more harmful at higher levels of the food chain. Hence, option A is correct.

149. Fungi are living organisms, so they are biotic components of the biosphere. Abiotic components include non-living elements like soil and minerals. Therefore, fungi is not an abiotic component.

150. The headquarters of Greenpeace International is located in Amsterdam, Netherlands. It is a global environmental organization. It works for environmental protection and sustainability.

Previous Paper (Solved)

UP-TET (PRIMARY LEVEL), 2019

(Exam held on 08-01-2020)

PART-I

CHILD DEVELOPMENT AND TEACHING METHOD

1. Human development starts from:
A. Pre-childhood stage B. Post-childhood stage
C. Stage of infancy D. Pre-natal stage

2. 'The Conditions of Learning' book is written by:
A. B.F. Skinner B. R.M. Gagne
C. I.P. Pavlov D. E.L. Thorndike

3. "Adolescence is the period of great stress, strain, storm and strike" is the statement of:
A. Stanley Hall B. Simpson
C. Crow & Crow D. Jersield

4. Total time taken in Indian Model of Micro Teaching is:
A. 40 minute B. 45 minute
C. 30 minute D. 36 minute

5. "Plateaus of learning are a characteristic feature of the learning process indicating a period where no improvement in performance is made". Who said this?
A. Hollingworth B. Ross
C. Skinner D. Gates and others

6. If a teacher finds a problematic child in the class, what should he does?
A. Ignore the child
B. Provide counselling to the child
C. Send the child back to home immediately
D. Punish the child

7. Co-curricular activities are mostly related to:
A. All round development of students
B. Professional development of students
C. Mental development of students
D. Development of educational institutions

8. Whom of the following has ***not*** propounded the learning theory?
A. Skinner B. B.S. Bloom
C. Thorndike D. Kohler

9. Meaning of stagnation in education is:
A. Not going to school by the child
B. Leave the school by the child
C. Retention of a child in a same class for more than one year
D. Taking not admission in school by the child

10. In which of the following skill, testing of previous knowledge comes?
A. Skill of introduction
B. Skill of closure
C. Skill of demonstration
D. Skill of stimulus-variation

11. Who gave the concept of multiple intelligence?
A. Spearman B. John Mayor
C. Gardner D. Golman

12. Dyslexia has difficulty in:
A. Expressing B. Standing
C. Speaking D. Reading/ Spelling

13. Which of the following is ***not*** the role of teacher in inclusive classroom?
A. Teacher should not pay attention to differently abled child
B. Teacher should encourage the children
C. Teacher should devote extra time to teach learning disabled
D. Make adequate seating arrangements according to the requirement of the child

14. In the class, questioning by students:
A. Should be encouraged
B. Should be stopped
C. Should not be allowed
D. Should be discouraged

15. Growth of a child is mainly related to:
A. Social Development
B. Emotional Development
C. Moral Development
D. Physical Development

16. 'Learning is any change in behaviour, resulting from behaviour' who said it?
A. Guilford B. Skinner
C. Crow & Crow D. Woodworth

17. Match the List–A and List–B.

List–A	List–B
(*a*) Bruner	(*i*) Basic teaching model
(*b*) Ausubel	(*ii*) Synectics teaching model
(*c*) Glasser	(*iii*) Advance organiser teaching model
(*d*) Gordon	(*iv*) Concept attainment teaching model
	(*v*) Inquiry training model

Codes:

	(*a*)	(*b*)	(*c*)	(*d*)
A.	(*iv*)	(*iii*)	(*ii*)	(*i*)
B.	(*i*)	(*ii*)	(*iii*)	(*v*)
C.	(*iii*)	(*i*)	(*ii*)	(*v*)
D.	(*iv*)	(*iii*)	(*i*)	(*ii*)

18. The first step of problem solving is:
A. Identification of problem
B. Testing of hypothesis
C. Formulation of hypothesis
D. Data collection

19. Learning of children will be most effective when:
A. Development of cognitive, affective and psycho-motor domain of children will take place
B. Teaching system will be autocratic
C. Teacher will lead the learning process and keep the children passive
D. Emphasis will be only on reading, writing and mathematical skills

20. Which step is prominent in the syntax of teaching model of memory level and under-standing level?
A. Exploration
B. Presentation
C. Planning
D. Generalization

21. Which of the following theory is also known as Theory of Reinforcement?
A. Stimulus Response Theory
B. Theory of Insight
C. Operant Conditioning Theory
D. Classical Conditioning Theory

22. Which of the following stages is ***not*** the part of Bruner's Cognitive Development Theory?
A. Iconic stage
B. Symbolic stage
C. Enactive stage
D. Intuitive stage

23. Morrison has described five steps in his teaching model at understanding level which are:
(*a*) Presentation (*b*) Exploration
(*c*) Organisation (*d*) Assimilation
(*e*) Recitation

The correct sequence is:
A. (*b*), (*a*), (*d*), (*c*), (*e*) B. (*b*), (*a*), (*c*), (*d*), (*e*)
C. (*a*), (*b*), (*c*), (*d*), (*e*) D. (*d*), (*e*), (*c*), (*a*), (*b*)

24. Which of the following is ***not*** related with cognitive domain?
A. Application
B. Understanding
C. Knowledge
D. Valuing

25. Which of the following is ***not*** the curve of learning?
A. Combination type
B. Longitudinal
C. Convex
D. Concave

26. Match the Column–A and Column–B.

Column–A	Column–B
(*a*) Animal Intelligence	(*i*) Gestalt
(*b*) Schedule of reinforcement	(*ii*) Piaget
(*c*) Law of pragnanz	(*iii*) Thorndike
(*d*) Adaptation	(*iv*) Skinner

Codes:

	(*a*)	(*b*)	(*c*)	(*d*)
A.	(*ii*)	(*iv*)	(*iii*)	(*i*)
B.	(*ii*)	(*iv*)	(*i*)	(*iii*)
C.	(*iii*)	(*iv*)	(*i*)	(*ii*)
D.	(*i*)	(*iv*)	(*iii*)	(*ii*)

27. "Development is a never ending process". This statement is related to which principle of development?
A. Principle of integration
B. Principle of inter-relationship
C. Principle of continuity
D. Principle of interaction

28. Through which Amendment of Constitution education has become fundamental right?
A. 25th Amendment
B. 52nd Amendment
C. 22nd Amendment
D. 86th Amendment

29. Instinct Theory of motivation was propounded by:
A. Abraham Maslow
B. Simpson
C. William James
D. McDougall

30. Which of the following stages of development is called as "A unique stage of emotional development" by Cole and Bruce?
A. Childhood
B. Adulthood
C. Adolescence
D. Infancy

PART-II

भाषा-I : हिन्दी

31. निम्नलिखित में से कौन-सा शब्द तद्भव है?
A. खेत B. प्रभु
C. नाथ D. त्रिकुटी

32. निम्नलिखित में से कौन-सा शब्द देशज है?
A. लाश B. औरत
C. पतलून D. धड़ाम

33. छछूँदर के सिर पर चमेली का तेल का अर्थ है-
A. मिथ्या आडम्बर
B. अधिक पाने की लालच करना
C. योग्य व्यक्ति को अच्छी चीज देना
D. अयोग्य व्यक्ति को अच्छी चीज देना

34. 'ऋग्वेद' का सन्धि विच्छेद क्या है?
A. ऋक् + वेद B. ऋ + गवेद
C. ऋग + वेद D. ऋ + वेद

35. 'आपबीती' शब्द में समास है :
A. द्वन्द्व समास B. द्विगु समास
C. तत्पुरुष समास D. कर्मधारय समास

36. 'घोंसले में चिड़िया है' में कौन-सा कारक है?
A. सम्बन्ध कारक B. सम्प्रदान कारक
C. अधिकरण कारक D. अपादान कारक

निर्देश (प्रश्न सं. 37 और 38) : दिए गए गद्यांश को पढ़कर निम्नलिखित प्रश्नों के सही विकल्प छाँटिए।

गांधीवाद में राजनीतिक और आध्यात्मिक तत्वों का समन्वय मिलता है। यही इस वाद की विशेषता है। आज संसार में जितने भी वाद प्रचलित हैं वह प्रायः राजनीतिक क्षेत्र में सीमित हो चुके हैं। आत्मा से उनका सम्बंध-विच्छेद होकर केवल बाह्य संसार तक उनका प्रसार रह गया है। मन की निर्मलता और ईश्वर निष्ठा से आत्मा को शुद्ध करना गांधीवाद का प्रथम आवश्यकता है। ऐसा करने से निःस्वार्थ बुद्धि का विकास होता है और मनुष्य सच्चे अर्थों में जन सेवा के लिए तत्पर हो जाता है। गांधीवाद में साम्प्रदायिकता के लिए कोई स्थान नहीं है। इसी समस्या को हल करने के लिए गांधीजी ने अपने जीवन का बलिदान कर दिया था।

37. उपर्युक्त गद्यांश के आधार पर बताइये कि संसार के सारे वाद सीमित हैं :
A. साम्प्रदायिकता तक B. आत्मा तक
C. धर्म तक D. राजनीतिक क्षेत्र तक

38. उपर्युक्त गद्यांश में गांधीवाद का आधार किसे बताया गया है?
A. जनसेवा और अध्यात्म को
B. ईश्वर निष्ठा और मन की निर्मलता को
C. राजनीतिक अध्यात्म और साम्प्रदायिकता को
D. राजनीतिक और आध्यात्मिक तत्व को

39. 'कनुप्रिया' के रचनाकार कौन हैं?
A. रांगेय राघव B. भगवतीचरण वर्मा
C. नागार्जुन D. धर्मवीर भारती

40. प्लुत स्वर कौन-सा है?
A. ओउम् B. ओम्
C. ओम D. अउम

41. प्रकाशन वर्ष की दृष्टि से डॉ. हरिवंश राय बच्चन की रचनाओं का सही अनुक्रम है :
A. मधुशाला, मधुबाला, मधुकलश, निशा निमन्त्रण
B. निशा निमन्त्रण, मधुबाला, मधुकलश, मधुशाला
C. मधुबाला, मधुशाला, निशा निमन्त्रण, मधुकलश
D. मधुकलश, मधुबाला, मधुशाला, निशा निमन्त्रण

42. सुमेल कीजिए :

(*a*) हिन्दी साहित्य सम्मेलन	(*i*) 1893
(*b*) काशी नागरी प्रचारिणी सभा	(*ii*) 1918
(*c*) राष्ट्रभाषा प्रचार समिति, वर्धा	(*iii*) 1910

कूट :

	(*a*)	(*b*)	(*c*)
A.	(*iii*)	(*ii*)	(*i*)
B.	(*ii*)	(*i*)	(*iii*)
C.	(*iii*)	(*i*)	(*ii*)
D.	(*i*)	(*ii*)	(*iii*)

43. 'तुलसीदास' के रचनाकार हैं :
A. केशवदास B. सूर्यकान्त त्रिपाठी 'निराला'
C. डॉ. रामविलास शर्मा D. महादेवी वर्मा

44. 'अन्या से अनन्या' आत्मकथा किसकी है?
A. प्रभा खेतान B. सुषम वेदी
C. उषा प्रियंवदा D. मन्नू भंडारी

45. 'प्रभु जी तुम चंदन हम पानी' किसका वाक्य है?
A. दादू B. नानक
C. रैदास D. कबीर

निर्देश (प्रश्न सं. 46 और 47) : दिए गए गद्यांश को पढ़कर निम्नलिखित प्रश्नों के सही विकल्प छाँटिए।

वरदन्त की पंगति कुंदकली अधराधर पल्लव लोचन की।
चपला चमकै घन बीच जगै छवि मोतिन माल अमोलन की।।
घुँघरारि लटें लटकैं मुख ऊपर कुण्डल लाल कपोलन की।
निवछावर प्राण करैं 'तुलसी' बलि जाऊँ ललाइन बोलन की।।

46. इस पद्यांश में कौन-सा रस है?
A. वात्सल्य रस B. शृंगार रस
C. शान्त रस D. करुण रस

47. उपरोक्त पद्य किस कवि का है?
A. सूरदास B. तुलसीदास
C. कबीर D. जायसी

48. उच्चारण स्थान की दृष्टि से कौन-सा विकल्प शुद्ध है?
A. स – दन्त्य B. च – कंठ्य
C. ष – तालव्य D. श – मूर्धन्य

49. निम्नलिखित में कौन-सा कथन अशुद्ध है?
A. हिन्दी में 'ज्ञ' का उच्चारण परम्परा से भिन्न हो गया है।
B. 'क्ष' संयुक्त व्यंजन है।
C. विसर्ग कंठ्य वर्ण है।
D. दो महाप्राण व्यंजनों का उच्चारण एक साथ हो सकता है।

50. 'मेरे लड़के ने मेरी आज्ञा का पालन नहीं किया' वाक्य में 'लड़के' के विषय में कौन-सा विकल्प अशुद्ध है?
A. कर्त्ता B. बहुवचन
C. एकवचन D. पुल्लिंग

51. 'राम आम खाता है' में वाच्य का कौन-सा रूप है?
A. भाववाच्य B. उभयवाच्य
C. कर्तृवाच्य D. कर्मवाच्य

52. *'रहिमन पानी रखिए बिन पानी सब सून।*
पानी गए न ऊबरे मोती मानस चून।'
इस दोहे में कौन-सा अलंकार है?
A. रूपक B. उत्प्रेक्षा
C. श्लेष D. उपमा

53. निम्नलिखित में से कौन-सा शब्द शुद्ध है?
A. चांद B. आंख
C. अँक D. अंगना

54. निम्न में से किस शब्द की वर्तनी सही है?
A. सम्निधि B. सन्निधी
C. सन्निधि D. संनिधि

55. उपचारात्मक शिक्षण की सफलता निर्भर करती है :
A. समय व अवधि पर
B. समस्याओं के कारणों की सही पहचान पर
C. उपचारात्मक शिक्षण की सामग्री पर
D. भाषिक नियमों के ज्ञान पर

56. 'प्रयोजन' का समानार्थी शब्द नहीं है :
A. हेतु B. नियोजन
C. उद्देश्य D. लक्ष्य

57. 'ऋजु' का विलोम शब्द है :
A. त्रिकोण B. वक्र
C. सीधा D. सरल

58. निम्नलिखित विकल्पों में किस विकल्प में विशेषण का निर्देश अशुद्ध है?
A. दूसरा – क्रमवाचक
B. वह नौकर – कोई विशेषण नहीं है
C. छब्बीस – पूर्णांक बोधक
D. ढाई – अपूर्णांक बोधक

59. 'आप भला तो जग भला' वाक्य में सर्वनाम के किस भेद का बोध होता है?
A. अनिश्चय वाचक सर्वनाम B. प्रश्नवाचक सर्वनाम
C. सम्बन्ध वाचक सर्वनाम D. निजवाचक सर्वनाम

60. निम्नलिखित में से कौन-सा शब्द पुल्लिंग है?
A. कढ़ी B. सरसों
C. संतान D. चील

PART-III

LANGUAGE-II : ENGLISH

61. Which of the following words is ***not*** a co-ordinating conjunction?
A. if B. for
C. and D. but

62. Fill in the blanks with appropriate prepositions:
His thirst ______ knowledge left him no leisure ______ anything else.
A. on, on B. for, for
C. by, by D. at, at

63. The word 'fast' in the sentence
'He is fast writer' is:
A. an adverb
B. an adjective
C. a conjunction
D. a noun

64. Which of the following is ***not*** a simple sentence?
A. She reads what she likes.
B. He is a man of great knowledge.
C. I have a very costly book in my house.
D. She does not know good manners.

65. The sentence
'He will be playing the piano in the concert day after tomorrow' is in

A. Future Imperfect Tense
B. Future Perfect Continuous Tense
C. Future Indefinite Tense
D. Present Indefinite Tense

66. In which of the following sentences is the subject of verb a feminine gender noun?
A. All the young men have arrived.
B. All the old men have arrived.
C. All the female members have arrived.
D. All the male members have arrived.

67. The method of teaching in which the teacher tries to establish a link between the foreign language word and the object without the interference of the learner's mother tongue is called:
A. the bilingual method
B. the grammar-translation method
C. the direct method
D. the structural method

68. If you are testing your students' comprehen-sion of written English, you are testing their understanding of what they have just:
A. listened to B. spoken
C. written D. read

69. Choose the correct sentence:
A. Please listen towards your teacher.
B. Please listen of your teacher.
C. Please listen to your teacher.
D. Please listen your teacher.

70. Find out the correct sentence/sentences:
A. Both of the above B. None of the above
C. I don't believe him. D. I am not believing him.

71. Which of the following sentences is in Passive voice?
A. Some boys were helping the wounded man.
B. My watch was lost.
C. Someone may steal the bicycle.
D. The teacher scolded him for being late.

72. Which of the following alternatives is the correct passive voice form of the following sentence?
'Do it'
A. It will be done B. Let it be done
C. It be done D. It is done

73. Which of the following words is plural?
A. Analysis B. Criteria
C. Index D. Crisis

74. Which of the following nouns is in plural?
A. Electronics B. Billiards
C. News D. Mice

75. He was an orphan and lived with his uncle.
In the above given sentence identify the gender of the word 'orphan'.
A. Common Gender B. Neuter Gender
C. Masculine Gender D. Feminine Gender

Direction (Qs. No. 76 and 77): *Read the passage given and answer the Questions that follow it.*

To forgive an injury is often considered to be a sign of weakness; it is really a sign of stength. It is easy to allow oneself to be carried away by resentment and hate into an act of vengeance but it takes a strong character to restrain those natural passions. The man who forgives an injury proves himself to be superior of the man who wronged him, and puts the wrong-doer to shame. Forgiveness may even turn a foe into a friend. So mercy is the noblest form of revenge.

76. The word strength is a:
A. Abstract noun B. Collective noun
C. Common noun D. Material noun

77. One who ***does not*** take revenge is:
A. a foolish man B. a foe
C. a weak man D. a strong man

Direction (Qs. No. 78 and 79): *Read the following poem and answer the questions set below it.*

She dwelt among the untrodden ways
Beside the spring of Dove;
A maid whom there were none to praise
And very few to love.

A violet by mossy stone
Half-hidden from the eye!
Fair as star when only one
is shining in the sky

78. What is the meaning of the word 'untrodden'?
A. Hidden B. Explicit
C. Unexplored D. Explored

79. Identify the correct figure of speech used in the second stanza.
A. Alliteration B. Simile
C. Metaphor D. Pun

80. Which of the following sentence/sentences is/are correct?
(*a*) There is few hope of his recovery.
(*b*) He showed few concern for his nephew.
(*c*) He showed little mercy to the vanquished.
A. (*a*), (*b*) and (*c*) B. None of the above
C. Only (*a*) D. Only (*c*)

81. Point out the sentence which is in past perfect tense.
A. We were listening to the radio all evening.
B. It was getting darker.
C. He studied many hours everyday.
D. I had written my letter before he arrived.

82. Fill in the blanks with the correct article:
Neil Armstrong was ______ first man to walk on ______ moon.
A. the, the B. an, a
C. a, the D. an, the

83. Fill in the blank in the following sentence:
The teacher has been teaching for ______ hour.
A. two B. three
C. a D. an

84. Add the right suffix to pluralize the word 'OX'.
A. – ies B. – s
C. – en D. – es

85. Change the word 'grow' into a noun by adding one of the suffixes given below.
A. – s B. – n
C. – ing D. – th

86. Which of the following alternatives is grammatically correct?
A. All these man are gentle.
B. All these mans are gentle.
C. All these men are gentle.
D. All this men are gentle.

87. Fill in the blank with appropriate preposition:
He came to me ______ midnight.
A. on B. upon
C. in D. at

88. Which of the following sentence ***does not*** have an adjective clause?
A. I met him where he li.ed.
B. I met him in Prayagraj which is a holy city.
C. The man who is truthful is loved by all.
D. I love the man who is truthful.

89. Fill in the blank with correct prepostion:
He is junior ______ me.
A. with B. to
C. than D. from

90. Fill in the blank with correct conjunction:
Either he is mad ______ he feigns madness.
A. nor B. or
C. and D. so

PART-IV

MATHEMATICS

91. Find Pythagorean triplet of which smallest number is 8.
A. 8, 9, 10 B. 8, 64, 512
C. 6, 8, 10 D. 8, 15, 17

92. Find the value of Z for which the number 417Z8 is divisible by 9.
A. 7 B. 9
C. 3 D. 6

93. If $2160 = 2^a \times 3^b \times 5^c$, then find the value of $3^a \times 2^{-b} \times 5^{-c}$.
A. $\frac{81}{40}$ B. $\frac{37}{39}$
C. $\frac{1}{2}$ D. 0

94. Find using side figure; the value of x is:

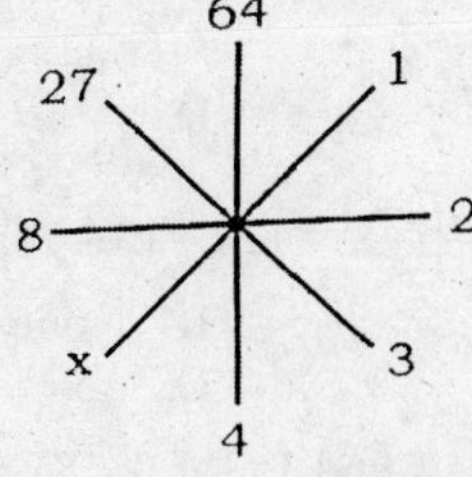

A. 5 B. 6
C. 0 D. 1

95. Mode of distribution can be obtained from:
A. More than type ogives
B. Frequency polygon
C. Histogram
D. Less than type ogives

96. The length of rectangle is increased by 60%. By what per cent would the width have to be decreased to maintain the same area?
A. 125% B. 37.5%
C. 50% D. 75.5%

97. The volume of a cube is numerically equal to sum of the length of its edges. The total surface area of cube in square units is:
A. 72.0 B. 44.2
C. 12.4 D. 64.5

98. Amit's salary in 2018 is ₹ 1,26,500. His salary for 2016 has risen annually by 10% and 15% respectively to reach 2018 salary figures. What was his salary in 2016?
A. ₹ 1,25,000 B. ₹ 1,00,000
C. ₹ 95,000 D. ₹ 1,15,000

99. The HCF of two numbers is 6 and their LCM is 432. If one of the number is 48, the other number is:
A. 42 B. 54
C. 52 D. 27

100. If third Friday is on 16th of month, then what will be the date of fourth (4th) Tuesday of same month?
A. 27 B. 29
C. 20 D. 22

101. Diagonal of a rectangular field is 17 metre and perimetre is 46 metre then area of the field will be:
A. 132 m^2 B. 289 m^2
C. 112 m^2 D. 120 m^2

102. On simplification $\{(2^{-1})\}^{-1}$, the number will be:
(*a*) Prime number (*b*) Even number
(*c*) Multiple of 2 (*d*) Odd number
A. (*a*), (*c*), (*d*) B. (*a*), (*b*), (*d*)
C. (*a*), (*b*), (*c*) D. (*b*), (*c*), (*d*)

103. Which one is correct in the following statements?
A. A composite number may be odd number.
B. Even prime number does not exist.
C. Sum of two prime numbers always prime number.
D. Least prime number is 1.

104. The difference between the interior and exterior angles of a regular polygon is 60°. The number of sides in the polygon is:
A. 6 B. 7
C. 4 D. 5

105. The number of points present on a straight line is:
A. 2 B. 1
C. infinite D. 0

106. If the length of a room is decreased by 10% and breadth is decreased by 20%, while height is increased by 5%, then what percentage changed in the volume of the room?
A. 24.4% B. 24.6%
C. 24% D. 24.2%

107. If length and breadth of a room is 15 m 17 cm and 9 m 2 cm respectively. What is the minimum number of square tiles which is fit for that?
A. 841 B. 840
C. 814 D. 820

108. Unit digit of the multiplication of $(2153)^{167}$ is:
A. 7 B. 9
C. 1 D. 3

109. If we increased 20% in numerator and 25% in denominator of a fraction then it is $\frac{3}{5}$, then the original fraction is
A. $\frac{8}{5}$ B. $\frac{8}{3}$
C. $\frac{3}{8}$ D. $\frac{5}{8}$

110. The numbers divisible by 8 are:
(*a*) 5240 (*b*) 5220
(*c*) 97128 (*d*) 97124
A. (*a*), (*c*) and (*d*) B. (*a*) and (*c*)
C. (*a*) and (*b*) D. (*b*) and (*c*)

111. How many vertices are there in a triangular prism?
A. 6 B. 8
C. 4 D. 5

112. What will be the loss percentage, if bananas purchased 6 for ₹ 10 and sold 4 for ₹ 6?
A. 5% B. 20%
C. 10% D. 6%

113. Which one is correct in the filling space?
1 gram = ______ kilogram.
(*a*) $\frac{1}{1000}$kg (*b*) 10^{-3} kg
(*c*) 0.0001 kg (*d*) 1000 kg
A. (*a*), (*b*) B. (*c*), (*d*)
C. (*b*), (*c*) D. (*a*), (*c*)

114. $(0.01)^2$ can be written in the percentage form
(*a*) 0.01% (*b*) $\frac{1}{100}$
(*c*) 1% (*d*) $\frac{1}{100}$%
A. (*b*), (*c*) B. (*a*), (*d*)
C. (*a*), (*b*) D. (*a*), (*c*)

115. If difference and product of two numbers are 5 and 36 respectively, then find the difference of their reciprocals.
A. $\frac{5}{9}$ B. $\frac{9}{5}$
C. $\frac{5}{36}$ D. $\frac{31}{36}$

116. If $\frac{a+b}{c}=\frac{b+c}{a}=\frac{c+a}{b}=$ K, then the value of K is:
A. $\frac{1}{2}$ B. $\frac{3}{2}$
C. 1 D. 2

117. The number of possible triangles with any three of the lengths 1.2 cm, 4.2 cm, 5.9 cm and 8.1 cm is:
A. Three B. Four
C. One D. Two

118. The denominator of a fraction is 1 more than double the numerator. On adding 2 to the numerator and subtracting 3 from the denominator, we obtain 1. Find the original fraction.
A. $\frac{2}{5}$ B. $\frac{1}{3}$
C. $\frac{4}{9}$ D. $\frac{1}{9}$

119. Simplify $(-9)-\{(-8)+(24\div\overline{13-7})\}$
A. –8 B. None of these
C. 5 D. –5

120. If HCF (*a*, 8) = 4 and LCM (*a*, 8) = 24, then '*a*' is:
A. 14 B. 8
C. 10 D. 12

PART-V

ENVIRONMENTAL STUDIES

121. In which of the following regions Reindeer are found?
A. Monsoon B. Taiga
C. Tundra D. Hot Desert

122. Which one of the following is ***not*** a temperate grassland?
A. Downs B. Prairies
C. Pampas D. Compas

123. According to population size, the largest Continent is:
A. Asia B. Africa
C. Europe D. North America

124. Where does Tharu tribe live in India?
A. Uttarakhand
B. Jharkhand
C. Thar Desert
D. Tarai region of Uttar Pradesh

125. Bhilai Steel Plant is situated in:
A. Chhattisgarh B. Odisha
C. Madhya Pradesh D. Jharkhand

126. Reservation for women in India is available in:
A. Cabinet
B. Panchayati Raj Institutions
C. Lok Sabha
D. Vidhan Sabha

127. In order to be appointed as the Governor of a State, one must have attained the age of:
A. 50 years B. 30 years
C. 35 years D. 45 years

128. Choose the right Code after comparing List–I with List–II.

List–I	List–II
(*a*) Indian Union	(*i*) Prime Minister
(*b*) State	(*ii*) Sarpanch
(*c*) Corporation	(*iii*) Governor
(*d*) Village Panchayat	(*iv*) Mayor

Codes:

	(*a*)	(*b*)	(*c*)	(*d*)
A.	(*i*)	(*iii*)	(*iv*)	(*ii*)
B.	(*iii*)	(*iv*)	(*i*)	(*ii*)
C.	(*iv*)	(*i*)	(*ii*)	(*iii*)
D.	(*ii*)	(*iii*)	(*iv*)	(*i*)

129. When and where, Article 356 was used first?
A. Jammu and Kashmir 1956
B. Madhya Pradesh 1957
C. Bihar 1958
D. Kerala 1959

130. Which tax can be imposed by Nagar Nigam?
A. Toll Tax B. All the above
C. Entertainment Tax D. House Tax

131. In 1853, India's first passenger train runs between:
A. Calcutta to Alipur B. Calcutta to Damdam
C. Bombay to Pune D. Bombay to Thane

132. Asia's largest cattle fair is organised at:
A. Pushkar B. Nasik
C. Haridwar D. Sonepur

133. National Integration Council was established in the year:
A. 1971 B. 1981
C. 1951 D. 1961

134. In which of the following Articles of Constitution, the Right to Equality are mentioned?
A. Articles 23 – 24 B. Articles 25 – 28
C. Articles 19 – 22 D. Articles 14 – 18

135. Which country has a flexible Constitution?
A. America B. United Kingdom
C. India D. China

136. Which is the example of sessile animal among following?
A. *Chiton* B. *Echinus*
C. *Euplectella* D. *Leech*

137. Unit of protein molecule is:
A. Amino acid B. Vitamin
C. Glucose D. Fatty acid

138. Which organelle is absent in plant cell?
A. Vacuoles B. Centrosome
C. Cellulose cell wall D. Plastids

139. Largest gland in human body is:
A. Adrenal Gland B. Liver
C. Pancreas D. Pituitary Gland

140. State bird of Uttar Pradesh is:
A. House Sparrow B. Parrot
C. Sarus Crane D. Peacock

141. Hamlet is associated with which settlement?
A. Linear B. Urban
C. Fragmented D. Rural

142. Which is volcano mountain?
A. Appalachian B. Kilimanjaro
C. Aravali D. Ural

143. Elephanta Island is located at:
A. Mumbai Coast B. Ganga Delta
C. Kutch Coast D. Goa Coast

144. Monsoon forests are found where rainfall is:
A. 50 – 150 cm B. 70 – 100 cm
C. 70 – 200 cm D. 150 – 200 cm

145. Karbi Anglong Plateau is an extension of:
A. Tibet B. Shan plateau
C. Peninsular plateau D. Himalaya

146. The world's most problematic aquatic weed, also known as "Terror of Bengal" is:
A. *Eichhornia Crassipes* (Water hyacinth)
B. *Cynodone dactylon* (Doob grass)
C. *Lantana Camara*
D. *Parthenium hysterophorus* (Congress grass)

147. The abiotic property of virus is:
A. It cannot reproduce
B. It can be crystalized
C. It does not have the genetic material
D. It does not have protein

148. Plant hormone that help in the ripening of fruits is:
A. Cytokinin B. Ethylene
C. Auxin D. Gibberellins

149. Free living, anaerobic, nitrogen (N_2) fixing bacteria found in soil is:
A. Clostridium B. Vibrio
C. Azotobacter D. Rhizobium

150. Which type of DNA is commonly found inside the cell?
A. B-DNA B. Z-DNA
C. A-DNA D. C-DNA

ANSWERS

1	2	3	4	5	6	7	8	9	10
D	B	A	D	B	B	A	B	C	A
11	**12**	**13**	**14**	**15**	**16**	**17**	**18**	**19**	**20**
C	D	A	A	D	A	D	A	A	B
21	**22**	**23**	**24**	**25**	**26**	**27**	**28**	**29**	**30**
C	D	A	D	B	C	C	D	D	A
31	**32**	**33**	**34**	**35**	**36**	**37**	**38**	**39**	**40**
A	D	D	A	C	C	D	D	D	A
41	**42**	**43**	**44**	**45**	**46**	**47**	**48**	**49**	**50**
A	C	B	A	C	A	B	A	D	B
51	**52**	**53**	**54**	**55**	**56**	**57**	**58**	**59**	**60**
C	C	D	C	B	B	B	B	D	C
61	**62**	**63**	**64**	**65**	**66**	**67**	**68**	**69**	**70**
A	B	B	A	A	C	C	D	C	C
71	**72**	**73**	**74**	**75**	**76**	**77**	**78**	**79**	**80**
B	B	B	D	A	A	D	C	B	D
81	**82**	**83**	**84**	**85**	**86**	**87**	**88**	**89**	**90**
D	A	D	C	D	C	D	A	B	B
91	**92**	**93**	**94**	**95**	**96**	**97**	**98**	**99**	**100**
D	A	A	D	C	B	A	B	B	A
101	**102**	**103**	**104**	**105**	**106**	**107**	**108**	**109**	**110**
D	C	A	A	C	A	C	A	D	B
111	**112**	**113**	**114**	**115**	**116**	**117**	**118**	**119**	**120**
A	C	A	B	C	D	C	C	D	D
121	**122**	**123**	**124**	**125**	**126**	**127**	**128**	**129**	**130**
C	D	A	D	A	B	C	A	D	B
131	**132**	**133**	**134**	**135**	**136**	**137**	**138**	**139**	**140**
D	D	D	D	B	C	A	B	B	C
141	**142**	**143**	**144**	**145**	**146**	**147**	**148**	**149**	**150**
D	B	A	C	C	A	B	B	A	A

EXPLANATORY ANSWERS

1. Human development starts from the pre-natal stage, because development begins at conception inside the mother's womb. Physical growth and basic biological development begin before birth. Therefore, infancy is not the first stage of human development; it comes after birth.

2. 'The Conditions of Learning" was written by Robert M. Gagne. He is known for his theory of learning conditions and hierarchy of learning. His work explains different types of learning and the instructional conditions needed for them.

3. The statement that adolescence is a period of great "stress, strain, storm and strike" is associated with Stanley Hall. He described adolescence as a turbulent transitional stage. According to him, this period involves emotional instability, conflict, and rapid developmental changes.

4. In the Indian model of micro-teaching, the total time generally taken is 36 minutes. It includes planning, teaching, feedback, re-planning, re-teaching, and re-feedback. This cycle helps trainee teachers improve one teaching skill at a time.

5. Ross stated that plateaus of learning are a characteristic feature of the learning process. A learning plateau refers to a stage where progress temporarily stops despite continued practice. It does not mean learning has ended; improvement may resume after proper guidance or renewed effort.

6. If a teacher finds a problematic child in the class, the best step is to provide counselling. Punishment, ignoring, or sending the child home does not solve the root cause. Counselling helps understand the child's emotional, social, or learning-related difficulties.

7. Co-curricular activities are mainly related to the all-round development of students. They support physical, social, emotional, moral, and creative growth along with academic learning. Activities like sports, debate, drama, music, and clubs help develop personality.

8. B.S. Bloom is mainly associated with Bloom's Taxonomy of educational objectives, not with propounding a learning theory. Skinner, Thorndike, and Kohler are directly associated with learning theories. Therefore, Bloom is the one who did not propound a learning theory among the given options.

9. Stagnation in education means a child remains in the same class for more than one academic year. It usually happens when the child fails to progress to the next class. It is different from dropout or non-enrolment.

10. Testing of previous knowledge comes under the skill of introduction. A teacher uses this skill at the beginning of a lesson to connect new content with what students already know. This creates readiness, interest, and a proper base for learning the new topic.

11. The concept of multiple intelligences was given by Howard Gardner. He proposed that intelligence is not a single general ability but consists of different types like linguistic, logical-mathematical, spatial, musical, etc. This theory broadened the understanding of human capabilities beyond traditional IQ.

12. Dyslexia is a specific learning disorder mainly related to difficulty in reading and spelling. Children with dyslexia may struggle with word recognition, decoding, and writing. It is not related to intelligence but to language processing difficulties.

13. In an inclusive classroom, ignoring differently abled children is not the role of a teacher. Instead, teachers must provide equal opportunities and support to all learners. Inclusion requires sensitivity, adaptation, and active involvement of the teacher.

14. Questioning by students should be encouraged in the classroom. It promotes curiosity, critical thinking, and active participation. It also helps the teacher understand students' thinking and clarify doubts effectively.

15. Growth of a child is mainly related to physical development. Growth refers to measurable changes like height, weight, and body structure. Development, on the other hand, includes qualitative aspects like emotional, social, and moral growth.

16. J.P. Guilford defined learning as a change in behaviour resulting from behaviour itself. This definition highlights that an individual's actions and experiences directly bring about modification in future behaviour patterns. It focuses on the idea that behaviour acts as both the cause and result of learning.

    Guilford's perspective differs from strict behaviorists by linking behavioural change with internal cognitive processing, yet the wording of the statement exactly matches his definition.

17. Bruner is associated with the concept attainment model, Ausubel with the advance organiser model, Glasser with the basic teaching model, and Gordon with the synectics teaching model. These models represent different approaches to teaching and learning processes.

18. The first step in problem solving is identifying the problem. Without clearly defining the problem, further steps like hypothesis formulation or data collection cannot be effectively carried out. It sets the direction for the entire process.

19. Learning is most effective when all three domains-cognitive (thinking), affective (feeling), and psychomotor (doing)-are developed. This ensures holistic education. Limiting learning to only one domain reduces effectiveness.

20. In both memory level and understanding level teaching models, presentation is a prominent step. It involves organizing and delivering content to students. This step ensures that learners receive information clearly before processing or applying it further.

21. Theory of Reinforcement is directly associated with Operant Conditioning given by B.F. Skinner. This theory explains that behaviour is strengthened or weakened through reinforcement and punishment. Learning occurs when responses are followed by satisfying consequences, making reinforcement central to the process.

22. Bruner's Cognitive Development Theory includes three stages-Enactive (action-based), Iconic (image-based), and Symbolic (language-based). Intuitive stage is not a part of Bruner's stages; it is more related to Piaget's theory. Hence, it is the correct option.

23. Morrison's understanding-level teaching model follows the sequence: Exploration, Presentation, Assimilation, Organisation, and Recitation. First, the teacher explores previous knowledge and readiness, then presents the new content clearly. After that, students assimilate the content, organise it meaningfully, and finally recite or express what they have understood.

24. The cognitive domain includes knowledge, understanding, application, analysis, synthesis, and evaluation. Valuing belongs to the affective domain, which deals with emotions, attitudes, and values. Therefore, it is not part of the cognitive domain.

25. Learning curves generally include concave, convex, and combination types, showing different patterns of progress. Longitudinal is a research method used to study changes over time, not a type of learning curve. Hence, it is not related to learning curves.

26. Animal Intelligence is associated with Thorndike, Schedule of reinforcement with Skinner, Law of Pragnanz with Gestalt psychology, and Adaptation with Piaget. These pairings correctly match the contributions of each psychologist to their respective concepts.

27. The statement "Development is a never ending process" reflects the principle of continuity. Development begins at conception and continues throughout life without stopping. It highlights that growth and development are ongoing and progressive processes.

28. Education became a fundamental right in India through the 86th Constitutional Amendment Act, 2002. It inserted Article 21A, making free and compulsory education a right for children aged 6 to 14 years.

29. The Instinct Theory of motivation was propounded by William McDougall. He emphasized that human behaviour is driven by innate instincts. These instincts act as internal forces motivating individuals to act in certain ways.

30. Cole and Bruce described childhood as a unique stage of emotional development because it is the period when basic emotional patterns are formed and shaped. During this stage, children begin to understand, express, and regulate their emotions in response to family and social environment.

It is considered unique because it lays the foundation for later emotional maturity, including development of self-concept, emotional control, and social behaviour, which continue to evolve in later stages of life.

31. 'खेत' शब्द तद्भव है क्योंकि यह संस्कृत के 'क्षेत्र' से विकसित हुआ है। तद्भव शब्द वे होते हैं जो समय के साथ ध्वनि परिवर्तन के माध्यम से प्राकृत और अपभ्रंश से होते हुए आधुनिक भाषा में आए हैं। 'प्रभु', 'नाथ' और 'त्रिकुटी' तत्सम शब्द हैं क्योंकि वे सीधे संस्कृत से लिए गए हैं।

32. 'धड़ाम' देशज शब्द है क्योंकि यह स्थानीय बोलचाल से उत्पन्न ध्वन्यात्मक शब्द है और किसी विदेशी या संस्कृत स्रोत से नहीं लिया गया है। 'लाश' (फारसी), 'औरत' (अरबी) और 'पतलून' (अंग्रेजी) विदेशी मूल के शब्द हैं।

33. 'छछूँदर के सिर पर चमेली का तेल' का अर्थ है किसी अयोग्य व्यक्ति को मूल्यवान वस्तु देना। इसमें व्यंग्यात्मक भाव है कि जो व्यक्ति योग्य नहीं है, वह उस चीज का सही उपयोग या महत्व नहीं समझ पाएगा।

34. 'ऋग्वेद' का सन्धि-विच्छेद 'ऋक् + वेद' होता है। यहाँ 'क' और 'व' के मेल से 'ग्व' ध्वनि बनती है। यह व्यंजन सन्धि का उदाहरण है।

35. 'आपबीती' में तत्पुरुष समास है, जिसका अर्थ है 'अपने ऊपर बीती हुई बात'। इसमें 'आप' (स्वयं) और 'बीती' (घटित घटना) का संबंध स्पष्ट होता है, जहाँ दूसरा पद प्रधान होता है।

36. 'घोंसले में चिड़िया है' वाक्य में 'घोंसले में' स्थान का बोध कराता है, इसलिए यह अधिकरण कारक है। अधिकरण कारक उस स्थान को दर्शाता है जहाँ क्रिया घटित होती है।

37. गद्यांश में स्पष्ट कहा गया है कि आज के अधिकांश वाद केवल राजनीतिक क्षेत्र तक सीमित हो गए हैं। उनका आत्मा से संबंध समाप्त हो गया है और वे केवल बाह्य संसार तक सीमित रह गए हैं।

38. गद्यांश की शुरुआत में ही स्पष्ट रूप से कहा गया है कि गांधीवाद में राजनीतिक और आध्यात्मिक तत्वों का समन्वय मिलता है और यही इसकी प्रमुख विशेषता है। यह दर्शाता है कि गांधीवाद केवल राजनीति तक सीमित नहीं है बल्कि उसमें आध्यात्मिक मूल्यों का भी समावेश है। इसी समन्वय के कारण गांधीवाद अन्य वादों से अलग है, क्योंकि यह बाह्य (राजनीतिक) और आंतरिक (आध्यात्मिक) दोनों पक्षों को संतुलित रूप से महत्व देता है।

39. 'कनुप्रिया' के रचनाकार धर्मवीर भारती हैं। यह एक प्रसिद्ध काव्य कृति है जिसमें राधा और कृष्ण के प्रेम को आधुनिक दृष्टिकोण से प्रस्तुत किया गया है। इसमें राधा की भावनाओं और आंतरिक संघर्ष को गहराई से व्यक्त किया गया है।

40. प्लुत स्वर वह होता है जिसका उच्चारण तीन मात्राओं तक खींचकर किया जाता है। 'ओउम्' में दीर्घ से भी अधिक लंबा उच्चारण होता है, इसलिए यह प्लुत स्वर का उदाहरण है। यह विशेष रूप से वैदिक उच्चारण में प्रयोग होता है।

41. डॉ. हरिवंश राय बच्चन की रचनाओं का प्रकाशन क्रम इसी प्रकार है। 'मधुशाला' सबसे पहले प्रकाशित हुई, इसके बाद 'मधुबाला', फिर 'मधुकलश' और अंत में 'निशा निमन्त्रण' प्रकाशित हुई। यह क्रम उनके काव्य विकास को भी दर्शाता है।

42. हिन्दी साहित्य सम्मेलन की स्थापना 1910 में हुई, काशी नागरी प्रचारिणी सभा की स्थापना 1893 में हुई, और राष्ट्रभाषा प्रचार समिति, वर्धा की स्थापना 1918 में हुई। इसलिए सही मिलान *(a)*-*(iii)*, *(b)*-*(i)*, *(c)*-*(ii)* है।

43. 'तुलसीदास' नामक कृति के रचनाकार सूर्यकान्त त्रिपाठी 'निराला' हैं। यह काव्य कृति तुलसीदास के जीवन और उनके व्यक्तित्व को प्रस्तुत करती है, जिसमें उनके संघर्ष और आध्यात्मिकता का चित्रण मिलता है।

44. 'अन्या से अनन्या' प्रसिद्ध लेखिका प्रभा खेतान की आत्मकथा है। इस कृति में उन्होंने अपने निजी जीवन, संघर्ष, संबंधों और आत्मनिर्भरता की यात्र का विस्तृत वर्णन किया है। यह नारी-चेतना और आत्मबोध की महत्वपूर्ण रचना मानी जाती है।

45. ''प्रभु जी तुम चंदन हम पानी'' संत रैदास का प्रसिद्ध पद है। इसमें भक्त और भगवान के संबंध को अत्यंत विनम्रता और भक्ति भाव से व्यक्त किया गया है। रैदास ने इसमें समर्पण और आध्यात्मिक प्रेम का सुंदर चित्रण किया है।

46. प्रस्तुत पद्यांश में बाल स्वरूप का अत्यंत स्नेहपूर्ण और कोमल चित्रण किया गया है, जैसे दाँतों की पंक्ति, अधरों की कोमलता, लटों का लटकना और विशेष रूप से ''ललाइन बोलन'' का उल्लेख। यह सब एक बालक की निश्छलता और आकर्षण को दर्शाता है। जहाँ बालक के रूप, हाव-भाव और बोलचाल पर स्नेह व्यक्त किया जाता है तथा उस पर न्योछावर होने की भावना प्रकट होती है, वहाँ वात्सल्य रस होता है। अतः इस पद्यांश में प्रमुख रूप से वात्सल्य रस ही व्यक्त हुआ है।

47. पद्य में 'तुलसी' शब्द का प्रयोग अंत में हुआ है, जो कवि का संकेत है। यह तुलसीदास की रचना है, जिसमें उन्होंने सौंदर्य का काव्यात्मक वर्णन किया है। उनके काव्य में भक्ति के साथ-साथ अलंकारिक सौंदर्य भी मिलता है।

48. 'स' का उच्चारण दन्त्य स्थान से होता है, जहाँ जीभ दाँतों के पास रहती है। अन्य विकल्प गलत हैं क्योंकि 'च' तालव्य होता है, 'ष' मूर्धन्य होता है और 'श' तालव्य होता है। इसलिए 'स – दन्त्य' सही है।

49. यह कथन अशुद्ध है क्योंकि दो महाप्राण व्यंजनों का एक साथ उच्चारण सामान्यतः संभव नहीं होता। अन्य कथन सही हैं जैसे 'क्ष' संयुक्त व्यंजन है और विसर्ग कंठ्य वर्ण है।

50. वाक्य में 'लड़के' एकवचन कर्ता है, जो पुल्लिंग है। यहाँ 'लड़के' शब्द एकवचन रूप में प्रयुक्त हुआ है, न कि बहुवचन में। इसलिए 'बहुवचन' विकल्प अशुद्ध है।

51. वाक्य ''राम आम खाता है'' में कर्ता 'राम' स्वयं क्रिया कर रहा है। यहाँ क्रिया का कार्य सीधे कर्ता द्वारा किया जा रहा है और उसी पर जोर है। इसलिए यह कर्तृवाच्य का उदाहरण है जहाँ कर्ता प्रधान होता है।

52. इस दोहे में 'पानी' शब्द का विभिन्न अर्थों में प्रयोग हुआ है—जैसे जल, मान-सम्मान और जीवन। एक ही शब्द से अनेक अर्थ निकलते हैं, जो श्लेष अलंकार की विशेषता है। इसलिए यहाँ श्लेष अलंकार विद्यमान है।

53. 'अंगना' शब्द की वर्तनी शुद्ध है। अन्य विकल्पों में वर्तनी दोष है जैसे 'चांद' की जगह 'चाँद', 'आंख' की जगह 'आँख', और 'अँक' की जगह 'अंक' सही रूप होता है। इसलिए 'अंगना' सही विकल्प है।

54. 'सन्निधि' शब्द की वर्तनी शुद्ध है। इसका अर्थ है 'निकटता' या 'पास होना'। अन्य विकल्पों में वर्तनी की त्रुटि है जैसे 'सम्निधि', 'सन्निधी', और 'संनिधि' अशुद्ध रूप हैं।

55. उपचारात्मक शिक्षण की सफलता इस बात पर निर्भर करती है कि विद्यार्थी की समस्या का वास्तविक कारण क्या है। जब कारण सही पहचाना जाता है, तभी उचित समाधान दिया जा सकता है। इसलिए यह सबसे महत्वपूर्ण आधार है।

56. 'प्रयोजन' का अर्थ उद्देश्य, हेतु या लक्ष्य होता है। 'नियोजन' का अर्थ योजना बनाना या व्यवस्थित करना होता है, जो 'प्रयोजन' का समानार्थी नहीं है। इसलिए यह सही उत्तर है।

57. 'ऋजु' का अर्थ सीधा या सरल होता है। इसका विलोम 'वक्र' है, जिसका अर्थ टेढ़ा या मुड़ा हुआ होता है। इसलिए 'वक्र' इसका सही विपरीतार्थक शब्द है।

58. 'वह नौकर' में 'वह' एक संकेतवाचक विशेषण है, जो 'नौकर' की विशेषता बता रहा है। इसलिए यह कहना कि इसमें कोई विशेषण नहीं है, अशुद्ध है। बाकी सभी विकल्पों में विशेषण का निर्देश सही है।

59. वाक्य ''आप भला तो जग भला'' में 'आप' शब्द का प्रयोग स्वयं के लिए किया गया है। यह व्यक्ति को स्वयं की ओर संकेत करता है और आत्म-सम्बन्ध को दर्शाता है। इसलिए यहाँ निजवाचक सर्वनाम का बोध होता है, जो अपने ही व्यक्ति की ओर संकेत करता है।

60. 'संतान' शब्द का प्रयोग व्याकरणिक दृष्टि से सामान्यतः पुल्लिंग के रूप में किया जाता है, जैसे–''उसकी संतान बहुत योग्य है''। यद्यपि यह उभयलिंगी अर्थ में प्रयुक्त हो सकता है, पर मानक हिन्दी में इसे पुल्लिंग माना जाता है। अन्य विकल्पों में 'कढ़ी' और 'सरसों' स्त्रीलिंग शब्द हैं, जबकि 'चील' भी नित्य स्त्रीलिंग माना जाता है। इसलिए दिए गए विकल्पों में 'संतान' ही पुल्लिंग शब्द के रूप में उपयुक्त है।

61. 'if' is not a co-ordinating conjunction; it is a subordinating conjunction used to introduce conditional clauses. Co-ordinating conjunctions like 'for', 'and', and 'but' join clauses of equal importance. Hence, 'if' does not belong to this group.

62. The correct sentence is "His thirst for knowledge left him no leisure for anything else." The preposition 'for' correctly expresses purpose or desire in both blanks. It is the standard and grammatically accepted usage.

63. In the sentence "He is a fast writer", the word 'fast' describes the noun 'writer'. Therefore, it functions as an adjective. It tells us about the quality or characteristic of the writer.

64. This is not a simple sentence because it contains a subordinate clause "what she likes". A simple sentence has only one clause, while this one has more than one. Hence, it is a complex sentence.

65. The sentence "He will be playing the piano in the concert day after tomorrow" is in future continuous (future imperfect) tense. It indicates an action that will be in progress at a specific time in the future. The structure "will be + verb-ing" confirms this.

66. The subject 'female members' clearly indicates feminine gender. Other options refer to masculine groups like 'men' or 'male members'. Hence, this is the correct choice.

67. In the direct method, the teacher directly associates words of the foreign language with objects or actions without using the mother tongue. This method emphasizes natural learning similar to first language acquisition. Translation is avoided in this approach.

68. Testing comprehension of written English means checking how well students understand what they have read. It evaluates their reading skills and ability to interpret written material. Therefore, 'read' is the correct answer.

69. The verb "listen" is always followed by the preposition "to" when referring to a person or thing being heard. Other options use incorrect prepositions or omit it entirely. Therefore, "listen to" is the correct grammatical structure.

70. This sentence is correct because "believe" is a stative verb and is generally not used in continuous tense. The sentence "I am not believing him" is grammatically incorrect. Hence, only option C is correct.

71. This sentence is in passive voice because the subject 'my watch' is receiving the action. The verb form "was lost" indicates that the action happened to the subject. Other sentences are in active voice.

72. The imperative sentence "Do it" changes into passive as "Let it be done". This structure is commonly used to express commands in passive voice. Other options do not correctly reflect the imperative passive form.

73. 'Criteria' is the plural form of 'criterion'. The other words-analysis, index, and crisis-are singular forms. Hence, 'criteria' is the correct plural noun.

74. 'Mice' is the plural form of 'mouse'. Other words like 'news', 'billiards', and 'electronics' appear plural in form but are treated as singular nouns in usage. Therefore, 'mice' is the correct answer.

75. The word 'orphan' can refer to both male and female without distinction. It does not specify gender, so it is classified as common gender. Hence, this is the correct option.

76. 'Strength' refers to a quality or state rather than a physical object. It cannot be seen or touched and represents an idea. Therefore, it is an abstract noun.

77. The passage clearly states that forgiveness is a sign of strength. A person who does not take revenge shows control and strong character. Hence, such a person is described as strong.

78. The word 'untrodden' means not walked upon or not visited. It refers to a place that has not been explored or traveled. Therefore, 'unexplored' is the correct meaning.

79. In the second stanza, comparison is made using the word "as" in expressions like "Fair as a star". This clearly shows a comparison between two unlike things. Such comparison using "as" or "like" is called a simile.

80. Sentence (c) is correct because "little" is used with uncountable nouns like "mercy". Sentences (a) and (b) are incorrect because "few" is used with countable nouns, whereas "hope" and "concern" require "little" in this context.

81. This sentence is in past perfect tense as it uses "had written". It indicates that one action was completed before another action in the past. The structure "had + past participle" confirms past perfect tense.

82. The correct sentence is "Neil Armstrong was the first man to walk on the moon". The definite article "the" is used before "first" and also before "moon" because it refers to something specific and unique.

83. The word "hour" begins with a vowel sound, so "an" is used instead of "a". Hence, the correct sentence is "The teacher has been teaching for an hour".

84. The plural of "ox" is "oxen," which is formed by adding the suffix "-en". This is an irregular plural form in English.

85. Adding "-th" to "grow" forms the noun "growth". This suffix changes the verb into a noun indicating the result or process.

86. "Men" is the correct plural form of "man", and it agrees with "these". The sentence is grammatically correct in number and structure.

87. The preposition "at" is used for specific points of time such as "midnight". Hence, the correct sentence is "He came to me at midnight".

88. This sentence does not contain an adjective clause; it has an adverbial clause of place ("where he lived"). The other sentences contain adjective clauses that describe a noun.

89. The correct usage is "junior to", not "junior than" or others. Therefore, the correct sentence is "He is junior to me".

90. The correct conjunction with "either" is "or". Hence, the correct sentence is "Either he is mad or he feigns madness".

91. A Pythagorean triplet must satisfy $a^2 + b^2 = c^2$.
Here, $8^2 + 15^2 = 64 + 225 = 289 = 17^2$.
So, the triplet with the smallest number 8 is 8, 15, 17.

92. If sum of all digits of any number is divisible by 9 then, the number is divisible by 9
$\because$ 417Z8 is divisible by 9
$\therefore$ 4 + 1 + 7 + Z + 8 is divisible by 9
$\therefore$ 20 + Z is divisible by 9
Z = 7
then 27 is divisible by 9.

93. Given, $2160 = 2^a \times 3^b \times 5^c$

$\Rightarrow \quad 2^4 \times 3^3 \times 5^1 = 2^a \times 3^b \times 5^c$

$\therefore a = 4, b = 3, c = 1$

$\therefore \quad 3^a \times 2^{-b} \times 5^{-c} = 3^4 \times 2^{-3} \times 5^{-1}$

$$= \frac{3^4}{2^3 \times 5^1} = \frac{81}{40}.$$

94. By using side figure:
$\because 1^3 = 1$
$\therefore x = 1$
$2^3 = 8$
$3^3 = 27$
$4^3 = 64.$

95. Mode of a distribution can be obtained graphically from a histogram. In a grouped frequency distribution, the modal class is identified from the tallest rectangle. Then the mode can be estimated using the histogram method.

96. Required % $= \frac{60}{160} \times 100\%$

$$= \frac{3}{8} \times 100\% = \frac{300}{8}\%$$

$$= 37\frac{1}{2}\% = 37.5\%.$$

97. Let the length of edge of a cube = x unit
Then, volume = x^3 unit cube
and the sum of the length of its edge = $12x$ unit
$\therefore x^3 = 12x$
$\Rightarrow x^2 = 12$
The total surface area of cube = $6(\text{edge})^2$
$= 6x^2 = 6 \times 12$
$= 72$ square units.

98. Let Amit's salary was ₹ x in 2016

Then, $x\left(1+\frac{10}{100}\right)\left(1+\frac{15}{100}\right) = 1,26,500$

$\Rightarrow \quad x \times \frac{11}{10} \times \frac{23}{20} = 1,26,500$

$\Rightarrow \quad x = \frac{1,26,500}{11 \times 23}$

$$= \frac{11500}{23} \times 10 \times 20$$

$= 500 \times 200 = 1,00,000$

$\Rightarrow \quad x =$ ₹ 1,00,000.

99. Given, HCF = 6, LCM = 432
and one of the number = 48
$\because$ one number × the other number = LCM × HCF
$\therefore$ 48 × the other number = 432 × 6

$\Rightarrow$ the other number $= \frac{432 \times 6}{48} = \frac{432}{8} = 54.$

100. Given, third Friday is on 16th of month
$\therefore$ First Friday = 16 – 14 = 2nd of month
$\therefore$ First Tuesday = 2 + 4 = 6th of month
$\therefore$ 4th Tuesday = 6 + 21 = 27th of month.

101. Length = l and breadth = b

$\therefore$ $l^2 + b^2 = 17^2$
$\Rightarrow$ $l^2 + b^2 = 289$ m
and $2(l + b) = 46$ m
$\Rightarrow$ $l + b = 23$ m
$\because$ $(l + b)^2 = l^2 + b^2 + 2lb$
$\therefore$ $(23)^2 = 289 + 2lb$
$\Rightarrow$ $529 - 289 = 2lb$
$\Rightarrow$ $2lb = 240$
$\Rightarrow$ $lb = 120$ m^2.

Hence, area of rectangular field = lb = 120 m^2.

102. $\{(2^{-1})\}^{-1} = \left\{\frac{1}{2}\right\}^{-1} = \left(\frac{1}{2}\right)^{-1} = \frac{1}{2^{-1}} = 2$

The number (2) will be
(*a*) Prime number
(*b*) Even number
(*c*) Multiple of 2

103. A composite number has more than two factors, and it may be odd, such as 9, 15, 21, etc. Option B is not accepted because 2 is an even prime number. The least prime number is 2, not 1.

104. In a regular polygon, exterior angle $= \frac{360°}{n}$, and

interior angle $= 180° - \frac{360°}{n}$.

Given difference = 60°:

$$180° - \frac{360°}{n} - \frac{360°}{n} = 60°$$

$$180° - \frac{720°}{n} = 60°$$

$$\frac{720°}{n} = 120°$$

$$n = 6.$$

105. A straight line extends endlessly in both directions. Therefore, it contains infinitely many points. It cannot be limited to 0, 1, or 2 points.

106. The volume of a room = lbh

Change volume $= \frac{9}{10}l \times \frac{80}{100}b \times \frac{105}{100}h$

$= \frac{9}{10}l \times \frac{4}{5}b \times \frac{21}{20}h = \frac{189}{250}lbh$

Now, change in the volume of the room

$= lbh - \frac{189}{250}lbh = \frac{61}{250}lbh$

$\therefore$ % change $= \dfrac{\frac{61}{250}lbh}{lbh} \times 100\%$

$= \frac{61}{5} \times 2\% = \frac{122}{5}\% = 24.4\%.$

107. Given, l = 15 m 17 cm = 1517 cm
and breadth = 9 m 2 cm = 902 cm
$\because$ Maximum size of square tile
= HCF of length and breadth

```
902 | 1517 | 1
    | -902 |
      615  | 902 | 1
           | -615|
             287 | 615 | 2
                 | -574|
                    41 | 287 | 7
                       | -287|
                         ×××
```

$\because$ HCF = 41 cm
$\therefore$ Maximum size of each tile = 41 cm
Minimum number of square tiles

$= \frac{\text{Area of room}}{\text{Area of each tiles}}$

$= \frac{1517 \times 902}{41 \times 41}$

= 37 × 22 = 814.

108. $\because$ $(2153)^{167} = (2153)^{41 \times 4 + 3}$

$= \{(2153)^4\}^{41} \times (2153)^3$

Unit digit of $\{(2153)^4\}41$ = 1
and unit digit of $(2153)^3$ = 7
$\therefore$ Unit digit of the multiplication of $(2153)^{167}$
= 1 × 7 = 7.

109. Let the original fraction $= \frac{x}{y}$

Then, $\dfrac{x \times \frac{120}{100}}{y \times \frac{125}{100}} = \frac{3}{5}$

$\Rightarrow$ $\frac{x}{y} = \frac{3}{5} \times \frac{125}{120} = \frac{25}{40} = \frac{5}{8}$

$\Rightarrow$ $\frac{x}{y} = \frac{5}{8}.$

110. If three digits from right side of any number are zero or multiple of 8

Then, the number will be divisible by 8

So, (*i*) 5240 and (*iii*) 97128 are divisible by 8.

111. A triangular prism has two triangular bases.

Each triangular base has 3 vertices.

Therefore, total vertices = 3 + 3 = 6.

112. Here, cost price of 1 banana = $₹\frac{10}{6} = ₹\frac{5}{3}$

and the selling price of 1 banana = $₹\frac{6}{4} = ₹\frac{3}{2}$

$$\text{Loss} = \text{CP} - \text{SP}$$
$$= \frac{5}{3} - \frac{3}{2} = \frac{10-9}{6} = \frac{1}{6}$$
$$\text{Loss\%} = \frac{\text{loss} \times 100}{\text{CP}}$$
$$= \frac{\frac{1}{6} \times 100}{\frac{5}{3}} = \frac{100}{6} \times \frac{3}{5} = 10\%.$$

113. $\because$ 1000 gram = 1 kg

$\therefore$ 1 gram = $\frac{1}{1000}$ kg = $\frac{1}{10^3}$ kg = 10^{-3} kg.

114. The percentage form

$$= (0.01)^2 \times 100\% = .0001 \times 100\%$$
$$= 00.0100\% = .0100\%$$
$$= .01\% = \frac{1}{100}\%.$$

115. Let the two numbers are x and y

Then, $x - y = 5$ ...(*i*)

and $xy = 36$

$\because$ $(x + y)^2 = (x - y)^2 + 4xy$

$\Rightarrow$ $(x + y)^2 = 5^2 + 4(36)$

$\Rightarrow$ $(x + y)^2 = 25 + 144$

$\Rightarrow$ $(x + y)^2 = 169 = 13^2$

$\Rightarrow$ $x + y = 13$ ...(*ii*)

Adding (*i*) and (*ii*), we get

$2x = 18$

$\Rightarrow$ $x = 9$

From (*i*), when $x = 9$, then $y = 4$

$\therefore$ $\frac{1}{x} - \frac{1}{y} = \frac{1}{9} - \frac{1}{4} = \frac{4-9}{36} = -\frac{5}{36}$

and $\frac{1}{y} - \frac{1}{x} = \frac{1}{4} - \frac{1}{9} = \frac{9-4}{36} = \frac{5}{36}.$

116. Given, $\frac{a+b}{c} = \frac{b+c}{a} = \frac{c+a}{b} = \text{K}$

$\therefore$ $a + b = c\text{K}$ ...(*i*)

$b + c = a\text{K}$ ...(*ii*)

$c + a = b\text{K}$ ...(*iii*)

From adding (*i*), (*ii*) and (*iii*), we get

$a + b + b + c + c + a = c\text{K} + a\text{K} + b\text{K}$

$\Rightarrow$ $2(a + b + c) = \text{K}(a + b + c)$

$\Rightarrow$ $2 = \text{K}$

Hence, K = 2.

117. For three lengths to form a triangle, the sum of any two smaller sides must be greater than the third side. Testing the possible sets, only 4.2 + 5.9 > 8.1, so 4.2, 5.9, 8.1 forms a triangle.

Hence, only one triangle is possible.

118. Let numarator = x

then denominator = $2x + 1$

$\therefore$ $\frac{x+2}{2x+1-3} = 1$

$\Rightarrow$ $x + 2 = 2x - 2$

$\Rightarrow$ $x = 2 + 2$

$= 4$

Then, original fraction

$$= \frac{x}{2x+1} = \frac{4}{2 \times 4 + 1} = \frac{4}{9}.$$

119. $(-9) - \{(-8) + (24 \div \overline{13 - 7})\}$

$= (-9) - \{(-8) + (24 \div 6)\}$

$= (-9) - \{(-8) + 4\}$

$= -9 + 4 = -5.$

120. $\because$ First number × second number = HCF × LCM

$\therefore$ $a \times 8 = 4 \times 24$

$\Rightarrow$ $a = \frac{4 \times 24}{8}$

$\Rightarrow$ $a = 4 \times 3 = 12$

$\Rightarrow$ $a = 12.$

121. Reindeer are mainly found in the Tundra region. This region has very cold climatic conditions and sparse vegetation. Reindeer are adapted to cold environments and are common in Arctic and sub-Arctic areas.

122. Prairies, Pampas, and Downs are temperate grasslands. "Campos" are tropical grasslands mainly found in Brazil, and "Compas" appears to refer to that. Hence, it is not a temperate grassland.

123. Asia is the largest continent according to population size. It contains countries like China, India, Indonesia, Pakistan, and Bangladesh, which together have a very large share of the world's population.

124. The Tharu tribe mainly lives in the Tarai region of Uttar Pradesh, especially near the India-Nepal border. They are also found in adjoining Terai areas. Their settlement is closely associated with forested and lowland regions.

125. Bhilai Steel Plant is situated in Bhilai, Chhattisgarh. It is one of India's major integrated steel plants. It was established with Soviet collaboration and is important for India's iron and steel industry.

126. In India, reservation for women is constitutionally provided in Panchayati Raj Institutions through the 73rd Constitutional Amendment. At least one-third of seats are reserved for women to ensure their participation in local self-government.

127. According to the Constitution of India, a person must be at least 35 years old to be appointed as the Governor of a State. This condition ensures maturity and experience for holding such a high constitutional office.

128. Indian Union is headed by the Prime Minister, State by the Governor, Corporation by the Mayor, and Village Panchayat by the Sarpanch. These are the respective executive heads at different administrative levels.

129. Article 356 was first used in Kerala in 1959 when the elected government was dismissed. This provision allows the central government to impose President's Rule in a state under certain conditions.

130. Nagar Nigam (Municipal Corporation) has the authority to impose various taxes such as toll tax, entertainment tax, and house tax. These taxes help in generating revenue for urban local governance.

131. India's first passenger train ran in 1853 between Bombay (Mumbai) and Thane. This marked the beginning of railway transport in India and was a significant milestone in infrastructure development.

132. Asia's largest cattle fair is held at Sonepur in Bihar. It is famous for trading animals and also has cultural and religious significance.

133. The National Integration Council was established in 1961 to address issues related to communalism, casteism, and regionalism. It works to promote unity and integrity in the country.

134. The Right to Equality is covered under Articles 14 to 18 of the Indian Constitution. These articles ensure equality before law, prohibition of discrimination, and abolition of untouchability and titles.

135. The Constitution of the United Kingdom is considered flexible because it can be amended easily by ordinary legislative procedures. It is not rigid like written constitutions of many other countries.

136. *Euplectella*, a type of sponge, is a sessile animal as it remains fixed to a surface throughout its life. Sessile animals do not move from place to place.

137. Proteins are made up of smaller units called amino acids. These amino acids link together in chains to form complex protein structures necessary for body functions.

138. Plant cells generally lack a centrosome, which is present in animal cells and helps in spindle formation during cell division. Plant cells instead use other structures for this function. Vacuoles, plastids, and cellulose cell wall are all characteristic features of plant cells.

139. The liver is the largest gland in the human body. It performs many vital functions such as metabolism, detoxification, and production of bile. It is much larger than other glands like pituitary or adrenal glands.

140. The state bird of Uttar Pradesh is the Sarus Crane. It is the tallest flying bird in the world and is known for its grace and long lifespan. It is also culturally significant in the region.

141. A hamlet is a very small human settlement, smaller than a village. It is typically found in rural areas and lacks many facilities. Therefore, it is associated with rural settlement patterns.

142. Mount Kilimanjaro is a volcanic mountain located in Africa. It is a dormant volcano and the highest peak on the continent. Other options are fold or block mountains, not volcanic.

143. Elephanta Island is located near the coast of Mumbai in the Arabian Sea. It is famous for its rock-cut caves and is a UNESCO World Heritage Site.

144. Monsoon forests, also known as tropical deciduous forests, are found in areas receiving rainfall between 70 and 200 cm. These forests shed leaves during dry seasons to conserve water.

145. Karbi Anglong Plateau is considered an extension of the Peninsular Plateau. It lies in Assam and is separated from the main plateau by the Garo-Rajmahal gap.

146. Water hyacinth is known as the "Terror of Bengal" because it spreads rapidly over water bodies. It blocks sunlight, reduces oxygen, and harms aquatic life.

147. Viruses show abiotic properties like crystallization outside a host cell. This means they can exist in a non-living form. However, they also show living characteristics inside a host.

148. Ethylene is a plant hormone responsible for fruit ripening. It promotes softening, color change, and conversion of starch into sugar. It is widely used in agriculture for artificial ripening.

149. Clostridium is a free-living anaerobic nitrogen-fixing bacterium found in soil. It fixes atmospheric nitrogen without requiring oxygen. Azotobacter is aerobic, and Rhizobium is symbiotic.

150. B-DNA is the most common form of DNA found inside living cells. It has a right-handed double helix structure. Other forms like A-DNA and Z-DNA occur under special conditions.

Previous Paper (Solved)

UP-TET (PRIMARY LEVEL), 2018

(Exam held on 18-11-2018)

PART-I

CHILD DEVELOPMENT AND PEDAGOGY

1. Kohler wanted to prove that learning is:
A. a situation in which individuals are superior to animals
B. an autonomous random activity
C. cognitive operation
D. the perception of different parts of the situation

2. From where to start in order to learn any new language?
A. Association between letters and words
B. Formation of sentences
C. Formation of words
D. None of the above

3. Which type(s) of students is/are included in inclusive class?
A. Only specific students
B. General and specific students
C. Only general students
D. Multilinguistic and gifted students

4. From the following, which term defines the mathematics related learning disability?
A. Dystopia B. Dyslexia
C. Dyscalculia D. None of the above

5. Successful inclusion needs:
A. lack of capacity building
B. no involvement of parents
C. segregation
D. sensitization

6. Which of the following is ***not*** the element of emotion?
A. Behavioural B. Physical
C. Cognitive D. Sensory

7. Which is the correct sequence of cognitive domain?
A. Knowledge-Application-Comprehension-Analysis-Synthesis-Evaluation
B. Evaluation-Application-Analysis-Synthesis-Comprehension-Knowledge
C. Evaluation-Synthesis-Analysis-Application-Comprehension-Knowledge
D. Knowledge-Comprehension-Application-Analysis-Synthesis-Evaluation

8. Which of the following is ***not*** a quality of good teaching?
A. Autocratic
B. Democratic
C. Sympathetic
D. Desirable information provider

9. Expectancy theory of motivation has been given by:
A. Victor Vroom B. Maslow
C. Herzberg D. Skinner

10. To which family advance organizer model is related with?
A. Personal
B. Social interaction
C. Information processing
D. Behaviour modification

11. Which is useful in the transformation of skills?
A. Skills transformation is a journey, not a destination
B. Linear Programme
C. Branching Programme
D. Preparation and acquisition

12. Which one is ***not*** the maxim of teaching from the following?
A. From simple to complex
B. From indefinite to definite
C. From seen to unseen
D. From deduction to induction

13. First step of microteaching cycle is:
A. feedback B. teaching
C. planning D. introduction

14. Which of the following is included in the teaching of understanding level?
A. Abstraction B. Application
C. Comparison D. Exploration

15. For educational reforms effective decentra-lization is possible by:
1. greater involvement of cluster and block resource centres
2. availability of local resource person
3. resource and reference material for the use of teachers

Choose the correct answer

A. 1 and 3 B. 1 and 2

C. 2 and 3 D. 1, 2 and 3

16. A student is reading, someone called him by name. By which sensation he (student) will respond from the following?

A. Visual sensation B. Tactual sensation

C. Auditory sensation D. Perceptual sensation

17. What is the age of pre-operational stage in Piaget theory?

A. Four to eight years B. Birth to two years

C. Two to seven years D. Five to eight years

18. Which of the following is ***not*** the characteristic of intellectual development of later childhood?

A. Operational planning of career

B. High interest in science fiction

C. Increased logical power

D. End of imaginary fears

19. Which of the following psychologists is associated with 'language development'?

A. Pavlov B. Binnet

C. Chomsky D. Maslow

20. Thorndike proved his theory titled:

A. cognitive learning

B. trial and error learning

C. sign learning

D. space learning

21. Gang age associated with age and delayed development is:

A. 16-19 years and morality

B. 3-6 years and language

C. 8-10 years and socialization

D. 16-19 years and cognitive

22. Which of the following is the third stage of cognitive development according to Piaget?

A. Formal operational stage

B. Pre-operational stage

C. Concrete operational stage

D. Sensory motor stage

23. Which is ***not*** included in psychological factors that contribute in learning from the following?

A. Learning desire B. Motivation

C. Interest D. Nature of content

24. Which of the following is a social value?

A. Altruism B. Primary goal

C. Instinct D. Aggression need

25. Backward exploration and means-end analysis are examples of which of the following?

A. Heuristics B. Algorithms

C. Mental sets D. Functional Fixedness

26. "Curves of learning give graphic representation of the amount, rate and limit of improvement brought about by practice." Who said it?

A. Skinner B. Ross

C. Ebbinghaus D. M. L. Bigge

27. Which one is ***not*** included in Thorndike's primary laws of learning from the following?

A. Law of associative shifting

B. Law of exercise

C. Law of effect

D. Law of readiness

28. Conditioned response theory lays emphasis on conditioning of:

A. reasoning B. behaviour

C. thinking D. motivation

29. The other name of operant conditioning is:

A. contiguous conditioning

B. instrumental conditioning

C. classical conditioning

D. trace conditioning

30. Which of the following is ***not*** a characteristic of learning?

A. Learning is directly observed

B. Learning is a relatively permanent change in behaviour

C. Learning is a growth of organism

D. Learning is a goal-directed process

PART-II

भाषा-I : हिन्दी

31. 'प्रागैतिहासिक' में किस उपसर्ग का प्रयोग है?

A. प्रा

B. प्राक्

C. प्राग

D. प्रागैति

32. 'तुलसीदास' किसकी कविता है?

A. हरिवंशराय बच्चन

B. मुक्तिबोध

C. अज्ञेय

D. सूर्यकांत त्रिपाठी 'निराला'

33. 'बहिष्कार' का संधि-विच्छेद क्या है?

A. बहिः + कार
B. वहिः + ष्कार
C. बहिष् + अकार
D. बहिर् + कार

34. 'वैदेही वनवास' किसकी रचना है?

A. मैथिलीशरण गुप्त
B. अयोध्या सिंह उपाध्याय 'हरिऔध'
C. रामधारी सिंह 'दिनकर'
D. श्रीधर पाठक

35. निम्न में से पुल्लिंग शब्द का चयन कीजिए :

A. पखावज
B. पहिया
C. लिखावट
D. मँझधार

निर्देश (प्रश्न सं. 36 और 37) : दिए गए गद्यांश को पढ़कर निम्नलिखित प्रश्नों के सही विकल्प छाँटिए।

स्पष्टता, आत्म-विश्वास, विषय की अच्छी पकड़ और प्रभावशाली भाषा में अपने विचारों और भावनाओं को व्यक्त करना ही सम्प्रेषण-कला है, जो निरंतर अभ्यास से निखारी जा सकती है। एक दिन में कोई अच्छा वक्ता नहीं बन सकता तथा भाषा पर अनायास ही किसी की पकड़ नहीं हो पाती। इसी अभ्यास से स्वामी विवेकानंद ने जिस सम्प्रेषण-कला का विकास किया था, उसने विश्वधर्म-सम्मेलन में लाखों अमेरिका-निवासियों को चकित और मोहित कर दिया था।

36. सम्प्रेषण-कला क्या **नहीं** है?

A. प्रभावशाली भाषा
B. अलंकरण
C. आत्म-विश्वास
D. विचारों और भावनाओं को व्यक्त करना

37. सम्प्रेषण-कला का विकास किससे होता है?

A. अनायास
B. अभ्यास
C. भाषण
D. विषय की अच्छी पकड़

38. निम्न में संयुक्त व्यंजन कौन-सा **नहीं** है?

A. त्र
B. य
C. क्ष
D. ज्ञ

39. 'मृत्युंजय' पद में कौन-सा समास है?

A. बहुव्रीहि
B. द्विगु
C. कर्मधारय
D. द्वंद्व

40. 'अलंकार' में किस उपसर्ग का प्रयोग है?

A. अलन्
B. अल्
C. अल
D. अलम्

41. <u>यह</u> पुस्तक किसकी है? में रेखांकित शब्द का पद-परिचय दीजिए :

A. गुणवाचक विशेषण (पुस्तक विशेष्य), एकवचन
B. सार्वनामिक विशेषण (पुस्तक विशेष्य), एकवचन, स्त्रीलिंग
C. सर्वनाम, एकवचन, स्त्रीलिंग
D. सम्बोधन अव्यय

42. 'विश्लेषण' शब्द का विलोम होगा :

A. व्याख्या
B. विवेचन
C. संश्लेषण
D. विभाजित

43. जिनका उच्चारण ऊपर के दाँतों पर जीभ लगाने से होता है, उसे क्या कहते हैं?

A. मूर्धन्य
B. कंठ्य
C. दन्त्य
D. अनुनासिक

44. निम्नलिखित में से 'ऊष्म व्यंजन' कौन-से हैं?

A. च-छ-ज
B. श-ष-स
C. अ-ब-स
D. य-र-ल

45. 'अत्यधिक' का विलोम क्या है?

A. अनधिगत
B. अत्यल्प
C. अत्याधिक
D. अनधीन

46. 'ऋत' का विलोम क्या है?

A. विकीर्ण
B. अनृत
C. वक्र
D. अनैक्य

47. 'संकल्प' शब्द में उपसर्ग बताइए :

A. सन्
B. सम्
C. सक्
D. सन्क

48. मुझसे खड़ा भी हुआ नहीं जाता। इस वाक्य का वाच्य होगा :

A. कर्तृवाच्य
B. भाववाच्य
C. कर्मवाच्य
D. अन्य

49. तद्भव और उसके तत्सम का कौन-सा मेल **गलत** है?

A. लुनाई-लावण्यता
B. लौंग-लवंग
C. आँत-अंत्र
D. आयसु-आदेश

50. लेखक और उसकी रचना का कौन-सा जोड़ा **गलत** है?

A. स्कन्दगुप्त–लक्ष्मीनारायण मिश्र
B. संस्कृति के चार अध्याय–रामधारी सिंह 'दिनकर'
C. रसज्ञ-रंजन–आचार्य महावीर प्रसाद द्विवेदी
D. अशोक के फूल–आचार्य हजारी प्रसाद द्विवेदी

51. कवि और उसकी रचना का कौन-सा जोड़ा सही **नहीं** है?

A. परिमल–सूर्यकांत त्रिपाठी 'निराला'
B. शिवराज भूषण–भूषण
C. शब्द रसायन–देव
D. उद्धव शतक–भारतेन्दु हरिश्चंद्र

52. लेखक और उसकी कृति के युग्म में कौन-सा युग्म **गलत** है?

A. आर्यों का आदि देश–डॉ. सम्पूर्णानंद
B. बोल्गा से गंगा–राहुल सांकृत्यायन
C. सूरज का सातवाँ घोड़ा–धर्मवीर भारती
D. दर्शन दिग्दर्शन–रामचंद्र शुक्ल

53. विराम-चिह्न की दृष्टि से कौन-सा वाक्य **अशुद्ध** है?
A. हाँ मेरा यही विचार है।
B. वह ईमानदार, परिश्रमी, कर्मठ और मृदुभाषी है।
C. उसके पास धन-वैभव, नौकर-चाकर आदि सभी कुछ था।
D. आप हमारे घर आना चाहते हैं, तो आइए; ठहरना चाहते हैं, तो ठहरिए।

54. कौन-सा शब्द भिन्न अर्थ और प्रकृति का है?
A. सनातन B. चिरंतन
C. शाश्वत D. अधुनातन

55. 'अर्वाचीन' शब्द का विलोम होगा :
A. अधुनातन B. प्राचीन
C. अद्यतन D. सनातन

56. व्याकरण की दृष्टि से कौन-सा शब्द **अशुद्ध** है?
A. विभीषण B. विरहणी
C. गृहिणी D. जगद्गुरु

57. निम्न में से कौन-सा युग्म गलत है?
A. मुट्ठी गरम करना–रिश्वत देना
B. लुटिया डूबना–सारा काम चौपट होना
C. सब्ज बाग दिखलाना–हरा-भरा करना
D. माई का लाल–साहसी व्यक्ति

58. मेरी भव बाधा हरो, राधा नागरि सोय।
जातन की झाँई परै, स्याम हरित दुति होय।।
उपर्युक्त दोहे में कौन-सा अलंकार है?
A. श्लेष B. अन्योक्ति
C. यमक D. रूपक

59. 'गौशाला' में कौन-सा समास है?
A. बहुव्रीहि B. तत्पुरुष
C. द्वंद्व D. द्विगु

60. 'देशभक्ति' में कौन-सा समास है?
A. तत्पुरुष B. द्वंद्व
C. कर्मधारय D. द्विगु

PART-III

LANGUAGE-II : ENGLISH

61. What is the main purpose of poetry recitation in a language classroom?
A. To give their opinions about poem
B. To know the historical background of the poem
C. To enjoy and appreciate the poem
D. To become aware of the poet and his/her work

62. Fill in the blanks with the correct article:
Yesterday I saw .... European riding on .... elephant.
A. a, a B. the, the
C. a, an D. a, the

63. Choose the correct sentence:
A. Please describe of the story.
B. Please describe about the story.
C. Please describe the story.
D. Please describe to the story.

64. Fill in the blank with correct preposition:
A prisoner was accused_______murder.
A. to B. of
C. for D. off

65. The antonym of 'innocent' is:
A. active B. clever
C. ignorant D. guilty

66. The synonym of 'significant' is:
A. efficient B. prominent
C. magnificent D. important

67. Which one of the following words can be made plural by adding a suffix 'en'?
A. Max B. Box
C. Tax D. Ox

68. Change the correct pronoun to complete the following sentence:
This dress is________and that one is mine.
A. your B. our book
C. yours D. your book

69. Change the following sentence into passive voice:
Have the girls asked this question?
A. Has this question asked by the girls?
B. This question have asked by girls.
C. Has this question been asked by the girls
D. Have this question asked by the girls

Directions (Qs. No. 70 and 71): *Read the passage given and answer the questions that follow it.*

Yesterday, two brave children of Gangapur were awarded Brave Hearts Award. They have exhibited a great spirit of selflessness and courage. Harsh, a twelve-year-old boy, saved a little girl from drowning in the river that flows along has village. Garima has been awarded for her presence of mind.

70. Which kind of noun is Gangapur?
A. Material noun B. Common noun
C. Collective noun D. Proper noun

71. Which part of speech as the word 'brave'?
A. Adjective B. Noun
C. Pronoun D. Preposition

72. Which of the following words is a material noun?
A. Air B. Cow
C. Gold D. Class

73. Which of the following words is an abstract noun?
A. Woman B. Connection
C. Boy D. Plough

74. Which kind of noun is 'adversity'?
A. Abstract noun
B. Common noun
C. Proper noun
D. Collective noun

75. Which part of speech is the word 'hard' in the sentence 'He is working hard'?
A. Preposition B. Adverb
C. Conjunction D. Noun

76. Which of the following sentences has a 'conjunction'?
A. She is poor but she is by nature hospitable
B. She is awfully busy
C. I am nobody for you
D. My grandfather is not well

77. Point out the sentence which is in present perfect tense.
A. Your sister visited us yesterday
B. I shall go to Jaunpur tomorrow
C. She is very intelligent
D. I have finished my work

78. Which of the following is misspelt word?
A. Derogatary
B. Desiccation
C. Descendant
D. Dermatitis

79. Which of the following sentences has transitive verb?
A. She writes well
B. She walks in the morning daily
C. He is running very fast
D. I killed a snake last night

80. Which of the following sentences is negative?
A. He does not listen to me
B. I come from a rich family
C. You can do all this in no time
D. They are very gentle people

81. Which of the following sentences is exclamatory?
A. Which is your favourite book
B. What a piece of work is man
C. What do you know about ancient India
D. His cruelty knew no bounds

82. Point out the complex sentence:
A. She does not sing
B. They are very wise people
C. You know me well
D. One who does not love one's country is wretched person

83. Which of the following words is 'plural'?
A. Goat
B. Dog
C. Fox
D. Mice

84. Which of the following words is regarded as singular?
A. Cats
B. Dogs
C. Mathematics
D. Cars

85. Which of the following sentences is in active voice?
A. I requested him to come in time
B. He was asked to keep quiet
C. A house was bought for fifty lacs
D. He was hit badly

86. Which of the following sentences is in passive voice?
A. He was assisted by a group of students
B. Please mind your business
C. I kept quiet throughout the meeting
D. They came late and lost the match

87. "That is the man the police was seeking".

In the above sentence, what is the status of the two the's?
A. Conjunction
B. Verb
C. Noun
D. Definite article

88. "These students are most disobedient"
In the above sentence, point out the gender of the word 'students':
A. Masculine gender
B. Feminine gender
C. Common gender
D. None of the above

89. In the sentence 'He was going along the road', point out the tense.
A. Past continuous
B. Present perfect
C. Past perfect
D. Future indefinite

90. Language learning starts from:
A. listening B. writing
C. reading D. speaking

PART-IV

MATHEMATICS

91. In the given figure, PAQ is the tangent of the circle at point A and ABCD is cyclic quadrilateral.

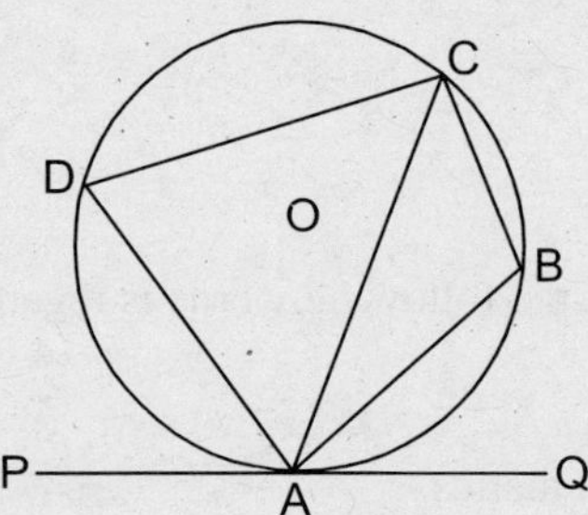

If $\angle CAQ = 70°$, then $\angle ABC$ is:

A. 110° B. 70°
C. 80° D. 90°

92. If the cost price of 8 pens is same as the selling price of 6 pens, then the gain per cent is:

A. $33\frac{1}{3}\%$ B. $11\frac{1}{2}\%$
C. $13\frac{1}{3}\%$ D. 25%

93. Which of the following rational number **does not** lie between $\frac{3}{5}$ and $\frac{4}{5}$?

A. $\frac{7}{10}$ B. $\frac{19}{30}$
C. $\frac{2}{3}$ D. $\frac{16}{30}$

94. If the price of 3 pens, 2 pencils and 4 erasers is ₹ 92 and the price of 8 pencils and 16 erasers is ₹ 68, then the price of 24 pens is:

A. ₹ 675 B. ₹ 625
C. ₹ 500 D. ₹ 600

95. We cannot construct a triangle, if we are given:

A. only three angles
B. two angles and one side
C. only three sides
D. two sides and included angle

96. If the length and breadth of a rectangular plot are increased by 50% and 20% respectively, then how many times will its area be increased?

A. $\frac{4}{5}$ B. $1\frac{4}{5}$
C. $1\frac{1}{5}$ D. $\frac{1}{5}$

97. The temperature of a normal human body is 37°C. In Fahrenheit scale, this temperature is:

A. 98°F B. 98.4°F
C. 98.6°F D. 98.8°F

98. If $1^2 + 2^2 + ... + 9^2 = 285$, then the value of $(0.11)^2 + (0.22)^2 + ... + (0.99)^2$ is:

A. 3.4485 B. 2.4485
C. 0.24485 D. 0.34485

99. A sum of money at simple interest doubles in 10 years. In how many years, at the same rate, it will be tripled?

A. 20 years B. 30 years
C. 25 years D. 15 years

100. In a circular park of diameter 80 m, there is a square-shaped playground of maximum area. The area of the playground is:

A. 3200 m^2 B. 6400 m^2
C. 1600 m^2 D. 12800 m^2

101. In an examination of 240 marks, a student scored 52 marks. In pie-chart, the corresponding angle is:

A. 63° B. 75°
C. 78° D. $\left(21\frac{2}{3}\right)^{\circ}$

102. If P% of P is 36, then P is equal to:

A. 15 B. 3600
C. 600 D. 60

103. If $2352 = 2^x \times 3^y \times 7^z$, then the value of $x + y + z$ is:

A. 8 B. 5
C. 7 D. 9

104. The number of even divisors of 100 will be:

A. 7 B. 6
C. 5 D. 8

105. How many cubes of side 3 cm can be separated from a cube of side 15 cm?

A. 125 B. 25
C. 27 D. 144

106. If 3^{1989} is divided by 7, then remainder is:

A. 8 B. 7
C. 6 D. 10

107. The sum of interior angles of a polygon is 216°. The number of sides of the polygon is:

A. 14 B. 12
C. 13 D. 15

108. The least non-negative prime integer is:
A. 2 B. 0
C. 1 D. 3

109. $\left(1\frac{1}{2}+11\frac{1}{2}+111\frac{1}{2}+1111\frac{1}{2}\right)$ is equal to:
A. 1263 B. 1236
C. 1233 D. 1239

110. If $a * b = a^2 + b^2 - ab$ for all natural numbers a and b, then the value of 9 * 10 is:
A. 181 B. 90
C. 91 D. 182

111. If x and y are non-zero real numbers, then $x^2 + xy + y^2$
A. is always positive
B. is always negative
C. takes the value zero for some x and y
D. takes both positive and negative values

112. The number at the place of * in adjoining figure will be:

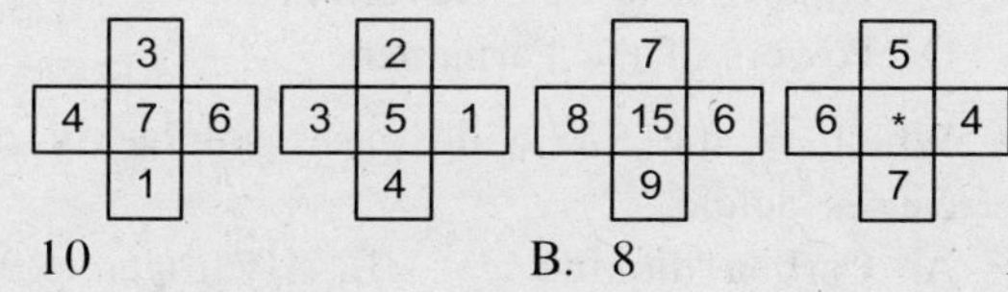

A. 10 B. 8
C. 9 D. 11

113. If for any two natural numbers a and b, $a^b = 125$, then b^a is:
A. 243 B. 241
C. 242 D. 247

114. The least number, divisible by all the natural numbers from 1 to 10, is:
A. 1000 B. 5040
C. 2520 D. 100

115. If it is Friday on 4/8/2017, then what will be the day after 61 days?
A. Thursday B. Tuesday
C. Wednesday D. Friday

116. In the given figure

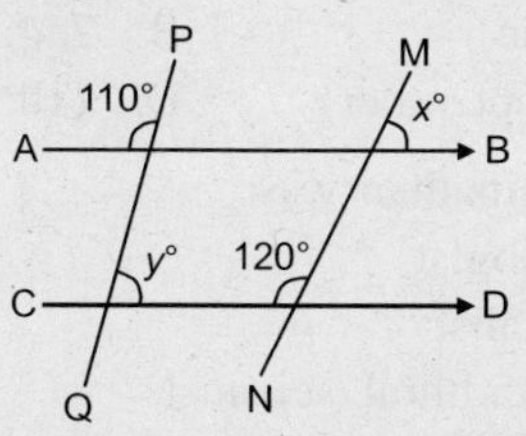

AB || CD, then the value of $y°-x°$ is:
A. 30° B. 10°
C. 20° D. 40°

117. If by selling an article for ₹ 390, a shopkeeper gains 20%, then the cost price of article is:
A. ₹ 324 B. ₹ 321
C. ₹ 323 D. ₹ 325

118. If the population of a town has increased from 60000 to 65000, then the increase in population (in per cent) is:
A. $7\frac{1}{4}$ B. $7\frac{9}{13}$
C. $8\frac{1}{3}$ D. $8\frac{1}{9}$

119. 40 persons consume 200 kg of rice in 30 days. In how many days will 30 persons consume 500 kg of rice?
A. 90 B. 120
C. 80 D. 100

120. In a rhombus, the lengths of diagonals are 16 cm and 12 cm. The side of the rhombus is:
A. 9 cm B. 7 cm
C. 8 cm D. 10 cm

PART-V

ENVIRONMENTAL EDUCATION

121. Plants are green due to the presence of which pigment?
A. Anthocyanin B. Carotenoid
C. Lycopene D. Chlorophyll

122. Human activities that cause climate change on the earth include:
A. use of aerosol cans B. burning of forests
C. agricultural activities D. All of the above

123. Which crop belonging to the family Euphorbiaceae is known for producing biodiesel?
A. Copper leaf B. Jatropha
C. Candlenut tree D. Sarpagandha

124. 'The Queen of Herbs' is the most sacred herb of India. This medicinal plant has importance in Hindu mythology and has the scientific name *Ocimum Sanctum*. What is it commonly called?
A. Thyme B. Tulsi
C. Rosemary D. Coriander

125. The water that is safe to drink is called:
A. fresh water
B. potable water
C. distilled water
D. tap water

126. The Bhopal Gas Tragedy of 1984 was due to the leakage of which of the following gases?
A. Methane B. Methyl isocyanate
C. Nitrous oxide D. Carbon monoxide

127. The World Environment Day falls on:
A. 5th June B. 2nd December
C. 16th September D. 11th July

128. M.S. Swaminathan was:
A. an ecologist
B. a journalist
C. an agricultural scientist
D. an ornithologist

129. Where is Wildlife Institute of India (WII) located?
A. Ahmedabad B. New Delhi
C. Coimbatore D. Dehradun

130. During photosynthesis, which of the following is absorbed by green plants?
A. Carbon dioxide B. Helium
C. Nitrogen D. Oxygen

131. The organism which feed on the waste products are called:
A. herbivores B. detrivores
C. carnivores D. chemovores

132. What type of energy is derived from heated ground-water?
A. Geothermal energy B. Hydroelectric energy
C. Solar energy D. Nuclear energy

133. Shola grasslands are found in:
A. the Himalayas B. the Western Ghats
C. the Eastern Ghats D. the Vindhyas

134. In India, pelicans breed in:
A. Kokkare Bellur B. Nelapattu
C. Koonthankulam D. All of the above

135. 'Minamata disease' was caused by eating fish which have high levels of:
A. cadmium B. arsenic
C. mercury D. all of the above

136. Maximum ozone depletion has been observed in which of the following?
A. The Equator B. The North Pole
C. The South Pole D. None of the above

137. Who among the following was the first Chief Justice of India?
A. Hiralal J. Kania B. M. Patanjali Sastri
C. Mehr Chand Mahajan D. S.R. Das

138. The 'Red Data Book' is related to:
A. animals near extinction
B. pollution in rivers
C. decreasing underground water level
D. air pollution

139. Who among the following is the present Chairperson of the National Commission for Women?
A. Malini Bhattacharya B. Girija Vyas
C. Rekha Sharma D. Yasmeen Abrar

140. The joint sitting of the Lok Sabha and the Rajya Sabha of states is summoned by:
A. the Parliament
B. the President
C. the Speaker of the Lok Sabha
D. the Chairman of the Rajya Sabha

141. Which Part of the Constitution has the provisions for Panchayati Raj System?
A. III B. IX
C. VI D. IV

142. 74th Amendment of the Constitution is related to:
A. Powers of the President
B. Rural Local Self-Government
C. Urban Local Self-Government
D. Powers of the Parliament

143. Which of the following gases soluble in rainwater causes acidic?
A. Carbon dioxide B. Hydrogen peroxide
C. Nitrogen monoxide D. Sulphur dioxide

144. 'Rule of Law' concept has been taken in the Indian Constitution from:
A. Switzerland B. USA
C. England D. Ireland

145. Who carries out notification for the election of the Lok Sabha?
A. Home Ministry
B. Election Commission of India
C. The President
D. Lok Sabha Secretariat

146. The first hour of business of the Lok Sabha is known as:
A. Zero hour B. Public hour
C. Privileges hour D. Question hour

147. What is Rainwater Harvesting?
A. Distribution of water
B. Collection and storage of used water
C. Collection and storage of rainwater
D. None of the above

148. Indian Rhinoceros is protected in:
A. Bandipur National Park
B. Corbett National Park
C. Kaziranga National Park
D. Gir National Park

149. Which of the following series is true about energy flow in an ecosystem?

A. Producers → Consumers → Decomposers
B. Producers → Decomposers → Consumers
C. Decomposers → Consumers → Producers
D. Consumers → Producers → Decomposers

150. Greenhouse gas, which is present in the highest quantity in atmosphere, is:

A. carbon dioxide
B. propane
C. ethane
D. methane

ANSWERS

1	2	3	4	5	6	7	8	9	10
C	A	A	C	D	D	D	A	A	C
11	**12**	**13**	**14**	**15**	**16**	**17**	**18**	**19**	**20**
A	D	C	D	D	C	C	A	C	B
21	**22**	**23**	**24**	**25**	**26**	**27**	**28**	**29**	**30**
C	C	D	A	A	C	A	B	B	A
31	**32**	**33**	**34**	**35**	**36**	**37**	**38**	**39**	**40**
B	D	A	B	B	D	B	B	A	D
41	**42**	**43**	**44**	**45**	**46**	**47**	**48**	**49**	**50**
B	C	C	B	B	B	B	B	A	A
51	**52**	**53**	**54**	**55**	**56**	**57**	**58**	**59**	**60**
D	D	A	D	B	B	C	A	B	A
61	**62**	**63**	**64**	**65**	**66**	**67**	**68**	**69**	**70**
C	C	C	B	D	D	D	C	C	D
71	**72**	**73**	**74**	**75**	**76**	**77**	**78**	**79**	**80**
A	C	B	A	B	A	D	A	D	A
81	**82**	**83**	**84**	**85**	**86**	**87**	**88**	**89**	**90**
B	D	D	C	A	A	D	C	A	A
91	**92**	**93**	**94**	**95**	**96**	**97**	**98**	**99**	**100**
A	A	D	D	A	A	C	A	A	A
101	**102**	**103**	**104**	**105**	**106**	**107**	**108**	**109**	**110**
C	D	C	B	A	C	A	A	B	C
111	**112**	**113**	**114**	**115**	**116**	**117**	**118**	**119**	**120**
A	D	A	C	A	B	D	C	D	D
121	**122**	**123**	**124**	**125**	**126**	**127**	**128**	**129**	**130**
D	D	B	B	B	B	A	C	D	A
131	**132**	**133**	**134**	**135**	**136**	**137**	**138**	**139**	**140**
B	A	B	D	C	C	A	A	C	B
141	**142**	**143**	**144**	**145**	**146**	**147**	**148**	**149**	**150**
B	C	D	C	B	D	C	C	A	A

EXPLANATORY ANSWERS

1. Kohler's insight learning theory emphasized that learning is not merely trial-and-error or random activity. He showed through experiments on chimpanzees that learning involves perception, understanding, and restructuring of the situation. Therefore, learning is treated as a cognitive operation.

2. Learning a new language generally begins with recognizing letters, sounds, and their association with words. Sentence formation comes later after vocabulary and word recognition develop. Hence, the initial stage is association between letters and words.

3. Inclusive education means education of all students, where all students are equal participants in the learning process. Provision of inclusive education involving students with disabilities is based on the belief that those with disabilities should not have to depend on specialised services alone, to benefit from educational resources, activities and practices that are otherwise available to all. Inclusivity is maintained when all members of a group are able to participate in its activities, which means, provisions made are considerate of all members and not just those from specific groups or, with special abilities, disabilities, and/or needs.

4. **Dyscalculia** is difficulty in learning or comprehending arithmetic, such as difficulty in understanding numbers, learning how to manipulate numbers, performing mathematical calculations and learning facts in mathematics. It is generally seen as the mathematical equivalent to dyslexia. It can occur in people from across the whole IQ range, along with difficulties with time, measurement, and spatial reasoning. Estimates of the prevalence of dyscalculia range between 3% and 6% of the population. In 2015, it was established that 11% of children with dyscalculia also have ADHD. Dyscalculia has also been associated with people who have Turner syndrome and people who have spina bifida. Mathematical disabilities can occur as the result of some types of brain injury, in which case the proper term, acalculia, is to distinguish it from dyscalculia which is of innate, genetic or developmental origin.

5. Inclusion of children with special education needs has become a matter of priority in many countries around the world. It is undoubted that reform towards inclusion of children with diverse needs continues across the globe. The implementation of inclusive education requires dedication and willingness on part of all stakeholders especially educators. Every educator must be aware of the concept of 'inclusion'. Sensitization towards inclusion is need of the hour.

6. The term emotion is derived from the Latin verb 'movere' means stir up, agitate, disturb or move. Woodworth has defined emotion as "conscious stirred up state of the organism".

   There are three components of emotions

   (*a*) **Cognition:** This component serves primarily to influence an evaluation of given situation, prompting us to become emotional in one way or another, or not at all.

   (*b*) **Feeling:** In daily life we think of feelings. The feelings are most readily evident changes in an aroused person. Feelings have immediate motivational significance. They give rise to many physiological processes in the cardiovascular system and produce increased blood pressure, changes in sexual urge. They also stimulate nervous system and prompt widespread electro-chemical activities.

   (*c*) **Behaviour:** The behavioural component involves facial, postural, gestures and vocal responses.

7. The cognitive domain involves knowledge and the development of intellectual skills (Bloom, 1956). This includes the recall or recognition of specific facts, procedural patterns, and concepts that serve in the development of inte-llectual abilities and skills. The original levels by Bloom et al. (1956) were ordered as follows: Knowledge-Comprehension-Application-Analysis-Synthesis-Evaluation.

8. Good teaching is generally democratic, sympathetic, learner-centred, and informative. An autocratic approach suppresses student participation and discourages free expression. Therefore, autocratic behaviour is not considered a quality of good teaching.

9. The expectancy theory was proposed by Victor Vroom of Yale School of Management in 1964. Vroom stresses and focuses on outcomes, and not on needs unlike Maslow and Herzberg. The theory states that the intensity of a tendency to perform in a particular manner is dependent on the intensity of an expectation that the performance will be followed by a definite outcome and on the appeal of the outcome to the individual.

10. The advance organizer model was developed by David Ausubel. It helps learners organize new information by relating it to prior knowledge. Since its main concern is reception, organization, and processing of knowledge, it belongs to the information processing family.

11. In programmed learning, linear programming (developed by B. F. Skinner) is specifically designed for shaping behaviours and skills through small, sequential steps with immediate reinforcement. Skill transformation requires gradual modification and strengthening of responses, which linear programmes do very effectively because every learner follows the same carefully structured path without deviation. Branching programmes (by Norman A. Crowder) are more suitable for diagnosis and remediation of errors rather than systematic transformation of skills.

12. Every teacher wants to make maximum involvement and participation of the learners in the learning process. He sets the classroom in such a way so that it becomes attractive for them. He uses different methods, rules,

principle sets in order to make his lesson effective and purposeful. He uses general rule or formula and applies it to particular example in order to make teaching-learning process easy and up to the understandable level of students. These settled principles, tenets, working rules or general truths through which teaching becomes interesting, easy and effective are called the maxims of teaching. They have universal significance. Every person who is expected to enter into the teaching profession have to familiarize himself with the maxims of teaching. Their knowledge helps him to proceed systematically.

The different maxims of teaching are:

- From known to unknown
- From simple to complex
- From concrete to abstract
- From analysis to synthesis
- From particular to general
- From empirical to rational
- From induction to deduction
- From psychological to logical
- From actual to representative
- From whole to parts
- From definite to indefinite
- From seen to unseen

13. Microteaching cycle:

1. PLAN
2. TEACH
3. FEEDBACK
4. RE-PLAN
5. RE-TEACH
6. RE-FEEDBACK

14. After rechecking, the better answer is exploration. In understanding-level teaching, the learner is not limited to memorization but tries to understand relationships, meanings, and principles. Exploration helps the learner discover or understand new ideas on the basis of previous knowledge, so it fits the understanding level most accurately.

15. Effective decentralization in educational reforms requires support at local levels. Cluster and block resource centres, local resource persons, and teaching-learning resource materials all strengthen decentralized educational planning and implementation. Hence all three statements are relevant.

16. The auditory sensation or the sensation of hearing is next in importance only to visual sensations. In a way, however, auditory sensations are even more important than visual sensations. They have the ability to respond to stimuli from a much longer distance than visual sensations.

From the point of view of evolution, auditory sensations are more primary than visual sensations. In fact, in some of the lower organisms where the visual sensation is not fully developed, auditory sensations are fairly well developed. The stimuli for auditory sensations are sound waves.

The human ear can respond to a wide range of sound waves ranging from sixteen decibels to nearly twenty-two thousand decibels. Sound waves below sixteen and above twenty two thousand are not generally heard.

17. Piaget has identified 4 sequential stages through which every individual progresses in cognitive development. Each stage has an age span with distinctive learning capabilities. This would be helpful in framing curriculum. And under-standing of this development sequence is indispensable for parents as well as for teachers because these influences a great deal during infancy, childhood and adolescence. The 4 developmental stages are discussed below:

(i) **Sensori-Motor Stage:** This stage begins at birth and lasts till the child is about 2 years old. It is called Sensori-Motor Stage, because children's thinking involves seeing, hearing, moving, touching, testing and so on.

(ii) **Pre-operational Stage (2 to 7 Years):** This stage is called Pre-operational because the children have not yet mastered the ability to perform mental operations. Children's thinking during this stage is governed by what is seen rather than by logical principles.

(iii) **Concrete Operational Stage (7 to 11 years):** At this stage a child is concerned with the integration of stability of his cognitive systems. He learns to add, subtract, multiply and divide. He is in a position to classify concrete objects. In short, children develop the abilities of rational thinking but their thinking is tied to concrete objects.

(iv) **Formal Operational Stage (11 & above):** This type is characterised by the emergence of logical thinking and reasoning. Other important cognitive attainments during this period are: the ability to think about the hypothetical possibilities and to solve problems through logical deductions and in a systematic manner.

18. Later childhood involves growth in logical thinking, curiosity, interest in factual and imaginative material like science fiction, and reduction of imaginary fears. Operational planning of career is more typical of adolescence, not later childhood. Therefore, it is not a characteristic of intellectual development of later childhood.

19. One of the greatest linguists of all times, Noam Chomsky asserts that language is innate. He wrote his famous book, "Language and Mind" in 1972, in which he proposed his famous theories on language acquisition. In this book Chomsky wrote, "When we study human language, we are approaching what some might call the 'human essence', the distinctive qualities of mind that are, so far as we know, unique to man". According to Chomsky, language is one characteristic that is unique to humans among all other living beings. Chomsky's theories have made it easier to understand the evolution and development of the languages.

Chomsky's theories on language are based upon the importance of linguistics in modern sciences. According to him, to study languages, it is important study human nature that lies in human mind.

20. Thorndike's major work is the three-volume series Educational Psychology. He postulated that the most fundamental type of learning involves the forming of associations (connections) between sensory experiences (perceptions of stimuli or events) and neural impulses (responses) that manifest themselves behaviourally. He believed that learning often occurs by trial and error (selecting and connecting). Thorndike began studying learning with a series of experiments on animals (Thorndike, 1911). Animals in problem situations try to attain a goal (e.g., obtain food, reach a destination). From among the many responses they can perform, they select one, perform it, and experience the consequences. The more often they make a response to a stimulus, the more firmly that response becomes connected to that stimulus.

21. Gang age refers to middle childhood when children strongly identify with peer groups. During 8-10 years, children develop group loyalty, cooperation, and social skills. Socialization becomes dominant, and children prefer group activities over individual play.

22. Piaget's Stages of Cognitive Development

Stage	Age Range	What happens at this stage?
Sensorimotor	0-2 years old	Coordination of senses with motor responses, sensory curiosity about the world. Language used for demands and cataloguing. Object permanence is developed.
Preoperational	2-7 years old	Symbolic thinking, use of proper syntax and grammar to express concepts. Imagination and intuition are strong, but complex abstract thoughts are still difficult. Conservation is developed.
Concrete Operational	7-11 years old	Concepts attached to concrete situations. Time, space, and quantity are understood and can be applied, but not as independent concepts.
Formal Operational	11 years old and older	Theoretical, hypothetical, and counterfactual thinking. Abstract logic and reasoning. Strategy and planning become possible. Concepts learned in one context can be applied to another.

23. Psychological Factors:

Readiness/Preparedness

- To be mentally ready to learn a skill is called readiness.
- "Bill Guard said teaching is a pleasant thing and it would be pleasant only if your students are internally ready for learning".

Interest

- Interest refers to the feeling of writing to know or learn about something.

Intelligence

- Intelligence is a natural capacity and ability which helps the man to understand and solve the problems according to the situation.

Motivation

- The internal process that activates guides and maintains behaviour over time, or influence of need and desires on the intensity and direction of behaviour.

Attitude

- Human attitude is constructed on the bases of one's personal thinking and ideologies he likes and dislikes these ideologies create feelings among the individual.

Feelings

- Feelings are the physical sensation we experience in our body and emotions are the labels we give those sensations in our minds.

24. Social values are those that promote welfare and harmony in society. Altruism means helping others without expecting personal gain, which directly reflects a social value. Other options like instinct or aggression are biological drives, not value-based behaviours.

25. Problem-Solving Strategies:

Method	Description	Example
Trial and error	Continue trying different solutions until problem is solved	Restarting phone, turning off WiFi, turning off bluetooth in order to determine why your phone is malfunctioning
Algorithm	Step-by-step problem-solving formula	Instruction manual for installing new software on your computer
Heuristic	General problem-solving framework	Working backwards; breaking a task into steps.

26. Hermann Ebbinghaus was a German psychologist who pioneered the experimental study of memory, and is known for his discovery of the forgetting curve and the spacing effect. He was also the first person to describe the learning curve. He was the father of the neo-Kantian philosopher Julius Ebbinghaus.

27. Thorndike's Primary Laws of Learning

1. Law of Readiness:

- The degree of preparedness and eagerness to learn
- Law of Action Tendency
- Individuals learn best when they are ready to learn, and they will not learn much if they see no reason for learning.

Educational Implications:

- The teacher should arouse curiosity for learning, so that the pupils feel ready to imbibe the new experiences.
- The teacher should, before taking up the new leasson arouse the interest and desire of the students to learn.

2. Law of Exercise:

- Things that are most often repeated are best remembered.
- Law of Use and Disuse
  - Law of Use: the learning are streng-thened with repeated trial or practice.
  - Law of Disuse : learning are weakened when trial or practice is discontinued.

Educational Implications:

- The teacher should provide different opportunities for learners to practice or repeat the task. (recall, manual drill, review etc.)
- The teacher should have constant practice in what has once been learnt. Delayed use or long disuse may cause forget-fullness.

3. Law of Effect:

- Learning is strengthened when it is accompanied by a pleasant or satisfying feeling.
- Learning is weakened when it is associated with an unpleasant feeling.
- The emotional state of the learner affect the learning.

Educational Implications:

- As a failure is accompanied by a dis-couraging emotional state, it should be avoided.
- Reward and recognition play a great role in encouraging the pupil.
- Punishments should be avoided as far as possible. Punishment produces a negative effect, and it causes discouragement.

28. Conditioned response theory focuses on observable behaviour changes through stimulus-response connections. It explains how behaviour is learned through conditioning processes like reinforcement. Cognitive elements like reasoning or thinking are not the main focus of this theory.

29. Operant conditioning (also called instrumental conditioning) is a learning process through which the strength of a behaviour is modified by reinforcement or punishment. It is also a procedure that is used to bring about such learning.

30. Nature and Characteristics of Learning

1. Learning is the change in behaviour.
2. Learning is a continuous life long process.
3. Learning is a universal process.
4. Learning is purposive and goal directed.
5. Learning involves reconstruction of experiences.
6. Learning is the product of activity and environment.
7. Learning is transferable from one situation to another.
8. Learning helps in attainment of teaching - learning objectives.

9. Learning helps in the proper growth and development.
10. Learning helps in the balanced develop-ment of the personality.
11. Learning helps in proper adjustment.
12. Learning helps in the realization of goals of life.
13. Learning does not necessarily imply improvement.

31. 'प्रागैतिहासिक' शब्द 'प्राक् + ऐतिहासिक' से बना है, जहाँ 'प्राक्' उपसर्ग का अर्थ होता है ''पूर्व'' या ''पहले का''। संधि के कारण 'क्' का 'ग' में परिवर्तन हुआ है। इसलिए सही उपसर्ग 'प्राक्' ही है।

32. 'तुलसीदास' कविता छायावादी कवि निराला की प्रसिद्ध रचना है। इसमें उन्होंने तुलसीदास के जीवन, संघर्ष और आध्यात्मिकता को दर्शाया है। यह कविता साहित्यिक और भावनात्मक दृष्टि से अत्यंत महत्वपूर्ण मानी जाती है।

33. 'बहिष्कार' शब्द का निर्माण 'बहिः + कार' से हुआ है, जहाँ 'बहिः' का अर्थ ''बाहर'' और 'कार' का अर्थ ''करना'' है। संधि के बाद 'बहिष्कार' शब्द बनता है, जिसका अर्थ है किसी को बाहर कर देना।

34. 'वैदेही वनवास' वास्तव में अयोध्या सिंह उपाध्याय 'हरिऔध' द्वारा रचित एक प्रसिद्ध प्रबंध काव्य है। यह रचना खड़ी बोली हिंदी के विकास में महत्वपूर्ण मानी जाती है और इसमें सीता के वनवास की करुण कथा का विस्तारपूर्वक चित्रण किया गया है। इस काव्य में भावनात्मक गहराई, करुण रस तथा आदर्श नारी के रूप में सीता के चरित्र का प्रभावशाली निरूपण मिलता है।

35. 'पहिया' पुल्लिंग शब्द है और इसका प्रयोग सामान्यतः पुल्लिंग रूप में किया जाता है। 'लिखावट' और 'मँझधार' स्त्रीलिंग शब्द हैं, जबकि 'पखावज' भी प्रायः स्त्रीलिंग माना जाता है। इसलिए 'पहिया' सही उत्तर है।

36. गद्यांश में स्पष्ट रूप से बताया गया है कि सम्प्रेषण-कला में स्पष्टता, आत्म-विश्वास, विषय की अच्छी पकड़ और प्रभावशाली भाषा के माध्यम से विचारों व भावनाओं को व्यक्त करना शामिल है। अलंकरण का कहीं उल्लेख नहीं है और यह केवल सजावट या अलंकारिक भाषा से जुड़ा तत्व है। इसलिए यह सम्प्रेषण-कला का आवश्यक अंग नहीं माना गया है।

37. गद्यांश में स्पष्ट कहा गया है कि सम्प्रेषण-कला निरंतर अभ्यास से निखारी जा सकती है। कोई भी व्यक्ति एक दिन में अच्छा वक्ता नहीं बन सकता, बल्कि लगातार अभ्यास से ही यह कौशल विकसित होता है। स्वामी विवेकानंद का उदाहरण भी इसी बात को सिद्ध करता है।

38. संयुक्त व्यंजन वे होते हैं जो दो या अधिक व्यंजनों के मेल से बनते हैं, जैसे 'त्र', 'क्ष', 'ज्ञ'। 'य' एक साधारण (एकल) व्यंजन है और इसमें किसी अन्य व्यंजन का संयोग नहीं है। इसलिए यह संयुक्त व्यंजन नहीं है।

39. 'मृत्युंजय' का अर्थ है ''जो मृत्यु को जीतने वाला है''। यहाँ शब्द का अर्थ उसके घटकों (मृत्यु + जय) से सीधे न होकर किसी अन्य (शिव) की ओर संकेत करता है। इसलिए यह बहुव्रीहि समास का उदाहरण है।

40. 'अलंकार' शब्द 'अलम् + कार' से बना है। 'अलम्' उपसर्ग का अर्थ होता है ''पर्याप्त, सुशोभित या युक्त''। संधि के कारण 'अलम्' से 'अलं' रूप बनता है, इसलिए सही उपसर्ग 'अलम्' है।

41. वाक्य में 'किसकी' शब्द 'पुस्तक' के बारे में जानकारी दे रहा है और 'किस' सर्वनाम से बना है। यह विशेषण की तरह संज्ञा 'पुस्तक' का बोध करा रहा है, इसलिए यह सार्वनामिक विशेषण है। 'पुस्तक' स्त्रीलिंग और एकवचन है, इसलिए 'किसकी' भी उसी के अनुसार प्रयोग हुआ है।

42. 'विश्लेषण' का अर्थ है किसी वस्तु को भागों में विभाजित करके समझना, जबकि 'संश्लेषण' का अर्थ है विभिन्न भागों को जोड़कर एक संपूर्ण रूप देना। दोनों शब्द परस्पर विपरीत अर्थ रखते हैं। इसलिए 'संश्लेषण' इसका उचित विलोम है।

43. जिन ध्वनियों का उच्चारण जीभ को ऊपर के दाँतों से लगाकर किया जाता है, उन्हें दन्त्य कहते हैं। जैसे त, थ, द, ध, न। यह उच्चारण स्थान के आधार पर वर्गीकरण है और इसमें जीभ दाँतों को स्पर्श करती है।

44. ऊष्म व्यंजन वे होते हैं जिनके उच्चारण में वायु का घर्षण अधिक होता है और हल्की गर्माहट जैसी ध्वनि निकलती है। 'श, ष, स' इसी श्रेणी में आते हैं। ये स्पर्श व्यंजनों से भिन्न होते हैं क्योंकि इनमें पूर्ण अवरोध नहीं होता।

45. 'अत्यधिक' का अर्थ है बहुत अधिक, जबकि 'अत्यल्प' का अर्थ है बहुत कम। दोनों शब्द मात्रा की दृष्टि से एक-दूसरे के विपरीत हैं। इसलिए 'अत्यल्प' इसका सही विलोम है।

46. 'ऋत' का अर्थ सत्य, नियम या धर्म से है, जबकि 'अनृत' का अर्थ असत्य होता है। दोनों शब्द एक-दूसरे के विपरीत अर्थ व्यक्त करते हैं। इसलिए 'अनृत' इसका सही विलोम है।

47. 'संकल्प' शब्द 'सम् + कल्प' से बना है। यहाँ 'सम्' उपसर्ग का अर्थ होता है 'पूर्णतः' या 'संपूर्ण रूप से'। संधि के कारण 'सम्' का 'संकल्प' रूप बन जाता है।

48. इस वाक्य में कर्ता स्पष्ट रूप से क्रिया नहीं कर रहा, बल्कि असमर्थता की भावना व्यक्त हो रही है– ''मुझसे खड़ा भी हुआ नहीं जाता।'' यहाँ क्रिया का केंद्र भाव है, इसलिए यह भाववाच्य है।

49. तद्भव-तत्सम संबंध में अर्थ और ध्वनि दोनों का संबंध होना आवश्यक होता है। 'लुनाई' का संबंध 'लवण' (नमक) से माना जाता है, जबकि 'लावण्यता' का अर्थ सौंदर्य या आकर्षण होता है, जो अलग मूल से आया है। इसलिए 'लुनाई' और 'लावण्यता' के बीच न तो ध्वन्यात्मक और न ही अर्थगत संबंध स्थापित होता है, अतः यह मेल गलत है।

50. यह जोड़ा गलत है क्योंकि 'स्कन्दगुप्त' नाटक जयशंकर प्रसाद की रचना है, न कि लक्ष्मीनारायण मिश्र की। अन्य सभी जोड़े सही लेखक और उनकी रचनाओं से संबंधित हैं।

51. 'उद्धव शतक' भारतेन्दु हरिश्चंद्र की रचना नहीं है। भारतेन्दु की प्रमुख रचनाओं में 'अंधेर नगरी' आदि शामिल हैं, जबकि 'उभव शतक' का संबंध अन्य कवि से है। इसलिए यह जोड़ा गलत है।

52. 'दर्शन दिग्दर्शन' रामचंद्र शुक्ल की कृति नहीं है। वे मुख्यतः 'हिंदी साहित्य का इतिहास' जैसी आलोचनात्मक रचनाओं के लिए प्रसिद्ध हैं। इसलिए यह लेखक-कृति युग्म गलत है।

53. यहाँ 'हाँ' के बाद अल्पविराम (,) होना चाहिए क्योंकि यह स्वीकृति सूचक पद है। सही वाक्य होगा– "हाँ, मेरा यही विचार है।" इसलिए विराम-चिह्न की दृष्टि से यह वाक्य अशुद्ध है।

54. 'सनातन', 'चिरंतन' और 'शाश्वत' तीनों का अर्थ है सदा रहने वाला या अनंत। जबकि 'अधुनातन' का अर्थ है आधुनिक या वर्तमान समय का, जो भिन्न अर्थ और प्रकृति का है।

55. 'अर्वाचीन' का अर्थ होता है आधुनिक या नवीन, इसलिए इसका विलोम 'प्राचीन' (पुराना) होगा। दोनों समय के संदर्भ में एक-दूसरे के विपरीत हैं।

56. 'विरहिणी' सही शब्द है, जिसमें 'इ' की मात्रा प्रयोग होती है। 'विरहणी' व्याकरण की दृष्टि से अशुद्ध रूप है। अन्य सभी शब्द शुद्ध हैं।

57. 'सब्ज बाग दिखाना' का अर्थ होता है झूठे सपने दिखाना या प्रलोभन देना, न कि सच में हरा-भरा करना। इसलिए यह युग्म गलत है।

58. इस दोहे में एक ही शब्द या पद से अनेक अर्थ निकलते हैं, जो श्लेष अलंकार की मुख्य विशेषता है। विशेष रूप से 'हरित दुति' पद के कई अर्थ लिए जा सकते हैं–रंग परिवर्तन, प्रसन्नता, प्रभाव का कम होना आदि। इसी प्रकार 'स्याम' और 'हरित' के संयोग से भाव, रंग और प्रतीक तीनों स्तरों पर अर्थ निकलते हैं। इसलिए यह दोहा श्लेष अलंकार का उत्कृष्ट उदाहरण है, जहाँ एक ही अभिव्यक्ति में बहुस्तरीय अर्थ निहित होते हैं।

59. 'गौशाला' = 'गौ + शाला' अर्थात् गायों की शाला। इसमें 'का/के/की' संबंध का लोप है और दूसरा पद प्रधान है। इसलिए यह तत्पुरुष समास है।

60. 'देशभक्ति' = 'देश के प्रति भक्ति'। यहाँ संबंध कारक (के प्रति) का लोप है। इसलिए यह तत्पुरुष समास का उदाहरण है।

61. The main aim of poetry recitation is to help learners feel rhythm, emotions, and beauty of language. It develops aesthetic sense and interest in literature. Hence, it focuses on enjoyment and appreciation.

62. 'European' begins with a consonant sound (/y/), so 'a' is used. 'Elephant' begins with a vowel sound, so 'an' is used. Therefore, the correct combination is "a European" and "an elephant".

63. The verb 'describe' does not take any preposition like of/about/to. It directly takes an object. Hence, this is the grammatically correct sentence.

64. The correct collocation is 'accused of', which means charged with a crime. Prepositions like 'to', 'for', or 'off' are incorrect in this usage.

65. 'Innocent' means not guilty or free from blame. The opposite meaning is 'guilty', which indicates responsibility for wrongdoing.

66. 'Significant' means something meaningful or important. 'Important' is the closest synonym among the given options as both convey similar importance.

67. The plural of 'ox' is 'oxen', formed by adding the suffix '-en'. This is an irregular plural form in English, unlike the others listed.

68. The sentence requires a possessive pronoun to replace "your dress" and avoid repetition. 'Yours' is the correct possessive pronoun form, while 'your' would need a noun after it. Hence, "This dress is yours and that one is mine" is grammatically correct.

69. In passive voice, the object becomes the subject and the correct tense structure must be maintained. Present perfect interrogative changes to "Has + subject + been + past participle". Therefore, option C is correct.

70. 'Gangapur' is the specific name of a place. Proper nouns always denote particular names of persons, places, or things. Hence, it is classified as a proper noun.

71. The word 'brave' describes the quality of the noun 'children'. Words that describe nouns or pronouns are called adjectives. Therefore, 'brave' is an adjective.

72. Material nouns refer to substances or materials from which things are made. 'Gold' is a metal and hence a material noun. Other options are not substances in this sense.

73. Abstract nouns represent ideas, qualities, or states that cannot be seen or touched. 'Connection' refers to a concept, not a physical object. Hence, it is an abstract noun.

74. 'Adversity' refers to a condition or state of hardship. It is not tangible and represents an idea. Therefore, it is an abstract noun.

75. In the sentence "He is working hard", 'hard' modifies the verb 'working'. Words that modify verbs are called adverbs. Hence, 'hard' is used as an adverb here.

76. The word 'but' joins two clauses and acts as a conjunction. Therefore, this sentence contains a conjunction.

77. Present perfect tense is formed using "have/has + past participle". The given sentence follows this structure. Hence, it is in present perfect tense.

78. The correct spelling is 'derogatory'. The given word is incorrectly spelt. The other options are correctly spelled words.

79. A transitive verb requires an object to complete its meaning. In this sentence, 'killed' has 'a snake' as its object. Therefore, it contains a transitive verb.

80. A negative sentence contains words like 'not', 'no', 'never' etc. which deny or negate the action. In this sentence, 'does not' clearly shows negation. The other sentences do not contain any negative marker.

81. Exclamatory sentences express strong feelings and usually begin with 'what' or 'how' and end with an exclamation. This sentence expresses admiration and emotion. The other options are interrogative or declarative in nature.

82. A complex sentence contains one main clause and one or more subordinate clauses. Here, "who does not love one's country" is a subordinate clause attached to the main clause. Hence, it is a complex sentence.

83. 'Mice' is the plural form of 'mouse'. The other options like 'goat', 'dog', and 'fox' are singular forms. Therefore, 'mice' is the correct plural noun.

84. Although 'mathematics' ends with 's', it is treated as a singular noun because it refers to a subject or field of study. The other options clearly indicate plural forms.

85. In active voice, the subject performs the action. Here, 'I' is performing the action of requesting. The other sentences are in passive voice as the subject receives the action.

86. In passive voice, the subject receives the action and the doer is often introduced by 'by'. Here, 'he' is receiving the action. Therefore, this is a passive voice sentence.

87. The word 'the' is used before specific nouns and is called a definite article. In both cases in the sentence, 'the' specifies particular nouns. Hence, both are definite articles.

88. The word 'students' can refer to both male and female persons. Such nouns that can denote either gender are called common gender. Therefore, 'students' is of common gender.

89. The structure "was going" indicates an action that was continuing in the past. It follows the pattern "was/were + verb-ing". Hence, it is in past continuous tense.

90. Language learning naturally begins with listening, as a learner first hears sounds and words before speaking, reading, or writing. This is the first stage in language acquisition.

91. $\angle CAQ = 70°$ (Given)

$\angle CAP + \angle CAQ = 180°$

$\angle CAP = 180° - \angle CAQ$

$= 180° - 70° = 110°$

$\because$ $\angle ABC = \angle CAP$

(Alternate Segment Angle)

$\therefore$ $\angle ABC = 110°$.

92. Given, C.P of 8 pens = S.P. of 6 pens

$$\therefore \quad \frac{\text{CP of pens}}{\text{SP of pens}} = \frac{6}{8}$$

Let CP and SP of a pen respectively ₹ $6x$ and ₹ $8x$

$$\text{Then, \% profit} = \frac{\text{SP} - \text{CP}}{\text{CP}} \times 100$$

$$= \frac{8x - 6x}{6x} \times 100$$

$$= \frac{2x}{6x} \times 100 = \frac{1}{3} \times 100 = 33\frac{1}{3}\%$$

93. $\because \frac{3}{5} = 0.6, \frac{4}{5} = 0.8$

(*a*) $\frac{7}{10} = 0.7 \Rightarrow 0.6 < 0.7 < 0.8$

(*b*) $\frac{19}{30} = 0.633 \Rightarrow 0.6 < 0.633 < 0.8$

(*c*) $\frac{2}{3} = 0.666 \Rightarrow 0.6 < 0.666 < 0.8$

(*d*) $\frac{16}{30} = 0.533 \Rightarrow 0.533 < 0.6$

$\therefore \frac{16}{30}$, will not be in between rational number $\frac{3}{5}$ and $\frac{4}{5}$.

94. Given, 3 Pens + 2 Pencils + 4 Rubbers

= ₹ 92 ...(1)

8 Pencils + 16 Rubbers = ₹ 68

4 × (2 Pencils + 4 Rubbers) = ₹ 68

2 Pencils + 4 Rubbers = ₹ 17 ...(2)

From eq. (1),

3 Pens + ₹ 17 = ₹ 92

[$\because$ From eq. (2), 2 Pencils + 4 Rubbers costs is ₹ 17]

3 Pens = ₹ 92 – ₹ 17

3 Pens = ₹ 75

1 Pen cost = ₹ 25

24 Pens costs = ₹ 25 × 24

= ₹ 600

So, 24 Pens cost is ₹ 600.

95. In triangle construction, having only three angles (AAA condition) determines the shape but not the size of the triangle. This means infinitely many similar triangles can be drawn, so a unique triangle cannot be constructed. On the other hand, conditions like SSS (three sides), SAS (two sides and included angle), and ASA (two angles and one side) give a unique triangle. Therefore, only three angles are insufficient for construction.

96. Let rectangular field length and breadth are x and y unit respectively.

Initial area of rectangular field $l \times b$

$= x \times y$ square unit

New length of rectangular field $= x \times 150\%$

$$= \frac{3x}{2} \text{ unit}$$

New breadth of rectangular field

$$= y \times 120\% = \frac{6y}{5} \text{ unit}$$

New area of rectangular field $= l \times b$

$$= \frac{3x}{2} \times \frac{6y}{5} = \frac{9}{5}xy \text{ square unit}$$

Increase in the area of rectangular field

$$= \frac{9}{5}xy - xy = \frac{4}{5}xy$$

$$= \frac{4}{5} \times \text{ initial area}$$

So, area will increase $\frac{4}{5}$ times.

97. As we

the relation between °C and F is,

$$\frac{°C}{5} = \frac{F-32}{9}$$

$$\frac{37}{5} = \frac{F-32}{9}$$

$$\therefore \quad F-32 = \frac{37 \times 9}{5} = 66.6$$

$F = 66.6 + 32$

$F = 98.6.$

98. Given, $1^2 + 2^2 + 3^2 + ... + 9^2 = 285$ ...(1)

$(0.11)^2 + (0.22)^2 + (0.33)^2 + ... + (0.99)^2$

$= (0.11)^2 [1^2 + 2^2 + 3^2 + ... + 9^2]$

$= (0.11)^2 \times 285$ [From eq. (1)]

$= 0.0121 \times 285 = 3.4485$

99. Let amount = ₹ x

Simple Interest $= 2x - x =$ ₹x

$$\because \text{Simple Interest} = \frac{p \times r \times t}{100}$$

$$\frac{x \times r \times 10}{100} = x$$

Let after t' years, amount will be three times.

Then, Simple Interest $= 3x - x = 2x$

$$\text{Simple Interest} = \frac{p \times r \times t}{100}$$

$$\frac{x \times 10 \times t'}{100} = 2x$$

$$t' = \frac{200}{10}$$

$t' = 20$ years

100. The squared playing field Area will be maxi-mum if

Diameter of circle = diagonal of square

$$\therefore \quad \sqrt{2}a = 80$$

D C 80 m a O A a B

$$a = \frac{80}{\sqrt{2}} = 40\sqrt{2} \text{ m}$$

$$\therefore \quad \sqrt{2}a = 80$$

$$a = \frac{80}{\sqrt{2}} = 40\sqrt{2} \text{ m}$$

The playing field area $= a^2 = \left(40\sqrt{2}\right)^2$

$= 3200 \text{ m}^2$

101. Corresponding angle in pie-chart $= \frac{52}{240} \times 360° = 78°$.

102. $p\%$ of $p\% = 36$

$$p \times \frac{p}{100} = 36$$

$$p^2 = 3600$$

$$p = \sqrt{3600} = 60$$

103.

2	2352
2	1176
2	588
2	294
3	147
7	49
7	7
	1

$2352 = 2 \times 2 \times 2 \times 2 \times 3 \times 7 \times 7$

$= (2)^4 \times (3)^1 \times (7)^2$

Compare with $2^x \times 3^y \times 7^z$, we get

$x = 4, y = 1, z = 2$

$\therefore \quad x + y + z = 4 + 1 + 2 = 7$

104.

2	100
2	50
5	25
5	5
	1

$100 = 2 \times 2 \times 5 \times 5$

$100 = (2)^2 \times (5)^2$

Total divisor of $100 = (2 + 1)(2 + 1)$

$= 3 \times 3 = 9$

Total odd divisor of $100 = (2 + 1) = 3$

Then, Total even divisor of $100 = 9 - 3 = 6$

105. Let 'n' cube can be cut.

Then, volume of 15 cm side cube

volume of $n \times 3$ cm side cube

$(15)^3 = n \times (3)^3$

$n = \dfrac{15 \times 15 \times 15}{3 \times 3 \times 3}$

$n = 5 \times 5 \times 5$

$n = 125$

So, 125 small cube can be cut from a 15 cm side cube.

106. $\dfrac{3^{1989}}{7} = \dfrac{\left((3)^3\right)^{663}}{7} = \dfrac{(27)^{663}}{7}$

$= (-1)^{663} = -1$

So, Remainder $= 7 - 1 = 6$.

107. The sum of internal angle of a polygon

$= (n - 2) \times 180°$

$(n - 2) \times 180° = 2160$

$n - 2 = 12$

$n = 14$

So the number of sides of polygon is 14.

108. The smallest Non-negative prime integer is 2 which is also only a even prime number.

109. $1\frac{1}{2} + 11\frac{1}{2} + 111\frac{1}{2} + 1111\frac{1}{2}$

$= (1 + 11 + 111 + 1111) + \left(\frac{1}{2} + \frac{1}{2} + \frac{1}{2} + \frac{1}{2}\right)$

$= 1234 + 2 = 1236.$

110. Given,

$a * b = a^2 + b^2 - ab$

$9 * 10 = (9)^2 + (10)^2 - 9 \times 10$

$= 81 + 100 - 90$

$= 181 - 90 = 91.$

111. $x^2 + xy + y^2 = x^2 + y^2 + 2xy - xy$

$= (x + y)^2 - xy$

$\because \quad (x + y)^2 \geq 4xy \qquad \left[\dfrac{x + y}{2} \geq \sqrt[2]{xy}\right]$

The value of $(x + y)^2$ always be positive whose value will be bigger than xy.

So, $x^2 + xy + y^2$ will always be positive.

112. As, $4 + 3 = 7$ and $1 + 6 = 7$

$3 + 2 = 5$ and $4 + 1 = 5$

$8 + 7 = 15$ and $9 + 6 = 15$

Similarly, $6 + 5 = 11$ and $7 + 4 = 11$

113. Given, a and b are two natural numbers.

$(a)^b = 125$

$(a^b) = (125)^1$ or $(a^b) = (5)^3$

$a = 125, b = 1$ | $a = 5, b = 3$

$(b)^a = (1)^{125} = 1$ | $(b)^a = (3)^5 = 243$

which is not given in options. | which is given in options.

114. The smallest number, which is divisible by 1 to 10 natural numbers will be the LCM of number from 1 to 10.

$1 = 1$

$2 = 1 \times 2$

$3 = 1 \times 3$

$4 = 1 \times 2 \times 2$

$5 = 1 \times 5$

$6 = 1 \times 2 \times 3$

$7 = 1 \times 7$

$8 = 1 \times 2 \times 2 \times 2$

$9 = 1 \times 3 \times 3$

$10 = 1 \times 2 \times 5$

L.C.M $= 1 \times 2 \times 2 \times 2 \times 3 \times 3 \times 5 \times 7$

$= 2520$

115. 4/8/2017 → Friday, after 61 days = 62nd day

62nd days = 8 weeks + 6 days

(Saturday, Sunday, Monday, Tuesday, Wednesday, Thursday)

So, after 61 days, the day will be Thursday.

116.

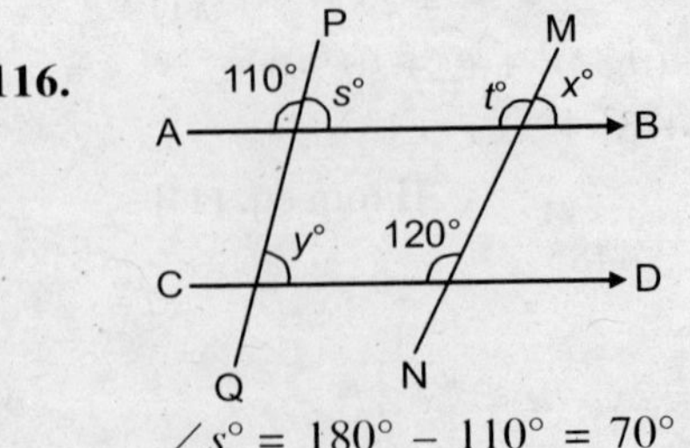

$\angle s° = 180° - 110° = 70°$

$\angle y = \angle s° = 70°$ (Corresponding angle)

$\angle t° = 120°$ (Corresponding angle)

$x° = 180° - \angle t°$

$= 180° - 120° = 60°$

$\therefore y° - x° = 70° - 60 = 10°$

117. Given, SP of article = ₹ 390

Profit % = 20%

$\because \quad CP = \frac{100}{(100 + \text{Profit}\%)} \times S.P.$

$= \frac{100}{100+20} \times 390 = \frac{100}{120} \times 390$

$=$ ₹ 325

So, CP of the article is ₹ 325.

118. % Increase in population

$= \frac{65,000 - 60,000}{60,000} \times 100$

$= \frac{5,000}{60,000} \times 100 = \frac{50}{6} = \frac{25}{3} = 8\frac{1}{3}\%$.

119. $\because \quad \frac{M_1 \times D_1}{W_1} = \frac{M_2 \times D_2}{W_2}$

$\frac{40 \times 30}{200} = \frac{30 \times D_2}{500}$

$D_2 = \frac{40 \times 30 \times 500}{200 \times 30}$

$D_2 = 100$ days.

120. We know that, the relation between the diagonals and side of rhombus is

$d_1^2 + d_2^2 = 4a^2$

Given that, $d_1 = 16$ cm, $d_2 = 12$ cm

$(16)^2 + (12)^2 = 4a^2$

$4a^2 = 256 + 144$

$4a^2 = 400$

$a^2 = 100$

$a = 10$ cm

So, side of rhombus is 10 cm.

121. Chlorophyll is any of several related green pigments found in the mesosomes of cyano- bacteria, as well as in the chloroplasts of algae and plants. Chlorophyll is essential in photosynthesis, allowing plants to absorb energy from light. Chlorophylls absorb light most strongly in the blue portion of the electromagnetic spectrum as well as the red portion. Conversely, it is a poor absorber of green and near-green portions of the spectrum, which it reflects, producing the green colour of chlorophyll-containing tissues. Two types of chlorophyll exist in the photosystems of green plants: chlorophyll *a* and *b*.

122. Human activities like use of aerosol cans release harmful gases such as CFCs, burning of forests increases carbon dioxide levels, and agricultural activities release methane and nitrous oxide. All these contribute to greenhouse effect and climate change. Therefore, all listed activities are responsible.

123. Jatropha *curcas* (Linnaeus) belongs to Euphorbiaceae family and widely planted as an economic crop. Jatropha is easy to grow and it is tolerant to stress and drought. Different parts of the plant such as bark, fruit and seeds were used for several applications in medicine and energy production. *Jatropha carcas seeds* are found to be the richest source of oil provides the highest productivity of biodiesel. Moreover, American and European standards organisation confirmed the quality of jatropha biodiesel and they are very well comparable with the commercially available fossil fuels. The productivity of biodiesel from crude jatropha oil can be improved by optimizing the conditions required for the conversion of seed oil to methyl ester of fatty acids.

124. Tulsi is an aromatic shrub in the basil family Lamiaceae (tribe ocimeae) that is thought to have originated in north central India and now grows native throughout the eastern world tropics. Within Ayurveda, tulsi is known as "The Incomparable One," "Mother Medicine of Nature" and "The Queen of Herbs," and is revered as an "elixir of life" that is without equal for both its medicinal and spiritual properties. Within India, tulsi has been adopted into spiritual rituals and lifestyle practices that provide a vast array of health benefits that are just beginning to be confirmed by modern science. This emerging science on tulsi, which reinforces ancient Ayurvedic wisdom, suggests that tulsi is a tonic for the body, mind and spirit that offers solutions to many modern day health problems.

125. Drinking water, also known as potable water, is water that is safe to drink or to use for food preparation. The amount of drinking water required to maintain good health varies, and depends on physical activity level, age, health-related issues, and environmental conditions. For those who work in a hot climate, up to 16 litres a day may be required. Liquid water, along with air pressure, nutrients, and solar energy, is essential for life.

126. Warren Anderson was the head of the Union Carbide when the Bhopal gas tragedy occurred on December 3, 1984. Bhopal gas tragedy is counted among the world's worst industrial and chemical disasters. On December 3, 1984, more than 40 tonnes of poisonous methyl isocyanate (MIC) has leaked and 4000 people were killed immediately. On December 7, 1984, Anderson was arrested and released on bail by the Madhya Pradesh Police. Later he fled to India and never returned. On February 1, 1992 he was declared a fugitive as he failed to appear before a court in Bhopal.

127. The United Nations, aware that the protection and improvement of the human environment is a major issue, which affects the well-being of peoples and economic development throughout the world, designated 5 June as World Environment Day. The celebration of this day provides us with an opportunity to broaden the basis for an enlightened opinion and responsible conduct by individuals, enterprises and communities in preserving and enhancing the environment. Since it began in 1974, it has grown to become a global platform for public outreach that is widely celebrated in more than 100 countries.

128. MS Swaminathan is an Indian geneticist and administrator, known for his role in India's Green Revolution, a program under which high-yield varieties of wheat and rice were planted. Swaminathan has been called the "Father of Green Revolution in India" for his role in introducing and further developing high-yielding varieties of wheat in India. He is the founder of the MS Swaminathan Research Foundation. His stated vision is to rid the world of hunger and poverty. Swaminathan is an advocate of moving India to sustainable development, especially using environmentally sustainable agriculture, sustainable food security and the preservation of biodiversity, which he calls an "evergreen revolution".

129. Established in 1982, Wildlife Institute of India (WII) is an internationally acclaimed Institution, which offers training program, academic courses and advisory in wildlife research and management. The Institute is actively engaged in research across the breadth of the country on biodiversity related issues. The institute is based in Dehradun, India. It is located in Chandrabani, which is close to the southern forests of Dehradun. The campus is 180 acres, from which 100 acres is wilderness and 80 acres is of institution.

130. During photosynthesis, green plants absorb carbon dioxide from the atmosphere through stomata. This carbon dioxide, along with water and sunlight, is used to synthesize glucose. Oxygen is released as a by-product, not absorbed.

131. A detritivore is a *heterotrophic* organism, which obtains its nutrition by feeding on *detritus*. Detritus is the organic matter made up of dead plant and animal material. Detritivores may also obtain nutrition by *coprophagy*, which is a feeding strategy involving the consumption of feces. Detritivores are often invertebrate insects such as mites, beetles, butterflies and flies; mollusks such as slugs and snails; or soil-dwelling earthworms, millipedes and woodlice.

132. The word geothermal comes from the Greek words geo (earth) and therme (heat). So, geothermal energy is heat from within the earth. We can use the steam and hot water produced inside the earth to heat buildings or generate electricity. Geothermal energy is a renewable energy source because the water is replenished by rainfall and the heat is continuously produced inside the earth.

133. Shola forests are tropical Montane forests found in the valleys separated by rolling grasslands only in the higher elevations. Generally they are patches of forests found mainly in the valleys where there is least reach of the fog and mist. They are usually separated from one another by undulating montane grassland. They are found only in South India in the Southern Western Ghats.

134. In India, pelicans are known to breed in multiple protected wetland areas such as Kokkare Bellur (Karnataka), Nelapattu (Andhra Pradesh), and Koonthankulam (Tamil Nadu). These sites provide suitable nesting and feeding conditions. Hence, all the given options are correct.

135. Minamata disease sometimes referred to as Chisso-Minamata disease is a neurological syndrome caused by severe mercury poisoning. Signs and symptoms include ataxia, numbness in the hands and feet, general muscle weakness, loss of peripheral vision, and damage to hearing and speech. In extreme cases, insanity, paralysis, coma, and death follow within weeks of the onset of symptoms. A congenital form of the disease can also affect fetuses in the womb. Minamata disease was first discovered in Minamata city in Kumamoto prefecture, Japan, in 1956. It was caused by the release of methylmercury in the industrial wastewater from the Chisso Corporation's chemical factory, which continued from 1932 to 1968.

136. The breakdown of ozone in the stratosphere results in reduced absorption of ultraviolet radiation. Consequently, unabsorbed and dangerous ultraviolet radiation is able to reach the Earth's surface at a higher intensity. Ozone levels have dropped by a worldwide average of about 4 percent since the late 1970s. For approximately 5 percent of the Earth's surface, around the north and south poles, much larger seasonal declines have been seen, and are described as "ozone holes". The discovery of the annual depletion of ozone above the Antarctic was first announced by Joe Farman, Brian Gardiner and Jonathan Shanklin, in a paper which appeared in Nature on May 16, 1985.

137. Hiralal Jekisundas Kania became the first Chief Justice of the Supreme Court of India after independence on August 14, 1947 and remained in office till November 5, 1951.

138. **Red Data Book :** The International Union for Conservation of Nature **IUCN**, is a global organization that works in the field of conservation of nature and sustainable use of natural resources. It is involved in gathering the data and also in analysis, research, field projects, support, and education. An objective of IUCN is to inspire, encourage and assist various organizations throughout the world to conserve nature and to ensure that any use of natural resources is reasonable and ecologically sustainable. The headquarters of IUCN are located in Gland, near Geneva, in Switzerland. IUCN was established in 1964, has formulated **Red List of Threatened Species** has evolved to become the world's most comprehensive source of information on the global conservation status of animal, fungi and plant species. **Red Data Book** is the book published by the IUCN, that provides all the information on **endangered species** of plants and animals.

139. Rekha Sharma has served as the Chairperson of the National Commission for Women. She has been associated with the commission in leadership roles and contributed to women-related policy and grievance redressal. Hence, this is the correct option.

140. As per Article 108 of Constitution, a Joint session of Parliament can be summoned in the following situations.

If after a Bill has been passed by one House and submitted to the other House:

(*a*) the Bill is rejected by the other House; or (*b*) the Houses have finally disagreed as to the amendments to be made in the Bill; or (*c*) more than six months elapse from the date of the reception of the Bill by the other House without the Bill being passed by it, the President may, unless the Bill has elapsed by reason of a dissolution of the House of the People, notify to the Houses by message if they are sitting or by public notification if they are not sitting, his intention to summon them to meet in a joint sitting for the purpose of deliberating and voting on the Bill.

However, in calculating period of six months, those days are not considered when house is prorogued or adjourned for more than 4 consecutive days.

If the above conditions are satisfied, the President of India may summon joint sitting of both the houses of parliament.

141-142. 73rd and 74th Constitutional Amendments were passed by Parliament in December, 1992. Through these amendments local self-governance was introduced in rural and urban India. The Acts came into force as the Constitution (73rd Amendment) Act, 1992 on April 24, 1993 and the Constitution (74th Amendment) Act, 1992 on June 1, 1993. These amendments added two new parts to the Constitution, namely, 73rd Amendment added Part IX titled "The Panchayats" and 74th Amendment added Part IXA titled "The Municipalities". The Local bodies—'Panchayats' and 'Municipalities' came under Part IX and IXA of the Constitution after 43 years of India becoming a republic.

143. Acid rain is a rain or any other form of precipitation that is unusually acidic, meaning that it has elevated levels of hydrogen ions (low pH). It can have harmful effects on plants, aquatic animals and infrastructure. Acid rain is caused by emissions of sulphur dioxide and nitrogen oxide, which react with the water molecules in the atmosphere to produce acids. Some governments have made efforts since the 1970s to reduce the release of sulphur dioxide and nitrogen oxide into the atmosphere with positive results. Nitrogen oxides can also be produced naturally by lightning strikes, and sulphur dioxide is produced by volcanic eruptions. Acid rain has been shown to have adverse impacts on forests, freshwaters and soils, killing insect and aquatic life-forms, causing paint to peel, corrosion of steel structures such as bridges, and weathering of stone buildings and statues as well as having impacts on human health.

144. The concept of 'Rule of Law' was developed by A.V. Dicey in England. It emphasizes equality before law and supremacy of law over arbitrary power. The Indian Constitution adopted this principle from the British legal system.

145. Functions of the Election Commission of India

- ECI is responsible for a free and reasonable election.
- It ensures that political parties and candidates adhere to the Model Code of Conduct.
- Regulates parties and registers them as per eligibility to contest in elections.
- Proposes the limit of campaign expenditure per candidate to all parties and monitors the same.
- It is mandatory for all political parties to submit annual reports to the ECI in order to be able to claim the tax benefit on the contributions.
- Guarantees that all political parties regularly submit audited financial reports.

146. **Question Hour:** The first hour of every parliamentary sitting is allotted for this. The concerned Minister is obliged to answer to the Parliament, either orally or in writing, depending on the type of question raised. Question Hour is not mentioned in the Constitution. It finds mention in the Rules of Procedure of the House.

147. Rain water harvesting is collection and storage of rain water that runs off from roof tops, parks, roads, open grounds, etc. This water runoff can be either stored or recharged into the ground water. A rainwater harvesting systems consists of the following components:

1. catchment from where water is captured and stored or recharged,
2. conveyance system that carries the water harvested from the catchment to the storage/recharge zone,
3. first flush that is used to flush out the first spell of rain,
4. filter used to remove pollutants,
5. storage tanks and/or various recharge structures.

148. Kaziranga Wildlife National Park is a title of a remarkable success story of conservation of the One Horned Indian Rhinoceros and other wild lives in the North East India. It is not only the homeland of the Great Indian One Horned Rhinoceros, but also provides shelter to a variety of wild lives. It is one of the significant Wildlife natural habitat for in situ conservation of biological biodiversity of universal value. The values and criteria made Kaziranga National Park to get inscribed in the World Heritage Site List 1985. The Wildlife Kaziranga National Park covered area consists of 429.93 sq.km. with an additional area of 429.40 sq.km. and situated in the two districts of Assam, namely Golaghat and Nagaon.

149.

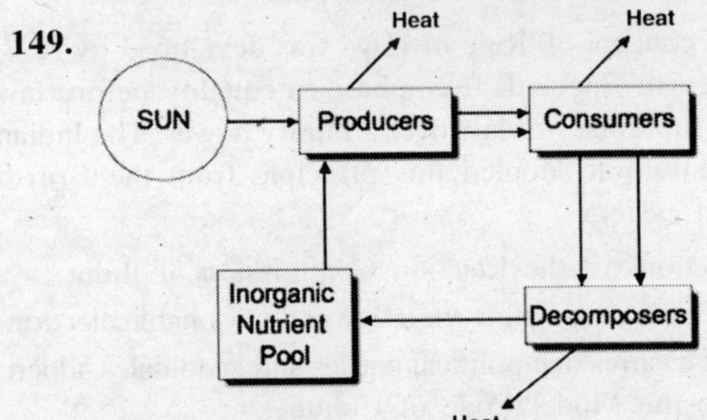

Energy and nutrient transfer through ecosystems

150. The greenhouse effect is a naturally occurring phenomenon that is responsible for heating of Earth's surface and atmosphere. You would be surprised to know that without greenhouse effect the average temperature at surface of Earth would have been a chilly −18°C rather than the present average of 15°C. In order to understand the greenhouse effect, it is necessary to know the fate of the energy of sunlight that reaches the outermost atmosphere. Clouds and gases reflect about one-fourth of the incoming solar radiation, and absorb some of it but almost half of incoming solar radiation falls on Earth's surface heating it, while a small proportion is reflected back. Earth's surface re-emits heat in the form of infrared radiation but part of this does not escape into space as atmospheric gases (e.g., carbon dioxide, methane, etc.) absorb a major fraction of it. The molecules of these gases radiate heat energy, and a major part of which again comes to Earth's surface, thus heating it up once again. This cycle is repeated many a times. The above-mentioned gases - carbon dioxide and methane - are commonly known as greenhouse gases (see below figure) because they are responsible for the greenhouse effect.

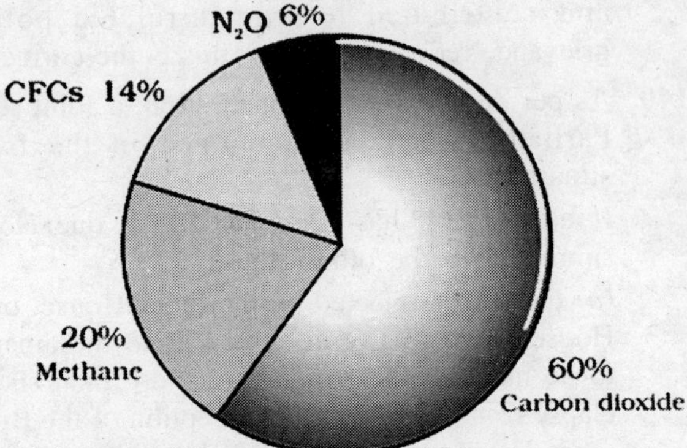

Figure: Relative contributions of various greenhouse gases to total global warming

Child Development & Pedagogy

SECTION-A

CHILD DEVELOPMENT

A. MEANING OF CHILD DEVELOPMENT

Child development refers to the progressive and orderly growth of a child in multiple areas including physical, mental, emotional, social, linguistic, and creative capacities. It is a continuous process through which children acquire skills, knowledge, attitudes, and behavior that shape their overall personality. Child development is not limited to age-based growth but involves the development of competencies and potential in different domains.

Necessity of Child Development

Understanding child development is essential for several reasons:

1. **Proper Guidance:** Helps parents, teachers, and caregivers provide age-appropriate support and education.
2. **Identifying Abilities:** Assists in recognizing a child's strengths, talents, and areas needing improvement.
3. **Balanced Growth:** Ensures physical, mental, emotional, and social development in harmony.
4. **Early Intervention:** Detects developmental delays or behavioral issues at an early stage for corrective measures.
5. **Preparation for Life:** Supports the child in becoming a confident, responsible, and skilled individual.

Development and Growth

Growth and Development are two important concepts related to changes that occur in individuals over time.

Growth refers to the physical changes in the body. It includes an increase in height, weight, size, and structure of the body. Growth is quantitative in nature, which means it can be measured easily using numbers, such as centimeters and kilograms. It mainly focuses on external and visible changes.

Development, on the other hand, refers to the overall changes in a person's abilities and skills. It includes physical, cognitive, emotional, social, and moral development. Development is qualitative in nature, meaning it is related to changes in functioning and behavior that cannot always be measured directly. It involves improvement in thinking, learning, communication, and emotional maturity.

Growth is a part of development, but development is broader and more comprehensive. While growth may stop after a certain age, development continues throughout life.

In simple terms, growth is about physical increase, whereas development is about overall progress and improvement in abilities.

Stages of Child Development

Child development occurs through a series of continuous and interconnected stages, each marked by distinct patterns of physical, cognitive, emotional, and social growth.

1. **Prenatal Stage (Conception to Birth):** The prenatal stage begins at conception and continues until birth. During this period, the foundation of life is established as the body's major organs and systems develop. The brain and nervous system grow rapidly, and the health, nutrition, and environment of the mother significantly influence the development of the fetus.
2. **Infancy Stage (0 to 2 Years):** The infancy stage covers the period from birth to two years of age and is characterized by rapid physical and psychological growth. Infants gradually gain control over their bodies, learning to sit, crawl, stand, and walk. Cognitive development begins as they recognize familiar faces and respond to sounds. Emotional bonds, especially with caregivers, form during this time, and early communication develops from crying and babbling to the use of simple words.
3. **Early Childhood (2 to 6 Years):** Early childhood, which spans from two to six years, is a time of increased independence and curiosity. Children improve their motor skills and become more coordinated in their movements. Their thinking becomes more imaginative, and they begin to understand the world through play and exploration. Language development progresses quickly, allowing

them to form sentences and express ideas. Socially, they learn to interact with others, share, and follow basic rules.

4. **Middle Childhood (6 to 12 Years):** Middle childhood, from six to twelve years, is marked by steady growth and the development of more structured thinking. Children begin to think logically and develop problem-solving skills. They gain knowledge through formal education and become more aware of their abilities and limitations. Friendships and peer relationships become important, and children learn cooperation, discipline, and responsibility.
5. **Adolescence (12 to 18 Years):** Adolescence, which ranges from twelve to eighteen years, is a transitional stage between childhood and adulthood. Physical changes occur due to puberty, leading to growth in height and changes in body structure. Cognitive abilities expand to include abstract thinking and reasoning. Emotionally, adolescents explore their identity and seek independence, while social relationships, particularly with peers, become more significant.
6. **Adulthood (18 Years and Above):** Adulthood follows adolescence and involves maturity in all aspects of development. Physically, individuals reach their peak and gradually experience changes associated with aging. Cognitive development includes advanced reasoning, decision-making, and problem-solving abilities. Emotionally, adults tend to develop stability and a clearer sense of self. Socially, they take on responsibilities such as careers, relationships, and family life, contributing actively to society.

JEAN PIAGET'S THEORY

Jean Piaget's Theory of Cognitive Development states that children are active learners who construct their understanding of the world through interaction with their environment. According to this theory, children progress through four distinct stages of cognitive development as they age. Piaget emphasized that mental development occurs through processes such as schemas (mental frameworks), assimilation (integrating new information into existing schemas), and accommodation (modifying schemas to incorporate new information).

Stage	Age Range	Characteristics / Cognitive Development
Sensorimotor Stage	0 – 2 years	- Learning through senses and motor activities - Develops object permanence (understanding that objects exist even when not seen) - Begins to coordinate sensory input with physical actions
Preoperational Stage	2 – 7 years	- Symbolic thinking develops (use of words, images, symbols) - Egocentric thinking (difficulty seeing things from others' perspective) - Imaginative and pretend play increases - Limited understanding of cause and effect
Concrete Operational Stage	7 – 11 years	- Logical thinking develops but mainly with concrete objects and situations - Understanding of conservation (quantity, mass, volume remain the same despite changes in shape) - Ability to classify and organize objects - Reduced egocentrism, improved perspective-taking
Formal Operational Stage	12 years and above	- Abstract and hypothetical thinking develops - Can reason logically about abstract concepts - Problem-solving and planning skills improve - Ability to think about possibilities, ideals, and future scenarios

B. BASIS OF CHILD DEVELOPMENT AND FACTORS INFLUENCING IT

Child development is a continuous, dynamic, and holistic process through which a child progresses physically, mentally, emotionally, socially, linguistically, and creatively. It involves the gradual acquisition of skills, knowledge, habits, attitudes, and behaviors that together form the foundation of the child's personality and life skills. Understanding child development is essential for parents, teachers, and caregivers, as it helps them provide appropriate guidance, create supportive environments, and nurture a child's potential in a balanced manner.

The development of a child primarily depends on two fundamental bases: heredity (inheritance) and environment. These factors work in tandem and influence every aspect of a child's growth, shaping abilities, behavior, temperament, and overall personality.

Heredity (Inheritance)

Heredity, or genetic inheritance, refers to the transmission of physical, mental, and psychological traits from parents to the child through genes. It plays a foundational role in determining a child's development potential.

Influence of Heredity

- **Physical Attributes:** Heredity influences physical characteristics such as height, body structure, facial features, eye color, hair type, and complexion. These traits form the biological framework within which the child develops.
- **Cognitive Abilities:** Intellectual capacity, learning potential, memory, and problem-solving aptitude are also influenced by genetic factors. Some children may inherit a natural inclination towards mathematics, music, or language.
- **Personality Traits:** Temperament, behavioral tendencies, and emotional responsiveness are often shaped by inherited traits. For example, some children may naturally be more introverted or extroverted, calm or energetic.
- **Health Predispositions:** Certain health conditions or tendencies, such as susceptibility to specific illnesses, are genetically inherited, influencing the child's physical and mental development.

Although heredity provides the potential and framework for development, it does not operate in isolation. A child's genes set the possibilities, but the actual growth, learning, and expression of these traits depend heavily on the environment.

Environment

Environment refers to the sum of all external conditions, influences, and experiences that a child encounters from birth onward. While heredity provides potential, the environment shapes, nurtures, and directs that potential into actual growth.

Types of Environmental Influence

1. **Family Environment:** The family environment is the primary and most influential context for a child's early development. Children learn their first lessons about love, care, security, and social norms within the family.
   - **Emotional Support:** A nurturing family helps the child develop emotional stability, self-confidence, and the ability to form healthy relationships.
   - **Parenting Styles:** Authoritative, supportive, or permissive parenting styles significantly affect behavior, discipline, moral values, and social skills.
   - **Habits and Values:** Daily routines, family interactions, and parental guidance help instill habits, ethical values, and coping mechanisms.
   - **Security and Motivation:** A safe and encouraging home environment fosters exploration, curiosity, and creativity.
2. **Social Environment:** The broader social environment includes society, culture, traditions, community, and peer groups. Social interactions play a vital role in shaping the child's social and emotional competencies.
   - **Social Skills:** Through engagement with others, children learn cooperation, teamwork, sharing, and conflict resolution.
   - **Cultural Values:** Traditions, customs, and societal expectations help the child understand norms and develop moral reasoning.
   - **Peer Influence:** Friendships and peer groups provide opportunities for social learning, enhancing self-esteem, communication, and negotiation skills.
   - **Empathy and Adjustment:** Exposure to diverse social situations teaches children empathy, tolerance, and adaptability.
3. **School Environment:** Schools are structured environments that contribute significantly to cognitive, social, and moral development. Education, teacher guidance, and co-curricular activities provide opportunities to practice learned skills and acquire new ones.
   - **Intellectual Development:** Schools develop logical thinking, problem-solving, and analytical skills through structured learning.
   - **Discipline and Responsibility:** Regular schedules, rules, and participation in activities promote discipline, responsibility, and time management.
   - **Social Interaction:** Interaction with teachers and peers enhances cooperation, leadership, and communication skills.
   - **Creativity and Expression:** Art, music, science projects, and other activities encourage creativity, innovation, and independent thinking.
4. **Communication Medium (Media Environment):** In modern times, media such as television, internet, social media, and books have become major environmental factors influencing child development.
   - **Knowledge and Awareness:** Educational content, documentaries, and books expose children to new ideas, cultures, and concepts.

- **Language and Expression:** Media improves vocabulary, comprehension, and the ability to communicate effectively.
- **Creativity and Imagination:** Interactive games, storytelling, and creative apps encourage imaginative thinking and problem-solving.
- **Risks of Overexposure:** Excessive screen time or inappropriate content may lead to behavioral problems, reduced attention span, or social withdrawal. Balanced and supervised use is crucial for positive development.

Interaction of Heredity and Environment: Child development is not determined solely by genes or environment alone. Heredity sets the potential, providing the blueprint for physical, cognitive, and emotional abilities. Environment acts as a nurturing agent, directing, shaping, and realizing this potential. A child with strong genetic potential requires a supportive, stimulating, and healthy environment to thrive fully. Likewise, a child with less innate potential can develop remarkable abilities through guidance, education, and environmental support.

The interplay between heredity and environment influences all domains of development—physical growth, mental and cognitive skills, emotional regulation, social adaptation, language acquisition, and creative expression.

IMPORTANT FACTS

- Child development is the process of physical, mental, emotional, social, and language growth in children.
- Understanding child development helps in effective teaching, guidance, and overall growth.
- Stages of development: Infancy (0–2 yrs), Early Childhood (3–6 yrs), Middle Childhood (7–11 yrs), Adolescence (12–18 yrs).
- Physical development – body growth, motor skills, coordination, health.
- Mental development – thinking, reasoning, problem-solving, cognitive skills.
- Emotional development – understanding, expressing, and managing emotions.
- Language development – speech, vocabulary, comprehension, communication.
- Expressive ability – conveying thoughts and feelings effectively.
- Creativity – imagination, originality, and innovative thinking.
- Basis of development – heredity (genetics) and environment.
- Environmental factors – family, social interactions, school, peers, communication medium.
- Influencing factors – heredity, environment, nutrition, health, education, culture, social context.

MEANING AND PRINCIPLES OF LEARNING

A. MEANING OF LEARNING

Learning is a complex, ongoing process through which an individual acquires knowledge, skills, attitudes, and values, leading to a relatively permanent change in behavior or understanding. It is the foundation of human development, enabling individuals to adapt to their environment, solve problems, and achieve personal and professional growth.

Key Characteristics of Learning

1. **Behavioral Change:** Learning results in visible or measurable changes in behavior, skills, or understanding. For example, a child learning to tie shoelaces or solve arithmetic problems.
2. **Acquisition of Knowledge and Skills:** Learning enables the individual to gain both theoretical understanding (like reading comprehension) and practical skills (like cycling or painting).
3. **Experience-Based:** Learning often occurs through life experiences, observation, experimentation, practice, and reflection.
4. **Lifelong Process:** Learning is not limited to formal education; it continues throughout life as individuals adapt to new situations, technologies, and environments.
5. **Influenced by Internal and External Factors:** Learning depends on personal abilities, motivation, and the surrounding environment.

Factors Affecting Learning

The process of learning is influenced by multiple interrelated factors. These can broadly be categorized as internal (personal) factors and external (environmental) factors.

1. **Internal Factors**
   - **Intelligence:** Children with higher cognitive abilities may grasp concepts faster and apply knowledge effectively. For example, a mathematically gifted child may solve problems more quickly.
   - **Motivation:** A motivated learner actively engages in learning. Motivation can be intrinsic (interest in the subject) or extrinsic (rewards or recognition).
   - **Interest:** Learning is more effective when the subject matter aligns with the learner's personal interests. For example, a child interested in animals will enjoy biology lessons more.
   - **Emotional State:** Anxiety, stress, or fear can hinder concentration and memory, while positive emotions like curiosity, excitement, and confidence enhance learning.

- **Physical Health:** Proper nutrition, adequate sleep, and general well-being are essential for sustaining attention and energy required for learning.
- **Previous Knowledge:** Prior understanding and experience create a foundation for new learning. For instance, knowledge of basic arithmetic helps in learning algebra.

2. **External Factors**
   - **Family Environment:** A supportive family encourages exploration, provides learning resources, and reinforces positive behavior. Parental guidance, encouragement, and values shape habits, attitudes, and motivation.
   - **School Environment:** Teachers, curriculum design, classroom management, and peer interactions significantly influence learning. Schools provide structured opportunities for cognitive, social, and emotional growth.
   - **Socio-Cultural Factors:** Social norms, culture, traditions, and community values guide the child's attitudes, behavior, and understanding of the world.
   - **Learning Materials:** Availability of books, digital tools, laboratory equipment, and educational toys improves comprehension and engagement.
   - **Media and Technology:** Educational media, online resources, and technology platforms can enhance learning by providing interactive, engaging, and innovative ways to understand complex topics.

Influential Methods of Learning

Learning is most effective when appropriate methods are applied. Different strategies and approaches influence how well knowledge, skills, and attitudes are acquired.

1. **Observation (Learning by Seeing):** Children and adults learn by observing the behavior, actions, and outcomes of others. For example, a child learns to cook by watching a parent or learns social skills by observing peers.
2. **Practice or Learning by Doing:** Active participation and hands-on experience reinforce learning. For example, practicing handwriting, solving math problems, or performing science experiments helps retain knowledge and develop skills.
3. **Reading and Writing:** Reading exposes the learner to ideas, facts, and theories, while writing helps consolidate understanding and improve expression. Journals, essays, and note-taking are practical examples.
4. **Discussion and Interaction:** Group discussions, debates, and collaborative projects encourage learners to think critically, articulate ideas, and evaluate multiple perspectives. This method enhances cognitive, social, and emotional skills simultaneously.
5. **Experimentation:** Learning through experimentation allows children to test hypotheses, make mistakes, and learn from them. For example, conducting science experiments or trial-and-error problem-solving improves analytical and creative thinking.
6. **Multimedia and Digital Learning:** Audio-visual aids, interactive apps, educational videos, and online platforms cater to different learning styles—visual, auditory, and kinesthetic. They make complex ideas more understandable and learning more engaging.
7. **Reward and Motivation-Based Learning:** Positive reinforcement, encouragement, and rewards increase motivation and engagement. For example, praising a child for completing a task correctly encourages consistent effort.

Key Insights

Learning is not a simple accumulation of facts; it is an active, participatory, and multidimensional process. Its effectiveness depends on:

- The learner's abilities, interest, and motivation.
- A supportive, stimulating, and resource-rich environment.
- Use of appropriate learning methods and strategies.
- Integration of experiences, practice, and reflection.

By understanding the meaning, influencing factors, and effective methods, educators, parents, and learners themselves can enhance the learning process, ensuring it is meaningful, deep, and long-lasting.

B. RULES OF LEARNING – THORNDIKE'S PRINCIPLES AND THEIR IMPORTANCE

Learning is the process through which an individual acquires knowledge, skills, attitudes, or behavior changes due to experience or practice. Psychologists have studied the mechanisms of learning to understand how humans and animals acquire new behaviors. One of the most influential contributors to the study of learning was Edward L. Thorndike (1874–1949), an American psychologist known for his "Connectionism" theory.

Thorndike proposed that learning is the formation of connections between stimuli and responses. His work primarily involved experiments with animals, such as cats in puzzle boxes, to study how behaviors are learned through trial and error. Based on his research, he formulated three main laws of learning, which are widely applied in education, psychology, and skill development.

Thorndike's Main Rules (Laws) of Learning

1. **Law of Readiness (Law of Preparedness):** Learning is most effective when the learner is ready and motivated to learn. A learner who is physically, mentally, and emotionally prepared is more likely to engage in the learning process.

- If a learner is eager, alert, and willing, the process of forming connections between stimulus and response occurs smoothly. Conversely, forcing learning when a learner is unwilling or unprepared can lead to resistance or frustration.
- A student who is curious about science will learn a new concept in physics more effectively than one who is disinterested or tired.

2. **Law of Exercise (Law of Practice):** Connections between stimulus and response are strengthened with repeated practice and weakened when not practiced. Repetition helps reinforce learning and improves retention.
   - **Explanation:** The more a learner practices a skill, the more automatic it becomes. This law emphasizes the role of habit formation in learning.
   - **Example:** Learning to write, play a musical instrument, or solve mathematical problems requires repeated practice to achieve proficiency.
3. **Law of Effect:** Responses that lead to satisfying or positive outcomes are more likely to be repeated, while those that produce discomfort or negative consequences are less likely to recur.
   - Learning is strengthened when rewards or positive reinforcement follow a correct response. Conversely, undesirable results discourage the behavior.
   - A student who is praised for solving a problem correctly will attempt similar problems again, whereas scolding for a mistake may reduce motivation.

Additional Considerations in Thorndike's Theory

- Thorndike emphasized trial-and-error learning, especially in early stages of skill acquisition.
- Learning is incremental; small successes gradually build mastery.
- He rejected the idea that learning is purely the result of insight or sudden realization; rather, learning is a process of forming and strengthening connections through experience.

Importance of Thorndike's Rules of Learning

1. **Enhances Effective Teaching**
   - Understanding the Law of Readiness helps teachers ensure students are attentive, motivated, and prepared to learn before introducing new concepts.
   - Using the Law of Exercise, teachers can design repetitive practice exercises to reinforce learning.
   - Positive reinforcement based on the Law of Effect ensures that students associate learning with satisfaction and motivation.
2. **Guides Curriculum Design**
   - Curriculum and teaching materials can be structured to progress from simple to complex topics, aligning with the learner's readiness and ensuring systematic practice.
3. **Improves Skill Acquisition**
   - Practical skills, like handwriting, sports, music, or vocational abilities, improve significantly when repeated practice is encouraged and errors are corrected with constructive feedback.
4. **Supports Behavioral and Emotional Development**
   - The Law of Effect highlights the importance of rewards and encouragement in shaping positive behaviors. This principle is applied in classrooms, therapy, and parenting to promote desirable behaviors.
5. **Provides a Scientific Basis for Learning Theories**
   - Thorndike's laws laid the groundwork for behaviorist learning theories, influencing later psychologists like B.F. Skinner and educational practices worldwide.

Thorndike's rules of learning—Law of Readiness, Law of Exercise, and Law of Effect—provide a practical and scientific framework for understanding how humans learn. These laws emphasize the importance of motivation, repetition, and reinforcement in learning. By applying these principles, educators, parents, and trainers can create effective, structured, and meaningful learning experiences that enhance knowledge, skills, and behavior in a lasting way.

C. KEY PRINCIPLES OF LEARNING AND THEIR PRACTICAL UTILITY IN CLASSROOM TEACHING

Learning is a structured process in which individuals acquire knowledge, skills, attitudes, and values, leading to a relatively permanent change in behavior. Several psychologists and educators have studied learning and formulated principles and theories that guide effective teaching. Understanding these principles helps teachers make learning meaningful, engaging, and long-lasting.

Key Principles of Learning

The principles of learning describe how knowledge and skills are acquired and retained:

- **Readiness:** Learning occurs most effectively when the learner is physically, mentally, and emotionally ready. A student who is alert, motivated, and interested in a topic will understand and retain information better. For instance, a student curious about astronomy will grasp a lesson on planets faster than one who is uninterested. In the classroom, teachers can enhance readiness by explaining the purpose of a lesson and connecting it to real-life experiences.

- **Exercise (Practice):** Repetition strengthens learning, while lack of practice weakens it. Skills such as writing, arithmetic, or performing experiments improve with consistent practice. In the classroom, assigning daily exercises or engaging activities ensures reinforcement and helps form habits and mastery.
- **Effect (Feedback and Reinforcement):** Learning is reinforced when responses lead to satisfying outcomes and weakened if outcomes are unpleasant. Praising a student for a correct answer encourages further effort, while scolding may reduce motivation. Positive reinforcement in classrooms enhances self-confidence and encourages desired behavior.
- **Individual Differences:** Every learner has unique abilities, interests, and learning pace. Teachers can accommodate these differences through differentiated instruction, flexible assignments, and personalized feedback, ensuring all students make progress.

Thorndike's Principle of Trial and Error

Thorndike's principle of trial and error is a fundamental concept in learning psychology, which states that learning occurs through a process of repeated attempts, mistakes, and gradual correction. When a learner faces a problem, they try multiple responses until the correct one is discovered. Successful responses are strengthened, while unsuccessful responses gradually disappear.

Key Concepts of Trial and Error Learning

1. **Law of Effect:** Responses that produce satisfying results are strengthened and repeated, while responses that produce discomfort or failure are weakened and gradually eliminated.
2. **Incremental Learning:** Learning is gradual, built step by step, rather than instantaneous.
3. **Active Participation:** The learner must actively engage with the problem to find a solution.
4. **Error Correction:** Mistakes are a natural part of learning, helping the learner discover correct responses.

Examples in Everyday Learning

- A child learning to ride a bicycle may fall multiple times, adjusting balance and pedaling techniques until they succeed.
- A student solving a math problem may make several calculation errors, but gradually learns the correct procedure through repeated practice.
- A programmer debugging code tries different solutions until the program works correctly.

Importance of Thorndike's Trial and Error Principle

- Encourages active learning and problem-solving rather than passive memorization.
- Highlights the role of experience and practice in mastering skills.
- Emphasizes reinforcement, where successful attempts are strengthened, forming habits and learning patterns.
- Provides a foundation for behavioral learning theories, influencing modern educational methods, habit formation, and skill development.

Pavlov's Relation Theory of Feedback

Pavlov's classical conditioning theory not only explains how associations are formed between stimuli, but it also lays the foundation for understanding feedback in learning. In educational contexts, Pavlov's ideas are often applied to describe how responses to stimuli can be strengthened or modified through reinforcement, which is essentially feedback.

The Relation Theory of Feedback refers to the process in which a learner's response to a stimulus is influenced and strengthened by subsequent feedback or reinforcement. Just as Pavlov's dogs learned to associate a neutral stimulus (bell) with food, humans can learn behaviors or knowledge when their responses are followed by appropriate feedback.

In other words, feedback acts as a conditioned stimulus that reinforces correct behavior or knowledge acquisition, promoting learning.

Key Concepts

1. **Stimulus-Response Relationship (S-R Relation):** Learning occurs when a specific stimulus leads to a predictable response. Feedback strengthens this S-R connection.
2. **Positive Feedback:** Praise, rewards, or encouragement given immediately after a correct response helps reinforce the association between the learning task (stimulus) and the correct response.
3. **Negative Feedback:** Constructive correction or highlighting errors helps the learner modify incorrect responses, preventing repetition of mistakes.
4. **Reinforcement Timing:** Immediate feedback after a response is more effective in strengthening the learning connection, similar to how Pavlov paired the bell with food simultaneously for faster learning.
5. **Association Building:** Through repeated feedback, the learner associates certain cues, actions, or stimuli with the expected response, just as Pavlov's dogs associated the bell with food.

Examples in Classroom Learning

- A teacher asks a student a math problem.
  - If the student answers correctly, immediate praise reinforces learning (positive feedback).
  - If the answer is wrong, the teacher provides hints or corrections, helping the student adjust their response (negative feedback).
- In language learning, repeating the correct pronunciation of a word and immediately correcting mistakes strengthens the association between the sound (stimulus) and the correct response.

Importance in Learning

- Helps strengthen correct responses and reduce errors.
- Promotes habit formation and consistency in learning.
- Encourages active participation, as learners see that their responses have consequences.
- Makes learning adaptive and progressive, similar to classical conditioning where repeated pairing strengthens the learned behavior.

Skinner's Action Learning Theory

B.F. Skinner (1904–1990), an American psychologist, proposed the Action Learning Theory, also known as Operant Conditioning, which explains learning as a process where behavior is influenced by its consequences. In simple terms, a learner's action is strengthened or weakened based on reinforcement or punishment. Unlike Pavlov's classical conditioning (which focuses on associations), Skinner emphasized active behavior and its outcomes.

Key Concepts of Skinner's Theory

1. **Operant Behavior:** Behavior that acts on the environment to produce a consequence. For example, a student raises a hand to answer a question; the response depends on previous outcomes.
2. **Reinforcement:** Any consequence that increases the likelihood of a behavior being repeated. Reinforcement can be:
   - **Positive Reinforcement:** Rewarding a correct response, e.g., praise, grades, stickers.
   - **Negative Reinforcement:** Removing an unpleasant stimulus when a correct response occurs, e.g., exempting a student from extra homework for good performance.
3. **Punishment:** Any consequence that reduces the likelihood of a behavior being repeated. Punishment can be:
   - **Positive Punishment:** Adding an unpleasant consequence, e.g., scolding.
   - **Negative Punishment:** Removing a pleasant stimulus, e.g., taking away privileges.
4. **Shaping:** Gradually reinforcing successive approximations of a desired behavior until the learner performs the complete behavior.

   Example: Teaching a child to write letters step by step, praising small improvements along the way.
5. **Schedules of Reinforcement:** Behavior can be reinforced at different intervals or ratios to strengthen learning:
   - **Continuous Reinforcement:** Every correct response is reinforced.
   - **Partial Reinforcement:** Only some correct responses are reinforced, e.g., weekly rewards, which make learning more resistant to extinction.

Examples in Learning

- A teacher gives praise or gold stars to students who answer questions correctly, increasing participation (positive reinforcement).
- A student loses recess time for incomplete homework, decreasing undesirable behavior (negative punishment).
- A computer-based learning program gives immediate feedback for correct answers, shaping correct learning habits gradually.

Importance in Learning

- Encourages active participation; learners act and learn from consequences.
- Reinforcement strengthens desired behaviors and skill acquisition.
- Helps in behavior modification, habit formation, and classroom management.
- Can be applied to both academic learning and social/behavioral skills.
- Provides a scientific method to measure and shape learning outcomes.

Kohler's Theory of Understanding (Insight Learning)

Wolfgang Köhler (1887–1967), a German psychologist, proposed the Theory of Insight Learning, which emphasizes sudden understanding or "aha" moments in the learning process. Unlike trial-and-error learning, insight learning occurs when a learner suddenly perceives the solution to a problem by reorganizing or restructuring the elements of the problem in their mind.

Insight learning is cognitive and mental, not merely behavioral, and shows that learning can be intelligent, immediate, and understanding-based rather than just repetitive.

Key Features of Insight Learning

1. **Sudden Recognition of Relationships:** The learner suddenly sees how various elements of a problem are related, leading to a solution.
2. **Mental Reorganization:** The learner mentally restructures the problem rather than relying on repeated trial and error.
3. **Problem Solving:** Insight occurs mostly in situations where direct experience alone is insufficient, requiring reasoning, imagination, and understanding.
4. **Retention of Learning:** Once insight occurs, the solution is usually retained longer, because it is based on understanding rather than rote learning.

Kohler's Experiments

Kohler conducted classic experiments with chimpanzees on the island of Tenerife:

- **Problem:** A banana was hung out of reach of the chimpanzee.
- **Observation:** Instead of trying randomly to reach the banana (trial-and-error), the chimpanzee suddenly stacked boxes or used a stick to reach it.
- **Conclusion:** The chimpanzee had a moment of insight, understanding the relationship between the objects and the goal.

Other experiments showed similar sudden problem-solving abilities in apes, highlighting cognitive processes in learning.

Key Principles

1. **Cognitive Processing:** Learning involves mental representation of the problem.
2. **Active Understanding:** Learners actively try to understand relationships and causality.
3. **Sudden Learning:** Solutions often appear suddenly rather than gradually.
4. **Transfer of Learning:** Once insight is gained, learners can apply similar solutions to new problems.

Examples in Human Learning

- A student suddenly figures out a shortcut to solve a complex math problem after understanding the underlying principle.
- A programmer realizes the logic error in a code after analyzing the program structure, without trying random fixes.
- A child uses objects creatively to build a toy or solve a challenge after understanding the function of each piece.

Importance in Learning

- Encourages creative thinking and problem-solving.
- Promotes cognitive development rather than rote memorization.
- Helps learners apply knowledge to new situations.
- Shows that learning can be rapid, intelligent, and long-lasting when insight occurs.

Vygotsky's Theory of Learning Curve

Lev Vygotsky (1896–1934), a Russian psychologist, emphasized the social and cultural context of learning. His theory of the learning curve focuses on how a learner progresses in acquiring knowledge or skills over time, highlighting that learning is not uniform but occurs in stages influenced by social interaction, guidance, and scaffolding.

According to Vygotsky, a learning curve represents the progression of learning and performance over time, showing the rate at which a learner acquires a new skill or knowledge. Learning is most effective when learners are supported in their Zone of Proximal Development (ZPD), i.e., the range between what a learner can do independently and what they can do with guidance.

Key Concepts of Vygotsky's Learning Curve

1. **Learning is Social:** Interaction with teachers, peers, and mentors significantly affects the learning pace.
2. **Zone of Proximal Development (ZPD):** The learning curve depends on tasks within the ZPD—too easy tasks lead to stagnation, while tasks that are too hard can cause frustration.
3. **Guidance and Scaffolding:** The rate of learning can be improved with appropriate support, prompting, and feedback from teachers or more capable peers.
4. **Gradual Improvement:** The learning curve typically shows initial slow progress, steady improvement, and sometimes plateaus, which reflect periods of consolidation before further progress.

Types of Learning Curves (as applied in Vygotsky's Theory)

1. **Steep Learning Curve:**
   - Rapid acquisition of knowledge or skills.

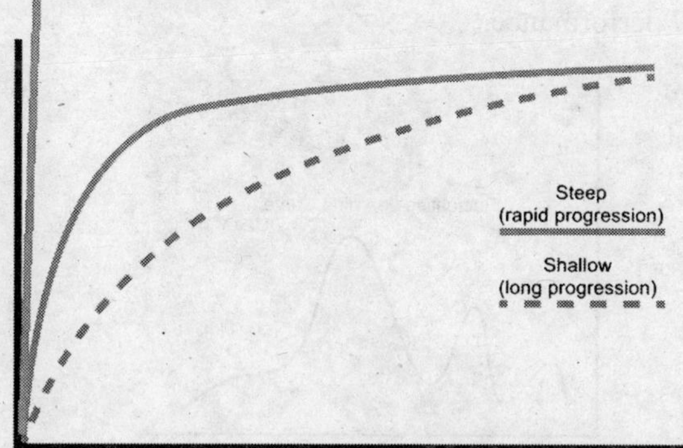

- Usually occurs when the learner is highly motivated and guidance/scaffolding is effective.
- Example: A student quickly mastering a simple computer skill with proper instruction.

2. **Gradual Learning Curve:**
- Slow and steady progress over time.
- Represents consistent effort, practice, and reinforcement.
- **Example:** Learning a musical instrument over months, gradually improving technique.

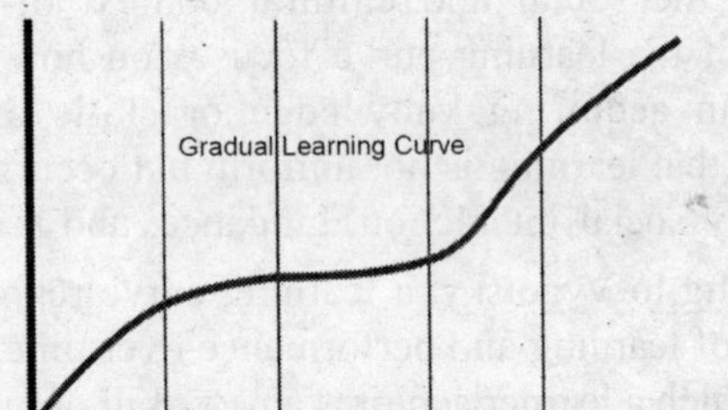

3. **Plateau in Learning Curve:**
- A temporary stagnation in progress where performance seems to stop improving.
- Common in complex learning tasks when the learner is consolidating knowledge or encountering obstacles.
- Causes include lack of motivation, fatigue, insufficient guidance, or difficulty of the material.
- Solution: Provide additional guidance, review concepts, encourage practice, or break tasks into smaller steps.

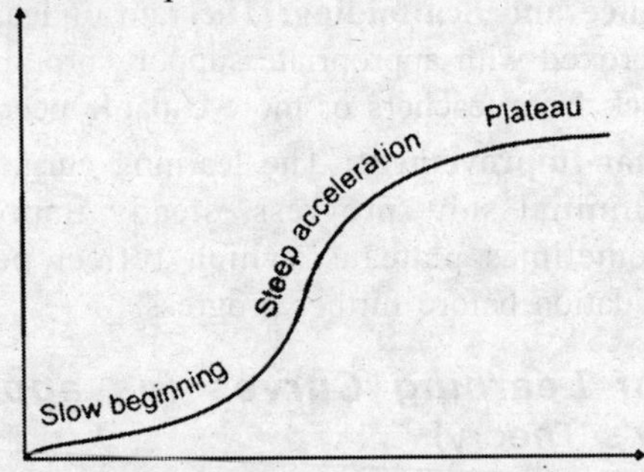

4. **Fluctuating Learning Curve:**
- Progress may rise and fall, showing variability in performance.

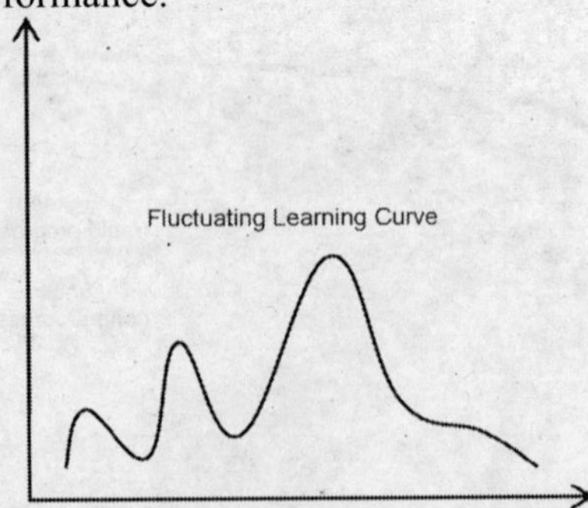

- Often seen when learners try new strategies or face varying levels of challenge.

Practical Implications in Education

- Teachers can monitor the learning curve to identify where learners need support.
- Instruction should be adapted to the learner's ZPD, providing guidance just beyond their independent capabilities.
- Plateaus should be recognized as normal, with interventions like reinforcement, scaffolding, or alternative strategies.
- Encourages active collaboration, peer learning, and social interaction, which accelerate the learning process.

Plateau in Learning – Meaning, Causes, and Solutions

In the context of learning, a plateau refers to a period during which a learner's progress temporarily stops or stagnates, despite continued effort. On a learning curve, this appears as a flat section where performance does not seem to improve. Plateaus are a natural and common part of the learning process, particularly in skill acquisition, cognitive development, or behavior learning.

Even though no visible progress occurs, internal consolidation and skill stabilization often take place during this period. A plateau does not indicate failure; it is usually temporary and can be overcome with appropriate strategies.

Causes of Plateau in Learning

1. **Fatigue or Mental Exhaustion:** Continuous learning without breaks can tire the learner, causing temporary stagnation.
2. **Lack of Motivation:** If the learner feels bored, unchallenged, or discouraged, progress slows.
3. **Complexity of Material:** Introducing advanced concepts or skills before mastering foundational ones can create a plateau.
4. **Insufficient Guidance or Feedback:** Learners may struggle if they do not receive adequate instruction, correction, or reinforcement.
5. **Overconfidence or Routine:** Learners may rely on habits or repetitive practice without actively seeking improvement, causing stagnation.
6. **Emotional or Environmental Factors:** Stress, distractions, poor learning environment, or personal issues can interrupt progress.
7. **Physical or Health Limitations:** In physical skill learning (sports, handwriting, motor skills), health or energy levels can cause temporary plateaus.

Solutions to Overcome Plateau

1. **Provide Guidance and Scaffolding:** Offer additional support, demonstrations, or strategies to help learners advance beyond the stagnation point.
2. **Set Clear, Incremental Goals:** Break complex tasks into smaller steps to make progress measurable and achievable.
3. **Introduce Variety in Practice:** Change exercises, tasks, or approaches to make learning more engaging and reduce monotony.
4. **Offer Feedback and Reinforcement:** Timely constructive feedback helps learners correct mistakes and regain motivation.
5. **Encourage Reflection and Problem-Solving:** Ask learners to analyze their approach, identify challenges, and experiment with new strategies.
6. **Maintain Motivation and Emotional Support:** Recognize effort, celebrate small achievements, and provide encouragement to overcome frustration.
7. **Allow Rest and Consolidation:** Temporary breaks or rest periods can help consolidate learning and prevent fatigue-related plateaus.
8. **Peer Learning and Collaboration:** Working with others can provide new insights, guidance, and motivation to overcome stagnation.

IMPORTANT FACTS

- Learning is a process, not a product.
- It involves change in behavior.
- Change must be relatively permanent.
- It occurs through experience and practice.
- Learning is universal (occurs in all humans).
- Readiness – Learning is best when the learner is mentally & physically ready.
- Practice (Exercise) – Repetition strengthens learning.
- Effect – Learning improves with satisfaction or reward.
- Motivation – Increases interest and efficiency.
- Reinforcement – Strengthens behavior (positive/negative).
- Attention – Concentration is necessary.
- Feedback – Immediate feedback improves performance.
- Individual Differences – Learners differ in ability and speed.
- Transfer of Learning – Previous learning affects new learning.
- Active Participation – Learning is better with active involvement.
- Ivan Pavlov – Classical Conditioning
- Dog Experiment: Food → salivation (natural response)
- Bell + Food → salivation
- Bell alone → salivation
- Concept: Learning by association
- B.F. Skinner – Operant Conditioning
- Skinner Box: Rat presses lever → gets food (reward)
- Behavior increases due to reward
- Concept: Learning by reinforcement and punishment
- Edward Thorndike – Trial and Error Theory
- Puzzle Box: Cat tries many methods → finally escapes
- Learning through repeated attempts
- Concept: Learning by trial and error
- Laws of Learning:
  - ❑ Law of Effect – Responses followed by satisfaction are strengthened
  - ❑ Law of Exercise – Practice strengthens learning
  - ❑ Law of Readiness – Learning occurs when the learner is ready
- Wolfgang Köhler – Insight Learning
- Chimpanzee Sultan: Uses sticks to get banana
- Sudden solution without trial-and-error
- Concept: Learning by insight (sudden understanding)
- Learning = Permanent change in behavior due to experience
- Key Principles = Readiness, practice, effect, motivation, reinforcement
- Learning improves with attention, feedback, participation
- Theories explain learning as association, reinforcement, insight, observation

TEACHING AND LEARNING METHODS

Teaching and learning are central processes in education. Effective teaching not only imparts knowledge but also develops skills, attitudes, and critical thinking in learners. Understanding the meaning, purpose, principles, sources, and methods of teaching is essential for educators to design impactful learning experiences.

1. **Meaning of Teaching:** Teaching is a systematic process through which a teacher facilitates learning by guiding, motivating, and supporting students. It involves presenting knowledge, explaining concepts, demonstrating skills, and encouraging learners to engage actively.

   In essence, teaching is helping someone learn. It is not merely transferring information, but creating an environment where learners can construct understanding, develop skills, and apply knowledge in real-life situations.

2. **Purpose of Teaching:** The primary purposes of teaching include:
   - **Knowledge Transmission:** To provide learners with factual, conceptual, and procedural knowledge.
   - **Skill Development:** To help learners acquire intellectual, physical, and practical skills.
   - **Attitude and Value Formation:** To guide learners in developing ethical values, positive attitudes, and social behavior.
   - **Critical Thinking and Problem-Solving:** To enable learners to analyze, reason, and apply knowledge creatively.
   - **Motivation for Lifelong Learning:** To encourage curiosity, inquiry, and self-directed learning.
3. **Communication in Teaching:** Communication is the foundation of effective teaching. A teacher communicates knowledge, instructions, and feedback, while learners express understanding, doubts, and responses.
   - **Types of Communication**
     - ❑ **Verbal Communication:** Using spoken words, lectures, discussions, and explanations.
     - ❑ **Non-Verbal Communication:** Gestures, body language, visual aids, and facial expressions.
   - **Importance:** Clear and effective communication ensures that learners understand concepts, remain engaged, and are motivated to learn.
4. **Principles of Teaching:** Teaching is guided by several established principles that enhance learning effectiveness:
   - **Principle of Interest:** Students learn better when the content is interesting and relevant to them.
   - **Principle of Participation:** Active involvement improves understanding and retention.
   - **Principle of Reinforcement:** Regular practice, feedback, and rewards strengthen learning.
   - **Principle of Progression:** Teaching should move from simple to complex concepts, ensuring gradual understanding.
   - **Principle of Individual Differences:** Teaching must accommodate different learning abilities, interests, and speeds.
   - **Principle of Motivation:** Encouraging and inspiring learners enhances learning outcomes.
5. **Sources of Teaching:** Effective teaching draws on various sources to provide knowledge and enrich learning:
   - **Textbooks and Reference Books:** Structured and verified information for classroom use.
   - **Teacher's Experience and Expertise:** Practical knowledge and illustrations from the teacher.
   - **Library and Internet Resources:** Access to up-to-date knowledge, multimedia, and research.
   - **Experiences and Real-Life Situations:** Field visits, experiments, observations, and practical exercises.
   - **Peer Learning:** Discussions, group activities, and collaborative learning among students.
6. **Teaching Methods:** Teaching methods are organized ways of presenting content to facilitate learning. They can be classified into traditional and modern methods:

   (a) Traditional Methods
   - **Lecture Method:** Teacher-centered explanation of concepts; efficient for large groups.
   - **Demonstration Method:** Showing practical application of skills or experiments; effective for skills learning.
   - **Discussion Method:** Interaction among teacher and students to explore ideas and clarify doubts.
   - **Project Method:** Students complete tasks or projects, promoting active and experiential learning.

   (b) Modern / New Methods (Approaches)
   - **Problem-Based Learning (PBL):** Students learn by solving real-life problems, encouraging critical thinking.
   - **Collaborative / Cooperative Learning:** Group activities to achieve shared learning goals.
   - **Inquiry-Based Learning:** Encourages questioning, exploration, and discovery.
   - **E-Learning / Digital Learning:** Use of multimedia, online platforms, and digital resources for flexible learning.
   - **Experiential Learning:** Learning through direct experiences, simulations, and hands-on activities.
7. **Basic Teaching:** Basic teaching refers to the fundamental process of instruction that ensures learning takes place effectively. It involves:
   - **Planning:** Preparing lessons, objectives, content, and materials.
   - **Presentation:** Delivering the content using appropriate methods and examples.
   - **Interaction:** Engaging students through questions, discussions, and activities.
   - **Evaluation:** Assessing understanding through questions, tests, or practical exercises.
8. **Basic Skills of Teaching:** Successful teaching requires mastery of basic teaching skills, which include:
   - **Explanation:** Clearly conveying concepts and ideas in simple language.
   - **Questioning:** Asking relevant and thought-provoking questions to stimulate thinking.

- **Listening:** Actively understanding students' responses, doubts, and feedback.
- **Blackboard / Visual Aid Skills:** Using diagrams, charts, and multimedia effectively.
- **Reinforcement:** Encouraging correct responses and providing constructive feedback.
- **Stimulating Interest:** Creating engaging and motivating learning experiences.
- **Classroom Management:** Maintaining discipline and a conducive environment for learning.

Teacher-Oriented Method (Teacher-Centered Method)

The teacher-oriented method is a traditional approach to teaching in which the teacher plays the central and dominant role in the learning process. In this method, the teacher controls the content, pace, and direction of learning, while students act mainly as passive listeners. The focus is on transmission of knowledge from teacher to students.

In this approach, the teacher explains concepts, gives instructions, and provides information, and students are expected to listen, take notes, and memorize the content. It is commonly used in lecture-based teaching, where the teacher delivers information and students have limited interaction.

Characteristics

- Teacher is the main authority and source of knowledge.
- Students have a passive role in learning.
- Emphasis on lecture, explanation, and memorization.
- Limited student participation and interaction.
- Uniform teaching method for all learners.

Advantages

- Useful for teaching large groups of students.
- Helps in covering syllabus quickly.
- Provides clear and structured information.
- Effective for introducing new concepts.

Disadvantages

- Students may become passive and less engaged.
- Less scope for creativity and critical thinking.
- Does not address individual differences effectively.
- Limited development of problem-solving skills.

Example: A teacher explaining a chapter on the board while students listen quietly and take notes.

Student-Oriented Method (Learner-Centered Method)

The student-oriented method is an approach to teaching in which the student is the central focus of the learning process. In this method, learning is active, and students participate, explore, and construct knowledge through their own experiences. The teacher acts as a facilitator or guide rather than the main source of information.

In this approach, students are encouraged to ask questions, solve problems, work in groups, and express their ideas. It promotes active learning, critical thinking, creativity, and independent learning.

Characteristics

- Student is the center of the learning process.
- Teacher acts as a facilitator or guide.
- Emphasis on active participation and interaction.
- Learning through activities, discussion, and experience.
- Focus on individual differences and needs.

Advantages

- Enhances understanding and long-term retention.
- Develops critical thinking and problem-solving skills.
- Encourages creativity and self-confidence.
- Promotes active participation and interest in learning.

Disadvantages

- Time-consuming compared to teacher-centered methods.
- Requires careful planning and skilled teachers.
- Difficult to manage in large classrooms.

Example: Students working in groups to solve a problem, perform an experiment, or participate in a discussion while the teacher guides them.

Comparison: Teacher-Oriented vs Student-Oriented Method

Basis	Teacher-Oriented Method	Student-Oriented Method
Focus	Teacher is the center	Student is the center
Role of Teacher	Authority, knowledge provider	Facilitator, guide
Role of Student	Passive listener	Active participant
Teaching Style	Lecture-based	Activity-based, interactive
Learning Process	One-way communication	Two-way communication
Participation	Limited	High
Thinking Skills	Focus on memorization	Focus on critical thinking
Individual Differences	Mostly ignored	Considered
Classroom Environment	Formal and controlled	Flexible and interactive
Outcome	Short-term learning	Deep and long-term learning

IMPORTANT FACTS

- Teaching and learning are interrelated processes that aim at bringing behavioral change in learners.
- Learning is student-centered, while teaching provides guidance and direction.
- Effective teaching depends on methods, strategies, and learner participation.
- Lecture Method – Teacher explains content; useful for large classes but less interactive.
- Demonstration Method – Learning by seeing (teacher shows, students observe).
- Discussion Method – Encourages thinking, interaction, and expression of ideas.
- Project Method – Learning by doing; based on real-life activities.
- Activity Method – Students actively participate in tasks and activities.
- Problem-Solving Method – Students learn by solving problems logically.
- Heuristic Method – Learners discover knowledge by themselves.
- Programmed Learning – Step-by-step learning with immediate feedback.
- Teaching should follow principles like motivation, reinforcement, readiness, and practice.
- Use of teaching aids (charts, models, audio-visual tools) improves learning.
- Learning becomes effective when there is active participation and feedback.
- Teaching should consider individual differences among learners.
- Good teaching develops thinking, reasoning, and creativity.
- Teaching-learning process should be continuous and interactive.

INCLUSIVE EDUCATION: GUIDANCE AND COUNSELING

A. EDUCATIONAL INCLUSION RESPECTS IDENTITY

Inclusive education is an educational approach that ensures all children, irrespective of their differences, have equal access to quality education. It focuses on equity, participation, and learning for all, adapting teaching, curriculum, and environment to meet each learner's needs. It is not merely placing children with different abilities in the same classroom but actively removing barriers to learning and promoting full participation.

1. **Meaning of Inclusive Education:** Inclusive education means integrating all children into mainstream schools and classrooms, including those who face physical, mental, social, or cultural barriers. It emphasizes that every child—regardless of gender, caste, religion, language, region, physical ability, or cognitive differences—has the right to learn in a supportive and accessible environment. It ensures that learners are accepted, valued, and supported to achieve their full potential.
2. **Identity and Types of Inclusion:** Inclusive education addresses diverse forms of exclusion. Some main types include:
   - **Socio-Cultural Inclusion:** Ensuring children are not excluded based on caste, religion, gender, language, region, or color.
   - **Economic Inclusion:** Providing opportunities for children from low-income or marginalized families.
   - **Disability Inclusion:** Including children with physical, sensory, or cognitive disabilities, such as:
     - ❑ **Visually Impaired (Blind or Low Vision):** Using braille books, audio materials, and tactile aids.
     - ❑ **Hearing Impaired (Deaf):** Using sign language, captioned content, and hearing devices.
     - ❑ **Speech/Bone Impairments:** Supporting communication with assistive devices, speech therapy, and adapted teaching.
     - ❑ **Physical Mobility Impairments:** Ensuring barrier-free classrooms, ramps, and accessible facilities.
   - **Mental and Cognitive Inclusion:** Supporting children with learning difficulties or lower mental efficiency through remedial teaching and personalized attention.
3. **Causes of Exclusion:** Certain groups of children may face barriers to education due to social, cultural, or personal factors, such as:
   - **Caste, Religion, or Language:** Children from minority communities may face discrimination or difficulties with the medium of instruction.
   - **Gender:** Girls in some regions may have limited access to education.
   - **Region or Socio-economic Status:** Children in rural or underdeveloped areas may lack resources, teachers, or infrastructure.
   - **Color or Ethnicity:** Social discrimination can limit participation.
   - **Physical and Mental Disabilities:** Sensory, motor, or cognitive impairments may restrict access without adaptive strategies.

4. **Strategies for Resolution and Inclusion:** Inclusive education requires planned strategies to address barriers and support all learners:
   - **Curriculum Adaptation:** Modify teaching content, methods, and assessment according to individual needs.
   - **Teacher Training:** Equip teachers with skills to manage diverse classrooms and apply inclusive teaching methods.
   - **Assistive Technology:** Provide tools like braille readers, hearing aids, speech devices, and adaptive software.
   - **Policy Implementation:** Enforce laws and policies, such as the Right to Education Act, that guarantee equitable education.
   - **Community and Peer Support:** Encourage peer mentoring, collaborative learning, and parental involvement.
5. **Guidance in Inclusive Education:** Guidance in inclusive education helps learners make informed decisions and overcome challenges:
   - **Academic Guidance:** Assists students in understanding subjects, learning strategies, and coping with difficulties.
   - **Career Guidance:** Helps adolescents identify interests, skills, and career opportunities suited to their abilities.
   - **Personal Guidance:** Supports social, emotional, and behavioral development, helping learners handle stress, anxiety, or low self-confidence.
   - **Special Needs Guidance:** Provides tailored support for children with disabilities, learning difficulties, or social disadvantages.
   - **Family and Community Guidance:** Involves parents and communities to actively participate in children's education and support inclusion.
6. **Counseling in Inclusive Education:** Counseling is a structured support system that addresses learners' emotional, psychological, and social needs:
   - **Emotional Support:** Helps children handle frustration, anxiety, or feelings of exclusion.
   - **Behavioral Counseling:** Guides children to develop positive behaviors, self-discipline, and social skills.
   - **Motivational Support:** Encourages students to actively participate and build self-confidence.
   - **Remedial Counseling:** Provides special strategies for students with learning difficulties, ensuring they are not left behind academically.
7. **Examples of Excluded Groups Addressed Through Inclusive Education**
   - Children from economically disadvantaged families who may lack learning materials.
   - Children from minority religions or castes facing social barriers.
   - Girls in regions with gender bias in education.
   - Children with physical disabilities such as mobility issues or sensory impairments.
   - Students with mental or cognitive challenges requiring tailored support.
   - Children whose language or cultural background differs from the medium of instruction.
8. **Importance of Inclusive Education in Practice:** Inclusive education ensures that every child has:
   - Access to quality education regardless of background or ability.
   - Opportunities to participate socially and academically in mainstream classrooms.
   - Support to develop skills, knowledge, and critical thinking.
   - A safe and supportive learning environment that fosters equity, respect, and cooperation.
   - Access to guidance and counseling that addresses personal, social, and academic needs.

B. EQUIPMENT, MATERIALS, METHODS, TLM, AND OBSERVATIONS REQUIRED FOR INCLUSIVE EDUCATION

Inclusive education ensures that all children, regardless of abilities, backgrounds, or learning challenges, participate fully in classroom learning. To achieve this, educators need to use special equipment, learning materials, teaching methods, and observation strategies to support diverse learners effectively.

1. **Equipment Required for Inclusive Education:** Equipment in inclusive education refers to physical or technological tools that help children with disabilities or learning challenges access education effectively. These include:
   - **Assistive Technology for Visual Impairments:**
     - ❑ Braille books and slates
     - ❑ Magnifying glasses and screen magnifiers
     - ❑ Audio books and text-to-speech devices
     - ❑ Tactile learning tools (maps, diagrams, charts with raised surfaces)
   - **Assistive Technology for Hearing Impairments:**
     - ❑ Hearing aids and amplification devices
     - ❑ FM systems for classrooms
     - ❑ Captioned videos and visual alert devices
     - ❑ Sign language interpreters

- **Equipment for Physical Disabilities:**
  - ❑ Wheelchairs, walking aids, and adjustable furniture
  - ❑ Ramps, accessible desks, and ergonomic seating
  - ❑ Adaptive keyboards or switches for computer use
- **Equipment for Speech and Communication Impairments:**
  - ❑ Speech-generating devices (communication boards, tablets with speech apps)
  - ❑ Alternative communication cards or sign language guides
- **General Classroom Equipment for Inclusion:**
  - ❑ Projectors and screens for visual learning
  - ❑ Interactive whiteboards for multisensory teaching
  - ❑ Comfortable seating arrangements to accommodate learners with mobility challenges

2. **Materials Required for Inclusive Education:** Materials are learning resources that support diverse learning needs. These materials must be adapted to the abilities and interests of students:

- **Visual Materials:**
  - ❑ Charts, pictures, diagrams, and illustrations
  - ❑ Flashcards, storybooks with large print or braille
  - ❑ Color-coded teaching aids for easier understanding
- **Audio Materials:**
  - ❑ Recorded lessons, audio books, and storytelling recordings
  - ❑ Podcasts and language tapes for listening and comprehension practice
- **Kinesthetic/Tactile Materials:**
  - ❑ Clay, blocks, and puzzles for hands-on learning
  - ❑ Braille maps, tactile diagrams, and models
  - ❑ Manipulative tools for mathematics and science
- **Digital Materials:**
  - ❑ E-books and learning apps with accessibility features
  - ❑ Interactive simulations and educational games
  - ❑ Videos with captions or sign language interpretation
- **Specialized Materials for Students with Disabilities:**
  - ❑ Adaptive pens and grips for children with fine motor challenges
  - ❑ Hearing-friendly classroom acoustics and visual cues for hearing-impaired students
  - ❑ Customized worksheets with simplified language for slow learners

3. **Methods Required for Inclusive Education:** Methods in inclusive education refer to teaching strategies that accommodate diverse learners. These methods focus on active engagement, differentiation, and individual support:

- **Differentiated Instruction:** Teaching the same concept in multiple ways to meet diverse learning needs.
- **Peer-Assisted Learning:** Pairing students to encourage collaboration, mentorship, and social learning.
- **Multisensory Teaching:** Using visual, auditory, and tactile methods to reinforce learning.
- **Activity-Based Learning:** Encouraging hands-on experiences, experiments, and practical demonstrations.
- **Collaborative and Cooperative Learning:** Group projects and discussion circles that involve all learners.
- **Remedial Teaching:** Providing extra instruction or alternative explanations for learners who struggle.
- **Scaffolding:** Offering step-by-step guidance, gradually reducing support as students gain independence.

4. **Teaching-Learning Materials (TLM) in Inclusive Education:** TLM are organized resources that support teaching and learning. They help students understand concepts better and participate actively:

- **Visual Aids:** Charts, flashcards, pictures, graphs, and mind maps
- **Models and Real Objects:** Mathematical models, science apparatus, maps, and globes
- **Audio-Visual Aids:** Videos, films, audio recordings, and multimedia presentations
- **Digital TLM:** Tablets, computers, educational software, online learning platforms
- **Hands-On Materials:** Puzzles, games, building blocks, manipulatives, and craft materials
- **Adaptive TLM:** Braille charts, sign language flashcards, tactile maps, and communication boards

Role of TLM

- Reinforces concepts through multiple senses
- Makes abstract ideas tangible
- Encourages interactive and student-centered learning
- Supports learners with special needs by providing alternative ways to understand information

5. **Observations Required for Inclusive Education:** Observation is critical in inclusive education to identify learner needs, monitor progress, and adapt teaching strategies. Observations help teachers make evidence-based decisions about learning support.
   - **Classroom Behavior Observation:**
     - ❑ Participation in activities
     - ❑ Interaction with peers and teachers
     - ❑ Response to instructions and learning materials
   - **Learning Progress Observation:**
     - ❑ Understanding of concepts
     - ❑ Completion of tasks and assignments
     - ❑ Accuracy, speed, and quality of work
   - **Social and Emotional Observation:**
     - ❑ Confidence, self-esteem, and motivation
     - ❑ Emotional responses to challenges and successes
     - ❑ Cooperation, empathy, and social interactions
   - **Physical and Health Observation:**
     - ❑ Physical mobility and posture
     - ❑ Use of assistive devices
     - ❑ Fatigue or discomfort during learning activities
   - **Cognitive Observation:**
     - ❑ Problem-solving skills
     - ❑ Attention span and memory
     - ❑ Ability to follow instructions and apply learning

   Observations should be continuous and systematic, enabling teachers to modify teaching methods, adapt materials, and provide guidance or counseling as needed for inclusive education.

C. NECESSARY TOOLS AND TECHNIQUES FOR TESTING THE LEARNING OF INCLUSIVE CHILDREN

Testing the learning of inclusive children involves assessing students with diverse abilities, backgrounds, and learning needs. The primary goal is to measure knowledge, skills, understanding, and progress while accommodating differences in cognitive, physical, sensory, or social abilities. Traditional testing methods may not be suitable for all learners, so specialized tools and techniques are required for inclusive education.

1. **Meaning of Assessment in Inclusive Education:** Assessment in inclusive education is a process of evaluating learning outcomes, understanding individual needs, and providing feedback to enhance learning. It is not limited to academic performance; it also evaluates social, emotional, cognitive, and functional abilities.

   Assessment must be flexible, personalized, and accessible, ensuring every child has an equal opportunity to demonstrate their learning.

2. **Tools Required for Testing Inclusive Children:** Testing tools for inclusive children are adapted to different abilities and may be categorized as follows:

   (a) Written and Printed Tools
   - **Modified Question Papers:** Large print, simplified language, braille versions, or visual representations.
   - **Worksheets and Task Sheets:** Adapted for fine motor abilities or cognitive levels.
   - **Graphic Organizers:** Charts, tables, or diagrams to help learners structure answers.

   (b) Oral and Verbal Tools
   - **Oral Examinations:** Teacher asks questions verbally, allowing children with writing difficulties to respond.
   - **Structured Interviews:** Individualized discussions to assess understanding and critical thinking.
   - **Story Retelling and Explanation Tasks:** Assess comprehension, language, and expression skills.

   (c) Practical and Performance-Based Tools
   - **Project Work:** Evaluates creativity, application of knowledge, and collaborative skills.
   - **Hands-On Activities:** Experiments, art, craft, or practical exercises to assess understanding.
   - **Role-Play and Simulation:** Helps evaluate problem-solving, social, and communication skills.

   (d) Digital and Technological Tools
   - **Computer-Based Testing:** Adapted software for children with mobility or learning challenges.
   - **Audio-Visual Tests:** Using videos or audio clips for comprehension and analysis.
   - **Assistive Technology:** Tools like screen readers, speech-to-text, and adaptive keyboards for students with disabilities.

   (e) Observation Tools
   - **Observation Checklists:** Track behavior, participation, and engagement in learning tasks.
   - **Rating Scales:** Evaluate skills, attention, and social-emotional development.
   - **Portfolio Assessment:** Collection of students' work over time to measure progress, creativity, and understanding.

3. **Techniques for Testing Inclusive Children:** Different techniques are applied to accommodate diverse learning needs, focusing on fair and accurate assessment:

   (a) Continuous and Formative Assessment
   - Regular monitoring of progress through daily classroom activities, homework, and participation.

- Provides feedback to improve learning and identify areas needing support.

(b) **Individualized Assessment**

- Assessing each child according to their abilities and learning pace.
- Using customized tasks or adapted exams for children with special needs.

(c) **Performance-Based Assessment**

- Focus on practical tasks, projects, or demonstrations rather than only written exams.
- Measures application, creativity, and critical thinking.

(d) **Peer and Self-Assessment**

- Encouraging children to evaluate their own work or that of peers.
- Promotes self-awareness, responsibility, and reflective learning.

(e) **Diagnostic Assessment**

- Identifying learning gaps, difficulties, and strengths before designing instructional strategies.
- Helps in remedial teaching, counseling, and support planning.

(f) **Adaptive and Alternative Techniques**

- **Multiple Modes of Response:** Students can respond orally, in writing, or using assistive devices.
- **Simplified Language:** Questions framed in clear, simple language to avoid misunderstanding.
- **Time Adaptation:** Allowing extra time for children who need it due to cognitive or physical challenges.
- **Non-Verbal Assessments:** Using gestures, symbols, pictures, or practical demonstrations to measure learning.

4. **Observational Techniques for Inclusive Assessment:** Observation is critical for understanding inclusive children's learning, behavior, and interaction. Key observational techniques include:
   - **Behavioral Observation:** Tracking attention, participation, motivation, and interaction with peers.
   - **Task Analysis Observation:** Watching how students approach a task, including problem-solving steps and strategy use.
   - **Checklist Observation:** Structured lists to record skills, abilities, and social behaviors.
   - **Anecdotal Records:** Short descriptive notes about significant learning behaviors or incidents.
   - **Portfolio Review:** Observing and evaluating the progress of work samples over time.

5. **Advantages of Using Specialized Tools and Techniques:** Using these tools and techniques allows educators to:
   - Accurately measure learning and understanding for all students.
   - Identify strengths, weaknesses, and learning gaps.
   - Provide personalized support and remediation.
   - Ensure equity and fairness in assessment, especially for children with disabilities or learning difficulties.
   - Monitor progress across academic, social, emotional, and practical domains.

D. SPECIAL TEACHING METHODS FOR INCLUDING CHILDREN

Special teaching methods ensure that children with physical, sensory, cognitive, or social challenges can actively participate in learning. Special teaching methods adapt instruction, learning materials, and classroom strategies to meet the unique needs of each learner. These methods are crucial for children with visual impairments, hearing impairments, physical disabilities, learning difficulties, and cognitive challenges.

1. **Braille Script and Tactile Methods for Visually Impaired Children:** Braille is a tactile writing system that allows visually impaired children to read and write independently. It consists of raised dots arranged in patterns representing letters, numbers, and symbols.
   - **Teaching Methods:**
     - ❑ Use of Braille slates and stylus for writing
     - ❑ Braille books for all subjects, including mathematics and science
     - ❑ Tactile diagrams, maps, and charts for understanding shapes, graphs, and spatial information
     - ❑ Audio-assisted reading to reinforce Braille learning
   - **Practical Techniques:**
     - ❑ Encourage finger tracing of letters and numbers
     - ❑ Pair Braille reading with verbal explanations to enhance comprehension
     - ❑ Integrate hands-on learning activities like clay modeling, tactile math tools, and interactive experiments
2. **Sign Language and Visual Communication for Hearing-Impaired Children:** For children with hearing impairments, sign language and visual communication methods are essential to facilitate understanding and expression.
   - **Teaching Methods:**
     - ❑ Use of Indian Sign Language (ISL) or other local sign languages

- ❑ Incorporating visual cues, gestures, and facial expressions
- ❑ Use of captioned videos, visual storytelling, and diagrams
- ❑ Amplified audio devices and hearing aids to reinforce residual hearing
- **Practical Techniques:**
  - ❑ Conduct peer-assisted learning where hearing students also learn basic signs
  - ❑ Visual schedules and cue cards to support classroom routines
  - ❑ Role-plays and simulations using gestures for interactive learning

3. **Adaptive Methods for Children with Speech and Communication Challenges:** Children with speech or communication impairments require alternative and augmentative communication methods.
   - **Teaching Methods:**
     - ❑ Use of communication boards or speech-generating devices
     - ❑ Picture exchange communication systems (PECS) for expressing needs
     - ❑ Structured oral exercises, voice modulation practices, and articulation therapy
     - ❑ Multisensory reinforcement with visual, auditory, and tactile cues
   - **Practical Techniques:**
     - ❑ Encourage expression through gestures, symbols, or drawings
     - ❑ Individualized instruction using step-by-step guidance
     - ❑ Peer interaction in controlled settings to build social communication skills

4. **Methods for Children with Physical Disabilities:** Children with mobility or motor challenges require adaptive teaching strategies and classroom modifications.
   - **Teaching Methods:**
     - ❑ Use of wheelchair-accessible seating and adjustable desks
     - ❑ Adaptive tools for writing, drawing, and computer use (special pens, keyboards, or switches)
     - ❑ Classroom activities adapted to their physical abilities, such as hands-on experiments or digital simulations
   - **Practical Techniques:**
     - ❑ Provide extra time for physical tasks
     - ❑ Encourage collaborative work where peers assist or share responsibilities
     - ❑ Include virtual or computer-assisted exercises to minimize physical strain

5. **Multisensory Teaching Methods for Children with Cognitive and Learning Difficulties:** Children with learning difficulties benefit from multisensory, interactive, and individualized instruction.
   - **Teaching Methods:**
     - ❑ **Visual methods:** charts, diagrams, videos, color-coded notes
     - ❑ **Auditory methods:** oral explanations, rhymes, songs, and storytelling
     - ❑ **Tactile methods:** hands-on activities, clay modeling, puzzle-solving
     - ❑ **Kinesthetic methods:** role-playing, movement-based learning, and physical demonstrations
   - **Practical Techniques:**
     - ❑ Break complex tasks into smaller, manageable steps
     - ❑ Use repetition and reinforcement to improve retention
     - ❑ Provide continuous feedback and encouragement
     - ❑ Combine games, quizzes, and interactive exercises to maintain engagement

6. **Technology-Assisted Teaching Methods:** Technology is increasingly used in inclusive education to support diverse learners.
   - **Teaching Methods:**
     - ❑ Digital learning platforms with adaptive content for different levels of learning
     - ❑ Tablets with text-to-speech or speech-to-text functions
     - ❑ Educational software with interactive simulations, audio-visual aids, and accessibility features
   - **Practical Techniques:**
     - ❑ Allow learners to complete assignments digitally to bypass physical or sensory limitations
     - ❑ Use multimedia presentations to explain abstract concepts visually and audibly
     - ❑ Integrate online collaborative projects to develop social and cognitive skills

7. **Peer and Cooperative Teaching Methods:** Inclusive classrooms benefit from peer-assisted and cooperative learning methods, which promote social skills and shared learning experiences.
   - **Teaching Methods:**
     - ❑ Pair students with and without disabilities for guided learning
     - ❑ Small group discussions and projects where each child contributes according to ability
     - ❑ Encourage mentorship roles, where capable learners help others understand concepts

- **Practical Techniques:**
  - ❑ Structured peer tutoring for literacy, numeracy, and communication skills
  - ❑ Collaborative problem-solving tasks that integrate multiple skills
  - ❑ Social-emotional learning activities to enhance empathy and cooperation

8. **Remedial and Individualized Teaching Methods:** Individualized approaches are crucial for children who require extra support or slower-paced instruction.

- **Teaching Methods:**
  - ❑ Personal learning plans tailored to the student's strengths and weaknesses
  - ❑ Remedial exercises for literacy, numeracy, or cognitive skills
  - ❑ Frequent one-on-one instruction and monitoring
- **Practical Techniques:**
  - ❑ Adjust learning content to suit individual abilities
  - ❑ Use alternative assessment methods to measure understanding
  - ❑ Implement scaffolding strategies to gradually reduce teacher support

9. **Summary of Key Special Teaching Approaches**

- Braille and tactile methods for visually impaired learners
- Sign language and visual methods for hearing-impaired learners
- Communication boards and speech devices for speech-impaired learners
- Adaptive physical tools for mobility or fine motor challenges
- Multisensory, interactive methods for cognitive or learning difficulties
- Technology-assisted methods for all special needs
- Peer-assisted and cooperative learning for social integration
- Individualized and remedial instruction for personalized learning

These methods ensure that children with varied abilities, disabilities, and learning challenges can actively participate in learning and achieve meaningful educational outcomes.

E. GUIDANCE AND COUNSELING FOR INCLUSIVE CHILDREN

Guidance and counseling in inclusive education are structured support systems designed to help children with diverse abilities, learning challenges, and social or emotional needs. Inclusive children may face difficulties due to physical disabilities, sensory impairments, learning differences, social exclusion, or emotional challenges. Guidance and counseling aim to facilitate personal, academic, and social development, ensuring that each child participates meaningfully in learning and achieves their potential.

1. **Meaning of Guidance and Counseling**

- Guidance refers to helping children make appropriate decisions regarding learning, career, social interactions, and personal development. It involves providing information, suggestions, and support to enable informed choices.
- Counseling is a more personalized, supportive process in which a trained counselor or teacher helps the child understand their feelings, overcome difficulties, resolve conflicts, and develop coping strategies.

In inclusive education, both guidance and counseling are essential to address academic, emotional, social, and behavioral needs.

2. **Purpose of Guidance and Counseling for Inclusive Children**

The purpose of guidance and counseling includes:

- **Academic Support:** Helping children identify learning strategies, overcome difficulties, and set academic goals.
- **Social Integration:** Supporting inclusion in peer groups and promoting social skills.
- **Emotional Development:** Assisting children in understanding and managing emotions such as anxiety, frustration, or low self-esteem.
- **Behavioral Guidance:** Helping children develop appropriate classroom behaviors and coping strategies.
- **Career and Vocational Planning:** For older students, guiding career choices according to abilities and interests.
- **Personal Development:** Enhancing self-awareness, confidence, and motivation.

3. **Types of Guidance and Counseling**

Guidance and counseling can be categorized based on needs and focus areas:

(a) Educational Guidance

- Focuses on helping children with learning strategies, study habits, and academic planning.
- Assists in selecting subjects, courses, or learning programs suitable for abilities.

(b) Vocational Guidance

- Helps children explore career interests and opportunities.
- Provides information about vocational training and skill development suitable for their strengths.

(c) Personal Guidance

- Deals with emotional, psychological, and social challenges.
- Supports children in building self-confidence, self-discipline, and coping with personal issues.

(d) Social Guidance

- Aims at integration with peers and society.
- Focuses on developing social skills, empathy, cooperation, and teamwork.

(e) Behavioral Counseling

- Addresses behavioral challenges, hyperactivity, aggression, or withdrawal.
- Uses strategies such as reinforcement, modeling, and structured routines.

4. Methods of Guidance and Counseling

Different methods are used depending on the child's needs, age, and abilities:

(a) Individual Counseling

- One-on-one interaction between the counselor/teacher and the child.
- Focuses on personal, emotional, and academic concerns.
- Techniques include active listening, questioning, reflection, and problem-solving exercises.

(b) Group Counseling

- Conducted in small groups for children with similar needs or challenges.
- Helps develop social skills, peer support, and collaborative problem-solving.
- Includes activities such as role-plays, group discussions, and cooperative games.

(c) Peer Counseling

- Trained students help other students cope with academic or social challenges.
- Encourages peer support, empathy, and collaborative learning.

(d) Career or Vocational Guidance

- Assessment of interests, abilities, and aptitudes to guide career choices.
- Uses aptitude tests, interest inventories, and counseling interviews.

(e) Remedial Counseling

- Specific support for children facing learning difficulties or developmental delays.
- Includes structured exercises, repetition, and tailored learning plans.

(f) Therapeutic Techniques

- Techniques such as behavior modification, cognitive-behavioral strategies, and relaxation exercises for children with emotional or behavioral challenges.

5. Requirements for Effective Guidance and Counseling

Effective guidance and counseling for inclusive children requires the following:

- **Trained Personnel:** Teachers, school counselors, or psychologists trained in inclusive education and special needs.
- **Resource Materials:** Counseling guides, assessment tools, storybooks, visual aids, and teaching-learning materials adapted for diverse learners.
- **Safe and Supportive Environment:** Confidential, non-judgmental space for children to express concerns.
- **Assessment Tools:** Psychological, academic, and social assessment tools to identify individual needs.
- **Collaborative Support:** Involvement of parents, peers, and other educators to reinforce guidance strategies.
- **Time and Scheduling:** Sufficient time allocated for individual or group counseling sessions.

6. Areas of Guidance and Counseling for Inclusive Children

Guidance and counseling cover multiple domains:

(a) Academic Area

- Helps children with study strategies, understanding concepts, homework completion, and exam preparation.

(b) Social Area

- Develops social skills, peer relationships, teamwork, conflict resolution, and empathy.

(c) Emotional Area

- Supports emotional regulation, self-confidence, stress management, and motivation.

(d) Career and Vocational Area

- Guides older students in career exploration, skill development, and vocational training.

(e) Behavioral Area

- Addresses classroom behavior, self-discipline, attention span, and adaptation to school routines.

(f) Physical and Health Area

- Provides guidance for children with physical disabilities, promoting mobility, health awareness, and self-care skills.

(g) Cognitive and Intellectual Area

- Helps children develop problem-solving skills, critical thinking, memory enhancement, and reasoning abilities.

(h) **Recreational and Creative Area**

- Encourages participation in art, music, sports, and creative activities to enhance overall development.

F. DEPARTMENTS / INSTITUTIONS SUPPORTING IN CONSULTATION

1. Psychology Department, Uttar Pradesh, Allahabad

The Psychology Department in Uttar Pradesh, Allahabad is a key institution providing specialized psychological services and guidance for children in the educational system, particularly those in inclusive education programs. Its role is crucial in assessing, supporting, and facilitating the overall development of children with special needs, learning difficulties, emotional or behavioral challenges.

Functions of the Department

1. **Psychological Assessment**
   - Conducts tests and evaluations to determine intellectual, emotional, and social development levels of children.
   - Identifies children with learning disabilities, developmental delays, behavioral issues, and mental health concerns.
   - Provides reports and recommendations for Individualized Education Plans (IEPs).
2. **Counseling Services**
   - Offers personalized counseling to children to address academic, emotional, and behavioral challenges.
   - Guides parents and teachers on effective strategies to support children in inclusive classrooms.
   - Helps children develop coping strategies, self-confidence, and problem-solving skills.
3. **Training and Capacity Building**
   - Organizes workshops and training programs for teachers and school counselors on child psychology, inclusive education, and special education strategies.
   - Trains educators to identify learning difficulties early and implement remedial strategies effectively.
4. **Research and Development**
   - Conducts research on child development, learning processes, and inclusive education methods.
   - Develops innovative psychological tools, assessment techniques, and intervention strategies for diverse learners.
5. **Referral Services**
   - Refers children to specialized institutions or medical facilities when additional support is needed for therapy, rehabilitation, or health-related concerns.

Role in Inclusive Education

- Provides psychological support to teachers for handling children with different abilities in mainstream classrooms.
- Assists in diagnosing and planning interventions for children with visual, hearing, cognitive, or behavioral impairments.
- Facilitates cooperation between parents, schools, and other support institutions to ensure holistic child development.
- Acts as a resource center for schools in Uttar Pradesh for consultation regarding inclusive education policies and strategies.

Practical Impact on Schools

- Schools can consult the department for child assessments, counseling sessions, and remedial guidance.
- Teachers can receive special training to handle children with learning difficulties effectively.
- Helps integrate children with special needs into mainstream classrooms by providing tailored strategies and support.

2. Divisional Psychology Centre (at Divisional Level)

The Divisional Psychology Centre operates at the divisional administrative level and plays a vital role in providing psychological and educational support to schools and children across multiple districts. It acts as a regional hub between district-level services and schools, ensuring that inclusive education policies are implemented effectively.

Functions of the Divisional Psychology Centre

1. **Assessment and Evaluation**
   - Conducts psychological and educational assessments for children referred by schools in the division.
   - Identifies children with learning disabilities, developmental delays, behavioral issues, and emotional challenges.
   - Provides diagnostic reports and recommendations for remedial programs or individualized interventions.
2. **Teacher Training and Capacity Building**
   - Organizes workshops and training programs for teachers and school counselors on:
     - ❑ Inclusive education strategies
     - ❑ Special education techniques
     - ❑ Child psychology and behavior management
   - Helps teachers understand how to implement individualized teaching strategies in classrooms.

3. **Supervision and Monitoring**
   - Monitors the implementation of inclusive education programs in schools within the division.
   - Evaluates whether schools are using appropriate teaching-learning materials (TLMs), adaptive teaching methods, and inclusive practices effectively.
   - Provides guidance for corrective measures to improve classroom learning for children with special needs.
4. **Consultation and Guidance**
   - Provides expert consultation to schools, parents, and district education authorities regarding children with special needs.
   - Recommends special interventions, assistive devices, or therapeutic programs when required.
   - Supports the development of Individualized Education Plans (IEPs) for children facing learning or developmental challenges.
5. **Research and Resource Development**
   - Conducts research on child development, inclusive education practices, and teaching-learning strategies.
   - Develops psychological assessment tools, learning modules, and educational resources suitable for regional needs.

Role in Inclusive Education

- Acts as a bridge between district-level hospitals, schools, and central psychology departments.
- Ensures that inclusive policies and programs reach all schools in the division effectively.
- Provides specialized psychological support to children with cognitive, emotional, social, or physical challenges.
- Facilitates training for teachers and counselors so that inclusive classrooms are more effective and adaptive.
- Supports coordination between parents, teachers, and local authorities to ensure a holistic approach to child development.

Practical Impact on Schools

- Enables schools to identify children with special needs early and provide timely interventions.
- Teachers receive practical strategies and tools to teach children with learning difficulties, sensory impairments, or behavioral challenges.
- Helps children benefit from structured guidance and counseling in alignment with their abilities.
- Ensures that inclusive education is standardized and consistently monitored across the division.

3. District Hospital and Its Role in Inclusive Education

The District Hospital is a key institution in providing medical, health, and rehabilitative support for children enrolled in inclusive education programs. It plays a vital role in diagnosing, treating, and managing physical, sensory, and developmental challenges, which are essential for ensuring that all children can participate meaningfully in learning activities.

Functions of the District Hospital in Inclusive Education

1. **Medical Assessment and Diagnosis**
   - Conducts comprehensive health check-ups for children with special needs or learning difficulties.
   - Diagnoses physical disabilities, visual or hearing impairments, orthopedic conditions, speech and language disorders, and chronic illnesses.
   - Provides referral services to specialized centers if further diagnosis or treatment is required.
2. **Treatment and Rehabilitation**
   - Offers medical treatment and rehabilitation services for children with physical, sensory, or neurological impairments.
   - Provides therapies such as physiotherapy, occupational therapy, speech therapy, and audiology services.
   - Supplies assistive devices, including wheelchairs, hearing aids, prosthetics, and visual aids, enabling children to participate fully in school activities.
3. **Nutritional and Health Support**
   - Monitors children for malnutrition, anemia, and other health deficiencies that may affect learning and development.
   - Provides guidance on diet, supplements, and lifestyle for overall physical and cognitive development.
   - Collaborates with school nutrition programs to ensure healthy meals and dietary support.
4. **Preventive and Curative Care**
   - Conducts immunization drives, routine screenings, and preventive health programs.
   - Addresses common health issues such as infections, vision problems, hearing deficits, and posture-related difficulties.
   - Ensures that children with health concerns can continue education without interruption.
5. **Coordination with Schools and Other Institutions**
   - Works closely with teachers, school counselors, and district education authorities to provide medical reports, recommendations, and interventions for children with special needs.

- Supports referral and follow-up systems for children requiring specialized treatment or therapies.
- Coordinates with NGOs and government programs to deliver health-related resources and services in schools.

Role in Inclusive Education

- Ensures that children with physical, sensory, or health-related challenges receive the medical attention needed to fully participate in classroom activities.
- Provides professional assessment and intervention that informs teachers and counselors about a child's abilities and limitations.
- Plays a vital role in the early detection of disabilities, which is crucial for planning individualized education strategies.
- Supports children in gaining independence, mobility, and communication skills necessary for successful learning.
- Acts as a central point for medical consultation, linking schools with specialized therapies and health services.

Practical Impact on Schools and Teachers

- Enables teachers to understand the medical needs and physical limitations of each child.
- Helps develop adapted classroom strategies based on a child's health or disability profile.
- Provides children with necessary interventions and assistive devices, reducing barriers to learning.
- Collaborates with parents and schools to monitor progress and maintain continuity in education despite health challenges.

4. Trained Diet Mentor in District Education and Training Institute

Nutrition plays a critical role in a child's cognitive, emotional, and physical development, particularly for children with special needs in inclusive education. The Trained Diet Mentor stationed in the District Education and Training Institute (DETI) is responsible for ensuring that children receive adequate, balanced, and specialized nutrition to support learning, growth, and overall health.

Functions of the Trained Diet Mentor

1. Assessment of Nutritional Status

- Evaluates the nutritional health of children in schools, identifying deficiencies or excesses that may affect learning and development.
- Uses tools like growth charts, BMI assessments, and dietary surveys to track nutritional progress.
- Focuses on children with special health needs, disabilities, or chronic illnesses that require customized dietary interventions.

2. Development of Diet Plans

- Designs individualized or group diet plans based on the child's age, health status, and specific needs.
- Considers allergies, metabolic disorders, and physical impairments when recommending meals or supplements.
- Ensures that children receive adequate calories, vitamins, minerals, and proteins for optimal cognitive and physical development.

3. Guidance to Schools and Parents

- Provides training and guidance to school staff on the importance of nutrition in learning and behavior.
- Advises parents on healthy meal preparation, balanced diets, and special dietary requirements for children with disabilities or learning difficulties.
- Promotes awareness about hydration, meal timings, and nutritional hygiene.

4. Monitoring and Evaluation

- Monitors the effectiveness of school meal programs, midday meal schemes, and dietary interventions.
- Evaluates whether the nutritional needs of children, especially those with special health conditions, are being met.
- Provides recommendations for adjustments or improvements in school nutrition programs.

5. Integration with Educational Plans

- Coordinates with teachers, school counselors, and special educators to ensure that nutrition supports learning outcomes.
- Works alongside psychologists, medical staff, and inclusive education experts to link diet with cognitive, emotional, and physical development goals.
- Helps children with disabilities overcome fatigue, concentration issues, or behavioral challenges related to nutritional deficiencies.

Role in Inclusive Education

- Ensures that children with physical, sensory, or cognitive challenges receive proper nutrition that supports their learning and development.
- Helps reduce the impact of malnutrition, anemia, or dietary deficiencies on academic performance and school participation.
- Provides scientific dietary guidance for children with special needs, enabling them to thrive in mainstream classrooms.

- Acts as a resource for teachers and school administrators, helping them understand the link between diet and effective learning.

Practical Impact on Schools

- Children receive healthy, balanced meals that improve concentration, energy, and participation in classroom activities.
- Teachers can tailor classroom activities knowing that students' nutritional needs are met.
- Parents receive guidance on preparing meals at home that support cognitive and emotional development.
- School administrators benefit from professional monitoring of nutrition programs to ensure compliance with health standards.

5. Supervision and Inspection System in Inclusive Education

The Supervision and Inspection System plays a critical role in ensuring that inclusive education policies, practices, and standards are implemented effectively in schools. It acts as a quality control and support mechanism for teachers, school administrators, and education authorities, ensuring that children with diverse needs receive equitable educational opportunities.

Functions of the Supervision and Inspection System

1. Monitoring Teaching Practices

- Observes classroom teaching to ensure that inclusive teaching strategies are properly applied.
- Evaluates whether teachers are using child-centered, adaptive, and differentiated teaching methods.
- Checks the effective use of Teaching-Learning Materials (TLMs) and assistive devices for children with special needs.

2. Ensuring Compliance with Policies

- Reviews whether schools adhere to government regulations, inclusive education guidelines, and safety norms.
- Ensures that children from excluded or marginalized groups receive access to quality education.
- Monitors the implementation of Individualized Education Plans (IEPs) and remedial programs.

3. Teacher Support and Guidance

- Provides on-site mentoring and coaching to teachers for improving teaching practices.
- Offers feedback on classroom management, lesson planning, and inclusive strategies.
- Identifies areas where teachers need additional training or resources.

4. Assessment and Evaluation of Learning Outcomes

- Evaluates student performance, participation, and engagement in inclusive classrooms.
- Helps identify children who are falling behind due to learning difficulties or special needs.
- Supports schools in developing intervention strategies for improving learning outcomes.

5. Resource Allocation and Recommendations

- Recommends the allocation of TLMs, assistive devices, and specialized teaching aids where necessary.
- Advises school management on classroom modifications, infrastructural changes, and accessibility improvements.
- Coordinates with other institutions (psychology centers, hospitals, NGOs) to ensure holistic support for students.

Role in Inclusive Education

- Ensures that inclusive education principles are consistently applied across all schools in the district or division.
- Guarantees that teachers are accountable for the quality of education delivered to children with special needs.
- Supports early identification of gaps in learning, teaching, or resource availability.
- Acts as a bridge between policy implementation and classroom practices, providing feedback for continuous improvement.
- Ensures equity and accessibility, so all children, regardless of abilities or backgrounds, receive quality education.

Practical Impact on Schools

- Teachers receive regular guidance, monitoring, and constructive feedback for improving classroom practices.
- Schools implement inclusive curricula and remedial programs effectively.
- Children benefit from personalized support, better learning materials, and adaptive teaching methods.
- Administrators can plan interventions and allocate resources efficiently based on inspection reports.
- The system promotes continuous professional development for teachers in inclusive education strategies.

6. Community and School Support Committees in Inclusive Education

Community and School Support Committees are critical mechanisms for ensuring that inclusive education programs are effectively implemented and sustained at the local level. These committees involve parents, community members, teachers, school administrators, and local authorities working collaboratively to support children with diverse learning needs. Their purpose is to create a supportive, participatory, and accountable framework for inclusive education.

Functions of Community and School Support Committees

1. Promoting Inclusive Education Awareness

- Educates the community about the importance of inclusive education for children of all abilities.
- Raises awareness about rights of children with disabilities and the need to prevent discrimination based on caste, gender, religion, language, or region.
- Encourages local participation in school activities and programs to create an inclusive learning environment.

2. Monitoring School Programs

- Monitors the implementation of inclusive education initiatives, ensuring that children from marginalized and disadvantaged backgrounds are not excluded.
- Evaluates whether schools are providing appropriate teaching-learning materials, accessibility, and remedial support.
- Tracks attendance, performance, and engagement of children with special needs in classrooms.

3. Supporting Teachers and Students

- Acts as a bridge between schools and families, providing support for teachers in managing classrooms with children of varied abilities.
- Assists in organizing special programs, extra classes, or remedial sessions for children who need additional help.
- Provides guidance and encouragement to children and parents, ensuring active participation in the learning process.

4. Resource Mobilization

- Facilitates the provision of financial, material, and human resources for inclusive education.
- Coordinates with government agencies, NGOs, and local organizations to provide necessary teaching aids, assistive devices, or therapy services.
- Encourages community contributions such as volunteers, mentors, or sponsorships for children with special needs.

5. Conflict Resolution and Advocacy

- Addresses issues of discrimination, exclusion, or neglect in schools.
- Acts as an advocacy body to ensure that children's onflicts between parents, teachers, and school authorities regarding inclusive practices.

6. Capacity Building

- Organizes training and workshops for community members, parents, and teachers on inclusive education practices.
- Provides knowledge on support strategies, adaptive teaching methods, and child development principles.
- Strengthens the capacity of the community to participate in and sustain inclusive educational programs.

Role in Inclusive Education

- Ensures that children from diverse socio-economic, cultural, and physical backgrounds receive access to quality education.
- Acts as a support network for schools, helping them overcome challenges in implementing inclusive classrooms.
- Bridges the gap between families, teachers, and local authorities, ensuring community ownership of education programs.
- Helps identify barriers to learning early, whether they are social, cultural, or infrastructural, and works to remove them.
- Facilitates active engagement of parents and community members in monitoring, planning, and decision-making for inclusive education.

Practical Impact on Schools

- Schools receive community support in organizing remedial classes, awareness programs, and extracurricular activities.
- Teachers gain local guidance and assistance for handling children with special needs.
- Children experience a welcoming and inclusive environment, where their learning and emotional needs are supported.
- Resources, volunteers, and local initiatives enhance the quality of education and participation of marginalized children.
- Creates accountability systems, ensuring that inclusive policies are effectively implemented and monitored.

7. Government and NGOs in Inclusive Education

Government agencies and Non-Governmental Organizations (NGOs) play a vital role in supporting inclusive education programs at local, district, state, and national levels. They provide policy guidance, financial support, resources, training, advocacy, and technical assistance, ensuring that children from all backgrounds—including those with disabilities or special needs—have access to quality education.

Functions of Government Agencies in Inclusive Education

1. **Policy Formulation and Implementation**
   - Develop laws, regulations, and policies that ensure inclusive education for all children, including those with physical, sensory, cognitive, or social challenges.
   - Oversee programs like Right to Education (RTE), Sarva Shiksha Abhiyan (SSA), and inclusive education schemes for children with disabilities.
   - Ensure schools comply with infrastructure accessibility, trained personnel, and curriculum adaptations.
2. **Financial and Material Support**
   - Allocate funds for inclusive education programs, including grants for special schools, assistive devices, and TLMs (Teaching-Learning Materials).
   - Provide infrastructure support, such as ramps, accessible toilets, and classrooms adapted for children with physical challenges.
   - Supply scholarships, uniforms, books, and nutritional support to marginalized children.
3. **Training and Capacity Building**
   - Conduct teacher training programs, workshops, and refresher courses for educators in inclusive classrooms.
   - Train school administrators and staff in adaptive teaching methods, behavioral interventions, and special education techniques.
   - Develop resource materials and guidelines for inclusive teaching practices.
4. **Monitoring and Evaluation**
   - Monitor schools to ensure compliance with inclusive education policies and standards.
   - Evaluate the effectiveness of inclusive education programs and recommend improvements.
   - Maintain databases on children with disabilities to facilitate planning and resource allocation.
5. **Collaboration and Coordination**
   - Coordinate with district hospitals, psychology centers, NGOs, and local support committees to ensure children receive comprehensive support.
   - Facilitate interdepartmental collaboration among education, health, social welfare, and rehabilitation sectors.

Functions of NGOs in Inclusive Education

1. **Awareness and Advocacy**
   - Advocate for the rights of children with special needs and marginalized groups.
   - Conduct community outreach programs to sensitize parents, teachers, and local leaders about inclusion.
   - Work to eliminate stigma and discrimination against children with disabilities.
2. **Support Services**
   - Provide remedial classes, counseling, speech therapy, and vocational training for children with special needs.
   - Supply assistive devices, educational kits, and teaching-learning materials to schools.
   - Offer psychological and social support to children and families facing challenges.
3. **Capacity Building and Training**
   - Organize teacher workshops, parent training, and volunteer orientation for effective inclusive practices.
   - Develop innovative teaching methods, digital tools, and learning modules for children with diverse needs.
4. **Research and Development**
   - Conduct research on inclusive education, child development, and learning strategies for children with disabilities.
   - Develop best practice models for teaching, assessment, and classroom management.
5. **Monitoring and Evaluation**
   - Collaborate with schools and government agencies to monitor program effectiveness.
   - Offer feedback and recommendations to improve inclusive education initiatives.

Role in Inclusive Education

- Ensures that children from excluded classes, marginalized communities, and children with disabilities have access to quality education.
- Provides policy support, funding, and technical resources to schools and local authorities.
- Bridges the gap between government schemes and ground-level implementation.
- Enhances the capacity of teachers, schools, and communities to implement inclusive practices.
- Strengthens community participation, advocacy, and accountability in inclusive education.

Practical Impact on Schools

- Schools gain access to funding, TLMs, assistive devices, and professional support for inclusive classrooms.
- Teachers receive training and guidance to meet the diverse needs of learners.
- Children benefit from holistic support, including health, nutrition, therapy, and adaptive learning resources.
- Programs supported by NGOs and government agencies ensure sustainability and effectiveness of inclusive education initiatives.
- Encourages active community engagement and parental involvement, enhancing learning outcomes for all children.

G. IMPORTANCE OF GUIDANCE AND COUNSELING IN CHILD LEARNING

Guidance and counseling are essential educational processes that help children identify their strengths, weaknesses, interests, and potential, and provide them with support, direction, and strategies to overcome personal, academic, emotional, and social challenges. These processes play a vital role in enhancing learning, motivation, and overall development.

1. Academic Development

- Guidance and counseling help children understand their learning styles, aptitudes, and areas of interest, allowing teachers and parents to support them effectively.
- Through academic counseling, children can set realistic goals, plan study schedules, and improve their learning strategies.
- Counseling provides support for children who face difficulties in specific subjects, helping them develop remedial plans and strategies for better comprehension.
- It ensures that children maintain consistent academic performance and reduce stress or anxiety related to schoolwork and examinations.

2. Emotional and Psychological Support

- Counseling provides children with a safe environment to express emotions, fears, and frustrations that may affect their learning.
- It helps them manage stress, anxiety, and emotional disturbances, which are common barriers to effective learning.
- Guidance equips children with coping strategies for handling peer pressure, family issues, and social challenges, enhancing emotional resilience.
- It assists children in building self-confidence, self-esteem, and motivation, which are directly linked to improved concentration and learning outcomes.

3. Social Development

- Counseling and guidance promote positive social behavior and interpersonal skills, which are essential for collaborative learning in classrooms.
- Children learn conflict resolution, empathy, cooperation, and communication skills, allowing them to participate more effectively in group activities.
- Social counseling helps integrate children from diverse cultural, linguistic, or socio-economic backgrounds, making classrooms more inclusive.
- It assists in reducing behavioral problems, bullying, or isolation, creating a conducive learning environment for all children.

4. Career and Vocational Guidance

- Guidance helps children understand their strengths, talents, and interests, enabling informed career choices.
- Vocational counseling assists older children in selecting appropriate subjects, courses, and skill-based programs aligned with their abilities.
- Early career guidance develops goal-setting skills and planning capabilities, which enhance motivation and focus in academic learning.
- It encourages children to develop skills relevant to future employment, fostering practical application of knowledge learned in school.

5. Special Needs and Inclusive Education Support

- Guidance and counseling are critical for children with special needs, including physical, cognitive, or sensory disabilities.
- Counselors help identify learning barriers, design individualized educational plans, and recommend specialized teaching methods or assistive tools.
- Counseling ensures that children with disabilities receive appropriate emotional support, motivation, and adaptive strategies for effective learning.
- It facilitates communication between teachers, parents, therapists, and other professionals, ensuring coordinated support.

6. Behavioral Management

- Counseling assists children in understanding the consequences of their actions, promoting self-discipline and responsible behavior.
- Guidance helps in reducing disruptive behaviors that interfere with learning, fostering a positive classroom climate.

- Behavioral counseling enables children to set personal goals, develop routines, and follow structured learning habits, which improve academic performance.
- It supports children in developing decision-making and problem-solving skills, essential for independent learning and personal growth.

7. Motivation and Self-Development

- Guidance and counseling enhance intrinsic motivation by helping children identify meaningful learning goals.
- Counseling supports the development of self-awareness, critical thinking, and creativity, contributing to deeper and more effective learning.
- Children learn to reflect on their progress, recognize achievements, and overcome challenges, which fosters lifelong learning habits.
- It helps children adapt to changes, handle failures, and persevere in the face of difficulties, which are essential skills for personal and academic success.

8. Coordination with Parents and Teachers

- Guidance and counseling serve as a bridge between children, teachers, and parents, providing insights into a child's learning needs and progress.
- Counselors advise teachers on adapted teaching methods, behavioral strategies, and learning aids for individual students.
- Parents receive support and guidance to encourage a healthy learning environment at home, aligned with the child's strengths and needs.
- Effective counseling ensures continuous monitoring and adjustment of learning strategies based on the child's development.

IMPORTANT FACTS

- Inclusive education means educating all children together, including those with disabilities, in the same classroom.
- It promotes equality, diversity, and a non-discriminatory environment.
- Every child has the right to quality education regardless of ability, background, or needs.
- The focus is on removing barriers and providing equal learning opportunities.
- Inclusive classrooms respect individual differences in ability, learning style, and pace.
- Teachers use flexible teaching strategies to accommodate all learners.
- Use of teaching aids, assistive devices, and a supportive environment is important.
- It encourages social interaction, cooperation, and acceptance among students.
- Inclusive education builds confidence, self-esteem, and independence in learners.
- Guidance is a process that helps individuals make proper decisions and adjustments.
- It supports students in educational, personal, and vocational areas.
- Guidance helps in solving academic and behavioral problems.
- Its aim is the overall development of personality.
- Counseling is a professional service that helps individuals understand and solve problems.
- It involves face-to-face interaction between the counselor and the student.
- Counseling focuses on emotional, social, and psychological well-being.
- It helps students manage stress, anxiety, and conflicts.
- Educational guidance helps students in studies and subject selection.
- Vocational guidance helps students in career selection.
- Personal guidance helps students in personal and social adjustment.
- Individual counseling involves one-to-one interaction.
- Group counseling provides guidance in group settings.
- Teachers identify individual needs of learners.
- They provide equal opportunities to all students.
- Child-centered teaching methods are used.
- A supportive and positive classroom environment is created.
- Students are helped to adjust in an inclusive environment.
- Mental health and emotional balance are promoted.
- Dropout rates and learning difficulties are reduced.
- Self-confidence and decision-making skills are developed.
- Inclusive education, guidance, and counseling together ensure the holistic development of every learner.

KEY TERMS

- **Child Development** – Continuous, orderly growth in physical, mental, emotional, social areas from birth to adolescence.
- **Physical Development** – Changes in height, weight, strength, coordination, motor skills.
- **Mental Development** – Thinking, reasoning, memory, problem-solving, decision-making.
- **Emotional Development** – Understanding, expressing, managing feelings and emotions.
- **Social Development** – Interaction with others, building relationships, learning social norms.
- **Language Development** – Speaking, listening, reading, writing, communication skills.
- **Educational Importance** – Understanding development helps design suitable teaching methods and learning environments.
- **Creativity & Expressive Ability** – Imagination, artistic skills, self-expression.
- **Orderly Development** – Follows predictable sequence (e.g., crawling before walking).
- **Continuous Development** – Gradual, steady growth throughout childhood.
- **Holistic Development** – Interconnected growth of physical, mental, emotional, social areas.
- **Stages of Development** – Infancy, early childhood, middle childhood, adolescence.
- **Heredity** – Genetic factors from parents influencing development.
- **Environment** – External conditions and experiences affecting growth and learning.
- **Nutrition** – Intake of food and nutrients essential for physical and mental development.

SECTION-B

CONCEPT OF INCLUSIVE EDUCATION AND UNDERSTANDING CHILDREN WITH SPECIAL NEEDS

INCLUSIVE EDUCATION: DEFINITION AND CONCEPT

Inclusive Education denotes that all children irrespective of their strengths and weaknesses will be part of the mainstream education. Thus, inclusive education means, "the act of ensuring that all children despite their differences, receive the opportunity of being part of the same classroom as other children of their age, and in the process get the opportunity to being exposed to the curriculum to their optimal potential."

Every child is special for his/her parent and, every child has a special need for love, acceptance and a feeling of belongingness. Here, we call **children with special needs** to those who are "different" from their cohorts. They are born equal with some limitations and with the help of inclusion be able to actively participate as equal citizens in all aspects of society and community life. Thus, children with special needs refer to "all those children who require adaptations to the normal process of education due to problems of vision, hearing, movement, learning and intellect." In other words, these children have some kind of **disability**.

Disability: Definitions

Disability refers to any limitations experienced by the disabled in comparisons to able persons of similar age, sex and culture. The UN Declaration on the Rights of Disabled Persons has defined disabled person as "any person unable to ensure by himself or herself, wholly or partly, the necessities of a normal individual and/or social life, as a result of a deficiency, either congenital or not, in his or her physical or mental capabilities".

DISTINCTIONS AMONG IMPAIRMENT, DISABILITY AND HANDICAP

The World Health Organisation (WHO) has made distinctions between the definitions of impairment, disability and handicap as follows:

- Impairment is any loss or abnormality of psychological, physiological or anatomical structure or function generally taken to be at organ level. Impairment is a damage to tissue due to disease or trauma.
- A disability is any restriction or lack of ability (resulting from an impairment) to perform an activity in the manner or within the range considered normal for a human being.
- A handicap is a disadvantage for an individual, resulting from impairment or disability that limits or prevents fulfilment of a role that is normal (depending on age, sex and social cultural factors) for that individual. Handicap is a condition or burden, which is imposed on the person confronted with the disability.

Types of Disability According to PWD Act, 1995

The PWD Act, 1995 has given the following seven types of disability as:

1. Blindness
2. Low Vision
3. Leprosy-cured
4. Hearing impairment
5. Locomotor disabilities
6. Mental retardation
7. Mental illness

EDUCATIONAL PROVISIONS FOR CHILDREN WITH SPECIAL NEEDS

The last two decades of the 19th century has witnessed the knowledge and processes of educating the disabled children through Christian Missionaries. The first school for the deaf was established in Mumbai in 1883 and the first school for the blind in Amritsar in 1887. At that time, it was believed that children with disabilities could not be educated alongwith normal children. Therefore, education to disabled children was offered through special school. This trend continued early sixties of the last century with the help of some international agencies who developed programme of integrated education. Here, children disabilities were placed in regular school so that they could study alongwith their non-disabled 'peers". The integrated education adopts various models for service deliver. Presently the emphasis is on the need to provide education for all in appropriate environment with inclusive philosophy through inclusive education.

Integrated Education for the Disabled Children (IEDC)

With the development of science and technology and improvement in Medical Services and Aggressive neo-natal intervention has ensured that a large number of babies who would earlier have not survived but often with different abilities. The number of differently abled children is on the increasing trend but it is not possible to create the required number of special schools throughout the country to meet this challenge due to the high cost and also due to the fact that the population is so scattered. The best alternative under these situations is to make use of the infrastructural facilities already present in terms of regular schools and integrate children into the mainstream of education.

Consequent on the success of international institutions in introducing differently abled children in regular schools, the planning commission, Govt. of India, in 1971 includes in its plan a programme for integrated education. In 1974, the Union Government introduced a scheme called "Integrated Schools" to do just this. This scheme was later revised and a plan of action formulated. The important aims of IEDC includes:

- Provide educational opportunity to differently abled children in regular schools.
- Facilitate retention of differently abled in the school system.
- Integrate children from special school to common schools.

The scope of the scheme of IEDC includes pre-school training, counselling for the parents, and special training in skills for all kinds of differently abled children. It provides facilities in the form of books, stationary, uniforms and allowances for transport, reader and escort etc.

Project Integrated Education for the Disabled (PIED)

This scheme was launched by MHRD Govt. of India in collaboration with UNICEF in 1987 to strengthen the integration of differently abled into regular schools. Under this scheme, a cluster instead of individual school is given importance. This scheme is an improvement over the special schools in one or many ways and provides a way towards universalisation of elementary education and Education for All including for differently abled children.

ASSUMPTION ABOUT INTEGRATED EDUCATION

Integrated education assumes a process of bringing disabled children into mainstream schools, where the system remains the same. As per the system, the child is the problem. So, it is essential to change the child where the resources are focused on the individual child. The failure is due to the child's problem; he is not able, not ready, not good enough to cope up with the system.

In integrated education; it is the children with disabilities who are seen as the problem, who must be "fixed", "changed" & "adapted" to suit the existing regular, mainstream school. It is the disabled child who is seen as a square peg in a round table. The system remains the same. The onus for successful integration therefore, is on the disabled child.

ASSUMPTION ABOUT INCLUSIVE EDUCATION

Assumptions of inclusive education is opposite to integrated education. Inclusive education assumes that changes the system to fit the child. It is essential to addresses all types of individual needs, not just disability. Teachers and schools are held responsible for children's learning. It focuses on flexibility of curriculum, teacher training and change in environmental. Failure is the problem with the system not with the child. It is quite essential to assumes that all children can learn and that all children need their learning to be supported in diverse ways.

In this model of inclusive education, it is not the child, but the education system, which is seen as a problem. Therefore, it is the system (with all its components) with should be changed, modified & made flexible enough to accommodate the diverse needs of all learners, including children with disabilities. The onus for success is therefore on the flexibility of the system. It focuses on the environment, as the "disabling" cause because it fails to provide appropriate access to equal opportunities for all persons to participate fully in social life.

Though integrated education of differently abled children has gained momentum all over the country since 1974, there are some other possibilities too for these children to get education. For example, the NIOS (National Institute of Open Schooling) offers education which have the advantage of being specially adopted to the needs of every child as well as aimed at giving the child every opportunity to progress at his/her pace. Another example is alternative schooling and community-based rehabilitation programmes.

EDUCATION FOR A COHESIVE SOCIETY

Despite more than half a century of independence, India is struggling for freedom from various kinds of biases and imbalances such as rural/urban, rich/poor, and differences on the basis of caste, religion, ideology, gender etc. Education can play a very significant role in minimising and finally eliminating these differences by providing equality of access to quality education and opportunity.

Equality of opportunity means ensuring that every individual receives suitable education at a pace and through methods suited to his/her being. Children of the disadvantaged, and socially discriminated groups and also those suffering from specific challenges must be paid special attention.

Provision for equal opportunity to all not only in access, but also in the conditions for success is a precondition for the promotion of equality. The curriculum must create an awareness of the inherent equality of all with a view to removing prejudices and complexes transmitted through the social environment and the factor of birth.

EDUCATION OF GIRLS

Equality among sexes is a fundamental right under the constitution of India. The state, however, also has the right to exercise positive protective discrimination in favour of the disadvantaged population groups including women. Emphasis in education has moved from 'Equality of Educational Opportunity' (NPE, 1968) to 'Education for Women's Equality and Empowerment' (1986). As a result, the curricular and training strategies for the education of girls now demand more attention. Besides, making education accessible to more and more girls, especially rural girls, removing all gender discrimination and gender bias in school curriculum, textbooks and the process of transaction is absolutely necessary. There is a need to develop and implement gender inclusive and gender sensitive curricular strategies to nurture a generation of girls and boys who are equally competent and are sensitive to one another, and grow up in a caring and sharing mode as equals, and not as adversaries.

EDUCATION OF LEARNERS FROM DISADVANTAGED GROUPS

For achieving a cohesive society it would be essential to respond to specific educational needs of learners from different sections of the society with special emphasis on the Scheduled Castes, the Scheduled Tribes and the other socially and economically disadvantaged groups. In order to do so, there is a need for integrating the socio-cultural perspectives partly by showing concern for their linguistic specificities and pedagogic requirements. Implications of the multilingual and multicultural environment shall have to be taken care of through specifically devised methodology. Contextualisation of curriculum shall have to be effected through curricular materials. The fundamental rights of the disadvantaged groups have to be consciously in- corporated in the curriculum. Even the problem of educating the migrating population shall have to be handled through specific condensed educational programmes based on the main ingredients of the national curriculum.

EDUCATION OF THE GIFTED AND TALENTED

An educational system has the dual role of promoting equality as well as excellence. Education is increasingly called upon to liberate all the creative potentialities of human consciousness. Man essentially fulfils himself in and through creation. It is in the context of this, that education of gifted and talented children assumes great importance. A curricular programme while on the one hand should identify such children, on the other it should also nurture their diverse creative abilities by paying them special attention. It is also important that the identification and nurturance begins right from the earliest stage of education. Moreover, the task of identifying the gifted and talented must be accomplished on the basis of a broad conceptualisation of the process from multiple perspectives rather than as a search for a unitary human attribute. Not only their IQ (Intelligence Quotient) but also their EQ (Emotional Quotient) and SQ (Spiritual Quotient) ought to be assessed.

NATIONAL LEVEL POLICY AND LEGISLATION

National Level Policy and Legislation refers to the rules, laws, and formal plans created by a country's government to guide, regulate, and improve specific sectors, such as education, health, child welfare, or social services. These policies and legislations ensure standardized practices across the nation and protect the rights of citizens.

At the national level, policies are broad frameworks or guidelines that outline the goals, priorities, and strategies of the government. Legislation refers to formal laws passed by the legislature that are legally binding and enforceable.

For example, in the context of education or children:

- Policies may focus on inclusive education, child development, or universal access to schooling.
- Legislation may enforce rights, like the Right to Education Act, or safeguard children against discrimination, abuse, or neglect.

In short, national policies provide direction and vision, while legislation provides legal authority and protection.

Kothari Commission (1964-66)

The Kothari Commission first suggested that the education of handicapped children has to be organised not merely on humanitarian grounds, but also an aspects of utility. The commission emphasised that the education of children with disability should be "an inseparable part of the general education system. The commission also specifically emphasised that the education of children with disability should be "an inseparable part of the general education system. The commission also specifically emphasised the importance of integrated education in meeting this target as it is cost effective and useful in developing mutual understanding between children with and without disabilities.

National Policy on Education (1986)

The National Policy on Education was adopted by Indian Parliament in 1986. The policy emphasized the removal of disparities, and ensuring equalisation of educational opportunity under its para education of the disabled.

National Education Policy (NEP) 2020

The National Education Policy (NEP) 2020 was approved by the Government of India on 28 July 2020. It aims to transform the Indian education system by making it more holistic, flexible, multidisciplinary, and skill-oriented with 21st-century needs.

1. **New Structure of School Education (5+3+3+4)**

   NEP 2020 replaces the old 10+2 system with a new 5+3+3+4 structure:

   - **Foundational Stage (5 years):** 3 years of pre-primary + Classes 1–2 (Play-based learning)
   - **Preparatory Stage (3 years):** Classes 3–5 (Activity-based learning)
   - **Middle Stage (3 years):** Classes 6–8 (Conceptual learning)
   - **Secondary Stage (4 years):** Classes 9–12 (Critical thinking)

   This structure focuses on the developmental stages of children.

2. **Early Childhood Care and Education (ECCE)**
   - Covers children aged 3–6 years
   - Aims for universal access to quality early education by 2030
   - Focus on play-based, activity-based, and discovery-based learning

3. **Foundational Literacy and Numeracy (FLN)**
   - Priority to ensure all children achieve basic reading and arithmetic skills by Grade 3 (by 2025)
   - Introduction of National Mission for Foundational Literacy and Numeracy (National FLN Mission).

4. **Medium of Instruction**
   - Mother tongue/regional language as medium of instruction till at least Grade 5 (preferably till Grade 8)
   - Promotes multilingualism and better understanding among students

5. **Curriculum and Pedagogy**
   - Emphasis on experiential learning, critical thinking, and skill development
   - Reduction of syllabus content to focus on core concepts
   - Introduction of coding from Grade 6
   - Flexibility in subject choices (no strict separation of arts, science, and commerce) .

6. **Assessment and Examination Reforms**
   - Board exams to be made easier and more flexible
   - Focus on competency-based assessment
   - Introduction of 'PARAKH' (Performance Assessment, Review, and Analysis of Knowledge for Holistic Development)
   - Regular assessments in Classes 3, 5, and 8

7. **Teacher Education and Training**
   - Minimum qualification: 4-year integrated B.Ed. degree by 2030
   - Continuous Professional Development (CPD) of 50 hours per year
   - Focus on merit-based recruitment and promotions

8. **Inclusive and Equitable Education**
   - Special focus on disadvantaged groups (SC, ST, OBC, minorities)
   - Establishment of Gender Inclusion Fund
   - Support for children with special needs

9. **Use of Technology in Education**
   - Promotion of digital learning platforms (DIKSHA, e-content)
   - Encouragement of online and blended learning
   - Focus on bridging the digital divide

10. **Key Objectives of NEP 2020**
    - Achieve 100% Gross Enrolment Ratio (GER) by 2030
    - Promote holistic and multidisciplinary education
    - Develop critical thinking and creativity
    - Reduce dropout rates

NEP 2020 is a transformative policy that focuses on quality, equity, and accessibility in education. Its success depends on effective implementation and active participation of teachers.

National Policy for Persons with Disabilities (2006)

The National Policy for Persons with Disabilities (2006) aims to empower persons with disabilities (PwDs) and ensure their full participation in society. It promotes equal opportunities, rights protection, inclusive education, and economic empowerment. The policy emphasizes early intervention, rehabilitation services, barrier-free environments, and support for women and children with disabilities. Key supporting laws include the Rights of Persons with Disabilities Act, 2016 and the National Trust Act, 1999. The policy ensures that PwDs can lead a dignified, independent, and productive life.

Persons with Disabilities (Equal Opportunities, Protection of Rights & Full Participation) Act, 1995

Landmark legislation in the history of special education in India is the persons with Disabilities Act, 1995. This comprehensive Act covers seven disabilities, namely blindness, low vision, hearing impaired, loco-motor impaired, mental retardation, leprosy cured and mental illness.

The Rehabilitation Council of India (RCI) Act, 1992

This Act was passed in 1992 for the purpose of constituting the Rehabilitation Professionals and for maintenance of a Central Rehabilitation Register. It was amended by Rehabilitation Council of India (Amendment) Act, 2000 to provide for monitoring the training of rehabilitation professionals and personal, promoting research in rehabilitation and special education as additional objectives of the council.

SECTION-C

LEARNING AND PEDAGOGY

HOW CHILDREN THINK AND LEARN

Children learn from anything and everything they see and act upon. They have learnt a lot before they join school, and they continue to learn outside the school hours. If we believe that children learn only in school, it is because of what we wrongly regard as learning. When a child spends hours on trying to solve a Jigsaw puzzle (say), he/she is often reprimanded by adults for wasting study time. Little do the grown-ups realise that it is through such interesting games that this child may be increasing his/her understanding of shapes and size. And, this learning is taking place outside the school hours, without formal instruction. A curriculum built upon assumptions about children's learning, that ignore this aspect, is also responsible for children losing interest in mathematics or in any formal learning.

From the time a child is born, his/her interaction with the world around his/her starts. He/she perceives things around his/her, and gradually makes sense of them. He/she slowly begins to recognise people and objects, relate more and more to the environment, and observe things through the senses of touch, sight, taste, smell and sound. There are **four different stages** of learning or development that each child goes through.

Sensorimotor

This is from the ages of birth to about two years old. During this time the child's primary mode of learning occurs through the five senses. He/she learns to experience environment. The child touches things, holds, looks, listens, tastes, feels, bangs, and shakes everything in sight. When the child adds motor skills such as creeping, crawling and walking, his/her environment expands by leaps and bounds. The child is now exploring their environment with both senses and the ability to get around.

Preoperational

This is the stages between ages two and seven. During this stage the child is busy gathering information or learning, and then trying to figure out ways that they can used what they have learned to begin solving problems.

During this stage of his/her life child will be thinking in specifics and will find it very difficult to get generalise anything. This is the time when a child learns by asking questions. The child generally will not want a real answer to his question at this point. When he asks why do we have grass .... He simply wants to know that it is for him to play in. No technical answers for know. The child in this age group judges everything on the 'me' basis—How does it affect me? Do I like it?

Concrete Operations Period

This is the period of time when child is between the ages of seven to ten. This is a wonderful age as this is when children begin to manipulate data mentally. They take the information at hand and begin to define, compare and contrast it. They, however, still think concretely.

The concrete operational child is capable of logical thought. This child still learns through their senses, but no longer relies on only them to teach him. He now thinks as well. A good teacher for this age group would start each lesson at a concrete level and then more toward a generalised level. The child, during this period, is very literal in their thinking.

Formal Operations Period

The period begins at about age eleven. At this time the child will break through the barrier of literalism and more on to thinking in more abstract terms. He no longer restricts thinking to time and space. This child now starts to reflect, hypothesize and theorize. In the formal operation period, children need to develop cognitive abilities. The following is a list of six simple categories of cognitive abilities. The following is a list of six simple categories of cognitive abilities:

1. **Knowledge of facts and principals:** This is the direct recall of facts and principals. **Examples:** memorisation of dates, name, definition, vocabulary words.
2. **Comprehension:** Understanding of facts and ideas.

3. **Application:** Needs to know, rules, principles, and procedures and how to use them.
4. **Analysis:** Breaking down concepts into parts.
5. **Synthesis:** Putting together information or ideas.
6. **Evaluation:** Judging the value of information.

BASIC PROCESSES OF TEACHING AND LEARNING

Teaching-learning process is the heart of education. On it depends the fulfilment of the aims & objectives of education. It is the most powerful instrument of education to bring about desired changes in the students. Teaching learning are related terms. In teaching-learning process, the teacher, the learner, the curriculum & other variables are organised in a systematic way to attain some pre-determined goal.

Essential Aspects of the Teaching-learning Process

According to Diana Laurillard, there are four aspects of the teaching-learning process:

1. **Discussion**—between the teacher and learner.
2. **Interaction**—between the learner and some aspect of the world defined by the teacher.
3. **Adaptation**—of the world by the teacher and action by the learner.
4. **Reflection**—on the learner's performance by both teacher and learner.

According to **Burton** in the figure given below

1. Teaching can become effective only by relating it to process of learning.
2. Teaching objective cannot be realised without being related to learning situation.
3. We may create and use teaching aids to create some appropriate learning situation.
4. The strategies and devices of teaching may be selected in such a manner that the optimal objectives of learning area achieved.
5. To understand principles, goals, objectives of education in right perspective.
6. Appropriate learning situation condition may be created for congenial and effective teaching.

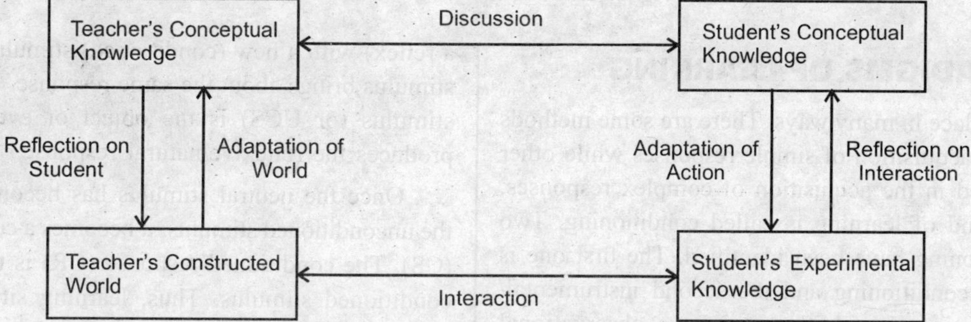

Fig. 1: *Essential aspects of the ideal teaching-learning process*

Approaches to Learning Theories

Aspect	Behaviourist	Cognitivist	Humanist
Learning theorists	Thorndike, Pavlov, Watson, Guthrie, Hull, Tolman, Skinner	Koffka, Kohler, Lewin, Piaget, Ausubel, Bruner, Gagne	Maslow, Rogers
View of the learning process	Change in behaviour	Internal mental process (including insight, information processing, memory, perception)	A personal act to fulfil potential
Locus of learning	Stimuli in external environment	Internal cognitive structuring	Affective and cognitive needs
Purpose in education	Produce behavioural change in desired direction	Develop capacity and skills to learn better	Become self-actualized autonomous
Educator's role	Arranges environment to elicit desired response	Structures content of learning activity	Facilitates development of the whole person
Manifestations in adult learning	Behavioural objectives	Cognitive development	Andragogy
	Competency-based education	Intelligence, learning and memory as function of age	Self-directed learning
	Skill development and training	Learning how to learn	

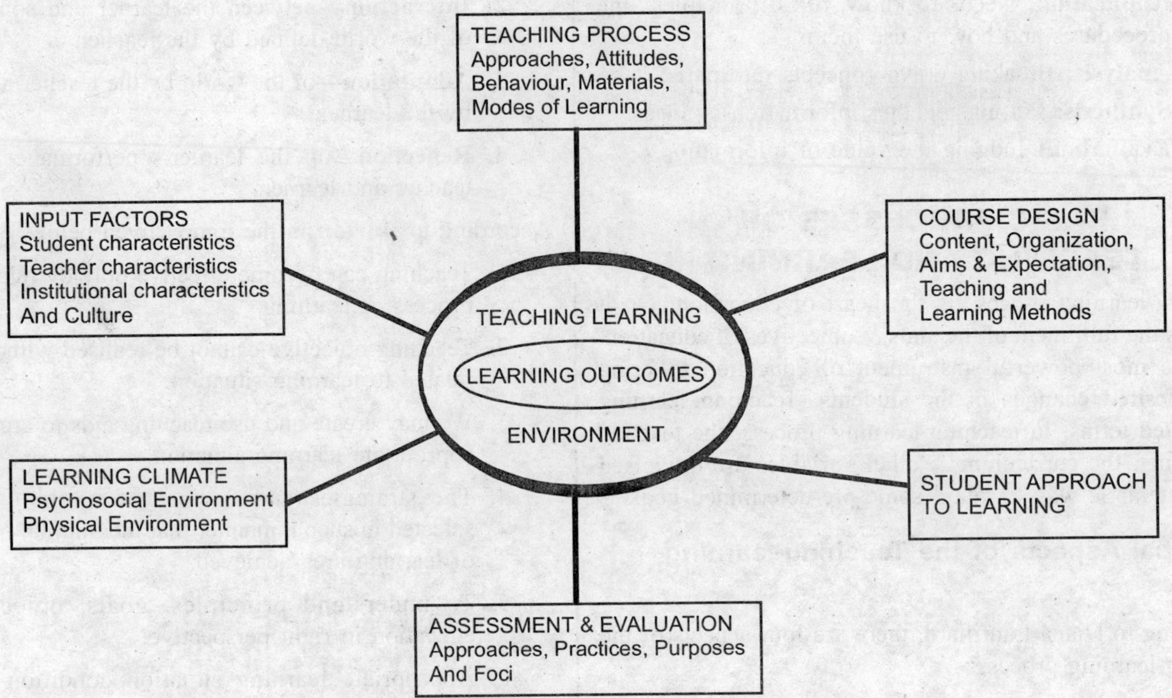

Fig. 2: *Teaching-Learning Environment*

PARADIGMS OF LEARNING

Learning takes place in many ways. There are some methods that are used in acquisition of simple responses while other methods are used in the acquisition of complex responses. The simplest kind of learning is called conditioning. Two types of conditioning have been identified. The first one is called classical conditioning and the second instrumental/ operant conditioning. In addition, we have observational learning, cognitive learning, verbal learning, concept learning and skill learning.

Classical Conditioning

This type of learning was first investigated by Ivan P. Pavlov. Like many great scientific advances, classical conditioning was discovered accidentally. The nineteenth-century Russian physiologist Ivan Pavlov was looking at salivation in dogs in response to being fed, when he noticed that his dogs would begin to salivate whenever he entered the room, even when he was not bringing them food. However, when Pavlov discovered that any object or event which the dogs learnt to associate with food (such as the food bowl) would trigger the same response, he realised that he had made an important scientific discovery, and he devoted the rest of his career to studying this type of learning.

Classical conditioning is 'classical' in that it is the first systematic study of basic laws of learning. Classical conditioning involves learning to associate an unconditioned stimulus that already brings about a particular response (*i.e.* a reflex) with a new (conditioned) stimulus, so that the new stimulus brings about the same response. The unconditioned stimulus (or UCS) is the object or event that originally produces the reflexive/natural response.

Once the neutral stimulus has become associated with the unconditioned stimulus, it becomes a conditioned stimulus (CS). The conditioned response (CR) is the response to the conditioned stimulus. Thus, learning situation in classical conditioning is one of S-S learning in which one stimulus becomes a signal of another stimulus.

Determinants of Classical Conditioning

How quickly and strongly acquisition of a response occurs in classical conditioning depends on several factors. Some of the major factors influencing learning a CR are described below:

1. Time Relations between Stimuli: The classical conditioning procedures, discussed below, are basically of four types based on the time relations between the onset of conditioned stimulus (CS) and unconditioned stimulus (US). The first three are called forward conditioning procedures, and the fourth one is called backward conditioning procedure. The basic experimental arrangements of these procedures are as follows:

(*a*) When the CS and US are presented together, it is called simultaneous conditioning.

(*b*) In delayed conditioning, the onset of CS precedes the onset of US. The CS ends before the end of the US.

(*c*) In trace conditioning, the onset and end of the CS precedes the onset of US with some time gap between the two.

(*d*) In backward conditioning, the US precedes the onset of CS.

It is now well established that delayed conditioning procedure is the most effective way of acquiring a CR. Simultaneous and trace conditioning procedures do lead to acquisition of a CR, but they require greater number of acquisition trials in comparison to the delayed conditioning procedure. It may be noted that the acquisition of response under backward conditioning procedure is very rare.

2. Type of Unconditioned Stimuli: The unconditioned stimuli used in studies of classical conditioning are basically of two types, *i.e.* appetitive and aversive. Appetitive unconditioned stimuli automatically elicits approach responses, such as eating, drinking, caressing, etc. These responses give satisfaction and pleasure. On the other hand, aversive US, such as noise, bitter taste, electric shock, painful injections, etc. are painful, harmful, and elicit avoidance and escape responses. It has been found that appetitive classical conditioning is slower and requires greater number of acquisition trials, but aversive classical conditioning is established in one, two or three trials depending on the intensity of the aversive US.

3. Intensity of Conditioned Stimuli: This influences the course of both appetitive and aversive classical conditioning. More intense conditioned stimuli are more effective in accelerating the acquisition of conditioned responses. It means that the more intense the conditioned stimulus, the fewer are the number of acquisition trials needed for conditioning.

Operant/Instrumental Conditioning

B.F. Skinner is regarded as the father of operant conditioning, but his work was based on **Thorndike's law of effect.** In the late nineteenth century, psychologist Edward Thorndike proposed the law of effect. The law of effect states that any behaviour that has good consequences will tend to be repeated, and any behaviour that has bad consequences will tend to be avoided. In the 1930s, B.F. Skinner, extended this idea and began to study operant conditioning. Operant conditioning is a type of learning in which responses come to be controlled by their consequences.

Operants are those behaviours or responses, which are emitted by animals and human beings voluntarily and are under their control. The term operant is used because the organism operates on the environment. Conditioning of operant behaviour is called operant conditioning. Skinner conducted his studies on rats and pigeons in specially made boxes, called the Skinner Box.

Determinants of Operant Conditioning

The operant or instrumental conditioning is a form of learning in which behaviour is learned, maintained or changed through its consequences. Such consequences are called **reinforcers**. A reinforcer is defined as any stimulus or event, which increases the probability of the occurrence of a (desired) response. A reinforcer has numerous features, which affect the course and strength of a response. They include its type—positive or negative, number or frequency, quality—superior or inferior, and schedule—continuous or intermittent (partial).

Reinforcement may be positive or negative. Positive reinforcement involves stimuli that have pleasant consequences. They strengthen and maintain the responses that have caused them to occur. Positive reinforcers satisfy needs, which include food, water, medals, praise, money, status, information, etc. Negative reinforcers involve unpleasant and painful stimuli. Responses that lead organisms to get rid of painful stimuli or avoid and escape from them provide negative reinforcement. Thus, negative reinforcement leads to learning of avoidance and escape responses. For instance, one learns to put on woollen clothes, burn firewood or use electric heaters to avoid the unpleasant cold weather. One learns to move away from dangerous stimuli because they provide negative reinforcement. It may be noted that negative reinforcement is not punishment. Use of punishment reduces or suppresses the response while a negative reinforcer increases the probability of avoidance or escape response. For instance, drivers and co-drivers wear their seat belts to avoid getting injured in case of an accident or to avoid being fined by the traffic police.

Classical and Operant Conditioning : Differences

1. In classical conditioning, the responses are under the control of some stimulus because they are reflexes, automatically elicited by the appropriate stimuli. Such stimuli are selected as US and responses elicited by them as UR. Thus Pavlovian conditioning, in which US elicits responses, is often called respondent conditioning. In instrumental conditioning, responses are under the control of the organism and are voluntary responses or 'operants'. Thus, in the two forms of conditioning different types of responses are conditioned.
2. In classical conditioning, the CS and US are well-defined, but in operant conditioning CS is not defined. It can be inferred but is not directly known.
3. In classical conditioning, the experimenter controls the occurrence of US, while in operant conditioning the occurrence of the reinforcer is under the control of the organism that is learning. Thus, for US in classical conditioning the organism remains passive, while in operant conditioning the subject has to be active in order to be reinforced.

4. In the two forms of conditioning, the technical terms used to characterise the experimental proceedings are different. Moreover what is called reinforcer in operant conditioning is called US in classical conditioning. An US has two functions. In the beginning, it elicits the response and also reinforces the response to be associated and elicited later on by the CS.

OBSERVATIONAL LEARNING

The other form of learning takes place by observing others. Earlier this form of learning was called **imitation**. Bandura and his colleagues in a series of experimental studies investigated observational learning in detail. In this kind of learning, human beings learn social behaviours, therefore, it is sometimes called **social learning**. In many situations individuals do not know how to behave. They observe others and emulate their behaviour. This form of learning is called **modelling**.

Examples of observational learning abound in our social life. Fashion designers employ tall, pretty, and gracious young girls and tall, smart, and well-built young boys for popularising clothes of different designs and fabrics. People observe them on televised fashion shows and advertisements in magazines and newspapers. They imitate these models. Observing superiors and likeable persons and then emulating their behaviour in a novel social situation is a common experience.

The children observe adults' behaviours, at home and during social ceremonies and functions. They enact adults in their plays and games. For instance, young children play games of marriage ceremonies, birthday parties, thief and policeman, house keeping, etc. Actually they enact in their games what they observe in society, on television, and read in books.

Children learn most of the social behaviours by observing and emulating adults. The way to put on clothes, dress one's hair, and conduct oneself in society are learned through observing others. It has also been shown that children learn and develop various personality characteristics through observational learning. Aggressiveness, prosocial behaviour, courtesy, politeness, diligence, and indolence are acquired by this method of learning.

COGNITIVE LEARNING

Some psychologists view learning in terms of cognitive processes that underlie it. They have developed approaches that focus on such processes that occur during learning rather than concentrating solely on S-R and S-S connections. Thus, in cognitive learning, there is a change in what the learner knows rather than what he/she does. This form of learning shows up in insight learning and latent learning.

Insight Learning

Kohler demonstrated a model of learning which could not be readily explained by conditioning. He performed a series of experiments with chimpanzees that involved solving complex problems. Kohler placed chimpanzees in an enclosed play area where food was kept out of their reach. Tools such as poles and boxes were placed in the enclosure. The chimpanzees rapidly learned how to use a box to stand on or a pole to move the food in their direction. In this experiment, learning did not occur as a result of trial and error and reinforcement, but came about in sudden flashes of insight. The chimpanzees would roam about the enclosure for some time and then suddenly would stand on a box, grab a pole and strike a banana, which was out of normal reach above the enclosure. The chimpanzee exhibited what Kohler called insight learning—the process by which the solution to a problem suddenly becomes clear.

In a normal experiment on insight learning, a problem is presented, followed by a period of time when no apparent progress is made and finally a solution suddenly emerges. In insight learning, sudden solution is the rule. Once the solution has appeared, it can be repeated immediately the next time the problem is confronted. Thus, it is clear that what is learned is not a specific set of conditioned associations between stimuli and responses but a cognitive relationship between a means and an end. As a result, insight learning can be generalised to other similar problem situations.

Latent Learning

Another type of cognitive learning is known as latent learning. In latent learning, a new behaviour is learned but not demonstrated until reinforcement is provided for displaying it. Tolman made an early contribution to the concept of latent learning. To have an idea of latent learning, we may briefly understand his experiment. Tolman put two groups of rats in a maze and gave them an opportunity to explore. In one group, rats found food at the end of the maze and soon learned to make their way rapidly through the maze. On the other hand, rats in the second group were not rewarded and showed no apparent signs of learning. But later, when these rats were reinforced, they ran through the maze as efficiently as the rewarded group.

Tolman contended that the unrewarded rats had learned the layout of the maze early in their explorations. They just never displayed their latent learning until the reinforcement was provided. Instead, the rats developed a cognitive map of the maze, *i.e.* a mental representation of the spatial locations and directions, which they needed to reach their goal.

LEARNING AS A SOCIAL ACTIVITY

Learning is a social activity. Our learning is intimately associated with our connection with other human beings, our teachers, our peers, our family as well as casual acquaintances, including the people before us or next to us. We are more likely to be successful in our efforts to educate, if we recognise this principle rather than try to avoid it. Much of traditional education, as Dewey pointed out, is directed towards isolating the learner from all social interaction, and towards seeing education as a one-on-one relationship between the learner and the objective material to be learned. In contrast, progressive education (to continue to use Dewey's formulation) recognizes the social aspect of learning and uses conversations interaction with others, and the application of knowledge as an integral aspect of learning.

SOCIAL CONTEXT OF LEARNING

Social Learning Theory

Social learning theory focuses on the learning that occurs within a social context. It considers that people learn from one another, including such concepts as observational learning, imitation, and modelling. Among others **Albert Bandura** is considered the leading proponent of this theory.

General Principles of Social Learning Theory Follows:

1. People can learn by observing the behaviour of others and the outcomes of those behaviours.
2. Learning can occur without a change in behaviour. Behaviourists say that learning has to be represented by a permanent change in behaviour, in contrast social learning theorists say that because people can learn through observation alone, their learning may not necessarily be shown in their performance. Learning may or may not result in a behaviour change.
3. Cognition plays a role in learning. Over the last 40 years social learning theory has become increasingly cognitive in its interpretation of human learning. Awareness and expectations of future reinforcements or punishments can have a major effect on the behaviours that people exhibit.
4. Social learning theory can be considered a bridge or a transition between behaviourist learning theories and cognitive learning theories.

How the Environment Reinforces and Punishes Modelling:

People are often reinforced for modelling the behaviour of others. Bandura suggested that the environment also reinforces modelling. This is in several possible ways:

1. The observer is reinforced by the model. For example, a student who changes dress to fit in with a certain group of students has a strong likelihood of being accepted and thus reinforced by that group.
2. The observer is reinforced by a third person. The observer might be modelling the actions of someone else, for example, an outstanding class leader or student. The teacher notices this and compliments and praises the observer for modelling such behaviour thus reinforcing that behaviour.
3. The imitated behaviour itself leads to reinforcing consequences. Many behaviours that we learn from others produce satisfying or reinforcing results. For example, a student in my multimedia class could observe how the extra work a classmate does is fun. This student in turn would do the same extra work and also receive enjoyment.
4. Consequences of the model's behaviour affect the observers behaviour vicariously. This is known as vicarious reinforcement. This is where in the model is reinforced for a response and then the observer shows an increase in that same response. Bandura illustrated this by having students watch a film of a model hitting a inflated clown doll. One group of children saw the model being praised for such action. Without being reinforced, the group of children began to also hit the doll.

Contemporary Social Learning Perspective of Reinforcement and Punishment

1. Contemporary theory proposes that both reinforcement and punishment have indirect effects on learning. They are not the sole or main cause.
2. Reinforcement and punishment influence the extent to which an individual exhibits a behaviour that has been learned.
3. The expectation of reinforcement influences cognitive processes that promote learning. Therefore, attention pays a critical role in learning. And attention is influenced by the expectation of reinforcement. An example would be, where the teacher tells a group of students that what they wiil study next is not on the test. Students will not pay attention, because they do not expect to know the information for a test.

Cognitive Factors in Social Learning

Social learning theory has cognitive factors as well as behaviourist factors (actually operant factors).

1. **Learning without performance:** Bandura makes a distinction between learning through observation and the actual imitation of what has been learned.
2. **Cognitive processing during learning:** Social learning theorists contend that attention is a critical factor in learning.
3. **Expectations:** As a result of being reinforced, people form expectations about the consequences that future

behaviours are likely to bring. They expect certain behaviours to bring reinforcements and others to bring punishment. The learner needs to be aware however, of the response reinforcements and response punishment. Reinforcement increases a response only when the learner is aware of that connection.

4. **Reciprocal causation:** Bandura proposed that behaviour can influence both the environment and the person. In fact each of these three variables, the person, the behaviour, and the environment can have an influence on each other.
5. **Modelling:** There are different types of models. There is the live model, and actual person demonstrating the behaviour. There can also be a symbolic model, which can be a person or action portrayed in some other medium, such as television, videotape,. computer programs.

Behaviours that can be learned through modelling:

Many behaviours can be learned, at least partly, through modelling. Examples that can be cited are, students can watch parents read, students can watch the demonstrations of mathematics problems, or seen someone acting bravely and a fearful situation. Aggression can be learned through models. Much research indicate that children become more aggressive when they observed aggressive or violent models. Moral thinking and moral behaviour are influenced by observation and modelling. This includes moral judgments regarding right and wrong which can in part, develop through modelling.

Conditions Necessary for Effective Modelling to Occur:

Bandura mentions four conditions that are necessary before an individual can successfully model the behaviour of someone else:

1. **Attention:** the person must first pay attention to the model.
2. **Retention:** the observer must be able to remember the behaviour that has been observed. One way of increasing this is using the technique of rehearsal.
3. **Motor reproduction:** the third condition is the ability to replicate the behaviour that the model has just demonstrated. This means that the observer has to be able to replicate the action, which could be a problem with a learner who is not ready developmentally to replicate the action. For example, little children have difficulty doing complex physical motion.
4. **Motivation:** the final necessary ingredient for modelling to occur is motivation, learners must want to demonstrate what they have learned. Remember that since these four conditions vary among individuals, different people will reproduce the same behaviour differently.

Effects of Modelling on Behaviour:

Modelling teaches new behaviours.

Modelling influences the frequency of previously learned behaviours.

Modelling may encourage previously forbidden behaviours.

Modelling increases the frequency of similar behaviours. For example, a student might see a friend excel in basketball and he tries to excel in football because he is not tall enough for basketball.

Educational Implications of Social Learning Theory:

Social learning theory has numerous implications for classroom use.

1. Students often learn a great deal simply by observing other people.
2. Describing the consequences of behaviour is can effectively increase the appropriate behaviours and decrease inappropriate ones. This can involve discussing with learners about the rewards and consequences of various behaviours.
3. Modelling provides an alternative to shaping for teaching new behaviours. Instead of using shaping, which is operant conditioning, modelling can provide a faster, more efficient means for teaching new behaviour. To promote effective modelling a teacher must make sure that the four essential conditions exist; attention, retention, motor reproduction, and motivation.
4. Teachers and parents must model appropriate behaviours and take care that they do not model inappropriate behaviours.
5. Teachers should expose students to a variety of other models. This technique is especially important to break down traditional stereotypes.
6. Students must believe that they are capable of accomplishing school tasks. Thus, it is very important to develop a sense of self-efficacy for students. Teachers can promote such self-efficacy by having students receive confidence-building messages, watch others be successful, and experience success on their own.
7. Teachers should help students set realistic expectations for their academic accomplishments. In general in my class that means making sure that expectations are not set too low. I want to realistically challenge my students. However, sometimes the task is beyond a student's ability, example would be the cancer group.
8. Self-regulation techniques provide an effective method for improving student behaviour.

CHILD AS A PROBLEM SOLVER AND A SCIENTIFIC INVESTIGATOR

Problem solving is the foundation of a young child's learning. It must be valued, promoted, provided for and sustained in the early childhood classroom. Opportunities for problem solving occur in the everyday context of a child's life. By observing the child closely, teachers can use the child's social, cognitive, movement and emotional experiences to facilitate problem solving and promote strategies useful in the lifelong process of learning.

Problem solving is thinking that is goal-directed. Almost all our day-to-day activities are directed towards a goal. Here, it is important to know that problems are not always in the form of obstacles or hurdles that one faces. It could be any simple activity that you perform to reach a defined goal, for example, preparing a quick snack for your friend who has just arrived at your place. In problem solving there is an initial state (*i.e.* the problem) and there is an end state (the goal). These two anchors are connected by means of several steps or mental operations. Following table would clarify our understanding of various steps through which one solves a problem.

Table: Mental Operations Involved in Solving a Problem

Let us look at the problem of organising a play in school on the occasion of Teachers' Day. Problem solving would involve the following sequence.

	Mental operation	Nature of problem
1.	Identify the problem	A week is left for teachers' day and you are given the task of organising a play.
2.	Represent the problem	Organising a play would involve identification of an appropriate theme, screening of actors, actresses, arranging money, etc.
3.	Plan the solution: Set sub-goals	Search and survey various available themes for a play, and consult teachers and friends who have the expertise. The play to be decided, based on such considerations as cost, duration, suitability for the occasion, etc.
4.	Evaluate all solutions (plays)	Collect all the information/stage rehearsal.
5.	Select one solution and execute it	Compare and verify the various options to get the best solution (the play).
6.	Evaluate the outcome	If the play (solution) is appreciated, think about the steps you have followed for future reference for yourself as well as for your friends.
7.	Rethink and redefine problems and solutions	After this special occasion you can still think about ways to plan a better play in future.

Learning Through Problem Solving

By exploring social relationships, manipulating objects, and interacting with people, children are able to formulate ideas, try these ideas out, and accept or reject what they learn. Constructing knowledge by making mistakes is part of the natural process of problem solving. Through exploring, then experimenting, trying out a hypothesis, and finally, solving problems, children make learning personal and meaningful. Piaget states that children understand only what they discover or invent themselves. It is this discovery within the problem solving process that is the vehicle for children's learning. Children are encouraged to construct their own knowledge when the teacher plans for problem solving; bases the framework for learning in problem solving; and provides time, space, and materials.

Teacher's Role

Changing through problem solving is modelled by adults and facilitated by the teacher in the classroom environment. When teachers articulate the problems they face and discuss solutions with children, children become more aware of the significance of the problem-solving process. Being a problem solver is modelled by the teacher and emulated by the children. The teacher's role is two-fold: first, to value the process and be willing to trust the learner, and second, to establish and maintain a classroom environment that encourages problem solving. It is the attitude of the teacher that must change first in the problem-solving classroom. Values and goals must be clearly defined to include a child-centered curriculum, the development of communication skills, promotion of cooperative learning, and inclusion of diverse ideas.

The teacher must be willing to become a learner, too. By being curious, observing, listening, and questioning, the teacher shares and models the qualities that are valued and promoted by the problem-solving process.

Planning for Problem Solving

A curriculum that accommodates a variety of developmental levels as well as individual differences in young children sets the stage for problem solving. Choices, decision-making, and a curriculum framework that integrates learning, such as Katz and Chard's project method, are especially appropriate for young learners. The project approach facilitates cooperative learning and promotes diverse ideas. Donna Ogle's K-W-L (what you KNOW, what you WANT to know, and what you have LEARNED) is another method of organizing work that promotes problem solving. Themes, units, webbing, and the KWL method are all ways of organizing curriculum that can support problem solving. Beginning with the needs and interests of the children, problem solving develops from meaningful experiences important to the children. The teacher-designed curriculum provides the classroom basis for these experiences.

For example, a second grade investigation of waste materials from a classroom led one group of young children to explore the topic in an integrated way. Reading, writing, counting, measuring, interviews of community people, and science experiments were planned, initiated and reported. Solutions to many problems posed during the investigation were tried out and some were found to be successful. Through group work, individuals were able to participate and communicate as cognitive and social needs were met. Each child, at individual levels and in individual ways, was successful within the group experience. Problem solving empowers children.

Providing for Problem Solving

Problem solving is a skill that can be learned and must be practiced. It is facilitated by a classroom schedule that provides for integrated learning in large blocks of time, space for ongoing group projects, and many open-ended materials. The teacher provides the time, space, and materials necessary for in-depth learning.

1. Time: Teachers can provide for problem solving by enlarging blocks of learning time during the school day. Because making choices, discussing decisions, and evaluating mistakes takes time, large time blocks best suit the problem-solving process. It is important that children know they have time to identify and solve problems.

2. Space: Projects and group meetings may require an assessment of classroom space. Moving desks and tables together facilitates communication and cooperation in the classroom. Once the teacher has observed the patterns of traffic in the classroom, equipment can be moved or eliminated to promote problem solving.

3. Materials: The open-ended materials that are needed for the construction and concrete solving of problems should be safe, durable, and varied. Well-marked storage units should be easily accessible to children, and materials should be available for ongoing exploration and manipulation. Access to a variety of materials encourages children to use materials in new and diverse ways. This freedom promotes problem solving.

The Problem-Solving Model

Individuals or groups can solve problems. Group problem solving is important to young children because many diverse ideas are generated. Both individual and group processes should be included in the early childhood classroom. Becoming skillful at problem solving is based on the understanding and use of sequenced steps. These steps are:

1. Identifying the problem,
2. Brainstorming a variety of solutions,
3. Choosing one solution and trying it out, and
4. Evaluating what has happened.

Choosing Good Problems

Goffin provides teachers with guiding questions that will help them identify appropriate problems for young children. Some of these are:

1. Is the problem meaningful and interesting?
2. Can the problem be solved at a variety of levels?
3. Must a new decision be made?
4. Can the actions be evaluated?

Problem solving is a way to make sense of the environment and, in fact, control it. The process allows children in an increasingly diverse world to be active participants and to implement changes. By including problem solving in the early childhood classroom, we equip children with a life-long skill that is useful in all areas of learning.

Obstacles to Solving Problems

Two major obstacles to solving a problem are mental set and lack of motivation.

Mental Set

Mental set is a tendency of a person to solve problems by following already tried mental operations or steps. Prior success with a particular strategy would sometimes help in solving a new problem. However, this tendency also creates a mental rigidity that obstructs the problem solver to think of any new rules or strategies. Thus, while in some situations mental set can enhance the quality and speed of problem solving, in other situations it hinders problem solving. You might have experienced this while solving mathematical problems. After completing a couple of questions, you form an idea of the steps that are required to solve these questions and subsequently you go on following the same steps, until a point where you fail. At this point you may experience difficulty in avoiding the already used steps. Those steps would interfere in your thought for new strategies. However, in day-to-day activities we often rely on past experiences with similar or related problems.

Like mental set, **functional fixedness** in problem solving occurs when people fail to solve a problem because they are fixed on a thing's usual function. If you have ever used a hardbound book to hammer a nail, then you have overcome functional fixedness.

Lack of Motivation

People might be great at solving problems, but all their skills and talents are of no use if they are not motivated. Sometimes people give up easily when they encounter a problem or failure in implementing the first step. Therefore, there is a need to persist in their effort to find a solution.

ALTERNATIVE CONCEPTIONS OF LEARNING

When teachers provide instruction on concepts in various subjects, they are teaching students who already have some pre-instructional knowledge about the topic. Student knowledge, however, can be erroneous, illogical or misinformed. These erroneous understandings are termed alternative conceptions or misconceptions (or intuitive theories). Alternative conceptions (misconceptions) are not unusual. In fact, they are a normal part of the learning process. We quite naturally form ideas from our everyday experience, but obviously not all the ideas we develop are correct with respect to the most current evidence and scholarship in a given discipline. Moreover, some concepts in different content areas are simply very difficult to grasp. They may be very abstract, counterintuitive or quite complex. Hence, our understanding of them is flawed. In addition, things we have already learned are sometimes unhelpful in learning new concepts/theories. This occurs when the new concept or theory is inconsistent with previously learned material. Accordingly, as noted, it is very typical for students (and adults) to have misconceptions in different domains (content knowledge areas). Indeed, researchers have found that there is a common set of alternative conceptions (misconceptions) that most students typically exhibit. There is one class of alternative theories (or misconceptions) that is very deeply entrenched. These are "ontological misconceptions," which relate to ontological beliefs (*i.e.*, beliefs about the fundamental categories and properties of the world).

Alternative conceptions (misconceptions) can impede learning for several reasons. First, students generally are unaware that the knowledge they have is wrong. Moreover, misconceptions can be very entrenched in student thinking. In addition, new experiences are interpreted through these erroneous understandings, thereby interfering with being able to correctly grasp new information. Also, alternative conceptions (misconceptions) tend to be very resistant to instruction because learning entails replacing or radically reorganizing student knowledge. Hence, conceptual change has to occur for learning to happen. This puts teachers in the very challenging position of needing to bring about significant conceptual change in student knowledge. Generally, ordinary forms of instruction, such as lectures, labs, discovery learning, or simply reading texts, are not very successful at overcoming student misconceptions. For all these reasons, misconceptions can be hard nuts for teachers to crack. However, several instructional strategies have been found to be effective in achieving conceptual change and helping students leave their alternative conceptions behind and learn correct concepts or theories.

Instructional strategies that can lead to change in students' alternative conceptions (misconceptions) and learning of new concepts and theories

1. Present new concepts or theories that you are teaching in such a way that students see as plausible, high-quality, intelligible and generative.
2. Use students' correct conceptions and build on those by creating a bridge of examples to the new concept or theory that students are having trouble learning due to misconceptions they hold.
3. Use model-based reasoning, which helps students construct new representations that vary from their intuitive theories.
4. Use diverse instruction, wherein you present a few examples that challenge multiple assumptions, rather than a larger number of examples that challenge just one assumption.
5. Help students become aware of (raise student metacognition about) their own alternative conceptions (misconceptions).
6. Present students with experiences that cause cognitive conflict in students' minds. Experiences (as in strategy 3 above) that can cause cognitive conflict are ones that get students to consider their erroneous (misconception) knowledge side-by-side with, or at the same time as, the correct concept or theory.
7. Engage in Interactive Conceptual Instruction (ICI).
8. Develop students' epistemological thinking, which incorporates beliefs and theories about the nature of knowledge and the nature of learning, in ways that will facilitate conceptual change. The more naive students' beliefs are about knowledge and learning, the less likely they are to revise their misconceptions.
9. Help students "self-repair" their misconceptions.
10. Once students have overcome their alternative conceptions (misconceptions).

Presenting new concepts or theories

In presenting new concepts or theories, teachers should be sure to show these theories or concepts as:

1. Plausible: The new information should be shown to be consistent with other knowledge and able to explain the available data. Learners must see how the new conception (theory) is consistent with other knowledge and a good explanation of the data.

2. High quality: Of course, the theory/concept to be taught is of high quality from a scientific point of view, since it is a correct theory. However, the presented theory should take a better account of the data than what students currently have available to them. For example, the instructor should deal with the problem from the perspective of the students (*e.g.*, students for whom a "flat earth" theory provides a better account of the data available than does a "spherical earth" theory). Hence, the quality of the new theory must be considered along with the kind of data that students know about.

3. Intelligible: Teachers should do what they can to increase the intelligibility of the new theory. Learners must be able to grasp how the new conception works. To increase intelligibility, teachers can use methods such as use of:

(*a*) analogies,

(*b*) models, and

(*c*) direct exposition.

4. Generative/fruitful: Teachers should show that the new concept/theory can be extended to open up new areas of inquiry. Learners must be able to extend the new conception to new areas of inquiry. Teachers might accomplish this by illustrating the application of the new concept/theory to a range of problems. These problems can include familiar ones and new ones.

UNDERSTANDING CHILDREN'S 'ERRORS' AS SIGNIFICANT STEPS IN THE LEARNING PROCESS

The legacy of Jean Piaget to the world of early childhood education is that he fundamentally altered the view of how a child learns. And a teacher, he believed, was more than a transmitter of knowledge she was also an essential observer and guide to helping children build their own knowledge.

As a university graduate, Swiss-born Piaget got a routine job in Paris standardizing Binet-Simon IQ tests, where the emphasis was on children getting the right answers. Piaget observed that many children of the same ages gave the same kinds of incorrect answers. What could be learned from this?

Piaget interviewed many hundreds of children and concluded that children who are allowed to make mistakes often go on to discover their errors and correct them, or find new solutions. In this process, children build their own way of learning. From children's errors, teachers can obtain insights into the child's view of the world and can tell where guidance is needed. They can provide appropriate materials, ask encouraging questions, and allow the child to construct his own knowledge.

Piaget's continued interactions with young children became part of his life-long research. After reading about a child who thought that the sun and moon followed him wherever he went, Piaget wanted to find out if all young children had a similar belief. He found that many did indeed believe this. Piaget went on to explore children's countless "why" questions, such as, "Why is the sun round?" or "Why is grass green?" He concluded that children do not think like adults. Their thought processes have their own distinct order and special logic. Children are not "empty vessels to be filled with knowledge" (as traditional pedagogical theory had it). They are "active builders of knowledge-little scientists who construct their own theories of the world."

SENSE AND FEELINGS

Meaning of Sense

Sense refers to the physiological and psychological ability through which human beings receive information from their environment. It is the process by which stimuli from the external world are detected, transmitted, and interpreted by the brain. The five main sense organs—eyes, ears, nose, tongue, and skin—help in vision, hearing, smell, taste, and touch respectively.

Senses play a fundamental role in the early stages of life as they provide the first means of interaction with the environment. Through sensory experiences, children begin to explore, discover, and understand the world around them. Sensory input forms the basis of perception, concept formation, and learning.

Characteristics of Sensory Development in Children

1. Infancy (0–2 years): During infancy, sensory development is rapid but not fully mature at birth. Infants rely mainly on touch, taste, and smell. Vision and hearing gradually improve over time. They respond to bright lights, loud sounds, and familiar voices, especially of caregivers.

Touch plays a crucial role in emotional bonding and security. Activities like holding, cuddling, and gentle stroking help in developing trust and attachment. Sensory stimulation during this stage is essential for brain development and lays the foundation for future learning.

2. Early Childhood (2–6 years): In early childhood, sensory abilities become more refined and coordinated. Children actively explore their environment using all senses. Vision and hearing improve significantly, enabling recognition of objects, colors, shapes, sounds, and language patterns.

Children engage in activities such as drawing, building, playing, and experimenting. These experiences enhance creativity, language development, and problem-solving skills. Learning at this stage is highly dependent on sensory experiences, and children learn best through play and hands-on activities.

3. Middle Childhood (6–12 years): At this stage, sensory development is well organized and integrated with cognitive abilities. Children can observe details, compare objects, and analyze sensory information more effectively.

Vision supports reading and visual learning, hearing aids in understanding instructions and communication, and touch helps in writing, crafts, and physical activities. Children also develop aesthetic appreciation, such as interest in art, music, and sports. Sensory experiences are now combined with logical thinking and reasoning.

Meaning of Feelings

Feelings refer to the emotional states or internal experiences that arise in response to situations, thoughts, or sensory inputs. They include emotions such as happiness, sadness, fear, anger, love, curiosity, excitement, and anxiety.

Feelings are subjective in nature and play a significant role in influencing behavior, personality, and learning. They are an essential part of emotional development and help individuals respond appropriately to different situations.

Role of Feelings in Learning and Teaching

Feelings have a direct impact on the learning process. Positive emotions such as interest, curiosity, confidence, and satisfaction promote active participation and improve understanding. A child who feels secure and motivated is more likely to engage in learning activities and achieve better outcomes.

On the other hand, negative emotions such as fear, anxiety, frustration, and boredom can hinder learning. These emotions reduce concentration, participation, and memory retention. Therefore, emotional well-being is essential for effective learning.

Relationship between Senses and Feelings

Senses and feelings are closely interconnected. Sensory experiences often trigger emotional responses. For example, a pleasant classroom environment with colorful charts, engaging activities, and friendly interaction can create positive feelings.

Conversely, a noisy, stressful, or uncomfortable environment can generate negative emotions and reduce interest in learning. Thus, effective learning occurs when both sensory and emotional aspects are properly addressed.

Impact on Social and Emotional Development

Feelings play a crucial role in shaping social behavior and emotional development. Children learn to recognize, express, and regulate their emotions over time. This helps them build relationships, cooperate with others, and adjust in social situations.

Proper emotional development leads to self-confidence, empathy, and resilience. It also helps children deal with challenges, stress, and conflicts effectively.

Role of Teacher in Developing Sense and Feelings

Teachers have an important responsibility in nurturing both sensory and emotional development. They should:

- Provide a stimulating and activity-based learning environment.
- Use teaching aids such as charts, models, audio-visual tools, and real objects.
- Encourage observation, exploration, and hands-on learning.
- Create a safe, supportive, and fear-free classroom atmosphere.
- Understand students' emotions and respond with empathy and patience.
- Motivate students and build their confidence.
- Encourage expression of feelings through activities like storytelling, drawing, and group work.

Educational Implications

Understanding senses and feelings helps in designing effective teaching-learning processes. It promotes child-centered education and ensures holistic development.

Learning becomes more meaningful when it involves both sensory experiences and emotional engagement. It improves participation, retention, and overall personality development of learners.

MOTIVATION AND LEARNING

Motivation

Motivation is the heart of the learning process. It generates the will in an individual to do something. Adequate motivation not only engages the student in an activity which results in learning, but also sustains and directs learning. Two types of motivation are commonly recognised. These are: intrinsic and extrinsic motivation.

Intrinsic motivation arises when the resolution of tension is to be found in mastering the learning task itself; the material learned provides its own reward. For example, the student who studies the construction of model aeroplanes diligently so that he can make a model, is experiencing a kind of intrinsic motivation.

Extrinsic motivation occurs when a student pursues a learning task, but for reasons which are external. If a student engages in construction of model aeroplanes because he thinks it will please his father, who is an ex-pilot, rather than because of intrinsic motivation. We should remember that in most learning situations motivation can not be dichotomised so neatly. It is the function of the total learning situation and hinges on some blend of personal concern for the work itself and the concern for some extrinsic factors as well. As a working principle, motivation is probably a function of an interactive situation where reward to a particular action acts as an incentive. Some of the common forms of extrinsic motivation are:

- **Purposive striving, goals and ideals:** The goal and purposes of learning clearly perceived by the individual, provide strong motivation for better action and learning.
- **Knowledge of results:** Knowledge of results in terms of success and failure provides incentive for greater efforts on the part of the student. If a student practices a task without knowing the accuracy or inaccuracy of his performance, he may practise wrong task. In such a case, all learning will be futile. Therefore, if results of performance are known to the student, he learns better as compared to when he does not know about the results. Mere repetition of a task without knowledge of its results fails to bring about learning. Knowledge of results serves two purposes: (i) it enables the subject to evaluate his efficiency and to change his responses in the direction of greater accuracy, and (ii) it adds to the satisfaction in reaching a goal, one tends of repeat rewarded responses.
- **Punishment and rewards:** Punishment can be understood as an act of inflicting pain deliberately with the purpose of affecting the future conduct of an individual being punished. Punishment is based on fear of physical pain, embarrassment and loss of status. Thus, punishment of fear of being punished is one of the common and obvious methods of keeping under control and guiding the students. Punishment or fear is a very strong stimuli, a negative incentive to learning especially when errors occur. Thorndike showed that generally punishment speeds up learning and reduces the number of errors as it produces emotional excitement which tends to fix at punished response. But it does not mean that punishment under all the circumstances and with all the students is equally effective. For example, it may prove disastrous and destructive when task is very difficult.
- Contrary to punishment, rewards are certainly better and positive incentives to learning. They are responsible for initiative, energy, competition, self-expression and creative ability. According to law of effect, reward is satisfying and pleasant, thus reward strengthens learning. Rewards may in the form of gifts, prizes, money, badges, cups, certificates of merit, or other objects of some value. Motivation through such objects feeds the natural drive in all the human beings. But, when these rewards are too much strived for, they degenerate the whole learning.
- **Praise and blame:** These are also strong incentives for effective learning. Praise stimulates average and inferior children, but has less effect on those of superior intelligence. Reproof is felt most by superior children, but girls seem more susceptible to praise than do boys. Regardless of age sex, or initial ability, praise is the most effective of the incentives. Reproof seems to be less effective for all students. Chase (1932) reported praise to be less effective than blame with young children, but Hurlock (1920) generalised, still accepted by contemporary investigators, that praise is more effective stimulus in motivating both immediate and long-continued tasks.
- **Rivalry:** The rivalry between students which leads to resentment, jealousy, etc., or rivalry between groups of students which creates hatred, is the least desirable type of incentive to be encouraged in the schools. Self-rivalry or rivalry in the form of healthy competition is the most valuable type. This tendency should be developed in the student. Though experimental researchers have shown rivalry to be a powerful motivation influence, the emotional and social consequences of rivalry must be considered by the teacher.

Functions of Motivation

The major functions of motivation in learning are as follows:

- To energies the students in learning
- To direct behaviour
- To select behaviour
- To help capture the attention
- To help in acquiring knowledge
- To help in character formation
- To develop social qualities

Attention in Relation to Motivation

Attention is the basic pre-requisite of all learning in the classroom. Learning is possible only if students concentrate their attention on the object or stimuli to be learnt. Attention increases the amount and rate of learning, and also the efficiency of work.

Attention is closely related to motivation. Attention is motivated behaviour, in which the student makes a variety of efforts for achieving the goal. Thus motivation helps in capturing attention. You can help your students by motivating them to concentrate their attention on the tasks to be learnt by them.

Between the two types of motivation, intrinsic motivation should be preferred to extrinsic motivation. It produces better learning because it is related to interest. The learner pursues the activity in which he has interest without waiting for any external pressure. When the learner does not show any intrinsic motivation or interest in learning we have to resort to extrinsic motivation by the use of 'incentives'—whether financial or non-financial (monetary or non-monetary)—such as rewards, awards, prizes, competitions, praise, etc.

In-built Motivation

Another type of motivation is called in-built motivation. Whatever may be the type of motivation, it should be an in-built component of the whole programme of education/training. Right type of trainers, attractive and need-based reading materials, supportive training methodologies, constant awareness of the new dimensions of the programme will facilitate motivation in an in-built manner.

Theories of Motivation

The main theories of motivation are: (a) Psycho-analytic Theory, (b) Maslow's Theory of Self-actualisation, (c) Physiological Theory and (d) Achievement-Motivation Theory.

Psycho-Analytic Theory

According to this theory, motivation gives the vital life forces which are the prime mover of life and its activities. 'It is will power that motivates a person', *i.e.,* 'no will power—no activity'. All these versions agree on one point *i.e.,* 'building ego of man'.

Maslow's Theory of Self-Actualisation

This theory is based on human needs and their satisfaction. Maslow (1998) has arranged man's basic needs in a hierarchy, *i.e.,* some needs are strong or more important than others. According to him the five basic needs, progressing from physiological needs through safety needs, love, esteem needs and the need for self-actualisation. These basic needs are described here under:

- **Physiological needs:** Maslow states that physiological needs are undoubtedly the most powerful of all needs. Examples are the needs for food, sleep or rest. Until the biological needs are met, an individual may lack awareness of other needs. When a person is gratified he/she is released and higher needs can emerge. Some potential adult learners from low-economic background actually have unmet physiological needs, such as hunger, which prevent them from learning. An old person may not be able to see or hear well and he might not be open to satisfying other needs.
- **Safety Needs:** When physiological needs are satisfied, safety needs emerge, such as need for security, for physical safety, for stability in one's life. Safety needs are seen when a person prefers the familiar over the unfamiliar. An adult would rather go to a meeting in a building with which he is familiar than in a building new to him.
- **Love or Belongingness:** If both the physiological and safety needs are gratified, the needs for love, affection and belongingness emerge. Love needs involve both giving and receiving love. They involve the feeling of being wanted. The person who does not feel he belongs, no matter what the reason, probably will not continue with the group and discontinue his participation in adult education programme. The teacher should be affectionate towards adult learners and develop a group spirit among learners.
- **Esteem:** All people in our society have a need, a desire, for self-respect or self-esteem and for the esteem of others. There are two types: The desire for achievement and the desire for prestige or recognition from others. Satisfaction of the need for self-esteem leads to feelings of self-confidence and of being useful to the society. Thwarting of these needs produce feelings of inferiority or weakness. Fear or failure or lack of self-esteem might prevent an adult from participating in educational activities.
- **Self-Actualisation:** Even after the earlier needs are satisfied a person might still feel restless unless he becomes everything he is capable of becoming. This is called self-fulfilment or self-actualisation. The specific form of this needs varies from person-to-person. One person might desire to be an ideal mother or an ideal leader.
- **Implications for Adult Learning:** Before starting the adult education class, the basic needs of the learners should be studied. It may be possible that due to poverty and less per capita income, the basic biological needs of the learners may not be fulfilled. Then the main aim of adult education should be to provide regular income to the learners. This can be done by starting various income generating projects. The educators should also help by marketing of such products produced by the learners. The officials connected with adult education should take steps to start such programmes. This will make the classes

more interesting to the learners. The teacher needs to strengthen the group spirit among learners and should identify himself/herself with the group. The learning experiences in the centres should promote the talents, attitudes capacities and potentialities of adults.

Physiological Theory of Motivation

This theory has been developed by Clifford Morgan and William James. According to this theory of the body determines attitudes and interests and explains activities and behaviour of people.

Implications for Adult Education: Participation in physical activities decrease with age so also interests change as a person becomes older. Many physical limitations affect the amount of time an adult has for educational activities. After working all day at a job, some adults are too tired to participate in educational activity, such people can be motivated giving them work which gives them relaxation. Hearing and vision also decrease with age. The ages of the group members will determine the size of letters that a teacher writes on a black board, the colour of the chalk used, the size of the articles he holds for the adults to see, and how loudly and distinctly he speaks. The size, type and quality of handout material are also important.

Achievement-Motivation Theory

This theory has been developed by McClelland (1985). According to this theory all human behaviour is intended to reduce tension and reach a state of physiological and psychological equilibrium. It is a desire to do better, to achieve unique accomplishment, to compete with a standard of excellence and to involve oneself with long term achievement goals. It can be identified on the basic of individual expectation of success. It applies only when the individual knows that his/her performance will be evaluated by himself or by others in terms of excellence, and that the consequences of his action will either succeed or fail.

FACTORS CONTRIBUTING TO LEARNING

Introduction

Learning, can be considered as the process by which skills, attitudes, knowledge and concepts are acquired, understood, applied and extended. All human beings, whether grown ups or children engage in the process of learning, either consciously, sub-consciously or subliminally. It is through learning that their competence and ability to function in their environment get enhanced. It is important to understand that while we learn some ideas and concepts through instruction or teaching, we also learn through our feelings and experiences. Feelings and experiences are a tangible part of our lives and these greatly influence what we learn, how we learn and why we learn.

Learning has been considered partly a cognitive process and partly a social and affective one. It qualifies as a cognitive process because it involves the functions of attention, perception, reasoning, analysis, drawing of conclusions, making interpretations and giving meaning to the observed phenomena. All of these are mental processes which relate to the intellectual functions of the individual. Learning is a social and affective process, as the societal and cultural context in which we function and the feelings and experiences which we have, greatly influence our ideas, concepts, images and understanding of the world. These constitute inner subjective interpretations and represent our own unique, personalized constructions of the specific universe of functioning. Our knowledge, ideas, concepts, attitudes, beliefs and the skills which we acquire are a consequence of these combined processes.

CLASSIFICATION OF FACTORS: PERSONAL & ENVIRONMENTAL

To understand how we categorise the factors affecting learning, let us begin by considering the following examples:

- Ravi is sixteen year old and wants to please his mother by getting good results in his board examinations. He is so eager to please her, that he spends long hours of concentrated time and energy on his studies. He consciously tries to control other sources of distraction in his life and reduces the time spent on watching television, playing games and chatting with his friends.
- Rita Williams wants to be a famous tennis player. To achieve her goal, she practices tennis whenever she can, even though she gets no encouragement from her family. She makes it a point to watch tennis matches and maintain a good rapport with her sports teacher.
- Yuvraj is a good student, but lately he has been scoring very low marks at school. He is not able to concentrate or pay attention and his class work and home assignments reflect a very poor quality. Sources revealed that his parents fight a lot with each other and are about to get divorced.
- Arti and Kavita are two sisters. Arti is very good at art and craft and can sketch just about anything she sees. Kavita has a ear for music. She knows most songs and can sing them even if she has heard them only once. Both of them spend hours together pursuing their respective interest areas.

- Sayeeda is tall, attractive and has a very good figure. She wants to be a model or an air-hostess and nurtures this secretly as her dream. She is too scared to share her wishes with her family, since she belongs to an orthodox family, where girls at best can pursue teaching as a career. When she tries telling her mother what she wants, she is firmly told that she can only do her B.Ed and can go to the coaching classes for these.

The above cited examples illustrate that learning is a universal phenomenon mediated by a number of factors, both personal and environmental in nature. The dictum "everybody learns" is as true as its corollary, *i.e.*, everybody learns in accordance with his/her unique, individualized blend of personal and environmental factors. For example, in case of Ravi, the desire to please his mother, striving to do well in his board exams and managing his life situations appropriately constitute the key factors which influence him. For Rita Williams, it is her intrinsic desire to be a good tennis player which is paramount. She is not deterred by the lack of family support and continues to make efforts to promote her love for tennis on her own and fulfil her desire to be successful.

In case of Yuvraj, in spite of his innate capacity to study and perform well, his lack of achievement can be attributed to the emotional insecurity stemming from his parents' divorce. As far as Arti and Kavita are concerned, their special interests and talent in art and music respectively, seem to guide their activities.

For Sayeeda, the home environment and family culture and values determine her professional choice. Her own inner interests, desires and wishes are not to be taken into cognizance.

In all the examples cited, we can find evidence of both personal and environmental factors influencing the process of learning. Learning can thus be defined as a function of the interaction of personal and environmental factors.

$$L = f\,(EF \times PF)$$

L = learning; f = function; EF = environmental factors; PF = personal factors.

Personal factors are the intra individual factors like motivation, interests, abilities etc which predispose an individual towards learning as in the case of Rita Williams, Arti and Kavita. Environmental factors on the other hand, are those contextual factors which highlight the role of the environment in learning, such as the socio-emotional, societal and cultural factors as seen in the case of Yuvraj and Sayeeda. Although the two factors represent different categories, they operate in a common system. The environmental factors provide the context within which the personal factors, operate. The learner and the learning process can only be completely understood with reference to the interaction of both environmental and personal factors. This may be diagrammatically represented as follows:

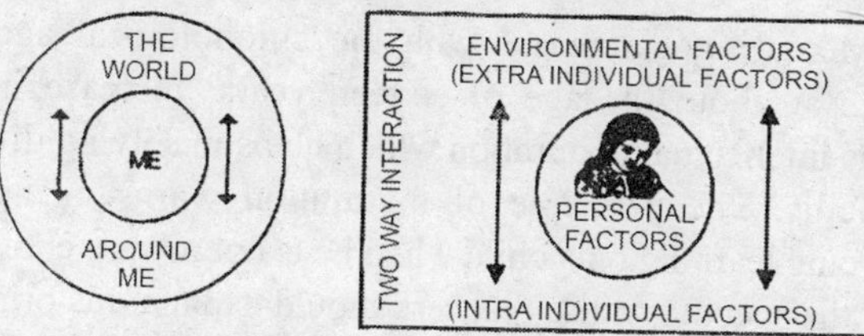

Fig: *Factors affecting learning*

Personal Factors Influencing Learning

The process of learning is influenced by a variety of personal factors. A thorough knowledge of these factors will prove very helpful for teachers and parents in understanding and guiding their children's learning. Some of the personal factors that influence the learning process may be classified as under : sensation and perception, fatigue and boredom, maturation, emotional condition, needs, interests, motivation, attention, intelligence, aptitude, attitude, etc. Let us discuss the important personal factors in the following sub-sections.

Sensation and Perception

Apart from the general health of the students, sensation and perception are the psychological factors which help in learning. Sensation is at the core of perception. There are five sense organs *i.e.*, skin, ears, tongue, eyes and nose. These sense organs are the gateways of knowledge and help in perception of various stimuli in the environment. Any defect in any of the sense organs will affect learning and hence acquisition of knowledge. For example, defects of vision such as myopia, hypermetropia, astigmatism, etc., cause headaches, nausia and general disinclination to study. A blind person depends upon the sense of touch or skin for learning and thus acquires knowledge and skills, as he can not visualise the objects. The stimuli are preceived and assimilated, and hence learnt through various sense organs. In this way we can say that sensation and perception is the bases of knowledge and learning.

Fatigue and Boredom

It is virtually boredom or lassitude rather than fatigue which bothers the students. The difference between the two is that fatigue is mental or physical tiredness which decreases in efficiency and competency to work. Boredom, on the other hand, is a lack of desire on an aversion to work. Such an aversion makes one feel fatigued without being actually fatigued. Studying seldom causes fatigue. It is mainly boredom which, besides causing the impression of fatigue, decreases student efficiency in learning.

Age and Maturation

Learning is directly dependent upon age and maturation. No learning can take place unless individual is matured enough to learn. Some children can learn better at earlier age while others take more time to learn the same content.

Mental age increases with the chronological age and ceases at about the age of sixteen years. Increase in age means intellectual maturation which helps in solving difficult problems. The principle of maturation warns us against enforcing learning on a child when he is not mature enough to learn the specific skills. Teachers should explain this principle to parents who are over ambitious or over enthusiastic in sending their children to school at the very early age.

Emotional Conditions

Desirable emotional conditions enhance the quality and speed of learning. Happiness, joy and satisfaction are always favourable for any type of learning. Adverse emotional conditions, on the other hand, hinder learning. Many studies have established the fact that emotional strain, stress, tensions, disturbances, etc., are extremely inimical to scholastic pursuits.

Needs

A need is the lack of something which, if provided, would facilitate child's usual behaviour. The lack of something is experienced by the child. The child then tries to perform that activity which culminates in the satisfaction of the need. Thus, the needs are associated with goals. Among human beings, the needs are relatively permanent tendencies which seek satisfaction in achieving certain specific goals. When these goals are achieved, the particular need is satisfied or met for the time being, but it recurs sooner or later and energises further activity. The needs in human beings can be physiological such as need for oxygen, food, water, etc. They may be social such as the need for affection, recognition, self-regard, etc. Social needs are however, quite different from physiological needs. Social needs might originate after physiological needs are satisfied. These needs have a complex structure and dominate the individual's behaviour.

There is not equal urgency in the satisfaction of all needs. Some have to be satisfied before others can manifest themselves.

In schools, children are not expected to do any intellectual thinking unless their physiological needs are satisfied. Poor, starved children may concentrate less on attainment of knowledge than on food. Similarly, very cold or hot classrooms or over-crowded seats will not be conducive to good learning. Likewise the need for safety, love and esteem, all act as powerful motives in the learning situations. If the child is afraid of the teacher or feels unsafe while in the school on account of too much beating or some other form of punishment, no learning can take place. Similarly, his needs for warmth and affection are very stimulating and hence results in effective learning.

Interests

Various types of interests of the students can be exploited to facilitate their learning. The interests during early infancy are mostly limited and short lived. As the child grows older his interests diversify and stabilize. You, a school teacher, should have thorough knowledge of children's interests. You can eliminate much drudgery, monotony and boredom from the school work if you make your instruction lively and stimulating and arouse student interest in it.

Once the students' interest is aroused in an activity you should expend more effort on it. No learning can be achieved without proper expenditure of effort on it. Students can even overcome distraction, fatigue and boredom if they feel interested in your instruction and class activities. It has often been found that, in most cases, fatigue in reality is loss of interest in the learning activity. Interest, should be exploited to yield results of greater quantity and quality learning in school.

Life is so exciting that many interesting things and activities often clamor to attract our attention. Children frequently face the dilemma of mutually conflicting interests. Immediate interests often seem to be clashing with the remoter ones. A student might be in a quandary at least for the time being when his interest in sports impels him towards the play-field and his interest in studies force him to concentrate on books.

In such cases of conflicting interests a lot of hesitancy, wastage, frustration and unhappiness is bound to follow. What is needed is education at home and school which helps/trains children to achieve a healthy balance in their interests. They should be trained to budget their time in such a manner as to pay a reasonable attention to various interests, scholastic, athletic, social etc., within the time at their disposal.

Motivation

Motivation is the heart of the learning process. It generates the will in an individual to do something. Adequate motivation not only engages the student in an activity which results in learning, but also sustains and directs learning. Two types of motivation are commonly recognised. These are: intrinsic and extrinsic motivation.

Intelligence

Intelligence as expressed by an I.Q. score on an intelligence test is positively related to learning. Generally, students with higher I.Q. learn rapidly. However, higher I.Q. in itself is no guarantee for rapid learning, since other factors such as needs, interest, motivation, etc., of the students and the methods used for learning are also important.

Aptitude

A student who possesses appropriate aptitude for a particular subject of study or skill, will learn better and retain it for a longer time. On the other hand, he will require relatively longer time to study a subject for which he lacks natural aptitude. He is liable to forget it soon besides feeling bored and unhappy all the time while learning it. Hence, it is extremely desirable to analyse the aptitude of students before prescribing courses of study for them.

Attitude

The learning process is also influenced considerably by the attitude of the student. If he is alert, attentive and interested in the material to be learnt, he is bound to have a favourable attitude towards it. Such an attitude will enable him to tackle the learning situation economically, pleasantly and effectively. Conversely, if he is inattentive and is uninterested in the material his attitude is bound to be unfavourable. This will hinder the smooth learning of the material in hand besides involving undue strain and tension in the learner.

Environmental Factors

Environmental influences begin since the time of the conception of the child in the womb of the mother. Mother's mental, physical and emotional conditions influence the development of foetus in the womb. The external environment starts from the time of birth of the child. It (external environment) refers to the surroundings which prevail in home, school and locality. At these places, the child interacts with members of the family, teachers, classmates or peers and neighbours and establishes relationship with them. The relationship with the members of the society, and the surroundings may affect the development of the child and also the way he learns. Some of the environmental factors are discussed as follows:

Surrounding : Natural, Social and Cultural

As the title of the sub-section indicates, we shall discuss here natural, social and cultural environment the child interacts with and get influenced.

Natural surrounding covers the climatic and atmospheric condition. These conditions affect learning directly. It has been found that high temperature and humidity reduces mental efficiency. For a limited time, humidity and high temperature can be tolerated but prolonged humidity and high temperature become unbearable and decrease mental efficiency. The intellectual productivity and creativeness of people living in hot regions are much low. Likewise, the morning time is always better for mastering difficult tasks. Mental efficiency decreases due to increased humidity and temperature. Studies on the academic progress of evening school students shows losses of efficiency varying from one to six per cent.

Social surrounding includes especially the environment of home, school and locality. Physical conditions at home such as large family, small family, (specific place of the study), insufficient ventilation, improper lighting, uncomfortable temperature, noisy home environment due to use of radio, TV, etc., noisy neighbourhood, constant visits by friends or relatives, etc., influence the intellectual learning of the student. The socio-emotional factors such as child rearing practices, reward and punishment, scope for freedom and independence in activities and decision making, play and study facilities, ambitions and aspirations of the parents, disorganisation and discord among birth positions such as eldest, youngest or single child have their definite influence on learning. For example, a student who comes from a very poor family and never had any intellectual stimulation at home remains dull and unresponsive in the class. In some societies there is a strong sex bias. Girls are directly or indirectly told that education is not meant for them. In the middle class families, on the other hand, parents are rather over-ambitious. They wish their children to make quick academic progress, grow-up and find a respectable vocation preferably a white collar job. Such children, therefore get sufficient incentive from their families. This, of course, is most favourable to scholastic learning, although an overdose of family emphasis on acquiring academic excellence might affect the child's mental and physical health adversely. Similarly, school activities, study facilities and teaching methods and behaviour of teachers, principals and non-teaching staff have an impact upon learning. If the school atmosphere is unconducive, it adversely affects the learning process. Locality also has an influence on a child. If the locality is bad, the learning will be ineffective to some extent.

Cultural demands and social expectations also influence learning. The spirit of culture is reflected in its social and educational institutions. Children's learning, therefore, is greatly determined by the demands and expectations of their culture. Thus, for instance, in an industrialized culture the emphasis mostly centres mechanical sciences and preparing children for highly mechanised vocations. In an agriculture based community, on the other hand, the educational process focusses on preparing its members for those skills which are suited to the needs of an agrarian community.

The philosophical elements of culture also influence the spirit of children's learning. Children in a democratic culture tend to acquire democrative and values and attitudes. A feudal, aristocratic or dictatorial culture, on the other hand, promotes autocratic modes of thought and behaviour.

Relationship with Teacher, Parents and Peers

The teacher is an important constituent in the instructional process. She/he plays an important role in shaping the behaviour of students. The way he teaches and manages the students has an affect on their learning. An authoritarian teacher will create an aggression and hostility among students while a democratic teacher will create a participatory climate for learning. The democratic environment leads students to constructive, thoughtful and cooperative behaviour. Generally, students learn better in a democratic set up because they like democratic procedures. The teacher is no more an instructor or the director of learning in a democratic set up. She/he helps his/her students in their learning. The teachers no more dominate the scene, they can get better results by decentralizing authority, increasing independence of students. They can attend to the comments and questions of the students. They can encourage students to participate in learning activities in and outside the class. There should be more emphasis on activity-centred classroom where student's active participation in the teaching-learning process is encouraged and the teacher acts as a guide to promote learning.

Relationship with parents plays a vital role in the learning process of the student. If the child-parents relationship is based on mutual respect and faith, it can provide the child a congenial atmosphere which in turn can facilitate his/her learning. A distorted and unhealthy environment, on the other hand, adversely affects the learning of the student. The upward mobility brings resistance on the part of the student to learn. Students in such families find themselves unable to cope up. A subtle but powerful influence on the growing child arises from his/her position among the children in the family. The parents of the first born expect the child to act like miniature adults and hence the first-born are found to encounter a variety of expectations and stresses. Whereas parents tend to be more relaxed in their do's and dont's with the last-born. Factors like traumatic events at home, separation or death can also precipitate learning problems in the normal child.

A healthy peer group relationship also plays an important role in learning. Student-student relationship in the classroom, school, society, etc., create a particular type of emotional climate. The climate solely depends upon their relationships. A sound relationships provides a tension free environment to the student to learn more and to compete in the class. If the relationship among peers is not good, it adversely affects their learning. Therefore, to improve the classroom learning climate, free discussion should be there. You should help your students understand each other in formal or informal meetings. They should be encouraged to meet each other and their teachers freely. If any mis-understanding is created or developed, it should be immediately clarified so as to maintain the healthy climate and cordial relationship among peers.

Media Influence on Learning

Media has been considered an important component of transmitting information. Media can be divided into two broad categories—print and non-print media. Print media refers to texts or printed materials. It is economical and has traditionally been used for pedagogical purposes.

But, it may not be the only or the perfect medium to impart education. Non-print media, also known as modern electronic media, have certain unique qualities which, in certain cases, facilitate learning much more faster than the print medium. These helps meet diverse learning objectives more efficiently than the printed matter.

Certain non-print media formats and delivery systems contribute well to student's learning actitivies, For example, audio tapes or computers can be used effectively to drill and practice in language and learning arithmatic. Electronic media can help promote the discovery approach to learning. For example, a film can be exploited for discovery teaching in the physical sciences. Students keep watching the various sections of the film until they perceive the relationships between the visuals. Then they are curious to find out the principles that explain those relationships. Likewise, in the social sciences various media can be used to present students with visual and auditory experiences that provide related inquiry. Films and stimulation are often used to present real-life or laboratory learning situations to students.

The role of the electronic media has proved effective for teaching students. These excite the student psychologically and prepare/motivate them to participate in teaching-learning activites. Non-print media perform following fuctions:

- direct attention,
- arouse motivation,
- increase student's concentration, and
- help them actively involve in the learning process.

PRACTICE PAPER

1. Mastery Oriented learners typically attribute success to _______ and failure to _______ .
   A. ability and good luck; task difficulty
   B. ability and effort; bad luck
   C. ability and good luck; low ability
   D. ability and effort; insufficient effort

2. Which of the following statement represents 'Proximodistal' principle of development?
   A. Development is multidirectional and multidimensional.
   B. Identical twins living in different cultures can develop at different rates.
   C. Children develop ability to grasp the ball before putting beads in thread.
   D. Children develop ability to sit up before standing.

3. According to Vygotsky children speak to themselves:
   A. To aid thought and for self-regulation.
   B. To provide self-reinforcement when adults are ignoring them.
   C. Because they are egocentrc.
   D. Because their thought is illogical.

4. Challenges in social communication are evident in:
   A. Attention deficit hyperactivity disorder
   B. Cerebral palsy
   C. Austism Spectrum Disorder
   D. Learning Disabilities

5. According to Vyogotsky's theory of learning and development, which of the following is an example of scaffolding?
   A. Breaking a task down into smaller steps and providing support as needed.
   B. Providing a student with a grade for their work as motivation.
   C. Providing a student with a reading assignment and asking them to answer questions independently.
   D. Demonstrating a skill to a student and then having them master it on their own.

6. Dysgraphia is characterised by:
   A. Delayed motor skills
   B. Difficulties in writing
   C. Lack of reading fluency
   D. Repetitive behavioural patterns

7. In order to help students to become good problem solvers, a teacher should emphasize on the practice of:
   A. focusing on information that confirms existing beliefs and preconceptions.
   B. approaching problems in a particular fixed fashion.
   C. breaking large complex problems into smaller manageable problems.
   D. centering only on one particular piece of information related to problem.

8. **Assertion (A):** Teachers should use multisensory materials to cater to needs of students in an inclusive classroom.

   Reason (R): Inclusive classrooms should adopt standardization of curricular materials as well as assessment strategies.

   Choose the **correct** option:
   A. (A) is true, but (R) is false.
   B. Both (A) and (R) are false.
   C. Both (A) and (R) are true and (R) is the correct explanation of (A).
   D. Both (A) and (R) are true, but (R) is not the correct explanation of (A).

9. In the constructivist view:
   A. Individuals are passively influenced by enviornmental events.
   B. Individuals are conditioned to learn new behaviours.
   C. Learning is extending and transforming the current understanding.
   D. Learning is simply writing associations on the blank slates of our brains.

10. **Assertion (A):** Effective teachers familiarize themselves with daily lives and socio-cultural backgrounds of learners.

    Reason (R): Learning takes place in a social context.

Choose the **correct** option:

A. (A) is true, but (R) is false.
B. Both (A) and (R) are false.
C. Both (A) and (R) are true and (R) is the correct explanation of (A).
D. Both (A) and (R) are true, but (R) is not the correct explanation of (A).

11. Meaningful learning is primarily NOT about:

A. memorizing information
B. understanding the concept
C. constructing knowledge
D. developing skills

12. **Assertion (A):** Teacher should encourage boys of her class to participate in sports while assigning art decoration to girls.

Reason (R): Children acquire gender roles primarily because of the underlying biological differences.

Choose the **correct** option:

A. (A) is true, but (R) is false.
B. Both (A) and (R) are false.
C. Both (A) and (R) are true and (R) is the correct explanation of (A).
D. Both (A) and (R) are true, but (R) is not the correct explanation of (A).

13. Kinesthetic learners prefer to learn through ....

A. seeing
B. touching
C. doing and moving
D. listening

14. According to Howard Gardner while a scientist would exhibit high .... Intelligence, a sculptor would have high .... Intelligence.

A. Naturalistic; Spatial
B. Transductive; Spatial
C. Logical-mathematical; Bodily Kinesthetic
D. Spatial; Bodily Kinesthetic

15. Inclusion needs to be promoted through:

(*i*) Flexible curriculum
(*ii*) Cooperative learning
(*iii*) Segregation and labelling
(*iv*) Accessibility of building

A. (*ii*), (*iii*), (*iv*)
B. (*i*), (*ii*), (*iii*), (*iv*)
C. (*i*), (*ii*), (*iii*)
D. (*i*), (*ii*), (*iv*)

16. Children learn better if they experience:

A. Low level of alertness during activity
B. Moderate level of excitement to learn
C. High degree of anxiety to perform
D. Learned helplessness

17. **Assertion (A):** Children below the ages of 5-6 years should not be pressurized to write 'properly' and 'within the lines'.

Reason (R): Children gain a control of finer motor skills from 5-6 years onwards.

Choose the **correct** option:

A. (A) is true, but (R) is false.
B. Both (A) and (R) are false.
C. Both (A) and (R) are true and (R) is the correct explanation of (A).
D. Both (A) and (R) are true, but (R) is not the correct explanation of (A).

18. Children often come up with their own explanations of events around them. On being probed as to why does it rain Sia says, "God was tired of carrying the buckets of water on his shoulders". Such explanations:

A. Depict that children have an egocentric view and cannot consider other's viewpoint.
B. Illustrate that children are not capable of any reasoning.
C. Prove that children's thinking is much lesser than adults quantitively.
D. Indicate that children have naive understanding rooted in their cultural context with which they try to understand events.

19. Piaget described cognitive development as occuring in:

A. A continuous continuum
B. Four overlapping culture specific stages
C. Four qualitatively different stages
D. Three progressive levels

20. During play time at school, Rishab, a 7-year—old boy picked a doll to play with. Some of his peers made fun of him for his choice of toy. As a teacher who wants his students to grow up with gender role flexibility, which of the following would be the best response to the situation by the teacher?

A. Talk to Rishabh that dolls are suitable for girls and boys should not play with dolls.
B. Tell Rishabh that he should play with something else because his friends won't approve of him playing with doll.
C. Let Rishabh play with doll and tell other children that they can also choose any toy of their choice.
D. Quitely take away the doll and give a car toy to Rishabh without saying anything.

21. In developmental terms, a time frame where an individual upholds an amplified sensitivity to particular incentives for developing particular skills to function in an efficient manner is referred to as .... of development.

A. Incentive period
B. Stimulus period
C. Critical period
D. Encoding period

22. In order to cater to needs of students struggling with Attention Deficit Hyperactivity Disorder teachers should avoid:

A. Creating distractions and making noises
B. Flexibility in curricular materials and instructions
C. Breaking the task into small easily manageable parts
D. Using multi-sensory materials

23. Lawrence Kohlberg argued that:

A. moral development in children occurs in a continuous manner.
B. there are cultural differences in moral reasoning of children.
C. moral development occurs progressively in stages.
D. there are gender differences in moral reasoning of children.

24. At which level of Kohlberg's moral development does individual's ethical behaviour mainly depends on the mindset that "What do people think of me"?

A. Post-conventional B. Non-conventional
C. Pre-conventional D. Conventional

25. According to Jean Piaget a child who is unable to understand the logic behind simple mathematical reversals such as 4 + 5 = 9 so 9 – 5 = 4, it is because of:

A. animistic thinking B. irreversibility
C. egocentrism D. perceptual centration

26. Assertion (A): Teachers should distance themselves from students and place primary responsibility for learning on them only.

Reason (R): Learning takes place affectively in an authoritative rather than a democratic environment.

Choose the **correct** option:

A. (A) is true, but (R) is false.
B. Both (A) and (R) are false.
C. Both (A) and (R) are true and (R) is the correct explanation of (A).
D. Both (A) and (R) are true, but (R) is not the correct explanation of (A).

27. Assertion (A): Scaffolding provided by the teachers hinders the learning process of children.

Reason (R): Lev Vygotsky proposed that children learn independently by acting upon and manipulating the environment.

Choose the **correct** option:

A. (A) is true, but (R) is false.
B. Both (A) and (R) are false.
C. Both (A) and (R) are true and (R) is the correct explanation of (A).
D. Both (A) and (R) are true, but (R) is not the correct explanation of (A).

28. Which of the following correctly describes extrinsic motivation?

A. Motivation that comes from environmental consequences.
B. Motivation that comes from a sense of personal satisfaction.
C. Motivation that comes from personal enjoyment of the task.
D. Motivation that comes from internal factors.

29. Two important cognitive development milestones of sensorimotor stage of Piaget's theory of cognitive development are:

A. Animism and Transformation
B. Classification and seriation
C. Object permanence and deferred limitation
D. Reversibility of thought and hypothetic-deductive reasoning

30. Children:

A. Are born unruly and need to be socialized.
B. Come into this world with genetic codes that determine their destiny.
C. Are greatly influenced by the social cultural context they grow up in.
D. Come into this world as *tabula rasa* or blank slate.

31. Dysgraphia is a:

A. Speech disorder characterized by stuttering and errors in articulation.
B. Locomotor disorder characterized by gross motor impairment.
C. Neurological disorder characterized by trouble in forming letters and shapes.
D. Psychological disorder characterized by lack of attention and impulsive behaviour.

32. The approach to educating gifted children which moves them through curriculum at an unusually rapid pace is known as:

A. Differentiated instruction
B. Enrichment
C. Acceleration
D. Immersion

33. Teachers who are working towards inclusive classrooms:

(*i*) Create curriculum adaptations
(*ii*) Incorporate diverse perspectives
(*iii*) Examine their own implicit bias
(*iv*) See diversity as an obstacle

Which of the above are correct?

A. (*i*), (*ii*), (*iii*), (*iv*) B. (*i*), (*ii*), (*iii*)
C. (*i*), (*iii*), (*iv*) D. (*ii*), (*iii*), (*iv*)

34. While __________ agencies of socialisation are predominantly important in infancy, __________ agencies of socialization also become important in early childhood.

A. tertiary; secondary B. primary; secondary
C. secondary; primary D. secondary; tertiary

35. According to Lev Vygotsky:

A. Social factors influence language development, but not cognitive development.
B. Cognitive development facilitates language development.
C. Language development and cognitive development advance independent from each other.
D. Language development facilitates cognitive development.

36. At which level of Lawrence Kohlberg's moral reasoning, do children typically believe that people should live up to the expectations of the society and behave in "good" ways?

A. Post-operational level
B. Pre-conventional level
C. Conventional level
D. Pre-operational level

37. Read the following statements and choose the correct option:

Assertion (A): Interaction with more knowledgeable others, such as teachers and peers, can provide the necessary support and guidance to help learners develop their understanding and skills.

Reason (R): Social interaction is a key component of learning and development.

A. Both (A) and (R) are false.
B. Both (A) and (R) are true and (R) is the correct explanation of (A).
C. Both (A) and (R) are true, but (R) is not the correct explanation of (A).
D. (A) is true, but (R) is false.

38. What is the main goal of 'assessment for learning'?

A. To identify students who can be categorised as 'slow learners'
B. To evaluate student performance and assign grades
C. To provide feedback to students that can be used to improve their learning
D. To compare student performance to a standard or benchmark

39. At which age can children engage in word play and like jokes and riddles that involve a play on words?

A. Twelve years B. One year
C. Three years D. Seven years

40. Carol Gilligan has critiqued Kohlberg's theory of moral development:

A. From a social cognitive perspective.
B. From a feminist perspective.
C. For not giving adequate importance to genetic factors.
D. For using case study as the research method.

41. One of the main characteristics of pre-operational thought according to Jean Piaget is __________ which refers to the tendency to focus on one aspect of a situation and neglect others.

A. Causation B. Centration
C. Decentration D. Transduction

42. In early childhood, growth _____ and thinking is _______, while in middle childhood, growth _______ and thinking is _______.

A. slows, somewhat egocentric; is steady, logical
B. is steady, somewhat egocentric; slows, logical
C. is steady, logical; slows, egocentric
D. slows, logical; is steady, egocentric

43. Which of the following is a gross motor skill?

A. Knitting
B. Swimming
C. Cutting along the outline of a circle on a paper
D. Cutting along the outline of a big rectangle on a paper

44. Physical growth and development follow the _______ and _______ principles of development.

A. integration (simple to complex); differentiation (complex to simple)
B. cephalocaudal (top-down); proximodistal (inner to outer)
C. proximodistal (top-down); cephalocaudal (inner to outer)
D. differentiation (simple to complex); integration (complex to simple)

45. According to Howard Gardner, a philosopher has __________ type of intelligence and a sculptor has more __________ type of intelligence.

A. linguistic; interpersonal
B. spatial; intrapersonal
C. intrapersonal; spatial
D. interpersonal; linguistic

46. Experiential learning stresses on:

A. Control of teacher on the learning of children.
B. The role of reinforcement in learning.
C. Importance of critical reflection.
D. Learning as a product rather than a process.

47. Which of the following is an effective method to enhance problem-solving skills in children?
   A. Discouraging independent thinking and focusing on declarative knowledge
   B. Encouraging them to avoid difficult problems
   C. Providing them with readymade solutions to problems
   D. Giving them opportunities to brainstorm and make intuitive guesses

48. Read the following statements and choose the correct option:

   Assertion (A): Teachers should create a meaningful environment which seeks active participation and engagement of all children.

   Reason (R): All children are intrinsically motivated to learn and are capable of learning.

   A. Both (A) and (R) are false.
   B. Both (A) and (R) are true and (R) is the correct explanation of (A).
   C. Both (A) and (R) are true, but (R) is not the correct explanation of (A).
   D. (A) is true, but (R) is false.

49. Which of the following process does ***not*** contribute to the course of learning?
   A. Organization B. Categorization
   C. Conceptualization D. Decontextualization

50. Which of the following is an example of a question that requires students to reflect on their own thinking?
   A. What is the relationship between nouns and verbs in a sentence?
   B. What is the definition of a verb?
   C. How do you change a verb to the present tense?
   D. How has your thinking about the use of verbs changed since the beginning of the class?

51. Which of the following is an example of an internal attribution for failure?
   A. I received a low grade because the teacher is a tough grader.
   B. I failed the test because I didn't study enough.
   C. I didn't get good marks because the teacher was biased.
   D. I failed the test because my friends were distracting me.

52. Read the following statements and choose the correct option:

   Assertion (A): At a very early age, girls in most cultures across the world choose dolls as toys while boys prefer to play with cars.

   Reason (R): Children organize information about what is considered appropriate for a boy or a girl on the basis of what a particular culture expects and behave accordingly.

   A. Both (A) and (R) are false.
   B. Both (A) and (R) are true and (R) is the correct explanation of (A).
   C. Both (A) and (R) are true, but (R) is not the correct explanation of (A).
   D. (A) is true, but (R) is false.

53. As per Lev Vygotsky, ____________ plays a significant role in the development of conceptual abilities among children.
   A. Tangible rewards
   B. Peer collaboration
   C. Social isolation
   D. Standardized curriculum

54. According to Lev Vygotsky's theory, inner speech:
   A. is a way for children to communicate with an imaginary friend.
   B. is a sign of cognitive immaturity.
   C. is a sign of developmental delay.
   D. is a way for children to regulate their own thinking.

55. Four-year-old Aparna says that a button is alive because it helps tie her shirt together. According to Jean Piaget, her thinking is characterized by:
   A. Transductive reasoning
   B. Animistic thinking
   C. Centration
   D. Hypothetical-deductive thinking

56. Which of the following is a typical characterstic of students having autism?
   A. Superior ability of differentiating fiction from fact
   B. Advanced socio-emotional reciprocity
   C. Frequent repetitive and recurring behaviour
   D. Higher level of communication skills

57. Read the following statements and choose the correct option:

   Assertion (A): To facilitate critical thinking among learners, teachers should expose them to diverse situations and differing perspectives.

   Reason (R): Students learn and enrich their abilities to think critically and creatively as they engage in conversations across differences.

   A. Both (A) and (R) are false.
   B. Both (A) and (R) are true and (R) is the correct explanation of (A).
   C. Both (A) and (R) are true, but (R) is not the correct explanation of (A).
   D. (A) is true, but (R) is false.

58. The primary goal of learning should be:

A. Memorization of facts.
B. Becoming excellent at rote rehearsal.
C. Competing with peers.
D. Development of critical thinking.

59. Children learn more effectively if a concept proceeds from:

A. Generic to Specific. B. Abstract to Concrete.
C. Complex to Simple. D. Rational to Empirical.

60. Variability in learning styles of students:

A. Should be valued and seen as a reflection of human diversity.
B. Should be ignored and attempts should be made to bring uniformity in learning styles.
C. Should not be taken into consideration during teaching-learning process.
D. Should be seen as a barrier and hindrance to teaching-learning process.

61. Which of the following is an example of use of gross motor skills?

A. Balancing on one foot
B. Squeezing a pea
C. Turning pages of a book
D. Holding a pencil

62. Development changes are a result of:

A. Unique combination of genetic and environmental circumstances.
B. Only genetic makeup of an individual.
C. Only socio-cultural factors.
D. Neither hereditary nor environmental factors.

63. The period from 2 years to 6 years is referred to as:

A. Infancy B. Early childhood
C. Middle childhood D. Adolescence

64. **Assertion (A):** A lot of children's play in the cities is based on reality T.V. shows that they see.

Reason (R): Apart from family and peers these days media is becoming an important agency of socialization of children.

Choose the correct options.

A. Both (A) and (R) are true and (R) is the correct explanation of (A)
B. Both (A) and (R) are true, but (R) is not the correct explanation of (A)
C. (A) is true, but (R) is false
D. Both (A) and (R) are false

65. Which of the following factors are considered important by Piaget to facilitate learning?

(*i*) Mobility of the teacher
(*ii*) Provisioning of diverse materials
(*iii*) Providing moderately novel experiences
(*iv*) Ensuring positive and negative reinforcement

A. (*ii*), (*iv*) B. (*i*), (*ii*), (*iii*)
C. (*ii*), (*iii*), (*iv*) D. (*i*), (*ii*), (*iii*), (*iv*)

66. At which stage do children have an animistic view of the larger world and believe that the trees and plants as well as moving clouds and rolling stones can have motives and intentions?

A. Sensori-motor stage
B. Pre-operational stage
C. Concrete operational stage
D. Formal operational stage

67. Language plays an important role in the cognitive development of children in the theory of:

A. Lev Vygotsky B. Jean Piaget
C. Howard Gardner D. Lawrence Kohlberg

68. According to Vygotsky, children learn by:

A. having competitions
B. interaction with peers
C. striving for rewards and avoiding punishments
D. making stimulus-response connections

69. In a child-centered classroom children:

A. are looked at as passive imitators.
B. are actively engaged in construction of knowledge.
C. are eager to copy answer from blackboard as it is.
D. have to be passive listeners only.

70. Which of the following is a correctly matched pair?

A. Punishment and Obedience orientation – Laws are not fixed but can be changed for the good of the society.
B. Good-Boy – Good-girl orientation – One earns approval by being nice.
C. Law and Order orientation – Ethical principles are self-chosen than on the basis of the value of human rights.
D. Social Contract orientation – Physical consequences of an action determine whether it is good/bad.

71. In Howard Gardner's theory person high on .... intelligence can recognize and are aware of the beauty of different species of flora and fauna.

A. spatial B. naturalistic
C. musical D. inter-personal

72. National Education Policy 2020 recommends:

A. Multilingualism
B. Monolingualism
C. Standardization of curriculum
D. Standardization of assessment

73. A teacher holds the perception that boys are more intelligent and risk taking and girls are obedient and sincere and treats them accordingly. This is an example of:

A. gender bias B. gender constancy
C. gender equity D. gender equality

74. Assertion (A): Teachers should use a wide variety of assessment tools and technique to assess children.

Reason (R): No single assessment tool is capable of providing information about a child's progress and learning in different areas of development.

Choose the correct option.

A. Both (A) and (R) are true and (R) is the correct explanation of (A)
B. Both (A) and (R) are true, but (R) is not the correct explanation of (A)
C. (A) is true, but (R) is false
D. Both (A) and (R) are false

75. Which of the following situation does NOT illustrate assessment for learning?

A. Students actively think about where they are, where they are going and how to get there.
B. Teachers give constructive qualitative feedback to facilitate learning.
C. Constant comparisons are made between the students to enhance performance.
D. Several methods of formative assessment such as peer and self-assessment are used.

76. Inclusive Education requires:

A. Flexible pedagogies
B. Inaccessible building
C. Rigid mindsets
D. Standardized curriculum

77. Which of the following disability causes challenges in 'social communication'?

A. Autism B. Dyscalculia
C. Dysgraphia D. Locomotor disability

78. Which of the following helps in inclusion of learners from disadvantaged and deprived groups?

A. Consideration of diversity
B. Decontextualized curriculum
C. Pedagogy centered towards dominant group
D. Standardized testing

79. Provision of multiple modes of representation of content will help in inclusion of:

(*i*) students with hearing impairment
(*ii*) students with visual impairment
(*iii*) students facing learning difficulties
(*iv*) students facing locomotor difficulties

A. (*i*) B. (*ii*), (*iii*)
C. (*i*), (*ii*), (*iv*) D. (*i*), (*ii*), (*iii*), (*iv*)

80. Which of the following is a correctly matched pair of appropriate accommodation strategy for inclusion of students which specified disability?

A. Dyscalculia : Provision of calculator
B. Dyslexia : Assigning lengthy written assignments
C. Hearing Impairment : Giving audio tapes
D. Visual Impairment : Providing picture books

81. In early grades, which of the following approaches is preferable for teaching-learning process?

A. Imitation without understanding
B. Learning by doing
C. Passive listening
D. Rote-memorisation

82. Assertion (A): Participation in the social life of the school is significant for learning to occur.

Reason (R): Learning is primarily a social activity.

Choose the correct option.

A. Both (A) and (R) are true and (R) is the correct explanation of (A)
B. Both (A) and (R) are true, but (R) is not the correct explanation of (A)
C. (A) is true, but (R) is false
D. Both (A) and (R) are false

83. Teachers can make classroom activities meaningful by:

A. dividing them in disconnected chunks
B. giving ambiguous instructions about them
C. presenting them in decontextualized manner
D. situating them in the authentic context

84. Which of the following pedagogical practices does NOT contribute positively in teaching-learning process?

A. Curriculum adaptation as per needs
B. Experiential learning for students
C. Innovation in curricular planning
D. Rigid exam-centered teaching strategies

85. Assertion (A): A teacher should connect content to be taught with students' daily life experiences.

Reason (R): Children come to school with valuable life experiences that teachers need to pay attention to.

Choose the correct option.

A. Both (A) and (R) are true and (R) is the correct explanation of (A)
B. Both (A) and (R) are true, but (R) is not the correct explanation of (A)
C. (A) is true, but (R) is false
D. Both (A) and (R) are false

86. Which of the following helps learners evaluate their own learning and check their understanding?

A. Forgetting B. Imitation
C. Metacognition D. Rote-memorization

87. Misconception among children are:

A. Abnormal B. Atypical
C. Natural D. Rare

88. A student experiencing 'learned helplessness' is likely to:

A. show enthusiasm in learning
B. focus on mastery-oriented goals
C. focus on performance-oriented approach goals
D. withdraw from learning activities

89. Which of the following is an example of intrinsic motivation?

A. learning a new language out of interest
B. drawing a picture to win a cash prize
C. participating in a sport to win an award
D. studying to get praise of parents

90. Which of the following is an environmental factor which impact learning?

A. Attitude B. Motivation
C. Personality traits D. School

91. In order to address learners from diverse backgrounds, a teacher should:

A. use standardized assessment for all.
B. use statements that strengthen negative stereotypes.
C. avoid talking about aspects related to diversity.
D. draw examples from diverse settings.

92. Problem-solving abilities can be facilitated by:

A. encouraging use of analogies.
B. generating fear among students.
C. focusing on drill and practice.
D. encouraging fixed process of solving the problems.

93. In order to address the needs of students who are facing learning difficulties, a teacher should NOT:

A. do individualized educational planning.
B. practice rigid structures for pedagogy and assessment.
C. use multiple audio-visual aids.
D. use constructive pedagogical approaches.

94. _______ is the primary Identifying feature of creativity.

A. Hyperactivity B. Inattentiveness
C. Low comprehension D. Divergent thinking

95. Which of the following is most effective mode of teaching-learning?

A. Observation without analysis
B. Imitation and repetition
C. Rote memorization of content
D. Exploration of relationships between concepts

96. A teacher should analyse the various errors made by students on a given task because:

A. she can segregate those who made more errors in comparison to others.
B. learning is solely based on correction of errors.
C. she can decide degree of punishment accordingly.
D. understanding of errors are meaningful in the teaching-learning process.

97. Motivation to learn can be sustained by:

A. giving very easy tasks to children.
B. focusing on rote-memorisation.
C. punishing the child.
D. focusing on mastery-oriented goals.

98. Shame _________

A. is very effective to motivate the children to learn.
B. should be generated frequently in teaching-learning process.
C. has no relation to cognition.
D. can have negative impact on cognition.

99. Constructivist view of learning suggests that children _______ construction of their own knowledge.

A. play an active role in
B. are solely dependent on textbooks in
C. have no role to play in
D. are solely dependent on adults for

100. Which of the following belief is good for learning?

A. Efforts don't make any difference.
B. Failure is uncontrollable.
C. Ability is improvable.
D. Ability is fixed.

101. Conceptual understanding among students is likely to improve in the settings which emphasise on:

A. frequent examinations.
B. inquiry and dialogue.
C. competitions.
D. textbook-centric pedagogy.

102. It is difficult for children to learn when:

A. learning is socially contextualized.
B. content is represented through multiple ways.
C. information is presented in disconnected chunks.
D. they are intrinsically motivated.

103. Best state of learning is:

A. moderate arousal, no fear.
B. no arousal, no fear.
C. high arousal, high fear.
D. low arousal, high fear.

104. Individual differences in development of children can be attributed to:

A. neither heredity nor environment.
B. interplay of heredity and environment.
C. heredity only.
D. environment only.

105. During a task, Saina is talking to herself about ways she can proceed on the task. According to Lev Vygotsky's ideas on language and thought; this kind of 'private speech' is a sign of:

A. Ego-centricism. B. Psychological disorder.
C. Cognitive immaturity. D. Self-regulation.

106. Evaluation practices should aim at:

A. identifying students' needs and requirements.
B. identification of high-achievers for prize distribution.
C. labelling of students.
D. segregation of students for ability-based groups.

107. After observing that students are struggling to proceed further on an ongoing activity, a teacher decides to provide cues and hints in form of what, why, how. According to Lev Vygotsky's theory, this strategy of teacher will:

A. cause withdrawal tendency among students.
B. be meaningless in process of learning.
C. demotivate the children to learn.
D. act as a scaffold for learning.

108. After getting hurt during a play activity, Rohan started crying. Seeing this, his father responded, "Don't behave like girls, boys don't cry". This statement by the father:

A. reduces gender bias.
B. promotes gender equality.
C. reflects gender stereotype.
D. challenges gender stereotype.

109. In a progressive classroom:

A. ample opportunities should be provided for construction of knowledge.
B. students should be labelled on the basis of their academic scores.
C. a teacher should follow fixed curriculum.
D. the emphasis should be on competition among students.

110. According to Lawrence Kohlberg's theory, "Performing an act and doing something because others approves it", represents ________ stage of morality.

A. Post-conventional B. Formal conventional
C. Pre-conventional D. Conventional

111. Which of the following is correct in the context of socialization of children?

A. Peers are primary socialization agents and family is a secondary socialization agent.
B. Family and mass-media both are secondary socialization agents.
C. School is a secondary socialization agent and family is a primary socialization agent.
D. School is a primary socialization agent and peers are secondary socialization agents.

112. Theory of multiple intelligence emphasizes that:

A. There are several forms of intelligences.
B. There are no individual differences in intelligence.
C. Intelligence Quotient (IQ) can be measured only by objective tests.
D. Intelligence in one domain ensures intelligence in all other domains.

113. Pre-operational stage in Jean Piaget's theory of cognitive development characterizes ________.

A. Hypothetico deductive thinking
B. Ability to conserve and seriate objects.
C. Development of abstract thinking
D. Centration in thought

114. Which of the following statement is correct in context of development?

A. Development occurs only during the period of childhood.
B. Development is multi-dimensional.
C. Development has the same rate of growth across cultures for everyone.
D. Development occurs only through learning that takes place in school.

115. Lev Vygotsky's social-cultural perspective of learning emphasizes importance of ______ in the learning process.

A. Motivation B. Equilibration
C. Cultural tools D. Attribution

116. In his theory of cognitive development, Jean Piaget explains cognitive structures in terms of ________.

A. Zone of proximal development
B. Schemas
C. Psychological tools
D. Stimulus-response association

117. In on Inclusive classroom emphasis should be on:

A. segregation of students based on their social identity.
B. providing opportunities aiming at maximizing potential of individual children.
C. performance oriented goals.
D. undifferentiated instructions

118. According to Right of Persons with Disabilities Act (2016), which of the following term is appropriate to use?

A. Student with physical disability
B. Student with crippled body
C. Retarded student
D. Handicapped student

119. Sequence of development among children from birth to adolescence is:

A. concrete, abstract, sensory.
B. abstract, concrete, sensory.
C. sensory, concrete, abstract.
D. abstract, sensory, concrete.

120. Individual differences in a progressive classroom should be treated as:

A. criteria for making ability-based groups.
B. important for planning of teaching-learning process.
C. a hindrance to the process of learning.
D. a failure on the part of teacher.

121. The most critical period of acquisition and development of language is:

A. pre-natal period B. early childhood
C. middle childhood D. adolescence

122. Which of the following is a stage of moral development proposed by Lawrence Kohlberg?

A. Latency Stage
B. The social contract orientation
C. Concrete operational stage
D. Industry vs. Inferiority stage

123. During classroom discussions, a teacher often pays more attention to boys than girls. This is an example of:

A. Gender bias B. Gender identity
C. Gender relevance D. Gender constancy

124. Which of the following is an effective strategy to reduce children's gender stereotyping and gender-role conformity?

A. Discussion about gender bias
B. Emphasizing gender-specific roles
C. Gender-segregated play groups
D. Gender-segregated seating arrangement

125. Which of the following theorists while viewing children as active seekers of knowledge emphasized the influence of social and cultural contents on their thinking?

A. John B. Watson B. Lev Vygotsky
C. Jean Piaget D. Lawrence Kohlberg

126. While working on a jig-saw puzzle, 5 years old Najma says to herself, "Where is the blue piece? No, not this one, darker one that would go here and make this shoe". This kind of talk is referred to by Vygotsky as:

A. private speech B. talk aloud
C. scaffolding D. egocentric speech

127. Giving cues to children and offering support as and when needed is an example of:

A. reinforcement B. conditioning
C. modelling D. scaffolding

128. Which of the following behaviours characterize the 'concrete operational stage' as proposed by Jean Piaget?

A. Hypothetico-deduction reasoning; propositional thought
B. Conservation; class inclusion
C. Deferred imitation; object permanence
D. Make-believe play; irreversibility of thought

129. Which of the following is a Piagetian construct in the context of cognitive development of children?

A. Schemas B. Observational learning
C. Conditioning D. Reinforcement

130. Primary objective of Assessment should be:

A. assigning rank to students.
B. understanding children's clarity and confusions about related concepts.
C. labelling students as per their score.
D. marking pass or fail in the report cards.

131. Which of the following statements about intelligence is correct?

A. Intelligence is a fixed ability determined at the time of birth only.
B. Intelligence can be accurately measured and determined by using standardized tests.
C. Intelligence is a unitary factor and a single trait.
D. Intelligence is multi-dimensional and a set of complex abilities.

132. Ruhi always thinks of multiple solutions to a problem many of which are original solutions. Ruhi is displaying characteristics of a/an:

A. creative thinker B. convergent thinker
C. rigid thinker D. egocentric thinker

133. In a situation of less participation of students belonging to a deprived group in teaching-learning process, a teacher should:

A. ask the children to withdraw from school.
B. accept this situation as it is.
C. lower her expectations from such students.
D. reflect on her own teaching and find ways to improve student's involvement.

134. In an inclusive classroom, a teacher ________ Individualized Education Plans.

A. should not prepare
B. should occasionally prepare
C. should actively prepare
D. should discourage the preparation of

135. The primary characteristic of children with 'dyslexia' includes:
A. attention deficit disorders
B. divergent thinking; fluency in reading
C. inability to read fluently
D. engaging in repetitive locomotor actions

136. The concept of 'Inclusive Education' as advocated in the Right to Education Act, 2009 is based on:
A. the behaviouristic principles
B. a sympathetic attitude towards disabled
C. a rights-based humanistic perspective
D. mainstreaming of the disabled by offering them primarily vocational education

137. In the constructivist framework, learning is primarily:
A. based on rote-memorization.
B. centered around reinforcement.
C. acquired through conditioning.
D. focused on the process of meaning-making.

138. 'Naive theories' that children construct about various phenomenon:
A. should be ignored by the teacher.
B. should be punished by the teacher.
C. should be 'replaced' by correct one through repetitive memorization.
D. should be challenged by presenting counter evidence and examples.

139. Child-centered pedagogy promotes:
A. exclusive reliance on text books.
B. giving primacy to children's experiences.
C. rote memorisation.
D. labelling and categorization of students base on ability.

140. Emotions and cognition are _______ each other.
A. completely separate from
B. independent of
C. inter-woven with
D. not related to

141. Which of the following statements about learning is correct from a constructivist perspective?
A. Learning is the process of reproduction and recall.
B. Learning is the process of rote memorization.
C. Learning is conditioning of behaviours by repetitive association.
D. Learning is the process of construction of knowledge by active engagement.

142. Presenting students with clear examples and non-examples:
A. is an effective way to encourage conceptual change.
B. leads to confusion in the minds of students.
C. causes gaps in their understanding of concepts.
D. focuses on procedural knowledge rather than conceptual understanding.

143. Repeatedly asking children to engage in learning activities either to avoid punishment or to gain a reward:
A. decreases extrinsic motivation.
B. increases intrinsic motivation.
C. would encourage children to focus on mastery rather than performance goals.
D. decreases children's natural interest and curiosity involved in learning.

144. Which of the following practices promote meaningful learning?
(*i*) Corporal punishment
(*ii*) Co-operative learning environment
(*iii*) Continuous and comprehensive evaluation
(*iv*) Constant comparative evaluation
A. (*i*), (*ii*)
B. (*ii*), (*iii*)
C. (*i*), (*ii*), (*iii*)
D. (*ii*), (*iii*), (*iv*)

145. How can teachers facilitate understanding of complex concepts in children?
A. By delivering a lecture
B. By organizing competitive events
C. By repetitive mechanical drill
D. By providing opportunities for exploration and discussion

146. A primary school teacher can encourage children to become effective problem solvers by:
A. offering materialistic rewards for every small tasks.
B. emphasizing only on procedural knowledge.
C. dismissing and penalizing 'incorrect answers'.
D. encouraging children to make intuitive guesses and then brainstorming on the same.

147. In which of the following periods does physical growth and development occur at a rapid pace?
A. Infancy and early childhood
B. Early childhood and middle childhood
C. Middle childhood and adolescence
D. Adolescence and adulthood

148. Which of the following is NOT a principle of development?
A. Development is lifelong.
B. Development is modifiable.
C. Development is influenced by both heredity and environment.
D. Development is universal and cultural contents do not influence it.

149. The primary cause of individual variations is:

A. the genetic code received by the individuals from birth parents
B. the inborn characteristics
C. the environmental influences
D. the complex interplay between the heredity and the environment

150. Which of the following are examples of secondary socializing agency?

A. Family and neighbourhood
B. Family and media
C. School and media
D. Media and neighbourhood

151. Human development starts from:

A. Pre-childhood stage B. Post-childhood stage
C. Stage of infancy D. Pre-natal stage

152. 'The Conditions of Learning' book is written by

A. B.F. Skinner B. R.M. Gagne
C. I.P. Pavlov D. E.L. Thorndike

153. "Adolescence is the period of great stress, strain, storm and strike" is the statement of

A. Stanley Hall B. Simpson
C. Crow & Crow D. Jersield

154. Total time taken in Indian Model of Micro Teaching is

A. 40 minute B. 45 minute
C. 30 minute D. 36 minute

155. "Plateaus of learning are a characteristic feature of the learning process indicating a period where no improvement in performance is made". Who said this?

A. Hollingworth B. Ross
C. Skinner D. Gates and others

156. If a teacher finds a problematic child in the class, what should he does?

A. Ignore the child
B. Provide counselling to the child
C. Send the child back to home immediately
D. Punish the child

157. Co-curricular activities are mostly related to:

A. All round development of students
B. Professional development of students
C. Mental development of students
D. Development of educational institutions

158. Whom of the following has *not* propounded the learning theory?

A. Skinner B. B.S. Bloom
C. Thorndike D. Kohler

159. Meaning of stagnation in education is:

A. Not going to school by the child
B. Leave the school by the child
C. Retention of a child in a same class for more than one year
D. Taking not admission in school by the child

160. In which of the following skill, testing of previous knowledge comes?

A. Skill of introduction B. Skill of closure
C. Skill of demonstration D. Skill of stimulus-variation

161. Who gave the concept of multiple intelligence?

A. Spearman B. John Mayor
C. Gardner D. Golman

162. Dyslexia has difficulty in

A. Expressing B. Standing
C. Speaking D. Reading/ Spelling

163. Which of the following is ***not*** the role of teacher in inclusive classroom?

A. Teacher should not pay attention to differently abled child
B. Teacher should encourage the children
C. Teacher should devote extra time to teach learning disabled
D. Make adequate seating arrangements according to the requirement of the child

164. In the class, questioning by students:

A. Should be encouraged
B. Should be stopped
C. Should not be allowed
D. Should be discouraged

165. Growth of a child is mainly related to:

A. Social Development B. Emotional Development
C. Moral Development D. Physical Development

166. 'Learning is any change in behaviour, resulting from behaviour' who said it?

A. Guilford B. Skinner
C. Crow & Crow D. Woodworth

167. Match the List–A and List–B.

List–A	List–B
(*a*) Bruner	(*i*) Basic teaching model
(*b*) Ausubel	(*ii*) Synectics teaching model
(*c*) Glasser	(*iii*) Advance organiser teaching model
(*d*) Gordon	(*iv*) Concept attainment teaching model
	(*v*) Inquiry training model

Codes:

	(*a*)	(*b*)	(*c*)	(*d*)
A.	(*iv*)	(*iii*)	(*ii*)	(*i*)
B.	(*i*)	(*ii*)	(*iii*)	(*v*)
C.	(*iii*)	(*i*)	(*ii*)	(*v*)
D.	(*iv*)	(*iii*)	(*i*)	(*ii*)

168. The first step of problem solving is:
A. Identification of problem
B. Testing of hypothesis
C. Formulation of hypothesis
D. Data collection

169. Learning of children will be most effective when:
A. Development of cognitive, affective and psychomotor domain of children will take place
B. Teaching system will be autocratic
C. Teacher will lead the learning process and keep the children passive
D. Emphasis will be only on reading, writing and mathematical skills

170. Which step is prominent in the syntax of teaching model of memory level and understanding level?
A. Exploration B. Presentation
C. Planning D. Generalization

171. Which of the following theory is also known as Theory of Reinforcement?
A. Stimulus Response Theory
B. Theory of Insight
C. Operant Conditioning Theory
D. Classical Conditioning Theory

172. Which of the following stages is ***not*** the part of Bruner's Cognitive Development Theory?
A. Iconic stage B. Symbolic stage
C. Enactive stage D. Intuitive stage

173. Morrison has described five steps in his teaching model at understanding level which are
(*a*) Presentation (*b*) Exploration
(*c*) Organisation (*d*) Assimilation
(*e*) Recitation
The correct sequence is:
A. (*b*), (*a*), (*d*), (*c*), (*e*) B. (*b*), (*a*), (*c*), (*d*), (*e*)
C. (*a*), (*b*), (*c*), (*d*), (*e*) D. (*d*), (*e*), (*c*), (*a*), (*b*)

174. Which of the following is ***not*** related with cognitive domain?
A. Application B. Understanding
C. Knowledge D. Valuing

175. Which of the following is ***not*** the curve of learning?
A. Combination type B. Longitudinal
C. Convex D. Concave

176. Match the Column–A and Column–B.

Column–A	Column–B
(*a*) Animal Intelligence	(*i*) Gestalt
(*b*) Schedule of reinforcement	(*ii*) Piaget
(*c*) Law of pragnanz	(*iii*) Thorndike
(*d*) Adaptation	(*iv*) Skinner

Codes:

	(*a*)	(*b*)	(*c*)	(*d*)
A.	(*ii*)	(*iv*)	(*iii*)	(*i*)
B.	(*ii*)	(*iv*)	(*i*)	(*iii*)
C.	(*iii*)	(*iv*)	(*i*)	(*ii*)
D.	(*i*)	(*iv*)	(*iii*)	(*ii*)

177. "Development is a never ending process". This statement is related to which principle of development?
A. Principle of integration
B. Principle of inter-relationship
C. Principle of continuity
D. Principle of interaction

178. Through which Amendment of Constitution education has become fundamental right?
A. 25th Amendment B. 52nd Amendment
C. 22nd Amendment D. 86th Amendment

179. Instinct Theory of motivation was propounded by
A. Abraham Maslow B. Simpson
C. William James D. McDougall

180. Which of the following stages of development is called as "A unique stage of emotional development" by Cole and Bruce?
A. Childhood B. Adulthood
C. Adolescence D. Infancy

181. Kohler wanted to prove that learning is:
A. a situation in which individuals are superior to animals
B. an autonomous random activity
C. cognitive operation
D. the perception of different parts of the situation

182. From where to start in order to learn any new language?
A. Association between letters and words
B. Formation of sentences
C. Formation of words
D. None of the above

183. Which type(s) of students is/are included in inclusive class?
A. Only specific students
B. General and specific students
C. Only general students
D. Multilinguistic and gifted students

184. From the following, which term defines the mathematics related learning disability?
A. Dystopia B. Dyslexia
C. Dyscalculia D. None of the above

185. Successful inclusion needs:
A. lack of capacity building
B. no involvement of parents
C. segregation
D. sensitization

186. Which of the following is ***not*** the element of emotion?

A. Behavioural B. Physical
C. Cognitive D. Sensory

187. Which is the correct sequence of cognitive domain?

A. Knowledge-Application-Comprehension-Analysis-Synthesis-Evaluation
B. Evaluation-Application-Analysis-Synthesis-Comprehension-Knowledge
C. Evaluation-Synthesis-Analysis-Application-Comprehension-Knowledge
D. Knowledge-Comprehension-Application-Analysis-Synthesis-Evaluation

188. Which of the following is ***not*** a quality of good teaching?

A. Autocratic
B. Democratic
C. Sympathetic
D. Desirable information provider

189. Expectancy theory of motivation has been given by:

A. Victor Vroom B. Maslow
C. Herzberg D. Skinner

190. To which family advance organizer model is related with?

A. Personal
B. Social interaction
C. Information processing
D. Behaviour modification

191. Which is useful in the transformation of skills?

A. Skills transformation is a journey, not a destination
B. Linear Programme
C. Branching Programme
D. Preparation and acquisition

192. Which one is ***not*** the maxim of teaching from the following?

A. From simple to complex
B. From indefinite to definite
C. From seen to unseen
D. From deduction to induction

193. First step of microteaching cycle is:

A. feedback B. teaching
C. planning D. introduction

194. Which of the following is included in the teaching of understanding level?

A. Abstraction B. Application
C. Comparison D. Exploration

195. For educational reforms effective decentralization is possible by:

1. greater involvement of cluster and block resource centres
2. availability of local resource person
3. resource and reference material for the use of teachers

Choose the correct answer

A. 1 and 3 B. 1 and 2
C. 2 and 3 D. 1, 2 and 3

196. A student is reading, someone called him by name. By which sensation he (student) will respond from the following?

A. Visual sensation B. Tactual sensation
C. Auditory sensation D. Perceptual sensation

197. What is the age of preoperational stage in Piaget theory?

A. Four to eight years B. Birth to two years
C. Two to seven years D. Five to eight years

198. Which of the following is ***not*** the characteristic of intellectual development of later childhood?

A. Operational planning of career
B. High interest in science fiction
C. Increased logical power
D. End of imaginary fears

199. Which of the following psychologists is associated with 'language development'?

A. Pavlov B. Binnet
C. Chomsky D. Maslow

200. Thorndike proved his theory titled:

A. cognitive learning B. trial and error learning
C. sign learning D. space learning

201. Gang age associated with age and delayed development is:

A. 16-19 years and morality
B. 3-6 years and language
C. 8-10 years and socialization
D. 16-19 years and cognitive

202. Which of the following is the third stage of cognitive development according to Piaget?

A. Formal operational stage
B. Pre-operational stage
C. Concrete operational stage
D. Sensory motor stage

203. Which is ***not*** included in psychological factors that contribute in learning from the following?

A. Learning desire B. Motivation
C. Interest D. Nature of content

204. Which of the following is a social value?

A. Altruism B. Primary goal
C. Instinct D. Aggression need

205. Backward exploration and means-end analysis are examples of which of the following?

A. Heuristics B. Algorithms
C. Mental sets D. Functional Fixedness

206. "Curves of learning give graphic representation of the amount, rate and limit of improvement brought about by practice." Who said it?

A. Skinner B. Ross
C. Ebbinghaus D. M. L. Bigge

207. Which one is ***not*** included in Thorndike's primary laws of learning from the following?

A. Law of associative shifting
B. Law of exercise
C. Law of effect
D. Law of readiness

208. Conditioned response theory lays emphasis on conditioning of:

A. reasoning B. behaviour
C. thinking D. motivation

209. The other name of operant conditioning is:

A. contiguous conditioning
B. instrumental conditioning
C. classical conditioning
D. trace conditioning

210. Which of the following is ***not*** a characteristic of learning?

A. Learning is directly observed
B. Learning is a relatively permanent change in behaviour
C. Learning is a growth of organism
D. Learning is a goal-directed process

211. The period of learning, where no improvement in performance is made, is called:

A. learning curve B. plateau of learning
C. memory D. attention

212. The formula for calculating IQ is:

A. Mental age × Chronological age
B. $\dfrac{\text{Chronological age}}{\text{Mental age}}$
C. $\dfrac{\text{Mental age}}{\text{Chronological age}} \times 100$
D. Chronological age + Mental age

213. Who has propounded the law of trial and error of learning?

A. Kohler B. Pavlov
C. Thorndike D. Gestalt

214. In a normal zygote, the number of chromosomes in pair is:

A. 22 B. 23
C. 24 D. None of the above

215. Operant conditioning theory is propounded by:

A. Hull B. Thorndike
C. Hegarty D. Skinner

216. Kohler is associated with which of the following?

A. Theory of motivation B. Theory of development
C. Theory of personality D. Theory of learning

217. Fluid mosaic model of intelligence was proposed by:

A. Cattell B. Thorndike
C. Vernon D. Skinner

218. Brainstorming model of teaching is used to improve which of the following?

A. Understanding B. Application
C. Creativity D. Problem solving

219. Goleman is associated with which of the following?

A. Social intelligence B. Emotional intelligence
C. Spiritual intelligence D. General intelligence

220. Find the odd one out.

A. Theory of learning to learn
B. Theory of identical elements
C. Drive reduction theory
D. Theory of generalization

221. The lowest level of cognitive achievement is:

A. knowledge B. understanding
C. application D. analysis

222. A boy who can ride a cycle is going to drive a motorbike. This is an example of:

A. horizontal transfer of learning
B. vertical transfer of learning
C. bilateral transfer of learning
D. No transfer of learning

223. Which of the following is **not** the cause of plateau of learning?

A. Limit of motivation
B. Non-cooperation of school
C. Physiological limit
D. Limit of knowledge

224. "Learning is the modification of behaviour through experience and training." This statement was given by:

A. Gates and others B. Morgan and Gilliland
C. Skinner D. Cronbach

225. 'Stanford-Binet Test' measures:

A. personality B. reading efficiency
C. intelligence D. None of the above

226. Who has classified introvert personality and extrovert personality?

A. Freud B. Jung
C. Munn D. Allport

227. The factors affecting the social development of children are:

A. economic elements

B. social-environmental elements
C. physical elements
D. hereditary elements

228. Which of the following is a primary law of physical development?
A. Law of difference from mental development
B. Law of irregular development
C. Law of rapid growth
D. Law of relation from imagination and emotional development

229. Which of the following is ***not*** the theory of development?
A. Theory of conditioned reflex
B. Theory of continuous growth
C. Theory of interrelation
D. Theory of uniform pattern

230. "Development result in new characteristic and new abilities." This Statement is given by:
A. Gesell B. Hurlock
C. Meredith D. Douglas and Holland

231. Instincts are classified in fourteen types by:
A. Drever B. McDougall
C. Thorndike D. Woodworth

232. "Attention is the concentration of consciousness upon one object rather than upon another." This statement is given by:
A. Dumville B. Ross
C. Munn D. McDougall

233. Which is ***not*** included in primary law of learning?
A. Law of readiness
B. Law of exercise
C. Law of multiple response
D. Law of effect

234. Which test is propounded by Dr. S. Jalota in Hindi for the children of 12 to 16 years?
A. Non-verbal intelligence test
B. General mental ability test
C. Army alpha test
D. Picture drawing test

235. Who propounded the two-factor theory of intelligence?
A. Thorndike B. Spearman
C. Vernon D. Stern

236. Which of the following pairs is not true?
A. Stimulus-response theory of learning—Thorndike
B. Operant conditioning theory of learning—B. F. Skinner
C. Classical theory of learning—Pavlov
D. Holistic theory of learning—Hull

237. Whose name is associated with 'Father of the Eugenics'?
A. Crow and Crow B. Galton
C. Ross D. Woodworth

238. Who described different types of personality based on glands?
A. Kretschmer B. Jung
C. Cannon D. Spranger

239. "Creativity is a mental process to express the original outcomes." This statement is given by:
A. Cole and Bruce B. Drevahal
C. Dehan D. Crow and Crow

240. The tendency of 'Feeling of Revolt' is concerned with which of the following ages?
A. Childhood B. Infancy
C. Early adolescence D. Middle adolescence

241. Thematic Apperception Test (T.A.T.) was developed by
A. Symond B. Holtzman
C. Murray D. Bellak

242. The greatest contribution of psychology to education is
A. Subject-oriented education
B. Teacher centred education
C. Activity based education
D. Child-centred education

243. Which of the following is not related to principles of growth and development?
A. Principle of continuity
B. Principle of classification
C. Principle of integration
D. Principle of individuality

244. In class teaching the step of introducing a lesson is based on which law of learning?
A. Law of effect B. Law of analogy
C. Law of readiness D. Law of association

245. The first step of concept formation is
A. Generalisation B. Abstraction
C. Perception D. Differentiation

246. Concept of observational learning was given by ______
A. Tolman B. Bandura
C. Thorndike D. Kohler

247. In learning, law of effect was given by ______
A. Pavlov B. Skinner
C. Watson D. Thorndike

248. Which of the following method is not used to measure memory?
A. Recall method B. Reasoning method
C. Recognition method D. Re-learning method

249. Scope of Child Psychology is
A. study the characteristics of Infancy stage only
B. study the characteristics of conception period only
C. study the characteristics of childhood only
D. study the characteristics from conception to adolescence

250. The situation usually caused by a failure of mother's twenty-first chromosome pair to separate is known as
A. Down's syndrome B. Klinefelter's syndrome
C. Turner's syndrome D. Wilson's syndrome

251. According to Kohlberg, at which level, morality is externally controlled?
A. Pre-conventional level
B. Conventional level
C. Post-conventional level
D. None of the above

252. Which one of the following is correct development sequence?
A. Ovum-sperm, blastocyst, zygote
B. Blastocyst, ovum-sperm, zygote
C. Blastocyst, zygote, ovum-sperm
D. Ovum-sperm, zygote, blastocyst

253. Introvert, extrovert and ambivert kinds of personality is classified by
A. Kretacher B. Jung
C. Shaldon D. Sprenger

254. Example, observation, analysis classification and generalization are the steps of which method of the following?
A. Deductive method B. Inductive method
C. Introspection method D. Extrospection method

255. The internal or subjective determinants of attention are
A. Interest, air, attitude
B. Stimulus, objects, device
C. Light, sound, smell
D. Reward, punishment, incentive

256. Behaviourist ______ has said, "Give me the newborn infant. I can make him doctor, advocate, thief or whatever I wish."
A. Freeman B. Newman
C. Watson D. Holzinger

257. _____ plays important role in drawing attention.
A. Intensity of stimulus B. Utility of stimulus
C. Reliability of stimulus D. Activity of stimulus

258. "_______ is the art of stimulating interest in the pupil."
A. Teaching B. Sympathy
C. Impartial view D. Motivation

259. According to Freud
A. "Forgetting is failing to retain or to be able to recal what has been acquired."
B. "Forgetting means failure at any time to recall an experience, when attempting to do so or to perform an action previously learned."
C. "Forgetting is a tendency to ward off from memory that which is unpleasant."
D. None of the above

260. S-O-R is proposed by
A. Watson B. Kofka
C. Kohler D. Gestalt Psyhologists

261. The scale which has all the properties of an interval scale and in addition has an absolute zero.
A. Nominal Scale B. Ordinal Scale
C. Interval Scale D. Ratio Scale

262. According to Freud, our values are internalized within the ____
A. id B. ego
C. superego D. situations

263. Modification of behaviour through experience is called
A. Memory B. Learning
C. Motivation D. Thinking

264. In statistics the bar graph of a frequency distribution is called
A. Histogram
B. Frequency Polygon
C. Cumulative Frequency
D. Graph

265. At which stage of development, maximum development of intelligence takes place?
A. Childhood B. Infancy
C. Adolescence D. Adulthood

266. Maximum behaviour of the child is based upon
A. Instinct B. Morality
C. Reality D. Attention

267. In theory of learning by insight Kohler did his experiment on
A. Dog B. Chimpanzees
C. Cat D. Rats

268. It is not essential that children with high intelligence quotient will be higher in ______.
A. creativity B. studies
C. analysing D. getting good marks

269. Internal condition attracting attention is
A. Duration B. Novelty
C. Interest D. Size

270. When acquired knowledge in one situation is used in another situation, is called
A. Methods of learning
B. Transfer in learning
C. Plateau in learning
D. Interest in learning

271. Which of the following would support continuous and comprehensive evaluation?
A. Best works portfolio
B. Growth and learning progress portfolio
C. Standardized achievement test
D. Standardized intelligence test

272. While talking about her poor marks in mathematics Avi says "I just don't have the sense for numbers" Avi is attributing his performance to:
A. Luck
B. Task difficulty
C. Lack of effort
D. Lack of ability

273. Which of the following statement best describes the role of the teacher in progressive education?
A. The teacher is the primary source of knowledge.
B. The teacher serves as a facilitator.
C. The teacher implements the prescribed curriculum 'as it is'.
D. The teacher leaves the children on their own to work independently.

274. Howard Gardner's concept of Intelligence implicates that:
A. everyone processes and understands the world in the same way.
B. human beings differ in their abilities in different domains.
C. intelligence has only one dimension.
D. intelligence is only about 'practical' learning.

275. Which of the following statement about development is correct?
A. Development is a discontinuous process.
B. Development occurs in a spiral manner, not linear.
C. Development proceeds from specific to general.
D. Different aspects of development are independent to each other.

276. According to Lev Vygotsky, children regulate their own behaviour through the:
A. Processes of adaptation
B. Use of inner speech
C. Process of equilibration
D. Use of self-reinforcement

277. Which pedagogical approach would be adopted by teachers who firmly believe in constructivism to teach concepts of floating and sinking to class V children?
A. Lecture method
B. Showing videos
C. Showing power point presentation
D. Guided discovery

278. Which of the following is not an effective memory technique for meaningful learning?
A. Rote Rehearsal B. Mnemonics
C. Concept Mapping D. Elaborative Rehearsal

279. Heredity totally determine an individual's:
(*i*) Sex (*ii*) Gender
(*iii*) Academic Success (*iv*) Learning Style
A. (*i*) B. (*ii*)
C. (*i*), (*iii*), (*iv*) D. (*ii*), (*iii*), (*iv*)

280. Repetitive and ritualistic behaviour is an identifying characteristic of:
A. Autism Spectrum Disorder
B. Learning Disabilities
C. Attention Deficit Hyperactivity Disorder
D. Cerebral palsy

ANSWERS

1	2	3	4	5	6	7	8	9	10
D	C	A	C	A	B	C	A	C	C
11	**12**	**13**	**14**	**15**	**16**	**17**	**18**	**19**	**20**
A	B	C	C	D	B	C	D	C	C
21	**22**	**23**	**24**	**25**	**26**	**27**	**28**	**29**	**30**
C	A	C	D	B	B	B	A	C	C
31	**32**	**33**	**34**	**35**	**36**	**37**	**38**	**39**	**40**
C	C	B	B	D	C	B	C	D	B
41	**42**	**43**	**44**	**45**	**46**	**47**	**48**	**49**	**50**
B	B	B	B	C	C	D	B	D	D
51	**52**	**53**	**54**	**55**	**56**	**57**	**58**	**59**	**60**
B	B	B	D	B	C	B	D	A	A

61	62	63	64	65	66	67	68	69	70
A	A	B	A	B	B	A	B	B	B
71	72	73	74	75	76	77	78	79	80
B	A	A	A	C	A	A	A	D	A
81	82	83	84	85	86	87	88	89	90
B	A	D	D	A	C	C	D	A	D
91	92	93	94	95	96	97	98	99	100
D	A	B	D	D	D	D	D	A	C
101	102	103	104	105	106	107	108	109	110
B	C	A	B	D	A	D	C	A	D
111	112	113	114	115	116	117	118	119	120
C	A	D	B	C	B	B	A	C	B
121	122	123	124	125	126	127	128	129	130
B	B	A	A	B	A	D	B	A	B
131	132	133	134	135	136	137	138	139	140
D	A	D	C	C	C	D	D	B	C
141	142	143	144	145	146	147	148	149	150
D	A	D	B	D	D	A	D	D	C
151	152	153	154	155	156	157	158	159	160
D	B	A	D	B	B	A	B	C	A
161	162	163	164	165	166	167	168	169	170
C	D	A	A	D	A	D	A	A	B
171	172	173	174	175	176	177	178	179	180
C	D	A	D	B	C	C	D	D	A
181	182	183	184	185	186	187	188	189	190
C	A	A	C	D	D	D	A	A	C
191	192	193	194	195	196	197	198	199	200
A	D	C	D	D	C	C	A	C	B
201	202	203	204	205	206	207	208	209	210
A	C	D	A	A	C	A	B	B	A
211	212	213	214	215	216	217	218	219	220
B	C	C	B	D	D	A	C	B	C
221	222	223	224	225	226	227	228	229	230
A	B	B	A	C	B	B	C	A	B
231	232	233	234	235	236	237	238	239	240
B	A	C	B	B	D	B	C	D	C
241	242	243	244	245	246	247	248	249	250
C	D	B	C	C	B	D	B	D	A
251	252	253	254	255	256	257	258	259	260
A	D	B	B	A	C	A	D	C	A
261	262	263	264	265	266	267	268	269	270
D	C	B	A	C	A	B	A	C	B
271	272	273	274	275	276	277	278	279	280
B	D	B	B	B	B	D	A	A	A

GLOSSARY

Accommodation : Piaget used this term for modification or reorganisation of existing cognitive structure (schemata) to deal with environmental demands. Accommodation is the adjustment the individual makes when incorporating external reality. Piaget uses this concept in conjunction with assimilation, which is the individual's response to the immediate and compelling environmental demands that have been and are being assimilated.

Advance organisers : Introductory information intended to facilitate a student's learning by providing a framework and organisation for the material to be learned.

Affective domain : One of the categories of educational objectives for students attitudes, values and emotional growth. The affective domain includes five basic categories: receiving, responding, valuing, organisation and characterisation by a value.

Assimilation : Assimilation is the process of taking within or internalising, one's environmental experience. The term is used by Piaget for the process of making sense of experiences and perceptions by fitting them into previously established cognitive structure (schemata). Assimilation is used by Piaget in conjunction with the concept of accommodation. Piaget believes that assimilation is a spontaneous process on the part of the child.

Attitudes : A learned predisposition to respond either positively or negatively to persons, situations, or things. Attitudes carry a strong emotional component and therefore can never be neutral.

Attribution theory : The term attribution refers to the explanation a person gives for his or her own or another person's actions or beliefs. An attribution based on internal factors is called a dispositional attribution, and one based on external factors is called a situational attribution.

Behaviourism : A school of thought in Psychology usually considered to have originated in the work and writings of John B. Watson in 1913. Watson argued against the use of introspection in gathering psychological data. He considered observable behaviour the only valid data in Psychology. According to Watson, any concepts, like mind or consciousness, that have mentalistic overtones must be purged from the field of psychology. The most famous current representative of this tradition is Harvard University's B.F. Skinner.

Classical conditioning : A procedure in which the conditioned stimulus after being paired with the unconditioned stimulus often enough, can then be substituted for it. It is often called "stimulus substitution."

Cognition : The process of faculties by which knowledge is acquired and manipulated (*e.g.*, thinking or remembering).

Cognitive domain : A part of Bloom's Taxonomy of educational objectives. Bloom divided the objectives in the cognitive domain into six categories: knowledge, comprehension, application, analysis, synthesis and evaluation.

Cognitive style : The consistent way in which an individual responds to a wide range of perceptual tasks.

Computer-assisted instruction (CAI) : The use of a computer as tutor to present information, give students opportunities to practice what they learn, evaluate student achievement, and provide additional instruction.

Concept learning : The acquisition of pattern-recognition knowledge involving the learning of a rule or rules for classifying a number of objects into mutually exclusive categories based on one or more salient characteristics of the objects.

Conditioned response : A response elicited by a conditioned stimulus. The response is similar but not identical to its associated unconditioned response.

Cognitive learning : The view that learning is based on a restructuring of perceptions and thoughts occurring within the organism is called cognitive learning. This restructuring allows the learner to perceive new relationships, solve new problems and gain understanding of a subject area. Cognitive learning theorists stress the reorganisation of one's perceptions in order to achieve understanding, as opposed to the behaviourist theorists, who stress the importance of associations formed between stimuli and responses.

Conditioned response : The term is used both in classical conditioning, and in operant conditioning. In classical conditioning, the conditioned response is the response being elicited by the conditioned stimulus. The stronger the conditioning, the greater the magnitude of the conditioned response and the shorter its latency. In Pavlov's experiment the conditioned response was the dog's salivation to the tone. In operant conditioning, since the response must precede the reinforcer, the conditioned response is defined not in terms of magnitude or latency, but in terms of either the rate of response or its resistance to extinction. For example, a strongly conditioned operant will occur for more rapidly than one that has been only weakly conditioned. Also, a strongly conditioned operant will be far more difficult to extinguish.

Conditioned stimulus : In classical conditioning, the previously neutral stimulus takes on the power to elicit the response through association with an unconditioned stimulus. For this to occur, the conditioned stimulus must precede the unconditioned stimulus on enough occasions to cause the conditioned stimulus to serve as a signal that the unconditioned stimulus will follow. In Pavlov's experiment on conditioning the dog, the tone was used as the conditioned stimulus. The tone was consistently followed by the meat powder, until the dog began salivating to the tone alone.

Conditioning : Process of learning whereby stimuli and responses become associated through training. There are two general types of conditioning, classical and operant. In classical conditioning a conditioned stimulus is presented, followed by an unconditioned stimulus. Conditioning is exhibited when the organism learns to respond to the conditioned stimulus alone. In operant conditioning the operant is allowed to occur and then is followed by a reinforcing stimulus. Operant conditioning is exhibited when the rate of responding increases over the original, preconditioned rate.

Convergent thinking : A term used by Guilford to describe the type of thinking in which an individual produces a single response to a specific question or problem.

Creativity : The capacity of individuals to produce novel or original answers or products.

Culture : The ways in which a group of people think, feel, and react in order to solve problems of living in their environment.

Cumulative records : A file on a student that includes such information as family data, health, academic grades, standardized test scores, attendance and teacher comments.

Discovery learning : Term is used to describe a form of learning that results not from rote memorisation or conditioning but from the active exploration of alternatives on the part of the learner. This learning is largely a result of learner's own efforts. Learning attained through discovery is more meaningful and long-lasting than that from memorisation.

Divergent thinking : A term used by Guilford to describe the type of thinking wherein an individual produces multiple responses or solutions (often non-traditional) to a single question or problem. Divergent thinking is associated with creativity.

Egocentrism : Piaget's term for describing children in the preperational stage, who have difficulty in assuming the point of view of others.

Enactive : Bruner's first stage of cognitive development, in which children understand the environment through physical action on that environment.

Encoding : The short-term memory process of transforming incoming information into episodic or semantic form and associating it with old knowledge for storage in long-term memory.

Entry behaviour : The knowledge, skills, or attitudes that a learner brings into a new learning situation.

Formal-operations stage : This is a stage of cognitive development according to Jean Piaget, occurring during early adolescence. The period of formal operations (eleven to sixteen years) is the last of Piaget's stages and is characterised by the youth's ability to develop full, formal patterns of thinking based on abstract symbolism. The youth is able to reason things out logically at the abstract level, develop symbolic meanings, and generalize to other situations. This is the highest level of thinking and according to Piaget, must await the maturation of certain structures in the brain for its full development.

Equilibration : A motivation principle in Piaget's theory that identifies human beings as active and exploratory in attempting to impose order and meaningfulness on experiences. This order or balance occurs through the processes of assimilation and accommodation.

Evaluation : This is a process of obtaining information to form judgments so that educational decisions can be made.

External locus of control : A feeling that one has little control over one's and the failure to perceive a cause-and-effect relationship between actions and consequences.

Extrinsic motivation : Motivation influenced by external events such as grades, marks or money.

Gestalt psychology : A school of thought maintaining that the organised whole, configuration, or totality of psychological experience should be the proper object of study. Founded in Germany by Max Wertheimer in the early 1900s, gestalt psychology's first interest was in the field of perception. Later, under Wolfgang Kohler's direction, studies were done in the area of learning, and under Kurt Lewin's direction, in the area of motivation. Gestalt psychologists tend to emphasize cognitive processes in the study of learning. They stress that true understanding occurs only through the reorganisation of ideas and perceptions, not through memorisation or conditioning.

Information processing : Theory of learning and remembering that is based on the computer as a model. Information is seen as following into and within the organism. The sense organs respond to incoming information, and it is passed along and encoded in the memory and nervous system. The encoded information may then be stored and processed and finally retrieved and acted on. As with the computer, there is information input, storage and/or processing, and output.

Insight : A suddenly realised solution to a problem, sometimes called the "a-ha! phenomenon". Introduced by Wolfgang Kohler, the concept of insight is used to explain the apparently spontaneous appearance of a solution to a problem. Insight results from the reorganisation of ideas and perceptions rather than from simple trial-and-error behaviour. The concept of insight is used typically by gestalt psychologists.

Inquiry learning : A process that is similar to discovery learning. Students learn strategies to manipulate and process information, test hypothesis and apply their conclusions to new content or situations.

Intelligence : The capacity, or a set of capacities that allows an individual to learn, solve problems, and/or interact successfully with his or her environment. As hypothetical construct, intelligence has come to mean higher-level thought processes, or intellectual abilities. Statistical studies of intelligence utilise the concept of measured intelligence, which is the score received on a standardised intelligence test.

Intelligence Quotient (IQ) : Originally, a measure of intelligence calculated by dividing a student's mental age (MA) by the chronological age (CA) and multiplying by 100, that is, $IQ = MA/CA \times 100$. This is called the ratio method of obtaining an IQ. More recently, IQ has been computed by the deviation method. One's deviation IQ is defined by one's relative standing among peers. The deviation IQ is computed on the basis of how far one's score deviates from the mean score obtained for the entire group of individuals of the same chronological age. This technique is based on the standard, or z-score concept and assumes a normal distribution for each age group.

Law of effect : This is one of E.L. Thorndike's main laws of learning. It states that when an association between a stimulus and response is followed by a satisfying state of affairs, the association (or connection) is strengthened. When the association is followed by an annoying state of affairs, it is weakened. In brief, reward strengthens and punishment weakens any connection between stimuli and responses. In a later version of the law, Thorndike soft-pedaled the importance of punishment of a weakening agent. Thorndike's law of effect is considered by many psychologists to be the cornerstone on which B.F. Skinner built his system of operant conditioning.

Law of exercise : One of E.L. Thorndike's three main laws of learning. It states that the more frequently a stimulus response connection occurs, the stronger the resulting association and hence, the stronger the learning. The repetition of a learned response strengthens the bond between stimulus situation and the response. The law was later amended to incorporate the importance of the consequences of the action; thus, practice without knowledge of results is not nearly as effective as when the consequences become known to the learner.

Law of readiness : One of E.L. Thorndike's three main laws of learning. It states that learning occurs when the student is mentally ready to learn. The reference here is to momentary readiness rather than maturational readiness.

Learning : Learning is a very general term refering to a process that leads to a relatively permanent change in behaviour resulting from experience. Thus, such activities as acquiring physical skills, memorizing poems, acquiring attitudes, etc., are all examples of learning. Learning may be conscious or unconscious, adaptive or maladaptive, overt or covert. Although the learning process is typically measured on the basis of a change in performance, most psychologists agree that an accompanying change occurs within the nervous system. Though there are a great many theories and explanations concerning learning, there is general agreement regarding its definition.

Locus of control : The concept identifies the type of personal control used by an individual. When the locus of control is internal, individual views himself as personally in charge of his own destinies. When the locus of control is external, the person feels he is at the mercy of external circumstances.

Long-term memory (LTM) : In the information-processing system, LTM is the second of the two main storage systems. Information that is in short-term memory may, under certain conditions, be passed along for processing and consolidation into a more permanent storage site, long-term memory. Long-term memory has the potential for holding encoded information for long periods.

Mental age : Term first used by Alfred Binet as the unit for measuring intelligence. Binet defined mental age in terms of the age at which a given number of test items are passed by an average child. If, for example, the average six-year-old could correctly answer a certain number of items, then any other child correctly answering the same number of items would be assigned at least a mental age of six.

Motivation : A general psychological term used to explain behaviour initiated by needs and directed towards a goal. Motives may be biogenic (that is stemming from tissue needs within the organism) or acquired (that is, learned through interaction with the environment, especially the social environment). Among learning theorists, Jerome Bruner makes much of the principle of motivation, assuming that almost all children have a built-in "will to learn".

Nature-nurture controversy : Debate over which component, nature (heredity) or nurture (environment), is more influential in determining behaviour. In Psychology the behaviourists consistently argued on behalf of nurture, and the intelligence testers favoured nature. Educational Psychology has long been the battleground on which this issue has been fought, since the psychologists primarily concerned with this issue were the learning theorists (largely behaviourists).

Need hierarchy : Theory proposed by Abraham Maslow that suggests that human beings place their needs on the following universal, order-of-importance scale: (*i*) physiological needs, (*ii*) safety needs, (*iii*) love needs, (*iv*) esteem needs, and (*v*) self-actualising needs.

Needs : The part of the motivational cycle seen as deficits that lie within the individual. These may be physiological (*e.g.*, the needs for food) or psychological (*e.g.*, the need for approval).

Non-verbal behaviour : Body language. Based largely on the theroy of Charles Galloway and some research by Robert Rosenthal, the teacher's non-verbal behaviour represents an important avenue for the transmission of teacher expectations. Galloway has shown how non-verbal behaviour can promote or reduce student learning. Rosenthal has shown how his test (Profile of Non-verbal Sensitivity) can identify the channels for communicating how teachers really feel about their students.

Operants : Responses, according to B.F. Skinner, for which the original stimuli are either unidentified or non-existent are called operants. The consequences of operant behaviour can be observed even though the stimulus is not known. For example, if a rat presses the lever in a Skinner box and this results in reinforcement, an increase in operant rate will be observed despite the fact that no stimulus could be identified as initiating the original lever pressing. In operant conditioning, reinforcement is contingent on the operant's first being emitted. The organism must in some way "operate" on the environment in order that the reinforcement will follow. Operant responding at one time was called instrumental responding by some psychologists.

Operant conditioning : A type of learning that involves an increase in the probability that a response will occur as a function of reinforcement. This is a form of conditioning, described by B.F. Skinner, in which the free operant is allowed to occur and is followed by a reinforcing stimulus that is, in turn, followed by an increased likelihood of the operant's occurring again. For optimum conditioning the reinforcing stimulus should follow the operant immediately. The rate of responding for a conditioned operant may jump dramatically over the preconditioned rate (operant level).

Operant level : The original, or preconditioned, rate of operant responding before any reinforcing stimuli have been introduced. If a rat happens to press the lever in a Skinner box four times an hour (without being reinforced), the operant level for that response is established at four per hour. Thus, the operant level is the rate at which the free operant is typically emitted prior to conditioning.

Positive reinforcement : A procedure that maintains or increases the rate of a response by presenting a stimulus (a positive reinforcer) following the response.

Preoperational stage : The second stage in Piaget's theory of cognitive development, in which the lack of logical operations forces children to make decisions bases on their perceptions.

Primary reinforcement : The process of using a stimulus that is reinforcing in the absence of any learning. Such stimuli as food and water are primary reinforcers.

Programmed instruction (PI) : PI is an arrangement of instructional material in a step-by-step sequence designed to lead the student to a specified goal. The material being presented is broken down into small steps called frames. There are two general approaches to programming: (*i*) linear programmes, in which all students go through the entire programme and the frames gradually increase in difficulty, and (*ii*) branched programmes, in which the student skips forward or backward in the programme (the order of the frame presentation varies) as a result of the success or failure experienced in responding. PI can be in book form, or it can be presented through the use of a teaching machine and/or computer. The concept of programmed instruction is credited to B.F. Skinner.

Psychoanalytic theory : This reveals the theory/method of studying and treating mental illness presented by Sigmund Freud. The theory attempts to give a rational explanation for irrational thoughts and responses. Psychoanalytic theory states (*i*) that all behaviour is determined by specific motives; (*ii*) that most human motives lie at the unconscious level, and therefore people are unaware of the reasons for most of their own behaviour; (*iii*) that neurotic symptoms result from an individual's inner conflicts; and (*iv*) that inner conflicts are a product of childhood trauma and anxiety. The technique is based on the therapist's revealing to the patient the source of his or her anxiety and helping the patient achieve insight and emotional release.

Puberty : The biological changes that lead to reproductive maturity. Its onset is identified by such factors as the growth of body hair, voice changes in males, and menstruation and breast development in females.

Punishment : A method for controlling behaviour through the use of aversive stimulation. In other words, punishment is a procedure in which an aversive stimulus is presented immediately following a response, resulting in a reduction in the rate of response. Punishment, though not itself causing the extinction of a conditioned response, does severely reduce the rate of responding while the punishment is in force. Punishment should not be confused with negative reinforcement.

Reinforcement : Any stimulus that increases the likelihood of a response's recurring. Reinforcement, as a Skinnerian concept, should not be confused with reward, feelings of pleasure, or any other concept with subjective of mentalistic overtones. Reinforcement may be used in either classical (respondent) or operant conditioning. In respondent condition the unconditioned stimulus serves as the reinforcement. In operant conditioning the presentation of any stimulus following the emitted response can be considered a reinforcement if it results in a higher response rate.

Schemata : Cognitive structures created through the abstraction of previous experience. Schemata function in the comprehension and recall of data and can aid learning or be responsible for many types distortion in recall.

Secondary reinforcement : A process that uses a stimulus that is not originally reinforcing but that acquires reinforcing properties when paired with a primary reinforcer. Money is a secondary reinforcer.

Self-actualization : Maslow's term for the psychological need to develop one's capabilities and potential in order to enhance personal growth. It refer to a person's constant striving to realise the potential within and to develop inherent talents and capabilities.

Self-concept : The total organisation of the perceptions individuals have of themselves.

Self-esteem : The value, or judgement, individuals place on their behaviour. Self-esteem and self-concept are often used interchangeably in educational literature.

Self-reinforcement : A procedure in which individuals reinforce their own behaviour.

Sensitive period : This is a time period when an organism is susceptible to a change in behaviour due to certain kinds of environmental stimulation. The sensitive periods typically occur early in the organism's life and tend to produce behaviour changes that are relatively long-lasting. The process of mother-infant bounding is said to occur only during the baby's first three days of life.

Short-term memory (STM) : In the information processing system, STM is the first of two main storage systems. Sometimes it is called working or active memory. Estimates of how long information may be retained in short-term memory vary from about twenty seconds to over a minute.

Social facilitation : The concept from the field of social psychology is used to explain the fact that in some circumstances individuals perform more quickly when in a group situation than when alone. Social facilitation is most pronounced in the case of fairly simple mechanical tasks. The more difficult and the more intellectual the task, the less the effect of social facilitation.

Social learning theory : Theory, proposed by Albert Bandura, suggests that a large part of what a person learns occurs through imitation or modelling. Bandura's major concern is with learning that takes place in the context of a social situation in which individuals come to modify behaviour as a result of how others in the group respond. Social learning does not require primary reinforcement.

Stimulus-response : A theory that stresses the importance of the build up of stimulus response associations in defining learning. Most behaviourists adhere to stimulus response learning theories, the major exception being E.C. Tolman. The leading stimulus response theorists are E.L. Thorndike, Ivan Pavlov, J.B. Watson, Edwin Guthrie, C.L. Hull, and B.F. Skinner. Stimulus response theorists stress the importance of nurture in the nature-nurture debate. Most theories of learning during the first half of the twentieth century were stimulus response theories. The cognitive-gestalt position, however, was not based on a stimulus-response theory.

Stimulus variety : Variation, at all sensory modes, of stimulus inputs. Stimulus variety was seen by many early-experience theorists as the crucial ingredient in intellectual development. The more the child hears, sees, and touches, the more he or she will want to hear, see, and touch and the more intellectual growth will occur.

Teaching machine : A device used to present an instructional programme one step (or frame) at a time. The student either writes in answers or presses a button corresponding to the correct alternative. The advantages of the teaching machine are that (*i*) the student can proceed at his or her own pace; (*ii*) the student receives immediate feedback; (*iii*) for many students the machines are intrinsically motivating.

Unconditioned response : An unconditioned response is any response that can be elicited automatically by the presentation of a certain stimulus, without any training or learning. The term is used in classical conditioning and in Ivan Pavlov's original experiment the unconditioned response was salivation to the stimulus of meat powder being placed in the dog's mouth.

Unconditioned stimulus : Any stimulus that will elicit a given response automatically, without any training or learning. The term is used in classical conditioning and in the case of Ivan Pavlov's own experiment, the unconditioned stimulus was meat powder placed in the dog's mouth.

Mathematics

SECTION-A

MATHEMATICS

1 Numbers and Numeric System

The Hindu-Arabic and International numeral systems make use of the ten basic digits: 0, 1, 2, 3, 4, 5, 6, 7, 8 and 9. A number is denoted by a group of digits, called numeral.

The place-value chart for the Hindu-Arabic Numeral is as follows:

Ten Crores	Crores	Ten Lakhs	Lakhs	Ten Thousands	Thousands	Hundreds	Tens	Ones

The number 789345126 can be read as:

"Seventy-eight crores, ninety-three lakhs, fourty-five thousands, one hundred twenty six."

The place-value chart for the International Numeral is as follows:

Billions	Hundred Millions	Ten Millions	Millions	One Hundred Thousands	Ten Thousands	Thousands	Tens	Ones

The number 123115027 can be read as:

"One hundred twenty three million one hundred fifteen thousands twenty seven."

PLACE VALUE AND FACE VALUE OF A DIGIT

- **Place Value :** Numbers are written by using the symbols 0, 1, 2, 3, 4, 5, 6, 7, 8, 9 called digits, with each digit getting a value depending on the place it occupies. This value assigned to the digit due to its placement, is called place value. For example, in the number 56, digit 6 is placed in unit's place and 5 in ten's place. Therefore, place value of 6 in 56 is $6 \times 1 = 6$ and that of 5 is $5 \times 10 = 50$.
- **Face Value :** In a number face value of a digit is the digit itself. For example, in 42, the face value of digit 2 is 2 and that of digit 4 is 4.

Note: The place value of 0 in any number is 0, at whatever place it may be.

VARIOUS TYPES OF NUMBERS

- **Natural Numbers :** Counting numbers are called natural numbers. Thus 1, 2, 3, 4, 5, 6, 7, 8, ... are called natural numbers.
- **Whole Numbers :** The number '0' together with the natural numbers gives us the numbers which are called whole numbers.

  Thus 0, 1, 2, 3, 4, 5, 6, ... etc. are whole numbers.
- **Integers :** The negative numbers together with the whole numbers are called integers. Thus, ..., –3, –2, –1, 0, 1, 2, 3, ... are all integers.

  1, 2, 3, 4, ... are called positive integer.

  –1, –2, –3, –4, ... are called negative integer.

  The number 0 is simply an integer. It is neither positive nor negative.

- **Even Numbers :** All those numbers which are exactly divisible by 2, are called even numbers.

  Thus, 2, 4, 6, 8, 10, 12, 28, 32 etc. are even numbers.

- **Odd Numbers :** All those numbers which are not exactly divisible by 2, are called odd numbers.

  Thus, 1, 3, 5, 7, 9, 19, 21 etc. are called odd numbers.

- **Prime Numbers :** The numbers which have only two factors, 1 and the number itself are called prime numbers. Thus, 2, 3, 5, 7, 11, 19, 23, 31, ... etc. are called prime numbers.

- **Composite Numbers :** The numbers which have more than two factors are called composite numbers. Thus, 4, 9, 15, 18, 27, ... are called composite numbers.

KEY POINTS

☛ 1 is neither a prime nor a composite.

☛ 2 is the lowest prime number.

☛ 2 is the only even prime number.

- **Co-Primes :** Two natural numbers a and b are said to be co-primes if their H.C.F. is 1. Thus, (2, 3), (4, 5), (7, 9), (8, 11), etc. are pairs of co-primes.

- **Twin Primes:** Two consecutive odd prime numbers are called twin primes.

  Example: (*i*) 3 and 5, (*ii*) 5 and 7, (*iii*) 17 and 19.

TEST OF DIVISIBILITY

- **Divisibility by 2 :** A number is divisible by 2 if its units digit is 0, 2, 4, 6, 8. For example each of the numbers 130, 244, 566, 278 ...... is divisible by 2.

- **Divisibility by 3 :** A number is divisible by 3 if the sum of its digits is divisible by 3. For example: 89642 is divisible by 3. because sum of digits (8 + 9 + 6 + 4 + 2) = 27 which is divisible by 3.

  In the number 234561, the sum of digits (2 + 3 + 4 + 5 + 6 + 1) = 21 which is divisible by 3. Hence the given number is also divisible by 3.

- **Divisibility by 4 :** A number is divisible by 4 if the number formed by its last two digits is divisible by 4. For example : 634728 is divisible by 4 because 28 is divided by 4.

- **Divisibility by 5 :** A number is divisible by 5 if its unit's digit is either 0 or 5. For example, each of the numbers 100, 205, 12340, 72345 is divisible by 5 because unit's digit in each of these numbers is either 0 or 5.

- **Divisibility by 6 :** A number is divisible by 6 if it is divisible by both 2 and 3. For example : 243534 is divisible by 6 because its last digit is 4 which is divisible by 2 and sum of digits 2 + 4 + 3 + 5 + 3 + 4 = 21 which is divisible by 3. Hence the given number is divisible by 6.

- **Divisibility by 8 :** A number is divisible by 8 if the number formed by hundred's, ten's and unit's digit of the given number is divisible by 8. For example : In the number 16789352, the number formed by last three digits, namely 352 is divisible by 8.

  ∴ 16789352 is divisible by 8.

- **Divisibility by 9 :** A number is divisible by 9 only when the sum of its digits is divisible by 9. For example : In the number 246591, the sum of digits (2 + 4 + 6 + 5 + 9 + 1) = 27, which is divisible by 9.

  ∴ 246591 is divisible by 9.

- **Divisibility by 10 :** A number is divisible by 10 if its unit's digit is zero. For example, each of the numbers 50, 80, 1310, 1400 is divisible by 10 because unit's digit in each of these numbers is 0 (zero).

- **Divisibility by 11 :** A number is divisible by 11 if the difference between the sum of its digits at odd places and the sum of its digits at even places is either 0 or a number divisible by 11.

  Consider the number 29435417.

  (Sum of its digits at odd places) – (Sum of its digits at even places)

  = (7 + 4 + 3 + 9) – (1 + 5 + 4 + 2)

  = (23 – 12) = 11

  Which is divisible by 11.

  ∴ 29435417 is divisible by 11.

SOLVED EXAMPLES

Example 1 : What is the sum of first four prime numbers?

Solution : Sum of first four prime numbers = 2 + 3 + 5 + 7 = 17.

Example 2 : What is the number of prime factors of $(6)^{10} \times (7)^{17} \times (55)^{27}$?

Solution : $(6)^{10} \times (7)^{17} \times (55)^{27} = 2^{10} \times 3^{10} \times 7^{17} \times 5^{27} \times 11^{27}$

∴ No. of prime factors = 10 + 10 + 17 + 27 + 27 = 91

Example 3 : Is 979 a prime number?

Solution : The approximate square root of 979 is 32.

Prime numbers less than 32 are 2, 3, 5, 7, 11, 13, 17, 19, 23, 29, 31. We observe that 979 is divisible by 11, so it is not a prime number.

Example 4 : What is the sum of all primes between 70 and 100?

Solution : Prime numbers between 70 and 100 are 71, 73, 79, 83, 89 and 97.

$\therefore$ Sum of $71 + 73 + 79 + 83 + 89 + 97 = 492$.

Example 5 : What is the difference in face value and local value of 5 in 7501?

Solution : The local value of 5 in 7501 = 500 and intrinsic value of 5 in 7501 = 5.

$\therefore$ Required difference = 500 – 5 = 495.

Example 6 : Which one of the following is the pair of twin primes?

(*i*) 5, 11 (*ii*) 7, 11 (*iii*) 11, 17 (*iv*) 1, 3 (*v*) 17, 19

Solution : Twin primes are the pairs of those prime numbers whose difference is 2. In the given alternatives, (17, 19) is such a pair of two prime numbers whose difference is 2.

Example 7 : What is at the unit place of $(742)^{75}$?

Solution : Here, $N^n = (742)^{75}$

Dividing the index 75 by 4 we have remainder 3.

$\therefore$ $(742)^{75}$ will have the same number at the unit place of $(742)^3$ and the number at the unit place of $(742)^3$ is 8 because, $2 \times 2 \times 2 = 8$.

Example 8 : A number when divided by 899 gives a remainder of 63. If the same number is divided by 29, then what will be the remainder?

Solution : Number $= D \times Q + R$

$= 899 \times K + 63$

$= 31 \times 29 \times K + 29 \times 2 + 5$

$= 29\,(31K + 2) + 5$

$\therefore$ The remainder when the number is divided by 29 is 5 Ans.

Example 9 : If 30 x 0103 is divisible by 11, then, what is the value of x?

Solution : If a number is divisible by 11, the difference between the sum of the digits at the even places and sum of digits at odd places should be zero or a multiple of 11.

The sum of the digits in the even places = 0 and the sum of the digits in the odd places

$= 3 + x + 1 + 3$

$= 7 + x$

$\therefore \quad (7 + x) - 0 = 11$

$x = 11 - 7 = 4.$

Example 10 : In a division sum, the divisor is ten times the quotient and five times the remainder. If the remainder is 46 determine the dividend.

Solution : Let the quotient be Q and the remainder be R.

According to the question,

Divisor $= 5 \times 46 = 230$

Quotient $= \dfrac{230}{10} = 23$

$\therefore$ Dividend = Divisor × Quotient + Remainder

$= 230 \times 23 + 46$

$= 5290 + 46 = 5336.$

EXERCISE

1. Find the value of Z for which the number 417Z8 is divisible by 9.

A. 7 B. 9 C. 3 D. 6

2. If $2160 = 2^a \times 3^b \times 5^c$, then find the value of $3^a \times 2^{-b} \times 5^{-c}$.

A. $\frac{81}{40}$ B. $\frac{37}{39}$ C. $\frac{1}{2}$ D. 0

3. On simplification $\{(2^{-1})\}^{-1}$, the number will be:

(*a*) Prime number (*b*) Even number
(*c*) Multiple of 2 (*d*) Odd number

A. (*a*), (*c*), (*d*) B. (*a*), (*b*), (*d*)
C. (*a*), (*b*), (*c*) D. (*b*), (*c*), (*d*)

4. Unit digit of the multiplication of $(2153)^{167}$ is:

A. 7 B. 9 C. 1 D. 3

5. The numbers divisible by 8 are:

(*a*) 5240 (*b*) 5220 (*c*) 97128 (*d*) 97124

A. (*a*), (*c*) and (*d*)
B. (*a*) and (*c*)
C. (*a*) and (*b*)
D. (*b*) and (*c*)

6. Which of the following rational number **does not** lie between $\frac{3}{5}$ and $\frac{4}{5}$?

A. $\frac{7}{10}$ B. $\frac{19}{30}$ C. $\frac{2}{3}$ D. $\frac{16}{30}$

7. If $2352 = 2^x \times 3^y \times 7^z$, then the value of $x + y + z$ is:

A. 8 B. 5 C. 7 D. 9

8. The number of even divisors of 100 will be:

A. 7 B. 6 C. 5 D. 8

9. If 3^{1989} is divided by 7, then remainder is:

A. 8 B. 7 C. 6 D. 10

10. If $a * b = a^2 + b^2 - ab$ for all natural numbers a and b, then the value of $9 * 10$ is:

A. 181 B. 90 C. 91 D. 182

11. If x and y are non-zero real numbers, then $x^2 + xy + y^2$

A. is always positive

B. is always negative

C. takes the value zero for some x and y

D. takes both positive and negative values

12. If for any two natural numbers a and b, $a^b = 125$, then b^a is:

A. 243 B. 241 C. 242 D. 247

13. The least number, divisible by all the natural numbers from 1 to 10, is

A. 1000 B. 5040 C. 2520 D. 100

14. The digit of unit place in $(378 \times 236 \times 459 \times 312)$ will be:

A. 6 B. 8 C. 2 D. 4

15. If 604__6 is divisible by 11, then the integer in the blank space is:

A. 1 B. 3 C. 7 D. 5

16. A two-digit number is such that the product of its digits is 6. If 9 is added to the number, the digits are reversed. The number is:

A. 16 B. 35 C. 43 D. 23

17. When 121012 is divided by 12, the remainder is:

A. 0 B. 2 C. 3 D. 4

18. The smallest prime number is:

A. 2 B. 3 C. 5 D. 7

19. The smallest number of four digits is:

A. 1001 B. 0001 C. 0010 D. 1000

20. The largest number of four digits is:

A. 1000 B. 9000 C. 9009 D. 9999

21. The product of two prime numbers is a:

A. prime number B. even number

C. odd number D. composite number

22. Prime factors of a number are 2, 2, 3, 7. The number is:

A. 14 B. 41 C. 48 D. 84

23. The number which when added to itself 10 times gives 264. The number is:

A. 20 B. 22 C. 24 D. 26

24. The difference between the squares of two consecutive numbers is 25. The numbers are:

A. 11, 12 B. 12, 13 C. 15, 14 D. 14, 13

25. If the number $(10^n - 1)$ is divisible by 11, then n is:

A. odd number B. even number

C. any number D. multiple of 11

26. Divide 48 into two parts such that 7 times the first part added to 5 times the second part is 246. Find the first part.

A. 2 B. 3 C. 4 D. 5

27. The sum of a number and its reciprocal is thrice the difference of the number and its reciprocal. Find the number.

A. $\sqrt{2}$ B. $\sqrt{3}$ C. $\sqrt{5}$ D. $\sqrt{7}$

28. Ram eats 8 bananas in the morning, 5 in the afternoon and 2 in the evening. How many dozens of bananas does he eat in a day.

A. $1\frac{1}{4}$ B. $\frac{1}{4}$ C. $\frac{3}{13}$ D. $14\frac{17}{30}$

29. The least value of K when 7K25 is divisible by 5 is:

A. 0 B. 1 C. 2 D. 3

30. A reception party was held in a five star hotel and the charges per plate were as many rupees as the number of plates used. The total charges came to be ₹ 15129. How many rupees were charged per plate?

A. 120 B. 121 C. 122 D. 123

31. The unit's digit in the product $(7^{71} \times 6^{59} \times 3^{65})$ is:

A. 6 B. 4 C. 2 D. 1

32. If the number 357 ★ 25 ★ is divisible by both 3 and 5, then the missing digits in the unit's place and thousandth place respectively are:

A. 0, 4 B. 5, 4 C. 5, 6 D. 0, 6

33. The difference between the squares of two consecutive odd integers is always divisible by:

A. 8 B. 7 C. 6 D. 3

34. Find the number which is nearest to 457 and exactly divisible by 11.

A. 462 B. 460 C. 451 D. 450

35. What least number must be subtracted from 427398 so that remaining number is divisible by 15?

A. 11 B. 6 C. 5 D. 3

36. The greatest number by which the product of three consecutive multiples of 3 is always divisible is:

A. 243 B. 162 C. 81 D. 54

37. In a division of a question with zero remainder, a candidate took 12 as divisor instead of 21. The quotient obtained by him was 35. The correct quotient is:

A. 20 B. 13 C. 12 D. 0

38. The difference between two numbers is 1365. When the larger number is divided by the smaller one, the quotient is 6 and the remainder is 15. The smaller number is:

A. 360 B. 295 C. 270 D. 240

39. When a number is divided by 31, the remainder is 29. When the same number is divided by 16, what will be the remainder?

A. 15 B. 13
C. 11 D. Data inadequate

40. When a number divided by 6 leaves a remainder 3. When the square of the same number is divided by 6, the remainder is:

A. 3 B. 2 C. 1 D. 0

ANSWERS WITH EXPLANATIONS

1. (A): If sum of all digits of any number is divisible by 9 then, the number is divisible by 9

$\because$ 417Z8 is divisible by 9

$\therefore$ 4 + 1 + 7 + Z + 8 is divisible by 9

$\therefore$ 20 + Z is divisible by 9

$$Z = 7$$

then 27 is divisible by 9.

2. (A): Given, $2160 = 2^a \times 3^b \times 5^c$

$\Rightarrow \quad 2^4 \times 3^3 \times 5^1 = 2^a \times 3^b \times 5^c$

$\therefore a = 4, b = 3, c = 1$

$\therefore \quad 3^a \times 2^{-b} \times 5^{-c} = 3^4 \times 2^{-3} \times 5^{-1}$

$$= \frac{3^4}{2^3 \times 5^1} = \frac{81}{40}.$$

3. (C): $\{(2^{-1})\}^{-1} = \left\{\frac{1}{2}\right\}^{-1}$

$$= \left(\frac{1}{2}\right)^{-1} = \frac{1}{2^{-1}} = 2$$

The number (2) will be

(*a*) Prime number (*b*) Even number

(*c*) Multiple of 2

4. (A): $\because \ (2153)^{167} = (2153)^{41 \times 4 + 3}$

$$= \{(2153)^4\}^{41} \times (2153)^3$$

Unit digit of $\{(2153)^4\}41 = 1$

and unit digit of $(2153)^3 = 7$

$\therefore$ Unit digit of the multiplication of $(2153)^{167}$

$$= 1 \times 7 = 7.$$

5. (B): If three digits from right side of any number are zero or multiple of 8 then, the number will be divisible by 8

So, (*i*) 5240 and (*iii*) 97128 are divisible by 8.

6. (D): $\because \ \frac{3}{5} = 0.6, \ \frac{4}{5} = 0.8$

(*a*) $\frac{7}{10} = 0.7 \Rightarrow 0.6 < 0.7 < 0.8$

(*b*) $\frac{19}{30} = 0.633 \Rightarrow 0.6 < 0.633 < 0.8$

(*c*) $\frac{2}{3} = 0.666 \Rightarrow 0.6 < 0.666 < 0.8$

(*d*) $\frac{16}{30} = 0.533 \Rightarrow 0.533 < 0.6$

$\therefore \ \frac{16}{30}$, will not be in between rational number $\frac{3}{5}$ and $\frac{4}{5}$.

7. (C):

2	2352
2	1176
2	588
2	294
3	147
7	49
7	7
	1

$$2352 = 2 \times 2 \times 2 \times 2 \times 3 \times 7 \times 7$$
$$= (2)^4 \times (3)^1 \times (7)^2$$

Compare with $2^x \times 3^y \times 7^z$, we get

$$x = 4, y = 1, z = 2$$

$\therefore \quad x + y + z = 4 + 1 + 2 = 7$

8. (B):

2	100
2	50
5	25
5	5
	1

$$100 = 2 \times 2 \times 5 \times 5$$
$$100 = (2)^2 \times (5)^2$$

Total divisor of 100 = (2 + 1) (2 + 1)

$$= 3 \times 3 = 9$$

Total odd divisor of 100 = (2 + 1) = 3

Then, Total even divisor of 100 = 9 – 3 = 6

9. (C): $\frac{3^{1989}}{7} = \frac{\left((3)^3\right)^{663}}{7} = \frac{(27)^{663}}{7}$

$= (-1)^{663} = -1$

So, Remainder = 7 – 1 = 6

10. (C): Given,

$a * b = a^2 + b^2 - ab$

$9 * 10 = (9)^2 + (10)^2 - 9 \times 10$

$= 81 + 100 - 90$

$= 181 - 90 = 91$

11. (A): $x^2 + xy + y^2 = x^2 + y^2 + 2xy - xy$

$= (x + y)^2 - xy$

$\because \quad (x + y)^2 \geq 4xy \qquad \left[\frac{x+y}{2} \geq \sqrt[2]{xy}\right]$

The value of $(x + y)^2$ always be positive whose value will be bigger than xy.

So, $x^2 + xy + y^2$ will always be positive.

12. (A): Given, a and b are two natural numbers.

$(a)^b = 125$

$(a^b) = (125)^1$	or $(a^b) = (5)^3$
$a = 125, b = 1$	$a = 5, b = 3$
$(b)^a = (1)^{125} = 1$	$(b)^a = (3)^5 = 243$
which is not given in options.	which is given in options.

13. (C): The smallest number, which is divisible by 1 to 10 natural numbers will be the LCM of number from 1 to 10.

1 = 1
2 = 1 × 2
3 = 1 × 3
4 = 1 × 2 × 2
5 = 1 × 5
6 = 1 × 2 × 3
7 = 1 × 7
8 = 1 × 2 × 2 × 2
9 = 1 × 3 × 3
10 = 1 × 2 × 5

L.C.M = 1 × 2 × 2 × 2 × 3 × 3 × 5 × 7

= 2520

14. (D): The digit of unit place in
378 × 236 × 459 × 312

= 8 × 6 × 9 × 2

= 864 = 4

Hence, unit place = 4.

15. (D): 604[5]6 is divisible by 11

$\therefore$ 6 + 4 + 6 – (0 + 5) = 16 – 5 = 11

Hence, the integer in the blank space = 5.

16. (D): Let ten's place digit number = x and unit's place digit number = y

$\therefore$ Number = $10x + y$

According to the question,

$xy = 6$

$10x + y + 9 = 10y + x$

$\Rightarrow 9x - 9y = -9$

$\Rightarrow x - y = -1$

$\Rightarrow x = y - 1$

$\because xy = 6$

$\Rightarrow (y - 1)y = 6$

$\Rightarrow y^2 - y - 6 = 0$

$\Rightarrow y^2 - 3y + 2y - 6 = 0$

$\Rightarrow y(y - 3) + 2(y - 3) = 0$

$\Rightarrow (y - 3)(y + 2) = 0$

$\Rightarrow y = 3$ or $y = -2$

$\therefore y = 3$

$x = 3 - 1 = 2$

$\therefore$ Number = $10x + y$

$= 10 \times 2 + 3 = 23.$

17. (D):

```
       10084
12)121012(
     12
    ×101
      96
     ×52
      48
       4
```

Hence, the remainder = 4.

18. (A): The smallest prime number = 2.

19. (D): The smallest number of four digits is 1000.

20. (D): The largest number of four digits is 9999.

21. (D): The product to two prime numbers is always a composite number.

22. (D): The number is equal to the product of prime factors.

$\therefore$ 2 × 2 × 3 × 7 = 84 is the required number.

23. (C): Let the number is x.

Then, $x + 10x = 264$

$\Rightarrow 11x = 264$

$\therefore x = \frac{264}{11} = 24$

24. (B): Let the numbers are x and $(x + 1)$

$\therefore \quad (x + 1)^2 - x^2 = 25$

$\Rightarrow \quad x^2 + 1 + 2x - x^2 = 25$

$\Rightarrow \quad 2x + 1 = 25$

$\Rightarrow \quad 2x = 25 - 1 = 24$

$\therefore \quad x = \frac{24}{2} = 12$

$\therefore \quad x + 1 = 12 + 1 = 13$

Hence, the numbers are 12, 13.

25. (B): n is even number.

26. (B): Let the first part $= x$ then 2nd part $= (48 - x)$

By question, $7x + 5(48 - x) = 246$

$\Rightarrow \quad 2x = 246 - 240$

$\therefore \quad x = 3$

27. (A): Let the no. $= x$ then its reciprocal $= \frac{1}{x}$

By the question, $\left(x + \frac{1}{x}\right) = 3\left(x - \frac{1}{x}\right)$

$\Rightarrow \quad \frac{x^2 + 1}{x} = \frac{3(x^2 - 1)}{x}$

$\Rightarrow \quad x^2 + 1 = 3x^2 - 3$

$\Rightarrow \quad 3x^2 - x^2 = 3 + 1$

$\therefore \quad x = \sqrt{2}$.

28. (A): Total dozen of bananas Ram eats in a day

$= \frac{8}{12} + \frac{5}{12} + \frac{2}{12} = \frac{15}{12} = 1\frac{1}{4}$

29. (A): A number is divisible by 5 if its last digit (the units digit) is either 0 of 5.

In the number 7K25, the last digit is 5.

K is the single digit.

∴ Among the given options (0, 1, 2 and 3), the smallest (least) possible value for K is 0.

30. (D): Let the no. of plates $= x$

then cost of one plate $= x$

∴ Cost of total plate $= x \times x = x^2$

By the question $x^2 = 15129$

$\therefore \quad x = \sqrt{15129} = \sqrt{123 \times 123} = 123.$

31. (B): $(7^{71} \times 6^{59} \times 3^{65}) = [7^{(17 \times 4 + 3)} \times 6^{(14 \times 4 + 3)} \times 3^{(16 \times 4 + 1)}]$

Hence, required digit = Unit digit in $(3 \times 6 \times 3) = 4$

32. (C): 357 ★ 25 ★

For divisible by 5, the last digit must be either 0 or 5.

If last digit is 0, then other required digit will be 2 or 5 or 8

Hence, the numbers are (0, 2) or (0, 5) or (0, 8)

If last digit is 5, then other required digit will be 0 or 3 or 6 or 9

Hence, the numbers are (5, 0) or (5, 3) or (5, 6) or (5, 9)

So, correct option is (C)

33. (A): Let two consecutive odd numbers are $(2n + 1)$ and $(2n + 3)$

Hence, $(2n + 3)^2 - (2n + 1)^2 = 4n^2 + 12n + 9 - 4n^2 - 4n - 1$

$= 8n + 8 = 8(n + 1)$

which is always divisible by 8.

34. (A): The numbers 451 and 462 are divisible by 11, in which 462 is nearest to 457.

35. (D): $427398 = 15 \times 28493 + 3$

Hence, required number to be subtracted = 3

36. (B): Let the three consecutive multiples of 3 are $3n$, $3(n + 1)$, $3(n + 2)$

Now, $3n \times 3(n + 1) \times 3(n + 2) = 27n\,(n^2 + 3n + 2)$

Putting, $\quad n = 1$ then, $27 \times 1\,(12 + 3 \times 1 + 2)$

$= 27 \times 6 = 162$

Hence, required number = 162

37. (A): The number $= 12 \times 35 = 420$

Hence, correct quotient $= 420 \div 21 = 20$

38. (C): Here, $(x + 1365) = 6x + 15$

$\Rightarrow \quad 5x = 1350$

$\therefore \quad x = \frac{1350}{5} = 270$

Hence, the smaller number = 270

39. (D): The number $= 31x + 29$

Here, given data is inadequate.

40. (A): The number $= 6x + 3$

Now, $\quad (6x + 3)^2 = 36x^2 + 36x + 9$

$= (36x^2 + 36x + 6) + 3$

$= 6(6x^2 + 6x + 1) + 3$

Hence, required remainder = 3

2 Operations on Numbers
(Addition, Subtraction, Multiplication and Division)

When zero is included with the set of natural numbers, it is called the set of whole numbers. It is denoted by W.

Whole numbers : W = {0, 1, 2, 3, 4, ...}

In this chapter we will read the four basic operations with whole numbers : addition, subtraction, multiplication and division.

ADDITION

Addition is the process of calculating the total of two or more numbers or amounts. The numbers being added are called addends, and the result is called the sum.

For example : $3 + 5 + 8 = 16$

$10 + 15 + 6 = 31$

Properties of Addition

(*i*) Addition of whole numbers is commutative. If a and b any two whole numbers, then

$$a + b = b + a$$

Example: $4 + 6 = 6 + 4$.

(*ii*) Addition of whole numbers is associative. If a, b, c are any three whole numbers

then, $(a + b) + c = a + (b + c)$

Example: $(6 + 4) + 5 = 6 + (4 + 5)$

(*iii*) The sum of any whole number and 0 is the whole number itself.

If a is any whole number,

then, $a + 0 = 0 + a = a$

Example: $6 + 0 = 0 + 6 = 6$

0 is called the identity element of addition (or additive identity) of whole numbers.

(*iv*) The sum of two integers is always an integer.

SUBTRACTION

Subtraction is the process of finding the difference between two numbers by removing the value of one (called the subtrahend) from another (called the minuend). The result is known as the difference.

Properties of Subtraction

Such that

(*i*) Not Commutative $a - b \neq b - a$,

(*ii*) Not Associative $a - (b - c) \neq (a - b) - c$

and

(*iii*) Not Identity $a - 0 \neq 0 - a \neq a$

(although $a - 0 = a$ is true)

(*iv*) The difference of two integerss is always an integer.

For example : Subtract 51 from 79.

Solution : Here, minuend = 79 and subtrahend = 51

$$79 - 51 = 28$$

Thus subtraction represents the idea of "undoing" addition.

In general, if $a + b = c$,

then $c - a = b$ and

$c - b = a$.

For example: $58 - 36 = 22$.

MULTIPLICATION

In a multiplication operation, the number that is being multiplied is called the multiplicand, and the number that multiplies it is known as multiplier. And, the result of multiplication is called product.

For example:

$3 \times 4 = 12$ or $4 + 4 + 4 = 12$

$4 \times 3 = 12$ or $3 + 3 + 3 + 3 = 12$

Properties of Multiplication

- The product of two whole numbers is again a whole number. (Closure property of multiplication)

- Multiplication of whole numbers is commutative. If a and b are any two whole numbers, then $a \times b = b \times a$
  Example : $8 \times 6 = 6 \times 8$
- Multiplication of whole numbers is associative. If a, b, c are any three whole numbers, then $a \times (b \times c) = (a \times b) \times c$
  Example: $6 \times (2 \times 4) = (6 \times 2) \times 4$
- The product of 1 and any whole number is the whole number itself. If a is any whole number, then
  $a \times 1 = 1 \times a = a$
  Example : $8 \times 1 = 1 \times 8 = 8$
  1 is called the identity element for multiplication of whole numbers (or the multiplicative identity).
- Multiplication of whole number is distributive over addition. (Distributive property)
  If a, b, c are any three whole numbers, then $a \times (b + c) = a \times b + a \times c$
  Example: $4 \times (5 + 6) = 4 \times 5 + 4 \times 6$

DIVISION

In division, the number that is being divided is known as the dividend. The number that divides it is called the divisor. The result of the division is the quotient, and any amount left after the division is the remainder.

Properties of Division

(*i*) $a \div b \neq b \div a$

(*ii*) $(a \div b) \div c \neq a \div (b \div c)$

(*iii*) The quotient of two integers is not always an integer (e.g. $1 \div 2 = 0.5$)

For example: $32 \div 8 = 4$

Since $32 - 8 - 8 - 8 - 8 = 0$

Division is more commonly thought of as the inverse operation for multiplication.

For example:

$32 \div 8 = 4$

since $4 \times 8 = 32$

$32 \div 4 = 8$

since $8 \times 4 = 32$

In general, if $a \times b = c$, then

$c \div a = b$

and $c \div b = a$

Example: Divide 240 by 16

```
16) 240 (15
    16
    ×80
     80
      ×
```

Thus, $240 \div 16 = 15$

We can say that quotient is 15 and remainder is 0.

An important formula in respect of division of whole numbers

$$\text{Dividend} = \text{Divisor} \times \text{Quotient} + \text{Remainder}$$

$$\text{Divisor} = \frac{\text{Dividend} - \text{Remainder}}{\text{Quotient}}$$

$$\text{Quotient} = \frac{\text{Dividend} - \text{Remainder}}{\text{Divisor}}$$

Things to remember while solving problems on whole numbers:

(*i*) Sum of numbers from 1 to $n = \frac{n(n+1)}{2}$

(*ii*) Sum of odd numbers from 1 to n = (Number of odd numbers)^2

(*iii*) Number of odd numbers from 1 to $n = \left(\frac{\text{Last odd number} + 1}{2}\right)$.

(*iv*) Number of even numbers from 1 to $n = \left(\frac{\text{Last even number}}{2}\right)$

(*v*) Sum of even numbers from 1 to n = Number of even numbers × (Number of even numbers + 1)

SOLVED EXAMPLES

Example 1 : Add 6367402 from 547639.

Solution :

```
  6367402
+  547639
  6915041
```

∴ The sum of the given numbers = 6915041.

Example 2 : Subtract 52681 from 97432.

Solution :

```
  97432
 –52687
  44751
```

∴ 97432 – 52681 = 44751.

Example 3 : Multiply 546 by 100.

Solution : To multiply a given number by 100, insert two zeros on the right of the given number as:

$\therefore$ 546 × 100 = 54600.

Example 4 : Multiply 5672 by 746.

Solution :

```
      5 6 7 2
      × 7 4 6
    ---------
      3 4 0 3 2   ← (5672 × 6)
    2 2 6 8 8×    ← (5672 × 4)
  3 9 7 0 4××     ← (5672 × 7)
  -----------
  4 2 3 1 3 1 2   ← (addition)
```

Example 5 : Divide 37568 by 14.

Solution : Dividend = 37568 and Divisor = 14.

```
14) 37568 (2683
   -28
   ---
     95
    -84
    ---
     116
    -112
    ----
       48
      -42
      ---
        6
```

$\therefore$ Quotient = 2683 and Remainder = 6.

EXERCISE

1. Which of the following is not equal to 24?
   A. 18 + (13 –7) B. (12 – 4) + (13 – 5)
   C. (11 – 3) + 16 D. (14 – 5) + (19 – 4)
2. In a division sum, it the divisor, quotient and remainder are 54, 14 and 7 respectively, then the dividend is:
   A. 803 B. 753 C. 763 D. 767
3. The product of two numbers is 980. If one number is five times the other, the smaller number is:
   A. 14 B. 20 C. 28 D. 35
4. The product of two numbers is 3136. If one number is four times the other, the greater number is:
   A. 96 B. 108 C. 112 D. 128
5. On dividing 17662 by a certain number, the quotient is 78 and the remainder is 34, the divisor is:
   A. 221 B. 226 C. 228 D. 234
6. When a certain number is multiplied by 13, the product consists entirely of the digit 8. What is the smallest such number?
   A. 68376 B. 68888 C. 68686 D. 68876
7. When (–1) is multiplied by itself 40 times, the product is:
   A. 40 B. –40 C. –1 D. 1
8. When (–1) is multiplied by itself 25 times, the product is:
   A. 1 B. –1 C. –25 D. 25
9. If 9587 – A = 7429 – 4358, then what is the value of A?
   A. 6516 B. 5616 C. 6156 D. 6616
10. If 7589 – P = 3434, then find the value of P.
    A. 4242 B. 4155 C. 1123 D. 11023
11. On dividing 12401 by a certain number, we get 76 as quotient and 13 as remainder. What is the divisor?
    A. 163 B. 165 C. 173 D. 153
12. On dividing a certain number by 342, we get 47 as remainder. If the same number is divided by 18, what will be the remainder?
    A. 8 B. 9 C. 10 D. 11
13. 8001 + 7909 + 5190 = ?
    A. 21100 B. 20100 C. 21090 D. 20090
14. What is the product of 981 and 100?
    A. 0 B. 981 C. 9810 D. 98100
15. Find the product 797 × 0.
    A. 797 B. 0
    C. 7970 D. None of these
16. The value of the following expression is:
    6784 × 53 + 6784 × 47
    A. 783700 B. 678840 C. 678400 D. 678040
17. Find the following product:
    637 × 105
    A. 66785 B. 66985 C. 66815 D. 66885
18. Find the following product:
    532 × 1002
    A. 533064 B. 532064 C. 534064 D. 533024
19. 55555 + 5665 + 565 – ? = 4334 + 434
    A. 57017 B. 57007 C. 56017 D. 58017
20. What is the product of 23208 × 254 × 0 × 126?
    A. 15351470 B. 189765
    C. 0 D. 232080

ANSWERS WITH EXPLANATIONS

1. (B): (A) 18 + (13 – 7) = 18 + 6 = 24
(B) (12 – 4) + (13 – 5) = 8 + 8 = 16
(C) (11 – 3) + 16 = 8 + 16 = 24
(D) (14 – 5) + (19 – 4) = 9 + 15 = 24
Hence, option (B) is not equal to 24.

2. (C): Given: divisor = 54, quotient = 14, remainder = 7
∴ Dividend = (Divisor × Quotient) + Remainder
= (54 × 14) + 7 = 756 + 7 = 763.

3. (A): Let the smaller number be x.
Then, the greater number is $5x$
∴ $x \times 5x = 980 \Rightarrow 5x^2 = 980$
$\Rightarrow x^2 = 196 \Rightarrow x = \sqrt{196} = 14$
Hence, the smaller number = x = 14.

4. (C): Let the smaller number be x
Then, the greater number is $4x$
∴ $x \times 4x = 3136 \Rightarrow 4x^2 = 3136$
$$x^2 = \frac{3136}{4} = 784$$
$$\Rightarrow x = \sqrt{784} = 28$$
Hence, the greater number = $4x = 4 \times 28 = 112$.

5. (B): $\text{Divisor} = \dfrac{\text{Divident} - \text{Remainder}}{\text{Quotient}}$
$$\therefore \text{Divisor} = \frac{17662 - 34}{78} = \frac{17628}{78} = 226$$

6. (A): It is clear that, we keep on dividing 8888 ..... by 13 till we get 0 as remainder.

```
      68376
13 ) 888888....
      78
      108
      104
       48
       39
        98
        91
         78
         78
          ×
```

Hence, the required number is 68376.

7. (D): (–1) × (–1) × (–1) × (–1) × ..... 40 times
$= (-1)^{40} = 1$
$$\left[\because (-1)^n = \begin{cases} 1, \text{ when } n \text{ is even} \\ -1, \text{ when } n \text{ is odd} \end{cases}\right]$$

8. (B): (–1) × (–1) × (–1) × (–1) × ..... 25 times
$= (-1)^{25} = -1$
$$\left[\because (-1)^n = \begin{cases} 1, \text{ when } n \text{ is even} \\ -1, \text{ when } n \text{ is odd} \end{cases}\right]$$

9. (A): 9587 – A = 7429 – 4358
⇒ 9587 + 4358 – 7429 = A
⇒ 13945 – 7429 = A ⇒ 6516 = A
∴ A = 6516.

10. (B): 7589 – P = 3434
⇒ 7589 – 3434 = P ⇒ 4155 = P
∴ P = 4155

11. (A): Divisor × Quotient + Remainder = Dividend
$$\therefore \text{Divisor} = \frac{\text{Dividend} - \text{Remainder}}{\text{Quotient}}$$
$$= \frac{12401 - 13}{76} = \frac{12388}{76} = 163.$$

12. (D): Suppose that on dividing the given number by 342, we get
Quotient = K and remainder = 47
Then, Number = 342 × K + 47
Divide by 18 = (18 × 19K) + (18 × 2) + 11
= 18 (19K + 2) + 11
Hence, the number when divided by 18 gives remainder = 11.

13. (A): 8001 + 7909 + 5190 = 21100

14. (D): To multiply a given number by 100, insert two zeroes on the right of the given number.
Hence, 981 × 100 = 98100.

15. (B): Multiplying a number by 0 makes the product equal to zero.
∴ 797 × 0 = 0.

16. (C): Using the property, $a \times b + a \times c = a \times (b + c)$, we get
6784 × 53 + 6784 × 47 = 6784 × (53 + 47)
= 6784 × 100 = 678400.

17. (D): 637 × 105 = 637 × (100 + 5)
= 637 × 100 + 637 × 5 = 63700 + 3185 = 66885.

18. (A): 532 × 1002 = 532 × (1000 + 2)
= 532 × 1000 + 532 × 2 = 532000 + 1064 = 533064.

19. (A): 55555 + 5665 + 565 – x = 4334 + 434
⇒ 61785 – x = 4768
⇒ x = 61785 – 4768 = 57017

20. (C): 23208 × 254 × 0 × 126 = 0
Because any number multiplied by zero always becomes zero.

3 LCM and HCF of Numbers

LEAST COMMON MULTIPLE (L.C.M.)

The least number which is exactly divisible by each one of the given numbers is called their L.C.M.

L.C.M. of two or more given numbers is determined by following two methods:

(*i*) By prime factorization method.

(*ii*) By division method.

(i) Finding L.C.M. by Prime Factorization Method

Resolve each one of the given numbers into a product of prime factors. Then, L.C.M. is the product of highest power of all the factors.

Example : Determine the L.C.M. of 24, 36 and 90.

Solution : $24 = 2 \times 2 \times 2 \times 3$

$36 = 2 \times 2 \times 3 \times 3$

$90 = 2 \times 3 \times 3 \times 5$

It is clear from the above that 2 appears as prime factor maximum three times, 3 two times and 5 one time.

$\therefore$ L.C.M. of the given numbers

$= 2 \times 2 \times 2 \times 3 \times 3 \times 5 = 360$

(ii) Finding L.C.M. by Division Method

Arrange the given numbers in a row in any order. Divide by a number which divides exactly at least two of the given numbers and carry forward the numbers which are not divisible. Repeat the above process till no two of the numbers are divisible by the same number except 1. The product of the divisors and the undivided numbers is the required L.C.M. of the given numbers.

Example : Find the L.C.M. of 16, 24, 36 and 54.

Solution :

2	16,	24,	36,	54
2	8,	12,	18,	27
2	4,	6,	9,	27
3	2,	3,	9,	27
3	2,	1,	3,	9
	2,	1,	1,	3

$\therefore$ L.C.M. $= 2 \times 2 \times 2 \times 3 \times 3 \times 2 \times 3 = 432.$

Highest Common Factor (H.C.F.)

The H.C.F. of two or more given numbers is the largest or the highest among common factors of the given numbers. In other words H.C.F. of the given numbers is the greatest common divisor of the given numbers.

There are two methods of finding the Highest Common Factor of two or more given numbers.

(*i*) Prime factorization method.

(*ii*) Continued division method.

(i) Finding H.C.F. by Prime Factorization Method

Express each one of the given numbers as the product of Prime factors. The product of least powers of Common Prime factors gives H.C.F.

Example : Find the H.C.F. of 28, 32 and 40.

Solution : $28 = \underline{2 \times 2} \times 7$

$32 = \underline{2 \times 2} \times 2 \times 2 \times 2$

$40 = \underline{2 \times 2} \times 2 \times 5$

We note that 2 occurs as a prime factor atleast two times in any of the given numbers.

$\therefore$ Required H.C.F. $= 2 \times 2 = 4.$

(ii) Finding the H.C.F. by Continued Division Method

Divide the greater number by the smaller number, divide the divisor by the remainder, divide the remainder by the next remainder, and so on until no remainder is left. The last divisor is the required H.C.F.

Example : Find the H.C.F. of 48, 168 and 324.

Solution :

48) 168 (3
     144
     24) 48 (2
          48
          ×

Thus, the H.C.F. of 48 and 168 is 24. Now, we find out the H.C.F. of 24 and 324.

$$\begin{array}{l} 24\,)\,324\,(13 \\ \underline{24} \\ 84 \\ \underline{72} \\ 12\,)\,24\,(2 \\ \underline{24} \\ \times \end{array}$$

∴ Required H.C.F. = 12.

L.C.M. AND H.C.F. OF FRACTIONS

$$\text{L.C.M.} = \frac{\text{L.C.M. of numerators}}{\text{H.C.F. of denominators}}$$

$$\text{and H.C.F.} = \frac{\text{H.C.F. of numerators}}{\text{L.C.M. of denominators}}$$

Relationship between two numbers and their L.C.M. and H.C.F.

Product of the H.C.F. and the L.C.M. of two numbers is equal to the product of the given two numbers.

∴ L.C.M. × H.C.F. = 1st Number × 2nd Number

Important Notes:

- The H.C.F. of two co-prime numbers is always 1. This is because co-prime numbers are defined as numbers that share no common factors other than 1.
- The L.C.M. of two co-prime numbers is always equal to the product of the numbers.

SOLVED EXAMPLES

Example 1 : Find the L.C.M. of 4, 8 and 12 by prime factorization method.

Solution :

$$\begin{array}{r|l} 2 & 4 \\ \hline 2 & 2 \\ \hline & 1 \end{array} \qquad \begin{array}{r|l} 2 & 8 \\ \hline 2 & 4 \\ \hline 2 & 2 \\ \hline & 1 \end{array} \qquad \begin{array}{r|l} 2 & 12 \\ \hline 2 & 6 \\ \hline 3 & 3 \\ \hline & 1 \end{array}$$

$4 = 2 \times 2 = 2^2$

$8 = 2 \times 2 \times 2 = 2^3$

$12 = 2 \times 2 \times 3 = 2^2 \times 3^1$

∴ The L.C.M. of 4, 8 and 12

$= 2^3 \times 3^1 = 8 \times 3 = 24.$

Example 2 : Find the L.C.M. of 9, 18 and 27 by common division method.

Solution :

$$\begin{array}{r|l} 3 & 9,\ 18,\ 27 \\ \hline 3 & 3,\ 6,\ 9 \\ \hline & 1,\ 2,\ 3 \end{array}$$

∴ The L.C.M. of 9, 18 and 27

$= 3 \times 3 \times 2 \times 3 = 54.$

Example 3 : Find the H.C.F. of 12 and 18 by prime factorization method.

Solution :

$$\begin{array}{r|l} 2 & 12 \\ \hline 2 & 6 \\ \hline 3 & 3 \\ \hline & 1 \end{array} \qquad \begin{array}{r|l} 2 & 18 \\ \hline 3 & 9 \\ \hline 3 & 3 \\ \hline & 1 \end{array}$$

$12 = 2 \times 2 \times 3$

$18 = 2 \times 3 \times 3$

∴ The H.C.F. of 12 and 18 = 2 × 3 = 6

Example 4 : Find the H.C.F. of 24 and 36 by division method.

Solution :

$$\begin{array}{l} 24\,)\,36\,(1 \\ \underline{24} \\ 12\,)\,24\,(2 \\ \underline{24} \\ \times \end{array}$$

Since, the last divisor is 12

∴ The H.C.F. of 24 and 36 = 12.

Example 5 : Find the L.C.M. of $\frac{2}{5}, \frac{3}{10}$ and $\frac{6}{25}$.

Solution : L.C.M. of $\frac{2}{5}, \frac{3}{10}$ and $\frac{6}{25}$

$$= \frac{\text{L.C.M. of 2, 3 and 6}}{\text{H.C.F. of 5, 10 and 25}} = \frac{6}{5}.$$

Example 6 : What is the H.C.F. of $\frac{4}{9}, \frac{10}{21}$ and $\frac{20}{63}$?

Solution : H.C.F. of $\frac{4}{9}, \frac{10}{21}$ and $\frac{20}{63}$

$$= \frac{\text{H.C.F. of 4, 10 and 20}}{\text{L.C.M. of 9, 21 and 63}} = \frac{2}{63}.$$

Example 7 : The L.C.M. and H.C.F. of two numbers are 72 and 6 respectively. If one of the numbers is 18, determine the other.

Solution : First no. × 2nd no.

= L.C.M. × H.C.F.

∴ 18 × 2nd no. = 72 × 6

∴ 2nd number = $\frac{72 \times 6}{18} = 24.$

EXERCISE

1. What is the L.C.M. of 84, 140 and 70?
   A. 210 B. 420 C. 630 D. 294

2. If product of two co-prime numbers is 117, then the L.C.M. is:
   A. 9 B. 13 C. 39 D. 117

3. Greatest number, which is to be divided by 280 and 1245 leaves the remainder 4 and 3 respectively, is
   A. 138 B. 148 C. 145 D. 178

4. Find the greatest number which divides 1277 and 1368 to give the remainder 3 in each case.
   A. 68 B. 77 C. 91 D. 97

5. What is the largest number which divides 270 and 426, leaving remainder 6 in each case?
   A. 22 B. 30 C. 12 D. 36

6. The product of H.C.F. and L.C.M. of two numbers is 348. If one of them is 24, then other number is:
   A. 18 B. 6 C. 32 D. 16

7. Three bells ring at intervals of 12, 15 and 18 minutes respectively. They started ringing simultaneously at 9:00 am. What will be the next time when they all ring simultaneously?
   A. 10:00 am B. 11:00 am
   C. 12:00 pm D. 1:00 pm

8. Three bells ring respectively at an interval of 16 minutes, 20 minutes and 24 minutes. They rang together at 9:30 in the morning. At what time will they ring together again?
   A. 12:00 noon B. 1:00 pm
   C. 1:30 pm D. 3:00 pm

9. The H.C.F and L.C.M. of two numbers are 4 and 48 respectively. If one of these numbers is 12, the second number is:
   A. 16 B. 12 C. 8 D. 4

10. The H.C.F. of $\frac{5}{6}, \frac{6}{7}, \frac{7}{8}, \frac{8}{9}$ and $\frac{9}{10}$ is:
    A. $\frac{1}{2420}$ B. $\frac{1}{2520}$ C. $\frac{1}{2660}$ D. $\frac{1}{2540}$

11. The L.C.M. and H.C.F. of two numbers are 4284 and 32 respectively. If one of the numbers is 204, the other number is:
    A. 672 B. 576 C. 676 D. 572

12. The largest three-digit number, when divided by 6, 9 and 12 leaves 1 as remainder in each case, will be:
    A. 887 B. 987 C. 973 D. 730

13. There are two electrical wires, one is 9 m 60 cm long aluminium wire and the other is 5 m 12 cm long copper wire. Find the maximum length that can be equally cut from each wire in such a way that the total length of each wire is exactly divisible by it.
    A. 40 cm B. 46 cm C. 64 cm D. 60 cm

14. Five bells begin to toll together and toll at intervals of 24, 40, 64, 72 and 120 seconds. After what interval to time will they toll again together?
    A. 42 min. B. 36 min. C. 48 min. D. 54 min.

15. The traffic lights at three different road crossings changes after every 48, 72 and 108 seconds respectively. If they change simultaneously at 9 am, at what time will they change again simultaneously?
    A. 10 minutes 10 seconds
    B. 7 minutes 12 seconds
    C. 7 minutes 10 seconds
    D. 12 minutes 10 seconds

16. Find the greatest possible length which can be used to measure 4 m 3 cm, 4 m 34 cm and 4 m 65 cm respectively.
    A. 31 cm B. 29 cm C. 28 cm D. 32 cm

17. Three bells start ringing together at 8:30 a.m. If they ring after 4, 5 and 6 minutes respectively each time, the next time they will ring together at:
    A. 8:45 a.m. B. 9:30 a.m.
    C. 9:45 a.m. D. 10:15 a.m.

18. Four traffic signals glow at the intervals of 5, 10, 15 and 20 minutes. After what time will they glow together?
    A. 30 minutes B. 90 minutes
    C. 60 minutes D. 120 minutes

19. What is the H.C.F of two or more consecutive even numbers?
    A. 0 B. 1
    C. 2 D. None of these

20. The L.C.M. of the two numbers is 48. If the numbers are 16 and 24, then their H.C.F. is:
    A. 4 B. 6 C. 8 D. 12

ANSWERS WITH EXPLANATIONS

1. (B):

$$\begin{array}{r|l} 2 & 84,\ 140,\ 70 \\ \hline 2 & 42,\ 70,\ 35 \\ \hline 3 & 21,\ 35,\ 35 \\ \hline 5 & 7,\ 35,\ 35 \\ \hline 7 & 7,\ 7,\ 7 \\ \hline & 1,\ 1,\ 1 \end{array}$$

$\therefore$ L.C.M. of 84, 140 and 70 = $2 \times 2 \times 3 \times 5 \times 7 = 420$.

2. (D): 13 and 9 are two co-prime numbers whose product $= 13 \times 9 = 117$

$\therefore$ L.C.M. of 13 and 9 = 117.

3. (A): $280 - 4 = 276$

$1245 - 3 = 1242$

H.C.F. of 276 and 1242

$$\begin{array}{l} 276)\ 1242\ (4 \\ \quad\ \ 1104 \\ \hline 138)\ 276\ (2 \\ \qquad\ \ 276 \\ \hline \qquad\ \ \times \end{array}$$

Hence, required number = 138.

4. (C): $1277 - 3 = 1274$

$1368 - 3 = 1365$

$$\begin{array}{r|l} 2 & 1274 \\ \hline 7 & 637 \\ \hline 7 & 91 \\ \hline 13 & 13 \\ \hline & 1 \end{array} \qquad \begin{array}{r|l} 3 & 1365 \\ \hline 5 & 455 \\ \hline 7 & 91 \\ \hline 13 & 13 \\ \hline & 1 \end{array}$$

$1274 = 2 \times 7 \times 7 \times 13$

$1365 = 3 \times 5 \times 7 \times 13$

H.C.F. of 1274 and 1365 = $7 \times 13 = 91$.

5. (C): $270 - 6 = 264$

$426 - 6 = 420$

$$\begin{array}{r|l} 2 & 264 \\ \hline 2 & 132 \\ \hline 2 & 66 \\ \hline 3 & 33 \\ \hline 11 & 11 \\ \hline & 1 \end{array} \qquad \begin{array}{r|l} 2 & 420 \\ \hline 2 & 210 \\ \hline 3 & 105 \\ \hline 5 & 35 \\ \hline 7 & 7 \\ \hline & 1 \end{array}$$

$264 = 2 \times 2 \times 2 \times 3 \times 11$

$420 = 2 \times 2 \times 3 \times 5 \times 7$

$\therefore$ Required number = H.C.F. of 264 and 420

$= 2 \times 2 \times 3 = 12$.

6. (D): First number × Second number = L.C.M. × H.C.F.

$24 \times$ Second number $= 384$

$\therefore$ Second number $= \dfrac{384}{24} = 16$

7. (C): L.C.M, of 12, 15 and 18 minutes

$$\begin{array}{r|l} 2 & 12,\ 15,\ 18 \\ \hline 2 & 6,\ 15,\ 9 \\ \hline 3 & 3,\ 15,\ 9 \\ \hline 3 & 1,\ 5,\ 3 \\ \hline 5 & 1,\ 5,\ 1 \\ \hline & 1,\ 1,\ 1 \end{array}$$

$= 2 \times 2 \times 3 \times 3 \times 5$

$= 180$ minutes

$= \left(\dfrac{180}{60}\right)$ hours $= 3$ hours

$\therefore$ Required time = 9 : 00 am + 3 hrs = 12.00 pm.

8. (C): L.C.M. of 16, 20 and 24 minutes

$$\begin{array}{r|l} 2 & 16,\ 20,\ 24 \\ \hline 2 & 8,\ 10,\ 12 \\ \hline 2 & 4,\ 5,\ 6 \\ \hline & 2,\ 5,\ 3 \end{array}$$

$= 2 \times 2 \times 2 \times 2 \times 5 \times 3$

$= 240$ minutes

$= \left(\dfrac{240}{60}\right)$ hours $= 4$ hours

$\therefore$ The bells will ring together again = 9:30 am + 4 hrs

= 1:30 pm.

9. (A): The second number $= \dfrac{\text{H.C.F.} \times \text{L.C.M.}}{\text{First number}}$

$= \dfrac{4 \times 48}{12} = 4 \times 4 = 16$

10. (B): H.C.F. of $\dfrac{5}{6}, \dfrac{6}{7}, \dfrac{7}{8}, \dfrac{8}{9}$ and $\dfrac{9}{10}$

$$\text{H.C.F.} = \frac{\text{H.C.F. of numerators}}{\text{L.C.M. of denominators}}$$

$$= \frac{\text{H.C.F. of } 5, 6, 7, 8, 9}{\text{L.C.M. of } 6, 7, 8, 9, 10} = \frac{1}{2520}.$$

11. (A): $\because$ First number × 2nd number = L.C.M. × H.C.F.

$\Rightarrow 204 \times$ 2nd number $= 4284 \times 32$

$\therefore$ 2nd number $= \dfrac{4284 \times 32}{204} = 42 \times 16$

$\therefore$ Required number = 672.

12. (C): L.C.M. of 6, 9 and 12

$\therefore$ L.C.M. $= 2 \times 3 \times 3 \times 2 = 36$

$\because$ Largest 3-digit number = 999

$$36\overline{)999}(27$$
$$\begin{array}{r} 72 \\ \hline 279 \\ 252 \\ \hline 27 \end{array}$$

2	6,	9,	12
3	3,	9,	6
	1,	3,	2

∴ Largest 3-digit no. which is exactly divisible by 6, 9 and 12

$= 999 - 27 = 972$

∴ Required number $= 972 + 1 = 973$.

13. (C): 9m 60 cm = 960 cm
and 5 m 12 cm = 512 cm
H.C.F. of 960 and 512

$$512\overline{)960}(1$$
$$512$$
$$448\overline{)512}(1$$
$$448$$
$$64\overline{)448}(7$$
$$448$$
$$\times$$

∴ The required largest piece = 64 cm.

14. (C): L.C.M. of 24, 40, 64, 72 and 120

2	24,	40,	64,	72,	120
2	12,	20,	32,	36,	60
2	6,	10,	16,	18,	30
3	3,	5,	8,	9,	15
5	1,	5,	8,	3,	5
	1,	1,	8,	3,	1

L.C.M. $= 2 \times 2 \times 2 \times 3 \times 5 \times 8 \times 3 = 2880$

2880 seconds $= \dfrac{2880}{60} = 48$ min.

∴ Required time = 48 min.

15. (B): L.C.M. of 48, 72 and 108 = 432 seconds.
Traffic lights will change simultaneously after 432 seconds
= 7 min. 12 seconds.

∴ Required time = 7 min. 12 seconds.

16. (A): 4 m 3 cm = 403 cm
4 m 34 cm = 434 cm
4 m 65 cm = 465 cm
H.C.F. of 403, 434 and 465

$$403\overline{)434}(1$$
$$403$$
$$\times 31\overline{)403}(13$$
$$31$$
$$\times 93$$
$$93$$
$$\times$$

$$31\overline{)465}(15$$
$$\begin{array}{r} 31 \\ \hline 155 \\ 155 \\ \hline \times \end{array}$$

∴ Required measure
= H.C.F. of 403, 434 and 465 = 31 cm.

17. (B): L.C.M. of 4, 5 and 6

2	4,	5,	6
	2,	5,	3

L.C.M. $= 2 \times 2 \times 5 \times 3 = 60$ min.
60 min. = 1 hour

∴ Required time = 8:30 a.m. + 1 hour = 9:30 a.m.

18. (C): Required time = L.C.M. of 5, 10, 15 and 20 minutes

5	5, 10, 15, 20
2	1, 2, 3, 4
	1, 1, 3, 2

$= (5 \times 2 \times 3 \times 2)$ minutes
= 60 minutes

19. (C): For two or more consecutive even numbers, the H.C.F. is always 2.

20. (C): H.C.F. $= \dfrac{\text{First number} \times \text{Second number}}{\text{L.C.M.}}$

∴ Required H.C.F. $= \dfrac{16 \times 24}{48} = 8$

4 Fractional Numbers

FRACTIONAL NUMBERS

A fraction consists of two numbers, an upper number (called the numerator, denoted by N_r) and a lower number (called the denominator, denoted by D_r). *i.e.,* a fraction = $\frac{N_r}{D_r}$.

Thus a fraction is a number that represents a ratio or division of two whole numbers. A fraction is written in the form $\frac{x}{y}$, the number on the top, 'x' is called numerator; the number on the bottom, 'y' is called denominator. The denominator tells how many equal parts there are; and the numerator tells how many of these equal parts are taken.

It is of the form $\frac{p}{q}$, where p and q are whole numbers and $q \neq 0$, such a number is also called a rational number.

Types of Fractions

Fractions are of different kinds, such as proper fractions, improper fractions and mixed fractions.

Proper fraction : A fraction whose numerator is less than its denominator is called a proper fraction.

For example : $\frac{1}{8}, \frac{3}{11}, \frac{14}{23}$... are all proper fractions.

Improper fraction : A fraction whose numerator is greater than its denominator is called an improper fraction.

For example : $\frac{8}{5}, \frac{12}{7}, \frac{25}{16}$,... are all improper fractions.

A fraction of this type can be written as a mixed number easily.

Take for example; $\frac{19}{12}$. On dividing 19 by 12, we get 1 as the quotient and 7 as remainder.

We call 1 as the integral part and 7 as the fractional part of $\frac{19}{12}$ and write $\frac{19}{12}$ as $1\frac{7}{12}$. Such a mixed number is called a mixed fraction. A mixed fraction can be written as an improper fraction and vice-versa.

For example : $4\frac{5}{7} = \frac{4 \times 7 + 5}{7} = \frac{33}{7}$, an improper fraction and $\frac{23}{17} = 1\frac{6}{17}$ a mixed fraction.

LIKE AND UNLIKE FRACTIONS

Like fractions: Fractions which have the same denominator are called like fractions.

For example : $\frac{3}{13}, \frac{5}{13}, \frac{9}{13}, \frac{11}{13}$ are all like fractions.

Unlike fractions : Fractions which have different denominators are known as unlike fractions.

For example: $\frac{2}{3}, \frac{5}{7}, \frac{7}{9}$ are unlike fractions.

Equivalent fractions : Two or more fractions are called equivalent fractions, if they have the same value.

For example : $\frac{1}{2}, \frac{4}{8}, \frac{6}{12}, \frac{15}{30}$ are equivalent fractions.

FOUR FUNDAMENTAL OPERATIONS ON FRACTIONS

As with integers, the operations of addition, subtraction, multiplication and division.

(A) Addition

(*i*) **Addition of like fractions :** Like fractions can be added very easily. We have to keep the denominator the same and add only the numerators.

For example : $\frac{2}{13} + \frac{5}{13} + \frac{4}{13} = \frac{2+5+4}{13} = \frac{11}{13}$.

***(ii)* Addition of unlike fractions :** To add unlike fractions, we first convert them to equivalent fractions, having the same denominators. For finding this common denominator, we use the L.C.M. of the denominators of the given fractions.

For example :

(i) $\frac{2}{3}+\frac{3}{5} = \frac{2\times5+3\times3}{15} = \frac{10+9}{15} = \frac{19}{15}$

$= 1\frac{4}{15}$

(ii) $\frac{1}{2}+\frac{2}{3}+\frac{5}{6}$

L.C.M. of 2, 3 and 6 = 6

$= \frac{3+4+5}{6} = \frac{12}{6} = 2.$

(B) Subtraction

Subtraction of like fractions, unlike fractions and mixed fractions are done in a way similar to those for addition. The methods can be explained by the following examples.

For example : Find $1-\frac{3}{7}$

Solution : $1-\frac{3}{7} = \frac{7-3}{7} = \frac{4}{7}.$

(C) Multiplication

A fraction of any type can be multiplied by a whole number or by another fraction.

***(i)* Multiplication of fraction by a whole number :** For multiplying a fraction by a given whole number, we multiply the numerator of the fraction by the whole number. The denominator is kept the same and the result is then simplified.

Example : Multiply $\frac{3}{5}$ by 8

Solution : The required result is

$\frac{3}{5}\times8 = \frac{24}{5} = 4\frac{4}{5}.$

***(ii)* Multiplication of a fraction by another fraction:** To multiply a given fraction by another fraction, we multiply the numerators of the two fractions together and the denominators of the two fractions together and simplify the result.

Example : Multiply $\frac{3}{5}$ by $\frac{7}{8}$

Solution : The required result = $\frac{3}{5}\times\frac{7}{8} = \frac{21}{40}.$

(D) Division of fractions

This can be done either by multiplying by the L.C.M. of the denominators of the fractions or by multiplying by such a number which can make the denominator 1.

It may be noted that one fraction is a reciprocal of another if their product is 1. So $\frac{1}{3}$ and 3 are reciprocals.

To find the reciprocal of a fraction, simply interchange the numerator and denominator. This is known as inverting fractions.

Thus, to divide one fraction by another fraction, invert the divisor and multiply.

Example : Divide $\frac{3}{8}$ by $\frac{1}{2}$.

Solution : $\frac{3}{8}\div\frac{1}{2} = \frac{3}{8}\times\frac{2}{1} = \frac{6}{8} = \frac{3}{4}.$

Example : Divide $\frac{2}{3}$ by $\frac{8}{9}$.

Solution : $\frac{2}{3}\div\frac{8}{9} = \frac{2}{3}\times\frac{9}{8} = \frac{18}{24} = \frac{3}{4}.$

Properties of Fraction

Addition $\rightarrow \frac{a}{b}+\frac{c}{d} = \frac{ad+bc}{bd}$

Subtraction $\rightarrow \frac{a}{b}-\frac{c}{d} = \frac{ad-bc}{bd}$

Multiplication $\rightarrow \frac{a}{b}\times\frac{c}{d} = \frac{ac}{bd}$

Division $\rightarrow \frac{a}{b}\div\frac{c}{d} = \frac{a}{b}\times\frac{d}{c}$

Dividing by a fraction is the same as multiplying by its inverse.

Cross product $\rightarrow \frac{a}{b} = \frac{c}{d} \Leftrightarrow ad = bc$

Additive Identity: $\frac{a}{b}+0 = \frac{a}{b}$

Multiplicative Identity: $\frac{a}{b}\times1 = \frac{a}{b}$

Multiplicative Inverse: The reciprocal of a fraction, when multiplied by the original fraction, give 1.

$\frac{a}{b}\times\frac{b}{a} = 1$

SOLVED EXAMPLES

Example 1 : Which of the following fractions is the largest?

$\frac{3}{7}, \frac{1}{7}, \frac{8}{7}$ and $\frac{2}{7}$

Solution : The given fraction are like fractions whose denominator is 7.

In like fractions, the fraction whose numerator is greatest will be the largest fraction.

Hence, the largest fraction among the given fraction is $\frac{8}{7}$.

Example 2 : Which of the following fractions is the smallest?

$\frac{2}{7}, \frac{3}{5}, \frac{1}{5}$ and $\frac{4}{5}$

Solution : The given fractions are like fractions whose denominator is 5.

∴ The fraction whose numerator is smallest will be the smallest fraction.

Hence, the smallest fraction among the given fractions is $\frac{1}{5}$.

Example 3 : Find the smallest and the greatest fraction from the following fractions:

$\frac{1}{4}, \frac{2}{3}, \frac{4}{7}$ and $\frac{1}{2}$

Solution : The given fractions are unlike fractions.

$\frac{1}{4} = 0.25;\ \frac{2}{3} = 0.66;\ \frac{4}{7} = 0.57$ and $\frac{1}{2} = 0.50$

$0.25 < 0.50 < 0.57 < 0.66$

∴ The smallest fraction = 0.25 or $\frac{1}{4}$

And the greatest fraction = 0.66 or $\frac{2}{3}$.

Example 4 : Convert $2\frac{3}{5}$ into the improper fraction.

Solution : $2\frac{3}{5} = 2 + \frac{3}{5} = \frac{2}{1} + \frac{3}{5} = \frac{2 \times 5 + 3}{5} = \frac{10+3}{5} = \frac{13}{5}$

Example 5 : Find the sum of $\frac{5}{7}, \frac{2}{7}$ and $\frac{6}{7}$.

Solution : The given fractions are like fractions.

$\frac{5}{7} + \frac{2}{7} + \frac{6}{7} = \frac{5+2+6}{7} = \frac{13}{7}$

Example 6 : Find the sum of $\frac{1}{4}$ and $\frac{3}{5}$.

Solution : The given fractions are unlike fractions.
L.C.M. of denominators 4 and 5
$= 2 \times 2 \times 5 = 20$

$\frac{1}{4} = \frac{1 \times 5}{4 \times 5} = \frac{5}{20}$ and $\frac{3}{5} = \frac{3 \times 4}{5 \times 4} = \frac{12}{20}$

$\therefore \frac{1}{4} + \frac{3}{5} = \frac{5}{20} + \frac{12}{20} = \frac{5+12}{20} = \frac{17}{20}$

Example 7 : Subtract $\frac{3}{7}$ from $\frac{5}{7}$.

Solution : The given fraction are like fractions.

$\therefore \frac{5}{7} - \frac{3}{7} = \frac{5-3}{7} = \frac{2}{7}$

Example 8 : Find the product of $\frac{3}{5}$ and $\frac{5}{7}$ in the simplest form.

Solution : $\frac{3}{5} \times \frac{5}{7} = \frac{3 \times 5}{5 \times 7} = \frac{15}{35} = \frac{15 \div 5}{35 \div 5} = \frac{3}{7}$

Example 9 : Find the reciprocal of $3\frac{1}{5}$.

Solution : Given fraction is $3\frac{1}{5} = \frac{16}{5}$

∴ The reciprocal of $\frac{16}{5} = \frac{5}{16}$

Example 10 : Find the sum of $\frac{3}{7}$ and its reciprocal.

Solution : The reciprocal of $\frac{3}{7} = \frac{7}{3}$

∴ The required sum $= \frac{3}{7} + \frac{7}{3}$

$= \frac{9+49}{21} = \frac{58}{21}$ or $2\frac{16}{21}$

EXERCISE

1. Which of the following fractions is the smallest?

A. $\frac{11}{17}$ B. $\frac{9}{16}$ C. $\frac{13}{19}$ D. $\frac{10}{18}$

2. Which of the following fractions is the greatest?

A. $\frac{14}{25}$ B. $\frac{11}{19}$ C. $\frac{17}{28}$ D. $\frac{13}{22}$

3. Which of the following is not a proper fraction?

A. $\frac{21}{29}$ B. $\frac{38}{40}$ C. $\frac{47}{44}$ D. $\frac{36}{39}$

4. Which of the following is an improper fraction?

A. $\frac{15}{9}$ B. $\frac{11}{15}$ C. $\frac{19}{21}$ D. $\frac{5}{11}$

5. What is the fraction equivalent to $\frac{48}{60}$ with denominator 5?

A. $\frac{2}{5}$ B. $\frac{4}{5}$ C. $\frac{6}{5}$ D. $\frac{3}{5}$

6. Arrange the following fractions in ascending order:

$\frac{17}{3}, \frac{17}{11}, \frac{17}{9}, \frac{17}{15}$

A. $\frac{17}{15} < \frac{17}{11} < \frac{17}{9} < \frac{17}{3}$ B. $\frac{17}{11} < \frac{17}{15} < \frac{17}{9} < \frac{17}{3}$

C. $\frac{17}{15} < \frac{17}{9} < \frac{17}{11} < \frac{17}{3}$ D. $\frac{17}{3} < \frac{17}{9} < \frac{17}{11} < \frac{17}{15}$

7. Arrange the fractions $\frac{6}{7}, \frac{5}{7}, \frac{11}{7}, \frac{9}{7}$ in descending order:

A. $\frac{9}{7} > \frac{11}{7} > \frac{6}{7} > \frac{5}{7}$ B. $\frac{5}{7} > \frac{11}{7} > \frac{9}{7} > \frac{6}{7}$

C. $\frac{6}{7} > \frac{9}{7} > \frac{11}{7} > \frac{5}{7}$ D. $\frac{11}{7} > \frac{9}{7} > \frac{6}{7} > \frac{5}{7}$

8. The difference of $1\frac{3}{16}$ and its reciprocal is equal to:

A. $1\frac{1}{8}$ B. $\frac{4}{3}$

C. $\frac{15}{16}$ D. None of these

9. By how much is three-fifth of 350 greater than four-seventh of 210?

A. 90 B. 110 C. 120 D. 210

10. One-fifth of a number exceeds one-seventh of the same by 10. The number is;

A. 125 B. 150 C. 175 D. 200

11. Two-fifth of one-fourth of three-seventh of a number is 15. What is half of that number?

A. 94 B. 175 C. 188 D. 196

12. A man spends $\frac{2}{5}$ of his salary on house rent, $\frac{3}{10}$ of his salary on food and $\frac{1}{8}$ of his salary on conveyance. If he has ₹ 1400 left with him, find his expenditure on food.

A. ₹ 2000 B. ₹ 2200 C. ₹ 2400 D. ₹ 2500

13. If $\frac{1}{8}$ of a pencil is black, $\frac{1}{2}$ of the remaining is white and the remaining $3\frac{1}{2}$ cm is blue, find the total length of the pencil.

A. 6 cm B. 7 cm C. 8 cm D. 9 cm

14. How many one-fourths are there is 18?

A. 96 B. 72 C. 84 D. 18

15. The reciprocal of the fraction $3\frac{5}{17}$ is:

A. $\frac{17}{56}$ B. $\frac{17}{15}$ C. $\frac{17}{50}$ D. $\frac{56}{17}$

16. The sum of $3\frac{2}{5}$ and its reciprocal is:

A. $\frac{314}{85}$ B. $\frac{305}{85}$

C. $\frac{289}{85}$ D. $\frac{325}{85}$

17. The difference between $4\frac{2}{3}$ and its reciprocal is:

A. $\frac{181}{42}$ B. $\frac{181}{42}$ C. $\frac{187}{42}$ D. $\frac{189}{42}$

18. What fraction of an hour is 36 minutes?

A. $\frac{2}{5}$ B. $\frac{3}{5}$ C. $\frac{4}{5}$ D. $\frac{2}{3}$

19. What fraction of 7 days is 12 hours?

A. $\frac{1}{7}$ B. $\frac{1}{60}$ C. $\frac{1}{5}$ D. $\frac{1}{14}$

20. A piece of wire $\frac{2}{5}$ m long broke into two pieces. If One of the pieces is $\frac{3}{8}$ m long, then the length of the other piece is:

A. $\frac{1}{20}$ m B. $\frac{3}{5}$ m C. $\frac{5}{8}$ m D. $\frac{1}{40}$ m

21. Amit had $\frac{5}{9}$th part of a cake. He ate $\frac{3}{4}$th part of it. What part of the cake was remained to be eaten?

A. $\frac{5}{24}$ B. $\frac{5}{32}$ C. $\frac{5}{28}$ D. $\frac{5}{36}$

22. If we increased 20% in numerator and 25% in denominator of a fraction then it is $\frac{3}{5}$, then the original fraction is

A. $\frac{8}{5}$ B. $\frac{8}{3}$ C. $\frac{3}{8}$ D. $\frac{5}{8}$

23. The denominator of a fraction is 1 more than double the numerator. On adding 2 to the numerator and subtracting 3 from the denominator, we obtain 1. Find the original fraction.

A. $\frac{2}{5}$ B. $\frac{1}{3}$ C. $\frac{4}{9}$ D. $\frac{1}{9}$

24. $\left(1\frac{1}{2}+11\frac{1}{2}+111\frac{1}{2}+1111\frac{1}{2}\right)$ is equal to:

A. 1263 B. 1236 C. 1233 D. 1239

25. If $\frac{a}{3}=\frac{b}{4}=\frac{c}{7}$, then the value of $\frac{a+b+c}{c}$ is:

A. $\sqrt{2}$ B. 7 C. 2 D. $\frac{1}{\sqrt{7}}$

ANSWERS WITH EXPLANATIONS

1. (D): $\frac{11}{17} = 0.647;$ $\frac{9}{16} = 0.5625;$

$\frac{13}{19} = 0.684;$ $\frac{10}{18} = 0.556$

Clearly, 0.556 i.e. $\frac{10}{18}$ is the smallest fraction.

2. (C): $\frac{14}{25} = 0.56;$ $\frac{11}{19} = 0.579;$

$\frac{17}{28} = 0.607;$ $\frac{13}{22} = 0.591$

Clearly, 0.607 i.e. $\frac{17}{28}$ is the greatest fraction.

3. (C): The fraction $\frac{47}{44}$ is not a proper fraction because its numerator is greater than its denominator.

4. (A): The fraction $\frac{15}{9}$ is an improper fraction because its numerator is greater than its denominator.

5. (B): Let $\frac{48}{60}=\frac{x}{5}$

$\Rightarrow$ $60x = 5 \times 48$

$\Rightarrow$ $x = \frac{5\times 48}{60} = 4$

Hence, the required fraction is $\frac{4}{5}$.

6. (A): For fractions with the same numerators,

- A fraction with the smallest denominator is the greatest fraction.
- A fraction with the greatest denominator is the smallest fraction.

So, ascending order of the fraction is $\frac{17}{15}<\frac{17}{11}<\frac{17}{9}<\frac{17}{3}$.

7. (D): Out of the fractions having the same denominator, the fractions having the greatest numerator is greater.

$\therefore$ The required descending order: $\frac{11}{7}>\frac{9}{7}>\frac{6}{7}>\frac{5}{7}$.

8. (D): $1\frac{3}{16} = \frac{1\times 16+3}{16} = \frac{19}{16}$

Its reciprocal $= \frac{16}{19}$

Difference $= \frac{19}{16}-\frac{16}{19}=\frac{19\times 19-16\times 16}{304}$

$= \frac{361-256}{304}=\frac{105}{304}$.

9. (A): $\frac{3}{5}\times 350-\frac{4}{7}\times 210$

$= 3 \times 70 - 4 \times 30 = 210 - 120 = 90.$

10. (C): $\frac{1}{5}\times x-\frac{1}{7}x = 10$

$\Rightarrow \quad \frac{7x-5x}{35} = 10$

$\Rightarrow \quad 2x = 35 \times 10$

$\Rightarrow \quad x = \frac{350}{2} = 175.$

11. (B): Let the number be x. Then,

$\frac{2}{5}$ of $\frac{1}{4}$ of $\frac{3}{7}$ of $x = 15$

$\Rightarrow \quad \frac{2}{5}\times\frac{1}{4}\times\frac{3}{7}\times x = 15$

$\Rightarrow \quad \frac{3x}{70} = 15$

$\Rightarrow \quad x = \frac{70\times 15}{3} = 70\times 5 = 350$

$\therefore \quad \frac{1}{2}$ of $350 = \frac{1}{2}\times 350 = 175.$

12. (C): Part of the salary left

$= 1-\left(\frac{2}{5}+\frac{3}{10}+\frac{1}{8}\right)$

$= 1-\left(\frac{16+12+5}{40}\right) = \frac{40-33}{40} = \frac{7}{40}$

Let the monthly salary = ₹x

Then, $\frac{7}{40}$ of $x = 1400$

$\Rightarrow \quad x = \frac{40\times 1400}{7} = 8000$

$\therefore$ Expenditure on food = $\frac{3}{10}\times 8000 =$ ₹ 2400

13. (C): Let the total length of the pencil = x cm

$\therefore$ Black part = $\left(\frac{x}{8}\right)$cm

Remaining part = $x-\frac{x}{8} = \frac{7x}{8}$ cm

White part = $\left(\frac{1}{2}\times\frac{7x}{8}\right) = \frac{7x}{16}$ cm

Remaining part = $\frac{7x}{8}-\frac{7x}{16} = \frac{14x-7x}{16} = \frac{7x}{16}$

$\therefore \quad \frac{7x}{16} = \frac{7}{2} \Rightarrow x = \frac{16\times 7}{2\times 7} = 8$

Hence, total length of the pencil = 8 cm.

14. (B): The number of one-fourths in 18

$= \left(18\div\frac{1}{4}\right) = \left(18\times\frac{4}{1}\right) = 72$

15. (A): $3\frac{5}{17} = \frac{3\times 17+5}{17} = \frac{51+5}{17} = \frac{56}{17}$

$\therefore$ The reciprocal of $3\frac{5}{17}$ *i.e.* $\frac{56}{17} = \frac{17}{56}$

16. (A): $3\frac{2}{5} = \frac{3\times 5+2}{5} = \frac{15+2}{5} = \frac{17}{5}$

Then, the reciprocal of $3\frac{2}{5}$ *i.e.* $\frac{17}{5} = \frac{5}{17}$

$\therefore$ Required sum = $\frac{17}{5}+\frac{5}{17} = \frac{289+25}{85} = \frac{314}{85}$.

17. (C): $4\frac{2}{3} = \frac{4\times 3+2}{3} = \frac{12+2}{3} = \frac{14}{3}$

Then, the reciprocal of $4\frac{2}{3}$ *i.e.* $\frac{14}{3} = \frac{3}{14}$

$\therefore$ Required difference = $\frac{14}{3}-\frac{3}{14} = \frac{196-9}{42} = \frac{187}{42}$.

18. (B): 60 minutes = 1 hour

1 minute = $\frac{1}{60}$ hour

$\therefore$ 36 minutes = $\left(\frac{1}{60}\times 36\right)$ hour = $\frac{3}{5}$ hour.

19. (D): Required fraction = $\frac{12 \text{ hours}}{7 \text{ days}} = \frac{12 \text{ hours}}{(7\times 24) \text{ hours}}$

$= \frac{12}{7\times 24} = \frac{1}{14}$

20. (D): Total length of the piece of wire = $\frac{2}{5}$m

Length of the piece = $\frac{3}{8}$m

$\therefore$ The length of the other piece = $\left(\frac{2}{5}-\frac{3}{8}\right)$m

$= \left(\frac{16-15}{40}\right)$m $= \frac{1}{40}$m

21. (D): Part of the cake, Amit had eaten

$$= \frac{3}{4} \text{ of } \frac{5}{9} = \left(\frac{3}{4}\times\frac{5}{9}\right) = \frac{5}{12}$$

∴ Remaining part of the cake to be eaten

$$= \left(\frac{5}{9}-\frac{5}{12}\right) = \left(\frac{20-15}{36}\right) = \frac{5}{36}.$$

22. (D): Let the original fraction $= \dfrac{x}{y}$

Then, $$\frac{x\times\frac{120}{100}}{y\times\frac{125}{100}} = \frac{3}{5}$$

$$\Rightarrow \quad \frac{x}{y} = \frac{3}{5}\times\frac{125}{120}$$

$$= \frac{25}{40} = \frac{5}{8}$$

$$\Rightarrow \quad \frac{x}{y} = \frac{5}{8}$$

23. (C): Let numerator $= x$

then denominator $= 2x + 1$

$$\therefore \quad \frac{x+2}{2x+1-3} = 1$$

$$\Rightarrow \quad x + 2 = 2x - 2$$

$$\Rightarrow \quad x = 2 + 2$$

$$= 4$$

Then, original fraction

$$= \frac{x}{2x+1}$$

$$= \frac{4}{2\times4+1}$$

$$= \frac{4}{9}.$$

24. (B): $1\frac{1}{2}+11\frac{1}{2}+111\frac{1}{2}+1111\frac{1}{2}$

$$= (1 + 11 + 111 + 1111) + \left(\frac{1}{2}+\frac{1}{2}+\frac{1}{2}+\frac{1}{2}\right)$$

$$= 1234 + 2$$

$$= 1236$$

25. (C): $\because \quad \dfrac{a}{3} = \dfrac{b}{4} = \dfrac{c}{7} = k$

$$\therefore \quad a = 3k,\ b = 4k,\ c = 7k$$

Value of $$\frac{a+b+c}{c} = \frac{3k+4k+7k}{7k}$$

$$= \frac{14k}{7k} = 2.$$

5 Decimal System

DECIMAL FRACTION

Fractions in which denominators are power of 10 are called decimal fractions.

Example : $\frac{1}{10}, \frac{1}{100}, \frac{7}{1000}$ *etc.*

Here, $\frac{1}{10}$ is 1 tenths, written as 0.1

$\frac{1}{100}$ = 1 hundredths = 0.01

$\frac{7}{1000}$ = 7 thousandths = 0.007

Like and Unlike Decimals

(i) **Like Decimals:** Decimals having the same number of decimal places are called like decimals. For example, 3.01, 15.78, 112.30 are like decimals. Each of these decimal numbers has two decimal places.

(ii) **Unlike Decimals:** Decimals having different number of decimal places are called unlike decimals.

For example, 0.71, 1.2, 205.1014 and 0.004 are all unlike decimals.

Note:
- The addition of zeros to the extreme right of a decimal part does not change the value of the decimal number, *i.e.* 2.5 = 2.50 = 2.5000.
- If both numerator and denominator of a fraction contain decimals, then we first convert both into like decimals and then we remove the decimal signs from both,

i.e. $\frac{1.535}{0.21} = \frac{1.535}{0.210}$

$= \frac{1535}{210} = \frac{307}{42} = 7\frac{13}{42}$

FUNDAMENTAL OPERATIONS ON DECIMAL FRACTIONS

Addition and Subtraction of Decimal Fractions

First of all write down the numbers under one another. Other than the decimal point lies in one column. After arranging in this way, we add or subtract in usual fashion.

Multiplication of Decimal Fractions

Multiply the given numbers considering them without the decimal point. Now, in the product, the decimal point is marked off to obtain as many places of decimal as is the sum of the number of decimal places in the given numbers.

For example, 2.41 × 0.45 = 241 × 45 = 10845

Sum of decimal places = 2 + 2 = 4

∴ 2.41 × 0.45 = 1.0845

To multiply a decimal number by 10 is equivalent to moving the decimal point to the right one place, to multiply by 100 is equivalent to moving the decimal point to the right two places and so on. In other words, we move the decimal point to the right by as many places as there are zeros after 1 in the multiplier.

For example, 4.16 × 10 = 41.6,

0.065 × 100 = 6.5

Dividing a Decimal Fraction by a Counting Number

Divide the given number without considering the decimal point, by the given counting number.

Now, in the quotient, put the decimal point to give as many places of decimal as there are in the dividend.

Example : Find the quotient (0.0204 ÷ 17)

Solution : 204 ÷ 17 = 12

Dividend contains 4 places of decimal

So, 0.0204 ÷ 17 = 0.0012

Dividing a Decimal Fraction by a Decimal Fraction

Multiply both the dividend and the divisor by a suitable power of 10 to make divisor a whole number.

Now proceed as above;

thus, $\frac{0.00066}{0.11} = \frac{0.00066 \times 100}{0.11 \times 100}$

$= \frac{0.066}{11} = 0.006$

Approximation of Decimal Fractions

Add one to the last retained digit if the digit to the right of it is 5 or greater than 5, else ignore all the digits to the right of the last retained digit.

For Example: 0.486753

Its approximate value up to five decimal places is 0.48675, up to four decimal places is 0.4868, upto three decimal places is 0.487 and so on.

CONVERSION OF DECIMAL NUMBER INTO MIXED NUMBER

Write the integral part of the decimal number as it is and draw a horizontal line on its right side. Write the digits in the fractional part as numerator above the line. Below the line write 1 and put as many zeros as there are digits in the fractional part of the decimal number and this will form the denominator.

In the integral part consists of only zeros, we can ignore it.

For example: $7.23 = 7\frac{23}{100} = \frac{723}{100}$

$0.45 = \frac{45}{100} = \frac{9}{20}$

$0.0013 = \frac{13}{10000}$

Recurring Decimal

If in a decimal number a digit or a set of digits is repeated again and again the decimal is known as recurring decimal.

For example: (*i*) $2.666..... = 2.6 \text{ or } 2.\overline{6}$

(*ii*) $1.363636... = 1.\dot{3}\dot{6} \text{ or } 1.\overline{36}$

(*iii*) $7.3424242... = 7.3\dot{4}\dot{2} \text{ or } 7.3\overline{42}$

Recurring decimal numbers are of two types: (*i*) pure and (*ii*) mixed

(*i*) **Pure recurring decimals :** A decimal fraction in which all the figures after the decimal point are repeated is called a pure recurring decimal. For example, $0.\overline{3}$, $0.\overline{37}$, $3.\overline{4579}$ etc.

(*ii*) **Mixed recurring decimals:** A decimal fraction in which atleast one figure after the decimal point is not repeated is called a mixed recurring decimal.

For example: $0.3\overline{59}$, $0.2\overline{954}$, $0.2\overline{7}$ etc.

CONVERSION OF RECURRING INTO VULGAR FRACTION

(i) Pure Recurring Decimals

Rule: Put as many 9's in the denominator at the number of digits under recurring and delete the recurring sign.

For example: $0.\overline{5} = \frac{5}{9}$, $0.\overline{35} = \frac{35}{99}$

$0.\overline{24} = \frac{24}{99} = \frac{8}{33}$

(ii) Mixed Recurring Decimals

For example:

(*a*) $0.1\overline{8}$

Here, numerator = 18 − 1 = 17

and denominator = 9 × 10 = 90

$\therefore \quad 0.1\overline{8} = \frac{18-1}{90} = \frac{17}{90}$

(*b*) $0.2\overline{79} = \frac{279-2}{990} = \frac{277}{990}$

(*c*) $0.43\overline{213} = \frac{43213-43}{99900} = \frac{43170}{99900} = \frac{4317}{9990}$

SOLVED EXAMPLES

Example 1 : Add 521 + 52.1 + 5.21 + 0.521

Solution :

$$\begin{array}{r} 521.000 \\ 52.100 \\ 5.210 \\ +\ 0.521 \\ \hline 578.831 \\ \hline \end{array}$$

After adding we get 578.831

Example 2 : What is the simplified value of the following expression? (1.1 + 10.01 + 101.0101)

Solution : 1.1 + 10.01 + 101.0101 = 112.1201

$$\begin{array}{r} 1.1000 \\ 10.0100 \\ +101.0101 \\ \hline 112.1201 \\ \hline \end{array}$$

Example 3 : Find 31.004 – 17.2386

Solution :

$$\begin{array}{r} 31.0040 \\ -\ 17.2386 \\ \hline 13.7654 \\ \hline \end{array}$$

Example 4 : Find the product .2 × .02 × .002.

Solution : 2 × 2 × 2 = 8

Sum of decimal places = 1 + 2 + 3 = 6

∴ .2 × .02 × .002 = 0.000008

Example 5 : Multiply 6.32 × 0.59

Solution : 632 × 59 = 37288

Sum of decimal places = 2 + 2 = 4

∴ 6.32 × 0.59 = 3.7288

Example 6 : Divide 0.052 by 1.3.

Solution : $\frac{0.052}{1.3} = \frac{0.052 \times 10}{1.3 \times 10} = \frac{0.52}{13} = 0.04$

Example 7 : If 4.73 × 0.6 = 2.838, then the value of 473 × 0.6 is:

Solution : 4.73 × 0.6 = 2.838

⇒ 4.73 × 0.6 × 100 = 2.838 × 100

⇒ (4.73 × 100) × 0.6 = 283.8

∴ 473 × 0.6 = 283.8

Example 8 : If $\frac{1}{3.128} = 0.31969$, then the value of $\frac{1}{0.003128}$ is:

Solution : We have: $\frac{1}{3.128} = 0.31969$

$$\therefore \frac{1}{0.003128} = \frac{1}{0.003128} \times \frac{1000}{1000} = \frac{1}{3.128} \times 1000 = 0.31969 \times 1000 = 319.69$$

Example 9 : Multiply $0.\overline{09}$ by 7.3

Solution : $0.\overline{09} \times 7.\overline{3} = \frac{9}{99} \times \frac{73-7}{9} = \frac{1}{11} \times \frac{66}{9} = \frac{2}{3} = 0.\overline{6}.$

Example 10 : Divide $0.\overline{6}$ by 7.5

Solution : $0.\overline{6} \div 0.75 = \frac{6}{9} \div \frac{75}{100} = \frac{2}{3} \div \frac{3}{4} = \frac{2}{3} \times \frac{4}{3} = \frac{8}{9} = 0.\overline{8}.$

EXERCISE

1. $x \times 0.015 = 0.0075 \times 0.147$, Find the value of x.
   A. 0.735 B. 0.0735 C. 0.0675 D. 0.675

2. Find the sum of 337.62 + 8.591 + 34.4.
   A. 370.611 B. 380.511 C. 380.611 D. 426.97

3. The value of 34.95 + 240.016 + 23.98 is equal to:
   A. 298.0946 B. 298.111
   C. 298.946 D. 299.09

4. 4.036 divided by 0.04 gives:
   A. 1.009 B. 10.09 C. 100.9 D. 1009

5. $\frac{1}{0.04}$ is equal to:
   A. $\frac{1}{40}$ B. $\frac{2}{5}$ C. 2.5 D. 25

6. How many digits will be there to the right of the decimal point in the product of 95.75 and .02554?
   A. 5 B. 6 C. 7 D. 3

7. If $\frac{144}{0.144} = \frac{14.4}{x}$, then the value of x is:
   A. 0.0144 B. 1.44 C. 14.4 D. 144

8. A tailor has 37.5 metres of cloth and he has to make 8 pieces out of a metre of cloth. How many pieces can he make out of this cloth?
   A. 320 B. 360
   C. 400 D. None of these

9. 892.7 – 573.07 – 95.007 = ?
   A. 224.623 B. 224.777 C. 233.523 D. 414.637

10. Find the product .4 × .04 × .004 × 40.
    A. 25600 B. .002560 C. 2560 D. .00264

11. If 522 ÷ 29 = 18, then 5.22 ÷ 0.0018 = ?
    A. 0.29 B. 2900 C. 2.9 D. 290

12. If $\frac{1}{4.126} = 0.24236$, then the value of $\frac{1}{0.004126}$ is:
    A. 24.236 B. 2.4236 C. 2423.6 D. 242.36

13. The product of two decimals is 0.768. If one of the decimal number is 1.6, find the other number.
A. 0.48 B. 0.47 C. 0.42 D. 0.37

14. What decimal of an hour is a second?
A. 0.0256 B. 0.0025 C. 0.00027 D. 0.000225

15. What decimal of an hour is 45 minutes?
A. 0.05 B. 0.75 C. 0.25 D. 0.5

16. A vessel weights 5.48 kg when empty and 17.36 kg when full of water. What is the weight of the water in it?
A. 10.88 kg B. 11.48 kg
C. 22.84 kg D. 11.88 kg

17. Samir bought 10.25 m of cloth for ₹ 471.50. Find the price of the cloth per metre.
A. ₹ 42 B. ₹ 48 C. ₹ 46 D. ₹ 36

18. Riya scored 56.73 points and Asha scored 74.92 points in a university exam. How many points less did Riya score than Asha?
A. 1.8 B. 18.19 C. 18.10 D. 18.15

19. The rainfall in a city in first 5 days of a month was 1.27 cm, 3.25 cm, 2.79 cm, 2.57 cm and 1.37 cm. How much did it rain altogether?
A. 11.25 cm B. 9.98 cm
C. 11.00 cm D. 11.98 cm

20. A tailor takes 2.5 m of cloth for making a curtain. He received an order of making 25 curtains from Mrs Puri. How much cloth will he require to fulfill the order?
A. 65 m B. 51 m C. 62.5 m D. 625.50 m

21. The smallest decimal among the following is:
A. $\frac{2.4}{4}$ B. 5.2×0.1
C. $\frac{4.6}{10}$ D. $(0.6)^2$

22. Convert 0.75 into the fraction in its lowest terms:
A. $\frac{5}{8}$ B. $\frac{1}{4}$ C. $\frac{3}{4}$ D. $\frac{3}{8}$

23. Seven-tenths is written in the decimal form as:
A. 0.7 B. 7×10 C. 70.0 D. $\frac{7}{20}$

24. The fractional form of $2.1\overline{36}$ is:
A. $2\frac{3}{22}$ B. $2\frac{1}{22}$ C. $\frac{47}{220}$ D. $\frac{68}{495}$

25. What is the value of $6.\overline{46}$ in the fractional form?
A. $\frac{640}{99}$ B. $\frac{640}{100}$ C. $\frac{64640}{1000}$ D. $\frac{646}{99}$

ANSWERS WITH EXPLANATIONS

1. (B): $x \times 0.015 = 0.0075 \times 0.147$

$$\Rightarrow x = \frac{0.0075 \times 0.147}{0.015}$$

$$= \frac{0.0075 \times 0.147}{0.015} \times \frac{10000000}{10000000}$$

$$\Rightarrow x = \frac{75 \times 147}{15 \times 10000} = \frac{5 \times 147}{10000} = \frac{735}{10000} = 0.0735$$

2. (C):

$$\begin{array}{r} 337.62 \\ 8.591 \\ +\ 34.4 \\ \hline 380.611 \end{array}$$

3. (C):

$$\begin{array}{r} 34.95 \\ 240.016 \\ +\ 23.98 \\ \hline 298.946 \end{array}$$

4. (C): $\frac{4.036}{0.04} = \frac{4036}{1000} \times \frac{100}{4}$

$$= \frac{1009}{10} = 100.9.$$

5. (D): $\frac{1}{0.04} = \frac{100}{4} = 25.$

6. (B): Sum of decimal places = 7

Since the last digit to the extreme right will be zero ($\because 5 \times 4 = 20$), So there will be 6 significant digits to the right of the decimal point.

7. (A): $\frac{144 \times 1000}{144} = \frac{144}{10x}$

$$\Rightarrow 1000 \times 10x = 144$$

$$\Rightarrow x = \frac{144}{10000} = 0.0144.$$

8. (D): Required no. of pieces = 37.5×8

$$= \frac{375 \times 8}{10} = \frac{3000}{10}$$

$$= 300.$$

9. (A): $892.7 - 573.07 - 95.007$

$$\begin{array}{r} 892.700 \\ -668.077 \\ \hline 224.623 \end{array}$$

$= 892.7 - 668.077$

$= 224.623$

10. (B): $.4 \times .04 \times .004 \times 40$

$$= \frac{4 \times 4 \times 4 \times 40}{10 \times 100 \times 1000} = \frac{256}{100000}$$

$= 0.00256 = .002560.$

11. (B): $522 \div 29 = 18$

Now, $5.22 \div 0.0018 = ?$

$$? = \frac{522}{100} \div \frac{18}{10000}$$

$$? = \frac{522}{18} \times \frac{10000}{100}$$

$= 29 \times 100 = 2900$

12. (D): Given: $\frac{1}{4.126} = 0.24236$

$$\therefore \quad \frac{1}{0.004126} = \frac{1}{0.004126} \times \frac{1000}{1000}$$

$$= \frac{1}{4.126} \times 1000$$

$= 0.24236 \times 1000 = 242.36$

13. (A): Let the other decimal number be x.

$x \times 1.6 = 0.768$

$$\Rightarrow \quad x \times \frac{16}{10} = \frac{768}{1000}$$

$$\therefore \quad x = \frac{768}{1000} \times \frac{10}{16} = \frac{48}{100} = 0.48$$

14. (C): 1 hour = (60 × 60) seconds = 3600 seconds

$\therefore$ Required decimal $= \frac{1\,\text{sec}}{3600\,\text{sec}} = 0.00027$ (approx.)

15. (B): 1 hour = 60 minutes

$\therefore$ Required decimal $= \frac{45\text{ minutes}}{1\text{ hour}} = \frac{45\text{ min}}{60\text{ min}} = \frac{3}{4}$

$= 0.75$

16. (D): Weight of the vessel when it is full of water = 17.36 kg

Weight of the empty vessel = 5.48 kg

$\therefore$ The weight of the water in the vessel = (17.36 – 5.48) kg = 11.88 kg

17. (C): Price of 10.25 m of cloth = ₹ 471.50

$\therefore$ Price of 1 m of cloth = ₹$\left(\frac{471.50}{10.25}\right)$ = ₹ 46

18. (B): Riya's score = 56.73 points

Asha's score = 74.92 points

Points less Riya scored than Asha = 74.92 – 56.73 = 18.19

$\therefore$ Riya scored 18.19 points less than Asha.

19. (A): Total rain = (1.27 + 3.25 + 2.79 +2.57 + 1.37) cm = 11.25 cm

20. (C): Cloth per curtain = 2.5 m

Number of curtains = 25

Total cloth required = (2.5 × 25) m = 62.5 m

21. (D): $\frac{2.4}{4} = 0.60$; $5.2 \times 0.1 = 0.52$;

$\frac{4.6}{10} = 0.46$; $(0.6)^2 = 0.36$

Clearly, $0.60 > 0.52 > 0.46 > 0.36$

$$\Rightarrow \quad \frac{2.4}{4} > 5.2 \times 0.1 > \frac{4.6}{10} > (0.6)^2$$

$\therefore (0.6)^2$ is the smallest decimal among the given ones.

22. (C): $0.75 = \frac{75}{100} = \frac{75 \div 25}{100 \div 25} = \frac{3}{4}$

23. (A): Seven-tenths $= \frac{7}{10} = 0.7$

24. (A): $2.1\overline{36} = 2 + 0.1\overline{36} = 2 + \frac{136-1}{990}$

$$= 2 + \frac{135}{990} = 2 + \frac{3}{22} = 2\frac{3}{22}.$$

25. (A): $6.\overline{46} = 6 + 0.\overline{46} = 6 + \frac{46}{99}$

$$= \frac{594+46}{99} = \frac{640}{99}.$$

6 Square Roots

The square root of a number is the number which when multiplied by itself produces the number in question. We use the radical sign '$\sqrt{\ }$' for the 'positive square root'.

Square root of a given number may be obtained by following two methods:

1. By Prime Factorization Method
2. By Division Method

1. SQUARE ROOT OF A PERFECT SQUARE NUMBER BY PRIME FACTORIZATION METHOD

This method is most suitable when the given number is a small perfect square number. In this method we adopt the following steps:

(*a*) Find the prime factors of the given number.

(*b*) Make pairs of similar factors.

(*c*) Take one number from each pair and multiply together.

Given below are a few examples to illustrate the method explained above.

Square root of 9

$= \sqrt{9} = \sqrt{3 \times 3} = 3$

Similarly,

Square root of 25 = $\sqrt{25} = \sqrt{5 \times 5} = 5$

Square root of 36 = $\sqrt{36} = \sqrt{2 \times 2 \times 3 \times 3}$

$= 2 \times 3 = 6$

2. SQUARE ROOT OF A PERFECT SQUARE NUMBER BY DIVISION METHOD

When numbers are very large or can not easily be factorised we use this method. This method is also applicable when the factors do not form complete pairs or the numbers are given in decimal form. In this method we divide the given square number into pairs of two digits beginning with the unit's digit. For example.

Find the square root of 1681.

We first divide the number into pairs of two digits beginning with the unit's digit and then apply division method for finding the square root of the given number.

Thus,

```
        41
    ---------
 4 | 16  81
   | 16
   ---------
81 |     81
   |     81
   ---------
   |     ×
```

Hence, Square root of 1681 is 41.

3. SQUARE ROOT OF DECIMAL FRACTIONS

Division method is quite appropriate for finding the square root of decimal fractions. For example:

Find the square root of .001849.

```
       .043
    ----------
 4 | 00 18 49
   |    16
   ----------
83 |    249
   |    249
   ----------
   |     ×
```

$\therefore$ Square root of .001849 is .043.

SOLVED EXAMPLES

Example 1 : Find the square root of $32 + \sqrt{5 + \sqrt{121}}$.

Solution : Square root of $32 + \sqrt{5 + \sqrt{121}}$

$= \sqrt{32 + \sqrt{5 + \sqrt{121}}} = \sqrt{32 + \sqrt{5 + 11}}$

$= \sqrt{32 + \sqrt{16}}$

$= \sqrt{32 + 4} = \sqrt{36}$

$= \sqrt{2 \times 2 \times 3 \times 3}$

$= 2 \times 3 = 6$

Example 2 : Find the square root of $128 + \sqrt{261-\sqrt{25}}$.

Solution : Square root of $128 + \sqrt{261-\sqrt{25}}$

$= \sqrt{128+\sqrt{261-\sqrt{25}}}$

$= \sqrt{128+\sqrt{261-5}} = \sqrt{128+\sqrt{256}}$

$= \sqrt{128+16} = \sqrt{144} = 12$

Example 3 : Find the square root of 104976.

Solution :

$$\begin{array}{r|l} & \quad 324 \\ \hline 3 & \overline{10}\ \overline{49}\ \overline{76} \\ & \ 9 \\ \hline 62 & \ \ 149 \\ & \ \ 124 \\ \hline 644 & \ \ 2576 \\ & \ \ 2576 \\ \hline & \quad \times \end{array}$$

∴ Square root of 104976 is 324.

Example 4 : Find the Square root of 180625.

Solution :

$$\begin{array}{r|l} & \quad 425 \\ \hline 4 & \overline{18}\ \overline{06}\ \overline{25} \\ & 16 \\ \hline 82 & \ \ 206 \\ & \ \ 164 \\ \hline 845 & \ \ 4225 \\ & \ \ 4225 \\ \hline & \quad \times \end{array}$$

∴ Square root of 180625 is 425.

Example 5 : Find the greatest number of four digits which is a perfect square.

Solution : The greatest four digit number is 9999

$$\begin{array}{r|l} & \quad 99 \\ \hline 9 & \overline{99}\ \overline{99} \\ & 81 \\ \hline 189 & 1899 \\ & 1701 \\ \hline & \ \ 198 \end{array}$$

∴ The greatest perfect square number of four digits is 9999 – 198 = 9801.

Example 6 : Find the least number of six digits which is a perfect square.

Solution : The least six-digit number = 100000

$$\begin{array}{r|l} & \quad 316 \\ \hline 3 & \overline{10}\ \overline{00}\ \overline{00} \\ & \ 9 \\ \hline 61 & \ 100 \\ & \ \ 61 \\ \hline 626 & \ 3900 \\ & \ 3756 \\ \hline & \ \ 144 \end{array}$$

∴ $100000 = (316)^2 + 144$ which is not a perfect square number.

∴ The least perfect square number of six digits $= (317)^2$

∴ The required number is $317 \times 317 = 100489$.

EXERCISE

1. The square root of $5\frac{4}{9}$ is:

A. $\frac{8}{3}$ B. $\frac{7}{3}$ C. $\frac{5}{3}$ D. $\frac{1}{2}$

2. What will be value of the square root of 15625?

A. 115 B. 135 C. 125 D. 145

3. Square root of $\sqrt{1296}$ of will be:

A. 6 B. 36 C. 16 D. 26

4. What will be the square root of 72 upto three decimal places?

A. 8.485 B. 6.465
C. 8.845 D. 8.465

5. If $\frac{x}{7} = \frac{28}{x}$, what will be the value of x?

A. 12 B. 21 C. 18 D. 14

6. The value of $\sqrt{95+\sqrt{13+\sqrt{144}}}$ is:

A. 12 B. 11 C. 10 D. 19

7. By what smallest number 675 be multiplied so that the product becomes a perfect square number?

A. 2 B. $\frac{3}{5}$ C. 4 D. 3

8. If the approximate square root of 80 is 8.94. What will be the value of $\sqrt{20}$?

A. 3.37 B. 4.47 C. 4.87 D. 4.40

9. If $\frac{\sqrt{?}}{4} = \frac{1}{3}$, what will be in place of (?)?

A. $\frac{16}{3}$ B. $\frac{16}{9}$ C. $\frac{21}{16}$ D. $\frac{4}{3}$

10. Find the least number of four digits which is a perfect square.

A. 1025 B. 1125
C. 1016 D. 1024

11. What least number should be subtracted from 11125 so that the resulting number becomes a perfect square?

A. 100 B. 99 C. 81 D. 90

12. In an orchard 4624 plants have been arranged in such a way that the number of plants in each row is the same as the number of rows. How many plants have been arranged in a row?

A. 63 B. 68 C. 78 D. 58

13. An Army General arranges his soldiers in such a way that the number of rows is the same as the number of columns. In doing so, he finds that 100 soldiers are left out. If the total number of soldiers is 14500, find the number of soldiers in each row.

A. 110 B. 105 C. 120 D. 115

14. Kanchan had 537 toffees. On her birthday she distributed among her friends the toffees in such a way that her each friend got as many toffees as was the number of her friends. In doing so, 8 toffees were left with her. Total number of her friends is:

A. 22 B. 23 C. 24 D. 27

15. A sum of ₹ 676 was deposited with a co-operative society by its members in a certain month. If each member of the society deposited as much amount (in paise) as was the number of members of the society, what was the number of members of the society?

A. 270 B. 260 C. 272 D. 280

16. $\left(\frac{\sqrt{625}}{11} \times \frac{14}{\sqrt{25}} \times \frac{11}{\sqrt{196}}\right)$ is simplified to

A. 11 B. 8 C. 6 D. 5

17. Simplify : $\sqrt{41 - \sqrt{21 + \sqrt{19 - \sqrt{9}}}}$

A. 6.4 B. 6 C. 5 D. 3

18. Simplify: $\sqrt{\frac{25}{81} - \frac{1}{9}}$

A. $\frac{25}{81}$ B. $\frac{16}{81}$ C. $\frac{4}{9}$ D. $\frac{2}{3}$

19. $\sqrt{(272)^2 - (128)^2} = ?$

A. 256 B. 240
C. 200 D. 144

20. How many two-digit numbers satisfy this property : The last digit (unit's digit) of the square of the two-digit number is 8?

A. 3 B. 2
C. 1 D. None of these

ANSWERS WITH EXPLANATIONS

1. (B): Square root of $5\frac{4}{9}$ = Square root of $\frac{49}{9}$

$$= \sqrt{\frac{49}{9}} = \frac{\sqrt{7 \times 7}}{\sqrt{3 \times 3}} = \frac{7}{3}.$$

2. (C):

```
          125
     ___________
  1 | 1 56 25
    | 1
    |______
 22 |   56
    |   44
    |______
245 |   1225
    |   1225
    |______
    |     ×
```

∴ Square root of 15625 = 125.

3. (A): Square root of $\sqrt{1296} = \sqrt{\sqrt{1296}}$

$$= \sqrt{\sqrt{6 \times 6 \times 6 \times 6}}$$

$$= \sqrt{6 \times 6} = 6$$

4. (A): 72 = 72.000000

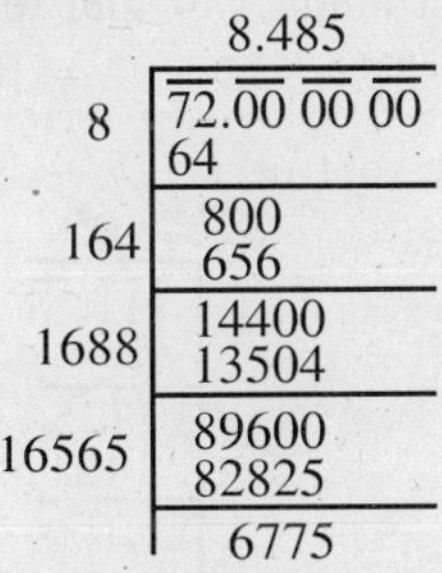

Square root of 72.000000 upto three decimal places = 8.485

5. (D): $\frac{x}{7} = \frac{28}{x}$

$\Rightarrow \quad x^2 = 7 \times 28$

$\Rightarrow \quad x^2 = 7 \times 7 \times 2 \times 2$

$\Rightarrow \quad x = \sqrt{7 \times 7 \times 2 \times 2}$

$\Rightarrow \quad x = 7 \times 2 = 14.$

6. (C): $\sqrt{95+\sqrt{13+\sqrt{144}}} = \sqrt{95+\sqrt{13+12}} = \sqrt{95+\sqrt{25}}$

$= \sqrt{95+5} = \sqrt{100} = \sqrt{10\times10} = 10$

7. (D): $675 = 3 \times 3 \times 3 \times 5 \times 5 = 3 \times 3^2 \times 5^2$

From the above, we find that only a factor 3 is left unpaired

∴ If we multiply 675 by 3 the product would be $\underline{3 \times 3} \times 3^2 \times 5^2$ which is a perfect square.

∴ The required smallest number is 3.

8. (B): $\sqrt{80} = 8.94$ (given)

$\therefore \sqrt{20} = \sqrt{\frac{20\times4}{4}} = \sqrt{\frac{80}{4}} = \frac{8.94}{2} = 4.47$

∴ Value of $\sqrt{20} = 4.47$.

9. (B): $\frac{\sqrt{?}}{4} = \frac{1}{3} \Rightarrow \sqrt{?} = \frac{4}{3}$

$\Rightarrow ? = \frac{4}{3}\times\frac{4}{3} = \frac{16}{9}$

∴ Sign of interrogation (?) should be replaced by $\frac{16}{9}$.

10. (D): The least number of four digits = 1000

Square root of 1000

```
        31
    -----------
 3 | 10 00
   |  9
   |-------
61 | 100
   |  61
   |-------
   |  39
```

∴ $1000 = (31)^2 + 39$ which is not a perfect square number

∴ The least number of four digits is

$32^2 = 32 \times 32 = 1024$.

11. (A): Square root of 11125

```
         105
     -----------
  1 | 111 25
    |  1
    |--------
205 |  1125
    |  1025
    |--------
    |   100
```

The remainder 100 shows that if we subtract 100 from 11125, the resulting number will be a perfect square.

∴ 100 is to be subtracted from 11125.

12. (B): Number of plants that have been arranged in a row will be square root of 4624.

$\therefore \sqrt{4624} =$

```
          68
      -----------
   6 | 46 24
     | 36
     |--------
 128 | 1024
     | 1024
     |--------
     |   ×
```

∴ Number of plants arranged in a row will be 68.

13. (C): Number of soldiers in each row will be square root of 14500 – 100 = 14400

∴ Square root of 14400 = $\sqrt{14400}$

$= \sqrt{12\times10\times12\times10} = 12 \times 10 = 120$.

14. (B): Total number of Kanchan's friends = Square root of (537 – 8 = 529)

```
        23
    ---------
 2 | 5 29
   | 4
   |-------
43 | 129
   | 129
   |-------
   |  ×
```

∴ Total number of her friends = 23.

15. (B): ₹ 676 = 676 × 100 = 67600 Paise

∴ Number of members of the society = Square root of 67600

```
         260
     -----------
  2 | 6 76 00
    | 4
    |---------
 46 | 276
    | 276
    |---------
520 |  ×
```

∴ Number of members = 260.

16. (D): $\left(\frac{\sqrt{625}}{11}\times\frac{14}{\sqrt{25}}\times\frac{11}{\sqrt{196}}\right) = \frac{25}{11}\times\frac{14}{5}\times\frac{11}{14} = 5$

17. (B): $\sqrt{41-\sqrt{21+19-\sqrt{9}}} = \sqrt{41-\sqrt{21+\sqrt{19-3}}}$

$= \sqrt{41-\sqrt{21+\sqrt{16}}} = \sqrt{41-\sqrt{21+4}}$

$= \sqrt{41-\sqrt{25}} = \sqrt{41-5} = \sqrt{36} = 6$

18. (C): $\sqrt{\frac{25}{81}-\frac{1}{9}} = \sqrt{\frac{25-9}{81}} = \sqrt{\frac{16}{81}} = \frac{\sqrt{16}}{\sqrt{81}} = \frac{4}{9}$

19. (B): $\sqrt{(272)^2-(128)^2} = \sqrt{(272+128)(272-128)}$

$= \sqrt{400\times144} = 20\times12 = 240$

20. (D): A two-digit number having 8 at its unit place cannot be a perfect square because square of digits from 1 to 9 do not give 8 as unit digit in the results.

7 Simplification

BODMAS RULE

When an expression involves multiple mathematical operations, the order in which these operations are performed is determined by:

B $\rightarrow$ Bracket
O $\rightarrow$ Of
D $\rightarrow$ Division
M $\rightarrow$ Multiplication
A $\rightarrow$ Addition
S $\rightarrow$ Subtraction

Note:

- The brackets are removed in the order ( ), { } and [ ].
- When executing 'Of', it is substituted with '×' and then solved as a multiplication.

Some Important Formulae

$$(a + b)^2 = a^2 + b^2 + 2ab$$
$$(a - b)^2 = a^2 + b^2 - 2ab$$
$$a^2 - b^2 = (a + b)(a - b)$$

SOLVED EXAMPLES

Example 1 : Simplify: $16 + 12 \div 4 \times 5 - 2$

Solution : $16 + 12 \div 4 \times 5 - 2 \quad \leftarrow D$

$= 16 + 3 \times 5 - 2 \quad \leftarrow M$

$= 16 + 15 - 2 \quad \leftarrow A$

$= 31 - 2 \quad \leftarrow S$

$= 29$

Example 2 : Simplify: $30 - (12 - 6 \div 3)$

Solution : $30 - (12 - 6 \div 3)$

$= 30 - (12 - 2) = 30 - 10 = 20.$

Example 3 : Simplify: $90 - [90 - \{45 + (45 \div 15)\}]$

Solution : $90 - [90 - \{45 + (45 \div 15)\}]$

$= 90 - [90 - \{45 + 3\}]$

$= 90 - [90 - 48] = 90 - 42 = 48.$

Example 4 : Simplify: $60 - [46 - \{14 \div (8 - 1)\}]$

Solution : $60 - [46 - \{14 \div (8-1)\}]$

$= 60 - [46 - \{14 \div 7\}]$

$= 60 - [46 - 2] = 60 - 44 = 16.$

Example 5 : $84 + 16 \div 2 - 6 \text{ of } 7 + 3 \times 2 = ?$

Solution: $? = 84 + 16 \div 2 - 6 \text{ of } 7 + 3 \times 2$

$? = 84 + 8 - 42 + 3 \times 2$

$= 84 + 8 - 42 + 6 = 98 - 42 = 56.$

Example 6 : $\dfrac{16 - 6 \times 2 + 3}{23 - 3 \times 2} = ?$

Solution : $? = \dfrac{16 - 6 \times 2 + 3}{23 - 3 \times 2}$

$= \dfrac{16 - 12 + 3}{23 - 6} = \dfrac{19 - 12}{23 - 6} = \dfrac{7}{17}.$

Example 7 : Simplify: $\dfrac{4}{5} + \left[\dfrac{3}{4} - \left\{\dfrac{3}{2} \text{ of } \dfrac{2}{6} \div \left(\dfrac{1}{4} + \dfrac{1}{2}\right)\right\}\right]$

Solution :

Given expression

$$= \frac{4}{5} + \left[\frac{3}{4} - \left\{\frac{3}{2} \text{ of } \frac{2}{6} \div \left(\frac{1}{4} + \frac{1}{2}\right)\right\}\right]$$

$$= \frac{4}{5} + \left[\frac{3}{4} - \left\{\frac{3}{2} \text{ of } \frac{2}{6} \div \frac{3}{4}\right\}\right]$$

$$= \frac{4}{5} + \left[\frac{3}{4} - \left\{\frac{3}{2} \times \frac{2}{6} \times \frac{4}{3}\right\}\right]$$

$$= \frac{4}{5} + \left[\frac{3}{4} - \frac{2}{3}\right] = \frac{4}{5} + \left[\frac{9 - 8}{12}\right] = \frac{4}{5} + \frac{1}{12}$$

$$= \frac{48 + 5}{60} = \frac{53}{60}.$$

EXERCISE

1. The value of 8 + 8 ÷ 2 + 2 is:
A. 9 B. 8
C. 10 D. 14

2. Find the value of (700 ÷ 10) – {(12 × 8) ÷ (34 – 10)} is:
A. 69 B. 68
C. 67 D. 66

3. Find the value of 7789 × 48 + 7789 × 52.
A. 19846372 B. 407524
C. 778900 D. 778999

4. Simplify: 2.5 + 2.5 ÷ 0.5 × 2 – 4
A. 8 B. 8.5
C. 6 D. 10.5

5. The value of: –{3 – (2 – 3) + 5 – 7} is:
A. –2 B. 3
C. 4 D. –4

6. Naina was given $1\frac{1}{2}$ piece of cake and Najma was given $1\frac{1}{3}$ piece of cake, then the total amount of cake given to both of them is:
A. $\frac{19}{6}$ B. $\frac{17}{6}$
C. $\frac{13}{6}$ D. $\frac{11}{6}$

7. A piece of wire $\frac{7}{8}$ metre long broke into two pieces. One piece was $\frac{1}{4}$ metre long, then length of other piece is:
A. 3/8 m B. 7/8 m
C. 5/8 m D. 9/8 m

8. Jaidev takes $2\frac{1}{5}$ minutes to walk across the school ground. Rahul takes $\frac{7}{5}$ minutes to do the same. Who takes less time and by what fraction?
A. Jaidev 2/3 minute B. Jaidev 4/3 minute
C. Rahul 4/5 minute D. Rahul 3/5 minute

9. The solution of 75 × {25 + (3 × 10)} ÷ 3 is:
A. 1075 B. 1275
C. 1375 D. 1575

10. Simplify : 6 ÷ 6 + 6 × 6 – 6
A. 1 B. 7
C. 31 D. 36

11. Simplify: $1\frac{1}{24} - 1 + \frac{7}{36}$
A. $\frac{17}{72}$ B. $1\frac{17}{72}$
C. $\frac{7}{60}$ D. $\frac{5}{60}$

12. Solve (106 × 106 – 94 × 94) = ?
A. 2400 B. 2000
C. 1904 D. 1906

13. The total weight of brinjal, lady-finger and onion is 48.057 kg. If brinjal and lady-finger weigh 5.35 kg and 24.52 kg respectively, find the weight of onion.
A. 17.187 kg B. 18.187 kg
C. 17.180 kg D. 18.180 kg

14. 9 + [6 + 7 of 3 – (9 + 2 – 6 ÷ 2)]
A. 25 B. 26
C. 27 D. 28

15. If the cost of 420 oranges is ₹ 2,520, then the cost of 8 dozen oranges, is:
A. ₹ 480 B. ₹ 528
C. ₹ 540 D. ₹ 576

16. If 16 bags cost ₹ 1,520, then the cost of 3 bags will be:
A. ₹ 240 B. ₹ 255
C. ₹ 270 D. ₹ 285

17. Simplification of $\frac{1}{13}[7+2\times5\times11+12\times13]$ equals:
A. 13 B. 9
C. 11 D. 12

18. On simplification of
$10\times10+\left[400\div\left\{100-\left(50-\overline{3\times10}\right)\right\}\right]$ we get:
A. 265 B. 65
C. 310 D. 105

19. Simplify: 19 – [4 + 16 – (12 – 2)].
A. 9 B. 17
C. 21 D. 23

20. Simplify: $27 - [18 - \{16 - (5 - \overline{4 - 1})\}]$.

A. 27 B. 25
C. 23 D. 21

21. $\dfrac{(7967)^2 - (4137)^2}{(7967 - 4137)} = ?$

A. 3830 B. 12104
C. 7968 D. 7969

22. If difference and product of two numbers are 5 and 36 respectively, then find the difference of their reciprocals.

A. $\dfrac{5}{9}$ B. $\dfrac{9}{5}$
C. $\dfrac{5}{36}$ D. $\dfrac{31}{36}$

23. If $\dfrac{a+b}{c} = \dfrac{b+c}{a} = \dfrac{c+a}{b} = K$, then the value of K is

A. $\dfrac{1}{2}$ B. $\dfrac{3}{2}$
C. 1 D. 2

24. Simplify $(-9) - \{(-8) + (24 \div \overline{13 - 7})\}$

A. –8 B. None of these
C. 5 D. –5

25. $\dfrac{4}{7}$ of a pole is in the mud. When $\dfrac{1}{3}$ of it is pulled out, an 8 meters long piece of the pole still remains in the mud. What is the total length of the pole?

A. 21 meters B. 25 meters
C. 30 meters D. 12 meters

ANSWERS WITH EXPLANATIONS

1. (D): $8 + 8 \div 2 + 2 = 8 + \dfrac{8}{2} + 2 = 8 + 4 + 2 = 14.$

2. (D): $(700 \div 10) - \{(12 \times 8) \div (34 - 10)\}$
$= 70 - \{96 \div 24\}$
$= 70 - 4 = 66.$

3. (C): $7789 \times 48 + 7789 \times 52$
$= 7789 \times (48 + 52)$
$= 7789 \times 100 = 778900.$

4. (B): $2.5 + 2.5 \div 0.5 \times 2 - 4$
$= 2.5 + 2.5 \times \dfrac{1}{0.5} \times 2 - 4$
$= 2.5 + 5 \times 2 - 4$
$= 2.5 + 10 - 4 = 12.5 - 4 = 8.5.$

5. (A): $-\{3 - (2 - 3) + 5 - 7\}$
$= -\{3 - (-1) + 5 - 7\}$
$= -\{3 + 1 + 5 - 7\}$
$= -\{9 - 7\} = -2.$

6. (B): Total amount of cake
$= 1\dfrac{1}{2} + 1\dfrac{1}{3}$
$= \dfrac{3}{2} + \dfrac{4}{3} = \dfrac{9+8}{6} = \dfrac{17}{6}$

7. (C): Length of other piece
$= \dfrac{7}{8} - \dfrac{1}{4} = \dfrac{7-2}{8} = 5/8$ m.

8. (C): Jaidev takes $= 2\dfrac{1}{5} = \dfrac{11}{5}$ minutes

Rahul takes = 7/5 minutes

Rahul takes less times by
$= \dfrac{11}{5} - \dfrac{7}{5} = \dfrac{44 - 28}{20} = \dfrac{16}{20}$
$= \dfrac{4}{5}$ minute

9. (C): $75 \times \{25 + 30\} \div 3$
$= 75 \times 55 \div 3$
$= 75 \times 55 \times \dfrac{1}{3}$
$= 25 \times 55 = 1375.$

10. (C): $6 \div 6 + 6 \times 6 - 6 = 1 + 36 - 6 = 37 - 6 = 31.$

11. (A): $1\dfrac{1}{24} - 1 + \dfrac{7}{36}$
$\Rightarrow \dfrac{25}{24} - 1 + \dfrac{7}{36} = \dfrac{75 - 72 + 14}{72} = \dfrac{17}{72}.$

12. (A): $106 \times 106 - 94 \times 94 = 11236 - 8836 = 2400$

13. (B): The total weight of brinjal, ladyfinger and onion
= 48.057 k.g.

and the total weight of brinjal and ladyfinger
$= 5.35 + 24.52 = 29.87$

Hence, the weight of onion
$= 48.057 - 29.87 = 18.187$ kg

14. (D): $9 + [6 + 7 \times 3 - (9 + 2 - 3)]$
$= 9 + [6 + 21 - 8]$
$= 9 + 19 = 28.$

15. (D): $\because$ Cost of 420 oranges = ₹ 2520

$\therefore$ Cost of 96 oranges = ₹ $\dfrac{2520}{420} \times 96$ = ₹ 576.

16. (D): Cost of 16 bags = ₹ 1520

Cost of 3 bags = $\frac{1520}{16} \times 3$ = ₹ 95 × 3 = ₹ 285.

17. (C): $\frac{1}{13}[7+2\times5\times11+2\times13]$

$= \frac{1}{13}[7+110+26] = \frac{1}{13}[143] = 11.$

18. (D): $10\times10+\left[400\div\left\{100-\left(50-\overline{3\times10}\right)\right\}\right]$

$= 100 + [400 \div \{100 - (50 - 30)\}]$
$= 100 + [400 \div \{100 - 20\}]$
$= 100 + [400 \div 80]$
$= 100 + 5 = 105.$

19. (A): $19 - [4 + \{16 - (12 - 2)\}]$
$= 19 - [4 + \{16 - 10\}] = 19 - [4 + 6]$
$= 19 - 10 = 9.$

20. (C): $27-\left[18-\left\{16-\left(5-\overline{4-1}\right)\right\}\right]$
$= 27 - [18 - \{16 - (5 - 3)\}]$
$= 27 - [18 - \{16 - 2\}]$
$= 27 - [18 - 14] = 27 - 4 = 23.$

21. (B): $? = \frac{(7967)^2 - (4137)^2}{(7967 - 4137)}$

$= \frac{(7967 + 4137)(7967 - 4137)}{(7967 - 4137)}$

$[\because a^2 - b^2 = (a + b)(a - b)]$

$= (7967 + 4137) = 12104.$

22. (C): Let the two numbers are x and y

Then, $x - y = 5$ ...(*i*)

and $xy = 36$

$\because (x + y)^2 = (x - y)^2 + 4xy$

$\Rightarrow (x + y)^2 = 5^2 + 4(36)$

$\Rightarrow (x + y)^2 = 25 + 144$

$\Rightarrow (x + y)^2 = 169 = 13^2$

$\Rightarrow x + y = 13$ ...(*ii*)

Adding (*i*) and (*ii*), we get

$2x = 18$

$\Rightarrow x = 9$

From (*i*), when $x = 9$, then $y = 4$

$\therefore \frac{1}{x} - \frac{1}{y} = \frac{1}{9} - \frac{1}{4}$

$= \frac{4-9}{36}$

$= -\frac{5}{36}$

and $\frac{1}{y} - \frac{1}{x} = \frac{1}{4} - \frac{1}{9}$

$= \frac{9-4}{36}$

$= \frac{5}{36}.$

23. (D): Given, $\frac{a+b}{c} = \frac{b+c}{a} = \frac{c+a}{b} = \text{K}$

$\therefore a + b = c\text{K}$ ...(*i*)

$b + c = a\text{K}$ ...(*ii*)

$c + a = b\text{K}$ ...(*iii*)

From adding (*i*), (*ii*) and (*iii*), we get

$a + b + b + c + c + a = c\text{K} + a\text{K} + b\text{K}$

$\Rightarrow 2(a + b + c) = \text{K}(a + b + c)$

$\Rightarrow 2 = \text{K}$

Hence, K = 2.

24. (D): $(-9)-\left\{(-8)+(24\div\overline{13-7})\right\}$

$= (-9) - \{(-8) + (24 \div 6)\}$
$= (-9) - \{(-8) + 4\}$
$= -9 + 4$
$= -5.$

25. (A): Let total length of the pole = $7x$ m

Remaining part when $\frac{1}{3}$ part pulled out from the mud

$= 1 - \frac{1}{3} = \frac{2}{3}$

According to the question,

$\frac{2}{3} \times 4x = 8 \Rightarrow x = 3$

Hence, total length of the pole

$= 7x = 7 \times 3 = 21$ m.

8 Unitary Method

The unitary method is the method by which we find the value of a single unit from the value of multiple units and then use this value to find the value of required number of units.

The two operations generally used in the unitary method are multiplication (when we find out the cost of many quantities) and division (when we find out the cost of one quantity).

SOLVED EXAMPLES

Example 1 : If 15 oranges cost ₹ 105, what is the cost of 33 oranges?

Solution : The cost of 15 oranges = ₹ 105

$\Rightarrow$ The cost of 1 orange = ₹ $\left(\frac{105}{5}\right)$

[Less oranges, Less cost]

$\therefore$ The cost of 33 oranges

= ₹ $\left(\frac{105}{15}\times 33\right)$ = ₹ 231.

[More oranges, More cost]

Example 2 : A man buys two dozen mangoes for ₹ 216. What is the cost of 42 such mangoes?

Solution : The cost of two dozen mangoes i.e., 24 mangoes = ₹ 216

$\Rightarrow$ The cost of 1 mango = ₹ $\frac{216}{24}$

$\therefore$ The cost of 42 mangoes = ₹ $\left(\frac{216}{24}\times 42\right)$

= ₹ (9 × 42) = ₹ 378.

Example 3 : A man earns ₹ 4200 by working for one week. How much will he earn at the same rate it he works for 18 days?

Solution : Earning for one week i.e., 7 days = ₹ 4200

$\Rightarrow$ Earning for 1 day = ₹ $\left(\frac{4200}{7}\right)$

$\therefore$ Earnings for 18 days = ₹ $\left(\frac{4200}{7}\times 18\right)$

= (600 × 18) = ₹ 10800.

Example 4 : A bike consumes 28 litres of petrol, covering a distance of 1904 km. How much petrol will be needed to cover a distance of 5712 km?

Solution : 1904 km can be covered in 28 litres of petrol

$\Rightarrow$ 1 km can be covered in $\left(\frac{28}{1904}\right)$ litres

$\therefore$ 5712 km can be covered in $\frac{28}{1904}\times 5712$

= 84 litres.

[More distance, More petrol]

Example 5 : If 21 men can finish a piece of work in 14 days, in how many days will 42 men finish it?

Solution : 21 men can finish the work in 14 days

$\Rightarrow$ 1 men can finish the work in (14 × 21) days

[Less men, More days]

$\therefore$ 42 men can finish the work in $\left(\frac{14\times 21}{42}\right)$ days

= $\left(\frac{14}{2}\right)$ days = 7 days.

[More men, Less day]

EXERCISE

1. The cost of 16 apples is ₹ 80, what is the cost of 30 apples?
   A. ₹ 140 B. ₹ 150 C. ₹ 146 D. ₹ 160

2. The cost of 18 pens is ₹ 153, what is the cost of 32 pens?
   A. ₹ 272 B. ₹ 232 C. ₹ 262 D. ₹ 292

3. If the cost of 12 books is ₹ 144, then the cost of 18 books is:
   A. ₹ 180 B. ₹ 198 C. ₹ 216 D. ₹ 206

4. If a person travels 150 km in 5 hours, then the time taken by him to travel 180 km is:
   A. 3 hours B. 6 hours
   C. 4 hours D. 8 hours

5. The cost of 6 bowls is ₹ 90, what is the cost of 10 bowls.
   A. ₹ 120 B. ₹ 125 C. ₹ 150 D. ₹ 175

6. 6 dozen eggs are bought for ₹ 108. How much will 108 eggs cost?
   A. ₹ 162 B. ₹ 152 C. ₹ 172 D. ₹ 182

7. If the cost of 15 mangoes is ₹ 180, then what is the cost of 25 mangoes?
   A. ₹ 200 B. ₹ 220 C. ₹ 300 D. ₹ 360

8. The cost of 25 pencils is ₹ 75, what is the cost of 75 pencils?
   A. ₹ 100 B. ₹ 150 C. ₹ 180 D. ₹ 225

9. If the price of 12 packets of biscuits is ₹ 240, then the price of 8 packets of biscuits will be:
   A. ₹ 160 B. ₹ 140 C. ₹ 120 D. ₹ 240

10. Cost of 12 kg of potatoes is ₹ 360. Find the cost of 8 kg of potatoes.
    A. ₹ 180 B. ₹ 240 C. ₹ 300 D. ₹ 120

11. If the cost of 120 m of cloths is ₹ 9600, then what will be the cost of 147 m of that cloth?
    A. ₹ 16170 B. ₹ 11670
    C. ₹ 11760 D. ₹ 17160

12. If the cost of 18 chocolates is ₹ 540, what is the cost of 25 chocolates?
    A. ₹ 450 B. ₹ 500 C. ₹ 750 D. ₹ 900

13. If 49 m of a cloth costs ₹ 1225, how many metres of cloth can be bought for ₹ 7500?
    A. 280 m B. 300 m C. 320 m D. 350 m

14. If the cost of 33.5 m silk is ₹ 8375, how many metres of silk can be purchased for ₹ 5000?
    A. 20 m B. 22 m C. 24 m D. 36 m

15. If 17 m of a uniform iron rod weigh 53.2 kg, what will be the weight of 23 m such rod?
    A. 70.01 kg B. 71.2 kg
    C. 71.97 kg D. 72.1 kg

16. 60 cows can graze a field in 17 days, how many cows will graze the same field in 12 days?
    A. 85 B. 102 C. 68 D. 80

17. If 36 men can finish a piece of work in 16 days, how many days will 9 men take to finish the work?
    A. 32 B. 36 C. 54 D. 64

18. 42 men can dig a trench in 16 days, how long will 7 men take to dig the similar trench?
    A. 98 B. 96 C. 104 D. 108

19. Travelling 800 km by rail costs ₹ 4520, what will be the fare of a journey of 200 km when a person travels by train?
    A. ₹ 1170 B. ₹ 2140 C. ₹ 1130 D. ₹ 3250

20. The price of 75 quintals of goods is ₹ 375. Find the price of 42 quintals of goods.
    A. ₹ 200 B. ₹ 210 C. ₹ 220 D. ₹ 230

21. Tarun types 450 words in half an hour. How many words would he type in 7 minutes?
    A. 90 words B. 105 words
    C. 100 words D. 110 words

22. An aeroplane takes 12 hours to fly a distance of 6000 km. How much distance can it cover in 1 hour?
    A. 400 km B. 450 km C. 500 km D. 600 km

23. A worker is paid ₹ 750 for 6 days of work. If he works for 23 days, how much money will he get?
    A. ₹ 2825 B. ₹ 2875 C. ₹ 2850 D. ₹ 2890

24. For a shirt, cloth required must be 2 m 75 cm. Then, how much cloth would be taken to have such 6 shirts?
    A. 15 m 50 cm B. 16 m 50 cm
    C. 18 m D. 21 m

25. 15 men can do a piece of work in 36 hours. How many will be required to finish the work in 20 hours?
    A. 23 men B. 25 men
    C. 27 men D. 30 men

ANSWERS WITH EXPLANATIONS

1. (B): The cost of 16 apples = ₹ 80

$\Rightarrow$ The cost of 1 apple = ₹ $\left(\frac{80}{16}\right)$

$\therefore$ The cost of 30 apples = ₹ $\left(\frac{80}{16}\times 30\right)$

= ₹ (5 × 30) = ₹ 150.

2. (A): The cost of 18 pens = ₹ 153

$\Rightarrow$ The cost of 1 pen = ₹ $\left(\frac{153}{18}\right)$

$\therefore$ The cost of 32 pens = ₹ $\left(\frac{153}{18}\times 32\right)$

= ₹ (17 × 16) = ₹ 272.

3. (C): The cost of 12 books = ₹ 144

$\Rightarrow$ The cost of 1 book = ₹ $\left(\frac{144}{12}\right)$

$\therefore$ The cost of 18 books = ₹ $\left(\frac{144}{12}\times 18\right)$

= ₹ (12 × 18) = ₹ 216.

4. (B): The time taken to cover 150 km distance = 5 hours

$\Rightarrow$ The time taken to cover 1 km distance

= $\left(\frac{5}{150}\right)$ hours

$\therefore$ The time taken to cover 180 km distance

= $\left(\frac{5}{150}\times 180\right)$ hours

= $\left(\frac{1}{30}\times 180\right)$ hours = 6 hours.

5. (C): The cost of 6 bowls = ₹ 90

$\Rightarrow$ The cost of 1 bowl = ₹ $\left(\frac{90}{6}\right)$

$\therefore$ The cost of 10 bowls = ₹ $\left(\frac{90}{6}\times 10\right)$

= ₹ (15 × 10) = ₹ 150.

6. (A): 6 dozen = 6 × 12 = 72

The cost of 72 eggs = ₹ 108

$\Rightarrow$ The cost of 1 egg = ₹ $\left(\frac{108}{72}\right)$

$\therefore$ The cost of 108 egg = ₹ $\left(\frac{108}{72}\times 108\right)$

= ₹ (18 × 9) = ₹ 162.

7. (C): The cost of 15 mangoes = ₹ 180

$\Rightarrow$ The cost of 1 mango = ₹ $\left(\frac{180}{15}\right)$

$\therefore$ The cost of 25 mangoes = ₹ $\left(\frac{180}{15}\times 25\right)$

= ₹ (12 × 25) = ₹ 300.

8. (D): The cost of 25 pencils = ₹ 75

$\Rightarrow$ The cost of 1 pencil = ₹ $\left(\frac{75}{25}\right)$

$\therefore$ The cost of 75 pencils = ₹ $\left(\frac{75}{25}\times 75\right)$

= ₹ (3 × 75) = ₹ 225.

9. (A): The cost of 12 packets = ₹ 240

$\Rightarrow$ The cost of 1 packet = ₹ $\left(\frac{240}{12}\right)$

$\therefore$ The cost of 8 packets = ₹ $\left(\frac{240}{12}\times 8\right)$

= ₹ (20 × 8) = ₹ 160

Hence, cost of 8 packets of biscuits = ₹ 160.

10. (B): The cost of 12 kg of potatoes = ₹ 360

$\Rightarrow$ The cost of 1 kg of potato = ₹ $\left(\frac{360}{12}\right)$

$\therefore$ The cost of 8 kg potatoes = ₹ $\left(\frac{360}{12}\times 8\right)$

= ₹ (30 × 8) = ₹ 240.

11. (C): The cost of 120 m of cloth = ₹ 9600

$\Rightarrow$ The cost of 1 m of cloth = ₹ $\left(\frac{9600}{120}\right)$

$\therefore$ The cost of 147 m of cloth = ₹ $\left(\frac{9600}{120}\times 147\right)$

= (80 × 147) = ₹ 11760.

12. (C): The cost of 18 chocolates = ₹ 540

$\Rightarrow$ The cost of 1 chocolates = ₹ $\left(\frac{540}{18}\right)$

$\therefore$ The cost of 25 chocolates = ₹ $\left(\frac{540}{18}\times 25\right)$

= ₹(30 × 25) = ₹ 750.

13. (B): For ₹ 1225, clothes purchased = 49 m

⇒ For ₹ 1, cloths purchased = $\left(\frac{49}{1225}\right)$ m

∴ For ₹ 7500, cloths purchased = $\left(\frac{49}{1225}\times 7500\right)$ m

$= \left(\frac{7500}{25}\right)$ m = 300 m.

14. (A): For ₹ 8375, silk purchased = 33.5 m

⇒ For ₹ 1, silk purchased = $\left(\frac{33.5}{8375}\right)$ m

∴ For 5000, silk purchased = $\left(\frac{33.5}{8375}\times 5000\right)$ m

$= \left(\frac{335}{8375\times 10}\times 5000\right)$ m

$= \left(\frac{1}{25\times 10}\times 5000\right)$ m = 20 m.

15. (C): Weight of 17 m uniform rod = 53.2 kg

⇒ Weight of 1 m uniform rod = $\left(\frac{53.2}{17}\right)$ kg

∴ Weight of 23 uniform rod = $\left(\frac{53.2}{17}\times 23\right)$ kg

$= \left(\frac{532}{17\times 10}\times 23\right)$ kg = 71.97 kg.

16. (A): 60 cows can graze a field in 17 days
1 cow can graze a field in 17 × 60 days

∴ Cow required to graze the field in 12 days = $\frac{17\times 60}{12}$

= 17 × 5 = 85 cows.

17. (D): 36 men can finish the work in 16 days.
⇒ 1 man can finish the work in (16 × 36) days

∴ 9 men can finish the work in $\left(\frac{16\times 36}{9}\right)$ days

= 64 days

18. (B): 42 men can dig a trench in 16 days
⇒ 1 man can dig a trench in (16 × 42 days)

∴ 7 men can dig a trench in $\left(\frac{16\times 42}{7}\right)$ days

= (16 × 6) days = 96 days.

19. (C): The fare for 800 km by rail = ₹ 4520

⇒ The fare for 1 km by rail = ₹ $\left(\frac{4520}{800}\right)$

∴ The fare for 200 km by rail = ₹ $\left(\frac{4520}{800}\times 200\right)$

= ₹ $\left(\frac{4520}{4}\right)$ = ₹ 1130.

20. (B): The price of 75 quintals of goods = ₹ 375

⇒ The price of 1 quintal of goods = ₹ $\left(\frac{375}{75}\right)$

∴ The price of 42 quintals of goods = ₹ $\left(\frac{375}{75}\times 42\right)$

= ₹ (5 × 42) = ₹ 210.

21. (B): The words typed in half an hour (30 minutes)
= 450 words

⇒ The words typed in 1 minute = $\left(\frac{450}{30}\right)$ words

∴ The words typed in 7 minutes = $\left(\frac{450}{30}\times 7\right)$ words

= (15 × 7) words = 105 words.

22. (C): Distance covered by an aeroplane in 12 hours
= 6000 km

∴ Distance covered by an aeroplane in 1 hour

$= \left(\frac{6000}{12}\right)$ km = 500 km.

23. (B): Earning for 6 days = ₹ 750

Daily wages = ₹ $\left(\frac{750}{6}\right)$

∴ Earning for 23 days = ₹ $\left(\frac{750}{6}\times 23\right)$

= ₹ (125 × 23) = ₹ 2875.

24. (B): Cloth required for a shirt = 2.75 m
Cloth required for 6 shirt = (2.75 × 6) m = 16.50 m
Hence, required length of cloths for 6 shirts = 16 m 50 cm.

25. (C): 15 men can do a piece of work in 36 hours.
Total man-hours required to finish the job
= (15 × 36) man-hours

∴ To finish the work in 20 man-hours, the number of men required

$= \left(\frac{15\times 36}{20}\right)$ = 27 men.

9 Measurement of Length, Mass, Capacity, Time and Temperature

MEASUREMENT EXPERIENCES

Length

Length is the measure of something from end to end. The concept of the standard units for length, the metre (m), the centimetre (cm) and the kilometre (km) are introduced.

This table shows the common metric units for length:

1000 millimetres (mm) = 1 metre (m)

10 millimetres (mm) = 1 centimetre (cm)

100 centimetres (cm) = 1 metre (m)

1000 metres (m) = 1 kilometre (km)

Mass

The focus with mass should be on the heaviness of the object and not its size. The standard units for mass are the kilogram (kg) and the gram (g).

This table shows the common metric units for weight or mass:

1000 micrograms (mcg) = 1 milligram (mg)

1000 milligrams (mg) = 1 gram (g)

1000 grams (g) = 1 kilogram (kg)

1000 kilograms (kg) = 1 tonne

Capacity

Capacity refers to how much a container can actually hold and often relates to volume. For example, the capacity of a hot water tank is the volume of water that can fit inside the tank. The capacity of a petrol tank is the volume of petrol that can fit inside the tank. An empty one-litre Jug has a capacity of one litre, but because it is empty it has nil volume. The standard units for volume are the litre (*l*) and the millilitre (ml).

1000 millilitre (ml) = 1 litre (*l*)

1000 litre (*l*) = 1 kilolitre (kl)

1000 cubic centimetre (cc) = 1 litre (*l*)

Time

Time is an abstract and complex concept. The calendar is also a measure of time. Children need to be able to order months and seasons and describe duration of time using days, weeks and months. They should be encouraged to use the calendar to identify the date and determine the number of days in each month.

60 seconds = 1 minute

60 minutes = 1 hour

24 hours = 1 day

7 days = 1 week

4 weeks or 30 days = 1 month

12 months = 1 year

365 days = 1 year

366 days = 1 leap year

Temperature

Temperature is the measure of hotness or coldness of a body Temperature is measured in degree Celsius (°C) or degree Fahrenheit (°F). To measure the temperature an instrument is used, called thermometer. Doctors use degree Fahrenheit thermometer.

(*i*) Comparison between Celsius and Fahrenheit

$$\frac{C}{5} = \frac{F-32}{9}$$

(*ii*) Conversion of Fahrenheit to Celsius and vice-versa

$$°C = (°F - 32) \times \frac{5}{9}; \quad °F = \frac{9}{5} \times °C + 32$$

SOLVED EXAMPLES

Example 1 : Convert 7 metres into millimetres.

Solution : 1 m = 1000 mm

$\therefore$ 7 m = (7 × 1000) mm = 7000 mm

Example 2 : Convert 21 centimetres into decametres.

Solution : 1 dam = 1000 cm $\Rightarrow$ 1 cm = $\frac{1}{1000}$ dam

$\therefore 21 \text{ cm} = \left(21 \times \frac{1}{1000}\right) \text{dam} = 0.021 \text{ dam}$

Example 3 : Convert 5 kilograms into grams.

Solution : 1 kg = 1000 gm

$\therefore$ 5 kg = (5 × 1000) gm = 5000 gm

Example 4 : Convert 3 litres into mililitres.

Solution : 1 *l* = 1000 ml

$\therefore$ 3 *l* = (3 × 1000) ml = 3000 ml

Example 5 : Convert 36 seconds into minutes.

Solution : 1 minute = 60 seconds

$\Rightarrow$ 1 second = $\frac{1}{60}$ minutes

$\therefore 36 \text{ seconds} = \left(36 \times \frac{1}{60}\right) \text{ minutes}$

$= \frac{6}{10}$ minutes = 0.6 minutes

Example 6 : 12 minutes past 1 in the afternoon, is written as:

Solution : 12 minutes past 1 in the afternoon = 1 : 12 pm.

Example 7 : Convert 113°F temperature into °C.

Solution : $°C = (°F - 32) \times \frac{5}{9}$

$\therefore = (113 - 32) \times \frac{5}{9}$

$= 81 \times \frac{5}{9} = 9 \times 5 = 45°C$

Example 8 : Convert 35°C temperature into °F.

Solution : $°F = \frac{9}{5} \times °C + 32 = \frac{9}{5} \times 35 + 32$

$= 9 \times 7 + 32 = 63 + 32 = 95°F$

EXERCISE

1. 4850 grams is equal to:
   A. 4 kg 85 g B. 4 kg 850 g
   C. 48 kg 50 g D. 48 kg 5 g
2. Four-tenth of a centimetres when written in the fractions of metre, is equal to:
   A. 0.04 B. 0.0004 C. 0.004 D. 0.00004
3. Five-hundredth of a metre, when written in the fractions of kilometres, is equal to:
   A. 0.2 B. 0.000002 C. 0.002 D. 0.0005
4. 20 minutes past 7, in the morning is written as:
   A. 7:02 p.m. B. 7:20 p.m.
   C. 7:02 a.m. D. 7:20 a.m.
5. What is the total number of seconds in a day?
   A. 24 B. 60 C. 3600 D. 86400
6. How many seconds are there in 7 hours and 40 minutes?
   A. 27600 B. 2860 C. 26600 D. 26700
7. 3 kilometre is equal to:
   A. 3000 cm B. 30000 cm
   C. 300000 cm D. $\frac{3}{1000}$ cm
8. 6 dam is equal to:
   A. 6000 cm B. $\frac{1}{600}$ cm
   C. 600 cm D. $\frac{1}{6000}$ cm
9. 2 dam 45 cm is equal to:
   A. 20045 cm B. 2045 cm
   C. 2450 cm D. 24500 cm
10. Convert 568 minutes into hours and minutes.
    A. 8 hr 48 min B. 9 hr 28 min
    C. 10 hr 8 min D. 9 hr 38 min
11. How many millimetres are there in 8 centimetres?
    A. 0.08 B. 0.008 C. 80 D. 800
12. Convert 4 hectares to square metres.
    A. 40000 m^2 B. 4000 m^2
    C. 400 m^2 D. 400000 m^2
13. The value of 185°F in degree celsius is:
    A. 83°C B. 85°C C. 84°C D. 86°C

14. Convert 428°F into degree celsius.

A. 230°C B. 210°C C. 220°C D. 202°C

15. Convert 75 degree celsius into degree fahrenheit.

A. 167°F B. 176°F C. 187°F D. 197°F

16. Convert 116 degree celsius into degree fahrenheit.

A. 204.8°F B. 240.8°F
C. 242.8°F D. 244.8°F

17. How many months are there in 6 years and 3 months?

A. 57 months B. 76 months
C. 75 months D. 77 months

18. How many months are there in 13 years and 7 months?

A. 136 months B. 143 months
C. 153 months D. 163 months

19. What is the number of days in a leap year?

A. 365 days B. 362 days
C. 366 days D. 364 days

20. Convert 5 years 178 days into days.

A. 2030 days B. 2003 days
C. 2300 days D. 2078 days

21. Convert 4 metres 2604 centimetres into centimetres.

A. 3040 cm B. 3400 cm
C. 3004 cm D. 6604 cm

22. 5 minutes past 3, in the afternoon, is written as:

A. 5:30 a.m. B. 5:30 p.m.
C. 3:50 p.m. D. 3:05 p.m.

23. 5 cm is expressed in kilometres as:

A. 0.005 km B. 0.0005 km
C. 0.00005 km D. 0.000005 km

24. How many hours are there in a week?

A. 168 hrs B. 156 hrs C. 172 hrs D. 164 hrs

25. The number of minutes in 12 weeks is:

A. 1276 min B. 1296 min
C. 12960 min D. 120960 min

ANSWERS WITH EXPLANATIONS

1. (B): $1000 \text{ g} = 1 \text{ kg} \Rightarrow 1 \text{ g} = \frac{1}{1000}\text{kg}$

$\therefore 4850 \text{ g} = \left(\frac{1}{1000} \times 4850\right) \text{kg} = 4 \text{ kg } 850 \text{ g}$

2. (C): $1 \text{ metre} = 100 \text{ cm} \Rightarrow 1 \text{ cm} = \frac{1}{100}\text{m}$

∴ Four tenths of a centimetre

$= \left(\frac{4}{10} \times \frac{1}{100}\right) \text{m} = \frac{4}{1000}$

$= 0.004 \text{ m}$

3. (B): $1 \text{ km} = 1000 \text{ m} \Rightarrow 1 \text{ m} = \frac{1}{1000} \text{ km}$

∴ Five-hundredth of a metre $= \left(\frac{1}{500} \times \frac{1}{1000}\right) \text{km}$

$= \frac{1}{500000} = 0.000002$

4. (D): 20 minutes past 7, in the morning is written as 7:20 a.m.

5. (D): The number of hours in a day = 24 hours

∴ 24 hour = (24 × 60) minutes
= (24 × 60 × 60) seconds
= (24 × 3600) seconds
= 86400 seconds

6. (A): 7 hours = (7 × 60 × 60) seconds
= (7 × 3600) seconds
= 25200 seconds

40 minutes = (40 × 60) seconds
= 2400 seconds

∴ 7 hours and 40 minutes = (25200 + 2400) seconds
= 27600 seconds

7. (C): 1 m = 100 cm

1 km = 1000 m
= (1000 × 100) cm
= 100000 cm

∴ 3 km = (3 × 100000) cm
= 300000 cm

8. (A): 1 m = 100 cm

1 dam = 10 m = (10 × 100) cm = 1000 cm

∴ 6 dam = (6 × 1000) cm = 6000 cm

9. (B): 1 dam = 10 m = (10 × 100) cm = 1000 cm

∴ 2 dam 45 cm = (2 × 1000) cm + 45 cm
= (2000 + 45) cm = 2045 cm

10. (B): 1 hour = 60 minutes

∴ 568 min = 9 hr 28 min

$$\begin{array}{r} 60\overline{)\,568\,}(9 \\ \underline{540} \\ 28 \end{array}$$

11. (C): 1 cm = 10 mm

∴ 8 cm = (8 × 10) mm = 80 mm

12. (A): 1 hectare = 100 m × 100 m = $10000\ m^2$

$\therefore$ 4 hectare = $(4 \times 10000)\ m^2 = 40000\ m^2$

13. (B): $°C = (°F - 32) \times \frac{5}{9}$

$= (185 - 32) \times \frac{5}{9} = 153 \times \frac{5}{9}$

$= 17 \times 5 = 85°C$

$\therefore$ 185°F = 85°C

14. (C): $°C = (°F - 32) \times \frac{5}{9}$

$= (428 - 32) \times \frac{5}{9} = 396 \times \frac{5}{9}$

$= 44 \times 5 = 220°C$

$\therefore$ 428 °C = 220°C

15. (A): $°F = \frac{9}{5} \times °C + 32$

$= \frac{9}{5} \times 75 + 32 = 9 \times 15 + 32$

$= 135 + 32 = 167\ °F$

$\therefore$ 75 °F = 167 °F

16. (B): $°F = \frac{9}{5} \times °C + 32$

$= \frac{9}{5} \times 116 + 32 = 9 \times 23.2 + 32$

$= 208.8 + 32 = 240.8\ °F$

$\therefore$ 116°C = 240.8 °F

17. (C): 6 years 3 months = 6 years + 3 months
= (6 × 12) months + 3 months
= 72 months + 3 months
= 75 months

18. (D): 13 years 7 months = 13 years + 7 months
= (13 × 12) months + 7 months
= 156 months + 7 months
= 163 months

19. (C): A Leap year has 366 days because the month of February has 29 days in it during a leap year.

20. (B): 5 years 178 days
= 5 years + 178 days
= (5 × 365) days + 178 days
= 1825 days + 178 days
= 2003 days

21. (C): 1 m = 100 m

$\therefore$ 4 m 2604 cm = 4 m + 2604 cm
= (4 × 100 + 2604) cm
= (400 + 2604) cm = 3004 cm

22. (D): 5 minutes past 3, in the afternoon is written as 3:05 p.m.

23. (C): $1\ cm = \frac{1}{100}$ m and $1\ m = \frac{1}{1000}$ km

$\therefore$ $5\ cm = \frac{5}{100} m = \left(\frac{5}{100} \times \frac{1}{1000}\right) km$

$= \frac{5}{100000} km = 0.00005\ km$

24. (A): 1 week = 7 days
1 day = 24 hours

$\therefore$ 1 week = (7 × 24) hrs = 168 hrs

25. (D): 1 week = 7 days
1 day = 24 hours
1 hour = 60 minutes

$\therefore$ 12 weeks = (12 × 7) days
= (12 × 7 × 24) hrs
= (12 × 7 × 24 × 60) minutes
= 120960 minutes

10 Percentage

The term 'per cent' means 'out of a hundred'. A per cent is a fraction that always has 100 as its denominator. It is denoted by per cent sign (%).

To convert a per cent to a fraction, we have to remove the per cent sign and divide the given number by 100.

For example:

(*i*) $4\% = \frac{4}{100} = \frac{1}{25}$

(*ii*) $10\% = \frac{10}{100} = \frac{1}{10}$

To convert fractions into percentages, first divide the numerator by the denominator and then multiply it by 100 and place the % sign after it.

For example: $\frac{3}{5} = \left(\frac{3}{5} \times 100\right)\% = 60\%$

If the value of a variable X increases by a%, then the resulting value is equal to $(100 + a)\%$ of X.

If the value of a variable X decreases by a%, then the resulting value is equal to $(100 - a)\%$ of X.

$$\% \text{ Increase} = \left(\frac{\text{Increase in the value}}{\text{Initial value}} \times 100\right)\%$$

$$\% \text{ Decrease} = \left(\frac{\text{Decrease in the value}}{\text{Initial value}} \times 100\right)\%$$

SOLVED EXAMPLES

Example 1 : Express the following as per cent:

(*i*) $\frac{3}{25}$ (*ii*) $\frac{9}{40}$ (*iii*) $8\frac{2}{3}$

Solution : (*i*) $\frac{3}{25} \times 100 = 12\%$

(*ii*) $\frac{9}{40} \times 100 = 22.5\%$

(*iii*) $\frac{26}{3} \times 100 = 866\frac{2}{3}\%$

Example 2 : Express the following into fraction:

(*i*) 25% (*ii*) 75% (*iii*) 240%

Solution : (*i*) $25\% = \frac{25}{100} = \frac{1}{4}$

(*ii*) $75\% = \frac{75}{100} = \frac{3}{4}$

(*iii*) $240\% = \frac{240}{100} = \frac{12}{5}$

Example 3 : Find 75% of 400.

Solution : $400 \times \frac{75}{100} = 300$

Example 4 : Population of a town increases 25% per year. If the population of the town this year is 3,50,000, find the population of the town after two years.

Solution : Increase in population = 25%

It means that if the population of the town is 100, its population will be 125 after one year

∴ If population of the town is 3,50,000 this year

Its population after one year will be

$= \frac{125 \times 3,50,000}{100} = 4,37,500$

∴ Population of the town after one more year

$= \frac{125}{100} \times 437500 = 546875.$

Example 5 : The population of a certain town has increased from 70,000 to 75,000. Find the increase per cent.

Solution : Increase in population = 75000 – 70000 = 5000

Percentage increase

$= \frac{5000 \times 100}{70,000} = \frac{50}{7}\% = 7\frac{1}{7}\%.$

Example 6 : In a school, there are 300 students. Out of them, there are 40% girls. Find the number of boys and girls in the school.

Solution : Girls students = 40%

Number of girls $= \frac{40}{100} \times 300 = 120$

$\therefore$ Number of boys = 300 – 120 = 180.

Example 7 : Neeraj's salary is 15% more than Dheeraj's salary. If Dheeraj's salary is ₹ 1200, find Neeraj's salary.

Solution : Neeraj's salary is 15% more than Dheeraj's salary.

If Dheeraj's salary is ₹ 100 Neeraj's salary = ₹ 115

$\therefore$ If Dheeraj's salary is Re 1, Neeraj's salary $= ₹ \frac{115}{100}$

$\therefore$ When Dheeraj's salary is ₹ 1200, Neeraj's salary

$= \frac{115 \times 1200}{100} = ₹ 1380.$

EXERCISE

1. Which number is 60% less than 80?
   A. 48 B. 42 C. 32 D. 12
2. In an examination 93% of students passed and 259 failed. The total number of students is:
   A. 3700 B. 500
   C. 3950 D. None of these
3. The population of a village is 6700. If 30% of them are men, 25% are women, find the number of children in the village.
   A. 3015 B. 3105 C. 3501 D. 3005
4. What is the 40% of 2 hours?
   A. 24 min B. 36 min C. 48 min D. 30 min
5. A student secured 30% marks out of total marks of 600. If he failed by 60 marks, the total marks required to pass exam are:
   A. 75 B. 180 C. 240 D. 220
6. What is 75% of one hour?
   A. 45 min B. 30 min
   C. 40 min D. 60 min
7. What is 7.5% of ₹ 2000?
   A. ₹ 1.50 B. ₹ 15.00
   C. ₹ 1500 D. ₹ 150
8. A boy gets 25 marks our of 80 and fails by 15 marks. Find the percentage of pass marks.
   A. 40% B. 30% C. 33% D. 50%
9. Anju scored 39 marks out of 60 in Maths test. What % is this?
   A. 75% B. 35% C. 60% D. 65%
10. If 75% of a number is 15. Find the number.
    A. 20 B. 25 C. 40 D. 35
11. Monthly income of Rama was ₹ 6000. If her income is increased by 10% then her income after increase is:
    A. ₹ 6100 B. ₹ 6200 C. ₹ 6500 D. ₹ 6600
12. The population of India is about 100 crore. If annual increase is 2 per cent per year, then population after one year will be:
    A. 100 crore B. 101 crore
    C. 102 crore D. 105 crore
13. In an examination, Suresh scored 89% marks out of 750 marks. How many marks did he get?
    A. 667.5 B. 668.5 C. 669.5 D. 670.5
14. On a rainy day 35% of a class of 40 students were absent. Then the number of absentees:
    A. 16 B. 15 C. 14 D. 13
15. The population of a village is 2400. If 12% were children, then the number of adults is:
    A. 2552 B. 2652 C. 2752 D. 2112
16. Manju's weight is 14 % more than Anju's weight. If Anju's weight is 63 kg, then Manju's weight is:
    A. 71.82 kg B. 72.82 kg
    C. 73.82 kg D. 74.82 kg
17. After spending 69% of her money, a lady has ₹ 93 left. How much had she first?
    A. ₹ 250 B. ₹ 350 C. ₹ 300 D. ₹ 800
18. Out of 200 candidates who appeared in a certain examination, 25% were not successful. How many candidates were successful?
    A. 150 B. 145 C. 140 D. 160
19. A's salary is 50% more than B's salary. If B's salary is ₹ 1500, find the salary of A.
    A. ₹ 2500 B. ₹ 2400 C. ₹ 2250 D. ₹ 2350

20. 6% of the soldiers of an army were killed in a war. If 282 soldiers are still alive, find the number of soldier killed in the war.
A. 15 B. 18 C. 16 D. 17

21. The price of butter is ₹ 25 per kg. Find the cost of 4 kg. butter if the price increases by 40% per kg.
A. ₹ 140 B. ₹ 145 C. ₹ 150 D. ₹ 135

22. The population of a city has increased from 50,000 to 60,000. Find the increase per cent.
A. 18% B. 20% C. 25% D. 15%

23. A earns 20% more than B. If B earns ₹ 40, find the earnings of A.
A. ₹ 40 B. ₹ 50 C. ₹ 45 D. ₹ 48

24. A labourer gets ₹ 10 per day. He saves 20% of his monthly earnings. Find his savings in a year.
A. ₹ 690 B. ₹ 720 C. ₹ 735 D. ₹ 700

25. The population of a village is 4,500. If 11/18th of them are males and the rest females; find the percentage of females.
A. $38\frac{8}{9}\%$ B. $37\frac{8}{9}\%$ C. $39\frac{8}{9}\%$ D. $35\frac{8}{9}\%$

26. A trader weighs 800 gm. in place of a kg. weight. Find the error per cent committed by the trader.
A. 15% B. 18% C. 20% D. 25%

27. Amit's salary in 2018 is ₹ 1,26,500. His salary for 2016 has risen annually by 10% and 15% respectively to reach 2018 salary figures. What was his salary in 2016?
A. ₹ 1,25,000 B. ₹ 1,00,000
C. ₹ 95,000 D. ₹ 1,15,000

28. If P% of P is 36, then P is equal to:
A. 15 B. 3600 C. 600 D. 60

29. If the population of a town has increased from 60000 to 65000, then the increase in population (in per cent) is:
A. $7\frac{1}{4}$ B. $7\frac{9}{13}$
C. $8\frac{1}{3}$ D. $8\frac{1}{9}$

30. If $\frac{3}{5}$th part of 60% of a number is 36, then that number is:
A. 100 B. 75 C. 80 D. 90

ANSWERS WITH EXPLANATIONS

1. (C): $80 - 80 \times \frac{60}{100} = 80 - 48 = 32.$

2. (A): Let the total number of students = x
given, the number of passed students = 93%
∴ The number of failed students = 100 – 93 = 7%

$$\because \quad x \times 7\% = 259$$
$$\therefore \quad x \times \frac{7}{100} = 259$$
$$\Rightarrow \quad x = \frac{259 \times 100}{7} = 37 \times 100 = 3700$$

Hence, the total number of students = 3700.

3. (A): Population of a village = 6700
Men = 30%
Women = 25%
Children = 100 – (30 + 25)
= 100 – 55 = 45%
∴ The number of children in the village
$$= 6700 \times \frac{45}{100} = 67 \times 45 = 3015.$$

4. (C): 40% of 2 hours
= 40% of 2 × 60 minutes [1 hour = 60 minutes]
$$= \frac{40}{100} \times 120 = 48 \text{ min.}$$

5. (C): Total marks = 600
$$\text{Marks obtained} = \frac{30}{100} \times 600 = 180$$
According to the question,
Passing marks = 180 + 60 = 240.

6. (A): 75% of one hour = 60 minutes $\times \frac{75}{100}$
$$= 60 \times \frac{3}{4} = 45 \text{ minutes.}$$

7. (D): 7.5% of ₹ 2000 = $2000 \times \frac{7.5}{100} = 20 \times 7.5 =$ ₹ 150.

8. (D): Total marks = 80
Passing marks = 25 + 15 = 40
$$\therefore \% \text{ of passing marks} = \frac{40}{80} \times 100 = 50\%.$$

9. (D): Required % $= \frac{39}{60} \times 100 = \frac{13}{20} \times 100$
= 13 × 5 = 65%.

10. (A): Let number be x
Then, 75% of x = 15
$$\Rightarrow \quad x \times \frac{75}{100} = 15 \Rightarrow x \times \frac{3}{4} = 15$$
$$\Rightarrow \quad x = \frac{15 \times 4}{3} = 5 \times 4 = 20.$$

11. (D): Monthly income after increase

$$= 6000 + 6000 \times \frac{10}{100} = ₹\ 6600$$

12. (C): Population increase $= 100 \times \frac{2}{100} = 2$ crore

∴ Population after one year = 100 + 2 = 102 crore.

13. (A): Marks obtained = 89 % of 750

$$= \frac{89}{100} \times 750 = 89 \times 7.5 = 667.5.$$

14. (C): No. of absent students $= 40 \times \frac{35}{100} = 14$

15. (D) The nos. of adults = 88% of 2400

$$= \frac{88}{100} \times 2400 = 88 \times 24 = 2112.$$

16. (A): Manu's weight $= 63 + 63 \times \frac{14}{100}$

= 63 + 8.82 = 71.82 kg.

17. (C): Expenditure = 69%

Saving = 100 – 69 = 31%

If savings are ₹ 31 total amount = ₹ 100

∴ When savings are ₹ 93 total amount

$$= \frac{100 \times 93}{31} = ₹\ 300$$

18. (A): Number of successful candidates $= \frac{75 \times 200}{100} = 150$

19. (C): A's salary = 50% more than B's salary

∴ When B earns ₹ 100, A earns ₹ 150

∴ When B's salary is ₹ 1500, A's salary

$$= \frac{150 \times 1500}{100} = ₹\ 2250$$

20. (B): Soldiers killed = 6%

Soldiers alive = 100 – 6 = 94%

When 94 soldiers are alive number of soldiers killed = 6

When number of soldiers alive is 282, number of soldiers killed in the war $= \frac{6 \times 282}{94} = 18$

21. (A): Increase in price = 40%

Original price of 1 kg. butter = ₹ 25

New price of 1 kg. butter $= \frac{140 \times 25}{100} = ₹\ 35$

Cost of 4 kg. butter = 35 × 4 = ₹ 140

22. (B): Increase in population = 6000 – 5000 = 1000

∴ Increase per cent $= \frac{1000 \times 100}{5000} = 20\%$

23. (D): A's earning = 20% more than B's earning

∴ When B earns ₹ 100, A earns ₹ 120

When B earns ₹ 40, A earns $= \frac{120 \times 40}{100} = ₹\ 48$

24. (B): Monthly earning = 30 × 10 = ₹ 300

Monthly saving $= \frac{20 \times 300}{100}$

∴ Labourer's yearly saving = 12 × 60 = ₹ 720.

25. (A): Population of the village = 4500

No. of males $= \frac{11}{18} \times 4500 = 2750$

∴ No. of females = 4500 – 2750 = 1750

∴ Percentage of females $= \frac{1750 \times 100}{4500} = 38\frac{8}{9}\%$

26. (C): 1 kg. = 1000 gms.

Error = (1000 – 800) gms = 200 gms.

On weighing 1000 gms. error = 200 gms.

∴ Per cent error $= \frac{200 \times 100}{1000} = 20\%$

27. (B): Let Amit's salary was ₹ x in 2016

Then, $x\left(1+\frac{10}{100}\right)\left(1+\frac{15}{100}\right) = 1{,}26{,}500$

$$\Rightarrow \quad x \times \frac{11}{10} \times \frac{23}{20} = 1{,}26{,}500$$

$$\Rightarrow \quad x = \frac{1{,}26{,}500}{11 \times 23} = \frac{11500}{23} \times 10 \times 20$$

= 500 × 200 = 1,00,000

⇒ x = ₹ 1,00,000.

28. (D): $p\%$ of $p\%$ = 36

$$p \times \frac{p}{100} = 36, \quad p^2 = 3600, \quad p = \sqrt{3600} = 60$$

29. (C): % Increase in population

$$= \frac{65{,}000 - 60{,}000}{60{,}000} \times 100$$

$$= \frac{5000}{60000} \times 100$$

$$= \frac{50}{6} = \frac{25}{3} = 8\frac{1}{3}\%$$

30. (A): Let number = x

$$\therefore \quad \frac{3}{5} \times \frac{60}{100} \times x = 36$$

$$\Rightarrow \quad x = \frac{36 \times 5 \times 10}{3 \times 6} = 100$$

Hence, number = 100.

11 Simple Interest

- **Principal:** The money you deposit or put in the bank is called the principal (P).
- **Interest:** The extra money you get from the bank is called the interest (I).
- **Amount:** Total money you get after a fix time is called the amount (A).
- **Simple Interest:** If the interest is paid annually and not compounded after one year and so on, then such interest is called simple interest (S.I.).

FORMULA

$$\text{Simple Interest (S.I.)} = \frac{P \times R \times T}{100}$$

$$\text{Principal (P)} = \frac{S.I. \times 100}{R \times T}$$

$$\text{Rate (R)} = \frac{S.I. \times 100}{P \times T}$$

$$\text{Time (T)} = \frac{S.I. \times 100}{P \times R}$$

Amount (A) = P + I

Principal (P) = A – I

Interest (I) = A – P

Where, P = Principal, T = Time

R = Rate, I = Interest

SOLVED EXAMPLES

Example 1 : In how many years, will ₹4,000 amount to ₹4,480 at 6% per annum?

Solution : Here P = ₹4,000; R = 6%; T = ?

A = ₹4,480

∴ I = ₹4480 – 4000 = ₹480

$$\text{Hence, } T = \frac{I \times 100}{P \times R} = \frac{480 \times 100}{4,000 \times 6} = 2 \text{ years}$$

Example 2 : Find the interest on ₹500 for 4 years at 6% per annum.

Solution : P = ₹500, R = 6%,

T = 4 years.

$$\therefore \text{Simple Interest} = \frac{P \times R \times T}{100}$$

$$= \frac{500 \times 6 \times 4}{100} = ₹\ 120.$$

Example 3 : ₹1,800 amounts to ₹2,250 in 2½ years. Find the rate percent.

Solution : P = ₹1,800

A = ₹2,250

∴ I = A – P

= 2250 – 1800 = ₹450

$$\text{Time} = 2\frac{1}{2} \text{ years} = \frac{5}{2} \text{ years.}$$

$$R = \frac{100 \times S.I.}{P \times T} = \frac{100 \times 450 \times 2}{1,800 \times 5} = 10\%.$$

Example 4 : What sum of money lent for 3 years at 4% per year will amount to ₹392?

Solution : Time= 3 years, R = 4%

Let principal be ₹100

$$I = \frac{P \times R \times T}{100} = \frac{100 \times 4 \times 3}{100} = ₹\ 12$$

∴ Amount = ₹100 + 12 = ₹112

∴ When amount is ₹112, principal = ₹100

∴ When amount is ₹392, principal

$$= \frac{100 \times 392}{112} = ₹350.$$

Example 5 : In what time will ₹500 amount to ₹1,000 at 5% per year?

Solution : P = ₹500, Amount = ₹1000

∴ I = A – P = 1000 – 500 = ₹500

R = 5%

$$\text{Time} = \frac{100\times I}{P\times R} = \frac{100\times 500}{500\times 5} = 20 \text{ years.}$$

Example 6 : Find the simple interest on ₹1,000 from 2nd July to 12 September, 2006 at 4% per year.

Solution : Number of days from 2nd July to 12 September, 2006:

July + August + September = 30 + 31 + 12 = 73 days.

Principal = ₹1000, Rate = 4%

$$\text{Time} = \frac{73}{365}\text{ year} = \frac{1}{5}\text{ year}$$

$$\because \quad \text{S.I.} = \frac{P\times R\times T}{100} = \frac{100\times 4\times 1}{5\times 100} = ₹8$$

Example 7. Pramod took ₹1,100 from Ajay at 8% interest per year. How much will he return to Ajay after six months?

Solution: Here, P = ₹1,100; R = 8%

$$T = 6 \text{ months} = \frac{1}{2}\text{ years}$$

$$\therefore \quad I = \frac{P\times R\times T}{100} = \frac{1100\times 8\times 1}{100\times 2} = ₹\,44$$

∴ A = P + S.I. = 1100 + 44 = ₹1144.

Example 8 : Find the principal that shall earn interest of ₹60 at 6% per annum in 5 years.

Solution : I = ₹60, R = 6%,

T = 5 years.

$$P = \frac{100\times I}{R\times T}$$

$$\Rightarrow \quad P = \frac{100\times 60}{6\times 5} = ₹\,200.$$

EXERCISE

1. At what rate, a sum of ₹ 6000 will amounts to ₹ 7800 in 5 years?

A. 3% B. 4% C. 5% D. 6%

2. Find the simple interest on ₹ 5000 at the rate of 7½% for a period of 3 years.

A. ₹ 5000 B. ₹ 6125 C. ₹ 2000 D. ₹ 1125

3. How much time will it take for an amount of ₹ 450 to yield ₹81 as interest at 4.5% per annum of simple interest?

A. 3 years B. 4 years C. 6 years D. 5 years

4. Joseph borrowed ₹ 25,000 on simple interest at the rate of 6% per annum for 4 years. How much did the pay at the end of 4 years?

A. ₹ 30,000 B. ₹ 31,000 C. ₹ 31,800 D. ₹ 31,920

5. In how many years will a sum of ₹ 1,800 become ₹ 2,610 on simple interest at the rate of 9% per annum?

A. 4 years B. 5 years C. 6 years D. 4½ years

6. What sum of money lent out at 9% for 3 years will produce ₹81 simple interest?

A. ₹225 B. ₹250 C. ₹300 D. ₹325

7. A sum of ₹200 is deposited in the post office at the rate of 5½% simple interest per annum. What will be the total amount after 2 years?

A. ₹550 B. ₹345 C. ₹255 D. ₹222

8. Find the simple interest on ₹120 for 7 months at 5% per annum.

A. ₹2.50 B. ₹3.50 C. ₹4.50 D. ₹5.50

9. If in 10 years ₹150 amounts ₹200, find the rate of simple interest.

A. $3\frac{1}{3}\%$ B. $4\frac{1}{2}\%$

C. $3\frac{1}{2}\%$ D. $4\frac{1}{3}\%$

10. Satyendra borrowed ₹450 from Raju. After two years, he cleared the account by paying ₹549 to Raju. Find the rate of interest.

A. 8% B. 9% C. 10% D. 11%

11. Abhishek borrowed ₹750 for a period of 6 years at the rate of 4% per annum. After fixed time, he cleared of his debt by paying ₹300 in cash and a radio set. Find the price of the radio set.

A. ₹580 B. ₹630 C. ₹625 D. ₹595

12. A sum of money amounts to ₹910 at 5% per year in 6 years. Find the principal.

A. ₹500 B. ₹600 C. ₹700 D. ₹400

13. Manoj borrowed ₹1,500 at 8% per annum from his friend and returned the whole amount after 10 months. What amount did he repay?

A. ₹1200 B. ₹1400 C. ₹1500 D. ₹1600

14. What is the rate of simple interest when ₹1,875 amounts to ₹2,325 in 4 years?

A. 3% B. 4% C. 6% D. 5%

15. The simple interest for ₹ 1050 for 2 years at the rate of 12% per annum is:

A. ₹ 1102 B. ₹ 52 C. ₹ 352 D. ₹ 252

16. Salma borrowed ₹ 2500 from someone. After 2½ years she paid ₹ 3000 and cleared her debt, then the rate of interest is:

A. 5% B. 6% C. 7% D. 8%

17. If principal is ₹ 250, rate 8% per annum and time 3 years, then simple interest is:

A. ₹ 60 B. ₹ 70 C. ₹ 75 D. ₹ 85

18. If simple interest is ₹ 200, rate 3% per annum and time is 20 months, then the principal is:

A. ₹ 6000 B. ₹ 5000 C. ₹ 4000 D. ₹ 3000

19. If principal is ₹ 1000, simple interest ₹ 250 and time is 2 years, then rate is:

A. 10.5% B. 11.5% C. 13.5% D. 12.5%

20. Find the time if, principal is ₹ 400, simple interest ₹ 100 and rate is 12½% per annum:

A. 6 years B. 5 years
C. 3 years D. 2 years

21. If the principal is ₹ 2000, simple interest ₹ 510 and rate is 8½% per annum, then time is:

A. 3 years B. 2 years
C. 7 years D. 5 years

22. A sum of money doubles itself at simple interest in 5 years, then the rate of interest is:

A. 10% B. 15% C. 20% D. 25%

23. Sonam borrowed ₹ 2200 from Meena at the rate of 7% p.a. for 5 years. At the end of five years Sonam returned ₹ 2100 and a Hand Mixie, then the price of the Hand Mixie is:

A. ₹ 670 B. ₹ 770
C. ₹ 870 D. ₹ 970

24. In how many years does the sum of ₹ 1,200 become ₹ 1,800 at the rate of simple interest of 5% per annum?

A. 10 years B. 20 years
C. 15 years D. 25 years

25. A sum of money will double itself in 16 years at simple interest with a yearly rate of:

A. 10% B. 6¼% C. 8% D. 16%

ANSWERS WITH EXPLANATIONS

1. (D): S.I. = Amount – Principle

$= 7800 - 6000 = ₹\ 1800$

$\because$ $\text{S.I.} = \frac{P \times R \times T}{100}$

$1800 = \frac{6000 \times r \times 5}{100}$

$R = \frac{1800 \times 100}{6000 \times 5} = 6\%.$

2. (D): $\text{S.I.} = \frac{P \times R \times T}{100} = \frac{500 \times \frac{15}{2} \times 3}{100}$

$= \frac{5000 \times 15 \times 3}{200}$

$= \frac{225000}{200} = ₹\ 1125$

3 (B): Here, P = ₹ 450, R = 4.5%,

Simple Interest = ₹ 81

$\therefore$ $\text{Time} = \frac{\text{S.I.} \times 100}{P \times R}$

$= \frac{81 \times 100}{450 \times 4.5} = \frac{81 \times 1000}{450 \times 45}$

$= \frac{9 \times 100}{45} = \frac{1 \times 20}{5} = 4$ years.

4. (B): $\text{S.I.} = \frac{P \times R \times T}{100} = \frac{25000 \times 6 \times 4}{100} = ₹\ 6000$

Amount = P + S.I. = 25000 + 6000 = ₹ 31000

Hence, ₹ 31000 Joseph paid at the end of 4 years.

5. (B): S.I. = 2610 – 1800 = ₹ 810

$\text{Time} = \frac{\text{S.I.} \times 100}{P \times R} = \frac{810 \times 100}{1800 \times 9} = 5$ years.

6. (C): Simple Interest = ₹81, R = 9%, T = 3 years

$P = \frac{100 \times \text{S.I.}}{T \times R} = \frac{100 \times 81}{3 \times 9} = 300$

$\therefore$ P = ₹300.

7. (D): P = ₹200, $R = \frac{11}{2}\%$, T = 2 years

$\therefore$ Simple Interest $= \frac{200 \times 11 \times 2}{2 \times 100} = ₹22$

A = P + S.I. = ₹200 + ₹22

$\therefore$ Amount = ₹222.

8. (B): P = ₹120, R = 5%, $T = \frac{7}{12}$ years.

$\therefore$ $\text{S.I.} = \frac{120 \times 5 \times 7}{12 \times 100} = ₹3.50.$

9. (A): $P = ₹150$, Amount $= ₹200$

$$S.I. = 200 - 150 = ₹50$$

Time = 10 years

$$R = \frac{100 \times S.I.}{P \times T} \Rightarrow R = \frac{100 \times 50}{150 \times 100} = 3\frac{1}{3}\%.$$

10. (D): $P = ₹450$, $A = ₹549$

Simple Interest $= 549 - 450 = ₹99$

Time = 2 years

$$R = \frac{100 \times S.I.}{P \times T} = \frac{100 \times 99}{450 \times 2} = 11\%.$$

11. (B): $P = ₹750$, $R = 4\%$, $T = 6$ years.

$$\text{Simple Interest} = \frac{750 \times 4 \times 6}{100} = ₹180$$

Amount $= 750 + 180 = ₹930$

Now ₹300 + Cost of radio set = ₹930

∴ Cost of radio set $= 930 - 300 = ₹630$.

12. (C): Let, $P = ₹100$

$$S.I. = \frac{100 \times 5 \times 6}{100} = ₹30$$

Amount $= 100 + 30 = ₹130$

When amount ₹130 then $P = ₹100$

When amount ₹910 then $P = \frac{100}{130} \times 910$

∴ $P = ₹700$.

13. (D):

$$S.I. = \frac{P \times R \times T}{100} = \frac{15000 \times 8 \times 10}{100 \times 12} = ₹100$$

Amount $= 1500 + 100 = ₹1600$.

14. (C): S.I. = Amount – principal

$= 2325 - 1875 = ₹450$

$$R = \frac{S.I \times 100}{P \times T} = \frac{450 \times 100}{1875 \times 4} = 6$$

∴ $R = 6\%$.

15. (D):

$$\text{Simple interest} = \frac{P \times R \times T}{100} = \frac{1050 \times 12 \times 2}{100}$$

$= 21 \times 12 = ₹ 252$.

16. (D): $P = ₹ 2500$, $A = ₹ 3000$,

$$T = 2\frac{1}{2} \text{ years} = \frac{5}{2} \text{ years}$$

$S.I. = A - P = ₹ (3000 - 2500) = ₹ 500$

$$R = \frac{S.I. \times 100}{P \times T} = \frac{500 \times 100 \times 2}{2500 \times 5}$$

∴ $R = 8\%$.

17. (A): $P = ₹250, R = 8\%$ p.a., $T = 3$ years

$$S.I. = \frac{P \times R \times T}{100} = \frac{250 \times 8 \times 3}{100} = ₹ 60.$$

18. (C): S.I. = ₹ 200, R = 3% p.a.

$$T = 1 + \frac{8}{12} = \frac{5}{3} \text{ years}$$

$$P = \frac{S.I. \times 100}{R \times T} = \frac{200 \times 100 \times 3}{3 \times 5} = ₹ 4000.$$

19. (D): P = ₹ 1000, S.I. = ₹ 250, T = 2 years

$$R = \frac{S.I. \times 100}{P \times T} = \frac{250 \times 100}{1000 \times 2} = 12.5\%.$$

20. (D): P = ₹ 400, S.I. = ₹ 100

$$R = \frac{25}{2}\%, \quad T = \frac{100 \times 100 \times 2}{400 \times 25} = 2 \text{ yrs.}$$

21. (A): P = ₹ 2000, S.I. = ₹ 510

$$R = \frac{17}{2} \text{ p.a.}, \quad T = \frac{5100 \times 100 \times 2}{2000 \times 17} = 3 \text{ years.}$$

22. (C): Let P = ₹ 100, A = ₹ 200,

S.I. = 200 – 100 = ₹ 100

$$R = \frac{S.I. \times 100}{P \times T} = \frac{100 \times 100}{100 \times 5} = 20\%.$$

23. (C):

$$S.I. = \frac{2200 \times 7 \times 5}{100} = 22 \times 35 = ₹ 770$$

A = 2200 + 770 = ₹ 2970

Price of Hand mixie = 2970 – 2100 = ₹ 870.

24. (A): Here, P = ₹ 1200, A = ₹ 1800, $r = 5\%$

∴ Simple interest = A – P

= ₹ 1800 – ₹ 1200 = ₹ 600

$$T = \frac{S.I. \times 100}{P \times R}$$

$$= \frac{600 \times 100}{1200 \times 5} = \frac{6 \times 20}{12} = \frac{20}{2} = 10.$$

∴ Time = 10 years.

25. (B): Let Principal = ₹ P

Then, Amount = ₹ 2P

∴ Simple Interest = Amount – Principal

= 2P – P = ₹ P.

Given, Time = 16 Years

$$\text{Rate} = \frac{\text{Interest} \times 100}{\text{Principal} \times \text{Time}}$$

$$= \frac{P \times 100}{P \times 16}\% = \frac{25}{4} = 6\frac{1}{4}\%.$$

12 Profit & Loss

A consumer is that person who goes to the market and buys certain goods. The buyer is called a customer and the shopkeeper who sells the goods to him is called a retailer. The retailer purchases goods in turn in bulk from a wholesaler who keeps a large stock of good and in this case, the retailer becomes the customer.

1. Cost price (C.P.) : Cost price is that price at which a particular article is bought. Profit and loss both are marked at cost price.

2. Selling Price (S.P.) : Selling price is that price at which a particular article is sold.

3. Profit or Gain : Whenever a person sells an article at price greater than the cost price he is said to have made a profit or gain.

Profit or Gain = S.P. – C.P.

4. Loss : If S.P. is less than the C.P. there is loss.

Loss = C.P – S.P.

Some Basic Formulae:

(*i*) Gain = S.P. – C.P.

(*ii*) Loss = C.P. – S.P.

(*iii*) $\text{Gain \%} = \dfrac{\text{Gain} \times 100}{\text{C.P.}}$

(*iv*) $\text{Loss \%} = \dfrac{\text{Loss} \times 100}{\text{C.P.}}$

From these we can write direct expressions for S.P. and C.P.

(*v*) $\text{S.P.} = \left(\dfrac{100 + \text{Gain\%}}{100}\right) \times \text{C.P.}$ in case of gain or profit

(*vi*) $\text{S.P.} = \left(\dfrac{100 - \text{Loss\%}}{100}\right) \times \text{C.P.}$ in case of loss

These can be rewritten as

$\text{C.P.} = \dfrac{100}{100 + \text{Gain\%}} \times \text{S.P.}$ in case of profit

$\text{C.P.} = \dfrac{100}{100 - \text{Loss\%}} \times \text{S.P.}$ in case of loss

(*vii*) If the C.P. of x goods = S.P. of y goods, then

(*a*) $\text{Gain \%} = \dfrac{x - y}{y} \times 100$ [In case of $x > y$]

(*b*) $\text{Loss \%} = \dfrac{y - x}{y} \times 100$ [In case of $y > x$]

(*viii*) When a man sells two things at the same price each and in this process his loss on first things is x% and gain on second things is x%, then in such a type question, there is always a loss.

$\text{Loss \%} = x\% \text{ of } x = \dfrac{x^2}{100} = \left(\dfrac{x}{10}\right)^2.$

and $\text{Loss} = \dfrac{2 \times \text{S.P.}}{\left(\dfrac{100}{x}\right)^2 - 1}$

(*ix*) An article is sold at a profit of x%. Had it been sold for Rs. a some more, y% would have gained. Then,

$\text{C.P. of an article} = \dfrac{\text{More gain} \times 100}{\text{Difference in percentage profit}}$

(*x*) $\text{M.P.} = \left(\dfrac{100}{100 - \text{Discount\%}}\right) \times \text{S.P.}$

(*xi*) Discount = M.P. – S.P.

(*xii*) A dishonest shopkeeper prefers to sell goods at his cost price but uses a false weight of x grams for each kilogram. Then his gain per cent,

$\text{gain \%} = \dfrac{\text{Error}}{\text{True value} - \text{Error}} \times 100$

$= \dfrac{1000 - x}{x} \times 100$

or, $\text{gain \%} = \dfrac{\text{True weight} - \text{False weight}}{\text{False weight}} \times 100.$

SOLVED EXAMPLES

Example 1 : A dishonest dealer professes to sell his goods at cost price, but he uses a weight of 950 gm for the kg. weight. Find his gain per cent.

Solution : $\text{Gain \%} = \frac{\text{Error}}{\text{True value} - \text{Error}} \times 100$

$= \frac{50}{950} \times 100 = 5.26\%$

Example 2 : A man losses 10% by selling a watch for ₹ 630. Find the cost price of the watch.

Solution : Loss = 10 %

$\because$ When S.P. is ₹ 90, C.P. = ₹ 100

$\therefore$ When S.P. is ₹ 630,

$\text{C.P.} = \frac{100}{90} \times 630 = ₹\,700.$

Example 3 : Vikas bought a transistor for ₹ 500 and sold it for ₹ 550. What is loss or gain per cent?

Solution : C.P. = ₹ 500

S.P. = ₹ 550

Profit = 550 – 500 ₹ 50

$\text{Profit \%} = \frac{50}{500} \times 100 = 10\%.$

Example 4 : Devendra purchased a motor cycle for ₹ 10,000. He paid ₹ 150 for road tax and ₹ 100 as license fee. What price must he shell it to gain 20 %?

Solution : Actual cost price of the motor cycle

= 10,000 + 150 + 100 = ₹ 10,250

Gain = 20%

$\text{S.P.} = \frac{120}{100} \times 10,250 = ₹\,12,300.$

Example 5 : A watch maker bought an old watch for ₹ 80. He spent ₹ 10 on its repair and then sold it for ₹ 117. Find his gain or loss percent.

Solution : C.P. of the watch = ₹ 80

Expenditure or repairs = ₹ 10

Actual C.P. = ₹ 80 + ₹ 10 = ₹ 90

S.P. = 117

$\therefore$ Profit = ₹ 117 – ₹ 90 = ₹ 27

Hence, profit percentage $= \frac{27}{90} \times 100 = 30\%$

Example 6 : Some mangoes were bought at the rate of 1.50 per dozen and sold at the rate of 2.25 per dozen. If there is profit of ₹ 2.25, how many mangoes were bought?

Solution : C.P. = ₹ 1.50 per dozen

S.P. = ₹ 2.25 per dozen

Profit = 2.25 – 1.50 then, no. of mangoes

= ₹ 0.75 per dozen.

$\therefore$ When profit was ₹ 0.75 one dozen mangoes were purchased.

$\therefore$ When profit is ₹ 2.25 then no. of mangoes purchased

$= \frac{2.25}{.75} = \frac{225}{75} = 3$

= 3 dozen mangoes were purchased.

EXERCISE

1. By selling an article for ₹ 165, a man losses 4%. Find the S.P. of the article in order to gain 28%.

A. ₹ 220 B. ₹ 180 C. ₹ 225 D. ₹ 195

2. Ramesh buys 50 metre cloth at the rate of ₹ 120 per metre. At what rate should he sell the cloth in order to get 20% gain?

A. ₹ 180 B. ₹ 144 C. ₹ 150 D. ₹ 154

3. An electronics dealer buys a radio for ₹ 475 and spends ₹ 25 on its repairs. If he sells the radio for ₹ 600, find his profit per cent?

A. 20% B. 8% C. 12% D. 9%

4. By selling 60 oranges for ₹ 30 a man loses 25%. Find the cost price of 30 oranges.

A. ₹ 25 B. ₹ 30 C. ₹ 20 D. ₹ 15

5. A profit of 25% is made when an article is sold for ₹ 625. Find the profit per cent if the article is sold for ₹ 550.

A. 15% B. 18% C. 8% D. 10%

6. Sunil purchased a motor–cycle for ₹ 28,500. He spent ₹ 500 on repairs. He sold the motor–cycle at a gain of 15%. Find the selling price of the motor–cycle.

A. ₹ 10520 B. ₹ 10350 C. ₹ 10820 D. ₹ 10440

7. Sohan sold his television for ₹ 5,067 and lost 10%. If he sold television for ₹ 5,630, find his gain or loss per cent?

A. 20% B. 30%
C. 25% D. Neither loss nor gain

8. A man bought 6 oranges for a rupee and sold them at a profit of 20%. How many oranges for a rupee did he sell?

A. 6 Oranges B. 5 Oranges
C. 4 Oranges D. 3 Oranges

9. A shopkeeper buys a fan for ₹ 225. He wants to earn a profit of 8 per cent. At what price should he sell it?

A. ₹ 243 B. ₹ 250 C. ₹ 255 D. ₹ 240

10. A man purchased an old car for ₹ 6,200 and he spent ₹ 1700 on repairs. He resold the car for ₹ 8,200. How much profit he got?

A. ₹ 400 B. ₹ 500 C. ₹ 200 D. ₹ 300

11. Karishma bought two necklace for ₹ 1,39,500.00. She sold one of them for ₹ 75,000.00 and the other one for ₹ 80,000.00. How much money did she gain?

A. ₹ 25,500.00 B. ₹ 15,500.00
C. ₹ 20,500.00 D. ₹ 15,000.00

12. A person purchased an old bicycle for ₹ 450 and spends ₹ 50 on its maintenance. If he sold the old bicycle for ₹ 600 then his profit percentage is

A. 15% B. 18% C. 20% D. 25%

13. Rahul purchases a chair for ₹ 600 and uses ₹ 200 for repairs. If he sells it for ₹ 1000 then he has:

A. no profit no loss B. 25% loss
C. 25% profit D. cannot be calculated

14. A mobile phone is sold for ₹ 1650 after purchasing it for ₹ 1500. What is the percentage of profit?

A. 10 B. 15 C. 20 D. 16

15. A certain brand of soap-powder is sold at ₹ 15 per packet. It costs ₹ 144 a dozen. What is the profit in per cent on 8 dozen packets?

A. 20 B. 25 C. 24 D. 36

16. A man sells one speaker for ₹ 7,500 at a profit of 20% and another speaker for ₹ 8,100 at a loss of 10%. Find his total loss or profit.

A. Loss = ₹ 300 B. Loss = ₹ 350
C. Profit = ₹ 300 D. Profit = ₹ 350

17. A dealer purchased 50 tables for ₹ 4570 each. Nine tables got damaged in transit. He sold the remaining tables at ₹ 5000 each. Choose the most appropriate statement for this case?

A. He was able to recover the cost of the damaged tables.
B. He made a profit of ₹ 25000.
C. He incurred a loss of ₹ 23500.
D. He made a profit of ₹ 23500.

18. Jaspal purchased an old car for ₹ 1,18,000 and spent ₹ 7,000 on its maintenance. If he sold the car for ₹ 1,40,000, then his profit percentage is:

A. 10% B. 11% C. 12% D. 12.5%

19. A sweet seller declares that he sells sweets at the cost price. However, he uses a weight of 450 gm instead of 500 gm. His percentage profit is:

A. 10 B. $11\frac{1}{9}$
C. 12 D. $12\frac{2}{9}$

20. What should be the selling price of a cow whose cost is ₹ 1500 to get 20% profit?

A. ₹ 1530 B. ₹ 1600 C. ₹ 2000 D. ₹ 1800

21. What will be the loss percentage, if bananas purchased 6 for ₹ 10 and sold 4 for ₹ 6?

A. 5% B. 20% C. 10% D. 6%

22. If the cost price of 8 pens is same as the selling price of 6 pens, then the gain percent is:

A. $33\frac{1}{3}\%$ B. $11\frac{1}{2}\%$
C. $13\frac{1}{3}\%$ D. 25%

23. If by selling an article for ₹ 390, a shopkeeper gains 20%, then the cost price of article is:

A. ₹ 324 B. ₹ 321 C. ₹ 323 D. ₹ 325

24. If the cost price of an article is $\frac{3}{2}$ of its selling price, then the profit or loss per cent is:

A. $33\frac{1}{3}\%$ profit B. $33\frac{1}{3}\%$ loss
C. $33\frac{1}{8}\%$ loss D. $33\frac{1}{8}\%$ profit

25. If selling price is doubled then profit become tripled. Therefore profit per cent is

A. $66\frac{2}{3}$ B. 100
C. $105\frac{1}{3}$ D. 120

ANSWERS WITH EXPLANATIONS

1. (A): S.P. for an article = ₹ 165, Loss = 4%

When S.P. is ₹ 96, C.P. for the article = ₹ 100

∴ When S.P. is ₹ 165, C.P. for the article

$$= \frac{100 \times 165}{96} = \frac{25 \times 55}{8}$$

Gain = 28%

When C.P. for the article is ₹ 100

S.P. = ₹ 128

When C.P. for the article is $\frac{25 \times 55}{8}$ then

$$\text{S.P.} = \frac{128 \times 25 \times 55}{100 \times 8} = ₹\ 220$$

2. (B): Cost price of 50 metre cloth at the rate of ₹ 120 per metre = 50 × 120 = ₹ 6000

Gain = 20%

$$\therefore \quad \text{Selling price} = \frac{120 \times 6000}{100} = ₹\ 7200$$

It means that 50 metre cloth should be sold for ₹ 7200

∴ Selling price for 1 metre cloth

$$= \frac{7200}{50} = ₹\ 144.$$

3. (A): C.P. for radio = ₹ 475

Repair charges = ₹ 25

Actual cost price for radio = ₹ 500

Selling price = ₹ 600

Profit = ₹ 600 – ₹ 500 = ₹ 100

$$\text{Profit per cent} = \frac{100 \times 100}{500} = 20\%$$

4. (C): S.P. for 60 oranges = ₹ 30

Loss = 25%

$$\therefore \text{C.P. for 60 oranges} = \frac{100 \times 30}{75} = ₹\ 40$$

$$\therefore \text{C.P. for 30 oranges} = \frac{40 \times 30}{60} = ₹\ 20$$

5. (D): Selling price for an article = ₹ 625

Gain = 25%

$$\text{Cost price for the article} = \frac{100 \times 625}{125} = ₹\ 500$$

Now selling price = ₹ 550

∴ Profit = ₹ 550 – ₹ 500 = ₹ 50

$$\therefore \quad \text{Profit \%} = \frac{50 \times 100}{500} = 10\%.$$

6. (B): Total cost price of motor cycle

= ₹ 8500 + ₹ 500 = ₹ 9000

Gain = 15%

∴ When C.P. is ₹ 100 S. P. = ₹ 115

$$\therefore \text{When C.P. is ₹ 9000, S. P.} = \frac{115 \times 9000}{100} = ₹\ 10350.$$

7. (D): S.P. for a television = ₹ 5067

Loss = 10%

$$\text{when S.P. is ₹ 5067; C.P.} = \frac{100 \times 5067}{90} = ₹\ 5630$$

Cost price of the television = ₹ 5630

∴ Selling price of the television = ₹ 5630

It means, there will be no loss or gain in this transaction.

8. (B): C.P. for 6 oranges = ₹ 1

Profit = 20%

$$\therefore \text{S.P. for 6 oranges} = \frac{120 \times 1}{100} = ₹\ 1.20$$

It means he sold 6 oranges for ₹ 1.20

$$\therefore \text{In a rupee he sold} = \frac{6 \times 1}{1.20} = 5 \text{ Oranges}.$$

9. (A): C.P. of the fan = ₹ 225

$$\text{Profit} = \frac{8}{100} \times 225 = ₹\ 18$$

S.P. of the fan = 225 + 18 = ₹ 243.

10. (D): C.P. of the car = 6200 + 1700 = ₹ 7900

S.P. of the car = ₹ 8200

Profit = 8200 – 7900 = ₹ 300.

11. (B): C.P. = ₹ 1,39,500

S.P. = ₹ 75,000 + ₹ 80,000 = ₹ 1,55,000

Gain = ₹ 1,55,000 – ₹ 1,39,500

= ₹ 15,500.

12. (C): Total C.P. = ₹ 450 + ₹ 50 = ₹ 500

Total S.P. = ₹ 600

Profit = S.P. – C.P. = 600 – 500 = ₹ 100

$$\text{Profit \%} = \frac{\text{Profit}}{\text{CP}} \times 100 = \frac{100}{500} \times 100 = 20\%.$$

13. (C): Total cost price of the chair = ₹ 600 + ₹ 200

= ₹ 800

Selling price of the chair = ₹ 1000

∵ SP > CP → Profit

$$\text{Required profit \%} = \frac{\text{SP} - \text{CP}}{\text{CP}} \times 100$$

$$= \frac{1000 - 800}{800} \times 100 = \frac{200 \times 100}{800}$$

= 25% profit

14. (A): Here, Selling price of a mobile phone = ₹ 1650 and Cost price = ₹ 1500

∴ Profit = S.P. – C.P.

= 1650 – 1500 = ₹ 150

Now, the percentage of profit = $\frac{\text{Profit} \times 100}{\text{Cost price}}$

$= \frac{150 \times 100}{1500} = \frac{150}{15} = 10\%$

15. (B): Selling price of per packet shoap powder = ₹ 15

S.P. of 1 dozen packet = 12 × 15 = ₹ 180

S.P. of 8 dozen packets = 8 × 180 = ₹ 1440

and cost price of 8 dozen packets

= 8 × 144 = ₹ 1152

Profit = S.P. – C.P.

= 1440 – 1152 = 288

∴ Profit per cent = $\frac{\text{Profit} \times 100}{\text{C.P.}}$

$= \frac{288 \times 100}{1152} = \frac{28800}{1152} = 25\%.$

16. (D): The cost price of one speaker

$= 7500 \times \frac{100}{100+20}$

$= 7500 \times \frac{100}{120} = 7500 \times \frac{5}{6}$

= 1250 × 5 = ₹ 6250

and, the cost price of another speaker

$= 8100 \times \frac{100}{100-10}$

$= 8100 \times \frac{100}{90} = 8100 \times \frac{10}{9}$

= 900 × 10 = ₹ 9000

∴ Total cost price = 6250 + 9000 = ₹ 15250

and total selling price

= 7500 + 8100 = ₹ 15600

Hence, Profit = S.P. – C.P.

= 15600 – 15250 = ₹ 350.

17. (C): C.P. of 50 tables = ₹ 4570 × 50 = ₹ 228500

∵ The number of remaining tables after 9 tables got damage in transit

= 50 – 9 = 41

Now, S.P. of 41 table

= ₹ 5000 × 41 = ₹ 205000

Hence, loss = C.P. – S.P.

= ₹ 228500 – ₹ 205000

= ₹ 23500.

18. (C): C.P. of an old car = ₹ 118,000 + ₹ 7000

= ₹ 125,000

and S.P. of an old car = ₹ 140,000

∴ profit = S.P. – C.P.

= 140,000 – 125,000 = ₹ 15,000

Hence, profit percentage = $\frac{\text{Profit} \times 100}{\text{C.P.}}$

$= \frac{15,000 \times 10}{125,000} = \frac{1500}{125}$

$= \frac{60}{5} = 12\%.$

19. (B): Cost price of 1 kg sweets = ₹ 1000

True value = cost of 500 gm = ₹ 500

and cost of 450 gm = ₹ 450

∴ Error = ₹ 500 – ₹ 450 = ₹ 50

∴ Percentage profit

$= \left[\frac{\text{Error}}{\text{True value} - \text{Error}} \times 100\right]\%$

$= \left[\frac{50}{500-50} \times 100\right]\%$

$= \frac{50}{450} \times 100\% = \frac{1}{9} \times 100\% = 11\frac{1}{9}\%.$

20. (D): Given, cost price = ₹ 1500

and profit = 20%

∴ Selling price = ₹ $1500 \times \frac{120}{100}$

= ₹ 15 × 120 = ₹ 1800.

21. (C): Here, cost price of 1 banana = ₹$\frac{10}{6}$ = ₹$\frac{5}{3}$

and the selling price of 1 banana = ₹$\frac{6}{4}$ = ₹$\frac{3}{2}$

Loss = C.P. – S.P.

$= \frac{5}{3} - \frac{3}{2}$

$= \frac{10-9}{6}$

$= \frac{1}{6}$

Loss% = $\frac{\text{loss} \times 100}{\text{C.P.}}$

$= \frac{\frac{1}{6} \times 100}{\frac{5}{3}}$

$= \frac{100}{6} \times \frac{3}{5} = 10\%.$

22. (A): Given, C.P of 8 pens = S.P. of 6 pens

$$\therefore \quad \frac{\text{C.P. of pens}}{\text{S.P. of pens}} = \frac{6}{8}$$

Let C.P. and S.P. of a pen respectively ₹ $6x$ and ₹ $8x$

$$\text{Then, \% profit} = \frac{\text{S.P.} - \text{C.P.}}{\text{C.P.}} \times 100$$

$$= \frac{8x - 6x}{6x} \times 100$$

$$= \frac{2x}{6x} \times 100 = \frac{1}{3} \times 100 = 33\frac{1}{3}\%$$

23. (D): Given, S.P. of article = ₹ 390, Profit % = 20%

$$\therefore \quad \text{C.P.} = \frac{100}{(100 + \text{Profit \%})} \times \text{S.P.}$$

$$= \frac{100}{100 + 20} \times 390$$

$$\Rightarrow \quad = \frac{100}{120} \times 390 = ₹\ 325$$

So, C.P. of the article = ₹ 325.

24. (B): Let, S.P. = ₹ x

$$\therefore \quad \text{C.P.} = \frac{3x}{2} = \frac{3x}{2}$$

Clearly, C.P. > S.P.

$$\therefore \quad \text{Loss} = \text{C.P.} - \text{S.P.}$$

$$= \frac{3x}{2} - x = \frac{x}{2}$$

$$\text{Loss\%} = \frac{\text{Loss}}{\text{C.P.}} \times 100 = \frac{\frac{x}{2}}{\frac{3x}{2}} \times 100$$

$$= \frac{x}{2} \times \frac{2}{3x} \times 100 = \frac{100}{3} = 33\frac{1}{3}\%.$$

25. (B): Let C.P. = ₹ x

S.P. = ₹ $2x$

Profit = $2x - x = x$

$$\text{Profit\%} = \frac{\text{Profit}}{\text{C.P.}} \times 100 = \frac{x}{x} \times 100 = 100\%$$

13 Money

This chapter focuses on basic calculations using Indian currency (₹). It helps students understand real-life situations like buying and selling:

- Understanding rupees and paise (1 rupee = 100 paise)
- Doing addition, subtraction, multiplication, and division with money
- Solving word problems about total cost and change

SOLVED EXAMPLES

Example 1 : Priya buys a pencil box for ₹ 85.50 and a water bottle for ₹ 124.75. She pays ₹ 250. How much change does she get?

Solution : Cost of pencil box = ₹ 85.50

Cost of water bottle = ₹ 124.75

Total cost = 85.50 + 124.75 = ₹ 210.25

Money paid = ₹ 250

Change = 250 – 210.25 = ₹ 39.75.

Example 2 : Aman buys 5 kg of rice at ₹ 60 per kg and 3 kg of sugar at ₹ 45 per kg. Find the total cost.

Solution : Cost of rice = 5 × 60 = ₹ 300

Cost of sugar = 3 × 45 = ₹ 135

Total cost = 300 + 135 = ₹ 435.

Example 3 : 12 pencils cost ₹ 60. What is the cost of 1 pencil? What will 8 pencils cost?

Solution : Cost of 1 pencil = 60 ÷ 12 = ₹ 5

Cost of 8 pencils = 8 × 5 = ₹ 40

Hence, 1 pencil costs ₹ 5; 8 pencils cost ₹ 40.

Example 4 : Meera's lunch bill: 2 idlis at ₹ 15 each, 1 dosa at ₹ 40, and 1 coffee at ₹ 25. Find the total bill.

Solution : Idlis = 2 × 15 = ₹ 30

Dosa = ₹ 40

Coffee = ₹ 25

Total bill = 30 + 40 + 25 = ₹ 95

Hence, the total bill is ₹ 95.

EXERCISE

1. A person withdrew ₹ 4,560 from his bank account on 4th of a month and deposited ₹ 2,567 on 20th of the same month. If at the end of the month, balance is ₹ 3,125, then money (in ₹) at the start of the month in his account was:

A. 5,128
B. 5,118
C. 4,998
D. 5,213

2. Which one of the following costs least?

A. 750 packets of ₹ 7.50 each
B. 7.5 dozen items of ₹ 750 each item
C. 75 dozen items of ₹ 7.50 each item
D. 75 packets of ₹ 750 each

3. Sangeeta wants to buy a soap that costs ₹ 10. She has a five-rupee coin, 2 one-rupee coins and 5 fifty-paise coins. How much more money does she need to buy the soap?

A. ₹ 2.50 B. ₹ 0.50 C. ₹ 1.50 D. ₹ 2.00

4. Priya went to a shop with a ₹ 500 note. She purchased one soap, one toothpaste, one hair oil, one shampoo and one comb for ₹ 36, ₹ 85, ₹ 110, ₹ 160 and ₹ 13 respectively. She gave to the shopkeeper ₹ 500 note and he returned her ₹ 95. She checked and found that:

A. Shopkeeper has returned ₹ 1 less.
B. Shopkeeper has returned ₹ 1 more.
C. Returned amount is correct.
D. Returned amount is ₹ 9 less.

5. Savita went to ATM to withdraw some money. She got five notes of ₹ 2000, four notes of ₹ 500 and nine notes of ₹ 100. On counting she found that 1 note of ₹ 2000 and 1 note of ` 100 are less in the whole amount. How much amount did she enter for withdrawal?

A. 14000 B. 14500 C. 15000 D. 16500

6. The rates of various stationery items are given below:

A packet of crayons – ₹ 15.50
A packet of pencils – ₹ 14.00
A packet of sketch pens – ₹ 22.50
One scissors – ₹ 17.00
One eraser – ₹ 2.00
One sheet of glazed paper – ₹ 2.50
A pack of decorative stickers – ₹ 5.00

Sohail buys one packet of crayons, two packets of pencils, one packet of sketch pens, one scissors, 5 sheets of glazed papers and one pack of decorative stickers. How much would he be required to pay?

A. ₹ 100.50 B. ₹ 102.00
C. ₹ 98.00 D. ₹ 86.50

7. Ayesha has only ₹ 5 and ₹ 10 coins with her. If the total number of coins she has 25 and the amount of money with her is ₹ 160, then the number of ₹ 5 and ₹ 10 coins with her are:

A. 18 and 7 respectively
B. 10 and 15 respectively
C. 15 and 10 respectively
D. 20 and 5 respectively

8. The price list of vegetables in a super market is given as follows:

Item	Quantity	Price (₹)
Tomato	1 kg	40
Potato	2 kg	25
Carrot	250 g	20
Bottlegourd	1 kg	10
Chillies	100 g	10
Lemon	4 pieces	10

Sanjay buys $\frac{1}{2}$ kg tomatoes, 1 kg potatoes, $\frac{1}{2}$ kg carrot, 250 g chillies and 6 lemons. He gives a note of ₹ 200 to the bill clerk at the counter. How much money will he get back?

A. ₹ 112.50 B. ₹ 87.50
C. ₹ 86.50 D. ₹ 97.50

9. Find the value of ₹ 10.40 + ₹ 15.30 + ₹ 8.20.

A. ₹ 33.90 B. ₹ 34.00
C. ₹ 30.90 D. ₹ 339.

10. You have ₹ 50. You buy an ice-cream for ₹ 15.75 and a chocolate for ₹ 18.30. Money left = ₹ ______.

A. 15.95 B. 16.95 C. 14.95 D. 17.95

11. The cost of a daily newspaper is ₹ 4. What is the cost of newspaper in the month of January?

A. ₹ 12 B. ₹ 124 C. ₹ 35 D. ₹ 25

12. Hari saves ₹ 5 daily from his pocket expenses. How many rupees has he saved in the month of March ?

A. ₹ 36 B. ₹ 31 C. ₹ 155 D. ₹ 150.

13. The cost of 8 meter cloth is ₹ 680. What is the cost of 1 meter cloth ?

A. ₹ 80 B. ₹ 85 C. ₹ 70 D. ₹ 90.

14. If 1 kg of rice costs ₹ 45.75, what will be the cost of 5 kg rice?

A. ₹ 228.75 B. ₹ 229.75
C. ₹ 227.75 D. ₹ 230.75

15. A pen costs ₹ 12.25 and a notebook costs ₹ 24.75. How much more does the notebook cost than the pen?

A. ₹ 12.75 B. ₹ 13.00 C. ₹ 12.50 D. ₹ 13.25

16. A 5-rupee coin weighs 6 grams. What is the total weight of 10 such coins?

A. 60 g B. 55 g C. 65 g D. 70 g

17. A bag costs ₹ 450. A purse costs ₹ 275. Find their total cost.

A. ₹ 715 B. ₹ 720 C. ₹ 730 D. ₹ 725

18. The cost of one pencil is ₹ 3.65. What is the cost of 12 such pencils?

A. ₹ 42.80 B. ₹ 43.80 C. ₹ 44 D. ₹ 42

19. Mr. Bhatia bought 18 kg of mangoes for ₹ 267.30. At what rate per kg did he buy mangoes?

A. ₹ 13.85 B. ₹ 14.50 C. ₹ 15.00 D. ₹ 14.85

20. A man has ₹ 320 in coins of 1-rupee, 2-rupee, and 5-rupee. If the number of coins of each denomination is equal, what is the total number of coins?

A. 100 B. 120 C. 150 D. 90

ANSWERS WITH EXPLANATIONS

1. (B): Let ₹ x was in his acount at the start of the month

Then, ₹ x + ₹ 2567 – ₹ 4560 = ₹ 3125

⇒ ₹ x + ₹ 2567 = ₹ 4560 + ₹ 3125

⇒ x + ₹ 2567 = ₹ 7685

⇒ ₹ x = 7685 – 2567 = ₹ 5118.

2. (A): To determine which of the following costs the least, we'll calculate the total cost for each option:

(A) 750 packets of ₹ 7.50 each = ₹ 5625.00

(B) 7.5 dozen items (90 items) of ₹ 750 each item = ₹ 67500.00

(C) 75 dozen items (900 items) of ₹ 7.50 each item = ₹ 6750.00

(D) 75 packets of ₹ 750 each = ₹ 56250.00

On comparing we see that least cost is ₹ 5625.00 which is of 750 packets of ₹ 7.50 each.

3. (B): Cost of a soap = ₹ 10

She has total money = ₹ 5 + ₹ 2 + ₹ 2.5 = ₹ 9.5

₹ 10 – ₹ 9.5 = ₹ 0.50

∴ Required money = ₹ 0.50.

4. (A): Total cost = ₹ 36 + ₹ 85 + ₹ 110 + ₹ 160 + ₹ 13 = ₹ 404

₹ 500 – ₹ 404 = ₹ 96

The shopkeeper returned ₹ 95

Clearly, Shopkeeper has returned ₹ 1 less.

5. (C): Let amount enter for withdrawal = ₹ x

Then, ₹ x – [₹ 2000 + ₹ 100]

= ₹ [5 × 2000 + 4 × 500 + 9 × 100]

⇒ ₹ x – ₹ 2100 = 10000 + 2000 + 900

⇒ ₹ x = ₹ 2100 + ₹ 12900

⇒ ₹ x = ₹ 15000.

6. (A): The sum required to pay

= 15.50 + 2 × 14 + 22.50 + 17 + 5 × 2.50 + 5

= ₹ 100.50.

7. (A): Given, the total number of coins = 25

Let the number of ₹ 5 coins = x

Then, the number of ₹ 10 coins = $(25 - x)$

Therefore,

$5x + 10(25 - x)$ = ₹ 160

$\Rightarrow 5x + 250 - 10x = 160$

$\Rightarrow 250 - 5x = 160$

$\Rightarrow 5x = 250 - 160$

$\Rightarrow 5x = 90 \Rightarrow x = 18$

∴ The number of ₹ 5 coins = x = 18

and the number of ₹ 10 coins = $(25 - x)$

= 25 – 18 = 7.

8. (B): Cost of item [$\frac{1}{2}$ kg tomotoes + 1 kg potatoes + $\frac{1}{2}$ kg carrot + 250 g chillies + 6 lemons]

= ₹ (20 + 12.50 + 40 + 25 + 15) = ₹ 112.50

∴ money will be get back

= ₹ 200 – ₹ 112.50 = ₹ 87.50.

9. (A): Total value = 10.40 + 10.30 + 8.20

= ₹ 33.90.

10. (A): Total money = ₹ 50

Cost of Ice-cream = ₹ 15.75

Cost of chocolate = ₹ 18.30

Total money spent = 15.75 + 18.30 = ₹ 34.05

∴ Remaining amount = 50 – 34.05 = ₹ 15.95

Hence, the money left is ₹ 15.95.

11. (B): Cost of 1 newespaper = ₹ 4

Total days in January = 31 days

∴ Total cost = 4 × 31 = ₹ 124.

12. (C): Hari save daily = ₹ 5

Total days in March = 31 days

∴ Total savings = ₹ 5 × 31 = ₹ 155.

13. (B): The cost of 8 m clothes = ₹ 680

∴ The cost of 1 m clothes = $\frac{680}{8}$ = ₹ 85.

14. (A): The cost of 1 kg of rice = ₹ 45.75

∴ The cost of 5 kg of rice = 45.75 × 5 = ₹ 228.75.

15. (C): The cost of a notebook = ₹ 24.75

The cost of a pen = ₹ 12.75

∴ Required difference = 24.75 – 12.25

= ₹ 12.50.

16. (A): Weight of a coin = 6 grams

Number of coins = 10

∴ Total weight = 6 × 10 = 60 grams.

17. (D): The cost of a bag = ₹ 450

The cost of a purse = ₹ 275

∴ Total cost = 450 + 275

= ₹ 725.

18. (B): The cost of 1 pencil = ₹ 3.65

∴ The cost of 12 pencil = 12 × 3.65 = ₹ 43.80.

19. (D): The cost of 18 kg mangoes = ₹ 267.30

∴ The cost of 1 kg mango = $\frac{267.30}{18}$ = ₹ 14.85.

20. (B): Let the number of coins for each denomination (1-rupee, 2-rupee and 5-rupee) = x

$\Rightarrow 8x = 320$

$\Rightarrow x = \frac{320}{8} = 40$

∴ Total coins = $3x = 3 \times 40 = 120$

Hence, the total number of coins is 120.

14 Area & Perimeter

In this part of mensuration we often have to deal with the problem of finding the areas and perimeters of plane figures.

Triangle

1. Perimeter = 3 × side (Equilateral triangle)

2. Area $= \frac{1}{2} \times \text{base} \times \text{height}$, or

Area $= \sqrt{s(s-a)(s-b)(s-c)}$

where *a, b, c,* are the lengths of the sides of triangle and

$s = \frac{a+b+c}{2}$

Right Angled Triangle : It is one whose one of the angles is right angle, *i.e.*, 90°.

1. $(\text{Hypotenuse})^2 = (\text{Perpendicular})^2 + (\text{Base})^2$

2. Area $= \frac{1}{2} \times \text{Base} \times \text{Perpendicular}$

Equilateral Triangle : All three sides are equal in length and all three angles are equal to 60°.

1. Area $= \frac{\sqrt{3}}{4} \times (\text{Side})^2$

2. Area $= \frac{(\text{Height})^2}{\sqrt{3}}$

3. Height $= \frac{\sqrt{3}}{2} \times \text{side}$

4. Perimeter = 3 × side

Isosceles Triangle : Two sides are equal in lengths.

1. Area $= \frac{b}{4}\sqrt{4a^2 - b^2}$

where a = lengths of equal sides

b = length of unequal side

2. In an isosceles right triangle,

(*a*) Hypotenuse $= \sqrt{2} \times \text{congruent side } (a)$

(*b*) Area $= \frac{1}{2} \times a^2$

(*c*) Perimeter $= \sqrt{2} \times a\left(\sqrt{2}+1\right)$

Rectangle

1. Area = length(l) × breadth(b)

2. Perimeter = $2(l + b)$

3. Diagonal $= \sqrt{l^2 + b^2}$

Square

1. Area = $(\text{Side})^2$

2. Perimeter = 4 × side

3. Diagonal $= \text{side} \times \sqrt{2}$

Parallelogram

In parallelogram opposite sides are parallel and equal. The two diagonals are not always equal but they bisect each other at the point of intersection.

Area = Base × Height.

Trapezium

It is a quadrilateral whose one pair of opposite sides is parallel. Other two opposite sides are oblique.

Area $= \frac{1}{2} \times \text{Height} \times (\text{Sum of parallel sides})$.

Here, height is the distance between the two parallel sides.

Rhombus

It is parallelogram whose all sides are equal and diagonals bisect each other at right angle.

1. Area $= \frac{1}{2} \times \text{Product of diagonals}$

2. Side $= \sqrt{\left(\frac{d_1}{2}\right)^2 + \left(\frac{d_2}{2}\right)^2}$, where d_1 and d_2 are diagonals

3. Perimeter = 4 × side

Quadrilateral

Area $= \frac{1}{2} \times$ One diagonal $\times$ (Sum of perpendicular to it from the opposite vertices)

$$= \frac{1}{2} \times d \times (a+b)$$

Circle

1. Diameter = 2 × Radius
2. Area $= \pi r^2 = \frac{\pi}{4} d^2$;

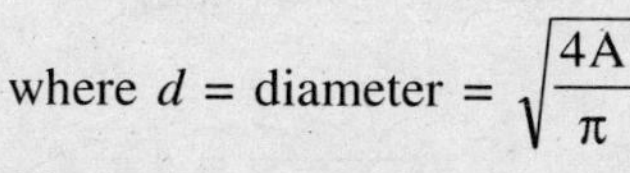

where d = diameter $= \sqrt{\frac{4A}{\pi}}$

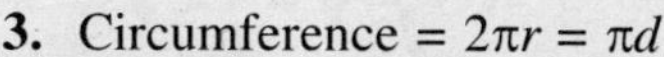

3. Circumference $= 2\pi r = \pi d$
4. Radius $= \frac{\text{Circumference}}{2\pi} = \frac{\sqrt{\text{Area}}}{\pi}$
5. Length of an Arc $= \frac{\theta}{360°} \times 2\pi r$
6. Area of sector $= \frac{\theta}{360°} \times \pi r^2 = \frac{1}{2} \times \text{Arc} \times r$

Polygon

1. Interior angle + Exterior angle = 180°
2. Each interior angle $= \left(\frac{2n-4}{n}\right) \times 90°$

   where n = number of sides
3. Sum of Exterior angles = 360°
4. Perimeter = Number of sides × Length of side.
5. For an equilateral triangle of side 'a'

   (a) radius of inscribed circle $= \frac{a}{2\sqrt{3}}$

   and side of the triangle $= 2\sqrt{3}r$,

   (b) radius of circumcircle $= \frac{a}{\sqrt{3}}$
6. Area of regular polygon $= \frac{1}{2}$(No. of sides) (Radius of the inscribed circle)
7. Area of regular hexagon $= \frac{3\sqrt{3}}{2}(\text{side})^2 = 2.598\ (\text{side})^2$
8. Area of a regular octagon $= 2\left(\sqrt{2}+1\right)(\text{side})^2$

   $= 4.828\ (\text{side})^2$
9. Area of quadrilateral,

   $$A = \sqrt{s(s-a)(s-b)(s-c)(s-d)}$$

   where, $s = \frac{a+b+c+d}{2}$

SOLVED EXAMPLES

Example 1 : Area of a rectangular field is 1600 sq. metre. If its length is four times its width, find the length of this rectangular field.

Solution : Suppose the length and the width of this field is $4x$ metres and x metres respectively.

∴ Area of the field

$= 4x \times x = 4x^2$ sq. metre

Since, $4x^2 = 1600 \Rightarrow x^2 = 400$

$\Rightarrow x = \sqrt{400} \Rightarrow x = 20$

∴ Length of the rectangular field = 4 × 20 = 80 m.

Example 2 : Perimeter of the rectangular floor of a room is 100 m. If its length and breadth are in the ratio 3 : 2, find the area of this rectangular floor.

Solution : Suppose the length and the breadth of this rectangular floor are $3x$ metre and $2x$ metre respectively.

The perimeter of the floor $= 2 \times (l + b)$

$= 2(3x + 2x) = 2 \times 5x = 10x$ metre

Since $10x = 100$

$\therefore x = \frac{100}{10} = 10$

∴ Length of the floor = 3 × 10 = 30 m

And breadth of the floor = 2 × 10 = 20 m

∴ Area of the floor

= 30 × 20 = 600 sq. m.

Example 3 : If the two diagonals of a rhombus are 72 cm and 30 cm respectively, find its perimeter.

Solution : Suppose the rhombus ABCD,

diagonal AC = 72 cm and

diagonal BD = 30 cm

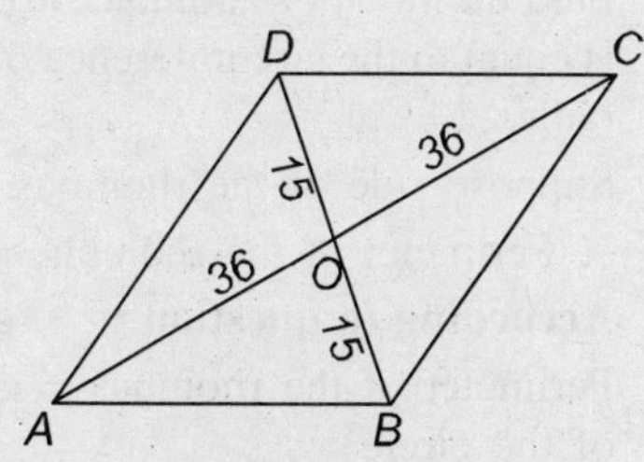

$\therefore$ OB = OD $= \frac{\text{BD}}{2} = \frac{30}{2} = 15$ cm and $OA = OC = \frac{AC}{2} = \frac{72}{2} = 36$ cm

$\therefore$ $AB = BC = CD = DA = \sqrt{36^2 + 15^2}$

$= \sqrt{1296+225} = \sqrt{1521} = 39$

$\therefore$ Perimeter of the rhombus = 4 × 39

= 156 cm.

Example 4 : A rectangular field is 50 metre long and 40 metre wide. There is a path 5 metre wide outside the field along its sides. Find the cost of growing grass in this path at ₹ 10.50 per sq. metre.

Solution : Area of the field = 50 × 40 = 2000 sq. m.

And area of the field including the path = 60 × 50 = 3000 sq. m.

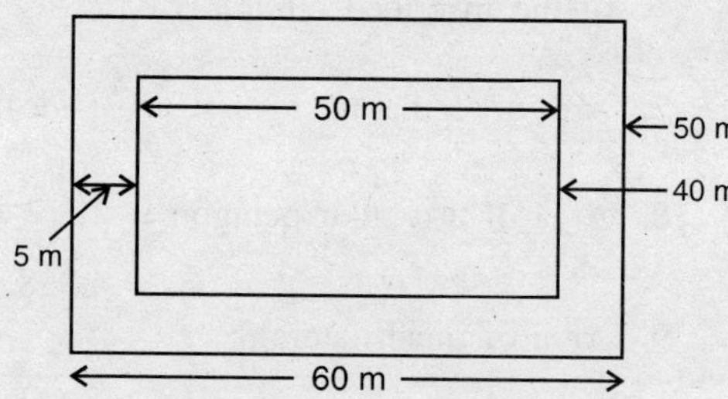

$\therefore$ Area of the path = 3000 – 2000

= 1000 sq. m.

$\therefore$ Cost of growing grass in the path

= ₹ 1000 × 10.50 = ₹ 10500.

Example 5 : The diagonal of a quadrilateral is 140 m and the offsets on it are 100 m and 30 m respectively. Find the area of this quadrilateral.

Solution : Area of the quadrilateral = $\frac{1}{2}$ × diagonal × sum of the offsets

$= \frac{1}{2} \times 140 \times (100+30)$

$= \frac{1}{2} \times 140 \times 130 = 9100$ sq. m.

Example 6 : Find the side of a rhombus whose perimeter is equal to the circumference of the circle of radius 14 cm.

Solution : Suppose side of the rhombus = x cm

$\therefore$ Perimeter of the rhombus = $4x$ cm

According to question :

Perimeter of the rhombus = circumference of the circle

$\Rightarrow 4x = 2\pi \times 14$

($\because$ radius of the circle = 14 cm)

$\Rightarrow \quad 4x = 2 \times \frac{22}{7} \times 14$

Hence, $x = \frac{2 \times 22 \times 2}{4} = 22$ cm

$\therefore$ Side of the rhombus = 22 cm.

Example 7 : Area of an equilateral triangle is $\sqrt{3}$ sq. cm. Find the length of its sides.

Solution : Area of equilateral triangle = $\frac{\sqrt{3}}{4} \times (\text{side})^2$

$\therefore \frac{\sqrt{3}}{4} \times (\text{side})^2 = \sqrt{3} \Rightarrow (\text{side})^2$

$= \frac{\sqrt{3} \times 4}{\sqrt{3}} = 4$

$\Rightarrow$ side = $\sqrt{4} = 2$

Hence, side of the triangle = 2 cm.

Example 8 : A rectangular tank is 25 m long, 12 m wide and 6 m high. Find the cost of plastering its walls and bottom at 75 paise per sq. metre.

Solution : Area of the four walls of the tank

= 2 × height (length + breadth)

= 2 × 6 × (25 + 12)

= 12 × 37 = 444 sq. m.

And area of the bottom of the tank

= length × breadth

= 25 × 12 = 300 sq. m.

Total area = 444 + 300 = 744 sq. m.

$\therefore$ Cost of plastering = $744 \times \frac{75}{100}$ = ₹ 558.

Example 9 : What will be the area of a right angled triangle whose height is double that of base of 13 cm?

Solution : Area of right angled triangle = $\frac{1}{2} \times 13 \times 26$

$= 169$ cm^2

Example 10: What will be the area of a circle whose circumference is 132 cm?

Solution : Radius of the circle, $r = \frac{\text{circumference}}{2\pi}$

$= \frac{132 \times 7}{2 \times 22} = 21$ cm

Hence, Area of the circle = $\frac{22}{7} \times 21 \times 21$

$= 1386$ cm^2.

EXERCISE

1. A field is in the form of a square whose perimeter is 580 m. Area of this field is
   A. 21025 sq. m. B. 20225 sq. m.
   C. 30025 sq. m. D. 19975 sq. m.

2. Find the area of the square whose each side measures 20 cm.
   A. 300 sq. cm. B. 380 sq. cm.
   C. 360 sq. cm. D. 400 sq. m.

3. Area of a circle is 154 sq. cm. Its circumference will be
   A. 44 cm B. 48 cm C. 54 cm D. 68 cm

4. The base and the height of a triangle is 8 cm and 10 cm respectively. Its area will be
   A. 40 sq. cm. B. 20 sq. cm.
   C. 49 sq. cm. D. 64 sq. cm.

5. If it is given that the parallel sides of a trapezium are 15 m and 25 m while the distance between them is 10 m. Its area will be:
   A. 150 sq. m. B. 225 sq. m.
   C. 200 sq. m. D. 270 sq. m.

6. If side of a square is reduced by 50%, its area will be reduced by
   A. 50% B. 75% C. 80% D. 60%

7. The perimeter of a square is 24 m and that of another is 32 m. Find the perimeter of a third square, area of which is equal to sum of the areas of these two squares
   A. 40 m B. 51 m C. 37 m D. 42 m

8. If the perimeter of an equilateral triangle is 72 cm, its area will be
   A. $144\sqrt{3}$ sq. cm B. $142\sqrt{3}$ sq. cm
   C. $154\sqrt{2}$ sq. cm. D. $144\sqrt{2}$ sq. cm.

9. The radii of two circles are 5 cm and 12 cm respectively. Find the radius of a circle which is equal in area to these two circles.
   A. 15 cm B. 13 cm C. 10 cm D. 8 cm

10. If the length of a rectangle is increased by 20% and width is decreased by 15%, then its area
    A. decreases by 4% B. increases by 2%
    C. decreases by 2% D. increases by 3%

11. If area of a traingle whose base is 6 cm is equal to the area of a square of side 6 cm, find the height of this triangle.
    A. 10 cm B. 22 cm C. 12 cm D. 18 cm

12. A garden is 24 m long and 14 m wide. There is a path 1 m wide outside the garden along its sides. If the path is to be constructed with square marble tiles 20 cm × 20 cm, find the number of tiles required to cover the path.
    A. 1800 B. 2200
    C. 2000 D. 2150

13. The radius of a circular wheel is 1.75 m. The number of revolutions that it will make in travelling 11 km, is
    A. 10 B. 100
    C. 1000 D. 10,000

14. The diameter of a wheel of a cycle is 70 cm. It moves slowly along a road. How far will it go in 24 complete revolutions?
    A. 38.9 m B. 52.8 m C. 56.6 m D. 60 m

15. A room having length 15m and breadth 12 m. What will be the total cost if the floor is made at ₹ 125 per m^2?
    A. ₹ 20,050 B. ₹ 20,500
    C. ₹ 22,050 D. ₹ 22,500

16. A circular ground has area equal to 616 m^2. Inside the circle a small circle is there whose radius equal to half of the radius of circle. Find the remaining area of the circle.
    A. 154 m^2 B. 156 m^2 C. 460 m^2 D. 462 m^2

17. The area of a circle is 1386 m^2. Find its circumference.
    A. 124 m B. 132 m C. 136 m D. 140 m

18. The length of a rectangle is increased by 60%. By how many per cent its breadth will be reduced so that its area remains the same?
    A. 37.5% B. 50% C. 60% D. 75%

19. The length of a rectangle is increased by 30% and breadth is decreased by the same per cent, the effective change in area will be
    A. 6% decrease B. 6% increase
    C. 9% decrease D. 9% increase

20. The circumference of a circle is 88 cm. Find its area.
    A. 544 cm^2 B. 616 cm^2 C. 724 cm^2 D. 849 cm^2

21. The area of an equilateral triangle of side 20 cm is
    A. $\left(100/\sqrt{3}\right)$ cm^2 B. $100\sqrt{3}$ cm^2
    C. $100\sqrt{3}/2$ cm^2 D. $100\sqrt{3}/4$ cm^2

22. If the perimeter of a square is $(4a + 8)$ unit, then its area will be

A. $(a^2 + 4a + 4)$ square unit
B. $(10a^2 - a - 8)$ square unit
C. $(a + 2a^2 + 4)$ square unit
D. $(4a^2 + 4a - 4)$ square unit

23. A rectangular park is 45 m long and 30 m wide. A path 2.5 m wide is constructed outside around the park. The area of the path is

A. 200 m^2 B. 300 m^2
C. 400 m^2 D. 375 m^2

24. The total area of four walls of a room is 660 m^2 and the length is twice its width. If the height of the room is 11 m, then the area of its ceiling is:

A. 200 m^2 B. 150 m^2 C. 100 m^2 D. 75 m^2

25. If the length and breadth of a rectangular plot are increased by 50% and 20% respectively, then how many times will its area be increased?

A. $\frac{4}{5}$ B. $1\frac{4}{5}$ C. $1\frac{1}{5}$ D. $\frac{1}{5}$

26. In a circular park of diameter 80 m, there is a square-shaped playground of maximum area. The area of the playground is:

A. 3200 m^2 B. 6400 m^2
C. 1600 m^2 D. 12800 m^2

27. In a rhombus, the lengths of diagonals are 16 cm and 12 cm. The side of the rhombus is:

A. 9 cm B. 7 cm C. 8 cm D. 10 cm

28. The length of rectangle is increased by 60%. By what per cent would the width have to be decreased to maintain the same area?

A. 125% B. 37.5% C. 50% D. 75.5%

29. Diagonal of a rectangular field is 17 metre and perimetre is 46 metre then area of the field will be:

A. 132 m^2 B. 289 m^2 C. 112 m^2 D. 120 m^2

30. If length and breadth of a room is 15 m 17 cm and 9 m 2 cm respectively. What is the minimum number of square tiles which is fit for that?

A. 841 B. 840 C. 814 D. 820

ANSWERS WITH EXPLANATIONS

1. (A): Here, $4 \times \text{side} = 580 \Rightarrow \text{side} = \frac{580}{4} = 145$ m

$\therefore$ Area $= (\text{side})^2 = (145)^2 = 21025$ sq. m.

2. (D): Area of the square $= (\text{side})^2 = (20)^2 = 400$ sq. cm.

3. (A): Area of the circle $= \pi r^2 \Rightarrow \pi r^2 = 154$

$\Rightarrow r^2 = \frac{154 \times 7}{22} \Rightarrow r = 7$ cm

$\therefore$ Circumference of the circle $= 2\pi r = 2 \times \frac{22}{7} \times 7$

$= 44$ cm.

4. (A): Area of the triangle $= \frac{1}{2} \times 8 \times 10 = 40$ sq. cm.

5. (C): Area of the trapezium $= \frac{1}{2} \times (15 + 25) \times 10 = 200$ sq. m.

6. (B): Area of the square $= x^2$ sq. m.

Side of the new square $= x - 50\%$ of $x = \frac{x}{2}$ m

$\therefore$ Area of the new square $= \left(\frac{x}{2}\right)^2 = \frac{x^2}{4}$ sq. m.

$\therefore$ Reduction in area of the square $= x^2 - \frac{x^2}{4}$

$= \frac{3x^2}{4}$ sq. m.

$\therefore$ Percentage reduction $= \frac{3x^2/4}{x^2} \times 100 = 75\%$

7. (A): Side of the 1st square $= \frac{24}{4} = 6$ m

And side of the 2nd square $= \frac{32}{4} = 8$ m

Now, area of the third square $= 6^2 + 8^2$

$= 36 + 64 = 100$ sq. m.

$\therefore$ Side of the third square $= \sqrt{100} = 10$ m

Hence, Perimeter of the third square $= 4 \times$ side

$= 4 \times 10 = 40$ m.

8. (A): Here, $3x = 72 \Rightarrow x = \frac{72}{3} = 24$ cm.

$\therefore$ Area of the equilateral triangle $= \frac{\sqrt{3}}{4} \times x^2$

$= \frac{\sqrt{3}}{4} \times (24)^2 = 144\sqrt{3}$ sq. cm.

9. (B): Area of the new circle $= \pi.5^2 + \pi.12^2$

$= 25\pi + 144\pi = 169\pi$ sq. cm.

$= \pi(13)^2$ sq. cm

Hence, it is clear that the radius of the new circle will be 13 cm.

10. (B): Area of the rectangle $= xy$ sq. metre

Area of the new rectangle $= \frac{120}{100} x \times \frac{85}{100} y$

$= 1.020\, xy$ sq. metre

$\therefore$ Increase in the area $= 1.02\,xy - xy$
$= .02\,xy$ sq. m.

$\therefore$ Percentage increase $= \dfrac{.02xy}{xy} \times 100 = 2\%$

11. (C): Area of the square = 36 sq. cm

Now, $\dfrac{1}{2} \times \text{base} \times \text{height} = 36 \Rightarrow \dfrac{1}{2} \times 6 \times \text{height} = 36$

$\therefore$ Height of the triangle $= \dfrac{36 \times 2}{6} = 12$ cm.

12. (C): Area of the garden = 24 × 14 = 336 sq. m

Area of the (garden + path) = 26 × 16 = 416 sq. m

$\therefore$ Area of the path = 416 – 336 = 80 sq. m

Area of 1 tile = 20 × 20 = 400 sq. cm
= .04 sq. m

$\therefore$ Number of tiles required to cover the path

$$= \frac{80}{.04} = 2000.$$

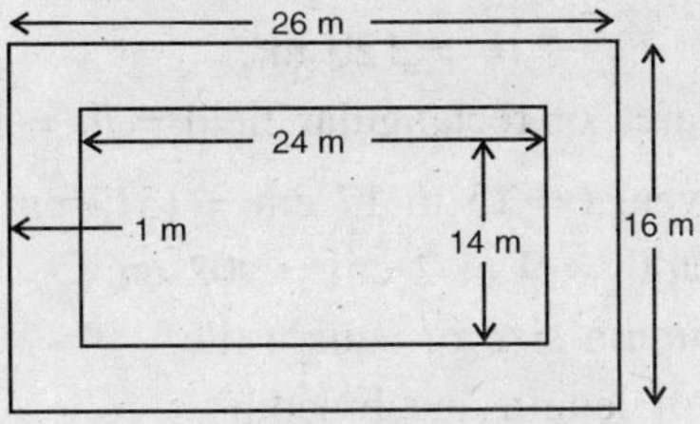

26 m
24 m
1 m
14 m
16 m

13. (C): The number of revolutions $= \dfrac{11 \times 1000}{2 \times \dfrac{22}{7} \times 1.75}$

$$= \frac{11 \times 1000 \times 7}{2 \times 22 \times 1.75} = 1000.$$

14. (B): Distance, travelled in 24 revolutions

$$= 24 \times 2 \times \frac{22}{7} \times 35$$
$= 5280$ cm $= 52.8$ m

15. (D): Area of the floor = 15 × 12 = 180 m^2

Hence, total cost of flooring = 180 × ₹ 125 = ₹ 22,500

16. (D): Radius of the circular ground $= \sqrt{\dfrac{616 \times 7}{22}} = \sqrt{28 \times 7}$
$= 14$ m

Area of the remaining portion $= 616 - \dfrac{22}{7} \times 7^2$
$= 616 - 154 = 462\ m^2$

17. (B): Radius of the circle $= \sqrt{\dfrac{1386 \times 7}{22}} = \sqrt{63 \times 7} = 21$m

Circumference of the circle $= 2 \times \dfrac{22}{7} \times 21 = 132$ m

18. (A): Let breadth be reduced by $x\%$, then,

$$60 - x - \frac{60 \times x}{100} = 0 \quad \Rightarrow x + \frac{3x}{5} = 60$$

$$\Rightarrow \frac{8x}{5} = 60 \qquad \therefore x = \frac{5 \times 60}{8} = 37.5\%$$

19. (C): Effective change in area $= 30 - 30 - \dfrac{30 \times 30}{100} = -9$

Hence, area is decreased by 9%.

20. (B): Radius of the circle $= \dfrac{88 \times 7}{2 \times 22} = 14$ cm

Area of the circle $= \dfrac{22}{7} \times 14 \times 14 = 616\ \text{cm}^2$

21. (B): Area of equilateral triangle

$$= \frac{\sqrt{3}}{4}(\text{side})^2$$

$$= \frac{\sqrt{3}}{4} \times (20)^2 = \frac{\sqrt{3}}{4} \times 400$$

$$= 100\sqrt{3}\ \text{cm}^2$$

22. (A): Perimeter of square = 4 × side

$\Rightarrow$ 4 × side = $4a + 8 = 4(a + 2)$

side of square = $a + 2$

Area of square = $(a + 2)^2$
= $(a^2 + 4a + 4)$ unit^2

23. (C): Area without path = 45 × 30 = 1350 m^2

Area with path = 50 × 35 = 1750 m^2

$\therefore$ Area of the path = 1750 – 1350 = 400 m^2

24. (A): Area of the four walls = $2(l + b) \times h$

$2(l + b) \times h = 660$

$\Rightarrow 2(2b + b) \times 11 = 660$

$\Rightarrow 3b = 30$

$\Rightarrow b = 10$ m

$\therefore$ length = 10 × 2 = 20 m

Area of the ceiling = $l \times b$
= 20 × 10 = 200 m^2.

25. (A): Let rectangular field length and breadth are x and y unit respectively.

Initial area of rectangular field $l \times b$
$= x \times y$ square unit

New length of rectangular field = x × 150%

$$= \frac{3x}{2} \text{ unit}$$

New breadth of rectangular field

$$= y \times 120\% = \frac{6y}{5} \text{ unit}$$

New area of rectangular field = $l \times b$

$$= \frac{3x}{2} \times \frac{6y}{5} = \frac{9}{5}xy \text{ square unit}$$

Increase in the area of rectangular field

$$= \frac{9}{5}xy - xy = \frac{4}{5}xy$$

$$= \frac{4}{5} \times \text{initial area}$$

So, area will increase $\frac{4}{5}$ times.

26. (A): The squared playing field Area will be maximum if Diameter of circle = diagonal of square

$\therefore \quad \sqrt{2}a = 80$

$$a = \frac{80}{\sqrt{2}} = 40\sqrt{2} \text{ m}$$

$\therefore \quad \sqrt{2}a = 80$

$$a = \frac{80}{\sqrt{2}} = 40\sqrt{2} \text{ m}$$

The playing field area = $a^2 = \left(40\sqrt{2}\right)^2 = 3200 \text{ m}^2$

27. (D): We know that the relation between the diagonals and side of rhombus is

$$d_1^2 + d_2^2 = 4a^2$$

Given that, $d_1 = 16$ cm, $d_2 = 12$ cm

$$(16)^2 + (12)^2 = 4a^2$$

$$4a^2 = 256 + 144$$

$$4a^2 = 400$$

$$a^2 = 100$$

$$a = 10 \text{ cm}$$

So, side of rhombus is 10 cm.

28. (B): Required % $= \frac{60}{160} \times 100\%$

$$= \frac{3}{8} \times 100\%$$

$$= \frac{300}{8}\%$$

$$= 37\frac{1}{2}\%$$

$$= 37.5\%.$$

29. (D): Length = l and breadth = b

$\therefore \quad l^2 + b^2 = 17^2$

$\Rightarrow \quad l^2 + b^2 = 289$ m

and $\quad 2(l + b) = 46$ m

$\Rightarrow \quad l + b = 23$ m

$\because \quad (l + b)^2 = l^2 + b^2 + 2lb$

$\therefore \quad (23)^2 = 289 + 2lb$

$\Rightarrow \quad 529 - 289 = 2lb$

$\Rightarrow \quad 2lb = 240$

$\Rightarrow \quad lb = 120 \text{ m}^2.$

Hence, area of rectangular field = $lb = 120 \text{ m}^2$.

30. (C): Given, l = 15 m 17 cm = 1517 cm

and breadth = 9 m 2 cm = 902 cm

$\because$ Maximum size of square tile

= HCF of length and breadth

902) 1517 (1
−902
615) 902 (1
−615
287) 615 (2
−574
41) 287 (7
−287
×××

$\because$ HCF = 41 cm

$\therefore$ Maximum size of each tile = 41 cm

Minimum number of square tiles

$$= \frac{\text{Area of room}}{\text{Area of each tiles}}$$

$$= \frac{1517 \times 902}{41 \times 41}$$

$$= 37 \times 22 = 814.$$

15 Volume and Surface Area

In mensuration we often have to deal with the problem of finding the volume of solid figure.

Cuboid

A cuboid has six faces, each one a ractangle. It has 12 edges. For example, a rectangular brick.

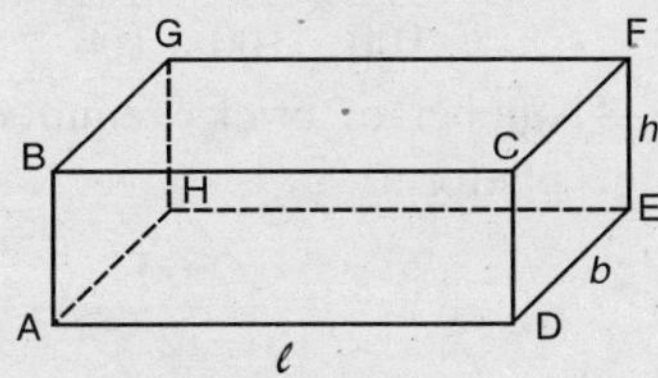

Let Length = l, Breadth = b and Height = h, then,

1. Volume = (Length × Breadth × Height)
2. Whole Surface Area = $2(lb + bh + lh)$
3. Diagonal = $\sqrt{l^2 + b^2 + h^2}$
4. Area of 4 walls of a room = $2 \times h\ (l + b)$

Cube

In a cube, Length = Breadth = Height

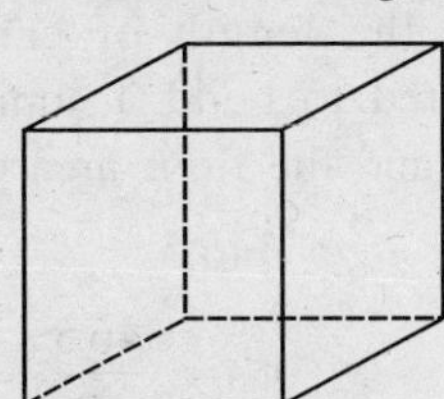

1. Volume = $(l)^3$
2. Length = $\sqrt[3]{\text{Volume}}$
3. Whole Surface Area = $6\ l^2$
4. Diagonal = $l \times \sqrt{3}$
5. Lateral Surface Area = $4\ l^2$

Cylinder

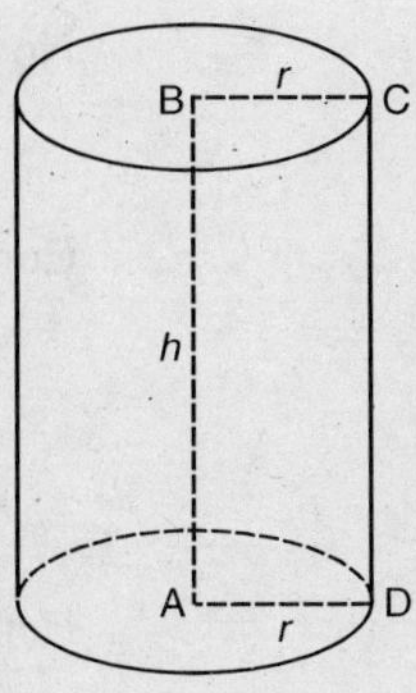

1. Volume = $\pi r^2 h$
2. Curved Surface Area = $2\pi rh$
3. Total Surface Area = $2\pi r(r + h)$
   where r = radius, h = height

Spherical Cell

1. Volume = $\frac{4}{3}\pi\left(R^3 - r^3\right)$
2. Total Surface Area = $4\pi(R^2 - r^2)$
   where R = Outer radius
   r = Inner radius

Sphere

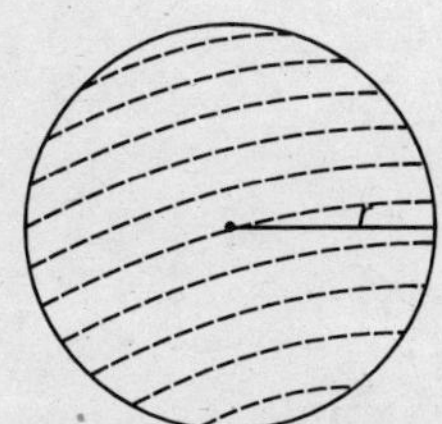

1. Volume = $\frac{4}{3}\pi r^3$
2. Surface Area = $4\pi r^2$

Semi-sphere

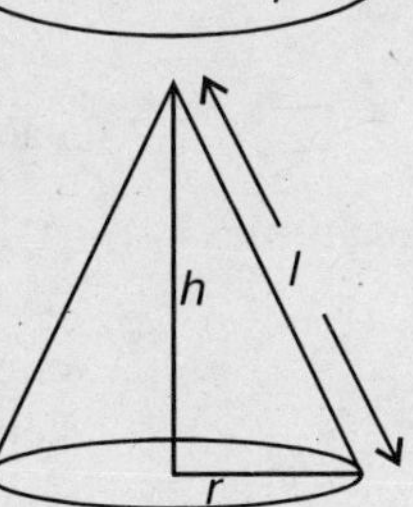

1. Volume = $\frac{2}{3}\pi r^3$
2. Curved surface area = $2\pi r^2$
3. Total surface area = $3\pi r^2$

Cone

1. Slant height (l) = $\sqrt{r^2 + h^2}$
2. Volume = $\frac{1}{3}\pi r^2 h$
3. Curved surface area = πrl
4. Total surface area = $\pi r\ (l + r)$
5. If the depth of the frustum of a cone be k and the radii of its ends are r_1 and r_2, then
   (*i*) Slant height of the frustum of a cone
   $= \sqrt{k^2 + (r_1 - r_2)^2}$
   (*ii*) Curved surface of the frustum = $\pi(r_1 + r_2)\ l$.
   (*iii*) Volume = $\frac{\pi k}{3}\left(r_1^2 + r_1 r_2 + r_2^2\right)$

SOLVED EXAMPLES

Example 1 : Find the side and surface area of a cube whose volume is 729 cu cm.

Solution : Here, $(\text{side})^3 = 729$

$\Rightarrow \quad (\text{side})^3 = (9)^3$

$\Rightarrow \quad \text{side} = 9$ cm

Since, surface area $= 6 \times (9)^2$

$= 6 \times 81 = 486$ sq. cm.

Example 2 : Diagonal of a rectangular solid figure is 17 cm long. If its two edges are 8 cm and 9 cm respectively, find its third edge.

Solution : Suppose, the length of the third edge = x cm

Diagonal = 17

$= \sqrt{(8)^2 + (9)^2 + x^2}$

$\Rightarrow \quad (17)^2 = (8)^2 + (9)^2 + x^2$

$\Rightarrow \quad 289 = 64 + 81 + x^2$

$\Rightarrow \quad 289 = 145 + x^2$

$\Rightarrow \quad x^2 = 289 - 145 = 144$

$\Rightarrow \quad x = \sqrt{144} = 12$

$\therefore$ Third edge is 12 cm long.

Example 3 : How many cubical blocks can be packed in a carton of size 10 m × 6 m × 4 m, if the volume of each cubical block is 15 cu metre?

Solution : Volume of the carton $= l \times b \times h$

$= 10 \times 6 \times 4 = 240$ cu m

$\therefore$ Number of cubical blocks that can be packed in the carton $= \dfrac{240}{15} = 16$

Example 4 : A 1100 cu cm iron cube is to be melted and recast into a iron rod in the form of a right circular cylinder. If diameter of the rod is kept 4 cm, what will be the length of this rod?

Solution : Suppose length of the rod = h cm

Radius of the rod $= \dfrac{4}{2} = 2$ cm

Here, Volume of the rod = Volume of the iron cube

$\therefore \quad \dfrac{22}{7} \times (2)^2 \times h = 1100$

$\Rightarrow \quad h = \dfrac{1100 \times 7}{22 \times 4} = 87.5$ cm

$\therefore$ Rod will be 87.5 cm long.

Example 5 : How many spherical bullets of radius 2 cm can be made from a metallic sphere whose radius is 8 cm?

Solution : Here, Number of bullets

$= \dfrac{\text{Volume of metallic sphere}}{\text{Volume of each bullet}}$

$= \dfrac{\frac{4}{3}\pi(8)^3}{\frac{4}{3}\pi(2)^3} = (8)^2 = 64$

Example 6 : How many bricks of size 6 cm × 5 cm × 4 cm will be required to construct a platform 15 m long, 8 m wide and 5 m high.

Solution : Volume of the platform $= 15 \times 8 \times 5$

$= 600$ cu m

Volume of one brick

$= \dfrac{6}{100} \times \dfrac{5}{100} \times \dfrac{4}{100} = \dfrac{12}{100000}$ cu m

$\therefore$ Number of bricks required to construct the platform

$= \dfrac{600}{\frac{12}{100000}} = 5000000$

$= 5 \times 10^6$.

Example 7 : Find the volume of a cone, whose height (h) is twice the radius (r) of its base.

Solution : Here, $h = 2r$

Since, volume of the cone

$= \dfrac{1}{3}\pi r^2 . 2r = \dfrac{2}{3}\pi r^3$

Example 8 : Find the length of canvas 1.1 m wide required to build a conical tent of height 14m and the floor area of 346.5 m^2.

Solution : Here, $\pi r^2 = 346.5$

$\Rightarrow \quad r^2 = \dfrac{346.5 \times 7}{22} = 110.25$

$\therefore \quad r = 10.5$ m

Now, slant height, $l = \sqrt{(14)^2 + (10.5)^2}$

$\sqrt{306.25} = 17.5$ m

Curved surface area of conical tent

$= \dfrac{22}{7} \times 10.5 \times 17.5$

$= 577.5\ m^3$.

Hence, length of canvas required $= \dfrac{577.5}{1.1}$

$= 525$ m

EXERCISE

1. A solid in the form of a cuboid is 4 cm × 3 cm × 2 cm. Its volume will be

A. 20 cu cm B. 22 cu cm
C. 28 cu cm D. 24 cu cm

2. A reservoir is 3 m long, 2 m wide and 1 m deep. Its capacity in litres is

A. 8000 litres B. 10000 litres
C. 6500 litres D. 6000 litres

3. Surface area of a cube is 1014 sq. cm. Its volume will be

A. 2197 cu cm B. 2297 cu cm
C. 2179 cu cm D. 2117 cu cm

4. Two spheres have their surface areas in the ratio 9 : 16. Their volumes are in the ratio of

A. 64 : 27 B. 27 : 64 C. 16 : 27 D. 11 : 27

5. The length of the longest rod that can be placed in a room 12 m long, 9 m broad and 8 m high is

A. 17 m B. 18 m C. 25 m D. 16 m

6. The radius and the height of a right circular cone are in the ratio of 3 : 5. If its volume is 120 π cu m, its slant height is

A. $3\sqrt{34}$m B. $2\sqrt{28}$m C. $2\sqrt{44}$m D. $2\sqrt{34}$m

7. Circumference of the base of a cylinder is 88 cm and height of the cylinder is 42 cm. Its volume is

A. 25872 cu cm B. 28572 cu cm
C. 25870 cu cm D. 22584 cu cm

8. If two cubes each of 10 cm side are kept close to each other, then the cuboid so formed will have surface area equal to

A. 1200 sq. cm B. 5000 sq. cm
C. 1000 sq. cm D. 1250 sq. cm

9. A room is in the form of a cube of side 10 m. How many bales of cotton can be kept in it if each bale covers 5 cu m space?

A. 100 B. 175 C. 200 D. 225

10. The surface area of a cube is 600 sq. m. Its diagonal is

A. $10\sqrt{3}$ cm B. $5\sqrt{3}$ cm
C. $4\sqrt{2}$ cm D. $10\sqrt{2}$ cm

11. If the radius of a sphere is decreased by 50%, then by how much per cent will the surface area of this sphere be decreased?

A. 50% B. 40% C. 60% D. 75%

12. A cone and a sphere have the same radius and the same volume. The ratio of the diameter of the sphere to the height of the cone is

A. 1 : 3 B. 3 : 2 C. 1 : 2 D. 2 : 3

13. Find the length of the longest rod that can be placed in a room 30m long, 24m broad and 18m high.

A. $15\sqrt{2}$ m B. 30 m
C. $30\sqrt{2}$ m D. 60 m

14. If the volume of a cube is 512 cm^3, then find its total surface area.

A. 192 cm^2 B. 256 cm^2
C. 329 cm^2 D. 384 cm^2

15. The volume of a cube is numerically equal to sum of the length of its edges. The total surface area of cube in square units is:

A. 72.0 B. 44.2 C. 12.4 D. 64.5

16. If the length of a room is decreased by 10% and breadth is decreased by 20%, while height is increased by 5%, then what percentage changed in the volume of the room?

A. 24.4% B. 24.6% C. 24% D. 24.2%

17. How many cubes of side 3 cm can be separated from a cube of side 15 cm?

A. 125 B. 25 C. 27 D. 144

18. A cube of side 5 cm is painted on all its faces. If it is sliced into 1 cm^3 cubes, how many 1 cm^3 cubes will have exactly one of their faces painted?

A. 142 B. 27 C. 42 D. 54

19. The length, breadth and height of a cuboid are in the ratio of 6 : 5 : 4. If the total surface area is 5328 cm^2, then the length, breadth and height of the cuboid will be

A. 20 cm, 22 cm, 23 cm
B. 38 cm, 25 cm, 23 cm
C. 36 cm, 30 cm, 24 cm
D. 22 cm, 23 cm, 21 cm

20. A godown is in the shape of a cuboid of measure 60 m × 40 m × 30 m. How many cuboidal boxes can be stored in this godown, if the volume of one box is 0.8 m^3?

A. 40,000 B. 60,000
C. 90,000 D. 72,000

ANSWERS WITH EXPLANATIONS

1. (D): Volume of the cuboid = $l \times b \times h = 4 \times 3 \times 2$
$= 24$ cu. cm.

2. (D): Volume of the reservoir = $l \times b \times h = 3 \times 2 \times 1$
$= 6$ cu. m
($\because$ 1 cu m = 1000 litre)
$\therefore$ Capacity of the reservoir = 6 × 1000 = 6000 litre.

3. (A): Here, $6 \times (\text{side})^2 = 1014$

$\Rightarrow \quad (\text{side})^2 = \frac{1014}{6} = 169$

$\therefore \quad \text{side} = \sqrt{169} = 13$ cm

Hence, Volume of the cube = $(\text{side})^3 = (13)^3$
$= 2197$ cu.cm.

4. (B): Here, $4\pi r_1^2 : 4\pi r_2^2 = 9 : 16$

$\Rightarrow \quad r_1^2 : r_2^2 = 9 : 16$

$\Rightarrow \quad \left(\frac{r_1}{r_2}\right)^2 = \left(\frac{3}{4}\right)^2$

$\Rightarrow \quad r_1 : r_2 = 3 : 4$

$\Rightarrow \quad \frac{r_1^3}{r_2^3} = \frac{27}{64}$

$\Rightarrow \quad r_1^3 : r_2^3 = 27 : 64.$

Therefore, ratio of their volumes = $\frac{4}{3}\pi r_1^3 : \frac{4}{3}\pi r_2^3$

$= r_1^3 : r_2^3 = 27 : 64$

5. (A): The longest rod that can be placed in the cuboidal room = Length of the diagonal

$= \sqrt{l^2 + b^2 + h^2}$

$= \sqrt{(12)^2 + (9)^2 + (8)^2}$

$= \sqrt{144 + 81 + 64}$

$= \sqrt{289} = 17$ m

6. (D): Suppose the base radius and the height of the right circular cone are $3x$ m and $5x$ m respectively.

$\therefore$ Volume of the cone = $\frac{1}{3}\pi r^2 h$

$= \frac{1}{3}\pi(3x)^2 \times 5x$ cu m

Now, $\frac{1}{3}\pi \times 9x^2 \times 5x = 120\pi \Rightarrow x^3 = \frac{120 \times 3}{9 \times 5}$

$\Rightarrow \quad x^3 = 8 \Rightarrow x^3 = (2)^3 \Rightarrow x = 2$ m

$\therefore$ The radius and the height of the cone will be $3 \times 2 = 6$ m and $5 \times 2 = 10$ m respectively.

$\therefore$ Slant height of the cone = $\sqrt{r^2 + h^2}$

$= \sqrt{(6)^2 + (10)^2}$

$= \sqrt{36 + 100} = \sqrt{136} = 2\sqrt{34}$ m.

7. (A): Here, $2\pi r = 88$

$\therefore \quad r = \frac{88}{2\pi} = \frac{88 \times 7}{2 \times 22} = 14$ cm

Since, volume of the cylinder = $\pi r^2 h$

$= \frac{22}{7} \times (14)^2 \times 42 = 22 \times 2 \times 14 \times 42 = 25872$ cu cm.

8. (C): Here, length of the cuboid = Edge of the first cube + Edge of the second cube
= 10 + 10 = 20 cm

$\therefore$ Surface area of the cuboid
= 2(20 × 10 + 10 × 10 + 10 × 20)
= 2(200 + 100 + 200)
= 2 × 500 = 1000 sq. cm.

9. (C): Volume of the cubical room = $(10)^3 = 1000$ cu m
Number of cotton bales which can be placed in the room

$= \frac{\text{Volume of the room}}{\text{Volume of each cotton bale}} = \frac{1000}{5} = 200.$

10. (A): Here, $6 \times (\text{side})^2 = 600$

$\Rightarrow \quad \text{side}^2 = 100$

$\Rightarrow \quad \text{side} = \sqrt{100} = 10$ cm

$\therefore$ Diagonal of the cube = $\sqrt{3} \times \text{side}$

$= \sqrt{3} \times 10 = 10\sqrt{3}$ cm.

11. (D): Change in surface area of the sphere = $\left(-50 - 50 + \frac{-50 \times -50}{100}\right)\%$

$= (-100 + 25)\% = -75\%$

Hence, surface area of the sphere will be decreased by 75%.

12. (C): Here, $4/3\pi r^3 = \frac{1}{3}\pi r^2 h$

$\Rightarrow \quad 4r = h$

$\Rightarrow \quad 2d = h \quad \therefore \frac{d}{h} = \frac{1}{2}$

Hence, required ratio = 1 : 2

13. (C): Length of the longest rod = $\sqrt{30^2+24^2+18^2}$

$= \sqrt{1800} = 30\sqrt{2}$ m

14. (D): Side of the cube = $(512)^{1/3}$ = 8 cm

Total surface area = 6 × 8^2 = 384 cm^2

15. (A): Let the length of edge of a cube = x unit

Then, volume = x^3 unit cube

and the sum of the length of its edge = $12x$ unit

$\therefore \quad x^3 = 12x$

$\Rightarrow \quad x^2 = 12$

The total surface area of cube = $6(\text{edge})^2$

$= 6x^2$

$= 6 \times 12$

= 72 square units.

16. (A): The volume of a room = lbh

$$\text{Change volume} = \frac{9}{10}l \times \frac{80}{100}b \times \frac{105}{100}h$$

$$= \frac{9}{10}l \times \frac{4}{5}b \times \frac{21}{20}h$$

$$= \frac{189}{250}lbh$$

Now, change in the volume of the room

$$= lbh - \frac{189}{250}lbh$$

$$= \frac{61}{250}lbh$$

$$\therefore \quad \% \text{ change} = \frac{\frac{61}{250}lbh}{lbh} \times 100\%$$

$$= \frac{61}{5} \times 2\%$$

$$= \frac{122}{5}\%$$

$= 24.4\%$.

17. (A): Let 'n' cube can be cut.

Then, volume of 15 cm side cube

volume of n × 3 cm side cube

$(15)^3 = n \times (3)^3$

$$n = \frac{15 \times 15 \times 15}{3 \times 3 \times 3}$$

$n = 5 \times 5 \times 5$

$n = 125$

So, 125 small cube can be cut from a 15 cm side cube.

18. (D): There are six faces in a cube. If the cube of 5 cm side is painted on all its faces and sliced into 1 cm^3 cubes, then number of 1 cm^3 cubes painted with only one side is each faces = 3 × 3 = 9

So, total number of cubes of 1 cm^3 painted only one side = 9 × 6 = 54

19. (C): Surface area of cuboid = $2(lb + bh + hl)$

$\Rightarrow 5328 = 2(6x \times 5x + 5x \times 4x + 4x \times 6x)$

$\Rightarrow 74x^2 = 2664$

$\Rightarrow \quad x^2 = 36$

$\Rightarrow \quad x = 6$

Length = 6 × 6 = 36 cm,

breadth = 5 × 6 = 30 cm

and height = 4 × 6 = 24 cm.

20. (C): No. of boxes = $\frac{60 \times 40 \times 30 \times 10}{8}$ = 90,000

16 Geometry

(*i*) **Point:** A minute geometrical figure that only determines a location is known as point. Point is a tiny dot which has no lenght or breadth.

Example: Tip of a compass, the pointed end of a needle etc.

(*ii*) **Line Segment:** A geometrical figure which has length but no breadth. It has two end points. Line segment is a part of line. It is the shortest route between two points. If a line segment has two end points X and Y then it is denoted as $\overline{XY}$ or $\overline{YX}$.

Example: An edge of box, An edge of book, pencil etc.

(*iii*) **Line:** If a line segment is extended endlessly in both directions is known as line. We can not draw a complete line and also can not determine its length because it has no end point in the both directions. So we put arrow marks to indicate its endlessness.

e.g., A B

We put minimum two points to determine the line and indicate the line as $\overleftrightarrow{AB}$ or $\overleftrightarrow{BA}$.

(*iv*) **Ray:** A ray is a portion of a line. It has only one end point. It start from a point and goes endlessly to the another direction. Length of ray is also can not be determined. Ray is drawn as A B and indicated as $\overline{AB}$.

Examples: Sun rays, Ray of light from a torch etc.

(*v*) **Intersecting line:** If two lines have a common point they are called intersecting lines.

Examples: X (the letter of english alphabet; the sign of mathematical operation.)

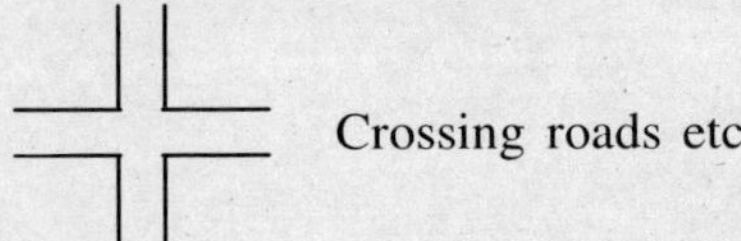

Crossing roads etc.

(*vi*) **Parallel lines:** If two lines do not intersect up to thier endless points is called parallel lines. In other words, lines like these which do not meet to each-other are said to be parallel; these lines are called parallel lines.

Examples: Railway tracks, opposite edges of scale, opposite edges of table etc.

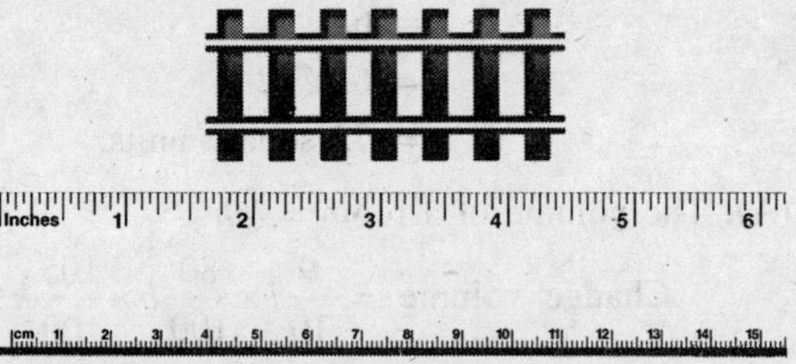

(*vii*) **Curves:** The doodling line is called curve. If we draw some drawing without lifting the pencil from the paper and without using a rular, all are curves.

(*a*) **Simple curve:** If a curve does not cross itself. It is also known as open curve.

(*b*) **Closed curve:** If a curve crosses to each other and surround some space is called closed curve.

(*viii*) **Concurrent Lines:** The point where three or more lines intersect.

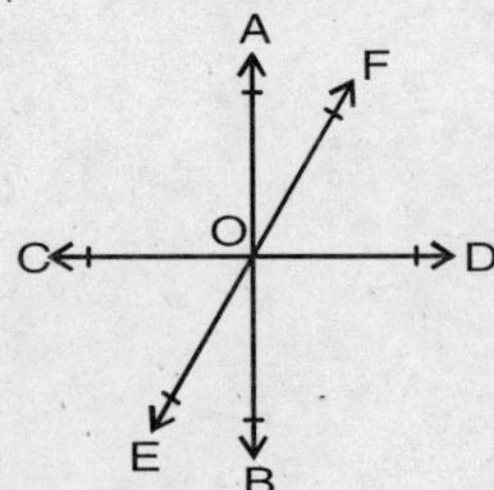

(*ix*) **Angle:** A geometrical figure which have two rays with single end point is called angle.

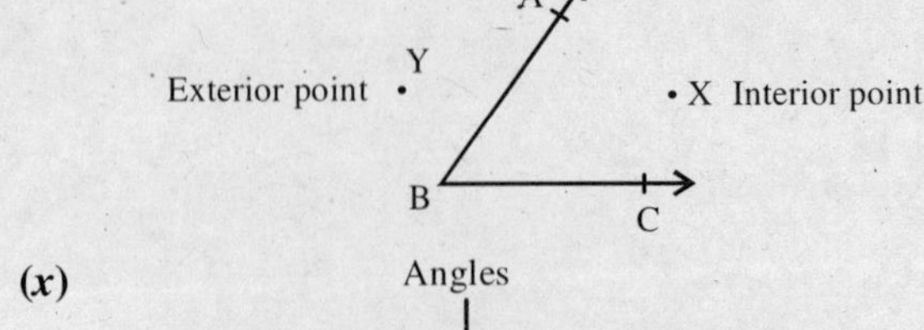

(*x*)

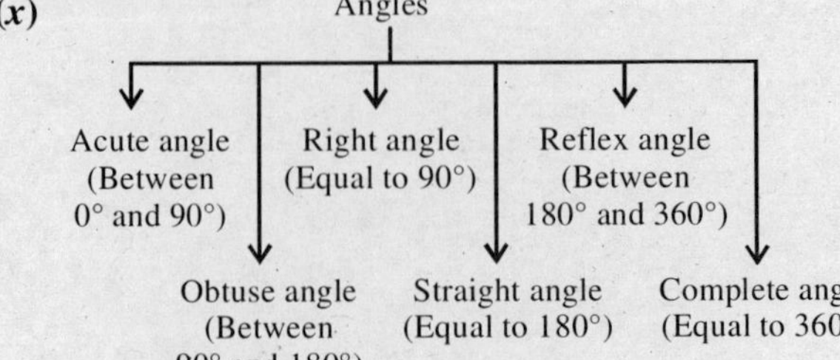

(xi) Complementary Angles: Two angles whose sum is 90º is said to be complementary to each other *i.e.*, complement of θ = (90º – θº).

(xii) Supplementary Angles: Two angles whose sum is 180º is said to be supplementary to each other. *i.e.*, supplementary of θ = (180º – θº).

(xiii) Adjecent Angles: If two angles have a common vertex then they are said to be adjecent.

Here, ∠BAC and ∠CAD are adjacent angles.

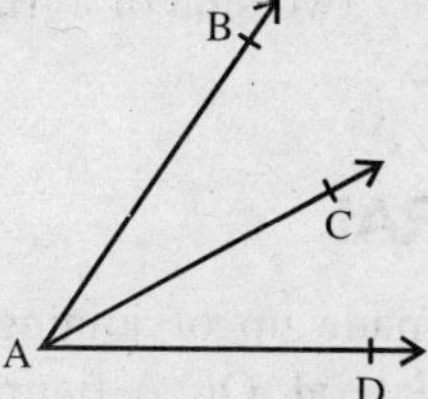

(xiv) Linear pair: If the pair of adjacent angles are also the supplementary to each-other then it is said to be a linear pair.

Here, ∠ABC and ∠CBD are adjacent and ∠ABC + ∠CBD = 180º

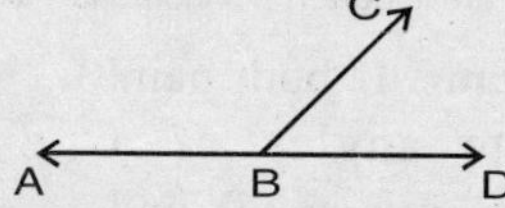

Hence, both the angles are linear pair.

(xv) Vertically opposite Angles: If two lines intersect at a point, the pair of alternative angles is called vertically opposite angles.

Vertically opposite angles are always equal.

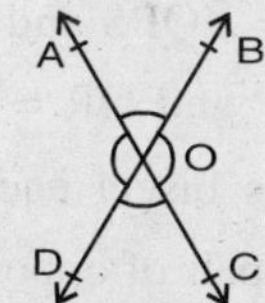

Here, ∠AOB and ∠DOC

also ∠AOD and ∠BOC are vertically opposite angles.

Hence, ∠AOB = ∠DOC and ∠AOD = ∠BOC

(xvi) Angles on parallel lines:

Transversal: If a straight line crosses two or more than two parallel lines then it is called transversal.

When a transversal crosses a pair of parallel lines then it forms eight angles.

(*a*) **Corresponding Angles:** Let AB and CD are two parallel lines and *l* is transversal, then, pair of corresponding angles are equal *i.e.*,

∠1 = ∠6 ∠3 = ∠8 ∠2 = ∠5 ∠4 = ∠7

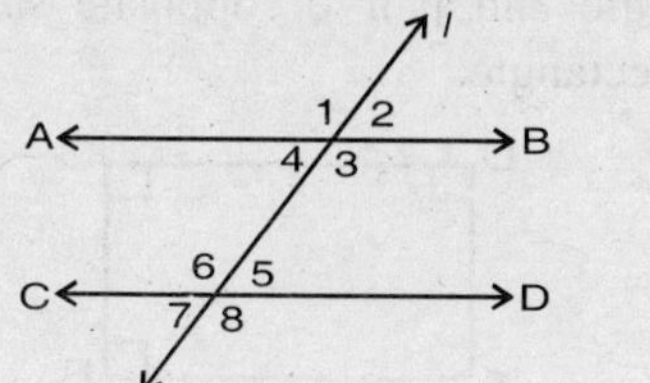

(*b*) **Alternate Interior Angles:** In the above figure ∠4 and ∠5 also ∠3 and ∠6 are the pairs of alternate interior angles. The pair of alternate interior angles are equal.

Hence, ∠4 = ∠5 and ∠3 = ∠6

* **The sum of interior angles on the same side of transversal is 180°.**

i.e., ∠3 + ∠5 = 180° also ∠4 + ∠6 = 180°.

TRIANGLE

A closed figure with three sides which has three angles and three vertices is called triangle.

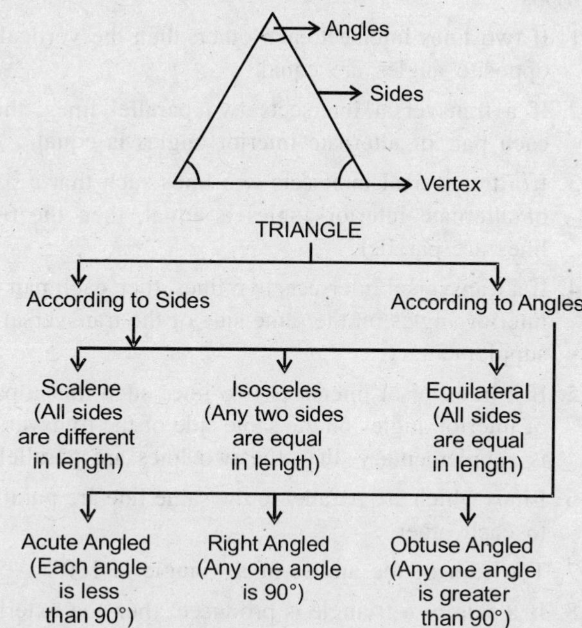

Pythagoras Theorem: In a right angled triangle the square of the hypotenuse equals the sum of the square of its sides.

i.e., $AC^2 = AB^2 + BC^2$

$\Rightarrow$ $b^2 = c^2 + a^2$

$= a^2 + c^2$

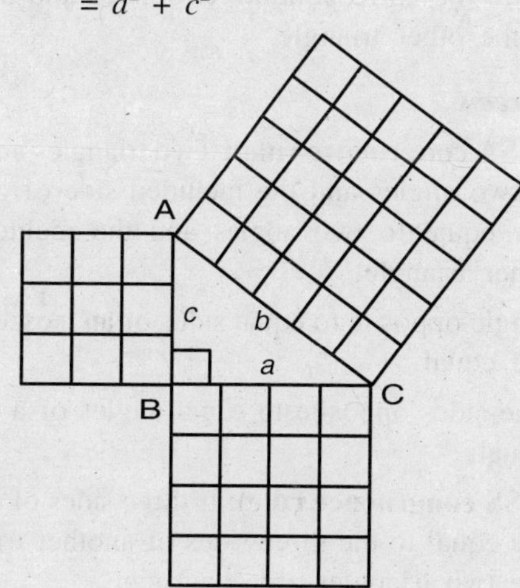

Axiom & Theorems on lines and angles

Axioms:

1. If a ray stands on a line, then the sum of two adjacent angles so formed is 180º.
2. If the sum of two adjacent angles is 180º, then the non-common arms of the angles form a line.
3. If a transversal intersects two parallel lines, then each pair of corresponding angles is equal.
4. If a transversal intersects two lines such that a pair of corresponding angles is equal, then the two lines are parallel to each other.

Theorems

1. If two lines intersect each other, then the vertically opposite angles are equal.
2. If a transversal intersects two parallel lines, then each pair of alternate interior angles is equal.
3. If a transversal intersects two lines such that a pair of alternate interior angles is equal, then the two lines are parallel.
4. If a transversal intersects two lines, then each pair of interior angles on the same side of the transversal is supplementary.
5. If a transversal intersects two lines such that a pair of interior angles on the same side of the transversal is supplementary, then the two lines are parallel.
6. Lines which are parallel to the same line are parallel to each other.
7. The sum of the angles of a triangle is 180º.
8. If a side of a triangle is produced, then the exterior angle so formed is equal to the sum of the two interior opposite angles.

Axiom and Theorems on Triangles

Axiom 1. (SAS congruence rule) : Two triangles are congruent if two sides and the included angle of one triangle are equal to the corresponding two sides and the included angle of the other triangle.

Theorems

1. **(ASA congruence rule):** Two triangles are congruent if two angles and the included side of one triangle are equal to two angles and the included side of other triangle.
2. Angle opposite to equal sides of an isosceles triangle are equal.
3. The sides opposite to equal angles of a triangle are equal.
4. **(SSS congruence rule):** If three sides of one triangle are equal to the three sides of another triangle, then the two triangles are congruent.
5. **(RHS congruence rule):** If in two right triangles the hypotenuse and one side of one triangle are equal to the hypotenuse and one side of the other triangle, then the two triangles are congruent.
6. If two sides of a triangle are unequal, the angle opposite to the longer side is larger (or greater).
7. In any triangle, the side opposite to the larger (greater) angle is longer.
8. The sum of any two side of a triangle is greater than the third side.

QUADRILATERAL

A figure which is made up of joining four non-collinear points called quadrilateral. Or, A figure which is made up of four sides, angles and four vertices is called quadrilateral. The sum of all angles of a quadrilateral is 360°.

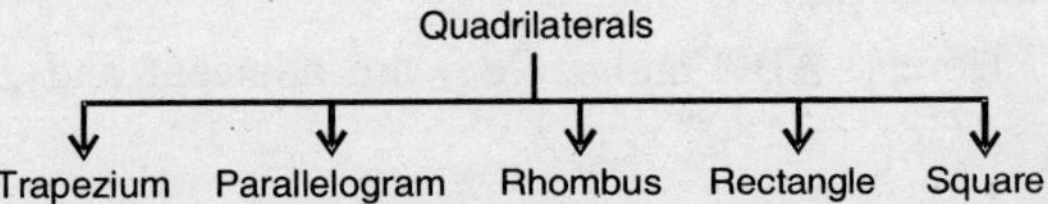

(*i*) **Parallelogram:** If both pairs of opposite angles of a quadrilateral are equal and both pair of opposite sides are equal and parallel is called parallelogram.

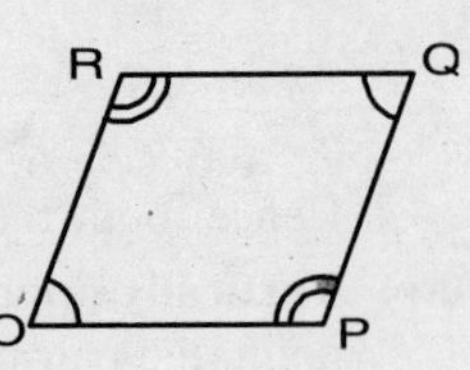

Here, (*a*) QR || OP and OR || PQ

(*b*) ∠ORQ = ∠QPS and ∠ROP = ∠PQR

(*c*) RQ = OP and OR = PQ

(*d*) diagonals bisect each other.

(*ii*) **Trapezium:** If one pair of opposite sides are parallel of a quadrilateral, then it is called a trapezium.

Here, AD || BC

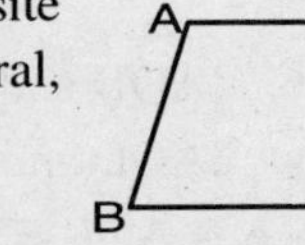

(*iii*) **Rhombus:** A parallelogram in which all the sides are equal is called a rhombus.

Here, (*a*) □ ABCD is a parallelogram

(*b*) AB = BC = CD = AD

(*c*) Diagonals bisect each-other at 90°.

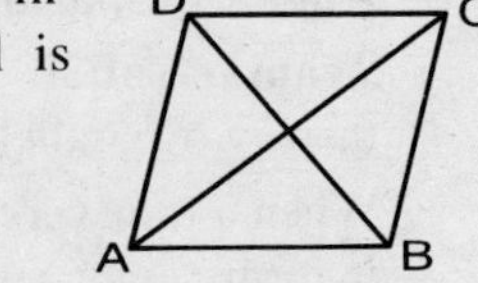

(*iv*) **Rectangle:** A parallelogram in which each angles is right angle and pair of opposite sides are equal is called rectangle.

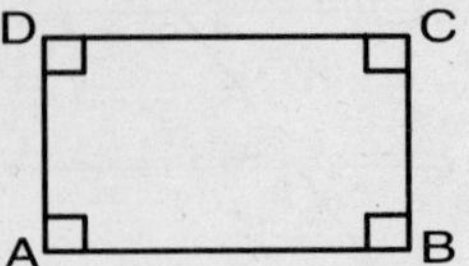

Here, (*a*) ABCD is a parallelogram.

(*b*) AB = CD and AD = BC

(*c*) Angles are right angle

(*d*) Diagonals are equal and bisects each-other.

(*v*) **Square:** A parallelogram which have all sides equal and each angle is right angle is called a square.

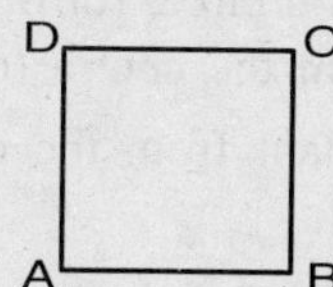

Here, (*a*) AB = BC = CD = AD

(*b*) AB || CD and AD || BC

(*c*) Angles are right angle

(*d*) Diagonals are equal and bisects each-other at 90°.

Theorems on Quadrilateral

Theorems

1. A diagonal of a parallelogram divides it into two congruent triangles.
2. In a parallelogram, opposite sides are equal.
3. If each pair of opposite sides of a quadrilateral is equal, then it is a parallelogram.
4. In a parallelogram, opposite angles are equal.
5. If in a quadrilateral, each pair of opposite angles is equal, then it is a parallelogram.
6. The diagonals of a parallelogram bisect each other.
7. If the diagonals of a quadrilateral bisect each other, then it is a parallelogram.
8. A quadrilateral is a parallelogram if a pair of opposite sides is equal and parallel.
9. The line segment joining the mid-points of two sides of a triangle is parallel to and half of the third side.
10. The line drawn through the mid-point of one side of a triangle, parallel to another side bisects the third side.

Theorems on Areas of Parallelograms and Triangles

Theorems

1. Parallelograms on the same base and between the same parallels are equal in area.
2. Two triangles on the same base (or equal bases) and between the same parallels are equal in area.
3. Two triangles having the same base (or equal bases) and equal areas lie between the same parallels.

CIRCLE

A circle is a set of points in a plane which are at a constant distance from a given fixed point.

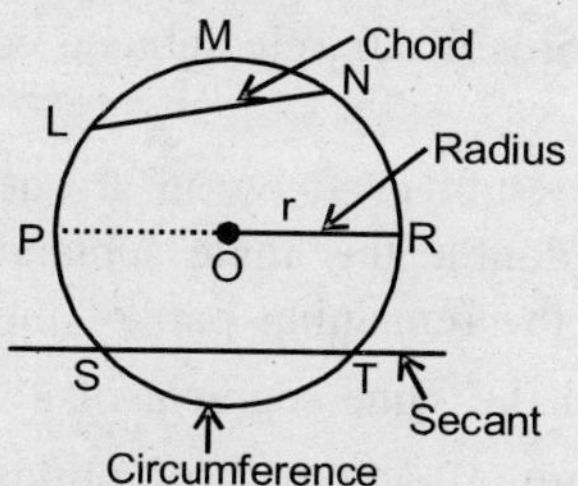

Here, The Fixed point O is called the centre.

The constant distance is called radius. PR is the diameter of the circle.

Diameter is twice of radius.

Arch: A continuous part of a circle.

Secant: A line which intersect a circle in two distinct points.

Chord: A line segment joining any two points on the circle.

Segment: A chord divides the circle into two parts and each parts is called segment.

Semicircle: A diameter divides the circle into two equal parts and each part is called semicircle.

Central Angle: An angle whose vertex is centre of a circle is called central angle.

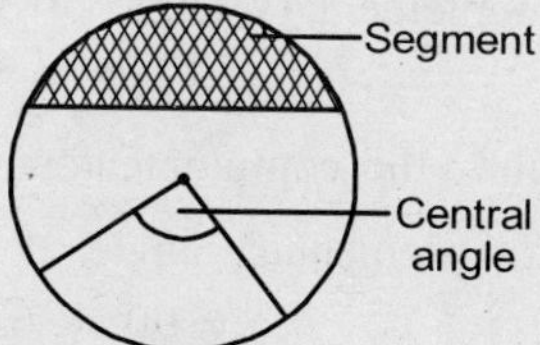

Cyclic Quadrilateral: If all four vertices of a quadrilateral lie on the circumference of a circle, then such a quadrilateral is called a cyclic quadrilateral.

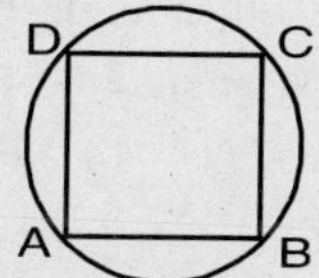

SOME IMPORTANT RESULTS

- The perpendicular from the centre to any chord bisects the chord.
- The line joining the centre of the mid point to any chord of a circle is perpendicular to the chord.
- Equal chords of congruent circles are equidistant from the corresponding centres.

- Chords of congruent circles which are equidistant from the corresponding centres, are equal.
- Equal chords of a circle are equidistant from the centre.
- Equal chords of a circle subtend equal angle at the centre.
- The angle subtended by an arc at the centre of a circle is double the angle subtended by it at any point on the remaining part of the circle.
- Angles in the same segment of a circle are equal.
- If the sum of any pair of opposite angles of a quadrilateral is 180°, then the quadrilateral is cyclic.
- The angle made in a semicircle is always a right angle.
- The arc of a circle subtending a right angle at any point of the circle in its alternate segment is a semicircle.

Theorems on Circles

1. Equal chords of a circle subtend equal angles at the centre.
2. If the angles subtended by the chords of a circle at the centre are equal, then the chords are equal.
3. The perpendicular from the centre of a circle to a chord bisects the chord.
4. The line drawn through the centre of a circle to bisect a chord is perpendicular to the chord.
5. There is one and only one circle passing through three given non-collinear points.
6. Equal chords of a circle (or of congruent circle) are equidistant from the centre (or centres).
7. Chords equidistant from the centre of a circle are equal in length.
8. The angle subtended by an arc at the centre is double the angle subtended by it at any point on the remaining part of the circle.
9. Angles in the same segment of a circle are equal.
10. If a line segment joining two points subtends equal angles at two other points lying on the same side of the line containing the line segment, the four points lie on a circle (*i.e.* they are concyclic).
11. The sum of either pair of opposite angles of a cyclic quadrilateral is 180°.
12. If the sum of a pair of opposite angles of a quadrilateral is 180°, the quadrilateral is cyclic.

SOLVED EXAMPLES

Example 1 : Find the supplementary angle of 57°.

Solution : Supplementary angle of 57°

$= 180° - 57° = 123°$.

Example 2 : Find the complementary angle of 63°.

Solution : Complementary angle of 63°

$= 90° - 63° = 27°$.

Example 3 : If one of the complementary angles is 14° smaller than the other, then find the greater angle.

Solution : Let the other angle be x. Then,

The first angle $= (x - 14°)$

Now, $x + (x - 14°) = 90°$

$\Rightarrow \quad 2x = 90° + 14°$

$2x = 104°$

$\Rightarrow \quad x = \dfrac{104°}{2} = 52°$

First angle $= (x - 14°)$

$= (52° - 14°) = 38°$

Other angle $= 52°$

$\therefore$ Greater angle $= 52°$.

Example 4 : If AB || CD and CD || EF. Also EA ⊥ AB. If ∠ BEF = 55°, find the values of x, y and z.

Solution : $y + 55° = 180°$

(Interior angles on the same side of the transversal ED)

Hence, $y = 180° - 55° = 125°$

Again $x = y$

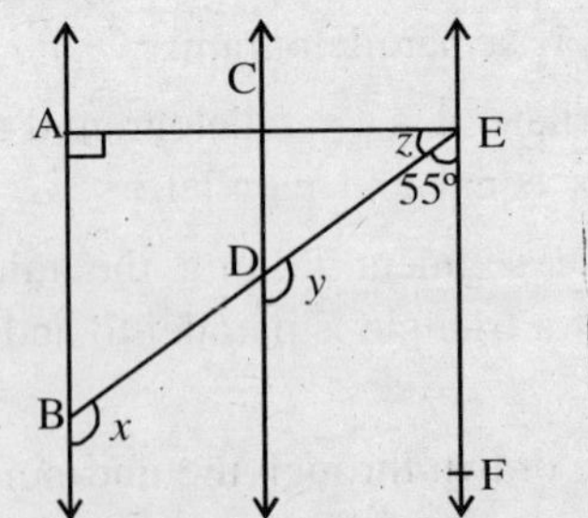

(AB || CD, Corresponding angles axiom)

Hence $x = 125°$.

Now, since AB || CD and CD || EF,

so, AB || EF,

So, $\angle EAB + \angle FEA = 180°$

Hence, $90° + z + 55° = 180°$

Which gives $z = 35°$

Example 5 : If ABCD is a cyclic quadrilateral and ∠ DBC = 55° and ∠ BAC = 45°, find ∠ BCD.

Solution : $\angle CAD = \angle DBC = 55°$

(Angles in the same segment)

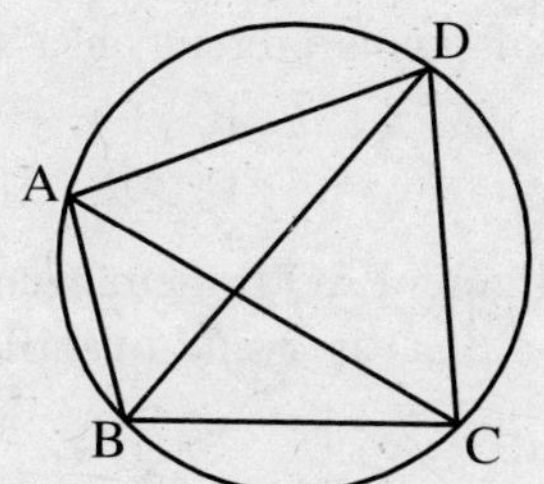

Hence, $\angle DAB = \angle CAD + \angle BAC$
$= 55^\circ + 45^\circ$
$= 100^\circ$

But $\angle DAB + \angle BCD = 180^\circ$

(Opposite angles of a cyclic quadrilateral)

So, $\angle BCD = 180^\circ - 100^\circ = 80^\circ$

Example 6 : Measure x in given figure.

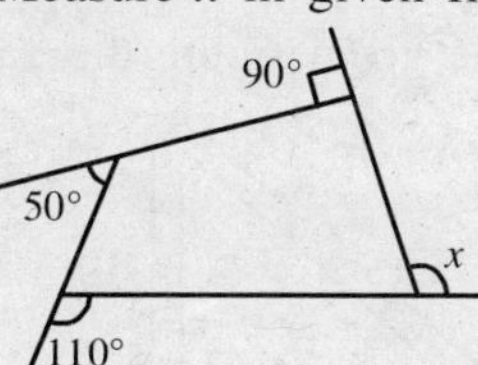

Solution : $x + 90^\circ + 50^\circ + 110^\circ = 360^\circ$
$x + 250^\circ = 360^\circ$
$x = 110^\circ$.

EXERCISE

1. Lines l and m intersect at O, forming angles as shown in figure. If $x = 45^\circ$, then values of y, z and u are

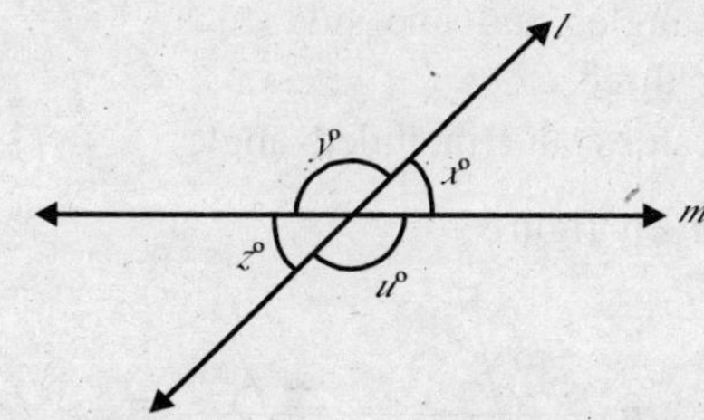

A. 45°, 135°, 135° B. 135°, 135°, 45°
C. 135°, 45°, 135° D. 115°, 45°, 115°

2. In the given figure, the value of x and y are

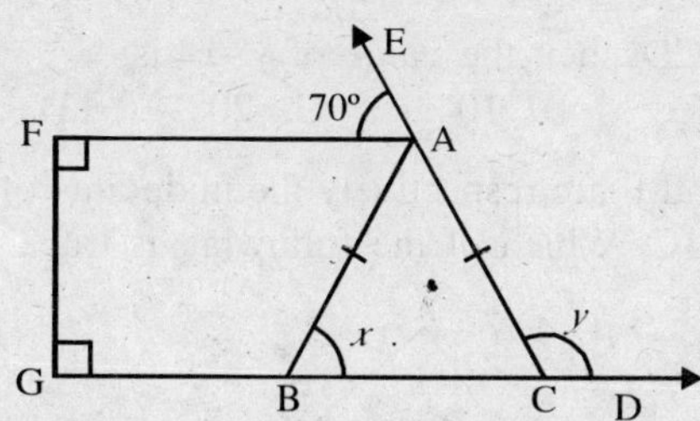

A. 70°, 110° B. 110°, 70°
C. 120°, 60° D. 70°, 90°

3. Which of the following statements is false?

A. A line segment can be produced to any desired length
B. Through a given point, only one straight line can be drawn
C. Through two given points, it is possible to draw one and only one straight line
D. Two straight lines can intersect in only one point

4. The number of sides of a regular polygon whose each exterior angle has a measure of 45° is:

A. 7 B. 5
C. 10 D. 8

5. ABCD is a parallelogram. The values of x, y and z are:

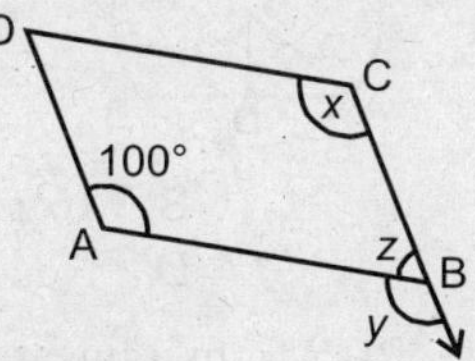

A. 80°, 100°, 100° B. 80°, 80°, 100°
C. 80°, 100°, 180° D. 100°, 100°, 80°

6. In a parallelogram RSTU if $m\,\angle R = 70^\circ$, then all the other angles x, y, z are:

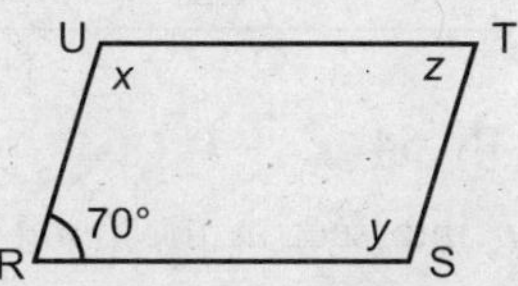

A. 101°, 101°, 70° B. 110°, 70°, 110°
C. 110°, 110°, 70° D. None of these

7. If ABCD is a parallelogram, OB = 4 and AC is 5 more than BD. Then OA equal to:

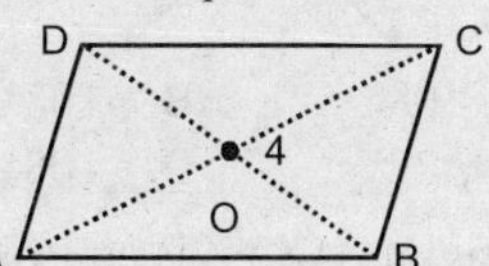

A. 6.6 B. 6.5 C. 5.5 D. 5.6

8. ABCD is a rectangle. Its diagonals meet at O. Find x, if OA = $2x + 4$ and OD = $3x + 1$.

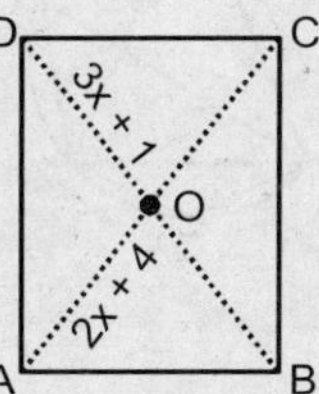

A. 3 B. 4
C. 5 D. None of these

9. If an angle equals to two-third of its complementary then the measurement of the angle is:

A. 45° B. 63° C. 90° D. 36°

10. According to the given figure the value of x is:

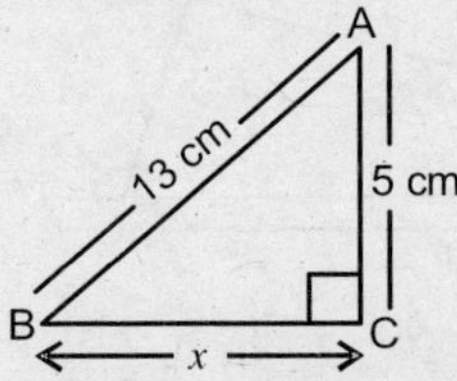

A. 13 cm B. 5 cm

C. 12 cm D. None of these

11. The length of the chord which is at a distance of 6 cm from the centre of the circle and the radius of the circle is 10 cm is:

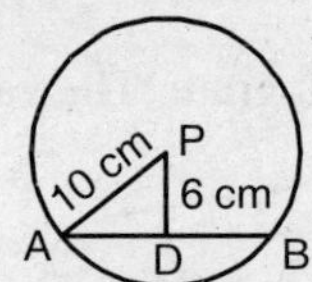

A. 8 cm B. 16 cm

C. 6 cm D. None of these

12. If, ∠PQR and ∠RQS form a linear pair then the value of x is:

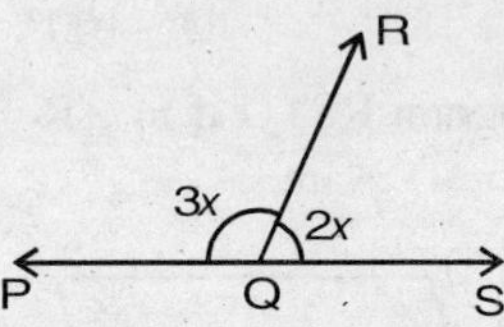

A. 45° B. 54° C. 63° D. 36°

13. Lines l and n intersect at the point O. The value of x, y and z if a = 72° is:

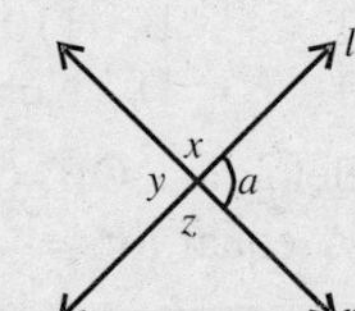

A. 72°, 72°, 108° B. 108°, 108°, 72°

C. 72°, 108°, 72° D. 108°, 72°, 108°

14. In the given figure, ΔXYZ is an isosceles triangle with XY = XZ and ∠XYZ = 60°. Then ∠YPZ equal to:

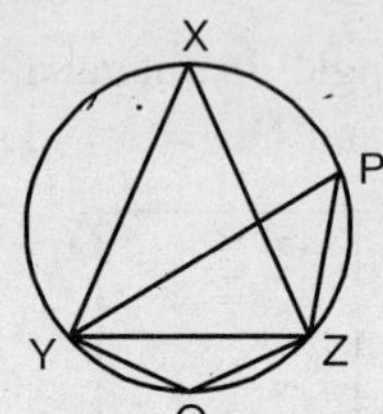

A. 120°

B. 60°

C. can not be determined

D. None of these

15. The number of points present on a straight line is

A. 2 B. 1

C. infinite D. 0

16. In the given figure, PAQ is the tangent of the circle at point A and ABCD is cyclic quadrilateral.

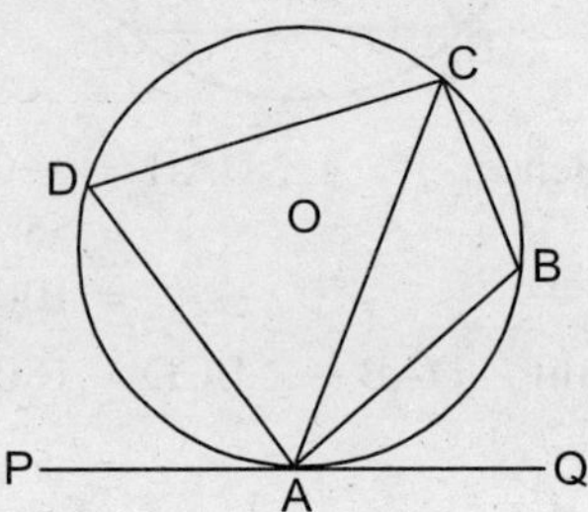

If ∠CAQ = 70°, then ∠ABC is:

A. 110° B. 70° C. 80° D. 90°

17. We cannot construct a triangle, if we are given:

A. only three angles

B. two angles and one side

C. only three sides

D. two sides and included angle

18. In the given figure

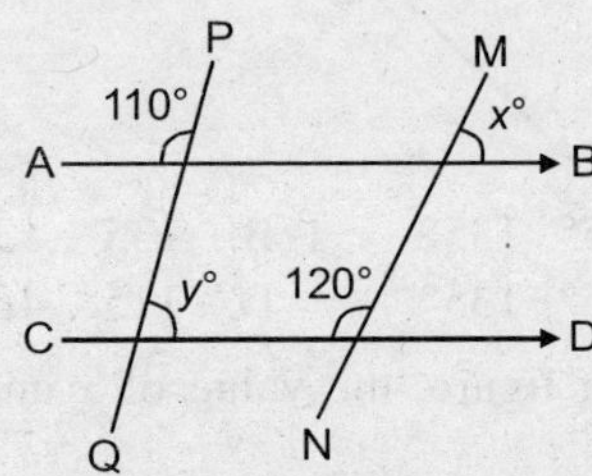

AB ∥ CD, then the value of $y°$-$x°$ is:

A. 30° B. 10° C. 20° D. 40°

19. D, E and F are respectively the midpoints of the sides of ΔABC, Which of the following is true?

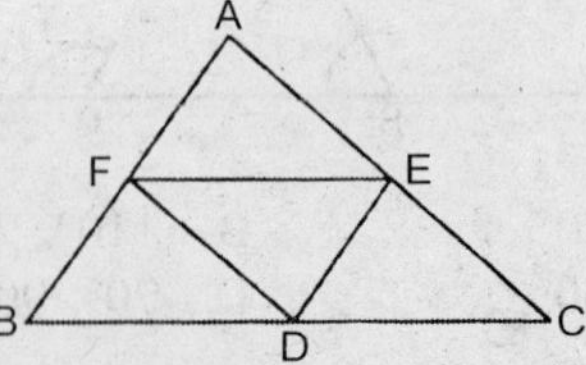

A. Area of ΔDEF = Area of ΔABC

B. Area of ΔDEF = $\frac{1}{2}$ Area of ΔABC

C. Area of ΔDEF = $\frac{1}{3}$ Area of ΔABC

D. Area of ΔDEF = $\frac{1}{4}$ Area of ΔABC

20. The difference of two complementary angles is 40°. The angles are:

A. 65°, 35° B. 70°, 30°

C. 25°, 65° D. 70°, 110°

ANSWERS WITH EXPLANATIONS

1. (C): $x = z$ [$\because$ vertically opposite angles]

$\Rightarrow$ $x = 45°$ $\Rightarrow z = 45°$

$y + x = 180°$ [$\because$ linear pair]

$\Rightarrow$ $y = 180° - 45°$

$\therefore$ $y = 135°$

Also, $y = u$ [$\because$ vertically opposite angles]

$\Rightarrow$ $u = 135°$.

2. (A): In Δ ABC,

$\angle ABC = \angle ACB = x$

and $x + y = 180°$

Now, $\angle EAF = \angle ACB = 70°$

[corresponding angles]

$\therefore$ $x = 70°$

$\Rightarrow$ $y = 180° - 70°$

$\therefore$ $y = 110°$.

3. (B): Since, an infinite number of straight lines can be drawn through a given point.

Hence, (B) is false statement.

4. (D): Total measure of all exterior angles = 360°

Measure of each exterior angles = 45°

Therefore, the number of exterior angles

$$= \frac{360}{45} = 8$$

Hence, The polygon has 8 sides.

5. (D): C is opposite to A.

Hence, $x = 100°$ (opposite angles property)

$y = 100°$ (measure of angle corresponding to $\angle x$)

$z = 80°$ (since $\angle y$, $\angle z$ is a linear pair).

6. (C): Given $m\angle R = 70°$

Then $m\angle T = 70°$

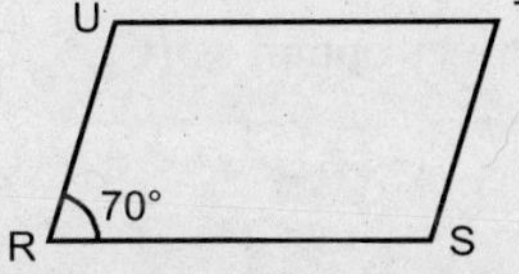

Since, $\angle$R and T are opposite angles of a parallelogram. and $\angle$R and $\angle$S are supplementary,

$m\angle S = 180° - 70° = 110°$

Also, $m\angle U = 110°$ since – $\angle$U is opposite to $\angle$S

Thus, $m\angle R = m\angle T = 70°$ and

$m\angle S = m\angle U = 110°$.

7. (B): OB = 4 then OD also is 4

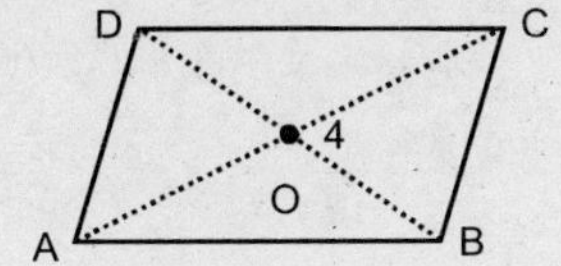

So, PB = 8,

Hence, AC = 8 + 5 = 13

Hence, $OA = \frac{1}{2} \times 13 = 6.5$

8. (A): $\overline{OD}$ is half of the diagonal $\overline{DB}$, $\overline{OA}$ is half of the diagonal $\overline{AC}$.

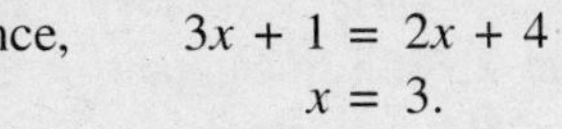

Diagonals are equal.

Hence, their halves are also equal.

Hence, $3x + 1 = 2x + 4$

or $x = 3$.

9. (D): Let the angle be $x°$

According to question, $x° = \frac{2}{3}(90° - x)$

$$\Rightarrow \quad x = \frac{180° - 2x°}{3}$$

$\Rightarrow$ $3x° = 180° - x°$

$\Rightarrow$ $5x° = 180°$

$$\therefore \quad x° = \frac{180°}{5} = 36°.$$

10. (C): From Pythagoras theorem,

$AC^2 + BC^2 = AB^2$

$\Rightarrow$ $5^2 + x^2 = 13^2$

$\Rightarrow$ $x^2 = 169 - 25$

$\therefore$ $x = \sqrt{144} = 12$ cm.

11. (B): Let AB is the chord of the circle with centre P and radius 10 cm.

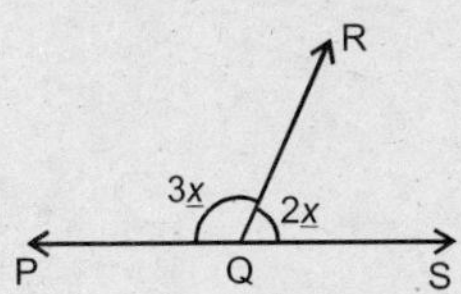

According to figure,

PD = 6 cm and PA = 10 cm.

As we know that perpendicular from centre bisect the chord.

Now in right angled triangle ADP,

$$AD = \sqrt{AP^2 - PD^2}$$

$$= \sqrt{10^2 - 6^2} = \sqrt{100 - 36}$$

$$= \sqrt{64} = 8 \text{ cm}$$

Hence, Length of chord AB = 2AD

= 2 × 8 = 16 cm.

12. (D): Since $\angle$PQR and $\angle$RQS form a linear pair

R
3x
2x
P
Q
S

Hence, $\angle PQR + \angle RQS = 180°$

$\Rightarrow \quad 3x + 2x = 180°$

$\Rightarrow \quad 5x = 180°$

$\therefore \quad x = 36°.$

13. (D): Since, y and a also, x and z are the pairs of vertically opposite angles and it is always equal to each - other

Hence, $\angle y = 72°$

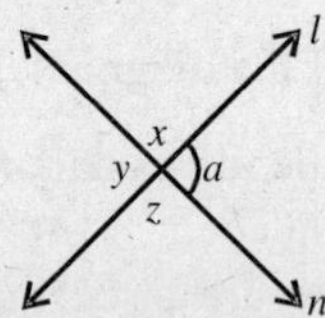

Again since, $\angle x$ and $\angle y$ are linear pair

Hence, $\angle x + \angle y = 180°$

$\therefore \quad x = 180° - 72° = 108°$

And $\quad \angle z = 108°$ (Vertically opposite angle).

14. (B): Since $\quad XY = XZ$

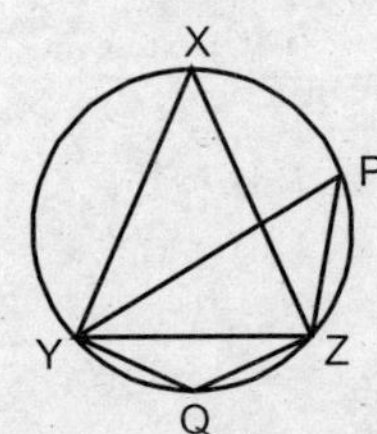

$\Rightarrow \quad \angle XYZ = \angle XZY = 60°$

In ΔXYZ,

$\angle YXZ = 180° - (60° + 60°) = 60°$

$\therefore \quad \angle YPZ = \angle YXZ = 60°$

(angle in the same segment).

15. (C): Infinite.

16. (A): $\quad \angle CAQ = 70°$ (Given)

$\angle CAP + \angle CAQ = 180°$

$\angle CAP = 180° - \angle CAQ$

$= 180° - 70° = 110°$

$\because \quad \angle ABC = \angle CAP$

(Alternate Segment Angle)

$\therefore \quad \angle ABC = 110°$

17. (A): Only three angles

18. (B):

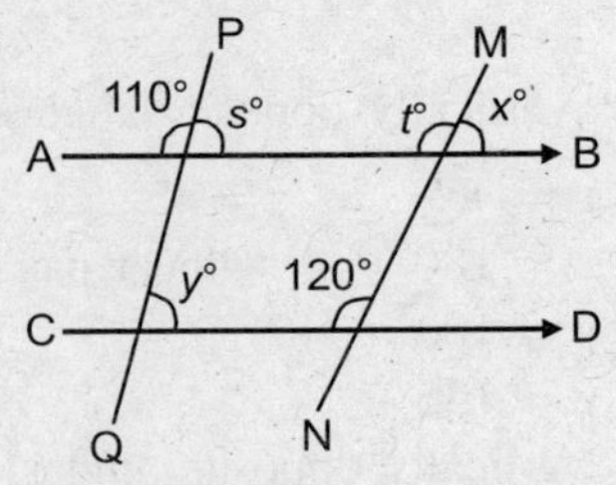

$\angle s° = 180° - 110° = 70°$

$\angle y = \angle s° = 70°$ (Corresponding angle)

$\angle t° = 120°$ (Corresponding angle)

$x° = 180° - \angle t°$

$= 180° - 120° = 60°$

$\therefore y° - x° = 70° - 60° = 10°$

19. (D):

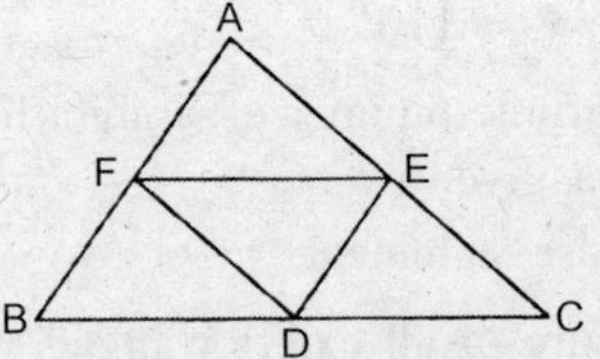

$\because$ D, E, F are the mid points of the sides of ΔABC

$\therefore \quad ar\Delta AFE = ar\Delta DEF$

(|| gm AFDE, EF is diagonal)

$ar\Delta BFD = ar\Delta DEF$

(|| gm BFED, FD is diagonal)

$ar\Delta ECD = ar\Delta DEF$

(|| gm FDCE, DE is diagonal)

Hence, area of $\Delta DEF = \frac{1}{4}$ area of ΔABC.

20. (C): The complement of $25° = 65°$

The complement of $65° = 25°$

Difference $= 65° - 25° = 40°$

Hence, the correct option is (C).

17 Railway / Bus Time-table

In this chapter, students learn to interpret 24-hour schedules to calculate journey durations, determine departure and arrival times, and plan travel effectively. The core skills include adding and subtracting hours and minutes, converting between 12-hour and 24-hour formats, and understanding stop durations and intervals in time-table.

SOLVED EXAMPLES

Example 1 : A train travels 600 km. For the first half, it goes at 60 km/h, and for the second half at 90 km/h. The train stops 3 times for 15 min each. What is the total journey time?

Solution : **First half:** Time $(t_1) = 300 \div 60 = 5$ hr

Second half: Time $(t_2) = 300 \div 90$

= 3 hr 20 min

Stops = 3

Duration time = 3 × 15 = 45 min

Total journey time = 5 hr + 3 hr 20 min + 45 min

= 8 hr + 65 min

= 9 hr and 05 min

Example 2 : Two buses start simultaneously from the same station. Speed of bus A is 40 km/h and Bus B is 50 km/h. Bus B starts 30 minutes later. How long will it take Bus B to catch Bus A?

Solution : Given: Bus A speed = 40 km/h, Bus B speed = 50 km/h

Bus B starts 30 minutes later,

30 min = 0.5 hr

Distance = Speed × Time

= 40 × 0.5 = 20 km

So Bus A has a 20 km head start.

Since both buses are moving in the same direction,

Relative speed = 50 – 40 = 10 km/h

Time for Bus B to catch Bus A

= Distance ÷ Relative speed

= 20 ÷ 10 = 2 hr

Example 3 : A bus for Agra leaves every 25 minutes. The clerk says the bus left 15 minutes ago and the next bus will leave at 9:00 a.m.. At what time was the information given?

Solution : Time when the previous bus left

= Next bus time – Interval time

= 9:00 a.m. – 25

= 8:35 a.m.

Time when the information was given

= Previous bus time + 15 min

= 8:35 a.m. + 15

= 8:50 a.m.

Example 4 : Train A leaves Delhi for Jaipur at 07:00 a.m. and travels at 60 km/h. Train B leaves Delhi for Jaipur at 09:00 a.m. and travels at 80 km/h. At what time will Train B catch up with Train A?

Solution : Distance covered by Train A before Train B starts:

Time difference = 09:00 – 07:00 = 2 hours

Distance = 60 km/h × 2 hr

= 120 km

Relative speed of Train B with respect to Train A = 80 – 60

= 20 km/h

Time taken by Train B to catch Train A

= Distance ÷ Relative speed

= 120 ÷ 20 = 6 hr

Time = 09:00 + 6 hr

= 15:00 hours (3:00 p.m.)

EXERCISE

1. A bus from Delhi leaves every half an hour from a bus terminal. An enquiry clerk told a passenger that the bus had left ten minute ago and the next bus will leave at 9:25 a.m. At what time did the enquiry clerk give this information to the passenger?
   A. 9:10 a.m. B. 9:15 a.m.
   C. 8.55 a.m. D. 9:05 a.m.

2. A bus for Jaipur leaves every forty minutes from a bus stand. An enquiry clerk told a passenger that the bus has already left 20 minutes ago and the next bus will leave at 11:35 a.m. At what time did the enquiry clerk give this information to the passenger?
   A. 11:15 a.m. B. 11:08 a.m.
   C. 10:55 a.m. D. 10:10 a.m.

3. A train leaves Mumbai on 30th April 2025 at 20:45 hours and reached Bokaro on 2nd May at 09:15 hours. What is the total travel time of the train?
   A. 30 hours 30 minutes B. 35 hours 15 minutes
   C. 34 hours 30 minutes D. 29 hours 45 minutes

4. A bus leaves station A at 8:15 a.m. and reaches station B at 12:45 p.m. If the distance between A and B is 270 km, what is the average speed of the bus?
   A. 55 km/h B. 60 km/h
   C. 65 km/h D. 70 km/h

5. The average speed of a train without stoppages is 48 kmph and average speed with stoppages is 40 kmph. How many minutes per hour does the train stop?
   A. 8 minutes B. 10 minutes
   C. 12 minutes D. 15 minutes

6. A train travels from Station P to Q. If it stops for 5 minutes at each of the 4 intermediate stations, and the average speed including stoppages is 50 km/h, what is the total travel time if the total distance is 200 km?
   A. 3 hours B. 3 hours 20 minutes
   C. 4 hours D. 4 hours 20 minutes

7. A passenger train leaves a station 2 hours after a freight train. The passenger train overtakes the freight train in 4 hours. If the speed of the freight train is 40 km/h, what is the speed of the passenger train?
   A. 60 km/h B. 70 km/h
   C. 80 km/h D. 90 km/h

8. A bus for Delhi leaves every 30 minutes from a bus stand. An inquiry clerk tells a passenger that the bus left 10 minutes ago and the next bus will leave at 11:00 a.m. At what time did the inquiry clerk give this information?
   A. 10:20 a.m. B. 10:30 a.m.
   C. 10:40 a.m. D. 10:50 a.m.

9. A bus leaves the bus station at 5:15 in the morning and reaches its destination after 11 hours 35 minutes. The time at the destination is:
   A. 4:50 pm B. 5:05 pm
   C. 4:45 pm D. 5:55 pm

10. A train departs from Station A at 06:15 AM and arrives at Station B at 11:45 AM. It stops for 3 minutes at each of 4 intermediate stations. If the train runs at a uniform speed between stops, what is the average time taken between two consecutive stations?
    A. 1 hr 3 min 36 sec B. 1 hr 9 min 38 sec
    C. 1 hr 15 min 40 sec D. 1 hr 12 min 45 sec

11. A bus leaves at 09:00 AM and reaches its destination at 02:00 PM, stopping for 5 minutes at every hour mark. What is the effective average speed if the bus covers 300 km?
    A. 57 km/h B. 60 km/h
    C. 62 km/h D. 65 km/h

12. A bus covers a journey of 180 km in 4 hours, including 3 breaks of 10 minutes each. What is the bus's average speed excluding breaks?
    A. 51 km/h B. 55 km/h
    C. 60 km/h D. 65 km/h

13. Rubina started her journey by car at 16:50 hours and finished at 21:15 hours on the same day. The time taken in completing the journey is:
    A. 4 hours 35 minutes B. 3 hours 25 minutes
    C. 4 hours 25 minutes D. 3 hours 35 minutes

14. A train starts from Patna on 30th May, 2010 at 23:40 hours and reaches Mumbai on 1st June, 2020 at 5:15 hours. What is the total travel time of train?
    A. 29 hours 15 minutes
    B. 28 hours 25 minutes
    C. 28 hours 20 minutes
    D. 29 hours 35 minutes

15. A train leaves Delhi on 29th August, 2019 at 16 : 30 hours and reaches its destination on 31st August at 08 : 45 hours. The total travel time of the journey is:
    A. 36 hours 15 minutes B. 38 hours 45 minutes
    C. 39 hours 45 minutes D. 40 hours 15 minutes

ANSWERS WITH EXPLANATIONS

1. (D): Bus departure time from the bus terminal

$= \frac{1}{2}$ hours = 30 minutes

The next bus will leave = 9:25 a.m.

The previous bus left = 9:25 a.m. – 30 minutes

= 8:55 a.m.

∴ Time when the passenger asked the enquiry clerk

= 8:55 a.m. + 10 minutes

= 9:05 a.m.

2. (A): Time when the previous bus left

= 11:35 a.m. – 40 minutes

= 10:55 a.m.

∴ Time when the passenger asked the enquiry clerk

= 10:55 a.m. + 20 minutes

= 11:15 a.m.

3. (C): Time taken by train on 30th April 2025

= 1 hour 15 minutes

Time taken by train on 1st May 2025 = 24 hours

Time taken by train on 2nd May 2025

= 9 hour 15 minutes

∴ Total time taken by train to reach Bokaro

= (1 hour 15 min.) + (24 hours) + (9 hour 15 min.)

= 34 hours 30 minutes.

4. (B): Time taken = 12:45 – 8:15 = 4 hours 30 minutes

= 4.5 hours

$\therefore \quad \text{Average speed} = \frac{\text{Distance}}{\text{Time}}$

$= \frac{270}{4.5} = \frac{270 \times 10}{45} = 60 \text{ km/h.}$

5. (B): Difference in speed = 48 – 40 kmph = 8 kmph

$\text{Stop time per hour} = \left(\frac{\text{Difference}}{\text{Speed without stoppages}}\right) \times 60 \text{ minutes}$

$= \left(\frac{8}{48}\right) \times 60 = \frac{1}{6} \times 60 = 10 \text{ minutes}$

Hence, the train stops for 10 minutes per hour.

6. (D): $\text{Total travel time excluding stops} = \frac{\text{Distance}}{\text{Speed}}$

$= \frac{200}{50} = 4 \text{ hours}$

Total stoppage time = 4 stations × 5 minutes

= 20 minutes

∴ Total time = 4 hours + 20 minutes

= 4 hours 20 minutes

7. (A): The freight train traveled for 2 + 4 = 6 hours

Distance covered by freight train = 40 × 6 = 240 km

Passenger train covers the same 240 km in 4 hours.

$\therefore \quad \text{Speed} = \frac{240}{4} = 60 \text{ kmh}$

Hence, the speed of the passenger train is 60 kmph.

8. (C): The time of the next bus = 11:00 a.m.

Time when the previous bus left

= 11:00 – 30 minutes

= 10:30 a.m.

∴ Time when the passenger asked the enquiry clerk

= 10:30 a.m. + 10 minutes

= 10:40 a.m.

9. (A): Departure time = 5:15 a.m.

Travel time = 11 hours 35 minutes

Add hours = 5:15 + 11 hours

= 16:15 (or 4:15 p.m.)

Add minutes = 4:15 + 35 minutes

= 16:50 (or 4:50 p.m.)

Hence, the time at the destination is 4 : 50 p.m.

10. (A): Total journey time = 11:45 – 06:15

= 5 hrs 30 minutes = 330 minutes

Total stoppage time = 4 × 3 = 12 minutes

Actual Time spent in travelling

= 330 – 12 = 318 minutes

Number of intervals = 5

$\therefore \text{ Average time per between two stations} = \frac{318}{5}$

= 63.6 minutes

= 1 hr 3 min 36 seconds

11. (D): Total travel time = From 9:00 a.m. to 2:00 p.m.

= 5 hours = 300 minutes

Stops = 1 stop per hour → 5 stops

Stop duration = 5 × 5 = 25 minutes

Travel time = 5 hours – 25 minutes

= 4 hr 35 min

$= 4 + \frac{35}{60} = 4.583 \text{ hr}$

$\therefore \quad \text{Average speed} = \frac{300}{4.583} = 65.45 \text{ km/h} \approx 65 \text{ km/h}$

12. (A): Total breaks time = 3 × 10 = 30 min = 0.5 hr

Travel time = 4 – 0.5 hrs = 3.5 hrs

$$\therefore \quad \text{Average speed} = \frac{180}{3.5} = 51.43 \approx 51 \text{ km/h.}$$

13. (C): Journey started by car at 16:50 hours

Finishing time = 21:15 hours

Time taken in completing the journey

= 21:15 hours – 16:50 hours = 4:25 hours

= 4 hours 25 minutes.

14. (D): The total travel time of train

= From 30th May, 2020 at 23 : 40 to 31th May, 2020 at 23 : 40 + from 31st May, 2020 at 23.40 to 5.15 am 1st June, 2020

= 24 hour + 5 hours 15 minutes + 20 minutes

= 24 hours + 5 hours 35 minutes

= 29 hours 35 minutes.

15. (D): Total travel time of the journey as the train leaves 16:30 pm

Total time taken on 29 August

= 24 hours – 16:30 hours

= 7:30 hours

Total time taken on 30 August

= 24 hours

Total time taken on 31st August

= 8:45 hours

Total travel time of the journey

= 7:30 hours + 24 hours + 8:45 hours

= 40 hours 15 minutes.

18 Calendar

(*i*) 1 year = 365 days = 52 weeks + 1 day
($\therefore$ An ordinary year contains 1 odd day) .

(*ii*) 1 leap year = 366 days = 52 weeks + 2 days
($\therefore$ A leap year contains 2 odd days)

(*iii*) 100 years = 76 ordinary years + 24 leap years
= 76 odd days + 24 × 2 odd days = 124 odd days
= 17 weeks + 5 days
$\therefore$ 100 years contain 5 odd days.

(*iv*) 200 years contain 3 odd days.

(*v*) 300 years contain 1 odd day.

(*vi*) 400 years contain no odd day because since there are 5 odd days in 100 years, there will be 20 days in 400 years. But every 4th century is a leap year.

(*vii*) First January 1 AD was Monday. Therefore we must count days from Sunday.
i.e. Sunday for 0 odd day, Monday for 1 odd day, Tuesday for 2 odd days and so on.

(*viii*) The first day of a century must either be Monday, Tuesday, Thursday or Saturday.

(*ix*) Last day of a century cannot be either Tuesday, Thursday or Saturday.

SOLVED EXAMPLES

Example 1 : What was the day on August 15, 1947.

Solution : August 15, 1947 = 1946 + 1947th year upto August 15
= 1600 + 300 + 46 + Days up to August 15 in lhe year 1947.

No. of odd days in 1600 years	= 0
No. of odd days in 300 years	= 1
No. of odd days in 35 ordinary years	= 35
No. of odd days in 11 leap years	= 22
No. of odd days in January	= 3
No. of odd days in February	= 0
No. of odd days in March	= 3
No. of odd days in April	= 2
No. of odd days in May	= 3
No. of odd days in June	= 2
No. of odd days in July	= 3
No. of odd days in August	= 15
Total No. of odd days	= 89

= 89 days = 12 weeks 5 days

$\therefore$ It was 5th day *i.e.* 'Friday' on August 15, 1947.

Example 2 : Gandhiji was born on Oct. 2, 1869, it was Saturday on that day. What was the day on Oct 2, 1870.

Solution : The difference between Oct 2, 1869 and Oct. 2, 1870 is of one year. No. of days in February is 28. After completion of one year 1 odd day increases. Therefore, it was Sunday on Oct., 2, 1870.

Example 3 : What was the day on December 31, 1917 ?

Solution : It is not necessary to repeat the whole process. It will be slightly easier to find the day on Jan. 1, 1918. Then Dec. 31, 1917 will be the previous day.

Jan. 1, 1918 = 1900 years + 17 years + 1 day of 1918th year

No. of odd days in 1900 years	= 1
No. of odd days in 13 years	= 13
No. of odd days in 4 leap years	= 8
No. of odd days in January	= 1
Total No. of odd days	= 23

23 days = 3 weeks + 2 days

$\therefore$ Tuesday was on January 1, 1918 and Monday was on December 31, 1917.

Example 4 : Why last day of a century can not be either Tuesday, Thursday or Saturday.

Solution : No. of odd days in 1st century = 5
$\therefore$ Last day of 1st century will be Friday

No. of odd days in 2 centuries = 3

∴ Last day of IInd century will be Wednesday

No. of odd days in 3 centuries = 1

∴ Last day of IIIrd century will be Monday

No. of Odd days in 4 centuries = 0

∴ 'Last day of IVth century will be Sunday

The same process will be repeated again after it. Therefore last day of any century cannot be either Tuesday, Thursday or Saturday.

Example 5 : How calendar of the year 1981 can be used in the year 1987.

Solution : The difference between Jan. 1, 1981 and Jan. 1, 1987 is 6 years in which 1984 is a leap year.

∴ No. of odd days in these 6 years = 6 + 1 = 7 = 1 week + 0 days.

So, in these 6 years no. of odd days are 0. There will be same day on Jan 1, 1981 and Jan 1, 1987.

Thus, calendar of 1981 can be used in the year 1987.

Example 6 : If day-after tomorrow is Sunday, what was day-before-Yesterday?

Solution :

Day-after-tomorrow	—	Sunday
Tomorrow	—	Saturday
Today	—	Friday
Yesterday	—	Thursday
Day-before-yesterday	—	Wednesday

EXERCISE

1. If the day before yesterday was Wednesday, then what day will it be the day after tomorrow?
A. Sunday B. Monday
C. Tuesday D. Thursday

2. If today is Monday, what day was it the day before yesterday?
A. Friday B. Saturday
C. Sunday D. Wednesday

3. If tomorrow is Thursday, what day was it three days ago?
A. Sunday B. Monday
C. Tuesday D. Saturday

4. If the day after tomorrow is Tuesday, what day was Yesterday?
A. Friday B. Monday
C. Sunday D. Saturday

5. How many leap years are there in 400 years?
A. 98 B. 99 C. 100 D. 97

6. How many odd days are there in the month of July?
A. 1 B. 2 C. 3 D. 4

7. The calendar for the year 1846 was same as that of the year.
A. 1840 B. 1841 C. 1836 D. 1835

8. The calendar for the year 1740 was same as that of the year.
A. 1741 B. 1768 C. 1746 D. 1747

9. If 'Friday' is 17th September, then 17th of which month of the same year will be Friday?
A. January B. July
C. December D. March

10. If the 2nd of a month falls on Sunday, then what day will the 31st of that month be?
A. Tuesday B. Saturday
C. Friday D. Monday

11. Which days cannot be the first day of a century?
A. Sunday, Tuesday, Friday
B. Sunday, Wednesday, Friday
C. Tuesday, Thursday, Saturday
D. None of these

12. Which days cannot be the last day of a century?
A. Sunday, Tuesday, Friday
B. Sunday, Wednesday, Friday
C. Tuesday, Thursday, Saturday
D. None of these

13. If 3rd December 1999 is Sunday, what day is 3rd January 2000?
A. Tuesday B. Wednesday
C. Thursday D. Friday

14. What was the day on 31st December 1, AD?
A. Monday B. Friday
C. Tuesday D. Sunday

15. Which of the following is not a leap year?
A. 1860 AD B. 1900 AD
C. 2000 AD D. All are leap years

16. What was the day on 31st December, 1800 AD.?
A. Friday B. Tuesday
C. Wednesday D. Sunday

17. How many times does the 29th days of the month occur in 400 consecutive years?

A. 97 times B. 4400 times
C. 4497 times D. None of these

18. What was the day on 28th June 2025 if 31st May 2025 was Saturday?

A. Sunday B. Wednesday
C. Saturday D. Monday

19. If it is Friday on 4/8/2017, then what will be the day after 61 days?

A. Thursday B. Tuesday
C. Wednesday D. Friday

20. If third Friday is on 16th of month, then what will be the date of fourth (4th) Tuesday of same month?

A. 27 B. 29 C. 20 D. 22

ANSWERS WITH EXPLANATIONS

1. (A): Day before Yesterday — Wednesday
Yesterday — Thursday
Today — Friday
Tomorrow — Saturday
∴ Day after tomorrow — Sunday

2. (B): Today — Monday
Yesterday — Sunday
∴ Day before Yesterday — Saturday

3. (A): Tomorrow — Thursday
Today — Wednesday
Yesterday — Tuesday
Two days ago — Monday
∴ Three days ago — Sunday

4. (B): Day after Tomorrow — Tuesday
Tomorrow — Monday
Today — Sunday
∴ Yesterday — Saturday

5. (D): 1 to 300 years $= 3 \times 24 = 72$
301 to 400 years $= 25$
∴ Total leap years $= 72 + 25 = 97$

6. (C): Total days in July month $= 31$
∴ Odd days $= 31 \div 7 = 3$ (remainder)
Hence, the month of July has 3 odd days.

7. (D): Calendar of an ordinary year repeats after 11 years.
∴ Required year $= 1846 - 11 = 1835$.

8. (B): Calendar of a leap year repeats after 28 years.
∴ Required year $= 1740 + 24 = 1768$.

9. (C): Months with same month code will have the same calendar.
Month code of September and December are same.

10. (D): 2nd of a month → Sunday
Number of odd days from 2nd to 31st of a month $= 29 \div 7 = 1$ (remainder) odd day
31st of that month = (Sunday + 1 day) = Monday

11. (B): The first day of a century can be Monday, Tuesday, Thursday and Saturday. So remaining days Wednesday, Friday and Sunday cannot be the first day of a century.

12. (C): The last day of a century are Sunday, Monday, Wednesday and Friday. So remaining days Tuesday, Thursday and Saturday cannot be the last day of a century.

13. (B): 3rd December 1999 is Sunday. Number of days in-between 3rd December 1999 and 3rd January 2000 $= 28 + 3 = 31$ days. $31 \div 7$ gives 3 as remainder.
So, 31st December 1999 will be Sunday and 3rd January 2000 will be 3 days ahead i.e. Wednesday.

14. (A): We know that 1st January, 1 AD was Monday. Now, number of days between 1st January, 1 AD to 31 December, 1 AD are 364 = 52 weeks.
So, 31 December 1, AD was Monday.

15. (D): All are leap years.

16. (C): 31 December, 1800 AD = 1600 years + 200 years
Now, 1600 years has zero odd days
and 200 years has 3 odd days
Hence, total odd days = 3
Hence, 31 December, 1800 AD was Wednesday.

17. (C): First three 100 years has 76 ordinary years each but last 100 years of 400 years has only 75 ordinary years. Hence, number of months of February in 400 consecutive years in which have only 28 days
$= 3 \times 76 + 75 = 303$
Hence, required number of months $= 12 \times 400 - 303 = 4497$

18. (C): Number of days between 31st May, 2025 and 28 June, 2025 = 28 days = 4 weeks + zero odd day
Hence, 31 May, 2025 was Saturday, so, 28 June, 2025 was also Saturday.

19. (A): 4/8/2017 → Friday, after 61 days = 62nd day
62nd days = 8 weeks + 6 days
(Saturday, Sunday, Monday, Tuesday, Wednesday, Thursday)
So, after 61 days, the day will be Thursday.

20. (A): Given, third Friday is on 16th of month
∴ First Friday $= 16 - 14 =$ 2nd of month
∴ First Tuesday $= 2 + 4 =$ 6th of month
∴ 4th Tuesday $= 6 + 21 =$ 27th of month.

19 Numerical and Geometric Figures

In this chapter, students learn to analyze numerical and geometric figures such as number squares, triangles, circles and other patterns. They develop the ability to identify relationships, between numbers and shapes using basic mathematical operations like addition, subtraction, multiplication, and division.

SOLVED EXAMPLES

Example 1 : Select the right option which can be placed at the sign of interrogation?

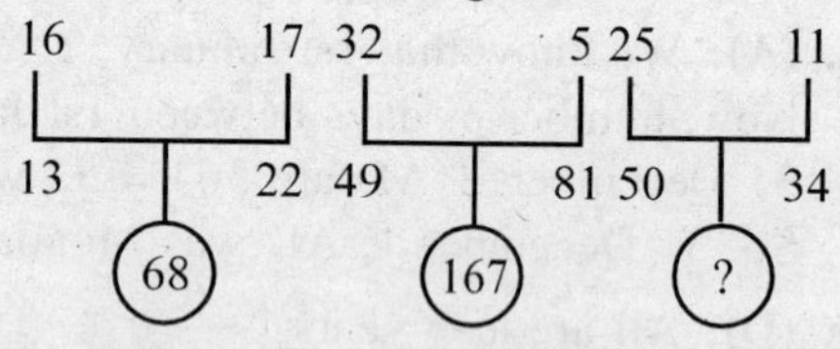

A. 65 B. 120

C. 116 D. 192

Solution (B): The number inside the circle is the sum of the other four numbers, *i.e.*,

$16 + 17 + 13 + 22 = 68$

$32 + 5 + 49 + 81 = 167$

Similarly,

$25 + 11 + 50 + 34 = 120$

Example 2 : Which one number can be placed at the sign of interrogation?

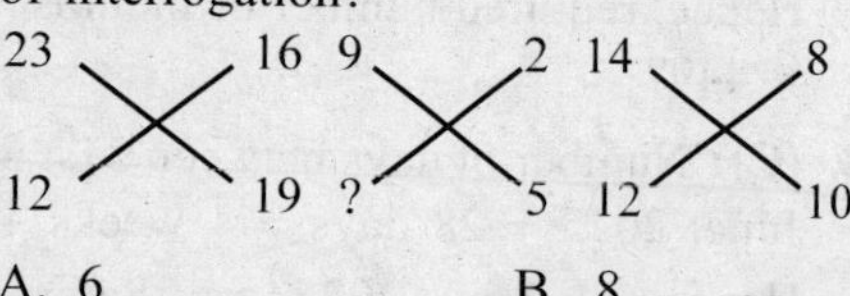

A. 6 B. 8

C. 7 D. 3

Solution (A): The difference between two opposite numbers is 4, *i.e.*,

$23 - 19 = 4$ and $16 - 12 = 4$

$14 - 10 = 4$ and $12 - 8 = 4$

Similarly,

$9 - 5 = 4$ and $6 - 2 = 4$.

Example 3 : Find the missing character in the following question:

1 9 9 16 9 25

16 49 ?

A. 49 B. 64

C. 25 D. 36

Solution (B): It is clear from the figure that square of sum of square roots of top two number is equal to bottom number

We have, $\left(\sqrt{1}+\sqrt{9}\right)^2 = (1 + 3)^2$

$\Rightarrow \quad (4)^2 = 16$

$\left(\sqrt{9}+\sqrt{16}\right)^2 = (3 + 4)^2$

$\Rightarrow \quad (7)^2 = 49$

Missing number

$= \left(\sqrt{9}+\sqrt{25}\right)^2$

$(3 + 5)^2 = (8)^2 = 64$

Example 4 : Find the missing number in the following question:

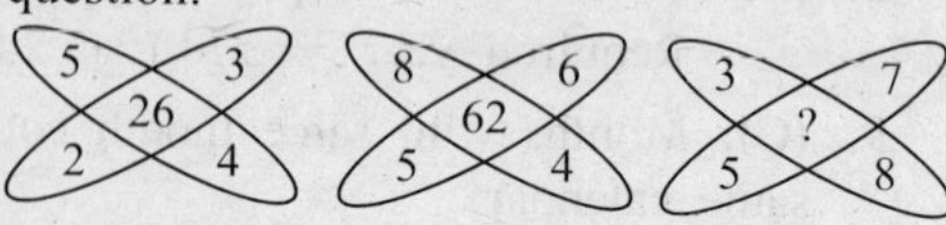

A. 55 B. 62

C. 59 D. 71

Solution (C): The middle number will be obtained by multiplying and adding the diagonal digits.

$(5 \times 4) + (3 \times 2) = 20 + 6 = 26$

$(8 \times 4) + (6 \times 5) = 32 + 30 = 62$

So, missing number $= (3 \times 8) + (7 \times 5)$

$= 24 + 35 = 59$

EXERCISE

Directions (Qs. No. 1 to 20): *In each the following questions, a set of figures carrying certain numbers is given. Assuming that the numbers in each set follow a similar pattern, find the missing number in each case.*

1.

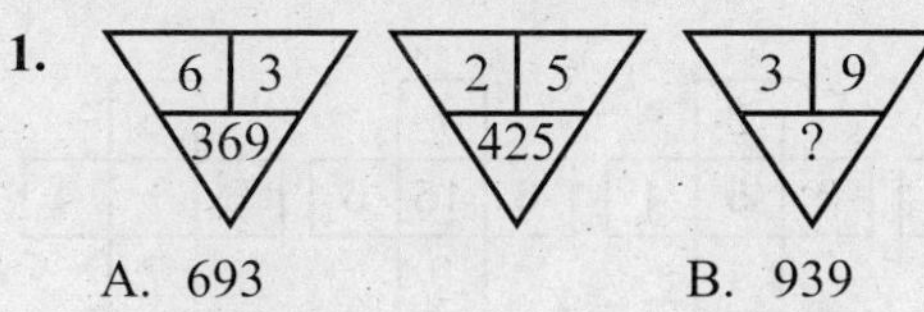

A. 693 B. 939
C. 981 D. 993

2.

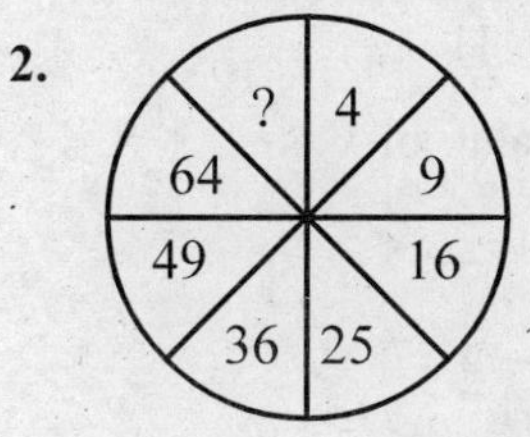

A. 68 B. 100 C. 72 D. 81

3.

7 16 | 8 12 | 21 25

207 | 80 | ?

A. 425 B. 184 C. 241 D. 210

4.

3 5 (39) 6 3 | 4 7 (51) 5 4 | 3 5 (?) 5 4

A. 35 B. 37 C. 45 D. 48

5.

7 5 / 6 | 5 21 / 13 | 24 4 / ?

A. 4 B. 8 C. 20 D. 14

6.

14	9	4
12	7	2
10	5	0
16	11	?

A. 9 B. 6 C. 3 D. 7

7.

29 27 39 (80) 33 45 43 | 29 30 42 (70) 31 43 44 | 59 40 ? (80) 10 39 20

A. 69 B. 49 C. 50 D. 60

8.

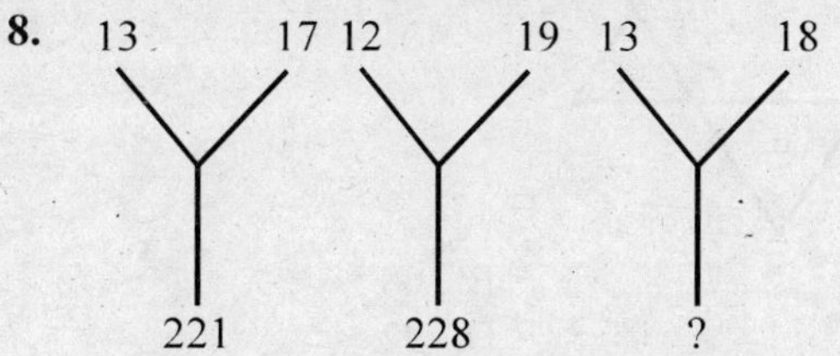

A. 31 B. 229 C. 234 D. 312

9.

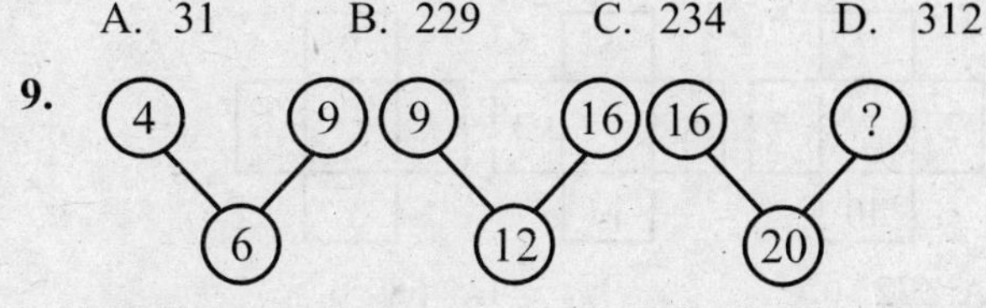

A. 21 B. 25 C. 50 D. 60

10.

51	(11)	61
64	(30)	32
35	(?)	43

A. 25 B. 27 C. 32 D. 37

11.

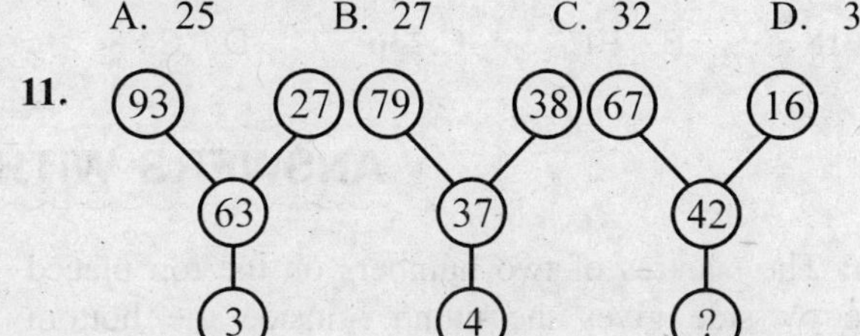

A. 5 B. 6 C. 8 D. 9

12.

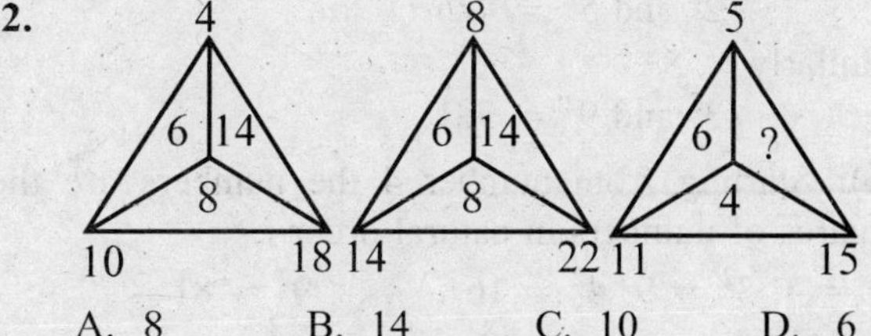

A. 8 B. 14 C. 10 D. 6

13.

2 4 / 20 | 3 9 / 90 | 1 5 / ?

A. 20 B. 25 C. 26 D. 75

14.

5 3 (19) 4 | 7 5 (?) 6 | 6 4 (29) 5

A. 25 B. 47 C. 37 D. 41

15.

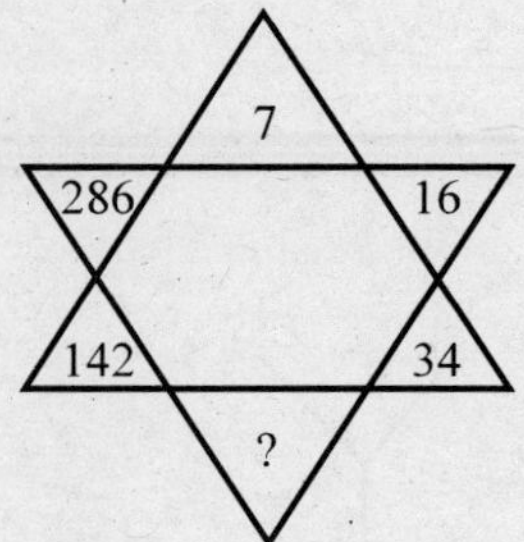

A. 70
B. 68
C. 56
D. 92

16.

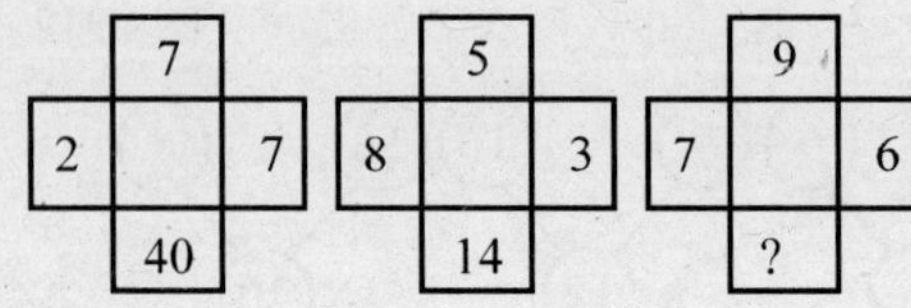

A. 72
B. 68
C. 82
D. 96

17.

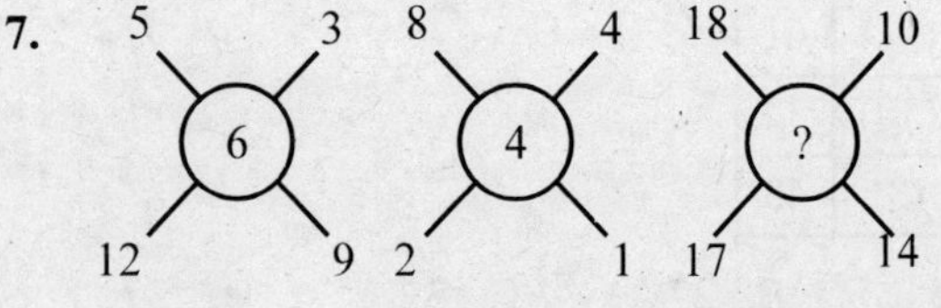

A. 18 B. 10 C. 36 D. 24

18. Which number replaces the question mark?

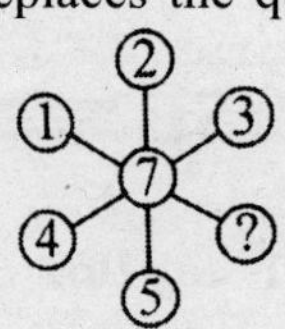

A. 8 B. 3 C. 4 D. 6

19. The number at the place of * in adjoining figure will be:

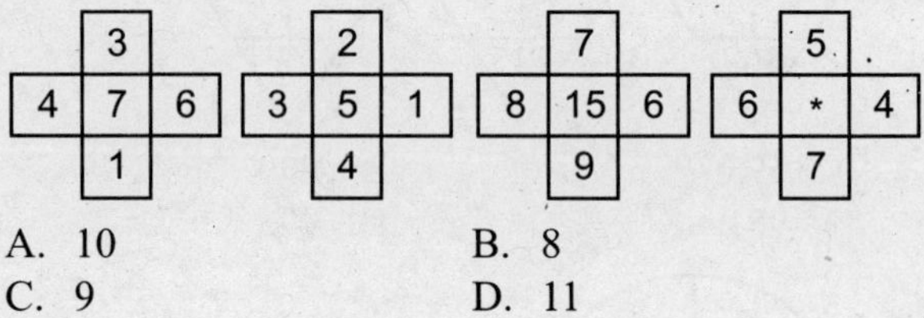

A. 10
B. 8
C. 9
D. 11

20. Find using side figure; the value of x is

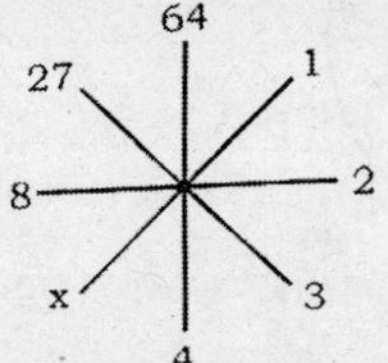

A. 5 B. 6 C. 0 D. 1

ANSWERS WITH EXPLANATIONS

1. **(C):** The squares of two numbers on the top placed side by side gives the number inside the bottom triangle, *i.e.*,

6^2 and $3^2 = 369$

2^2 and $5^2 = 425$

Similarly,

3^2 and $9^2 = 981$.

2. **(D):** Starting from number 4 the numbers are the squares of numbers in natural order *i.e.*,

$2^2 = 4,\ 3^2 = 9,\ 4^2 = 16 \ldots\ldots 9^2 = 81$

3. **(B):** The number at the bottom is the difference of the squares of two numbers at the top, *i.e.*,

$16^2 - 7^2 = 256 - 49 = 207$

$12^2 - 8^2 = 144 - 64 = 80$

Similarly,

$25^2 - 21^2 = 625 - 441 = 184$

4. **(B):** The number in the centre is the sum of the products of diagonal numbers, *i.e.*,

$(3 \times 3) + (5 \times 6) = 39$

$(4 \times 4) + (7 \times 5) = 51$

Similarly,

$(3 \times 4) + (5 \times 5) = 37$

5. **(D):** Sum of two numbers on the top divided by 2 gives the third number, *i.e.*,

$(7 + 5) \div 2 = 6$

$(5 + 21) \div 2 = 13$

Similarly,

$(24 + 4) \div 2 = 14$

6. **(B):** The numbers in 2nd and 3rd columns are 5 less than the numbers in 1st and 2nd columns respectively, *i.e.*,

$14 - 5 = 9$ and $9 - 5 = 4$

$12 - 5 = 7$ and $7 - 5 = 2$

Similarly,

$16 - 5 = 11$ and $11 - 5 = 6$.

7. **(A):** The sum of 3 numbers in each line in one figure is same, *i.e.*,

$29 + 80 + 43$ or $39 + 80 + 33$

or $45 + 80 + 27 = 152$

$29 + 70 + 44$ or $42 + 70 + 31$

or $43 + 70 + 30 = 143$

Similarly,

$59 + 80 + 20$ or $39 + 80 + 40 = 159$.

The missing number is :

$159 - (80 + 10) = 69$

8. **(C):** The number at the bottom is the product of two numbers at the top, *i.e.*,

$$13 \times 17 = 221$$
$$12 \times 19 = 228$$

Similarly,

$$13 \times 18 = 234$$

9. (B): Square of number at the bottom is equal to the product of two numbers at the top, *i.e.*,

$$6^2 = 4 \times 9, \textit{ i.e.}, 36$$
$$12^2 = 9 \times 16, \textit{ i.e.}, 144$$

Similarly,

$$20^2 = 16 \times ?, \textit{ i.e.}, 400.$$

The missing number is $400 \div 16 = 25$

10. (B): The sum of the products of the digits of numbers in 1st and 3rd columns is the number in the 2nd column, *i.e.*,

$$(5 \times 1) + (6 \times 1) = 11$$
$$(6 \times 4) + (3 \times 2) = 30$$

Similarly,

$$(3 \times 5) + (4 \times 3) = 27$$

11. (D): The sum of numbers on right and centre subtracted from the number on the left gives the number at the bottom, i.e.,

$$93 - (27 + 63) = 3$$
$$79 - (38 + 37) = 4$$

Similarly,

$$67 - (16 + 42) = 9$$

12. (C): The number inside each triangle is the difference of the numbers at its base *i.e.*,

$10 - 4 = 6$, $18 - 4 = 14$ and $18 - 10 = 8$

$14 - 8 = 6$, $22 - 8 = 14$ and $22 - 14 = 8$

Similarly,

$11 - 5 = 6$, $15 - 5 = 10$ and $15 - 11 = 4$.

13. (C): The sum of squares of two numbers at the top gives the third number below, *i.e.*,

$$2^2 + 4^2 = 20$$
$$3^2 + 9^2 = 90$$

Similarly,

$$1^2 + 5^2 = 26$$

14. (D): The product of numbers on either side of the triangle plus the number at the base is the number inside the triangle, *i.e.*,

$$(5 \times 3) + 4 = 19$$
$$(6 \times 4) + 5 = 29$$

Similarly,

$$(7 \times 5) + 6 = 41$$

15. (A): Clockwise starting from number 7, the next number is obtained by doubling the number and adding 2, *i.e.*,

$$(7 \times 2) + 2 = 16$$
$$(16 \times 2) + 2 = 34$$

Similarly,

$$(34 \times 2) + 2 = 70$$
$$(70 \times 2) + 2 = 142$$
$$(142 \times 2) + 2 = 286$$

16. (B): The number at the bottom is obtained by subtracting the sum of two numbers in the centre grid line from the square of the number at the top, *i.e.*,

$$7^2 - (2 + 7) = 40$$
$$5^2 - (8 + 3) = 14$$

Similarly,

$$9^2 - (7 + 6) = 68$$

17. (D): The number inside the circle is the product of difference of two numbers above and difference of two numbers below, *i.e.*,

$$(5 - 3)(12 - 9) = 2 \times 3 = 6$$
$$(8 - 4)(2 - 1) = 4 \times 1 = 4$$

Similarly,

$$(18 - 10)(17 - 14) = 8 \times 3 = 24$$

18. (D): We have,

$$2 + 5 = 7$$
$$4 + 3 = 7$$

Similarly,

$$1 + ? = 7$$
$$\therefore \quad ? = 7 - 1 = 6$$

Hence, the missing number is 6.

19. (D): As, $4 + 3 = 7$ and $1 + 6 = 7$

$3 + 2 = 5$ and $4 + 1 = 5$

$8 + 7 = 15$ and $9 + 6 = 15$

Similarly, $6 + 5 = 11$ and $7 + 4 = 11$

20. (D): By using side figure:

$\because 1^3 = 1$

$\therefore x = 1$

$$2^3 = 8$$
$$3^3 = 27$$
$$4^3 = 64.$$

20 Data Handling

Data handling is a tool to express or depict the given information using various types of symbols. In our day to day life we come across several kinds of information such as—

(*i*) Distance covered by a car in 10 hours.

(*ii*) Books sold by a shopkeeper in the last week.

(*iii*) Runs scored by Sachin in World Cup. etc.

The information collected in all such cases is called 'data'. In other words, "Data is a collection of numbers gathered to give some information." It is usually gathered in the context of a situation that we want to study. To give a clear idea of what it represents the data is represented in graphic form.

Organising Data

Generally data is given in unorganised or raw form. We organise it systematically to draw meaningful conclusions. *e.g.*, the temperature of 30 days of a city was given as : 30°, 25°, 29°, 28°, 25°, 30°, 30°, 26°, 29°, 28°, 30°, 30°, 28°, 26°, 30°, 28°, 22°, 29°, 28°, 30°, 26°, 28°, 30°, 27°, 30°, 25°, 28°, 29°, 30° and 29° then how many days the city faced the highest temperature?

It's not easy to answer the question looking at the given temperatures which are written haphazardly. So we arrange the data using tally marks. Thus we easily give the answer.

Temperatures	Tally makrs	No. of Days
25°	|||	3
26°	|||	3
27°	|	1
28°	~~||||~~ |||	8
29°	~~||||~~	5
30°	~~||||~~ ~~||||~~	10
		N = 30

Thus, we can easily determine that the city faced the highest temperature 30° till 10 days.

Grouping Data

In the above example we have seen that same degree of temperatures occurs frequently *e.g.*, 30° occurs 10 days, 28° occurs 8 days, 29° occurs 5 days and so on. This information can depicted graphically.

In our daily life we often deal with different type of data. Some of them are small but some of them are large data. For example, following is the daily attendence of employees of an office in April. 14, 16, 46, 24, 22, 43, 25, 24, 32, 43, 14, 30, 27, 31, 32, 28, 18, 19, 30, 27, 16, 25, 11, 12, 31, 30, 17, 48, 19, 23.

The frequency distribution table of the above observations would be so long. So, it is convenient to prepare groups of observations *e.g.*, 0-10, 10-20, 20-30 and so on. Then we obtain a frequency distribution of the groups of observations using tally marks.

Groups	Tally Marks	Frequency
10-20	~~||||~~ ~~||||~~	10
20-30	~~||||~~ ||||	9
30-40	~~||||~~ ||	7
40-50	||||	4
		N = 30

Data arranged in this manner is known as the grouped and the distribution is called a grouped frequency distribution. Now we can derive many meaningful inferences like—

(*i*) Most of the days the attendences were poor.

(*ii*) Only four days the attendence were maximum and so on.

Variate: The quantity that we measure from observation to observation is called a variate.

Class Interval: Every data is generally divided into small group using some interval is said to be in class-interval, *e.g.*, 0-5, 5-10, 10-15, etc.

Class-size: The difference between the true upper limit and true lower limit of a class gives the size of the class-interval, *e.g.*, class-size of the class interval 0-5 is 5.

Mid-value: The variable value which is midway between the lower and upper limit of a class is called its mid-value, *e.g.*, mid-value of class interval 0-5 is $\frac{0+5}{2} = 2.5$

Frequency: The number of observations corresponding to particular class is said to be the frequency of that class, *e.g.*, frequency of the interval 5-10 is 6. It means 6 persons have got 5 or more articles but less than 10.

Cumulative Frequency: The sum of the preceding frequencies is called cumulative frequency. Last frequency of cumulative frequency column is equal to the sum of the frequencies.

Class Limits: Every interval has two limits. Lower number of the interval is called lower limit while upper number of the interval is called upper limit, *e.g.*, in interval 0-5, 0 is the lower limit while upper number of the interval 5 is called upper limit.

Diagrammatic representation of data

(a) One-dimensional diagrams are (i) Bar diagram, (ii) Sub-divided bar diagram, (iii) Multiple bar diagram.

(b) Two-dimensional diagrams are (i) Squares, (ii) Circles, (iii) Pie-diagrams.

(c) Three-dimensional diagrams are (i) Cubes, (ii) Cylinders, (iii) Spheres.

(d) Pictograms.

(e) Cartograms.

Graphical representation of data

(a) Histogram

(b) Frequency polygon

(c) Frequency curve

(d) Cumulative frequency curve or ogive.

Histogram

A statistical graph that represents by the height of a rectangular column the number of times that each class of result occurs in a sample or experiment, *e.g.*, the following table presents the number of matured persons in the age group (15-50) in a city.

Age Group	No. of Persons
15-20	200
20-25	350
25-30	475
30-35	600
35-40	750
40-45	900
45-50	100

Then the histogram of the data is given below:

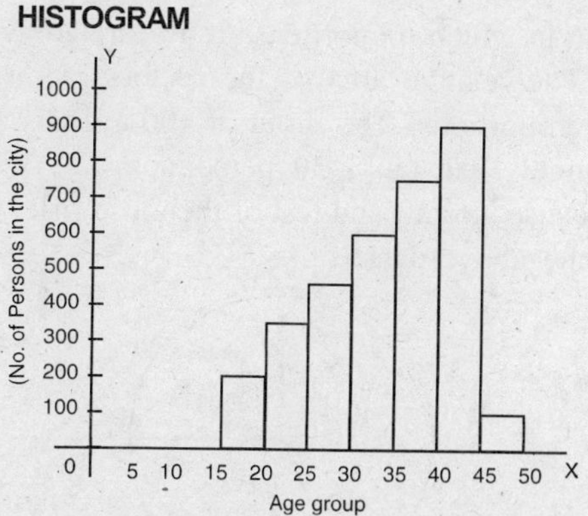

Frequency Polygon

The graph obtained when the mid-point of the tops of the rectangle in a histogram with equal class interval are joined by line segment. The area under the polygon is equal to the total area of the rectangle, *e.g.*, the frequency polygon of above given data is shown in figure.

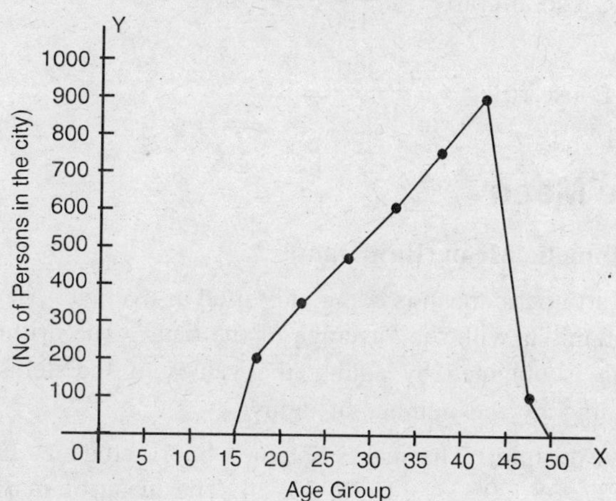

Bar Graph

A graph consisting of bars whose lengths are proportional to quantities in a set of data. It can be used when one axis cannot have a numerical scale, *e.g.*, to show how many different columns of flowers grow from a packet of mixed seeds given in figure.

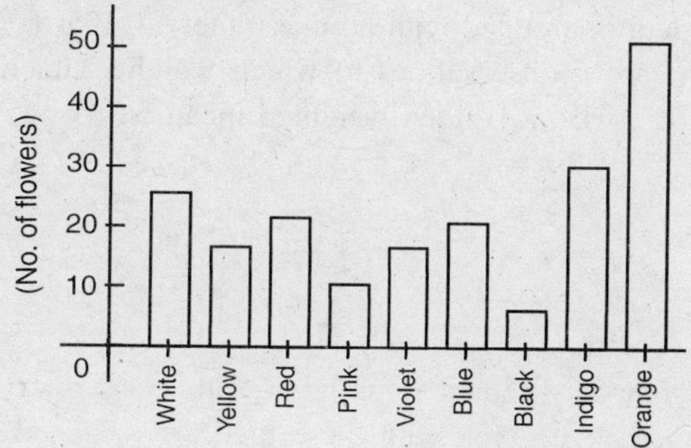

Pie-chart

A diagram in which proportions are illustrated as sectors of a circle. The relative area of the sectors representing the different proportions, *e.g.*, if out of 100 military personnels 25 personnels use tank, 30 personnels use warship, 40 personnels use aircraft and rest of them use rifles. Then pie-chart of the above data is

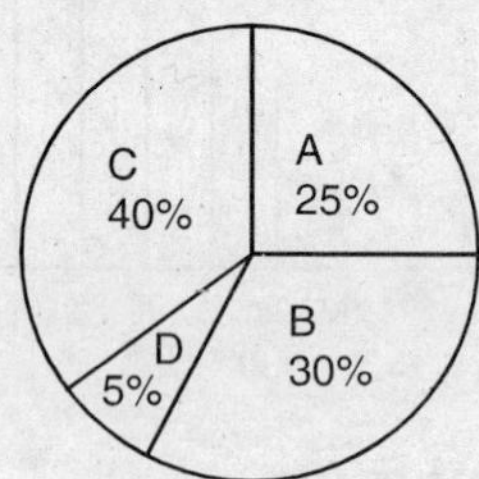

A use tank $= \frac{25 \times 360}{100} = 90°$

B use warship $= \frac{30 \times 360}{100} = 108°$

C use aircraft $= \frac{40 \times 360}{100} = 144°$

D use rifles $= \frac{5 \times 360}{100} = 18°$

The Mean

Arithmetic Mean (Raw Data)

The arthmetic mean is commonly used as average. All of us are familiar with the "average of the data". The arithmetic mean is obtained by adding the values of the items and dividing by the number of items.

For example : The marks obtained by 10 students are 22, 35, 37, 38, 29, 27, 34, 36, 28, 34. The mean of marks is:

Solution: No. of students = 10

$$\text{Mean } (\overline{x}) = \frac{22+35+37+38+29+27+34+36+28+34}{10}$$

$$= \frac{320}{10} = 32 \text{ marks.}$$

Arithmetic Mean (Grouped Data)

If the data is grouped with no class interval. If x_i $(i = 1, 2, 3 \ldots n)$ are n observations to which weights attached are f_i $(i = 1, 2, 3 \ldots n)$, then weighted mean is:

$$\overline{x} = \frac{\sum_{i=1}^{n} f_i x_i}{\sum_{i=1}^{n} f_i}$$

Again, if the data is grouped with class interval and frequencies are given with these then,

$$\text{mean } \overline{x} = \frac{\Sigma fx}{\Sigma f} \quad \text{where, } f = \text{frequency}$$

$$x = \text{mid-value}$$

For example: Calculate the mean for the following distribution:

Marks	Frequency
10-20	6
20-30	8
30-40	15
40-50	7
50-60	3
60-70	0
70-80	1

Solution:

Marks	Mid-value (x)	Frequency (f)	$f \times x$
10-20	15	6	15 × 6 = 90
20-30	25	8	25 × 8 = 200
30-40	35	15	35 × 15 = 525
40-50	45	7	45 × 7 = 315
50-60	55	3	55 × 3 = 165
60-70	65	0	65 × 0 = 0
70-80	75	1	75 × 1 = 75
		$\sum f = 40$	$\sum fx = 1370$

$$\text{Mean } \overline{x} = \frac{\sum fx}{\sum f} = \frac{1370}{40} = 34.25$$

The Median

It is defined as the value of that item of the arrayed series which divides the whole series into two equal parts. The middle item of the array is called the median. For example, in the 3, 5, 9, 13, 15, 21, 22, 25, 29, the median is 15. When the data is ungrouped and the number of items is odd, the median is $\left(\frac{n+1}{2}\right)$th value. If n is even, there will be two central items, *i.e.*, $\left(\frac{n}{2}\right)$th item and $\left(\frac{n}{2}+1\right)$th item. The average value of these two items will be median in such case.

When the data is grouped,

$$\text{Median} = l + \frac{\frac{N}{2} - C}{f} \times i$$

Where l is the lower limit of the class in which median lies. N is the sum of frequencies, i is the magnitude of class interval, f is the frequency of the median class and C is the cumulative frequency of the class preceding the median class.

Example: 1. The median of the scores 25, 28, 20, 8, 10, 15, is:

Solution: Ascending order:
8, 10, 15, 20, 25, 28

$$\text{Median} = \frac{15+20}{2} = \frac{35}{2} = 17.5$$

Example: 2. Calculate the median of the following:

Income in Rs. :	20	21	22	23	24
No. of persons :	2	4	4	3	6

Solution:

Income (x)	Frequency (f)	C. frequency (c)
20	2	2
21	4	6
22	4	10
23	3	13
24	6	19

Here N = 19, which is odd.

$$\therefore \text{ Median} = \text{Income of } \left(\frac{n+1}{2}\right)\text{th term}$$

$$= \text{Income of } \left(\frac{19+1}{2}\right)\text{th term}$$

$=$ Income of 10th term
$= $ Rs 22.

The Mode

Mode is defined as that item of the series which occurs most frequently. In a frequency distribution, mode is that variable which has the maximum frequency. When we say that average age of Indians is 60 years, it means that model age of the people in India is 60 years *i.e.* most of the people in India die after 60 years.

For example: Find the mode of given set of numbers: 2, 2, 3, 5, 4, 3, 2, 3, 3, 3, 5

Solution: Arranging the number with same value together, we get, 2, 2, 2, 3, 3, 3, 3, 4, 5, 5 mode of this data is 3 because it occurs more frequently then other observations.

In case of grouped data the formula to be used is

$$l + \frac{f - f_1}{2f - (f_1 + f_2)} \times i$$

Where l = lower limit of the model class
f = frequency of the model class
f_1 = frequency of the class preceding the model class
f_2 = frequency of the class succeeding of the model class
i = class interval

For example: Find the mode of the following frequency distribution.

Class interval	Frequency
24.5-29.5	1
29.5-34.5	1
34.5-39.5	3
39.5-44.5	4
44.5-49.5	7
49.5-54.5	9
54.5-59.5	3
59.5-64.5	8
64.5-69.5	4

Solution: Mode $= l + \frac{f - f_1}{2f - (f_1 + f_2)} \times i$

$$= 49.5 + \frac{9-7}{2 \times 9 - 7 - 3} \times 5$$

$= 49.5 + 1.2 = 50.7.$

EXERCISE

1. Rain fall (in mm) of 25 days of a city is given below: 38, 27, 36, 40, 20, 24, 36, 28, 22, 25, 36, 40, 27, 38, 26, 30, 28,, 32, 37, 38, 39, 27, 25, 28, 30. The average daily rainfall is:
   A. 30.08 mm
   B. 32.08 mm
   C. 31.80 mm
   D. 31.08 mm

2. The temperature (in degree) of 30 days is given below:
   38, 36, 26, 42, 38, 27, 40, 30, 36, 35, 28, 25, 42, 40, 28, 38, 41, 28, 25, 32, 38, 36, 26, 30, 38, 30, 36, 40, 32.
   The mean of the temperature (in degree) is:
   A. 33.366 B. 33.663
   C. 33.633 D. None of these

3. The number of observation corresponding to particular class is called:
A. Class-Interval B. Class-Limit
C. Class-Size D. Frequency

4. The median of 7, 11, 23, 36, 42, 50, 61, 73, 110 and 120 is:
A. 54.5 B. 5.55
C. 55.5 D. None of these

5. The mode of the data 14, 11, 16, 22, 14, 23, 17, 14, 26, 28, 11, 14, 26 is:
A. 0.14 B. 1.4 C. 14.0 D. 140

6. In a frequency distribution, the variable which has the maximum frequency is called:
A. Mean B. Histogram
C. Mid value D. Mode

Directions (Qs. No. 7-9): *The pie chart, drawn here, shows the spending of a country on various sports during a particular year. Study the pie-chart carefully and answer the questions that follow:*

Per cent of Money Spent on Various Sports for One Year

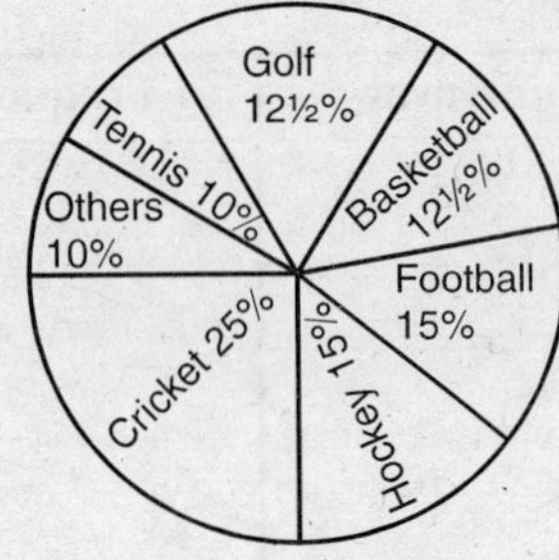

7. Graph shows that the most popular game of the country is:
A. Football B. Hockey
C. Cricket D. Tennis

8. Out of the following the country spent the same amount on:
A. Hockey and Cricket B. Hockey and Football
C. Hockey and Golf D. Tennis and Golf

9. The ratio of the total amount spent on football to that spent on hockey is:
A. 2 : 1 B. 1 : 1 C. 1 : 2 D. 3 : 2

Directions (Qs. No. 10-12): *The following bar graph shows the production of food grains in India during certain year. Study the graph carefully and answer the questions given below:*

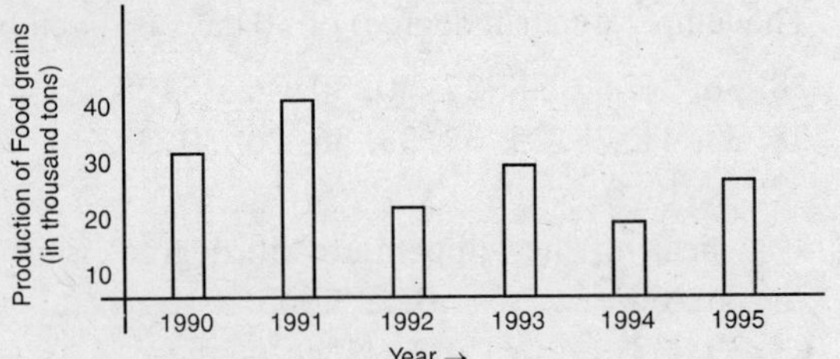

10. Total food grain production in 1992 and 1994 is equal to the production during which of the following years?
A. 1990 B. 1991 C. 1993 D. 1995

11. The difference between the foodgrain productions of 1991 and 1995 is:
A. 500 tons B. 1000 tons
C. 5000 tons D. 10000 tons

12. Percentage increase in the production of foodgrains in the year 1995 over the year 1994 is:
A. 15% B. 30% C. 50% D. 100%

13. To arrange the data we use:
A. tally mark B. mean
C. median D. None of these

14. Difference between upper limit and lower limit is called:
A. Class interval B. Class-size
C. Mid-value D. Class-limit

15. The heights of 10 girls are measured in cms and the results are as follows:

143, 148, 135, 150, 128, 139, 149, 146, 151, 132

The mean height of girls is
A. 141.1 cm B. 142.1 cm
C. 143.1 cm D. 140.2 cm

16. Which of the following is not a measure of central tendency?
A. Mean B. Median
C. Mode D. Range

17. The range of data 25, 15, 23, 40, 27, 25, 23 and 42 is
A. 37 B. 17 C. 27 D. 27.5

18. Which measures of central tendency get affected if the extreme observations on both the ends of a data arranged in descending order are removed?
A. Mean and median
B. Mean, median and mode
C. Mean and mode
D. Mode and median

19. The height of a rectangle in a histogram shows:
A. frequency of the class
B. width of the class
C. upper limit of the class
D. lower limit of the class

20. In an examination of 240 marks, a student scored 52 marks. In pie-chart, the corresponding angle is:

A. 63° B. 75° C. 78° D. $\left(21\frac{2}{3}\right)^{\circ}$

21. Mode of distribution can be obtained from
A. More than type ogives
B. Frequency polygon

C. Histogram
D. Less than type ogives

22. Which of the following statements are true with respect to 'Data handling'?
A. A line graph is used to show comparison among categories of data.
B. A histogram is used to compare the parts of a whole.
C. A graphical representation of data is easier to understand when there is a trend or comparison to be shown.
D. A bar graph displays data that changes continuously over period of time.

23. Which of the following is most appropriate to introduce 'Data Handling' at primary stage?
A. Within classroom, collecting statistics of students' height; favourite food; colour; cartoon etc. and asking questions related to data.
B. Showing population census of a city for five years and asking students to compare population growth.
C. Drawing a bar graph on the blackboard and asking students to read the data from it.
D. Asking the students to read time tables of bus and train timings

24. Which of the following statements is true for teaching of Data Handling in primary classes?
A. It should not be introduced as students of primary classes won't be able to handle the data.
B. It doesn't relate to mathematical concepts in arithmetic and geometry.
C. It can be introduced informally in primary classes as students of primary classes can relate it to their daily life experiences.
D. It demands higher cognitive skills which are not possessed by students of primary classes.

25. Which of the following statements is true for the mean and median of the scores

15, 8, 13, 1, 23, 15, 20, 1
A. Mean is greater than the median
B. Median is greater than the mean
C. Both mean and median are equal
D. Median cannot be determined as there are even number of scores

ANSWERS WITH EXPLANATIONS

1. (D): Average daily rainfall

$$= \frac{\begin{gathered}20\times1+22\times1+24\times1+25\times2+26\times1\\+27\times3+28\times3+30\times2+32\times1+36\times3\\+37\times1+38\times3+39\times1+40\times2\end{gathered}}{1+1+1+2+1+3+3+2+1+3+1+3+1+2}$$

$$= \frac{777}{25} = 31.08 \text{ mm.}$$

2. (C): Mean of the temperature

$$= \frac{\begin{gathered}25\times2+26\times2+27\times1+28\times4\\+30\times3+32\times2+35\times1+36\times4\\+38\times5+40\times3+41\times1+42\times2\end{gathered}}{2+2+1+4+3+2+1+4+5+3+1+2}$$

$$= \frac{1009}{30} = 33.633 \text{ degree.}$$

3. (D): The number of observations in a particular class is called its frequency.

4. (C): Number of observation (n) = 10

$$\text{Median} = \frac{1}{2}(\text{5th observation} + \text{6th observation})$$

$$= \frac{1}{2}\times(50+61) = \frac{111}{2} = 55.5$$

5. (C): The observation '14' occurs maximum (4) times, Hence, mode = 14.

6. (D)

7. (C): According to the graph, expenditure on cricket is the maximum. Therefore cricket is the most popular game.

8. (B): According to the graph, equal amount has been spent on Hockey and Football.

9. (B): Expenditure on the game of Football = 15% of total amount spent

Expenditure on the game of Hockey = 15% of total amount spent

Therefore the ratio of the expenditure on the two games = 1 : 1.

10. (B): Total production in 1992 and 1994 = 20 + 15 = 35 thousand tons

This total production is equal to the production in the year 1991.

11. (C): Difference between the production of foodgrains during 1991 and 1995

= 35 – 30 = 5 thousand tons.

12. (D): Percentage increase in foodgrain production

$$= \frac{30-15}{15} \times 100 = 100\%.$$

13. (A): Tally marks are used to organize and arrange raw data in a simple counting form before further analysis. Mean and Median are used after data is arranged.

14. (B): The difference between the upper limit and the lower limit of a class interval is called the class-size.

15. (B): The mean height of girls

$$= \frac{143+148+135+150+128+139+149+146+151+132}{10}$$

$$= \frac{1421}{10} = 142.1 \text{ cm}$$

16. (D): Range is not a measure of central tendency.

17. (C): The range of data = maximum – minimum
= 42 – 15 = 27

18. (C): If the extreme observations on both the ends of a data arranged in either ascending or descending order are removed, only mean and mode get affected while there is no affect on median.
Hence, correct option is (C). Mean and Mode.

19. (A): The height of a rectangle in a histogram shows frequency of the class.

20. (C): Corresponding angle in pie-chart $= \frac{52}{240} \times 360^\circ$
$= 78^\circ$

21. (C): Histogram can be used to obtain Mode of distribution.

22. (C): Graphical representations like line graphs, bar graphs, or pie charts help in visualizing data trends and comparisons effectively. They simplify complex numerical information, making it easier to interpret patterns and relationships in data.

23. (A): Introducing 'Data Handling' at the primary stage is most appropriately done through activities that are relatable and engaging for young learners. Collecting simple statistics within the classroom environment, such as students' heights, favorite foods, colors, cartoons, etc., and then asking questions related to this data, makes the concept tangible and relevant to their everyday experiences. This approach allows students to actively participate in the collection, analysis, and discussion of data, fostering their understanding of basic data handling concepts in a meaningful context.

24. (C)

25. (B): Scores in ascending order:

1, 1, 8, 13, 15, 15, 20, 23

Here, n = 8 (even number)

$$\therefore \quad \text{Median} = \frac{1}{2}\left[\frac{n}{2}\text{th term} + \left(\frac{n}{2}+1\right)\text{th term}\right]$$

$$= \frac{1}{2}[\text{4th term} + \text{5th term}]$$

$$= \frac{1}{2}[13+15] = \frac{1}{2}[28] = 14$$

$$\text{and Mean} = \frac{1+1+8+13+15+15+20+23}{8} = 12$$

Hence, Median is greater than the mean

$\Rightarrow$ Median (14) > Mean (12).

SECTION-B

PEDAGOGICAL ISSUES

1 Nature of Mathematics

WHAT IS MATHEMATICS?

Mathematics is the science of measurement and calculations. It is the science of logical reasoning. It is a systesmatically organised and exact branch of science.

A universal definition of mathematics can not be given due to its immensity (wide extent). Many mathematicians have defined the mathematics as a subject. But they could not even touched the every factors of mathematics.

e.g., ''Mathematics is the science of measurement, quantity and magnitude''

—Oxford dictionary

''Mathematics may be defined as the subject in which we never know what we are talking about nor wheather what we are saying true.''

—Bertrand Russel

''Mathematics is the language in which God has written the universe.''

—Galeleo

''Mathematics is the study of abstract system built of abstract elements. These elements are not described in concrete fashion.''

—Marshal H. Stone

''Mathematics is a way to settle in mind of children a habit of reasoning.''

—Locke

''Mathematics is the science that draws necessary conclusions.''

—Benjamin Peirce

''As far as the laws of mathematics refer to reality they are not certain; and as far as they are certain, they do not refer to reality.''

—Albert Einstien

According to above definitions we can conclude that

(*i*) Mathematics is the science that draws necessary conclusions.

(*ii*) It is a systematic, organised and exact branch of science.

(*iii*) It settles in the mind a habit of reasoning.

(*iv*) It is a science of logical reasoning.

(*v*) It is a science of number and calculation also.

(*vi*) Mathematics is the science of space, measurement, magnitude and quantity.

(*vii*) It deals with relationships and quantitative facts.

(*viii*) Mathematics is an abstract experimental and inductive science.

IMPORTANCE OF MATHEMATICS

Mathematical thinking is a very significant factor in a modern society as a habit of mind for its usage at the workplace, business and finance; and for personal decision-making. Mathematics is essential for the prosperity of a nation in providing devices for comprehending science, engineering, technology and other related subjects. It is a very important tool in public decision-making and for involvement in the knowledge economy. Mathematics provides students with great and powerful ways to describe, analyse and transform the world. It has the power to create moments of pleasure and wonder for all students when they solve a problem for the very first time, discover a better solution, or observe hidden links. Pupils who are very good at mathematics and capable of intelligent thinking are able to think independently in applied and abstract ways, and can reason, solve problems and calculate risk. In fact education should always begin with mathematics because it creates well designed brains that are capable of reasoning right. It is even proved that those who have learned math from their childhood should be trusted, for they have procured solid foundation for arguing which becomes to them a kind of second nature.

Mathematics is not a mere subject that prepares students for higher academic attainment or job qualification in the future. It is not all about practicing calculations in algebra, statistics and algorithms that, after all, computers are capable of doing. It is more about how it compels the human brain to formulate problems, theories and methods of solutions. It prepares children to face a variety of simple to multifaceted challenges every human being encounters on a daily basis. Irrespective of your status in life and however basic your skills are, you apply mathematics. Daily activities including the mundane things you do memorizing phone numbers, buying groceries, cooking food, balancing a budget, paying bills, estimating gasoline consumption, measuring distance and managing your time. In the fields of business and economy, including the diverse industries existing around you, basic to complex math applications are crucial.

Anywhere in the world, mathematics is employed as a key instrument in a diversity of fields such as medicine, engineering, natural science, social science, physical science, tech science, business and commerce, etc. Application of mathematical knowledge in every field of study and industry produces new discoveries and advancement of new disciplines. All innovations introduced worldwide, every product of technology that man gets pleasure from is a byproduct of Science and Math. The ease and convenience people enjoy today from the discoveries of computers, automobiles, aircraft, household and personal gadgets would never have happened if it were not for this essential tool used in technology.

Every branch of Mathematics has distinct applications in different types of careers. The skills enhanced from practicing math such as analyzing patterns, logical thinking, problem solving and the ability to see relationships can help you prepare for your chosen career and enable you to compete for interesting and high-paying jobs against people around the globe. Even if you do not take up math-intensive courses, you have the edge to compete against other job applicants if you have a strong mathematical background, as industries are constantly evolving together with fast-paced technology.

Since mathematics encompasses all aspects of human life, it is unquestionably important in education to help students and all people from all walks of life perform daily tasks efficiently and become productive, well-informed, functional, independent individuals and members of a society where Math is a fundamental component.

NATURE OF MATHEMATICS

Students must understand aims and objectives of the subjects which are included in the curriculum. Because it decides the nature of the subject. Mathematics has an unbreakable and strong position as compared to other subjects. It is more stable and important also than the other subjects which is taught in school curriculum. These are the factors which decide the structure, truthfulness, prediction and reliability of the subject. The nature of mathematics is also determined on the basis of these factors like the other subjects.

Mathematics relies on both logic and creativity, and it is pursued both for a variety of practical purposes and for its intrinsic interest. For some people, and not only professional mathematicians, the essence of mathematics lies in its beauty and its intellectual challenge. For others, including many scientists and engineers, the chief value of mathematics is how it applies to their own work. Because mathematics plays such a central role in modern culture, some basic understanding of the nature of mathematics is requisite for scientific literacy. To achieve this, students need to perceive mathematics as part of the scientific endeavor, comprehend the nature of mathematical thinking, and become familiar with key mathematical ideas and skills.

Mathematics is the science of patterns and relationships. As a theoretical discipline, mathematics explores the possible relationships among abstractions without concern for whether those abstractions have counterparts in the real world. The abstractions can be anything from strings of numbers to geometric figures to sets of equations. In addressing, say, "Does the interval between prime numbers form a pattern?" as a theoretical questions, mathematicians are interested only in finding a pattern or providing that there is none, but not in what use such knowledge might have. In deriving, for instance, an expression for the change in the surface area of any regular solid as its volume approaches zero, mathematicians have no interest in any correspondence between geometric solids and physical objects in the real world.

A central line of investigation in theoretical mathematics is identifying in each field of study a small set of basic ideas and rules from which all other interesting ideas and rules in that field can be logically deduced. Mathematicians, like other scientists, are particularly pleased when previously unrelated parts of mathematics are found to be derivable from one another, or from some more general theory. Part of the sense of beauty that many people have perceived in mathematics lies not in finding the greatest elaborateness or complexity but on the contrary, in finding the greatest economy and simplicity of representation and proof. As mathe-matics has progressed, more and more relationships have been found between parts of it that have been developed separately — for example, between the symbolic representations of algebra and the spatial representations of geometry. These cross-connections enable insights to be developed into the various parts; together, they strengthen belief in the correctness and underlying unity of the whole structure.

Mathematics is also an applied science. Many mathematicians focus their attention on solving problems that originate in the world of experience. They too search for patterns and relationships, and in the process they use techniques that are similar to those used in doing purely theoretical mathematics. The difference is largely one of intent. In contrast to theoretical mathematicians, applied mathematicians, in the examples numerical information, rather than as an abstract problem. Or they might tackle the area/volume problem as a step in producing a model for the crystal behavior.

The results of theoretical and applied mathematics often influence each other. The discoveries of theoretical mathematicians frequently turn out—sometimes decades later—to have unantici-pated practical value. Studies on the mathematical properties of random events, for example, led to knowledge that later made it possible to improve the design of experiments in the social and natural sciences. Conversely, in trying to solve the problem of billing long-distance telephone users fairly, mathematicians made fundamental discoveries about the mathematics of complex networks. Theoretical mathematics, unlike the other sciences, is not constrained by the real world, but in the long run it contributes to a better understanding of that world.

Because of its abstractness, mathematics is universal in a sense that other fields of human thought are not. It finds useful applications in business, industry, music historical scholarship, politics, sports, medicine, agriculture, engineering, and the social and natural sciences. The relationship between mathematics and the other fields of basic and applied science is especially strong. This is so for several reasons, including the following:

- The alliance between science and mathematics has a long history, dating back many centuries. Science provides mathematics with interesting problems to investigate, and mathematics, provides science with powerful tools to use in analyzing data. Often, abstract patterns that have been studied for their own sake by mathematicians have turned out much later to be very useful in science. Science and mathematics are both trying to discover general patterns and relationships, and in this sense they are part of the same endeavor.
- Mathematics is the chief language of science. The symbolic language of mathematics has turned out to be extremely valuable for expressing scientific ideas unambiguously. The statement that $a = F/m$ is not simply a shorthand way of saying that the acceleration of an object depends on the force applied to it and its mass; rather, it is a precise statement of the quantitative relationship among those variables. More important, mathematics provides the grammar of science—the rules for analyzing scientific ideas and data rigorously.
- Mathematics and science have many features in common. These include a belief in under-standable order; and interplay of imagination and rigorous logic; ideas of honesty and openness; the critical importance of peer criticism; the value placed on being the first to make a key discovery; being international in scope; and even, with the development of powerful electronic computers, being able to use technology to open up new fields of investigation.
- Mathematics and technology have also developed a fruitful relationship with each other. The mathematics of connections and logical chains, for example, has contributed greatly to the design of computer hardware and programming techniques. Mathematics also contributes more generally to engineering, as in describing complex systems whose behaviour can then be simulated by computer. In those simulations, design features and operating conditions can be varied as a means of finding optimum designs. For its part, computer technology has opened up whole new areas in mathematics, even in the very nature of proof, and it also continues to help solve previously daunting problems.

It is not necessary that all subjects should be same nature. Comparatively mathematics has unique nature thus on the basis of which we generally compare it with other subjects. Of course, the basis of comparision of two or more subjects is their nature. Understanding the nature of mathematics may be easy on the basis of following features—

(*i*) Mathematics relies on logic and creativity.

(*ii*) It is pursued for a variety of practical purposes and for its intrinsic interest.

(*iii*) Mathematics plays a central role in modern culture.

(*iv*) It is the science of patterns and relationships.

(*v*) Mathematics explores the possible relation- ships among abstractions as a theoretical discipline.

(*vi*) It is an applied science.

(*vii*) The result of theoretical and applied mathematics influence each - other.

(*viii*) Mathematics is universal in a sense that other fields of human thought are not.

(ix) It finds useful applications in business, music industry, politics, sports, medicines, agriculture, engineering, historical scholar-ship, social and natural science and many other region of human life.

(x) The relationship between mathematics and the other fields of basic and applied science is especially strong.

(xi) Mathematics is the chief language of science.

(xii) Mathematics and science have many common features.

(xiii) It involves conversion of abstract concepts into concrete form.

(xiv) It draws numerical inferences on the basis of given information and data.

(xv) Mathematical rules, law and formulae are universal.

(xvi) It has its own language and the language is well defined useful and clear. The language consists mathematical terms, concepts, formulae, theories, principles and signs etc.

(xvii) It helps to develop the habit of self confidence and self reliance.

(xviii) It provides doubtless and errorless theories, principles, concepts etc.

(xix) It helps in the development of sense of appreciation and scientific attitude.

(xx) It provides the training of scietific method.

(xxi) It provides accurate and reliable knowledge based on sense-organs.

Now, we can understand the nature of mathematics and conclude that really the structure of mathematics is the basis of its nature. It is stronger than the other subjects. Roger Becon has also said that Mathematics is the gateway and key of all sciences.

LOGICAL THINKING

Logical thinking is the process in which one uses reasoning consistently to come to a conclusion. Problems or situations that involve logical thinking call for structure, for relationships between facts, and for chains of reasoning that make sense.

According to Dr. Karl Albrecht sequential thought is the basis of all logical thinking. The process involves taking the important ideas, facts, and conclusions involved in a problem and arranging them in a chain-like progresssion that takes on a meaning in and of itself. To think logically is to think in steps.

It has been proven that specific training in logical thinking processes can make people smarter. Logical thinking allows a child to reject quick answers, such as "I don't know", or "this is too difficult", by empowering them to delve deeper into their thinking processes and understand better the methods used to arrive at a solution and even the solution itself.

Logical thinking is also an important foundational skill of math. Learning mathematics is a highly sequential process. If you don't grasp a certain concept, fact, or procedure, you can never hope to grasp others that come later, which depend upon it. For example, to understand fractions you must first understand division. To understand simple equations in algebra requires that you understand fractions. Solving 'world problems' depends on knowing how to set up and manipulate equations, and so on.

Logical thinking is not a magical process or a matter of genetic endowment, but a learned mental process.

One of the aims of the mathematics is to teach a child to think logically. Logical thinking exercises are carefully graded. For example, in the first example of *Logical Thinking exercise* a child would be asked to arrange a sequence of coloured blocks in front of them, from left to right.

One would then ask the child : "If you had to add one more colour to the above sequence, which colour would you choose?" The answer, of course, is dark.

UNDERSTANDING CHILDREN'S THINKING

One of the fundamental characteristics of "mathematics reform pedagogy is that teachers are encouraged to understand the mathematics thinking of each of their students and then use that knowledge in instructional planning. As compared to typical pedagogy of 25 years ago, explanation/demonstration by the teacher is relatively less important and using questions to probe students' thinking is relatively more important. One implication of this shift is that teachers have the burden of making sense of what students say in their explanations of their thinking. Making sense requires understanding not only the relevant mathematics that might underlie an explanation but also the trajectory of develop-ment of students' (*i.e.*, novices') mathematical understanding. Understanding each student's mathematical development becomes a critical focus of a teacher's attention.

Questioning

Teachers can get information about students' thinking in a variety of ways, for example, questioning, observation, analysis of students' writing, tests, and project work.

Probably the most important of these is questioning, since that is the most interactive of these techniques. Through a series of questions, a teacher can accomplish one or more of several different goals. First, carefully sequenced questions can lead students to a correct answer. Indeed, many teachers are very good at getting students to say almost anything desired, by "leading the student down the garden path." The down side of this, though, is that it may not be clear to the student why those questions were asked or what the final, correct answer means.

Second, questions can help a student process, or even self-correct, an answer. Teachers regularly recognize when a mistake has been made in computing or processing or choice of operation, etc. Asking a question about the student's work may have the effect of "slowing the student down" in order to re-analyze that work. That rethinking may be sufficient reflection for the student to see the error and correct it.

Third, questions can help expose a student's thinking so that the teacher can understand it. Sometimes teachers really don't see immediately how a student is thinking or what mathematics a student is using to generate a response. In that situation, questions can help reveal a student's thinking so that the teacher can determine whether the thought process is acceptable. It is this kind of questioning that is probably most useful for teachers to use as they learn to understand students' thinking, but this is also the kind of questioning that is least familiar to teachers. It is this kind of questioning that teachers need the most help at learning how to do.

Questioning has to occur in real time during face-to-face interactions; teachers have to create questions immediately and with very little reflection time. Teachers, obviously, have more time outside of class than they do in class, so an alternate, though perhaps not as effective, technique for understanding students' thinking is analysis of students' writing. Students might record solutions to problems in a journal, respond to specific prompts posed by the teacher, create reports of projects, or maintain portfolios of their work over time. In many ways, the easiest way for teachers to get students to respond to prompts, particularly in middle and high school classes, is to include those prompts on a test. Probably the most frequently used of these prompts is "show your work." The difficulty with this prompt is that teachers and students often do not share a common perspective on what constitutes work. It is important that as part of instruction, teachers and students reach an agreement on what should be written down so as to allow the teacher to understand the thinking that lies behind the solution to a particular problem.

The usefulness of writing as a window into thinking is influenced by the language and writing ability of the students. It is less useful in primary grades than in high school, and it is less useful when students are expected to write in their second language. We must consider, however, that mathematical symbolism is itself a second language for most students. Effort must be put forth, both by teachers in teaching and by students in learning, to master this form of written communication.

Professional Development Focused on Understanding Students' Thinking

There are several professional development projects that have helped teachers gain the skill and knowledge of processes for understanding students' thinking. The one we are most familiar with is Cognitively Guided Instruction (CGI). CGI is an approach to teaching mathematics in which knowledge of children's thinking is central to instructional decision making. Teachers use research-based knowledge about children's mathematical thinking to help them learn specifics about individual students and then to adjust instruction to match students' performance. Teachers learn to assess students' thinking and then use that knowledge to plan instruction.

Learning as development seems critical if teachers are going to help students increase the level of sophistication of their thinking. Teachers need to have both a vision of what level of sophistication they want students to attain and a sense of where each student is along the path toward that vision. In addition, teachers need to be thinking about how to organize instruction so that students move in the direction of the desired goals.

Reflective abstraction is important as a mechanism by which teachers can improve their instruction. It is also important for children, in the sense that the children must reflect on their own mathematical development. Thus, teachers have to reflect on their own work and to help students reflect on their thinking. In grades K-3, there would seem to be a special obligation to help students develop the skills necessary for reflection; for example, through listening to their peers explain solutions, learning to ask questions to clarify those presentations of solutions, and keeping written records of their solutions that can form data for reflection.

Dialogue is especially important in CGI classrooms, but for dialogue (as opposed to multiple monologues) to occur, all parties involved must listen to each other. Within the implementation of CGI, teachers have special responsibilities for listening. During early implementation of CGI, teachers tend to listen to children's explanations with the expectation that they (the teachers) are supposed to understand children's thinking simply on the basis of what the children say; this type of listening can be called "passive listening." In contrast, teachers who are especially effective at implementing CGI seem to understand that making sense of children's thinking is a joint responsibility; both the teacher and the children must contribute to generating shared knowledge about that thinking. These teachers often engage children in conversation about solution strategies so that both the teacher and the children come to understand how what is being said reflects real thinking. This type of listening can be called "active listening." A teacher's development of either passive or active listening skills is consistent with allowing students to develop personal meaning.

One other advantage of listening is that it provides time, both for the students and the teacher. When a teacher chooses to listen, all of the children in the class have time to think and to develop meaning. When listening is combined with questioning, the time required increases further, since students need time to respond to those questions. The teacher has the opportunity to use the questions to focus students' attention on particular aspects of a solution, so that their reflection on those aspects of thinking is more intense. Having patience to allow students to internalize deep understanding of mathematics concepts is an essential characteristic of effective teachers.

Recent curriculum projects have also attempted to help teachers understand students' thinking; these materials can be an effective vehicle for professional development. For example, in Investigations materials there are dialogue boxes, which illustrate how children might respond to particular questions, lists of questions that teachers can use to probe students' thinking, and suggestions for what to look for during observations. In Connected Mathematics Project materials a launch/explore/summarize strategy is suggested for the activities, and within the notes for each of these there are numerous suggestions for ways to assess what students know and can do. These aids for teachers are designed to help teachers use classroom interactions to deepen their understanding of children's thinking, with the hope that teachers will then use this information to make better instructional decisions. This process is what has been called classroom assessment. The pay-off for helping teachers become better at classroom assessment is better instructional planning, which in turn should lead to greater student learning.

Much research has tried to help understand the trajectory of students' thinking. The research underlying CGI, for example, indicates a consistent pattern of development of students' thinking as revealed in their solution strategies. When teachers understand this path of development, they can interpret where a child's thinking is and can project ways of helping that child move to a more sophisticated level of thinking. Making instructional decisions based on a clear understanding of children's thinking seems to have significant pay-off for improved learning of mathematics. Unfortunately, not much seems to be known about how to recreate these effects across all levels of mathematics instruction.

Professional development materials and programs should help teachers understand more about students' thinking. In addition to the obvious pay-off for student learning, teachers themselves also seem to be renewed and become more excited about being successful teachers. Such renewal is certainly a worthy goal in itself, but the more important outcome is better student learning that follows from teachers' renewed excitement about teaching.

2 Place of Mathematics in Curriculum

CURRICULUM EXPECTATIONS

The expectations identified for each course describe the knowledge and skills that students are expected to acquire, demonstrate, and apply in their class work, on tests, and in various other activities on which their achievement is assessed and evaluated. Two sets of expectations are listed for each strand, or broad curriculum area, of each course.

- The overall expectations describe in general terms the knowledge and skills that students are expected to demonstrate by the end of each course.
- The specific expectations describe the expected knowledge and skills in greater detail. The specific expectations are arranged under subheadings that reflect particular aspects of the required knowledge and skills and that may serve as a guide for teachers as they plan learning activities for their students. The organization of expectations in subgroupings is not meant to imply that the expectations in any subgroup are achieved independently of the expectations in the other subgroups. The subheadings are used merely to help teachers focus on particular aspects of knowledge and skills as they develop and present various lessons and learning activities for their students.

Importance of Mathematics in Curriculum

''Science and Mathematics should be taught on a compulsory basis to all pupils as a part of general education during first ten years of schooling.

—Kothari Commission (1964-66)

''The progress of Mathematics is linked to the prosperity of the state.''

—Nepolean

''Mathematics is a queen of all sciences without any king.''

—Unknown

Mathematics is most important subject in curriculum. Actually except our mother tongue there is no other subject which is such closely related to our daily life but mathematics. Now-a-days it has been given an important position in curriculum. Because it not only has the utility in daily life but also the social and cultural importance. It is helpful in the development of mental descipline. Mathematics has own desciplinary value and it does not need any special evaluation or testing to get a place in curriculum. When one sends his or her child to school he or she generally expects that the child will be able to cash the knowledge, skills, attitude and ideas. Parents expects that the child will earn intellectual habits and different powers *i.e.* discipline, value, morality etc. Of course matematics helps the child to achieve the aforesaid qualities. Moreover there are many advantage of giving due importance to mathematics and making it compulsory subject.

PLACE OF MATHEMATICS IN CURRICULUM

Everybody stands in need of some knowledge of mathematics. But in the case of an ordinary citizen, it is felt that the knowledge acquired during the primary and middle stage will suffice. Consequently there is some controversy over the place of mathematics in the school curriculum.

Some people are also of the view that mathematics is an exceptionally difficult subject, *i.e.,* its study demands special ability and intelligence. It is felt that everybody is not able enough to learn it successfully. Therefore, everybody should not be burdened with the study of this tough subject. References are also made to low pass percentage and heavy failures in this subjects in examinations. These poor results also support the view that mathematics should be made an optional subject.

There appears some justification for the view that mathematics should be made an optional subject at the high school stage. Since mathematics is primarily taught for its disciplinary value and mental discipline being a myth, no mathematics need be taught beyond the middle school stage.

It is also true that mathematics is indispensable in various sciences and professions. But everybody is not going to become an engineer or a statistician. Only those who have to go to such vocations may continue to study it. There is no need of burdening an average student with the study of this subjects, especially when an average citizen can lead to a successful life with the help of an elementary knowledge of mathematics and without any specialised or advanced knowledge in it.

If we take a broader view of the situation, we can infer that the belief of the critics is erroneous.

So far as the need of special ability in the learning of mathematics is concerned, it has been established with the help of experiments that in mathematics more of general intelligence (G) than specific ability (S) is needed.

Mathematics is a useful subject for most of the vocations and specialised courses. Although everybody studying in the school is not going to become an engineer or a scientist, but at a very early stage, it may not be possible to determine finally as to who is not going to join a profession like that. Therefore, the duty of the school is to give to the high school student a broad view of what he is capable of achieving in future. He should get a broader view of what he is capable of achieving in future. To deprive the student of the knowledge of this subject at the high school stage means narrowing the choice of semi-vocational courses, preparatory courses, vocational courses and vocations for him. Ignorance of mathematics will be a great handicap in the way of his future studies and occupations.

Educationists have begun to feel that education upto middle standard is not sufficient for the citizen of today. The period of compulsory education needs to be extended from the middle to the high school standard. After this extension of the period of compulsory education from eight to ten or eleven years, mathematics will have to be retained as a compulsory subject for as many number of years.

When foreigners talk of making this subject optional, they do so on a different fotting. Their pupils are two years older at the high school stage. In India, the pupils at high school stage are too young and immature to choose subjects and vocations for themselves. The parents being mostly illiterate are also not in a position to make any final choice at this stage regarding the future education and occupation.

While keeping it compulsory the interests of both types of students will have to be safeguarded. So the syllabus shall contain such subject matter as it useful for those who are going to discontinue their education after the high school stage and are entering into life. It shall also contain such knowledge as elucidates mathematical principles and processes so that the students who will later join a university course, shall not feel handicapped because of sudden rise in standard.

However, there cannot be any two opinions about the necessity of diversification and specialization in the final year of the higher secondary school stage. Here mathematics has to be treated as an optional or specialized subject like other subject of study.

The unprecedented changes that are taking place in today's world will profoundly affect the future of today's students. To meet the demands of the world in which they will live, students will need to adapt to changing conditions and to learn independently. They will require the ability to use technology effectively and the skills for processing large amounts of quantitative information. Today's mathematics curriculum must prepare students for their future roles in society. It must equip them with essential mathematical knowledge and skills; with skills of reasoning, problem solving, and communication; and, most importantly, with the ability and the incentive to continue learning on their own. This curriculum provides a framework for accomplishing these goals.

The choice of specific concepts and skills to be taught must take into consideration new applications and new ways of doing mathematics. The development of sophisticated yet easy-to-use calculators and computers is changing the role of procedure and technique in mathematics. Operations that were an essential part of a procedures-focused curriculum for decades can now be accomplished quickly and effectively using technology, so that students can now solve problems that were previously too time-consuming to attempt, and can focus on underlying concepts. "In an effective mathematics program, students learn in the presence of technology. Technology should influence the mathematics content taught and how it is taught. Powerful assistive and enabling computer and handheld technologies should be used seamlessly in teaching, learning, and assessment." This curriculum integrates appropriate technologies into the learning and doing of mathematics, while recognizing the continuing importance of students' mastering essential numeric and algebraic skills...

The development of mathematical knowledge is a gradual process. A coherent and continuous program is necessary to help students see the "big pictures", or underlying principles, of mathematics... These courses reflect the belief that students learn mathematics effectively when they are initially given opportunities to investigate ideas and concepts and are then guided carefully into an understanding of the abstract mathematics involved...

A balanced mathematics program at the secondary level includes the development of algebraic skills. This curriculum has been designed to equip students with the algebraic skills they need to understand other aspects of mathematics that they are learning, to solve meaningful problems, and to continue to meet with success as they study mathematics in the future. The algebraic skills required in each course have been carefully chosen to support the other topics included in the course. Calculators and other appropriate technology will be used when the primary purpose of a given activity is the development of concepts or the solving of problems, or when situations arise in which computation or symbolic manipulation is of secondary importance.

WHY MATHEMATICS IS KEPT IN CURRICULUM?

Before starting to teach a particular subject it is essential to know why we are goint to teach the subject. Aimlessness makes a work uninteresting and it is wastage of time, energy and other resourses. Hence we first determine aims and objectives of a work. Thus, teaching mathematics also has some aims and objectives. Because aimless teaching of mathematics may be uninteresting and it will be wastage of time, energy and other resourses for both the pupil and the teacher. Some aims of teaching mathematics are as follows—

(*i*) To develop their intellectual powers and disciplines.

(*ii*) To enable to make use of the learning in mathematics in their daily life.

(*iii*) To help the student in recieving social and moral virtues.

(*iv*) To help in the study of other subjects and future learning in mathematics.

(*v*) To give the insight to recognise relationships between different branches and topics of mathematics.

(*vi*) To meet this different interests, to develop their aesthetic abilities and to help them in their power of utilisation of their leisure time.

(*vii*) To help them in becoming self-dependent for mastering new topics and problems of mathematics.

(*viii*) To make them understand the contribution of mathematics in the development of culture and civilizaiton.

(*ix*) To prepare for the future vocation or occupation.

3 Language of Mathematics

WHAT IS A LANGUAGE?

Here are some definitions of language:

1. A set (finite or infinite) of sentences, each finite in length and constructed out of a finite set of element
—Noam Chomsky
2. The code we all use to express ourselves and communicate to others
—Speech & Language Therapy Glossary of Terms
3. A systematic means of communicating by the use of sounds or conventional symbols
—Word Net
4. A system of words used in a particular discipline
—Word Net

These definitions describe language in terms of the following components:

- A vocabulary of symbols or words
- a grammar consisting or rules or how these symbols may be used
- A community of people who use and understand these symbols
- A range of meanings that can be communicated with these symbols

Each of these components also found in the language of mathematics.

The language of mathematics is the system used by mathematicians to communicate mathematical ideas among themselves. This language consists of a substrate of some natural language (for example English) using technical terms and grammatical conventions that are peculiar to mathematical discourse, supplemented by a highly specialized symbolic notation for mathematical formulas.

Like natural languages in general, discourse using the language of mathematics can employ a scala of registers. Research article in academic journals use a more formal tone than oral exchanges over a scribbled-upon napkin in the university cafeteria.

THE VOCABULARY OF MATHEMATICS

Mathematical notation has assimilated symbols from many different alphabets and typefaces. It also includes symbols that are specific to mathematics, such as $\forall\exists\nabla\wedge\infty$

Mathematical notation is central to the power of modern mathematics. Though the algebra of Al-Khwarizmi did not use such symbols, it solved equations using many more rules than are used today with symbolic notation, and had great difficulty working with multiple variables (which using symbolic notation can simply be called x, y, z, etc.). Sometimes formulas cannot be understood without a written or spoken explanation, but often they are sufficient by themselves, and sometimes they are difficult to read aloud or information is lost in the translation to words, as when several parenthetical factors are involved or when a complex structure like a matrix is manipulated.

Like any other profession, mathematics also has its own brand of technical terminology. In some cases, a word in general usage has a different and specific meaning within mathematics—example are group, ring, field, category, term, and factor etc.

In other cases, specialist terms have been created which do not exist outside of mathematics—examples are tensor, fractal, functor. Mathematical statements have their own moderately complex taxonomy, being divided into axioms, conjectures, theorems, lemmas and corollaries. And there are stock phrases in mathematics, used with specific meanings, such as "*if and only if*", "*necessary and sufficient*" and "*without loss of generality*". Such phrases are known as mathematical jargon.

When mathematicians communicate with each other informally, they use phrases that help to convey ideas. Examples of some of the more idiomatic phrases are "kill this term", "vanish this interval" and "grow this variable".

The vocabulary of mathematics also has visual elements. Diagrams are used informally on blackboards, as well as more formally in published work. When used appropriately, diagrams display schematic information more easily. Diagrams also help visually and aid intuitive calculations. Sometimes, as in a visual proof, a diagram even serves as complete justification for a proposition. A system of diagram conventions may evolve into a mathematical notation.

THE GRAMMAR OF MATHEMATICS

The grammar used for mathematical discourse is essentially the grammar of the natural language used as substrate, but with several mathematics-specific peculiarities.

Most notably, the mathematical notation used for formulas has its own grammar, not dependent on a specific natural language, but shared internationally by mathematicians regardless of their mother tongues. This includes the conventions that the formulas are written predominantly left to right, also when the writing system of the substrate language is right-to-left, and that the Latin alphabet is commonly used for simple variables and parameters. A formula such as

$\sin x + a \cos 2x \geq 0$ is understood by Chinese and Israeli mathematicians alike.

Such mathematical formulas can be a part of speech in a natural-language phrases, or even assume the role of a full-fledged sentence. For example, the formula above, an equation, can be considered a sentence or sentential phrase in which the greater than or equal to symbol has the role of a verb. In careful speech, this can be made clear by pronouncing "≥" as "is greater than or equal to", but in an informal context mathematicians may shorten this to "greater or equal" and yet handle this grammatically like a verb.

Mathematical formulas can be vocalized (spoken aloud). The vocalization system for formulas has to be learned, and is dependent on the underlying natural language. For example, when using English, the expression "$f(x)$" is conventionally pronounced "eff of eks", where the insertion of the preposition "of" is not suggested by the notation per se. The expression "$\frac{dy}{dx}$" on the other hand, is vocalized like "dee-why-dee-eks", with complete omission of the fraction bar, in other contexts often pronounced "over".

Characteristic for mathematical discourse – both formal and informal – is the use of the inclusive first person plural "we" to mean: "the audience (or reader) together with the speaker (or author)".

MATHEMATICS IS A LANGUAGE

''My own attitude, which I share with many of my colleagues is simply that mathematics is a language. Like English, Latin or Chinese, these are certain concepts for which mathematics is particularly well suited, it would be as foolish to attempt to write a love poem the fundamental theorem of Algebra using the English language.''

—RLE Schwarzenberger (2000)

Mathematics can communicate a range of meanings that is as wide as (althought different from) that of a natural language. Here are there broad categories:

- **Mathematics describes the real world:** Many areas of mathematics originated with attempts to describe and solve real world phenomena from measuring farms (geometry) to falling apples (calculus) to gambling (probability). Mathematics is widely used in modern physics and engineering, and has been hugely successful in helping us to understand more about the universe around us from its largest scales (physical cosmology) to its smallest (quantum mechanics). Indeed, the very success of mathematics in this respect has been a source of puzzlement for some philosophers.
- **Mathematics describes abstract structures:** On the other hand, there are areas of pure mathematics which deal with abstract structures, which have no known physical counterparts at all. However, it is difficult to give any categorical examples here, as even the most abstract structures can be co-opted as models in some branch of physics.
- **Mathematics describes mathematics:** Mathematics can be used reflexively to describe itself—this is an area of mathematics called metamathematics.

As a language mathematics has own symbols, word and rules of sentence. Which is based on a certian consistant set of assumptions and built up from there according to the rules of logic. Such logic is necessary for developing mathematical thought. It's understanding and applications depend upon the level of development of ordinary language. *e.g.,* ''Every rectangle is a parallelogram but every parallelogram is not a rectangle. Here, only after developing the use of conjuctions *i.e.* but, hence, so therefore, or and etc. the children become ready for or ordinary language are also used in mathematics. But these words have an exact mathematical meaning. For example — sum, difference, addition, power, multiplication, division, subtraction etc.

Alternative Views

Some definitions of language, emphasize the spoken nature of language. Mathematics would not qualify as a language under these definitions, as it is primarily a written form of communication. However, these definitions would also disqualify sign languages, which are now recognized as languages in their own right, independent of spoken language.

Other linguists believe no valid comparison can be made between mathematics and language, because they are simply too different.

4 Community Mathematics

Community mathematics is an aspect of mathematics education that does not limit children to the confines of the classroom, but enables them to experience mathematics in social, cultural, and local contexts. This approach does not restrict children to merely memorizing formulas or solving problems; instead, it introduces them to practical, experiential, and life-oriented mathematics. The objective of community mathematics is for children to recognize, apply, and understand mathematics in everyday life situations.

Nature and Approach of Community Mathematics

The fundamental principle of community mathematics is that learning mathematics should not be confined to classrooms and books. Instead, children should understand mathematical concepts through local events, surroundings, and community experiences. For example, the prices of items in a local market, scores in games, local statistical data, or measurement activities in the environment connect children with mathematical concepts.

According to Jean Piaget's constructivist approach, children construct new concepts based on experiences and prior knowledge. In community mathematics, this process becomes even more effective because children encounter real-life problems and use active thinking, planning, and decision-making to solve them.

According to Lev Vygotsky's socio-cultural approach, a child's cognitive development occurs through social interactions. In community mathematics, communication with peers, teachers, and family makes the learning process meaningful and lasting.

Major Educational Approaches

Approach	Thinker	Contribution to Community Mathematics
Developmental / Constructivist	Jean Piaget	Creating new concepts through experiences and prior knowledge
Socio-cultural	Lev Vygotsky	Learning through social interaction and Zone of Proximal Development (ZPD)
Experiential Education	John Dewey	Learning through direct experiences, experiments, and projects
Multi-source / Cultural	Vernon	Mathematics = Books + Local/Cultural experiences

Factors Contributing to Learning

(i) Individual Factors

Individual factors relate to the child's internal abilities, mental structure, motivation, and experiences.

- **Cognitive ability:** A child's intelligence, attention, memory, and reasoning ability help in understanding and applying mathematical concepts.
- **Prior knowledge and experience:** A child's previous knowledge helps in linking and internalizing new concepts. For instance, if a child has experience in a game or market activity, they will better understand the use of mathematics there.
- **Motivation and curiosity:** Both intrinsic curiosity and external encouragement activate the learning process. Intrinsic motivation drives the child to learn independently, while extrinsic motivation enhances learning through rewards and praise.
- **Emotional and personality traits:** Self-esteem, confidence, patience, enthusiasm, and perseverance encourage active and sustained learning.

(ii) Environmental Factors

Environmental factors relate to the child's educational, social, and physical surroundings.

- **Teacher and teaching methods:** The teacher acts as a facilitator, providing opportunities for experiential learning, experiments, and active participation. A proactive, empathetic, and motivating teaching style enhances the child's learning ability.
- **Peers and social interaction:** Group activities, discussions, and collaborative learning help develop social skills and a sense of cooperation.
- **Physical and educational resources:** Laboratories, libraries, digital tools, and teaching materials deepen experiential learning and mathematical understanding.
- **Family and cultural environment:** Family support, language, culture, and values influence the child's learning perspective and motivation.

Major Teaching Issues

Effective teaching of community mathematics faces several challenges:

- **Localization of content:** Providing examples connected to the children's community and daily life.
- **Availability of resources:** Lack of sufficient tools, digital mediums, and teaching materials can affect learning.
- **Teacher's role:** Teachers must act as facilitators, motivating children to explore, experiment, and find solutions.
- **Social diversity:** Attention to children's social, cultural, and linguistic backgrounds is necessary.
- **Assessment:** Assessment should not be solely exam-based but should evaluate the ability to apply mathematics in real-life problems.

Learning Process

Learning in community mathematics is active, experiential, and collaborative. Children identify problems, test options, reflect on results, and implement solutions. Throughout this process, cognitive, emotional, and social development occurs simultaneously.

Teachers guide and encourage children's curiosity, creativity, and experiential learning through feedback. Children internalize mathematical principles through experiences and social interactions and apply them in real life.

Modern Approach

In contemporary education, learning community mathematics in the context of real-life problems is considered more effective. Through digital media, local community involvement, and project-based learning, children acquire mathematical concepts in a meaningful, lasting, and practical manner.

Community mathematics does not confine children to textbook-based learning; rather, it develops them as active problem-solvers and experiential explorers.

5 Evaluation

"Evaluation is systematic, continuous process of determining the effectiveness of the learning experiences provided in the class room."

—NCERT

"Evaluation is a continuous process; it forms an integral part of the total system of education and is intimately related to educational objectives. It exercises a good influence on pupils study habits and the teacher's methods of instruction and thus helps not only to measure educational achievement but also to improve it. The techniques of evaluation are means of collecting evidences about the students' development in desirable directions."

—Kothari Commission

"Evaluation is relatively a new technical term, introduced to designate a more comprehensive concept of measurement that is implied in conventional test and examinations."

—The Encyclopaedia of Education Research

"Evaluation may be defined as a systematic process of determining the extent to which educational objectives are achieved by the pupils."

—Dandekar

"Evaluation is an inclusive concept which indicates all kinds of means to ascertain the quality, value and effectiveness of desired outcomes. It is a compound of objective evidence and objective observation. It is total and final estimate. It is a valuable, an indispensable guide to the modification of policies and to further action."

—Wesley

Evaluation is consistently identified in the professional literature as both a critical component and a weak link in the delivery of professional development, but it must not be overlooked. Any effective evaluation should concern itself with changes that take place in instructional practices.

Both formal and informal methods of evaluation can be employed in determining the impact of the Workshop/ Presentation on instructional behaviour. More formal methods use some type of instrument to assess changes in instructional behaviour, before and after the workshop. Practitioners can complete self-evaluations, or a peer or supervisor can complete an evaluation instrument after classroom observations. Analysis of the completed instruments enables practitioners and supervisors to identify areas of strength and weakness and to work on improving instruction. Other less formal or more qualitative approaches include maintaining records/journals of an instructor's own reflections of what occurs in the classroom, or conducting ethnographic studies that describe what happens in the classroom when new instructional strategies are implemented.

In the Indian education system, the term evaluation is associated with examination, stress and anxiety. All efforts at curriculum definition and renewal come to naught if they cannot engage with the bulwark of the evaluation and examination system embedded in schooling. We are concerned about the ill effects that examinations have on efforts to make learning and teaching meaningful and joyous for children. Currently, the board examinations negatively influence all testing and assessment through out the school years, beginning with pre-school.

At the same time, a good evaluation and examination system can become an integral part of the learning process and benefit both the learners themselves and the educational system by giving credible feedback. This section addresses evaluation and assessment as they are relevant to the normal course of teaching-learning in the school, as a part of the curriculum.

RELATIONSHIP BETWEEN OBJECTIVES, LEARNING EXPERIENCES AND EVALUATION

The objectives, learning experiences and evaluation are all interrelated to each other. Evaluation is based on objectives of teaching and learning experiences and also evaluates the objectives at the same time. Thus, in the classroom teaching the teacher organises suitable teaching- learning activities in order to promote desired expected changes in behaviour. It is much broader term than text or examination. It concerned not only with assessment of the students but also with the whole process of education. After deciding what to teach? (content) and how to teach? (Methods). Why to teach? (object). The question arises what has been achieved? Thus evaluation helps to answer the question what has been achieved by the student? Thus evaluation is the process through which assessment, achievement and effectiveness of educational programme is determined.

Objectives
[Knowledge, Understanding
Application, Skills]

Learning Experiences
[Lecture, Problem Solving
Discussion, Text book]

Evaluation
[Essay type, Oral, Written,
Rating scale etc.]

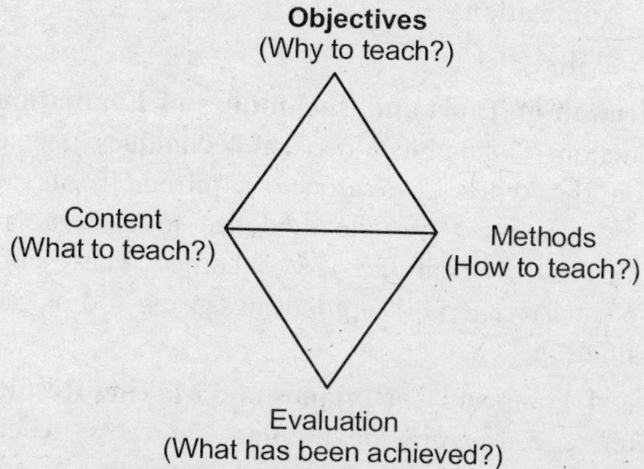

IMPORTANT FEATURES OF EVALUATION

1. It may be used to emprove curriculum, instructions, methods and examination etc.
2. It is diagnostic so that it may provide basis for remedial teaching.
3. It measures the direction and extent behavioural change.
4. Evaluation offers feedback to the entire educational system.
5. It is pupil oriented and activity based programme.
6. It is directly related with the teaching process.
7. It is continuous process.
8. It helps in determining the potentialities and interests of children.
9. It not only measures the educational achievement of the students but also helps in their progress.
10. There is a close relationship between instructional objectives, teaching process and evaluation.
11. It is helpful to a teacher in diagnosing children's difficulties.
12. It makes the reaching-learning process dynamic and innovative.
13. It is a wider concept than testing examination and measurement.
14. It becomes easy to know the present status of the children from their day-to-day record.
15. Evaluation is comprehensive (complete) as it includes everything that can be evaluated.
16. Evaluation is systematic and scientific.
17. Evaluation is both quantitative and qualitative aspects.
18. It is a judgment giving process.
19. Evaluation makes education purpose-centred.
20. Evaluation is concerned with growth and development of the student and not with the status in the group.

PURPOSE & FUNCTION OF EVALUATION

1. **Motivation :** To motivate the children for better learning.
2. **Present Status of the Children :** Evaluation helps in determining the present status of the children in the teaching-learning process.
3. **Guidance and Counselling :** Evaluation provides basis for guidance and counselling to children, by recognising individual differences of children.
4. **To Diagnose the Problems :** Evaluating procedures help the teacher to know the shortcomings of his students, and to diagnose children's weaknesses and strength for further instructions.
5. **Measure Examination System :** Evaluation helps the teacher to measure examination system *i.e.* the topper in the class or failure in the class, etc.
6. **Rate of Progress in Children :** Evaluation helps to determine the rate of progress in children *i.e.* how much marks did Ritu achieved in her 1st term examination and final examinations etc.
7. **Classification of Students :** Evaluation helps in the classification of students into different categories *i.e.* gifted, backward or average students.
8. **Basis for Selection :** With the help of various aptitude and attitude test for selection in various course of study, placement etc. evaluation plays a vital role.

9. **Discover Innovative and Effective Teaching Methods :** Evaluation helps to discover innovative and effective teaching methods by diagnosing children's weakness and strengths.
10. **Improvement in Curriculum :** By evaluation the teacher collect evidences for improvement in curriculum.
11. **Success in Teaching :** Evaluation helps the teacher to assess the success in her teaching.
12. **Improvement in Teaching-learning Process :** Evaluation helps to know the teacher the weaknesses of the student and on those base she brings improvements in teaching-learning process.
13. **Grading the Students :** Evaluation helps in grading the students on the basis of their quarterly, half-yearly and annual examinations and thus knowing the rank of the students of a class.
14. To measure behavioural changes of the children *i.e.* their interest, physical, emotional, moral and social development, etc.
15. **Encourage Teachers for Action Research :** The teacher adopt new strategies for action research on the basis of evaluation.
16. **Feedback to Teacher & Students :** Evaluation helps to give reinforcement and feedback to both the teacher and pupils.
17. **For Remedial Work :** Evaluation helps the students to find out remedies for the problems, so that better results can be achieved.
18. **Clarification of Objectives of Education :** Evaluation is based on objectives. The teacher tries to understand the objectives of each topic in the light of their utility in education.
19. **Basis of Admission :** The students's progress is evaluated by various method *i.e.* tests, annual examination and on its basis the students is given admission in the next class.
20. **In Giving Scholarships :** Evaluation helps in judging the progress of the students and on the basis of this scholarships are provided to students with very high grade.

PROCESS OF EVALUATION

Evaluation process involves the following steps:

1. Selection and formulation of objectives.
2. Defining objectives in terms of behavioural changes.
3. Selection of tools and techniques of evaluation.
4. Interpretation and generalisation of results.
5. Feedback the results for improvement of teaching learning process.

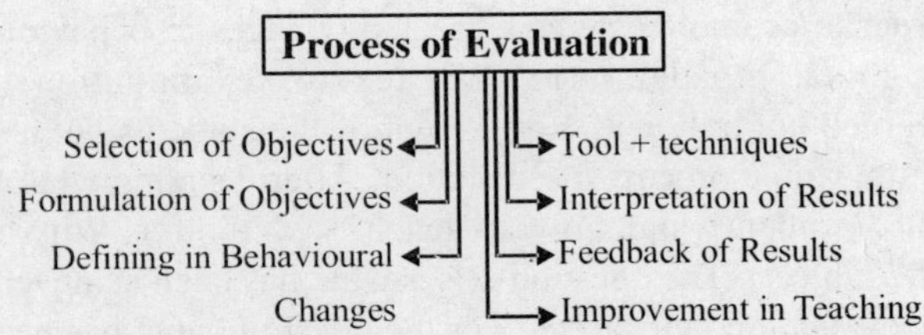

1. **Selection and Formulation of Objectives :** The objectives to be tested are selected in advance before conducting evaluation. The teacher must be very careful in the instructions. On the basis of instructions for objectives given the test items are constructed.
2. **Formulation of Objectives :** A teacher has to be very careful about the instructional objectives of various classes and on that basis of the objective specified various test items are formed for various classes, etc.
3. **Defining Objectives in Behavioural Terms :** After determining and formulation of objectives to be tested teacher should define the objectives clearly in terms of expected changes in pupils' behaviour *i.e.*
   (a) Knowledge
   (b) Understanding
   (c) Application
   (d) Skills
4. **Selection of Tools and Techniques of Evaluation :** Selection of suitable tools and techniques depends upon the types of evidence required. Tools and techniques must provide evidence to the teaching objectives to which they are concerned. They should also satisfy criteria of a good measuring rod or good evaluation.
5. **Use of Tools and Techniques and Making Results :** After selecting and developing the tools, teacher applies them in testing situations, she scores or other evidence regarding the behavioural changes are recorded. On the basis of recorded evidences and information conclusions are drawn.
6. **Interpretation and Generalisation of Results :** The evidence which we get through various tools and technique of evaluation are not meaningful to the learner, the teacher or the parents unless the scores are interpreted properly. Then the results are analysed in terms of objective to rate the progress of an individuals's comparative performance in the class. This collected data helps to generalise the level of achievements required for each class or individual student etc.
7. **Feedback of the Results for Improvement of Teaching Learning Process :** On the basis of analysis of test results or evidences recorded, pupil's progress is made and shown to the parents. This is necessary

for parents to know child's self-evaluation strengths and weakness of their ward for proper diagnosis.

8. **Improvements in Teaching-Learning Process:** On the basis of the feedback of the results, and after for diagnostic measures, re-teaching and remedial teaching is arranged and the teacher tries to adopt some new strategies in her teaching-learning process for better achievements in student's progress.

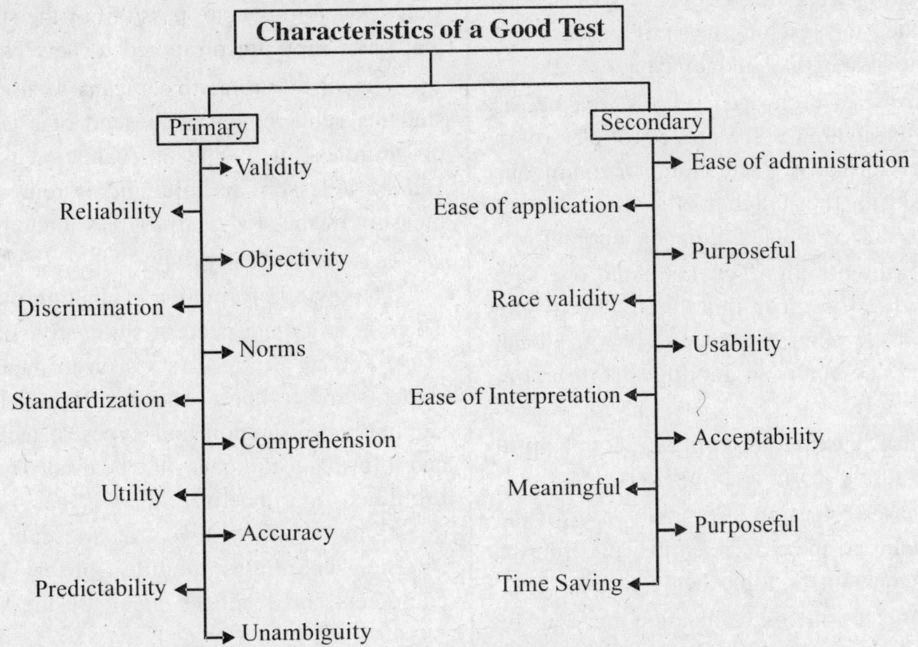

BASIC PRINCIPLES OF EVALUATION

The foundation or base of any building should be very strong, if the building is very beautiful but the foundation or base *i.e.* the pillars on which the building stands are weak, the building will collapse. Similarly, if evaluation is not based on certain basic principles, the evaluation system cannot said to be effective and teaching aims will not be achieved. Some of the basic principles of evaluation are:

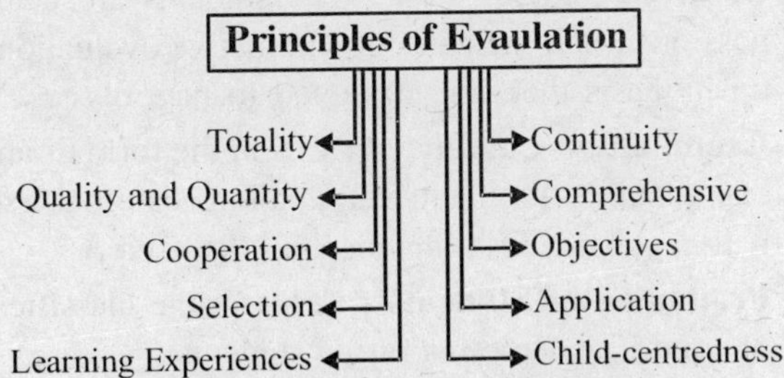

TYPES OF EVALUATION

1. Diagnostic Evaluation
2. Prognosis Evaluation
3. Formative Evaluation
4. Summative Evaluation
5. Comprehensive Evaluation
6. Continuous Evaluation

FORMATIVE EVALUATION

When a teacher has taught a part of unit or some topics or content or any learning concepts he or she wants to judge the outcome of the students. In the same manner the student also need to know their progress in the path of learning. The formative evaluation is a great help to the teacher as well as student as it provides the information to both about the strength and weakness of their teaching and learning.

The term formative means the ongoing or systematic assessment of student's achievement in the course of teaching programme. Formative evaluation occurs between the formative stage that it when the process of teaching and learning is going on and not after it is completed.

According to New Education Policy (1986)—Formative evaluation is an integral part of teaching-learning process. The formative evaluation also is helpful in the process of curriculum construction at the formative stage.

The formative evaluation is carried out both in formal [*i.e.*, question-answer, assignments, tests, quizzes, draft-work, concept maps, peer response, groups porfolio, reviews, conference etc) as well as informal (*e.g.*, listening students comments, conversations, observations etc.)

FEATURES/NEED/IMPORTANCE OF FORMATIVE EVALUATION

1. **Minimum Level of Learning :** The formative evaluation can be used by the teachers to ensure that the minimum levels of learning are attained by all children in the classroom teaching.

2. **Monitor the Teaching Process :** The purpose of formative evaluation is to monitor the teaching process to know that learning process is taking place or not.
3. **Enhance Teaching Learning Process :** It is mainly meant to enhance the teaching-learning process and not designed to make final judgements.
4. **Pupils Weaknesses Diagnosed :** Pupils weaknesses are diagnosed throughout in the process of classroom teaching. Hence formative evaluation is a continuous feedback to both the teacher and the student determining the success and failure of learning.
5. **Feedback to Students and Teacher :** On one side formative evaluation provides feedback to the children and on the other hand it provides feedback to the teacher also and can modify her teaching process accordingly.
6. **Monitoring Pupil's Learning Process :** It is helpful in monitoring pupils learning progress.
7. **Helps to Increase Retention :** It makes easy for the students and helps to increase retention and transfer of learning of the unit or topic being taught.
8. **Self Evaluation :** Formative evaluation can also be used as a self-evaluation. Can also be used as a self-evaluation devices by the children.
9. **Correcting Learning Deficiencies :** It also helps the teacher for correcting her learning deficiencies and weaknesses.
10. **Keep Students Attentive :** Formative test also keep the students attentive.
11. **Immediate Decision Making :** Formative evaluation is most useful for the immediate decision making that students face.
12. **Variety of Techniques Used :** This is a continuous and integral part of teaching where one uses variety of techniques *i.e.* attitude, aptitude, inventories, rating scale, checklists, etc. and alert listeners, and students remain informative for the topic being taught.
13. **Assimilation of Various Concepts:** Formative evaluation determines how well the students are assimilating various concepts, skills and behavioural changes.
14. **Helps to Improve Instructional Behaviour:** Formative evaluation helps to improve the instructional behaviour in the development phase, rather than being in trouble over its failure after the programme is completed.
15. **No Reason for Failure:** When student is continuously evaluated and guided through formative evaluation, there is no reason for the failure in the final summative evaluation.

SUMMATIVE EVALUATION

When the students become fully familiar with the whole syllabus, summative evaluation is conducted. Thus summative evaluation occurs in the end of the academic year session to declare pass/fail of the student result and on that basis they are promoted to new classes.

The turm summative means to assigning a grade for students achievement at the end of a term of the teaching programme. Such type of evaluation is carried out at the end of a lesson or unit, and it represent a find test or measure of the students progress made by him as the result of his progress of teaching.

Thus where formative evaluation reaches its last stage. There is an urgent need of summative evaluation. It occurs at the end of a term or a sesson to measure the success of students and to know what has been achieved by him. For summative evaluation both types of techniques *i.e.*, formal and informal techniques may be used. The formal techniques includes—standardised as well as teacher made test, questionaire, interviews, rating scale, assignments etc. Internal techniques include—observations, discussions, comments and feedback given by the student etc.

FEATURES/NEED/IMPORTANCE OF SUMMATIVE EVALUATION

1. **Final Progress :** It tells about the final progress of the students as a result after the course of full units or topic.
2. **Feedback is Less :** Interaction of the teacher and pupil is very limited and the feedback is much less as compared to formative evaluation.
3. **End of the Academic Year :** It occurs at the end of the academic year of the session.
4. **Declared Pass or Fail :** The students are declared pass or fail on the basis of summative evaluation and on its basis they are promoted to new classes.
5. **Examination Conducted :** It is in the form of annual examination, terminal examination, external examination (board examination *i.e.* CBSE etc.).
6. **Promotion of Students :** Helps in the classification of grades and promotion of students.
7. **End of Course :** It is treated as an end of the course activity.
8. **Results Help to Choose Career :** The result of the students helps them to choose their careers, placements and are predictions for their future success.

On the basis of above description it is clear that formal and informal methods are techniques which are equally used in formative and summative evaluation. But objectives of the techniques are different in both the evaluations.

Why Evaluate?

Effective teachers use a variety of means, some formal and others informal, to determine how much and how well their students are learning. For example, to formally evaluate student learning, most teachers use quizzes, tests, examinations, term papers, lab reports, and homework.These formal evaluation techniques help the instructor to evaluate student achievement and assign grades.

To evaluate classroom learning informally, teachers also use a variety of techniques. For example, teachers pose questions, listen carefully to student questions and comments, and monitor body language and facial expressions. Informal, often implicit evaluations permit the teacher to make adjustments in their teaching: to slow down or review material in response to questions, confusion, and misunderstandings; or to move on when student performance exceeds expectations.

When teaching at a distance, educators must address a different teaching challenge than when teaching in a traditional classroom. For example, instructors no longer have:

- A traditional, familiar classroom.
- A relatively homogeneous group of students.
- Face-to-face feedback during class (*e.g.*, students' questions, comments, body language, and facial expressions).
- Total control over the distance delivery system.
- Covenient opportunities to talk to students individually.

For these reasons, distance educators may find it useful to not only formally evaluate students through testing and homework, but to use a more informal approach in collecting data determine.

6 Problems of Teaching

Any analysis of mathematics education in our schools will identify a range of issues as problematic. We structure our understanding of these issues around the following four problems which we deem to be the core areas of concern:

1. A sense of fear and failure regarding mathematics among a majority of children,
2. A curriculum that disappoints both a talented minority as well as the non-participating majority at the same time,
3. Crude methods of assessment that encourage perception of mathematics as mechanical computation, and
4. Lack of teacher preparation and support in the teaching of mathematics.

Each of these can and need to be expanded on, since they concern the curricular framework in essential ways.

Fear and Failure

If any subject area of study evokes wide emotional comment, it is mathematics. While no one educated in Tamil would profess (or at the least, not without a sense of shame) ignorance of any Tirukkural, it is quite the social norm for anyone to proudly declare that (s)he never could learn mathematics. While these may be adult attitudes, among children (who are compelled to pass mathematics examinations) there is often fear and anxiety. Mathematics anxiety and 'math phobia' are terms that are used in popular literature.

In the Indian context, there is a special dimension to such anxiety. With the universalisation of elementary education made a national priority, and elementary education a legal right, at this historic juncture, a serious attempt must be made to look into every aspect that alienates children in school and contributes towards their non-participation, eventually leading to their dropping out of the system. If any subject taught in school plays a significant role in alienating children and causing them to stop attending school, perhaps mathematics, which inspires so much dread, must take a big part of the blame.

Such fear is closely linked to a sense of failure. By Class III or IV, many children start seeing themselves as unable to cope with the demands made by mathematics. In high school, among children who fail only in one or two subjects in year-end examinations and hence are detained, the maximum numbers fail in mathematics. This statistic pursues us right through to Class X, which is when the Indian state issues a certificate of education to a student. The largest numbers of Board Exam failures also happen in mathematics.

There are many perceptive studies and analyses on what causes fear of mathematics in schools. Central among them is the cumulative nature of mathematics. If you struggle with decimals, then you will struggle with percentages; if you struggle with percentages, then you will struggle with algebra and other mathematics subjects as well. The other principal reason is said to be the predominance of symbolic language. When symbols are manipulated without understanding, after a point, boredom and bewilderment dominate for many children, and dissociation develops.

Failure in mathematics could be read through social indicators as well. Structural problems in Indian education, reflecting structures of social discrimination, by way of class, caste and gender, contribute further to failure (and perceived failure) in mathematics education as well. Prevalent social attitudes which see girls as incapable of mathematics, or which, for centuries, have associated formal computational abilities with the upper castes, deepen such failure by way of creating self-fulfilling expectations.

A special mention must be made of problems created by the language used in textbooks, especially at the elementary level. For a vast majority of Indian children, the language of mathematics learnt in school is far removed from their everyday speech, and especially forbidding. This becomes a major force of alienation in its own right.

Disappointing Curriculum

Any mathematics curriculum that emphasises procedure and knowledge of formulas over understanding is bound to enhance anxiety. The prevalent practice of school mathematics goes further a silent majority give up early on, remaining content to fail in mathematics, or at best, to see it through, maintaining a minimal level of achievement. For these children, what the curriculum offers is a store of mathematical facts, borrowed temporarily while preparing for tests.

On the other hand, it is widely acknowledged that more than in any other content discipline, mathematics is the subject that also sees great motivation and talent even at an early age in a small number of children. These are children who take to quantisation and algebra easily and carry on with great facility.

What the curriculum offers for such children is also intense disappointment. By not offering conceptual depth, by not challenging them, the curriculum settles for minimal use of their motivation. Learning procedures may be easy for them, but their understanding and capacity for reasoning remain underexercised.

Crude Assessment

We talked of fear and failure. While what happens in class may alienate, it never evokes panic, as does the examination. Most of the problems cited above relate to the tyranny of procedure and memorization of formulas in school mathematics, and the central reason for the ascendancy of procedure is the nature of assessment and evaluation. Tests are designed (only) for assessing a student's knowledge of procedure and memory of formulas and facts, and given the criticality of examination performance in school life, concept learning is replaced by procedural memory. Those children who cannot do such replacement successfully experience panic, and suffer failure.

While mathematics is the major ground for formal problem solving in school, it is also the only arena where children see little room for play in answering questions. Every question in mathematics is seen to have one unique answer, and either you know it or you don't. In Language, Social Studies, or even in Science, you may try and demonstrate partial knowledge, but (as the students see it), there is no scope for doing so in mathematics. Obviously, such a perception is easily coupled to anxiety.

Amazingly, while there has been a great deal of research in mathematics education and some of it has led to changes in pedagogy and curriculum, the area that has seen little change in our schools over a hundred years or more is evaluation procedures in mathematics. It is not accidental that even a quarterly examination in Class VII is not very different in style from a Board examination in Class X, and the same pattern dominates even the end-of chapter exercises given in textbooks. It is always application of some piece of information given in the text to solve a specific problem that tests use of formalism. Such antiquated and crude methods of assessment have to be thoroughly overhauled if any basic change is to be brought about.

Inadequate Teacher Preparation

More so than any other content discipline, mathematics education relies very heavily on the preparation that the teacher has, in her own understanding of mathematics, of the nature of mathematics, and in her bag of pedagogic techniques. Textbook-centred pedagogy dulls the teacher's own mathematics activity.

At two ends of the spectrum, mathematics teaching poses special problems. At the primary level, most teachers assume that they know all the mathematics needed, and in the absence of any specific pedagogic training, simply try and uncriti-cally reproduce the techniques they experienced in their school days. Often this ends up perpetuating problems across time and space.

At the secondary and higher secondary level, some teachers face a different situation. The syllabi have considerably changed since their school days, and in the absence of systematic and continuing education programmes for teachers, their fundamen-tals in many concept areas are not strong. This encourages reliance on 'notes' available in the market, offering little breadth or depth for the students.

While inadequate teacher preparation and support acts negatively on all of school mathematics, at the primary stage, its main consequence is this: mathematics pedagogy rarely resonates with the findings of children's psychology. At the upper primary stage, when the language of abstractions is formalised in algebra, inadequate teacher preparation reflects as inability to link formal mathematics with experiential learning. Later on, it reflects as incapacity to offer connections within mathematics or across subject areas to applications in the sciences, thus depriving students of important motivation and appreciation.

Other Systematic Problems

We wish to briefly mention a few other systematic sources of problems as well. One major problem is that of compartmentalisation. There is very little systematic communication between primary school and high school teachers of mathematics, and none at all between high school and college teachers of mathematics. Most school teachers have never even seen, let alone interacted with or consulted, research mathematicians. Those involved in teacher education are again typically outside the realm of college or research mathematics.

Another important problem is that of curricular acceleration: a generation ago, calculus was first encountered by a student in college. Another generation earlier, analytical geometry was considered college mathematics.

But these are all part of school curriculum now. Such acceleration has naturally meant pruning of some topics: there is far less solid geometry or spherical geometry now. One reason for the narrowing is that calculus and differential equations are critically important in undergraduate sciences, technology and engineering, and hence it is felt that early introduction of these topics helps students proceeding further on these lines. Whatever the logic, the shape of mathematics education has become taller and more spindly, rather than broad and rounded.

While we have mentioned gender as a systematic issue, it is worth understanding the problem in some detail. Mathematics tends to be regarded as a 'masculine domain'. This perception is aided by the complete lack of references in textbooks to women mathematicians, the absence of social concerns in the designing of curricula which would enable children questioning received gender ideologies and the absence of reference to women's lives in problems. A study of mathematics textbooks found that in the problem sums, not a single reference was made to women's clothing, although several problems referred to the buying of cloth, etc.

Classroom research also indicates a fairly systematic devaluation of girls as incapable of 'mastering' mathematics, even when they perform reasonably well at verbal as well as cognitive tasks in mathematics. It has been seen that teachers tend to address boys more than girls, which feeds into the construction of the normative mathematics learner as male. Also, when instructional decisions are in teachers' hands, their gendered constructions colour the mathematical learning strategies of girls and boys, with the latter using more invented strategies for problem-solving, which reflects greater conceptual understanding. Studies have shown that teachers tend to attribute boys' mathematical 'success' more to ability, and girls' success more to effort. Classroom discourses also give some indication of how the 'masculinising' of mathematics occurs, and the profound influence of gender ideologies in patterning notions of academic competence in school. With performance in mathematics signifying school 'success', girls are clearly at the losing end.

RECOMMENDATIONS

While the litany of problems and challenges magnifies the distance we need to travel to arrive at the vision articulated above, it also offers hope by way of pointing us where we need to go and what steps we may/must take.

We summarise what we believe to be the central directions for action towards our stated vision. We group them again into four central themes:

1. Shifting the focus of mathematics education from achieving 'narrow' goals to 'higher' goals,
2. Engaging every student with a sense of success, while at the same time offering conceptual challenges to the emerging mathematician,
3. Changing modes of assessment to examine students' mathematisation abilities rather than procedural knowledge,
4. Enriching teachers with a variety of mathematical resources.

7 Error Analysis

ERRORS BY STUDENTS

Identification of students' specific errors is especially important for students with learning disabilities and low performing students. By pinpointing student errors, the teacher can provide instruction targeted to the student's area of need. In general, students who have difficulty learning math typically lack important conceptual knowledge for several reasons, including an inability to process information at the rate of the instructional pace, a lack of adequate opportunities to respond (*i.e.*, practice), a lack of specific feedback from teachers regarding misunderstanding or non-understanding, anxiety about mathematics, and difficulties in visual and/or auditory processing.

Lack of Knowledge

Students' lack of knowledge could be a major reason why they cannot solve certain problems consistently. As noted above, there are three types of errors: procedural, factual, and conceptual. When a student has not followed the correct steps (or procedures) to solve a problem, this is a procedural error. Factual errors are mistakes that students make when they cannot recall a fact required to solve a problem or if they have not mastered basic facts. Procedural and factual errors (also known as 'slips') are generally not due to inherent misunderstandings; slips may be due to memory deficits, impulsivity, or visual-motor integration problems and are easier to identify than conceptual errors. Conceptual errors (or 'bugs') may look like procedural errors, but they occur because the student does not fully understand a specific math concept, such as place value. As such, bugs are more serious errors. To determine if an error is conceptual, teachers should check by asking the student to represent the problem with concrete objects or show and explain the steps used to solve the problem.

Poor Attention and Carelessness

Other possible causes of student error are poor attention and carelessness. To address this issue, teachers should first consider the alignment between the instruction, student ability, and the task. For example, lack of attention is more likely to occur during a long-division lesson when the students have not learned division or mastered necessary pre-requisite skills (*i.e.*, there is a mismatch between the instruction and student ability). Inattention could occur during parts of lesson where students are required to listen for an extended period of time. In such cases, teachers should consider delivering the materials in a brisk, enthusiastic manner, making sure that students are given ample opportunities to engage and respond to questions. When lack of attention occurs during independent work, teachers should provide clear expectations for completing tasks, monitor student work, and provide corrective feedback.

To Conduct Error Analysis

The following steps describe the error analysis process, applied to mathematics:

1. Collect a sample of student work for each type of problem (*e.g.*, single-digit addition; two-digit multiplication with regrouping), with at least three to five items for each problem type.
2. Have the student verbalize or think aloud as s/he solves the problems without providing any type of cues or prompting.
3. Record all student responses in written and verbal format.
4. Analyse the responses and look for patterns among common problem types.
5. Look for examples of "exceptions" to an apparent pattern (accurate "exceptions" could signal that the student does not fully understand the procedure or concept).
6. Describe the patterns observed in simple language and the possible reasons for the student's problems (*e.g.*, if a student did not regroup double-digit addition problems, it could be a sign that the student does not understand the concept of place value).
7. Interview the student by asking him/her to explain how s/he solved the problem to confirm suspected error patterns.

ERRORS IN EVALUATION

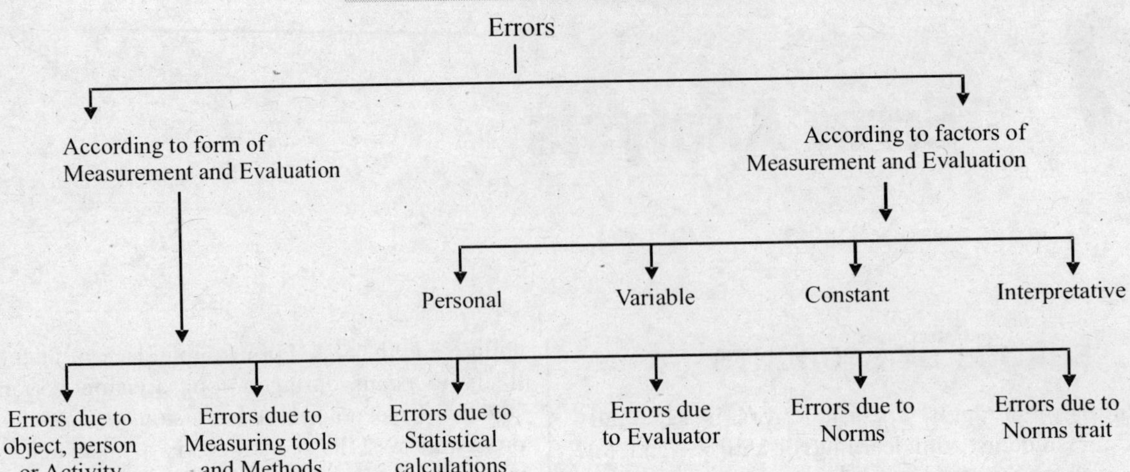

Subject-Related Errors (Object, Person, or Activity)

Errors caused by the physical or mental state of the student (e.g., fatigue, fear, illness, or lack of experience with the test).

Solution: Provide clear instructions beforehand and treat students with empathy.

Tool and Method Errors

Inaccuracy resulting from using the wrong instrument or an inadequate testing method for the specific quality being measured.

Solution: Develop and use objective, valid, and reliable tools.

Evaluator and Personal Errors

Biases, prejudices, or the mental state of the person grading the test. This is common in subjective, descriptive assessments.

Solution: Ensure evaluators remain objective and shift toward objective testing formats.

Technical and Statistical Errors

Statistical: Errors in choosing or calculating data.

Solution: Mastery of statistical methods.

Interpretative: Misinterpreting the final results or data.

Solution: Use correct norms and precise calculations.

Knowledge-Based Errors (Trait and Norms)

Trait: Lack of clarity on what specific quality is being measured.

Solution: Clearly define the traits to be assessed before testing.

Norms: Lack of understanding of the standards (norms) used to analyze results.

Solution: Ensure evaluators are trained on standardized norms.

Procedural Errors

Variable Errors: Random inconsistencies in administration or student state.

Solution: Standardize administration and use suitable methods.

Constant Errors: Systematic flaws in tools that affect all students equally (e.g., a poorly phrased question).

Solution: Refine tools to ensure high validity.

8 Diagnostic Testing & Remedial Teaching

Our main role as a teacher is to promote quality learning among the students. This is possible only when we act as a guide and the students actively participate in the process of lĕarning. During the teaching-learning process, we have to locate and identify the areas where the learner commits mistakes. It is the crucial stage of the teaching-learning process where we have to diagnose and prepare instructional material for Remedial Teaching to ensure the desired quality of learning.

At this stage the role of a teacher is just like a doctor's. The doctor takes all the steps necessary to diagnose the disease by performing different tests and then prescribes medicines for the particular disease.

In the case of education the process of diagnostic testing is the step and remedial teaching is the prescription. Hence diagnostic testing and remedial teaching are very essential for ensuring effective learning and in improving the quality of education.

TYPES OF DIAGNOSTIC TESTS

- **Educational**
  [These tests diagnose disorder of study material according to level of class.]
- **Physical/Clinical**
  [These tests diagnose the hearing, vision and other thing that cause hindrance in the course of learning.]

OBJECTIVES OF DIAGNOSTIC TESTING

- To understand the meaning and importance of diagnostic testing;
- To understand the nature and purpose of diagnostic testing;
- To follow the steps and stages of diagnostic testing in the classroom teaching-learning process; and
- To conduct remedial teaching in mathematics in classroom situations

FEATURES OF DIAGNOSTIC TEST

- It is an effective tool for teachers that helps in planning and organising remedial teaching.
- If finds out deficiency and weakness of student in learning of a contents.
- It is a base to form tutorial groups so as helps the poor students to develop their performance removing their differences.
- It is a qualitative test not a quantitative.
- In these tests no scores are made for correct answers only wrong responses are taken into view in the sequence of contents.
- It adopts objective type tests only.
- In needs an expert or specialist to identify the cause for wrong answers.
- It fully emphasises on all learning and teaching points.
- It arranges the items in hearing sequence so as to help transfer of learning position.

FUNCTIONS OF DIAGNOSTIC TEST

- Classification
  - (*i*) Aptitude/Musical level
  - (*ii*) Vocational level
  - (*iii*) Intellectual level
- Assessment of Specific Abilities with Regard to
  - (*i*) Level of Abnormality
  - (*ii*) Level of Adjustment
  - (*iii*) Level of Depression and Anxiety
- Remediation
  - (*i*) Special education for handicapped
  - (*ii*) Counselling for mental Ailment
  - (*iii*) Remedial teaching for learning weakness
  - (*iv*) Clinical treatment for Physical Ailment
- Etology
  - (*i*) Study of diagnosis

DIAGNOSTIC TESTING : MEANING AND IMPORTANCE

In general, after completing a particular unit/topic we conduct a test to assess the achievements of learners. After evaluation we draw some conclusions and we find that some of the students have fared very well and a particular group of students have achieved below your expectations. Now we will have to find out the causes for this low achievement or slow learning. There would be certain reasons for this low achievement. Now it is very essential to find out the particular area where the difficulty lies or the particular concept where the learner commits errors. To locate and identify the areas of learning difficulties leads to Diagnostic Testing.

After identifying the areas where the error lies, we have to find out the reasons due to which the particular child/group of students have not responded well. At this stage we have to play the role of a doctor. If a patient visits the doctor's clinic he suggests different tests relevant to the symptoms observed by him. After getting reports he is in a position to identify and diagnose the disease and then prescribe the medicine for it.

Likewise, as a teacher, we have to first identify and locate the area where the error lies. The process adopted for this purpose in educational situations is known as diagnostic testing. We may say that diagnostic testing implies a detailed study of learning difficulties.

In diagnostic testing the following points must be kept in mind:

(*i*) Who are the pupils who need help?

(*ii*) Where are the errors located ?

(*iii*) Why did the error occur ?

Suppose we have taught the simple method of subtraction of two-digit numbers without borrowing and then conducted a test which indicates the solutions as follows :

Student's name—Anshu.

98	77	85	81	97
– 62	– 52	– 35	– 40	– 67
36	25	5(5)	41	3(7)

After conducting test we are in a position to assess the whole group. This assessment is followed by an analysis *i.e.*, we have to find out about each individual the area of difficulty or the concept where the learner commits errors. For example, Student 'Anshu' has solved all the questions of subtraction of two-digit numbers without borrowing correctly except for the subtraction of one digit from another one-digit number. We find that her answers are 5 – 5 = 5, 7 – 7 = 7. We are in a position to diagnose the particular concept which Anshu could not understand. This is known as diagnostic testing.

While performing a diagnostic test you have the specific aim to analyse the exact nature of the progress made by the learner in a particular topic/unit and to know the particular area of weakness/error which requires a series of carefully graded tests. The main aim of diagnostic testing is to analyse not to assess. It will be more clear in the following example.

Student's name – Ashish

370	590	860	870
– 210	– 230	– 330	– 353
160	360	530	52(0)

513	654	845
– 206	– 352	– 203
307	(2)02	6(0)2

Careless slip

260	280	370
– 109	– 140	– 143
1(0)(0)	240	23(0)

Skill analysis of subtraction performance

We have conducted a test in the classroom to assess subtraction skill. After this assessment we have to find out how many students have not acquired this skill and who they are. For that particular group we will have to prepare a list to find the concept which is not clear to the learner or the particular step where the learner makes mistakes. For instance, in Ashish's case we have found that he makes a mistake when the question involves subtraction of zero from a number or of a number from zero through borrowing from the next digit. Ashish knows how to subtract zero from zero. You can conclude from this analysis that Ashish's makes a mistake only when the concepts of zero and a number come together in subtraction. This is identification of the area of learning difficulties, and the process involved in identifying and testing the problem is called diagnostic testing.

CONSTRUCTION OF DIAGNOSTIC TEST

- Formulate the objectives or outline of contents.
- Analyise the contents into subtopics and its elements.
- Identify the difficulties in the orders of sub-topics.
- Analyse the items and modify them.
- Prepare the final draft of the test.
- Prepare manual of test.
- Remedial devices and measures.

NATURE AND PURPOSE OF DIAGNOSTIC TESTING

If we consider arithmetical attainments from both a qualitative and quantitative standpoints, we can distinguish four main points (*i*) accuracy, (*ii*) speed of writing, (*iii*) methods of work and (*iv*) extent of the arithmetic process mastered.

It is obvious that we will try to find the feedback through the medium of class work or through weekly or monthly tests which indicate pupils' ability in each of the four aforesaid directions. But it is not enough for teaching purposes particularly with those pupils/learners who are slow learners. With this group of learners we are required to have a more analytical estimate of their achievements. Let us take the following example :

After teaching basic operations (addition, subtraction, multiplication and division) to a group of students, we conduct a test of say 10 items and the results are summarized as below :

Items	Errors	Items	Errors
1	2	6	10
2	1	7	8
3	3	8	9
4	2	9	32
5	3	10	32

From the above data it is possible to analyse the test items. It is clear that items 9 and 10 have been missed by most of the students. At this stage we have to re-think to make some modifications in items 9 and 10. This is the stage where we have identified and located the problem and hence diagnosed the area of error committed by the learners. Similarly, for items 6, 7 and 8, we will re-think and evolve instructional material to improve the quality of learning.

The above example suggests that Diagnostic Testing is analytical in nature where the teacher has to look at the performance of pupils in order to examine why they have not learned or mastered the particular concept or competency. For each pupil individually one has to pinpoint the specific kind of mistake he makes. This analysis is based on the date of performance rather than the general opinion of the teacher. It may be interpreted in terms of each students, a group of students, each concept/competency and for each of the questions.

Why should the teacher undertake this kind of probe into the performance of pupils? The obvious response is that he/she wants to ensure the quality of learning (at the level of mastery) and is curious to know what specific action should be taken to obtain the desired results. Thus the main purpose of diagnostic testing is to spot the learning difficulties of pupils with a view to developing corrective measures, termed as remedial teaching.

STEPS AND STAGES IN DIAGNOSTIC TESTING

The essential steps in educational diagnosis are:

(*i*) Identifying the students who are having trouble or need help.

(*ii*) Locating the errors or learning difficulties.

(*iii*) Discovering the causal factors of slow learning.

(*i*) Identifying the students who are having trouble or need help

First, one must know the learners who require help. For this we can administer a general achievement test based on the topics already taught. After evaluation we will be in a position to make lists of students who are below average, average or above average. Next, one has to locate the area where the error occurs in order to have a deeper insight into the pupils' difficulties.

(*ii*) Locating the errors or learning difficulties

After identifying the students who need help and visualising the necessity of additional instructional material to improve the quality of learning, our main role is to find out the area where the learner commits mistakes or which is the area where learning difficulties lie. For example we examine the pupils' responses as follows:

(*i*) $\frac{3}{4}+\frac{5}{4}=\frac{8}{4}$ (*ii*) $\frac{7}{12}+\frac{4}{12}=\frac{11}{12}$

(*iii*) $1+\frac{3}{4}=\frac{④}{4}$ (*iv*) $5+\frac{1}{7}=\frac{⑦}{7}$

(*v*) $\frac{1}{2}+\frac{1}{3}=\frac{②}{⑤}$ (*vi*) $\frac{3}{7}+\frac{4}{5}=\frac{⑦}{⑫}$

From the above example we would realise that the learner has the knowledge of adding fractions having the same denominator but the concept of addition of fractions having different denominators is not clear to him even though it was taught in the classroom. Thus we have located the area where the learning difficulty lies.

(*iii*) Discovering the causal factors of slow learning

In some cases of learning difficulties, the causal factors are relatively simple. A student may be inattentive during teaching-learning or may be committing errors due to insufficient practice or irregular attendance.

Sometimes the cause is ill-health or faulty work habits etc. It has also been observed sometimes that the basic cause of low achievement is a feeling of helplessness or the complexity of the subject-matter which perhaps is much above the level of their comprehension.

Sequential presentation in below shows how diagnosis leads to improved quality of learning.

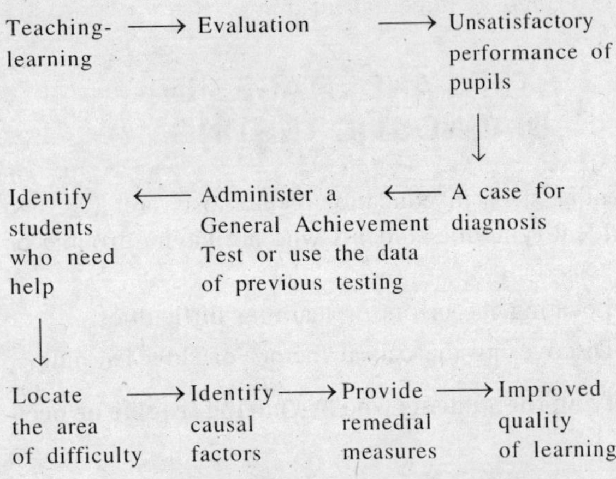

REMEDIAL TEACHING

While diagnosis is the process of investigating the learners' difficulties and the reasons for this, its follow up leads to actions that may help children make up their deficiencies. This step is generally termed Remedial Teaching. So you have to be skilled in preparing or arranging for such materials which may be used to undertake corrective instruction and thus enhancing the quality of learning.

Selection of Materials

The following points should be kept in mind while selecting appropriate instructional material:

(*i*) The corrective material should be designed to correct the students' individual difficulties.

(*ii*) You have to analyse the work of slow learners by means of observation, interview and diagnostic testing. A careful consideration of the three may help decide what kind of corrective material is to be designed and whether material will be adequate to correct the specific difficulties of learners.

(*iii*) The corrective material should be graded, self-directive and should permit students to work independently. Written directions, which accompany the material, should be easily readable and comprehensible by the students.

(*iv*) The corrective material must permit individuals to progress according to their pace.

(*v*) The material should encourage systematic recording of evidence of pupils' progress.

The following examples will illustrate the points discussed above.

For preparing the material for remedial teaching, let us explain the example discussed above. (steps and stages in dignostic testing) In this we had diagnosed that the learners had not understood the concept of adding fractions of the following type:

$$1+\frac{3}{4}, 2+\frac{5}{7}, 3+\frac{6}{7}, \text{ etc.}$$

On the other hand, they had attained mastery over adding fractions of the type

$$\frac{1}{2}+\frac{3}{2}; \frac{3}{2}+\frac{5}{2}; \frac{3}{4}+\frac{5}{4}; \frac{4}{5}+\frac{7}{5}; \text{ etc.}$$

Accordingly, now, we will have to prepare material where the learner should have plenty of opportunity to exercise on equalization of denominators in the given fractions.

$$(i)\ 1+\frac{3}{4}=\frac{1}{1}+\frac{3}{4}=\frac{1\times 4}{1\times 4}+\frac{3}{4}=\frac{4}{4}+\frac{3}{4}=\frac{4+3}{4}=\frac{7}{4}$$

$$(ii)\ 2+\frac{5}{7}=\frac{2}{1}+\frac{5}{7}=\frac{2\times 7}{1\times 7}+\frac{5}{7}=\frac{14}{7}+\frac{5}{7}=\frac{14+5}{7}=\frac{19}{7}$$

Enough practice should be provided to pupils on similar questions until they attain mastery. While selecting and implementing the instructional material the most important thing is the individual need of the student in a particular area. We have to give differential treatment. Different methodologies have to be adopted for different kinds of students. Other modes of interaction such as learner-learner interaction and learner-material interaction may also be utilized, besides the traditional teacher-learner interaction, using appropriate instructional material.

We have learnt about diagnostic testing which is the most important part of the teaching-learning process. It implies a detailed study of learning difficulties. Its aim is to analyse, not to assess. The nature and purpose of diagnostic testing is to identify the areas of difficulties where the learner commits errors.

After locating the area where the difficulty lies, as a teacher we will devise some strategy to remove problems in learning and the causes due to which the learner has faced the difficulties. The strategy used by us to remove the weakness of the learner is known as remedial teaching. Diagnostic testing leads to remedial teaching in which we have to prepare instructional material for quality learning, adopting different methodologies as per needs of the individual or a particular group.

PRACTICE PAPER

1. Which of the following is least appropriate about Formative Assessment in mathematics classrooms?

A. It helps to identify students' misconceptions

B. It provides cumulative evaluations that helps to rank children

C. To check the progress of students during instructional activities

D. To identify students' conceptual understanding

2. What is the most appropriate cognitive skill that help students to recognize and group shapes according to their attributes and properties?

A. Conservation B. Decomposition

C. Classification D. Seriation

3. Students feel difficulty in solving division problems because:

A. Division problems have no utility in daily life.

B. There are no informal ways of solving division problems.

C. For solving division problems students need to know addition, subtraction and multiplication thoroughly.

D. Students do not like the sign of division.

4. Most II graders are able to add two quantities like four candies and three candies, but when asked to do 4 + 5 on a worksheet a large number of the same set of learners is unable to do so. What is the most appropriate explanation of this observation according to National Curriculum Framework 2005?

A. Learners are not interested in learning real-life mathematics

B. The learners are not ready for the use of abstract mathematical symbols

C. Learners are not taught addition properly

D. Some learners are poor in mathematical skills

5. Which of the following is most appropriate for including open ended questions in mathematics class?

A. These questions develop critical thinking in students

B. Answers to these questions are not given in the book

C. These questions take more time to solve

D. These questions are not easy to copy from each other

6. According to National Education Policy 2020 Mathematics and Computational Thinking is to be given increased importance as:

A. It is foundational to evolving technologies like Artificial Intelligence (AI), machine learning and Data Science etc.

B. It can be a substitute for a teacher

C. It is the most difficult aspect of learning in school

D. It is foundational to human survival

7. According to National Curriculum Framework 2005 mathematics teachers need to shift towards:

(*a*) Promoting memorization and rigorous algorithms

(*b*) Mathematical reasoning and logic

(*c*) Becoming sole authority for right answers

Choose the **correct** options:

A. Only (*b*) B. (*b*) and (*c*)

C. Only (*a*) D. (*a*) and (*b*)

8. In order to identify individual differences of students in the mathematics class, which of the following assessment technique will not be appropriate?

A. Summative assessment

B. Formative assessment

C. Diagnostic assessment

D. Peer assessment

9. Which of the following resources is **best** suited to explain the concept of decimals?

(*a*) Number Chart (*b*) Dienes Blocks

(*c*) Taylor's Abacus (*d*) Graph Paper

Choose the **correct** option:

A. Only (*b*) B. (*b*) and (*d*)

C. (*a*) and (*c*) D. (*a*) and (*b*)

10. Which of the following learning experiences for children does not reflect the contribution of mathematics to everyday life and society?

A. Communication of mathematical ideas in writing using both formal and informal languages.

B. Meeting people from different areas of employment and exploring how they use mathematics in their work.
C. Collecting, organising, representing and interpreting data in day-to-day life.
D. Play small group games that draw on mathematical skills and concepts.

11. Which of the following represents the features of a mathematics laboratory?
(*a*) It is a place to enjoy mathematics through informal exploration.
(*b*) It provides opportunities to prove mathematical theorems through experiments.
(*c*) It provides opportunity to make conjectures, test them and to generalise observed patterns.
(*d*) It is used to assess students' knowledge of mathematics and grade them accordingly.
Choose the **correct** option.
A. (*a*) and (*d*) B. (*a*) and (*c*)
C. (*b*) and (*d*) D. (*b*) and (*c*)

12. Which of the following Indian mathematicians are known as founders of 'numerical analysis'?
(*i*) Ramanujan (*ii*) Bhaskaracharya
(*iii*) Varahmihir (*iv*) Aryabhatta
Choose the **correct** option.
A. (*i*) and (*iii*) B. (*ii*) and (*iv*)
C. (*ii*) and (*iii*) D. (*i*) and (*iv*)

13. National Curriculum Framework For Foundational Stage (NCFFS), 2022 highlighted the importance of the following components while teaching an abstract mathematical concept:
(*a*) Written Symbols (*b*) Experience
(*c*) Spoken Language (*d*) Picture
Which of the following is the appropriate sequence of these components while teaching an abstract mathematical concept?
A. $(c) \rightarrow (a) \rightarrow (d) \rightarrow (b)$
B. $(b) \rightarrow (c) \rightarrow (a) \rightarrow (d)$
C. $(c) \rightarrow (d) \rightarrow (a) \rightarrow (b)$
D. $(b) \rightarrow (c) \rightarrow (d) \rightarrow (a)$

14. Which of the following are correct examples of the statement "mathematics is hierarchical in levels that are logically structured"?
(*a*) The concept of integers needs to be developed before the concept of multiplication and division of numbers.
(*b*) Multiplication follows and builds on the concept of addition.
(*c*) Number sense needs to be developed before the concepts of addition and subtraction.
Choose the **correct** option:
A. (*a*) and (*b*) B. (*b*) and (*c*)
C. (*a*) and (*c*) D. only (*b*)

15. A mathematics teacher discusses the concept of open and closed curve in class. For better understanding of students she gave an example with four points. If the curve is open then nature of four points is:
A. All are collinear
B. Two of them must be collinear
C. Three of them must be collinear
D. Three of them must be non-collinear

16. The main approach suggested by National Curriculum Framework (NCF) 2005 in teaching learning of mathematics is:
A. Instructivism B. Pragmatism
C. Behaviourism D. Constructivism

17. Which of the following statement is most appropriate?
A. Charts are used in mathematics class as an effective teaching-learning material
B. Use of teaching-learning material in mathematics class consume students' time for practice
C. Students do not enjoy riddles in mathematics class
D. Mathematics lab is essential as it provides opportunities for hands on activities for students

18. Which of the following is true for word problems in school mathematics?
A. Word problems are not examples of mathematical modelling
B. Word problems are important in secondary classes only
C. Word problems focus more on procedural knowledge in mathematics
D. Word problems refer to exercises where the child formalises the situation into a form where a specific mathematical technique can be applied

19. According to National Education Policy (NEP) 2020, assessment of learners include:
A. Cognitive, affective and psychomotor domains
B. Cognitive, social and spiritual domains
C. Physical and psychological domains
D. Cognitive and physical domains

20. National Education Policy (NEP) - 2020 talks about "Knowledge of India". Which of the following are not included in it?
A. Tribal knowledge, indigenous and traditional ways of learning as part of various subjects like Mathematics, Astronomy, Medicine, Agriculture etc.
B. Field visits to different states as part of cultural exchange programmes.

C. Formal examination to assess the knowledge gained by the students.
D. Knowledge from ancient India and its contributions to modern India

21. According to National Curriculum Framework, 2005, which of the following processes are least relevant in a primary mathematics classroom?
A. Use of patterns
B. Visualization
C. Making connections and representations
D. Memorising formulae

22. Which of the following statements is/are most appropriate for the idea of cognitive conflict in teaching mathematics?
(*a*) Thoughtful efforts of a teacher to expose children to cognitive conflict can enhance their mathematical understanding.
(*b*) It is not useful for promoting mathematical understanding in children.
(*c*) Children get confused so cognitive conflict must be avoided.

Choose the correct option:
A. (*a*) and (*c*) B. Only (*a*)
C. Only (*c*) D. (*b*) and (*c*)

23. Which of the following is not true about 'multiplicity of approaches' in teaching mathematics?
A. It hampers the learning of child as it leads to confusion
B. Offering such a choice allows children to explore and use the approach that is most natural and easy for them
C. It is crucial for liberating school mathematics from the tyranny of the one correct answer
D. Very often, there are many ways of solving a problem

24. Which of the following should be the characteristics of mathematical language at primary level?
(*a*) It should be precise.
(*b*) It must be ambiguous as it can add openness in the subject.
(*c*) It should be reinforced through child's language used in everyday life.
(*d*) It must be highly technical as it will help students to communicate accurately in mathematics.

Choose the correct option:
A. (*a*), (*b*) and (*c*) B. (*a*) and (*c*)
C. (*a*), (*c*) and (*d*) D. (*a*) and (*d*)

25. Which aspect of evaluation is used when a teacher ensures that test made by her fulfils the objectives and criteria of that test?
A. Practicality B. Reliability
C. Consistency D. Validity

26. Which of the following statements about nature of mathematics are most appropriate?
(*a*) It helps the child to be creative.
(*b*) It helps in nurturing the child's imagination.
(*c*) It is based on deductive reasoning.
(*d*) It is always convergent.

Choose the correct option:
A. (*a*), (*b*) and (*c*) B. (*b*) and (*c*)
C. (*a*) and (*c*) D. (*a*) and (*b*)

27. To develop appreciation for mathematics among children, a teacher performs the following activities in the class. Choose the one which is ***not*** effective to achieve her objective.
A. She always praises the student who achieves highest marks in the class in the term-end examination.
B. She shows to children the videos on Indian mathematicians and their contributions.
C. She gives mathematical puzzles and magic squares to be solved in the class.
D. She establishes a mathematics corner in her class where students can perform various mathematical activities.

28. Which of the following statements is ***not*** correct?
A. Errors of the students give information about their thought process.
B. Errors in mathematics are part of learning.
C. Errors in mathematics help teachers in planning their lessons.
D. Errors of the students should be overlooked as pointing errors will demotivate them.

29. Which of the following statements is ***not*** correct about assessment?
A. Norm-referenced assessment is useful in diagnostic testing and remedial teaching.
B. Criterion-referenced assessment is to evaluate the mastery learning of the students.
C. Criterion-referenced assessment is useful in diagnostic testing and remedial teaching.
D. Norm-referenced assessment tells us where a student stands as compared to other students in his/her performance.

30. Mathematical learning material:
(*a*) Helps teachers in demonstrating the formulae.
(*b*) Helps students in self-learning.
(*c*) Helps teachers in providing instructions.
(*d*) Develops learning environment in the class.

Choose the correct option:

A. (*c*) and (*d*) B. (*a*) and (*b*)

C. (*b*) and (*d*) D. (*b*) and (*c*)

31. According to the National Education Policy (NEP) 2020, olympiads and competitions in various subjects will be __________ across the country.

A. made easier B. strengthened

C. discouraged D. reduced

32. Concepts like more-less, long-short, far-near, big-small, etc. are:

A. Vague terms for comparison.

B. Antonyms, not necessary for learning mathematics.

C. Simply English language adjectives.

D. Important pre-number concepts.

33. According to the National Curriculum Framework, 2005, classroom researches have indicated a fairly systematic devaluation of girls as incapable of mastering mathematics even when they perform well in mathematics. What is the most appropriate reason for this?

A. Poor performance of girls in mathematics is due to the fear of mathematics prevalent in them.

B. Mathematics, by its nature, is a male-dominated subject.

C. Gendered constructs of society have led to the belief that boys use more innovative strategies for problem-solving and thus have better conceptual understanding.

D. The mathematical abilities in boys are innate.

34. Classroom researches have shown that most of the students find mathematics more difficult than the other subjects they study in the same class. Which of the following aspects of the nature of mathematics adds to this fear?

A. The vast knowledge base of mathematics

B. The scope of multiple answers to a given question in mathematics

C. The scope of a number of different methods to solve a problem in mathematics

D. The abstract nature of primary concepts in mathematics

35. Who among the following has worked in the field of mathematical astronomy?

A. Aryabhatta B. Bhaskara I

C. Ramanujan D. Mahavira

36. Which of the following depicts a situation where children are constructing knowledge on their own?

A. The best student in the class reads aloud the multiplication tables and rest of the students repeat after him/her.

B. Children are reciting multiplication tables in a chorus.

C. Children are given manipulatives like number grids, tokens arranged in rectangular arrays and they are exploring multiplication patterns using them.

D. Teacher has written incomplete multiplication tables on blackboard and children are completing the tables by writing them on blackboard.

37. A teacher uses role play method in mathematics class. Her aim is:

A. Keeping children busy.

B. Projecting ideas.

C. Entertaining children.

D. Maintaining discipline.

38. According to National Curriculum Framework, 2005, the mathematics curriculum should be:

A. Coherent and Static

B. Ambitious and Static

C. Static and activity-oriented

D. Ambitious and Coherent

39. Which of the following can be considered as a base to develop "algebraic thinking" among primary grade learners?

A. Starting with simple patterns of repeating shapes and then moving to complex patterns involving numbers.

B. Using graphical method to introduce algebraic equations.

C. Introducing algebraic identities to solve the problems.

D. Emphasizing the use of algebra in daily life.

40. Children's mathematical reasoning abilities at primary level can most appropriately be inferred by:

A. step-by-step completion of questions given as home task

B. achievement in regular MCQ-based tests

C. analysing their errors

D. memorising of formal algorithms

41. Which of the following is/are responsible for fear and failure in mathematics according to National Curriculum Framework, 2005?

(*a*) Predominance of symbolic language

(*b*) Cumulative nature of mathematics

(*c*) Gender-Specific abilities

(*d*) Formative assessment techniques

Choose the correct option:

A. Only (*d*) B. (*a*) and (*b*)

C. (*b*) and (*c*) D. (*a*) and (*c*)

42. While deducing the area of a parallelogram from a rectangle, the most common transformation that a teacher does to relate the formula of area of these two shapes is:
A. Flip
B. Rotation
C. The transformation is not possible
D. Translation

43. Which of the following is **not** true for the use of manipulative aids in mathematics at upper-primary level?
A. They help in understanding complex concepts in mathematics.
B. They are used to utilize leisure time in a mathematics classroom.
C. They act as a pedagogical resource for assessment.
D. They help in concrete representation of abstract concepts in mathematics.

44. Following is the conversation between two students about their mathematics class:
A : Lots of questions were going round in my head but I was too scared to ask them.
B : I feel scared of asking questions in mathematics as I would look stupid if I got it wrong.
The situation depicts:
(*a*) A teacher-centered classroom
(*b*) Lack of fearless environment in the mathematics class
(c) Excuses made by most of the students in a mathematics classroom
(*d*) Lack of conceptual understanding of the teacher

Choose the correct option:
A. (*a*) and (*c*) B. (*b*) and (*d*)
C. Only (*c*) D. (*a*) and (*b*)

45. According to the National Education Policy (NEP), 2020, the important principle for imparting quality education and making children self-learners is
A. Learning what to learn
B. Learning where to learn from
C. Learning how to learn
D. Learning whom to learn from

46. Which of the following is important for a teacher while teaching "Estimation"?
A. Teacher must explain that there is one best way to estimate.
B. Teacher should neglect the answers of students whose answers are farthest off from the estimated answer.
C. Teacher should motivate the students with the closest estimate.
D. Teacher should give space for a range of reasonable answers followed by a discussion.

47. The primary objective of a diagnostic test in mathematics is
A. To emphasize parents to keep home tuitions for the child
B. To prepare report-cards of the children
C. To understand the child's learning gaps in mathematics
D. To distribute children in different sections of a class

48. A student in a mathematics class says that a square is both a parallelogram and a rectangle. He further says all rectangles are also parallelograms. According to Van Hiele's theory of geometric thinking, the student is at which level of geometric thinking ?
A. Relationships B. Analysis
C. Visualization D. Axiomatic

49. Teacher gave some objects to children that include a matchbox, a ball, a book, a steel glass and a rope. She asked them to identify the objects which have the most numbers of corners. Which of the following statements is correct for the above situation?
A. Rope should be selected as it is the longest among all the given objects
B. Book should be selected as it has more number of corners than the matchbox
C. Matchbox and book should be related as both of them can be classified in the same category of objects having edge, faces and corners
D. Ball should be selected as it has infinite corners

50. "Continuous and comprehensive" evaluation in mathematics would include:
(*a*) Detailed feedback on the students conceptual understanding
(*b*) Only the collective progress of the class in terms of percentage of students failed or passed
(*c*) Progress of the students throughout the year
(*d*) Minimum levels of learning in mathematics

Choose the correct options:
A. (*b*) and (*d*) B. (*a*), (*b*) and (*d*)
C. (*a*) and (*c*) D. only (*b*)

51. While teaching about measurement of length, a teacher asked the students to measure their table using hand spans and paper clips instead of measuring directly by a scale. What is the most appropriate reason for during this activity?
A. She wants to engage the children in hands-on activity because it is interesting for students
B. She wants her students to learn how to measure length correctly using paper clips
C. She wants her students to practise old ways of measurements using objects

D. She wants the students to understand the need for standard units for measurement

52. A primary school mathematics teacher asked the students to take out 'Ruler' as she was going to teach the topic on length measurement. Students got confused how can they take out a king or queen. Such words are called Homonyms. How can teachers address this challenge in classroom?

A. By asking the English language teacher to teach the word meanings of such words in English class
B. Teacher should draw the attentions of students to the specific meaning being used in mathematical context whenever such words appear in teaching
C. Teacher should prepare a list of such words with their meanings and ask students to memorise them
D. Teacher should ignore this as students eventually would learn many such words when they would practice more question

53. A class III teacher reads out the following problem to her students

"If I subtract '2 ones' from '2 tens' what will be the answer"

One students responded the answer is zero.

Which of the following statement is correct for the above context?

A. The answer given by the student is correct
B. Teacher should use concrete materials to strengthen the concept of place value in student
C. Teacher should give 10 similar problems to practice
D. Teacher should ignore the response of the student and should herself give the right answer and move to next problem to solve

54. While planning a lesson on the concept of addition of fractions a teacher is using the activity of rectangular strip folding. The above activity is a:

A. Content activity
B. Post content activity
C. Pre content activity
D. Wastage of time

55. Which one of the following is the most important characteristic of a good mathematics text book at primary level?

A. Concepts should be introduced through contexts
B. It should only contain numerous questions for practice
C. It should be attractive and colourful
D. Concepts should be introduced through formal algorithms

56. The National curriculum framework (2005) considers that mathematics involves 'a certain way of thinking and reasoning'. The vision can be realized by:

A. Giving special coaching to students
B. Adopting exploratory approach, use of manipulatives connecting concepts to real life, involving students in discussions
C. Rewriting all the text book of mathematics
D. Emphasizing on solving problems given in text book

57. As a mathematics educator what advice will you give to prospective teachers to improve children's performance in mathematics.

A. Get children as many books as possible for practice work
B. Advice parents for tutoring children at home
C. Help children make connections between conceptual and procedural knowledge
D. Plan remedial classes for children at the end of the year

58. The statement 'Teacher acts as a Facilitator, helps students to discover relationships and seek pattern for themselves' is most suited with:

A. Role play
B. Inductive method
C. Analytical method
D. Demonstration

59. A primary class teacher asks his students to collect data on number of boys and girls studying in class V in their neighbourhood (including at least five households). Which of the following most appropriately describes the purpose of this activity?

A. To make students aware of gender differences in their neighbourhood
B. To introduce the topic of data handling
C. To make children familiar with their community
D. To give holiday home work to students

60. Which of the following is least likely to impact teaching-learning in mathematics?

A. Knowing ways in which assessment affected the confidence of learners
B. Providing complete solutions to students' wrong answers
C. Enhanced quality of feedback
D. Using results of assessment to modify teaching

61. Which of the following statements regarding mathematics teaching-learning is **incorrect**?

A. Mathematical knowledge can be created in primary class students through observation of pattern and generalisations.
B. Argumentation and negotiation play an important role in creating mathematical knowledge.

C. Mathematical learning is a social process involving dialogue.
D. Culture and context has no role in constructing mathematical knowledge.

62. Which of the following is the most important aspect of teaching of mathematics at primary level?
A. Preparing for higher education and employment.
B. Promoting and preparing for technology.
C. Making mathematics part of children's life experiences.
D. Developing rigour in calculations.

63. Which of the following statements is **NOT correct** with regard to nature of mathematics?
A. Primary level mathematics is concrete and does not require abstraction.
B. Mathematics uses special vocabulary to communicate ideas precisely.
C. Argumentation skill is important in construction of mathematical knowledge.
D. Mathematical concepts are hierarchical in nature.

64. Which of the following activities is **most likely** to develop spatial reasoning among students?
A. Identifying tessellating figures
B. Drawing bar graphs to represent data
C. Identifying patterns in a number-chart
D. Solving Sudoku puzzles

65. Which of the following is a desirable teaching-learning practice in the context of Mathematics?
A. Open book tests should be avoided.
B. Students should be told to follow the prescribed steps of solving problems.
C. Open ended questions should be avoided to prevent confusion.
D. Intuitive understanding of concepts should be encouraged.

66. The main purpose of introducing 'mapping' in the primary Mathematics curriculum is/are:
(*a*) to promote spatial thinking.
(*b*) to promote proportional reasoning.
(*c*) to make subject easy and interesting.
(*d*) to break the monotony of numbers.
A. (*a*) & (*c*) B. (*a*) & (*d*)
C. (*a*) & (*b*) D. (*b*) & (*c*)

67. Which of the following topics are not part of primary school Mathematics curriculum as per NCF 2005?
A. Tessellation B. Symmetry
C. Patterns D. Ratio

68. Which of the following could be contributing factor to under-achievement in mathematics?
A. Gender
B. Socio-cultural background
C. Nature of Mathematics
D. Innate ability of person

69. Which of the following is the most important aspect of making lesson plan while teaching Mathematics to primary school children?
A. following the sequence of text-book.
B. presenting mathematical concepts in structured manner.
C. providing opportunities to students to allow construction of concepts.
D. writing activities and questions for reference.

70. Which of the following can NOT be considered a feature of a constructivist Mathematics classroom?
A. The role of language and dialogue in learning Mathematics is given due attention.
B. The teacher acknowledges that students may construct multiple understandings from a given interaction.
C. Objective type test items are used as the primary means of assessment.
D. Connections between Mathematics and other curricular areas are highlighted.

71. Which of the following statements is in agreement with the constructionist view of Mathematics?
A. Mathematics is about learning facts.
B. Mathematicians are required to discover the 'truths'.
C. Mathematics is entirely objective.
D. Visualisation is an important aspect of Mathematics.

72. Which of the following activities is best suited for the development of spatial understanding among children?
A. Drawing the top view of a bottle
B. Locating cities on a map
C. Noting the time of moon rise
D. Representing numbers on a number line

73. Which of the following is NOT true with respect to the learning of Mathematics?
A. Ability to perform and excel in Mathematics is innate.
B. Teachers' beliefs about learners have powerful impact on learning outcomes.
C. Students' socio-economic background impacts their performance in Mathematics.
D. School's language of instruction can impact a child's performance in Mathematics.

74. Identify the type of the following word problem:
"I have 6 pencils. Manish has two more than me. How many pencils does Manish have?"
A. Comparison addition B. Comparison subtraction
C. Takeaway addition D. Takeaway subtraction

75. Which material can you use for teaching reading at primary stage?
A. Flannel Board B. Lecture by experts
C. Flash cards D. All of these

76. Objective type questions have
A. reliability B. validity
C. coverage D. All of these

77. Which is not related to affective domain?
A. Knowledge B. Characterisation
C. Valueing D. Receiving

78. Which one is the teaching technique?
A. Interview B. Note making
C. Review D. All of the above

79. The devices used to make teaching method more effective are known as
A. principle of teaching
B. techniques of teaching
C. methodology of teaching
D. None of the above

80. We, as mathematics teacher, evaluate pupil performance for
A. upgrading the students
B. motivating the students
C. assessing teacher's performance
D. All of the above

81. The introductory questions should
A. be based on previous knowledge of the students
B. be easy and not difficult
C. have linkage
D. All of the above

82. Internal qualities of a good mathematics book are
A. good printing
B. psychological presentation of the subject-matter
C. suitable font type and size
D. All of the above

83. Which one of the following is not the principle of teaching
A. exposure B. gradation
C. review D. phonology

84. Solving mistakes take place due to
A. poor text books
B. lack of writing exercises
C. defective pronunciation
D. All of the above

85. Main defects of essay type questions are that
A. they evaluate theory aspect only
B. they are not so reliable
C. they are not so valid
D. All of the above

86. At primary level, we should use .... method for teaching reading.
A. Story method B. Sentence method
C. Phonic method D. All of these

87. Which is not a method of teaching mathematics?
A. Grammar B. Translation
C. Direct method D. Enquiry method

88. Giving assignment of the students is a
A. Technique
B. A.V. Aids
C. Principle of teaching
D. Maxim of teaching

89. What are the points of informative and summative assessment?
A. Objectives
B. Tests
C. Level of Generalisation
D. All of the above

90. The teacher should ask the questions
A. Standing amidst the pupils
B. Speaking loudly
C. Following the principle of variety
D. All of the above

91. Which one of the following is not a teaching technique?
A. Seminar B. Symposium
C. Film and Chart D. Interview

92. At Primary stage, which method for teaching of writing is useful?
A. French method
B. Kindergarten method
C. Play way method
D. All of the above

93. Which teaching technique is not suitable for primary stage?
A. Symposium B. Explanation
C. Drill D. Questioning

94. For evaluation, teacher should use
A. essay type questions
B. oral testing
C. objective type questions
D. All of the above

95. The administration of a teaching unit involves
A. introduction B. presentation
C. evaluation D. All of these

96. An ideal lesson plan is
A. Objective based
B. Based on Previous knowledge
C. Based on Teaching levels
D. All of the above

97. The curriculum means
A. Courses of Study
B. Race Course
C. Syllabus
D. Educational Programme

98. Type of curriculum used in our education is
A. Learner-centred B. Teacher-centred
C. Objective-centred D. Content-centred

99. The curriculum is developed in view of
A. Educational objectives
B. Child development
C. National development
D. All of the above

100. What is characteristic of essay type examination?
A. Validity
B. Reliability
C. Objectivity
D. Depends on memory

101. Which is the main remedial teaching strategy?
A. Tutorial B. Supervised
C. Both 'A' and 'B' D. None of these

102. The more comprehensive plan is
A. Resource Plan B. Unit Plan
C. Lesson Plan D. All of these

103. A unit Plan should
A. be flexible
B. provide a variety
C. consists of familiar topics
D. All of the above

104. Preparation of daily lesson planning includes
A. determination of objectives
B. selection of content
C. determination of methods
D. All of the above

105. Achievement tests are
A. teacher-made B. standardised
C. Both 'A' and 'B' D. None of these

106. What is the basis of remedial teaching?
A. Diagnosis
B. Weakness of the students
C. Individual difference
D. All of the above

107. The function of measurement is
A. prognosis B. diagnosis
C. research D. All of these

108. In team teaching, the participant teachers decide their
A. objectives B. activities
C. ideas D. All of these

109. Error of evaluation is
A. personal error B. constant error
C. variable error D. All of the above

110. Evaluation is a process of
A. qualitative B. quantitative
C. Both 'A' and 'B' D. None of these

111. Mathematics is the sciences of
A. space B. numbers
C. calculations D. All of these

112. Who said that, 'Mathematics is the science which draws necessary conclusions'?
A. Hogben B. Locke
C. Benjamin Peirce D. None of these

113. The nature of mathematics is
A. ornamental B. logical
C. difficult D. not for common

114. Which work is not related with a teacher?
A. Planning B. Teaching
C. Guidance D. Budgeting

115. What is characteristic of the unit approach of curriculum?
A. Child centred B. Content centred
C. Objective centred D. Teacher centred

116. The team teaching is a method of
A. playing game B. teaching
C. physical exercise D. None of these

117. Characteristics of good questions are
A. realisation of aims
B. thought provoking
C. brief and direct
D. All of the above

118. What is the basis of teaching method?
A. Objective B. Content
C. Both 'A' and 'B' D. None of these

119. The most effective teaching aid
A. Non-projected B. Direct experience
C. Projected D. None of these

120. The most useful teaching aid in mathematics is
A. visual aid B. audio aid
C. audio visual aid D. None of these

121. The most use of teaching aids are in
A. arithmetic B. algebra
C. science D. trigonometry

122. A good objective should be
A. related to teacher
B. testable
C. small
D. attractive

123. Introductory questions are asked
A. in the beginning of the lesson
B. in midway
C. at the end
D. at every stage

124. Memory questions are used to test
A. previous knowledge of pupils
B. present knowledge of pupils
C. interest of the pupils
D. discipline

125. The aims of questioning are
A. to motivate the pupils
B. to create interest and curiosity
C. to test the previous knowledge
D. All of the above

126. Which is the teacher-centred method?
A. Source method
B. Lecture method
C. Project method
D. Socialised Recitation

127. Micro-teaching helps in
A. controlling indiscipline
B. encouraging indiscipline
C. Both 'A' and 'B'
D. None of the above

128. Achievement test for
A. test of minimum performance
B. test of maximum performance
C. test of natural performance
D. test of performance

129. Which problem in classroom is due to curriculum?
A. Cleanliness B. Indiscipline
C. Teaching D. Discipline

130. In the scope of educational diagnosis use is made of
A. interview B. diagnostic test
C. observation D. All of these

ANSWERS

1	2	3	4	5	6	7	8	9	10
B	C	C	B	A	A	A	A	B	A
11	**12**	**13**	**14**	**15**	**16**	**17**	**18**	**19**	**20**
B	A	D	B	A.	D	D	D	A	C
21	**22**	**23**	**24**	**25**	**26**	**27**	**28**	**29**	**30**
D	B	A	B	D	A	A	D	A	C
31	**32**	**33**	**34**	**35**	**36**	**37**	**38**	**39**	**40**
B	D	C	D	B	C	B	D	A	C
41	**42**	**43**	**44**	**45**	**46**	**47**	**48**	**49**	**50**
B	A	B	D	C	D	C	A	C	C
51	**52**	**53**	**54**	**55**	**56**	**57**	**58**	**59**	**60**
D	B	B	C	A	B	C	B	B	B
61	**62**	**63**	**64**	**65**	**66**	**67**	**68**	**69**	**70**
D	C	A	B	D	C	D	B	C	C
71	**72**	**73**	**74**	**75**	**76**	**77**	**78**	**79**	**80**
D	A	A	A	C	D	A	D	B	D
81	**82**	**83**	**84**	**85**	**86**	**87**	**88**	**89**	**90**
D	D	C	D	A	B	D	A	D	D
91	**92**	**93**	**94**	**95**	**96**	**97**	**98**	**99**	**100**
C	D	A	D	D	D	B	C	C	D
101	**102**	**103**	**104**	**105**	**106**	**107**	**108**	**109**	**110**
C	C	D	D	C	D	D	B	D	B
111	**112**	**113**	**114**	**115**	**116**	**117**	**118**	**119**	**120**
D	C	B	D	B	D	D	B	A	A
121	**122**	**123**	**124**	**125**	**126**	**127**	**128**	**129**	**130**
C	B	A	A	D	B	A	D	B	D

Environmental Studies

SECTION-A

ENVIRONMENTAL STUDIES

FAMILY

The basic unit of the social structure in every society is the family. The easy and classical definitions emphasized that the family was a group based on marriage, common residence, emotional bonds, and stipulation of domestic services. The family has also been defined as a group based on marital relations, right and duties of parenthood, common habitation and reciprocal relations between parents and children. Some sociologists feel that the family is a social group characterised by common residence, economic cooperation and reproduction.

Nowadays the concept of a family is viewed in terms of certain criteria applicable to all societies. For instance, it is felt that the family is a primary kinship unit which carries out aspects of the sexual, reproductive, economic and educational functions. Keeping in mind these definitions, we generally picture a family as a durable association of husband and wife with or without children. The wide variety of family forms, noticed in societies throughout the world in the course of human history is a cultural phenomenon of considerable interest. For example, with regard to residence in some societies, family are 'matrilocal', where a young married couple takes up residence at the home of the bride's parents. While in 'patrilocal' family, the couple takes up residence at the home of bridegroom's parents.

Another distinction is made between the conjugal family which is also called family of procreation, and consanguineous family which is also called family of orientation.

One can also classify families into nuclear, extended and joint types based on the way they are organised.

The nuclear family consists of a married couple and their children. The extended family is commonly defined as the nuclear family plus all kinds belonging to either side, living together. It may be pointed out that a consanguineous family implies ties of blood.

Universal Nature of Family

The family is the most permanent and pervasive of all social institutions. There is no human society without any family system. All societies both large and small, primitive and civilised, ancient and modern have institutionalised the process of procreation of the species and the meaning of the young.

The same type of family is not found everywhere. There are several types of family. In the west nuclear family is found. This comprises the husband and wife together with their children. In Indian villages and in small towns the extended or joint family is found. This has people in it of two to three or more generations under the same roof.

Main Characteristics of Family

1. **Universality:** There is no human society in which some form of the family does not appear. Malinowski writes the typical family a group consisting of mother, father and their progeny is found in all communities, savage, barbarians and civilized. The irresistible sex need, the urge for reproduction and the common economic needs have contributed to this universality.
2. **Emotional basis:** The family is grounded in emotions and sentiments. It is based on our impulses of mating, procreation, maternal devotion fraternal love and parental care. It is built upon sentiments of love, affection, sympathy, cooperation and friendship.
3. **Limited size:** The family is smaller in size. As a primary group its size is necessarily limited. It is a smallest social unit.
4. **Formative influence:** The family welds an environment which surrounds trains and educates the child. It shapes the personality and moulds the character of its members. It emotionally condition the child.
5. **Nuclear position in the social structure:** The family is the nucleus of all other social organizations. The whole social structure is built of family units.
6. **Responsibility of the members:** The members of the family has certain responsibilities, duties and obligations. MacIver, points out that in times of crisis men may work and fight and die for their country but they toil for their families all their lives.

7. **Social regulation:** The family is guarded both by social taboos and legal regulation. The society takes precaution to safeguard this organisation from any possible breakdown.

Functions of a Family

The function can be discussed as under:

1. According to Kingsley, there are four major social functions of family. These are: reproduction, maintenance, placement, and socialization. MacIver divided the functions of the family into two categories—essential and non-essential. Under the essential he includes three functions:
   (a) stable satisfaction of sex need,
   (b) production of rearing of children, and
   (c) provision of a home.
   Under the non-essential functions he mentions religious, educational, economic, health and recreation. These, he says, have now been transferred to specialized agencies in society.
2. Lundberg has enumerated four basic functions of family:
   (a) The regulations of sexual behaviour and reproductions,
   (b) Care and training of children,
   (c) Co-operation and division of labour, and
   (d) Primary group satisfactions, etc.
3. Ogburn and Nimkoff have divided family functions into six categories:
   (a) Affectional,
   (b) Economic,
   (c) Recreational,
   (d) Protective,
   (e) Religious, and
   (f) Educational.

FOOD

It is a nutritive substance taken by an organism for growth, work, repair and maintaining life processes. It provides energy to do work and maintain body heat, provides materials for the growth of the body, makes necessary materials for reproduction and provides materials for the repair of damaged cells and tissues of our body. Food has many different components and each one is necessary for one or the other function. Major ones are — carbohydrates, fats, proteins, minerals, vitamins, water and roughage.

- **Carbohydrates:** They are made up of three elements - carbon, hydrogen and oxygen, the proportion of hydrogen and oxygen being the same as in water. Glucose ($C_6H_{12}O_6$), Sucrose ($C_{12}H_{22}O_{11}$) and Starch $(C_6H_{10}O_5)_n$ are examples of carbohydrates. They are the main source of energy in our body, with 1 gm of carbohydrates producing about 17 kilojoules of energy upon oxidation. For a normal person, 400 to 500 gms of carbohydrates are required daily but for sportspersons, growing children and nursing mothers, it is on higher side. Cellulose, which forms the cell walls of plants is also a carbohydrate but not a food for human because the enzyme capable of digesting cellulose is not produced in human beings. Cellulose, however, helps in maintaining a healthy digestive system. Sugar is a type of carbohydrate which is sweet in taste. Glucose, Fructose and Sucrose are examples of sugar. The carbohydrates in our food is obtained mainly from plant sources like wheat, rice, maize, potatoes, peas, beans and fruits. During respiration, oxidation of carbohydrates takes place. It is represented as

$$C_6H_{12}O_6 + 6O_2 \rightarrow 6CO_2 + 6H_2O + \text{Energy}$$

- **Fats:** They are esters of long chain fatty acids and an alcohol called glycerol. Fats also contain atoms of carbon, hydrogen and oxygen. However, fats contain less proportion of oxygen as compared to carbohydrates. The main function of fats in the body is to provide a steady source of energy and for this purpose, they are deposited within the body. One gm of fat gives 37 kilojoules of energy which is more than double of that given by carbohydrates. Fats, the richest source of energy to our body, can be stored in the body for subsequent use. Fats, soluble in organic solvents and insoluble in water, also supply fat-soluble vitamins to our body. Fats, as such cannot be absorbed by our body due to insolubility in water and needs to be hydrolysed into simpler substances, soluble in water. A normal diet should contain about 75 gms of fat per day. Fats are supplied to our body by butter, ghee, cheese, milk, egg-yolk, meat, nuts, soyabean and cooking oils. Fats containing saturated fatty acids are solid at ordinary room temperature while those containing. unsaturated fatty acids are in the liquid form. Saturated fats are stable and hence get deposited in the body. Our body can convert carbohydrates into some fatty acids but a few others have to be taken with the food as they cannot be synthesised within the body. These fatty acids, which have to be supplied through the food, are called essential fatty acids. These are unsaturated in nature. Therefore, it is better to use unsaturated fats in our diet.
- **Energy Requirements:** The energy requirement of a body varies according to age, sex, lifestyle, occupation, climate and special situations like pregnancy and lactation. Lesser intake of food gives insufficient energy and leads to sickness. Excess intake of food also creates problems. Following table gives average daily requirements of energy, with women generally needing less energy than men of the same age group.

Age	Energy requirements
5 years	6000 kJ per day
11 years	9000 kJ per day
18 years	11000 kJ per day
Adult (normal work)	9600 kJ per day
Adult (heavy work)	12000 kJ per day
Adult (very heavy work)	16000 kJ per day

- **Proteins:** They are complex organic compounds made up of carbon, hydrogen, oxygen and nitrogen. The building blocks of Protein are Amino acids and there are large number of amino acids. Some proteins also contain sulphur and phosphorus. Proteins are essential for the growth of children and teenagers, and for maintenance and making good the wear and tear of the body tissues in adults. Proteins are made up of nitrogen containing compounds called amino acids. An adult needs about 1 gm of protein per kg of body weight. Proteins can be obtained from the plant as well as animal sources, with groundnuts, beans, whole cereals like wheat and maize and pulses belonging to the former category and fish, eggs, milk, cheese and lean meat belonging to the latter. Milk, meat and eggs contain all the amino acids required by our body.
- **Minerals:** Our body also needs some inorganic substances like metals, non-metals and their salts, though in small amounts. These minerals are needed to build bones, teeth, formation of Red Blood Corpuscles, coagulation of blood, functioning of muscles, nerves and glands, etc. Some of the important minerals needed by our body are — iron, iodine, calcium, phosphorus, sodium, potassium, zinc, copper, magnesium, chloride, fluoride and sulphur. We get most of the minerals in combined form from plant sources. Deficiency of these minerals causes many diseases. The quantity of minerals required vary with about 30 milligram of iron requirement, 1 milligram of iodine requirement and 1 gm of calcium and phosphorus requirement daily for a normal person.
- **Vitamins:** They are complex organic compounds which are necessary for normal growth, good health, good vision, proper digestion and healthy teeth, gums and bones. They act as catalysts in certain chemical reactions of metabolism in our body. They don't provide energy to our body nor form body tissues. Vitamins are needed in small quantities and their deficiency effects eyes, skin, bones, hair and general growth. More than 15 types of vitamins are known and only 2 vitamins — D and K can be formed in our body. Rest are either provided through our diet or taken separately in synthetic form. Vitamin B-complex and C are water soluble vitamins while vitamin A, D, E and K are oil soluble. Vitamin B-Complex is a mixture of 11 vitamins. Following table gives necessity and sources of vitamins.

Vitamin	Necessity	Source
Vitamin A	For maintaining healthy eyesight, normal skin and hair	Cod liver oil, fish, eggs, milk, carrot, leafy vegetables.
Vitamin B_1	For growth, carbohydrate metabolism, functioning of heart, nerves and muscles.	Milk, soya-food, meat, whole cereals, green vegetables.
Vitamin C	For keeping teeth, gums and joints healthy, for increasing resistance of body to infection	Citrus fruits, guava, tomatoes.
Vitamin D	For normal growth of bones and teeth	Milk, eggs, butter, cod liver oil, sun light.
Vitamin E	For normal reproduction, functioning of muscles and protection of liver	Green leafy vegetables, milk, butter, tomato.
Vitamin K	For normal clotting of blood and normal functioning of liver	Green leafy vegetables, soyabean, tomato.

- **Water:** It is essential for our body because it helps in the assimilation of food. About two-thirds of a man's body is the water in his tissues. Water also helps in digestion, transport, excretion and regulating body temperatures. The survival time without water is very short. Amount of water needed depends on one's age, type of work and the climate. Dehydration is caused by excessive loss of water from the body.
- **Roughage:** It is the fibrous material present in plants and their products. It mainly consists of the indigestible plant carbohydrates called cellulose. Though it does not provide any energy to the body, yet keeps the digestive system in order, by helping in retaining water in the body and preserving constitution. The main source of roughage are salads, cabbage, corn cob, porridge, vegetables and fruits with stems.

DISEASES

Communicable Diseases

They are the diseases which can be transmitted from reservoirs of infection or infected person to the healthy but susceptible persons. The disease causing agent or the pathogen can be transmitted directly or indirectly. Direct transmission occurs:

(*i*) By direct contact with an infected person, e.g., chickenpox, smallpox, measles, leprosy, ringworm, gonorrhea, syphilis etc.

(*ii*) Through sneezing, coughing, talking with infected person or spitting, e.g., diphtheria, influenza, common cold, measles, tuberculosis, pneumonia, mumps, whopping cough.

(*iii*) Through contact of injuries with soil, e.g., tetanus.

(*iv*) Through animal bites, e.g., rabies.

(*v*) Through placenta from mother to the foetus, e.g., German measles.

Indirect transmission takes place through some intermediate agents:

(*i*) Through agency of some vectors, e.g., African sleeping sickness is spread by Tse Tse fly, Kala-azar by sand fly, malaria by female Anopheles, Yellow fever by Aedes mosquito, Filariasis by Culex mosquito, Bubonic plague by Rat flea and Typhoid, cholera, amoebic dysentery by housefly.

(*ii*) By agencies like blood, water, food, e.g., cholera, dysentery, typhoid, AIDS.

(*iii*) Through contaminated articles like towels, handkerchief, toys, soap, utensils, surgical instruments.

(*iv*) By wind currents, aerosol sprays and dust.

(*v*) Through unclean hands, e.g., Enterobiesis.

Deficiency Diseases

These occur due to deficiency of some nutrients in the diet or some hormone due to hypo activity or damage to endocrine glands.

Diet Deficiency	*Disease*	*Symptoms*
Protein	Kwashiorkor	Swelling of abdomen and feet; enlarged liver; skin becomes dark and scaly.
Protein-energy malnutrition	Marasmus	Rapid weight loss; body growth and brain weight lowered.
Vitamin A	Night-blindness, Xerophthalmia	Inability to see in dim light; extreme dryness of eyes; defective teeth formation; dry skin; retarded growth in children.
Vitamin B_1	Beri-Beri	Swelling and Pain in legs, loss of appetite; weakness; palpitation; headache.
Vitamin B_2	Cheilosis	Cracking of skin; inflammation of mouth and tongue; retarded growth.
Vitamin B_5	Pellagra	Skin eczema; swelling of gums; mental disturbances; disturbance of digestive tract.
Vitamin C	Scurvy	Swelling and bleeding of gums; pain in the muscles and joints; General weakness and fatigue; decreased resistance to cold; long time for wound healing.
Vitamin D	Rickets (inchildren), (in adult) Osteomalacia	Twisting of bones; bending of bones.
Vitamin K	Hypothrombinemia	Reduced capacity of clotting.
Iron	Anaemia	Loss of appetite; loss of weight; body looks pale; early tiredness.
Iodine	Goitre	Retarded growth; mental disability; enlargement of thyroid gland.
Fluoride	Dental caries	Loosing of teeth; swelling and bleeding of gums.
Calcium and phosphorus	Affects formation of bones and teeth	Weakening of bones; loss of teeth enamel; pain in the bones
Insulin	Diabetes	Sugar level in blood increases; person becomes more susceptible to infections.
Thyroxine	Cretinism (child), Goitre	Mental retardation; physical growth stunted; small skeleton.
STH	Dwarfism	Diminished growth of the bones; person becomes dwarf, caused by lower activity of pituitary gland.
	Gigantism	Hyperactivity of pituitary gland causes excessive growth of the bones; person becomes abnormally tall.

Allergic Disease

In these diseases, body becomes hypersensitive to some foreign agents, allergens, which cause inflammation when come in contact with the body or enter inside the body. Foreign agents can be dust, pollens, certain-foods, serum, certain drugs or fabrics. The unfavourable response of the body to allergens is called allergic reaction. Asthma and hay fever are allergic diseases.

Degenerative Diseases

These occur due to degenerative changes in some vital organs of the body. Deposition of calcium salts or cholesterol in the walls of the blood vessels, hypertension or high blood pressure, reduced blood supply to heart muscles, clot formation in the coronary artery and back flow of blood from the ventricles to auricles are degenerative diseases of heart and blood vessels of the body. Obstruction of blood circulation to brain and stroke, epilepsy and inflammation of joints (arthritis) also belong to this category of diseases.

Cancer: It is characterised by uncontrolled growth and division of certain body tissues, forming a tumour. The rate of cell division is much higher than that of normal cells. All tumours are not cancerous. These cells have less survival capability than the normal cells and due to less adhesiveness, generally wander through the tissues to cause cancerous growth in different parts of the body. Cancer is neither contagious nor hereditary disease. The agents inducing cancer growth fire called carcinogens. Cancer can be caused by radiations (X-rays, gamma rays and particulate radiations); physical irritants (certain foods causing continued abrasion of the linings of the intestinal tract), chemical agents (caffeine, polycyclic hydrocarbons, heavy metallic ions, hormones), biological agents (viruses). The body organs, affected by cancerous cells are breast, stomach, lung, skin, pancreas, bones, muscles, lymph nodes, urinary bladder, vagina, liver and blood. Blood cancer is called Leukaemia. It is characterised by increased WBC count of the blood. The malignant tumour that grow rapidly and damage the normal cells, needs to be removed immediately otherwise could cause death. Danger signs of cancer are: persisting tumour, any wound not healing, any wound with continuous bleeding, persistent indigestion, rapid change in appearance of warts, persistent changes in bowel movements, persistent hoarseness in voice or coughing or swallowing or unexpected loss of weight.

Congenital Diseases

These are inborn diseases which are present from the birth. These are inheritable and are generally caused by gene or chromosomal mutations. These are Albinism, Sickle cell anaemia, Thalassemia, Hemophilia, Wilson's diseases and Anophthalmia. Some genetic disorders are caused due to changes in chromosomes number in the offsprings e.g. Dow's syndrome (mongolism), Klinefelter's syndrome, Turner's syndrome or super males/females.

Bacterial Diseases

Bacteria are minute organisms which are known to cause a number of diseases:

Disease	*Incubation period*	*Spread through*	*Symptoms*
Tuberculosis	2-10 weeks	Air-borne, droplet infection	Fever, coughing, chest pain and bloody sputum. Any part of body can be effected but lung is most common.
Diptheria	2-6 days	Air-borne droplet infection	Inflammation of mucus membrane of nose, throat and tonsils. In severe cases respiratory tract is blocked. Generally affects children below the age of 5 years.
Cholera	6 hours to 2-3 days	Contaminated food and water. House flies are the vectors	Acutc diarrhoea, muscular cramps, sunken eyes, low blood pressure, dehydration, loss of minerals in urine.
Leprosy	Upto 5 years	Prolonged and intimate contact	Deformity of fingers and toes, formation ulcers, scaly and nodulated skins, infected skin becomes senseless.
Whopping cough	7-14 days	Droplet infection	Mild fever, severe coughing, vomiting, accumulation of muscles in respiratory tract, interfering in respiration.
Tetanus	3-21 days	Entry of cysts through any wound made by sharp object, dog bite or fall on the road	Restlessness, pulling pain in the wound, convulsions, stiffness of neck, rigid jaw muscles, contraction of muscles and paralysis.
Typhoid	1-3 weeks	Directed and Contact	Headache, classic typhoid fever, haemorrhage and ulceration of intestines, lashes on chest and upper abdomen.
Plague	2-6 days	Rats and bedbugs transmit the germs	High fever, extreme weakness, enlargement of lymph nodes, haemorrhage of bronchi and lungs.
Pneumonia	1-3 days	Air-borne	Collection of lymph, mucus in the bronchioles and alveoli. Reduced respiratory efficiency.

Gonorrhoea, syphilis, diarrhoeal diseases, food poisoning and meningitis are also caused by bacterias.

Viral Diseases

Disease	Incubation period	Spread through	Symptoms
Chicken-pox	12-20 days	Direct contact with infected persons or infected objects	Fever, headache, loss of appetite followed by dark red coloured rashes on the whole body. After some days rashes dry forming crusts which finally fall and patient recovers. Children below age of 5 years are more likely to catch the virus.
Smallpox	12 days	Droplet infection	Sudden high fever, headache, painful whole body followed by rashes. Rashes change into postulates with fluid. Rashes dry up leaving permanent pockmarks.
Poliomyelitis	7-14 days	Direct and oral	Headache and fever followed by stiffness of neck and convulsions. Finally, legs become paralysed. If respiratory centres are damaged, breathing fails and causes death.
Measles	10 days	Droplet infection	Common cold, headache, fever followed by coughing, sneezing, skin eruptions, conjunctivitis.
Mumps	12-26 days	Droplet infection	Painful enlargement of salivary gland high fever, difficulty in the movement of jaws and opening of mouth.
Rabies	1-3 months	Bite of rabied animal like dogs, monkeys, cates	100% fatal disease, causes severe headache, high fever and painful contraction of muscles of throat and chest. Patient fears from water. So, the disease is also called hydrophobia.
Influenza	24-28 hours	Air-borne	Bronchitis, coughing, bronchopneumonia.

AIDS

Acquired Immuno Deficiency Syndrome (AIDS) is caused by a virus which weakens the human body's immunity or self defence mechanism. Since natural immunity of the body gets reduced, AIDS makes body prone to many other infections. The patient suffering from AIDS actually die from other infections or diseases. AIDS disease usually spreads through sexual contact, transfusion of infected blood, use of infected needles for injections or from infected mother to the foetus. No medicine or vaccine has been developed to cure AIDS. Precaution is recommended to avoid AIDS.

Diseases Caused by Protozoa

Amoebiasis (Amoebic dysentery), Malaria, Kala-azar, Trypanosomiasis and Giardiasis are main diseases caused by protozoans. Malaria is a parasitic infection. When mosquito bites man to suck blood, it introduces the saliva containing the malarial parasite into blood stream of the man.

FOOD CHAIN

Flow of energy in an ecosystem is one way process. The sequence of organism through which the energy flows, is known as food chain. Plants are eaten by insects, insects are eaten by frogs, the frogs are eaten by fish and fishes are eaten by humans. The pattern of eating and being eaten forms a linear chain called food chain. Such a food chain can always be traced back to the producers.

The primary producers trap radiant energy of the sun and transfers to chemical or potential energy of organic compounds like proteins, fats and carbohydrates. The formation of ATP during photosynthesis is the first nutritional level. ATP is stored in food matter which is utilized by herbivores, the plant eaters. This process constitutes the second trophic level. When a herbivores animal eats the plant, the organic compounds are oxidised and the energy is liberated. Some of the energy is produced as heat which is not a useful energy. Flow of energy is greatly reduced at each successive level of nutrition because of the energy utilisation by the organisms and heat loses at each step in transformation of energy. This accounts for the decrease in biomass at each successive levels.

A typical food chain of an Indian rivers is as follows :

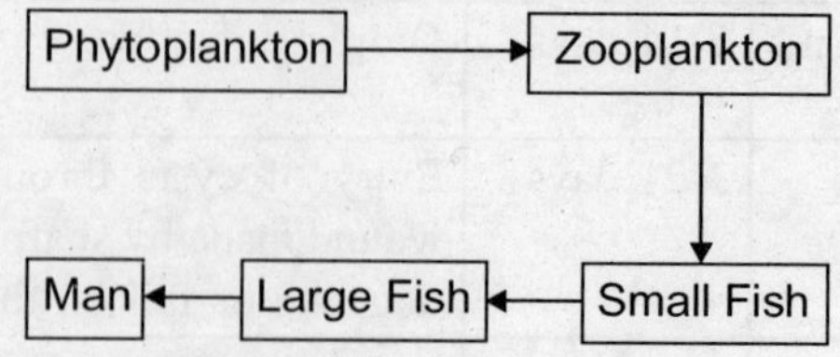

A typical food chain of an Indian river.

It should be noted that the number of steps in a food chain are always restricted to maximum four or five steps. Humans are at the end of a number of food chains.

Types of Food Chain

There are three types of food chain in the nature.

(i) Grazing Food Chain

The consumers (which starts the food chain) utilising the plant as their food, constitute grazing food chain. This food chain begins from green plants and the primary consumer is herbivore. Most of the ecosystem in nature follows this type of food chain. From energy view point such chains are very important. For example:

Grass → Grasshopper → Birds → Falcon.

(ii) Detritus Food Chain

The organic wastes exudates, and dead matter derived from grazing food chain are termed as detritus. This type of food chain starts from dead organic matter of decaying animals and plant bodies to the micro-organisms and then to detritus feeding organism and to other predators.

The food chain depends mainly on the influx of organic matter produced in another system. It represent an important component in the energy flow of an ecosystem. The organism of the food chain include algae, bacteria, fungi, protozoa, insects, nematodes etc.

In a community of organisms in a shallow sea, about 30% of the total energy flows via detritus food chain. However, in a forest with large biomass of plants and a relatively small biomass of animals even larger portion of energy flow may be obtained via detritus pathways.

Significance of Food Chain

The knowledge of food chain helps in understanding the feeding relationship as well as the interaction between organism and ecosystem. Besides its also help in understanding the mechanism of energy flow and circulation of matter in ecosystem. In addition to these, it also helps to understand the movement of toxic substance and the problem associated with biological magnification in the ecosystem.

Food chains are not always as simple as it looks. Quite often several different species of food organism.

FOOD WEB

A food chain represents only one part of energy flow through an ecosystem, whereas the ecosystem may consist of several interrelated food chains. But for simplicity, in general, a food chain implies a simple isolated relationship which rarely occurs in ecosystems. The same food resource may be a part of more than one chain. This is possible when the resource is at the lower trophic level. Accordingly the inter connected networks of feeding relationships is known as food webs. Most animals in nature utilize more than one species for their food. Therefore, food chains in an ecosystem become interconnected with each other which are summarised in Fig. below.

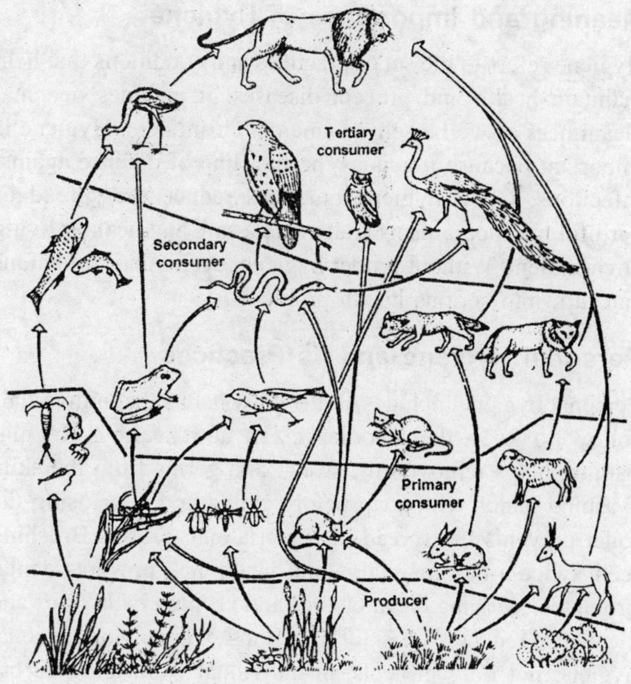

Food web

Several different trophic levels are recognised in any complex food webs. This is mentioned as under:

(*i*) Producer	Green plants	First trophic level
(*ii*) Primary consumers	Herbivores	Second trophic level
(*iii*) Secondary consumers	Carnivores	Third trophic level
(*iv*) Tertiary consumers	Higher carnivores	Fourth trophic level

An example of food web may consist of as many as food chain.

For example:

(*i*) Grass → Grasshopper → Hawk
(*ii*) Grass → Grasshopper → Lizard → Hawk
(*iii*) Grass → Rabbit → Hawk
(*iv*) Grass → Mouse → Hawk
(*v*) Grass → Mouse → Snake → Hawk

HEALTH AND HYGIENE

Meaning and Concept of Health

Health is a state of complete physical, mental, and social well-being, and not merely the absence of disease or illness. Physical health refers to the proper functioning of the body and its organs. Mental health includes emotional stability, positive thinking, and the ability to handle stress. Social health involves the ability to interact effectively with others and maintain healthy relationships. Thus, health is a comprehensive concept that includes all aspects of human life and ensures overall development.

Meaning and Importance of Hygiene

Hygiene refers to the set of practices and conditions that help maintain health and prevent diseases. It includes personal cleanliness as well as environmental cleanliness. Hygiene is important because it acts as the first line of defense against infections. Good hygiene practices reduce the spread of harmful microorganisms and create a safe and healthy living environment. Without proper hygiene, even minor infections can turn into serious health problems.

Personal Hygiene and Its Practices

Personal hygiene includes all the daily habits that individuals follow to keep their bodies clean and healthy. Regular bathing helps remove dirt, sweat, and germs from the skin. Washing hands with soap before eating and after using the toilet prevents the spread of bacteria and viruses. Brushing teeth twice a day maintains oral health and prevents dental problems. Wearing clean clothes and keeping nails short and clean also reduce the risk of infections. Maintaining personal hygiene not only protects an individual from diseases but also improves confidence and social acceptance.

Environmental Hygiene and Clean Surroundings

Environmental hygiene refers to maintaining cleanliness in the surroundings where people live, study, and work. It includes proper disposal of waste, use of clean drinking water, maintenance of toilets and drainage systems, and control of pollution. Clean surroundings prevent the breeding of disease-causing organisms such as bacteria, viruses, and insects. For example, stagnant water can become a breeding ground for mosquitoes, leading to diseases like malaria and dengue. Therefore, maintaining environmental hygiene is essential for community health.

Diseases Caused by Poor Hygiene

Lack of proper hygiene can result in the spread of various communicable diseases. Water-borne diseases such as cholera, typhoid, and diarrhea are caused by contaminated water. Air-borne diseases like tuberculosis and the common cold spread through the air by coughing and sneezing. Vector-borne diseases such as malaria and dengue are transmitted through insects like mosquitoes. These diseases can be controlled and prevented by following proper hygiene practices and maintaining cleanliness in the environment.

Role of Balanced Diet in Health

A balanced diet plays a crucial role in maintaining good health. It provides the body with essential nutrients such as carbohydrates for energy, proteins for growth and repair, fats for energy storage, and vitamins and minerals for proper functioning of the body. Drinking sufficient clean water is also necessary for digestion and removal of waste from the body. A well-balanced diet strengthens the immune system and helps the body resist infections and diseases.

Role of Schools and Teachers in Promoting Health and Hygiene

Schools and teachers have a significant role in developing awareness about health and hygiene among children. Teachers can educate students about the importance of cleanliness, proper nutrition, and healthy habits. Schools should provide clean drinking water, proper sanitation facilities, and a hygienic environment. Activities such as health education programs, cleanliness drives, and handwashing campaigns can help inculcate good habits in students. When children learn these practices at an early age, they are more likely to follow them throughout their lives.

ACCOMMODATION

Accommodation refers to the place or arrangement where people live or stay. It is a fundamental human necessity, along with food, water, and clothing. Accommodation provides shelter, protection, and safety from natural forces such as rain, wind, sun, cold, and storms. A proper and well-planned accommodation ensures comfort, security, privacy, and a healthy living environment for individuals and families.

Importance of Accommodation

Accommodation plays a vital role in human life. Its significance can be described in multiple ways:

1. **Protection from Natural Hazards:** Well-built houses safeguard people from storms, floods, extreme heat or cold, and other environmental threats.
2. **Health and Hygiene:** Proper accommodation with clean water, sanitation, drainage, and ventilation prevents the spread of diseases such as cholera, typhoid, respiratory infections, and malaria.
3. **Privacy and Security:** Accommodation provides personal space, ensures safety from strangers or wild animals, and promotes a sense of mental security.
4. **Social and Cultural Significance:** The type of house often reflects traditions, culture, social status, and lifestyle of the residents.
5. **Stability and Productivity:** Comfortable accommodation supports regular routines, education, work, and social interactions, allowing individuals to lead a productive and balanced life.

Types of Accommodation

Accommodation can be classified based on structure, materials, purpose, and duration:

1. **Traditional Houses**
   - Made of natural materials like mud, bamboo, wood, leaves, or thatch.

- Commonly found in villages and rural areas.
- Adapted to local climate and resources.

2. **Modern Houses**
   - Constructed using bricks, cement, concrete, and steel.
   - Equipped with modern facilities such as electricity, water supply, and sanitation.
   - Found mainly in urban and semi-urban areas.
3. **Apartments / Flats**
   - Multi-storey buildings designed to accommodate a large population in cities.
   - Efficient use of limited urban space with facilities like lifts, water supply, and parking.
4. **Temporary Shelters**
   - Tents or makeshift structures used during emergencies, disasters, or by nomadic communities.
   - Provide short-term protection and mobility.
   - Choice of accommodation depends on climate, availability of materials, socio-economic conditions, and cultural practices.

Accommodation and Climate

Houses are often designed according to the local climate to provide comfort and durability:

1. **Hot Regions:**
   - Thick walls to block heat
   - Small windows to reduce sunlight
   - Ventilated roofs to allow air circulation
2. **Cold Regions:**
   - Insulated walls to retain warmth
   - Smaller openings to prevent heat loss
   - Sloped roofs to allow snow to slide off
3. **Flood-Prone Areas:**
   - Houses built on stilts or raised platforms to avoid water damage
   - Durable materials resistant to water
4. **Windy / Stormy Areas:**
   - Aerodynamic design to reduce wind pressure
   - Reinforced walls and roofs for safety

Health and Hygiene in Accommodation

Proper housing ensures physical and mental well-being. Essential elements include:

- Clean drinking water
- Proper drainage and sewage systems
- Adequate ventilation
- Sanitation facilities (toilets, bathrooms)

Risks of Poor Accommodation

- Overcrowding and unhygienic conditions lead to the spread of infectious diseases.
- Lack of clean water or toilets increases waterborne diseases.

Maintaining cleanliness inside and outside the house is essential for a healthy living environment.

Role of Accommodation in Society

Accommodation is not just a shelter; it reflects culture, lifestyle, and economic status:

1. **Quality of Life:** Safe and comfortable housing improves well-being, social stability, and community development.
2. **Support for Vulnerable Groups:** Governments and organizations provide housing for disaster-affected people, urban slum dwellers, and marginalized communities.
3. **Education and Growth:** Secure housing allows children to attend school regularly and families to engage in work and social activities.
4. **Cultural Identity:** Traditional houses reflect regional culture, architecture, and local customs, preserving heritage and social values.

TREES AND PLANTS

Trees and plants are living organisms that form the foundation of life on Earth. They are primary producers in the ecosystem, which means they can make their own food through photosynthesis, using sunlight, water, and carbon dioxide. Plants include a wide variety of forms such as trees, shrubs, herbs, climbers, and creepers. They provide food, oxygen, and shelter for humans, animals, and other organisms, and are essential for maintaining ecological balance. Without plants, life on Earth would not be possible.

Importance of Trees and Plants

Trees and plants are vital for life and the environment. They produce oxygen, which is essential for all living beings, and absorb carbon dioxide, thus helping to reduce greenhouse gases and combat climate change. Plants provide food in the form of fruits, vegetables, grains, and leaves. They also provide raw materials for clothing, paper, medicines, timber, and fuel. Trees protect soil from erosion, conserve water, and maintain soil fertility. Additionally, they improve air quality, regulate the climate, and make the surroundings beautiful and pleasant.

Types of Plants

Plants can be classified based on size, structure, and their use:

- **Trees:** Large, woody plants with a single main stem, such as mango, neem, and banyan. Trees provide shade, timber, and fruits.

- **Shrubs:** Medium-sized woody plants with multiple stems, like hibiscus and rose. Shrubs are often used for decoration and medicinal purposes.
- **Herbs:** Small, soft-stemmed plants, such as coriander, spinach, and tulsi. Herbs are important for food and medicine.
- **Climbers:** Plants that grow by climbing on supports, like money plant, grapevine, and sweet pea.
- **Creepers:** Plants that spread along the ground, such as pumpkin and watermelon. Creepers help in soil protection and provide food.

Role of Trees and Plants in the Environment

Trees and plants play a crucial role in protecting the environment. They reduce air pollution by absorbing harmful gases, dust, and smoke. Trees provide shelter and food for birds, insects, and small animals, supporting biodiversity. They act as windbreakers, prevent floods by controlling water flow, and reduce heat in urban areas. Forests help in maintaining rainfall patterns and stabilize the climate. Green spaces with more trees improve mental health, reduce stress, and provide recreational areas for humans.

Economic and Social Importance

Plants and trees contribute significantly to the economy. Timber, paper, fruits, vegetables, medicinal plants, and raw materials for industries come from trees and plants. They also play a role in traditional medicine and cultural practices. Socially, trees are considered sacred in many cultures, and festivals and rituals often involve planting or worshiping trees. Urban plantations in parks, roadsides, and schools improve aesthetics and awareness about the importance of greenery.

Ways to Protect Trees and Plants

Protection and conservation of trees and plants are essential for environmental sustainability. People should avoid cutting trees unnecessarily, participate in afforestation programs, and plant more trees in schools, homes, and public areas. Protecting plants from pests and diseases, maintaining gardens, and creating awareness about their importance can help ensure a green and healthy environment. Communities and governments must work together to preserve forests and natural habitats.

Trees and plants are the backbone of life on Earth. They maintain ecological balance, provide essential resources like food, oxygen, and shelter, and improve the quality of life for humans and animals. Protecting and planting trees is not only a responsibility but also a necessity to ensure a sustainable, healthy, and pollution-free environment for present and future generations. Every individual must contribute to conserving and nurturing the green cover of the Earth.

BIOMES

A biome is a large community unit characterized by the kinds of plants and animals present. This may be contrasted to the ecosystem, which is a natural unit of living and non-living components that interact to form a stable system in which the exchange to materials follows a circular path. Thus, an ecosystem might be a small pond or a large area coextensive with a biome, but it includes the physical environment as well as populations of animals, plants and microorganisms.

The definition of biome includes not only the actual climax community of a region, but also the several intermediate communities that precede the climax community. Further, there is usually no sharp line of demarcation between adjacent biomes; instead each blends with the next through a fairly broad transition region termed as **ecotone.** There is, for example, an extensive region in Northern Canada where the tundra and coniferous forest blend in the tundra-coniferous ecotone. Some of the biomes recognized by ecologists are **tundra biome, alpine biome, forest biome, grassland biome, desert biome.**

Tundra Biome

Tundra presents the most common example of "fragile ecosystem". Tundra which means "marshy plain" lies largely north of latitude 60°N (*i.e.,* between the Arctic ocean and polar ice-caps and the forests to the south) and is characterizes by the absence of trees, the presence of dwarfed plants, and an upper ground surface that is wet, spongy and uneven, or hummocky, as a result of freezing and thawing of this poorly drained land. Some five million acres of tundra stretch across Northern America, Northern Europe and Siberia. Although there is variation from place to place within the biome, temperature, precipitation, and evaporation are characteristically slow, the warmest months averaging below 10°C and the wettest with about 25 mm of precipitation. Despite the small amount of precipitation, water is usually not a limiting factor because the rate of evaporation is also very low.

The ground usually remains frozen except for the uppermost 10 to 20 cm, which thaw during the brief summer seasons. The permanently frozen deeper soil layer is called **permafrost**. The permafrost line which may exist at a depth of a few centimetres to several metres, is the ultimate limit of plant root growth, but the immediate control is the depth to which soil is thawed in summer. The rather thin carpet of vegetation of tundra biome includes few species : grasses and sedges are characteristic of numerous marshes and poorly drained areas, but large areas consist of ericaceous heat plants (bilberries and dwarf huckleberries), low flowering herbs, and lichens. Perhaps the most characteristic arctic tundra plant is the lichen known as "reindeer moss" *(Cladonia)*. The animals that have adapted to survive in the tundra are caribou or reindeer, the arctic hare, arctic fox, polar bear, wolves, lemmings, snowyowls ptarmigans and during the summer, swarms of flies, mosquitoes and a host of migratory birds.

Further, certain animals such as caribou and reindeer are highly migratory because there is not enough vegetation produced in any one local area to support them. Though tundras are barren areas yet a surprisingly large number of organisms have become adapted to survive the cold. During the long daylight hours of the brief summer, the rate of primary production is quite high. The production from the vegetation on the land, from the plants in the many shallow ponds that dot the landscape and from the phytoplankton in the adjacent Arctic Ocean provides enough food to support a variety of resident mammals and many kinds of migratory birds and insects. Diversity is very low, and despite the extreme hardiness of the tundra organisms, their growth rate tends to be very low, and the community as a structural unit is exceedingly vulnerable.

Alpine Biome

The region of mountain above the timber line contains a distinct flora and fauna and is referred to as the **alpine zone.** Alpine zone remains conspicuous in those mountains whose peaks reach up to the niveal or snow zone, as in the Himalayas. The alpine zone (zone which lies between timber line and snow zone) includes in the descending order, a **sub-snow zone** immediately below the snow zone a **meadow zone** in the centre and a **shrub zone** which gradually merges into the timber zone. According to **Mani** (1957) snow zone of Himalayas lies over 5100 m above mean sea level and alpine zone exists at a height of 3600 m. From an ecological view point, the zone above the limits of tree growth (timber line) exhibits extreme environmental conditions which greatly influence the biota of this region.

The characteristic features of high altitude environment are following– a low air density, low oxygen and carbon dioxide contents and water vapour, high ozone content, high atmospheric transparency affording greater penetration of light, cold, snow cover, increased rate of desiccation, high, wind velocity, insolation of high intensity during the day and rapid radiation during the night, the high glare from the sky and snow, high intensity of ionizing rediation and the exclusion of trees. Alpine zone of Himalayas is characterized by a sparseness of animal groups, the scarcity being relatively important as far as tropical Indian, South Chinese, Indo-Chinese and Malayan derivatives are concerned. Important constituents of the fauna of this zone are cold-adapted palaearctic forms.

A large number of insects and arachnids remain best adapted to Himalayan alpine zone and at 6900 metres height. The torrential streams which are the products of melting snow contain many mayflies, stoneflies and caddisflies. Some of common insects of this zone are—stonefly *Rhabdiopteryx lunata;* grasshoppers like *Bryodema* and *Gomphomastax;* apterous species *Conophyma; Dicranophyma; Sphingonotus;* tettigonid *Hypsinomus fasciata;* earwigs like *Anechura;* bugs like *Dolmacoris, Tibetocoris,* and *Nysius ericae;* aquatic beetle *Amphizoa;* carbides like *Bembidion.*

Forest Biomes

The word **forest** is derived from Latin *'foris'* meaning outside, the reference being to village boundary fence, and must have included all uncultivated and uninhabitated land. Today a forest is any land managed for the diverse purposes of forestry whether covered with trees, shrubs, climbers, etc., or not. The forest biomes include a complex assemblage of different kinds of biotic communities. Optimum conditions of temperature and ground moisture responsible for the growth of trees contribute greatly to the establishment of forest communities. In addition, 50 mm rainfall is a pre-requisite for the growth of trees. The nature of soil, wind and air currents determines the distribution (abundance or sparseness) of forest vegetation. Normally ecologists recognise among forest communities such features as their evergreen nature, whether deciduous or indeciduous, as well as their shape, whether broad-leaved as in temperate forests of more needle-like as in the conifers. On the basis or these features the forest biomes of the world have been classified into following biomes- **coniferous forest, tropical forest,** and **temperate forest.** All these forest **biomes** are generally arranged on a gradient from north to south or from high altitude to lower altitude.

Coniferous Forest: Cold regions with high rainfall and strongly seasonal climates with long winters and fairly short summers are characterized by boreal conifer forest which is transcontinental. For example, adjacent to the tundra region either at latitude or high altitude is the **northern coniferous** or **boreal forest,** which stretches across both North America and Eurasia just south of the tundra *(i.e.,* Canada, Sweden, Finland, Siberia and Mussoorie). The term **taiga** is applied to the northern range of coniferous forests. This is characterized by evergreen plant species. Large size is common, both in the trees, which range up to some 40 m in height, and in vertebrates, which include the giants of several groups of animals, such as moose, caribou, elk, grizzly bear, wolverine beaver, and several large species of birds. Species diversity is low, and pure stands of trees and shrubs are common, as are outbreaks of defoliating insects of several sorts (*e.g.,* bark beetles, saw flies, geometrid moths, etc.). Understory trees are uncommon as a result of the continual low light penetration. Among common understory associates are orchids and ericaceous shrubs like the blue berry.

Boreal forest soils are thin podozols, and are rather poor both because the weathering of rock proceeds slowly in the cold environments, and because the litter derived from conifer needle is broken down very slowly and is not particularly rich in nutrients. These soils are acidic and mineral deficient, the result of the movement of a large amount of water through the soil; in the absence of a significant counter upward movement of evaporation, soluble essential nutrients like calcium, nitrogen, and potassium are leached sometimes beyond the reach of roots thereby leaving no alkaline-oriented cations to encounter the organic acids of the accumulating litter. The productivity and community stability of a boreal coniferous forest are lower than those of any other biome.

Temperate Deciduous Forest: The temperate forest biomes are characterized by a moderate climate and broad-leaved deciduous trees, which shed their leaves in fall, are bare over winter and grow new foliage in the spring. These forests are the characteristics of North America, Europe, Eastern Asia, Chile, part of Australia and Japan, with a cold winter and an annual rainfall of 75–150 cm and a temperature of 10–20°C. In these biomes the precipitation may be fairly uniform throughout the year. In India, at elevations of 9000–12,000 feet in Himalayas occur temperate vegetation including pines, fir, yew and juniper trees with and undergrowth of scrubby rhododendrons.

Soils of temperate forests are podozolic and fairly deep. Trees are quite tall—about 40–50 m in height their leaves are thin and broad. the predominant genera of this biome are maple, beech, oak, hickory, basswood, Chestnut, cottonwood, sycamore, elm and willow. There are not many epiphytes or lianas save for some species of mosses, algae and lichens growing on tree trunks, and a few vines, notably *Vitis,* the grape. The understory of shrubs and herbs in the deciduous forest is typically well-developed and richly diversified, with a considerable portion of the photosynthesis and flowering attuned to the short days of the spring season, prior to the leafing out of and consequent shading by the tree canopy. One consists of spring flowers, which bloom before the trees have expanded their leaves and are gone by summer, and the other is adapted to the low light levels of the forest floor and lasts into the fall.

The animals originally present in temperate forests are deer, bears, squirrels, gray foxes, bobcats, wild turkey and wood peckers. Other common animals of this region are invertebrates like earthworms, snails, millipedes, Coleoptera and Orthoptera and vertebrates like amphibians such as newts, salamanders, toads, and cricket frogs; reptiles such as turtles, lizards and snakes; mammals such as racoon opossum, pigs, mountain lion, etc., and birds like horned owl, hawks, etc. All these animals and plants show a profound seasonality; some may even hibernate throughout the winter. The range of animal size and adaptations is wide; the largest animals include such forms as the deer and black bear. The dominant carnivores are large, including the wolf and mountainlion, although smaller carnivores such as fox and skunk are also common. Diversity of fauna is lower than in any of the rain forests and a few species seems clearly to the dominant.

Temperate Evergreen Woodland: Many parts of the world have a Mediterranean-type climate with warm, dry summers and cool, moist winters. These are commonly inhabited by low evergreen trees with small hard needles or slightly broader leaves. The most important area of tropical evergreen woodland in North America is the **'Chaparral'** of the Pacific Coast, the Mediterranean **'maquis',** Spanish **'encinar'** and **'melle scrab'** on Australia's South Coast are the same type of community. In such a woodland, trees are essentially lacking, although shrubs may range upto 3–4 m in height. Species diversity is roughly intermediate between that of a temperate deciduous forest and a drier grassland. Fire is an important factor in this ecosystem, and the adaptations of the plants enable them to regenerate quickly after being turned. The characteristic animals of temperate evergreen woodland or chaparral are mule deer, brush rabbits, wood rats, chipmunks, lizards wem-tits and brown towhees. Small-hooved cursorial ungulates are the dominant herbivores. Saltatorial (jumping) animals and many fast moving ungulates are also common in this fauna.

Temperate Rainforests: The temperate rainforest is a colder ecosystem than any other rainforest. Such a forest has a definite seasonality, with both temperatures and rainfall varying throughout the year. Rainfall is high, but fog may be very heavy and actually more important as a source of water than rainfall. The diversity is much lower, both in plants and animals, in comparison to warmer rainforests, yet it remains still higher than other temperate forest types. The dominant trees (canopies) are coast redwood of the Pacific coast of North America and the alpine ash of Australia and Tasmania, both of which reach more than 100 m in height. Epiphytes and lianas are common but are not abundant like those of other rainforests. The animals of temperate rainforests are similar to those of deciduous forests, but show a somewhat higher-diversity.

Tropical Rainforests: Tropical rainforests occur near Southeast Asia (parts of India and Malaysia), Malaya, Borneo, New Guinea and Northwest Australia. Tropical rainforests are among the most diverse communities on earth. Both temperature and humidity are high and constant. The annual rainfall which exceeds 200 to 225 cm is generally evenly distributed throughout the year.

The flora is highly diversified: a square mile may contain 300 different species of trees, a diversity unparalleled in any other biome. The extremely dense vegetation of the tropical rainforests remains vertically stratified with tall trees often covered with vines, creepers, lianas, epiphytic orchids and bromeliads. Under the tall trees is a continuous evergreen carpet, the canopy layer, some 25 to 35 metres tall. The lowest layer is an understory of trees, shrubs, herbs like ferns and palms, all of which become dense where there is a break in the canopy. Nearly all plants are evergreen, and those that do lose their leaves entirely do so at irregular intervals with no apparent regard to the climatic regime. The leaves of most plants are of moderate size, leathery and dark green in colour.

Soils of tropical rainforests are red latosols, and they may be exceedingly thick. The high rate of leaching makes these soils virtually useless for agriculture purposes, but if they are left undisturbed the extremely rapid cycling of nutrients within the litter layer (due to decomposition) can compensate for the natural poverty of the soil. It is the nature of the soil, both its potential for high leaching as well as its chemical composition that promotes a rock-like quality when exposed to air, that largely has prevented western style agriculture from being applied to the tropical forests.

Invertebrate density and abundance are very high in tropical rainforests, but while vertebrates are diverse, they are not as abundant as in many other communities. The common invertebrates of these forests are worms, snails, millipedes, centipedes, scorpions, isopods, spiders, insects, planarians and leeches. Among insects, heteropterans, orthopterans, blattids, mantids, phasmids, bees, termites and ants are most common. Nocturnal and arboreal habits are most common in many mammals such as insectivores, leopards, jungle cats, ant-eaters, giant flying squirrels, monkeys and sloths. But in New Guinea and Northern Queensland, where monkeys are absent, there are arboreal kangaroos despite the fact that the basic anatomy of the kangaroo is not particularly well-suited to arboreal life. Further, in the foot hills of the forest zone of peninsular India covered with dense tropical vegetation, we have the tiger, the elephant samber deer swamp deer as the major ground dwelling mammals.

Tropical Seasonal Forests: Tropical seasonal forests occur in region whose total annual rainfall is very high, but segregated into pronounced wet and dry periods. Tropical seasonal forests are found in Southeast Asia, Central and South America, Northern Australia, Western Africa and the tropical islands of the pacific as well as India and Southeast Asia. In exceedingly wet tropical seasonal forests, commonly known as **monsoon forests,** the annual precipitation may be several times that of the tropical rainforests. Trees may reach heights over 40 m, but are more commonly 20–30 m high. Stratification is of a relatively simple type with a single understory tree layer, canopy is deciduous and understory is evergreen. Teak is often a major large tree in the best-known tropical seasonal forests, those of India (Central India) and Southeast Asia. Bamboo is also an important climax shrub in these areas although in other areas it is important only in earlier stages of the succession.

Tropical Savanna Biomes

Savannas are tropical **grasslands** with scattered, drought-resistant trees which generally do not exceed above ten metres in height and do not form a canopy. Thus, a savanna is an intermediate between a forest and a grassland. Savannas constitute extensive areas in Eastern Africa, which support the richest diversity of grazing mammals in the world, and also occur in Australia, South America and Asia. The climate is generally characterized by a rainy (May to October) and dry (November to April) season; in the llanos of Venezuela, for example, nearly 90 per cent of the annual rainfall of 130 cm falls during the rainy season. The latosol soil of savannas are nutrient poor owing a heavy leaching. Quite widely distributed in savannas are soils called literite which when dried harden to rock-like consistency thereby precluding their use in western style agriculture. Although climate and soil are significant regulating factors in this biome, the controlling factor appears to be fire, which gives grass and certain species of trees a powerful advantage over other tree species.

The trees of savannas are resistant of desiccation, and may be either deciduous or evergreen. Their leaves are often hard and drought-resistant. Grasses are the most conspicuous plants, and may reach heights of 1.5–2 m. Gigantism of certain animal groups in these tropical savannas is as pronounced as it is in the boreal forest including such giants as many antelope, giraffes, elephants, buffalo and lions. In addition, a rich insect an fauna especially those with strong mandibles capable of mastication are conspicuous in this biome. Grasshoppers and termites are encountered in large numbers.

Grassland Biomes

The grassland biome is found where rainfall is about 25 to 75 cm per year, not enough to support a forest, yet more than of a true desert. The seasonality of grasslands is pronounced, both with respect to rainfall, which is concentrated in the summer and to temperature. The grassland communities are open land communities with limited moisture conditions irregular rainfall, sharp seasonal and diurnal variations and very high radiation. Since tall trees or other thick vegetations are excluded from these communities there is a free movement of air. These winds carry the particles of sand or dust. These open habitats provide natural pasture for grazing animals (herbivore) which are excluded from predation by predators which hide in thick vegetation and prey upon them.

In grasslands, the stratification is reduced essentially to a single story, but within that level, species diversity may be as high as in a deciduous forest-especially for the tall grass prairies. Only along the streams are trees to be found, but the "gallery forests" within a few metres of stream bank are characteristics of grasslands. The grasses comprising of the grasslands can be divided into two basic groups, the tall grasses more than 1 m high, which are found in moist portions of the grassland, and the short grasses less than 1 m high, which are found in the drier regions.

Since the precipitation–evaporation ratio is below 1 in the grassland, leaching is considerably less. The soils of the grasslands are rich, fertile prairie soils (black-earths) and chernozems. Organic matter (humus) accumulates in the upper portion of the soil, rendering it dark; this upper portion remains neutral to slightly alkaline because of the continued replenishment of cations like calcium and potassium through the upward movement associated with evaporation.

Typical animals of grasslands tend to be quite small, with the exception of a few very large cursorial herbivore mammals such as the bison and pronghorn in North America, the wild horse, ass, and saiga antelope of Eurasia and zebra and antelops of Southern Africa. The large herbivores are no where near as diverse as they are in savanna areas. Likewise, carnivores are relatively small such as are coyotes, weasels, badgers, foxes, ferrets, owls and rattle snakes, Rodents such as prairie dogs, rabbits, and ground squirrels are common. Most herbivores characteristically aggregate into herds or colonies; this aggregation provides some protection against predators. The characteristic birds of grasslands are prairie chickens, meadow larks, and rodent hawks. Further, saltatorial motion is widespread, not only in mammals such as rabbits and kangaroo rats, but also in insects, such as grasshoppers and crickets. This probably has to do with increasing rate at which animal can move through or over the tall grassess, as well as making it harder for a predator to catch the animal. Visibility in the grasslands is exceedingly good and the premium placed on efficiency including predators is very high.

The common insects of steppes are termites, locusts, bees, burrowing wasps, mutilid wasps, bumble bees and blister bees. The steppes also harbour an undisturbed reptilian fauna. Lizards and steppes also harbour an undisturbed reptilian fauna. Lizards and snakes are met with in large numbers and possess, remarkable diversity. Most of them are fossorial, insectivorous and carnivorous.

Desert Biomes

Deserts are the biome formed in the driest of environments. Temperature may range from very hot as in **hot deserts** to very cold as in **cold deserts.** Major hot deserts of the world are situated near the tropics of cancer and capricon, with a rainfall of less than 10 mm. The most important hot deserts of world is the Sahara-Arabia-Gobi desert complex extending from Africa to Central Asia and contains highly irregular and very insignificant rainfall, and low humidity due to excessive evaporation. Fairly extensive hot deserts also occur in India (Sind-Rajasthan deserts), South America (Chile), North America and Australia. The cold deserts occur at high elevations where the temperatures are low and rainfall scanty as the air losses all its moisture content as it ascends higher and higher. Cold deserts occur in Ladakh regions of Himalayas, Tibet, and Bolivia Arctic. The hot and cold deserts may also be distinguished by differences in plant population which are mostly succulent type (*e.g.*, cactus, palo verde trees, creosote bush, etc.). Most cold deserts have sage bush.

Low erratic precipitation coupled with soil and air temperatures that are extremely high by day and drop abruptly by night, low humidity, and high insulation are the major desiccating environmental factors to which desert vegetation and animals have adapted. Desert plants which tend to be shrubs are adapted to drought conditions through reduced leaf size and the dropping or leaves in dry conditions, both reducing water loss via evapotranspiration. The roots of most desert plants remain well developed and occur in the top metre of the soil to take maximum possible advantage of any rainfall. Further, the root hairs on many desert plants are ephemeral, drying back under drought conditions and thereby reducing potential water loss by osmosis. Yet other species are short lived annuals that complete their life cycles during the short-moist period. In most hot deserts, there occur plants such as cacti, water-storing succulents such as acacias, euphorbias, cacti, prickly pears, etc., which are adapted by their protoplasmic colloids, which enable the accumulation of substantial water reserves, as well as by a reduced leaf surface, which obviates water loss via evapotranspiration.

The animals present in the desert are reptiles, insects and burrowing rodents. All these animals possess special morphological, physiological and ethological adaptations for deserts. In general, large animals are very uncommon except mule, dear and some species of gazelle and all animals have cursorial, fossorial and or saltatorial adaptations. Some desert animals are nicely adapted for high extremes of temperature. For example, the lethal the temperature for different species of insects found to be following–for the canal spider *Galcodes granti* it is 50°C, for the *Gryllus domesticus* it is 40°C and for the forficulid *Labidura riparia* is is 38°C. Diurnal rhythms are perhaps the best method of avoiding the heat. While some desert plants close their petals at night, manu blossom only at night. Some insects like tenebrionid bettle *Akis spinosa* remain active during the day, and the centipede *Scolopendra clavipes* restricts its activities to night time.

Further, certain reptiles and certain insects are well adapted for survival in deserts because of their thick, impervious integuments and the fact they excrete dry waste matter. A few species of mammals have become secondarily adapted to the desert by excreting very concentrated urine.

They avoid the sun by remaining in their burrows during the day. Kangaroo rat and pocket mouse, both are able to live without drinking water by extracting the moisture from the seeds and succulent cactus they eat. The camel and the desert birds (Ostrich, etc.) must have an occasional drink of water but can go for long periods of time using the water stored in the body. Most insects of deserts are herbivores and as a correlation the number of small insectivorous lizards found in the desert is usually high.

THREATS TO BIODIVERSITY

One of the measure threat to Biodiversity is space, food and raw material for expanding human and plant establishment. Wilson 1985 described the losses of biodiversity as "*Crisis*' and this is more serious for developing countries like India. Since 1600 there have been over 1000 recorded extinctions of plants and animals species. Probably early humans were directly reponsible for extinction of many large and smaller mammals. But the elimination of species is a normal process of the natural world. When species die or extinct, they will replace by others. Due to human population and its impact an ecosystems, thousands of species and sub-species become extinct every year. According to E.O. Wilson, we are losing 10,000 organisms a year i.e. 27 per day. If this will continue, we may destroy millions of plants, animals and microbes in next few decades. It is studied that 99% of all species of fossil that ever existed are now extinct.

Before man's appearance on this planet the rate of extinction was one species per thousand years. However, the pressure of human activity has drastically changed the picture. Between 1650 AD and 1950 AD about 30 species of higher animals were lost. Studies show that about 50,000 invertebrates species are losing every year. Almost one recorded as threatened. Indian wild life act 1972 schedule-I provides a list of about 150 endangered species. Disappearance of Dinosaurs along with about 50% of exististing species at the end of Cretaceous period is the best example of extinction. In India 33% of reptiles and 42 of bird species are endemic. It is said that, the current extinction rates are possibly 4 or 5 times more than the rates in the fossil record.

Habitat Loss

Habitat loss due to human activities and other disturbances are welknown factor. Varying human disturbances are changing ecosystems and are thus threatening the biodiversity. Due to habitat degradation wild population become more volnerable to predators and diseases. This is especially true for wildlife, which suffer due to habitat loss and fragmentation. Habitat loss is in instalments so that the habitat is divided into small and scattered patches i.e. *habitat fragmentation*. The natural forests and grasslands, which were the natural homes of thousands species including wild life species, are going cleared day by day for conversion into agriculture lands, pastures, settlements or for development projects. Thus these species are perished due to loss of their habitat.

Due to pollution and the presence of toxic and hazardous pollutants, our fresh water resources have suffered and many species of aquatic birds, fish and mammals have been threatened. Electric power plants, which causes thermal pollution in biosphere affected all aquatic communities and their natural food chains. Marine biodiversity is also under serious threat due to human intervention. If the present rate of deforestation continue, there will be loss of about 12% birds species and about 15% plant species in South and Central America. Huge amount of habitat are lost each year as the world's forests are cut down. Rain forests, tropical dry forests, wet lands, mangroves and grasslands are threatened habitats and leading to desertification. Problems of acid rains and global climate change are also wellknown for habitat loss.

Poaching of Wildlife

Poaching is another threat to wildlife. As an ancient period, hunters, collectors, and smugglers (traders) are the measure threat to a number of species including endangered species. They collected furs, hides, horns, tusks, and some live specimens, herbal products and smuggled to others for millions of dollars. The alarming point in this case is that for one animal they killed more than one. It is an illegal trade and internationally banned.

The cost of these animal parts are surprising. The cost of Bengal tiger coat is more than one lac dollars. South American ocelot costs more than 50,000 dollars, a single orchid cost more than 5000 dollars, horns of rhinoceros cost their weight in gold. These are some examples by which we can understand the situation of trading wildlife products, which is highly profit making for poachers.

Over collection and over exploitation are the main causes of disappearance of plants of scientific and medicinal value. The reduction of genetic diversity among the cultivated species drastically limit possibilities of creating new cultivar in the future, which could be disastrous for human race. It is advisable that do not purchase the parts and products made from wild animals specially endangered species.

Man-Wildlife Conflicts

Struggle for existence. This is applicable for both, man and wild animal. Due to habit loss animals come out of the forest and destroy the crops later on they become danger to human being. Villagers and affected people kill them. There are so many cases of conflict between man and wild life. In these cases forest department could not pacify, resulted to lack of non co-operation for wild life conservation from affected people.

Animals are prone to infection when they are under stress. Animals held in captivity are also more prone diseases. The elephants and other wild animals suffer pain and turn violent when they come to destroy the electric fancied crop field. It is noted that ill, weak and injured animals have tendency to attack man. Man and wild life conflicts also occur during human encroachment into forest area.

There are number of cases, when man eating tiger was reported several men because they like human flesh rather than animals flesh.

CONSERVATION OF BIODIVERSITY

The geological history of biodiversity is about 3.5 to 4 billion years old. The first appearance of multicellular organism was perhaps a mile stone in the history of biodiversity which did not diversify until about 600 million years ago. It is true that biodiversity is a source, once extinct can not be regenerated again. Due to human activities and over exploitation of ecosystem, the most severe extinction has occurred. This is our one of the first and most important requirement *i.e.*, conservation. From biological point of view, its our responsibility to conserve plants, animals (including cultivated plants and domestic animals, and their wild relatives).

In view of the importance of biodiversity (economic, environmental, scientific and medical) the urgent need for conservation of biodiversity was felt in Rio conference. The World Summit on sustainable development held in Johannesburg in August 2002 reiterated that the conservation of biodiversity was necessary for the survival of human race on this earth. In the Convention on Biodiversity (CBD), which has 42 Articles, Articles, 8 and 9 are about in-situ conservation and *ex-situ* conservation respectively. The objectives of CBO clearly stated the conservation of biological diversity, the sustainable use of its components, and the fair and equitable sharing of the benefits arising from the utilization of genetic resources. The conservation has to be *ex-situ* as also in-situ. Both are complimentary to each other.

Conservation of Biodiversity in India

Dr. M.S. Swaminathan (1983) reviewed the scientific aspects of conservation. He suggested that the first step in conservation should be defining the categories of materials (plants/ genes) for preservation and the major methods preserving them. He suggested that the following categories should be usually regarded as important.

1. Cultivated varieties in current use.
2. Obsolete cultivars.
3. Primitive cultivars or land races.
4. Wild species and weedy species closely related to cultivated varieties.
5. Wild species of potential value to man.
6. Special genetic stock developed by man.

The principle of any technology designed for germplasm conservation should be to preserve the maximum possible genetic diversity of a particular plant or genetic stock for future use. Diversity in plants is at the level of species, varieties and individuals. Special genetic stocks may include the material (mutant or breed lines with identified gene or gene combination) developed and used in on going breeding programme. It has been estimated that the survival of approximately 9,000 wild species of plants is some way threatened and that the majority of these are from tropical regions. This further highlights the need for a positive approach to conservation of endangered plants. When new cultivars replace the primitive or conventionally used agricultural crops, it becomes especially important that the crop be properly documented and conserved.

According to Swaminathan (1983) conservation methodologies can take the following three forms :

1. Entire biomass
2. *In situ* preservation
3. *Ex situ* preservation

Many ways are being suggested for preserving biodiversity:

1. No undisturbed land use.
2. Catalogues of genetic resources and national biological inventories be prepared.
3. Measures should be taken to reduce emission of green house gases and ozone destroying compounds. Some of them include following:
4. Effective measures for the conservation of biodiversity be developed and strengthened in all countries.

The details of these conservation methods made a separate sub-discipline of biodiversity studies called *conservation biology*. These techniques of conservation of biodiversity include:

1. *In situ* conservation
2. *Ex situ* conservation

Conservation of biodiversity can be achieved in a number of complementary ways. These methods, all of them falling within the broader concepts of gene banks.

Ex-situ Conservation

"*Ex-situ*" conservation: It means the wild-life conservation in captivity under human care. In this, the endangered plants and animals are collected and bred under controlled conditions in gardens, zoos, sanctuaries etc., wild-life management in captivity have the following advantages:

(*i*) The organisms are assured of food, water, shelter and security and hence can have longer life span and longer span of breeding activity, thereby increasing the possibility of having more number of offsprings.

(*ii*) The chances of survival of endangered species increase because of human care under secure conditions.

(*iii*) This offers the possibility of using genetic techniques to improve the species concerned.

However, there are some disadvantages and limitations of wild-life management is captivity:

(*i*) Since maintenance and breeding of plants and animals under captivity is very expensive, it can be adopted only for a few selected species.

(*ii*) Wild-life captivity only under a set of favourable environmental conditions deprives the organisms the opportunity to adopt to ever-changing natural environment. Therefore, new life forms cannot evolve and thus the gene-pool gets stagnant.

Ex-situ conservation, using sample populations, is done through establishment of gene banks which include genetic resource centres, zoo's, botanical gardens, culture collections etc.

Ex-situ conservation, is the chief mode for preservation of genetic resources, which may include both cultivated and wild material. Generally seeds or in-vitro maintained plant cells, tissue and organs are preserved under appropriate conditions for long term storage as gene banks. This requires considerable knowledge of the genetic structure of population sampling techniques, methods of regeneration and maintenance of varietal genepools, particularly in cross pollinated plants.

The Methods of *Ex-situ* Conservation

The practice of *ex-situ* conservation involves technique which are essentially meant to maintain, multiply or help the species to survive under natural conditions. These include—

(*i*) Long term captive breeding

(*ii*) Short term propagation and release

(*iii*) Animal translocations

(*iv*) Animal Reintroduction

Instead of the above methods there are three techniques also used for *ex-situ* conservation. They are —

(*i*) Seed banks

(*ii*) Gene banks

(*iii*) *In-vitro*

(*iv*) *In-vivo*

Certain conservation agencies, botanical gardens and many research institutions are also working in this field. Establishment of "Central Zoo Authority" by Govt. of India is another milestone in the way of *Ex-situ* conservation.

In-situ Conservation

In-situ conservation is the conservation of ecosystem where all the flora, fauna and wildlife survive in tandem with nature. Development of gene sanctuaries, biosphere reserves, national parks, protected areas and reserve forests, where wildlife could grow and multiply, constitutes the vital forms of *in-situ* conservation. Development of biosphere reserves (*in-situ* conservation) has more than one advantage. It allows natural agencies of creating variation to act unabatedly, thus the range of natural variation continues to reshuffling and replenishing the plantation is never exhausted. The reserves are instrumental in preserving much of wildlife in the vicinity of human establishments.

Approximately 42% of the total geographical area of the country has been earmarked for extensive in-situ conservation of habitats and ecosystem. A protected area network of 104 National Parks and 550 wildlife sanctuaries has been created. The results of this network have been significant in restoring viable population of large mammals such as tiger, lion rhinoceros, crocodiles, elephants etc. Ten biodiversity rich areas of the country have been designated as biosphere reserves.

In-situ means in the natural, original place or position, as in the location of the explant on the mother plant prior to excision. *In-situ* conservation which include conservation of plant and animals in their native ecosystems or even in man made ecosystem, where they naturally occur. This type of conservation applies only of wild fauna and flora and not to the domesticated animals and plants, because conservation is achieved by protection of populations in nature. This method of conservation mainly aims at preservation of land races with wild relatives in which genetic exists and/or in which the weedy/wild forms present hybrids with related cultivars. These are evolutionary systems that are difficult of plant breeders to stimulate and should not be knowingly destroyed.

The *in-situ* conservation of habitats has received high priority in the world conservation strategy programmes launched since 1980. Institutional, arrangement, especially in countries of the developing world, have been emphasized. This mode of conservation has some limitations however, there is risk of material being lost due to environmental hazards. Further the cost of maintaining a large portion of available genotypes in nurseries or fields may be extremely high.

In-situ conservation includes a system of protected areas of different categories e.g. National parks, Sanctuaries, National Monument, Cultural landscape, Biosphere Reserves etc. One of the best methods to save wildlife species, which is on the road to extinction, is to put it in a special enclosure to reproduce. Sanctuaries and National Parks, whose legal definition varies from country to country, best illustrate this.

National Parks, Wildlife Sanctuaries and Biosphere Reserves

National Parks or a Sanctuary may be defined *as an area, declared by state, for the purpose of protecting, propagating or developing wild life therein, or its natural environment for their scientific educational and recreational value. Human activities like hunting, firewood, collection, timber harvesting etc. are restricted in these areas.*

The creation of National Parks, Wildlife Sanctuaries and Biosphere Reserves in an attempt to manage wildlife by defining protected areas. Wildlife therein is regularly monitored and necessary management strategies for their perpetuation and preservation are formulated and implemented. These protected areas not only benefit wildlife, but indirectly humans too. Their protection means the protection of entire ecosystem, which is necessary to continue to enjoy the benefits that we may now receive from it. A National Park is an area dedicated to conserve the scenery (or environment) and natural objects and the wildlife therein. In national parks, all private rights are non-existent and all forestry operations and other usages such as grazing of domestic animals are prohibited.

Important National Parks and Wildlife Sanctuaries in India

States	National Parks and Wildlife Sanctuaries
Andhra Pradesh	Coringa Wildlife Sanctuary, Kolleru Wildlife Sanctuary, Rollapadu Wildlife Sanctuary
Arunachal Pradesh	Namdapha Pelicanary Wildlife Sanctuary
Assam (Asom)	Kaziranga National Park Manas Wildlife Sanctuary
Jharkhand	Hazaribagh National Park, Betla National Park
Goa	Mollen Wildlife Sanctuary
Gujarat	Gir National Park, Velavader National Park Wild Ass
Haryana	Sultanpur Lake Bird Sanctuary
J & K	Dechigam Wildlife Sanctuary
Karnataka	Bandipur National Park, Nagarhole National Park, Ranganthitto Bird Sanctuary, Silent Valley National Park
Kerala	Periyar Wildlife Sanctuary Wynad Wildlife Sanctuary
Madhya Pradesh	Kanha National Park, Shivpuri National Park, Bandhavgarh National Park, Panna National Park

States	National Parks and Wildlife Sanctuaries
Maharashtra	Tadoda National Park, Yawal Wildlife Sanctuary
Manipur	Keibul Lamjao National Park
Meghalaya	Balpakram Sanctuary
Mizoram	Dampa Wildlife Sanctuary
Nagaland	Intangki Wildlife Sanctuary
Orissa	Simlipal National Park, Chilka Lake Bird Sanctuary
Punjab	Abohar Wildlife Sanctuary
Rajasthan	Ranthambore National Park, Sariska Wildlife Sanctuary Ghana Bird Sanctuary
Sikkim	Kanchenjunga National Park
Tamil Nadu	Mudumalai Wildlife Sanctuary, Vedanthangal Water Bird Sanctuary
Uttar Pradesh	Dudhwa National Park
Uttarakhand	Corbett National Park, Rajaji National Park
West Bengal	Jaldapara Wildlife Sanctuary

Biosphere Reserves in India

S.No.	Name	Area (km^2)	Date of Est.	Location
1.	Nilgiri*	5520	1986	Part of Wynad, Nagarhole, Bandipur and Madumalai, Nilambur, Silent Valley and Siruvani hills in Tamil Nadu, Kerala and Karnataka.
2.	Nanda Devi*	5860.69	1988	Part of Chamoli, Pithoragarh and Almora districts in Uttarakhand.
3.	Nokrek*	820	1988	Part of East, West and South Garo Hill districts in Meghalaya.
4.	Manas	2837	1989	Part of Kokrajhar, Bongaigaon, Barpeta, Nalbari, Kamprup and Darang districts in Assam.
5.	Sunderban*	9630	1989	Part of delta of Ganges & Brahamaputra river system in West Bengal.
6.	Gulf of Mannar*	10500	1989	India part of Gulf of Mannar extending from Rameswaram island in the North to Kanyakumari in the South of Tamil Nadu.
7.	Great Nicobar*	885	1989	Southern most island of Andaman and Nicobar Islands.
8.	Similipal*	4374	1994	Part of Mayurbhanj district in Orissa.
9.	Dibru-Saikhova	765	1997	Part of Dibrugarh and Tinsukia districts in Assam.
10.	Dehang-Dibang	5111.5	1998	Part of Upper Siang, West Siang and Dibang Valley districts in Arunachal Pradesh.
11.	Pachmarhi*	4981.72	1999	Part of Betul, Hoshangabad and Chhindwara districts in Madhya Pradesh.
12.	Khangchendzonga*	2931.12	2000	Part of North and West districts in Sikkim.

S.No.	Name	Area (km²)	Date of Est.	Location
13.	Agasthyamalai*	3500.36	2001	Part of Thirunelveli and Kanyakumari districts in Tamil Nadu and Thiruvanthapuram, Kollam and Pathanmthitta districts in Kerala.
14.	Achanakmar-Amarkantak*	3,835. 51	2005	Part of Anuppur and Dindori districts of Madhya Pradesh and Bilaspur district of Chattisgarh.
15.	Kachchh	12,454	2008	Part of Kachchh, Rajkot, Surendranagar and Patan districts in Gujarat.
16.	Cold Desert	7,770	2009	Pin Valley National Park and surroundings; Chandratal & Sarchu; and Kibber Wildlife sanctuary in Himachal Pradesh.
17.	Seshachalam	4755.99	2010	Seshachalam hill ranges in Eastern Ghats encompassing part of Chittoor and Kadapa districts in Andhra Pradesh.
18.	Panna	2998.98	2011	Part of Panna and Chhattarpur districts in Madhya Pradesh

** Sites with * have been included in the World Network of Biosphere Reserves of UNESCO.*

WORD FILE - NATIONAL PARKS

Key Facts: India's Protected Areas

- National parks in India are classified as IUCN Category II protected areas. The first national park in India was established in 1936 as Hailey National Park, which is now known as Jim Corbett National Park in Uttarakhand.
- By 1970, India had only five national parks. In 1972, the Wildlife Protection Act was enacted, and Project Tiger was launched to safeguard the habitats of species dependent on conservation.
- As of April 2025, India has 107 national parks covering a total area of 44,402.95 km², which falls under IUCN Category II, accounting for approximately 1.35% of India's total geographical area.
- States like Madhya Pradesh and Andaman & Nicobar Islands have a high number of national parks.
- **Oldest National Park:** Jim Corbett National Park (established 1936 as Hailey National Park) in Uttarakhand.
- **Largest National Park:** Hemis National Park in Ladakh, known for snow leopards.
- **Smallest National Park:** South Button Island National Park in the Andaman & Nicobar Islands.
- **Only Floating National Park:** Keibul Lamjao National Park (Manipur), located on Loktak Lake.
- **Only Asiatic Lion Habitat:** Gir National Park and Wildlife Sanctuary (Gujarat).
- **UNESCO World Heritage Sites:** Include Kaziranga (Assam), Manas (Assam), Keoladeo (Rajasthan), and Sundarbans (West Bengal).
- **Project Tiger:** Initiated to protect tiger habitats, with parks like Corbett and Ranthambore being critical sites.

Key Facts About Biosphere Reserves in India

- **First Biosphere Reserve:** Nilgiri (1986).
- **Largest Biosphere Reserve:** Great Rann of Kutch (Gujarat).
- **Smallest Biosphere Reserve:** Dibru-Saikhowa (Assam).
- **UNESCO Recognition:** As of early 2026, 13 of the 18 biosphere reserves are recognized internationally under the UNESCO MAB Programme.
- **Funding:** The scheme is implemented by the Government of India with 90:10 ratio for North-Eastern/ Himalayan states and 60:40 for other states.

Status of Protected Areas in India & World

- Protected areas in India are the principal mechanism of conservation of biodiversity on Earth and serve as the most important units for in-situ biodiversity conservation.
- With only 2.4% of the world's land area, 16.7% of the world's human population and 18% livestock, it contributes about 8% of the known global biodiversity.
- Over 120,000 designated protected areas cover about 13% of the Earth's land surface.
- Marine protected areas cover 6.3% of territorial seas and 0.5% of the high seas.

Total Protected Areas in India 2026

India has a rich network of protected areas to conserve its biodiversity. The country has 107 National Parks, 573 Wildlife Sanctuaries, 96 Ramsar Sites, 58 Tiger Reserves, and 18 Biosphere Reserves, taking the total number of protected areas to 852 across India.

Category	Number
National Parks	107
Wildlife Sanctuaries	573
Ramsar Sites in India	96
Tiger Reserves in India	58
Biosphere Reserve in India	18
Total	**852**

OUR ENVIRONMENT (SURROUNDINGS)

Environment or Surroundings refers to everything around us – both natural and human-made – that affects our life and the life of other living organisms. It includes air, water, land, plants, animals, humans, and all interactions between them.

A clean and healthy environment is essential for life, health, development, and overall well-being.

Types of Our Environment

Type	Description	Examples
Natural Environment	Elements provided by nature	Rivers, forests, mountains, lakes, air, soil
Human-made Environment	Elements created by humans	Houses, roads, schools, markets, factories

Components of Our Environment

1. **Air (Atmosphere)** – Needed for breathing and survival.
2. **Water** – Used for drinking, cooking, cleaning, agriculture, and industry.
3. **Land (Soil)** – Supports agriculture, buildings, and human activities.
4. **Plants / Vegetation** – Provide oxygen, food, medicine, and shelter.
5. **Animals** – Part of the ecosystem; provide food, help in agriculture, maintain ecological balance.
6. **Humans** – Influence the environment through culture, technology, and social activities.

All these components interact to form a balanced environment.

Importance of Our Environment

- Provides basic resources for survival (air, water, food, shelter).
- Maintains climate and weather balance.
- Supports biodiversity and ecological balance.
- Offers space for education, recreation, and cultural activities.
- Protects against natural disasters like floods and soil erosion.

Pollution of Our Environment

Pollution occurs when harmful substances or factors contaminate the environment, making it unsafe for life.

Types of Pollution

Type	Causes	Effects
Air Pollution	Vehicle smoke, factory emissions, burning fuels	Respiratory problems, smog, acid rain
Water Pollution	Industrial waste, sewage, chemicals	Waterborne diseases, death of aquatic life
Soil Pollution	Pesticides, plastics, industrial waste	Poor crop yield, soil infertility
Noise Pollution	Loud traffic, construction, machines	Hearing loss, stress, sleep problems

Ways to Protect Our Environment

1. **Plant Trees (Afforestation)** – Improves air quality and prevents soil erosion.
2. **Save Water (Water Conservation)** – Avoid wastage, collect rainwater.
3. **Proper Waste Management** – Dispose garbage in dustbins, avoid littering.
4. **Reduce Plastic Use** – Prevent soil and water pollution.
5. **Save Energy (Energy Conservation)** – Use electricity and fuels wisely.

Role of Humans in Protecting the Environment

- Maintain cleanliness at home, school, and surroundings.
- Plant and protect trees and greenery.
- Use water and energy responsibly.
- Reduce pollution by cycling, walking, or using public transport.
- Avoid throwing garbage in rivers, lakes, or open areas.

Important Facts

Topic	Key Points
Meaning of Environment	Everything around us, both natural and human-made
Natural Components	Air, water, land, plants, animals
Human-made Components	Roads, buildings, schools, markets, industries
Types of Pollution	Air, water, soil, noise
Conservation Methods	Plant trees, conserve water, manage waste, reduce plastics
Importance	Provides resources, protects life, maintains biodiversity, supports health

FAIR

A fair, or Mela, is a gathering of people organized for social, cultural, religious, or recreational purposes. It is usually held on special occasions such as festivals, harvests, or religious events. Fairs serve as places where people meet, celebrate, enjoy entertainment, trade goods, and showcase local traditions, crafts, and foods.

Types of Fairs

Fairs can be classified based on their purpose:

1. **Religious Fairs:** Held to celebrate religious occasions or festivals. For example:
   - **Kumbh Mela** in India, which occurs every 12 years and attracts millions of pilgrims.
   - **Pushkar Fair** in Rajasthan, associated with a holy lake and temple.
2. **Seasonal or Harvest Fairs:** Organized to celebrate agricultural cycles or harvests. Farmers and villagers participate to buy, sell, and trade goods. Example: Lohri Mela, Baisakhi Fair.
3. **Trade and Commerce Fairs:** Held to promote local industries, crafts, and businesses. Traders display and sell products such as handicrafts, clothes, food items, and household goods. Example: Surajkund Mela in Haryana.
4. **Cultural Fairs:** Focus on music, dance, art, and performance. Folk traditions are showcased, and competitions are often organized. Example: Sonepur Fair in Bihar.

Importance of Fairs

1. **Social Importance**
   - People from different villages and towns come together, promoting friendship and unity.
   - Fairs help in passing cultural traditions to the next generation.
   - They provide opportunities for recreational activities, games, and entertainment.
2. **Economic Importance**
   - Traders and artisans earn income by selling goods and handicrafts.
   - Promote local industries and tourism, boosting the economy.
   - Farmers can sell agricultural products directly to buyers.
3. **Cultural and Educational Importance**
   - Folk music, dance, and arts are preserved and promoted.
   - Children and youth learn about their heritage, crafts, and traditional occupations.
   - Fairs often include educational exhibitions or awareness programs about health, hygiene, and environment.

Features of a Fair

- Large gatherings of people, often lasting for 1–10 days.
- Stalls selling goods, toys, clothes, food items, and handicrafts.
- Rides, games, and cultural performances.
- Religious rituals and ceremonies in some fairs.
- Temporary marketplaces and arrangements for accommodation and sanitation.

Environmental and Health Aspects of Fairs

- Fairs generate waste such as plastics, leftover food, and paper. Proper management is necessary.
- Temporary arrangements for clean drinking water and toilets are essential to prevent diseases.
- Planting trees and maintaining green areas around fairgrounds can reduce pollution.
- Awareness about hygiene, sanitation, and waste disposal should be promoted.

Role of Students and Community in Fairs

- Students can participate in cleanliness drives and awareness campaigns during fairs.
- Communities can organize cultural programs to showcase local heritage.
- Promote eco-friendly practices, such as using cloth bags instead of plastics.
- Encourage participation in educational exhibitions and workshops during fairs.

INDIVIDUALS AND BUSINESSES ASSOCIATED WITH LOCAL PROFESSIONS

Local professions are occupations, trades, or businesses that are practiced within a particular community, village, or town, often based on local resources, skills, and traditions. These professions provide employment, fulfill the needs of the local population, and support the local economy.

Importance of Local Professions

- Promote self-employment and income generation.
- Preserve traditional skills and crafts passed from generation to generation.
- Support local markets by providing goods and services.
- Reduce dependence on external goods and services, fostering economic sustainability.
- Help in maintaining the cultural and social identity of the community.

Types of Local Professions

1. **Agriculture and Farming**
   - Farmers cultivate crops such as wheat, rice, vegetables, and fruits.
   - Allied professions include dairy farming, poultry farming, and fishery.
   - **Businesses:** Local agricultural supply stores, seed shops, and fertilizer suppliers.

2. **Handicrafts and Artisans**
   - Local artisans create items like pottery, weaving, embroidery, jewelry, and woodwork.
   - **Businesses:** Shops selling handicrafts locally and to tourists, export businesses.
   - Examples: Carpet weaving in Kashmir, pottery in Khurja, bamboo crafts in Northeast India.
3. **Trade and Commerce**
   - Shopkeepers, grocers, vegetable vendors, and local markets serve the community.
   - Small-scale industries and family-run businesses also contribute.
   - **Examples:** Kirana shops, small clothing stores, and local eateries.
4. **Services and Professions**
   - Local services include teachers, barbers, tailors, carpenters, electricians, and plumbers.
   - Healthcare professionals like local doctors, nurses, and pharmacists.
   - **Transport services:** Rickshaw pullers, taxi drivers, and small logistics businesses.
5. **Cultural and Religious Professions**
   - Priests, folk artists, musicians, and traditional performers.
   - **Local businesses:** Event organizing, festivals, and religious fairs.

Role of Individuals in Local Professions

- **Skill Preservation:** Passing traditional knowledge and techniques to younger generations.
- **Community Support:** Providing essential goods and services locally.
- **Economic Contribution:** Generating income and employment for themselves and others.
- **Innovation:** Introducing new methods and products while maintaining local relevance.

Challenges Faced by Local Professionals and Businesses

- Competition from mass-produced and imported goods.
- Limited access to modern technology and markets.
- Insufficient financial support or credit facilities.
- Lack of awareness about quality standards and marketing.
- Migration of younger generation to cities, leading to decline in traditional skills.

Ways to Support Local Professions

- Promote buying local goods and services.
- Government support: subsidies, training programs, and exhibitions.
- Encourage skill development and vocational education.
- Set up cooperative societies for collective marketing and better profits.
- Awareness campaigns to preserve cultural heritage and traditional crafts.

WATER

Water is a precious natural resource and is essential for all forms of life on Earth. Humans, animals, and plants cannot survive without water. It is also vital for agriculture, industries, energy production, and daily activities. Despite covering 71% of the Earth's surface, only about 3% of water is freshwater, and even less is available for direct human use.

Sources of Water

Water comes from natural and underground sources:

A. Natural Sources

- **Rivers** – Flowing fresh water used for drinking, irrigation, and industries.
- **Example:** Ganga River, Yamuna, Brahmaputra.
- **Lakes and Ponds** – Still water bodies storing water for local use.
- **Example:** Dal Lake (Jammu & Kashmir), Chilika Lake (Odisha).
- **Rainfall** – The primary source of freshwater; replenishes rivers and groundwater.
- **Glaciers** – Store huge amounts of freshwater in mountains; slowly release water through melting.
- **Oceans and Seas** – Store saltwater, not drinkable but important for marine life and transportation.

B. Underground Sources

- **Wells** – Man-made holes to extract groundwater.
- **Tube wells** – Use pumps to bring water to the surface.
- **Springs** – Natural water flowing from underground.

Types of Water

Type of Water	Description	Example
Freshwater	Water with very little salt; suitable for drinking	Rivers, lakes, ponds
Saltwater	Contains high salt concentration; not drinkable	Oceans like Indian Ocean
Groundwater	Water found beneath Earth's surface	Wells, hand pumps, tube wells
Rainwater	Collected directly from rainfall	Roof water harvesting systems

Water Cycle (Hydrological Cycle)

The water cycle is the continuous movement of water through the environment, ensuring a balance of water on Earth.

Stages of Water Cycle

1. **Evaporation** – Heat from the sun converts water from rivers, lakes, and oceans into water vapor.
2. **Condensation** – Water vapor cools and forms clouds.
3. **Precipitation** – Water falls as rain, snow, hail, or sleet.
4. **Collection** – Water gathers in rivers, lakes, ponds, and underground reservoirs.

This cycle recycles water and maintains the Earth's water balance.

Uses of Water

Water is essential for life and human development. Its main uses are:

Use	Description
Domestic	Drinking, cooking, bathing, washing clothes
Agriculture	Irrigation for crops, watering animals
Industry	Factories, production, cooling machinery
Hydroelectricity	Producing electricity through water flow
Transportation	Boats, ships, and waterways
Recreation	Swimming, boating, water sports
Environmental	Maintaining rivers, lakes, and ecosystems

Importance of Water

- Necessary for survival of all living beings
- Supports agriculture and food production
- Maintains ecological balance
- Regulates climate and temperature
- Provides habitats for aquatic animals
- Generates hydroelectric power
- Important for domestic, industrial, and recreational activities

WATER POLLUTION

Water Pollution is a phenomenon that is characterized by the deterioration of the quality of land water (rivers, lakes, marshes and ground water) or sea water as a result of various human activities. In the past, if we take a look then as long as the human pollution was small and communication was scattered over large areas of land, the disposal of human waste created no problems. But as communities became more concentrated and villages and towns grew, such a mode of disposal by natural agencies got replace by organized disposal, though again through the agency of natural land and soil columns.

Water pollution is any physical or chemical change in the water that can adversely affect organisms. It is a global problem, affecting both the industrialized and the developing nations. Heat, toxic metals, acids, sediment, animal and human wastes, and synthetic organic compounds foul the waterways of developed nations. Human and animal wastes, sediment and pathogenic organisms head the list in the industrialized nations. In these countries, unsanitary water and malnutrition account for most of the illness and death. Like air pollutants, water pollutants come from mumerous natural and anthropogenic sources. Likewise, water pollutants produced in one nation may take into others, creating complex international control problems that may take decades to solve.

Sources of Water Pollution

Water, the most abundant and wonderful natural resource, is extremely essential for survival of all living organisms. But today clean water has become a precious commodity and its quality is threatened by numerous sources of pollution which are as follows:

1. **Sewage and Domestic Wastes:** Sewage is commonly a cloudy dilute aqueous solution containing minerals and organic matter. About 75% of water pollution is caused by sewage, domestic wastes and food processing plants. It also includes human excreta, soap, detergents, metals, glass, rubbish, garden waste and sewage sludge. Domestic sewage and other wastes are often untreated or partially treated and dumped into the water bodies such as ponds, lakes, streams and rivers. Since the dumping is uncontrolled especially near big cities, the water bodies are not able to recycle them and lose their self regulating capacity.

   If domestic waste of sewage is not properly handled after it is produced or if the sewage received at the end of sewage treatment plants is not of the adequate standards, there are chances of the water being polluted. The indiscriminate method of handling the domestic sewage may also cause pollution of underground sources of water such as wells. If sewage or partially treated sewage is directly discharged into water bodies such as rivers, the water of such gives is polluted or contaminated.

2. **Industrial Effluents:** Industrial Effluents discharged into water bodies contain toxic chemicals, hazardous compounds, phenols, aldehydes, ketones, amines, cyanides, metallic wastes, plasticizers, toxic acids, corrosive alkalies, oils, greases, dyes, biocides, suspended solids and thermal pollutants from numerous industries. The effluents *i.e.* discharges from the industries such as that of pharmaceuticals, breweries, tanneries, dyeing, textiles, paper, plastic, chemicals, metallurgical, fertilizers etc. are some of the most important agents of water pollution. These effluents when discharged through

the sewage system poison the biological purification mechanism of sewage treatment and pose several pollution problems.

3. **Agricultural Discharges:** Plant nutrients, pesticides, fertilizers, farm wastes, manure slurry, sediments, drainage from silage, plant and animal debris, soil erosion containing mostly the inorganic materials are reported to cause heavy pollution to water sources. In modern agricultural pesticides NPK fertilizers containing nitrates and phosphates are added to soil. Some of these are washed off through the rainfall irrigation and drainage into water bodies, where they severely disturb the aquatic ecosystem. The excessive use of plant nutrients leads to the disruption of nitrogen and phosphorus balance in water affecting plant growth. Organic wastes increase the BOD of receiving water.
4. **Fertilizers:** Modern agriculture relies heavily on artificial fertilizers, including several biocides. Although these chemicals enhance vegetation but they disrupt the entire natural aquatic ecosystem. They acutely pollute the water. Indiscriminate and excessive use of fertilizers on land has also created on adverse ecological effect on aquatic ecosystem because some of them are washed off land into rivers and lakes through irrigation, rain, seepage and drainage. One of the ingredients of fertilizers is phosphate salts which cause algal bloom.
5. **Detergents:** Detergents are of recent origin, used as cleansing agents and derived from surfactants (10-30%), builder (15%) and other ingredients. Household detergents contain several pollutants which severely affect the water bodies. They contain surface active agents and contribute to phosphates of Sodium (Na), sodium silicates, sodium sulphates etc. the most important disadvantage of detergents is the environmental pollution caused by the factory refuse discharged of nearby water sources.
6. **Toxic Metals:** Amongst the industries with the highest emission of heavy metals are the mining industry, metallurgical industry, leather industry, distilleries, battery industry and thermal power plants. Toxic metals are added in aquatic system from industrial processes and domestic sewage discharge.

Harmful Effects of Water Pollution

1. **Harmful Effects of Sewage and Domestic Waste**
   (*a*) Sewage is an excellent medium for the growth of pathogenic bacteria, viruses and protozoa.
   (*b*) Domestic sewage, which is primarily composed of spent water containing wine, soapy water, food material, makes water completely unfit for drinking and domestic use.
   (*c*) Several pathogenic microorganism introduced into the water cause deleterious effects and chronic diseases in man and animals.
2. **Harmful Effects of Industrial Pollutants**
   (*a*) It causes deleterious effects on living organisms and may bring about death of sub lethal pathology of kindness, liver, brains, lungs.
   (*b*) Disinfectants, which are added in water to control algal growth and bacteria may persist in water bodies and may cause mortality of fish.
   (*c*) Effluents containing acids and alkalies make the water corrosive.
3. **Effects of Fertilizers**
   (*a*) Effects on Humans and Animals—Excessive application of nitrogen fertilizers to the soil often leads to accumulation of nitrates in the water which when drunk by cattle and man get reduced to toxic nitrates by the intestinal bacteria. Nitrates enter the blood stream and react with haemoglobin which has a stronger affinity for nitrates than for oxygen to form methemoglobin. This causes damage to the respiratory and vascular systems, because of which suffocation and death may occur.
   (*b*) Effects of plants—Agricultural fertilizers crowd out essential nutrients present in the top soil layers. The microbe enriched humus enhances plant growth. But fertilizer enriched soil cannot support the microbial life for a long time. Fertilizers used to increase in growth of crops also increase the algal growth in surface water into which they are washed.
4. **Effects of Thermal Pollutants in Water**
   The rise in temperature in aquatic system has a profound effect on organisms as well as on water quality. These detrimental effects are as follows:
   (*a*) Reduction in dissolved oxygen
   (*b*) Increase in BOD
   (*c*) Excessive eutrophication
   (*d*) Decrease in solubility of gases in water
   (*e*) Rapid setting of sediment load in water affecting aquatic food supply
5. **Effects of Radioactive Pollutants in Water**
   (*a*) Polluted water containing radioisotopes produces a set of syndromes characterized by nausea, vomiting, diarrhoea, epilation and general weakness which is known as radiation sickness.
   (*b*) It destroys biological immune system *i.e.*, body becomes less resistant towards a variety of diseases.
   (*c*) It causes somatic genetic disorders, gene mutations and blood abnormalities in higher animals including man.
   (*d*) Radioactive elements present in water accumulate in soil sediments, air and aquatic ecosystems.

Strategies for Water Pollution Control

We are now in a state when water pollution has become a global problem partly because of the population explosion and partly due to the phenomenal advancement in industrialization. Pollution control methods are an investment that ensures long time profits. It is fact that damage caused by pollution is much greater than the investment required to setting up adequate and sustainable pollution control measures. Pollution is an indication of an inefficient process. It represents wastage of world resources, an economic burden on a nation and a financial loss to an enterprise. The pollution can be reduced and minimized by reducing the inefficiencies. The overall efficiency of an energy use in most industrialized or developed countries is 40%. Over 50% of the energy used is wasted and appears in one form or the other as other as waste heat that has an impact on the climate as well as aquatic ecosystems. As a result, industries are facing increasing opposition from the civic society.

A great deal to time and money is wasted in building effluent treatment plants and systems. In many cases, a change of process or raw materials would ensure the problem is removed with minimum costs and without affecting the quality of the product. But the traditional pollution control system does not solve the problem. It may however, complicate it. For example, purification of wastewater creates sludge, but on incineration of chemical wastes creates toxic gases as well as particulate matter. Thus what emerges is an environmental paradox. It takes resources to remove pollution. Pollution removal generates residues. It takes more resources to dispose of this residue and disposal or residue also gives rise to pollution.

So certain strategies are to be adapted to control and prevent water pollution, which are the following:

1. The structural dimensions of non-waste technology requires to be improved and should consist of a linking up of several different industrial, agricultural and urban activities in such a manner that the waste of one industry becomes the raw material to another. Such technology will rely on multiple use of resources and internal transfer if wastes from one section to become the raw materials for another.

   The objectives should be:

   (*a*) Prevention of waste.

   (*b*) Minimizing that wastes which cannot be prevented, and

   (*c*) Rendering harmless the waste ultimately released into the environment.

2. Pollution prevention through cleaner production techniques should be adopted, as they are safer because polluting waste is eliminated at the source.
3. The most reliable way to prevent and control water pollution is undoubtedly to stabilize the aquatic ecosystem by balancing the input and output of energy and nutrients. Practical devices to increase the stability of ecosystem include reduction of waste inputs, controlling hazardous industrial effluents and municipal sewage, harvesting of Biomass, trapping of nutrients, aeration and fish management to protect aquatic flora and fauna.
4. Wastes can be treated by inexpensive as well as efficient methods. For example; where sufficient land is available, by taking the advantage of plentiful sunshine and hot climate that exist in most areas in India, oxidation or stabilization ponds can also be used. In oxidation ponds, domestic or industrial wastes are stored in large, well-detined shallow ponds and kept in it for a few days. Because of the presence of sufficient sunlight and organic nutrients in waste, a healthy bloom of algae flourishes along with colonies of bacteria. In this mutual process, the bacteria speedily digest the organic waste and render it harmless.
5. Treatment of sewage yields irrigation water that contains all the essential nutrients such as nitrogen, phosphorous and potassium to make it a good fertilizer. Now metals like Zn can be extracted from the wastewater of rayon manufacturing industry and lignosulphonate can be recovered from paper and pulp wastewater. The treated sewage can also be used for air-conditioning purpose.

Ground Water Pollution

Over 98% of the fresh water earth lies below the surface. The remaining 2% is what we see in lakes, rivers, streams and reservoirs. Of the fresh water below about 90% satisfies the description of ground water, that is water that occurs in saturated materials below the water table. About 2% water occurs as soil moisture in the unsaturated zone above the water table and is essential for plant growth.

Ground water acts as a reservoir by virtue of Large pore space in earth materials, as a conduit which can transport water over long distances and as a mechanical filter that improves water quality by removing suspended solids and bacterial contamination. It is the source of water for wells and springs that is the recommended source of rural domestic use. It is replenished by precipitation through rain, snow, sleet and hail. Today, Human activities are constantly adding industrial, domestic and agricultural waters to ground water reservoirs at an alarming rate. Ground water contamination is generally irreversible *i.e.* once it is contaminated; it is difficult to restore the original water quality of the aquifer. Although the soil mantle through which water passes acts as an adsorbent retaining a large part of colloidal and soluble ions with its cation exchange capacity, but ground water is not completely free from the menace of chronic pollution.

India has a good industrial infrastructure in core industries like metals, chemicals, fertilizers, drugs and petroleum, industries like plastics, pesticides, detergents, fuels, solvents, paints, dyes and food additives, released effluents and emissions, polluting soil water-plant ecosystem. The disposal of solid and liquid wastes containing heavy metals like lead, nickel, chromium, molybdenum and mercury in land or water bodies, leads to heavy metal contamination of the soil-water-plant-animal ecosystems.

Factors Affecting Ground Water Pollution

1. Rainfall Pattern
2. Depth of water table
3. Distance from the source to contamination
4. Soil properties such as Texture, structure and filtration rate

Sources of Contamination in Ground Water

1. Domestic wastes
2. Industrial wastes
3. Agricultural wastes
4. Run off from urban areas

1. **Domestic Wastes:** Domestic wastes and methods of their disposal are of primary concern in urban areas. Prime factors responsible for deteriorating the water quality include pathogenic organisms, oxygen demand, nutrients and solids from domestic wastes. Solid wastes are the potential source of contamination as they are partly burned and partly incorporated into the soil and pose serious danger to the ground water.
2. **Industrial Wastes:** Most industries generally produce wastes containing toxic heavy metals along with hazardous organic and inorganic effluents. These chemicals contaminate with the ground water and severely pollute it. Over 500 factories in North Delhi are severely polluting the ground water, which is used for domestic purposes. The steel re-rolling mills and pickling factories are dumping heavy metals and acids into open cesspools or drains, and from here these pollutants permeate into the water table. The worst affected are the people which work in these factories or live around them, most of whom depend on hand pumps for potable water.
3. **Agricultural Wastes:** Fertilizers, pesticides, insecticides, herbicides, processing wastes and animal wastes etc. are constantly added to the water. Leachates from agricultural land containing nitrates, phosphates and potash, move downward with percolating water and join the aquifers below posing danger to the ground water. Nitrate causes eutrophication of the rivers also although in India phosphate is more blamed for this asphyxiation of water bodies.

Recent researchers showed that all pesticides were found in higher concentrations in ground water compared to surface water. The report explains that the high pesticide residue concentration in ground water might be because ground water flows non-turbulently and experiences limited dilutions as compared to surface water and also due to higher stability of organochlorine pesticides residue concentration in ground water. The soil becomes a reservoir for these pesticides thereby steadily transferring them to ground water. This is a dangerous condition and must be prevented because, people depend on groundwater more than sources particularly rural people because they believe it to be safer than surface water.

4. Urban Areas

1. Effluents from urban areas contain large concentration of oils, greases, nutrients, heavy metals and detergents. The detergents being soluble can pass through the soil and pollute ground water.
2. Raw sewage dumped in shallow soak pits and seepage from polluted lake, pond or stream also pollutes water.
3. Rainfall could pick up substantial contaminants from dust and air and join the aquifer below. The infiltration of liquids containing toxic pollutants may cause pollution in sandy soils and well waters.

5. Soluble Effluents

1. Several soluble effluents pollute the ground water critically. The extent of pollution is more in sandy soils and humid regions having high water table conditions.
2. A direct impact of this has been on the levels of ground water. Increasing use of groundwater has pushed the water table lower.
3. Along the coasts, increasing ground water withdrawals have led to the ingress of saline water into ground water.
4. Pollution is another major factor that is reducing water quality and thereby the availability of clean water.
5. The amounts and types of wastes discharged have outstripped nature's ability to breakdown pollutants into less harmful elements.

Sewage Irrigation

Sewage irrigation is one of the method by which land treats the sewage. The water of the sewage percolates in the ground and the suspended solids remain on the surface of the ground. The organic suspended solids remain at the surface of the ground. The organic suspended solids, are partly acted upon by bacteria, and are partly oxidized by exposure to atmosphere actions of heat, light and air.

Irrigation Water Quality

The quantity of water for irrigation is determined by the effect of its constituents both on the crop and the soil. The deleterious effect on the constituents of the irrigant on plant growth can result from:

(*i*) Direct chemical effects upon the metabolic reactions in the plants.

(*ii*) Direct osmotic effects of salts in preventing water uptake by plants.

(*iii*) Any indirect effect through changes in soil structures, permeability and aeresation.

Sewage Farming

When the sewage is used for growing corps, it is called sewage farming. The roots of the corps consume the fertilizing elements of sewage. The mineral salts of sewage such as nitrates, sulphates and phosphates are the main fertilizing constituents of sewage. By the sewage farming a good income can be done, which is always profitable.

The nutrients of sewage like nitrogen, phosphorus and potassium along with micro-nutrients as well as organic matter present in it could be advantageously employed for sewage farming to add to the fertility of the fields, along with the irrigation potential of water content. Even the application of the treated effluent to land should be carried out with certain precautions, because it is not completely free from this risk. The good sewage farm should run on scientific lines with effluent supervision with the primary objective of disposal of sewage combined with its utilization to the possible extent in a good sanitary manner without polluting the soil, open watercourses or under ground water or contamination of the crops, or impairing the productivity of the farm. The sewage farming should be done such that hygienic safety to the staff is protected against the infection by pathogenic organisms and helminthes. Though the sewage after primary treatment can be applied to the farm, the main reason of providing only primary treatment and eliminating secondary treatment merely depends on cost consideration.

Important Facts

Topic	Important Fact
Total water on Earth	71% of surface
Freshwater	Less than 3% of total water
Main source	Rainfall
Water cycle	Evaporation, Condensation, Precipitation, Collection
Polluted water	Causes diseases like cholera, typhoid
Conservation methods	Rainwater harvesting, drip irrigation, careful use

Quick Points

- Water is a renewable but limited resource
- Freshwater is mainly available in rivers, lakes, glaciers, and groundwater
- Water cycle maintains life and climate
- Pollution makes water unsafe for humans and animals
- Conservation is essential for future generations

TRAFFIC AND COMMUNICATION

Traffic and communication are two fundamental aspects of human civilization that allow the movement of people, goods, and information across different regions. They form the backbone of economic, social, and cultural development. While traffic refers to the physical movement of people and goods using various modes of transport, communication involves the exchange of information through verbal, written, broadcast, or digital means. Both are interlinked, as effective communication often enhances the efficiency of traffic systems, and smooth traffic facilitates timely communication and delivery of resources.

TRAFFIC

Traffic includes the movement of vehicles, people, and commodities on land, water, and air routes. Roadways, railways, waterways, and airways are the primary channels for transportation. Roads form the most common and widely used mode, connecting cities, towns, and villages. Railways are essential for transporting heavy goods and large numbers of passengers over long distances efficiently. Waterways, including rivers, canals, and seas, provide economical transport for bulk cargo, while air transport is crucial for fast movement of people and perishable goods across national and international boundaries.

Efficient traffic systems contribute to trade, commerce, industry, and tourism, while also supporting essential services such as healthcare, emergency response, and disaster management. However, rapid urbanization and increased vehicular traffic have led to several environmental challenges, including air and noise pollution, greenhouse gas emissions, soil contamination, and fragmentation of natural habitats. The growing number of vehicles and unplanned urban expansion can disrupt ecosystems and adversely affect human health.

COMMUNICATION

Communication refers to the transfer of information, ideas, and knowledge from one individual or group to another. It can occur through spoken words, written text, broadcast media, or digital technologies. Verbal communication includes face-to-face conversations and telephone calls, while written communication covers letters, newspapers, books, and official documents. Broadcast communication, such as television and radio, allows information to reach a large audience simultaneously. Digital communication through the internet, mobile apps, and video conferencing has revolutionized information exchange, making it faster, interactive and global.

Communication plays a crucial role in education, governance, business, and social integration. It enables people to stay informed, make decisions, and collaborate effectively. However, modern communication technologies also present environmental concerns, particularly in the form of electronic waste, energy consumption, and the ecological impact of infrastructure development, such as mobile towers and data centers. Improper disposal of electronic devices can contaminate soil and water with toxic substances, while excessive energy use contributes to carbon emissions.

Interconnection Between Traffic and Communication

Traffic and communication are deeply interconnected. Efficient traffic systems depend on timely communication for scheduling, route planning, and safety management. Similarly, communication relies on traffic for the delivery of messages, goods, and services. For instance, postal services, courier deliveries, and emergency services combine both traffic and communication networks to function effectively. Together, they ensure the smooth operation of societies, economies, and governance systems.

Environmental Impacts

While traffic and communication are essential for development, they also contribute to environmental degradation if not managed responsibly. Vehicle emissions, industrial traffic, and air transport increase air pollution and greenhouse gas emissions. Noise from roads, railways, and airports affects human health and wildlife. Waste from communication technologies, such as discarded electronics, pollutes land and water. Sustainable solutions, such as public transport, electric vehicles, renewable energy for digital networks, and proper e-waste management, are necessary to mitigate these impacts.

Final Insights

Traffic and communication are indispensable for modern life, enabling the movement of people, goods, and ideas efficiently. At the same time, their environmental implications cannot be ignored. Balancing development with sustainability requires careful planning, technological innovation, and public awareness. Responsible traffic management and environmentally conscious communication systems can ensure that human progress coexists with a clean, safe, and sustainable environment.

SPORTS AND SPORTSMANSHIP

Sports are physical activities that involve skill, competition, and teamwork. They are an essential part of education and daily life, helping individuals stay healthy, disciplined, and socially active. Sports can be played at various levels – local, national, or international – and include activities like football, cricket, athletics, badminton, chess, and yoga. Participation in sports not only strengthens the body but also develops mental alertness, patience, and social values.

Sportsmanship refers to the ethical and fair behavior expected of players during sports. It includes respect for opponents, following rules, accepting victories and defeats gracefully, and promoting fairness and equality. True sportsmanship ensures that competition becomes a learning experience rather than just a fight for victory.

Importance of Sports

Sports play a crucial role in physical, mental, and social development. They improve strength, stamina, and flexibility, keeping the body fit and healthy. Regular participation in sports reduces stress, improves concentration, and develops problem-solving abilities.

Socially, sports bring people together, encourage teamwork, and foster cooperation. They create opportunities for students and communities to learn leadership, communication, and collaboration skills. At the national level, sports promote unity, patriotism, and pride when athletes represent their country in competitions.

Classification of Sports

Sports can be classified into different categories based on their nature:

1. **Indoor and Outdoor Sports**
   - Indoor sports are played inside closed spaces such as halls or rooms. Examples include billiards, table tennis, badminton, and bowling. These sports require precision, concentration, and quick reflexes.
   - Outdoor sports are played in open areas like fields or grounds. Examples include cricket, hockey, soccer, golf, and baseball. These sports often require greater physical strength, stamina, and teamwork.
2. **Individual and Team Sports**
   - Individual sports are played by a single player competing against another individual, such as athletics, boxing, tennis, and golf.
   - Team sports involve a group of players working together, such as cricket, basketball, volleyball, hockey, and soccer. These sports emphasize coordination and cooperation.

Detailed Description of Major Sports

Athletics

Athletics is one of the oldest and most fundamental forms of sport, consisting of track and field events such as running races, jumping (long jump, high jump), and throwing (javelin, discus). It is mainly an individual sport and forms a major part of international competitions like the Olympic Games. Athletics develops speed, strength, endurance, and agility.

Badminton

Badminton is a fast-paced indoor sport played using a racket and a shuttlecock. It can be played in singles or doubles. The objective is to hit the shuttlecock over the net so that it lands in the opponent's court. It requires quick reflexes, agility, and hand-eye coordination.

Baseball

Baseball is an outdoor team sport played between two teams of nine players each. Players take turns batting and fielding. The aim is to score runs by hitting the ball and running around bases. It requires strategy, coordination, and timing.

Basketball

Basketball is played on a rectangular court between two teams of five players each. The objective is to score points by shooting the ball through the opponent's hoop. It is a dynamic game that requires speed, teamwork, coordination, and decision-making skills.

Billiards

Billiards is an indoor cue sport played on a rectangular table covered with cloth. Players use a cue stick to strike balls and score points. It demands accuracy, concentration, and strategic thinking.

Bowling

Bowling is played by rolling a ball down a lane to knock over a set of pins. It can be played individually or in teams. The player scoring the highest points wins. It requires control, precision, and consistency.

Boxing

Boxing is a combat sport in which two participants compete using their fists while wearing protective gloves. The match takes place in a ring and is divided into rounds. Boxing requires strength, stamina, discipline, and tactical skill.

Cricket

Cricket is one of the most popular sports in India. It is played between two teams of eleven players each. One team bats to score runs, while the other bowls and fields to restrict runs and dismiss players. Cricket requires patience, teamwork, strategy, and technical skill.

Hockey

Hockey is played with a stick and a ball between two teams of eleven players each. The aim is to score goals by hitting the ball into the opponent's goalpost. It requires speed, coordination, and teamwork.

Table Tennis

Table tennis, also known as ping-pong, is an indoor sport played on a table using small paddles and a lightweight ball. It can be played in singles or doubles. The game requires fast reflexes, concentration, and precise control.

Soccer

Soccer is the most popular sport in the world. It is played between two teams of eleven players each. Players aim to score goals by kicking the ball into the opponent's net. It requires stamina, teamwork, and strategic planning.

Tennis

Tennis is played with rackets and a ball, either in singles or doubles format. Players hit the ball over a net into the opponent's court. It requires strength, agility, concentration, and endurance.

Volleyball

Volleyball is played between two teams of six players each. The objective is to send the ball over the net and ground it in the opponent's court. It emphasizes team coordination, quick reflexes, and communication.

Golf

Golf is an outdoor individual sport in which players use clubs to hit a ball into a series of holes on a course in the fewest number of strokes. It requires precision, patience, and focus.

Sportsmanship and Its Values

Sportsmanship teaches important life values such as fairness, respect, honesty, and patience. A good sportsperson never cheats or breaks rules, encourages teammates, and applauds opponents' efforts. Accepting defeat gracefully is as important as celebrating victory humbly.

Sportsmanship also promotes emotional control and discipline. Players learn to handle pressure, develop patience, and show empathy and encouragement toward others. These values are transferable to everyday life, helping children become responsible and ethical individuals.

Basic Rules and Equipment of Sports

Sport	Basic Rules	Equipment
Athletics	Follow track lanes; no false start; includes running, jumping, throwing	Track, running shoes, javelin, discus
Badminton	Shuttle must cross net; played to 21 points; singles/doubles	Racket, shuttlecock, net
Baseball	9 players per team; score by running bases	Bat, ball, gloves, helmet
Basketball	5 players per team; dribble while moving; score in hoop	Basketball, hoop, court
Billiards	Strike balls with cue; score points by hitting targets	Cue stick, balls, table
Bowling	Roll ball to knock down pins; played in turns	Bowling ball, pins, lane
Boxing	Punch above waist; played in rounds; win by points/knockout	Gloves, mouthguard, ring
Cricket	11 players per team; score runs; bowlers take wickets	Bat, ball, stumps, pads
Hockey	Use stick to hit ball; score goals in post	Hockey stick, ball, shin guards
Table Tennis	Ball must bounce; played to 11 points	Paddle, ball, table, net
Soccer (Football)	No hands (except goalkeeper); score goals	Football, goalpost, shin guards
Tennis	Ball over net; played as singles/doubles; scoring system	Racket, ball, net
Volleyball	6 players per team; max 3 touches; ball over net	Volleyball, net, court
Golf	Hit ball into holes in fewest strokes	Golf club, ball

Role of Sports in Education and Society

Schools and educational institutions play a vital role in promoting sports. Physical education classes, annual sports events, and inter-school competitions encourage students to participate actively. Sports clubs, playgrounds, and coaching centers help identify and train talented individuals.

At the societal level, sports unite people across communities and regions. Major sporting events like the Olympics, World Cup, and Commonwealth Games foster international cooperation and friendly competition. Participation in sports also discourages negative habits, promotes mental health, and inspires youth to lead disciplined lives.

Challenges in Sports and Sportsmanship

Despite their importance, sports face several challenges. Lack of proper infrastructure, insufficient training facilities, and inadequate coaching limit opportunities for children and youth. Excessive focus on winning, commercialization, and unethical practices like doping harm the spirit of true sportsmanship. Social and economic barriers may prevent talented individuals from accessing training and competition opportunities.

Measures to Promote Sports and Sportsmanship

To encourage sports and sportsmanship, schools and communities can organize regular games, tournaments, and physical activities. Teachers, coaches, and parents should emphasize skill development, teamwork, and ethical conduct rather than just winning. Government and private initiatives to build sports facilities, provide scholarships, and train coaches help nurture talent at the grassroots level.

Education about fair play, respect for opponents, and discipline should be integrated into school curricula. Promoting local sports and traditional games also preserves cultural heritage while encouraging participation.

Significance of Sports and Sportsmanship

Sports and sportsmanship are essential for developing healthy, disciplined, and socially responsible individuals. Participation in sports improves physical fitness, sharpens the mind, and strengthens character. Through sports, children learn teamwork, patience, and respect for rules and opponents. Promoting sports and ethical behavior in competitions ensures a balanced and inclusive environment, contributing to personal growth, national pride, and social harmony.

INDIA - RIVERS, PLATEAUS, FORESTS, TRAFFIC, CONTINENTS, AND OCEANS

India is a diverse country with a rich geographical and ecological landscape. It is located in South Asia and has varied terrain, including mountains, plains, plateaus, forests, rivers, and coastlines. These physical features play a vital role in agriculture, climate regulation, and biodiversity. With well-developed transport and communication systems, India is internally well-connected and linked to the rest of the world.

Rivers of India

India is endowed with many rivers that serve as lifelines for agriculture, drinking water, and industry. Major rivers include the Ganga River, Yamuna River, Brahmaputra River, Godavari River, Krishna River, and Narmada River.

The Ganga, considered sacred, supports millions of people along its banks. Rivers provide water for irrigation, hydroelectric power, and domestic use. They also support fisheries, wetlands, and diverse ecosystems. Many rivers originate from the Himalayas or the Western Ghats, flow across plains, and finally empty into the sea.

Major Rivers of India

River	Type	Origin	Flows Into	Key Feature
Ganga River	Himalayan	Himalayas	Bay of Bengal	Most sacred, longest in India
Yamuna River	Himalayan	Himalayas	Ganga	Tributary of Ganga
Brahmaputra River	Himalayan	Tibet (near Himalayas)	Bay of Bengal	Largest river by volume
Godavari River	Peninsular	Western Ghats	Bay of Bengal	Longest peninsular river
Krishna River	Peninsular	Western Ghats	Bay of Bengal	Important for irrigation
Narmada River	Peninsular	Central India	Arabian Sea	Flows westward

Plateaus of India

India has several important plateaus, which are elevated areas of land with relatively flat tops. The Deccan Plateau in the south is rich in minerals and supports agriculture. The Chotanagpur Plateau in eastern India is known for coal, iron, and other mineral resources. Plateaus influence climate, soil fertility, and human settlement patterns. They also act as natural water reservoirs, as many rivers and streams originate from them.

Plateaus of India

Plateau	Location	Resources	Importance
Deccan Plateau	Southern India	Minerals, black soil	Agriculture, industries, forestry
Chotanagpur Plateau	Eastern India	Coal, iron, mica	Major industrial region, mining
Malwa Plateau	Central India	Fertile soil, manganese	Agriculture, mineral resources
Rajasthan Plateau (Aravalli Region)	Western India	Gypsum, copper	Mining, agriculture
Mewar Plateau	Rajasthan	Granite, minerals	Building materials, mining
Karnataka Plateau	Southern India	Iron ore, gold	Industrial and agricultural development

Forests of India

India's forests are home to diverse flora and fauna. They are classified into tropical rainforests, deciduous forests, thorn forests, and mangroves. Tropical rainforests in the Western Ghats and northeastern states have dense vegetation and high biodiversity. Deciduous forests cover central India and are important for timber and medicinal plants. Mangroves, such as the Sundarbans, protect coastal regions and support aquatic life. Forests maintain ecological balance, prevent soil erosion, and regulate the climate.

Types of Forests in India

Forest Type	Region	Features	Examples / Typical Species
Tropical Evergreen	Western Ghats, Northeast	Dense, evergreen, receives very high rainfall	Teak, Rosewood, Bamboo
Tropical Deciduous	Central India (Madhya Pradesh, Chhattisgarh, Odisha)	Trees shed leaves seasonally; moderate rainfall	Teak, Sal, Neem
Thorn Forest / Scrub	Rajasthan, Semi-arid regions	Dry, sparse vegetation, adapted to drought	Cactus, Acacia, Euphorbia
Mangrove Forest	Coastal areas, Sundarbans	Salt-tolerant, grow in tidal waters	Sundari tree, Avicennia, Rhizophora
Montane / Hill Forest	Himalayan region	Evergreen or coniferous; cooler climate	Deodar, Pine, Silver Fir
Littoral and Swamp Forests	Coastal plains, wetlands	Water-logged, aquatic plants	Coconut palms, Water lilies

Traffic in India

Traffic refers to the movement of people, vehicles, and goods across India. Roads, railways, airways, and waterways connect villages, towns, and cities.

Road transport—cars, buses, trucks, and two-wheelers—is the most common mode. Railways are essential for long-distance travel and freight transport. Airways connect cities at national and international levels, while rivers and seas support water transport.

Efficient traffic systems promote trade, education, healthcare, tourism, and overall national development.

Modes of Transport (Traffic)

Mode	Examples	Advantage
Roadways	Cars, buses	Flexible, door-to-door
Railways	Trains	Cheap, long-distance
Airways	Aeroplanes	Fastest
Waterways	Ships, boats	Cheapest for heavy goods

Continents and Oceans

India is part of Asia, the largest continent in the world. It is bordered by the Indian Ocean in the south, the Arabian Sea in the west, and the Bay of Bengal in the east.

India's location between these water bodies significantly influences its climate, trade routes, and marine life. Globally, continents and oceans are interconnected through trade, communication, and ecosystems, making India an integral part of the world's geography.

Continents

Continent	Special Feature
Asia	Largest and most populous
Africa	Rich in wildlife
North America	Developed countries
South America	Amazon rainforest
Antarctica	Coldest continent
Europe	Industrialized region
Australia	Smallest continent

Significance of Geographical Features

The rivers, plateaus, and forests of India support agriculture, provide natural resources, and maintain ecological balance. Traffic systems enable mobility, trade, and communication, connecting people across the country.

India's location in Asia and its proximity to major oceans enhance its strategic, economic, and cultural importance globally. Understanding the interconnection of these geographical features helps in appreciating India's natural wealth, environmental significance, and role in global development.

OUR REGION: RIVERS, MOUNTAINS, STONES, FORESTS, TRAFFIC

Uttar Pradesh, located in northern India, is one of the largest and most populous states. It is known for its fertile plains, cultural heritage, and diverse natural resources. The state has a variety of geographical features such as rivers, hills, stones, and forests, which influence agriculture, industry, climate, and daily life. Traffic and transportation systems ensure connectivity, trade, and development throughout the state. Understanding these aspects helps in appreciating the environment, economy, and lifestyle of Uttar Pradesh.

Rivers of Uttar Pradesh

Uttar Pradesh is blessed with several important rivers that are vital for agriculture, drinking water, industry, and cultural activities.

- **Ganga River:** The Ganga is the most sacred and prominent river of the state, flowing through cities such as Varanasi, Kanpur, Allahabad (Prayagraj), and Patna. It provides water for irrigation, supports fisheries, and sustains millions of people along its banks. The Ganga is also used for religious ceremonies, making it culturally significant.
- **Yamuna River:** The Yamuna flows through Agra, Mathura, and other towns. It supports agriculture in western Uttar Pradesh and provides water for industries and households.
- **Ghaghara and Gomti Rivers:** Ghaghara, a tributary of the Ganga, brings water from the Himalayan region, while Gomti flows through Lucknow and surrounding areas, supporting irrigation and daily use.
- **Other Rivers:** Betwa, Chambal, Ken, and Rapti rivers are important for local irrigation, fishery, and soil fertility. Many rivers form fertile alluvial plains, making Uttar Pradesh one of the richest agricultural regions in India.

Rivers also help maintain groundwater levels, support wetlands, and provide habitats for aquatic plants and animals. During monsoon seasons, proper river management is required to prevent flooding in low-lying areas.

Mountains and Hills in Uttar Pradesh

While most of Uttar Pradesh is part of the Indo-Gangetic plains, the Shivalik Hills in the northern districts like Saharanpur and Pilibhit form small hilly regions.

- These hills influence local climate by increasing rainfall and affecting temperature patterns.
- Streams originating from these hills supply water to nearby villages and rivers.

- Hills and small mountains are home to forests and wildlife, contributing to ecological balance.
- The terrain also supports activities such as trekking, tourism, and small-scale agriculture on terraced fields.

Although Uttar Pradesh does not have very high mountains, these hilly regions play an important role in water conservation, biodiversity, and cultural significance.

Stones and Minerals

Uttar Pradesh has various types of stones and mineral resources used in construction, roads, and industries:

- **Limestone:** Found in districts like Lalitpur and Mirzapur, limestone is used for cement production and construction.
- **Sandstone and Granite:** Used in building temples, monuments, and public infrastructure.
- **Marble:** The state has some marble deposits used in decorative purposes and flooring.

These resources contribute to local economies by providing employment and supporting industries. Proper mining and resource management are essential to prevent environmental degradation and maintain ecological balance.

Forests of Uttar Pradesh

Forests are vital for environmental balance, wildlife conservation, and human livelihood in Uttar Pradesh.

- **Dudhwa National Park:** Located in Lakhimpur Kheri district, this forest area is rich in tigers, elephants, and other wildlife species.
- **Katarniaghat Wildlife Sanctuary:** Known for its dense vegetation and endangered species.
- **Other Forest Areas:** Western Uttar Pradesh and Bundelkhand regions have smaller forest patches, supporting biodiversity and local livelihoods.

Forests provide timber, firewood, medicinal plants, fruits, and grazing areas for livestock. They prevent soil erosion, maintain rainfall patterns, regulate climate, and act as carbon sinks. Many communities depend on forests for income and sustenance. Afforestation programs and forest protection initiatives are crucial for sustainability.

Traffic and Transportation

Traffic and transportation systems connect Uttar Pradesh internally and with other states, facilitating trade, communication, and mobility:

- **Roadways:** National highways, expressways like the Yamuna Expressway, and state highways connect major cities, towns, and rural areas. Roads support the movement of goods, agricultural produce, and commuters.
- **Railways:** Uttar Pradesh has one of the largest railway networks in India. Major stations in Lucknow, Varanasi, Kanpur, and Allahabad (Prayagraj) support passenger and freight transport, linking rural and urban areas.
- **Air Transport:** Airports in Lucknow, Varanasi, Kanpur, and Agra facilitate domestic and international connectivity.
- **Waterways:** Rivers like Ganga are being developed for inland water transport in some areas, improving trade and reducing pressure on roads and railways.

Efficient traffic systems support economic growth, healthcare access, education, tourism, and trade. Proper planning and management ensure safety and sustainability.

Significance of Rivers, Mountains, Stones, Forests, and Traffic in Uttar Pradesh

The rivers, hills, stones, and forests of Uttar Pradesh sustain agriculture, support industries, and maintain ecological balance. Traffic and transportation systems connect people, promote trade, and enable access to essential services. Together, these natural and human-made features shape the economy, lifestyle, and culture of the state. Awareness and proper management of these resources ensure sustainable development, environmental protection, and social progress in Uttar Pradesh.

THE CONSTITUTION OF INDIA

The Constitution of India is the supreme law of the country. It defines the framework of the government, the powers and duties of its organs, and the fundamental rights and duties of citizens. The Constitution establishes India as a sovereign, socialist, secular, and democratic republic. It serves as the guiding document for law-making, governance, and protection of citizens' rights.

Importance of the Constitution

The Constitution is important for the following reasons:

- It provides a legal framework for the functioning of the government.
- It ensures justice, equality, liberty, and freedom for all citizens.
- It safeguards fundamental rights and prescribes duties for citizens.
- It maintains harmony between the central and state governments.
- It protects the sovereignty and integrity of the country.

History of the Indian Constitution

- **British Rule:** During British colonial rule, India had various laws like the Government of India Acts of 1919 and 1935. These acts laid the groundwork for governance but did not provide full democracy.

- **Constituent Assembly:** After independence, the Constituent Assembly was formed on 9 December, 1946 to draft a Constitution for free India. Dr. B.R. Ambedkar was appointed as the Chairman of the Drafting Committee.
- **Adoption and Enforcement:** The Constitution was adopted on 26 November, 1949 and came into effect on 26 January, 1950, a day now celebrated as Republic Day in India.

Salient Features of the Constitution

The Indian Constitution is unique due to its combination of federal and unitary features, flexibility, and comprehensiveness. Key features include:

1. **Lengthiest Constitution:** India has the longest written constitution in the world with 448 articles and 12 schedules.
2. **Sovereign, Socialist, Secular, Democratic, Republic:** It declares India's political system and ideology.
3. **Federal Structure with Unitary Bias:** Powers are divided between the central government and state governments, but the center has supremacy in emergencies.
4. **Fundamental Rights and Duties:** Citizens are guaranteed basic rights, and they also have duties to uphold the Constitution.
5. **Directive Principles of State Policy:** Guidelines for the government to ensure social, economic, and political justice.
6. **Separation of Powers:** Clear division between the legislature, executive, and judiciary.
7. **Independent Judiciary:** The Supreme Court and High Courts protect the Constitution and act as a check on the legislature and executive.
8. **Amendment Procedure:** The Constitution can be amended to meet changing needs while maintaining its basic structure.
9. **Universal Adult Franchise:** Every citizen above 18 has the right to vote.

Preamble of the Constitution

The Preamble reflects the objectives and philosophy of the Constitution. Key points include:

- **Justice:** Social, economic, and political justice for all.
- **Liberty:** Freedom of thought, expression, belief, faith, and worship.
- **Equality:** Equality of status and opportunity, removal of discrimination.
- **Fraternity:** Promotes national unity and integrity.
- **Sovereign:** India is free from foreign control.
- **Socialist:** Ensures equitable distribution of resources and opportunities.
- **Secular:** No religion is given preference; all religions are respected.
- **Democratic Republic:** Head of state is elected, and governance is by representatives of the people.

Fundamental Rights

Fundamental Rights are guaranteed under Articles 12–35 and protect citizens from discrimination and exploitation:

1. **Right to Equality (Articles 14–18):** Prohibits discrimination based on religion, caste, gender, or place of birth.
2. **Right to Freedom (Articles 19–22):** Includes freedom of speech, expression, assembly, movement, and association.
3. **Right against Exploitation (Articles 23–24):** Prohibits human trafficking, forced labor, and child labor.
4. **Right to Freedom of Religion (Articles 25–28):** Ensures freedom to practice, propagate, and manage religious affairs.
5. **Cultural and Educational Rights (Articles 29–30):** Protects the rights of minorities to preserve culture, language, and educational institutions.
6. **Right to Constitutional Remedies (Article 32):** Allows citizens to move the Supreme Court or High Courts to enforce fundamental rights.

Directive Principles of State Policy

- Found in Part IV (Articles 36–51), these are guidelines for the government to ensure social, economic, and political justice.
- Examples include promoting education, providing adequate livelihood, ensuring health and nutrition, reducing inequalities, and protecting the environment.
- While not enforceable by courts, they guide the state in policy-making.

Fundamental Duties

- Added by the 42nd Amendment in 1976, under Article 51A.
- Duties include respecting the Constitution, promoting harmony, protecting the environment, and safeguarding public property.

Union and State Government

- **Union Government (Central):** Headed by the President and Prime Minister, includes the Parliament (Lok Sabha and Rajya Sabha).

- **State Government:** Headed by the Governor and Chief Minister, includes State Legislature.
- **Division of Powers:** Listed in Union List, State List, and Concurrent List (7th Schedule).

Judiciary in India

- **Supreme Court:** The highest court, guardian of the Constitution, protector of Fundamental Rights.
- **High Courts:** Present in each state, supervise lower courts.
- **Subordinate Courts:** Handle civil and criminal matters at district and local levels.
- **Judicial Review:** Courts can declare laws unconstitutional if they violate the Constitution.

Amendments to the Constitution

- The Constitution is flexible but rigid in some provisions.
- Article 368 allows amendments, requiring different levels of approval depending on the subject.
- Amendments have been used to introduce changes such as Fundamental Duties, reservation policies, and decentralization.
- The Basic Structure Doctrine ensures that the essential principles of the Constitution cannot be altered.

Schedules of the Constitution

- 12 schedules organize administrative and governmental matters:
  - ❑ Union & State lists, tribal areas, allocation of seats, powers, and responsibilities.
- They provide clarity in governance and smooth functioning of government machinery.

Significance of the Constitution

- Acts as a supreme law guiding governance and citizen behavior.
- Protects democracy, equality, justice, and liberty.
- Ensures unity, integrity, and sovereignty of India.
- Balances power between Union and states.
- Guides social, economic, and cultural development.

Indian Constitution

Topic	Details
Definition	The Constitution is the Supreme law of India that lays down the framework of governance and rights of citizens.
Adopted On	26 November 1949
Came Into Force	26 January 1950
Drafting Committee Chairman	B.R. Ambedkar
Length	Longest written Constitution in the world
Sources	Borrowed from various countries like the UK, USA, Ireland, Canada, etc.
Preamble	Introduces the Constitution; declares India as Sovereign, Socialist, Secular, Democratic Republic
Parts	Originally 22 Parts; now 25 Parts
Articles	Originally 395 Articles; now 450+ Articles
Schedules	Originally 8 Schedules; now 12 Schedules
Fundamental Rights	Rights guaranteed to citizens (Part III, Articles 12–35)
Fundamental Duties	Duties of citizens (Part IVA, Article 51A)
Directive Principles	Guidelines for the government (Part IV)
Federal System	Division of power between Centre and States
Parliamentary System	Government responsible to Parliament
Amendment Procedure	Defined in Article 368
Citizenship	Defined in Part II (Articles 5–11)
Emergency Provisions	National, State, and Financial Emergencies (Part XVIII)
Independent Judiciary	Supreme Court is the highest judicial authority
Secularism	No official religion; equal respect for all religions

Important Points

- The Preamble is considered the "soul" of the Constitution.
- Fundamental Rights are enforceable in court.
- Directive Principles are non-justiciable (not enforceable by courts).
- Fundamental Duties were added by the 42nd Amendment (1976).

GOVERNANCE SYSTEM IN INDIA

Governance refers to the system through which a country or region is administered and managed. In India, governance is based on the Constitution, which defines the structure, powers, and functions of the government at three levels: national, state, and local. Effective governance ensures law and order, development, citizen participation, justice, and public welfare. India follows a democratic system, allowing people to participate through voting and local representation.

LOCAL SELF-GOVERNMENT

Local Self-Government is the system in which local people manage their own affairs in villages, towns, and cities. It ensures participatory democracy, development, and accountability at the local level.

There are two types:

1. Rural Local Bodies (Panchayati Raj)
2. Urban Local Bodies (Municipalities)

Rural Local Self-Government (Panchayati Raj)

- Introduced by the 73rd Constitutional Amendment Act, 1992
- Follows a three-tier system:
  1. **Gram Panchayat** – Village Level
  2. **Panchayat Samiti / Block Panchayat** – Block Level
  3. **Zila Parishad** – District Level

Features:

- Elected representatives
- Regular elections every 5 years
- Reservation for SCs, STs, and women
- State Finance Commission constituted for grants

a. Village Panchayat (Gram Panchayat)

- Lowest level of rural governance
- Composed of elected representatives, including a Pradhan / Sarpanch
- **Functions:**
  - ❑ Maintenance of village roads and public buildings
  - ❑ Drinking water supply
  - ❑ Primary education and healthcare
  - ❑ Agricultural development and welfare schemes
- **Gram Sabha:** Assembly of all adult villagers, responsible for approving plans and budgets

b. Block Panchayat (Panchayat Samiti)

- Middle level in the three-tier system
- Coordinates activities of Gram Panchayats in the block
- Implements development schemes related to education, health, and irrigation

c. District Panchayat (Zila Parishad)

- Highest rural body at the district level
- Supervises Block Panchayats and Gram Panchayats
- Plans and manages district-level development projects (roads, hospitals, schools)
- Receives funds from the state and central governments

Urban Local Self-Government (Municipalities)

- Introduced by the 74th Constitutional Amendment Act, 1992
- Applies to towns and cities

Types of Urban Local Bodies:

1. **Municipal Corporation** – For large cities
2. **Municipal Council / Municipality** – For smaller cities and towns
3. **Nagar Panchayat** – For areas transitioning from rural to urban

Features:

- Elected representatives
- Responsible for urban planning, public health, sanitation, water supply, and related services

a. Nagar Panchayat

- Governs areas transitioning from rural to urban
- Provides basic facilities like water supply, sanitation, street lighting, and public health

b. Municipality (Municipal Council)

- Governs smaller towns and cities
- **Functions include:**
  - ❑ Urban planning and housing
  - ❑ Waste management and sanitation
  - ❑ Water supply and street lighting
  - ❑ Education and healthcare

c. Municipal Corporation

- Governs large cities like Lucknow, Kanpur, etc.
- **Responsibilities:**
  - City planning and infrastructure development
  - Public transportation and traffic management
  - Health, sanitation, and social welfare
  - Tax collection and budget planning

DISTRICT ADMINISTRATION

- Represents the state government at the district level
- Headed by District Magistrate / Collector
- **Functions:**
  - Maintenance of law and order
  - Revenue collection
  - Coordination of development schemes
  - Disaster management and public services
- Works alongside the Zila Parishad for rural development

Functions of Local Self-Government

a. Rural Areas (Panchayati Raj)

- Construction and maintenance of roads, bridges, and public buildings
- Drinking water supply
- Primary education
- Health and sanitation services
- Agricultural development and welfare programs

b. Urban Areas (Municipalities)

- Planning and development of urban infrastructure and housing
- Public health and sanitation
- Water supply and street lighting
- Regulation of markets and slum development
- Welfare programs for weaker sections

Importance / Advantages

1. **Democratic Participation** – Citizens actively participate in governance
2. **Efficient Administration** – Decisions are made faster at the local level
3. **Economic Development** – Promotes local projects according to community needs
4. **Empowerment of Marginalized Groups** – Women and weaker sections are represented
5. **Accountability and Transparency** – Local leaders are answerable to citizens

Challenges

- Lack of awareness among citizens
- Financial dependency on state governments
- Political interference
- Corruption and mismanagement
- Shortage of trained personnel

Term	Meaning
Gram Sabha	Assembly of all adult members of a village
Gram Panchayat	Elected body at village level
Zila Parishad	District-level governing body
Nagar Panchayat	Transitional urban local body
Municipality	Governing body for small towns
Municipal Corporation	Governing body for large cities

STATE GOVERNANCE

A state in India has its own government, administration, and judiciary, functioning under the framework of the Indian Constitution. Each state is responsible for managing law and order, development, and public services within its territory.

Executive

The executive is responsible for implementing laws and policies made by the legislature and managing day-to-day administration.

Key Components

1. **Governor**
   - Constitutional head of the state
   - Appointed by the President of India for a 5-year term
   - **Powers:**
     - Summon and dissolve the state legislative assembly
     - Approve bills before they become law
     - Appoint the Chief Minister and other ministers
2. **Chief Minister (CM)**
   - Head of the state government (real executive power)
   - Leader of the majority party in the state assembly
   - **Responsibilities:**
     - Formulates policies and plans
     - Heads the council of ministers
     - Coordinates between the state and central government
3. **Council of Ministers**
   - Appointed by the Governor on the advice of the CM
   - Assists the CM in policy implementation and administration

4. **State Secretariat and Departments**
   - Administrative wing that executes government decisions
   - Departments: Education, Health, Agriculture, Finance, Police, etc.

Legislature

The state legislature is responsible for making laws.

Types:

1. **Unicameral** – Only one house (Legislative Assembly/Vidhan Sabha)
2. **Bicameral** – Two houses (Legislative Assembly/ Vidhan Sabha + Legislative Council / Vidhan Parishad)

Functions:

- Pass laws on state subjects (Education, Agriculture, Health, etc.)
- Approve the state budget and expenditure
- Hold the executive accountable

Judiciary

The judiciary ensures justice, law enforcement, and constitutional compliance.

Key Components:

1. **High Court**
   - Highest court in a state or group of states
   - Headed by Chief Justice
   - Hears appeals from lower courts and protects citizens' rights
2. **Subordinate Courts**
   - Include District Courts, Tehsil / Taluka Courts, and Civil/Criminal Courts
   - Handle civil and criminal cases at local levels

Functions:

- Interpret and enforce laws
- Settle disputes between citizens and the state
- Protect Fundamental Rights

Administrative Structure

The administration manages the implementation of policies and public services.

Key Officials:

1. **District Collector / District Magistrate**
   - Head of district administration
   - Responsibilities: Revenue collection, law and order, disaster management
2. **Superintendent of Police (SP)**
   - Maintains law and order in the district
3. **Block and Tehsil Officers**
   - Oversee local administration, development programs, and public welfare schemes
4. **Local Governance Bodies**
   - **Rural:** Gram Panchayat, Panchayat Samiti, Zila Parishad
   - **Urban:** Nagar Panchayat, Municipality, Municipal Corporation

State Governance

Branch	Head / Key Officials	Responsibilities
Executive	Governor, Chief Minister, Council of Ministers	Implement laws, policy execution, day-to-day administration
Legislature	Vidhan Sabha / Vidhan Parishad	Make laws, approve budget, oversee executive
Judiciary	High Court, District Courts	Enforce laws, settle disputes, protect rights
Administration	District Collector, SP, Tehsil Officers	Revenue, law & order, development programs

NATIONAL GOVERNANCE

At the national level, governance is carried out by the Union Government, which manages defense, foreign affairs, finance, and national security. It consists of:

- **Executive:** President (constitutional head), Prime Minister, and Council of Ministers.
- **Legislature:** Parliament with Lok Sabha (House of the People) and Rajya Sabha (Council of States).
- **Judiciary:** Supreme Court of India, the highest court, protects the Constitution, interprets laws, and ensures justice.

National governance coordinates with state governments for implementing laws, policies, and national development programs.

NATIONAL SYMBOLS

National symbols represent India's identity, culture, and heritage. They inspire unity and pride among citizens:

- **National Flag:** Tricolor with saffron, white, and green, symbolizing courage, peace, and prosperity, with the Ashoka Chakra at the center.
- **National Emblem:** Adapted from the Lion Capital of Ashoka, representing power, courage, and justice.
- **National Anthem:** "Jana Gana Mana," played during official events and national functions.

- **National Song:** "Vande Mataram," symbolizes patriotism.
- **National Animal:** Bengal Tiger, representing strength.
- **National Bird:** Peacock, symbolizing beauty and grace.
- **National Flower:** Lotus, symbolizing purity.
- **National Fruit:** Mango, representing richness.

These symbols unite the citizens and reflect India's culture, diversity, and values.

VOTING AND DEMOCRACY

Democracy is a system of government where the power rests with the people. In a democracy, citizens have the right to choose their representatives and participate in decision-making processes. Voting is the most important tool through which citizens exercise their democratic rights. It ensures that government policies and leadership reflect the will of the people.

Meaning of Voting

Voting is the process of expressing one's choice or opinion in elections. Every citizen above 18 years of age in India has the right to vote, as guaranteed by the Constitution. Voting empowers citizens to select leaders at the local, state, and national levels, influencing governance and public policies.

Importance of Voting

Voting is the cornerstone of democracy for several reasons:

- It ensures representation of the people in governance.
- It allows citizens to hold leaders accountable for their actions and decisions.
- It helps in maintaining the balance of power in the government.
- It gives every individual the right to influence decisions that affect their daily lives.
- Voting encourages political awareness and civic responsibility among citizens.

Democracy in India

India is the largest democracy in the world. The Indian democratic system is based on the principles of equality, freedom, and justice. Democracy in India is representative, meaning citizens elect representatives to make decisions on their behalf. Key features include:

- **Universal Adult Franchise:** Every citizen above 18 years has the right to vote, regardless of gender, religion, caste, or social status.
- **Free and Fair Elections:** Conducted by the Election Commission of India, which ensures transparency and fairness.
- **Regular Elections:** Elections are held periodically at local, state, and national levels to maintain a representative government.
- **Separation of Powers:** Power is divided among the Legislature, Executive, and Judiciary to prevent misuse of authority.

Types of Elections in India

1. **Local Elections:** These elections are conducted for urban and rural local bodies, such as Village Panchayats, Nagar Panchayats, Municipalities, and Municipal Corporations. Local elections empower citizens to manage governance at the grassroots level.
2. **State Elections:** State elections are held for the State Legislative Assemblies and, in some states, the Legislative Council. Citizens elect representatives who make laws and policies for the state.
3. **National Elections:** National elections are conducted for the Lok Sabha (House of the People), which is the lower house of Parliament. These representatives make decisions and laws for the entire country.

The Election Process

The election process in India is carefully structured to ensure fairness and transparency:

- **Voter Registration:** Citizens must be registered on the electoral roll.
- **Nomination of Candidates:** Individuals can contest elections after fulfilling eligibility criteria.
- **Campaigning:** Candidates and parties communicate their policies and plans to voters.
- **Voting:** Citizens cast their votes using Electronic Voting Machines (EVMs) or ballot papers.
- **Counting and Results:** Votes are counted, and winners are declared based on majority votes.

Significance of Democracy and Voting

- Democracy ensures equal rights and opportunities for all citizens.
- Voting strengthens national unity by making citizens feel responsible for governance.
- It promotes accountability, as elected representatives are answerable to the people.
- Active participation in voting helps in social, economic, and political development.

Challenges in Voting and Democracy

While India has a strong democratic system, some challenges remain:

- Low voter turnout in some regions.
- Influence of money, caste, and religion in elections.

- Misinformation and fake news affecting voter choices.
- Ensuring the participation of marginalized groups like women and the poor.

Civic Responsibility

Voting is not only a right but also a duty. Citizens must participate responsibly to strengthen democracy, ensure fair governance, and shape the future of the nation. A strong democratic system reflects an informed and active citizenry, making India a vibrant and inclusive democracy.

NATIONAL UNITY

National unity refers to the sense of oneness and togetherness among the citizens of a country. It is the feeling of belonging to one nation, despite differences in religion, language, culture, caste, region, or social background. National unity is essential for the stability, progress, and development of a country. In India, a country known for its diversity, national unity is the foundation of its strength and democracy.

Importance of National Unity

National unity plays a vital role in the growth and security of a nation:

- It ensures **peace and harmony** among diverse communities.
- It strengthens **national integrity** and reduces the risk of conflicts.
- A united nation is able to **face external threats** more effectively.
- It fosters **economic and social development** as people work together for common goals.
- National unity promotes **social justice and equality,** ensuring that every citizen feels valued.

Factors Contributing to National Unity

1. **Constitution and Laws:** The Indian Constitution provides a framework for equality, justice, and liberty, ensuring that all citizens are treated fairly. Constitutional values like democracy, secularism, and rule of law unite people under a common system of governance.
2. **Democracy and Voting:** Active participation in democracy, such as voting and involvement in civic activities, helps citizens feel responsible for the nation. Democratic rights give every individual a voice, which strengthens the sense of unity.
3. **National Symbols:** Symbols like the National Flag, National Emblem, National Anthem, and National Song promote patriotism and pride in the country. They remind citizens of shared heritage, culture, and values.
4. **Education and Awareness:** Education plays a crucial role in fostering national unity. Schools teach children about the country's history, culture, diversity, and the importance of tolerance, respect, and cooperation among citizens.
5. **Cultural Integration:** India's rich diversity—different languages, religions, festivals, and traditions—is a source of strength. Respecting and celebrating this diversity while maintaining a common identity strengthens unity.
6. **Media and Communication:** Mass media, social media, and communication platforms play a role in spreading awareness about national issues, achievements, and the importance of working together as one nation.

Threats to National Unity

Even in a democratic and diverse country like India, certain factors can weaken national unity:

- Casteism and communalism that divide people based on religion or social status.
- Regionalism where local interests are prioritized over national interests.
- Corruption and inequality leading to resentment and distrust among citizens.
- Misinformation and propaganda that spread false narratives about communities or the nation.

Ways to Promote National Unity

- Encourage respect for all religions, languages, and cultures.
- Promote education and awareness about the Constitution and democratic rights.
- Encourage voluntary social service, helping citizens feel connected to the country and fellow citizens.
- Celebrate national festivals and events like Independence Day and Republic Day to foster patriotism.
- Strengthen law and order to protect citizens and maintain peace.

Significance of National Unity

National unity is the backbone of a strong and prosperous nation. A united citizenry ensures stability, encourages economic growth, protects sovereignty, and enables social harmony. In a diverse country like India, national unity is not just a feeling but a responsibility for every citizen to work together for the greater good of the nation.

ENVIRONMENT: NEED, PROTECTION, IMPORTANCE, AND SOCIAL RESPONSIBILITY

The environment refers to the surroundings in which living organisms exist. It includes both biotic components (plants, animals, humans) and abiotic components (air, water, soil, climate). The environment provides essential resources necessary for survival and development.

Need of Environment

The environment forms the basic foundation for the existence of life on Earth. It surrounds all living organisms and provides the essential conditions required for their survival and growth. Every living being, including humans, animals, and plants, depends directly or indirectly on the environment for fulfilling its needs.

Environment as a Life Support System

The environment acts as a life-support system by supplying air for breathing, water for drinking, and food for nourishment. Without these essential elements, survival would not be possible. It also provides shelter and suitable living conditions that help organisms grow and reproduce. The availability of these resources ensures continuity of life on the planet.

Maintenance of Ecological Balance

Another important aspect of the environment is its role in maintaining ecological balance. Natural systems operate through interconnected processes such as food chains, food webs, and natural cycles. These processes ensure that energy flows smoothly and nutrients are recycled within ecosystems. Any disturbance in this balance can lead to serious environmental problems.

Source of Natural Resources

The environment is the primary source of natural resources. It provides renewable resources like forests and water, as well as non-renewable resources such as minerals and fossil fuels. These resources are essential for agriculture, industry, and overall economic development. Human progress and technological advancement depend largely on these resources.

Regulation of Climate

The environment plays a vital role in regulating climate and weather conditions. It controls temperature, rainfall, and seasonal changes, which are crucial for agriculture and sustaining life. A stable climate ensures proper crop production and supports living organisms.

Support for Biodiversity

The environment supports a wide variety of plants and animals by providing natural habitats. This biodiversity is essential for maintaining ecological stability and resilience. Each species plays a specific role in the ecosystem and contributes to its proper functioning.

Cultural and Social Importance

The environment has significant cultural, social, and aesthetic value. It influences human lifestyles, traditions, and beliefs. Natural surroundings provide opportunities for recreation, mental peace, and overall well-being, making life more balanced and meaningful.

Need for Environmental Protection

Environmental protection refers to the conservation and safeguarding of natural resources and ecosystems from damage and degradation. In the present time, increasing human activities have caused serious harm to the environment, making its protection a necessity rather than a choice.

Rising Environmental Degradation

Rapid industrialization, urbanization, and population growth have led to excessive exploitation of natural resources. This has resulted in deforestation, pollution, and loss of biodiversity. Environmental protection is needed to control and reduce this degradation and restore natural balance.

Control of Pollution

Air, water, and soil pollution have increased significantly due to human activities such as industrial waste, vehicle emissions, and improper waste disposal. These pollutants not only harm the environment but also affect human health. Protecting the environment helps in reducing pollution and ensuring a cleaner and healthier life.

Conservation of Natural Resources

Natural resources such as water, forests, minerals, and fossil fuels are limited. Overuse and misuse of these resources can lead to their depletion. Environmental protection is necessary to conserve these resources and ensure their availability for future generations.

Protection of Biodiversity

Many species of plants and animals are becoming endangered or extinct due to habitat destruction and environmental changes. Protecting the environment helps in preserving biodiversity and maintaining ecological balance.

Climate Change and Global Warming

Human activities have increased greenhouse gas emissions, leading to climate change and global warming. This causes extreme weather conditions, melting glaciers, and rising sea levels. Environmental protection is essential to reduce these effects and maintain a stable climate.

Ensuring Sustainable Development

Environmental protection promotes sustainable development, which means meeting present needs without compromising the ability of future generations to meet their own needs. It ensures balanced growth while preserving natural resources.

Human Health and Well-being

A clean and healthy environment is directly related to human health. Pollution and environmental degradation can cause diseases and reduce quality of life. Protecting the environment helps in improving overall health and well-being.

Concept overview

Need	Explanation
Control of Degradation	Reduces environmental damage
Pollution Control	Ensures clean air, water, and soil
Resource Conservation	Prevents depletion of resources
Biodiversity Protection	Saves plants and animals
Climate Stability	Reduces global warming
Sustainable Development	Ensures future security
Health Protection	Improves quality of life

IMPORTANCE, UTILITY AND PROTECTION OF ENVIRONMENT

The environment is essential for the existence and development of life on Earth. It provides the necessary conditions and resources for living organisms to survive, grow, and function effectively. Its importance and utility can be understood through various aspects of human life, natural systems, and ecosystems.

Importance of Environment

The environment plays a crucial role in sustaining life by providing basic necessities such as **air, water, food, and shelter**. These resources ensure the survival and growth of all living beings. Without a healthy environment, life on Earth would not be possible.

It also maintains **ecological balance** by regulating natural processes such as food chains, nutrient cycles, and energy flow. This balance is vital to prevent environmental disturbances and maintain stability in ecosystems.

Additionally, the environment regulates **climate and weather conditions,** including temperature, rainfall, and seasonal changes. These factors are essential for agriculture, water availability, and overall life support systems.

Another critical aspect is the preservation of **biodiversity**. The environment provides habitats for a variety of species, helping conserve plants, animals, and microorganisms. Biodiversity strengthens ecosystems, increases resilience, and ensures ecological stability.

Utility of Environment

The environment serves as a major source of **natural resources** essential for human life. It provides water for drinking and irrigation, fertile soil for agriculture, forests for timber and oxygen, and minerals for industrial development. These resources form the backbone of economic growth and development.

It supports **agriculture** by providing fertile soil, suitable climate, and water resources. Agricultural production depends entirely on environmental conditions, highlighting the environment's practical utility.

The environment also facilitates **industrial development** by supplying raw materials and energy resources required for manufacturing and production.

Beyond material resources, the environment has **recreational and aesthetic utility**. Natural landscapes, forests, rivers, and mountains provide opportunities for tourism, relaxation, and mental well-being, enhancing the quality of human life.

Additionally, it holds **cultural and spiritual significance,** as many traditions, customs, and beliefs are closely connected with nature. The environment shapes human values and lifestyles, contributing to social and cultural well-being.

Important Facts

Aspect	Importance	Utility
Life Support	Provides air, water, and food	Ensures survival and growth
Ecological Balance	Maintains natural systems	Prevents environmental disturbances
Climate	Regulates weather and seasons	Supports agriculture and life
Resources	Conserves biodiversity	Supplies raw materials
Economy	Supports human development	Drives agriculture and industry
Social Value	Maintains traditions and culture	Provides recreation and mental well-being

Reasons for Environmental Protection

Human activities such as industrialization, urbanization, deforestation, and pollution have caused serious harm to natural resources and ecosystems. Environmental protection is necessary to:

- Control pollution (air, water, and soil)
- Conserve natural resources
- Protect biodiversity and endangered species
- Regulate climate and reduce the effects of global warming
- Ensure sustainable development for future generations
- Safeguard human health by providing clean air, water, and a safe living environment

Measures of Environmental Protection

- Afforestation and Reforestation – Planting trees to restore green cover
- Pollution Control – Reducing air, water, and soil pollution
- Waste Management – Practicing Reduce, Reuse, Recycle
- Water and Energy Conservation – Efficient use of natural resources
- Wildlife Protection – Conserving endangered species and natural habitats
- Use of Renewable Energy – Solar, wind, and hydropower

Concept Overview

Aspect	Importance / Utility	Protection Measures
Air	Essential for respiration	Reduce emissions, plant trees
Water	Drinking, irrigation, industry	Treat wastewater, conserve water
Soil	Agriculture, habitat	Prevent erosion, use organic farming
Forests	Oxygen production, biodiversity	Afforestation, prevent deforestation
Wildlife	Maintains ecological balance	Protected areas, anti-poaching
Natural Resources	Supports economy and development	Sustainable use, renewable energy
Climate	Supports agriculture and life	Reduce pollution, climate awareness

SOCIAL RESPONSIBILITY TOWARDS THE ENVIRONMENT

Social responsibility towards the environment refers to the moral duty of individuals, communities, and organizations to protect, conserve, and sustainably use natural resources. Every person is part of the environment, and human actions directly affect its quality and sustainability. Taking responsibility ensures that the environment remains healthy for present and future generations.

Role of Individuals

Individuals play a vital role in environmental protection. By adopting eco-friendly habits, each person can contribute to a cleaner and greener environment. Some key responsibilities include:

- **Reducing Waste:** Minimizing the use of plastics, paper, and non-biodegradable materials.
- **Water and Energy Conservation:** Using water and electricity wisely to reduce wastage.
- **Tree Plantation:** Planting trees and protecting existing greenery.
- **Pollution Reduction:** Using public transport, avoiding unnecessary vehicle use, and supporting clean energy.
- **Awareness and Education:** Educating others about environmental issues and promoting sustainable practices.

Role of Society and Communities

Communities and societies collectively influence environmental quality. Social responsibility at the community level includes:

- **Supporting Environmental Campaigns:** Participating in initiatives like cleanliness drives and tree plantation programs.
- **Promoting Sustainable Practices:** Encouraging recycling, renewable energy, and eco-friendly industries.
- **Protection of Local Ecosystems:** Conserving water bodies, forests, and wildlife habitats.
- **Waste Management:** Proper disposal and segregation of solid and liquid waste.
- **Advocacy and Policy Support:** Supporting laws and policies that protect the environment.

Role of Organizations and Businesses

Organizations and businesses also have social responsibilities towards the environment:

- **Adopting Green Practices:** Reducing emissions, using renewable energy, and minimizing industrial waste.
- **Corporate Social Responsibility (CSR):** Funding environmental projects such as reforestation, water conservation, and wildlife protection.
- **Sustainable Production:** Manufacturing products using eco-friendly processes and materials.
- **Employee Awareness Programs:** Educating staff about environmental conservation and sustainable practices.

Key Principles of Environmental Responsibility

1. **Reduce, Reuse, Recycle** – Minimizing waste and conserving resources.
2. **Sustainable Use of Resources** – Using natural resources wisely without overexploitation.
3. **Biodiversity Conservation** – Protecting plants, animals, and ecosystems.

4. **Pollution Prevention** – Reducing air, water, and soil pollution.
5. **Climate Action** – Supporting efforts to reduce global warming and environmental hazards.

Important Facts

Level	Responsibilities
Individual	Reduce waste, save water and energy, plant trees, reduce pollution, raise awareness
Society / Community	Participate in environmental campaigns, manage waste, protect local ecosystems, promote sustainability
Organizations / Businesses	Green practices, CSR projects, sustainable production, employee environmental education

SCHEMES OPERATED FOR ENVIRONMENTAL PROTECTION IN INDIA

Environmental protection has become a top priority in India due to rapid industrialization, urbanization, and the over-exploitation of natural resources. The government has launched various **schemes and programs** to conserve biodiversity, reduce pollution, restore ecosystems, and promote sustainable development. These schemes also aim to increase public awareness and encourage community participation in protecting the environment.

Major Schemes and Their Objectives

1. **Swachh Bharat Abhiyan (Clean India Mission)**
   - **Objective:** To ensure cleanliness, proper sanitation, and waste management in urban and rural areas.
   - **Key Features:**
     - ❑ Elimination of open defecation
     - ❑ Promotion of solid waste segregation, recycling, and management
     - ❑ Awareness campaigns encouraging citizen participation
2. **National Afforestation Programme (NAP)**
   - **Objective:** To increase forest cover and restore degraded lands.
   - **Key Features:**
     - ❑ Planting trees in urban and rural areas
     - ❑ Community involvement in protecting forests
     - ❑ Prevention of soil erosion and conservation of biodiversity
3. **Namami Gange Programme**
   - **Objective:** To clean and conserve the Ganga River.
   - **Key Features:**
     - ❑ Sewage treatment and river cleaning projects
     - ❑ Afforestation along river banks
     - ❑ Public awareness and sustainable water management
4. **Project Tiger**
   - **Objective:** Protection and conservation of tigers and their habitats.
   - **Key Features:**
     - ❑ Creation of tiger reserves
     - ❑ Anti-poaching measures and wildlife protection
     - ❑ Monitoring of tiger populations
5. **National Air Quality Monitoring Programme (AQI)**
   - **Objective:** To monitor and improve air quality across Indian cities.
   - **Key Features:**
     - ❑ Real-time air quality indexing
     - ❑ Identification of pollution sources
     - ❑ Awareness campaigns to reduce air pollution
6. **Jal Jeevan Mission**
   - **Objective:** To provide safe and sustainable drinking water to households.
   - **Key Features:**
     - ❑ Promotes rainwater harvesting and water conservation
     - ❑ Provides piped drinking water in rural and urban areas
     - ❑ Encourages community participation in water management
7. **Renewable Energy and Energy Efficiency Schemes**
   - **Objective:** Reduce dependence on fossil fuels and promote sustainable energy.
   - **Key Features:**
     - ❑ Promotion of solar, wind, and hydro energy
     - ❑ Encouragement of energy-efficient appliances and industrial practices
     - ❑ Reduces carbon emissions and environmental pollution
8. **National Biodiversity Action Plan (NBAP)**
   - **Objective:** To conserve India's rich biodiversity.
   - **Key Features:**
     - ❑ Conservation of endangered species
     - ❑ Protection of ecosystems and habitats
     - ❑ Sustainable use of natural resources

At a Glance: Environmental Protection Schemes

Scheme / Programme	Objective / Focus	Key Activities
Swachh Bharat Abhiyan	Cleanliness and sanitation	Waste management, awareness campaigns
National Afforestation Programme	Increase forest cover	Tree plantation, soil conservation
Namami Gange Programme	Clean and conserve Ganga	River cleaning, afforestation, sewage treatment
Project Tiger	Tiger conservation	Tiger reserves, anti-poaching, monitoring
National Air Quality Monitoring Programme	Monitor air pollution	Real-time AQI, pollution control campaigns
Jal Jeevan Mission	Safe drinking water	Piped water supply, water conservation
Renewable Energy & Energy Efficiency	Promote sustainable energy	Solar, wind, hydro energy, energy-efficient appliances
National Biodiversity Action Plan	Biodiversity conservation	Protect species, ecosystems, sustainable use

Significance of These Schemes

1. **Conservation of Natural Resources:** Ensures sustainable use of water, forests, and biodiversity.
2. **Pollution Control:** Reduces air, water, and soil pollution, improving public health.
3. **Climate Regulation:** Promotes renewable energy and reduces greenhouse gas emissions.
4. **Community Awareness:** Encourages citizen participation in environmental protection.
5. **Biodiversity Preservation:** Protects endangered species and maintains ecological balance.
6. **Sustainable Development:** Supports long-term economic and ecological stability.

Final Insights

India's environmental protection schemes are critical for preserving natural resources, controlling pollution, conserving biodiversity, and promoting sustainable development. These programs not only safeguard ecosystems but also ensure a healthier, safer, and greener environment for all. Active participation by individuals, communities, and organizations strengthens these efforts, creating a sense of shared responsibility toward nature. By engaging in these initiatives, every citizen contributes to long-term ecological balance, sustainable growth, and the well-being of present and future generations.

IMPORTANT FACTS

- Environment is the surroundings of living and non-living things.
- Components: abiotic – air, water, soil, sunlight, temperature; biotic – plants, animals, humans, microbes.
- Ecosystem is interaction of organisms with their environment.
- Food chain shows energy flow: producer → primary consumer → secondary consumer → decomposer; food web is interconnected chains.
- Individuals can protect the environment – plant trees, avoid plastics, conserve water and energy, eco-friendly habits.
- Family – roles, care, support, values, responsibilities, respect for elders, cooperation.
- Food, health, hygiene – balanced diet, nutrition, cleanliness, handwashing, oral care, exercise, vaccination, disease prevention.
- Water – sources (river, well, rainwater), uses (drinking, irrigation), conservation (rainwater harvesting, avoid wastage), preventing pollution.
- Traffic & communication – road safety, signals, public transport, pedestrian rules, telephone, internet, postal services.
- Sports & sportsmanship – physical activity, indoor & outdoor games, rules, teamwork, fair play, discipline, cooperation.
- India – rivers, plateaus, forests, traffic systems, continents, oceans, climate zones, landmarks.
- Our region – local rivers, mountains, stones, forests, transport, local industries, cultural heritage.
- Constitution – fundamental rights & duties, equality, law, justice, citizenship, secularism, freedom.
- Governance – local self-government (village panchayat, Nagar-panchayat, district panchayat), urban governance (municipality, municipal corporation), state governance (administrative, judiciary, executive), national governance (Parliament, President, Prime Minister, national symbols, voting, national unity).
- Environment – need & importance of protection, air/water/soil conservation, reduce-reuse-recycle, planting trees, social responsibility, environmental awareness programs, government schemes (Swachh Bharat, Green India Mission), sustainability, climate change awareness.

SECTION-B

PEDAGOGICAL ISSUES

CONCEPT AND SCOPE OF EVS

The word environment is derived from French word *'environ'*, means to encircle or surround. It is a composite word for the surrounding in which organism or group of organisms live. The environment consists of *biotic* and *abiotic* substances, *i.e.*, consists of air, water, food, sunlight, temperature, electricity etc. So, one can define the environment as, *"it is the sum of all social, economical, biological, physical or chemical factors which constitute all surroundings of men or living organism, who is both creater and modular of this environment."*

As other organisms, man is also affected by environmental changes. These changes in environment may harm or benefit the man or other organisms living in it. *Environmental Science is the application of all fields of natural science toward solving environmental problems.* Biology, Geology, Chemistry, Physics, Meteorology and many other disciplines are included in the environmental science. Economics, Sociology, Education and Mass-Communication do help in understanding the socio-economic aspects of environment. Mathematics, Statistics and Computer Science also help in modeling and management of environment.

The *Environmental Science* is, therefore, a multidisciplinary science, which may require attention of experts from different branches of science when decisions regarding environmental matters have to be taken. The craze of progress in agriculture, industry, transportation and technology is taken as the general criterion of development of any nation. Such activities of man has created adverse effects on all living organisms in the biosphere. Today environment has become very unpleasant, contaminated and harmful for living organisms.

Environmental Science courses at both the basic and the advanced level are the most rapidly growing courses at many universities in the India. Individual disciplines are developing Environmental Chemistry, Environmental Biology, Environmental Geology and many similar courses to address society's changing needs. Many colleges now recognise majors in *Environmental Science* and CBSE has also started this course at senior secondary level.

History of Environmental Impact and Movements

Considering the age of the Earth and even the human species, the massive environmental impact of humans is a very recent development. Indeed, our relationship with the environment has evolved as we and our technology have evolved.

Environmental historians often identify five basic stages in this evolution. These stages are largely determined by the economic activity in which humans engage using the technologies available. This activity, in turn, affects how humans impact the environment.

1. Hunting and gathering: Early humans were largely at the mercy of their environment, so they generally viewed it in adversarial terms. Weather, predators, food shortages, and disease were constant threats.

2. Agriculture and conservationism: The shift from hunting and gathering to cultivating food is one of the most profound milestones in human evolution. It allowed a great increase in population size and permitted people to settle down in large towns and cities. But agriculture also had a major impact on the environment. People began to view land as a resource to be exploited wherever needed. As land was cleared and cultivated, however, the wilderness vanished. Toward the end of the agricultural stage, the loss of wilderness became so great that alarmed citizens began conservation movements to set up preserves for the remaining wilderness. Today many developing countries still have agricultural economics, and their vanishing wilderness, especially tropical rainforests, has stimulated the growth of conservationism.

3. Industry and environmentalism: The Industrial Revolution began in England around 1800. As nations industrialize, population grows faster, and the environment is perceived more and more as a place to dispose of the concentrated waste by-products of industry. The result is a rapid increase in air and water pollution, as well as problems with solid and hazardous waste disposal. Toward the end of the stage, pollution becomes so widespread that antipollution social movements emerge. In many countries, these social movements began in the early 1960s and peaked in the

1970s. When people talk about "environmentalismm," this antipollution movement is often what they mean. Several early books heralded this new awareness including *Silent Spring* (1962) by Rachel Carson, which warned of pesticide pollution; *The Population Bomb* (1968) by Paul Ehrlich; and *The Limits to Growth* (1972) by Donella H. Meadows and others. These efforts and rising public concern led to the passage of landmark environmental legislation throughout the world.

4. Transition and sustainability: Although some forms of pollution have been reduced, many other environmental problems have increased. In India, for example, species of wildlife are becoming imperiled at increasing rates as habitat is destroyed. Groundwater contamination has worsened, and there are many thousands of hazardous and radioactive waste sites that will likely not be cleaned up for centuries. Despite recycling and precycling efforts, the amount of solid waste produced per person continues to climb. Globally, we see global warming, ozone depletion, and increasing species extinction as the greatest environmental threats to future generations. These problems are caused in large part by rapidly increasing population in developing countries, which also leads to local food shortages and the loss of billions of tons of soil to erosion each year.

We are currently in this fourth stage—the transition. Environmental problems have become so widespread that they demand large-scale solutions that involve many aspects of society. Beginning in the early nineties, a sustainability movement has emerged to try to deal with these problems. Unlike the conservation and antipollution movements of the past, which emphasized specific problems, this movement seeks long-term coexistence with the environment. **Sustainability** means meeting the needs of today without reducing the quality of life for future generations. This includes not reducing the quality of the future environment. Sustainability is achieved through sustainable ("green") technologies that use renewable resources such as solar power and recycle many materials. These technologies allow a **sustainable economy** that produces wealth and provides jobs for many human generations without degrading the environment.

The sustainability movement uses three approaches not attempted by previous environmental movements. First, it focuses explicitly on trying to reduce society's use of all resources. Emphasis is thus on input reduction, as opposed to end-of-pipe solutions *Waste is viewed as a symptom, not a cause, of the environ-mental crisis.*

Second, the sustainability movement is more holistic. It realizes the necessity of addressing the social, and especially economic, causes environmental degradation. This has led to at increasing appreciation of the role of poverty and other economic factors that cause people to deplete resources and pollute. Market-based solutions are becoming more popular, and less emphasis is placed on the legal solutions used in that past. For example, many experts now agree that it is often more effective and cheaper for society to tax coal, gasoline, and other polluting substances than to pass laws specifying how much pollution may be emitted. The higher gasoline prices encourage people to drive less or buy fuel-efficient cars, for instance. Such economic approaches acknowledge that, far from being anti-environmental business can greatly benefit the environment. It is what people produce and sell that can cause environmental problems, not the acts of producing and selling in themselves. Producing and selling furniture made from tropical rainforest timber will harm the environment whereas Brazil nut, rubber, and many other rainforest product may be extracted and sold with little or nil long-term damage.

Components of the Environment

Environment consists of all living and non-living things which surround us. Therefore, the basic components of the environment are:

1. Atmosphere
2. Hydrosphere
3. Lithosphere
4. Biosphere

Atmosphere

Atmosphere consists of a complex mixture of a number of gases, water vapour and a variety of fine particulate matter. The gaseous mantle which surrounds the globe is constituted by about 5.15×10^{15} metric tonnes of gas which exerts a pressure of about 1 kg per sq.cm. on earth's crust. Most of these gases are compressed in the lowermost layer due to the pressure of lower layer above it. Pressure decreases as we move upward.

The composition of earth's atmosphere

Gas	Parts per million	Relative percentage
Nitrogen	780832.00	78.08
Oxygen	209460.00	20.95
Argon	9340.00	00.93
Carbon dioxide	403.00	00.03
Neon	18.00	00.0018
Ozone	0.07	00.000007

Structure of Atmosphere

Based primarily on the temperature pattern, earth's atmosphere can be roughly divided into four major zones:—

1. **The troposphere:** The zone immediately above earth's surface is known as the *troposphere* which extends upto

a height of about 20 kms above the equator and about 8 kms over the poles. The temperature in this zone drops with height being as low as –60°C at its upper extremity.

2. **The stratosphere:** The layer next to troposphere is called the *stratosphere*. It is about 30 kms in thickness and is a very important zone of atmosphere as it contains the vital ozone layer. The temperature in this zone rises from –60°C to about 0°C in its upper layers. The rise in temperature is due to the formation of ozone under the influence of ultra-violet radiation.
3. **The mesosphere:** It is a zone of about 40 kms in thickness which lies next to the stratosphere. This zone is characterised by gradual decline in temperatures to about –90°C.
4. **The thermosphere:** It is the zone next to mesosphere in which temperature increases with height. Most of the constituents of this zone are in ionized state.

Importance of Atmosphere

It is the typical structure and composition of earth's atmosphere which is responsible for creating conditions suitable for the existence of a healthy biosphere on this planet. Atmosphere's role in maintenance of the biosphere in a healthy state can be summed up as follows:

1. Atmosphere regulates the temperature of earth's crust. The presence of gases capable of absorbing long wavelength radiations, is responsible for maintaining the temperatures under which life activities are possible. Moon for example, has no atmosphere. At its equator, surface temperatures rise to 101°C in the day. In nights they drop down to –180°C. No life can survive at these temperatures.
2. The incoming solar radiations are filtered high above earth's surface. Harmful ultra-violet radiations are absorbed in the stratosphere by the vital ozone layer. These rays can severely damage the terrestrial life.
3. Constant mixing of the contents of atmosphere occurs due to air currents and the vertical temperature gradient. This prevents accumulation of harmful gases and vapours at any particular spot. Atmosphere is therefore, a quick and effective media for transfer, transport and dissemination of gaseous wastes.
4. Pollutants in the atmosphere are removed by a much more effective mechanism than that operating on land or in water. As the troposphere derives its heat from earth's surface, warm air being lighter rises and cools down adiabetically. Cooling condenses water vapours. The entire load of pollutants is brought down with snow, dew or rains which cleans the atmosphere.

Hydrosphere

Water is absolutely essential for life on this planet. It is a natural resource of fundamental importance. The atomic structure and unique properties of water seem to be especially designed for the biosphere.

Importance of Water for the Biosphere

Without water life as it exists on our planet is impossible. The importance of water in sustaining a healthy biosphere on our planet can be summed up as follows:

1. Water is the very medium in which all biochemical reactions within a living organism and a large number of chemical reactions involving components of rocks, soil and pollutants of environment occur. It is the availability of water which determines the nature, composition and abundance of terrestrial life. Regions with very low rainfall become deserts. Lush green vegetation develops where water is in abundance.
2. Due to its high specific heat, changes in its temperature need large amounts of heat energy or its withdrawal as compared to other objects. This causes temperature differences between land and sea when heated by solar radiations and an active air circulation is maintained. The air circulation in turn determines precipitation pattern and climatic conditions of locality.
3. A high latent heat of vaporisation causes a large amount of solar energy to be used up in evaporation of water. The solar heat could have, otherwise, raised global temperatures significantly.
4. The unique property of expansion, when cooled below 4°C causes water to freeze from top downwards as aquatic bodies lose or gain most of their heat energy from the surface in contact with air above. Aquatic life stays safe under the ice-sheet.
5. Water is an efficient means of transfer and transport of the material dissolved or suspended in it. Low lying regions of the world, river basins, land along sea coasts are, therefore, much more productive than upland areas. Water transports dissolved materials, silt, debris, nutrients and pollutants etc. from upland areas to low lying regions. Nearly 90% of world population is, therefore, concentrated in these areas.
6. Water also plays an important role in reducing the atmosphere burden of particulate matters and gaseous pollutants. Water vapours condense around fine particulate matter and gaseous materials dissolve in water and the entire load of waste materials and gases is brought down with rains or snow. This cleans the atmospheric air.

Lithosphere

Earth's crust consists of rocks the loose materials derived from these rocks, most of which is modified into soil. There are about a dozen elements which constitute the bulk of earth's crust-nearly 99% by weight. These elements go into the formation of minerals which in turn form rocks from which all soils are derived.

Elementary Composition of Earth's Crust

	Elements	Percentage
1.	Oxygen	46.6
2.	Silicon	27.7
3.	Aluminium	8.1
4.	Iron	5.0
5.	Calcium	3.6
6.	Sodium	2.8
7.	Potassium	2.6
8.	Magnesium	2.0
9.	Hydrogen	0.9
10.	Titanium	0.41
11.	Chlorine	0.20
12.	Carbon	0.19
13.	Others	1.00

SIGNIFICANCE OF EVS

The environment studies enlighten us, about the importance of protection and conservation of our indiscriminate release of pollution into the environment.

At present a great number of environment issues, have grown in size and complexity day by day, threatening the survival of mankind on earth. We study about these issues besides and effective suggestions in the Environment Studies. Environment studies have become significant for the following reasons:

1. **Environment Issues Being of International Importance:** It has been well recognised that environment issues like global warming and ozone depletion, acid rain, marine pollution and biodiversity are not merely national issues but are global issues and hence must be tackled with international efforts and cooperation.
2. **Problems Cropped in the Wake of Development:** Development, in its wake gave birth to Urbanization, Industrial Growth, Transportation Systems, Agriculture and Housing etc. However, it has become phased out in the developed world. The North, to cleanse their own environment has, fact fully, managed to move 'dirty' factories of South. When the West developed, it did so perhaps in ignorance of the environmental impact of its activities. Evidently such a path is neither practicable nor desirable, even if developing world follows that.
3. **Explosively Increase in Pollution:** World census reflects that one in every seven persons in this planted lives in India. Evidently with 16 per cent of the world's population and only 2.4 per cent of its land area, there is a heavy pressure on the natural resources including land. Agricultural experts have recognized soils health problems like deficiency of micronutrients and organic matter, soil salinity and damage of soil structure.
4. **Need for An Alternative Solution:** It is essential, specially for developing countries to find alternative paths to an alternative goal. We need a goal as under:
   1. A goal, which ultimately is the true goal of development an environmentally sound and sustainable development.
   2. A goal common to all citizens of our earth.
   3. A goal distant from the developing world in the manner it is from the over-consuming wasteful societies of the "developed" world.
5. **Need to Save Humanity from Extinction:** It is incumbent upon us to save the humanity from extinction. Consequent to our activities constricting the environment and depleting the biosphere, in the name of development.
6. **Need for Wise Planning of Development:** Our survival and sustenance depend. Resources withdraw, processing and use of the product have all to by synchronised with the ecological cycles in any plan of development our actions should be planned ecologically for the sustenance of the environment and development.

INTEGRATED ENVIRONMENT STUDIES

An ever-increasing world population demanding food, water, energy, health care, and education puts unprecedented pressure on both, the "Earth System" that is its natural environment and resource, and the institutions that design the framework organizing access to and distribution of resources and education. Successful sustainable management of these global challenges, therefore, requires an integrated approach which combines elements from the natural and engineering sciences with those from social, political and economics studies. The Integrated Environmental Studies provides a broad and interdisciplinary education in these diverse fields within the multicultural environment.

ENVIRONMENTAL STUDIES AND ENVIRONMENTAL EDUCATION

Status of Environmental Education in School Education

The education system in India had incorporated certain aspects of environment in school curricula as early as 1930. The Kothari Commission (1964-66) also suggested that basic education had to offer EE and relate it to the life needs and aspirations of the people and the nation. At the primary stage, the report recommended that "the aims of teaching science in the primary schools should be to develop proper understanding of the main facts, concepts, principles and processes in physical and biological environment". Environmental education at primary, secondary, higher secondary levels was treated in a different way. Environmental education is an essential part of every pupil's learning. It helps to encourage awareness of the environment, leading to informed concern for active participation in resolving environmental problems. It was introduced without any delay from class –1 as EVS, as a subject so that right from their childhood, the right attitudes towards environment will be nurtured in the young minds.

It is important that we capture this enthusiasm and that no opportunity is lost to develop knowledge, understanding and concern for the environment through school education. The curricular, cross-curricular attempt of environmental education also should be a joy for the learner. In this direction, NCERT has published in collaboration with the Centre for Environmental Education, Ahemadabad a book titled "Joy of learning" with lot of environmental activities, a handbook for teachers. Similarly, several workshops were conducted to orient school teachers and educational functionaries of the state boards on various aspects of environmental education. Strategies for successful implementation of EE in schools were discussed in detail in these interactions.

A curricular framework of environmental education

- It envisages the place of EE in the school curriculum.
- Place of EE vis-à-vis other subjects of study.
- Mode and strategy of inclusion of chapters at different levels.
- EE in terms of time and allocation of marks.
- Development of syllabi and instructional material for dissemination at different levels of school education.

In order to supplement the analysis of individual and institutional consultations it was decided to organise two face-to-face National Consultations on Environmental Education in Schools. The First Consultation on the academic aspects of Environmental Education (EE) in schools was organised by NCERT on 13-14 February 2004 in New Delhi . Seventy participants comprising eminent scientists, environmentalists, officials of central and state govt. departments dealing with environment, senior academicians attached to Departments/ Centres of environmental studies, environmental science, environmental ecology, botany, regional development, geography, marine biology, etc. of different universities, teacher educators, principals of teacher training colleges, prominent Non-Governmental Organisations (NGOs) and NCERT faculty took part in deliberations. The second consultation on the implementation of EE in schools was held on 13th March 2004 . Seventy-two officials comprising Presidents/Chairpersons of Boards/Councils of school education, Directors of State Councils of Educational Research and Training (SCERTs), Directors of Education in the states, eminent scientists, environmentalists and NCERT faculty participated. The initial draft prepared by NCERT faculty presented in the First Consultation was revised as per the suggestions received. This revised version was presented in the Second Consultation and suggestions for further improvement were received. Various issues were deliberated in these Consultations through plenary presentation, open house discussion, interaction in groups and consolidation of recommendations.

Aims & Objectives of Environmental Education

The objectives of environmental education is to increase public awareness about environmental issues, explore possible solutions, and to lay the foundations for a fully informed and active participation of individual in the protection of environment and the prudent and rational use of natural resources. The resolutions provide the following guiding principles for environmental education:

- The environment as a common heritage of mankind.
- The common duty of maintaining, protecting & improving the quality of environment, as a contribution to the protection of human health and safeguarding the ecological balance;
- The need for a prudent and rational utilisation of resources;
- The way in which each individual can, by his own behavior and action, contribute to the protection of environment;
- The long-term aims of environmental education are to improve management of environment and provide satisfactory solutions to environmental issues.
- Provide opportunities to acquire the knowledge, values, attitudes, commitment and skills needed to protect and improve the environment.
- Encourage pupils to examine and interpret the environment from a variety of perspectives-physical, geographical, biological, sociological, economic, political, technological, historical, aesthetic and ethical.
- Arouse pupil's awareness and curiosity about the environment and encourage active participation in resolving environmental problems.
- Environmental education is closely linked to the other cross circular themes of other subject areas.

LEARNING PRINCIPLES

The Learning principles of environmental education are:

1. Environmental education should consider the environment in its totality – natural and man-made, ecological, political, economic, technological, social, legislative, cultural and esthetic.
2. Environmental education should be a continuous life-long process, both in-school and out-of-school.
3. Environmental education should be interdisciplinary in its approach.
4. Environmental education should emphasise active participation in preventing and solving environmental problems.
5. Environmental education should examine major environmental issues from a world point of view, while paying due regard to regional differences.
6. Environmental education should focus on current and future environmental situations.
7. Environmental education should examine all development and growth from an environmental perspective.
8. Environmental education should promote the value and necessity of local, national and international cooperation in the solution of environmental problems.

RELATION TO SCIENCE & SOCIAL SCIENCE

Environmental Studies is a student- centred syllabus drawing together the disciplines History, Geography and Civics in a thematic approach to learning. This systematic study of environmental and social issues will enable young people to reflect on the world in which they live and to develop the skills and competencies required for active participation in society.

Environmental studies is the academic field which systematically studies human interaction with the environment. It is a broad interdisciplinary field of study that includes the natural environment, built environment, and the sets of relationships between them. While distinct from ecology and environmental science, the discipline encompasses study in the basic principles of those two fields of learning as well as the associated subjects, such as: policy, politics, law, economics, sociology and other social aspects, planning, pollution control, natural resources, and the interactions of human beings and nature.

A big aspect of environmental studies is the sciences. Students in this discipline may study things like biology, chemistry, geology, and engineering in order to understand more about the natural environment. Some people may also pick a specific field, like forestry or fisheries management, probing more deeply into this facet of interaction between humans and the natural world. Most environmental studies programs have a very demanding science component, to ensure that students have a thorough grounding in the sciences and to show them how to think like scientists.

ESS is a multidisciplinary course with an integrated methodology. Themes are used to provide a context within which the knowledge and understanding of History, Geography and Civic Education can be applied and within which young people are introduced to the work of historians, geographers, archaeologists, cartographers, meteorologists, ecologists and town planners.

ESS is constructed on the rationale that:

- themes of immediate and obvious relevance to students can provide important motivation for further learning;
- the multi-focal perspective provided by the thematic approach allows concepts from the separate disciplines to interact in mutually enriching ways;
- each concept is explored both in space and time by coordinating the geography and history inputs;
- the study of real-world issues requires an integrated approach since many disparate disciplines must be simultaneously brought to bear to understand such issues. Thus an integrated methodology is relevant to the vocational needs and life-experience of students;
- the pedagogical principle of integration, introduced in the Primary school can be continued into second level and used as a springboard for specific disciplines;
- integration of the separate subjects allows the expertise of teachers of the disparate disciplines to interact positively;
- a multidisciplinary approach based on a small number of well-defined subjects can provide the basis for the further development of links with other areas of the curriculum;
- the specific skills of the integrated subjects can be taught in an issues-focused manner, so that their relevance is clear to students.

APPROACHES OF PRESENTING CONCEPTS

What are some strategies to teach environmental topics, particularly controversial ones, without coming up against affective barriers to learning? How can you help students learn the science and the policy without getting weighed down by feeling guilty or defiant?

- **Teach the science first:** Even though most environmental topics are a blend of science, policy, economics and human impacts, it may be helpful to separate these into three distinct sub-topics. First, present the science objectively, using data and relevant examples. Next, discuss the policy and economic issues related to this topic. Once those subjects are covered thoroughly, students will often be interested to learn what their own personal stake may be. By setting the stage deliberately, students are more likely to be receptive to the information and are less likely to get turned off.
- **Teach with data:** Statements like *"species are going extinct at an alarming rate," "wetlands are being turned into strip malls,"* and *"the climate is getting hotter"*are emotional statements (even if true) and will elicit emotional responses in your students. Rather than risk sounding like an alarmist, let the data speak for itself. Have students work through data sets, and they can discover for themselves the rate and extent of environmental change. In some cases, they still may end up being surprised or emotional, but it's because they reached their own conclusion, not because you told them to be alarmed.
- **Use active Learning Techniques:** Students learn better when they can learn it for themselves, and this is especially true for topics that are potential turnoffs for students. Environmental issues lend themselves to teaching techniques like using local examples, gathering data from the field, using role-playing or debates, or participating in environmental projects.
- **Controversy, ambiguity, and topics with incomplete or missing evidence can be used constructively (but need to be introduced judiciously):** Engaging controversial topics, or topics that have no clear-cut answers, can create an environment where students are motivated to learn more out of curiosity or imminent need. Students can be encouraged to review what is known, to identify what additional information is needed to solve the problem, and to continue the search to find and critically examine new information. Learning goals for students can include development of "scientific habits of the mind", to be critical consumers of information, and to be able to create, present and rebut arguments based on evidence. A supportive environment needs to be created to encourage scholarly and open review of the arguments and ideas, and provisions need to be put in place to prevent interpersonal (ad hominem) attacks in reporting results in class activities.
- **It's not all doom and gloom:** Certain environmental topics can be downright depressing. However, there are also many environmental success stories. Strive for a balance in which students do not feel overwhelmed by a preponderance of "bad news." After all, environmental successes provide relevant examples of how problems can be overcome.
- **Clearly define your role and your teaching approach:** There are many ways to teach environmental issues. Before jumping into your curriculum, consider what your desired outcomes are and what approach you will take. Is your intent to teach just the relevant scientific processes, to promote an awareness of environmental issues, or to lead students toward a shift in their own environmental behavior? In the classroom, do you assume the role of environmental guardian, a free-marketeer, or a devil's advocate? There are advantages to various approaches, but it's important to consciously consider what your goals are and how you can best achieve them.
- **Lead by example, but don't preach:** We all know the stereotype that college professors drive tiny, efficient cars and live an eco-minded lifestyle. Regardless of whether or not this describes you, it's best to avoid talking down to your students for their own personal choices. Preaching to the class about what's "good" and what's "bad" will likely have the opposite effect than you intended; it can be a major turn-off for students. If your goal is to promote environmentally-favorable behavior in your students, consider a hands-on project that will challenge students to consider the environmental impacts of their own actions.

ACTIVITIES

Human activities are deeply related to environment and its degradation. In many ways environment decides human behaviour. To make the child aware of environment many activities should be included—

1. Aforestation and Gardening: The knowledge of flora and fauna, their uses, importance and effects should easily be given to child.
2. Arranging debate and seminars on environmental issues of social importance like Earthquake, Tsunami, Flood, Pollution, Global Warming, Deforestation, Acid Rain and Ozone Depletion.
3. Prepare Chart and Models related to environment related topics.
4. Travelling of environmental sites.

EXPERIMENTATION/ PRACTICAL WORK

1. Observe a newly grown potted plant for 20 days. Observe the changes that take place. Record your observations in the table give below:

Number of Days	Changes in the Plant		
	Height of the Plant	Number of Leaves	Other Changes
1st day			
3rd day			
5th day			
7th day			
10th day			
13th day			
15th day			
17th day			
20th day			

Plant also give rise to new plants. New plants are generally grown from seeds. Find out in what other ways we can grown new plants?

2. **Make a list of thirteen natural things which you see in and around your house. Group them into living and non-living things.**

	Living things	*Non-living things*
(i)		
(ii)		
(iii)		
(iv)		
(v)		
(vi)		
(vii)		
(viii)		
(ix)		
(x)		
(xi)		
(xii)		
(xiii)		

3. **Select five plants from your surrounding. Carefully look at each plant. Feel the stem. It is hard or soft. does it stand erect? What is the colour? Observe other parts.**

Note down your observations in the table given below.

Local Name of the Plant	Type of stem: hard/ soft and erect/ not erect	Flowers: colour and shape	Leaves: colour and shape	Fruits: Present/ Absent	Seeds: Present/ Absent
1					
2					
3					
4					
5					

4. **Observe the animals in your surrounding. Which of these animals are four footed? compare these with five common types of birds. In what way are the four footed animals different from the birds? In what way are they similar?**

5. **Given below are names of some parts of a plant and an animal. Group them into parts of a plant and parts of an animal.**

Neck, flower, root head, stem, leg, chest, fruit.

Parts of a plant	*Parts of an animal*

6. **Draw a picture of any local plant. Write down the names of different parts of the plant.**

DISCUSSION

Sustainable Development

Sustainable development is the concept of needs and limitations imposed by technology and society on the environment's ability to meet the present and future need. The term sustainable development was brought into common use by the world commission on environment and development in its reports (WCED). According to WCED sustainable development means a process of change in which the exploitation of resources, the direction of investments, the orientation of technological development and institutional change are all in harmony and enhance both current and future potentiality to meet human needs and aspirations.

Sustainable development is a development that meets needs of the present without compromising the ability of future generations to meet their own needs. For achieving sustainable development what is needed in global movement as well as significantly increased political will and public pressure in order to persuade industry, governments and institutions to take responsibility for their action.

It must be borne in mind that development should not endanger the natural system that support life on earth. With this attitude towards nature technological advances increase our ability to use earth resources and thus increase the damage. However, the realisation is growing fast that we are in a world of limits and ever increasing growth of material consumption can only damage the life giving physical components of the environment.

The concept of sustainable development was highly appreciated at the United Nations Conference on Environment and Development (UNCED) at a Rio de Janero in Brazil, commonly known as Earths Summit.

Sustainable development also needs understanding the basic needs of deprived people of the world. It is necessary to provide opportunities in order to satisfy their aspirations for a better and secured life. Sustainable development can be successfully achieved by (I) conservation or reduction of excessive resource use (II) recycling and reuse of materials and (III) more use of renewable resources like solar energy, rather than non-renewable resources such as oil and coal.

Urban Problems Related to Energy

Urbanisation is a global phenomenon in the developed countries of the world. It is now taking a steady stride in developing countries. The degree of urbanisation has increased tremendously. It means that (A) the proportion has increased (B) the population density of towns has increased and (C) the percentage of growth of population has increased in countries like India.

These three parameters which are related with volume, spatial spread and growth from the three indices of degree of urbanisation is largely due to a steady migration of rural population from rural to urban areas.

The main reason for heavy concentration of urban population in large metropolitan cities is that they are the centres of major industrial and commercial activities. They offer much attraction for migration of people and this accounts for rapid increase in their population.

Factors contributing to urbanisation are (A) Industrialisation (B) Transportation (C) Socio-economic changes all of which have impact on environment and health. The management of urbanisation involves an extremely range of problems and thus effecting all aspects of social life.

The urbanisation and proliferation of urban slums presents a challenge to public health. This situation has become a global concern and future of entire mankind is at stake due to phenomenal rise in population, rapid urbanisation, degradation, of environment, ever increasing pollution and over exploitation of natural and non-renewable resources.

Urbanisation has brought into associated problems related with the energy. Energy is an essential impact for urban development. Energy is produced from commercial sources like cow dung, fuel wood and agricultural wastes. Per capita consumption of commercial energy is sometimes used as an index of the consumption of economic advancement. India's per capita commercial energy, however is very low. It is one eighth of the world average commercial energy accounts for a little over of the total energy used in the country, the rest coming from non-commercial sources.

Global Warming

The accumulation of global warming coincides with a rise in the concentration of green house gases in the atmosphere. More heat and infrared reactions are trapped by the gaseous mantle around the globe which accelerates the pace of global warming.

The globe system and atmosphere is a state of dynamic equilibrium with the rate of absorption of solar radiation and its emission back to space as infrared and heat waves, which balance each other. Such gases and vapours which allow free passage to radiations are of relatively shorter wave length (2900-7000 Å) onwards, play very important role in maintaining surface temperature within a range in which heat can exist. They form a blanket around the globe which checks the passage of infrared and heat wave from earth crust back to space and keep it warm. The word green house is nothing but a glass house which is constructed to grow specific tropical plants in cold areas of tropical climate.

Green House Gases

There are number of gases present in the atmosphere which are capable of absorbing effectively heat waves and infrared rays while being transparent to radiation of lower wave lengths. Trace gases such as water vapour, carbondioxide, methane, chloroflurocarbons, ozone, nitrous oxide are some of the gases which constitutes troposphere. Amongst these five gases having rising concentration's of which has been implicated in causing noticeable rise in the mean global temperature. These gases are carbondioxide, methane, chlorofluorocarbons, nitrous oxide and water vapours, other gases such as sulphur dioxide, ozone are not able to contribute much as they are quickly cleared from atmosphere.

The sources of major green house gases are given below.

The Sources of Major Green House Gases

S. No.	Green House Gases	Sources
1.	Carbon dioxide	Fossil fuels combustion, deforestation and land use changes.
2.	Methane	Enteric fermentation in cattle and insects. Biomass burning and garbage, land, fuels, coal mines and natural gas leaks, rice, paddies, swamps, bogs.
3.	Chlorofluorocarbons	Aerosol, refrigeration and air conditioning, plastic foams, industrial solvents.
4.	Nitrous oxide	Fertiliser use, fossil fuel combustion, biomass burning.

An additional 1.1 to 2.2 billion tones (1–2 billion metric tonnes) of carbon (4–8 billion tonnes [3.6–7.3 billion metric tonnes] of CO_2) are emitted into the atmosphere each year due to deforestation. Like the fossil fuels, which were once living organisms, the extant forests hold vast stores of carbon. When the trees and other plants die and are either burned or allowed to decay, this carbon is converted into CO_2. Furthermore, trees serve the vital function of removing CO_2 from the atmosphere as they grow, unless deforested areas are quickly replanted, not only is CO_2 emitted directly into the atmosphere, but a vital mechanism for removing excess CO_2 from the atmosphere is also destroyed.

Although not yet considered a serious threat, there is another aspect of excess CO_2 production: the oxygen portion of CO_2 comes from the atmosphere, and we (along with all living aerobic creatures) need this oxygen to breathe. For every tonne of carbon burned, 2.66 tonnes of oxygen are taken from the atmosphere. Since the atmosphere is composed of about 20.9% oxygen, the supply may seem virtually unlimited. Yet measurements indicate that the oxygen content of the atmosphere is currently decreasing at a rate of about 13 ppm annually. Oxygen is being lost from the atmosphere, and as more plants are destroyed, it is not being replaced as fast as it once was. The most serious immediate concern is that falling oxygen levels may adversely affect oxygen concentrations in the oceans and other standing bodies of water. Slight decreases in oxygen concentrations could have severely disruptive effects on many marine organisms. Although carbon dioxide is blamed for 50 to 70% of the current abnormal global warming, (depending on the authority consulted and how "global warming" is calculated), it is not the only major greenhouse gas. The other major culprits are chloroflurocarbon (CFCs), methane (natural gas, CH_4), tropospheric ozone, and nitrogen oxide (NO_x).

The chlorofluorocarbons that promote global warming are the same CFCs that are destroying stratospheric ozone. Indeed, they are up to thousand of times more efficient at absorbing heat and promoting global warming than CO_2. At present, CFCs account for 15 to 25% of the human contribution to global warming. This number would have been even higher if steps had not been taken to reduce the CFCs released into the atmosphere. Thus, there are two good reasons to reduce our reliance on CFCs: to save the ozone layer and to reduce global warming. Methane accounts for an estimated 15 to 20% of current global warming.

It has been estimated that carbon dioxide will account for about half of the temperature increase while methane, nitrous oxide and chloroflurocarbons will be responsible for the rest.

Green house gases are provided both by industrial and biological processes but the industrial emission are fairly well documented but the knowledge of the production rates of green house gases through biological processes and the factors regulating emissions are still in adequate.

Consequence of Global Warming

The earth surface temperature has increased by about 0.5°C but it is suggested that mean global temperature will rise by 2-6°C. During the next century and the concentration of CO_2 will reach 600 ppm.

The rise in global temperature and consequently unfavourable climatic conditions will also affect number of species. The loss of genetic resources may take place on a large scale. The change in wind a precipitation pattern will play an important role in altering the biotic communities. Insects and pests may increase and coupled with higher humidity, pathogenic diseases will multiply. The increase in temperature will also affect agriculture in different parts of the world. In order to cape with alteration in cropping pattern, pest resistance varieties will have to developed. Some of the serious consequences of global warming are:

(*i*) Increase in surface temperature of earth.

(*ii*) Sudden changes in rainfall and temperature pattern.

(*iii*) Rise in sea level causing increased wave attacks and inundation of waste lands.

(*iv*) Changes in rainfall and temperature patterns.

(*v*) Increase in frequency of hurricanes, floods and erosion.

(*vi*) Increase in tropical fever diseases and other health problems.

- **Green House Effect and Ozone Layer Depletion:** The green house gases in the troposphere provides thermal insulation while these gases are considered responsible in causing ozone depletion in the stratosphere. The depletion of ozone layer could neutralise some of the warming effect caused by higher concentration of green house gases.
- **Global Warming and Human Health:** Temperature changes may have an impact on several categories of diseases including cardiovascular, cerebrovascular and respiratory diseases. High temperature overload the thermoregulating system of the body.
- **Communicable Diseases:** The distribution of range of diseases which correlated with temperature could be affected by global climate changes. It occurs likely that communicable diseases problems will be aggravated by climate change.
- **Immune System:** The UV Radiation affects the immune system of the skin and hence these might be an increased number of cases of skin cancer.
- **Water, Food and Changing Climate:** The ability of the earth to produce food depends heavily on elements such as ground water, the genetic diversity of human species and productive soil. Fertilise soil is losing its productivity in many parts of the world because of erosion and salinization. The direct effect of CO_2 on plant growth and use of water complicate efforts how future climate change effect, agriculture, forests and other ecosystems.
- **Rise in Sea Level:** Rising sea level may be one of the most widely felt and easily recognized consequences of warmer global climate. Currently, sea level rising, it is estimated that sea level may rise from about 0.5 to 1.5 metres in response to 3 to 5° C increase in temperature. The issue of global warming is important because an increase in the average temperature of only a few degrees could lead to the melting of glacial ice, a rise in sea level, and flooding of coastal regions.

Acid Rain

Acid rain refers to any precipitation hence a pH value less than that of a normal rain water, when pH value is around 5 or 6. Normal rain water is weakly acidic, because atmospheric carbon dioxide combines with rain water to form weak carbonic acid.

The severe acidic nature of water occurs due to massive pollution caused by industrialisation. Oxides of sulphur, nitrogen and hydrocarbons are the major contributing factors to acid rain.

The gases and aerosols accumulate high up in the atmosphere, water vapours condense on aerosol surface and form a fine film providing suitable level as catalysts for the oxide of sulphur and nitrogen to dissolve in water and react to form corresponding acids which form salts such as nitrates and sulphates when come in contact with basic aerosols. As water vapours continue to condense on these aerosols, large droplets of water are produced which rain down as acid rains.

Sulphuric acid, nitric acid and various sulphates and nitrates are the major chemical constituents of acid rain, small amount of hydrochloric acid and its salt may also be present.

Most areas are susceptible to acid rain. The buffering capacity of water or soil determines its susceptibility. In general, lower the buffering capacity of soil or water are produced which rain down as acid rains.

Effects of Acid Rain

The effects of acid rain depends on the route of deposition (Wet/Dry) as well as on the level of contact with plants, building and water course. Acid rain exerts both direct and indirect influence on organisms and materials. The direct effects are determined by the concentration of pollutants in air and generally they decline with increasing distances from the source of emission. On the other hand the indirect effects include its secondary and tertiary products. They are known to affects and material with more harmful consequences at a distance upto hundreds and some times thousand kilometers.

Dry deposition has direct effects on the environment. It attacks building materials such as sand stone, lime stone, marble, steel while/wet deposition has both direct and indirect effects. It increases the acidity of lakes and rivers, aquatic and terrestrial ecosystem. Acidity kills fish, bacteria and algae.

Acid rain has several effects on fish and fishery resources. Fish kills are a common feature in highly acidified water. A sublethal levels fishes may fail to reproduce. The population may gradually extinct because of negligible recruitment of young fish to replace older ones as they die. They die because of accumulation of heavy metals.

Many direct and indirect effects of acid rain on productivity and survival of wildlife population have been documented. Wildlife is affected indirectly because of loss of alteration of food habit resources. Acid rain can directly affect eggs and tadpoles of frogs and salamanders that breed in small forest ponds. As plants and wildlife are directly related any affect on the former will be disadvantageous to the later.

Ozone Layer Depletion

Ozone is a gas which is composed of three atoms of oxygen. The ozone concentration at earth surface is usually present in the range of 0.02 ppm to 0.04 ppm. Ozone varies globally with concentration of more than 1 ppm and is continuously present on upper atmosphere.

The pressure of ozone in the atmosphere plays as dual role. At ground level ozone enters the body through inhalation and exerts toxic effects directly on the lung. Exposure of ozone has been associated with being cancer, DNA breakage and visual impairment. However, the stratosphere ozone forms a protective shield against harmful UV radiation.

The atmospheric ozone is obtained in its two layers. The bottom layer extends up to 15 km from the earth and is known as troposphere, where as the top layer which extends from 15 to 50 km is known as stratosphere ozone.

Depletion of ozone layer has appeared, first over Antarctica in Northern hemisphere and polar regions. The primary cause for ozone loss is due to chloroflurocarbons (CFC's). During the year 1980 and 1987 it was established that direct involvement of chlorine and some heterogenous chemicals were responsible for depletion of ozone.

It has been established that various kinds of gases which are released in the atmosphere by human activity are main causes for depletion of ozone layer.

Depletion of Ozone Layers Over Poles

The stratosphere ozone is formed mist of equator which is displaced over the polar regions. It is because of this reason that the concentration of ozone is found to be maximum at poles. At these poles and Antarctic and Arctic regions the depletion of ozone has been found to be fastest. This is due to strong westerly winds around the poles moving at a speed of 90 to 100 metre per second.

Depletion of Ozone Layer by Chlorofluorocarbons (CFC's)

Out of many reactions sequences which lead to the destruction of ozone, one of the most important reaction is associated with the breakdown of stable organic chlorine compounds of CFC's where air active chlorine atom can catalytically destroy ozone.

Its Impact on Earth

Accelerating ozone layer depletion has serious impact on most of the life forms. For every 10% depletion of the ozone layer, one can expect 20% increase in U.V. radiation arriving on earth. This radiation could change genetic character, after immune systems, damage crops, disrupt marine food web and enhance green house warming by affecting the CO_2 absorption capacity of planktons in the ocean. The incidence of human cancer would increase and the sight of millions could be affected as more intense UV radiation damages eyes and causes cataracts. Immune response may be depressed in people exposed to increased radiation levels, vaccination programmes may become less effective and infectious diseases may become more common and more severe. Plant growth may be inhibited and crop yields may be reduced. Adverse effects on nitrogen fixing bacteria in rice paddies may result in drastic drops in production.

Immune System and Vaccination

UV radiation suppresses allergic reaction of the skin and affects the immune system. As a result skin cancer is developed along with many infectious diseases. These include measles and other viral diseases, herpes, parasite diseases, malaria, tuberculosis leprosy and fungal infection.

Skin Cancer

It has been estimated that five per cent decrease in ozone would mean 14% increase basal cell carcinoma and 25% increase in the carcinoma. It has also been estimated that every one per cent decrease in stratosphere ozone could mean that 2% of world population will develop the type of cancer.

Cataracts and Blindness

Cataracts and blindness are also expected to increase with depletion of ozone layer. Ultra violet radiation damages cornea, lens and to a lesser extent the retina. It has been estimated that one per cent radiation of the ozone layer can cause 150 thousands cataracts. Exposure to sunlight has been established as factor in the development of intraocular in melanoma.

Impacts on Oceans

Depletion of ozone layer disrupts oceans life. The most significant effect of increasing amounts of UV radiation is on plankton and other tiny marine organisms. Planktons produce more than one-half of earth biomass. UV radiation reduces the amount of phytoplankton and zooplankton. In addition it leads to 5% disease in fish yield.

Damage to Materials

Depletion of ozone layer causes many materials to degrade more rapidly. Plastic outdoors will have much shorter life times. Polyacrmyl shedings, window pipes, gullies and trims used in buildings are likely to degrade faster along with cable coverings. Developing countries will suffer the most because plastics are cheap and popular in building materials.

Green House Effect

The haloalkanes not only deplete ozone layer but they are also known as potential green house gases. Phytoplanktons in the oceans normally absorb half of the CO_2 of the atmosphere. Such quality of phytoplankton is considerably decreased when exposed to UV radiation such a process result in the increased level of CO_2 in the atmosphere which in effect will contribute to global warming and hence will have house effect.

CONTINUOUS AND COMPREHENSIVE EVALUATION

Continuous and Comprehensive Evaluation refers to a system of school based assessment that covers all aspects of student's development. It emphasizes two fold objectives. Continuity in evaluation and assessment of broad based learning.

CCE helps in reducing stress of students by :

- Identifying learning progress of students at regular time intervals on small portions of content.
- Employing a variety of remedial measures of teaching based on learning needs and potential of different students.
- Desisting from using negative comments on the learner's performance.
- Encouraging learning through employment of a variety of teaching aids and techniques.
- Involving learners actively in the learning process.
- Recognizing and encouraging specific abilities of students, who do not excel in academics but perform well in other co-curricular areas.

Teachers should Keep in Mind

- Use a variety of tools (oral, projects, presentations).
- Understand different learning styles and abilities.
- Share the assessment criteria with the students.
- Allow peer and self assessment.
- Give an opportunity to the student to improve.

Important Points

- CCE will cover the scholastic and co-scholastic areas of school education.
- The two types of assessment referred to in the circular are formative and summative. The periodicity of the two types of assessment are four and twice a year respectively.
- Formative Assessment totals to 40% weightage.
- Summative Assessment totals to 60% weightage.
- There are nine grades in Part A of Scholastic assessment and Part B of the same assessment has five grades.
- Summative assessment covers non academic areas like attitudes and skills and there are three grades.
- If a student secures Grade 6 in the academic areas his/her marks would range from 51% to 60%.
- CCE advocates absolute grading. This means that Grade 9 would imply an A2 grade.
- The academic term will be divided into two terms.

TEACHING MATERIAL/EQUIPMENT

Text Book

Text book is the area in which the language material is presented prescribed for teaching and learning English.

Characteristics of Good Text Books

A good text books not only teaches but it also tests. A few essential characteristics of good text books are given below:

1. The size of text book should be handy for the students.
2. The binding should be proper and strong.
3. The subject matter should be printed on good quality paper.
4. Heading and subheading should be printed on title page in bold form.
5. Illustration should be attractive. For every young pupil, the picture should be well drawn and realistically coloured and not in black and white.
6. Clear and unambiguous instruction should be given along side the test and practice and exercise.
7. The introduction at the beginning and conclusion at the end of the chapter should be given in the text book.
8. The words and structure are carefully graded.
9. No difficult words and new words are given in good text book.
10. The words and structure already learnt are repeated in the coming pages so that the students could revise them making them stable in their memory.
11. The subject matter of text book should provide new information so that students could get new knowledge.
12. There should be both practice and text exercise at the end of the chapter.
13. The practice should be low which the majority of students could solve them easily.

Chalkboard

It is the closest friend of a teacher in the class and about 50% teaching task is completed with the help of the blackboard. Advantages of using a chalkboard in the class are as follows :

(*i*) It is a cheap material aid which does not cost much on its maintenance.

(*ii*) When a teacher writes important points of the lesson on the chalkboard along with his oral teaching and lectures, aural and visual both the senses of students work simultaneously. It increases learning many times.

(*iii*) Writing meaning of difficult words, drawing graphs or diagrams, solving the sums of mathematics, preparing the summary of the lesson, all these works can be done on the chalkboard and they help the students understand the facts, events or terminologies.

(*iv*) Blackboard works as a model for students. This can help the students mend their ways if they imitate the model.

Models

Models are the reflection or copy of the real objects. They are used in the class to clarify the concepts when either real objects are not available or it is not possible to bring real objects to the class. They are also the abbreviated version of real objects. Elephants, lions or other animals or birds can not be brought to the class, hence, it is better to use the models of these objects. Globe is the best example of model to be used in the class.

Through models knowledge of all types of historical, geographical and scientific facts and concepts can be given to students. Models are especially useful for teaching visually handicapped children who perceive the objects by touch. Since, clear dimensions of length, breadth and height are given in the model in a proportionate manner, they are more useful for concept formation than pictures.

How to Use Models

(*i*) Scale should be used for showing size, shape or structure of the real objects. Apart from this, teacher should also clarify the real shape, size or structure of the real object.

(*ii*) Students should be given opportunity to have a critical view on the model and their views on it.

(*iii*) All students should be given chance to have a close look at the model in the class.

(*iv*) Models should have direct relevance to the lesson and they should develop scientific temperament among learners.

(*v*) Models should be properly explained in the class in order to make the use of models effective.

Pictures

Pictures are used in the class as material aids when neither real objects nor models can be arranged. They are cheap and easily available in the market, therefore, a teacher should not be miserly in using them. Pictures are actually the outlines of the real objects and when they are shown in the class, they give clear concepts about the colour, physique, shape and size of the real objects. Attention of students can easily be drawn to the lesson through them. If pictures related to the lesson are not available in the market, the teacher should sketch them by using pencils and water colours. Pictures are used as material aids for teaching all the school subjects.

Diagrams

They are another option and used when even pictures can not be arranged. They can also clarify the concepts like models or pictures but at a lesser degree. Diagrams are drawn on the chalkboard by using coloured chalks and then students copy it on their notebooks. The biggest advantage of this material aid is that teacher need not spend even a single pie in using this material aid.

They help in clarifying the concepts, laws and principles of science and social sciences. Their role in teaching languages is very limited.

Graphs

Graphs are especially used in history, geography, science and mathematics. They help the teacher and the students to study, analyse and compare the data, facts or events. Whenever action research is made by a teacher in the class, graphs are used to show the data.

Maps

Maps are the flat representation of the surface of the earth on a paper where many informations are presented through lines, symbols dots, points or letters. They have special significance in teaching history and geography. We can also get information about the size and physical features of a country, state or continent through these maps and distance between different parts of the country or the world can also be read from them. Though printed maps of all states or countries are available in the market yet a teacher draws them also on roler boards. This will enable the students to draw such maps themselves.

Slide Projector

Simple 'slide projector' was known as "magic lantern" in the olden days. The principle here is that when we put the transparent slide on the socket and throw light from behind, the light passes through it and projects the image on the screen.

A slide projector typically consists of a quart, three halogen lamps, light to be reflected by the reflector, a heat filter and lastly, condenser lenses. The heat filter is a thermo crystal which absorbs most of the heat produced by three lamps. A cooling system is also needed which consists of a fan for convecting off the heat, filter and other components. The fan is thermostatically controlled. When projector is switched off, the fan is also switched off.

Classroom uses of the Slide Projector : Slides are prepared for selected topics and the informations contained by them may be in the form of written words, pictures, graphs, sketches, etc. The topic selected should be arranged frame by frame. The ideal ratio of length and breadth of slides is 2 : 3. Each frame should have only one concept for the ease of understanding.

The slides and the film strips are arranged in a sequential order. This arrangement is also coordinated with the teaching learning activity of the class. When slides are shown in the class, curtains are drawn on the windows in order to reduce the entry of natural light in the class.

Before showing these slides, teacher elaborates important points. Once the film is over, the teacher gives his own comments and relates the aid with the lesson to be taught.

Film Strips

They are used before a large group of students either for introducing a lesson or for elaborating some minute object not seen in ordinary situations. Film strips are projected on a big screen through a film projector and then the projector is switched on. Here, very minute objects look very big on the screen and we can study their parts. For example, knowledge about bacteria and viruses can be given to students through these film strips. Sometimes, sound recording is also used along with the film to clarify important points.

Advantages of Film Strips

(*i*) The order or sequence of film strips is fixed and a teacher can prepare the relevant material to supplement the film according to the sequence.

(*ii*) We can have any part of the film on the screen as long as we desire so. As a result, a teacher can discuss a single topic as long as he needs. Thus, complete control over the equipment and the material is possible.

(*iii*) Handling of film projectors is also not complex. There is no problem of storing them because of their small size. Precautions are, however, needed against fungi or physical damage.

(*iv*) They have become very cheap today and any school can afford the cost of these projectors.

(*v*) They do not require complete darkness in the room as we do in using epidiascope or motion film projectors.

Limitations of Film Strips

(*i*) They can be used only in small sized classes because of limited focal length. Modern projectors are, however, having large focal length.

(*ii*) Slide projection is not as effective as film projection. Inventions of 3D films have reduced the use of slides even further. In spite of this, fixed order of the film strips creates problem in handling individual frames.

(*iii*) Many schools do not have audio-visual workshops and thus, they depend on the cheap and unstandardized materials available in the market.

Film Projector

16 mm films are generally used for the purpose of training or teaching. These films are planned and executed by a pannel of experts who endeavour to prepare films of good quality.

As far as use of film projector for classroom teaching is concerned, it is very easy. Everything is automatic here. If electricity supply is not restricted, the film will not stop in the middle, after it is put on the projector.

Advantages of Motion Pictures

(*i*) Motion pictures can especially be used for training purposes. Take the example of games and sports. If some actions of a player is wrong leading to defeat in the game, it can be corrected by viewing the films. After the game is over, the film of the game is later analysed to be discussed by the experts to bring in new strategies and tactics to counterplay.

(*ii*) In all training courses, perfection is needed everywhere. If action is recorded on films, we can see our own performance and remove our defects.

(*iii*) In the classroom teaching, motion pictures can highlight those aspects also that would have otherwise been missed. For example, by enlarging, close up and action replay techniques, motion pictures can highlight those movements also which are very minute and can be missed in ordinary situations.

(*iv*) Motion pictures are **multi-sensory technique** of instruction. It is because a combination of light, sound and actions are seen here.

(*v*) Motion pictures can develop imaginative and observational capacities of students simultaneously.

(*vi*) Whatever ideals are shown by the models in motion pictures are imitated by pupils and thus, good ideals and etiquettes can be developed in them.

(*vii*) They are helpful in giving clarity of concepts through concreteness and accuracy.

(*viii*) Facts and events related to industry, politics, history and geography and knowledge about scientific inventions, discoveries, laws and principles can be communicated to pupils very effectively through these motion pictures.

Kinescope

It is a sight and sound recording that can be made in the studio from the television screen for repeated use. What transcription is to radio, the kinescope is to TV. They are used for the following purposes :

(*i*) For delayed telecast.

(*ii*) For retelecast of the same programme.

(*iii*) For repeating the telecast when programme could not be seen due to failure of network.

(*iv*) For sending programmes abroad.

Only limitation of kinescope is that live element or spontaneity does not exist here.

It can be used in teaching learning process in the same way as television is used.

Epidiascope

Epidiascope is an equipment that can project all types of materials whether transparent or non-transparent (opaque). It has thus a twin facility and separate mechanism for projecting transparent and opaque materials.

In epidiascope, the word epi means 'upon' dia means 'through' and scope means 'projected material to be seen'.

While projecting a slide, beams pass through the slide and projects its image on the screen. In this way, transparent material is projected.

While projecting the opaque material the light bits upon the object which reflects the image on a very sensitive mirror and reflects the image of the opaque objects on the screen.

Despite the multipurpose functioning of this device, it is not very popular in educational institutions because of its poor quality image, total room darkening, very high need of energy, complexity of its use and poor range. It is to be installed in the middle of the class due to its low range, therefore, causing more interference than aiding something to the lesson. Because of its ability to project opaque objects on the screen, it is also known as opaque projector.

Overhead Projector (OHP)

Built on the basic principle of periscope, OHP is an important audio visual equipment. In the classroom it is placed in front of the teacher above his head to reflect an image on the screen (blackboard). This device consists of a strong energy source, (bulbs), fixed reflectors (mirrors), projection lens and a platen. This projector is called over head because the image goes over the head of the teacher and falls on the screen behind him. The teacher puts one slide over the other in order to give a sense of continuity of the subject matter projected on the screen.

Advantages of OHP : Its advantages lie in its special characteristics given below :

(*i*) No special training is required by the teacher to operate a projector.

(*ii*) OHPs are not very costly as compared to computers or film projectors.

(*iii*) It is handy and portable.

(*iv*) The image formed by the projector is also very bright and every pupil can see it. A 4 × 4 inches slide gives an image of 4 × 4 feet. This enlarged image is very easy to understand.

(*v*) It can create interests in pupils and hence it is a good motivator.

(*vi*) It is the best visual aid available to a teacher to supplement his oral teaching. He uses the screen of OHP as a blackboard without looking back. Transparencies, drawing, diagrams, figures and outlines etc. can be shown on the screen.

Television

TV differs from the radio in the sense that it is audio and visual both. We can see the incident occurring round the globe on it immediately after the occurrence of the incident through telecast. Thus, it is bisensory (multisensory) media. We get news, views and recreation through television in the same way as we do through the transistor but in a more compact and concrete way due to the facility of vision here.

As far as application of TV in education is concerned, it is still in the stage of infancy in India. It was only in 1961 that Indian television (Doordarshan) started a special service for schools in collaboration with the directorate of Education. This programme aimed at supplementing the regular classroom teaching in selected subjects. By 1972 only 400 schools of the capital received this telecast and two lakh students benefited from them. These programmes were telecast in the evening and on Sundays but there was no mechanism developed at that time to measure the effectiveness of such transmitting programmes.

After the introduction of distance education system in India, television is now regularly used as an instructional media. The enactment of Prasar Bharti Act is expected to boost the role of TV in the teaching learning process.

Advantages of Television

(*i*) It heightens the reality more than the physical presence. For example, if someone is watching a cricket match in a stadium, even then he can not see certain situations despite being present there. On the other hand, if he is viewing a match on a TV, he can see and analyse every situation by close up action replay. Thus, television experience may be more real than the actual one. It can show even those details which we can not see with the help of direct experiences. Thus, television can be used for all training programmes and behaviour of the trainees can be modified in the desired manner.

(*ii*) TV experiences are new and versatile. So, they can bring variety to classroom teaching by breaking monotony and strengthening the learning structures by its multisensory approach.

(*iii*) It widens the horizon of pupils' experiences by giving them upto date knowledge of the real situation and by making them conversant with the opinions of others.

(*iv*) It can motivate the pupils for learning by arousing and retaining their interest in the learning situation.

Limitations of Television

(*i*) Speed of a television can not be changed as we can do in motion pictures.

(*ii*) A TV programme can not be adjusted to teaching and vice versa will have to be done. A teacher can take the help of video recording in such cases.

Tape Recorder and Audio Cassettes

Cassette type audio taps are available now which can play for 90 minutes on both sides. We can listen to our own recorded voice, recorded speeches of politicians and learned people, recorded poems of great composers, songs, music etc by the tape recorder.

Audio cassette recorder is used for the following purposes :

Such types of recording serve the following purposes:

(*i*) Analysis of verbal messages : Accuracy, speed and tone of verbal messages are studied here and if perfection is seen, reinforcement to the presenter is given.

(*ii*) Drill and practice : Accurate verbal messages are presented before the trainee for drill and practice.

(*iii*) Teaching of specific skills : Impressive oral presentation is actually a skill. This skill is taught to students through audio-recording in the individual and group situations.

(*iv*) Speech improvement : Style of speaking and phonetics can also be improved by using this technology.

(*v*) Improvement in vocabulary : Recorded verbal messages are full of many new words which pupils can learn by listening to the message.

(*vi*) Recreation : Many recorded songs and music entertain the listeners and remove their fatigue.

Radio

It is an important and easily accessable audio aid serving three important general purposes "news, views and recreation". It is the cheapest equipment of all and radio broadcast is now reachable to 100% population of the country. Pupils can get information about the incidents in any part of the globe immediately through radio. This increases their general awareness of the world. Students listen the ideas of learned people, politicians and educationists from across the world on the radio. This extends their own views and way of thinking. Apart from these, there are hundreds of programmes of music, songs and plays broadcast on the radio which entertain them round the clock.

Instructional Value of the Radio

(*i*) It is a powerful means of developing listening comprehension.

(*ii*) It can also help the pupils to acquire correct pronunciation and phonetics like tape recorders.

(*iii*) Conversational style and language can be learned on the radio.

(*iv*) It improves word power of learners.

(*v*) Mass education goals can be achieved through radio broadcast. It was the realization of the people when radio came into being in 1917.

(*vi*) News listened on the radio can improve our general knowledge.

(*vii*) Radio listening does not require literacy. Even illiterates can take the benefit of it.

Radio Broadcast in India : The first radio station was established in India in July 1927 in Mumbai followed by one more station in Kolkata in the same year. This media is now able to penetrate to the remotest villages of the country and is covering more than 99% of the population.

School broadcasting in India was started in 1937. Radio broadcasting is now very much used for mass education as well as the education of school going children in selected areas. Central Institute for educational technology (CIET) under the supervision and control of NCERT produces quality radio broadcast programmes. Adult education Radio Programmes also started in 1956 to educate the adults in the age group of 15-35 in the vicinity of Pune as a project sponsored by UNESCO. Today, broadcast of adult education programmes are many under different titles. When Consumer Protection Act was passed in 1986, consumer education through radio was also given recognition. Today, it is a regular programme of all the radio stations in India. One more regular radio programme is the radio counseling programme of IGNOU which is broadcast from 4-5 pm on every Sunday.

Apart from these, radio broadcast is also making the people aware about various social and economic problems and people are also educated about how they can solve these problems.

Computer

It is the latest electronic device that is audio and visual both. It accepts data, performs operations on that data in sequence (decided by a programme) and outputs the results.

Computer in education : From input devices to output and its storage, computer has a wide range of applicability in education. In computers inputs are converted into output by a programme. Thus, input (data) plus programme form software or instructional programme. Inputs are converted into output in the CPU of the computer.

Computer always works according to the programme given to it. Whatever instruction or programme the students gives to the computers, it will always act accordingly and output will also come out on the same line. Application of computers in education can be understood by the following lines.

Videodiscs

This system is comprised of videodisc, where the information is stored, a video player and a TV set.

It is helpful in teaching learning process in the following ways :

(*i*) Students can get more informations through effective way of presentation.

(*ii*) By forwarding or reversing the CD player, learners can have access to any informations as many times as possible. This repeated action is necessary in understanding complex materials.

(*iii*) Live coverage given by the CD player can provide higher degree of motivation.

(*iv*) Auto stop system provided in the system can help those learners who study till late hours of night.

(*v*) The materials prepared by the effective teachers can be made available in the market for wide use.

Videotext

This system provides an interactive information retrieval service. It allows the home television to work as a computer terminal, which retrieves the textual material and graphic information from a remote data base.

Advantages of Videotext

(*i*) It is useful for downloading the required information from a remote data base.

(*ii*) It raises the general awareness of learners.

(*iii*) The principal of a school can have access to any information about his or other schools any time if this system is available in the school.

(*iv*) It is especially useful for distance learning. A learner can connect himself with his study centre or regional office any time.

(*v*) It is free from time schedule. We can have any information any time.

(*vi*) Two way interaction between the teacher and the taught is possible here with the help of alphanumeric keyboard. The learner can address to his tutor by typing questions and sending it to the tutor. Once he receives the answer, he gets immediate feedback.

(*vii*) It is faster than telephone or telegram because user need not wait here in queue.

Teleconferencing

Teleconferencing is a two way broadcast system in which learners can interact with the programme through a local telephone. It is a powerful medium of instruction for distance education. In this system three or four subject experts sit at different places and participate in the discussion on the given subject matter. Here learners do not take part in the teaching-learning process directly. They only hear the programme on their radio set or TV. They can however, interact with the experts through telephone which is connected to the radio or TV station where the discussion is being organised.

Thus, teleconferencing involves the use of many media and allows interactive group communication by means of a two way broadcast. All such conferencing need good quality audio device to facilitate immediate interaction among the participants for exchange of views.

Advantages of Teleconferencing

(*i*) **Effective for distance learning :** When groups of students are scattered over a large area of the country and it is not possible for them to interact with their teachers personally, then learning through teleconferencing is the best option for them.

(*ii*) **Interaction between the teacher and the taught possible :** As far as interaction between teachers and learners are concerned, this approach does not differ in any way from classroom teaching.

(*iii*) **High quality instruction :** Since, very learned people and experts of the subject take part in these discussions, the quality of the programme is never questionable.

(*iv*) **Immediate feedback :** Learners get answer of their questions immediately from the experts and their problem is solved. In this way, they get immediate feedback.

(*v*) **Flexibility :** Experts do not teach here on a pre-determined track. Their instruction and its way of presentation always changes according to the questions asked by learners. Thus, this approach is very flexible.

Internet

It is the abbreviation of international network. The computers connected to this system are automatically connected to world wide website(www). Due to this we can hear and see any programme available on website any time when we want to do so. If we have missed any television or radio programme, we can not have access to that programme again but if that programme is loaded on the website, we can repeatedly hear and see the programme. We will only have to log on the website of the programme producer and it will be available for us. The major advantage of this system is that it has made 24 hour communication possible especially between those countries which have great differences in their local timings such as India and America have a time difference of 10 ½ hours. When there is day time in India, offices are closed in America.

Applications of internet in education

(*i*) We can get any information any time at home through internet on one hand and we can store the information by creating our own website on the other. Thus, it is not necessary to have immediate print out of the textual matter.

(*ii*) The two talking persons can see each other in face to face situations also through internet. Thus, a teacher can teach millions of students scattered across the world together.

(*iii*) Many educational institutions have created their educational websites. We can download any information about them any time by logging on these websites.

(*iv*) Internet has also its role to play in classroom teaching. Teacher can show any educational programme through internet any time according to his own convenience and he will not have to adjust his time table according to the programme as he does while using radio or television as aids.

(*v*) Latest teaching strategies and latest researches in different fields can be obtained through internet immediately and we need not have to wait for their publication in magazines and journals.

(*vi*) Books, magazines and newspapers are also published on internet and it has made our access to them easy. Any Indian living in Canada even can read "Amar Ujala" or "Times of India" daily.

(*vii*) Research material and encyclopaedias are also published on internet to facilitate learning process.

PROBLEMS

Teaching of Environmental Studies is a complex human activity. At the one end it is related to fixation of national goal and on the other end it is related to the daily activity of a minor child in the classroom.

Environmental study is not only related to a particular subject but a group of subjects. Therefore its content is so wide and varied. The major problems of Environmental studies are—

1. The Syllabus of Environmental Study is not properly arranged.
2. Community Resources are not properly used.
3. Lack of Resources.
4. No scope for Personal experiences in environmental Curriculum.
5. Attitude of Students towards the subject.
6. Lack of well experienced teachers.
7. Methods of teaching is not adequate.
8. Lack of Practical experiences.

PRACTICE PAPER

1. In which of the following regions Reindeer are found?
A. Monsoon B. Taiga
C. Tundra D. Hot Desert

2. Which one of the following is ***not*** a temperate grassland?
A. Downs B. Prairies
C. Pampas D. Compas

3. According to population size, the largest Continent is:
A. Asia B. Africa
C. Europe D. North America

4. Where does Tharu tribe live in India?
A. Uttarakhand
B. Jharkhand
C. Thar Desert
D. Tarai region of Uttar Pradesh

5. Bhilai Steel Plant is situated in:
A. Chhattisgarh
B. Odisha
C. Madhya Pradesh
D. Jharkhand

6. Reservation for women in India is available in:
A. Cabinet
B. Panchayati Raj Institutions
C. Lok Sabha
D. Vidhan Sabha

7. In order to be appointed as the Governor of a State, one must have attained the age of:
A. 50 years B. 30 years
C. 35 years D. 45 years

8. Choose the right Code after comparing List–I with List–II.

List–I	List–II
(*a*) Indian Union	(*i*) Prime Minister
(*b*) State	(*ii*) Sarpanch
(*c*) Corporation	(*iii*) Governor
(*d*) Village Panchayat	(*iv*) Mayor

Codes:

	(*a*)	(*b*)	(*c*)	(*d*)
A.	(*i*)	(*iii*)	(*iv*)	(*ii*)
B.	(*iii*)	(*iv*)	(*i*)	(*ii*)
C.	(*iv*)	(*i*)	(*ii*)	(*iii*)
D.	(*ii*)	(*iii*)	(*iv*)	(*i*)

9. When and where, Article 356 was used first?
A. Jammu and Kashmir 1956
B. Madhya Pradesh 1957
C. Bihar 1958
D. Kerala 1959

10. Which tax can be imposed by Nagar Nigam?
A. Toll Tax B. All the above
C. Entertainment Tax D. House Tax

11. In 1853, India's first passenger train runs between:
A. Calcutta to Alipur
B. Calcutta to Damdam
C. Bombay to Pune
D. Bombay to Thane

12. Asia's largest cattle fair is organised at:
A. Pushkar B. Nasik
C. Haridwar D. Sonepur

13. National Integration Council was established in the year:
A. 1971 B. 1981
C. 1951 D. 1961

14. In which of the following Articles of Constitution, the Right to Equality are mentioned?
A. Articles 23 – 24 B. Articles 25 – 28
C. Articles 19 – 22 D. Articles 14 – 18

15. Which country has a flexible Constitution?
A. America B. United Kingdom
C. India D. China

16. Which is the example of sessile animal among following?
A. *Chiton* B. *Echinus*
C. *Euplectella* D. *Leech*

17. Unit of protein molecule is:

A. Amino acid B. Vitamin
C. Glucose D. Fatty acid

18. Which organelle is absent in plant cell?

A. Vacuoles B. Centrosome
C. Cellulose cell wall D. Plastids

19. Largest gland in human body is:

A. Adrenal Gland B. Liver
C. Pancreas D. Pituitary Gland

20. State bird of Uttar Pradesh is:

A. House Sparrow B. Parrot
C. Sarus Crane D. Peacock

21. Hamlet is associated with which settlement?

A. Linear B. Urban
C. Fragmented D. Rural

22. Which is volcano mountain?

A. Appalachian B. Kilimanjaro
C. Aravali D. Ural

23. Elephanta Island is located at:

A. Mumbai Coast B. Ganga Delta
C. Kutch Coast D. Goa Coast

24. Monsoon forests are found where rainfall is:

A. 50 – 150 cm B. 70 – 100 cm
C. 70 – 200 cm D. 150 – 200 cm

25. Karbi Anglong Plateau is an extension of:

A. Tibet B. Shan plateau
C. Peninsular plateau D. Himalaya

26. The world's most problematic aquatic weed, also known as "Terror of Bengal" is:

A. *Eichhornia Crassipes* (Water hyacinth)
B. *Cynodone dactylon* (Doob grass)
C. *Lantana Camara*
D. *Parthenium hysterophorus* (Congress grass)

27. The abiotic property of virus is:

A. It cannot reproduce
B. It can be crystalized
C. It does not have the genetic material
D. It does not have protein

28. Plant hormone that help in the ripening of fruits is

A. Cytokinin B. Ethylene
C. Auxin D. Gibberellins

29. Free living, anaerobic, nitrogen (N_2) fixing bacteria found in soil is:

A. Clostridium B. Vibrio
C. Azotobacter D. Rhizobium

30. Which type of DNA is commonly found inside the cell?

A. B-DNA B. Z-DNA
C. A-DNA D. C-DNA

31. Plants are green due to the presence of which pigment?

A. Anthocyanin B. Carotenoid
C. Lycopene D. Chlorophyll

32. Human activities that cause climate change on the earth include:

A. use of aerosol cans B. burning of forests
C. agricultural activities D. All of the above

33. Which crop belonging to the family Euphorbiaceae is known for producing biodiesel?

A. Copper leaf B. Jatropha
C. Candlenut tree D. Sarpagandha

34. 'The Queen of Herbs' is the most sacred herb of India. This medicinal plant has importance in Hindu mythology and has the scientific name *Ocimum Sanctum*. What is it commonly called?

A. Thyme B. Tulsi
C. Rosemary D. Coriander

35. The water that is safe to drink is called:

A. fresh water B. potable water
C. distilled water D. tap water

36. The Bhopal Gas Tragedy of 1984 was due to the leakage of which of the following gases?

A. Methane B. Methyl isocyanate
C. Nitrous oxide D. Carbon monoxide

37. The World Environment Day falls on:

A. 5th June B. 2nd December
C. 16th September D. 11th July

38. M.S. Swaminathan was:

A. an ecologist
B. a journalist
C. an agricultural scientist
D. an ornithologist

39. Where is Wildlife Institute of India (WII) located?

A. Ahmedabad B. New Delhi
C. Coimbatore D. Dehradun

40. During photosynthesis, which of the following is absorbed by green plants?

A. Carbon dioxide B. Helium
C. Nitrogen D. Oxygen

41. The organism which feed on the waste products are called:

A. herbivores B. detrivores
C. carnivores D. chemovores

42. What type of energy is derived from heated groundwater?

A. Geothermal energy B. Hydroelectric energy
C. Solar energy D. Nuclear energy

43. Shola grasslands are found in:

A. the Himalayas B. the Western Ghats
C. the Eastern Ghats D. the Vindhyas

44. In India, pelicans breed in:

A. Kokkare Bellur B. Nelapattu
C. Koonthankulam D. All of the above

45. 'Minamata disease' was caused by eating fish which have high levels of:

A. cadmium B. arsenic
C. mercury D. All of the above

46. Maximum ozone depletion has been observed in which of the following?

A. The Equator B. The North Pole
C. The South Pole D. None of the above

47. Who among the following was the first Chief Justice of India?

A. Hiralal J. Kania
B. M. Patanjali Sastri
C. Mehr Chand Mahajan
D. S.R. Das

48. The 'Red Data Book' is related to:

A. animals near extinction
B. pollution in rivers
C. decreasing underground water level
D. air pollution

49. Who among the following is the present Chairperson of the National Commission for Women?

A. Malini Bhattacharya B. Girija Vyas
C. Rekha Sharma D. Yasmeen Abrar

50. The joint sitting of the Lok Sabha and the Rajya Sabha of states is summoned by:

A. the Parliament
B. the President
C. the Speaker of the Lok Sabha
D. the Chairman of the Rajya Sabha

51. Which Part of the Constitution has the provisions for Panchayati Raj System?

A. III B. IX
C. VI D. IV

52. 74th Amendment of the Constitution is related to:

A. Powers of the President
B. Rural Local Self-Government
C. Urban Local Self-Government
D. Powers of the Parliament

53. Which of the following gases soluble in rainwater causes acidic?

A. Carbon dioxide B. Hydrogen peroxide
C. Nitrogen monoxide D. Sulphur dioxide

54. 'Rule of Law' concept has been taken in the Indian Constitution from:

A. Switzerland B. USA
C. England D. Ireland

55. Who carries out notification for the election of the Lok Sabha?

A. Home Ministry
B. Election Commission of India
C. The President
D. Lok Sabha Secretariat

56. The first hour of business of the Lok Sabha is known as:

A. Zero hour B. Public hour
C. Privileges hour D. Question hour

57. What is Rainwater Harvesting?

A. Distribution of water
B. Collection and storage of used water
C. Collection and storage of rainwater
D. None of the above

58. Indian Rhinoceros is protected in:.

A. Bandipur National Park
B. Corbett National Park
C. Kaziranga National Park
D. Gir National Park

59. Which of the following series is true about energy flow in an ecosystem?

A. Producers → Consumers → Decomposers
B. Producers → Decomposers → Consumers
C. Decomposers → Consumers → Producers
D. Consumers → Producers → Decomposers

60. Greenhouse gas, which is present in the highest quantity in atmosphere, is:

A. carbon dioxide B. propane
C. ethane D. methane

61. 'AGMARK' is related with:

A. quality B. packaging
C. processing D. production

62. The problem of water pollution with arsenic is maximum in

A. Uttar Pradesh B. Madhya Pradesh
C. Bihar D. West Bengal

63. The Wildlife Protection Act was passed in:
A. 1960 B. 1962
C. 1972 D. 1975

64. The process of curd production from milk is known as:
A. photosynthesis B. distillation
C. fermentation D. sterilization

65. Fundamental Duties are adopted from the Constitution of which country?
A. Germany B. United Kingdom
C. USA D. USSR

66. The Polestar is:
A. North star B. South star
C. East star D. West star

67. 'Project Tiger' was started in India in:
A. 1972 B. 1973
C. 1981 D. 1985

68. The Valley of Flowers is located in:
A. Jammu & Kashmir B. Himachal Pradesh
C. Sikkim D. Uttarakhand

69. How many bones are present in an adult human being?
A. 305 B. 275
C. 206 D. 175

70. The Headquarters of Greenpeace International is located in:
A. New York B. Sydney
C. Amsterdam D. Nagasaki

71. During light phase of photosynthesis, ______ is oxidized and ______ is reduced.
A. water, NADP B. $NADPH_2$, CO_2
C. CO_2, water D. CO_2, $NADPH_2$

72. What is **not** true for LPG?
A. It is a clean fuel
B. It has high calorific value
C. It burns with blue flame
D. It is methane emitting

73. *The Origin of Species* is a work of:
A. Aristotle B. Charles Darwin
C. Mendel D. Robert Hooke

74. The Tropic of Capricorn is:
A. $23\frac{1}{2}°$ B. $23\frac{1}{2}°N$
C. $23\frac{1}{2}°S$ D. 23° S

75. The Head Office of The International Court of Justice is situated in:
A. Geneva B. The Hague
C. New York D. Paris

76. The Constituent Assembly adopted National Anthem on:
A. 20th January, 1950 B. 24th January, 1950
C. 21st May, 1949 D. 13th November , 1949

77. Where is Pushkar Fair held?
A. Jaipur B. Udaipur
C. Jodhpur D. Ajmer

78. Which of the following ultraviolet rays more dangerous?
A. UV-A B. UV-B
C. UV-C D. None of the above

79. Which of the following is ***not*** an abiotic component of biosphere?
A. Protein B. Soil
C. Fungi D. Phosphorus

80. 'Gir Lion Project' is situated in:
A. Gujarat B. Maharashtra
C. Uttar Pradesh D. Madhya Pradesh

81. WWF stands for:
A. World Wide Fund B. World War Fund
C. World Wildlife Fund D. World Watch Fund

82. The river Ganga rises from:
A. Aravalli range B. Ladakh glacier
C. Gangotri glacier D. Milap glacier

83. Which of the following agencies is primarily concerned with the measurement of pollution in India?
A. Green Tribunal
B. Central Pollution Control Board
C. Central Water Commission
D. Survey of India

84. 'Cotopaxi' is an active volcano situated in:
A. Sicily B. Hawaii
C. Andes D. Rockies

85. Tsangpo river of Tibet, in India, is known as:
A. Ganga B. Yamuna
C. Brahmaputra D. Indus

86. In a food chain of grassland ecosystem the top consumers are:
A. herbivorous
B. carnivorous
C. bacteria
D. either carnivorous or herbivorous

87. The main atmospheric layer near the surface of the earth is:
A. stratosphere B. troposphere
C. mesosphere D. ionosphere

88. The number of permanent members of the UN Security Council is:
A. 3 B. 4
C. 5 D. 6

89. Sariska National Park is situated in:
A. West Bengal B. Gujarat
C. Rajasthan D. Assam

90. The main source of energy in an ecosystem is:
A. ATP B. sunlight
C. DNA D. RNA

91. Chipko Andolan was inspired by
A. Hemvati Nandan Bahuguna
B. Sunder Lal Bahuguna
C. Mother Teresa
D. Mahatma Gandhi

92. Chemical nature of insulin is
A. Vitamin B. Protein
C. Lipid D. Carbohydrate

93. In plants, meiosis occurs in
A. Root up B. Pollen grain
C. Stem tip D. Anther

94. In biotic community the primary consumers are
A. Carnivores B. Omnivores
C. Herbivores D. Detritivores

95. Name the drug most commonly used in fever control
A. Brufen B. B-complex
C. Paracetamol D. Liv-52

96. Microorganism responsible for curd formation is
A. *Aspergillus* B. *Streptococcus*
C. *Retrovirus* D. *Lactobacillus*

97. Who discovered the blood group in human being?
A. Landsteiner B. Jennings
C. Pantien and Mast D. Karl Marx

98. Onion, Potato and Ginger are
A. Root B. Stem
C. Adventitious root D. Scale leaves

99. Which is the unicellular microorganism?
A. Spirogyra B. Virus
C. Paramecium D. Hydra

100. Of the following which plant product is a substitute of soap?
A. Rudraksha B. Reetha
C. Tendu D. All of the above

101. Among the following automobile fuel which one is considered to be eco-friendly?
A. Diesel B. Petrol
C. LPG D. CNG

102. In an ecosystem mineral cycling is called as
A. Biogeochemical cycle
B. Geological cycle
C. Chemical cycle
D. None of the above

103. Which of the following plants are dispersed widely?
A. Those dispersed as spores
B. Those dispersed as seed
C. Those dispersed as fruit
D. Those dispersed by vegetative propagation

104. When an organism takes benefit from an associated partner without harming the latter, it is called ______
A. Parasite B. Commensal
C. Saprophyte D. Symbiont

105. When peacock eats a snake which eats insects thriving on green plants the peacock is
A. Primary consumer
B. Final decomposer
C. Primary decomposer
D. At the apex of food pyramid

106. Which of the following is an example of Metamorphic rock?
A. Sandstone B. Granite
C. Marble D. Limestone

107. Which of the following salts is found in maximum quantity in the oceans?
A. Magnesium sulphate B. Calcium sulphate
C. Magnesium chloride D. Sodium chloride

108. Who presides over the meetings of the Rajya Sabha?
A. Vice President B. President
C. Prime Minister D. Chief Justice of India

109. Which of the following soils covers the maximum area in India?
A. Black soil B. Alluvial soil
C. Red soil D. Sandy soil

110. Such herbivorous animals which are only depend on green plants
A. First level consumers
B. Second level consumers
C. Third level consumers
D. Consumers

111. Plague is
A. Viral disease B. Fungal disease
C. Bacterial disease D. Mineral disease

112. Gaseous waste is
- A. Peel of fruits and vegetables
- B. Dirty water of house drainage
- C. Waste of farms and stores
- D. Smoke of burning coal and woods

113. The correct definition of ecosystem is
- A. mutually interacting biotic community
- B. abiotic component of an area
- C. the area of earth and atmosphere inhabited by life
- D. a balanced system of biotic community and its environment

114. Greatest advantage of bipedal movement in the evolution of man is
- A. supports the body properly
- B. loss of weight
- C. forearms becoming free for carrying out order of brain
- D. greater speed

115. What is the instrument to record the intensity of Earthquake?
- A. Physiograph B. Seismograph
- C. Cardiograph D. Barograph

116. Which planet is the nearest to the Sun?
- A. Mars B. Jupiter
- C. Venus D. Mercury

117. 'Gir' National Park is situated in
- A. Rajasthan State
- B. Gujarat State
- C. Madhya Pradesh State
- D. Maharashtra State

118. The quality of observation method is not
- A. It is psychological method.
- B. It is based on practical experience.
- C. It is child centered method in which a teacher is only an administrator.
- D. It is adopted by different surveys.

119. Merits of problem-solving method in environment education is
- A. goal oriented method
- B. creative method
- C. selectivity
- D. All of the above

120. Limitation of observation method is
- A. This method is not economical
- B. The result are not more legal minute observation.
- C. The study of internal behaviour of individual is not possible
- D. All of the above

121. Name the instrument used for measuring air pressure.
- A. Barometer B. Thermometer
- C. Seismograph D. Hygrometer

122. Bt cotton is
- A. a hybrid plant B. a transgenic plant
- C. a natural plant D. a medicinal plant

123. Acid rain is chiefly due to atmospheric pollution by
- A. SO_2 B. H_2S
- C. HCl D. N_2

124. Which of the following is the most productive ecosystem?
- A. Tropical rain forests B. Tundra
- C. Savanna D. Desert

125. Which of the following chemicals are used for ripening of mangoes?
- A. Calcium carbonate B. Calcium hydroxide
- C. Calcium carbide D. Calcium chloride

126. Which of the following diseases spread through contaminated drinking water?
- A. AIDS B. Typhoid
- C. Anaemia D. Tetanus

127. Green house gases do not include
- A. CO_2 B. N_2O
- C. CO D. CH_4

128. Which of the following is a dicotyledonous plant?
- A. Bamboo B. Banana
- C. Sugarcane D. Mustard

129. Uptake of water in plants takes place by
- A. Xylem B. Phloem
- C. Cambium D. Palisade

130. Which one is the first literary source?
- A. Rigveda B. Samveda
- C. Yajurveda D. Atharvaveda

131. Which two gases make up 99% of the atmosphere?
- A. Ozone and Oxygen
- B. Oxygen and Nitrogen
- C. Carbon dioxide and Ozone
- D. Argon and Ozone

132. The basic objective of educational excursion in EVS is
- A. To develop the energy of children
- B. First hand experience to the students
- C. Promote socialisation
- D. Promote team spirit

133. How to recognize the characteristic of physiologically dry soil?

A. It has plenty of water
B. Light available to plant is not enough
C. Salt concentration is very high in soil
D. The soil is hard stony

134. Why are continuous and comprehensive evaluation necessary?

A. To know how much learner have not learnt.
B. To maintain the progress of learners discontinuously.
C. No unnecessary fear of examination is seen among learner by continuous evaluation.
D. To give importance to examination system.

135. Grazing animals change vegetation by

A. seed dispersal B. cross pollination
C. selective grazing D. spreading disease

136. Which of the following is required for healthy bones?

A. Potassium and Vitamin K
B. Calcium and Vitamin E
C. Calcium and Vitamin C
D. Calcium and Vitamin D

137. Name the highest peak of the Himalayas in India.

A. Mt. K_2 B. Mt. Everest
C. Mt. Kanchenjunga D. Mt. Dhaulagiri

138. At lower classes play-way method of teaching is based on

A. Psychological principles of development
B. Sociological principles of teaching
C. Theory of physical education programmes
D. Principles of method of teaching

139. Name the lowest layer of the atmosphere.

A. Stratosphere B. Ozonosphere
C. Ionosphere D. Troposphere

140. Name the disease caused due to deficiency of Vitamin-C.

A. Scurvy B. Beri Beri
C. Night blindness D. Fatigue

141. Who is the first woman IPS officer in India?

A. Pratibha Patil B. Padmaja Naidu
C. Kiran Bedi D. Hansa Mehta

142. Name the famous 'one-horn rhinoceros' Wild-life Sanctuary in Assam.

A. Manas B. Kaziranga
C. Gir forest D. Kanha-Kisli

143. Which of the following is an example of igneous rock?

A. Basalt B. Limestone
C. Slate D. Graphite

144. Ozone layer is found in earth's atmospheric layer

A. Troposphere B. Stratosphere
C. Mesosphere D. Ionosphere

145. Who is the founder of Sikh religion?

A. Guru Teg Bahadur B. Guru Govind Singh
C. Guru Arjun Dev D. Guru Nanak

146. The instrument to record the intensity of Earthquake is

A. Physiograph B. Seismograph
C. Cardiograph D. Barograph

147. 'The longest day' in the southern hemisphere is on

A. 21st March B. 21st June
C. 23rd September D. 22nd December

148. Who is the author of 'Satyartha Prakash'?

A. Swami Dayanand Saraswati
B. Swami Vivekanand
C. Raja Ram Mohan Roy
D. Madan Mohan Malviya

149. 'Bihu' is a folk dance of which of the following States in India?

A. Rajasthan B. Tamil Nadu
C. Assam D. Uttar Pradesh

150. A group of interconnected food chains is called

A. Food cycle B. Chain reaction
C. Food web D. Pyramid of biomass

151. Which of the following best reflects child-centred strategies in teaching EVS at primary level?

(*a*) Discussion
(*b*) Demonstration
(*c*) Lecture
(*d*) Survey

A. (*b*) and (*c*) B. (*c*) and (*d*)
C. (*a*) and (*d*) D. (*a*) and (*b*)

152. Which of the following strategies promotes inquiry while teaching the theme 'Food'?

A. Demonstrating fireless cooking of sandwiches, shikanji (lemon water) etc.
B. Asking students to find out food preferences of their family members.
C. Showing pictures of various preserved food items used in different regions of India.
D. Asking students to collect pictures of various food items.

153. Which of the following sets depicts the themes of EVS at primary level?

A. Food, Material, Shelter
B. Family and Friends, Travel, Natural resources

C. Shelter, Travel, Things we make and do
D. Weather, Water, Travel

154. Read statements (A) and (R) properly and then answer the following questions.

(A) : Silkworm can find his female worm from many kilometers away by her smell.

(R) : Some female insects release 'Pheromones' which can be recognised by their males by smell.

Choose the correct answer:

A. Both (A) and (R) are correct, but (R) does not explains (A)
B. (A) is correct, but (R) is incorrect
C. (A) is incorrect, but (R) is correct
D. Both (A) and (R) are correct and (R) explains (A)

155. Doctors prescribed blood test for patients to confirm malaria. Blood test is done to:

A. check iron in blood
B. check for eggs of female anopheles mosquitoes in blood
C. check for microbes in blood
D. check for haemoglobin in blood

156. Students conduct a survey in their homes and neighbourhood to find out the number of members and approximate amount of water used in each family. What skills and processes are developed through this activity?

A. questioning, inferring, expression
B. hypothesising, inferring, expression
C. prediction, experimentation, observing
D. questioning, experimentation, sensitivity towards environment

157. An EVS teacher asks her students to think and answer "Why do we feel comfortable in woollens clothes during winter". This question is a:

A. analytical question
B. hypothetical question
C. factual question
D. convergent question

158. A teacher wants to select synchronous communication with her students for teaching EVS. Which of the following will she choose?

A. Phone calls, pre-recorded videos, tele-conferencing
B. E-mail, social media posts, phone calls
C. Instant messaging, blogs, tele-conferencing
D. Video conferencing, online chat sessions, phone calls

159. While teaching EVS, a teacher's statement/question, which encourages students to elaborate on an answer either on their own or from the response of their peers, is:

A. Probing B. Conditioning
C. Chaining D. Trial and error

160. Read the following statements and choose the correct option:

Assertion (A): Learning of EVS needs to be oriented to process skills relating to observation, identification, classification, etc.

Reason (R): Through acquiring various process skills, the learning outcomes of EVS learning are expected to be achieved.

A. (A) is false, but (R) is true.
B. Both (A) and (R) are true and (R) is the correct explanation of (A).
C. Both (A) and (R) are true, but (R) is not the correct explanation of (A).
D. (A) is true, but (R) is false.

161. Which of the following is ***not*** a learning outcome in EVS for students of Class III?

A. Voices opinion on good and bad touch
B. Voices opinion on issues observed/experienced and relates to social practices such as discrimination in ownership of resources
C. Observes rules in few local, indoor, outdoor games
D. Identifies directions of classroom

162. You want to encourage hands-on activities for students of EVS. Which of the following is the most appropriate activity?

A. Map reading from a globe
B. Collecting coins of different countries
C. Developing an EVS kit from available material
D. Drawing parts of different plants on a chart

163. Formative assessment of EVS is ______.

(*a*) Assessment for learning
(*b*) Assessment of learning
(*c*) Assessment as learning
(*d*) Assessment about learning

Choose the correct option:

A. (*c*) and (*d*) B. (*a*) and (*b*)
C. (*a*) and (*c*) D. (*b*) and (*c*)

164. When we burn fuels we get:

A. Only light energy
B. Heat and light energy
C. Mechanical and light energy
D. Light and sound energy

165. Consider the following statements about snakes and identify the ***incorrect*** one from the following:

A. They swallow their food whole.
B. Snakes have sharp teeth.
C. Poisonous snakes have fangs.
D. They chew up their prey.

166. Deficiency of <u>A</u> causes anaemia. <u>B</u> and <u>C</u> are rich sources of A. A, B and C respectively are:

A. Calcium, Milk, Eggs
B. Iron, Milk, Eggs
C. Iron, Spinach, Dates
D. Calcium, Spinach, Dates

167. Assertion (A): A boiled egg put in a mug of water sinks whereas it floats when put in salt water.

Reason (R): The density of egg increases on boiling.

Choose the correct option:

A. Both (A) and (R) are correct and (R) is correct explanation of (A)
B. Both (A) and (R) are correct, but (R) is not correct explanation of (A)
C. (A) is correct and (R) is incorrect
D. Both (A) and (R) are incorrect

168. Assertion (A): Earthworm is referred to as a farmer's best friend.

Reason (R): Earthworms destroy the weeds.

Choose the correct option:

A. Both (A) and (R) are true and (R) is correct explanation of (A)
B. Both (A) and (R) are true, but (R) is not correct explanation of (A)
C. (A) is true, but (R) is false
D. Both (A) and (R) are false

169. Which of the following is an important feature in school field trip in EVS teaching?

A. Awakens students' interest to learn and get new learning information.
B. Both teacher and students get a break from regular teaching-learning practice.
C. The funds for teaching-learning are properly utilized.
D. Parents feel happy to see their children going on picnic.

170. EVS curriculum has followed a theme-based approach to:

A. cover wide range of concepts in one go.
B. save resources.
C. help in assessing knowledge of children holistically.
D. enable students to be concerned about society and nature both.

171. Environmental studies education for primary students intends that:

A. Students become less inquisitive.
B. Students become more inquisitive.
C. Students make fewer mistakes.
D. Students develop good drawing and writing skills.

172. EVS pedagogy advocates the following practices *except*:

A. Capacitating students for critical thinking and problem solving.
B. Acknowledging textbooks are superior over actual life experiences.
C. Promoting collaboration amongst students.
D. Nurturing the creativity and curiosity of students.

173. Why is 'Community' important for teaching-learning in EVS at primary level?

A. It is an easily available resource.
B. It comprises wise and elderly people.
C. It provides learning opportunities in a real setting.
D. It does not need any funds for expenditure.

174. A competent EVS teacher uses pedagogical processes which are:

A. True to child's life.
B. True to subject.
C. True to school.
D. True to child's life and subject.

175. Which one of the following should be minimized in the EVS classroom?

A. Free debates
B. Picture reading
C. Narratives
D. Descriptions

176. Real challenge for EVS learning at primary level is:

A. Definitions and information
B. Rote learning
C. Descriptions of concepts
D. Opportunities for childrens to express themselves

177. Which of the following themes consists of subthemes in the syllabus of EVS at primary level?

A. Family and friends
B. Water
C. Work and play
D. Food

178. Socio-cultural issues related to Water Theme can be effectively learnt through:

(*a*) Role-play
(*b*) Real dialogue among students
(*c*) Field trip
(*d*) Demonstration and home work

A. (*a*), (*b*) and (*c*) only
B. (*c*) and (*d*) only
C. (*d*) only
D. (*c*) only

179. Self-assessment in EVS is:
(*a*) assessment as learning
(*b*) learning about learning
(*c*) judgements about achievements and the outcome of learning.
(*d*) assessment of learning.

A. (*a*), (*b*) and (*c*) only B. (*c*) only
C. (*a*) and (*c*) only D. (*a*), (*c*) and (*d*) only

180. Learning of EVS is based on the principle of:
A. simple to complex B. complex to simple
C. global to local D. abstract to concrete

ANSWERS

1	2	3	4	5	6	7	8	9	10
C	D	A	D	A	B	C	A	D	B
11	**12**	**13**	**14**	**15**	**16**	**17**	**18**	**19**	**20**
D	D	D	D	B	C	A	B	B	C
21	**22**	**23**	**24**	**25**	**26**	**27**	**28**	**29**	**30**
D	B	A	C	C	A	B	B	A	A
31	**32**	**33**	**34**	**35**	**36**	**37**	**38**	**39**	**40**
D	D	B	B	B	B	A	C	D	A
41	**42**	**43**	**44**	**45**	**46**	**47**	**48**	**49**	**50**
B	A	B	D	C	C	A	A	C	B
51	**52**	**53**	**54**	**55**	**56**	**57**	**58**	**59**	**60**
B	C	D	C	B	D	C	C	A	A
61	**62**	**63**	**64**	**65**	**66**	**67**	**68**	**69**	**70**
A	D	C	C	D	A	B	D	C	C
71	**72**	**73**	**74**	**75**	**76**	**77**	**78**	**79**	**80**
A	D	B	C	B	B	D	C	C	A
81	**82**	**83**	**84**	**85**	**86**	**87**	**88**	**89**	**90**
C	C	B	C	C	B	B	C	C	B
91	**92**	**93**	**94**	**95**	**96**	**97**	**98**	**99**	**100**
B	B	D	C	C	D	A	B	B	B
101	**102**	**103**	**104**	**105**	**106**	**107**	**108**	**109**	**110**
D	A	C	B	D	C	D	A	B	A
111	**112**	**113**	**114**	**115**	**116**	**117**	**118**	**119**	**120**
C	D	D	C	B	D	B	C	D	D
121	**122**	**123**	**124**	**125**	**126**	**127**	**128**	**129**	**130**
A	B	A	A	C	B	C	D	A	A
131	**132**	**133**	**134**	**135**	**136**	**137**	**138**	**139**	**140**
B	B	C	C	C	D	A	D	D	A
141	**142**	**143**	**144**	**145**	**146**	**147**	**148**	**149**	**150**
C	B	A	B	D	B	D	A	C	C
151	**152**	**153**	**154**	**155**	**156**	**157**	**158**	**159**	**160**
C	B	C	D	C	A	A	D	A	B
161	**162**	**163**	**164**	**165**	**166**	**167**	**168**	**169**	**170**
B	C	C	B	D	C	B	C	A	C
171	**172**	**173**	**174**	**175**	**176**	**177**	**178**	**179**	**180**
B	B	C	D	D	D	A	A	A	A

English Language

SECTION-A

COMPREHENSION AND ENGLISH GRAMMAR

1 COMPREHENSION

INTRODUCTION

Reading Comprehension determines the ability of an examinee to grapple with abstract thoughts hidden in the text. It also judges his ability to draw conclusions from the given set of information that is in the form of running text. This test can be solved by reading the given paragraph and answering the questions that are given below it. Answers may be given either by ticking the right choices in the question paper or filling the relevant boxes (showing options) in the answer sheet with pencil. The passage can vary in length; it could be as small as a paragraph of 50 words or, it could be a type of small essay of nearly 500 words, conveniently divided into some paragraphs. Single paragrpahs are also given in many a test. The topic of the paragraph generally deals with abstract subjects whereas figures or tables are generally avoided.

Reading Comprehension is an art. Our readers will do well to answer this test by:

(*a*) developing a broad frame of reference;

(*b*) reading as many passages as is possible and answer questions given below them;

(*c*) developing the reading habit and imbibing the "flow of English language" thoroughly to understand its style and grammatic intricacies.

While treating the test from an artistic viewpoint, readers will have to develop the sense of making logical conclusions. These conclusions must be based on the text given in the passage; they cannot imagine phenomenon, conclusions or facts. They have to limit their imagination and the power to comprehend the abstract points (the "fine things" stated in the topic) to the passage only.

Reading Comprehension is a science too. In order to solve this test in a scientific manner, readers will have to proceed according to the following steps:

(1) Read the passage at fast pace.

(2) Now, read the passage again at slow pace and also underline important points.

(3) Read those words carefully that are in bold face letters. Try to connect them to the lines in which, they have been carefully embedded.

(4) Now, read the first question given below the passage. If you know the answer fully well, tick the relevant option in the answer sheet.

(5) Now, go to next question and answer it. Proceed in a similar manner and answer all the questions.

(6) If you find a question to be too difficult to answer, skip it and go to the next question. In the end, you can read the passage (only in parts) and answer these question that were left by you.

(7) If the examination has a system of negative marking, do not answer the difficult questions through guess- work or your imagination. It is better not to answer those questions if negative marks are likely to be earned by you by answering them.

(8) Many passages have tests of antonyms and synonyms appended in the end of their questions. Do not imagine the antonym or synonym of the given word or the bold-faced word of the passage. Instead, link that word to the line in which, it is embedded. Try to find out what the author is saying in that line. Now, answer the question (antonym or synonym) keeping in mind the "true spirit" of the word in its sentence.

(9) In many tests, you may be asked to give a suitable title to the passage. Scan through the passage quickly and read the underlined phrases carefully. Give such a title to the passage as would encompass all the vital points of the passage. Do not go beyond the "real essence" of the given passage. Do not use difficult words in the title decided by you.

As an artist, you have to comprehend the fine aspects of the text that you will read. As a logician, you will be required to deduct and conclude.

Practice will make you perfect.

PASSAGE–1

The impact of technical advancement in armaments on man, needs to be analyzed with a rational mind, and heart free from prejudices of any kind towards modernisation. The most noticeable impact of this development certainly has been the loss of immunity from violence for successive generations ever since the invention of gunpowder. In modern times, the presence of technically advanced arms, not only at the fronts but also among the civilian population, has vastly undermined the value of human life, and endangered the very entity of those virtues of self restraint and discretion, on which a peaceful and amiable society rests. However, an unbiased view of the present scenario, would refrain one from attributing the rising trends of violence to the availability of technically superior weapons, for one must not overlook the fact that "Necessity is the mother of invention".

Every stage in the development of armaments has been marked by its distinct impact on society. When man fought with stones and his bare hands, the society was not yet compact. The discovery of metal and the use of spears, knives and arrows indicate the stage of the formation of small kingdoms. Fire continued to be an effective weapon of destruction. When man introduced the cavalry into the army and improved the strategies of making war, some small kingdoms gave away to form empires, but with no revolutionary advances in armaments forthcoming, the political structure of society remained more or less stagnant for the many coming centuries.

The next significant development was the use of gunpowder, which could be used to perform acts which were then thought to be impossible. Gunpowder was used to form the ammunition of several guns and canons. This sudden advances in weaponry not only facilitated the control of a large mass of people by relatively few armed men that helping to form strong empires, but the availability of the new technology to a select few nations enabled the formation of colonies in continents which did not have access to the modernized technologies of warfare. Modern technological advances in armaments aided the formation of nation states in Europe. The extensive use of the fire-power lent a lethal edge to the naval power which proved to be the greatest asset to any nation in the 19th century. Small United Nations States of Europe with strong navies, modern arms and disciplined men gained control of lands in foreign continents far greater in areas than the parent countries.

1. Necessity is the mother of invention means
   A. where there is mother there is invention
   B. when necessity arises invention is done
   C. most of the invention are pre-planned
   D. nothing happens without creating congenial environment

2. The invention of modern weapons have resulted into
   A. loss of immunity from war in the society
   B. successive wars for the last two centuries
   C. arms race among the nations
   D. loss of life and property every now and then

3. Small kingdoms turned into big empires, after
   A. the invention of cavalry and canons and its introduction into the army
   B. the introduction of nuclear arms into the army
   C. the end of the use of knives, arrows and swords
   D. the end of the 19th century

4. The style of the passage is
   A. informative   B. analytical
   C. retrospective   D. provocative

PASSAGE–2

It was during one of the most dreadful smallpox epidemics in England that Edward Jenner, a country doctor, made a discovery which was to alter the course of history. Jenner noticed that the disease seldom struck those who lived in rural areas and worked around cattle. Most farmers and dairy workers had contracted cowpox and had recovered with nothing more serious than a putsule which left a scar. This observation led Dr. Jenner to think: Why not vaccinate people with cowpox to protect them from smallpox ? On May 14, 1876, Dr. Jenner took a healthy boy, James Phillips, to a dairy maid, Sarah Nelmes, who had a cowpox putsule on her hand resulting from an infection from her master's cow. Dr. Jenner made two shallow cuts on James Phillips' arm and inoculated them with matter taken from the cowpox sore. A putsule developed on the boy's arm formed a scab and healed. In July of the same year. Dr. Jenner inoculated James with matter from a smallpox putsule. During the next two weeks, the doctor watched for signs of smallpox. They did not develop. The vaccination was successful. Dr. Jenner wrote a paper explaining his method of vaccination. At first the doctors were hostile and would not listen to a ridiculous procedure. Many towns people organised anti vaccination campaigns. Gradually, however, the doctors and their patients accepted vaccination.

1. The fact that Edward Jenner was a country doctor, was important in the discovery of smallpox vaccine, because
   A. he had enough time to pursue his research in the rural areas
   B. he noticed that the disease was prevalent where people worked around cattle
   C. he noticed that the disease seldom struck people who worked around the cattle
   D. he found that he could convince rural people more easily than city people

2. Dr. Jenner was successful as cowpox virus produces
   A. severe infection in humans resulting in deaths
   B. a mild infection in humans which is not enough to produce active immunity
   C. a mild infection in humans which is enough to produce active immunity
   D. no infection in humans

3. Dr. Jenner made his experiment on a healthy boy who
   A. died after experimentation
   B. could not be relieved of his mark of putsule
   C. developed the sings of putsule on his body when he was injected the matter of cowpox
   D. was paid for it

4. Passage here is having a/an
   A. narrative style B. analytic style
   C. provocative style D. idiomatic style

PASSAGE–3

The Indian culture of our times is in the making. Many of us are striving to produce a blend of all cultures that seem today to be in clash with one another. No culture can live, if it attempts to be exclusive. There is no such things as pure Aryan culture in existence in India today. Whether the Aryans were indigenous to India or were unwelcome intruders, does not interest me much. What does interest me is the fact that may remote ancestors blended with one another with the utmost freedom and we of the present generation are a result of that blend. I do not want my house to be walled in, on all sides and my windows to be stuffed. I want the cultures of all lands to be blown about my house as freely as possible. But I refuse to be blown off my feet by any. I would have any young men and women with literary tastes to learn as much of English and other world-languages as they like, and then expect them to give the benefits of their learning to India and the world alike like a Bose, a Ray or Tagore. But I would not have a single Indian forget, neglect or be ashamed of his mother tongue, or feel that he or she cannot think or express the best thoughts in his or her own vernacular. Mine is not a religion of the prison house.

1. The author views Indian Culture as
   A. pure Aryan culture.
   B. a clash of cultures.
   C. a continual blend of cultures.
   D. the culture of remote ancestors.

2. The author thinks that
   A. the Aryans were indigenous to India.
   B. the Aryans were unwelcome intruders.
   C. the question whether the Aryans were indigenous or not is not of interest.
   D. the culture that we have inherited is the Aryan culture.

3. The author wants
   A. the cultures of others to be kept out.
   B. the cultures of others to replace our old culture.
   C. the freedom to blend other cultures with our own.
   D. the preservation of the culture of our ancestors.

4. The author wants Indians to
   A. learn only English, as much as they like.
   B. learn English and other world languages.
   C. learn only the mother tongue or the vernacular.
   D. English and other world languages in addition to the mother tongue.

PASSAGE–4

As civilization proceeds in the direction of technology, it passes the point of supplying all the basic essentials of life, food, shelter, clothes, and warmth. Then we are faced with a choice between using technology to provide and fulfil needs which have hitherto been regarded as unnecessary or, on the other hand, using technology to reduce the number of hours of work which a man must do in order to earn a given standard of living. In other words, we either raise our standard of living above that necessary for comfort and, happiness or we leave it at this level and work shorter hours. I shall take it as axiomatic that mankind has, by that time, chosen the latter alternative. Men will be working shorter and shorter hours in their paid employment.

1. "Then we are faced with a choice..." what does "then'' refer to?
   A. When automation takes over many aspects of human life
   B. The present state of civilization
   C. The past stage of civilization
   D. After having provided the basic essentials of life

2. What does the passage suggest about the use of technology?
   A. It creates new and essential needs for mankind
   B. It is opposed to the basic essentials of life
   C. It is complementary to a raised standard of living
   D. It is responsible for man's love of comfort and happiness

3. What does increased use of technology imply?
   A. An advanced stage in human civilization
   B. A backward step in human culture
   C. Unnecessary comfort and happiness for mankind
   D. Man's zest for more and more work

4. What does the author suggest?
   A. Man will gradually rise above his present stage in civilization
   B. Man will gradually settle down to the same stage with fewer hours of work
   C. Man will gradually raise his standard of living by working longer hours
   D. Man will gradually earn a given standard of living with the help of technology

PASSAGE–5

It is said that ideas are explosive and dangerous. To allow them unfettered freedom is, in fact, to invite disorder. But, to this position, there are at least two final answers. It is impossible to draw a line round dangerous ideas, and any attempt at their definition involves monstrous folly. If views, moreover, which imply disorder are able to disturb the foundations of the State, there is something supremely wrong with the governance of the State. For disorder is not a habit of mankind. We cling so eagerly to our accustomed ways that, as even Burke insisted; popular violence is always the outcome of a deep popular sense of wrong.

1. What is the central point that the passage emphasizes?
   A. It is unnecessary to define dangerous ideas
   B. Dangerous ideas are born out of the enjoyment of freedom
   C. A well-governed State is unaffected by dangerous ideas
   D. Dangerous ideas originate from man's preoccupation with politics

2. From a close study of the passage, which one of the following statements emerges most clearly?
   A. The author is against the exercise of political freedom
   B. He is indifferent to dangerous and explosive ideas
   C. He welcomes violence as a method to change governments
   D. He warns that violence is the outcome of popular dissatisfaction with the government

3. The author says, 'we cling eagerly to our accustomed ways'. Which one of the following statements may be considered as the assumption of the author?
   A. We are afraid of social changes
   B. Mankind is averse to any disorder
   C. We have developed inertia that makes us incapable of social action
   D. There is an all-round lack of initiative in the society

4. Which of the following statements may most correctly bring out the significance of the opinion of Burke quoted in the passage?
   A. Burke advocated violence against injustice
   B. Burke's opinion coincides with the author's opinion on explosive and dangerous ideas
   C. Burke hated any popular uprising
   D. Burke had no belief in political liberty

PASSAGE–6

The psychological causes of unhappiness, it is clear, are many and various. But all have something in common. The typical unhappy man is one who, having been deprived in youth of some normal satisfaction, has come to value this one kind of satisfaction more than any other, and has therefore given to his life a one-sided direction, together with a quite undue emphasis upon the achievement as opposed to the activities connected with it. There is, however, a further development which is very common in the present day. A man may feel so completely thwarted that he seeks no form of satisfaction, but only distraction and oblivion. He then becomes a devotee of "pleasure". This is to say, he seeks to make life bearable by becoming less alive. Drunkenness, for example, is temporary suicide - the happiness that it brings is merely negative, a momentary cessation of unhappiness.

1. Who is a typical unhappy man?
   A. One who has been deprived of normal satisfaction in youth
   B. One who finds life unbearable and attempts suicide
   C. One who does not mind momentary unhappiness
   D. One who seeks every form of satisfaction

2. "One sided direction" refers to the pursuit of which one of the following?
   A. Drinking and forgetfulness
   B. The satisfaction one had been deprived of
   C. Activities leading to happiness
   D. Every form of psychological satisfaction

3. Which one of the following is the correct statement? Drinking helps the unhappy only to
   A. forget their dissatisfaction
   B. get sublime happiness
   C. get the motivational needs fulfilled
   D. concentrate harder

4. What does "becoming less alive" imply?
   A. Neglect of health
   B. Decline in moral values
   C. Living in a make-believe world
   D. Leading a sedentary way of living

PASSAGE–7

What is to be the limit of forgiveness? It would probably have been allowed by many of the ancients that an unforgiving temper was not to be commended. They would have said, we are not to exact a penalty for every nice offence; we are to overlook some things; we are to be blind sometimes. But they would have said at the same time, we must be careful to keep our self-respect, and to be on a level with the world. On the whole, they would have said, it is the part of a man fully to requite to his friends their benefits and to his enemies their injuries.

1. Which one of the following is the correct statement? According to the writer we must
   A. ignore an offence if it is nice
   B. forgive people if they bring us nice presents
   C. forgive pretty offenders
   D. not punish each and every offence

2. Which one of the following is the correct statement? We must
   A. be blind if we want to forgive others
   B. be blind to the faults of our friends
   C. be indifferent to what others do
   D. overlook certain things

3. Which one of the following is the correct statement? In ancient times people were
   A. ordered to lose their tempers
   B. permitted to lose their tempers and not forgive their enemies
   C. told that it was not good to have an unforgiving temper
   D. advised to forgive each and every offence committed by both friends and foes

4. What is the underlying tone of the passage?
   A. We must be forgiving in general
   B. We must forgive our friends
   C. There is no limit whatsoever to our duty to forgive
   D. We must always punish the wrongdoer

PASSAGE–8

We should preserve Nature to preserve life and beauty. A beautiful landscape, full of green vegetation, will not just attract our attention but will fill us with infinite satisfaction. Unfortunately, because of modernization, much of nature is now yielding to towns, roads and industrial areas. In a few places some Natural reserves are now being carved out to avert the danger of destroying Nature completely. Man will perish without Nature, so modern man should continue this struggle to save plants, which give us oxygen, from extinction. Moreover, Nature is essential to man's health.

1. What does "Nature" in the passage mean?
   A. Countryside covered with plants and trees
   B. Physical power that created the world
   C. Inherent things that determine character
   D. Practical study of plants and animals

2. Which one of the following is the correct statement? According to the passage
   A. Beauty is only skin-deep
   B. Everything is beautiful in its natural state
   C. There is beauty in Nature
   D. Nature is a moral teacher

3. What does the writer suggest?
   A. We should not modernize, so that Nature can be preserved
   B. While modernizing we should be careful not to destroy Nature completely
   C. All Nature has been destroyed by modern living
   D. Carving out Natural reserves will hamper the growth of industries

4. What does "Struggle" in the passage mean?
   A. Man's Struggle to exist in the world
   B. Man's Struggle to save Nature
   C. Man's Struggle to catch up with modern trends
   D. Man's Struggle to conserve oxygen

5. Why a beautiful landscape will fill us with infinite satisfaction'?
   A. We love beauty
   B. It is full of green vegetation
   C. It will ensure our future existence
   D. It will show our command over Nature

PASSAGE–9

Finally, there arises the question as to our leadership potential. Although the entire younger generation by the very definition is a potential storehouse of leadership, I feel that our universities provide the richest reservoir from which the future leaders of this country will be forthcoming. I have had occasion to travel fairly extensively and to visit a number of university centres in the country. It is deeply encouraging to see that despite the economic and other difficulties which these young men and women have to face they are full of energy and idealism. The real question is whether we have the ability and imagination to tap this reservoir, to fan the sparks of youthful idealism into bright flames that would illumine the future of India — the India of our dreams for the building of which countless generations have struggled and sacrified; an India socially emancipated, economically prosperous, politically integrated, militarily strong and spiritually dynamic.

1. Which one of the following is correct?
The writer believes that India is
A. socially emancipated
B. economically prosperous
C. spiritually dynamic
D. None of the above

2. What is the author's tone in the passage?
A. Optimistic B. Autocratic
C. Pessimistic D. Partisan

3. Where will the future leaders of the country mainly come from?
A. The families of present political leaders
B. The community of social scientists
C. The universities
D. The entire younger generation

4. Which one of the following is correct?
For realizing the India of our dreams,
A. we should have the imagination to exploit our budding leadership potential
B. we should admire the sacrifices made by several generations
C. we should bring about more technological advancements
D. we should provide better facilities for sports

5. Which one of the following is correct?
What is deeply encouraging about educated young men and women of India is that
A. they come from the richest reservoirs of potential leaders
B. they are full of energy and idealism because of quality education
C. they are full of youthful idealism and imagination
D. they are full of energy and idealism in spite of economic and other difficulties they face as students

PASSAGE–10

My own recollection is that I had not had any high regard for my ability. I used to be astonished whenever I won prizes and scholarships. But, I very assiduously guarded my character. The least little blemish drew tears from my eyes. When I merited, or seemed to the teacher to merit, a rebuke, it was unbearable for me. I remember having once received corporal punishment. I did not so much mind the punishment, as the fact that it was considered my desert. I wept piteously. That was when I was in the first or second standard. There was another such incident during the time when I was in the seventh standard. Dorabji Edulji Gimi was the Headmaster then. He was popular among the boys, though he was a disciplinarian. He was a man of method and a good teacher. He had made gymnastics and cricket compulsory for the boys of the upper standards. I disliked both. I never took part in any exercise, cricket or football, before they were made compulsory. My shyness was one of the reasons for this aloofness, which I now see as wrong. I then had the false notion that gymnastics had nothing to do with education. Today I know that physical training should have as much place in the curriculum as mental training.

1. Why did the author say that he did not have any high regard for his ability?
A. He was a dunce
B. He always used to miss his classes
C. He never did well in studies or sports
D. He was full humility

2. The author's idea that character is a treasure is revealed in which of the statements?
A. "I won prizes and scholarships"
B. "When I merited, or seemed to the teacher to merit, a rebuke, it was unbearable for me"
C. "I very assiduously guarded my character"
D. "I wept piteously"

3. Why did the author weep piteously?
A. He felt insulted
B. Punishment was considered his due
C. He felt the physical pain
D. He took the punishment to heart

4. Why did the author dislike gymnastics and cricket?
A. They cut into his study time
B. He had to spend money in buying bats, etc.
C. He felt that physical education could cause injury
D. He was shy

PASSAGE–11

According to the research findings of a team of American scientists published recently, the sea waves contain as much energy as the world is consuming at present. Scientists have found that through the application of two major devices called land-based systems and offshore devices, this source of energy can provide huge amount of electricity without cooling towers and pollution.

Land-based systems include tapered channels and fixed oscillating water column (OWC) devices whereas offshore devices include floating OWC devices, buoys, etc. Through these devices the mechanical energy of ocean waves is absorbed and converted into electrical energy. The wave power potential depends on numerous factors such as the device's capability to harness long wavelengths, period of waves and depth of water where they arise.

Compared to conventional power stations which require greater space and are difficult to maintain in critical situations, wave power devices are highly modular, cost effective and easier to upgrade. As the recent findings suggest, sea wave energy has much greater potential to be used for electricity generation than the hitherto known sources of renewable energy. Moreover, most of the renewable energy systems require hundreds of square acres of useful land for their installation. But in case of wave energy devices, 'space crunch' can never be a serious problem.

1. Which one of the following statements is correct? Harnessing energy from sea waves
A. undermines ecological balance.
B. requires huge capital.
C. requires high technical expertise.
D. results in saving of useful land area.

2. Which one of the following statements is correct? Wave power devices
A. convert wind energy into mechanical power.
B. convert mechanical energy of ocean waves into electrical energy.
C. require costly transmission mechanism.
D. entail risk to human life.

3. Which one of the following statements is correct?
A. Fixed as well as floating oscillating water column devices are required to harness ocean wave energy.
B. Fixed oscillating water column devices are required for off shore based system.
C. Floating oscillating water column devices are required for land-based system.
D. Electricity generated from oceans is independent of the depth of water where waves arise.

4. Which one of the following statements is correct? The capacity of system to generate electricity from ocean waves
A. can be increased only at exorbitant cost.
B. can be easily upgraded.
C. can be increased but it requires a great space.
D. is only a few megawatts.

5. Which one of the following statements is **not** correct?
A. Conventional power stations require cooling towers.
B. Power generation from ocean waves also adds to pollution like conventional power stations.
C. Ocean wave energy can meet all the present energy of the world.
D. Period of waves is one of the relevant factors in power generation from ocean waves.

PASSAGE–12

The most important fact, which a leader who wishes to motivate others should bear in mind, is that an individual has an incessant and gnawing craving for importance. There is no exception to this psychological need. Barring his biological needs, practically all his actions are directed at satisfying his continuing need to feel important. According to William James, the deepest principle in human nature is the craving to be appreciated. The individual who can honestly satisfy this burning hunger for importance on the part of his fellow human beings can literally rule the world. He can motivate and influence any person, big or small, high or low, educated or uneducated, rich or poor, man or woman, provided he is capable of making the other person feel truly important. By discovering the special and particular gifts of an individual, by giving due recognition and sincere appreciation to that singular gift or talent, you can win him or her over to your side easily.

You have to create an eager want on the part of the other individual if you wish to motivate him. In other words, you have to make the horse feel thirsty if your aim is to make it drink. Fortunately for you, there is an inborn, ever-present, gnawing hunger on the part of every human being to gain recognition and appreciation. This want is already there and you don't have to create it. All you have to do is to satisfy this hunger. If you objectively analyse your own motives and needs you will find that this need for recognition is the strong driving factor behind your aspiration to become a leader. It was this urge for importance which made Alexander the Great embark on a world conquest, and made many emperors wage innumerable battles and wars. This urge has driven artists, authors, scientists, inventors and others to attain great heights in their chosen fields and produce the best results.

1. Which one of the following statements is correct?
   A. Many scientists and inventors have excelled because of the availability of research facilities.
   B. Artists and authors have made contribution to society because of their innate genius.
   C. Many athletes have won gold medals in the Olympics because of their coaches.
   D. People in different areas have been successful because of the need of recognition.

2. Which one of the following statements is **not** correct?
   A. Hunger for recognition has to be developed over the years in one's personality.
   B. Need to gain recognition is an inborn trait.
   C. Many wars have been waged to satisfy the need to get importance.
   D. Craving for importance is a natural psychological need of every human being.

3. Which one of the following statements is correct?
   A. A successful leader must be able to identify the need of importance of others.
   B. Need for recognition is a trait only of high professionals.
   C. To motivate a person, an increase of his salary is the best strategy.
   D. Monetary success is the driving force for a leader.

PASSAGE–13

Because goldfish can be kept easily in small ponds and aquariums, they make good pets, but like many other pets, they must have proper care and the right kind of place to live.

A two-inch fish requires a minimum of two gallons of water containing sufficient oxygen to support life. Some oxygen will make its way into the water of an aquarium from the air that touches the surface. Plants in an aquarium also help to furnish oxygen. Snails help to keep an aquarium clean. Thus, with plenty of plants and snails the water in an aquarium does not have to be changed frequently. A large lake may prove to be a quite unsuitable abode for goldfish.

It is important that goldfish not be overfed. They can be fed such things as dried insects in addition to commercially-prepared goldfish food, but they should never be fed more than once a day. Even then, they should not be given more food than can be consumed in about five minutes. This ensures prolonged life.

1. Which one of the following statements is correct?
   A. Snails eat up the goldfish in an aquarium
   B. A large lake may not be a suitable place for goldfish
   C. Plants provide food to the snails in an aquarium
   D. Goldfish come above the surface of water to get oxygen from air

2. Which one of the following statements is **not** correct?
   A. Goldfish can be made goods pets
   B. Plants in an aquarium provide oxygen to goldfish
   C. Goldfish must never be given too much food
   D. Snails make the aquarium clean by eating up goldfish

3. Which of the following helps supply goldfish with oxygen?
   A. Snails B. Dried insects
   C. Goldfish food D. Plants

4. Which one of the following statement is **not** correct?
   A. Water in an aquarium has to be changed frequently because of plants and snails
   B. Commercially-prepared goldfish is available
   C. The place for the goldfish should be selected with care
   D. Dried insects make good feed for goldfish

5. What is important to remember when feeding goldfish?
   A. Goldfish should be fed more than once a day at regular intervals
   B. Goldfish should be fed with plants and snails
   C. Goldfish should be fed only once a day
   D. Goldfish should be fed only in the evenings

PASSAGE–14

Ah ! whatever could be said was said. All held him guilty. Even his own mother who claimed to understand him the best. All had betrayed him in his hour of need. Yet, there he was, still with a sparkling hope and knew that the truth must prevail. In the cold, dark and damp cell he never for a moment lost faith in God and goodness and was waiting anxiously for an angel to come, plead non guilty for him and free him of his miseries.

1. Three of the following statements indicate that he had a sparkling hope. Which statement does not?
   A. He had never lost faith in God.
   B. He was sure there was goodness.
   C. He could have evidence in his favour.
   D. He knew that the truth must prevail.

2. Whatever others said about him, he
   A. betrayed no one.
   B. thought over the problem.
   C. never lost faith in goodness.
   D. raised his voice against injustice.

3. In the dark dungeon he always waited for
   A. his mother.
   B. the jailer.
   C. the verdict freeing him of his miseries.
   D. the angel to come and plead for him.

4. The truth must prevail means
   A. he was true.
   B. angel will reveal truth.
   C. truth always wins in the end.
   D. we must plead for the truth.

PASSAGE–15

Once while travelling by the local bus, I got a seat beside a very strange man. He seemed interested in every passenger aboard. He would stare at a person, scribble some odd mathematical notations on his long notebook and then move on to the next. Being quite interested in what he was doing I asked him what all those notations meant and then came the startling reply. He saw a man's face not as a single unit but as thousands of squares put together. He was in fact a statistical expert and a budding artist learning the art of graphics.

1. The man was scribbling down
   A. the figures of co-passengers.
   B. the details of thousands of squares put together.
   C. some mathematical formulae and calculations.
   D. some mathematical signs.

2. The man caught author's attention because
   A. he was sitting next to him.
   B. he was staring at every person in the bus.
   C. he would stare at every person and then scribble down some mathematical notation.
   D. he was a budding artist learning the art of graphics.

3. The author found that man's reply quite startling because
   A. a statistical expert cannot be a budding scientist.
   B. a budding artist cannot be a statistical expert.
   C. graphics is still a rare art form and he was learning it while travelling in a bus.
   D. the fact that "a man's face can be analysed as thousands of squares" was a strange concept.

4. From the passage we gather that
   A. the author is very inquisitive.
   B. the author tries to poke his nose in other people's business.
   C. the author is interested in mathematical notations.
   D. the author wants to talk to fellow passengers in the bus.

PASSAGE–16

With the inevitable growth of specialisation I see the universities facing two great dangers. First, it is very easy to get so involved in the technical details of education that the object of education is lost. And secondly, in an effort to condition a university to the needs of its students and to the needs of the state it may lose its power to make or mould those students into responsible men, capable of thinking for themselves and capable of expressing the results of their thoughts to others.

1. The author calls growth of specialisation 'inevitable'. Which one of the following statements is likely to be the most correct reason for this inevitability?
   A. Universities give grants only to do specialised work in different disciplines.
   B. The professors and researchers in universities are competent only for specialised work.
   C. Specialisation helps economic growth of the nation.
   D. In an age of science and technology specialisation becomes necessary.

2. Which one of the following statements most correctly suggests the central theme of the passage?
   A. The aim of education is specialisation.
   B. The aim of education is to mould the youth to work for the state.
   C. The aim of education is to make the youth capable of independent thought and expression.
   D. The aim of education is to enable the youth to earn a comfortable living.

3. Which one of the following statements most correctly suggests the warning implied in the passage?
   A. University education should not be concerned with technical details.
   B. Universities should not subordinate themselves to the interests of tile state.
   C. Universities should be concerned only with the needs of students.
   D. Universities should not go in for any specialisation.

PASSAGE–17

We shall go on to the end; we shall fight in France, we shall fight on the seas and oceans, we shall fight with growing confidence and strength in the air, we shall defend our island whatever the cost may be, we shall fight on the beaches, we shall fight on the landing grounds, we shall fight in the fields and in the streets, we shall fight in the hills. We shall never surrender, and even if this island or a large part of it were subjugated and starving, then our empire beyond the seas would carry on the struggle, untill the New World steps forth to the rescue and the liberation of the Old.

1. On the basis of the passage which of the following statements may be said to be correct?
A. The speaker is encouraging his men for the conquest of France
B. The speaker is aggressive and maniacal war-monger
C. The speaker is not satisfied with the conquest of the island
D. The speaker is a patriot urging the defence of his motherland

2. The speaker in the passage wants to go on fighting because
A. he is a raving lunatic
B. he is in a state of utter despair
C. he expects help from other quarters
D. he is the leader of a suicide squad

3. Which of the following pairs of the phrases helps best to bring out the intention of the speaker?
A. "Go on to the end"; "shall never surrender"
B. "Growing confidence"; " subjugated and starving"
C. "Subjugated and starving"; "fight on the landing ground"
D. "Fight in the streets"; "subjugated and starving"

4. The passage consists of repetitive patterns in syntax and vocabulary. The effect of this style is that it
A. reveals the speaker's defects in giving a speech
B. produces the impression of bad poetry
C. conveys the speaker's helpless situation
D. reinforces the speaker's basic intention

PASSAGE–18

It is said that once three old men set out on a Journey together. One of them was bald, the second was a philosopher and the third was a barber. At nightfall they decided that each one of them should sit for watch *turn* by turn. The *barber* was to keep watch first of all, the *philosopher* after that and the bald man last of all. So, the philosopher and the bald man went to sleep and the barber was on watch. For some time he kept awake but in the end, he felt tired of it and he thought of some *diversion* as otherwise it was difficult for him *to pass* time. Then he took out the razor from his box and shaved the head of the philosopher. At the fixed time he woke up the philosopher and himself went to sleep. when the philosopher got up and felt his head all over, he was startled and said in surprise, "It was my turn but this *wretched* fellow has *awakened* bald man."

1. Why did the philosopher get up?
A. He realised that his head was being shaved off
B. It was his turn to keep watch
C. He was awakened by the barber
D. he had a bad dream

2. Who went to sleep first?
A. The philosopher and the barber
B. The barber and the bald man
C. The bald man and the philosopher
D. The barber

3. Why did the barber shave off the head of the philosopher?
A. The barber was jealous of the philosopher
B. The barber wanted to indulge in some fun
C. The barber wanted the philosopher to keep watch
D. The barber was feeling drowsy

4. Which one of the following is the correct sequence decided upon the three to keep watch turn by turn?
A. Barber – bald man – philosopher
B. Bald man – philosopher – barber
C. Barber – philosopher – bald man
D. Bald man – barber – philosopher

5. Which one of the following statements is **not** correct?
A. All the three men decided to keep watch one by one
B. The barber woke up the bald man
C. The head of the philosopher was shaved off
D. The philosopher was startled on feeling his head all over

PASSAGE–19

There can be only two explanations why countries like UK, US, Germany and Japan are willing to spend up to 5.5 million to make the Next Generation Linear Collider (NGLC) : Intellectual snobbery or complete indifference to the problems of the real world. To plan a 20-mile-long tunnel merely to go about smashing atoms, so as to recreate the Big Bang, is a frightful waste of public money. The project has no foreseeable practical application. Already, cyber-savvy cosmologists are engaged in simulating the Big Bang, or the beginning of the universe, in the virtual world, through number crunching and reverse engineering. They have successfully created a black hole on the desktop. So why go in for prohibitively expensive experimentation, when the virtual world is just a mouse-click away? Scientific ingenuity, remember, is not confined to reallife experiments; many of today's break-throughs have been inspired by research conducted almost entirely in cyberspace. Moreover, virtual research is 'clean'— without such fallouts as lab accidents and chemical leakages—and costs next to nothing.

1. Countries like UK, US, Germany and Japan wish to spend lot of money
   A. to attend to the problems of humanity.
   B. to control AIDS.
   C. for defence research.
   D. to carry out atomic research.

2. Virtual research is carried out
   A. on computers.
   B. by experimentation in the field.
   C. by spending up billions of dollars.
   D. by experimentation in space.

3. Scientific research is not prohibitively costly when conducted
   A. by simulation in the virtual world.
   B. smashing atoms in a tunnel.
   C. making real-life models.
   D. using satellites.

4. Reverse engineering
   A. is commonly practised in research.
   B. is prohibitively expensive experimentation.
   C. is not used by cosmologists in the virtual world.
   D. is independent of analysis using computers.

PASSAGE–20

Failure and success are the ways of life. Constant efforts despite initial setbacks have brought us from the chrysalis of failures into the bright opportunity of triumphs. The conquest of Everest is a fitting example. Success eluded men for nearly twenty-five years. The leader of an unsuccessful expedition started, "Everest cannot add to its height, but spirit of man heightens even under repulse." Subsequent conquest of Everest has proved the truth of this. Indeed every newborn day is in itself an opportunity teeming with splendid chances for those who are alert, wide awake and aspiring.

1. According to the writer, the conquest of Everest proves that
   A. the spirit of man heightens under demanding circumstances.
   B. man cannot attain the unattainable.
   C. success is always elusive.
   D. the nature is most potent.

2. In this passage, "chrysalis of failure" means that
   A. failure involves a closed situation from which one cannot escape.
   B. failure can be compared to the pupa of the gold-coloured butterflies.
   C. failure is a transitional state.
   D. as an insect emerges in a different shape from chrysalis, so a human being changes after every failure.

3. The very style of the prose suggests that the writer intends the last sentence of the passage to be
   A. poetic
   B. inspiring
   C. vague
   D. contradictory to the first sentence of the passage.

4. The expression "teeming with" in the passage can be replaced by
   A. multiplying
   B. abounding
   C. fruitful
   D. promising

5. Every new day brings fresh challenges for a person
   A. who is young
   B. whose head is teeming with bright ideas
   C. who has come out of the chrysalis of failure
   D. who is watchful and daring.

PASSAGE–21

Pisa offers a quiet holiday. Apart from the Leaning Tower Square where the tourists flock, the city is free of the kind of crowds one sees at Florence. An 11-km bus ride brings us to Marina de Pisa, the coastal extension of the city, where the Ligurian Sea and quaint buildings provide a few hours of relaxed walks. However, there is not much of a beach.

Gone is the tension of the previous night, when, flying into Italy in the late hours, my wife and I were a little apprehensive. Compared to Germany where we had spent three weeks, Italy, one thought, was 'unsafe'. The fears were compounded when the night bus from the airport terminated at the railway station, instead of going all the way to our hotel. ''Ten Euros,'' said the cab driver at the station when asked how much the ride to the hotel would cost. Quite sure he was overcharging, we got in nevertheless. At 11.30 p.m. we anyway had little choice. The streets were dimly lit and the driver was uncommunicative. Stopping at a desolate building after we had clearly gone out of the city limits, he announced : "Your hotel." I gave him a 10-Euro bill and turned away. But the cabman stopped me. "Your change, sir," he said, pointing to the meter which read 8-20 Euros.

The small change I got back that day was like receiving the certificate of a nation's honesty. Italy, as it turned out, was just fine.

1. The author and his wife were
   A. thrilled at the idea of travelling to Italy.
   B. concerned about safety.
   C. worried because of high cost.
   D. worried because of language problem.

2. The author
   A. was cheated by the taxi driver.
   B. did not like the etiquette of the taxi driver.
   C. was pleasantly surprised by the rectitude of the driver.
   D. was irked because the driver was very talkative.

3. Pisa
   A. has many traffic jams.
   B. is full of business houses.
   C. is a quiet town.
   D. has major pollution problems.

4. Marina de Pisa
   A. is known for its beautiful beaches.
   B. is full of churches.
   C. has many shopping centres.
   D. is a coastal city.

PASSAGE–22

Much of our adult state of fear is linked up with the feeling that I, an individual, have to cope single-handed with a hostile world, the details of which have become far too complicated for me to understand. This feeling of isolation is in part a by-product of the way we have been educated and the stress that is pure on passing examinations. The more 'successful' your education, the more likely you are to feel alone, because the process of segregation has been more complete at every stage you proved how much cleverer you are than all those other fellows, until in the end you stand quite alone and afraid. It ought to be possible to manage things in a different way so that we go forward into the future, collaborating as a team instead of looking around for every possible opportunity to knife each other in the back.

1. An adult in the modern world is in a state of fear because
   A. he has developed an individuality.
   B. he feels lonely in an unfriendly world.
   C. his life has become complicated.
   D. he cannot understand the challenge.

2. The modern man feels isolated
   A. because he has passed through the stress of examinations.
   B. because he is the by-product of 'successful' social system.
   C. because he fails to receive education.
   D. because he nurses his feeling of isolation.

3. The writer thinks that fierce competitiveness in the modern educational system
   A. makes them neurotic.
   B. makes man clever.
   C. does not make man care for his fellows.
   D. makes man hostile to his environment.

4. Modern education makes man feel segregated
   A. because of its emphasis on materialism.
   B. by making him distrustful of others.
   C. by making him stand on his own.
   D. by inculcating the fear of society in him.

5. It would be a better educational system
   A. if it would manage things differently.
   B. if it inculcates the spirit of togetherness.
   C. if it teaches collaboration with a team.
   D. if it does not allows us to knife each other in the back.

PASSAGE–23

Diversity typically provides fresh perspectives on issues, but it makes it more difficult to unify the team and reach agreements. The strongest case for diversity on work teams is when these teams are engaged in problem-solving and decision-making tasks. Heterogeneous teams bring multiple perspective to the discussion, thus increasing the likelihood that the team will identify creative or unique solutions. Additionally, the lack of a common perspective usually means diverse teams spend more time discussing issues, which decrease the chances that a weak alternative will be chosen. However, keep in mind that the positive contribution that diversity makes to decision-making teams undoubtedly declines over time. Diverse groups have more difficulty working together and solving problems, but this dissipates with time expect the value-added component of diverse teams to decrease as members become more familiar with each other and the team becomes more cohesive.

1. Diversity on work team leads to
   A. human problems.
   B. creative solutions.
   C. economy in manufacturing.
   D. higher turnover.

2. With diversity in work-force there is
   A. difficulty in reaching a solution quickly.
   B. difficulty in designing wage formula.
   C. difficulty in managing international market.
   D. difficulty experienced in shop-floor management.

3. Advantages of diversity
   A. are sustained over long periods of time.
   B. lead to further increase with time.
   C. decline as the members come to know each other.
   D. decline as the absenteeism increases.

4. Problem-solving tasks can be handled by
   A. homogeneous groups.
   B. heterogeneous groups.
   C. management graduates.
   D. consultants.

PASSAGE–24

The world of today has achieved much, but for all its declared love for humanity it has based itself far more on hatred and violence than on the virtues that make man human. War is the negation of truth and humanity. War may be unavoidable sometimes but its progeny are terrible to contemplate. Not more killing, for man must die, but the deliberate and persistent propagation for hatred and falsehood, which gradually become the normal habits of the people. It is dangerous and harmful to be guided in our life's course by hatreds and aversions, for they are wasteful of energy and limit and twist the mind, and prevent it from perceiving the truth.

1. According to the author, the achievements of the world are not impressive because
   A. there is nothing much to boast of.
   B. they are mostly in the field of violence.
   C. its love of humanity is a pretence.
   D. the world has not made any achievement.
2. War is the negation of truth means
   A. wars do not exist.
   B. wars are evil.
   C. wars spread and advertise falsehood.
   D. wars kill human beings.
3. According to the author, the world's declared love of humanity is
   A. false.
   B. true.
   C. non-existent.
   D. not to be taken seriously.
4. Man should be guided by
   A. scientific discoveries.
   B. practical wisdom.
   C. generous human feelings.
   D. materialism.
5. Hatred and aversions are unwholesome as they are
   A. dangerous.
   B. harmful.
   C. narrow.
   D. barriers in seeing the truth.

PASSAGE–25

Few people ask from books what books can give us. Most commonly we come to books with blurred and divided minds, asking of fiction that it shall be true, of poetry that it shall be false, of biography that it shall be flattering, of history that it shall enforce our own prejudices. If we could banish all such preconceptions when we read, that would be an admirable beginning.

1. According to this passage, most readers think that poetry is essentially
   A. imagination B. unrealistic
   C. realistic D. didactic
2. The author's reference to biography being viewed as something 'flattering' suggests that he thinks that it should be
   A. offensive B. critical
   C. truthful D. subjective
3. According to the passage, most books of history are
   A. an objective of the past events
   B. the author's views on the past events
   C. reproduction of the records available from the past
   D. an objective interpretation of the past records
4. According to this passage, most readers
   A. expect too much from books
   B. ignore the objective of the writer
   C. do not know what to expect from a book
   D. are positively inclined towards the author
5. The main intention of the author is to
   A. point out the faults of the readers
   B. define what various kinds of books are
   C. suggest the correct approach to books
   D. enumerate the readers' preconceptions

PASSAGE–26

I couldn't sleep that night. A vague feeling of impending misfortune affected me. My sister and I were twins, and you know how subtle the links are between such people. It was a wild night. Suddenly, there bursts forth the wild scream of a terrified woman. I knew that it was my sister's voice. I rushed into the corridor. By the light of the corridor lamp, I saw my sister at the door of her room, her face pale with terror, and her hands groping for help, and her whole figure swaying unsteadily. I ran to her and threw my arms around her, but her knees gave way and she fell to the ground.

1. The author couldn't sleep because
   A. the night was wild
   B. she apprehended some trouble
   C. she knew that some calamity would befall her
   D. she felt uneasy
2. It was well known that
   A. she and her sister were twins
   B. twins have a special bond between them
   C. the relationship between twins is always cordial
   D. twins can sense danger more easily than others
3. She rushed into the corridor because
   A. she heard a terrifying cry
   B. her sister called her to the room
   C. she recognised the voice of the person who screamed
   D. she dreamt that her sister needed her help

4. She realised that her sister
   A. was in a state of excitement
   B. needed support
   C. was too weak to walk
   D. was gripped with fear

5. She threw her arms around her sister to
   A. express her affection
   B. prevent her from running away
   C. prevent her from falling down
   D. sȧve her from danger

PASSAGE–27

Because millions of years ago, a little tarsier-like creature began to use its hands and became inquisitive, the long trail of evolution towards man began. Those things are among man's characteristic features. Every year he delves deeper and deeper into the secrets of nature and his responsibilities grow more serious. In an age of mass production and machines, collective reason must control mass hysteria and mass instinct. That is the problem. The atomic bomb has only thrown it into higher relief. In the atomic bomb, man has used the fundamental energy process of the universe for destructive purposes, but that is largely an accident of the time and place. All around we have abundant evidence that without this energy, life itself could not exist.

1. The author believes, that man has evolved from a little tarsier-like creature because
   A. his face resembles that of a tarsier
   B. he uses his hands and walks like a tarsier
   C. he is curious and walks like a tarsier
   D. he is curious and uses his hands like a tarsier

2. The increasing human knowledge of the secrets of Nature has given rise to a problem which
   A. involves a huge expenditure
   B. makes man more and more irreligious and irreverential
   C. is both a boon and a bane
   D. necessitates a rational and humane approach to individual and social life

3. The invention of the atomic bomb has made this problem
   A. more obscure
   B. more prominent
   C. more controversial
   D. insignificant

4. Man has used atomic energy for destructive purposes because
   A. it has no constructive purposes at all
   B. he does not know how to sue it constructively
   C. its constructive use is too expensive to be practicable
   D. the force of circumstances compelled him to do so

5. The author thinks that the use of atomic energy
   A. will affect the society adversely
   B. is needed for the enrichment of life
   C. will ultimately destroy our civilization
   D. will lead to the end of the universe

PASSAGE–28

The jobs do not get changed around from time to time. I started off on one of the nicer ones. I sat at a conveyor belt slipping a piece of cardboard under each cake as it came down the line. At first it was difficult to keep up. An uneconomic movement, a fumble and four cakes have gone without cards. I got up to chase the four cakes, eight more appeared and for five minutes or so I had to work at twice the speed to work my way back to where I was sitting before. But it takes half a day or so to learn how it's done and soon it becomes quite automatic. The frenzy had quite worn off by the end of the first day and then there was only the monotony and the aching arms. Later I moved to another job on the line, as the girl who usually did it had left. I wasn't surprised. It was the nastiest job in that department. As the cake came out of a machine that had sliced it in three layers, two streams of artificial cream were poured over the layers. I had to stack the layers up again—a messy and very tiring job. The cakes are heavy and the cream is slippery. Anyone who has worked at all in a factory knows how deathly conveyor belt work is. At first it is difficult to keep up, and when you're tired it is quite merciless. After a while, when you have become fairly used to it, the fact that you can't work faster is also infuriating.

1. The writer's purpose in writing this piece is to
   A. make people who don't work in factories realise what it is like to work there
   B. plead to abolish manual labour from factories
   C. plead to get unskilled jobs made easier
   D. explain to young people how to handle a job in an automatized production unit

2. When the writer 'was moved to another job' she wasn't surprised to find that
   A. she had been moved
   B. her new job was very unpleasant
   C. the cream in the cakes was artificial
   D. the girl before her had left

3. The writer found it a messy job to
   A. separate the three layers of the cake
   B. pour artificial cream over the layers
   C. stack the layers up again
   D. put the cake back on the conveyor belt again

4. The writer calls the conveyor belt 'merciless' because it
   A. could cause an injury if one makes a mistake
   B. is devoid of human feelings
   C. does not slow down even when the worker is tired
   D. is a hard taskmaster

5. After some time the writer got annoyed at the conveyor belt because
   A. she found it dull and monotonous to work with it
   B. she wanted to change her profession
   C. she found it merciless
   D. it always had the same speed

PASSAGE–29

The arrival of the train did not disturb Sir Mohanlal's sang-froid. He continued to sip his Scotch and ordered the bearer to tell him when he had moved the luggage to a first class compartment. Excitement, bustle, and hurry were exhibition of bad breeding, and Sir Mohan was eminently well-bred. he wanted everything 'tickety-boo' and orderly. In his five years abroad, Sir Mohan had acquired the manners and attitudes of the upper classes. He rarely spoke Hindustani. When he did, it was like an Englishman's—only the very necessary words and properly anglicized. But he fancied his English, finished and refined at no less a place than the University of Oxford. He was fond of conversation and like a cultured Englishman he could talk on almost any subject—books, politics, people. How frequently had he heard English people say that he spoke like an Englishman!

1. Sir Mohan Lal is portrayed as
   A. an indophile
   B. a true Englishman
   C. a Hindu
   D. an anglophile

2. When Sir Mohan Lal spoke Hindustani it was
   A. Colloquial Hindi
   B. Literary Hindi
   C. Indian English
   D. Anglicized Hindi

3. According to Sir Mohan Lal, a well-bred person would
   A. remain aloof from the crowd
   B. like to drink only Scotch in public
   C. always be calm and orderly
   D. speak like an Englishman

4. From his description in this passage, Sir Mohan Lal appears to be
   A. a man of culture
   B. an aristocrat
   C. a snob
   D. a scholar

5. According to the passage, a cultured Englishman is able to talk effortlessly on
   A. art and culture
   B. human civilization
   C. modern science
   D. almost any subject

PASSAGE–30

The first and decisive step in the expansion of Europe overseas was the conquest of the Atlantic Ocean. That the nation to achieve this should be Portugal was the logical outcome of her geographical position and her history. Placed on the extreme margin of the old, classical Mediterranean world and facing the untraversed ocean. Portugal could adapt and develop the knowledge and experience of the past to meet the challenge of the unknown. From the seamen of Genoa and Venice, they had learned the organisation and conduct of a mercantile marine and from Jewish astronomers and map-makers the rudiments of navigation. Largely excluded from the share in Mediterranean commerce, at a time when her population was making heavy demands on her resources. Portugal turned southwards and westwards for opportunities of trade and commerce. But ocean navigation was not the same as navigating the land-locked Mediterranean. The earliest of the band had neither the benefit of sailing directions nor traditional lore. Even the familiar heavenly constellations had been left behind. The challenge was formidable.

1. According to the passage, the most important step in the expansion of European power was
   A. the emergence of Portugal as a power
   B. the growth of Mediterranean commerce
   C. the contact of Europeans with Jewish astronomers
   D. the conquest of the Atlantic Ocean

2. The most important advantage that Portugal had, was its
   A. geographical location
   B. contact with the Arabs
   C. contact with Genoa and Venice
   D. cultural history

3. The Portuguese sailors were ready to explore the world by sea because they
   A. knew about many countries
   B. had rich patrons to finance them
   C. were prepared for the hazards of sea voyage
   D. were in touch with seamen from Genoa and Venice

4. Portugal was motivated to pioneer ocean navigation because
   A. it was encouraged by other European powers
   B. it faced strong rivals in land-based trade
   C. it collaborated with Venetian merchants
   D. its limited resources could not support its growing population

5. The earliest group of Portuguese navigators going across the Atlantic did not find the venture
   A. different from land-locked navigation
   B. more difficult than coastal navigation
   C. easy and comfortable
   D. challenge and demanding

PASSAGE–31

Literature and history are twin sisters, inseparable. In the days of our own grandfathers and for many generations before them, the basis of education was the Greek and Roman classics for the educated, and the Bible for all. In the classical authors and in the Bible history and literature were closely intervolved and it is that circumstances which made the old form of education to stimulating to the thought and imagination of our ancestors. To read the classical authors and to read the Bible was to read at once the history and the literature of the three greatest races of the ancient world. No doubt the classics and the Bible were read in manner we now consider uncritical but they were read according to the best tenets of the time and formed a great humanistic education. Today the study both of the classics and of the bible has dwindled to small proportions. What has taken their place? To some extent the vacuum has been filled by a more correct knowledge of history and a wider range of literature. But I fear that the greater part of it has been filled up with rubbish.

1. Which of the following statements best reflects the underlying tone of the passage?
   A. Literature and history and mutually exclusive
   B. Literature and history and complementary to each other
   C. The study of literature is meaningless without any knowledge of history
   D. Literature and history are inseparably linked together in the classics and the Bible
2. The author of the above passage says that in the past the basis of education for all people, irrepsective of their intellectual calibre, was
   A. Greek and Roman Classics
   B. The Bible
   C. A correct knowledge of history
   D. A wider range of literature
3. The author of the above passage says that the classics and the Bible were read by his ancestors
   A. methodically and with discretion
   B. in a manner that broadened their view of life
   C. with great emphasis on their literacy values
   D. without critical discrimination but in the light of their humanistic culture
4. According to the author of the above passage the old form of education based the study of the classics and of the Bible, has
   A. succeeded in creating interest in history
   B. laid the basis of human civilization
   C. had a gradual decline in our time
   D. been rejuvenated in the context of modern education
5. The author of the above passage fears that the greater part of the vacuum created by lack of interest in the classic and the Bible has been filled up by
   A. a richer sense of history
   B. a wider range of literature
   C. worthless ideas
   D. a new philosophy of life

PASSAGE–32

During the early days as editor of the popular magazine, Saturday Evening Post, George Lorimer did much of the reading of unsolicited stories. This meant endless hours of sitting at the desk, pouring over big stacks of manuscripts, trying to decide which were worthy of publication and which were not. Lorimer became an expert at making these decisions.

One day he received a huffy letter from a would-be writer who had a complaint. "Last week you rejected my story," she wrote. "I am positive you did not read it, because, as a test, I pasted together pages 14, 15 and 16. The manuscript came back with the pages still pasted. There is no question in my mind but that you are a sham and a disgrace to your profession."

Lorimer's reply was succinct: "Madam, at breakfast when I crack open an egg, I don't have to eat the whole egg to know it is bad."

1. Lorimer did much reading of the stories
   A. if they were solicited ones
   B. when they appeared to be bad
   C. when they were from women writers
   D. when they came unsolicited
2. Lorimer was a good editor because
   A. his reply to the angry writer was polite
   B. he apologized for rejecting the story without reading it
   C. he could find the worth of a story with a little effort
   D. he was prompt in writing letters
3. The lady wrote a huffy letter because
   A. her story was rejected
   B. her story was rejected unread
   C. her story was rejected although it was good
   D. Lorimer was biased in his decision

4. Lorimer's reply was
   A. irrelevant B. rude
   C. wity D. funny

5. Lorimer read the stories
   A. because he enjoyed reading them
   B. in order to publish them
   C. only to find fault with them
   D. in order to review them

PASSAGE–33

As the tortoise tucks its feet and head inside the shell and will not come out even though you may break the shell into pieces, even so the character of the man who has control over his motives and organs, is unchangeably established. He controls his own inner forces, and nothing can draw them out against his will. By this continuous reflex of good thoughts and good impressions moving over the surface of the mind, the tendency to do good becomes strong, and in consequence, we are able to control the Indriyas or sense organs.

1. The author uses the phrase 'inner forces' in this passage. Which of the following would be its most correct meaning in the context?
   A. Emotional disturbances in man
   B. Strength of the internal organs
   C. Forces produced by sense organs
   D. Reflection of the intellect

2. Which of the following statements would illustrate the metaphor in the passage?
   A. Man is slow-moving and slow-witted
   B. A man of character refuses to be influenced by outside compulsions against his will
   C. Man confines himself to a life of isolation
   D. Man cannot have a good character or strong will

3. Which of the following statements may be assumed to reflect the central theme of the passage?
   A. Good thoughts lead to the control of the sense organs
   B. Control of the sense organs leads to good thoughts
   C. Character, though established, may be disturbed by outside forces
   D. No man can achieve success in destroying the inner forces

4. Which of the following statements would be most correct in explaining the metaphorical meaning of 'break the shell into pieces'?
   A. Destruction of the human body
   B. Breaking of the physical environment of man
   C. Attempt to destroy man's character
   D. Inflicting physical and mental agony on man

5. The passage consists of two long sentences and a short one. The purpose of this style should be to suggest that
   A. it is impossible for man to attain perfection of character
   B. the attainment of perfect character is the result of a long process of mental discipline
   C. the whole life process is clumsy
   D. there is a lot of confusion in our understanding of sense organs, character, etc.

PASSAGE–34

One of the most serious problems confronting our country is that of a fast-growing population. In fact, it is at the root of many other problems. At the moment, thanks to planning, we are able to produce food and cloth sufficient for our people and even in some excess. But if the population continues to grow at this rate, it will not be long before the surplus turns into a bare minimum and even a deficit. The position in regard to accommodation is even now far from satisfactory in spite of our efforts.

1. "It is at the root of many other problems" means that
   A. it is found along with many other problems
   B. it is caused by many other problems
   C. it gives rise to many other problems
   D. it is buried under many other problems

2. The present satisfactory position in regard to food and cloth is due to
   A. the fact that the population has been controlled
   B. our good lunch
   C. good rainfall
   D. our economic planning

3. If the population of India continues to increase at this rate, the situation in regard to food and cloth
   A. is likely to remain the same
   B. is likely to become less satisfactory
   C. is likely to improve
   D. is likely to vary up and down

4. The situation in respect of accommodation
   A. is less than satisfactory
   B. is quite satisfactory
   C. is improving rapidly
   D. is the result of total neglect

5. At present Indians have
   A. more provision for cloth than accommodation
   B. more provision for accommodation than cloth
   C. abundance of cloth and accommodation
   D. scarcity of cloth and accommodation

ANSWERS

Passage	1	2	3	4	5
PASSAGE 1—	B	A	A	C	
PASSAGE 2—	C	C	C	A	
PASSAGE 3—	C	C	C	D	
PASSAGE 4—	D	D	A	B	
PASSAGE 5—	B	D	C	B	
PASSAGE 6—	A	B	B	C	
PASSAGE 7—	D	D	C	C	
PASSAGE 8—	A	C	B	D	C
PASSAGE 9—	D	A	C	A	D
PASSAGE 10—	D	C	A	D	
PASSAGE 11—	D	B	A	B	B
PASSAGE 12—	D	A	A		
PASSAGE 13—	B	D	D	A	C
PASSAGE 14—	C	C	D	C	
PASSAGE 15—	A	C	D	A	
PASSAGE 16—	D	C	B		
PASSAGE 17—	D	C	A	D	
PASSAGE 18—	C	C	B	C	B
PASSAGE 19—	D	A	A	A	
PASSAGE 20—	A	D	B	B	D
PASSAGE 21—	B	C	C	D	
PASSAGE 22—	B	B	B	B	B
PASSAGE 23—	B	A	A	B	
PASSAGE 24—	C	C	A	C	D
PASSAGE 25—	C	B	D	B	C
PASSAGE 26—	B	B	C	D	C
PASSAGE 27—	D	D	B	D	B
PASSAGE 28—	D	B	C	C	D
PASSAGE 29—	D	D	C	A	D
PASSAGE 30—	D	A	D	D	C
PASSAGE 31—	D	B	D	C	C
PASSAGE 32—	D	C	A	C	D
PASSAGE 33—	D	B	A	C	B
PASSAGE 34—	C	D	B	A	A

❄ ❄ ❄ ❄ ❄

2 PARTS OF SPEECH

Parts of Speech form the foundation of a language. They are groups of words that share similar grammatical characteristics. There are eight parts of speech in traditional english grammar: Noun, Pronoun, Verb, Adjective, Adverb, Preposition, Conjunction and Interjection.

NOUN

A noun is a word that names a person, place, thing, quality or idea.

Proper Noun

A proper noun is the specific name of a particular person, place, organization, or thing, and it is always begins with a capital letter.

- **Names:** Abhay, Durgesh, Gopal, Ritesh, Sidhant, Tarun
- **Rivers:** Ganga, Godavari, Kavery, Narmada, Yamuna
- **Places:** Delhi, Jammu, Jodhpur, India, Canada
- **Mountains:** Himalayas, Dhaulagiri, Satpuras
- **Organizations:** Google, United Nations
- **Titles:** Harry Potter, The New York Times
- **Celestial bodies:** Earth, Moon, Jupiter, Mars

Common Noun

A common noun is a word that refers to a general person, place, thing, or idea, rather than a specific one.

Unlike proper nouns, common nouns are not capitalized unless they begin a sentence.

- Look at the following sentences,
  - (*i*) I saw a dog in the park. ("dog" is a common noun)
  - (*ii*) She read a book about history. ("book" is a common noun)
- Words like teacher, doctor, city, country, car, phone are common nouns.

Collective Noun

A collective noun is a word that refers to a group of people, animals, or things.

- The team is practicing for the final match.
- A flock of birds flew across the sky.
- She gave me a bouquet of flowers.

Some of the most useful collective noun

People	Animals	Things
A team of players	A block of birds/sheep	A bunch of grapes/keys
A class of students	A herd of cattle/deer/elephants	A stack of books/papers
A crowd of spectators	A pack of wolves/dogs	A collection of stamps/coins
A band of musicians	A swarm of bees/insects	A heap of rubbish/laundry
A staff of employees	A gaggle of geese (on land)	A pack of cards/lies
A choir of singers	A pride of lions	A fleet of ships/trucks
An army of soldiers	A shoal of fish	A group of islands/buildings
A gang of thieves	A litter of puppies/kittens	A library of books
A panel of judges	A troop of monkeys	A range of mountains

Abstract Noun

An abstract noun is a noun that refers to an idea, quality, state, or feeling—something that cannot be seen, touched, heard, or physically measured, but is understood by the mind.

- **Emotions:** love, anger, happiness
- **Qualities:** honesty, bravery, kindness
- **Concepts/States:** freedom, justice, knowledge, childhood

Noun — Abstract Noun

Noun	Abstract Noun	Noun	Abstract Noun
Brother	Brotherhood	Member	Membership
Friend	Friendship	Neighbour	Neighbourhood
King	Kingship	Owner	Ownership
Child	Childhood	Partner	Partnership
Mother	Motherhood	Citizen	Citizenship
Leader	Leadership	Poet	Poetry
Scholar	Scholarship	Hero	Heroism

Adjective — Abstract Noun

Adjective	Abstract Noun	Adjective	Abstract Noun
Angry	Anger	Strong	Strength
Happy	Happiness	Proud	Pride
Brave	Bravery	Loyal	Loyalty
Honest	Honesty	Lazy	Laziness
Kind	Kindness	Long	Length
Wise	Wisdom	Sad	Sadness
Patient	Patience	Creative	Creativity

Verb — Abstract Noun

Verb	Abstract Noun	Verb	Abstract Noun
Act	Action	Fail	Failure
Achieve	Achievement	Think	Thought
Decide	Decision	Choose	Choice
Grow	Growth	Discover	Discovery
Know	Knowledge	Move	Movement
Lose	Loss	Appear	Appearance
Suceed	Success	Believe	Belief
Sell	Sale	Obey	Obedience

Material Noun

A material noun is a type of noun that represents the raw substance, physical matter, or ingredient from which objects are made. Examples include gold, wood, water, iron, milk, cotton etc.

Classification of Noun on the Basis of Gender

Nouns are classified into four categories based on gender.

1. **Masculine Gender :** A noun that denotes a male is said to be of the masculine gender, as man, uncle, ox, boy etc.
2. **Feminine Gender :** A noun that denotes a female is said to be of feminine gender, as woman, aunt, princess, cow etc.
3. **Common Gender :** Nouns which denote both males and females are said to be of the common gender, as friend, cousin, person, parent, baby etc.
4. **Neuter Gender :** A noun that denotes the name of object without life is said to be of neuter gender, as file, table, pencil.

By using a different word from the masculine

Masculine	Feminine	Masculine	Feminine
Boy	Girl	Son	Daughter
Gentleman	Lady	Bachelor	Maid
Earl	Countess	Monk	Nun
Sir	Madam	Lad	Lass
Buck	Doe	Colt	Filly
Dog	Bitch	Horse	Mare
Stag	Hind	Nephew	Niece

By adding suffix (-ess, -ine, -a)

Masculine	Feminine	Masculine	Feminine
Murderer	Murderess	Sorcerer	Sorceress
Duke	Dutchess	Emperor	Empress
Hero	Heroine	Viceroy	Vicerine
Governor	Governess	Master	Mistress
Heir	Heiress	Sultan	Sultana
Lion	Lioness	Mayor	Mayoress
Actor	Actress	Count	Countess
Abbot	Abbess	God	Goddess
Author	Authoress	Tiger	Tigress
Priest	Priestess	Poet	Poetess
Shepherd	Shepherdess	Waiter	Waitress

By placing a word before or after

Masculine	Feminine	Masculine	Feminine
Son-in-law	Daughter-in-law	Father-in-law	Mother-in-law
Man-servant	Maid-servant	Pea-cock	Pea-hen
Step-father	Step-mother	Widower	Widow
Grand-father	Grand-mother	He-goat	She-goat

Classification of Noun on the Basis of Number

There are two noun numbers in English — the Singular and the Plural.

- **Singular Numbers :** A noun that denotes one person or one thing, is said to be in the Singular number. For example — book, pencil, bird, dog, hen etc. are in singular number.
- **Plural Number :** A noun that denotes more than one person or one thing is said to be in plural number. For example — boys, pens, lions, girls, men etc. are in plural number.

Singular	Plural	Singular	Plural
Cat	Cats	Room	Rooms
Pen	Pens	Bus	Buses
Tree	Trees	Dish	Dishes
Bush	Bushes	Glass	Glasses
Judge	Judges	Tax	Taxes
Watch	Watches	Calf	Calves
Thief	Thieves	Knife	Knives
Scarf	Scarves	Wife	Wives
Leaf	Leaves	Wolf	Wolves
Half	Halves	Monarch	Monarchs
Roof	Roofs	Hoof	Hoofs
Gulf	Gulfs	Staff	Staffs
Radio	Radios	Bamboo	Bamboos
Folio	Folios	Hero	Heroes
Volcano	Volcanoes	Mango	Mangoes
Potato	Potatoes	Photo	Photos
Piano	Pianos	Radius	Radii
Fly	Flies	Foot	Feet
Lady	Ladies	Boy	Boys
Monkey	Monkeys	Ox	Oxen
Axis	Axes	Tooth	Teeth
Goose	Geese	Basis	Bases
Vertex	Vertices	Stimulus	Stimuli

1. Note the plurals of the following nouns:

Singular	Plural	Singular	Plural
copy	copies	cry	cries
baby	babies	duty	duties
body	bodies	country	countries
family	families	diary	diaries
fly	flies	fairy	fairies
city	cities	spy	spies
army	armies	storey	storeys
bay	bays	monkey	monkeys

2. The following nouns do not undergo any change in plural form, in general:

Singular	Plural	Singular	Plural
deer	deer	sheep	sheep
thousand	thousand	pair	pair
hundred	hundred	score	score
dozen	dozen	gross	gross

3. The following nouns are usually used in plural forms. They take a plural verb after them:

eatables	fetters	surroundings
riches	alms	spectacles
trousers	pants	scissors
premises	thanks	annals
congratulations	goods	shorts
tongs	pains	arms
breeches	tropics	wages

4. The following are the nouns which are plural in appearance but are usually used in singular number. They are followed by a singular verb:

news	politics	physics
mathematics	economics	ethics
politics	classics	gallows
statistics	athletics	innings
mechanics	summons	mumps

5. Collective nouns often used as plurals:

public	police	cattle
audience	clergy	folk
people	poultry	nation
elite	gentry	glitterati

6. The nouns that are usually used in singular forms:

advice	hair	rice
fuel	alphabet	machinery
offspring	issue	furniture
mischief	stationery	luggage
bedding	information	abuse

7. Material nouns are always used in singular number:

gold	copper	milk
water	silk	wool

Note: They may be used in plural with a different meaning.

copper coins (coppers), chains or fetters (irons), cans made of tin (tins).

PRONOUN

The repetition of a noun in a sentence or a set of sentences is really boring. So, instead of repeating the noun, we can use a word (for that noun) called the pronoun.

"A pronoun is a word that we use instead of a noun".

Example: This is *Sachin*. *He* plays cricket.

Note: *He* is the pronoun used in place of *Sachin*.

Kinds of Pronoun

1. **Personal Pronoun :** A pronoun which is used instead of the name of a person is known as a 'Personal Pronoun'. A list of the 'Personal pronouns' is listed below :

   I, my, mine, me, we (First Person)

   You, your, yours (Second Person)

   He, his, him, she, her, hers, it, its, they, their, theirs, them (Third Person)

2. **Possessive Pronoun :** A possessive pronoun is a pronoun that shows ownership or possession. It replaces a noun phrase to avoid repetition and makes it clear who owns something.

   Types of Possessive Forms:

Type	Function	Examples
Possessive Adjectives	Come *before* a noun	my, your, his, her, our
Possessive Pronouns	Stand *alone* (replace noun phrases)	mine, yours, his, hers, ours, theirs

Examples:

- This book is *mine*.
- That house is *hers*, not yours.
- These seats are *ours*.
- The red car is *theirs*.
- Is this umbrella *yours*?

Note: Possessive pronouns *do not* use apostrophes.

- *Its* color is bright.
- *It's* color is bright. ("It's" = it is)

Comparison: Possessive Adjective vs. Possessive Pronoun

Sentence with Possessive Adjective	Sentence with Possessive Pronoun
This is my phone.	This phone is mine.
That is her notebook.	That notebook is hers.
These are our jackets.	These jackets are ours.

3. **Demonstrative Pronoun :** Pronouns used to point out the objects to which they refer are called Demonstrative Pronouns.

   Examples:

   (*i*) *This* is a present from my uncle.

   (*ii*) *These* are merely excuses.

   (*iii*) Bombay mangoes are better than *those* of Bengaluru.

4. **Indefinite Pronoun :** All pronouns which refer to persons or things in a general way and do not refer to any particular person or thing are called Indefinite Pronouns.

   Examples :

   (*i*) *Somebody* has stolen my watch.

   (*ii*) *Few* escaped unhurt.

   (*iii*) Did you ask *anybody* to come?

5. **Distributive Pronoun :** Each, either, neither are called distributive pronouns because they refer to persons or things one at a time. For this reason they are always singular and followed by the verb in singular.

   Examples :

   (*i*) *Each* of the men received a reward.

   (*ii*) *These* men received *each* a reward.

   (*iii*) *Either* of you can go.

6. **Relative Pronoun :** A relative pronoun refers or relates to some noun going before, which is called its Antecedent.

   Examples :

   (*i*) I met Hari *who* used to live here.

   (*ii*) I have found the pen *which* I had lost.

   (*iii*) Here is the book *that* you lent me.

7. **Interrogative Pronoun :** These pronouns are used for asking questions.

   Examples :

   (*i*) *Whose* book is this?

   (*ii*) *What* will all the neighbours say?

   (*iii*) *Which* do you prefer, tea or coffee?

   Note: Interrogative pronouns can also be used in asking indirect questions.

   Examples:

   (*i*) I asked *who* was speaking.

   (*ii*) Tell me *what* you have done.

   (*iii*) Say *which* you would like best.

VERB

A Verb is a word that tells something about the action or state of or happening to a person or thing.

A Verb tells the following:

1. What a person or thing does. e.g.,
   (*i*) Sachin *goes* to school daily.
   (*ii*) The bell *rang* loudly.
   (*iii*) Many birds *fly* in the sky.
   (*iv*) She *sang* a song.
2. What a person or thing is. e.g.,
   (*i*) India is the biggest democracy in the world.
   (*ii*) Ram Mehar *is* very rich.
   (*iii*) They *are* happy.
3. What is done to a person or thing. e.g.,
   (*i*) You are *liked* by all.
   (*ii*) Two thieves *were arrested*.
   (*iii*) Four students *were punished* by the teacher.
4. What happens to a person or thing. e.g.,
   (*i*) His maternal uncle *died* last week.
   (*ii*) Two ships *sank* yesterday.
   (*iii*) Leaves *turn* yellow in autumn.
5. What a person or thing has, had, and so on. e.g.,
   (*i*) I *have* a new car.
   (*ii*) He *had* a scooter last year.
   (*iii*) He *has* several cows and goats.

It goes without saying that a verb is the most important part of a sentence. No sentence is complete without a Verb.

Different Kinds of Verbs

1. Action Verbs and Stative Verbs

Action Verbs : Express physical or mental action.

Examples:

(*i*) She *runs* every morning. (physical action)

(*ii*) I *wrote* a letter. (physical action)

(*iii*) He *thought* about the problem. (mental action)

(*iv*) He *understands* the concept. (mental action)

Stative Verbs : Describe a state or condition rather than an action. Usually not used in continuous tenses.

Examples:

(*i*) I *know* the answer.

(*ii*) She *loves* music.

2. Transitive and Intransitive Verbs

Transitive Verbs : Require a direct object to complete their meaning.

Examples:

(*i*) She *wrote* a letter. (letter = direct object)

(*ii*) They *play* football.

Intransitive Verbs : Do not require a direct object.

Examples:

(*i*) He *sleeps* peacefully.

(*ii*) The baby *cried* loudly.

3. Finite and Non-Finite Verbs

Finite Verbs : A finite verb is a verb that changes according to the subject and shows tense (past, present, or future).

It acts as the main verb in a sentence and agrees with the subject in number and person.

Examples:

(*i*) She *drinks* coffee every morning. (3rd Person, singular, simple present)

(*ii*) They *play* football every evening. (3rd Person, Plural, Simple Present)

(*iii*) He *watched* a movie last night. (3rd Person, Singular, Simple Past)

(*iv*) The children *were laughing* loudly. (3rd Person, Plural, Past Continuous)

(*v*) I *was reading* a book when you called. (1st Person, Singular, Past Continuous)

Non-finite Verbs: A non-finite verb is a verb form that does not change with the subject or tense.

It cannot act as the main verb in a sentence and does not show tense.

They usually function as nouns, adjectives, or adverbs.

Examples:

(*i*) I enjoy *reading* novels.

(Reading = non-finite, acts as object of the verb enjoy)

(*ii*) Her hobby is *painting*.

(Painting = non-finite, acts as subject complement)

(*iii*) The man *wearing* a red hat is my uncle.

(Wearing = non-finite, modifies man)

(*iv*) We picked some *fallen* leaves.

(Fallen = non-finite past participle, describes leaves)

Modal Verbs

Modal verbs are special helping verbs that express ability, possibility, necessity, permission, obligation, or advice.

They are always used with a main verb (in its base form, without "to").

Can, Could, May, Might, Shall, Should, Will, Would, Must, Ought to are all the modal auxiliary verbs.

Can and Could

'Can' and 'Could' are both modal verbs used to express ability, possibility, permission, and requests, but they differ in tense, formality, and degree of certainty.

Examples:

(*i*) I *can* swim.

(*ii*) *Can* I use your phone?

(*iii*) Too much sugar *can* make you sick.

(*iv*) *Can* you help me?

(*v*) When I was younger, I *could* run fast.

(*vi*) He *could* read at age four.

(*vii*) *Could* I borrow your pen?

(*viii*) This *could* be dangerous.

(*ix*) You *could* get hurt if you're not careful.

May, Might, Must

'May' is a modal verb used to express Possibility and Permission (formal or polite). (Possibility can be high or low)

Examples:

(*i*) It *may* rain today.

(*ii*) You *may* leave early today.

'Might' is a modal verb used to express:

- A weaker or less certain possibility than may
- Polite suggestions or hypothetical situations

Examples:

(*i*) We *might* go to the zoo tomorrow.

(*ii*) She *might* have called if she knew you were home.

'Must' is a modal verb used to express:

- Strong necessity or obligation
- Logical certainty or strong belief

Examples:

(*i*) You *must* wear your seatbelt.

(*ii*) That *must* be his phone; it's ringing in his bag.

Shall and Will

'Shall' is a modal verb used mainly to:

- Express the future (especially in formal or British English)
- Make suggestions or offers
- Ask for instructions or decisions

Examples:

(*i*) I *shall* return tomorrow.

(*ii*) *Shall* I help you with that?

(*iii*) Where *shall* we sit?

'Will' is a modal verb used to:

- Express future actions
- Show willingness, promises, or decisions made at the moment
- Predict what is likely to happen

Examples:

(*i*) He *will* start college next year.

(*ii*) I *will* always love you.

(*iii*) She *will* never lie to you.

(*iv*) Don't worry, we *will* fix it.

Would

'Would' is a modal verb used to express:

- Polite requests or offers
- Hypothetical or imaginary situations
- Future in the past
- Preferences or habits (in the past)

Examples:

(*i*) *Would* you help me carry this?

(*ii*) I *would* travel the world if I had more money.

(*iii*) He said he *would* call me later.

Should

'Should' is a modal verb used to express:

- Advice or suggestions
- Expectation
- Mild obligation or duty
- Probability

Examples:

(*i*) He *should* apologize.

(*ii*) The train *should* arrive soon.

(*iii*) Students *should* wear uniforms.

(*iv*) That *should* be enough for everyone.

Ought to

'Ought to' is a modal verb (similar to "should") that is used to express:

- Moral duty or obligation
- Advice or recommendation
- Probability or expectation

It is always followed by the base form of a verb (without "to") — even though the modal itself includes "to".

Examples:

(*i*) You *ought to* help your parents.

(*ii*) He *ought to* study more before the test.

(*iii*) The train *ought to* arrive soon.

ADJECTIVE

An Adjective is a word which adds something to the meaning of a noun or a pronoun. e.g.,

(*i*) He talks *slowly*.

(*ii*) Mridula is an *intelligent* girl.

(*iii*) He has a *black* goat.

(*iv*) He is a *brilliant* student.

(*v*) She is a *clever* girl.

(*vi*) It is a *beautiful* picture.

In the sentences given above, the words in italics are adjectives.

Types of Adjectives

Here are the main types of adjectives:

1. **Descriptive Adjectives (Qualitative Adjectives) :** Descriptive adjectives (also known as qualitative adjectives) are words that describe the quality, characteristic, or nature of a noun or pronoun.

Examples:

(*i*) The *beautiful* painting was expensive.

(*ii*) He is a *brave* soldier.

(*iii*) They live in a *small* house.

2. **Quantitative Adjectives :** These adjectives show the amount or quantity of a particular noun.

Examples:

(*i*) I have *some* money.

(*ii*) She drank *little* water.

(*iii*) We need *more* sugar.

3. **Numeral Adjectives (Adjectives of Number):** Numeral adjectives, also called adjectives of number, are adjectives that indicate how many or in what order people or things are.

Types:

- Cardinal – one, two, three, etc.
- Ordinal – first, second, third, etc.

Examples:

(*i*) He has *two* brothers. (Cardinal)

(*ii*) This is my *first* car. (Ordinal)

4. **Demonstrative Adjectives :** A demonstrative adjective is a word that points out or indicates a specific noun or nouns and comes before a noun to modify it. It helps show which one(s) we are talking about.

Examples:

(*i*) *This* book is interesting.

(*ii*) *Those* shoes are new.

(*iii*) I like *that* movie.

5. **Possessive Adjectives :** Adjectives like my, your, his, her, our, its, their etc are known as possessive adjectives.

Examples:

(*i*) That is *my* bag.

(*ii*) *Her* dog is friendly.

(*iii*) *Their* house is big.

6. **Interrogative Adjectives :** What, Which, Whose are interrogative adjectives.

Examples:

(*i*) *Which* book do you prefer?

(*ii*) *What* time is it?

(*iii*) *Whose* pen is this?

7. **Distributive Adjectives :** A distributive adjective refers to individual members of a group separately, rather than collectively. It is used with singular nouns and always modifies a singular noun.

Examples:

(*i*) *Each* student must bring a notebook.

(*ii*) *Every* child needs love.

(*iii*) *Either* road leads to the station.

8. **Emphasizing Adjectives :** Emphasizing adjectives are adjectives used to highlight or stress a noun. They give special importance to the noun they modify and are often used to add force or emphasis to a statement.

Examples:

(*i*) I saw it with my *own* eyes.

(*ii*) He is the *very* man we need.

9. **Exclamatory Adjectives :** An exclamatory adjective is a word used to express strong emotion or surprise, and it is always used with a noun in exclamatory sentences.

Examples:

(*i*) *What* a beautiful day!

(*ii*) *What* a mess!

10. Proper Adjectives : A proper adjective is an adjective that is formed from a proper noun and is used to describe something in relation to a specific place, person, language, or culture.

It always begins with a capital letter, just like a proper noun.

Examples:

(*i*) I love *Italian* food.

(*ii*) She wore a beautiful *Chinese* dress.

(*iii*) He's studying *French* literature.

(*iv*) The *Christian* festival of Christmas is widely celebrated.

(*v*) We read a *Shakespearean* play in class.

(*vi*) The *Japanese* culture is very unique.

Degrees of Comparison

Adjectives have three degrees of comparison:

1. **Positive Degree :** It expresses the common form of an adjective.

   Example:

   Ram is a *tall* boy.

   In the above sentence *tall* is an adjective and expresses the common form.

2. **Comparative Degree :** It expresses the more of the same form.

   Example:

   Ram is *taller* than Mahesh.

   In the above sentence *taller* is an adjective that expresses the more of the common form of the adjective *tall*.

3. **Superlative Degree :** It expresses the most of the common form of an adjective.

   Example:

   He is the ablest man of the town.

How and when to use the Superlative Degree?

(*a*) The Superlative Degree is used when more than two persons or things are compared.

(*b*) The Superlative Degree is generally preceded by 'the' and followed by 'of' in most of the cases or otherwise.

(*c*) When an adjective of the superlative degree is preceded by a Possessive Adjective or a Noun in the Possessive case, 'the' should not be used before it.

Example:

Which is Kalidas' best play?

It will be a blunder to use 'the' before the Superlative Degree in such cases.

Don't say : Which is Kalidas' the best play.

(*d*) To intensify the degree of comparison, *by far* is used before the superlative degree.

Example:

India is *by far* the most beautiful country of the world.

Note: Always avoid the use of double superlatives.

Don't say : He is the most strongest boy in the class.

Say : He is the strongest boy in the class.

Positive Form	Comparative Form	Superlative Form
big	bigger	biggest
small	smaller	smallest
fast	faster	fastest
slow	slower	slowest
tall	taller	tallest
short	shorter	shortest
happy	happier	happiest
sad	sadder	saddest
beautiful	more beautiful	most beautiful
ugly	uglier	ugliest
good	better	best
bad	worse	worst
hot	hotter	hottest
cold	colder	coldest
rich	richer	richest
poor	poorer	poorest
strong	stronger	strongest
weak	weaker	weakest
bright	brighter	brightest
dark	darker	darkest
clean	cleaner	cleanest
dirty	dirtier	dirtiest
light	lighter	lightest
heavy	heavier	heaviest
early	earlier	earliest
late	later	latest
friendly	friendlier	friendliest
angry	angrier	angriest
loud	louder	loudest

General Rules Recap

1. **One-syllable adjectives:** Add *-er* for comparative, *-est* for superlative.

   Example: "big" → bigger → biggest

2. **Adjectives ending in "y":** Change the "y" to *-ier* and *-iest* for comparative and superlative forms.

   Example: "happy" → happier → happiest

3. **Two or more syllable adjectives (except those ending in "y"):** Use *more* for the comparative and *most* for the superlative.

   Example: "beautiful" → more beautiful → most beautiful

4. **Irregular adjectives (e.g., "good," "bad"):** Have completely different forms for comparative and superlative.

   Example: "good" → better → best

ADVERB

An Adverb is a word which qualifies the meaning of a Verb, an Adjective or another Adverb. e.g.,

(*i*) He talks slowly.

(*ii*) He is a very good student.

(*iii*) He talks very slowly.

In sentence (*i*), *slowly* qualifies the verb talks.

In sentence (*ii*), *very* qualifies the adjective good.

In sentence (*iii*), *very* qualifies the adverb slowly.

Use of some Important Adverbs

(*a*) **Also, Too, Enough:** 'Also' and 'too' suggest 'addition' and 'excess' while 'enough' is placed after the verb it qualifies. e.g.,

(*i*) He taught English. Also, he edited the school magazine.

(*ii*) He is a writer and also he is a painter.

(*iii*) He is too obstinate to listen to any reason.

(*iv*) This is too difficult a piece for the junior students.

(*v*) Sarla was kind enough to help the poor.

(*vi*) He is brave enough to help the truth.

(*b*) **Fairly and Rather:** Both suggest the meaning 'moderately'. But, mainly 'fairly' is used with the words that denote a positive meaning and rather is used with the words that denote a negative meaning, e.g.,

(*i*) Rita did fairly well in that competition, but her performance was rather poor in sports.

(*ii*) Mona is fairly rich, but she is rather stingy.

Note: 'Rather' can also be used in a positive sense.

(*i*) This is a rather interesting job.

(*ii*) That boy is rather smart.

(*c*) **Hardly, Barely, Scarcely:** These words mostly convey the negative suggestions and are almost similar. e.g.,

(*i*) I have hardly any strength now.

(*ii*) There was barely any supply to the township.

(*iii*) There were scarcely a hundred guests present.

Note: With slight variance in the meaning, the words given above convey the idea of 'very little', 'not enough', 'lack of quantity and number'.

(*d*) **Yet, Still:** These adverbs can often be used to connect the sentence units:

(*i*) Mona was sick; yet she went on doing her work.

(*ii*) He has been defeated many times in the contest; still he wants to be a competitor.

(*e*) **Alone:**

(*i*) He alone (none else) is capable of handling that fire,

(*ii*) He hunted all alone in the forest. (not in any company).

PREPOSITION

A preposition shows the relationship of a word to a noun or noun phrase, which is known as the object of the preposition. It also indicates position.

Examples:

(*i*) The book is **under** the table.

Here, the preposition **under** shows the relationship between *book* and table.

(*ii*) The cat hid **behind** the curtain.

The preposition **behind** shows the relationship between curtain and hid.

(*iii*) He walked **through** the park.

The preposition **through** shows the relationship between walked and park.

Prepositions can be used to denote

1. **Prepositions of Place:** Prepositions of place are used to show the location or position of a noun or pronoun. They help to answer the question "Where?" in a sentence. Some of the most common prepositions of place include in, on, at, under, behind, between, next to, above, and below.

   Examples:

   (*i*) She is *in* the room.

   (*ii*) The book is *on* the table.

   (*iii*) We are meeting *at* the cafe.

   (*iv*) The cat is *under* the bed.

2. **Prepositions of Time:** Prepositions of time are used to indicate when an action takes place, answering the question "When?" Common prepositions of time include in, on, at, since, for, during, before, and after.

   Examples:

   (*i*) He was born *in* 1990.

   (*ii*) The meeting is *on* Monday.

   (*iii*) The show starts *at* 7 p.m.

   (*iv*) They've been friends *since* childhood.

   (*v*) She studied *for* three hours.

   (*vi*) I always have breakfast *before* work.

3. **Prepositions of Direction or Movement:** Prepositions of direction indicate the movement of an object or person from one place to another. They help answer the question "Where to?" Some common prepositions of direction include to, toward, into, onto, through, and across.

   Examples:

   (*i*) She is going *to* the gym.

   (*ii*) He ran *toward* the exit.

   (*iii*) She walked *into* the room.

   (*iv*) The cat jumped *onto* the table.

   (*v*) The river flows *through* the city.

4. **Prepositions of Agency:** Prepositions of agency are used to show the agent or the doer of an action, often in passive constructions. The most common preposition of agency is by.

   Examples:

   (*i*) The book was written *by* Shakespeare.

5. **Prepositions of Instrument or Means:** Prepositions of instrument indicate the tool, method, or instrument used to perform an action. Some of the most commonly used prepositions of instrument include by, with, and on.

   Examples:

   (*i*) She travelled *by* train.

   (*ii*) He cut the paper *with* scissors.

   (*iii*) She's talking *on* the phone.

6. **Prepositions of Cause, Reason, or Purpose:** Prepositions of cause, reason, or purpose indicate why something happens or the purpose behind an action. Common prepositions in this category include for, because of, and due to.

   Examples:

   (*i*) She left early *for* a doctor's appointment.

   (*ii*) The game was cancelled *because of* the rain.

   (*iii*) The flight was delayed *due to* bad weather.

7. **Compound Prepositions:** Compound prepositions consist of two or more words combined to act as a single preposition. Some examples include according to, due to, because of, in front of, and in spite of.

   Examples:

   (*i*) *According to* the report, sales increased by 20%.

   (*ii*) He parked his car in *front of* the house.

8. **Prepositions of Concession:** Prepositions of concession highlight contrast or an exception to what is expected. Common examples include despite and in spite of.

   Examples:

   (*i*) She finished the race *despite* feeling unwell.

CONJUNCTION

A conjunction is a word which connects words, clauses or sentences.

Look at the following sentences:

(*i*) He bought apples *and* mangoes.

(*ii*) God made the country *and* man made the town.

(*iii*) The door was open *but* there was no one in the house.

(*iv*) He knows that I am here *and* that I want to see him.

In the sentence (*i*), *and* connects two words—*apples* and *mangoes*.

In the sentence (*ii*), *and* connects two sentences—*God made the country* and *man made the town*.

In the sentence (*iii*), *but* connects two sentences—*The door was open* and *there was no one in the house*.

In the sentence (*iv*), *and* connects two clauses—*that I am here* and *that I want to see him*.

Rules Related to the Correct Usage of Conjunctions

- **Rule 1:** Use coordinating conjunctions (FANBOYS - For, And, Nor, But, Or, Yet, So) to connect words, phrases, or independent clauses of equal rank.

  Examples:

  (*i*) She likes apples *and* oranges. (words)

  (*ii*) He wanted to stay, *but* he had to leave. (independent clauses)

- **Rule 2:** When two independent clauses are joined by a coordinating conjunction, place a comma before the conjunction.

  Examples:

  (*i*) I was hungry, *so* I made a sandwich.

  (*ii*) She tried to call, *but* no one answered.

- **Rule 3:** A subordinating conjunction introduces a dependent clause and connects it to an independent clause.

  Examples:

  (*i*) *Because* it was raining, we stayed inside.

  (*ii*) I'll wait here *until* you come back.

- **Rule 4:** If the dependent clause comes first, use a comma.

  Example: *Although* he was tired, he kept working.

  If the independent clause comes first, no comma is needed.

  Example: He kept working *although* he was tired.

- **Rule 5:** Correlative conjunctions like either…or, neither…nor, not only…but also, must appear in pairs.

  Examples:

  (*i*) *Either* you come now *or* you stay behind.

  (*ii*) *Not only* was she smart, *but* also very kind.

- **Rule 6:** Both parts of a correlative conjunction should join elements of the same grammatical type (noun to noun, clause to clause, etc.).

  Examples:

  (*i*) Wrong: *Either* you clean the room *or* the dishes.

  (*ii*) Correct: *Either* you clean the room *or* you wash the dishes.

- **Rule 7:** Don't use two conjunctions together unnecessarily.

  Examples:

  Incorrect: *Although* he was tired, *but* he went to work.

  Correct: *Although* he was tired, he went to work.

  OR: He was tired, *but* he went to work.

- **Rule 8:** In formal writing, starting a sentence with and, but, or so is discouraged, although it is acceptable in informal writing.

  Example:

  Informal: *But* I didn't know that.

  Formal: *However*, I didn't know that.

- **Rule 9:** Choose the conjunction based on the logical connection:

  - ❑ Cause: because, since, as
  - ❑ Contrast: although, but, yet
  - ❑ Time: when, before, after
  - ❑ Condition: if, unless, provided that

- **Rule 10:** Don't Use "Because" After "The Reason Is"

  Example:

  Wrong: The reason is *because* he was late.

  Correct: The reason is *that* he was late.

INTERJECTION

An interjection is a word used to express emotion. It is often followed by an exclamation point. Interjections do not have any grammatical use.

Examples:

(*i*) *Ouch!* That really hurt badly.

(*ii*) *Well*, what you just did was wonderful.

(*iii*) *Wow*! Your new bike is amazing.

Exclamation marks are generally used after an interjection.

Examples:

(*i*) *Wow!* That is a beautiful dress indeed.

(*ii*) *Oh my God!* That was unexpected.

(*iii*) *Ok!* You can go office.

EXERCISE

NOUN

Directions (Qs. No. 1 to 5): *In the following questions choose the correct option to fill in the blanks.*

1. The _____ is full of stars.
   A. sky B. skies
   C. skys D. skyline

2. We planted five _____ in the garden.
   A. tree B. trees
   C. trez D. treez

3. A group of _____ is called a herd.
   A. lions B. cows
   C. monkeys D. fish

4. The _____ is flying in the sky.
   A. airplane B. aeroplanes
   C. kites D. birds

5. I saw a _____ of birds in the sky.
   A. crowd B. swarm
   C. flock D. pack

6. What is the collective noun for a group of 'players'?
   A. crew B. team
   C. army D. pack

7. Which word has the same singular and plural form?
   A. deer B. dogs
   C. fox D. chairs

8. What is the feminine gender of 'Actor'?
   A. actress B. actess
   C. lady actor D. actorine

9. Choose the correct collective noun for 'bees'.
   A. gang B. flock
   C. swarm D. herd

10. What is the plural of 'Knife'?
    A. knifes B. knive
    C. knives D. knifves

11. What is the feminine gender of 'Prince'?
    A. princess B. princeess
    C. lady prince D. princi

12. Choose the correct plural of 'Box'.
    A. boxs B. boxes
    C. boxies D. boxez

13. What is the collective noun for 'Ships'?
    A. gang B. pack
    C. fleet D. bunch

14. Which one of the following words can be made plural by adding a suffix 'en'?
    A. Max B. Box
    C. Tax D. Ox

15. Which of the following words is a material noun?
    A. Air B. Cow
    C. Gold D. Class

16. Which of the following words is an abstract noun?
    A. Woman B. Connection
    C. Boy D. Plough

17. Which kind of noun is 'adversity'?
    A. Abstract noun B. Common noun
    C. Proper noun D. Collective noun

18. Which of the following words is 'plural'?
    A. Goat B. Dog
    C. Fox D. Mice

19. Which of the following words is regarded as singular?
    A. Cats B. Dogs
    C. Mathematics D. Cars

20. In which of the following sentences is the subject of verb a feminine gender noun?
    A. All the young men have arrived.
    B. All the old men have arrived.
    C. All the female members have arrived.
    D. All the members have arrived.

21. Which of the following words is plural?
    A. Analysis B. Criteria
    C. Index D. Crisis

22. Which of the following nouns is in plural?
    A. Electronics B. Billiards
    C. News D. Mice

23. H was an orphan and lived wth his uncle.
    In the above given sentence identify the gender of the word 'orphan'.
    A. Common Gender B. Neuter Gender
    C. Masculine Gender D. Feminine Gender

24. Add the right suffix to pluralize the word 'OX'.
    A. –ies B. –s
    C. –en D. –es

25. Which of the following alternatives is grammatically correct?
    A. All these man are gentle.
    B. All these mans are gentle.
    C. All these men are gentle.
    D. All this men are gentle.

PRONOUN

Directions: (Qs. No. 26 to 45): *In the following questions choose the correct options to fill in the blanks.*

26. The place was so dirty that _____ wished to run away from there.
A. everybody B. anybody
C. few D. some

27. _____ was there to help me.
A. Somebody B. Anything
C. Anybody D. Nobody

28. Is there _____ to eat?
A. some B. something
C. any D. few

29. _____ of the students were making a great noise.
A. Anyone B. Somebody
C. Many D. Nobody

30. _____ of the students can solve this sum.
A. Someone B. Anybody
C. Somebody D. None

31. _____ of us should try our best to make India a heaven.
A. Any B. Somebody
C. Anybody D. All

32. _____ of us do not know the real meaning of our lives.
A. Any B. Something
C. Several D. Many

33. The teacher is talking to ______.
A. me B. I
C. mine D. my

34. Can you give the book to ______?
A. me B. I
C. mine D. my

35. That notebook is ______.
A. mine B. my
C. me D. I

36. The two girls hugged ______ after the match.
A. themselves B. each other
C. one another D. them

37. ______ is available to help you with the task?
A. Anyone B. Someone
C. Nobody D. Everybody

38. ______ of these books belong to the library?
A. Every B. All
C. Each D. Few

39. ______ can enter the room after the meeting starts.
A. Anyone B. Someone
C. Nobody D. Everybody

40. They are always helping ______.
A. us B. one another
C. them D. each other

41. ______ student will be selected for the award.
A. Any B. Every
C. Each D. Both

42. Can you help ______ with this task?
A. we B. us
C. our D. ours

43. The two friends argued with ______ for hours.
A. each other B. themselves
C. one another D. them

44. My son and my daughter are very fond of ....
A. herself B. each other
C. themselves D. himself

45. This dress is .... and that one is mine.
A. your B. our book
C. yours D. your book

VERB

Directions (Qs. No. 46 to 69): *In the following questions choose the correct option to fill in the blanks.*

46. She _____ to school every day.
A. go B. goes
C. going D. gone

47. They _____ playing football when it started to rain.
A. is B. was
C. are D. were

48. I _____ help you if you ask me.
A. will B. shall
C. would D. can

49. He _____ tired after working all night.
A. must be B. can be
C. may be D. has

50. You _____ study harder for the exam.
A. might B. should
C. can D. could

51. She wants _____ a doctor.
A. become B. becoming
C. to become D. becomes

52. We _____ go to the zoo tomorrow.
A. might B. should
C. must D. shall

53. He _____ finished his homework.
A. has B. have
C. had D. having

54. The teacher _____ the students every day.
A. teach B. teaching
C. teaches D. taught

55. I _____ my grandparents every Sunday.
A. visiting B. visited
C. visit D. visits

56. She _____ be the new manager.
A. may B. musts
C. is D. does

57. The dog _____ at the strangers.
A. bark B. barking
C. barks D. barked

58. He _____ a book when I called him.
A. read B. was reading
C. is reading D. reads

59. You _____ respect your elders.
A. ought to B. could
C. would D. shall

60. I _____ dancing when I was a child.
A. love B. loved
C. loves D. loving

61. We _____ playing cricket in the field.
A. is B. are
C. was D. be

62. She _____ a great dancer.
A. is B. are
C. be D. were

63. The movie _____ by a famous director.
A. directed B. was directed
C. directs D. directing

64. Pen and ink _____ required for me.
A. are B. were
C. is D. has required

65. Neither prose nor poem _____ given.
A. were B. was
C. has D. have

66. Either Sulekha or Rekha _____ coming here.
A. are B. is
C. were D. have

67. You and I _____ neighbours.
A. am B. are
C. was D. has

68. She as well as I _____ guilty.
A. is B. are
C. am D. must be

69. We .... the matter yesterday.
A. discussed about B. discussed of
C. discussed D. discussed well

70. Which of the following sentences has transitive verb?
A. She writes well
B. She walks in the morning daily
C. He is running very fast
D. I killed a snake last night

ADJECTIVE, ADVERB

Directions: (Qs. No. 71 to 90): *In the following questions choose the correct options to fill in the blanks.*

71. It is _____ picture than the one we saw last Monday.
A. interesting B. much interesting
C. more interesting D. most interesting

72. She is clever _____ .
A. that her mother is B. as her mother is
C. to her mother is D. than her mother is

73. They will get _____ .
A. Red, green and black paper
B. Red, green black paper
C. Red and green and black paper
D. Red green black paper

74. Health is _____ wealth.
A. preferable to B. more preferable than
C. more preferable to D. most preferable then

75. He has not sung _____ songs.
A. much B. most
C. more D. many

76. Srishti has searched _____ office.
A. whole the B. the whole
C. a whole D. some whole

77. Premchand was _____ best and _____ famous writer.
A. a, the most B. the, a most
C. the, more D. the, the most

78. William Shakespeare is famous as _____ .
A. a poet and a dramatist
B. a poet and dramatist
C. the poet and the dramatist
D. a poet and the dramatist

79. What does _____ leader suggest?
A. other B. another
C. others D. anothers

80. He is _____ brave.
A. stronger than B. stronger then
C. more strong then D. more strong than

81. No sooner said _____ .
A. so done B. and done
C. than done D. but done

82. She returned _____ than I had thought.
A. quickly B. more quicker
C. more quickly D. quicker

83. He is _____ foolish person.
A. rather the B. a rather
C. rather a D. rather

84. This pen _____ rupees.
A. costs twenty B. twenty costs only
C. costs only twenty D. only costs twenty

85. This tea is _____ to drink.
A. too hot B. very hot
C. enough hot D. much hot

86. The sky looks very _____ today.
A. bright B. brightly
C. brightness D. brightens

87. We saw _____ elephants at the zoo.
A. much B. more
C. many D. most

88. John is my _____ brother. (Find out the correct adjective)
A. elder B. bigger
C. old D. young

89. Today is the _____ day of my life. (Choose the correct adjective)
A. more important B. less important
C. important D. most important

90. Choose the correct adjective.
Yesterday was the _____ day of our trip.
A. most worse B. more worse
C. worst D. worser

91. Which part of speech is the word 'hard' in the sentence 'He is working hard'?
A. Preposition B. Adverb
C. Conjunction D. Noun

92. Which of the following words is an adverb?
A. Apace B. Face
C. Meek D. Fury

93. Fill in the blank with the most suitable adverb from those provided:
It took us .... five hours to reach the airport.
A. nearly B. always
C. enough D. none of these

94. The word 'Fast' in the sentence.
'He is fast writer' is:
A. an adverb B. an adjective
C. a conjunction D. a noun

95. Which of the following sentence does not have an adjective clause?
A. I met him where he lived.
B. I met him in Prayagraj which is a holy city.
C. The man who is truthful is loved by all.
D. I love the man who is truthful.

PREPOSITION

Directions: (Qs. No. 96 to 124): *In the following questions choose the correct options to fill in the blanks.*

96. She is capable _____ handling the project.
A. for B. of
C. in D. with

97. He was absent _____ school yesterday.
A. at B. of
C. from D. in

98. I was tired _____ walking all day.
A. from B. with
C. by D. of

99. There is a bridge _____ the river.
A. under B. over
C. in D. across

100. He sat _____ the fire to warm himself.
A. under B. over
C. beside D. near

101. The manager is responsible _____ the project.
A. for B. of
C. with D. in

102. He divided the apples _____ the four children.
A. among B. between
C. into D. with

103. He applied _____ the manager.
A. for B. to
C. with D. by

104. Trust _____ God and do the right.
A. in B. for
C. to D. with

105. You are hard _____ hearing.
A. at B. of
C. with D. for

106. Preeti was warned _____ the danger ahead.
A. for B. at
C. of D. about

107. I am thankful _____ you for a good advice.
A. for B. with
C. to D. of

108. The small plant in your lawn is very sensitive _____ touch.
A. on B. with
C. to D. about

109. Divya was sure to succeed _____ the examination.
A. for B. in
C. to D. with

110. Geeta was jealous _____ Ravina's beauty.
A. to B. with
C. for D. of

111. He was ignorant _____ what was happening there.
A. for B. of
C. to D. with

112. Your pen is inferior _____ mine.
A. than B. with
C. from D. to

113. It is necessary _____ you to apply for this job.
A. on B. with
C. for D. to

114. I tried .... relieve them .... their poverty.
A. to, with B. to, of
C. by, from D. into, with

115. When she parted .... her parents, her eyes were full of tears.
A. off B. with
C. from D. to

116. The deaf learn to communicate with one another .... sign language.
A. according to
B. by means of
C. inspite of
D. but for

117. We have been living here .... six months.
A. ever B. at
C. since D. for

118. Are you sorry .... what you have done?
A. with B. by
C. for D. over

119. Why are you always so suspicious .... me?
A. to B. with
C. of D. for

120. A prisoner was accused .... murder.
A. to B. of
C. for D. off

121. His thirst .... knowledge left him no leisure .... anything else.
A. for, for B. on, on
C. by, by D. at, at

122. He came to me .... midnight.
A. on B. upon
C. in D. at

123. He is junior .... me.
A. with B. to
C. than D. from

124. The speaker is going .... the subject.
A. to B. from
C. off D. within

125. Which of the following words is a preposition?
A. Beyond B. And
C. Yet D. Now

CONJUNCTION

Directions: (Qs. No. 126 to 148): *In the following questions choose the correct options to fill in the blanks.*

126. You can have _____ tea _____ coffee.
A. neither, nor B. both, and
C. either, or D. not only, but also

127. I will call you _____ I arrive.
A. as soon as B. but
C. unless D. or

128. He is not only smart _____ also funny.
A. and B. or
C. but D. but also

129. She didn't come to the party _____ she was sick.
A. because B. so
C. but D. although

130. The game was cancelled _____ heavy rain.
A. due to B. but
C. unless D. or

131. We will go out _____ it stops raining.
A. unless B. or
C. if D. though

132. _____ the manager _____ the staff were absent.
A. Neither, nor B. Both, and
C. Either, or D. Not only, but also

133. He ran fast, _____ he missed the train.
A. but B. yet
C. however D. so

134. I don't know _____ he is coming or not.
A. while B. whether
C. that D. because

135. The officer asked the peon _____ why he was late.
A. that B. if
C. but D. No word needed

136. No Sooner did the thief see the public _____ he ran away.
A. then B. and
C. but D. than

137. Abhinav _____ his brothers was going to Mumbai.
A. but B. yet
C. No word needed D. together with

138. He behaves _____ he were the captain of the team.
A. as if B. as
C. No word needed D. that

139. Either Rupali _____ Sonali is going to attend the meeting.
A. and B. but
C. nor D. or

140. Neither Nirmal _____ Ashwinee is going to listen the speech.
A. and B. but
C. nor D. or

141. Hardly had he left _____ his brother came.
A. then B. than
C. when D. that

142. I would rather have a copy _____ a book.
A. then B. than
C. when D. that

143. The cellphone is both cheap _____ best.
A. than B. and
C. then D. or

144. Although he is rich, _____ he is unhappy.
A. but B. yet
C. so D. still

145. Wait here _____ I come back.
A. till B. until
C. before D. after

146. He is my friend _____ I shall help him.
A. so B. hence
C. that is why D. therefore

147. .... he had not paid his bill, his electricity was cut off.
A. But B. Either
C. Unless D. As

148. Either he is mad .... he feigns madness.
A. nor B. or
C. and D. so

149. Which of the following words is not a coordinating conjunction?
A. if B. for
C. and D. but

150. Which of the following sentences has a 'conjunction'?
A. She is poor but she is by nature hospitable.
B. She is awfully busy.
C. I am nobody for you.
D. My grandfather is not well.

INTERJECTION

Directions: (Qs. No. 151 to 155): *In the following questions choose the correct interjection.*

151. Aww! The baby is so cute.
A. Aww! B. The baby
C. Cute D. None of the above

152. Hey! Come here and play with us.
A. Come B. Play
C. Us D. Hey!

153. Oh! It is nice to meet you again.
A. Oh! B. Meet
C. Nice D. It

154. Congratulations! You have got the job.
A. You B. Got
C. The job D. Congratulations!

155. Well done! You have proved your worth.
A. Worth B. Proved
C. Well done! D. None of the above

Directions (Qs. No. 156 to 160): *In the following questions choose the correct options to fill in the blanks.*

156. ___! We have won the competition.
A. Hurrah B. Alas
C. Oops D. Ouch

157. ___! I forgot my umbrella.
A. Hurrah B. Wow
C. Oops D. Ouch

158. ___! I hate junk food items.
A. Hurrah B. Alas
C. Yuck D. Ouch

159. ___! We have done our first project.
A. No B. Cheers
C. Yuck D. Ouch

160. ___! I did not notice you coming.
A. Hurrah B. Aww
C. Bravo D. Sorry

ANSWERS

1	2	3	4	5	6	7	8	9	10
A	B	B	A	C	B	A	A	C	C
11	12	13	14	15	16	17	18	19	20
A	B	C	D	C	B	A	D	C	C
21	22	23	24	25	26	27	28	29	30
B	D	A	C	D	A	D	B	C	D
31	32	33	34	35	36	37	38	39	40
D	D	B	A	A	B	B	C	A	D
41	42	43	44	45	46	47	48	49	50
C	B	A	B	C	B	D	A	A	B
51	52	53	54	55	56	57	58	59	60
C	A	A	C	C	A	C	B	A	B
61	62	63	64	65	66	67	68	69	70
B	A	B	C	B	B	B	A	C	D
71	72	73	74	75	76	77	78	79	80
C	C	A	A	D	B	D	B	B	D
81	82	83	84	85	86	87	88	89	90
C	C	C	C	A	A	C	A	D	C
91	92	93	94	95	96	97	98	99	100
B	A	A	B	A	B	C	A	B	D
101	102	103	104	105	106	107	108	109	110
A	A	B	A	B	D	D	D	B	D
111	112	113	114	115	116	117	118	119	120
B	D	D	B	B	B	D	C	C	B
121	122	123	124	125	126	127	128	129	130
A	D	B	A	A	C	A	D	A	A
131	132	133	134	135	136	137	138	139	140
C	B	C	B	D	D	D	A	D	C
141	142	143	144	145	146	147	148	149	150
C	B	B	B	A	B	D	B	A	A
151	152	153	154	155	156	157	158	159	160
A	D	A	D	C	A	C	C	B	D

❊ ❊ ❊ ❊ ❊

3 ARTICLES

The family of the articles has only three members. They are : A, An and The. However, they fall under two groups :

(*a*) Definite Article (*b*) Indefinite Article

'The' is known as definite article whereas 'a' and 'an' are known as indefinite articles.

Use of the Definite Article 'The'

'The' is used before

1. The superlative degree, e.g.,

He is the ablest man of the town.

(ablest is a superlative degree)

2. The name of states, countries etc. having a descriptive name, e.g.,

(*i*) The J & K is a small state. (J & K is a descriptive name)

(*ii*) He lives in the U.S.A. (U.S.A. is a descriptive name)

(But the Delhi and the America are wrong because neither Delhi nor America is a descriptive name)

3. The names of the scriptures, e.g.,

The Gita is a holy book. (Gita is a scripture)

4. Name of newspapers:

The Tribune is published from Chandigarh.

5. Name of rivers, canals, seas, oceans, bays, gulfs, groups of islands etc. e.g.,

(*i*) The Ganga is a holy river.

(*ii*) The Indian Ocean is the deepest ocean.

(*iii*) The Persian Gulf is a narrow gulf.

6. The name of famous buildings, e.g.,

The Taj is one of the best buildings in India.

7. The names of nationals, sects and communities, e.g.,

(*i*) The English defeated the Germans in the World War.

(*ii*) The rich should help the poor.

(*iii*) The Hindus believe in the caste system.

8. Proper nouns used as common nouns, e.g.,

(*i*) Kalidas is the Shakespeare of India.

(*ii*) Delhi is the London of India.

9. Famous historical events, e.g.,

The Industrial Revolution changed the face of England.

10. The directions and the celestial bodies, e.g.,

The sun rises in the east.

11. Titles, e.g.,

Akbar, the Great was loved by his subjects.

Do not use 'the'

1. Before languages:

The English is an international language. (Incorrect)

English is an international language. (Correct)

2. Before the names of games:

The hockey is a popular game. (Incorrect)

Hockey is a popular game. (Correct)

Use of the Indefinite Articles 'A' and 'An'

'A' is used before :

1. All singular common nouns beginning with a consonant, e.g.,

(*i*) A boy sings a song.

(*ii*) A black and a white cow were grazing in the field.

2. If a word begins with a vowel but gives the sound of a consonant, 'a' should be used before it, e.g.,

(*i*) He was helped in his work by a European.

(*ii*) He is a one-eyed man.

(*iii*) It is a useful work.

'An' is used as follows :

1. All singular common nouns beginning with a vowel (i.e., a, e, i, o, u), e.g.,
   (*i*) He is an artist.
   (*ii*) He is an old man.
   (*iii*) I intend to buy an umbrella.
2. If a word starts with a consonant but gives the sound of a vowel, 'an' should be used before it, e.g.,
   (*i*) Brutus is an honourable man.
   (*ii*) He is an honour to his profession.
   (*iii*) He is an L.L.B.
   (*iv*) He is an M.A.
   (*v*) You will reach there in an hour.

Demonstratives, that, these and those

1. The demonstrative adjectives and pronouns are for objects nearby the speaker:
   this (singular), those (plural)
   and for objects far away from the speaker.
   That (singular), those (plural)
2. Demonstratives are the only adjectives that agree in number with their nouns. e.g.,
   (*i*) That hat is nice. (*ii*) Those hats are nice.
3. When there is the idea of selection, the pronoun 'one' (or 'ones') often follows the demonstrative. e.g., I want a book. I'll get this (one).
   If the demonstrative is followed by an adjective, 'one' (or 'ones') must be used.
   I want a book. I'll get this big one.

EXERCISE

Directions (Qs. No. 1 to 30): *In the following questions choose the correct options to fill in the blanks.*

1. I saw _____ eagle flying in the sky.
A. a B. an
C. the D. no article

2. She has _____ idea that might help us.
A. a B. an
C. the D. no article

3. There is _____ university in this town.
A. a B. an
C. the D. no article

4. He gave me _____ useful suggestion.
A. a B. an
C. the D. no article

5. She adopted _____ dog from the shelter.
A. a B. an
C. the D. no article

6. I need _____ umbrella because it's raining.
A. a B. an
C. the D. no article

7. They saw _____ owl in the garden.
A. a B. an
C. the D. no article

8. She wants to be _____ astronaut.
A. a B. an
C. the D. no article

9. We had dinner at _____ Italian restaurant.
A. a B. an
C. the D. no article

10. I saw _____ European tourist at the museum.
A. a B. an
C. the D. no article

11. _____ will have to be paid for this material.
A. Half rupee B. Half a rupee
C. A half rupee D. An half rupee

12. Only _____ can save our country.
A. the Hitler B. a Hitler
C. Hitler D. an Hitler

13. I can run for _____ .
A. hundred miles
B. the hundred miles
C. a hundred miles
D. an hundred miles.

14. _____ earth is moving around the sun.
A. An B. A
C. The D. No article

15. This is _____ house which was built during earthquake.
A. a B. an
C. the D. No article

16. _____ America is a rich country.
A. The B. An
C. A D. No article

17. _____ U.S.A. is a developed country.
A. A B. An
C. The D. No article

18. _____ Bible is a holy book.
A. A B. The
C. An D. No article

19. _____ Gold is a costly metal.
A. The B. A
C. An D. No article

20. Kalidas is _____ Shakespeare of India.
A. a B. an
C. the D. No article

21. How foolish _____ plan it is!
A. a B. an
C. the D. No article

22. There are _____ husband and wife.
A. a B. an
C. the D. No article

23. French is _____ easy language.
A. a
B. an
C. the
D. none

24. We studied about _____ Roman Empire in school.
A. a B. an
C. the D. no article

25. Rakesh is _____ excellent Science article.
A. an B. a
C. the D. no article

26. They are going to _____ Metro station.
A. a B. the
C. an D. no article

27. .... Taj Mahal is .... monuments symbolizing love.
A. The, a B. A, an
C. The, an D. A, the

28. We were watching .... news on BBC last evening.
A. a B. the
C. an D. None of these

29. Yesterday I saw .... European riding on .... elephant.
A. a, a B. the, the
C. a, an D. a, the

30. Neil Armstrong was .... first man to walk on .... moon.
A. the, the B. an, a
C. a, the D. an, the

ANSWERS

1	2	3	4	5	6	7	8	9	10
B	B	A	B	A	B	B	B	B	A
11	**12**	**13**	**14**	**15**	**16**	**17**	**18**	**19**	**20**
B	B	C	C	C	D	C	B	D	C
21	**22**	**23**	**24**	**25**	**26**	**27**	**28**	**29**	**30**
A	D	B	C	A	B	A	B	C	A

❄ ❄ ❄ ❄ ❄

4 SENTENCE

A sentence is a group of words that is arranged in a proper order and expresses a complete thought or meaning.

A sentence always begins with a capital letter and ends with a full stop, question mark, or exclamation mark.

(A) Subject and Predicate

Subject

The subject is the part of a sentence that tells who or what performs the action. It is the doer of the action in a sentence.

Example: Ram is reading a book.

"Ram" is the subject.

Predicate

The predicate is the part of the sentence that tells what the subject does or what is said about the subject. It includes the verb and all other details.

Example: Ram is reading a book.

"is reading a book" is the predicate.

(B) Kinds of Sentences

1. **Assertive (Declarative) Sentence:** An assertive sentence is a sentence that makes a statement or expresses a fact, opinion, or information.

   Example: The sun rises in the east.
2. **Interrogative Sentence:** An interrogative sentence is a sentence that asks a question and ends with a question mark (?).

   Example: Where are you going?
3. **Imperative Sentence:** An imperative sentence is a sentence that expresses a command, request, advice, instruction, or suggestion.

   Example: Please sit down.
4. **Exclamatory Sentence:** An exclamatory sentence is a sentence that expresses strong emotion such as joy, surprise, anger, or sorrow and ends with an exclamation mark (!).

   Example: What a beautiful scene!
5. **Optative Sentence:** An optative sentence is a sentence that expresses a wish, prayer, or blessing.

   Example: May you succeed in life!

EXERCISE

Directions (Qs. No. 1 to 25): *In the following questions, choose the correct option.*

1. A group of words that expresses a complete thought is called a:

A. Phrase B. Clause
C. Sentence D. Word

2. In the sentence "Ram is reading a book", the subject is:

A. is reading
B. Ram
C. book
D. reading

3. In the sentence "She is writing a letter", the predicate is:

A. She B. writing
C. is writing a letter D. letter

4. The subject of a sentence is the part that:

A. tells action B. shows emotion
C. performs the action D. ends the sentence

5. The predicate includes:

A. only subject
B. verb and rest of sentence
C. only noun
D. punctuation

6. Which sentence is assertive?
A. Where are you going?
B. Please sit down.
C. The sun rises in the east.
D. What a beautiful day!

7. Which sentence is interrogative?
A. Open the door. B. How are you?
C. The sky is blue. D. What a nice place!

8. Which sentence is imperative?
A. She is singing.
B. Please close the window.
C. Where is he?
D. Wow! It is amazing.

9. Which sentence is exclamatory?
A. He is a teacher.
B. What a wonderful game!
C. Are you coming?
D. Sit down.

10. Which sentence expresses a wish?
A. I am happy.
B. May you succeed in life!
C. Close the door.
D. Where are you going?

11. "The teacher is teaching English." The subject is:
A. teaching B. English
C. The teacher D. is teaching

12. "They are playing football." The predicate is:
A. They B. football
C. are playing football D. playing

13. Which sentence ends with a question mark?
A. Imperative B. Interrogative
C. Assertive D. Exclamatory

14. "What a beautiful flower!" is a:
A. Assertive B. Imperative
C. Exclamatory D. Interrogative

15. "Please help me." is a:
A. Imperative B. Assertive
C. Interrogative D. Exclamatory

16. The sentence "She sings a song." is:
A. Interrogative B. Assertive
C. Imperative D. Exclamatory

17. "Where are you going?" is a:
A. Imperative B. Assertive
C. Interrogative D. Exclamatory

18. The subject in "The children are playing" is:
A. are playing B. playing
C. The children D. children are

19. The predicate in "Ram writes a letter" is:
A. Ram B. writes
C. a letter D. writes a letter

20. "How beautiful the scenery is!" is a:
A. Imperative B. Assertive
C. Exclamatory D. Interrogative

21. Which is NOT a sentence type?
A. Assertive B. Interrogative
C. Fragment D. Exclamatory

22. "Sit down." is a:
A. Assertive B. Imperative
C. Interrogative D. Exclamatory

23. In "He is playing cricket", the subject is:
A. playing B. cricket
C. He D. is playing

24. A sentence must have:
A. only subject B. only verb
C. subject and predicate D. only object

25. "The Earth revolves around the Sun." is a:
A. Imperative B. Interrogative
C. Assertive D. Exclamatory

ANSWERS

1	2	3	4	5	6	7	8	9	10
C	B	C	C	B	C	B	B	B	B
11	**12**	**13**	**14**	**15**	**16**	**17**	**18**	**19**	**20**
C	C	B	C	A	B	C	C	D	C
21	**22**	**23**	**24**	**25**					
C	B	C	C	C					

❄ ❄ ❄ ❄ ❄

5 TENSE

The tense of a verb reflects the time at which an action or event occurs.

There are three types of tenses:

1. Present Tense
2. Past Tense
3. Future Tense

Present Tense

If a verb expresses something occurring at the current moment, it is in the Present tense.

Present Tense is of four types:

A. Simple Present Tense: We use the Simple Present tense for events taking place now or for actions that occur regularly.

Structural formula: Subject + verb (s/es) + object.

Examples:

(*i*) She *lives* in Spain.

(*ii*) Bob *drives* a taxi.

The Simple Present Tense is used in the following conditions:

- To express habitual actions or routines:

  Example: She *goes* to school every day.
- To state general truths or facts:

  Example: The sun *rises* in the east.
- To express fixed arrangements or scheduled events (especially in the near future):

  Example: The train *leaves* at 6 PM.
- To give instructions or directions:

  Example: First, you *boil* the water.
- In headlines or storytelling (to create a sense of immediacy):

  Example: Man *wins* lottery and *buys* island.
- To express feelings, thoughts, or states (stative verbs):

  Example: I *believe* in hard work.

B. Present Continuous Tense: The present continuous tense is used to talk about the ongoing actions, events, or conditions that are still not finished.

Structural formula: Subject + helping verb (is/am/are) + main verb (ing) + object.

Examples:

(*i*) She *is playing* basketball.

(*ii*) Birds *are flying* in the sky.

(*iii*) I'*m learning* English.

The Present Continuous Tense is used for the following purposes:

- Actions happening right now (at the moment of speaking):

  Example: She *is reading* a book.
- Temporary actions or situations:

  Example: I *am staying* with a friend this week.
- Planned future events or arrangements:

  Example: They *are meeting* the manager tomorrow.
- Repeated actions with "always" (often with annoyance or emphasis):

  Example: He *is always forgetting* his keys!
- Changing or developing situations:

  Example: The weather *is getting* colder.

C. Present Perfect Tense: A present perfect tense refers to an action or state that has taken place recently.

Structural formula: Subject + helping verb (have/has) + verb (3rd form) + object.

Examples:

(*i*) She *has not finished* her work yet.

(*ii*) I *have seen* that movie twice.

(*iii*) We *have visited* LA several times.

The Present Perfect Tense is used for:

- Actions that happened at an unspecified time in the past but are relevant to the present:

  Example: She *has visited* Paris.

- Actions that started in the past and continue up to the present:

  Example: They *have lived* here for ten years.

- Recent actions or events with present results:

  Example: I *have just finished* my homework.

- Life experiences:

  Example: He *has never eaten* sushi.

- Repeated actions at different times in the past:

  Example: We *have seen* that movie several times.

D. Present Perfect Continuous Tense: The present perfect continuous tense shows a situation that has started in the past and continues in the present.

Structural formula: Subject + helping verb (have/has) + been + verb (ing) + object (optional) + since/for + time duration + object.

Examples:

(*i*) I *have been learning* English for many years.

(*ii*) He *has been working* here since 2010.

(*iii*) We *have been saving* money.

"Since" is followed by a specific point in time, such as:

- A year: *since 2015*
- A day: *since Monday*
- A time: *since 8 a.m.*
- A past event: *since we met*

Examples:

(*i*) I *have been working* here *since* January.

(*ii*) They *have been studying since* morning.

"For" is followed by a period of time, such as:

- Seconds, minutes, hours: for 30 minutes
- Days, weeks, months, years: for two weeks, for five years
- A long time/a short time: for a long time

Examples:

(*i*) I *have been waiting for* an hour.

(*ii*) They *have been studying for* two hours.

Past Tense

The past tense is used when a verb refers to something that took place in the past.

Past Tense is of four types:

A. Simple Past Tense: The simple past tense is used to show an action that happened in the past or a condition that existed earlier.

Structural formula: Subject + verb (2nd form) + object.

Examples:

(*i*) We *met* yesterday.

(*ii*) He *bought* a new laptop last week.

Simple Past Tense is used for:

- Completed actions in the past:

  Example: She *visited* the museum yesterday.

- Actions that happened at a specific time in the past:

  Example: I *met* him in 2020.

- Series of past events (narration or storytelling):

  Example: He *woke up, brushed* his teeth, and left for work.

- Habits or repeated actions in the past:

  Example: They *played* cricket every weekend when they were kids.

- States or situations that existed in the past:

  Example: The house *was* very quiet.

B. Past Continuous Tense: Past continuous tense shows an action that was happening at a specific time in the past.

Structural formula: Subject + helping verb (was/were) + verb (ing) + object.

Examples:

(*i*) I *was watching* TV.

(*ii*) We *were sleeping*.

(*iii*) She *wasn't eating* her lunch.

Past Continuous Tense is used for:

- An action that was happening at a specific time in the past:

  Example: She *was reading* at 8 PM.

- Two actions happening at the same time in the past:

  Example: I *was cooking* while he *was watching* TV.

- An action in progress in the past interrupted by another action (usually in Simple Past):

  Example: They *were playing* when it *started* to rain.

- To show background actions in a story or description:

Example: The birds *were singing*, and the sun *was shining*.

C. Past Perfect Tense: The past perfect tense is used to describe an event that occurred before a completed action in the past.

Structural formula: Subject + had + verb (3rd form) + object.

Examples:

(*i*) He *had gone* when she became ill.

(*ii*) She *had not lived* in New York.

(*iii*) They *had not been married* long when I was born.

Past Perfect Tense is used for:

- To show an action completed before another past action:

  Example: She *had left* before I arrived.

- To indicate the earlier of two past actions:

  Example: They *had finished* dinner when the guests *came*.

- To describe a past action with present relevance in a narrative or reflection:

  Example: I couldn't believe I *had forgotten* her birthday.

- In reported speech (indirect speech):

  Example: He said that he *had seen* the movie.

D. Past Perfect Continuous Tense: The past perfect continuous tense represents any action or event that started in the past and sometimes continued into another action or another time.

Structural formula: Subject + had been + Verb (ing) + object (optional) + time of action.

Examples:

(*i*) We *had been playing* games for 6 hours when Dad came home.

(*ii*) She *had been reading* magazines for 1 month before she decided to apply for the job.

(*iii*) *Had she been washing* dishes all day?

Past Perfect Continuous Tense is used for:

- To show an action that was ongoing in the past and continued up until another point in the past:

  Example: She *had been studying* for two hours before the power went out.

- To emphasize the duration of a past activity before something else happened:

  Example: They *had been working* at the company for five years when it closed.

- To describe the cause of something in the past:

  Example: He was tired because he *had been running*.

Future Tense

The future tense is a tense used to describe an event or action that has not yet happened and is expected to happen in the future.

A. Simple Future Tense: Simple Future Tense is used to describe an action that will occur in the future.

Structural formula: Subject + shall/will + verb + object.

Example:

- He *will* be here soon.

Simple Future Tense is used for:

- Actions that will happen in the future:

  Example: She *will travel* to Paris next year.

  I *shall visit* my grandparents next week.

- Decisions made at the moment of speaking:

  Example: I *will call* you later.

  We *shall see* what happens.

- Predictions about the future:

  Example: It *will rain* tomorrow.

- Promises or offers:

  Example: I *will help* you with your homework.

B. Future Continuous Tense: The future continuous tense is used to describe an ongoing action that will occur or occur in the future.

Structural formula: Subject + shall/will be + verb (ing) + object.

Examples:

(*i*) He *will be coming* to visit us next week.

(*ii*) She *will be watching* TV.

(*iii*) He *will be writing* a letter to Mary.

C. Future Perfect Tense: The future perfect is used to describe an action that will be completed between now and a certain point in the future.

Structural formula: Subject + shall/will + have + verb (3rd form) + object.

Examples:

(*i*) They *will have finished* the film before we get home.

(*ii*) She *will have cleaned* the house by 9 pm.

D. Future Perfect Continuous Tense: We use the future perfect continuous to focus on the duration of an action before a specific time in the future.

Structural formula: Subject + shall/will + have been + verb (ing) + object (optional) + time instant.

Examples:

(*i*) He *will have been studying* hard for 2 weeks before the exam.

(*ii*) By the time the alarm goes off, we *will have been sleeping* for 8 hours.

(*iii*) We *shall have been living* in this city for five years by the end of this month.

EXERCISE

Directions (Qs. No. 1 to 30): *In the following questions choose the correct option to fill in the blanks.*

1. She always _____ to school on foot.
A. go B. goes
C. going D. gone

2. They _____ a new house last year.
A. buy B. buys
C. bought D. buying

3. He _____ his homework tomorrow.
A. will do B. do
C. does D. doing

4. Look! The children _____ in the garden.
A. are playing B. play
C. were playing D. played

5. She _____ a new book these days.
A. write B. writes
C. is writing D. has written

6. They _____ for the bus right now.
A. wait B. waited
C. are waiting D. were waiting

7. She _____ TV when I called her.
A. was watching B. watched
C. watches D. has watched

8. I _____ dinner when the phone rang.
A. am having B. had
C. was having D. have had

9. He ___ a letter when I entered the room.
A. is writing B. was writing
C. wrote D. has written

10. They _____ to a song when I met them.
A. are listening B. listened
C. were listening D. listen

11. This time tomorrow, I _____ for my exam.
A. will study B. study
C. will be studying D. studying

12. We _____ in the library in the evening.
A. will be reading B. read
C. have read D. reading

13. He _____ for his flight at this time next week.
A. waits B. is waiting
C. will be waiting D. waited

14. They _____ the project presentation at that moment.
A. give B. are giving
C. will be giving D. gave

15. She _____ never _____ to London.
A. has, been B. had, been
C. was, being D. have, be

16. They _____ their lunch already.
A. eats B. ate
C. have eaten D. had eaten

17. He _____ his wallet.
A. has lost B. lost
C. loses D. is losing

18. She _____ before I reached.
A. left B. has left
C. had left D. leaves

19. The train _____ when we reached the station.
A. has left B. had left
C. left D. leaves

20. I _____ my work by 6 PM.
A. will finish B. will have finished
C. finish D. have finished

21. They _____ in this company for 5 years by next July.
A. will be working
B. will work
C. will have been working
D. are working

22. She _____ for two hours when the power went out.
A. had studied B. studied
C. had been studying D. has been studying

23. I _____ for this opportunity all my life.
A. am waiting B. have waited
C. have been waiting D. waited

24. He _____ the report by the deadline.
A. will have submitted B. submits
C. submitted D. has submitted

25. Water _____ at 100 degrees Celsius.
A. boils B. is boiling
C. has boiled D. boil

26. She _____ already _____ her meal.
A. had, eaten B. has, eaten
C. have, eaten D. eats

27. While we _____ dinner, the lights went out.
A. have B. had
C. are having D. were having

28. Tomorrow, we _____ a guest speaker at our event.
A. had B. are having
C. will have D. have had

29. By next year, I _____ in this city for a decade.
A. live B. will live
C. will have lived D. had lived

30. The captain _____ along with the players.
A. was present B. was presenting
C. have been presenting D. has been presenting

Directions (Qs. No. 31 to 35): *Read each sentence carefully. From the four options given, choose the one that correctly identifies the tense used in the sentence.*

31. The sun sets in the west.
A. Present Indefinite B. Past Indefinite
C. Future Indefinite D. Present Perfect

32. We were playing football in the evening.
A. Present Perfect Continuous
B. Future Continuous
C. Past Continuous
D. Present Indefinite

33. He had left before I arrived.
A. Past Perfect B. Present Perfect
C. Future Perfect D. Past Indefinite

34. She will have completed the task by tomorrow.
A. Present Perfect
B. Future Perfect
C. Past Perfect
D. Future Indefinite

35. He is reading a book right now.
A. Present Indefinite
B. Present Continuous
C. Past Perfect
D. Future Continuous

ANSWERS

1	2	3	4	5	6	7	8	9	10
B	C	A	A	C	C	A	C	B	C
11	**12**	**13**	**14**	**15**	**16**	**17**	**18**	**19**	**20**
C	A	C	C	A	C	A	C	B	B
21	**22**	**23**	**24**	**25**	**26**	**27**	**28**	**29**	**30**
C	C	C	A	A	B	D	C	C	A
31	**32**	**33**	**34**	**35**					
A	C	A	B	B					

❄ ❄ ❄ ❄ ❄

6 ACTIVE & PASSIVE VOICE

Voice is an important part of English grammar that shows whether the subject performs the action or receives the action in a sentence. There are two types of voice: Active Voice and Passive Voice.

Active Voice

In Active Voice, the subject performs the action of the verb.

Structure: Subject + Verb + Object

Examples:

- Ram writes a letter.
- She is reading a book.
- They played football.
- The teacher explains the lesson.

In these sentences, the subject (Ram, She, They, Teacher) is doing the action.

Passive Voice

In Passive Voice, the object of the active sentence becomes the subject, and the action is performed on it.

Structure: Object + Helping Verb (be form) + Past Participle + (by Subject)

Examples:

- A letter is written by Ram.
- A book is being read by her.
- Football was played by them.
- The lesson is explained by the teacher.

Rules of Conversion (Active → Passive)

Rule 1: Present Indefinite Tense

Active: Subject + Verb (1st form + s/es) + Object
Passive: Object + is/am/are + 3rd form + by + Subject

Example:

- **Active:** She sings a song.
- **Passive:** A song is sung by her.

Rule 2: Past Indefinite Tense

Active: Subject + Verb (2nd form) + Object
Passive: Object + was/were + 3rd form + by + Subject

Example:

- **Active:** He wrote a letter.
- **Passive:** A letter was written by him.

Rule 3: Future Indefinite Tense

Active: Subject + will + Verb (1st form) + Object
Passive: Object + will be + 3rd form + by + Subject

Example:

- **Active:** They will play cricket.
- **Passive:** Cricket will be played by them.

Rule 4: Present Continuous Tense

Active: Subject + is/am/are + Verb-ing + Object
Passive: Object + is/am/are + being + 3rd form + by + Subject

Example:

- **Active:** She is writing a letter.
- **Passive:** A letter is being written by her.

Rule 5: Past Continuous Tense

Active: Subject + was/were + Verb-ing + Object
Passive: Object + was/were + being + 3rd form + by + Subject

Example:

- **Active:** They were playing football.
- **Passive:** Football was being played by them.

Rule 6: Future Continuous Tense

Active: Subject + will be + Verb-ing + Object
Passive: Object + will be + being + Verb(3rd form) + by + Subject

Example:

- **Active:** She will be writing a letter.
- **Passive:** A letter will be being written by her.

Rule 7: Present Perfect Tense

Active: Subject + has/have + 3rd form + Object
Passive: Object + has/have been + 3rd form + by + Subject

Example:

- **Active:** He has completed the work.
- **Passive:** The work has been completed by him.

Rule 8: Past Perfect Tense

Active: Subject + had + Verb(3rd form) + Object
Passive: Object + had been + Verb(3rd form) + by + Subject

Example:

- **Active:** He had completed the work.
- **Passive:** The work had been completed by him.

Rule 9: Future Perfect Tense

Active: Subject + will have + Verb(3rd form) + Object

Passive: Object + will have been + Verb(3rd form) + by + Subject

Example:

- **Active:** They will have finished the project.
- **Passive:** The project will have been finished by them.

Rule 10: Present Perfect Continuous Tense

Active: Subject + has/have been + Verb-ing + Object

Passive: Object + has/have been being + Verb(3rd form) + by + Subject

Example:

- **Active:** She has been reading the book.
- **Passive:** The book has been being read by her.

Rule 11: Past Perfect Continuous Tense

Active: Subject + had been + Verb-ing + Object

Passive: Object + had been being + Verb(3rd form) + by + Subject

Example:

- **Active:** They had been playing football.
- **Passive:** Football had been being played by them.

Rule 12: Future Perfect Continuous

Active: Subject + will have been + Verb(-ing) + Object

- Indicates an action that will be ongoing up to a certain point in the future.

Example:

- She will have been writing the report for two hours.

Passive: Object + will have been being + Verb(3rd form) + by + Subject

Example:

- The report will have been being written by her for two hours

Important Changes in Passive Voice

- Subject becomes object (after "by")
- Object becomes subject
- Verb changes to 3rd form (Past Participle)
- Helping verbs are added (is, am, are, was, were, been, being)

When "by" is omitted

"By" is often omitted when the doer is unknown, unimportant, or obvious.

Examples:

- **Active:** People speak English worldwide.
- **Passive:** English is spoken worldwide.

EXERCISE

Directions (Qs. No. 1 to 25): *In the following questions, choose the correct option for the passive or active form.*

1. She writes a letter. (Passive voice)
A. A letter is written by her
B. A letter was written by her
C. A letter is being written by her
D. A letter has written by her

2. A book is read by him. (Active voice)
A. He reads a book
B. He read a book
C. He is reading a book
D. He has read a book

3. They play football. (Passive voice)
A. Football is played by them
B. Football was played by them
C. Football will be played by them
D. Football is being played by them

4. A letter was written by Ram. (Active voice)
A. Ram writes a letter
B. Ram wrote a letter
C. Ram is writing a letter
D. Ram has written a letter

5. He is reading a book. (Passive voice)
A. A book is read by him
B. A book is being read by him
C. A book was read by him
D. A book has read by him

6. Cricket is played by them. (Active voice)
A. They play cricket
B. They played cricket
C. They are playing cricket
D. They have played cricket

7. She sings a song. (Passive voice)
A. A song is sung by her
B. A song was sung by her
C. A song has been sung by her
D. A song is being sung by her

8. A letter was written by him. (Active voice)
A. He writes a letter
B. He wrote a letter
C. He is writing a letter
D. He has written a letter

9. They will play football. (Passive voice)
A. Football is played by them
B. Football will be played by them
C. Football was played by them
D. Football is being played by them

10. The lesson is explained by the teacher. (Active voice)
A. The teacher explains the lesson
B. The teacher explained the lesson
C. The teacher is explaining the lesson
D. The teacher has explained the lesson

11. She was writing a letter. (Passive voice)
A. A letter is written by her
B. A letter is being written by her
C. A letter was being written by her
D. A letter has been written by her

12. A song was sung by him. (Active voice)
A. He sings a song B. He sang a song
C. He is singing a song D. He has sung a song

13. They were playing football. (Passive voice)
A. Football was played by them
B. Football was being played by them
C. Football is played by them
D. Football has been played by them

14. A letter has been written by her. (Active voice)
A. She writes a letter
B. She wrote a letter
C. She has written a letter
D. She is writing a letter

15. He wrote a novel. (Passive voice)
A. A novel is written by him
B. A novel was written by him
C. A novel has been written by him
D. A novel is being written by him

16. A book is being read by her. (Active voice)
A. She reads a book B. She is reading a book
C. She read a book D. She has read a book

17. The work has been completed by him. (Active voice)
A. He completes the work
B. He completed the work
C. He has completed the work
D. He is completing the work

18. He is writing a story. (Passive voice)
A. A story is written by him
B. A story is being written by him
C. A story was written by him
D. A story has been written by him

19. Football was played by them. (Active voice)
A. They play football
B. They played football
C. They are playing football
D. They have played football

20. A song is sung by her. (Active voice)
A. She sings a song
B. She sang a song
C. She is singing a song
D. She has sung a song

21. The letter is being written by Ram. (Active voice)
A. Ram writes a letter
B. Ram is writing a letter
C. Ram wrote a letter
D. Ram has written a letter

22. They are playing cricket. (Passive voice)
A. Cricket is played by them
B. Cricket is being played by them
C. Cricket was played by them
D. Cricket has been played by them

23. A cake was baked by her. (Active voice)
A. She bakes a cake
B. She baked a cake
C. She is baking a cake
D. She has baked a cake

24. He has written a letter. (Passive voice)
A. A letter is written by him
B. A letter was written by him
C. A letter has been written by him
D. A letter is being written by him

25. The teacher explains the lesson. (Passive voice)
A. The lesson is explained by the teacher
B. The lesson was explained by the teacher
C. The lesson is being explained by the teacher
D. The lesson has been explained by the teacher

ANSWERS

1	2	3	4	5	6	7	8	9	10
A	A	A	B	B	A	A	B	B	A
11	12	13	14	15	16	17	18	19	20
C	B	B	C	B	B	C	B	B	A
21	22	23	24	25					
B	B	B	C	A					

❄ ❄ ❄ ❄ ❄

7 PUNCTUATION

Punctuation marks are symbols used in writing to make sentences clear, meaningful, and well-structured. They indicate pauses, emotions, questions, emphasis, and the proper flow of ideas in written language. Without punctuation, the meaning of a sentence may become confusing or incorrect.

1. **Full Stop (.):** A full stop is used at the end of a complete sentence to show a full stop or completion of an idea.

   Examples:
   - Ram goes to school.
   - She is reading a book.

2. **Comma (,):** A comma is used to show a short pause in a sentence or to separate items in a list.

   Examples:
   - Ram, Shyam, and Mohan went to school.
   - He bought apples, bananas, and oranges.

3. **Semicolon (;):** A semicolon is used to connect two closely related independent clauses.

   Example:
   - He worked hard; he succeeded in the exam.

4. **Colon (:):** A colon is used before a list, explanation, or example.

   Example:
   - I have three colors: red, blue, and green.

5. **Question Mark (?):** A question mark is used at the end of interrogative sentences.

   Examples:
   - Where are you going?
   - Have you completed your homework?

6. **Exclamation Mark (!):** An exclamation mark is used to express strong emotions such as surprise, joy, anger, or excitement.

   Examples:
   - Wow! What a beautiful view!
   - Oh no! What happened!

7. **Quotation Marks (" "):** Quotation marks are used to show direct speech or exact words spoken by someone.

   Example: • He said, "I am coming."

8. **Brackets (Parentheses) – ( ):** Brackets are used to give extra information or clarification in a sentence.

   Example:
   - Mahatma Gandhi (the Father of the Nation) was born in 1869.

9. **Hyphen (-):** A hyphen is used to join two words or parts of words.

   Examples:
   - Mother-in-law
   - Well-known

EXERCISE

1. He is reading a book__

A. ? B. !
C. . D. ,

2. Where are you going__

A. . B. ?
C. ! D. ;

3. Wow__ What a beautiful day__

A. !, . B. . ,
C. ?, ! D. ; ,

4. I have three favorite subjects __ Math, Science and English.

A. , B. ;
C. . D. :

5. I bought apples__ bananas__ and oranges.
A. , ,   B. ; ;
C. : :   D. . ,

6. He said__ "I am ready."
A. :   B. ,
C. .   D. ;

7. Mahatma Gandhi __known as Father of Nation was born in 1869.
A. .   B. !
C. ?   D. ,

8. She is a well__known writer.
A. -   B. ,
C. .   D. :

9. He worked hard__ he succeeded.
A. ,   B. ;
C. .   D. :

10. Have you completed your homework__
A. .   B. ?
C. !   D. ,

11. Oh no__ What happened__
A. ! ?   B. ? !
C. , .   D. , ,

12. She said__ "I will come tomorrow."
A. :   B. ,
C. .   D. ;

13. The sun is shining brightly__
A. ?   B. !
C. .   D. :

14. We need pen__ paper__ and books.
A. , ,   B. . .
C. ; ;   D. : :

15. What a wonderful performance__
A. ?   B. !
C. .   D. ,

16. The train is late__
A. .   B. ?
C. !   D. ,

17. I have two brothers__ Raj and Amit.
A. :   B. ,
C. ;   D. .

18. She is honest__ kind__ and helpful.
A. , ,   B. ; ;
C. . .   D. : :

19. Are you coming with us__
A. .   B. ?
C. !   D. ,

20. He shouted__ "Stop there!"
A. :   B. ,
C. .   D. ;

21. My mother is a doctor__
A. ?   B. .
C. !   D. ,

22. She is a good girl__ she always helps others.
A. ;   B. ,
C. :   D. .

23. I like tea__ coffee__ and milk.
A. , ,   B. ; ;
C. . .   D. : :

24. He said__ "What are you doing?"
A. :   B. ,
C. .   D. ;

25. The Earth revolves around the Sun__
A. ?   B. !
C. .   D. ,

ANSWERS

1	2	3	4	5	6	7	8	9	10
C	B	A	D	A	A	D	A	B	B
11	**12**	**13**	**14**	**15**	**16**	**17**	**18**	**19**	**20**
A	A	C	A	B	A	A	A	B	A
21	**22**	**23**	**24**	**25**					
B	A	A	A	C					

❄ ❄ ❄ ❄ ❄

8 WORD FORMATION

Word Formation is an important topic in English grammar that deals with how new words are created from existing words.

It helps in understanding vocabulary building, spelling patterns, and meaning changes.

1. Suffixes

A suffix is a group of letters added at the end of a word to change its meaning or part of speech.

Examples:

- teach → teacher
- happy → happiness
- kind → kindness
- beauty → beautiful
- act → action

2. Prefixes

A prefix is a group of letters added at the beginning of a word to change its meaning.

Examples:

- happy → unhappy
- possible → impossible
- legal → illegal
- active → inactive
- correct → incorrect

3. Conversion of Words (Zero Derivation)

In this method, the same word is used as different parts of speech without changing its form.

Examples:

- run (verb) → a run (noun)
- walk (verb) → a walk (noun)
- drink (verb) → a drink (noun)
- call (verb) → a call (noun)

4. Compound Words Formation

Two or more words are combined to form a new word with a new meaning.

Examples:

- black + board = blackboard
- sun + flower = sunflower
- tooth + brush = toothbrush
- rain + bow = rainbow

5. Blending of Words

Two words are merged to form a new word.

Examples:

- breakfast + lunch = brunch
- motor + hotel = motel
- smoke + fog = smog
- television + marathon = telethon

6. Clipping (Shortening of Words)

A long word is shortened to form a new word.

Examples:

- advertisement → ad
- examination → exam
- laboratory → lab
- gymnasium → gym

7. Acronyms

Words formed from the first letters of a group of words.

Examples:

- UNICEF → United Nations International Children's Emergency Fund
- NASA → National Aeronautics and Space Administration
- PIN → Personal Identification Number
- LASER → Light Amplification by Stimulated Emission of Radiation

EXERCISE

1. What is the correct prefix for "possible"?
   A. im- B. un- C. dis- D. in-
2. What is the noun form of "happy"?
   A. happily B. happiness C. happier D. happiest
3. Choose the correct word: teach → ____
   A. teacher B. teaching C. teaches D. taught
4. What is the opposite of "legal"?
   A. legal B. illegal C. legible D. loyal
5. What is the noun form of "kind"?
   A. kindly B. kindness C. kinder D. kindest
6. Which is a compound word?
   A. happiness B. blackboard C. quickly D. running
7. sun + flower = ____
   A. sunflower B. sunflow C. sunflour D. flower-sun
8. What is the correct prefix for "active"?
   A. dis- B. in- C. un- D. all of these
9. examination → ____
   A. exam B. examine C. example D. execution
10. Which is a blended word?
    A. notebook B. smog C. blackboard D. classroom
11. smoke + fog = ____
    A. smog B. fogsmoke C. smokfog D. smake
12. run (verb) → a ____ (noun)
    A. runner B. running C. run D. ran
13. What is the opposite of "happy"?
    A. unhappy B. happily C. happiness D. hopeful
14. Which is a suffix in "beautiful"?
    A. be- B. ful C. beau D. it
15. What is the correct prefix for "correct"?
    A. in- B. un- C. dis- D. all of these
16. laboratory → ____
    A. lab B. late C. labor D. label
17. tooth + brush = ____
    A. toothbrush B. tooth-brushes C. brush-tooth D. teethbrush
18. What is the noun form of "act"?
    A. active B. action C. actor D. acted
19. Which is a prefix?
    A. -ful B. -ness C. un- D. -ly
20. walk (verb) → a ____ (noun)
    A. walking B. walker C. walk D. walked

ANSWERS

1	2	3	4	5	6	7	8	9	10
A	B	A	B	B	B	A	D	A	B
11	**12**	**13**	**14**	**15**	**16**	**17**	**18**	**19**	**20**
A	C	A	B	A	A	A	B	C	C

❄ ❄ ❄ ❄ ❄

SECTION-B

PEDAGOGY OF LANGUAGE DEVELOPMENT

English is not the most widely spoken language in the world in terms of the number of native speakers. There are many more Chinese speakers than native English speakers but Chinese is spoken little outside of Chinese communities. However English is the most widespread language in the world.

For Governance and Career

In many former British colonies, English is still used in the government and as a medium of communication among people who do not have another language in common. In some cases, it is a neutral language that is used to avoid giving any one indigenous language too much prestige. English is often used in India, because it is neutral.

It is the language of the government. People who speak English have a certain status in society. It is used for books, music and dance. In Singapore, English is a second language, but it is necessary for daily life. Many companies there use English.

In addition, sixteen countries in Africa have retained English as the language of the government. Now standard English is taught in schools in those countries, because it is necessary for careers.

For News and Information

English is commonly used as a medium for the communication of information and news. Three quarters of all telex messages and telegrams are sent in English. Eighty percent of computer data are processed and stored in English. Much satellite communication is carried in English. Five thousand newspapers, more than half of the newspapers published in the world, are published in English.

Even in many countries where English is a minority language, there is at least one newspaper in English. In India alone, there are three thousand magazines published in English.

In many countries, television news is broadcast in English. Because of the power of television, demonstrators in every country use signs printed in English for the benefit of the international press.

For Business, Diplomacy, and the Professions

English is a major language of international business, diplomacy, science and the professions. It is the language that an Iranian businessman and a Japanese businessman are likely to use to communicate. Important commodities such as silver, tin, and hard currency are traded in English. English is also an official language of many professional and international organizations including the United Nations.

For Entertainment

Popular culture has also played an important part in spreading English. American and British popular music are heard all over the world. American movies are seen in almost every country. Books in English are available even in countries where very few people actually use English. One reason that students give for learning English is to understand these songs, movies and books.

For Travel

English is also very important for international travel. Much of the information, countries disseminate about themselves outside of their borders, is in English. English is spoken in large hotels and tourist attractions, at airports, and in shops that tourists frequent. There are travel brochures printed in English, and TV news is available in English.

LEARNING

A considerable change in the behaviour of the organism is called learning. When organism comes in contact with his environment certain necessary adjustment in the behaviour is needed. This adjustment in behaviour is the result of acquisition of various habits, skills, attitudes and knowledge which is actually learning in simple term.

Thus, learning means change in response or behaviour (modification, elimination or acquisition of responses involving some degree of performance) caused partly or wholly by conscious or unconscious experiences. This learning does not include physiological changes such as fatigue, temporary sensory resistance or non functioning even after continued stimulation.

Definition of Learning

It is very difficult to give a universally acceptable definition of learning because psychologists have defined the concept from different angles on the basis of their experiments. The common feature among these definitions is that learning in psychology has the status of a construct which means an idea or image that can not be directly observed like electrons or genes but they are inferred from the behaviour of the organism.

Melvin H Marx has defined learning in the following words;

"Learning is a relatively enduring change in behaviour which is a function of prior behaviour (usually called practice).

Explanation : According to the definition given above learning has three attributes:

1. Learning is a some what permanent change in behaviour. Changes occurred due to illness, fatigue, maturation or the consumption of intoxicants is not learning.
2. Learning is not directly observable. It is inferred from the behaviour of the organism in the form of construct.
3. Learning is a function of practice and experience. Experiences adds learning and practice gives it an enduring nature.

Some other **definitions** of learning are given below;

"Learning is modification of behaviour through experiences." **—Gates**

"Learning involves the acquisition of habit knowledge and attitudes". **—Crow and Crow**

"Learning is any change in behaviour resulting from behaviour." **—Guilford**

"Learning includes both acquisition and retention." **—Skinner**

Characteristics of Learning

On the basis of the meaning and definitions given above following characteristics of learning can be derived:

1. **Learning is a relatively permanent change in behaviour :** Temporary changes in behaviour brought about due to some accidents or consuming any drugs is not learning at all. Learning is a relatively permanent change in behaviour. It is in this context we can say that reading some selected material to pass an examination is not learning. It is because learnt material is forgotten immediately after the exam.
2. **Learning is a progress or growth of the organism :** Learning is a fundamental need of life. Without it, no progress or growth is possible. This process of growth is unending also. One achievement of the organism motivates him to go for further achievement and thus excellence in many cases is achieved.
3. **Learning is a life long process :** An organism needs learning (behavioural change) at every moment of life to adjust to new situations at every moment. He can not sit idle at any time. Situations all the time force him for the acquisition of new learning.
4. **Learning is not directly observable :** How much learning has taken place in an organism can not be directly observed. It is inferred from his behaviour which is manifested by some activities, mental or physical.
5. **Learning is the result of experiences :** Experiences are gained at every moment of life. Learning is the other name of these experiences.
6. **Learning is a goal directed process :** Learning is a purposeful activity. It is a goal directed process. Learning which is the result of unconscious efforts of the individual is not learning in actual sense.
7. **Learning is retained through practice :** Practice or exercise is a must to retain learning. If practice is not made, learning will be forgotten and the nature of learning will no longer remain permanent. Thus, learning is acquisition and retention both.
8. **Learning is aroused by individual and social needs :** Learning depends upon our social needs, problems, desires, and ideals. There are certain persons who learn very fast whereas others are slow in learning. It should be noticed that social environment affects learning. It is impossible to learn in the absence of environment.
9. **Learning is active and creative :** Learning is active and creative i.e. learning depends upon the active involvement of the learner. It is said that if the learner is not self active, he cannot learn. It is, therefore, said that learning is the result of active involvement and experience from the sender and the receiver both.
10. **Learning is universal :** Humans are not the only organism that learn i.e., react to the environment for adjustment. Animals also go through the process of learning though their speed of learning may be slower than humans.

ACQUISITION

Language acquisition is the process by which the language capability develops in a human. It is the process by which a child acquires its mother tongue. It is the most wonderful feat we perform in our whole life and we do it at an age when we can hardly do anything else. It is an active process by which children, taking cues available to them, construct their own utterances and say things they have never heard of. Language learning is a behaviour acquired by making conscious efforts. It involves certain skills – learning to understand when it is spoken, speaking, reading and writing. It is also forming a certain set of habits. It is acquired by imitation and practice. Since language is a learned activity, we have to learn it and teach it properly.

Distinction between Acquisition and Learning

There are many distinctions between the processes of acquisition and learning.

1. Children within 5 years of age learn their mother tongue through acquisition. A second language, is through conscious effort of learning.
2. Acquisition is an unconscious process where no formal classroom instruction is involved. Learning, however is about conscious knowledge and the application of rules and structures.
3. In language acquisition, the focus is on communication or reception of a message. But in language learning the thrust is on syntax and grammar.
4. The context is usually crucial and meaningful in language acquisition but it need not be important to that extent in language learning.
5. Motivation is a matter of urgent necessity for acquisition. It is not so for second learning.
6. Most importantly, the usual outcome of language acquisition is fluency which is by no means guaranteed in language learning.

It is the process by which humans acquire the capacity to perceive, produce and use words to understand and communicate. This capacity involves the picking up of diverse capacities including syntax, phonetics and an extensive vocabulary. This language might be vocal as with speech or manual as in sign. Language acquisition usually refers to first language acquisition, which studies infants' acquisition of their native language, rather than second language acquisition, which deals with acquisition (in both children and adults) of additional languages.

The capacity to acquire and use language is a key aspect that distinguishes humans from other organisms. While many forms of animal communication exist, they have a limited range of non-syntactically structured vocabulary tokens that lack cross cultural variation between groups.

A major concern in understanding language acquisition is how these capacities are picked up by infants from what appears to be very input. A range of theories of language acquisition has been created in order to explain this apparent problem including innatism in which a child is born prepared in some manner with these capacities, as opposed to the other theories in which language is simply learned.

Social interactionist theory consists of a number of hypotheses on language acquisition. These hypotheses deal with written, spoken, or visual social tools which consist of complex systems of symbols and rules on language acquisition and development. The compromise between ''nature'' and ''nurture'' is the ''interactionist'' approach. In addition, for years, psychologists and researchers have been asking the same question. What are the language behaviours that nature provides innately and what are those behaviours that are realized by environmental exposure, which as nurture.

The relational frame theory (Hayes, Barnes-Holmes, Roche, 2001), provides a wholly selectionist/learning account of the origin and development of language competence and complexity. Based upon the principles of Skinnerian behaviorism the relational frame theory posits that children acquire language purely through interacting with the environment. The relational frame theorists introduced the concept of functional contextualism in language learning, which emphasizes the importance of predicting and influencing psychological events, such as thoughts, feelings and behaviours, by focusing on manipulable variables in their context. The relational frame theory distinguishes itself from Skinner's work by identifying and defining a particular type of operant conditioning known as derived relational responding, a learning process that to date appears to occur only in humans possessing a capacity for language. Empirical studies supporting the predictions of relational frame theory suggest that children learn language via a system of inherent reinforcements, challenging the view that language acquisition is based upon innate, language-specific cognitive capacities.

Emergentist theories, such as Mac Winney's competition model, posit that language acquisition is a cognitive process that emerges from the interaction of biological pressures and the environment. According to these theories, neither nature nor nurture alone is sufficient to trigger language learning; both of these influences must work together in order to allow children to acquire a language. The proponents of these theories argue that general cognitive processes subserve language acquisition and that the end result of these processes is language-specific phenomena, such as word learning and grammar acquisition. The findings of many empirical studies support the predictions of these theories, suggesting that language acquisition is a more complex process than many believe.

PRINCIPLES OF LANGUAGE TEACHING

1. Consider the whole person : Teacher should take into consideration who the student is. Know different aspects of the individual. (Student's psychology, social background, etc.) Consult with the guiding and class teachers. Don't grade only by looking at his learning English.
2. Language learning is both forming habit and also utilizing the student's innate capacity. Cognitive school of Psychology using the student's innate capacity for the language. The student uses his creative mental power.
3. Keep the students involved. Try to have a student centered class as far as possible. Keep the appropriate ratio of teacher talk and student talk.
4. Language learners learn to do by doing. Items of language should be practised. Practice is extermely important in foreign language learning. Practice, especially drilling, helps with habit formation.
5. Teach all 4 language skills : Listening, Speaking, Reading, Writing. Listening and reading are receptive, speaking and writing are productive skills. All four language skills should go hand-in-hand. They should be integrated. All people understand far more than they can produce. The child has the move following order in acquiring the four skills Listening-Spcaking-Reading-Writing.
6. All learning should be functional and have meaning for the students in terms of their needs and life values. Start with their experiences.
7. Go from the known to the unknown. Build on what the students know either in their native language or in English. Compare and Contrast where possible. As a principle, try to have as meaningful language material as possible.
8. Teach only one thing at a time. Don't teach vocabulary and structure at the same time. Teach a new grammatical pattern with the known vocabulary items. While teaching new vocabulary items, use known grammatical patterns in your illustrated sentences.
9. Teach beginning (elementary) students only the forms most frequently used in normal speech. Help them realize that there may be more than one way of expressing the same ideas. But in the beginning, teach them only one form. e.g. the most commonly used request pattern is : Please open the door, Open the door please.
10. Errors will naturally occur in language learning. It is not necessary to correct every error. Be selective in error correction. Be gentle in error correction. Errors are a natural, necessary, and inevitable part of learning. Never interrupt your student while he is talking or reading for a correction. Wait until he finishes his part of talking or reading. Gentle correction should be a principle. Correct only common mistakes.
11. Recognize individual differences. All students learn at different roles. In every class there will naturally be slow, average, and bright students. Give opportunity to all the students to participate in class activities. Do not let the bright students monopolize. You can give bright students difficult tasks to keep their interest alive. To form mixed ability groups we should do anything possible not to foster the feeling of impriority.
12. Keep the pace alive. Provide a variety of activities. Class activities should not go at a monotonous rate. There will be boredom and little or no learning. The activities should go dynamically not monotonously. If the students are not interested with the activity, stop that activity.
13. Teach with examples. Examples speak louder than language explanation. Examples can help the students learn much better than complicated explanations.
14. Relate form to meaning and contextualize. All class activities should be meaningful. Meaning should always be in the foreground. Whatever activity the students are involved in, the students should be able to understand the meaning of what they hear, say, read, or write. Teach new vocabulary items or a grammatical pattern or pronunciation in context. In teaching vocabulary give the meaning and pronunciation. Smallest context is a sentence meaning arises out of the situation. We can use dialogues, anectodes in the spoken form as context.
15. Assign tasks in class. Involve the students as much as possible. A variety of tasks can be assigned in class.
16. Give students a feeling of confidence and success and encourage them. Education should be geared on success. When the grading time comes at the first semester, if there is a student on borderline, pass him.

17. Use Audio-visual aid as much as possible.
18. Teach well before you test. Students often fail because of poor teaching, poor testing, poor evaluation of the exams.

ROLE OF LISTENING

Listening is an active process that has three basic steps.

- **Hearing:** Hearing just means listening enough to catch what the speaker is saying. For example, say you were listening to a report on horses, and the speaker mentioned that no two are alike. If you can repeat the fact, then you have heard what has been said.
- **Understanding:** The next part of listening happens when you take what you have heard and understand it in your own way. Let's go back to that report on horses. When you hear that no two are alike, think about what that might mean. You might think, "Maybe this means that the colour is different for each horse."
- **Judging:** After you are sure you understand what the speaker has said, think about whether it makes sense. Do you believe what you have heard? You might think, "How could the colour to be different for every horse.

How to Become a Good Listener

- Give your full attention on the person who is speaking. Don't look out the window or at what else is going on in the room.
- Make sure your mind is focused, too. It can be easy to let your mind wander if you think you know what the person is going to say next, but you might be wrong! If you feel your mind wandering, change the position of your body and try to concentrate on the speaker's words.
- Let the speaker finish before you begin to talk. Speakers appreciate having the chance to say everything they would like to say without being interrupted. When you interrupt, it looks like you aren't listening, even if you really are.
- Let yourself finish listening before you begin to speak! You can't really listen if you are busy thinking about what you want say next.
- Listen for main ideas. The main ideas are the most important points the speaker wants to get across. They may be mentioned at the start or end of a talk, and repeated a number of times.
- Ask questions. If you are not sure you understand what the speaker has said, just ask. It is a good idea to repeat in your own words what the speaker said so that you can be sure your understanding is correct.
- Give feedback. Sit up straight and look directly at the speaker. Now and then, nod to show that you understand. At appropriate points you may also smile, frown, laugh, or be silent. These are all ways to let the speaker know that you are really listening. Remember, you listen with your face as well as your ears!

ROLE OF SPEAKING

Speaking English is the main goal of many learners. Their personalities play a large role in determining how quickly and how correctly they will accomplish this goal. Those who are risk-takers unafraid of making mistakes will generally be more talkative, but with many errors that could become hard-to-break habits. Conservative, shy students may take a long time to speak confidently, but when they do, their English often contains fewer errors and they will be proud of their English ability. It's a matter of quantity vs. quality, and neither approach is wrong. However, if the aim of speaking is communication and that does not require perfect English, then it makes sense to encourage quantity in your classroom. Break the silence and get students communicating with whatever English they can use, correct or not, and selectively address errors that block communication.

Speaking lessons often tie in pronunciation and grammar which are necessary for effective oral communication. Or a grammar or reading lesson may incorporate a speaking activity. Either way, students will need some preparation before the speaking task. This includes introducing the topic and providing a model of the speech they are to produce. A model may not apply to discussion-type activities, in which case students will need clear and specific instructions about the task to be accomplished. Then the students will practice with the actual speaking activity.

These activities may include imitating (repeating), answering verbal cues, interactive conversation, or an oral presentation. Most speaking activities inherently practice listening skills as well, such as when one student is given a simple drawing and sits behind another student, facing away. The first must give instructions to the second to reproduce the drawing. The second student asks questions to clarify unclear instructions, and neither can look at each other's page during the activity.

Some ideas to keep in mind as you plan your speaking activities.

- **Content:** As much as possible, the content should be practical and usable in real-life situations. Avoid too much new vocabulary or grammar, and focus on speaking with the language the students have.

- **Correcting Error:** You need to provide appropriate feedback and correction, but don't interrupt the flow of communication. Take notes while pairs or groups are talking and address problems to the class after the activity without embarrassing the student who made the error. You can write the error on the board and ask who can correct it.
- **Conversation Strategies:** Encourage strategies like asking for clarification, paraphrasing, gestures, and initiating ('hey,' 'so,' 'by the way').
- **Teacher Intervention:** If a speaking activity loses steam, you may need to jump into a role-play, ask more discussion questions, clarify your instructions, or stop an activity that is too difficult or boring.
- **Quantity vs. Quality:** Address both interactive fluency and accuracy, striving foremost for communication. Get to know each learner's personality and encourage the quieter ones to take more risks.

It is very important that teachers are aware if the aim of a speaking activity is fluency or accuracy, because the role of the teacher is radically different in each activity type.

In accuracy activities, the teacher needs to correct the students if they make mistakes. The whole point of the activity is to form correct sentences, so if a student gets it wrong, it needs to be immediately addressed in the form of correction.

In process oriented fluency activities, however, correcting students can be very counter productive indeed. If we want our students to communicate, we need to give them time and space to do so, in order that they can start to learn to deal with all the demands of oral interaction.

In fluency activities, the teacher becomes more of an organiser, a facilitator, a manager, a guide, a guru. The teacher sets up the activity, explains what needs to be done, organises the necessary groupings, and then lets the learners get on with it.

FUNCTIONS OF LANGUAGE

Six major functions of the English language are:

- A means of conveying information, example, "The Kyneton train is now approaching on platform 4." This example is conveying to those waiting for the Kyneton train that it has now arrived.
- An instrument of action, example, "Don't forget to feed the dog." This example is telling the second person in the conversation to do something.
- To maintain social relationships example, "Good Morning, how are you?" Here we see that this function allows us to make and keep friends. This function is usually more informal than others.
- Acting as a marker of groups example, "He was out for a duck." This example would only be heard by someone talking about the cricket, therefore establishing that the people involved in the conversation are involved with cricket in one way or another, marking them as a group.
- As an instrument of cognitive and conceptual development. This is the power of language to influence thinking. This is why we have many words that mean basically the same thing, because they all have slight differences or are used in different circumstances. For example if you could only say you were happy, but not excited, thrilled, etc, then you would not be able to give as much detail.
- As an art form, language can be purposed towards beauty for beauty's sake.

THE ROLE OF GRAMMAR IN LEARNING A LANGUAGE

One question always arise in my mind is learning grammar necessary for picking up a new language? Some linguists think grammar rules are usually considered core of any language learning class, without which a student would be completely lost. However, a language acquisition theory from Dr. Stephen Krashen, a renowned linguistics professor, suggests picking up a new language doesn't require any conscious knowledge of grammar; instead, the best and most effective methods of acquiring a new language occur through regular and useful conversation.

Dr. Krashen actually separates the way people learn languages into two separate categories: the ''acquired system'' and the ''learned system''. The acquired points to learning a new language in an almost subconscious manner, mostly through regular communication and interaction using the target language. The learned system, on the other hand, points to the traditional method of learning that many of us are used to, in which we learn conjugations, grammar rules, tenses, etc. The most important conclusion of Krashen's hypothesis, however, is that the ''acquired system'' is more effective and indeed better the ''learned system'' used by most language schools worlwide.

Language, which includes grammar, would emerge as a result of interaction and communication or that it would emerge as a result of comprehensible input. Krashen holds that given a ''natural order'' in acquistion, grammar teaching is unnecessary.

However, the acquisition of a second language is usually achieved in an acquisition—rich environment. In an acquisition—poor environment like China, there isn't much natural exposure to the target language. We cannot expect the students to achieve grammatical competence solely through interaction and communication.

In communicative language teaching, students could assimilates new structures through active practice and use. However, some also felt that ''more able and/or elder pupils wanted, and could benefit from systematic and explicit presentation of grammatical rules and explanations, and also that grammatical expositions could assist pupils in shifting from rote learning to a more creative use of the target language''. Wilkins (1976) points out that acquiring the grammatical system of the target language is of central importance, because an inadequate knowledge of grammar would severely constrain linguistic creativity and limit the capacity for communication.

CHALLENGES OF TEACHING LANGUAGE IN A DIVERSE CLASSROOM

Language Difficulty

Students in bilingual and ESL classrooms manipulate more than one language and are influenced by more than one culture. Their experiences with these languages and cultures influence their learning. The more we understand the personal, socio-cultural, and linguistic backgrounds of bilingual students, the better equipped we will be to provide these students with an effective learning environment. This environment should be one that supports learning in a second language and culture, while fostering a positive attitude and respect for the other language and culture.

The responsibility for English language learning, academic progress, and integration of bilingual and ESL learners into the school community should be assumed by *all* personnel at the school, not just by the bilingual and ESL staff. School administrators should make certain that bilingual students have opportunities to integrate both socially and academically with monolingual English speakers. The following practices promote the inclusion of all students in a supportive, educational environment:

1. Create participatory, inquiry-based classrooms
2. Maintain high expectations for all students
3. Teach ESL through content-area instruction
4. Use thematic units
5. Incorporate culturally familiar learning strategies
6. Use a variety of strategies when teaching literacy
7. Provide appropriate and valid assessment
8. Recognize that students use both languages to learn

Errors

English is such a complex language, it is fraught with traps that we all frequently fall into. With this list I hope to clear up at least a few of the confusing words we use every day. This is a list of some of the more common errors people make with English.

- **Its / It's:** As in this case, the apostrophe denotes an abbreviation: it's = it is. Its means "belongs to it". The confusion arises here because we also use an apostrophe in English to denote possession - *except* in this case; if you want to say "the cat's bag" you say "its bag" not "it's bag". "It's" always means "it is" or "it has". "It's a hot day." "it's been fun seeing you."
- **Your / You're:** Your means "belonging to you". You're means "you are". The simplest way to work out the correct one to use is to read out your sentence.
- **Practice / Practise:** In US English, practice is used as either a verb (doing word), or noun (naming word). Hence, a doctor has a practice, and a person practices the violin. In UK english, practice is a noun, and practise is a verb. A doctor has a practice, but his daughter practises the piano.
- **Bought / Brought:** Bought relates to buying something. Brought relates to bringing something. For example, I bought a bottle of wine which had been brought over from France.
- **Desert / Dessert:** This is a confusing one because in English an 's' on its own is frequently pronounced like a 'z' and two 's's are usually pronounced as an 's' (for example: prise, prissy). In this case, desert follow the rule - it means a large stretch of sand. However, dessert is pronounced "dez-urt" with the emphasis on the second syllable - i.e., something wc cat as part of our meal. To make matters worse, when a person leaves the army without permission, it is spelt desert.
- **Dryer / Drier:** If your clothes are wet, put them in a clothes dryer. That will make them drier. A hair dryer also makes hair drier.
- **Chose / Choose:** This is actually quite an easy one to remember - in English we generally pronounce 'oo' as it is written - such as "moo". The same rule applies here: choose is pronounced as it is written (with a 'z' sound for the 's') - and chose is said like "nose". Therefore, if you

had to choose to visit Timbuktu, chances are you chose to fly there. Chose is the past tense, choose is the present tense.

- **Lose / Loose:** This one is confusing. In this case, contrary to normal rules of English, the single 's' in loose is pronounced like an 's' – as in wearing trousers that are too loose. Lose on the other hand, relates to loss – for example: "I hope we don't lose this game". A good way to remember this is that in the word "lose" you have lost the second 'o' from loose. If you can't remember a rule that simple, you are a loser!
- **Literally:** This one is not only often used in error, it is incredibly annoying when it is used in the wrong way. Literally means "it really happened" – therefore, unless you live on a parallel universe with different rules of physics, you can not say "he literally flew out the door".
- **Disorders:** Children who have a condition of incomplete or less than normal mental development so that they are unable to adjust to day to day living in a normally efficient, useful, productive and harmonious manner are called mentally retarded. They are, hence, in constant need or care, protection, supervision and help.

Thus, mental retardation is a serious disability. It creates a lot of learning problems before mentally retarded children. These learning problems create obstacle in other areas of life as well. Thus, total life activities are affected by mental retardation.

General Characteristics of Mentally Retarded

On the basis of the definitions given above following common characteristics of mentally retarded children (less than 18 years of age) can be derived:

1. **Limited functioning:** Their level of functioning is very limited. They have difficulty not only in learning but also doing routine life job due to significant loss of conceptual, practical and social intelligence.
2. **Sub average intellectual functioning:** Their intellectual functioning is less than average (below 80 IQ) on an intelligence test. This is the fundamental criterion of diagnosing a mentally retarded child.
3. **Poor performance level:** If someone falls short in his performance of certain tasks from the performance of the majority of children of his own age, he is said to have low mental age or sub-normal intellectual functioning. For example, If eight years old child performs equal to the child of 6 years, his IQ will be (Mental Age/ Chronological age × 100) or (6/8) × 100 = 75.
4. **Slow acquisition of skills:** Academic (content related) and non academic (action related) both types of skills are acquired by them at a very slow rate.
5. **Low level of adaptive skills:** They are not only slow in acquiring skills but they are always poor in adaptive skills also.
6. **Early manifestations:** Mental retardation manifests itself before the age of 18. From this perspective, mental retardation is viewed as a disorder of the life period characterized by the slow rate of development.

Identification (Diagnosis) of Mental Retardation

For early detection of mental retardation of a child, the parents and the teacher refer the cases to child guidance centres so that their mental level may be ascertained and they may be classified for the purpose of placement (education and training).

Following symptoms will help the teacher and the parents to decide whether the child should be sent to child study centres for screening or not. Screening test results must be interpreted and matched in terms of following clinical diagnostic symptoms.

1. **Social adjustment criterion:** If a person is functioning adequately in all socio-economic conditions as compared to his peers or age mates, there is no need of sending the person to child guidance centres (CGC) for proper screening. Mentally retarded person will surely exhibit adjustment problem in social situations.
2. **Learning ability criterion:** Failure in educational endeavours or low level of general aptitude is another criterion of mental retardation but effects of socio-economic and physical factors should also be taken into account because poor academic achievement is caused due to these factors also.
3. **Development criterion:** The developmental history of the suspected child should also be taken into account, e.g., when the child began to sit, crawl, stand, walk and talk, whether it is normal or not. Delayed development is generally seen in mentally retarded children so, retardation in these areas is certainly helpful in diagnosing the child.
4. **Academic achievement criterion:** These children are generally very slow in academic achievement due to low level of retention power

and understanding ability. When they constantly perform poorly in content related skills despite repeated remedial measures adopted by the teachers, they are suspected to be mentally retarded.

5. **Size of the family criterion:** Larger the size of the family, lower will be the IQ scores of the family. Hence, it should also be taken into consideration while taking a decision of M.R.
6. **Medical examination:** It is generally done by experts in the field in CGCs.

   Important physical symptoms of mentally retarded children are given below:

   I. He has lips fairly apart with his tongue visible in between the teeth with saliva.

   II. He has a vacant look and a clumsy gait.

   III. He has flattered skull, stanting eyes and broad nose.

   IV. He has unusually large heads.
7. **Proper screening:** After identifying all the above symptoms, suspected mentally retarded children are properly screened by using different tests.

   The description of some of these tests are given below:

   (*a*) **Siguin Form Board Test:** This form board test was developed by Seguin a French physician in 1907 to identify and screen mentally retarded children. Here ten boards of different sizes are kept in different shelves of respective sizes in a tray. These boards are taken out of the tray at the time of testing. Then testee is asked to put these boards in the tray again in the same sequence as it was before in as less time as possible. This process is repeated three times and least time taking effort is taken for the purpose of scoring.

   (*b*) **Developmental Screening Test:** This test is used to measure the mental development of children from the age of 3 months to 15 years.

   Here different types of activities are given to children according to their ages to do. Mental development of the child is calculated on the basis of performance on these activities. Children and their parents and relatives are also interviewed here to gather some more informations about the child.

   (*c*) **General Mental Ability Test:** This test was developed by RP Srivastava and Kiran Saxena in 1985. Verbal and non-verbal both types of items have been included here. Both these sections have 50 items each. These sections have further been divided into five sub sections namely, analogy, classification, number series, reasoning problems and absurdities. Each item has four multiple choice responses out of which only one option is correct.

   Time allotted for verbal and non-verbal items is 15 minutes and 10 minutes respectively. One mark is given for every correct response and thus a child can score maximum 100 marks. This test can be administered in individual and group situations both.

Purpose of Diagnosing Mental Retardation

Diagnosis of mental retardation serves the following purposes:

1. It provides an estimate of the individual's present level of functioning in terms of the test performance, social adjustment and so on.
2. It provides information regarding the cause of the individual's inadequacies.
3. It helps us to provide them proper care and treatment.
4. It provides some predictions of the probable outcomes in future.
5. It helps us to take decision regarding their placement in proper special educational programmes.

Mental Retardation and Age

Incidence of mental retardation rises with the increasing age, reaches at its peak at about 14-18 years and then drops off sharply.

Causes of Mental Retardation

Underlying causes of mental retardation can be divided into two categories:

(A) Endogenous causes

(B) Exogenous causes

(A) Endogenous causes

Endogenous literally means originating within the body of the organism, and should refer to those forms of mental retardation that are genetically determined. Heredity is the primary casual factor here. Important genetic factors active to cause mental retardation are given below :

1. **Action of dominant gene** : The transmission of defective dominant gene from one generation to the next is very rare but in some cases some of these conditions may occur in mild form in one generation or in certain members of the family

of that generation and in more severe form in another generation or in other members of the same family.

2. **Action of recessive gene** : Such defective children typically come of normal parents. This defect occurs due to child's receiving two similar recessive genes one from each parent.

(B) Exogenous causes

They are also known as secondary, acquired or environmental causes. Some of these causes of mental retardation are given below :

(*a*) **Prenatal causes:** They work before the birth of the child, and are related to pregnant mothers. Important prenatal causes of mental retardation are as follows:

1. **Physical trauma:** Unsuccessful attempt at trauma and accident to pregnant mother so injure the fetus as to lower the child's mental level.
2. **Nutrition:** Malnutrition during the period of pregnancy may lower mental level of the child.
3. **Infectious diseases:** Infectious diseases of the mother during pregnancy may affect physical and mental development of the fetus and lower mental ability of the child.
4. **Blood incompatibility:** Incompatibility between maternal and fetal blood may cause the child severely jaundiced and mental deficiency is a possible accompaniment.
5. **Radioactivity:** Radiation may affect the germ cells in three ways.
   - They may be killed.
   - Their chromosomes maybe broken up.
   - They may be mutated.

   All these changes may lower mental ability of the child.
6. **Toxic agents:** Toxins such as lead, nicotine, and morphine affect the developing embryo and lower the mental level of off springs.
7. **Consumption of drugs and alcohols:** Consumption of wine, LSD, heroine etc., by the mother during pregnancy is also very fatal for the fetus development and it may cause permanent mental retardation of the child after birth.

(*b*) **Perinatal (natal) causes:** These causes are associated with the delivery of the child. Important likely causes of mental retardation are as follows:

1. **Pre-mature-birth:** Studies have shown that a large number of people born pre-maturely are mentally retarded. The brain structure of the premature infant is more fragile and thus it can be very easily damaged.
2. **Traumatic Birth injuries:** It is estimated that birth injuries are responsible for 1.5% of the total mental retardation in western countries.
3. **Delivery Complications:** If complications have emerged during the period of delivery, it may cause mental retardation to some extent.

(*c*) **Post-natal causes:** Important post natal causes of mental retardation are given below :

1. **Brain injury:** Traumatic brain injury from gun shot, wounds or fall is a rare cause of mental retardation.
2. **Infections:** Brain infection causes permanent brain damage or mental retardation. They include encephalitis of various types, meningitis, hydrocephally and the like infections.
3. **Severe malnutrition:** Deficiency in any particular nutrient like vitamins or minerals causes deficiency diseases which may cause mental retardation in the long run.
4. **General health:** Mental and physical health are most of the time found associated though mental retardation due to poor physical health is not permanent. Heavy mental shock may also cause mental deficiency temporarily. However, good physical health does not necessarily mean good mental health.
5. **Cultural factors:** Low IQ does not always mean low level of intelligence. It is because intellectual level is influenced by the child's cultural background. If an intelligence test includes items representing a particular culture, children alien to that culture are not supposed to perform well on this test of intelligence and hence their IQ level will be low.
6. **Home and family background:** It also affects mental level and intellectual power but so far as mental retardation is concerned, its role is very limited.
7. **Social deprivation:** When a child is deprived of social environment for a very long period of time he is likely to become mentally retarded.

Methods of Identification of Mentally Retarded Children

Different criteria are used to classify mentally retarded into different categories. These criteria are given below:

1. **Normal distribution criterion:** In a normally distributed population, mentally retarded population

is found beyond 2SD from the mean, i.e., about 2% of the population is generally found mentally retarded. If this population is tested on intelligence test, their IQ will be less than 90.

2. **IQ criterion:** American Association of Mental Deficiency has classified mentally retarded children on the basis of their IQ scores. Several other educationists have also classified them on this basis. Four broad categories of mentally retarded children are given below:
   (*a*) Border line cases or dullers : (IQ = 70-90)
   (*b*) Morons or feeble minded (IQ = 50-70)
   (*c*) Imbeciles (IQ = 25-50)
   (*d*) Idiots (IQ less than 25)

3. **Medical criterion:** Medical personnel and physician classify mentally retarded children on the basis of their physical/mental characteristics caused by a damage in the functioning of the brain due to genetic or environmental reasons. Some of these categories are given below:
   (*a*) Brain damaged child: It is a type of organic malfunctioning in the body which is caused by any serious disease or damage of the brain.
   (*b*) Mongoloids: These slow learners are very peculiar in the physical characteristics and behaviour such as they are very humble and friendly, they are very poor in taking initiative, they are obstinate in behaviour and they are so simpleton in their behaviour that we call them as cow of the God. Mongols are moderately mentally retarded whose IQ ranges 50-70.
   (*c*) Cretin child: Mental retardation in these children are caused due to any deformation in thyroid gland. They can be cured by the physician by correcting thyroid gland provided that they are identified in the early stage. They are similar to monogoloids in behaviour and characteristics.
   (*d*) Phenylketonurin (PKU): This problem is caused due to metabolic disturbances but its incidence is very rare. When body fails to metabolise phelinylenin protein, a toxic material reaches the brain and enters it through blood circulation and brain cells are damaged resulting in mental retardation.
   (*e*) Microcephally and hydrocephally: The head becomes short in microcephally and large in hydrocephally, as a result cerebro spinal fluid which is responsible for mental action stops causing mental retardation permanently.
   (*f*) Cerebral palsy: It is a type of disease which causes uncontrolled action of some muscles and mental retardation is caused due to inadjustability of muscles.

4. **Social deprivation criteria:** Mental retardation is also caused when a person is deprived of social environment and interaction for a long period of time. When these children comes to the environment they fail to adjust there which again increases their mental retardation.

LANGUAGE SKILLS

There are, in general, four language skills, each based upon the modality of emphasis. These are the Listening, Speaking, Reading, and Writing skills.

Listening Skill

Listening in English is attending to and interpreting oral English. Listening is necessary to develop the speaking skill. The student listens to oral speech in English, then separates into segments the stretch of utterances he hears, groups them into words, phrases, and sentences, and, finally, he understands the message these carry. Listening prepares the students to understand the speech of the native speakers of English as they speak naturally in a normal speed and normal manner.

There are three approaches to listening: interactive (listening to a message and doing something as a consequence) and one-way communication or non-interactive (just listening and retaining the message, in activities such as conversations overheard, public address announcements, recorded messages, etc.) and self-talk. Listening to radio and watching TV and films, public performances, lectures, religious services, etc., generally reflect non-interactive listening. Responding to the commands given reflects interactive listening, which, in fact, is equally widespread in communicative situations. Self-talk is also an important process by which internal thinking and reasoning is carried out.

Role of Listening: In the classroom, students listen in order to repeat and to understand. In listening to repeat, students imitate and memorize linguistic items such as words, idioms, and sentence patterns. This is an important beginning task and focus of listening exercises. However, it is listening to understand that is real listening in its own right.

Students listen to understand as part of using English for communication purposes. In listening to understand, students may be involved in the question-oriented response model of learning or in the task-oriented model of learning. In the question-oriented response model, students may be asked to listen to a sentence, a dialogue, a conversation, a passage, or a lecture and asked to answer questions which may be presented in the form of true/false statements, multiple choice questions, fill in the blank, or short answers. In the task-oriented response model, students may be asked to listen to a passage and accomplish the task described in the passage through interaction with others or by themselves.

Listening Comprehension: The listening skill is the most neglected one, both in first and second language teaching. Teachers tend to focus on the rudimentary elements of listening briefly, and pass over to other aspects of language teaching. Discrimination of sounds and intonations often form the major part of listening practice in the classroom. Listening for content is often assumed. In reality, the listening skill is fundamental to the entire process of mastering and using a language, whether first or second or foreign.

In the past, listening was labeled as a passive skill, along with reading. No doubt, it is a receptive skill like reading. Speaking and writing were considered to be productive skills, but also active skills. While this categorization is somewhat justifiable because the focus of listening is on reception of information, listening itself cannot be fully and correctly characterized only as a passive skill.

There is a need for an active involvement of the self for the efficient performance of listening. The listener is often forced into guessing an approximation to what the speaker is communicating. The listener expects and anticipates what may be the form and content of the immediate message being delivered. He actively avoids the redundancies in the process of listening, focuses himself on the relevant, interesting and/or crucial points, and engages himself in some critical analysis of content. Listening becomes the stepping stone for action. In view of all these and other activities that are involved in listening, we should consider listening as an active skill demanding active participation of the listener.

In essence, listening is not mere recognition of linguistic units and their meanings. It comprises an ability to predict information based on linguistic context, and the situation and topic of the message conveyed by the linguistic code, as well as the expectations about the world. Listening helps also to understand and act according to the emotional state of the speaker.

No one should think that listening comprehension exercises are miniature tests. These generally come in the form of questions to be answered, action to be performed, or objects to be identified, etc. Because this format demands response in the form in which tests are generally prepared and presented, we tend to treat the exercise as a test. Consider listening comprehension only as practice and look for progress in student performance.

Brief listening comprehension exercises with content interesting to the student and which focus upon and incorporate his communicative needs will develop his listening comprehension to a satisfactory level. Students need to be attentive to the tone of the conversation, and should ask questions whenever they find it difficult to understand the conversation.

What is the generally followed form of listening comprehension exercises? Students are given a specific task such as answering questions or solving problems. They listen to the teacher or the recorded material and perform the task asked for. Thus the teacher as well as materials on tape/cassette recorders become the major means to train the students in listening comprehension.

Speaking Skill

Imitation and repetition are important elementary steps in developing speaking skill in English. Imitation and repetition are inter-related, and yet they are distinct.

Imitation helps students to pronounce and produce the English utterance they hear from the teacher as closely as possible to the utterance produced by her. Imitation is not restricted to mere production of the sounds, phrases, and sentences. It includes also the capacity to produce the utterances in the contexts in which the original utterances were produced.

Some of the imitation and repetition exercises may be organized in the following manner: Present some simple sentence, phrase, or word and ask students to repeat after you. If you want them to understand and repeat a conversation, say the questions and the answers and have the students repeat the latter, or perhaps both, signaling the meaning in some way. The meaning can be demonstrated with realia (real objects brought into the classroom), pictures, gestures, or translating.

The teacher may use pictures, gestures, pantomime, translation, guessing, and drawing on the board to make the students understand the meaning. It is important that you use only meaningful words, phrases, and sentences for imitation and repetition. The props you use to explain or demonstrate the meaning should enable the student to learn the meaning with ease, along with the pronunciation.

Substitution of a word, phrase, or sentence by another is an elementary method which helps students to produce new utterances and to develop speaking skill.

Expressions of greeting, gratitude, small talk, introductions and making acquaintance, leave-taking, appreciation, expressions of regret and asking to be excused, etc., are very important communicative acts students need to master. For one thing, such expressions may take on different form and import in English than the ones students are accustomed to in their language and culture.

Simple question-answer dialogues around a given context and object/objects is another elementary method to develop speaking skill in students.

How does a teacher teach a dialogue? There are three types of drills one could use in the class: **choral drill** in which the entire class participates in one voice with the teacher modelling the utterance; **chain drill** in which one student asks the question and another answers, and in this way the entire class participates as a chain; and **individual drill** in which individual students are pointed out and asked to produce the utterance modelled by the teacher.

Eliciting is an important process which teachers must employ to get the class involved in what is going on in the class. For speaking practice eliciting is highly essential. It helps students to focus their attention, to think, and to use what they already know. It helps teachers to assess what the class already knew.

Translation is another helpful device to encourage students to speak in English. The students may be given some sentences in their own native language and asked to translate them and use these to answer or ask questions. There are several other ways of using translation as a tool to develop speaking skill.

Reading Skill

Scholors classify reading into three kinds: extensive reading, intensive reading, and oral reading. Extensive reading is used "to refer to the teaching of reading through reading. In this approach, there is no overt focus on teaching reading. Rather, it is assumed that the best way for students to learn to read is by reading a great deal of comprehensible material." Intensive reading is used to refer to the actual teaching skills in an instructional setting. Students are exposed to a variety of materials and asked to perform activities such as answering comprehension questions on the passage read. They may be trained to look for critical information in the passage they read, and make inferences, etc. Intensive reading is instruction-based and forms the core of teaching reading in the classroom. Oral reading does attract much attention from many teachers, but it is "an integral part of of reading.

At the beginning level, the focus is on the mechanics of reading. The beginner needs to be taught the relationship and the correspondence between the letters of the alphabet and the spoken language.

In a sense, the letters are all abstract symbols. The letter functions as a tag to the sounds it represents. By seeing (reading) the letter, the beginner identifies the appropriate sound value for that letter in that context.

This is not an easy task even for the adult learner. It is possible that the learner may come from a language in which the Roman alphabet similar to the one used in English is being used. And yet the sound values of letters in his language may vary context to context in his language also, which in their turn may be in conflict with the sound values of the letters as used in English.

Or, the learner may come from a language background in which syllabaries are used. That is, he may be accustomed to reading the syllables which more or less retain the same values wherever they are used. However, he will find that in character and chat, cha needs to be read differently.

Or, he may come from a language background where pictograms are used, as in Chinese in which there is no easy and manifest correspondence between the "letter" and the sound.

Keep the following in mind when you begin teaching reading at the beginner's level.

1. The background of the beginner: a child, an illiterate, a moderately educated person.
2. The Reading task involves decoding the system of abstract symbols to discover its relation to the spoken language system.
3. The time taken to master this relationship varies with age, maturation, previous experience, and other social factors.
4. With primary emphasis on mechanics one may master the mechanics of reading in four months.
5. Some recognition problems in English: capital, small, italics, handwriting, left to right, distinction between letters, mirror image problems.
6. Choose the words which express familiar meanings or meanings which can be recognized and retained in memory.
7. Choose only those words which focus on the item to be learned.
8. Do not choose those words which may have the same spelling in English as well as in the learner's language, but are read (pronounced) differently.
9. Do not ignore the stress.

Writing Skill

Writing is an individual effort. Individuals compose their thoughts often in privacy and then reduce their thoughts to writing, using the strict conventions followed in the language. Writing is an individual effort or work, but it must follow the rules laid down. The development of writing even in native English speaking children is conscious and is thus non-spontaneous.

In writing, the discrete nature of linguistic signs should be appreciated consciously. The learner must recognize the sound structure of each word, dissect it and reproduce it in alphabetical symbols, which he must have studied and memorized before. This same deliberate preparedness is needed to put words in a certain sequence to form a sentence.

"Writing is more an individual effort than speaking, while at the same time more rule-bound and therefore more error-prone... The speaker does not have to pronounce each word exactly according to one standard of pronunciation or one model of structure, while the writer is expected to produce according to one model of spelling, and usually a reduced range of structures, with 100 percent accuracy".

The writing classes have the potential to help consolidate and improve the students' speaking and reading skills. However, it is important for us to remember that writing is an important skill which can be taught as an end in itself, although none of the language skills is far removed from the other language skills. Focusing on writing as an independent skill helps us to identify the specific problems faced by the learners, and to identify the specific needs of the learners relating to writing. Mechanics of writing are distinct from the mechanics of other skills such as speaking and reading. While reading involves seeing and pronouncing, writing involves association of sounds with mental composition of thoughts and their orderly presentation, and hand movements.

Raimes classifies approaches to teaching writing into five types: controlled to free, free writing, paragraph pattern, grammar-syntax-organization, communicative, and process approaches. In the controlled to free approach, "students are first given sentence exercises, then paragraphs to copy or manipulate grammatically by, for instance, changing questions to statements, present to past, or plural to singular. They might also change words or clauses or combine sentences" (Raimes 1983).

In the free writing approach, students are asked to "write freely on any topic without worrying about grammar and spelling for five or ten minutes. . . . The teachers do not correct these short pieces of free writing; they simply read them and perhaps comment on the ideas the writer expressed" (Raimes 1983). In the paragraph pattern approach, "students copy paragraphs, analyze the form of model paragraphs, and imitate model passages. They put scrambled sentences into paragraph order, they identify general specific statements, they choose or invent an appropriate topic sentence, they insert or delete sentences" (Raimes 1983). In the communicative approach to writing, students are asked to assume the role of a writer who is writing for an audience to read. Whatever is written by a student is modified in some way by other students for better communicative effect. In the process approach to writing, students "move away from a concentration on the written product to an emphasis on the process of writing" (Raimes 1983).

Note that a proper blend of these approaches to writing will give us best results. For example, the controlled to free approach to writing helps us to focus on proper mechanics in the beginning level, whereas communicative approach to writing will be very effective once our students have some control over the mechanics and have acquired a good number of words and sentence structures to help them match these with their thoughts. All successful texts and teachers have always tried to take the best and relevant aspects of every method to suit the learner's level and need.

EVALUATING LANGUAGE COMPREHENSION

Meaning of Evaluation

Evaluation is the criteria of success or failure of a task done. If it is done at the end of a task, total efforts, including the investment of time and money may be a failure but if it goes side by side of the task, immediate feedback received might alarm the performer to rectify his mistakes and thus there is 100% chance of success of the programme.

Education is also an investment in the sense that time, energy and money are spent to bring about behavioural change in learners. That is why when a teacher performs his teaching works in his class, he also simultaneously finds out whether the changes in behaviour of learners are in concurrence with the learning objectives or not. If it is not so there, then what types of modifications are needed and at what steps of teaching. He also finds out whether the problem lies in his teaching strategies or techniques or it is there in the students itself. Thus, teaching and evaluation run-hand in hand. Evaluation determines the behaviour of students on one hand and testifies to the teaching of the teacher on the other. This very purposeful behaviour of the teacher is called evaluation in education.

Characteristics of Evaluation

On the basis of the definitions given above, the following characteristics of evaluation can be derived.

1. **A Comprehensive Process:** All the three domains of human behaviour, cognitive, affective and psychomotor, can be accurately measured by

evaluation. Apart from student's behaviour, teacher's behaviour (his task of teaching) is also evaluated.

2. **A Systematic Process:** Evaluation is a preplanned and systematic process which goes ahead keeping in view the pre-determined objectives. By this process we find out how much change has occurred in the behaviour of students and teachers and how much change is yet to be brought about by the task ahead.
3. **A Continuous Process:** Evaluation process can not be separated from teaching and both go side by side. By this process whatever changes take place in the behaviour of learners, its proper record is maintained and on this very base students are either ranked in a particular class or decision is taken to promote them to the next higher class.
4. **A Social Process:** Education is a purposeful activity fulfilling the requirements of learners and the society. Evaluation tells us to what extent teaching is fulfilling the requirements of both.
5. **An Information Collection Process:** When students progress step by step in the school system, all the informations regarding their progress are gathered by using a number of tests and by going through various techniques of measurement. After that these informations are interpreted in terms of predetermined objectives.
6. **A Combined Process:** While taking the final decision regarding a student and declaring him fail or pass, the reports of all the concerned teachers of school are taken into account. No such decision is taken by the evaluation report of one or two teachers. Thus, evaluation becomes a comprehensive process.
7. **A Process of Value Judgement:** Scoring 60 or 70 percent in any subject by any of the students in a class does not have any meaning unless the scores of the student is compared either with other students of his own class or it is presented with reference to any outside criterion. When it is done and stated that student has secured first division by scoring 60% or more marks or his rank is third or tenth in his class it becomes evaluation. Thus, evaluation is a value judgement process and tells how far a student is away from his destination.
8. **Evaluation includes Measurement:** Evaluation actually starts from some sorts of measurement then symbols are assigned to students by comparing the performance with cultural or scientific standard. It shows that evaluation reports may vary from culture to culture.

Purpose of Evaluation

Evaluation has following purposes to serve:

1. **Giving Details of Students' Progress:** Evaluation tells where a student is standing on the way to his destination of learning, how much he is ahead or behind his classmates, to what extent the behavioural changes occurred in him are acceptable, how far he can apply his present acquired knowledge to his future life or learning situations, at what point he is facing any difficulty and why and so on. Thus, evaluation here works like the diagnostic function of measurement.
2. **Predicting Future Achievement:** When evaluation covers the aptitude aspect of behaviour, it can predict the future performance of a student or a teacher on the basis of his present performance.
3. **Guidance and Motivation:** When a student comes to know about the actual position of his achievement, he gets motivated to do better. Besides, strengths and weaknesses of students become manifest through evaluation and a teacher can guide them accordingly.
4. **Improvement in the System:** Once proper guidance is given to students by the teacher after evaluation, teaching-learning process gets improved. A teacher can also come to know his own strength and weakness by the process and can change his own behaviour accordingly. Once he gets acquainted with his own shortcomings, he can remove them. Thus, process of evaluation is concerned with inputs and output both.
5. **Discovery of Effective Teaching Strategies:** Evaluation opens the new avenues of action researches in the class. When a teacher does not get the desired result by adopting a particular combination of teaching strategies, he adopts another combination and this process continues until a final effective combination of teaching strategies is discovered.
6. **Classification of Students:** By evaluation process we can classify students into different groups like talented, bright, average, slow learners and poor and adopt different strategies of teaching for different groups. We can also give remedial treatment to weak students in the class only after thorough evaluation of them.
7. **Providing Feedback to Students and Teachers Both:** When a teacher comes to know the results of his efforts he gets feedback. If result is good, he is motivated if result is not satisfactory, feedback pushes him to change his behaviour. Similarly, knowledge of progress and the feedback received thereof motivate the students also.

Steps in Evaluation

An evaluation is comprised of the following steps to be followed in order :

1. **Identification of Objectives:** First of all, a teacher decides which domain of behaviour of a student and upto which level he has to cover by his tests and what advantages he wants to gain by these tests.
2. **Matching the Objectives with the Content:** After identification of objectives a teacher matches the objectives with the subject-matter that he has to teach in the class. He also determines the level of teaching accordingly.
3. **Writing Objectives in Terms of Behavioural Change of Learners:** In the third step objectives are written in such a language which is clear and represent the change of students' behaviour.
4. **Taking the Students to the Environment of Testing:** Teacher takes the students from teaching environment to the testing one very smoothly so that students express their behaviour freely.
5. **Selection of Tools and Techniques:** At this step the teacher decides whether the test will be written, oral or practical and if written test is to be administered, it will be objective or subjective.
6. **Construction of the Test:** Here teacher constructs the test keeping in view the objectives already determined by matching them with the content.
7. **Administration of the Test:** Students are given the test constructed by the teacher and they take the test in stipulated time.
8. **Scoring:** Whatever changes have occurred in the behaviour of students are converted into numerals or grade by scoring.
9. **Interpretation of Result:** At this stage the marks obtained by the students are analysed by the teacher in order to see whether the changes in behaviour are in accordance with the objectives or not.
10. **Value Judgement:** At this step, teacher compares the behaviour of students with any internal norm or outside criteria in order to give it a value judgement, i.e., upto what level the achievement of students is satisfactory, average, excellent or poor.
11. **Feedback:** After preparing the result, it is sent to students and their guardians in order to give them feedback. Teachers also get feedback by the results and they come to know the strengths and weaknesses of their teaching.

Techniques of Evaluation

Evaluation is broader concept than measurement but no exact evaluation is possible without going through the process of measurement. All the three domains of behaviour are covered by evaluation, e.g.,

1. **Cognitive Domain:** Oral, written, essay type, objective type tests, practical examinations and observation techniques etc. are used for evaluating cognitive domain.
2. **Affective Domain:** This domain is evaluated by interest inventory, attitude scale, check list, rating scales and observation techniques.
3. **Psychomotor Domain:** Performance tests, practical examinations and observation techniques are used to evaluate this domain.

There are basically two techniques of evaluation:

A. **Quantitative:** These techniques are highly reliable and valid. Important such techniques are as follows:

1. **Oral:** These techniques are basically used at lower grades of teaching. At higher level of education too viva voce is used to test the lower levels of cognitive behaviour. Debates or drama can also be used for this purpose.
2. **Written:** Objective type tests, essay type tests and short answer questions are important written techniques to evaluate cognitive achievement of students. They give more accurate results than oral tests.
3. **Performance Tests:** Here some works are assigned to students to accomplish them. Students practically do these works and then output is evaluated.

B. **Qualitative:** These techniques evaluate the quality of attributes and hence they are highly subjective. Important such techniques are given below:

1. **Cumulative Records:** Such records are prepared by the school to show all-round development of students individually. They reflect the total personality of the child, i.e., marks obtained by students in sessional tests and examinations, their participation in games, sports cultural programmes and other co-curricular activities, their regularity, punctuality, their etiquette.
2. **Anecdotal Records:** These records maintain the description of significant events or works of students. Here informations regarding the behaviour, attitudes or interests of students are systematically cumulated.

3. **Observation:** This is the most common technique of qualitative assessment of students. It is mostly used at lower grades of education. This is the only technique for the evaluation of classroom interaction.
4. **Check List:** This technique is used for evaluating attitude and affective domain of students. Here questions are given to students and they are asked to answer them in yes or no, e.g.,

   Item : 'Do you like doing mathematical sums-Yes/No.'
5. **Rating Scales:** Here some statements are given to students and agreed, indifferent or disagreed are written before the statements. Then students are asked to tick the option according to their own choice.

Types of Evaluation

1. Formative Evaluation: The purpose of formative evaluation is to monitor instructional process to know whether learning is taking place or not. It is designed to enhance and improve teaching-learning process and thus it becomes a continuous process in the school system.

These tests diagnose the weaknesses of students as well as teachers and thus, both of them can get feedback from these tests. Students and teachers both after identifying their difficulties change their behaviour and remove these difficulties. Thus, function of this evaluation is remedial in nature.

The second function of this evaluation is that if evaluation finds teaching-learning process satisfactory, it motivates the teachers and students to work harder for better results.

Tanner (1972) has defined formative evaluation in the following words :

"Formative evaluation refers to the use of tests and other evaluative procedures while the course and instructional programme is in progress."

Both criterion referenced and norm referenced tests are used to take the students to the mastery of the content. These tests are given in the following stages of learning.

(*i*) At the end of each unit of the lesson.

(*ii*) At the end of each whole lesson.

(*iii*) At the end of each unit of the total course.

Advantages of Formative evaluation :

(*i*) It provides sufficient information to teachers for modifying teaching.

(*ii*) It helps in formulating individual and group remedial programmes.

(*iii*) It provides feedback to students as well as teachers.

(*iv*) It facilitates retention and transfer of training.

(*v*) It enables the teacher to readjust his teaching according to the needs of the students.

(*vi*) Students can also modify their behaviour after getting feedback from this evaluation.

(*vii*) It gives reinforcement to high achievers.

(*viii*) It can work as a self-evaluation device for learners.

2. Summative Evaluation: This evaluation takes place at the end of the session to measure over all achievement of pupils. Annual, internal or external examinations are the examples of summative evaluation. The purpose of this evaluation is to certify fail or pass of the product. If formative evaluation is related to the process of teaching, it is related to the product of teaching. Here students are evaluated from the whole syllabus. On the basis of this evaluation, a decision is taken whether a student should be promoted to the next class or he should be kept in the same class again.

On the basis of above discussions we can say that summative evaluation works as a complement to formative evaluation and both of them combined together are necessary for all educational system.

TEACHING LEARNING MATERIALS

Text Book

Text book is the area in which the language material is presented prescribed for teaching and learning English.

Characteristics of Good Text Books

A good text books not only teaches but it also tests. A few essential characteristics of good text books are given below:

(*i*) The size of text book should be handy for the students.

(*ii*) The binding should be proper and strong.

(*iii*) The subject matter should be printed on good quality paper.

(*iv*) Heading and subheading should be printed on title page in bold form.

(*v*) Illustration should be attractive. For every young pupil, the picture should be well drawn and realistically coloured and not in black and white.

(*vi*) Clear and unambiguous instruction should be given along side the test and practice and exercise.

(*vii*) The introduction at the beginning and conclusion at the end of the chapter should be given in the text book.

(*viii*) The words and structure are carefully graded.

(*ix*) No difficult words and new words are given in good text book.

(*x*) The words and structure already learnt are repeated in the coming pages so that the students could revise them making them stable in their memory.

(*xi*) The subject matter of text book should provide new information so that students could get new knowledge.

(*xii*) There should be both practice and text exercise at the end of the chapter.

(*xiii*) The practice should be low which the majority of students could solve them easily.

Chalkboard

It is the closest friend of a teacher in the class and about 50% teaching task is completed with the help of the blackboard. Advantages of using a chalkboard in the class are as follows :

(*i*) It is a cheap material aid which does not cost much on its maintenance.

(*ii*) When a teacher writes important points of the lesson on the chalkboard along with his oral teaching and lectures, aural and visual both the senses of students work simultaneously. It increases learning many times.

(*iii*) Writing meaning of difficult words, drawing graphs or diagrams, solving the sums of mathematics, preparing the summary of the lesson, all these works can be done on the chalkboard and they help the students understand the facts, events or terminologies.

(*iv*) Blackboard works as a model for students. This can help the students mend their ways if they imitate the model.

Models

Models are the reflection or copy of the real objects. They are used in the class to clarify the concepts when either real objects are not available or it is not possible to bring real objects to the class. They are also the abbreviated version of real objects. Elephants, lions or other animals or birds can not be brought to the class, hence, it is better to use the models of these objects. Globe is the best example of model to be used in the class.

Through models knowledge of all types of historical, geographical and scientific facts and concepts can be given to students. Models are especially useful for teaching visually handicapped children who perceive the objects by touch. Since, clear dimensions of length, breadth and height are given in the model in a proportionate manner, they are more useful for concept formation than pictures.

How to use models

(*i*) Scale should be used for showing size, shape or structure of the real objects. Apart from this, teacher should also clarify the real shape, size or structure of the real object.

(*ii*) Students should be given opportunity to have a critical view on the model and their views on it.

(*iii*) All students should be given chance to have a close look at the model in the class.

(*iv*) Models should have direct relevance to the lesson and they should develop scientific temperament among learners.

(*v*) Models should be properly explained in the class in order to make the use of models effective.

Pictures

Pictures are used in the class as material aids when neither real objects nor models can be arranged. They are cheap and easily available in the market, therefore, a teacher should not be miserly in using them. Pictures are actually the outlines of the real objects and when they are shown in the class, they give clear concepts about the colour, physique, shape and size of the real objects. Attention of students can easily be drawn to the lesson through them. If pictures related to the lesson are not available in the market, the teacher should sketch them by using pencils and water colours. Pictures are used as material aids for teaching all the school subjects.

Diagrams

They are another option and used when even pictures can not be arranged. They can also clarify the concepts like models or pictures but at a lesser degree. Diagrams are drawn on the chalkboard by using coloured chalks and then students copy it on their notebooks. The biggest advantage of this material aid is that teacher need not spend even a single pic in using this material aid.

They help in clarifying the concepts, laws and principles of science and social sciences. Their role in teaching languages is very limited.

Graphs

Graphs are especially used in history, geography, science and mathematics. They help the teacher and the students to study, analyse and compare the data, facts or events. Whenever action research is made by a teacher in the class, graphs are used to show the data.

Maps

Maps are the flat representation of the surface of the earth on a paper where many informations are presented through lines, symbols dots, points or letters. They have special significance in teaching history and geography. We can also get information about the size and physical features of a country, state or continent through these maps and distance between different parts of the country or the world can also be read from them. Though printed maps of all states or countries are available in the market yet a teacher draws them also on roler boards. This will enable the students to draw such maps themselves.

Slide Projector

Simple 'slide projector' was known as "magic lantern" in the olden days. The principle here is that when we put the transparent slide on the socket and throw light from behind, the light passes through it and projects the image on the screen.

A slide projector typically consists of a quart, three halogen lamps, light to be reflected by the reflector, a heat filter and lastly, condenser lenses. The heat filter is a thermo crystal which absorbs most of the heat produced by three lamps. A cooling system is also needed which consists of a fan for convecting off the heat, filter and other components. The fan is thermostatically controlled. When projector is switched off, the fan is also switched off.

Classroom uses of the Slide Projector : Slides are prepared for selected topics and the informations contained by them may be in the form of written words, pictures, graphs, sketches, etc. The topic selected should be arranged frame by frame. The ideal ratio of length and breadth of slides is 2 : 3. Each frame should have only one concept for the ease of understanding.

The slides and the film strips are arranged in a sequential order. This arrangement is also coordinated with the teaching learning activity of the class. When slides are shown in the class, curtains are drawn on the windows in order to reduce the entry of natural light in the class.

Before showing these slides, teacher elaborates important points. Once the film is over, the teacher gives his own comments and relates the aid with the lesson to be taught.

Film Strips

They are used before a large group of students either for introducing a lesson or for elaborating some minute object not seen in ordinary situations. Film strips are projected on a big screen through a film projector and then the projector is switched on. Here, very minute objects look very big on the screen and we can study their parts. For example, knowledge about bacteria and viruses can be given to students through these film strips. Sometimes, sound recording is also used along with the film to clarify important points.

Advantages of Film Strips

(*i*) The order or sequence of film strips is fixed and a teacher can prepare the relevant material to supplement the film according to the sequence.

(*ii*) We can have any part of the film on the screen as long as we desire so. As a result, a teacher can discuss a single topic as long as he needs. Thus, complete control over the equipment and the material is possible.

(*iii*) Handling of film projectors is also not complex. There is no problem of storing them because of their small size. Precautions are, however, needed against fungi or physical damage.

(*iv*) They have become very cheap today and any school can afford the cost of these projectors.

(*v*) They do not require complete darkness in the room as we do in using epidiascope or motion film projectors.

Limitations of Film Strips

(*i*) They can be used only in small sized classes because of limited focal length. Modern projectors are, however, having large focal length.

(*ii*) Slide projection is not as effective as film projection. Inventions of 3D films have reduced the use of slides even further. In spite of this, fixed order of the film strips creates problem in handling individual frames.

(*iii*) Many schools do not have audio-visual workshops and thus, they depend on the cheap and unstandardized materials available in the market.

Film Projector

16 mm films are generally used for the purpose of training or teaching. These films are planned and executed by a panel of experts who endeavour to prepare films of good quality.

As far as use of film projector for classroom teaching is concerned, it is very easy. Everything is automatic here. If electricity supply is not restricted, the film will not stop in the middle, after it is put on the projector.

Advantages of motion pictures

(*i*) Motion pictures can especially be used for training purposes. Take the example of games and sports. If some actions of a player is wrong leading to defeat in the game, it can be corrected by viewing the films. After the game is over, the film of the game is later analysed to be discussed by the experts to bring in new strategies and tactics to counterplay.

(*ii*) In all training courses, perfection is needed everywhere. If action is recorded on films, we can see our own performance and remove our defects.

(*iii*) In the classroom teaching, motion pictures can highlight those aspects also that would have otherwise been missed. For example, by enlarging, close up and action replay techniques, motion pictures can highlight those movements also which are very minute and can be missed in ordinary situations.

(*iv*) Motion pictures are **multi-sensory technique** of instruction. It is because a combination of light, sound and actions are seen here.

(*v*) Motion pictures can develop imaginative and observational capacities of students simultaneously.

(*vi*) Whatever ideals are shown by the models in motion pictures are imitated by pupils and thus, good ideals and etiquettes can be developed in them.

(*vii*) They are helpful in giving clarity of concepts through concreteness and accuracy.

(*viii*) Facts and events related to industry, politics, history and geography and knowledge about scientific inventions, discoveries, laws and principles can be communicated to pupils very effectively through these motion pictures.

Kinescope

It is a sight and sound recording that can be made in the studio from the television screen for repeated use. What transcription is to radio, the kinescope is to TV. They are used for the following purposes :

(*i*) For delayed telecast.

(*ii*) For retelecast of the same programme.

(*iii*) For repeating the telecast when programme could not be seen due to failure of network.

(*iv*) For sending programmes abroad.

Only limitation of kinescope is that live element or spontaneity does not exist here.

It can be used in teaching learning process in the same way as television is used.

Epidiascope

Epidiascope is an equipment that can project all types of materials whether transparent or non-transparent (opaque). It has thus a twin facility and separate mechanism for projecting transparent and opaque materials.

In epidiascope, the word **epi** means 'upon' **dia** means 'through' and **scope** means 'projected material to be seen'.

While projecting a slide, beams pass through the slide and projects its image on the screen. In this way, transparent material is projected.

While projecting the opaque material the light bits upon the object which reflects the image on a very sensitive mirror and reflects the image of the opaque objects on the screen.

Despite the multipurpose functioning of this device, it is not very popular in educational institutions because of its poor quality image, total room darkening, very high need of energy, complexity of its use and poor range. It is to be installed in the middle of the class due to its low range, therefore, causing more interference than aiding something to the lesson. Because of its ability to project opaque objects on the screen, it is also known as opaque projector.

Overhead Projector (OHP)

Built on the basic principle of periscope, OHP is an important audio visual equipment. In the classroom it is placed in front of the teacher above his head to reflect an image on the screen (blackboard). This device consists of a strong energy source, (bulbs), fixed reflectors (mirrors), projection lens and a platen.

This projector is called over head because the image goes over the head of the teacher and falls on the screen behind him. The teacher puts one slide over the other in order to give a sense of continuity of the subject matter projected on the screen.

Advantages of OHP

Its advantages lie in its special characteristics given below:

(*i*) No special training is required by the teacher to operate a projector.

(*ii*) OHPs are not very costly as compared to computers or film projectors.

(*iii*) It is handy and portable.

(*iv*) The image formed by the projector is also very bright and every pupil can see it. A 4 × 4 inches slide gives an image of 4 × 4 feet. This enlarged image is very easy to understand.

(*v*) It can create interests in pupils and hence it is a good motivator.

(*vi*) It is the best visual aid available to a teacher to supplement his oral teaching. He uses the screen of OHP as a blackboard without looking back. Transparencies, drawing, diagrams, figures and outlines etc. can be shown on the screen.

Television

TV differs from the radio in the sense that it is audio and visual both. We can see the incident occurring round the globe on it immediately after the occurrence of the incident through telecast. Thus, it is bisensory (multisensory) media. We get news, views and recreation through television in the same way as we do through the transistor but in a more compact and concrete way due to the facility of vision here.

As far as application of TV in education is concerned, it is still in the stage of infancy in India. It was only in 1961 that Indian television (Doordarshan) started a special service for schools in collaboration with the directorate of Education. This programme aimed at supplementing the regular classroom teaching in selected subjects. By 1972 only 400 schools of the capital received this telecast and two lakh students benefited from them. These programmes were telecast in the evening and on Sundays but there was no mechanism developed at that time to measure the effectiveness of such transmitting programmes.

After the introduction of distance education system in India, television is now regularly used as an instructional media. The enactment of Prasar Bharti Act is expected to boost the role of TV in the teaching learning process.

Advantages of television

(*i*) It heightens the reality more than the physical presence. For example, if someone is watching a cricket match in a stadium, even then he can not see certain situations despite being present there. On the other hand, if he is viewing a match on a TV, he can see and analyse every situation by close up action replay. Thus, television experience may be more real than the actual one. It can show even those details which we can not see with the help of direct experiences. Thus, television can be used for all training programmes and behaviour of the trainees can be modified in the desired manner.

(*ii*) TV experiences are new and versatile. So, they can bring variety to classroom teaching by breaking monotony and strengthening the learning structures by its multisensory approach.

(*iii*) It widens the horizon of pupils' experiences by giving them upto date knowledge of the real situation and by making them conversant with the opinions of others.

(*iv*) It can motivate the pupils for learning by arousing and retaining their interest in the learning situation.

Limitations of Television

(*i*) Speed of a television can not be changed as we can do in motion pictures.

(*ii*) A TV programme can not be adjusted to teaching and vice versa will have to be done. A teacher can take the help of video recording in such cases.

Tape Recorder and Audio Cassettes

Cassette type audio taps are available now which can play for 90 minutes on both sides. We can listen to our own recorded voice, recorded speeches of politicians and learned people, recorded poems of great composers, songs, music etc by the tape recorder.

Audio cassette recorder is used for the following purposes :

Such types of recording serve the following purposes

(*i*) **Analysis of verbal messages :** Accuracy, speed and tone of verbal messages are studied here and if perfection is seen, reinforcement to the presenter is given.

(*ii*) **Drill and practice :** Accurate verbal messages are presented before the trainee for drill and practice.

(*iii*) **Teaching of specific skills :** Impressive oral presentation is actually a skill. This skill is taught to students through audio-recording in the individual and group situations.

(*iv*) **Speech improvement :** Style of speaking and phonetics can also be improved by using this technology.

(*v*) **Improvement in vocabulary :** Recorded verbal messages are full of many new words which pupils can learn by listening to the message.

(*vi*) **Recreation :** Many recorded songs and music entertain the listeners and remove their fatigue.

Radio

It is an important and easily accessable audio aid serving three important general purposes "news, views and recreation". It is the cheapest equipment of all and radio broadcast is now reachable to 100% population of the country.

Pupils can get information about the incidents in any part of the globe immediately through radio. This increases their general awareness of the world. Students listen the ideas of learned people, politicians and educationists from across the world on the radio. This extends their own views and way of thinking. Apart from these, there are hundreds of programmes of music, songs and plays broadcast on the radio which entertain them round the clock.

Instructional Value of the Radio

(*i*) It is a powerful means of developing listening comprehension.

(*ii*) It can also help the pupils to acquire correct pronunciation and phonetics like tape recorders.

(*iii*) Conversational style and language can be learned on the radio.

(*iv*) It improves word power of learners.

(*v*) Mass education goals can be achieved through radio broadcast. It was the realization of the people when radio came into being in 1917.

(*vi*) News listened on the radio can improve our general knowledge.

(*vii*) Radio listening does not require literacy. Even illiterates can take the benefit of it.

Radio Broadcast in India

The first radio station was established in India in July 1927 in Mumbai followed by one more station in Kolkata in the same year. This media is now able to penetrate to the remotest villages of the country and is covering more than 99% of the population.

School broadcasting in India was started in 1937. Radio broadcasting is now very much used for mass education as well as the education of school going children in selected areas. Central Institute for educational technology (CIET) under the supervision and control of NCERT produces quality radio broadcast programmes. Adult education Radio Programmes also started in 1956 to educate the adults in the age group of 15-35 in the vicinity of Pune as a project sponsord by UNESCO. Today, broadcast of adult education programmes are many under different titles. When Consumer Protection Act was passed in 1986, consumer education through radio was also given recognition. Today, it is a regular programme of all the radio stations in India. One more regular radio programme is the radio counseling programme of IGNOU which is broadcast from 4-5 pm on every Sunday.

Apart from these, radio broadcast is also making the people aware about various social and economic problems and people are also educated about how they can solve these problems.

Computer

It is the latest electronic device that is audio and visual both. It accepts data, performs operations on that data in sequence (decided by a programme) and outputs the results.

Computer in education

From input devices to output and its storage, computer has a wide range of applicability in education. In computers inputs are converted into output by a programme. Thus, input (data) plus programme form software or instructional programme. Inputs are converted into output in the CPU of the computer.

Computer always works according to the programme given to it. Whatever instruction or programme the students give to the computers, it will always act accordingly and output will also come out on the same line. Application of computers in education can be understood by the following lines.

Videodiscs

This system is comprised of videodisc, where the information is stored, a video player and a TV set.

It is helpful in teaching learning process in the following ways:

(*i*) Students can get more informations through effective way of presentation.

(*ii*) By forwarding or reversing the CD player, learners can have access to any informations as many times as possible. This repeated action is necessary in understanding complex materials.

(*iii*) Live coverage given by the CD player can provide higher degree of motivation.

(*iv*) Auto stop system provided in the system can help those learners who study till late hours of night.

(*v*) The materials prepared by the effective teachers can be made available in the market for wide use.

Videotext

This system provides an interactive information retrieval service. It allows the home television to work as a computer terminal, which retrieves the textual material and graphic information from a remote data base.

Advantages of Videotext

(*i*) It is useful for downloading the required information from a remote data base.

(*ii*) It raises the general awareness of learners.

(*iii*) The principal of a school can have access to any information about his or other schools any time if this system is available in the school.

(*iv*) It is especially useful for distance learning. A learner can connect himself with his study centre or regional office any time.

(*v*) It is free from time schedule. We can have any information any time.

(*vi*) Two way interaction between the teacher and the taught is possible here with the help of alphanumeric keyboard. The learner can address to his tutor by typing questions and sending it to the tutor. Once he receives the answer, he gets immediate feedback.

(*vii*) It is faster than telephone or telegram because user need not wait here in queue.

Teleconferencing

Teleconferencing is a two way broadcast system in which learners can interact with the programme through a local telephone. It is a powerful medium of instruction for distance education. In this system three or four subject experts sit at different places and participate in the discussion on the given subject matter. Here learners do not take part in the teaching-learning process directly. They only hear the programme on their radio set or TV. They can however, interact with the experts through telephone which is connected to the radio or TV station where the discussion is being organised.

Thus, teleconferencing involves the use of many media and allows interactive group communication by means of a two way broadcast. All such conferencing need good quality audio device to facilitate immediate interaction among the participants for exchange of views.

Advantages of Teleconferencing

(*i*) **Effective for distance learning :** When groups of students are scattered over a large area of the country and it is not possible for them to interact with their teachers personally, then learning through teleconferencing is the best option for them.

(*ii*) **Interaction between the teacher and the taught possible :** As far as interaction between teachers and learners are concerned, this approach does not differ in any way from classroom teaching.

(*iii*) **High quality instruction :** Since, very learned people and experts of the subject take part in these discussions, the quality of the programme is never questionable.

(*iv*) **Immediate feedback :** Learners get answer of their questions immediately from the experts and their problem is solved. In this way, they get immediate feedback.

(*v*) **Flexibility :** Experts do not teach here on a pre-determined track. Their instruction and its way of presentation always changes according to the questions asked by learners. Thus, this approach is very flexible.

Internet

It is the abbreviation of international network. The computers connected to this system are automatically connected to world wide website (www). Due to this we can hear and see any programme available on website any time when we want to do so. If we have missed any television or radio programme, we can not have access to that programme again but if that programme is loaded on the website, we can repeatedly hear and see the programme. We will only have to log on the website of the programme producer and it will be available for us. The major advantage of this system is that it has made 24 hour communication possible especially between those countries which have great differences in their local timings such as India and America have a time difference of 10 ½ hours. When there is day time in India, offices are closed in America.

Applications of internet in education

(*i*) We can get any information any time at home through internet on one hand and we can store the information by creating our own website on the other. Thus, it is not necessary to have immediate print out of the textual matter.

(*ii*) The two talking persons can see each other in face to face situations also through internet. Thus, a teacher can teach millions of students scattered across the world together.

(*iii*) Many educational institutions have created their educational websites. We can download any information about them any time by logging on these websites.

(*iv*) Internet has also its role to play in classroom teaching. Teacher can show any educational programme through internet any time according to his own convenience and he will not have to adjust his time table according to the programme as he does while using radio or television as aids.

(*v*) Latest teaching strategies and latest researches in different fields can be obtained through internet immediately and we need not have to wait for their publication in magazines and journals.

(*vi*) Books, magazines and newspapers are also published on internet and it has made our access to them easy. Any Indian living in Canada even can read "Amar Ujala" or "Times of India" daily.

(*vii*) Research material and encyclopaedias are also published on internet to facilitate learning process.

REMEDIAL TEACHING

Remedial Teaching (RT) means that help is offered to pupils who need (pedagogical/didactic) assistance. These are often children who function at a lower than average level because of a certain learning- or behavioural problem/disorder, but RT can also be offered to pupils who achieve at a higher than average level, they too can do with the extra attention and care. The best known learning disorder is dyslexia.

The help includes the pupil who is being put forward for RT to the remedial teacher is examined by means of an intake conversation, checks, tests and/or observations. The remedial teacher tries to form a picture of the pupil also by way of talks with the group teacher and the parents in order to discover where the problem lies. When this is clear (diagnosis) a therapy plan is drawn up. In a therapy plan it states amongst others which aims should be achieved. The treatment that ensues is called remedial teaching. It is help that is completely specialized in the problem of the pupil, it is custom-made.

The therapy plan is drawn up for a fixed period of time. Remedial teaching is usually given during 6 weeks to 3 months, once or twice a week at school or in the remedial teacher's own practice. The aim being that the pupil can join his own group again after this period of time (or possibly after a continuation).

Remedial teaching is offered at many schools. However, a school is allowed to establish its own priorities and is not obliged to offer remedial teaching. There has to be a course of care though, the organization of which is determined by the whole team, although the directives and rules are laid down by the Ministery of Education an Science (OC&W).

Quizzing students more often is another commonly used method in a well balanced remedial teaching program. Taking the extra time to check each individual's progress gives the teacher an opportunity to regroup if necessary. It can also take the overall test pressure off students who tend to "freeze" when tested on larger amounts of material. From elementary to college, the best remedial teaching programs will include constant feedback from its students. This kind of communication provides a comfort level between student and teacher which leads to a more proficient, positive and rewarding outcome for both.

Too often, a lack of understanding among parents, school administrators and teaching staff gets in the way. Proper training of teachers and administrators go beyond their degree of specialties.

Listening to each other, and to parents and children who live with specific special needs, is a huge first step in creating an exemplary remedial teaching program as opposed to another "one size fits all" classroom. Requesting conferences, discussing individual strengths and weaknesses, and respecting each others expertise and opinions are all important pieces, and are defining points of the best remedial teaching programs.

Remedial Teaching for Slow Learners

Remedial Teaching is identifying slow learners and giving them the necessary guidance to help them overcome their problems, after identifying their areas of difficulty. Contrary to what is said, remedial teaching is done perfunctorily without identifying their areas of difficulty and underlying cause for lagging behind. Some students are unsympathetically branded as 'block heads' without an earnest attempt to know the real cause of their slow learning.

In the present system of education, students are identified as slow learners purely on the basis of their poor performance in the examination, which, in most cases deviates from what is taught. Consequently even talented students are sometimes misconstrued as dullards. So, a slow learner is one whose performance is very dismal in the examination. He is neither mentally retarded nor is on the lower rungs of intelligence scale.

The reasons for some students learning slowly are innumerable. One of the main reasons is the 'no detention system' at the primary and upper primary level. Students are promoted to higher classes on the basis of attendance, even if they score low marks. The heterogeneous composition (mental age & physical age) of over crowded classes in all government run schools and private schools also produces slow learners. So the incapacity of the teacher to pay individual attention to a student over a long period makes a student a slow learner. A slow learner is thus a product of negligence of school at different stages of learning, inspite of his innate capacity to learn.

There are some problems very specific to the individual. Ill health, lack of concentration, less exposure to the subject taught and parental background are some causative factors for slow learning. Talents differ. A childs capacity to learn different subjects varies from student to student. For instance, learning mathematics is a knack. All students do not do well in mathematics just as they do in other subjects. While other subjects can be learnt at any stage, it is very difficult for students to learn mathematics without the basics. Students show interest in the subjects they like and neglect other subjects if not taken care of. An urban child learns languages like English well while a rural child cannot, however well the teacher tries to explain.

Remedial Measures

Learning takes place from simple to complex. If for some reason the student has not learnt the basics, it is futile to teach him the advanced topics. Remedial teaching is not revising the topics taught repeatedly. Careful analysis of the students' performance in the examination and diagnosing the areas of difficulty are key aspects in remedial teaching. Once the difficult areas are identified, the next task is to plan the learning experiences to teach the basics to understand the given topic.

Teachers often feel that what has not been learnt at the primary level, cannot be taught simultaneously with the prescribed topics at the secondary level as they are busy completing the syllabus. Experience shows that once the basics are taught, the learning process is accelerated and the slow learners comprehend and grasp the given topics of the class, since they have already attained the mental age.

In Jawahar Navodaya Vidyalayas nation wide, the students are admitted in class VI based on a selection test consisting of a variety of questions to test intelligence and aptitude of the students.

It has been observed that many students thus selected do not possess the basics which they are supposed to learn at the primary level. But these schools have produced excellent results over the years by introducing bridge courses in their academic planning.

Subjects like physics pose difficulty for students when compared to biology. In biological sciences, students can see and find meaning in what they study. Whereas physics is somewhat intricate and difficult for students without good knowledge of mathematics. Poor performance in physics can be remedied by first teaching the required basic mathematical operations. Sometimes language becomes a barrier for students to understand the vast areas in subjects like geography. The innumerable new words used to describe various phenomena baffle the students. Students do not find these words in English language textbooks although they learn English language to pursue others subjects in an inter- disciplinary approach. The teacher has to explain all the words and their usage related to his subject before he teaches the concept.

The new words used in questions could confuse students and elicit wrong answers from them. Students should be exposed to a variety of questions with antonyms and synonyms - all the words used to frame a question to test the topic taught. Merely tagging the slow learners with bright students or segregating them into separate sections will not help the slow learners. Slow learners harbour themselves unobtrusively in the group of bright students.

Students learn a lot from the peer group. Unconscious learning does not take place if students are segregated. Keeping the slow learners in the peer group of bright students and paying individual attention to them by the teacher will enable them to overocme their difficulties.

Student is central in the learning process. The learning experiences should be activity-oriented and the teaching should motivate and create interest in the student to learn on his own. When group discussions are held in the classroom, the slow learners are benefited much.

Suitably tailored lesson plan by the teacher and careful monitoring by the school administration will help slow learners have a better grasp of all lessons in schools.

Various Approaches and Tools

Give your older kids a second chance to master grade-level reading.

A comprehensive literacy intervention curriculum for grades 1-12, LANGUAGE ! prepares students to return to conventional curricula by advancing them from current performance levels to grade placement level.

Lindamood-Bell

Lindamood-Bell is an organization dedicated to enhancing human learning. It has developed the sensory-cognitive processes that underlie reading, spelling, language comprehension, math, and visual motor skills. Its Process-Based education programs are for individuals ranging from severely learning disabled to academically gifted–ages 5 years through adult.

Open Court Reading

"Open Court Reading 2002 is a complete elementary basal reading program for Grades K-6. It maintains strong instruction in the areas of decoding (learning how to read), comprehension (understanding what you read), inquiry and investigation (learning how to apply what you have read), and writing (how to communicate with others in print). There are also applications for teaching spelling, vocabulary, grammar, usage, and mechanics, penmanship, and listening, speaking, and viewing."

Orton-Gillingham Approach

"The Orton-Gillingham approach is appropriate for teaching individuals, small groups, and classrooms. It is appropriate for teaching in the primary, elementary, intermediate grades, and at the secondary and college level as well as for adults. The explicit focus of the approach has been and continues to be upon persons with the kinds of language processing problems associated with dyslexia. Early intervention is highly desirable, but it is never too late to begin!"

Phono-Graphix

"The theoretical underpinnings of Phono-Graphix are remarkably straightforward and sensible, no doubt encouraging its rapid spread and popularity among teachers. It is based simply on the nature of the English code, the three skills needed to access that code, and teaching these in keeping with the way children learn.

Project Read

''Project Read/Language Circle is a research based mainstream language arts program for students who need a systematic learning experience with direct teaching of concepts and skills through multisensory techniques.''

Reading Mastery Plus

''Reading Mastery Plus gives students the skills and the clear, explicit instruction and guidance they need to master the fundamentals of reading. Oral language, phonemic awareness, and systematic phonics are the starting point.

This program is set up so students are active participants throughout the learning process. Less-structured activities and opportunities for independent work help students develop self-reliance. Ongoing assessment tools are used by the instructor to ensure that no student "falls through the cracks.''

Slingerland Institute for Literacy

''The Slingerland Institute for Literacy is a non-profit organization that trains teachers to work with dyslexic students in their classrooms using the Slingerland Multisensory Approach. This methodology is a simultaneous, multisensory, structured approach for teaching language arts in the classroom. The Slingerland Multisensory Approach for Teaching Language Arts Training Course is accredited at the Teacher and Instructor of Teaching levels by the International Multisensory Structured Language Educational Council (IMSLEC).''

SFA Components -Reading and Writing Programs

During reading periods, students are regrouped across age lines for 90 minutes so that each reading class contains students reading at one level. This eliminates the need to have reading groups within the class and increases the amount of time for direct instruction. Also, use of tutors as reading teachers during reading time reduces the size of most reading classes. The reading program in grades K-1 emphasizes the development of language skills and launches students into reading using phonetically regular storybooks supported by careful instruction that focuses on phonemic awareness, auditory discrimination, and sound blending as well as meaning, context, and self-monitoring strategies. Students become fluent as they read and reread to one another in pairs.

Reading Wings

A comprehensive, research-based approach to reading and writing for grades two and beyond. Reading Wings consists of four principal elements: listening comprehension, story-related activities, direct instruction in reading comprehension, and integrated writing/language arts. In all of these activities, students work in heterogeneous learning teams. Students are assigned to pairs or triads; then the pairs are assigned to teams. Mainstreamed, academically handicapped, and Title I-identified students are evenly distributed among the teams. All activities follow a regular cycle that involves teacher presentation, team practice, independent practice, peer pre-assessment, additional practice, assessment, and team recognition.

Wilson Language Training

At Wilson Language Training many people, regardless of their age, have not been able to acquire reading and writing skills because their learning needs have never been properly assessed. The majority of these people are subject to a core deficit at the most basic level of language skill: that of phonological coding.

❄ ❄ ❄ ❄ ❄

PRACTICE PAPER

1. Language acquisition differs from language learning in that acquisition is:
   A. Rule-based and formal
   B. Conscious and effortful
   C. Subconscious and natural
   D. Grammar-oriented
2. Which situation best represents language acquisition?
   A. Memorizing grammar rules
   B. Practicing worksheets
   C. Natural interaction at home
   D. Learning definitions
3. The most effective language teaching principle is:
   A. Emphasis on correctness
   B. Emphasis on communication
   C. Emphasis on translation
   D. Emphasis on memorization
4. Language learning is most effective when it is:
   A. Contextual and meaningful
   B. Teacher-centered
   C. Based on repetition only
   D. Exam-oriented
5. Listening is important because it:
   A. Develops pronunciation only
   B. Builds comprehension and language input
   C. Improves handwriting
   D. Focuses on grammar
6. Speaking skill primarily helps learners to:
   A. Memorize texts
   B. Express thoughts and ideas
   C. Avoid errors
   D. Improve spelling
7. Language is best viewed as:
   A. A set of rules
   B. A subject to pass exams
   C. A tool for communication
   D. A literary system only
8. In modern pedagogy, grammar should be taught:
   A. Separately from language use
   B. Through memorization of rules
   C. In meaningful contexts
   D. Only at advanced levels
9. Which approach discourages excessive focus on grammatical errors?
   A. Grammar-translation method
   B. Communicative approach
   C. Direct method
   D. Structural method
10. A multilingual classroom should be seen as:
    A. A problem B. A barrier
    C. A resource D. A limitation
11. Language difficulties in children may arise due to:
    A. Lack of intelligence B. Linguistic diversity
    C. Overlearning D. High motivation
12. Errors made by learners are:
    A. Signs of failure
    B. Obstacles to learning
    C. Natural steps in learning
    D. To be strictly avoided
13. A teacher should respond to errors by:
    A. Immediate correction always
    B. Ignoring all errors
    C. Punishing the learner
    D. Providing constructive feedback
14. Which of the following is a receptive skill?
    A. Speaking B. Writing
    C. Listening D. Storytelling
15. Reading is classified as:
    A. Productive skill B. Receptive skill
    C. Mechanical skill D. Oral skill
16. Writing skill requires:
    A. Only grammar knowledge
    B. Only vocabulary
    C. Organization of ideas and expression
    D. Only spelling
17. Comprehensive language assessment includes:
    A. Only writing B. Only reading
    C. Only grammar D. All four skills

18. Formative assessment in language focuses on:
A. Final marks B. Continuous improvement
C. Ranking students D. Annual exams

19. Effective teaching-learning materials should be:
A. Teacher-centered
B. Rigid and fixed
C. Contextual and engaging
D. Only textbook-based

20. Use of multilingual resources helps learners to:
A. Connect prior knowledge
B. Get confused
C. Reduce participation
D. Avoid learning

21. The main purpose of remedial teaching is to:
A. Support struggling learners
B. Complete syllabus
C. Test students
D. Increase homework

22. Remedial teaching should be:
A. General for all
B. Based on individual needs
C. Grammar-focused only
D. Exam-oriented

23. The best classroom practice for language learning is:
A. Lecture method
B. Drill method only
C. Interaction and participation
D. Silent reading only

24. Which strategy promotes language development most effectively?
A. Copying notes B. Group discussion
C. Memorizing rules D. Translation

25. Integrated language teaching means:
A. Teaching grammar only
B. Teaching skills separately
C. Combining all language skills
D. Ignoring speaking

26. Language acquisition is best supported when learners are exposed to:
A. Isolated grammar rules
B. Rich and meaningful input
C. Only written texts
D. Translation exercises

27. The primary aim of language teaching at the primary level is to:
A. Build communicative competence
B. Develop literary appreciation
C. Teach grammar rules
D. Prepare for examinations

28. Which factor plays the most important role in language learning?
A. Fear of mistakes
B. Motivation and exposure
C. Strict discipline
D. Repetition only

29. In language teaching, input should be:
A. Difficult and complex
B. Slightly above the learner's level
C. Below the learner's level
D. Grammar-focused

30. Which classroom activity best promotes listening skills?
A. Silent reading
B. Grammar exercises
C. Copying notes
D. Storytelling by the teacher

31. Fluency in language is best developed through:
A. Memorization
B. Practice in real communication
C. Grammar drills
D. Translation

32. Which of the following best supports speaking skills?
A. Role play B. Dictation
C. Reading aloud only D. Copywriting

33. Language learning becomes effective when learners:
A. Remain silent
B. Actively participate
C. Focus only on accuracy
D. Avoid mistakes

34. In modern classrooms, the teacher's role is mainly that of a:
A. Lecturer B. Examiner
C. Facilitator D. Controller

35. Which approach emphasizes learning language through use?
A. Grammar-translation method
B. Communicative approach
C. Structural method
D. Audio-lingual method

36. A child learns language best when:
A. Punished for mistakes
B. Given opportunities to express
C. Made to memorize rules
D. Tested frequently

37. Code-switching in a classroom refers to:
A. Mixing languages for better understanding
B. Avoiding language use
C. Teaching grammar
D. Testing vocabulary

38. Which is an example of productive skill?
A. Listening B. Reading
C. Writing D. Understanding

39. Extensive reading means:
A. Reading for detailed understanding
B. Reading large amounts for general understanding
C. Reading grammar rules
D. Reading aloud

40. Intensive reading focuses on:
A. General idea B. Detailed comprehension
C. Speed D. Entertainment

41. Which method encourages habit formation through repetition?
A. Communicative method
B. Constructivist method
C. Direct method
D. Audio-lingual method

42. Scaffolding in language teaching means:
A. Ignoring learners
B. Providing support as needed
C. Testing frequently
D. Teaching grammar rules

43. Which activity develops writing skills most effectively?
A. Creative writing
B. Copying from the board
C. Memorization
D. Dictation only

44. The main purpose of using stories in language teaching is to:
A. Teach grammar
B. Engage learners and build language
C. Save time
D. Test students

45. Which of the following is a barrier to language learning?
A. Fear and anxiety B. Interaction
C. Practice D. Motivation

46. Which strategy helps in vocabulary development?
A. Rote memorization only
B. Contextual usage
C. Ignoring new words
D. Translation only

47. Peer interaction in language classrooms helps in:
A. Reducing learning
B. Enhancing communication skills
C. Increasing fear
D. Limiting participation

48. Continuous feedback helps learners to:
A. Feel discouraged B. Improve performance
C. Avoid learning D. Depend on teachers

49. Which is NOT a language skill?
A. Listening B. Speaking
C. Drawing D. Writing

50. Language learning is most effective in:
A. Isolated environments B. Interactive environments
C. Silent classrooms D. Exam halls

51. Which of the following improves pronunciation?
A. Listening to correct models
B. Writing practice
C. Grammar drills
D. Silent reading

52. Which approach supports learner autonomy?
A. Teacher-centered approach
B. Learner-centered approach
C. Lecture method
D. Drill method

53. The use of real-life situations in teaching language is called:
A. Artificial learning B. Contextual learning
C. Mechanical learning D. Passive learning

54. Which of the following is an example of formative assessment?
A. Final exam
B. Unit test
C. Classroom observation
D. Board exam

55. Which skill helps in understanding written texts?
A. Speaking B. Listening
C. Reading D. Writing

56. Language teaching should focus on:
A. Accuracy only
B. Fluency only
C. Both accuracy and fluency
D. Neither

57. Which of the following supports inclusive language teaching?
A. Ignoring diversity
B. Respecting all languages
C. Using one language only
D. Avoiding interaction

58. Error correction should be:
A. Immediate and harsh
B. Supportive and constructive
C. Ignored completely
D. Punitive

59. Which is the best indicator of language proficiency?
A. Grammar knowledge
B. Ability to communicate effectively
C. Writing speed
D. Memorization

60. The ultimate goal of language learning is:
A. Passing exams
B. Using language effectively
C. Memorizing rules
D. Writing essays

61. Which of the following is **not** a language skill?
A. Reading B. Writing
C. Thinking D. Speaking

62. By which method the students learn to the maximum extent?
A. By seeing B. By reading
C. By listening D. By doing themselves

63. Which quality of the teacher is liked the most by the students?
A. Punctuality B. Impartiality
C. Love for discipline D. Dominance

64. What should the teacher do to maintain the interest of students in class teaching?
A. Maximum use of blackboard
B. Extensive use of examples from the practical life
C. Extensive use of teaching materials/aids
D. Giving ample opportunity to students for discussion/delibrations

65. Children with disability must get education because—
A. They are vulnerable
B. They have special needs
C. It is a basic constitutional right
D. They are poor

66. Which of the following is a sensory disorder?
A. Hearing Impairment
B. Mental Retardation
C. Cerebral Palsy
D. Neuro Muscular Disorder

67. Learning depends on—
A. Intelligence B. Parental attitude
C. Peer attitude D. None of these

68. Which of the following can increase the quality of education?
A. To extend one hour time period
B. Service period teacher training
C. Solution and treatment teaching
D. By help-books

69. Which cannot be the stage of learning?
A. Procedure B. Difference perception
C. Exercise D. Imagination

70. Which of the following is decisive for teaching work?
A. To make effective the excellence
B. To educate
C. True management of classes
D. Communication with students

71. What will be the indication when a group of students gets more marks in the question paper made by any teacher?
A. It is a group of high achiever
B. Teacher has tought well
C. Question-paper is good
D. None of these

72. Choose the one which best expresses the meaning of the word 'Condone'.
A. Grieve B. Endure
C. Forgive D. Ignore

73. Change the following active voice into passive one: Does the noise disturb you?
A. You are disturb by the noise.
B. Are you disturbed by the noise?
C. You are disturbing by the noise.
D. Are you disturbing by the noise?

74. A statement that can have a double meaning—
A. Verbose B. Ambivalent
C. Epigraph D. Ambiguous

75. We should always observe from the stand point of others. This is a:
A. Simple sentence B. Complex sentence
C. Compound sentence D. Phrase

76. Schools should be concerned with the development of child, which should include:
A. Acquisition of knowledge by the child
B. Acquisition of life skills by the child
C. Acquisition of skills required by the nation
D. Acquisition of skills required by the healthy person

77. A student gives a partially correct respond to your question. Then you will—
A. Seek further information
B. Provide reinforcement
C. Reframe your question
D. Tell the correct information

78. Which of the following is/are productive skill/skills?
A. Speaking B. Writing
C. Both A and B D. None of the above

79. Language acquisition can be automatically attained favoured by—
A. Cognitivists B. Behaviourists
C. Both of the above D. None of the above

80. Which of the following grammar teaching method disturbs the teaching of a text book or composition writing at times?
A. Deductive Method
B. Inductive Method
C. Inductive Deductive Method
D. Incidental Method

81. Teaching aids are useful because they—
A. help teacher's work
B. activate all senses
C. help students to be attentive
D. make learning more meaningful

82. Teaching would be more effective if the teacher—
A. Makes his intent purposeful
B. Is master of the subject
C. Uses various instructional aids
D. Declares his objectives in the beginning

83. The word 'Tacit' means—
A. Formal B. Fear
C. Silent D. Celestial

84. One who is well-versed in the science of languages is called a—
A. Philosopher B. Theologist
C. Philologist D. Zoologist

85. Choose the correctly spelt word—
A. Coloqial B. Coloquial
C. Colloqial D. Colloquial

86. Choose what expresses the meaning of 'Pull the wool over one's eye'—
A. Delay B. Encourage
C. Suppress D. Deceive

87. Student's learning difficulties can be best addressed by—
A. Advising them to work hard
B. Suggesting private tuitions
C. Supervised study in the library
D. Remedial teaching

88. For being successful in life students should be encouraged to—
A. selective study
B. casual study
C. intensive study
D. learning by rote memorisation

89. Students who bring out alternative solutions and cite the books not prescribed by the teacher should be—
A. discouraged
B. encouraged
C. advised to talk to the teacher outside the class
D. advised to follow the class notes to score better in the examinations

90. Problem of school dropouts can be effectively tackled by—
A. reducing curriculum load
B. teachers empathy
C. attractive school environment
D. providing incentives

91. Choose the synonym of voracious—
A. Hungry B. Wild
C. Quick D. Angry

92. Choose the misspelt word—
A. Command B. Appraise
C. Behaviour D. Mentenance

93. Remedial teachers should observe the following when dealing with the behaviour problems of pupils—
A. should always pay attention to their misbehaviour
B. always observe the performance of pupils in class and their behaviour in groups
C. give positive reinforcement to pupils good behaviour
D. refer the cases to student Guidance Officers/ teachers for follow up action

94. Use stress and rhythmic patterns and intonation patterns of the language and 'use vocabulary appropriately' are the micro-skills involved in which of the following?
A. Speaking B. Listening
C. Reading D. Writing

95. Problems in language learning arise due to lack of—
A. methodology of teaching
B. availability of materials
C. teaching of mother tongue
D. teacher's competence

96. Usual teaching-learning processes can be supplemented by the following to improve the quality—
A. Extra coaching
B. Diagnostic and remedial teaching
C. Enrichment programmes
D. Inservice teacher education

97. School based evaluation can solve the problem of—
A. Mass copying
B. Student's indiscipline
C. Unrealistic assessment
D. Teacher's social reputation

98. Choose the correct meaning of the idioms: Hobson's choice—
A. feeling of insecurity
B. accept or leave the offer
C. excellent choice
D. no choice at all

99. Choose the meaning of the **bold** phrase in the sentence— He has been working **on and off** for several years on this project.
A. at intervals B. rarely
C. painstakingly D. continuously

100. Pedagogy is considered to be the—
A. Science of Teaching
B. Art of Learning

C. Science of Communication
D. Art of Assimilation

101. Inductive approach of teaching means—
A. initiating the child to new subject
B. teaching through specific instruction
C. group learning as opposed to individualised learning
D. arriving at generalisations with the help of examples

102. Which of the following is an appropriate order for learning of a language?
A. Listening → Speaking → Writing → Reading
B. Speaking → Listening → Writing → Reading
C. Listening → Speaking → Reading → Writing
D. Listening → Reading → Speaking → Writing

103. The primary functions of language are—
A. Expression of feeling, meaning, communication and thinking
B. To control over other people, as language is a social act
C. Both A and B
D. None of these

104. Which of the following conditions must be satisfied in order to designate a person mentally retarded?
A. Sub-normal intellectual functioning
B. Very poor adaptive ability
C. Dependability on others
D. All of these

105. The best measure of identifying mildly mentally retarded is—
A. Administration of standardized intelligence test
B. Administration of behaviour test
C. Administration of adjustment test
D. A combination of all

106. Physical trauma during pregnancy may cause
A. Mental retardation B. Blindness
C. Deafness D. All of these

107. All of the following may cause mental retardation except
A. Blood incompatibility B. Action of toxic agent
C. Radio-activity D. None of these

108. Dullers do not differ from normal children in—
A. Physical characteristics
B. Level of social expectancy
C. Both of these
D. None of these

109. Which of the following things is not required for educating mildly mentally retarded children?
A. Regular counselling
B. Remedial teaching
C. Modification in the curriculum
D. Regular evaluation

110. Teaching of which of the following skills is **not** suitable to borderline cases?
A. Electric fitting
B. Repairing of electric or electronic equipments
C. Oratory skills
D. Activity based skills

111. Morons are slow in—
A. Physical growth B. Thinking and planning
C. Taking initiative D. All of these

112. Unsatisfactory relation of a mentally retarded child with the environment is technically called—
A. Autism B. Maladjustment
C. Pseudo-dullness D. None of these

113. Learning disabled children are—
A. Deficient in using potentials
B. Low in intelligence
C. Slow in activity
D. None of these

114. Learning disability is related to—
A. low listening and comprehension power
B. poor ability of expression
C. poor ability of mathematical operation
D. All of these

115. Learning disabled children perform very poorly in—
A. Academic areas B. Technical areas
C. Both of these D. None of these

116. Problem of learning disability is more complex than that of other disabilities because—
A. Its causes can not be easily ascertained by applying usual tests
B. It is associated to behaviour problems
C. Both of these
D. None of these

117. Educationally, learning disabled look similar to—
A. Dullers B. Backward children
C. Both of these D. None of these

118. In which of the following physical characteristics learning disabled children differ from the normal ones?
A. They are all the time clumsy and awkward
B. Poor coordination of motor abilities
C. Height, weight and health
D. All of these

119. Which of the following methods is most suitable for learning disabled children?
A. Behaviour guidance method
B. Remedial teaching
C. Brain storming
D. None of these

120. In order to improve work habits of learning disabled what should be done?

A. Unattending behaviour should be penalized
B. Close monitoring of the behaviour is needed
C. Cues and prompt should be given
D. All of these

121. Which of the following situations may lead to educational backwardness?
A. Sensory impairment
B. Motor disability
C. Long diseases and health problems
D. All of these

122. Which of the following is an important cause of educational backwardness at primary level of education in India?
A. Poor school organisation
B. Lack of accountability
C. Attitude of the masses towards education
D. All of these

123. Which of the following measures should be adopted by the teacher to check educational backwardness?
A. Continuous evaluation and regular feedback
B. Remedial teaching
C. Adjustment and behaviour training
D. All of these

124. Teaching by small steps and frequent short assignment techniques are useful for—
A. Slow learners
B. Learning disabled
C. Educationally backward children
D. Children of all types of disabilities

125. Special schools are required for backward children when—
A. Backwardness is due to any serious physical handicap
B. The size of population of backward children in the society is very large as is the case of Gujarat where the achievement of students in mathematics is always seen very low
C. Both of these
D. None of these

ANSWERS

1	2	3	4	5	6	7	8	9	10
C	C	B	A	B	B	C	C	B	C
11	**12**	**13**	**14**	**15**	**16**	**17**	**18**	**19**	**20**
B	C	D	C	B	C	D	B	C	B
21	**22**	**23**	**24**	**25**	**26**	**27**	**28**	**29**	**30**
A	B	C	B	C	B	A	B	B	D
31	**32**	**33**	**34**	**35**	**36**	**37**	**38**	**39**	**40**
B	A	B	C	B	B	A	C	B	B
41	**42**	**43**	**44**	**45**	**46**	**47**	**48**	**49**	**50**
D	B	A	B	A	B	B	B	C	B
51	**52**	**53**	**54**	**55**	**56**	**57**	**58**	**59**	**60**
A	B	B	C	C	C	B	B	B	B
61	**62**	**63**	**64**	**65**	**66**	**67**	**68**	**69**	**70**
C	D	B	C	C	D	A	B	A	A
71	**72**	**73**	**74**	**75**	**76**	**77**	**78**	**79**	**80**
B	B	B	D	A	B	B	C	A	D
81	**82**	**83**	**84**	**85**	**86**	**87**	**88**	**89**	**90**
D	C	C	C	D	D	D	C	B	D
91	**92**	**93**	**94**	**95**	**96**	**97**	**98**	**99**	**100**
A	D	A	A	D	D	C	D	A	A
101	**102**	**103**	**104**	**105**	**106**	**107**	**108**	**109**	**110**
D	C	C	D	D	D	D	C	C	C
111	**112**	**113**	**114**	**115**	**116**	**117**	**118**	**119**	**120**
D	A	D	D	A	A	B	B	A	D
121	**122**	**123**	**124**	**125**					
D	D	D	D	C					

❄ ❄ ❄ ❄ ❄

हिन्दी भाषा

SECTION-A

भाषा बोधगम्यता एवं व्याकरण

1 भाषा बोध

परिचय

भाषा बोध के अंतर्गत व्यक्ति की समग्र अवबोधन क्षमता का मूल्यांकन किया जाता है। इससे अभ्यर्थी की समझ क्षमता एवं दिए गए अवतरण में छुपे गूढ़ विचारों को ग्रहण करने की क्षमता आंकी जाती है। इसके द्वारा अभ्यर्थी के निर्णय लेने की क्षमता की भी जांच की जाती है। ऐसा दिए गए प्रतिपाद्य के हृदयंगम द्वारा ही संभव है। इस प्रकार भाषा बोध व्यक्तित्व के बहुआयामी पहलुओं के परीक्षण की पद्धति है। इसके द्वारा भाषा-ज्ञान, निहितार्थ की समझ एवं अवबोधन क्षमता, निर्णय क्षमता एवं सही निष्कर्ष तक पहुंचने की क्षमता की जांच एक साथ की जाती है। जाहिर है, इतने सारे परीक्षणों के द्वारा व्यक्तित्व का समग्र उभार एवं निखार प्रकट हो जाता है। ऐसे में भाषा बोध के प्रश्नों को हल करने में अतिरिक्त सावधानी एवं सचेतता आवश्यक है। इस प्रकार के प्रश्नों के सही उत्तर देने के लिए निरंतर अभ्यास की आवश्यकता होती है।

सर्वप्रथम अवतरण (गद्यांश) को पढ़कर उसके मूलभाव या निहितार्थ को समझने की कोशिश करनी चाहिए। एक बार पढ़कर मूलभाव को समझने में कठिनाई हो तो उसे एक से अधिक बार पढ़ें। जबतक निहितार्थ समझ में न आए उसे दुबारा एवं तिबारा पढ़ें। निहितार्थ समझ लेने पर प्रश्नों का उत्तर देना आसान हो जाता है।

इस बात का ध्यान रखें कि प्रश्नों के उत्तर दिए गए अवतरण पर ही आधारित हों। अपनी पूर्व की जानकारी के आधार पर निष्कर्ष न निकालें। यह संभव है कि अवतरण में दी गई जानकारी आपकी पूर्व की जानकारी या राय से भिन्न हो। ऐसे में अपनी जानकारी को अवतरण में दी गई सूचना के साथ घालमेल न करें। ऐसा करना आत्मघाती कदम हो सकता है। अवतरण को पढ़ते समय महत्वपूर्ण बिंदुओं को रेखांकित करते चलें। ऐसे में मूल बिंदुओं को शीघ्रता से दुहरा सकते हैं। हो सकता है समयाभाव के कारण मूल अवतरण को बार-बार पढ़ना संभव न हो।

अवतरण में दिए गए मोटे (Bold) शब्द एवं वाक्यांशों पर विशेष ध्यान दें और उन्हें मूल अवतरण एवं वाक्य से जोड़ने का प्रयास करें। ऐसा करना अवतरण के मूल भाव को समझने में सहायक होगा।

कभी-कभी अवतरण में किसी शब्द के समानार्थक या विपरीतार्थक शब्द पूछे जाते हैं। ऐसे प्रश्नों के उत्तर देने में जल्दबाजी न करें। जाहिर है किसी एक शब्द के कई समानार्थक एवं विपरीतार्थक शब्द हो सकते हैं। ऐसे में उपयुक्त शब्द का चुनाव आवश्यक है। इसके लिए लेखक के मूल कथ्य और विचार को समझना आवश्यक है।

नकारात्मक अंक मिलने की स्थिति में प्रश्न का उत्तर अनुमान के आधार पर न दें। ऐसे प्रश्नों को छोड़ देना ही उचित होगा।

कभी-कभी दिए गए अवतरण के लिए उपयुक्त शीर्षक लिखना होता है। यह प्रश्न काफी आसान भी है और कठिन भी। आसान इसलिए कि इनका उत्तर दिए गए अवतरण के आधार पर ही देना होता है और कठिन इसलिए कि अवतरण के मूल भाव को समझे बिना विषयांतर हो जाने की संभावना अक्सर बनी रहती है।

अंत में, सबसे जरूरी चीज है—अभ्यास! अभ्यास के बिना आसान प्रश्न भी कठिन लगने लगते हैं। भाषा-बोध के प्रश्नों को हल करने के लिए भाषा में अभिरुचि एवं समझ विकसित करनी चाहिए।

गद्यांश-1

कर्त्तव्य एक नैतिक बंधन है। यह एक तरह से ऋणी होने के समान है, जिस सामाजिक प्राणी के साथ हम रह रहे होते हैं। हमें अपने साथ रहने वालों के लिए इसकी अनुमति मिलनी चाहिए। हमारे जीवनवृत्ति का अधिकार संकेत देता है कि यह हमारा कर्त्तव्य है कि हम उन साथ रहने वाले प्राणियों को भी अपने समान ही जीवन की परिस्थितियां उपलब्ध कराएं। वास्तव में अधिकार और कर्त्तव्य परस्पर संबद्ध हैं। किसी एक

के संबंध में अधिकार दूसरे का कर्त्तव्य हो सकता है। अधिकार और कर्त्तव्य एक सिक्के के दो पहलू हैं। हमें दूसरे के ओहदों का हमेशा ख्याल रखना चाहिए। नैतिक कर्त्तव्य, वैधानिक अधिकार की अपेक्षा ज्यादा प्रभावी होते हैं। नैतिक कर्त्तव्य वह कर्त्तव्य है जो लोगों को नैतिक स्तर पर बांध कर रखती है। यह हमारा नैतिक कर्त्तव्य है कि हम गरीबों की मदद करें क्योंकि वह एक प्राणी और समाज का अंग है।

हमें उन परिस्थितियों के निर्माण के लिए हमेशा प्रयास करना चाहिए जिनसे मानवता का कल्याण हो सके। यह हमारा अनुकरणीय कर्त्तव्य है कि हम अपने माता-पिता की आज्ञा मानें और उन्हें सम्मान दें। यह कर्त्तव्य जिम्मेवारी की चेतना से पैदा होता है जो कि प्रत्यक्षतः हमारे अंतःकरण से संबंधित है। इस प्रकार से यह एक नैतिक कर्त्तव्य है जिसमें कोई व्यक्ति बिना वैधानिक बंधन के ही ऋणी है।

कर्त्तव्य की चेतना, सही तरीके से सभ्यता के विकास की सर्वश्रेष्ठता है। पाखंड कर्त्तव्य की चेतना के एकदम विपरीत है। पाखंड में जहां दुरात्मा का समावेश है, वहीं कर्त्तव्य में यथार्थता और विश्वस्तता का समावेश है।

1. गद्यांश के अनुसार, अधिकार और कर्त्तव्य हैं :
A. एक सिक्के के दो पहलू
B. अंतःसंबद्ध
C. (A) और (B) दोनों
D. (A) और (B) में से कोई नहीं

2. गद्यांश के अनुसार वैधानिक कर्त्तव्य है :
A. नैतिक कर्त्तव्य की अपेक्षा अधिक महत्त्वपूर्ण
B. नैतिक कर्त्तव्य की अपेक्षा कम महत्त्वपूर्ण
C. नैतिक कर्त्तव्य की अपेक्षा अधिक प्रभावी
D. नैतिक कर्त्तव्य की अपेक्षा कम प्रभावी

3. कर्त्तव्य आता है :
A. जिम्मेवारी से
B. वैधानिक बंधन से
C. पाखंड से
D. इनमें से कोई नहीं

4. निम्न में से कौन-सा वाक्य गद्यांश के अनुसार सही नहीं है?
A. पाखंड में दुष्टता का समावेश
B. पाखंड का कर्त्तव्य के विपरीत होना
C. कर्त्तव्य में यथार्थता का समावेश
D. कर्त्तव्य की चेतना का सभ्यता के विकास के लिए महत्त्वपूर्ण न होना

5. निम्न में से किन नैतिक कर्त्तव्यों का उल्लेख गद्यांश में नहीं किया गया है?
A. नैतिक कर्त्तव्य हमारी मातृभूमि से बढ़कर है
B. नैतिक कर्त्तव्य हमारे माता-पिता से बढ़कर है
C. नैतिक कर्त्तव्य गरीब से बढ़कर है
D. नैतिक कर्त्तव्य मानव-कल्याण में योगदान है

6. निम्न में से कौन नैतिक कर्त्तव्य से संबंधित नहीं है?
A. जिम्मेवारी की चेतना B. सद्विचार
C. पाखंड D. यथार्थता

7. गरीबों की मदद करना एक कर्त्तव्य है, क्योंकि :
A. हम गरीब हैं
B. हम अमीर हैं
C. हम उस समाज से संबंध रखते हैं
D. हम उनकी अच्छाई चाहते हैं

8. हमें माता-पिता के प्रति आज्ञाकारी और सम्मानपूर्ण होना चाहिए, क्योंकि :
A. यह जिम्मेवारी की चेतना है
B. यह वैधानिक बाध्यता है
C. यह सभ्यता है
D. यह पाखंड है

9. 'हमें दूसरे के ओहदों का हमेशा ध्यान रखना चाहिए।' यह एक है :
A. साधारण वाक्य B. जटिल वाक्य
C. मिश्रित वाक्य D. मुहावरा

10. 'हमें दूसरे के ओहदों का हमेशा ध्यान रखना चाहिए।' इस वाक्य में प्रयुक्त 'हमेशा' है :
A. क्रिया-विशेषण B. विशेषण
C. संज्ञा D. क्रिया

गद्यांश-2

ऐसे महान् चिन्तकों को जिनकी शिक्षाएँ वैश्विक हैं, अपने समय के संदर्भ से ही समझा जा सकता है। बुद्ध को व्यापक रूप में गलत समझा गया है। व्यवहारवादियों, अज्ञेयवादियों, निरीश्वरवादियों तथा नैतिक मानवतावादियों ने उन्हें अपने दर्शन का प्रचार करने वाला माना है। बुद्ध की शिक्षाओं को भारत की ईसा-पूर्व छठी शताब्दी को समझकर ही ठीक प्रकार से समझा जा सकता है क्योंकि उनका आविर्भाव उसी शताब्दी में हुआ था किन्तु ऐसा करना अपेक्षाकृत कठिन कार्य है।

ईसा-पूर्व छठी शताब्दी के भारत में बहुत प्रकार की विचारधाराएँ और सम्प्रदाय थे तथापि सभी सम्प्रदाय आत्मा के पुनर्जन्म, कर्म के दर्शन एवं मानव के चरम लक्ष्य निर्वाण के विषय में सहमत थे। बुद्ध ने इन सिद्धान्तों को स्वीकार किया है, यद्यपि उन्होंने धार्मिक सिद्धान्तवाद को अस्वीकार किया है, किन्तु उनका योगदान नैतिकता तथा सदाचार की उत्कृष्टता को महत्वपूर्ण मानने में था। उन्होंने हृदय को शान्ति प्रदान करने की आवश्यकता तथा नैतिकता के नियमों के अनुसरण पर विशेष बल दिया। दुःखों का अन्त शरीर की भूख को शान्त करने तथा हमारे संवेगों पर दृढ़ता से नियंत्रण करने से हो सकता है।

बुद्ध की रुचि ईश्वर में नहीं थी बल्कि मनुष्य और मानव-प्रयासों में थी। अपनी साधना और अपने प्रयत्नों से मानव अपने आपको देवत्व

की ऊँचाई तक उठा सकता है, यद्यपि भक्ति-सम्बन्धी तत्त्वों के बिना भी बुद्ध की शिक्षाएँ मुख्य रूप से धार्मिक हैं। बुद्ध के अन्दर आध्यात्मिक गहराई, नैतिक दृढ़ता तथा बौद्धिक स्पष्टता का भण्डार समाहित है। समय के व्यतीत होने के साथ-साथ उनके द्वारा की गई मानवता की सेवा का विश्वव्यापी समादर हो रहा है। उनका संदेश सभी काल के लिए सार्थक है।

1. परिच्छेद के अनुसार क्या बुद्ध की शिक्षाओं को धार्मिक कहा जा सकता है?
A. नहीं, क्योंकि उन्होंने ईश्वर के बारे में शिक्षा नहीं दी
B. हाँ, अवश्य ही
C. नहीं, क्योंकि उनकी शिक्षाओं में भक्ति-तत्वों का अभाव है
D. इस विषय में सन्देह है

2. बुद्ध के समय में प्रचलित विचारों के विभिन्न सम्प्रदायों का विश्वास था
A. आत्मा के पुनर्जन्म (आवागमन) में
B. कर्म के सिद्धान्त में
C. निर्वाण में
D. उपर्युक्त सभी में

3. बुद्ध ने किस पर जोर दिया?
A. ईश्वर की भक्ति पर
B. कर्मकाण्ड पर
C. प्रार्थना पर
D. आचारशास्त्र तथा नैतिक नियमों पर

4. परिच्छेद के अनुसार बुद्ध की शिक्षाएँ मुख्य रूप से धर्मसम्बन्धी हैं :
A. आध्यात्मिक गहराई के कारण
B. नैतिक दृढ़ता के कारण
C. क्योंकि विशुद्ध रूप से बौद्धिक नहीं हैं
D. उपर्युक्त सभी के कारण

5. बुद्ध ने अधिक महत्व प्रदान किया
A. ईश्वर को न कि मनुष्य को
B. मनुष्य तथा ईश्वर दोनों को
C. न ईश्वर को और न मनुष्य को
D. मनुष्य-मात्र को न कि ईश्वर को

6. संवेगों पर उचित नियंत्रण से होगा
A. दुःखों का अन्त
B. सर्वश्रेष्ठ और सर्वोच्च बनेंगे
C. हठधर्मिता को बढ़ावा मिलेगा
D. व्यक्ति ईश्वर की सन्निकटता प्राप्त करेगा

7. "उनके संदेशों की सार्वकालिक सार्थकता है।" यह कथन है :
A. साधारण वाक्य B. मिश्रित वाक्य
C. संयुक्त वाक्य D. सूक्ति

8. "बुद्ध की शिक्षाएँ मुख्य रूप से धार्मिक हैं" - इस वाक्य में 'मुख्य रूप से' यह शब्द है :
A. संज्ञा B. क्रिया
C. विशेषण D. क्रिया-विशेषण

9. महान विचारकों को ठीक से किसके द्वारा समझा जा सकता है?
A. ई. पू. छठी शताब्दी के भारत को समझने से
B. जिस काल में वे रहे हैं उस काल की सापेक्षता में उन्हें समझने से
C. बुद्ध की शिक्षाओं का ठीक-ठीक समादर करने से
D. उनके विचारों और दर्शन का अध्ययन करने तथा समझने से

10. परिच्छेद के अनुसार
A. बुद्ध ने उन सिद्धान्तों को स्वीकार नहीं किया जो उनके समय प्रचलन में थे
B. बुद्ध का नैतिक शास्त्र में अधिक योगदान नहीं है
C. बुद्ध का विश्वास हठवादी सैद्धान्तिक दर्शन में नहीं था
D. बुद्ध के समय कर्म का सिद्धान्त स्वीकार नहीं किया गया था

गद्यांश-3

मनुष्य का सुखी जीवन संतुलित प्राकृतिक पर्यावरण पर निर्भर करता है। मानव की बढ़ती जनसंख्या और तज्जन्य आवश्यकताएँ प्रकृति के संतुलन को बिगाड़ रही हैं। पर्यावरण में दूषित तत्त्वों की मात्रा आवश्यकता से अधिक बढ़ जाती है तो पर्यावरण का यह असन्तुलन प्रदूषण का रूप ले लेता है। मानव की आवासीय, औद्योगिक नगरीकरण, कृषि उत्पादन में वृद्धि करने की समस्याओं ने प्रकृति के संतुलन को बिगाड़कर प्रदूषण को बढ़ाया है। यातायात-साधनों की वृद्धि, वृक्षों की अंधाधुंध कटाई से वातावरण में ऑक्सीजन की कमी और कार्बन डाइआक्साइड की वृद्धि हो गई है। पॉप संगीत और रॉक संगीत तथा हॉर्न बजाने से ध्वनि प्रदूषण बढ़ रहा है। वातावरण को प्रदूषित कर हम अपनी मृत्यु को स्वयं ही निमंत्रण दे रहे हैं। प्रदूषण की वृद्धि के लिए मानव ही उत्तरदायी है। अतः इसके निवारण के लिए सर्वप्रथम अपने मानसिक प्रदूषण को दूर करना होगा। वृक्षारोपण, पेयजल-शुद्धीकरण, रासायनिक विस्फोटों पर नियंत्रण, कर्णभेदी ध्वनि विस्तारक यंत्रों, वाहनों और संगीत को रोकने के उपायों से मानव जीवन को प्रदूषण मुक्त बनाना होगा, तभी मानव जीवन सुखमय हो सकता है।

1. पर्यावरण असन्तुलन के लिए कौन उत्तरदायी है?
A. मानसिक प्रदूषण B. ध्वनि प्रदूषण
C. वृक्षों की अंधाधुंध कटाई D. प्राकृतिक प्रकोप

2. कर्णभेदी संगीत से किस प्रकार का प्रदूषण होता है?
A. वायु प्रदूषण B. ध्वनि प्रदूषण
C. पर्यावरण प्रदूषण D. मानसिक प्रदूषण

3. 'अपनी मृत्यु को स्वयं निमंत्रण देने' का अभिप्राय क्या है?
A. आत्महत्या करना
B. जीने की इच्छा छोड़ देना
C. हताश हो जाना
D. वातावरण को प्रदूषित करना

4. 'वृक्षारोपण' से प्रमुख लाभ क्या है?
A. मृदा संरक्षण
B. जड़ी-बूटियों, औषधियों की पूर्ति
C. वातावरण में वायुशुद्धि
D. रेगिस्तान वृद्धि की रोकथाम

5. मानव जीवन को सुखी कैसे बनाया जा सकता है?
A. औद्योगीकरण से
B. जनसंख्या नियंत्रण से
C. संतुलित पर्यावरण से
D. यातायात साधनों की वृद्धि से

गद्यांश-4

विकसित देशों के लोगों की अपेक्षा अविकसित देशों के लोगों की सोच ग्राम्यता के उत्प्रेरकों के सम्बन्ध में एकदम भिन्न है। वहाँ यह एक प्रकार से मानव के जीवित रहने की क्रिया के लिए केवल भौतिक आवश्यकता है। तीसरी दुनिया के देशों में, जो मुख्य रूप से ग्रामीण हैं, उनका एकमात्र आधार ग्रामीण विकास ही है, जिसके द्वारा मानव जीवन को इसके वर्तमान अवमानव स्तर से ऊपर उठाया जा सकता है। उन देशों में शताब्दियों से ग्रामीण जीवन जहाँ का तहाँ खड़ा अवरोधित है। उस ग्रामीण जनसंख्या की दशाओं को सुधारने के लिए कुछ नहीं किया गया जो अन्य चार पैर वाले प्रतिरूपों की तुलना में मामूली ढंग से भिन्न है। अविकसित एवं अर्द्धविकसित देशों में अज्ञान, कुस्वास्थ्य तथा गरीबी ग्रामीण जीवन के पर्याय बन गये हैं। लेकिन सबसे दुःखद स्थिति यह है कि इस प्रकार की मानव जनसंख्या ने ऐसा स्वीकार कर लिया है कि यह दुर्व्यवस्था अपरिवर्तनीय है। यह एक ऐसी स्थिति है जिसकी कोई दवा नहीं है। उनके जीवन से आशा की सभी किरणें दूर हो गयी हैं। इस प्रकार के देशों में, ग्रामीण विकास किसी प्रकार की भौतिक अथवा अभौतिक विकास के लिए अपरिहार्य शर्त है। इसलिए इन सभी देशों का प्रबुद्ध वर्ग ग्रामीण विकास के प्रश्न पर निरन्तर बढ़-चढ़कर रुचि ले रहा है।

उनके स्वतंत्रता संघर्ष की विरासत का यह एक अंग भी था। भारत जैसे देश में, इस बात को सभी जानते हैं कि स्वतंत्रता आन्दोलन में ग्रामीण विकास की कोशिश एक अविभाज्य अंग था। गाँधीजी जैसे नेताओं को भली-भाँति यह एहसास था कि वास्तविक भारत अवरोधग्रस्त ग्रामों में निवास करता है। शहर जो ज्यादातर पश्चिमी उपनिवेशवाद की उपज हैं, केवल दिखावटी दर्शनीय वस्तुएँ हैं। तब भी दो प्रकार की दुनिया थी—एक वह जहाँ तड़क-भड़क के जीवन जीने वाले तथा शाही रुचियों के सुविधासम्पन्न कुछ गिने-चुने सम्भ्रान्त क्षेत्रवासी रहते थे। दूसरे, वे क्षेत्र जो छोटे-छोटे टापू जैसे थे जिनको धूल-मिट्टी और गंदगी के विशाल समुद्र ने घेर रखा था और बहुसंख्यक लोग उन स्थानों का प्रतिनिधित्व करते थे।

भारत नगरों से किसी भी तरह अपरिचित नहीं रहा। प्राचीन भारत में, नगर देश के अंगभूत भाग थे जो मूलरूप से शेष सारे देश और समग्र समाज से सम्बन्धित थे। वे संस्कृति के सुमन की भाँति तथा राष्ट्र की कलात्मक उत्कृष्टता के परिचायक थे। आधुनिक नगर केवल दूसरों के शिकार करने वाले परजीवीमात्र हैं जो देश को कमजोर बना रहे हैं।

इसीलिए गाँधीजी ने 'गाँवों की ओर लौट चलो' यह ग्राम आन्दोलन प्रारम्भ किया था। उनके मतानुसार यह आन्दोलन ही भारत को स्वतंत्रता दिलवा सकता था और स्वतंत्रता को सुरक्षित रख सकता था। राष्ट्र की स्वतंत्रता के लिए अपनायी गयी उनकी रणनीति में ग्रामीण विकास गर्व का स्थान रखता था। इस प्रकार ग्रामीण विकास का उद्‌गम स्वतंत्रता संग्राम के मूल में सन्निहित है।

1. लोग ग्रामीण विकास में अत्यधिक रुचि ले रहे हैं क्योंकि—
A. उन्हें इसकी अपरिहार्यता का अनुभव हो चुका है
B. वे घोर स्वास्थ्य-समस्याओं से दुःखी हैं
C. निकट भविष्य में कुछ भी सार्थक करना सम्भव नहीं है
D. अब वे इसके सम्बन्ध में आशावादी हो गए हैं

2. परिच्छेद के अनुसार निम्नलिखित में से कौन-सा 'सहारा' (उत्तोलक का काम करने वाला) है?
A. अभौतिक विकास
B. ग्रामीण जीवन में अवरोधन
C. ग्रामीण जनता के स्तर को ऊँचा उठाना
D. समाज के कुछ खास वर्गों को प्रबुद्ध बनाना

3. निम्नलिखित में से लेखक की दृष्टि से कौन-सी सर्वाधिक दुःखद घटना है?
A. ग्रामों में लोगों की अवमानवीय दशा
B. ग्रामीण लोगों में स्व की दुर्दशा की ओर से निराशावाद
C. ग्रामीण विकास के महत्त्व का एहसास होने की कमी
D. नगर निवासियों के द्वारा ग्रामीणजनों का शोषण

4. इस परिच्छेद के सन्दर्भ में निम्नलिखित में से कौन-सा कथन सत्य नहीं है?
A. तीसरी दुनिया के देशों की ग्रामीण जनता की यह सोच है कि उनकी अवमानवीय स्थिति सुधर नहीं सकती।
B. तीसरी दुनिया के देशों के लोगों का जीवन-स्तर केवल ग्रामीण विकास द्वारा उठाया जा सकता है।
C. आधुनिक नगरों में रहने वाले अधिकांश धनाढ्य लोग वास्तव में ग्रामीण विकास के सम्बन्ध में चिन्तित हैं।
D. किसी भी प्रकार की अन्य उन्नति और विकास के लिए ग्रामीण विकास सर्वप्रथम आवश्यक है।

5. ग्रामीण विकास को भारत के स्वातंत्र्य आन्दोलन का एक अंग समझा गया था, क्योंकि—
A. केवल ग्रामों में ही शाही रुचि निवास करती थी
B. देश मुख्य रूप से ग्रामों से बना था
C. गाँधीजी पश्चिमी उपनिवेशवाद के विरुद्ध थे
D. उस समय वास्तविक भारत ब्रिटिश हुकूमत के मातहत था

6. तीसरी दुनिया के देशों में लोगों के रहन-सहन के स्तर–
   A. बहुत शीघ्रता से सुधर रहे हैं
   B. किसी भी सुधार के लिए निरापद हैं
   C. सुधार लाने के बड़े से बड़े उपाय के बावजूद अवमानवीय है
   D. एक जानवर की स्थिति से किसी भाँति अच्छे नहीं हैं

7. निम्नलिखित में कौन-सा कथन आधुनिक नगरों वाली दो विपरीत दुनिया का सबसे उपयुक्त वर्णन करता है?
   A. कुछ धनी लोग और अधिक गरीब लोग
   B. चमक-दमक का क्षेत्र और धनाढ्य लोग
   C. वाणिज्यिक तथा औद्योगिक शोषण
   D. पश्चिमी उत्पादों के संरक्षक तथा शाही रुचियों के पोषक

8. परिच्छेद के सन्दर्भ में निम्नलिखित में से कौन-सा कथन सत्य है?
   A. तीसरी दुनिया के अधिकांश देशों का त्वरित गति से नगरीकरण हो रहा है।
   B. भारत का स्वतंत्रता आन्दोलन ग्रामीण विकास का अंगभूत समझा जाता है।
   C. ग्रामीण जनता अपनी दशा सुधारने के बारे में बहुत आशावादी है।
   D. वर्तमान सन्दर्भ में अज्ञान, निर्धनता तथा रुग्ण-स्वास्थ्य ग्रामीण जीवन के अविभाज्य अंग हैं।

9. वह शब्द चुनिए जो परिच्छेद में प्रयुक्त शब्द 'मुख्य रूप से' जैसा हो।
   A. रोगी
   B. असंदिग्ध रूप से
   C. अभाव रूप से
   D. स्पष्ट रूप से दिखायी देने वाला

10. परिच्छेद में प्रयुक्त 'सुधारने के लिए' शब्द का विपरीतार्थक शब्द चुनिए।
   A. खराब होना B. कम होना
   C. शीघ्र पूरा करना D. जल्दी करना

गद्यांश-5

शिष्टजनों द्वारा अनुष्ठित आचरण मात्र कल्पना-उद्भूत सामाजिक शिष्टाचार नहीं है अपितु गंभीर वैज्ञानिक रहस्यों से ओत-प्रोत ऐसा संस्कार है जो मानव जीवन में गुणाधान प्रक्रिया को प्रशस्त करता है। भारतीय संस्कृति में शिष्टाचार का श्रीगणेश सामाजिक व्यवहार के सिंहद्वार – अभिवादन से होता है। ईश्वराभिवादन, पूज्यजनों को प्रणाम, नमस्कार, प्राञ्जलि, अञ्जलिपुट, प्रणिपात, नामोच्चारणपूर्वक नमन, प्रदक्षिणापूर्वक सम्मान तथा साष्टांग प्रणाम पर्यायभेद से अभिवादन के ही विविध रूप हैं। प्रतिदिन या विशिष्ट अवसरों पर कर्म में सफलता और दीर्घायुष्य-प्राप्ति हेतु माता-पिता तथा गुरुजनों को अभिवादन करना केवल भारतीय संस्कृति में ही विद्यमान है। अध्यात्म-विज्ञान की मान्यता है कि किसी वरेण्य व्यक्ति के आगमन पर प्राणस्पन्दन की गति ऊर्ध्वमुखी होकर ऊर्जस्वित हो जाती है। उनका आशीर्वाद प्राप्त कर प्राण ऊर्जावान् बन जाते हैं। आज अन्य क्षेत्रों की भाँति शिष्टाचार के विधि-विधान में प्रदूषण और अवमूल्यन निर्बाध गति से हो रहा है। 'हाय', 'ही', 'हेलो' करने वालों को भला हाथ जोड़कर मस्तक झुकाना कैसे रास आ सकता है? त्याग-वैराग्यसम्पन्न अल्पवयस्क या वयोवृद्धों का अभिवादन करना हमारी पुरातन आचार-पद्धति है।

1. शिष्टाचार का प्रथम सोपान क्या है?
   A. कुशलक्षेम पूछना B. मुस्कराते हुए बात करना
   C. अभिवादन करना D. भेंट देना

2. गुरुजनों को अभिवादन करने का कौन-सा कृत्य विधिसम्मत नहीं है?
   A. चरण स्पर्श करना B. हाथ जोड़कर सिर झुकाना
   C. साष्टांग प्रणाम करना D. हाथ मिलाना

3. आशीर्वाद ग्रहण करने का वैज्ञानिक रहस्य क्या है?
   A. मन प्रसन्न हो जाता है
   B. प्राण ऊर्जस्वित हो जाते हैं
   C. असम्भव कार्य सम्भव हो जाता है।
   D. हमारा आत्मविश्वास बढ़ता है

4. सामाजिक कुशलता प्राप्त करने का सिंहद्वार क्या है?
   A. श्रीगणेश का पूजन
   B. सहभोज का आयोजन
   C. प्रत्येक व्यक्ति को अपना गुरु मानना
   D. विधिपूर्वक यथायोग्य अभिवादन

5. 'सबहिं मानप्रद आप अमानी' का अभिप्राय है–
   A. स्वयं सम्मान की चाह न कर सबको सम्मान देना
   B. सबके मान की परवाह करने से पहले अपनी चिन्ता करना
   C. मान पाकर आपा न खोना
   D. अपने सम्मान के समान दूसरों का भी सम्मान करना

गद्यांश-6

शैक्षिक योजना का उद्देश्य सभी उम्र के वर्ग समूहों की कुल जनसंख्या की शैक्षिक आवश्यकताओं की पूर्ति करना होना चाहिए। निस्संदेह प्राथमिक स्तर से विश्वविद्यालयी स्तर तक शिक्षा का तीन स्तरीय पदानुक्रम परम्परागत शिक्षा की संरचना का सार भाग है तथापि हमें परिधीय शिक्षा जो उतनी ही महत्त्वपूर्ण है, की अवहेलना नहीं करनी चाहिए। आधुनिक अवस्थाओं के अंतर्गत, कार्यकर्त्ताओं को अपने उत्साह को तरोताजा करने की आवश्यकता है अथवा उन्हें एक नई दिशा में बढ़ने या अपने कौशलों को विश्वविद्यालयी प्रोफेसर के स्तर तक बढ़ाने की आवश्यकता है। सेवानिवृत और वृद्धों की भी अपनी आवश्यकताएँ होती हैं। शैक्षिक योजना ऐसी होनी चाहिए जिसमें प्रत्येक की आवश्यकताओं को ध्यान में रखा जाए। शिक्षा की हमारी संरचना इस मान्यता पर आधारित है कि शिक्षा का एक सीमावर्ती बिन्दु होता है। आजकल यह मूलभूत त्रुटि और अधिक हानिकारक बन गई है।

एडगर फौरे तथा अन्य सदस्यों द्वारा रचित युनेस्को का 'लर्निंग टू बी' नामक प्रतिवेदन, जो 1973 में प्रकाशित हुआ, यह दावा करता है कि बच्चों की शिक्षा द्वारा स्व-अधिगम के विभिन्न रूपों के लिए भावी प्रौढ़ तैयार होने चाहिएँ। एक व्यवहार्य भावी शिक्षा पद्धति में ऐसे मोड्यूल होने चाहिए जिसमें विभिन्न प्रकार के प्रकार्य सम्मिलित हों और वह विविध सामाजिक अवयवों के लिए उपयोगी हों। और प्रमाण-पत्रों का आधार अध्ययन अवधि न होकर निष्पादन होना चाहिए। इसकी इबारत पहले से ही दीवार पर लिखी हुई है।

इस बात या तथ्य को ध्यान में रखते हुए कि जीवन-पर्यन्त अधिगम या आजन्म शिक्षा के प्रति प्रतिबद्धता के महत्त्व को आजकल शैक्षिक रूप से विकसित देशों में भी विवेचित किया जा रहा है, परंतु इस बात की सम्भाव्यता कि यह विचार शैक्षिक चिंतन का अभिन्न अंग बन जाए बहुत दूर की बात है। क्योंकि इस दिशा में आगे बढ़ने का अर्थ है वर्तमान शैक्षिक संगठनों की पुनर्व्यवस्था से कुछ अधिक करना। कम-से-कम विभिन्न वर्गों के वयस्क अध्येताओं के लिए मुक्त विश्वविद्यालयी प्रोग्राम विकसित करके और परम्परागत महाविद्यालयों और विद्यालयों में प्रसार-सेवाएँ आरंभ करके इसका शुभारंभ किया जा सकता है। साथ ही इन संस्थाओं को चाहिए कि असंख्य सामुदायिक संगठनों, जैसे पुस्तकालय, संग्रहालय, म्युनिसिपल मनोरंजन कार्यक्रम, स्वास्थ्य सेवाएँ आदि, के साथ सहयोग करते रहें।

1. लेखक का मुख्य बल किस बात पर है?
A. परम्परागत पद्धतियों को सुदृढ़ किया जाना चाहिए।
B. औपचारिक शिक्षा, गैर-औपचारिक शिक्षा से अधिक महत्त्वपूर्ण है
C. व्यक्ति को सीखना कभी बंद नहीं करना चाहिए
D. मुक्त शिक्षा प्रणाली का कोई विकल्प नहीं है

2. निम्नलिखित में से कौन-सा कथन लेखक के प्रयोजन को वर्णित करता है?
A. वर्तमान शैक्षिक प्रणाली की आलोचना करना
B. वर्तमान शैक्षिक प्रणाली को मजबूत बनाना
C. गैर-परम्परागत शैक्षिक संगठनों का समर्थन करना
D. इनमें से कोई नहीं

3. परिच्छेद के अनुसार, वर्तमान शैक्षिक संरचनाएँ निम्नलिखित में से किसको मान्यता देती हैं?
A. सभी व्यक्तियों को उनकी आवश्यकताओं के अनुसार शिक्षित किया जा सकता है
B. वर्तमान में शैक्षिक योजना बहुत अधिक व्यवहार्य है
C. शिक्षा एक निश्चित समय में पूर्ण होने वाली प्रक्रिया है
D. जीवन-पर्यन्त शिक्षा (अधिगम) पर चर्चाएँ चलती रहनी चाहिए

4. दिए गए परिच्छेद के संदर्भ में निम्नलिखित में से कौन-सा सही नहीं है?
A. जीवन-पर्यन्त शिक्षा एक आधुनिक अवधारणा है
B. कर्मियों का ज्ञान तथा उनके कौशलों का निरंतर रूप से अद्यतन होते रहना चाहिए
C. 'लर्निंग टू बी' नामक ग्रंथ इस बात का समर्थन करता है कि शिक्षा का एक सीमांत बिन्दु होता है
D. विद्यालयों तथा महाविद्यालयों में भी विस्तार सेवाएँ आरंभ की जानी चाहिए

5. लेखक के अनुसार, 'जीवन-पर्यन्त शिक्षा' की अवधारणा है :
A. इतनी पुरानी जितनी परम्परागत शिक्षा होती है
B. जो अभी भी निर्माण अवस्था में हो
C. जो विकसित देशों में प्रचलित है
D. जो व्यवहार्य अथवा वांछनीय न हो

6. जीवन-पर्यन्त शिक्षा को शैक्षिक संरचना के साथ समेकित करने का अभिप्रेत होगा–
A. परम्परागत विद्यालयों और महाविद्यालयों को बंद कर देना
B. सभी औपचारिक पाठ्यक्रमों के लिए अधिक समयावधि
C. वर्तमान शैक्षिक संगठनों का सामान्य पुनर्व्यवस्थापन
D. इनमें से कोई नहीं

7. परिच्छेद के संदर्भ में इस वाक्य का क्या अर्थ है "इसकी इबारत पहले से ही दीवार पर लिखी हुई है"?
A. आजकल सभी कुछ अनिश्चित है
B. परिवर्तन पहले से ही हो चुके हैं
C. परिवर्तन के संकेत पहले ही स्पष्ट हैं
D. आप भविष्य को परिवर्तित नहीं कर सकते

8. निम्नलिखित में से कौन-सा शब्द परिच्छेद में प्रयुक्त 'पूर्ति करना' शब्द के अर्थ के सबसे समीप है?
A. पहुँच　　B. संपर्क करना
C. आरंभ करना　　D. संतुष्ट करना

9. परिच्छेद में प्रयुक्त 'अभिन्न' शब्द का विपरीतार्थक शब्द निम्नलिखित में से कौन-सा है?
A. अनिवार्य　　B. स्वतंत्र
C. मुख्य या प्रधान　　D. लघु या अप्रधान

10. परिच्छेद में प्रयुक्त शब्द 'परिधीय' का विपरीतार्थक शब्द निम्नलिखित में से कौन-सा है?
A. वास्तविकता　　B. सैद्धांतिक सुझाव
C. बहुत मजाकिया　　D. लगभग असंभव

गद्यांश-7

मानव-जीवन के सौ वर्षों को चार भागों में बाँटा गया है। वास्तव में सम्पूर्ण जीवन सतत प्रयत्न करते हुए व्यक्तित्व का विकास करने के लिए है। व्यक्तित्व के विकास की दिशा अवस्था के अनुसार बदलती है। विशेष प्रकार की योग्यताओं को विकसित करने के लिए अनुकूल वातावरण की आवश्यकता पड़ती है। आश्रम-व्यवस्था के अनुसार जीवन-भार श्रम करते हुए मानव अधिकाधिक सफलता प्राप्त कर सकता है। जीवन का प्रथम

आश्रम ब्रह्मचर्य अधिक से अधिक ज्ञान करने के लिए था। ब्रह्मचर्याश्रम में जो ज्ञान प्राप्त किया जाता है उसी की मात्रा के अनुरूप जीवन की सफलता होती है। इसी के बल पर गृहस्थाश्रम में वह अधिक से अधिक धन कमा कर लोक-कल्याण कर सकता है। मनुष्य की आध्यात्मिक प्रवृत्तियाँ स्वान्तः सुखाय होती हैं। इनके द्वारा वह वानप्रस्थ और संन्यास में शान्ति प्राप्त करता है।

1. वास्तव में सम्पूर्ण जीवन किसलिए है?
A. सतत प्रयत्न करते हुए व्यक्तित्व के विकास के लिए
B. श्रम करते हुए सफलता प्राप्त करने के लिए
C. अधिक से अधिक धन कमाने के लिए
D. अधिक से अधिक ज्ञान प्राप्त करने के लिए

2. व्यक्तित्व के विकास की दिशा कैसे बदलती है?
A. योग्यताओं के विकास के अनुसार
B. अनुकूल वातावरण के अनुसार
C. अवस्था के अनुसार
D. सतत प्रयत्नों के अनुसार

3. प्राप्त ज्ञान की मात्रा के अनुरूप क्या होता है?
A. जीवन की सफलता B. सुख की प्राप्ति
C. धन की प्राप्ति D. शान्ति की प्राप्ति

4. लोक-कल्याण कब अधिक किया जा सकता है?
A. ब्रह्मचर्याश्रम में B. वानप्रस्थ में
C. गृहस्थाश्रम में D. संन्यास में

5. मनुष्य शान्ति किसके द्वारा प्राप्त करता है?
A. ज्ञान के द्वारा
B. धन के द्वारा
C. लोक-कल्याण के द्वारा
D. आध्यात्मिक प्रवृत्तियों के द्वारा

गद्यांश-8

भारत की सांस्कृतिक शक्ति लोगों को आकर्षित करती है। सिकन्दर पूरब की ओर आया, तो उसने राज कायम कर लौटने का रास्ता पकड़ा। बाबर आया, तो वह भी लौटने की तैयारी में था। फिर भी उसे भारत ने आकर्षित किया। भारत में पश्चिम के लोग अपने लिए बेहद शांतिप्रिय बसेरा पाते हैं। निकोलोई-श्वेतास्लाव रोरिख, नारा रिचर्ड, एल्फ्रेड बुर्फल ऐसे अनेक नामी गिरामी लोगों ने, जो बीसवीं शताब्दी में ऊँचाइयों पर पहुँचे, बिना किसी संकोच के भारत को अपना घर बनाया। सरला बहन और मीरा बहन गांधी जी की दो शिष्याएं थीं। मीरा बहन ने पक्षी कुंज में अपना निवास बनाया था, जहां से वह हर समय हिमालय की बर्फ से लदी चोटियां देखती थी। मुंबई शहर को एक जर्मन विद्वान लाइफर ने आवास चुना।

भारतीय संस्कृति अपनी शक्ति उस वैविध्य से पाती है, जिसे मोटे तौर पर हम बहुलतावाद के रूप में देखते हैं। तथापि वैविध्य में गुणसूत्रों में जो लोकव्यापी होने का सामर्थ्य रहता है, वही तत्व संस्कृति का जीवनदायी तत्व निर्धारित हो जाता है। यानी भारतीय संस्कृति को सजीव और सक्रिय रखने की प्रक्रिया के भीतर गुणों को आत्मसात कर अपना बनाने की जो प्रवृत्ति है, यही वह मूल बिंदु है, जिसका बोध कर हम आसानी से कह सकते हैं कि भारतीय संस्कृति वैश्वीकरण, विश्व बाजार या नयी प्रौद्योगिकी से जन्मे कल-पुर्जों के अति उपयोगकर्ता सभ्यता के हमले भी झेल लेगी।

1. पश्चिमी दुनिया के लोगों के भारत की ओर आकर्षित होने का मुख्य कारण क्या है?
A. भारत की संपदा
B. भारत की आकर्षक जलवायु
C. भारत की बहुलतावादी संस्कृति
D. उपरोक्त सभी

2. निम्न में से किसने मुम्बई को अपना आवास स्थल बनाया?
A. लाइफर B. सरला बहन
C. एल्फ्रेड बुर्फल D. उपरोक्त सभी

3. भारतीय संस्कृति को जीवनदायी तत्त्व मिलते हैं—
A. लोक जीवन से B. सांस्कृतिक आदान-प्रदान से
C. सांस्कृतिक विक्षेप से D. A एवं B दोनों से

4. उपरोक्त उद्धरण के आधार पर निम्न में से कौन-सा कथन सही है?
A. भारत की संस्कृति ने सर्वदा ही विदेशियों को अपनी ओर आकर्षित किया है।
B. भारत की संस्कृति अन्य संस्कृतियों से श्रेष्ठ है।
C. भारत की संस्कृति एक बंद संस्कृति रही है।
D. A एवं B दोनों

गद्यांश-9

अफ्रीका में चीन के बढ़ते हुए प्रभाव से अमेरिका को एक और चिंता ने घेर लिया है। इराक, ईरान और उत्तरी कोरिया के बारे में तो अमेरिकी शासक खुलकर बात करते आये हैं, किंतु चीन से मुचैटा लेने के मामले में वे भारी सावधानी बरतते हैं। आखिर वे चीन के भारी कर्जदार तो हैं ही और शायद ये भुलाना भी आसान नहीं है कि किस प्रकार दशकों तक चीन से शत्रुता रखने के बाद उन्हें शीतयुद्ध जीतने के लिए पाकिस्तान की मध्यस्थता के माध्यम से, चीन की ओर मित्रता का हाथ बढ़ाना पड़ा था। चीन जैसी बड़ी ताकत से अपने रिश्तों में विश्व की सोल-सुपरपावर भी वो रुख नहीं अपना सकती, जो वह इराक जैसे बरसों से पिटे-पिटाए देश के साथ अपना सका था, यह बात समझना कठिन नहीं है।

लेकिन फिर भी अगर खतरा बढ़ने लगे, प्रतिस्पर्धा से कतराना संभव न रहे और वामपंथियों का दबाव बढ़ता चला जाये तो आखिर कब तक उनका राष्ट्रपति हाथों पर हाथ रखकर बैठा रह सकता है? इसीलिए तमाम उलझनों के बावजूद पूर्व राष्ट्रपति बुश को चीन की चुनौती की ओर ध्यान देने के लिए विवश होना पड़ा।

1. अमेरिका के लिए सबसे बड़ी चुनौती क्या है?
   A. चीन का बढ़ता आर्थिक प्रभाव
   B. शीत युद्ध के बाद सुपर पावर बने रहने की चिंता
   C. दक्षिण पंथ का विस्तार
   D. उपरोक्त सभी
2. चीन से मुचैटा लेने में अमेरिका अक्सर सावधानी बरतता है, क्यों?
   A. चीन की बड़ी पूँजी अमेरिका के बाजार में लगी हुई है।
   B. अमेरिका चीन के साथ बेहतर संबंध बनाना चाहता है।
   C. चीन शीत युद्ध के दौरान तटस्थ रहा था।
   D. A एवं C दोनों
3. निम्न में कौन-सा कथन सही है?
   A. चीन एशिया एवं अफ्रीका में अपने प्रभाव क्षेत्र का विस्तार कर रहा है।
   B. अमेरिका चीन के साथ संबंध खराब न हो जाए, इसलिए उत्तरी कोरिया के खिलाफ खुलकर कुछ नहीं कहता।
   C. शीत युद्ध के दौरान अमेरिका ने चीन की ओर मित्रता का हाथ बढ़ाया था।
   D. अमेरिका को वास्तविक खतरा विश्व आतंकवाद से है।
4. अमेरिकी राष्ट्रपति बुश को चीन की चुनौती की ओर क्यों ध्यान देना पड़ा?
   A. चीन के बढ़ते आर्थिक प्रभाव के कारण
   B. चीन द्वारा पाकिस्तान को मिलने वाले समर्थन के कारण
   C. उत्तरी कोरिया का चीन द्वारा समर्थन के कारण
   D. वामपंथ के बढ़ते दबाव के कारण

गद्यांश-10

समकालीन विश्व राजनीति में पश्चिम एशिया एक ऐसे क्षेत्र के तौर पर कुख्यात हो चुका है जहां केवल आतंक, अशांति और अराजकता का बोलबाला है। दूसरे विश्व युद्ध के बाद से ही मिडिल ईस्ट या पश्चिम एशिया कई छोटे-बड़े युद्ध और अनगिनत हिंसक झगड़े झेल चुका है। हाल ही में फतह और हमास द्वारा फिलिस्तीन के अलग-अलग इलाकों पर कब्जा करने के बाद तो पश्चिम एशिया का सामरिक वातावरण और उलझ गया है। अगर आतंक के खिलाफ विश्वव्यापी जंग की बात करें तो वर्तमान हालात यही इशारा कर रहे हैं कि अगर अमेरिका यह जंग हार नहीं रहा तो जीत भी उससे कोसों दूर है। पूरा पश्चिम एशिया समस्याग्रस्त है और अमेरिकी विदेश नीति के पास इन समस्याओं से जूझने के लिए कोई ठोस रणनीति नहीं है।

फिलहाल सबसे विकट समस्या इराक को लेकर है। इराक पर हुए अमेरिकी हमलों के कई साल गुजर चुके हैं। लेकिन वहाँ अभी तक शांति कायम नहीं की जा सकी है। रोजमर्रा के शिया-सुन्नी झगड़ों और अमेरिकी आधिपत्य के खिलाफ जिहादी हिंसा ने इराक को जर्जर बना दिया है। दोनों प्रमुख सम्प्रदायों को समान रूप से स्वीकार्य एक राजनीतिक व्यवस्था अभी नहीं पनप पाई है। दरअसल इराक को शिया, सुन्नी और कुर्द इलाकों में बाँटने की केवल औपचारिक घोषणा होना ही शेष है। अमेरिका के लिए गले की फांस बन चुका इराक दुनिया भर में जिहादियों के लिए प्रशिक्षण केंद्र में तब्दील हो चुका है। सितम्बर 2010 में अमेरिकी राष्ट्रपति बराक ओबामा ने ऑपरेशन 'इराकी फ्रीडम' खत्म होने की घोषणा की है। अब वहाँ स्थिति और बिगड़ सकती है। आत्मघाती हमलों में बेगुनाह इराकियों का मरना जारी है। अलकायदा दिन-प्रतिदिन अपनी ताकत में इजाफा कर रहा है। कट्टरपंथियों की फौज खड़ी हो रही है।

1. इराक में अमेरिका के लिए सबसे बड़ी चुनौती क्या है?
   A. इराक में एक प्रतिनिधि सरकार स्थापित करना
   B. इराक में शांति कायम करना
   C. इराक में गठबंधन सेना के बीच समन्वय स्थापित करना
   D. उपरोक्त सभी
2. उपरोक्त उद्धरण के आधार पर सही कथन का चयन कीजिए।
   A. फतह एवं हमास गुट की सक्रियता के कारण पश्चिम एशिया की समस्या और भी उलझ गई है।
   B. इराक में अमेरिका विरोधी जिहादी गुट लगातार सक्रिय हैं।
   C. इराक पर अमेरिकी हमले के बाद वैश्विक आतंकवाद में कमी आई है।
   D. A एवं B दोनों
3. इराक में शांति स्थापना में सबसे बड़ी बाधा क्या है?
   A. अल कायदा की इस क्षेत्र में बढ़ती गतिविधियाँ
   B. शिया-सुन्नी झगड़े
   C. जिहादी हिंसा
   D. A एवं C दोनों
4. पश्चिमी एशिया की पहचान निम्न में से किसके कारण है?
   A. अरब-इजराइल युद्ध के कारण
   B. इराक युद्ध के कारण
   C. सीरिया में होने वाली शांति प्रक्रिया के कारण
   D. उपरोक्त सभी के कारण

गद्यांश-11

किसी भी लोकतांत्रिक समाज का भविष्य, उसकी प्रगतिशीलता, वैज्ञानिकता और संवेदनशीलता पर निर्भर करता है। लोकतंत्र में मताधिकार योग्य व्यक्ति के चयन की कारगर व्यवस्था नहीं है। मतदाता की बौद्धिकता, वैज्ञानिकता और संवेदनशीलता ही सही निर्णय लेने में सहायक हो सकती है वरना चुनाव में तमाम हत्यारे अपराधी और गुंडे चुने जा सकते हैं। हमारे देश के ज्यादातर मतदाताओं में इन गुणों का अभाव है। वह मोबाइल युग में परम अवैज्ञानिक है। हम मतदाताओं की बौद्धिकता का अंदाज ऐसे लोगों को देखकर आसानी से लगा सकते हैं जो ओझा-तांत्रिक

और नीम-हकीमों के चक्कर में फंसकर तिल-तिल मरने को मजबूर हैं। वह यह समझ पाने की स्थिति में नहीं है कि ओझा-तांत्रिक, नीम-हकीम वगैरह उनकी अज्ञानता का लाभ उठाकर, शोषण कर रहे हैं।

हम वर्तमान शिक्षा व्यवस्था में पनपे उस गरीब समाज को देखकर बौद्धिकता की असलियत जान सकते हैं, जो अपनी औलादों की बलि देकर कल्याण ढूंढ़ता है। जो पढ़ने-पढ़ाने का हक मांगने के बजाय, उन्हें 'मिड-डे-मिल' खाना खिलाकर धन्य हो रहा है। बौद्धिकता की असलियत समाज के उन वयस्क मतदाताओं से जानी जा सकती है, जो असामाजिक तत्वों, अपराधियों के गले में माला डालकर उनकी जय-जयकार करते हैं। ये मतदाता वैज्ञानिकों या समाजशास्त्रियों को चुनने के बजाय फूलनदेवी, मलखान सिंह, मुख्तार अंसारी या शहाबुद्दीन जैसे लोगों को चुनते हैं।

1. उपरोक्त उद्धरण के आधार पर सही कथन का चयन कीजिए।
A. भारतीय मतदाता पिछड़ी सोच वाला और अवैज्ञानिक है।
B. भारतीय लोकतंत्र में मताधिकार, योग्य व्यक्ति के चयन की कारगर व्यवस्था नहीं है।
C. भारतीय मतदाता अशिक्षित है।
D. उपरोक्त सभी।

2. लोकतंत्र का भविष्य किस पर निर्भर करता है?
A. समाज की प्रगतिशीलता पर
B. सामाजिक संवेदनशीलता पर
C. D एवं B दोनों पर
D. सामाजिक सुव्यवस्था पर

3. भारतीय लोकतांत्रिक व्यवस्था का सबसे बड़ा अंतर्विरोध क्या है?
A. भारत में गरीबी एवं असमानता व्याप्त है।
B. समाज में भूखमरी एवं अज्ञानता है।
C. बौद्धिकता के युग में ज्यादातर मतदाता घोर अवैज्ञानिक हैं।
D. उपरोक्त सभी।

4. चुनाव में अपराधी किस्म के लोगों का चुना जाना किस बात का संकेत है?
A. जनता की तटस्थता का
B. जनता की अबौद्धिक निर्णय क्षमता का
C. जनता की सक्रिय भागीदारी का
D. प्रशासनिक विफलता का

गद्यांश-12

देह-प्रदर्शन स्वेच्छा से किया जाए या सामाजिक दबाव के कारण, लेकिन उसके दुष्प्रभावों को नजरअंदाज नहीं किया जा सकता है। नारियों से छेड़छाड़, अश्लील हरकतें, बलात्कार, यौन अपराध, देह व्यापार आदि बुराइयों की जड़ देह प्रदर्शन है। यदि पुरुषों से यह पूछा जाए कि क्या नारी के देह-प्रदर्शन से तुम को लज्जा महसूस नहीं होती है तो उनका तर्क होता है कि जब नारी को देह-प्रदर्शन करने में लज्जा नहीं आती है तो हमको देखने में लज्जा क्यों आएगी? देह-प्रदर्शन करने वाली नारी को समाज में हेय दृष्टि से देखा जाता है। ऐसी नारी को सिर्फ देह मानकर उसे इस्तेमाल किया जा रहा है।

आजकल माता-पिता के लिए लड़की की परवरिश करना चुनौतीपूर्ण होता जा रहा है क्योंकि यौन अपराधों की संख्या में वृद्धि होती जा रही है। माता-पिता सोचते हैं कि यदि हम बेटी की इज्जत की रक्षा न कर पाए तो बेटी को जन्म देने का क्या फायदा होगा? माता-पिता की यह सोच कन्या भ्रूण-हत्या का महत्त्वपूर्ण कारण है। जो नारी आर्थिक लाभ के लिए अंग प्रदर्शन करती है उसका यौवन व आकर्षण समाप्त हो जाने पर वह कुंठित हो जाती है। विषादग्रस्त होकर वह आत्महत्या भी कर सकती है। नारी देह के प्रति पुरुषों का आकर्षण यौवनावस्था में होता है, इसमें स्थायित्व नहीं होता है। ऐसी नारियाँ आकर्षणहीन हो जाने पर स्वयं को एकाकी महसूस करती हैं तथा कई प्रकार के मानसिक रोगों से ग्रस्त हो जाती हैं।

1. नारी देह-प्रदर्शन का स्वाभाविक परिणाम है–
A. उनके साथ छेड़छाड़
B. अश्लील हरकतें
C. यौन अपराध
D. उपरोक्त सभी

2. नारी देह-प्रदर्शन की बढ़ती प्रवृत्ति का मुख्य कारण है–
A. नारी की स्व इच्छा
B. सामाजिक दबाव एवं लोलुपता
C. शिक्षा का माहौल
D. A एवं B दोनों

3. लेखक के अनुसार कन्या भ्रूण-हत्या का महत्वपूर्ण कारण क्या है?
A. महिलाओं के साथ होनेवाला यौन शोषण
B. बच्चियों का उचित परवरिश न हो पाना
C. सामाजिक असुरक्षा की भावना
D. उपरोक्त सभी

4. उपरोक्त उद्धरण के आधार पर सही कथन का चयन कीजिए।
A. आर्थिक लाभ के कारण नारी में शरीर-प्रदर्शन की प्रवृत्ति बढ़ती जा रही है।
B. नारी के देह-प्रदर्शन के पीछे सामाजिक दबाव एक मुख्य कारण है।
C. अंग-प्रदर्शन करनेवाली नारियों को यौवन का आकर्षण समाप्त हो जाने पर कुंठा का सामना करना पड़ता है।
D. उपरोक्त सभी।

गद्यांश-13

वर्तमान इतिहास में दो प्रवृत्तियां दिखाई देती हैं। एक प्रवृत्ति की दिशा वर्चस्व (हेजीमनी) की ओर है जो मानव-अस्तित्व (सरवाइवल) के लिए खतरा बन कर पागलपन के सैद्धांतिक चौखटे में तर्कपूर्ण ढंग से काम कर रही है। दूसरी प्रवृत्ति इस विश्वास को समर्पित है कि 'एक नयी दुनिया संभव है', जिन शब्दों से विश्व सामाजिक मंच प्रेरित है, जो शासक विचारात्मक प्रणालियों को चुनौती दे रहा है और जो विचार,

कर्म और संस्थाओं का नया सृजनात्मक विकल्प बनाना चाहता है। इनमें कौन-सी प्रवृत्ति जीतेगी, कोई इसकी भविष्यवाणी नहीं कर सकता है। यह प्रक्रिया समूचे इतिहास में दिखाई देती है।'

चोमस्की का कहना है कि अस्सी के दशक में मुख्यधारा के अमेरिका, खासकर मध्य अमेरिका से संबंधित जो मानव एकता आंदोलन चले उन्होंने साम्राज्यवाद के इतिहास में नयी जमीन जोड़ी। इससे पहले कभी भी शासक समाज के लोग बड़ी संख्या में दुष्टतापूर्ण हमले के शिकार लोगों के साथ रहने और उन्हें कुछ मात्रा में सुरक्षा प्रदान करने नहीं गये थे। वैसे आम जनता में मानव अधिकारों की यह जागरूकता 1960 के दशक में तेज हुई थी और कई क्षेत्रों में जन-सक्रियता ने अपना सभ्यताकारी प्रभाव डाला। इससे अल्पसंख्यक समूहों, स्त्रियों, भावी पीढ़ियों के अधिकारों के आंदोलन और फिर पर्यावरण सुरक्षा के आंदोलन विकसित हुए थे।

1. वर्तमान इतिहास की दो महत्वपूर्ण प्रवृत्तियाँ कौन-सी हैं?
A. आशा एवं निराशा की।
B. हिंसा एवं सभ्यता की।
C. विश्व वर्चस्व की एवं एक नई दुनिया बसाने की।
D. साम्राज्यवाद एवं उदारवाद की।

2. आज मानव अस्तित्व के लिए सबसे बड़ा खतरा क्या है?
A. वर्चस्व की प्रवृत्ति
B. हिंसा की प्रवृत्ति
C. अधीनस्थता की प्रवृत्ति
D. उपरोक्त सभी

3. मानव एकता आंदोलन ने किस रूप में सकारात्मक भूमिका निभाई?
A. इसने शासक वर्ग की मानसिकता में बदलाव लाया।
B. इसने साम्राज्यवाद के इतिहास में एक नई जमीन जोड़ी।
C. इसने मानव अधिकारों को और भी सशक्त बनाया।
D. उपरोक्त सभी।

4. उपरोक्त उद्धरण के आधार पर सही कथन का चयन कीजिए।
A. हेजीमनी मानव अस्तित्व को बनाए रखने में सहायक है।
B. 'एक नई दुनिया संभव है' का विचार शासक विचारात्मक प्रणाली के लिए खतरा है।
C. मानव एकता आंदोलन का आरंभ दक्षिण अमेरिका से हुआ।
D. उपरोक्त सभी।

गद्यांश-14

इंडिया के लिए कॉमनवेल्थ गेम्स की सफलता ने एक साथ कई काम किए हैं। गेम्स शुरू होने से पहले दुनिया भर में बनी देश की नेगेटिव छवि धुलकर पॉजिटिव हो गई। इंडिया में निवेश करने वाले इन्वेस्टर्स अब शायद बेधड़क यहां पैसा लगाएंगे। ऑस्ट्रेलियाई और अंग्रेज अब शायद एक हिंदुस्तानी को नीचे नजर से न देख पाएं। इस सफलता ने भविष्य में ओलंपिक गेम्स जैसे बड़े आयोजन को लेकर भारत की दावेदारी को भी पुख्ता किया है। भारतीय खिलाड़ियों ने 71 देशों में दूसरा स्थान हासिल कर देश के युवाओं को दिखाया है कि कैसे खेल भी उसके लिए नाम और रुतबे का जरिया बन सकते हैं। खेलों के आयोजन में हजारों करोड़ रुपये खर्च जरूर हुए मगर इससे देश की दो पीढ़ियों के करोड़ों लोगों में खेलों के प्रति नया जज्बा भी पैदा हुआ है। इन खेलों ने हमारे कई खिलाड़ियों को गुमनामी से निकाल कर रोशनी के घेरे में खड़ा कर दिया। दीपिका कुमारी, कृष्णा पूनिया, सुरंजय, ओंकार सिंह, जिन्हें मुट्ठी भर लोग ही जानते थे, अब नेशनल हीरो बन गए हैं। इनमें कई खिलाड़ी ऐसे हैं जिन्होंने अपने माता-पिता की सुरक्षित और बेहतर करियर अपनाने की नसीहतों के खिलाफ जाकर खेलों को अपनाया। गेम्स ने देश को उनकी कामयाबी दिखाई, उन्हें अपने देशवासियों के सामने अपनी मेहनत और अपनी जिद का उत्सव मनाने का मौका दिया।

देश की गरीब जनता की जरूरतों को भुलाकर एक सर्कस शो पर करोड़ों रुपये फूंकने की दलील देने वाले गेम्स के आलोचक आगे की बजाय पीछे देखते हुए ऐसा कह रहे हैं। वे दह नहीं समझ रहे कि भारत का एक बड़ी ताकत बनने का दावा सिर्फ आंकड़ों में कैद नहीं रहना चाहिए, तमाम क्षेत्रों में दिखना चाहिए। गेम्स की कामयाबी ने यही किया है। उसने इंडिया के फ्यूचर की तस्वीर पेश की है—आत्मविश्वास से भरा, बुनियादी सुविधाओं से लैस, सफलता का जश्न मनाता हुआ इंडिया।

1. कॉमनवेल्थ गेम्स की सफलता का सबसे बड़ा लाभ क्या हुआ है?
A. भारतीय खिलाड़ियों ने अंतर्राष्ट्रीय स्तर की खेल प्रतिभा का प्रदर्शन किया।
B. खेल के आयोजन में करोड़ों रुपये का घोटाला हुआ।
C. गेम्स के दौरान खिलाड़ियों को स्तरहीन सुविधाएँ उपलब्ध कराई गईं।
D. भविष्य में ओलंपिक खेल जैसे बड़े आयोजन को लेकर भारत की दावेदारी पुख्ता हुई है।

2. आलोचकों की नजर में कॉमनवेल्थ गेम्स एक सर्कस शो क्यों था?
A. क्योंकि इसमें सर्कस की तरह तमाशे हुए।
B. आयोजन की तैयारी पूरी न हो पाने के कारण गेम्स एक तमाशा बनकर रह गया।
C. इसमें देश की गरीब जनता की जरूरतों को भुलाकर अनावश्यक खर्च किए गए।
D. उपरोक्त सभी

3. 'गुमनामी से निकालकर रोशनी के घेरे में खड़ा कर दिया' पदबंध का अर्थ बताइए—
A. अचानक प्रसिद्धि मिलना
B. अचानक बड़ी धनराशि मिलना
C. रोशनी से चकाचौंध होना
D. ऊँचा पद प्राप्त होना

4. उपरोक्त उद्धरण के आधार पर सही कथन का चयन कीजिए।
   A. कॉमनवेल्थ गेम्स से दुनिया भर में देश की अच्छी छवि बनी है।
   B. इससे दुनिया भर के निवेशक भारत में निवेश के लिए प्रोत्साहित होंगे।
   C. इससे युवाओं में एक नई स्फूर्ति पैदा हुई है।
   D. उपरोक्त सभी।

गद्यांश-15

देश में खाद्यान्न भंडारण की समस्या ने विकराल रूप धारण कर लिया है। इसकी भयावहता का अंदाजा इसी बात से लगाया जा सकता है कि एफसीआई के गोदामों में 67,542 टन अनाज नष्ट हो गया। इसकी कीमत 60 हजार करोड़ रुपए बताई गई है। सुप्रीम कोर्ट ने इसमें दखल देते हुए कहा है कि गोदामों में अनाज सड़ाने की जगह इसे गरीबों में बाँट देना चाहिए। सुप्रीम कोर्ट ने 12 अगस्त, 2010 को केन्द्र सरकार को आदेश देते हुए कहा कि वह फूड कॉरपोशन ऑफ इंडिया के गोदामों में अनाज सड़ाने की जगह गरीबों को मुफ्त बाँट दें।

जस्टिस दलवीर भंडारी और जस्टिस दीपक वर्मा की बेंच ने कहा कि और अनाज न सड़ने पाए, इसके लिए सरकार तुरंत कदम उठाए। वह उतने ही अनाज की खरीदारी करे, जितने को संभाल सकती है। साथ ही कोर्ट ने केन्द्र से प्रत्येक राज्य में एक बड़ा गोदाम और अलग-अलग जिलों व संभागों में विभिन्न गोदाम बनाने की व्यवस्था करने को कहा। इसके अलावा सरकार से यह सुनिश्चित करने को भी कहा कि उचित मूल्य की दुकानें पूरे महीने खुली रहें। कोर्ट ने सरकार को निर्देश दिया है कि वह 2010 के आंकड़ों के आधार पर बीपीएल (गरीबी रेखा से नीचे), एबीपीएल (गरीबी रेखा से ऊपर), एएवाई (अंत्योदय अन्न योजना) परिवारों का नए सिरे से सर्वे कराए। अधिकारी फायदे बांटने के लिए एक दशक पुराने आंकड़े पर भरोसा नहीं कर सकते।

बेंच ने अपना पहले का आदेश दोहराया कि एबीपीएल परिवार सब्सिडी वाला अनाज न हासिल करने पाएं। अगर सरकार उन्हें लाभ देना ही चाहती है तो उन परिवारों को दे, जिनकी सालाना आय 3 लाख रुपये से कम हो।

सुप्रसिद्ध अर्थशास्त्री डॉ. अमर्त्य सेन द्वारा 1981 में लिखी गई 'पावर्टी एंड फैमीन एंड एस्से ऑन इनटाइटिलमेंट एंड डिप्राइवेशन' (गरीबी और अकाल और पात्रता और वंचना पर निबंध) कृति में तर्क दिया गया कि अधिकांश मामलों में भूख और अकाल अनाज की उपलब्धता की कमी के कारण नहीं पड़ते, बल्कि उनका कारण असमानता और वितरण व्यवस्था की कमी होती है। उन्होंने जो बात 1981 में कही थी, संभवतः वह 2010 में भी सही है। हालांकि स्वतंत्रता प्राप्ति के बाद विगत तिरसठ वर्षों में भूख और वंचना से लड़ने के क्रम में हमने काफी अनुभव प्राप्त किया है।

1. अनाजों के भंडारण को लेकर सर्वोच्च न्यायालय ने कौन-से आदेश दिए हैं?
   A. सरकार भंडारण के बराबर क्षमता के अनाज का ही क्रय करे।
   B. सरकार अलग-अलग जिलों एवं संभागों में गोदाम बनाने की व्यवस्था करे।
   C. उचित मूल्य की दुकानें महीने भर खुली रहें।
   D. उपरोक्त सभी

2. देश में खाद्यान्न भंडारण की समस्या का मुख्य कारण क्या है?
   A. खाद्यान्न भंडारण की सीमित क्षमता
   B. अत्यधिक खाद्यान्नों की खरीद
   C. समय पर खाद्यान्नों का वितरण न हो पाना
   D. उपरोक्त सभी

3. प्रसिद्ध अर्थशास्त्री अमर्त्य सेन के अनुसार भूख एवं अकाल का कारण है–
   A. राष्ट्रीय कृषि उपज में कमी
   B. कृषि निर्यात की असमानता
   C. अनाजों के उपयुक्त वितरण की समस्याएं
   D. A एवं C

4. कोर्ट ने किस आधार पर बीपीएल, एबीपीएल एवं एएवाई परिवारों का सर्वे कराने को कहा है?
   A. 2011 की जनगणना के आधार पर
   B. 2005 के आंकड़ों के आधार पर
   C. 2007 के योजना आयोग के आंकड़ों के आधार पर
   D. 2010 के आंकड़ों के आधार पर

गद्यांश-16

वैश्वीकरण की दौड़ में क्षेत्रीय संगठनों का महत्व बढ़ा है। आज विश्व की स्थिति यह है कि राष्ट्र अपने आपसी मतभेदों को भुलाकर व्यापार एवं आर्थिक क्षेत्रों में एक-दूसरे को सहयोग कर रहे हैं। राष्ट्रों की पारस्परिक निर्भरता पहले की अपेक्षा काफी बढ़ी है। सार्क विश्व की 22 प्रतिशत आबादी को अपने दामन में रखने वाला विश्व का सबसे बड़ा क्षेत्रीय संगठन है। भारत विश्व की उभरती हुई आर्थिक शक्ति है। सार्क के सदस्य देश आपस में एक-दूसरे का आर्थिक सहयोग करें तो इस क्षेत्र से गरीबी, भुखमरी, अशिक्षा को सदा के लिए समाप्त किया जा सकता है। आज यूरोपियन संघ एवं आसियान जैसे क्षेत्रीय संगठनों ने जो आर्थिक सफलता पायी है। उससे सार्क के नेताओं को प्रेरणा लेनी चाहिए। इन क्षेत्रीय संगठनों ने आर्थिक एकजुटता के बल पर काफी उपलब्धियाँ हासिल की हैं। अब यह स्थिति स्पष्ट हो चुकी है कि आर्थिक विकास में क्षेत्रीय वैश्वीकरण की भूमिका अतिमहत्वपूर्ण है।

जनवरी 2009 में इस्लामाबाद में हुए सम्मेलन में इस तरह की स्पष्ट अभिव्यक्ति सामने आई। इस सम्मेलन में सार्क देशों ने 2012 तक दक्षिण एशियाई स्वतंत्र व्यापार क्षेत्र (साफ्टा) बनाने की इच्छा व्यक्त की है, लेकिन इस दिशा में अभी तक कोई ठोस कार्य नहीं हुआ है। साफ्टा के बारे में छोटे-छोटे देशों को यह भ्रम पैदा हो गया कि इससे भारत को ही अधिक लाभ होगा, जबकि सच्चाई यह नहीं है। उदाहरणस्वरूप

अभी हम भारत, श्रीलंका के मुक्त व्यापार को देखें। दोनों देशों के बीच मुक्त व्यापार पिछले तीन वर्ष से चल रहा है। श्रीलंका का भारत को निर्यात 135 प्रतिशत सालाना की दर से बढ़ा है। इस तुलना में भारत का श्रीलंका को निर्यात 32 प्रतिशत की दर से बढ़ा है। अपितु मुक्त व्यापार के होने से श्रीलंका भारत की अपेक्षा अधिक लाभ की स्थिति में है। यही बात नेपाल एवं भूटान के साथ हैं। पाकिस्तान एवं बांग्लादेश के साथ भारत का व्यापार उतना नहीं बढ़ा है जितना बढ़ना चाहिए। इन देशों के असहयोग के कारण भी साफ्टा को लागू करने में कठिनाई है।

1. वैश्वीकरण के कारण क्षेत्रीय संगठनों का महत्व बढ़ा है–
A. क्योंकि वैश्वीकरण के दौरान विभिन्न देशों के बीच व्यापार बढ़ा है।
B. राष्ट्र अपने आपसी मतभेद को भूलाकर आर्थिक क्षेत्र में एक-दूसरे को सहयोग कर रहे हैं।
C. सभी राष्ट्रों ने व्यापार को सीमाकर मुक्त कर दिया है।
D. अंतर्राष्ट्रीय बाजार में डॉलर का मूल्य घटा है।

2. उपरोक्त उद्धरण के आधार पर सही कथन का चयन कीजिए।
A. हाल के वर्षों में राष्ट्रों के बीच पारस्परिक निर्भरता बढ़ी है।
B. सार्क दुनिया का सबसे बड़ा क्षेत्रीय संगठन है।
C. सार्क देशों में दुनिया की लगभग 1/4 आबादी रहती है।
D. उपरोक्त सभी।

3. सार्क देशों के बीच आपसी व्यापार में पर्याप्त वृद्धि नहीं हुई है, इसका क्या कारण है?
A. सार्क देशों के बीच व्यापार प्रतिबंध
B. आपसी सहयोग का अभाव
C. पश्चिमी देशों पर अत्यधिक निर्भरता
D. व्यापारिक निवेश का अभाव

4. साफ्टा को लेकर सार्क देशों में कौन-सा भ्रम फैला हुआ है?
A. इससे भारत को अधिक लाभ होगा।
B. भारत एक आर्थिक महाशक्ति बन जाएगा।
C. भारत का प्रभाव दुनिया के अन्य देशों में बढ़ जाएगा।
D. भारतीय रुपया और भी मजबूत होगा।

गद्यांश-17

महामशीन के महाप्रयोग का उद्देश्य परमाणु कणों की आपसी टक्कर को देखना है, जिनसे नए कण बन सकते हैं। उनका वेग और ऊर्जा मापकर मालूम हो सकता है कि आखिर शुरू में ब्रह्माण्ड कैसे बना और बाद में कैसे उसकी उत्पत्ति हुई। एलएचसी के इस प्रयोग में परमाणु कणों की बहुत अधिक वेग से अब तक की सबसे अधिक ऊर्जा से टक्कर हुई। आशा की जा रही है कि अब वैज्ञानिक भौतिकी की अनेक गुत्थियों को सुलझा लेंगे।

50,000 करोड़ रुपए की लागत से बना लार्ज हैड्रॉन कोलाइडर (LHC) 2008 में असफल हो गया था। उस समय इस सबसे बड़े एटम स्मैशर में दो शक्तिशाली चुम्बकों के बीच विद्युत कनेक्शन फ्यूज हो गया था। इन चुम्बक प्रोटॉनों को स्टीआर कहते हैं। इस खराबी से सुरंग में बड़े जोर का विस्फोट हुआ था, लेकिन इस बार का प्रयोग सफल रहा। एलएचसी प्रसिद्ध ईश्वरीय कण 'हिग्स बोसोन' के चिह्न की भी पहचान करेगा। बताया जाता है कि इसी कण के कारण ब्रह्माण्ड की सभी चीजों को पिण्ड भार मिलता है। इसके अलावा रहस्यमयी 'ब्लैक होल' की भी पहचान की जाएगी, जिससे काफी हद तक ब्रह्माण्ड बना है, लेकिन इसमें अंधेरा होने के कारण अब तक इसके दर्शन नहीं हुए हैं। वैज्ञानिकों का कहना है कि एलएचसी में जब कणों की टक्कर हुई, तब अनेक ऐसे मिनी बिग बैंग बने, जैसे आज से 13 अरब, 70 करोड़ वर्ष पहले बने थे।

इन असाधारण खोजों के अतिरिक्त मशीन बिग बैंग के पहले और बाद के कणों की नकल करेगी। गुरुत्वाकर्षण के रहस्य भी जानने के प्रयत्न किए जाएंगे। इस अनुसंधान में लगे वैज्ञानिकों का कहना है कि जब कणों की बीमों की टक्कर हुई तब सभी डिटेक्टरों ने अपने परमाणु कणों के बहुरंगी मार्गों की पहचान की। ये कण प्रत्येक दिशा में कार्यशील थे। भौतिकविद् का कहना है कि जब उप परमाणु कण बड़े वेग से आपस में टकराते हैं तो वे टूटकर नए तत्व बनाते हैं। आशा की जा रही है कि इसमें से एक तत्व हिग्स बोसोन होगा जिससे हमारे ब्रह्माण्ड बनने की गुत्थी सुलझेगी। वैज्ञानिकों का कहना है कि प्रयोग में उत्सर्जित ऊर्जा फील्ड को यदि ऊष्मा में बदल दिया जाए तो यह सूर्य की सतह से भी ज्यादा गर्म होगा।

1. महामशीन ब्रह्माण्ड की उत्पत्ति की जाँच किस आधार पर करेगा?
A. परमाणु कणों की आपसी टक्कर से उत्पन्न वेग के आधार पर
B. परमाणु कणों के बीच आपसी आकर्षण के आधार पर
C. परमाणु कणों की आपसी टक्कर से उत्पन्न वेग एवं ऊर्जा के आधार पर
D. परमाणु कणों के गुरुत्वाकर्षण के आधार पर

2. लार्ज हैड्रॉन कोलाइडर की पिछली असफलता का क्या कारण था?
A. चुम्बकीय विद्युत कनेक्शन का फ्यूज होना
B. हिग्स बोसोन कण का रिसाव
C. परमाणु कणों के बीच तीव्र विकर्षण
D. परमाणु कणों का विस्फोट

3. ब्रह्मांड के पिंडों का पिंड भार किस पर निर्भर करता है?
A. पिंड के द्रव्यमान पर
B. पिंड के घनत्व पर
C. हिग्स बोसोन कण पर
D. A एवं B दोनों पर

4. हिग्स बोसोन कण का निर्माण होता है–
A. जब उप परमाणु कण तीव्र वेग से आपस में टकराते हैं।
B. परमाणु कणों के बीच तीव्र आकर्षण बल के कारण।
C. परमाणु कणों के बीमों के साथ टक्कर से।
D. A एवं B दोनों

गद्यांश-18

विज्ञान शब्द की परिभाषा तथा इसके विस्तार, और प्रौद्योगिकी से इसके भेद को भी स्पष्ट रूप से समझ लेना जरूरी है। मानव जाति के भविष्य की कुंजी जिन कुछ शक्तिशाली ताकतों के हाथ में है, उनमें से विज्ञान संभवतः एकमात्र ऐसी ताकत है, जिसे एक अनूठा स्थान प्राप्त है क्योंकि वस्तुतः निरपवाद रूप से इसे सभी स्वीकार करते हैं। उन गिने-चुने व्यक्तियों के मामले में भी, जो विज्ञान के प्रति नफरत रखने वाले दिखाई देते हैं, उनके साथ भी एक बार बातचीत करने पर यह तथ्य उभरकर सामने आएगा कि वे वास्तव में विज्ञान के विरुद्ध नहीं हैं, बल्कि प्रौद्योगिकी के विरुद्ध हैं, जिसका सम्बन्ध मानव की विविध जरूरतों को पूरा करने के लिए विज्ञान के निष्कर्षों के अनुप्रयोगों से है।

वर्तमान समय में विज्ञान से हमारा अभिप्राय है हमारे विश्व तथा इसके परिवेश का मौलिक ज्ञान, उस ज्ञान का इसके सभी पहलुओं में, नियंत्रित तथा निरन्तर अनुसरण करना, इसके लिये जरूरी नहीं कि उसका प्रयोग सार्वजनिक प्रयोजनों के लिए किया जाए। प्रौद्योगिकी से हमारा आशय विज्ञान को मानव सेवा में लगाने के विभिन्न तरीकों से है, उन तरीकों का संकेन्द्रित अध्ययन जिनमें चीजों को मानव-प्रयोजन के लिए रचा या बदला जा सकता है। दोनों में स्पष्ट अन्तर करने के लिए इस समय आण्विक विज्ञान तथा टेक्नोलॉजी के सर्वाधिक लोकप्रिय क्षेत्रों से उदाहरण दिए जा सकते हैं। जब भारी धात्विक तत्व यूरेनियम के केन्द्रक का विखंडन या विस्फोटन होता है तब उससे निःसृत होने वाले कणों की संख्या तथा प्रकृति का मापन विज्ञान द्वारा ही किया जाता है। लेकिन, जब इस वैज्ञानिक ज्ञान का प्रयोग विद्युत उत्पादन के लिये परमाणु बिजली घर डिजाइन करने तथा बनाने अथवा एक परमाणु बम डिजाइन करने और बनाने के लिए किया जाता है तो यह प्रौद्योगिकी होती है। इस प्रकार, यह प्रौद्योगिकी ही होती है जो नैतिक रंग ले लेती है और इसे नैतिक या अनैतिक कहा जा सकता है। विज्ञान तटस्थ या नैतिकता से परे होता है और वह नैतिक-आचार या मानव कल्याण के विरुद्ध नहीं होता, हालांकि एक वैज्ञानिक एक मनुष्य तथा टेक्नोलाजिस्ट होने के नाते इसके विरुद्ध हो सकता है।

1. लेखक :
A. विज्ञान के प्रति बेहतर रवैया अपनाये जाने के लिए वकालत करने की कोशिश कर रहा है
B. यह सुझाव देने की कोशिश कर रहा है कि हम विज्ञान का सार्वजनिक हित के लिए प्रयोग करें
C. भौतिक विज्ञान के बजाय नैतिक विज्ञान का अध्ययन करने की कोशिश कर रहा है
D. विज्ञान तथा प्रौद्योगिकी (टेक्नोलाजी) के बीच भेद करने की कोशिश कर रहा है

2. लेखक के अनुसार, विज्ञान
A. एकमात्र ऐसी ताकत है, जो मानवजाति के भविष्य का निर्धारण करती है
B. मानव की नियति को निर्धारित करने वाली चन्द एक ताकतों में से एक है
C. भविष्य में मानवजाति की एकमात्र चिन्ता होगी
D. उन अनेक बाधाओं में से एक है जो मनुष्य की प्रगति में रुकावट डालती है

3. यह अवतरण
A. आलंकारिक है
B. वर्णनात्मक है
C. वृत्तात्मक है
D. व्याख्यात्मक है

4. यूरेनियम केन्द्रक के विस्फोट के अध्ययन को
A. आधुनिक प्रौद्योगिकी (टेक्नोलाजी) का एक उदाहरण कहा जा सकता है
B. विद्युत-सिद्धांतों का एक अनुप्रयोग कहा जा सकता है
C. ऐसा अध्ययन कहा जा सकता है जिसके कोई भौतिक निहितार्थ नहीं हैं
D. समूची मानवजाति के कल्याण के लिए महत्त्वपूर्ण कहा जा सकता है

गद्यांश-19

बच्चे किसी देश के सामाजिक तथा राजनीतिक दर्शन का अंग होते हैं। उनके प्रति जो रवैये अपनाये जाते हैं वे इस बात का निर्धारण करने में महत्त्वपूर्ण कारक होते हैं कि क्या उनकी जरूरतें पूरी होंगी तथा उनके अधिकार उन्हें मिलेंगे। भविष्योन्मुख कोई भी समाज इस बात का ध्यान रखेगा कि विपदा के समय बच्चों का ख्याल रखा जाये। इस समय विश्व के अनेक भागों में बच्चों को शांति तथा भाई-चारे की भावना के साथ पाले-पोसे जाने का कोई अवसर प्राप्त नहीं है। युद्ध तथा आतंकवाद के जो अत्यधिक भयावह रिकार्ड मिलते हैं वे हमेशा अपने घरों के खण्डहरों तथा अपने परिवारों के शवों के पास रोने के लिए बचे हुए शिशुओं या छोटे बच्चों की (या इतने सहमे हुए बच्चों की जो रो भी नहीं पाते) तस्वीरें होती हैं। ऐसे देशों में जहां लड़ाई-झगड़ा चल रहा हो या ऐसे समाजों में जहां ऐसी कार्यवाहियों को मनमोहक ढंग से पेश किया जाता हो, वहां बच्चों का निर्बाध रूप से खेलना जीवन की घटनाओं तथा/या ऐसी घटनाओं की सामाजिक स्वीकृति को परिलक्षित करेगा, जो हम सभी को यह सोचने पर मजबूर कर देगा कि क्या इस प्रकार के राष्ट्रीय दर्शनों से प्रभावित करोड़ों बच्चों को शांति की भावना के साथ बड़े होने के उनके अधिकार मिलने की कोई संभावना है। और निश्चय ही, ''जाति, रंग, लिंग, राष्ट्रीय या सामाजिक मूल के धर्म'' पर अकेले या कुछेक के मेल पर आधारित भेदभाव करोड़ों बच्चों को, जरूरतों की सार्वत्रिकता के बावजूद, जिन पर अधिकार आधारित होते हैं, इन अधिकारों से वंचित रखता है।

1. निम्नलिखित में से कौन-सा कथन बच्चों में शांति तथा भाई-चारे की भावना के विकास के लिए सहायक नहीं है?
A. जब वयोवृद्ध बच्चों को युद्ध के संत्रासों का अनुभव करने के लिए छोड़ देते हैं

B. जब प्रौढ़ लोग जातीय भेद-भाव का व्यवहार करते हैं
C. जब किसी देश का राजनीतिक दर्शन विश्वव्यापी भाई-चारे की वकालत करता है
D. जब समाज युद्ध के कार्यकलापों को मनमोहक ढंग से पेश करता है

2. प्रौढ़ों का बच्चों के प्रति एक कर्त्तव्य है। किसी समाज विशेष में बच्चों की देखभाल कितनी अच्छी तरह से होती है इसका पता इस बात से चल सकता है कि
A. विपदा के समय उनके लिए क्या किया जाता है
B. वे प्रौढ़ों का कितना ख्याल रखते हैं
C. प्रौढ़ उनके अधिकारों के प्रति कितने संवेदनशील हैं
D. समाज कितना समृद्ध है

3. लेखक की धारणा है कि
A. युद्धों के बावजूद बच्चे शान्तिपूर्वक रहने के अपने अधिकारों को प्राप्त कर लेते हैं
B. बच्चों के अधिकार सामाजिक दशाओं पर निर्भर होने चाहिए
C. बच्चों को शांति की भावना के साथ बड़ा होने का अधिकार है
D. राष्ट्रीय दर्शन बच्चों के अधिकारों का समर्थन करते हैं

4. युद्ध सम्बन्धी कार्यकलापों
A. का समाजों द्वारा परिहार किया जाता है
B. को समाजों द्वारा परिलक्षित किया जाता है
C. की समाजों द्वारा निन्दा की जाती है
D. को समाजों द्वारा स्वीकार किया जाता है

गद्यांश-20

हम सभी चिकित्सा विज्ञान के क्षेत्र में हुई कतिपय उल्लेखनीय खोजों से परिचित हैं। मिसाल के तौर पर, हम वैक्सीनों की खोज के बारे में जानते हैं। हम चेचक तथा पोलियो जैसे रोगों की रोकथाम को समझ सकते हैं। हम अनेक साधारण एंटीबायोटिक्स के बारे में भी जानते हैं। यह जानकारी कि हम उपदंश रोग पर पेनिसिलीन और तपेदिक पर आइसोनाइजिड से काबू पा सकते हैं, कुछ हद तक आश्वासनदायक है। हम इस विश्वास के आधार पर निश्चय ही अपने आपको झूठी तसल्ली दे सकते हैं कि संक्रामक रोग अब कोई खतरा नहीं रहे हैं। लेकिन यह सत्य नहीं है और समाचारों तथा मेडिकल जर्नलों में हाल में छपे समाचार हमें संक्रामक रोगों के विभिन्न तथा कभी-कभी 'नए' खतरों की याद दिलाते हैं।

ऐसे समाचारों में अपेक्षाकृत अधिक यथार्थवादी दृष्टिकोण को स्वीकार किया गया है। इस दृष्टिकोण का निहितार्थ यह है कि संक्रामक रोग बने रहेंगे और यह कि उनके अन्दर कुछ ऐसी क्षमताएं हैं कि वे उन्हें खत्म कर देने की हमारी कोशिशों के खिलाफ लड़ सकते हैं। कतिपय मानव-व्याधियों, जैसे सुजाक रोग, तत्त्व-गुण (Strains) विकसित हो गए हैं जिन पर कतिपय एंटीबायोटिक्स का कोई असर नहीं होता।

1. चेचक तथा पोलियो जैसे रोगों की रोकथाम किसकी खोज के कारण संभव हो सकी है?
A. पेनिसिलीन B. आइसोनाइजिड
C. वैक्सीन D. एंटीबायोटिक्स

2. चिकित्सा विज्ञान के क्षेत्र में खोजों के द्वारा अब तक क्या संभव नहीं हो पाया है?
A. चेचक तथा पोलियो की रोकथाम
B. पेनिसिलीन की सहायता से उपदंश रोग के फैलाव पर नियंत्रण करने की संभावना
C. संक्रामक रोगों का उन्मूलन
D. आइसोनाइजिड की सहायता से तपेदिक के फैलाव पर नियंत्रण करने की संभावना

3. कुछ संक्रामक रोग उन्हें खत्म कर देने के हमारे प्रयासों के खिलाफ कैसे लड़ते हैं?
A. अन्य क्षेत्रों में अंतरित होकर
B. वैक्सीनों को प्रभावहीन बनाने की शक्ति विकसित करके
C. पहले की तरह भ्रांतिजनक बने रहकर
D. मानव-तंत्रिका में गहरे पैठ कर

4. यह अवतरण
A. सूचना देने वाला है B. वृत्तात्मक है
C. नाटकीय है D. प्रोत्साहक है

गद्यांश-21

प्रत्येक व्यवसाय अथवा व्यापार, कला और विज्ञान की अपनी तकनीकी शब्दावली होती है, जिसका कार्य अंशतः उन प्रक्रियाओं और वस्तुओं को दर्शाना होता है जिनके नाम सामान्य अंग्रेजी में नहीं मिलते और अंशतः पारिभाषिक शब्दावली में पूर्ण यथार्थता प्राप्त करना होता है। किसी भी प्रकार की तकनीकी बातचीत में ऐसी विशिष्ट भाषिका अथवा शब्दजाल की आवश्यकता होती है। विज्ञान अथवा कला विशेष के अध्येताओं के लिए सर्वविदित होने के साथ-साथ गणितीय सूत्र जैसी सूक्ष्मता रखते हैं। साथ ही, वे समय बचाते हैं, किसी प्रक्रिया का वर्णन करने की अपेक्षा उसका नाम लेना अधिक किफायती है। ऐसे हजारों पारिभाषिक शब्द बहुत अच्छी तरह इन शब्दकोशों में संकलित किए गए हैं, फिर भी, कुल मिलाकर, वे अंग्रेजी भाषा की मूल शब्दावली के बजाय उसके आस-पास ही ठहरते हैं। फिर भी विभिन्न व्यवसाय अपनी विशिष्ट शब्दावली की दृष्टि से पर्याप्त भिन्नता लिए हुए हैं। व्यापार, हस्तकला, कृषि और मछलीपालन जैसे अन्य व्यवसायों में जहाँ लम्बे समय से भारी संख्या में लोग लगे हैं, तकनीकी शब्दावली बहुत पुरानी है। इसमें अधिकतर स्थानीय शब्द मिलते हैं अथवा ऐसे आयातित शब्द हैं जो हमारी भाषा में घुल-मिल गए हैं। अतः अनेक रूपों में पूर्णतः तकनीकी होते हुए भी ये शब्दावलियां बोलने में अधिक परिचित-सी हैं और अन्य अधिकांश तकनीकीय तुलना में अधिक सहजता से समझी जाती हैं।

कानून, औषधि, धर्मविज्ञान और दर्शन की विशिष्ट भाषिका भी अपने प्राचीन रूप में परिष्कृत व्यक्तियों में पर्याप्त परिचित हो गई है, और प्रचलित शब्दावली में काफी योगदान कर चुकी है फिर भी प्रत्येक व्यवसाय आज भी ऐसी बहुत-सी तकनीकी शब्दावली लिए हुए है जो मूलतः विदेशी हैं। यह अनुपात पिछले पचास वर्षों में अधिक बढ़ा है विशेषतः यांत्रिक कलाओं, प्राकृतिक विज्ञान और राजनीति विज्ञान के विभिन्न क्षेत्रों में। यहाँ पूरी आजादी से नए शब्दों को शामिल कर लिया गया है और व्यर्थ हो जाने पर छोड़ दिया गया है। अधिकतर नए पद विशिष्ट बातचीत तक सीमित रहे हैं, कभी-कभी ही सामान्य बातचीत अथवा साहित्य जुड़ पाए हैं। पर आज कोई भी व्यवसाय, जैसा कि पहले सभी थे बंद निकाय नहीं हैं। वकील, चिकित्सक, वैज्ञानिक और पादरी अपने साथी सृजनकर्त्ताओं से जुड़ता है और ऐसा नहीं है कि मात्र व्यावसायिक रूप से ही मिलता है। बल्कि आज का प्रचलित विज्ञान प्रत्येक व्यक्ति को आधुनिक विचारों और खोजों से जोड़ता है। कोई भी महत्त्वपूर्ण प्रयोग चाहे वह दूर अथवा क्षेत्रीय प्रयोगशाला में किया गया हो, समाचार-पत्रों में तुरंत प्रकाशित हो जाता है और हर एक व्यक्ति उसके बारे में ऐसे ही बात करना शुरू कर देता है जैसे विकिरण किरणों और बेतारी तार-संचार के बारे में बात करता है। अतः हमारी सामान्य बोली सदैव नए तकनीकी शब्दों को अपना रही है और उन्हें प्रचलित कर रही है।

1. तकनीकी शब्दावली बढ़ाई जा सकती है :
A. नए शब्द बनाकर, विदेशी भाषाओं से शब्द ग्रहण करके और पुराने हुए शब्दों को निकालकर
B. नई अवधारणाओं के लिए नए शब्द गढ़कर
C. नए शब्द ढालकर और विदेशी भाषाओं से शब्द आयात करके
D. विदेशी शब्दों का अपनी भाषा में अनुवाद करके

2. प्रचलित विज्ञान, प्रत्येक व्यक्ति को परिचित कराता है
A. आधुनिक विचारों और नवीन खोजों से
B. नवीन खोजों और आविष्कारों से
C. आधुनिक विचारों, नवीन खोजों और तकनीक से
D. विज्ञान और तकनीक में नए विकास से

3. तकनीकी शब्दावली सभी की भाषा का अंग बन गई है :
A. व्यावसायिकों के प्रयासों द्वारा
B. विदेशी भाषा पढ़कर
C. प्रचलित वैज्ञानिक लेखों और समाचारपत्रों द्वारा
D. भाषा के परिवर्तनों द्वारा

4. तकनीकी शब्द हैं :
A. संक्षिप्त, किफायती और नामात्मक
B. नवीन, कठिन पर आवश्यक
C. भाषा की मूल शब्दावली से चुने हुए
D. सभी द्वारा सामान्य रूप से समझे जाने वाले

गद्यांश-22

मैं इस अंधविश्वास को जानता हूँ कि आत्म-ज्ञान जीवन की चौथी अवस्था में ही सम्भव है और वह है संन्यास। पर इस बात को सभी जानते हैं कि जो इस अमूल्य अनुभव को जीवन के अन्तिम क्षणों के लिए टालते हैं वे आत्म-ज्ञान प्राप्त नहीं करते बल्कि द्वितीय और दयनीय बचपन के समान बुढ़ापे को प्राप्त करते हैं और पृथ्वी पर एक भार की तरह जीते हैं। मुझे पूरी तरह याद है कि जब मैं 1911-12 में पढ़ाता था तब भी इसी विचार को मानता था भले ही इसी तरह की भाषा में उसे अभिव्यक्त न किया हो।

तब किस प्रकार यह आध्यात्मिक प्रशिक्षण दिया जाना था? मैंने बच्चों को भजन याद कराये और उनका अभ्यास कराया और उन्हें नैतिक शिक्षा की पुस्तकों से पढ़कर सुनाया। पर यह सब मेरे लिए संतोषजनक नहीं था। जब मैं उनके और अधिक निकट आया तो पाया कि अध्यात्म का प्रशिक्षण केवल पुस्तकों के माध्यम से नहीं कराया जा सकता। उसी प्रकार जैसे शारीरिक प्रशिक्षण व्यायाम के माध्यम से दिया जाता है और बौद्धिक अभ्यास के द्वारा, अतः अध्यात्म का प्रशिक्षण भी अध्यात्म के अभ्यास से संभव था। और अध्यात्म का प्रशिक्षण पूर्णतः अध्यापक के जीवन और चरित्र पर निर्भर करता है। अध्यापक चाहे विद्यार्थियों के बीच में है अथवा नहीं उसे सदैव अपने व्यवहार और चरित्र का ध्यान रखना है।

1. ऊपर उद्धृत पाठ सामग्री के लिए सर्वाधिक उपयुक्त शीर्षक है :
A. बौद्धिक अभ्यास B. अंधविश्वास
C. आध्यात्मिक विकास D. प्रशिक्षण

2. व्यापक स्तर पर आत्म-ज्ञान के बारे में लोगों के बीच अंधविश्वास है कि यह
A. अनवरत प्रक्रिया है
B. केवल संन्यास द्वारा संभव है
C. केवल आरम्भिक जीवन में संभव है
D. एक मिथक है

3. लेखक के अनुसार बच्चों का आध्यात्मिक प्रशिक्षण मुख्यतः किसके चरित्र पर निर्भर है?
A. अभिभावकों के B. अभिजात वर्ग के
C. सामाजिक नेताओं के D. अध्यापकों के

4. लेखक का बुढ़ापे के बारे में पहले विचार था कि यह
A. एक गुण है B. एक अभिशाप है
C. विचारों की स्मृति है D. संतोष है

गद्यांश-23

क्या विद्यार्थियों द्वारा प्राप्त किये गये परिणामों से अध्यापन-कार्य का मूल्यांकन किया जा सकता है? कुछ हद तक अध्यापकों को इसी प्रकार आँका जाता है, प्रायः सामूहिक रूप से, किसी संस्थान की ख्याति के

रूप में। परन्तु इसमें कुछ कठिनाइयाँ हैं। विशेष रूप से उल्लेखनीय कठिनाई, जिसे स्क्राइवन (1988) ने 'हार्वर्ड फैलेसी (भ्रामकता)' के नाम से वर्णित किया है, इस प्रकार है :

...यह मान लेने की भ्रामकता कि हार्वर्ड में पढ़ाई अच्छी होती होगी क्योंकि यहां के स्नातक अपने बाद के जीवन में अच्छी तरक्की करते हैं ...इन आँकड़ों से यही परिणाम निकाला जा सकता है कि हार्वर्ड में मस्तिष्क को स्थायी हानि नहीं पहुँचाई जाती—सामान्यतया। बाकी की युक्ति केवल इतनी-सी है कि प्रतिभाशाली विद्यार्थियों का चयन कर कक्षाओं में भेजा जाए और उनके मार्ग में कोई रुकावट खड़ी न की जाए। उन्हें पुस्तकालय, प्रयोगशाला, पीयर ट्यूटरिंग और परिवार के प्रभाव या नाम के प्रति आदर का उपयोग करने दिया जाए। अध्यापकों का योगदान यदि कोई है तो वह अवशेष जो दूसरे कारणों से अलग करने के बाद बचता है जैसे कि ...'पुराने विद्यार्थियों के जाल' और नाम की मान्यता का नौकरी के लिए चयन और पदोन्नति पर प्रभाव। यद्यपि हार्वर्ड प्रमाण्यतः एक महान विश्वविद्यालय है तथापि निश्चित रूप से यह प्रमाण्यतः एक महान अध्यापन विश्वविद्यालय नहीं है बल्कि केवल एक भव्य रूप से सुसज्जित विश्वविद्यालय।

दूसरे देशों के विश्वविद्यालयों को स्पष्टतः हार्वर्ड के स्थान पर रखा जा सकता है। लेकिन फिर भी यदि एक जैसे संस्थानों के एक जैसे पाठ्यक्रमों के परिणामों की तुलना करना सम्भव हो तो भी सफलता का श्रेय दूसरे कारणों को देने की बजाय अध्यापन को देने के बारे में स्क्राइवन का तर्क विचारणीय रहेगा। किसी प्रकार के 'मूल्य-जुड़े' पैमाने से भी यह सम्भव नहीं होगा और ऐसे पैमाने या तो इतने अपक्व होंगे कि उनका कोई अर्थ ही नहीं होगा या फिर इतने जटिल होंगे कि जाँचने और आँकने के लिए पढ़ाने और सीखने की केन्द्रित गतिविधियों के मुकाबले में बहुत अधिक समय की आवश्यकता होगी। एक ही संस्थान में एक वर्ष के परिणामों की अगले वर्ष के परिणामों से तुलना करने में भी कठिनाइयाँ सामने आती हैं क्योंकि विभागों में और विद्यार्थियों में परिस्थितियाँ बदलती रहती हैं।

1. इस परिच्छेद का शीर्षक क्या हो सकता है?
   A. हार्वर्ड विश्वविद्यालय में अध्यापन
   B. विद्यार्थियों के परिणामों से अध्यापन-कार्य का मूल्यांकन
   C. संस्थानों की प्रतिष्ठा
   D. अध्यापकों के मूल्यांकन के लिए अवशिष्ट पद्धति

2. हार्वर्ड फैलेसी (भ्रामकता) का अर्थ है :
   A. यह मान लेना कि प्रतिष्ठित संस्थानों में पढ़ाई अच्छी होती है
   B. जो कुछ हार्वर्ड में भ्रामक रूप से किया जा रहा है
   C. कि हार्वर्ड में प्रतिभाशाली विद्यार्थियों को दाखिला दिया जाता है और अच्छे परिणाम प्राप्त किये जाते हैं
   D. कि हार्वर्ड में जो अध्यापन कार्य होता है उसमें बहुत-सी भ्रामकतायें हैं

3. विद्यार्थियों की उपलब्धियों में अध्यापकों के योगदान को स्क्राइवन के अनुसार किस बात से आँका जाना चाहिए?
   A. स्नातकों द्वारा बाद के जीवन में अर्जित उपलब्धियों से
   B. विद्यार्थियों के दाखिले के लिए संस्थानों द्वारा निर्धारित मानदण्डों से
   C. बाकी सभी कारणों को निकालने के बाद बचे अवशिष्ट प्रभाव से
   D. संस्थानों में उपलब्ध सुविधाओं से

4. स्क्राइवन के अनुसार हार्वर्ड की प्रतिष्ठा किस कारण से है?
   A. इसका प्रचुर मात्रा में सुविधाओं से सम्पन्न होना
   B. प्रतिभाशाली विद्यार्थियों को दाखिला और उनके मार्ग में रुकावट न डालना
   C. इसका एक महान अध्यापन विश्वविद्यालय होना
   D. इसके अपक्व और अर्थहीन तरीके जिनसे अध्यापन-कार्य की प्रभाविकता को माना जाता है

गद्यांश-24

भिखारी की भाँति गिड़गिड़ाना प्रेम की भाषा नहीं है। यहाँ तक कि मुक्ति के लिए भगवान् की उपासना करना भी अधम उपासना में गिना जाता है। प्रेम कोई पुरस्कार नहीं चाहता। प्रेम सर्वथा प्रेम के लिए ही होता है। भक्त इसलिए प्रेम करता है कि बिना प्रेम किए वह रह ही नहीं सकता। जब तुम किसी मनोहर प्राकृतिक दृश्य को देखकर उस पर मोहित हो जाते हो तो तुम किसी फल की याचना नहीं करते और न वह दृश्य ही तुमसे कुछ माँगता है। फिर भी उस दृश्य का दर्शन तुम्हारे मन को आनंद से भर देता है।

1. प्रेम का उद्देश्य क्या होता है?
   A. मुक्ति B. उपासना
   C. भक्ति D. प्रेम

2. मुक्ति का अर्थ है :
   A. आजादी B. स्वतंत्रता
   C. परतंत्र D. निर्वाण

3. कैसी उपासना अधम मानी गई है?
   A. प्रेम की उपासना B. भगवान की उपासना
   C. मुक्ति की उपासना D. भक्ति की उपासना

4. मनोहर शब्द है :
   A. विशेषण B. संज्ञा
   C. सर्वनाम D. अव्यव

5. प्राकृतिक शब्द का अर्थ है :
   A. ईश्वरीय B. मानव संबंधी
   C. प्रकृति संबंधी D. प्रेम संबंधी

गद्यांश-25

कुछ लोग भाग्यवादी होते हैं और सब-कुछ भाग्य के सहारे छोड़कर कर्म से विरत हो जाते हैं। ऐसे लोग समाज के लिए बोझ हैं। वे कभी कोई बड़ा काम नहीं कर पाते। बड़ी-बड़ी खोज, बड़े-बड़े आविष्कार और बड़े-बड़े निर्माण कार्य कर्मशील लोगों के द्वारा ही संभव हो सके हैं। हम अपनी बुद्धि और प्रतिभा तथा कार्य-क्षमता के बल पर सही मार्ग पर चल सकते हैं, किन्तु बिना कठिन श्रम के अपने लक्ष्य तक नहीं पहुँच सकते। कठिन परिश्रम करने के बाद पाई गई सफलता हमारे मन को अलौकिक आनंद से भर देती है। यदि हम अपने कार्य में अपेक्षित श्रम नहीं करते तो हमारा मन ग्लानि का अनुभव करता है।

1. ''आविष्कार'' शब्द का अर्थ है :

A. अनुसंधान B. खोज
C. निर्माण D. विनाश

2. अलौकिक शब्द का क्या अर्थ है?

A. संसारिक B. भौतिक
C. अमानुषी D. प्राकृतिक

3. सफलता का विलोम क्या है?

A. सफल B. असफल
C. सफलतापूर्वक D. असफलता

4. परिश्रम करने और न करने से हमारे जीवन पर क्या प्रभाव पड़ता है?

A. लोग भाग्यवादी बन जाते हैं
B. कर्म से विरत हो जाते हैं
C. मन में ग्लानि का अनुभव होता है
D. इनमें से कोई नहीं

5. किस प्रकार के लोग समाज के लिए बोझ हैं?

A. भाग्यवादी B. कर्मठ
C. परिश्रमी D. प्रतिभाशाली

गद्यांश-26

वैदिक काल से हिमालय के पहाड़ बहुत पवित्र माने जाते हैं। इसमें कोई सन्देह नहीं कि हिमालय के पहाड़ों का दृश्य अति सुन्दर है। उसकी विशालता को देखकर मन में आनन्द और कृतज्ञता की लहर उठती है। ऐसा लगता है कि यह विशाल सृष्टि प्रभु की अनुपम देन है। सारी सृष्टि के प्रति समभाव जाग्रत होता है। वस्तुतः यह दृष्टि कोरी कल्पनात्मक या आध्यात्मिक नहीं है। देखा जाए तो सारे भारत की जलवायु का समतोल करने वाले यह हिमालय के पहाड़ हैं, विशेषकर उत्तरी भारत को वर्षा और पानी देने वाले ये ही हैं। गंगोत्री, यमुनोत्री, बद्री, केदार को तीर्थ माना जाता है, जो व्यर्थ कल्पना नहीं है। उन स्थानों से निकलने वाली पवित्र नदियाँ ही वास्तव में हमारी प्राणदात्री रही हैं।

1. हिमालय के पर्वत बहुत पवित्र कब से माने जाते हैं?

A. पाषाण काल से B. वैदिक काल से
C. प्राचीन काल से D. आधुनिक काल से

2. विशालता शब्द है :

A. जातिवाचक B. भाववाचक
C. विशेषण D. सर्वनाम

3. भारत की जलवायु को समतोल कौन करता है?

A. गंगोत्री B. यमुनोत्री
C. केदार D. हिमालय

4. सृष्टि का समानार्थक शब्द है :

A. सृजन B. रचना
C. प्रकृति D. संसार

5. प्राणदात्री का क्या अर्थ है?

A. गंगोत्री B. यमुनोत्री
C. प्राणसंचार करने वाली D. समभाव जाग्रत करने वाली

गद्यांश-27

सच्चा मित्र एक शिक्षक की भाँति होता है। जिस प्रकार शिक्षक अपने छात्र को सन्मार्ग की ही ओर अग्रसर करता है, उसी प्रकार एक सच्चा मित्र अपने मित्र को पाप के गर्त में गिरने से बचाता है। मानव-जीवन अधिक रहस्यपूर्ण है। कभी-कभी जीवन में ऐसे अवसर उपस्थित हो जाते हैं, जब मनुष्य की धर्मबुद्धि नष्ट हो जाती है और उसका मन द्रुत गति से पाप की ओर दौड़ता है। ऐसे समय में मित्र का ही उपदेश अधिक कल्याणकारी सिद्ध होता है। मित्र के उपदेश का जितना प्रभाव हृदय पर पड़ता है, उतना और किसी का नहीं पड़ता है।

1. सच्चा मित्र किस प्रकार का होता है?

A. विपत्ति में सहायता देने वाला
B. गलत मार्ग पर चलने से रोकने वाला
C. शिक्षक की भाँति
D. धार्मिक गुरु की तरह

2. सन्मार्ग शब्द का विपरीत शब्द है :

A. अग्रसर B. कुमार्ग
C. सुमार्ग D. मार्गदर्शक

3. व्यक्ति को पाप के गर्त्त में गिरने से कौन बचाता है?

A. शिक्षक B. भाई
C. पिता D. सच्चा मित्र

4. मानव पाप की ओर कब दौड़ता है?

A. जब स्वार्थी बन जाता है
B. जब धर्म-बुद्धि नष्ट हो जाती है
C. जब सच्चामित्र साथ छोड़ देता है
D. जब धनवान बन जाता है

5. उपदेश में कौन-सा उपसर्ग है?

A. उ B. उप
C. दे D. देश

गद्यांश-28

सब तरह के भावों को प्रकट करने की योग्यता रखने वाली और निर्दोष होने पर भी यदि कोई भाषा अपना निज का साहित्य नहीं रखती, तो वह रूपवती भिखारिन की तरह कदापि आदरणीय नहीं हो सकती। उनकी शोभा, उसकी बडी सम्पन्नता, उसकी मान-मर्यादा उसके साहित्य पर ही अवलम्बित रहती है। उसके विचारों और राजनैतिक स्थितियों का प्रतिबिम्ब देखने को यदि कहीं मिल सकता है, तो उसके ग्रन्थ साहित्य में मिल सकता है। सामाजिक शक्ति या सजीवता, सामाजिक अशक्ति या निर्जीवता और सामाजिक सभ्यता तथा असभ्यता का निर्णायक एकमात्र साहित्य है।

1. साहित्य विहीन भाषा किस प्रकार की होती है?
A. आदरणीय B. भिखारिन
C. रूपवती D. रूपवती भिखारिन

2. रूपवती का पुल्लिंग रूप है :
A. रूपवान B. सुन्दर
C. सुन्दरी D. रूपवत

3. भाषा की मान मर्यादा किस पर निर्भर करती है?
A. लिपि पर B. साहित्यकार पर
C. भक्ति पर D. साहित्य पर

4. "सम्पन्नता" शब्द का विपरीत शब्द है :
A. गरीबी B. विपन्न
C. अमीर D. विपन्नता

5. राजनैतिक, सामाजिक शक्ति का दर्शन हमें किसमें मिलता है?
A. समाज B. राज्य
C. नेता D. साहित्य

गद्यांश-29

स्वतंत्र भारत का सम्पूर्ण दायित्व आज विद्यार्थियों के ही ऊपर है, क्योंकि आज जो विद्यार्थी हैं, वे ही कल स्वतंत्र भारत के नागरिक होंगे। भारत की उन्नति, उसका उत्थान उन्हीं की उन्नति और उत्थान पर निर्भर करता है। अतः विद्यार्थियों को चाहिए कि वे अपने भावी जीवन का निर्माण बड़ी सतर्कता और सावधानी के साथ करें। उन्हें प्रत्येक क्षण अपने राष्ट्र, अपने समाज अपने धर्म, अपनी संस्कृति को अपनी आँखों के सामने रखना चाहिए, जिससे उनके जीवन से राष्ट्र को कुछ बल प्राप्त हो सके। जो विद्यार्थी राष्ट्रीय दृष्टिकोण से अपने जीवन का निर्माण नहीं करते, वे राष्ट्र और समाज के लिए भार-स्वरूप हैं।

1. भारत की उन्नति किस पर निर्भर करती है?
A. युवाओं पर B. नेताओं पर
C. साहित्यकारों पर D. विद्यार्थियों पर

2. उन्नति का समानार्थक शब्द है :
A. पतन B. उत्थान
C. विकास D. उदय

3. उत्थान का विपरीत शब्द है :
A. उदय B. पतन
C. पराजय D. हार

4. किसे अपने जीवन का निर्माण सतर्कता और सावधानी से करना चाहिए?
A. युवाओं को B. नेताओं को
C. बच्चों को D. विद्यार्थियों को

5. धर्म, संस्कृति तथा समाज का रक्षक कौन है?
A. नागरिक B. ग्रामीण
C. विद्यार्थी D. युवा

गद्यांश-30

हास्य एक ऐसा माध्यम है, जो नीरस-जीवन को भी सुखद बना देता है। हास्य का जादू इतना प्रभावशाली होता है कि वह छूत के रोग की तरह चारों ओर फैल जाता है। जिसने कभी हँसना नहीं सीखा, सचमुच उसने जीना नहीं सीखा। सामान्यतः मनुष्य को जीवन में इतनी मुसीबतें झेलनी पड़ती हैं कि वह अपने जीवन को पहाड़ समझने लगता है। ऐसे दूभर जीवन को यदि जीने योग्य बनाना हो तो उसके लिए आवश्यक है कि जीवन में हँसने की गुंजाइश हो। हँसी के सहारे मनुष्य अपने कष्टों को भुलाने का प्रयत्न करता है। संघर्ष, तनाव, व्यस्तता, घुटन यदि आज के जीवन की सहज देन हैं, जिनसे बचने के लिए यह आवश्यक है कि हम हँसना सीखें।

1. नीरस जीवन को कौन सुखद बना देता है?
A. संगीत B. गीत
C. आमोद प्रमोद D. हास्य

2. नीरस का संधि विच्छेद है :
A. नी + रस B. नि + रस
C. निः + रस D. नीः + रस

3. किसका जीवन व्यर्थ है?
A. जिसने रोना नहीं सीखा B. जिसने हँसना नहीं सीखा
C. जिसने गाना नहीं सीखा D. इनमें से कोई नहीं

4. हँसना शब्द है :
A. संज्ञा B. विशेषण
C. क्रिया विशेषण D. क्रिया

5. तनाव और घुटन से बचने के लिए क्या करना चाहिए?
A. रोना चाहिए B. गाना चाहिए
C. हँसना चाहिए D. काम करना चाहिए

उत्तरमाला

गद्यांश	1	2	3	4	5	6	7	8	9	10
गद्यांश-1	C	D	A	D	A	C	C	A	A	A
गद्यांश-2	B	D	D	B	D	A	A	D	B	C
गद्यांश-3	A	B	D	C	C					
गद्यांश-4	A	C	B	C	B	D	A	D	D	A
गद्यांश-5	C	D	B	D	A					
गद्यांश-6	C	B	A	C	B	D	C	D	B	A
गद्यांश-7	A	C	A	C	D					
गद्यांश-8	C	A	A	A						
गद्यांश-9	A	D	C	D						
गद्यांश-10	B	D	B	A						
गद्यांश-11	D	C	C	B						
गद्यांश-12	D	D	A	D						
गद्यांश-13	C	A	D	B						
गद्यांश-14	D	C	A	D						
गद्यांश-15	D	A	C	D						
गद्यांश-16	B	D	B	A						
गद्यांश-17	C	A	C	A						
गद्यांश-18	A	B	D	C						
गद्यांश-19	B	C	C	B						
गद्यांश-20	C	C	B	A						
गद्यांश-21	C	A	C	A						
गद्यांश-22	C	B	D	B						
गद्यांश-23	B	A	C	B						
गद्यांश-24	D	D	C	A	C					
गद्यांश-25	B	D	D	C	A					
गद्यांश-26	B	B	D	A	C					
गद्यांश-27	C	B	D	B	B					
गद्यांश-28	B	A	D	D	D					
गद्यांश-29	D	B	B	D	C					
गद्यांश-30	D	C	B	D	C					

❊ ❊ ❊ ❊ ❊

2 भाषा, लिपि और बोलियाँ

भाषा वह साधन है जिसके द्वारा मनुष्य अपने विचार दूसरों के सामने प्रकट करता है या समझता है। 'भाषा' शब्द संस्कृत की 'भाष्' धातु से लिया गया है जिसका अर्थ है–'बोलना' या 'कहना'। जब हम अपने विचारों को लिखकर या बोलकर प्रकट करते हैं या दूसरे के विचारों को सुनकर या पढ़कर ग्रहण करते हैं, तो उसे भाषा कहते हैं। भाषा में सार्थक ध्वनि का ही समावेश होता है।

भाषा के रूप

भाषा रूपी साधन का प्रयोग मानव अपने विचारों के परस्पर संप्रेषण हेतु कई प्रकार से कर सकता है; जैसे–मौखिक भाषा, लिखित भाषा या सांकेतिक भाषा।

- **मौखिक भाषा :** जब हम अपने विचारों को बोलकर या सुनकर व्यक्त करते हैं, तो उसे 'मौखिक भाषा' कहते हैं।
- **लिखित भाषा :** जब हम अपने विचारों को लिखकर व्यक्त करते हैं, तो उसे लिखित भाषा कहते हैं। यह भाषा का स्थायी रूप होता है।
- **सांकेतिक भाषा :** जब हम अपने विचारों को ध्वनि या चिह्नों का प्रयोग न करके सांकेतिक संकेतों व हाव-भाव से प्रकट करते हैं, तो उसे सांकेतिक भाषा कहते हैं।

भारत के संविधान में वर्णित राजभाषाओं की सूची

भारतीय संविधान के भाग XVII में अनुच्छेद 343 से 351 तक आधिकारिक भाषाओं का वर्णन है, जो संघ, राज्यों, न्यायपालिका और भाषाई अल्पसंख्यकों से संबंधित है। मुख्य प्रावधानों में देवनागरी लिपि हिन्दी को संघ की राजभाषा (343) घोषित करना, क्षेत्रीय भाषाएँ (345) और हिन्दी के विकास के निर्देश (351) शामिल हैं, जो भाषाई विविधता को संतुलित करते हैं।

वर्तमान में संविधान की आठवीं अनुसूची में निम्नलिखित 22 भाषाएँ शामिल हैं :

असमिया, बांग्ला, गुजराती, हिन्दी, कन्नड़, कश्मीरी, कोंकणी, मलयालम, मणिपुरी, मराठी, नेपाली, उड़िया (ओडिया), पंजाबी, संस्कृत, सिंधी, तमिल, उर्दू, तेलुगू, बोडो, संथाली, मैथिली और डोगरी।

भारत में शास्त्रीय भाषाएँ

वर्तमान में ऐसी छह भाषाएँ हैं जिन्हें भारत में 'शास्त्रीय भाषा' का दर्जा प्राप्त है :

1. तमिल (2004)
2. संस्कृत (2005)
3. कन्नड़ (2005)
4. तेलुगू (2008)
5. मलयालम (2013)
6. ओडिया (2014)

ये सभी शास्त्रीय भाषाएँ संविधान की आठवीं अनुसूची में सूचीबद्ध हैं।

लिपि

लिपि ध्वनियों को लिखने के लिए उपयोग किए जाने वाले चिह्नों या प्रतीकों का एक व्यवस्थित समूह है, जो भाषा को लिखित रूप प्रदान करती है।

हिन्दी भाषा की लिपि 'देवनागरी लिपि' है; इसकी उत्पत्ति ब्राह्मी लिपि से हुई है। ब्राह्मी एक प्राचीन लिपि है, जिससे हिन्दी, बांग्ला, गुजराती आदि लिपियों का विकास हुआ है।

देवनागरी लिपि बायीं से दायीं ओर लिखी जाती है। भारत में अधिकतर भाषाएँ बायीं से दायीं ओर ही लिखी जाती हैं। केवल उर्दू भाषा ही दायीं से बायीं ओर लिखी जाती है।

विश्व की कुछ भाषाओं और उनकी लिपियों के नाम इस प्रकार हैं :

1.	हिन्दी, संस्कृत, मराठी, नेपाली	देवनागरी लिपि
2.	पंजाबी	गुरुमुखी लिपि
3.	उर्दू, अरबी, फारसी	फारसी लिपि
4.	अंग्रेजी, फ्रेंच, पोलिश, जर्मन, स्पेनिश	रोमन लिपि
5.	रूसी	रूसी लिपि

बोलियाँ

बोली भाषा का ही एक प्रारम्भिक रूप है। जब एक ही भाषा अलग-अलग क्षेत्रों में अलग-अलग प्रकार से बोली जाती है, तो उसे बोली कहते हैं। बोली में साहित्य की रचना नहीं होती। बोली, भाषा का स्थानीय/क्षेत्रीय रूप है।

हिन्दी की प्रमुख बोलियाँ और उनका क्षेत्रीय वितरण

हिन्दी भाषा में मुख्य रूप से 5 उपभाषाएँ और 18 बोलियाँ हैं, जो शौरसेनी, अर्धमागधी और मागधी अपभ्रंश से विकसित हुई हैं।

पश्चिमी हिन्दी (शौरसेनी अपभ्रंश)

- **खड़ी बोली (कौरवी) :** दिल्ली, मेरठ, रामपुर, सहारनपुर, मुरादाबाद।
- **ब्रज भाषा :** मथुरा, आगरा, अलीगढ़, एटा, मैनपुरी, बरेली।
- **हरियाणवी (बांगरू/जाटू) :** हरियाणा, दिल्ली का देहाती क्षेत्र।
- **बुंदेली :** बुंदेलखंड क्षेत्र (झांसी, बांदा, हमीरपुर, मध्य प्रदेश के कुछ क्षेत्र)
- **कन्नौजी :** कन्नौज, फर्रुखाबाद, इटावा, हरदोई, पीलीभीत।

पूर्वी हिन्दी (अर्धमागधी अपभ्रंश)

- **अवधी :** लखनऊ, इलाहाबाद, फैजाबाद, सीतापुर, सुल्तानपुर।
- **बघेली :** रीवा, बघेलखंड क्षेत्र (मध्य प्रदेश का पूर्वी भाग)।
- **छत्तीसगढ़ी :** छत्तीसगढ़ राज्य।

राजस्थानी (शौरसेनी अपभ्रंश)

- **मारवाड़ी (पश्चिमी राजस्थानी) :** जोधपुर, बीकानेर, जैसलमेर।
- **जयपुरी (ढूँढाड़ी) (पूर्वी राजस्थानी) :** जयपुर, अजमेर।
- **मेवाती (उत्तरी राजस्थानी) :** अलवर, भरतपुर।
- **मालवी (दक्षिणी राजस्थानी) :** मालवा (मध्य प्रदेश का हिस्सा)।

बिहारी हिन्दी (मागधी अपभ्रंश)

- **भोजपुरी :** वाराणसी, गोरखपुर, गाजीपुर, बिहार के पश्चिमी जिले।
- **मैथिली :** दरभंगा, मुजफ्फरपुर (उत्तरी बिहार)।
- **मगही :** पटना, गया, हजारीबाग (दक्षिणी बिहार)।

पहाड़ी हिन्दी (खस/शौरसेनी अपभ्रंश)

- **गढ़वाली :** उत्तराखंड (गढ़वाल क्षेत्र)।
- **कुमाऊँनी :** उत्तराखंड (कुमाऊँ क्षेत्र)।
- **हिमाचली :** हिमाचल प्रदेश।

हिन्दी की प्रमुख बोलियों के नामकरण कर्ता

बोली	नामकरण कर्ता
कौरवी	डॉ. राहुल सांकृत्यायन
ब्रज बोली	ईश्वर चन्द्र गुप्त
राजस्थानी	जॉर्ज ग्रियर्सन
डिंगल	बाँकी दास
बिहारी	जॉर्ज ग्रियर्सन
भोजपुरी	रेमण्ड
मैथिली	कोलब्रुक

अभ्यास प्रश्न

1. भाषा का प्राथमिक रूप क्या है?
A. पढ़ना B. बोलना
C. लिखना D. इनमें से कोई नहीं

2. लिपि किस भाषा का आधार है?
A. लिखित भाषा B. मौखिक भाषा
C. सांकेतिक भाषा D. मनोभाषा

3. हिन्दी कैसी भाषा है?
A. वियोगात्मक B. संयोगात्मक
C. दोनों D. इनमें से कोई नहीं

4. पूर्वी हिन्दी की बोली है :
A. बुन्देली B. मगही
C. बघेली D. भोजपुरी

5. पश्चिमी हिन्दी की बोली है :
A. अवधी B. बुन्देली
C. बघेली D. मेवाती

6. अपभ्रंश को 'पुरानी हिन्दी' किसने कहा?
A. ग्रियर्सन B. श्याम सुंदर दास
C. चन्द्रधर शर्मा 'गुलेरी' D. आचार्य रामचन्द्र शुक्ल

7. भाषा के ग्राह्यात्मक कौशल हैं :
A. सुनना, पढ़ना B. पढ़ना, लिखना
C. लिखना, बोलना D. बोलना, सुनना

8. लिखित भाषा के लिए अनिवार्य है :
A. लिपि का ज्ञान B. अंकों का ज्ञान
C. बाराखड़ी का ज्ञान D. व्याकरण का ज्ञान

9. भाषा एक .... विषय है।
A. सैद्धान्तिक B. व्यावहारिक
C. नीरस D. चुनौतीपूर्ण

10. भाषा के विषय में मूल सत्य क्या है?
A. भाषा मात्र लिखित होती है।
B. भाषा का ढाँचा संरचनाहीन होता है।

C. भाषा प्रतीकात्मक है।

D. भाषा अनुकरणहीन माध्यम है।

11. भाषा के बारे में कौन-सा कथन उचित है?

A. भाषा एक नियमबद्ध व्यवस्था है।

B. भाषा व्याकरण का अनुसरण करती है।

C. भाषा और बोली में कभी भी कोई भी संबंध नहीं होता।

D. भाषा अनिवार्यतः लिखित होती है।

12. निम्नलिखित में से किस देश में हिन्दी भाषा का प्रयोग लिखने एवं बोलने में किया जाता है?

A. ऑस्ट्रेलिया B. दक्षिण अमेरिका

C. पाकिस्तान D. मॉरीशस

13. निम्नलिखित में से कौन-सी भाषा व्याकरण और वर्तनी से शुद्ध भाषा कहलाती है?

A. साहित्यिक भाषा B. प्रांजल भाषा

C. व्याकरणिक भाषा D. मानक भाषा

14. 'सूरसागर' किस भाषा की रचना है?

A. अवधी B. बुन्देली

C. ब्रज D. छत्तीसगढ़ी

15. हिन्दी भाषा में कितनी बोलियाँ हैं?

A. 15 B. 25

C. 18 D. 22

16. देवनागरी लिपि का विकास किस लिपि से हुआ?

A. अपभ्रंश B. सिंधु

C. खरोष्ठी D. ब्राह्मी

17. 'संघ की भाषा हिन्दी और लिपि देवनागरी होगी', संविधान के किस अनुच्छेद में कहा गया है?

A. अनुच्छेद 372 B. अनुच्छेद 343

C. अनुच्छेद 354 D. अनुच्छेद 350

18. निम्नलिखित में से कौन-सी भाषा संस्कृत भाषा की अपभ्रंश है?

A. खड़ी बोली B. ब्रज भाषा

C. अवधी D. पालि

19. संविधान की आठवीं अनुसूची में कुल कितनी भारतीय भाषाएँ हैं?

A. 15 B. 22

C. 18 D. 24

20. पश्चिमी हिन्दी का उद्‌भव जिस क्षेत्रीय अपभ्रंश में हुआ है, उसका नाम है :

A. मागधी B. अर्धमागधी

C. शौरसेनी D. महाराष्ट्रीय

21. 'भोजपुरी' निम्नलिखित में से किस उपभाषा की बोली है?

A. पूर्वी हिन्दी B. पश्चिमी हिन्दी

C. पहाड़ी D. बिहारी

22. बांगरू किस उपभाषा वर्ग की बोली है?

A. पश्चिमी हिन्दी B. पूर्वी हिन्दी

C. पहाड़ी D. बिहारी

23. निम्नलिखित में से किस भाषा का विकास शौरसेनी अपभ्रंश से हुआ?

A. गुजराती B. पंजाबी

C. मराठी D. सिंधी

24. हिन्दी किस भाषा परिवार की भाषा है?

A. ऑस्ट्रिक B. भारोपीय

C. द्रविड़ D. चीनी-तिब्बती

25. भाषा लिखने के लिए प्रयुक्त चिह्नों के व्यवस्थित रूप को क्या कहते हैं?

A. व्याकरण B. बोली

C. लिपि D. भाषा

उत्तरमाला

1	2	3	4	5	6	7	8	9	10
B	A	A	C	B	C	A	A	B	C
11	**12**	**13**	**14**	**15**	**16**	**17**	**18**	**19**	**20**
A	D	D	C	C	D	B	D	B	C
21	**22**	**23**	**24**	**25**					
D	A	A	B	C					

❄ ❄ ❄ ❄ ❄

3 वर्ण विचार

वर्णमाला

मौखिक भाषा की अंतिम इकाई ध्वनि है। लिखित भाषा की अंतिम इकाई वर्ण है। वर्ण शब्द की व्युत्पत्ति संस्कृत के 'वर्ण' धातु से हुई है, जिसका अर्थ है—वर्णन करना। वर्णों के समूह को **वर्णमाला** कहते हैं। अंग्रेजी में इसे ही Alphabet कहते हैं। हिन्दी वर्णमाला को दो भागों में विभक्त किया जा सकता है—

स्वर

स्वर मूल ध्वनि है। इन्हें किसी अन्य ध्वनि की सहायता के बिना उच्चारित किया जा सकता है, जैसे—अ, इ, उ। स्वरों की संख्या 11 है—अ, आ, इ, ई, उ, ऊ, ऋ, ए, ऐ, ओ और औ। उच्चारण में लगने वाले समय के अनुसार स्वरों को तीन भागों में बांटा जा सकता है—*(i)* ह्रस्व स्वर, *(ii)* दीर्घ स्वर, और *(iii)* प्लुत स्वर। जिन स्वरों के उच्चारण में 'अ' के उच्चारण के बराबर समय लगता है, उन्हें ह्रस्व स्वर कहा जाता है। अ, इ, उ, ऋ ह्रस्व स्वर हैं। जिन स्वरों के उच्चारण में 'आ' के उच्चारण के बराबर समय लगता है, उन्हें दीर्घ स्वर कहा जाता है। आ, ई, ऊ, ओ और औ दीर्घ स्वर हैं। प्लुत स्वरों के उच्चारण में तीन मात्राओं के उच्चारण के बराबर समय लगता है। सतीश में 'ती' के उच्चारण और ओउम् में 'ओ' के उच्चारण में तीन मात्राओं के उच्चारण के बराबर समय लगता है। रचना के आधार पर स्वरों को दो भागों में बांटा जा सकता है—

(i) **मूल स्वर :** अ, इ, उ, ऋ

(ii) **संयुक्त स्वर :** अ + अ = आ, अ + इ = ए, अ + ए = ऐ, अ + उ = ओ आदि।

व्यंजन

व्यंजन उन वर्णों को कहते हैं, जिनके उच्चारण में स्वरों की सहायता ली जाती हैं। क् + अ = क, च् + अ = च, त् + अ = त—ये सब व्यंजन के उदाहरण हैं। यहाँ क, च और त के उच्चारण में 'अ' की सहायता ली गई है।

हिन्दी में तीन संयुक्त व्यंजन हैं—क्ष, त्र और ज्ञ। इनका निर्माण इस प्रकार होता है—

क् + ष = क्ष; त् + र = त्र और ज + ञ = ज्ञ।

व्यंजन तीन प्रकार के होते हैं—*(i)* स्पर्श, *(ii)* अन्तस्थ और *(iii)* ऊष्म। क से म तक 25 वर्ण स्पर्श कहलाते हैं; य, र, ल, व अन्तस्थ कहे जाते हैं और श, ष, स, ह ऊष्म कहे जाते हैं।

वर्णों के मेल से मात्रिक तथा अमात्रिक शब्दों की पहचान

जब कई वर्ण आपस में मिलते हैं तो शब्द का निर्माण होता है जिसमें कुछ शब्दों में मात्राओं का प्रयोग होता है और कुछ शब्दों में मात्राओं का प्रयोग नहीं होता है। इस प्रकार जो शब्द बनते हैं, उन्हें ही मात्रिक तथा अमात्रिक शब्द कहते हैं।

- **अमात्रिक शब्द :** जब वर्णों के मेल से शब्द का निर्माण होता है और उस शब्द में किसी भी मात्रा का प्रयोग नहीं होता है, तो उसे अमात्रिक शब्द कहते हैं। जैसे—घर → घ + र, कमल → क + म + ल, पलक → प + ल + क, तरकस → त + र + क + स।
- **मात्रिक शब्द :** जब वर्णों के मेल से शब्द का निर्माण होता है और उस शब्द में अलग-अलग प्रकार की मात्राओं का प्रयोग होता है, तो उसे मात्रिक शब्द कहते हैं। जैसे—माहेश्वरी, शामिल, चुनाव, कैसी आदि।
  माहेश्वरी → आ, ए, ई की मात्रा का प्रयोग हुआ है।
  शामिल → आ, इ की मात्रा का प्रयोग हुआ है।
  चुनाव → उ, आ की मात्रा का प्रयोग हुआ है।
  कैसी → ऐ, ई की मात्रा का प्रयोग हुआ है।

मुख्य अंतर

- **संरचना :** अमात्रिक शब्दों में केवल व्यंजन + 'अ' स्वर होता है। मात्रिक शब्दों में व्यंजन के साथ अ-स्वर के अलावा अन्य स्वर (आ, इ, ई आदि) जुड़ते हैं।
- **उच्चारण :** अमात्रिक शब्दों का उच्चारण सपाट होता है, जबकि मात्रिक शब्दों में मात्रा के अनुसार ध्वनि बदलती है।

हिन्दी की सभी ध्वनियों के पारस्परिक अंतर की जानकारी

उच्चारण स्थान के आधार पर वर्णों का वर्गीकरण इस प्रकार है—

- **कण्ठ्य :** अ, आ, कवर्ग (क, ख, ग, घ, ङ), ह और विसर्ग में जिह्वा कण्ठ छूती है। क, ख, ग—इनका उच्चारण कण्ठ और जिह्वा मूल से होता है।

- **तालव्य :** इ, ई, चवर्ग (च, छ, ज, झ, ञ), य और श केवल तालु से बोले जाते हैं।
- **मूर्धन्य :** ऋ, टवर्ग (ट, ठ, ड, ढ, ण), र, ष तथा ड़ और ढ़ का उच्चारण मूर्द्धा से होता है।
- **दन्त्य :** तवर्ग (त, थ, द, ध, न), ल और स का उच्चारण दाँतों के साथ जिह्वा के मेल से होता है।
- **ओष्ठ्य :** उ, ऊ, पवर्ग (प, फ, ब, भ, म) का उच्चारण ओठों से होता है।
- **कण्ठत्तालु :** ए, ऐ का उच्चारण कण्ठ और तालु के मेल से होता है।
- **कण्ठोष्ठ :** ओ, औ का उच्चारण कण्ठ और ओठों के मेल से होता है।
- **दन्तोष्ठ :** व (फ) का उच्चारण दाँत और ओठों से होता है।
- **अनुनासिक :** ङ, ञ, न, म का उच्चारण मुँह और नाक से होता है।
- **नासिका :** सभी अनुस्वार नाक से बोले जाते हैं।

सभी प्रकार की मात्राएँ

हिन्दी व्याकरण में मात्राएँ स्वरों के वे चिह्न हैं, जो व्यंजनों के साथ मिलकर शब्द बनाते हैं। कुल 11 स्वरों में से 10 की मात्राएँ होती हैं, 'अ' स्वर की अपनी कोई मात्रा नहीं होती, लेकिन यह हर व्यंजन में अंतर्निहित होता है। प्रमुख मात्राएँ हैं : आ (ा), इ (ि), ई (ी), उ (ु), ऊ (ू), ऋ (ृ), ए (े), ऐ (ै), ओ (ो), औ (ौ)।

अनुस्वार और अनुनासिक में अंतर

- **अनुस्वार :** यह एक नासिक्य व्यंजन है जिसका उच्चारण केवल नाक से होता है। अं का चिह्न (ं) होता है। जैसे–हंस, रंग।
- **अनुनासिक :** जिन स्वरों या वर्णों का उच्चारण मुख और नासिक दोनों से किया जाता है, वे अनुनासिक कहलाते हैं, इनका चिह्न चन्द्रबिंदु (ँ) है। जैसे–आँख, गाँव।

नोट–अनुस्वार और अनुनासिक (चन्द्रबिन्दु) के अंतर से शब्दों के अर्थ बदल जाते हैं। जैसे–हंस (जलपक्षी) और हँस (हँसने की क्रिया)।

चन्द्रबिन्दु वास्तव में स्वर का ही नासिक्य रूप है, जबकि अनुस्वार एक व्यंजन की ध्वनि है।

संयुक्ताक्षर एवं अनुनासिक ध्वनियों के प्रयोग से बने शब्द

संयुक्ताक्षर (दो व्यंजनों का मेल) और अनुनासिक (चन्द्रबिन्दु ँ) हिन्दी वर्तनी के महत्वपूर्ण हिस्से हैं। संयुक्ताक्षर शब्दों में अकसर एक आधा व्यंजन दूसरे पूरे व्यंजन से जुड़ता है, जबकि अनुनासिक स्वर नाक और मुख से उच्चारित होते हैं, जैसे–प्याला, मच्छर, चाँद, मुँह।

नोट–गुच्छे (अनुनासिक + संयुक्ताक्षर)
कम्पन (अनुस्वार / नासिका)।

अभ्यास प्रश्न

1. वर्ण किसे कहते हैं?
A. अक्षर को B. शब्द को
C. ध्वनि के लिखित रूप को D. इनमें से किसी को नहीं

2. हिन्दी वर्णमाला में कौन-से दो मुख्य वर्ण हैं?
A. स्वर - व्यंजन B. अनुस्वार - विसर्ग
C. संधि - समास D. विसर्ग - व्यंजन

3. हिन्दी वर्णमाला में ह्रस्व स्वरों की संख्या है :
A. चार B. पाँच
C. छः D. कोई नहीं

4. अनुस्वार क्या है?
A. स्वर है B. व्यंजन है
C. स्वर और व्यंजन दोनों हैं D. उपर्युक्त में से कोई नहीं

5. क से म तक के व्यंजन कहलाते हैं :
A. स्पर्श B. स्पर्श संघर्षी
C. कंठ्य D. ओष्ठ्य

6. श, ष, स, ह, वायुप्रक्षेप की दृष्टि से कैसे व्यंजन हैं?
A. अल्पप्राण B. महाप्राण
C. उपर्युक्त दोनों D. इनमें से कोई नहीं

7. वायु प्रक्षेप की दृष्टि से स्वर क्या होते हैं?
A. अल्पप्राण B. महाप्राण
C. उपर्युक्त दोनों D. इनमें से कोई नहीं

8. अधोलिखित में से अनुनासिक स्वर वाला शब्द चुनिए :
A. बंदर B. सुंदर
C. बंदरी D. नंदी

9. 'ह' व्यंजन उच्चारण की दृष्टि से क्या है?
A. कंठ्य B. कंठतालव्य
C. कण्ठोष्ठ D. इनमें से कोई नहीं

10. शब्द के बीच में या अंत में जब अ स्वर का उच्चारण पूरा नहीं होता तो इसके पूर्व स्वर पर :
A. व्यंजनाघात होता है। B. स्वराघात या बलाघात होता है।
C. मात्राघात होता है। D. वर्णाघात होता है।

11. संयोग की दृष्टि से क्या, क्यों अधोलिखित में से क्या हैं?
A. संयुक्त ध्वनि B. युग्मक ध्वनि
C. सामान्य संयुक्ताक्षर D. इनमें से कोई नहीं

12. निम्नलिखित ध्वनियों की निर्दिष्ट विशेषताओं में से कौन-सा अशुद्ध है?
A. च - तालव्य, महाप्राण B. ख - महाप्राण, कंठ्य
C. त - अल्पप्राण, दंत्य D. म - ओष्ठ्य, सघोष

13. प्लुत स्वर कौन-सा है?
A. ओउम् B. अउम
C. ओम D. ओम्

14. 'ट' वर्ग में किस प्रकार के व्यंजन हैं?
A. कंठ्य B. तालव्य
C. मूर्धन्य D. दन्त्य

15. 'ङ्' का उच्चारण स्थान होता है :
A. नासिक्य B. कण्ठोष्ठ
C. मूर्धन्य D. कण्ठतालव्य

16. 'श' ध्वनि का उच्चारण स्थान क्या है?
A. दन्त B. मूर्धा
C. तालु D. दंतालु

17. निम्न में से संयुक्त व्यंजन कौन-सा नहीं है?
A. त्र B. य
C. क्ष D. ज्ञ

18. जिसका उच्चारण ऊपर के दाँतों पर जीभ लगाने से होता है, उसे क्या कहते हैं?
A. मूर्धन्य B. कण्ठ्य
C. दन्त्य D. अनुनासिक

19. निम्नलिखित में से 'ऊष्म व्यंजन' कौन-से हैं?
A. च, छ, ज B. श, ष, स
C. अ, ब, स D. य, र, ल

20. उच्चारण स्थान की दृष्टि से कौन-सा विकल्प शुद्ध है?
A. स - दन्त्य B. च - कण्ठ्य
C. ष - तालव्य D. श - मूर्धन्य

21. इ, ई, उ, ऊ किस प्रकार के स्वर हैं?
A. संवृत B. असकृत
C. विवृत D. अर्द्धविवृत

22. 'य', 'र', 'ल', 'व' कौन-से व्यंजन कहलाते हैं?
A. स्पर्श व्यंजन B. संयुक्त व्यंजन
C. अंतःस्थ व्यंजन D. अय व्यंजन

23. उच्चारण की दृष्टि से व्यंजन 'ण' का स्थान है :
A. तालु B. जीभ
C. दाँत D. नासिका

24. वर्णमाला में स्पर्श व्यंजनों की संख्या कितनी है?
A. 25 B. 30
C. 20 D. 35

25. हिन्दी व्यंजनों में 'क' वर्ग की सभी ध्वनियाँ हैं :
A. कण्ठ्य B. अल्पप्राण
C. अनुनासिक D. अघोष

26. निम्नलिखित में से दंतोष्ठ्य ध्वनियाँ हैं :
A. य, र B. ल, व
C. प, फ D. व, फ

27. निम्नलिखित में दिए गए विकल्पों में से 'मूर्धन्य' वर्ण है :
A. द B. स
C. ट D. ध

28. 'घ' का उच्चारण स्थान क्या है?
A. मूर्धन्य B. कण्ठ्य
C. ओष्ठ्य D. तालव्य

29. इनमें से ह्रस्व स्वर नहीं है :
A. अ B. इ
C. उ D. ए

30. 'क' का उच्चारण स्थान क्या है?
A. दंतोष्ठ B. कण्ठ्य
C. तालु D. नासिक्य

उत्तरमाला

1	2	3	4	5	6	7	8	9	10
C	A	A	C	A	B	A	C	A	B
11	12	13	14	15	16	17	18	19	20
A	A	A	C	A	C	B	C	B	A
21	22	23	24	25	26	27	28	29	30
A	C	D	A	A	D	C	B	D	B

❊ ❊ ❊ ❊ ❊

4 शब्द विचार

शब्द

एक अथवा एक से अधिक वर्णों के मेल से बने सार्थक वर्ण-समूह को 'शब्द' कहते हैं, किन्तु केवल वर्णों का समूह ही शब्द नहीं होता, बल्कि उस वर्ण समूह का कोई-न-कोई अर्थ अवश्य होना चाहिए।

शब्द के प्रकार/भेद

व्याकरण के अनुसार शब्दों के निम्नलिखित चार प्रकार/भेद होते हैं, जो इस प्रकार हैं :

1. उत्पत्ति के आधार पर शब्द भेद

उत्पत्ति के आधार पर शब्दों के चार भेद हैं :

(*i*) **तत्सम शब्द :** संस्कृत भाषा के कुछ शब्द ऐसे होते हैं जो हिन्दी में भी बिना परिवर्तन के प्रयुक्त होते हैं, उन शब्दों को 'तत्सम शब्द' कहते हैं। जैसे–अग्नि, रात्रि, हस्त, क्षेत्र, कर्म, कृषि, पुष्प आदि। ऋ, ष, क्ष, त्र, ज्ञ, श्र आदि वर्णो का प्रयोग अधिकांशतः तत्सम शब्दों में ही पाया जाता है।

(*ii*) **तद्भव शब्द :** ऐसे शब्द जो संस्कृत भाषा के तो हैं, लेकिन हिन्दी भाषा में परिवर्तित करके प्रयोग में लाए जाते हैं, 'तद्भव शब्द' कहलाते हैं। जैसे–आग, रात, खेत, काम, फूल आदि।

कुछ तत्सम और तद्भव शब्द इस प्रकार हैं :

तत्सम	तद्भव	तत्सम	तद्भव	तत्सम	तद्भव
स्वर्ण	सोना	अमूल्य	अमोल	कदली	केला
आम्र	आम	अज्ञान	अजान	आश्रय	आसरा
कर्ण	कान	अक्षि	आँख	अष्ट	आठ
अग्नि	आग	कोकिल	कोयल	आलस्य	आलस

(*iii*) **देशज शब्द :** वे शब्द जो देश की अन्य बोलियों या क्षेत्रीय भाषा से हिन्दी में शामिल हुए, 'देशज शब्द' कहलाते हैं। जैसे–थैला, लोटा, टाँग, पगड़ी आदि।

(*iv*) **विदेशज शब्द :** विदेशों की भाषा से आए हुए शब्द जो हिन्दी में शामिल हुए, उन्हें 'विदेशज' या 'आगत शब्द' कहते हैं।

हिन्दी भाषा में प्रयुक्त किए जाने वाले कुछ विदेशी शब्द निम्नलिखित हैं :

- **अंग्रेजी शब्द :** डॉक्टर, स्कूल, स्टेशन, ट्रेन, कप्तान, प्रेस, कमीशन, जज, गेट, कमिश्नर आदि।
- **फ्रेंच शब्द :** पिकनिक, कूपन, लैम्प, बम आदि।
- **स्पैनिश शब्द :** सिगरेट, सिगार, कॉर्क आदि।
- **अरबी शब्द :** अखबार, अदालत, इंसाफ, रिश्वत, दफ्तर आदि।
- **फारसी शब्द :** आमदनी, सौदागर, खुराक, पेशा, चिराग आदि।
- **तुर्की शब्द :** कैंची, कुली, चाकू, तोप, बेगम, बन्दूक आदि।
- **पुर्तगाली शब्द :** आलपीन, अलमारी, कनस्तर, चाबी, तौलिया आदि।

2. व्युत्पत्ति या रचना के आधार पर शब्द भेद

व्युत्पत्ति या रचना के आधार पर शब्दों को तीन भागों में विभाजित किया गया है :

(*i*) **रूढ़ :** वे शब्द जो किसी विशेष अर्थ के लिए प्रसिद्ध होते हैं और जिनके टुकड़े करने पर उन टुकड़ों का कोई अर्थ नहीं निकलता, उन्हें 'रूढ़ शब्द' कहते हैं। जैसे–घर-रूढ़ शब्द है। घ + र = टुकड़े करने पर घ और र का कोई अर्थ नहीं निकल रहा है।

(*ii*) **यौगिक :** ऐसे शब्द जो एक से अधिक सार्थक शब्दों के योग से बने हों, उन्हें 'यौगिक शब्द' कहते हैं। इनके टुकड़े कर देने पर प्रत्येक शब्द का अर्थ भी निकलता है। जैसे–राजपुत्र = राज + पुत्र, अनपढ़ = अन + पढ़।

(*iii*) **योगरूढ़ :** ऐसे शब्द जो एक से अधिक सार्थक शब्दों के मेल से बने हों, लेकिन विशेष अर्थ की ओर संकेत करते हों, 'योगरूढ़ शब्द' कहलाते हैं।

जैसे–नीलकंठ = नील + कंठ (विशेष अर्थ–नीले कंठ वाले शिव जी), दशानन = दश + आनन (दस मुख वाला – रावण)

3. अर्थ के आधार पर शब्द भेद

अर्थ के आधार पर शब्दों के दो भेद हैं :

(*i*) **सार्थक शब्द :** वे शब्द जो एक निश्चित अर्थ को प्रकट करते हैं, 'सार्थक शब्द' कहलाते हैं।
जैसे—महल, पुस्तक, राजा आदि।

(*ii*) **निरर्थक शब्द :** ऐसे शब्द जिनका कोई अर्थ नहीं निकलता, 'निरर्थक शब्द' कहलाते हैं।
जैसे—खाना-वाना, पानी-वानी आदि।

4. प्रयोग के आधार पर शब्द भेद

प्रयोग के आधार पर शब्दों के दो भेद हैं :

(*i*) **विकारी शब्द :** जिन शब्दों का रूप लिंग, वचन, काल, कारक आदि के कारण बदल जाता है, उन्हें 'विकारी शब्द' कहते हैं। विकारी शब्द चार प्रकार के होते हैं—संज्ञा, सर्वनाम, क्रिया, विशेषण।

(*ii*) **अविकारी शब्द :** जिन शब्दों का रूप लिंग, वचन, काल, कारक आदि के कारण नहीं बदलता है, उन्हें 'अविकारी शब्द' कहते हैं। अविकारी शब्द चार प्रकार के होते हैं—क्रिया-विशेषण, संबंधबोधक, समुच्चयबोधक, विस्मयादिबोधक।

अभ्यास प्रश्न

1. तत्सम शब्द किस दृष्टि से शब्द का भेद है?
A. अर्थ की दृष्टि से
B. उद्गम की दृष्टि से
C. व्युत्पत्ति की दृष्टि से
D. इनमें से कोई नहीं

2. 'संध्या' का तद्भव रूप है :
A. साँझ
B. वंध्या
C. आराध्य
D. त्रिज्या

3. 'आम्र' का तद्भव रूप है :
A. नाम
B. ग्राम
C. आम
D. वाम

4. 'मयूर' का तद्भव रूप है :
A. मोर
B. यार
C. माया
D. मरण

5. 'सावन' शब्द का तत्सम रूप है :
A. वन
B. श्रावन
C. श्रावण
D. श्रवण

6. 'खेत' शब्द का तत्सम रूप है :
A. क्षेत्र
B. नेत्र
C. रेत
D. श्वेत

7. 'गाँव' इस शब्द का तद्भव रूप है :
A. ग्राम
B. काँव
C. छाँव
D. शहर

8. फरमाइश रेखांकित शब्द स्रोत की दृष्टि से है :
A. तद्भव
B. तत्सम
C. विदेशी
D. देशज

9. आवारा शब्द किस भाषा का है?
A. अरबी
B. फारसी
C. तुर्की
D. पुर्तगाली

10. लौकी कैसा शब्द है?
A. देशी
B. तद्भव
C. तत्सम
D. विदेशी

11. लालटेन किस भाषा का शब्द है?
A. देशी
B. अंग्रेजी
C. फ्रेंच
D. डच

12. 'चाकू' किस भाषा का शब्द है?
A. फारसी
B. अरबी
C. तुर्की
D. डच

13. 'गँवार' का तत्सम शब्द है:
A. मूर्ख
B. ग्रामीण
C. ग्राहक
D. गम्भीर

14. 'अलमारी' शब्द है:
A. अरबी
B. फारसी
C. पुर्तगाली
D. पश्तो

15. निम्नलिखित में से तद्भव शब्द हैं :
A. भ्रमर
B. अग्नि
C. मस्तक
D. मछली

16. इनमें से कौन-सा शब्द तद्भव है?
A. मधुप
B. भ्रमर
C. भंवरा
D. मधुकर

17. 'मुदरी' का तत्सम रूप है :
A. मुद्रिका
B. मुद्री
C. मुंदरी
D. मुदरिका

18. 'सीस' का तत्सम रूप क्या है?
A. शीशा
B. शीर्ष
C. सिरा
D. शीर्षक

19. 'गोधूम' शब्द का तद्भव है :
A. गेहूँ
B. गाय
C. गोबर
D. गोधन

20. तद्भव और उसके तत्सम का कौन-सा मेल गलत है?
A. आँत-अंत्र
B. लौंग-लवंग
C. लुनाई-लावण्यता
D. आयसु-आदेश

21. निम्नलिखित में से कौन-सा शब्द तद्भव है?
A. खेत
B. प्रभु
C. नाथ
D. त्रिकुटी

22. निम्नलिखित में से कौन-सा शब्द देशज है?
A. लाश
B. औरत
C. पतलून
D. धड़ाम

23. 'मेंढक' का तत्सम रूप क्या है?
A. मुष्टि
B. मंडूक
C. बंदूक
D. मुद्ग

24. 'कपोत' शब्द का तद्भव है :
A. काम
B. काज
C. कबूतर
D. गाल

25. निम्न में से देशज शब्द ज्ञात कीजिए :
A. परोपकार
B. छलछल
C. प्रसन्न
D. पुष्कल

26. निम्नलिखित में से तत्सम शब्द कौन-सा है?
A. दीपक
B. दाहिना
C. दामाद
D. दीवाली

27. निम्नलिखित में से 'लोटा' शब्द है :
A. तत्सम
B. तद्भव
C. देशज
D. विदेशज

28. 'ज्येष्ठ' शब्द का तद्भव शब्द है :
A. जयेष्ठ
B. जेठ
C. बड़ा
D. ज्येठ

29. 'चकवा' शब्द का तत्सम शब्द है :
A. चक्रवात
B. चक्षु
C. चक्रवाक
D. इनमें से कोई नहीं

30. 'चणक' शब्द का तद्भव शब्द है :
A. पलंग
B. खीर
C. खपरा
D. चना

उत्तरमाला

1	2	3	4	5	6	7	8	9	10
B	A	C	A	C	A	A	C	B	C
11	**12**	**13**	**14**	**15**	**16**	**17**	**18**	**19**	**20**
B	A	B	C	D	C	A	B	A	C
21	**22**	**23**	**24**	**25**	**26**	**27**	**28**	**29**	**30**
A	D	B	C	B	A	C	B	C	D

❄ ❄ ❄ ❄ ❄

5 उपसर्ग एवं प्रत्यय

उपसर्ग

ऐसे शब्दांश जो किसी शब्द के पूर्व जोड़े जाने पर उसके अर्थ को परिवर्तित कर देते हैं, वे उपसर्ग कहलाते हैं। ये स्वयं सार्थक नहीं होते, लेकिन जिस शब्द से पहले जुड़ते हैं, उसके अर्थ में विशेषता उत्पन्न कर देते हैं। जैसे 'ज्ञान' में 'वि' जोड़ने पर 'विज्ञान' बनकर ज्ञान शब्द का अर्थ पूरी तरह बदल जाता है। इसी प्रकार 'ज्ञान' में 'अ' जोड़ने पर भी पूर्णतः भिन्न शब्द 'अज्ञान' बन जाता है।

उपसर्गों को पाँच भागों में विभक्त किया जा सकता है—

1. **संस्कृत के उपसर्ग :** संस्कृत के उपसर्गों की संख्या 22 है। वे इस प्रकार हैं—प्र, परा, अप, सम्, अनु, अव, निस्, निर्, दुस्, दुर्, वि, आ, नि, अधि, अपि, अति, सु, उत्, अभि, प्रति, परि, उप।
2. **अंग्रेजी के उपसर्ग :** अंग्रेजी भाषा के निम्न उपसर्गों का प्रयोग किया जाता है। वे इस प्रकार हैं— हैड, वाइस, सब, हॉफ, हेड, चीफ, जनरल, डिप्टी।
3. **हिन्दी के उपसर्ग :** हिन्दी के उपसर्ग विशेकर तद्भव शब्दों के पूर्व अर्थात् पहले आते हैं। वे इस प्रकार हैं—अन, अध्, उन, भर, दु, नि, अ, क, कु, अब, सु, पर, बिन।
4. **उर्दू-फारसी के उपसर्ग :** उर्दू एवं फारसी के उपसर्ग इस प्रकार हैं— ला, बद, बे, कम, गैर, खुश, ना, अल, बर, बिल, हम, दर, फिल/फी, ब, बा, सर, बिला, हर, बेश, नेक आदि।
5. **उपसर्ग के समान प्रयुक्त किए जाने वाले संस्कृत के अव्यय :** संस्कृत के उपर्युक्त उपसर्गों के अतिरिक्त के अव्ययों को उपसर्ग की तरह ही हिन्दी में प्रयोग किया जाता है। वे इस प्रकार हैं— अन्तर्, मुनर्, प्रादुर्, पूर्ण, प्राक्, पुरस्, बहिर, बहिस्, आत्म, स्व, पुरा, का/कु, न, स, स्वयं, इति, अलम, तिरस्, तत्, सत्, सम, सह, अन आदि।

प्रत्यय

ऐसे शब्द या शब्दांश जो किसी शब्द के अंत में लगकर उस शब्द के अर्थ में परिवर्तन कर देते हैं, वे प्रत्यय कहलाते हैं। जैसे— सज + आवट = सजावट, दुकान + दार = दुकानदार, पालन + हार = पालनहार।

प्रत्यय मुख्यतः दो प्रकार के होते हैं—

1. कृत् प्रत्यय

क्रिया अथवा धातु के बाद जो प्रत्यय लगाए जाते हैं, उन्हें कृत् प्रत्यय कहते हैं। कृत् प्रत्यय के मेल से बने शब्द को 'कृदंत' कहते हैं।

जैसे—तैर + आक = तैराक, पठ + अनीय = पठनीय।

कृत् प्रत्यय चार प्रकार के होते हैं—

(क) **कर्तृ वाचक कृत् प्रत्यय :** कर्ता का बोध कराने वाले प्रत्यय कर्तृ वाचक कृत् प्रत्यय कहलाते हैं।

जैसे— पाठ + आक = पाठक, गाड़ी + वाला = गाड़ीवाला।

(ख) **कर्म वाचक कृत् प्रत्यय :** कर्म का बोध कराने वाले प्रत्यय कर्म वाचक कृत् प्रत्यय कहलाते हैं।

जैसे—ओढ़ + नी = ओढ़नी, पढ़ + ना = पढ़ना।

(ग) **करण वाचक कृत् प्रत्यय :** साधन का बोध कराने वाले प्रत्यय करण वाचक कृत् प्रत्यय कहलाते हैं।

जैसे—चट + नी = चटनी, ढक + ना = ढकना।

(घ) **भाववाचक कृत् प्रत्यय :** क्रिया के भाव का बोध कराने वाले प्रत्यय भाववाचक कृत् प्रत्यय कहलाते हैं।

जैसे—मिल + आप = मिलाप, चिल्ल + आहट = चिल्लाहट।

हिन्दी के कुछ कृत् प्रत्यय और उनसे निर्मित शब्द

प्रत्यय	धातु	शब्द रूप (कृदंत)
आक	तैरना	तैराक
आड़ी	खेलना	खिलाड़ी
इया	बढ़	बढ़िया
अक्कड़	पीना	पियक्कड़
सार	मिलन	मिलनसार
आऊ	टिकना	टिकाऊ
हरा	सोना	सुनहरा
एरा	लूट	लुटेरा
औना	खेलना	खिलौना
ई	रेतना	रेती

प्रत्यय	धातु	शब्द रूप (कृदंत)
ऊ	झाड़ना	झाड़ू
वट	मिलना	मिलावट
त	बचना	बचत
आहट	घबराना	घबराहट
औता	समझाना	समझौता
औती	मनाना	मनौती

2. तद्धित प्रत्यय

क्रिया को छोड़कर संज्ञा, सर्वनाम, विशेषण आदि में जुड़कर नए शब्द बनाने वाले प्रत्यय तद्धित प्रत्यय कहलाते हैं। तद्धित प्रत्यय के मेल से बने शब्द को **'तद्धितांत'** कहते हैं।

हिन्दी के कुछ तद्धित प्रत्यय और उनसे निर्मित शब्द

प्रत्यय	शब्द	शब्द रूप (तद्धितांत)
आर	सोना	सुनार
आरी	जूआ	जुआरी
दार	समझ	समझदार
पन	बच्चा	बचपन
हट	चिकना	चिकनाहट
आस	मीठा	मिठास
क	ढोल	ढोलक

प्रत्यय	शब्द	शब्द रूप (तद्धितांत)
री	छाता	छतरी
इया	बूढ़ी	बुढ़िया
एल	नाक	नकेल
हाल	नाना	ननिहाल
औती	बाप	बपौती
इक	शरीर	शारीरिक
इमा	लाल	लालिमा
इष्ठ	वर	वरिष्ठ
ईन	कुल	कुलीन
र	मधु	मधुर
ई	गुजरात	गुजराती
गाह	चारा	चारागाह
त्र	सर्व	सर्वत्र
ओं	कोस	कोसों
स	आप	आपस
भर	दिन	दिनभर
ड़ा	दुःख	दुःखड़ा
ई	टोप	टोपी
इत	शाप	शापित
ए	धीर, पीछा	धीरे, पीछे

अभ्यास प्रश्न

निर्देश (प्र.सं. 1 से 15 तक) : *निम्नलिखित प्रश्नों में दिए गए शब्दों में प्रयुक्त उपसर्ग के सही विकल्प का चयन कीजिए।*

1. संकलन
A. संक B. स
C. सम् D. सम

2. स्वभाव
A. स B. स्व
C. सर्व D. सा

3. निष्काम
A. निस् B. निर
C. निः D. निश

4. उपहार
A. उप् B. उप
C. उपा D. उ

5. पराजय
A. पर B. परा
C. जय D. प

6. संयोग
A. सं B. सु
C. सम् D. सम

7. अत्याचार
A. अति B. आ
C. अ D. ति

8. अध्यात्म
A. अ B. अधि
C. धि D. आ

9. सरताज
A. स B. सर्
C. सर्र D. इनमें से कोई नहीं

10. अल्मस्त
A. अ
B. अल्
C. आल्
D. इनमें से कोई नहीं

11. नपुंसक
A. न
B. ना
C. नपु
D. इनमें से कोई नहीं

12. उत्तम
A. उ
B. उत्
C. उत्त
D. ऊत

13. संन्यासी
A. सम्
B. सन्
C. सं
D. सम

14. हमदर्दी
A. हम्
B. हमद
C. हम
D. इनमें से कोई नहीं

15. निरभिमान
A. निः
B. निर्
C. निस
D. निर

निर्देश (प्र.सं. 16 से 30 तक) : *निम्नलिखित प्रश्नों में दिए गए शब्दों में प्रयुक्त प्रत्यय के सही विकल्प का चयन कीजिए।*

16. विद्यालय
A. लय
B. आलय
C. य
D. अलय

17. वैज्ञानिक
A. इक
B. क
C. आई
D. ईक

18. चतुराई
A. आई
B. राई
C. यी
D. ई

19. मरियल
A. ईयल
B. ल
C. रियल
D. इयल

20. रसोइया
A. रस
B. या
C. इया
D. आ

21. गमन
A. अन
B. मन
C. न
D. उन

22. कहावत
A. हावत
B. वत
C. आवत
D. कह

23. पुजारिन
A. इन
B. आइन
C. रिन
D. पु

24. कवित्व
A. व
B. त्व
C. तव
D. इत्व

25. कविता
A. आ
B. ता
C. त्व
D. इता

26. पांडित्य
A. अ
B. य
C. त्य
D. इत्य

27. गांगेय
A. य
B. एय
C. गेय
D. इनमें से कोई नहीं

28. ग्रामीण
A. अ
B. ण
C. ईन
D. ईण

29. मासिक
A. अ
B. क
C. इक
D. इनमें से कोई नहीं

30. मलीन
A. न
B. ईन
C. लीन
D. लीन्

उत्तरमाला

1	2	3	4	5	6	7	8	9	10
C	B	A	B	B	C	A	B	B	B
11	**12**	**13**	**14**	**15**	**16**	**17**	**18**	**19**	**20**
A	B	A	C	B	B	A	A	D	C
21	**22**	**23**	**24**	**25**	**26**	**27**	**28**	**29**	**30**
A	C	A	B	B	B	B	C	C	B

❄ ❄ ❄ ❄ ❄

6 संज्ञा, सर्वनाम, क्रिया एवं विशेषण

संज्ञा

संज्ञा का अर्थ नाम होता है। संसार में जितने भी व्यक्ति या वस्तुएँ हैं, उनका कोई-न-कोई नाम अवश्य होता है। ऐसी सभी वस्तुओं के नामों को 'संज्ञा' कहा जाता है, जैसे—विजय, विनय, भारत, पाकिस्तान, दूध, दही, सुन्दरता, मिठास, झुण्ड आदि।

संज्ञा के भेद

संज्ञा के निम्नलिखित पाँच भेद होते हैं :

- **जातिवाचक संज्ञा :** जातिवाचक संज्ञा किसी प्राणी या वस्तु की सम्पूर्ण जाति का बोध कराती है; जैसे—गाय, किसान, किताब, लेखक, लड़का आदि।
- **व्यक्तिवाचक संज्ञा :** व्यक्तिवाचक संज्ञा किसी एक विशेष व्यक्ति, वस्तु या स्थान का बोध कराती है; जैसे—कृष्ण, गंगा, पटना, मेरठ, दिल्ली आदि। व्यक्तिवाचक संज्ञाओं के अंतर्गत निम्नलिखित नामों का समावेश होता है— व्यक्तियों के नाम, दिशाओं के नाम, देशों के नाम, नदियों के नाम, समुद्रों के नाम, पर्वतों के नाम, नगरों के नाम, पुस्तकों एवं समाचार पत्रों के नाम, दिनों के नाम, महीनों के नाम, ग्रह-नक्षत्रों के नाम, त्योहारों एवं उत्सवों के नाम, भाषाओं के नाम, वस्तुओं के नाम आदि।
- **द्रव्यवाचक संज्ञा :** द्रव्यवाचक संज्ञा किसी धातु या द्रव (तरल) पदार्थ का बोध कराती है; जैसे—दूध, दही, सोना, चाँदी, लोहा आदि।
- **समूहवाचक संज्ञा :** समूहवाचक संज्ञा किसी समूह का बोध कराती है; जैसे—झुण्ड, भीड़, सभा, गुच्छा, सेना, जुलूस आदि।
- **भाववाचक संज्ञा :** भाववाचक संज्ञा किसी व्यक्ति या वस्तु के धर्म अथवा गुण का बोध कराती है; जैसे—बुढ़ापा, मिठास, अच्छाई, मित्रता, शत्रुता आदि।

भाववाचक संज्ञा का निर्माण

भाववाचक संज्ञाओं का निर्माण तद्धित और कृदन्त प्रत्ययों को विभिन्न शब्द भेदों में लगाकर किया जाता है।

जातिवाचक संज्ञा से

जातिवाचक संज्ञा	भाववाचक संज्ञा	जातिवाचक संज्ञा	भाववाचक संज्ञा
पशु	पशुता	विद्वान	विद्वता
मनुष्य	मनुष्यता	शत्रु	शत्रुता
लड़का	लड़कपन	बूढ़ा	बुढ़ापा
देहात	देहाती	बंधु	बंधुत्व
स्त्री	स्त्रीत्व	शहर	शहरी
साधु	साधुत्व	माता	मातृत्व
घर	घरेलू	मूर्ख	मूर्खता

विशेषण से

विशेषण	भाववाचक संज्ञा	विशेषण	भाववाचक संज्ञा
सुन्दर	सुन्दरता	ईमानदार	ईमानदारी
कठोर	कठोरता	निपुण	निपुणता
कुरूप	कुरूपता	वीर	वीरता
गर्म	गर्मी	शिष्ट	शिष्टता
सर्द	सर्दी	कायर	कायरता
चौड़ा	चौड़ाई	नीच	नीचता
काला	कालापन	सभ्य	सभ्यता
नीला	नीलापन	शांत	शांति
कड़वा	कड़वाहट/कड़वापन	नम्र	नम्रता
छोटा	छुटपन/छोटापन	मीठा	मिठास

क्रिया से

क्रिया	भाववाचक संज्ञा	क्रिया	भाववाचक संज्ञा
पढ़ना	पढ़ाई	सजाना	सजावट
लड़ना	लड़ाई	लिखना	लिखावट
चढ़ना	चढ़ाई/चढ़ाव	बनाना	बनावट

क्रिया	भाववाचक संज्ञा	क्रिया	भाववाचक संज्ञा
विचारना	विचार	मिलाना	मिलावट
उठना	उठाव	निकलना	निकास
बहना	बहाव	झाड़ना	झाड़
खींचना	खिंचाव	फूँकना	फूँक
झुकना	झुकाव	लूटना	लूट

सर्वनाम से

सर्वनाम	भाववाचक संज्ञा	सर्वनाम	भाववाचक संज्ञा
मम	ममता	अहं	अहंकार
स्व	स्वत्व	पराया	परायापन
अपना	अपनत्व/अपनापन	सर्व	सर्वस्व
आप	आपा	निज	निजता
एक	एकता		

अव्यय से

अव्यय	भाववाचक संज्ञा	अव्यय	भाववाचक संज्ञा
निकट	निकटता	शाबाश	शाबाशी
समीप	समीपता/सामीप्य	वाह	वाहवाही
दूर	दूरी	धिक्	धिक्कार
अधिक	अधिकता	तेज	तेजी
सहज	सहजता	नित्य	नित्यता
नीचे	निचाई	बहुत	बहुतायत
मना	मनाही	शीघ्र	शीघ्रता
परस्पर	पारस्परिक	जल्दी	जल्दबाजी
कम	कमी	देर	देरी
बराबर	बराबरी	धीरे	धीमापन
ऊपर	ऊपरी		

अभ्यास प्रश्न

1. संज्ञा बोध कराती है :
A. व्यक्तियों के नाम का B. वस्तुओं के नाम का
C. स्थानों के नाम का D. उपरोक्त सभी का

2. वस्तु अथवा व्यक्ति के नाम को कहते हैं :
A. प्रतीक B. चिह्न
C. संज्ञा D. पहचान

3. संज्ञा के भेद होते हैं :
A. चार B. पाँच
C. छः D. तीन

4. प्रधानमंत्री कौन-सी संज्ञा है?
A. व्यक्तिवाचक B. समूहवाचक
C. जातिवाचक D. भाववाचक

5. जातिवाचक संज्ञा बोध कराती है :
A. व्यक्ति या मनुष्य के जातिवर्ग का
B. व्यक्ति के संस्कार का
C. पशुओं के जाति गुण का
D. व्यक्ति के पद का

6. सोना, चाँदी, लोहा, पीतल किस संज्ञा से संबद्ध शब्द हैं?
A. जातिवाचक संज्ञा B. भाववाचक संज्ञा
C. द्रव्यवाचक संज्ञा D. किसी से नहीं

7. इनमें से कौन-सा संज्ञा का कार्य नहीं है?
A. समूहसूचक नामों का बोध कराना
B. धातु, द्रव्य और अनाजों के नाम का बोध कराना
C. दिनों, महीनों, ग्रह-नक्षत्रों का बोध कराना
D. व्यक्ति के भविष्य का बोध कराना

8. इनमें से क्या भाववाचक संज्ञा नहीं है?
A. ममता B. कृपा
C. क्षमा D. गुच्छा

9. 'जयचन्दों' ने ही देश का विनाश किया। यहाँ 'जयचन्द' क्या है?
A. व्यक्तिवाचक संज्ञा B. जातिवाचक संज्ञा
C. भाववाचक संज्ञा D. इनमें से कोई नहीं

10. 'कक्षा' कौन-सी संज्ञा है?
A. जातिवाचक B. भाववाचक
C. समूहवाचक D. व्यक्तिवाचक

11. 'पढ़ना' की भाववाचक संज्ञा क्या होगी?
A. पाठ B. पठनीय
C. पढ़ाई D. पाठक

12. 'पंडित' की भाववाचक संज्ञा है:
A. पंडित्व B. पंडिताइन
C. पंडिताऊ D. पांडित्य

13. डॉ. राजेन्द्र प्रसाद को देशरत्न कहा जाता है। रेखांकित शब्द में कौन-सी संज्ञा है?
A. जातिवाचक संज्ञा B. द्रव्यवाचक संज्ञा
C. व्यक्तिवाचक संज्ञा D. भाववाचक संज्ञा

14. 'बुढ़ापा' शब्द में कौन-सी संज्ञा है?
A. जातिवाचक B. व्यक्तिवाचक
C. भाववाचक D. समूहवाचक

15. 'गंगा' शब्द में कौन-सी संज्ञा है?
A. जातिवाचक B. व्यक्तिवाचक
C. द्रव्यवाचक D. भाववाचक

16. 'सेना' शब्द में कौन-सी संज्ञा है?
A. समूहवाचक B. भाववाचक
C. द्रव्यवाचक D. व्यक्तिवाचक

17. 'गेहूँ' शब्द में कौन-सी संज्ञा है?
A. भाववाचक B. व्यक्तिवाचक
C. समूहवाचक D. द्रव्यवाचक

18. 'लड़का' शब्द में कौन-सी संज्ञा है?
A. समूहवाचक B. भाववाचक
C. जातिवाचक D. व्यक्तिवाचक

19. निम्नलिखित में से कौन-सा शब्द भाववाचक संज्ञा नहीं है?
A. सुन्दरता B. प्रेम
C. राम D. ईमानदारी

20. 'हिमालय' में कौन-सी संज्ञा है?
A. जातिवाचक B. व्यक्तिवाचक
C. द्रव्यवाचक D. समूहवाचक

उत्तरमाला

1	2	3	4	5	6	7	8	9	10
D	C	B	C	A	C	D	D	B	C
11	12	13	14	15	16	17	18	19	20
C	D	C	C	B	A	D	C	C	B

❊ ❊

सर्वनाम

संज्ञा शब्दों की पुनरुक्ति को दूर करने हेतु उनके स्थान पर जो शब्द प्रयुक्त किए जाते हैं, उन्हें सर्वनाम कहते हैं; जैसे–राम आज बीमार है, इसलिए वह आज विद्यालय नहीं आया। इस वाक्य में 'वह' शब्द राम के लिए प्रयुक्त हुआ है। यदि 'वह' शब्द का प्रयोग न होता तो 'राम' शब्द की पुनरुक्ति होती और वाक्य का सौन्दर्य नष्ट हो जाता।

हिन्दी के मूल सर्वनाम 11 हैं–मैं, तू, आप, यह, वह, जो, सो, कौन, क्या, कोई, कुछ।

सर्वनाम के भेद

सर्वनाम के निम्नलिखित छः भेद होते हैं :

- **पुरुषवाचक सर्वनाम :** जो सर्वनाम बोलने वाले या सुनने वाले या जिसके विषय में कुछ कहा जाए–इन तीनों पुरुषों का बोध कराते हैं, उन्हें पुरुषवाचक सर्वनाम कहा जाता है। 'पुरुषवाचक' सर्वनाम से पुरुष और स्त्री दोनों का बोध होता है।

  पुरुषवाचक सर्वनाम निम्न हैं : मैं, हम, तू, तुम, आप, यह, ये, वह, वे आदि।

  उदाहरण : उसने मुझे बोला था कि **तुम** पढ़ रही हो।

  उपर्युक्त वाक्य में तीन तरह के पुरुषवाचक शब्द आए हैं। उसने, मुझे और तुम– अतः स्पष्ट होता है कि पुरुषवाचक सर्वनाम के तीन भेद होते हैं।

  पुरुषवाचक सर्वनाम तीन प्रकार के होते हैं–

  1. **उत्तम पुरुष :** जिन शब्दों का प्रयोग बोलने वाला खुद (स्वयं) के लिए करता है। जैसे– मैं, मेरा, मुझे, मुझको, मेरी, हम, हमारा, हमारी, हम सब, हमलोग, आदि।
  2. **मध्यम पुरुष :** जिन शब्दों का प्रयोग सुनने वाले के लिए किया जाता है जैसे–तू, तुम, तुम्हें, तुम्हारा, तुमको, आप, आपको, आपलोग, आदि।
  3. **अन्य पुरुष :** जिन शब्दों का प्रयोग किसी तीसरे व्यक्ति के बारे में बात करने के लिए किया जाता है। जैसे– यह, वह, ये, वे, उन, उनको, उनसे, इन्हें, उन्हें, ये लोग, वे लोग, आदि।

- **निजवाचक सर्वनाम :** निजवाचक सर्वनाम से निज या अपने आप का बोध होता है; जैसे–आप, अपने-आप, खुद, निज, स्वतः, स्वयं, आदि।

  उदाहरण : मैं **अपनी** गाड़ी से जाऊँगा।

  मैं अपना काम **आप** ही कर लूंगी।

  उपर्युक्त वाक्यों में **अपनी** और **आप** निजवाचक सर्वनाम हैं।

- **निश्चयवाचक सर्वनाम :** निश्चयवाचक सर्वनाम से पास या दूर (उपस्थित या अनुपस्थित) की वस्तु का निश्चित रूप से बोध होता है; जैसे–यह, वे, वह, ये आदि।

  उदाहरण : यह मेरी गाड़ी है, **वह** राम की गाड़ी है।

- **अनिश्चयवाचक सर्वनाम :** अनिश्चयवाचक सर्वनाम से अज्ञात या अनिश्चित व्यक्तियों या वस्तुओं का बोध होता है; जैसे– कुछ, कुछ भी, सब कुछ, बहुत कुछ, कुछ-न-कुछ और जो कुछ, कोई, सब कोई, हर कोई, कोई भी और कोई-न-कोई आदि।

  उदाहरण : दरवाजे पर **कोई** खड़ा है। **कोई** आ रहा है।

- **प्रश्नवाचक सर्वनाम :** प्रश्नवाचक सर्वनाम का प्रयोग किसी व्यक्ति या वस्तु के विषय में कुछ पूछने के लिए होता है; जैसे–कौन, क्या आदि।

  उदाहरण : तुम **क्या** कर रहे हो?
- **संबंधवाचक सर्वनाम :** संबंधवाचक सर्वनाम से किसी संज्ञा या सर्वनाम के संबंध का ज्ञान होता है; जैसे–जो, सो... वह पुनरुक्त सर्वनाम के कुछ उदाहरण निम्न हैं–जो, सो, उसे, जिसकी, उसकी, जैसा, वैसा आदि।

  उदाहरण : जो सोएगा, सो खोएगा।

  जैसा कर्म करोगे, **वैसा** ही फल मिलेगा।

  उपर्युक्त वाक्यों में **जो,** और **सो** तथा **जैसा** और **वैसा** संबंध वाचक सर्वनाम हैं।

अभ्यास प्रश्न

1. **वह** सर्वनाम **वे** के रूप में कब व्यवहृत होता है?
A. आदर भाव में B. प्रश्न भाव में
C. संबंध भाव में D. अनिश्चय भाव में

2. इनमें से कौन शब्द पुरुषवाचक सर्वनाम नहीं है?
A. मैं B. तुम
C. आप D. सभी हैं

3. अधोलिखित में से कौन-सा प्रश्नवाचक सर्वनाम है?
A. कोई B. कौन
C. कभी D. कुछ

4. निम्नलिखित में कौन-सा शब्द अनिश्चयवाचक सर्वनाम है?
A. कौन B. क्या
C. वही D. कुछ

5. प्रश्नवाचक सर्वनाम में **कौन** का प्रयोग किसके लिए होता है?
A. व्यक्ति के लिए B. वस्तु के लिए
C. प्रश्न के लिए D. किसी के लिए नहीं

6. कोई आ रहा है– वाक्य में 'कोई' किस प्रकार का सर्वनाम है।
A. अनिश्चयवाचक B. निश्चयवाचक
C. निजवाचक D. संबंधवाचक

7. जैसा करोगे, वैसा भरोगे में कौन-सा सर्वनाम है?
A. पुरुषवाचक सर्वनाम B. प्रश्नवाचक सर्वनाम
C. संबंधवाचक सर्वनाम D. निजवाचक सर्वनाम

8. निम्न में सर्वनाम शब्द है:
A. नींद B. सफाई
C. रोग D. कौन

9. निम्न में कौन शब्द सर्वनाम है?
A. मोहन B. आप
C. कमला D. गुड़िया

10. शायद कमरे में <u>कोई</u> छिपा हुआ है। इस वाक्य में रेखांकित शब्द है।
A. प्रश्नवाचक सर्वनाम B. संबंधवाचक सर्वनाम
C. अनिश्चयवाचक सर्वनाम D. निजवाचक सर्वनाम

11. <u>जो</u> परिश्रम करेगा सो पास होगा। रेखांकित सर्वनाम का भेद बताइए।
A. निश्चयवाचक B. अनिश्चयवाचक
C. संबंधवाचक D. प्रश्नवाचक

12. निम्नलिखित वाक्य को उचित सर्वनाम के साथ पूर्ण कीजिए:
.... काम कर रहा है।
A. वह B. वेह
C. वे D. इनमें से कोई नहीं

13. बाहर कोई रो रहा है, इस वाक्य में कौन-सा शब्द सर्वनाम है?
A. बाहर B. रो रहा
C. कोई D. है

14. तुम <u>क्या</u> खोज रहे हो? रेखांकित शब्द में कौन-सा सर्वनाम है?
A. अनिश्चयवाचक B. प्रश्नवाचक
C. संबंधवाचक D. निश्चयवाचक

15. निम्नलिखित में सर्वनाम है:
A. राजेन्द्र B. पुस्तक
C. मैं D. सीता

16. निम्नलिखित में से निश्चयवाचक सर्वनाम है:
A. क्या B. कुछ C. कौन D. यह

17. निम्नलिखित वाक्य को उचित सर्वनाम के साथ पूर्ण कीजिए:
.... बहुत बुद्धिमान हो।
A. मैं B. तू C. तुम D. वह

18. किस वाक्य में प्रश्नवाचक सर्वनाम का प्रयोग हुआ है?
A. आपको यह काम करना है। B. वह पढ़ता-लिखता है न?
C. आप कहाँ रहते हो? D. वहाँ कौन पढ़ रहा था?

19. 'ऐसा भी हो सकता है।' वाक्य में कौन-सा शब्द सर्वनाम के रूप में प्रयोग किया गया है?
A. सकता B. ऐसा
C. भी D. हो

20. निम्नलिखित में से कौन-सा शब्द सर्वनाम नहीं है?
A. नदी B. यह C. वह D. आप

उत्तरमाला

1	2	3	4	5	6	7	8	9	10
A	D	B	D	A	A	C	D	B	C
11	**12**	**13**	**14**	**15**	**16**	**17**	**18**	**19**	**20**
C	A	C	B	C	D	C	D	B	A

❋ ❋

क्रिया एवं विशेषण

क्रिया

जिस शब्द से किसी काम का होना या करना समझा जाए, उसे क्रिया कहते हैं, जैसे–खाना, पीना, सोना, जागना, पढ़ना-लिखना आदि।

क्रिया तीन प्रकार के शब्दों से बनती है :

- धातु से–पढ़ना = पढ़ + ना
- संज्ञा से–हथियाना = हाथ + आ + ना
- विशेषण से–चिकनाना = चिकना + आ + ना

हिन्दी की बहुत-सी क्रियाएँ धातु से ही बनती हैं अर्थात् दूसरे शब्दों में हम कह सकते हैं कि जिस मूल शब्द से क्रिया का निर्माण होता है, उसे धातु कहते हैं। धातु में 'ना' जोड़ने से क्रिया का सामान्य रूप बनता है। इसका अर्थ यह है कि सामान्य क्रिया से 'ना' हटा देने पर, जो शब्द रह जाता है, उसे धातु कहते हैं :

- धातु + ना = सामान्य क्रिया; पढ़ + ना = पढ़ना

क्रिया के भेद

क्रिया के दो प्रकार के भेद होते हैं:

1. **सकर्मक क्रिया :** जो क्रिया सदैव कर्म के साथ आती हो, तो उसे सकर्मक क्रिया कहा जाता है। जैसे–श्याम ने केला खाया। इस वाक्य में **श्याम कर्ता** है, **खाया क्रिया** है और केला यहाँ पर **कर्म** है।
2. **अकर्मक क्रिया :** जिन क्रियाओं में कर्म का बोध नहीं होता और क्रिया का प्रभाव कर्ता पर पड़ता है, उन्हें अकर्मक क्रिया कहते हैं। जैसे–रमेश गाता है। यहाँ **कर्म** का अभाव है तथा गाता है **क्रिया** का प्रभाव रमेश पर पड़ता है।

अकर्मक एवं सकर्मक में परिवर्तन

जब कार्य अपने लिए न करके दूसरे के लिए किया जाए अथवा दूसरे से कराया जाए तब अकर्मक क्रिया सकर्मक बन जाती है और सकर्मक क्रिया द्विकर्मक बन जाती है। जैसे–

सुरेखा पुस्तक पढ़ती है। (सकर्मक)
सुरेखा पढ़ती है। (अकर्मक)
नवीन हँस रहा है। (अकर्मक)
नवीन, गोपाल को हँसाता है। (सकर्मक)
रमेश पढ़ता है। (सकर्मक)
अध्यापक, रमेश को पढ़ाता है। (द्विकर्मक)

क्रिया के अन्य भेद

संरचना के आधार पर क्रिया पाँच प्रकार की होती है।

1. **सामान्य क्रिया :** जहाँ किसी एक क्रिया का प्रयोग हो, तो वह सामान्य क्रिया कहलाती है।

   जैसे–महेश आया। इस वाक्य में 'आया' शब्द एक क्रिया के रूप में प्रयुक्त हुआ है।
2. **संयुक्त क्रिया :** जहाँ दो अथवा दो से अधिक क्रियाओं का साथ-साथ प्रयोग हो, तो वह संयुक्त क्रिया कहलाती है। जैसे–सूरज सो गया है। इस वाक्य में 'सो गया' दो-दो क्रियाओं का एक साथ प्रयोग हुआ है।
3. **नामधातु क्रिया :** संज्ञा, सर्वनाम, विशेषण आदि शब्दों से बने क्रिया पदों को नामधातु क्रिया कहते हैं। जैस–हाथ से हथियाना, गर्म से गर्माना, खटखट से खटखटाना आदि।
4. **प्रेरणार्थक क्रिया :** जब कर्ता कोई काम स्वयं न करके दूसरे को उसे करने को प्रेरित करे, तो अकर्मक क्रिया सकर्मक बन जाती है। ऐसी क्रियाएं प्रेरणार्थक क्रियाएं कहलाती हैं। जैसे–अध्यापक छात्रों से पाठ पढ़वाता है।
5. **पूर्वकालिक क्रिया :** मुख्य क्रिया से पहले आने वाली क्रिया पूर्वकालिक क्रिया कहलाती है। जैसे–मैं अभी सोकर उठा। यहाँ 'सोकर' पूर्वकालिक क्रिया है। यहाँ मुख्य क्रिया 'उठा' है।

विशेषण

संज्ञा और सर्वनाम की विशेषता बताने वाले शब्द को विशेषण कहते हैं। जिस शब्द की विशेषता बताई जाए, उसे विशेष्य कहते हैं; जैसे–उजली गाय मैदान में खड़ी है। इस वाक्य में 'उजली' विशेषण तथा गाय विशेष्य है।

विशेषण के भेद

विशेषण के मुख्य चार भेद निम्नलिखित हैं :

- **गुणवाचक विशेषण :** जिस विशेषण द्वारा विशेष्य के गुण अथवा दोष (भाव, रंग, आकार, स्थान, समय आदि) का बोध होता है, उसे 'गुणवाचक विशेषण' कहते हैं।
- **परिमाणबोधक/परिमाणवाचक विशेषण :** जो विशेषण किसी वस्तु की मात्रा वजन, माप-तोल को बताते हैं, उन्हें परिमाणबोधक या परिमाणवाचक विशेषण कहते हैं; जैसे—**बहुत** पानी, **कितना** सोना, **कितनी** चाँदी, **सब** कुछ, **और** दूध आदि।
- **सार्वनामिक विशेषण :** सर्वनाम जब किसी संज्ञा के पूर्व आते हैं, तो सार्वनामिक विशेषण कहलाते हैं; जैसे—यह कलम, वह थोड़ा, कौन आदमी, मेरा आदि।
- **संख्यावाचक विशेषण :** जिन विशेषणों द्वारा संख्या का बोध होता है, उसे संख्यावाचक विशेषण कहते हैं; जैसे—**पाँच** आदमी, **दो** विद्यार्थी, **एक** पुस्तक आदि।

विशेषण की रचना

कुछ शब्द मूल रूप में ही विशेषण होते हैं, किंतु कुछ विशेषण शब्दों की रचना निम्नलिखित शब्दों से की जाती है—

1. संज्ञा, 2. सर्वनाम, 3. क्रिया, 4. अव्यय

1. संज्ञा से विशेषण बनाना

संज्ञा	विशेषण	संज्ञा	विशेषण	संज्ञा	विशेषण
सप्ताह	साप्ताहिक	मानव	मानवीय	दिन	दैनिक

संज्ञा	विशेषण	संज्ञा	विशेषण	संज्ञा	विशेषण
मिठाई	मीठा	लालच	लालची	गुलाब	गुलाबी
अंश	आंशिक	संकेत	सांकेतिक	नीति	नैतिक
अर्थ	आर्थिक	अज्ञान	अज्ञानी	पाप	पापी
चमक	चमकीला	नरक	नारकीय	वर्णन	वर्णनीय

2. सर्वनाम शब्दों से विशेषण बनाना

सर्वनाम	विशेषण	सर्वनाम	विशेषण	सर्वनाम	विशेषण
यह	ऐसा	आप	आप-सा	जो	जैसा
वह	वैसा	तुम	तुम-सा	कौन	कैसा

3. क्रिया शब्दों से विशेषण बनाना

क्रिया	विशेषण	क्रिया	विशेषण	क्रिया	विशेषण
पढ़ना	पढ़ाकू	चलना	चालू	भागना	भगोड़ा
गाना	गायक	मरना	मरियल	लड़ना	लड़ाकू
पूज	पूजनीय	वंद	वंदनीय	टिकना	टिकाऊ

4. अव्यय शब्दों से विशेषण बनाना

अव्यय	विशेषण	अव्यय	विशेषण	अव्यय	विशेषण
आगे	अगला	पीछे	पिछला	बाहर	बाहरी
अंदर	अंदरूनी	ऊपर	ऊपरी	नीचे	निचला
भीतर	भीतरी	सतह	सतही		

अभ्यास प्रश्न

1. क्रिया के सही रूप से वाक्य पूरा कीजिए:
ट्रेन अचानक से ....।
A. रुका है B. रुक गई
C. रुक रही थी। D. रुक चुकी है

2. अकर्मक क्रिया वाले वाक्य को चुनिए:
A. बच्चे पतंग उड़ाते हैं। B. चिड़ियाँ उड़ती हैं।
C. करीम ने दौड़ लगाई। D. उसने अपनी डायरी जला दी।

3. निम्नलिखित वाक्य में से क्रिया पहचानिए:
रमेश हर दिन बगीचे में खेलता है।
A. खेलता B. खिलौना
C. खिलाना D. इनमें से कोई नहीं

4. सही क्रिया चुनिए:
बच्चा कमरे में .... था।
A. सोना B. सो रहा
C. सोएगा D. सो रहा होगा

5. हम लोग आज बड़े मैदान में फुटबॉल मैच देखने जा रहे हैं। वाक्य में क्रिया क्या है?
A. देखने B. फुटबॉल मैच
C. बड़े D. रहे हैं

6. सही क्रिया चुनिए:
बच्चा दो घंटे से ....।
A. सो रहा है B. सो रहे हैं
C. सो चुका है D. सोएगा

7. सही क्रिया चुनिए : अशोक उसे कल ....।
A. मिलता है B. मिला
C. मिलेंगे D. मिल रहा है

8. सही क्रिया चुनिए:
भूमध्य रेखा के पास, सूर्य अधिक मात्रा में पानी ....।
A. वाष्पित कर रहा है B. वाष्पित करता है
C. वाष्पित कर चुका है D. वाष्पित करें

9. निम्न में से कौन-सी अकर्मक क्रिया है?
A. चुराना B. माँगना
C. लेना D. हँसना

10. निम्न में से कौन-सी सकर्मक क्रिया है?
A. सोना B. हँसना
C. रोना D. देखना

11. चिड़िया आकाश में उड़ रही है। इस वाक्य में 'उड़ रही' क्रिया किस प्रकार की है?
A. अकर्मक B. सकर्मक
C. सामान्य D. इनमें से कोई नहीं

12. विशेषण किसकी विशेषता बताता है?
A. संज्ञा की B. सर्वनाम की
C. संज्ञा, सर्वनाम दोनों की D. क्रिया की

13. जिस पद की विशेषता बतायी जाये, उसे कहते हैं :
A. विशेषण B. प्रविशेषण
C. विशेष्य D. प्रधानपद

14. यह किताब ठीक है। इस वाक्य में **यह** कौन-सा विशेषण है?
A. सार्वनामिक विशेषण B. परिमाण बोधक विशेषण
C. गुणवाचक विशेषण D. कोई नहीं

15. **पूजनीय** विशेषण पद बना है :
A. क्रिया में प्रत्यय लगाकर B. विशेषण में प्रत्यय लगाकर
C. संज्ञा में प्रत्यय लगाकर D. इनमें से कोई नहीं

16. तुलनात्मक विशेषण की कितनी अवस्थाएँ होती हैं?
A. दो B. तीन
C. चार D. पाँच

17. यह घोड़ा अच्छा है। वाक्य में **यह** कौन-सा विशेषण है?
A. गुणवाचक B. प्रविशेषण
C. क्रमवाचक D. सार्वनामिक

18. **मीठा** आम में मीठा कौन-सा विशेषण है?
A. गुणवाचक B. संख्यावाचक
C. परिमाणवाचक D. कोई नहीं

19. **चलता-फिरता, टेढ़ा-मेढ़ा** कैसा विशेषण हैं?
A. प्रत्यय लगने से विकारी विशेषण हैं
B. दो शब्दों के मेल से बने विकारी विशेषण हैं
C. दोनों के मेल से
D. कोई नहीं

20. दिए गए विकल्पों में से विशेषण पहचानिएः
A. ऊँचा B. पाया
C. चिड़ियाँ D. अवशेष

21. निम्नलिखित में से संकेतवाचक विशेषण को चुनिएः
A. वह मकान B. बीस मन अनाज
C. दस विद्यार्थी D. लंबी महिला

22. काला, पीला आदि शब्द किस प्रकार के विशेषण के उदाहरण हैं?
A. गुणवाचक विशेषण B. परिणामबोधक विशेषण
C. संख्यावाचक विशेषण D. सार्वनामिक विशेषण

23. 'मदनपुरी काली पतलून पहनकर खेलने आया' में विशेषण है।
A. पतलून B. खेलने
C. काली D. मदनपुरी

24. सात लीटर दूध है—इसमें विशेषण होगा।
A. संख्यावाचक B. परिमाणवाचक
C. गुणवाचक D. इनमें से कोई नहीं

25. 'वह नौकर नहीं आया' वाक्य में 'वह' कौन-सा विशेषण है?
A. संख्यावाचक B. सार्वनामिक
C. गुणवाचक D. परिमाणवाचक

निर्देश (प्र.सं. 26 से 30): *निम्नलिखित प्रश्नों में दिए गए विकल्पों में से सही विशेषण का चयन कीजिए।*

26. A. मीठा B. खाना C. बच्चा D. गाया
27. A. कुत्ता B. लंबा C. दौड़ D. सोया
28. A. पानी B. खाया C. हरा D. फल
29. A. पंख B. सुन्दर C. उड़ना D. बैठा
30. A. पेड़ B. चलना C. बड़ा D. बैठे

उत्तरमाला

1	2	3	4	5	6	7	8	9	10
B	B	A	B	A	A	B	B	D	D
11	**12**	**13**	**14**	**15**	**16**	**17**	**18**	**19**	**20**
A	C	C	A	A	B	D	A	B	A
21	**22**	**23**	**24**	**25**	**26**	**27**	**28**	**29**	**30**
A	A	C	B	B	A	B	C	B	C

❋ ❋ ❋ ❋ ❋

7 लिंग, वचन और कारक

लिंग

'लिंग' शब्द संस्कृत भाषा का शब्द है, जिसका अर्थ चिह्न होता है। जिस चिह्न द्वारा यह जाना जाए कि अमुक शब्द पुरुष जाति का है या स्त्री जाति का है। संज्ञा के जिस रूप से पुरुषत्व या स्त्रीत्व का बोध हो, उसे लिंग कहते हैं। हिन्दी में सृष्टि के समस्त पदार्थ, चाहे वे सजीव हों या निर्जीव, दो लिंगों में ही विभक्त किए गए हैं वे हैं—

- **पुल्लिंग :** जिन संज्ञा शब्द से (यथार्थ व कल्पित) पुरुषत्व का बोध होता है, उन्हें पुल्लिंग कहते हैं, जैसे—लड़का, बैल, पेड़, नगर इत्यादि। इन उदाहरणों में 'लड़का' और 'बैल' यथार्थ पुरुषत्व सूचक हैं और 'पेड़' तथा 'नगर' से कल्पित पुरुषत्व का बोध होता है।
- **स्त्रीलिंग :** जिस संज्ञा से (यथार्थ व कल्पित) स्त्रीत्व का बोध होता है, उसे स्त्रीलिंग कहते हैं, जैसे—लड़की, गाय, लता, पुरी इत्यादि। इन उदाहरणों में 'लड़की' और 'गाय' यथार्थ स्त्रीत्व का और 'लता' और 'पुरी' से कल्पित स्त्रीत्व का बोध होता है।

लिंग-परिवर्तन (पुल्लिंग से स्त्रीलिंग बनाने) के नियम

हिन्दी में पुल्लिंग से स्त्रीलिंग बनाने की कई विधियाँ प्रचलित हैं। इसके लिए शब्दों के अन्त में प्रत्यय जोड़े जाते हैं। इन्हें स्त्री प्रत्यय कहते हैं। हिन्दी में प्रमुख स्त्री प्रत्यय निम्नलिखित हैं— आ, ई, आइना, आनी, इका, इन, इया, नी।

नियम :

1. अकारान्त तथा आकारान्त पुल्लिंग संज्ञाओं के अंतिम 'अ' या 'आ' के स्थान पर 'ई' प्रत्यय जोड़ने से स्त्रीलिंग बनता है। जैसे—

पुल्लिंग	स्त्रीलिंग	पुल्लिंग	स्त्रीलिंग
नर	नारी	चाचा	चाची
देव	देवी	दादा	दादी
पुत्र	पुत्री	नाना	नानी
लड़का	लड़की	बेटा	बेटी
गदहा	गदही	छोटा	छोटी
घोड़ा	घोड़ी	लम्बा	लम्बी

2. पुल्लिंग संज्ञा शब्दों के अंतिम 'आ' के स्थान पर 'इया' जोड़कर स्त्रीलिंग बनाया जाता है। जैसे—

पुल्लिंग	स्त्रीलिंग	पुल्लिंग	स्त्रीलिंग
बेटा	बिटिया	चूहा	चुहिया
बूढ़ा	बुढ़िया	कुत्ता	कुतिया

3. कतिपय प्राणीवाचक अकारान्त पुल्लिंग संज्ञाओं के अन्त में 'नी' जोड़कर स्त्रीलिंग बनाया जाता है। जैसे—

पुल्लिंग	स्त्रीलिंग	पुल्लिंग	स्त्रीलिंग
मोर	मोरनी	ऊँट	ऊँटनी
शेर	शेरनी	राजपूत	राजपूतनी

4. वर्ण तथा व्यवसाय बोधक शब्दों के अन्त में 'आइन' प्रत्यय लगाकर स्त्रीलिंग बनाया जाता है। जैसे—

पुल्लिंग	स्त्रीलिंग	पुल्लिंग	स्त्रीलिंग
पण्डित	पण्डिताइन	बाबू	बबुआइन
ठाकुर	ठकुराइन	साधु	सधुआइन

5. कुछ पुल्लिंग संज्ञा शब्दों के अंतिम 'अक' प्रत्यय को इका करके भी स्त्रीलिंग बनाया जाता है। जैसे—

पुल्लिंग	स्त्रीलिंग	पुल्लिंग	स्त्रीलिंग
नायक	नायिका	सेवक	सेविका
गायक	गायिका	पाठक	पाठिका

6. पुल्लिंग संज्ञाओं के अन्त में 'आनी' प्रत्यय जोड़कर स्त्रीलिंग बनाया जाता है। जैसे—

पुल्लिंग	स्त्रीलिंग	पुल्लिंग	स्त्रीलिंग
मेहतर	मेहतरानी	देवर	देवरानी
सेठ	सेठानी	जेठ	जेठानी
नौकर	नौकरानी		

7. वर्ण और व्यवसाय सूचक शब्दों के अन्त में 'इन' लगाकर स्त्रीलिंग बनाया जाता है। जैसे—

पुल्लिंग	स्त्रीलिंग	पुल्लिंग	स्त्रीलिंग
माली	मालिन	तेली	तेलिन
लुहार	लुहारिन	कहार	कहारिन

8. कुछ आकारान्त पुल्लिंग शब्दों के अन्त में आये हुए 'आ' को 'अ' कर देने से स्त्रीलिंग बन जाता है। जैसे–

पुल्लिंग	स्त्रीलिंग	पुल्लिंग	स्त्रीलिंग
भैंसा	भैंस	भेंड़ा	भेंड़

9. कुछ आकारान्त पुल्लिंग शब्दों के अन्तिम 'आ' का 'ई' करके स्त्रीलिंग बनाया जाता है। जैसे–

पुल्लिंग	स्त्रीलिंग	पुल्लिंग	स्त्रीलिंग
फूफा	फूफी	चाचा	चाची
नाना	नानी	दादा	दादी
जीजा	जीजी		

10. कुछ पुल्लिंग संज्ञाओं के स्त्रीलिंग रूप बिल्कुल स्वतंत्र होते हैं। जैसे–

पुल्लिंग	स्त्रीलिंग	पुल्लिंग	स्त्रीलिंग
मर्द	औरत	ससुर	सास
राजा	रानी	मियाँ	बीबी
सम्राट्	सम्राज्ञी	वर	वधू
कवि	कवयित्री	पिता	माता
पुरुष	स्त्री		

वचन

शब्द के जिस रूप में एकत्व (एक संख्या) या अनेकत्व (अनेक संख्या) का बोध होता है, उसे वचन कहते हैं। वचन दो प्रकार के होते हैं :

- **एकवचन :** शब्द के जिस रूप में एक वस्तु का बोध होता है, उसे एकवचन कहते हैं, जैसे–कागज, कलम, घोड़ा, घड़ी इत्यादि।
- **बहुवचन :** शब्द के जिस रूप से अनेक वस्तुओं का बोध होता है, उसे बहुवचन कहते हैं, जैसे–कागजात, कलमें, घोड़े, घड़ियाँ इत्यादि।

सामान्यतः संज्ञा, सर्वनाम, विशेषण और क्रिया के ही रूप को एकवचन और बहुवचन में परिवर्तित किया जाता है।

विभक्ति रहित संज्ञाओं के बहुवचन बनाने के नियम

विभक्ति रहित संज्ञाओं का बहुवचन साधारणतः निम्नलिखित नियमों के अन्तर्गत बनाया जाता है–

1. पुल्लिंग संज्ञा के आकारान्त को एकारान्त कर बहुवचन बनाया जाता है। यथा–

एकवचन	बहुवचन	एकवचन	बहुवचन
घोड़ा	घोड़े	गधा	गधे
लड़का	लड़के		

अपवाद- मामा, नाना, बाबा, पिता, योद्धा, आत्मा, देवता, जामाता आदि। इन शब्दों के रूप दोनों वचनों में समान होते हैं।

2. पुल्लिंग आकारान्त शब्दों के अतिरिक्त अन्य मात्राओं से अन्त होने वाले शब्दों के रूप दोनों वचनों में एक समान रहते हैं। जैसे–

एकवचन	बहुवचन	एकवचन	बहुवचन
एक बालक	चार बालक	एक डाकू	चार डाकू
एक भाई	चार भाई	एक जौ	चार जौ

3. आकारान्त स्त्रीलिंग शब्दों के अन्त में 'एँ' जोड़ने से बहुवचन बनता है। जैसे–

एकवचन	बहुवचन	एकवचन	बहुवचन
शाखा	शाखाएँ	लता	लताएँ
माता	माताएँ	महिला	महिलाएँ

4. अकारान्त स्त्रीलिंग संज्ञा के बहुवचन शब्द में आगत अंतिम अ को यें कर देने से बनता है। जैसे–

एकवचन	बहुवचन	एकवचन	बहुवचन
गाय	गायें	रात	रातें
बात	बातें	आँख	आँखें
याद	यादें		

5. दीर्घ या ह्रस्व इकारान्त संज्ञाओं को ह्रस्व इकारान्त कर उनके अन्त में याँ जोड़ देने से बहुवचन बनता है। जैसे–

एकवचन	बहुवचन	एकवचन	बहुवचन
नारी	नारियाँ	पहेली	पहेलियाँ
लड़की	लड़कियाँ	सहेली	सहेलियाँ
नीति	नीतियाँ	नदी	नदियाँ
घड़ी	घड़ियाँ	छड़ी	छड़ियाँ
धोती	धोतियाँ	साड़ी	साड़ियाँ

6. जिन स्त्रीलिंग शब्दों के अन्त में 'या' आता है, 'या' पर चन्द्रबिन्दु लगाकर बहुवचन बनाया जाता है जैसे–

एकवचन	बहुवचन	एकवचन	बहुवचन
बुढ़िया	बुढ़ियाँ	चिड़िया	चिड़ियाँ
गुड़िया	गुड़ियाँ	डिबिया	डिबियाँ
दुनिया	दुनियाँ		

7. ह्रस्व या दीर्घ ऊकारान्त स्त्रीलिंग संज्ञाओं को ह्रस्व उकारान्त बनाकर अन्त में 'एँ' लगाने से बहुवचन का निर्माण होता है। जैसे–

एकवचन	बहुवचन	एकवचन	बहुवचन
धेनु	धेनुएँ	वस्तु	वस्तुएँ
बहू	बहुएँ	ऋतु	ऋतुएँ

8. कुछ शब्द समष्टि मूलक होते हैं। जैसे– गण, कुल, वृन्द, समूह, वर्ग, लोग, जन, मण्डल, दल, ग्राम, मण्डली आदि। ये शब्द विशेषतः वहाँ जोड़े जाते हैं, जहाँ दोनों वचनों में पुल्लिंग अथवा स्त्रीलिंग में एक ही रूप होते हैं।

उदाहरण :

एकवचन	बहुवचन	एकवचन	बहुवचन
पाठक	पाठकगण	आप	आप लोग
तुम	तुम लोग	छात्र	छात्रगण
विद्यार्थी	विद्यार्थीगण		

कारक

''क्रिया के साथ जिसका सीधा संबंध हो, उसे कारक कहते हैं– क्रियान्वायित्वं कारकत्वं।'' इस प्रकार वाक्य में जिस शब्द का संबंध क्रिया से होता है, कारक कहलाता है। कारक चिह्न अव्यय या संबंध के परिचायक होते हैं, इन्हें विभक्ति या परसर्ग (बाद में जुड़ने वाले) भी कहा जाता है। सामान्यतः ये स्वतंत्र होते हैं और संज्ञा या सर्वनाम के साथ प्रयुक्त होते हैं। हिन्दी के परसर्ग प्रत्ययों के विकसित रूप हैं। अतः इन्हें चरम कारक नहीं माना गया है, क्योंकि इनका क्रिया से कोई संबंध नहीं रहता है।

हिन्दी में 'संबंध' और 'संबोधन' को मिलाकर आठ कारक माने गए हैं। इनके नाम, विभक्तियाँ और विभक्तिबोधक चिह्न निम्नलिखित हैं–

विभक्ति	बोधक नाम	विभक्तिबोधक चिह्न
प्रथमा	कर्ता (कारक)	ने
द्वितीया	कर्म (कारक)	को
तृतीया	करण (कारक)	से, के द्वारा, द्वारा
चतुर्थी	सम्प्रदान (कारक)	को, के लिए, के वास्ते
पंचम	अपादान (कारक)	से
षष्ठी	संबंध	का, की, के, रा, री, रे
सप्तमी	अधिकरण (कारक)	में, पर
अष्टमी	सम्बोधन	ए, ऐ, हे, अजी, अरे, ओ

अभ्यास प्रश्न

1. 'आयुष्मान' का स्त्रीलिंग है:
   A. श्रीमती B. आयुष्मती
   C. आयुष्माती D. आयुमती

2. निम्न में से कौन-सा शब्द पुल्लिंग है?
   A. दया B. घटना
   C. जड़ता D. बुढ़ापा

3. निम्नलिखित में पुल्लिंग शब्द है:
   A. नदी B. देवी
   C. कविता D. चन्द्रमा

4. 'कवि' का स्त्रीलिंग है:
   A. कवित्व B. कविता
   C. कवयित्री D. कवियत्री

5. निम्न में से स्त्रीलिंग शब्द का चयन कीजिए:
   A. वेग B. मौन
   C. दही D. अहिंसा

6. 'मेहतरानी' का पुल्लिंग है:
   A. मेहतरी B. मेहतराइन
   C. मेहतर D. मेहतरा

7. निम्नलिखित में से स्त्रीलिंग शब्द का चयन कीजिए:
   A. धुआँ B. संध्या
   C. भत्ता D. धावा

8. 'भिखारिन' का पुल्लिंग शब्द कौन-सा है?
   A. सेवक B. भिखारी
   C. मजदूर D. इनमें से कोई नहीं

9. 'सम्राट' का स्त्रीलिंग शब्द कौन-सा है?
   A. साम्रज्ञी B. साम्राज्ञी
   C. सम्राटनी D. सम्राज्ञी

10. 'विद्वान' का स्त्रीलिंग शब्द है:
    A. विद्वान B. बुद्धिमती
    C. विदुषी D. विदुषिनी

11. 'तपस्वी' शब्द का सही स्त्रीलिंग है:
    A. तपस्विनी B. तपस्वीनी
    C. तपस्वनी D. इनमें से कोई नहीं

12. नदी शब्द है:
    A. स्त्रीलिंग B. पुल्लिंग
    C. उभयलिंग D. इनमें से कोई नहीं

13. 'सेवक' का स्त्रीलिंग है:
    A. सेवका B. सेवकाइन
    C. सेवकी D. सेविका

14. 'गायक' का स्त्रीलिंग है:
    A. गायकी B. गायिका
    C. गायिकी D. गायक

15. लिंग के अनुसार शुद्ध जोड़े का चयन कीजिए:
A. माली - मालिन B. माली - माला
C. माली - मालनी D. माली - मलिन

16. 'उसे' का बहुवचन है:
A. उसको B. उससे
C. उन्हें D. उसका

17. 'हमें' का एकवचन है:
A. हम B. हमको
C. मुझे D. मुझसे

18. 'लड़की' शब्द का बहुवचन रूप है:
A. लड़कियाँ B. लड़की
C. लड़कियें D. लड़कीएं

19. 'देवता' का बहुवचन है:
A. देवताएँ B. देवताओं
C. देवताइयों D. देवत्व

20. 'पक्षी' का बहुवचन है:
A. पक्षियों B. पक्षीय
C. पक्षि D. पक्षी

21. 'फूल' का बहुवचन है:
A. फुले B. फुल
C. फूल D. इनमें से कोई नहीं

22. इनमें से कौन-सा शब्द हमेशा बहुवचन के रूप में प्रयुक्त होता है?
A. माता B. प्राण
C. किताब D. भक्ति

23. 'गुरु' का बहुवचन होगा:
A. गुरुएँ B. गुरुआँ
C. गुरुजन D. गुरुवो

24. किस शब्द में बहुवचन बनाने में परिवर्तन होगा?
A. चाचा B. पिता
C. फूल D. भेड़िया

25. 'चाकू' का बहुवचन है:
A. चाकुएँ B. चाकूओं
C. चाकुवों D. चाकू

26. 'देव' का बहुवचन है:
A. देवता B. देवगण
C. देवजन D. देवमंडल

27. 'जाति' शब्द का बहुवचन रूप होगा?
A. जातीय B. जातियाँ
C. जातियो D. जातियों

28. इनमें सदैव एकवचन शब्दों का प्रयोग होता है?
A. कला B. भाषा
C. कथा D. वर्षा

29. 'बहन' का बहुवचन है:
A. बहनों B. बहनें
C. बहना D. बहनाएँ

30. निम्नलिखित में से कौन-सा युग्म सही है?
A. प्राण-प्राणों B. दर्शन-दर्शनों
C. भक्त-भक्तजन D. दाम-दामों

31. कारक के कितने भेद होते हैं?
A. सात B. आठ
C. छः D. नौ

32. 'मैंने' कौन-सा कारक है?
A. कर्त्ता B. कर्म
C. करण D. सम्प्रदान

33. 'को' और 'के लिए' किस कारक के चिह्न हैं?
A. कर्म B. सम्प्रदान
C. संबंध D. करण

34. 'बालक ने पुस्तक पढ़ी होगी।' वाक्य में प्रयुक्त कारक चिह्न है।
A. कर्म कारक B. अधिकरण कारक
C. करण कारक D. कर्ता कारक

35. 'हे राम! रक्षा करो।' वाक्य में कौन-सा कारक है?
A. कर्ता B. अपादान
C. सम्बोधन D. अधिकरण

36. 'वह अगले साल आएगा।' इस वाक्य में कौन-सा कारक है?
A. कर्म कारक B. अपादान कारक
C. संबंध कारक D. अधिकरण कारक

37. 'रमेश जयपुर से दिल्ली जा रहा है।' इस वाक्य में कारक है।
A. संबंध B. अपादान
C. करण D. सम्प्रदान

38. 'भूखे को अन्न दो और प्यासे को पानी' वाक्य किस कारक का है?
A. सम्प्रदान B. संबंध
C. अपादन D. अधिकरण

39. कर्म कारक के लिए प्रयुक्त होने वाला चिह्न है।
A. ने B. के लिए
C. को D. से

40. 'मैं काम से जा रहा हूँ।' वाक्य में 'से' कारक है।
A. सम्प्रदान B. करण
C. अपादान D. अधिकरण

41. 'पेड़ पर पक्षी बैठे हैं।' इस वाक्य में 'पेड़ पर' पद में कौन-सा कारक है?

A. करण B. अपादान
C. संबंध D. अधिकरण

42. राजा <u>सेवक</u> को कम्बल देता है, वाक्य में रेखांकित पद में कौन-सा कारक है?

A. कर्मकारक
B. संबंध कारक
C. सम्प्रदान कारक
D. कर्ता कारक

43. 'राम की गाय चरती है।' वाक्य में कौन-सा कारक है?

A. कर्ता B. कर्म
C. संबंध D. अधिकरण

44. निम्न में अधिकरण कारक का परसर्ग कौन-सा है?

A. पर B. ने
C. को D. से

45. गृहिणी ने <u>गरीबों</u> को कपड़े दिए। रेखांकित पद का कारक बताइए।

A. संबंध कारक B. सम्प्रदान कारक
C. अपादान कारक D. कर्ता कारक

उत्तरमाला

1	2	3	4	5	6	7	8	9	10
B	D	D	C	D	C	B	B	D	C
11	**12**	**13**	**14**	**15**	**16**	**17**	**18**	**19**	**20**
A	A	D	B	A	C	C	A	B	A
21	**22**	**23**	**24**	**25**	**26**	**27**	**28**	**29**	**30**
C	B	C	D	D	B	B	D	B	C
31	**32**	**33**	**34**	**35**	**36**	**37**	**38**	**39**	**40**
B	A	B	D	C	D	B	A	C	B
41	**42**	**43**	**44**	**45**					
D	C	C	A	B					

❄ ❄ ❄ ❄ ❄

8 विलोम, पर्यायवाची, तुकांत और अतुकांत शब्द

विलोम शब्द

जब दो शब्दों के अर्थ एक-दूसरे के विपरीत हों, तो उन्हें विलोम या विपरीतार्थी शब्द कहते हैं। शब्दों का सामर्थ्य बढ़ाने तथा भावों को स्पष्ट और सटीक अभिव्यक्ति में भी विलोम शब्द सहायक होते हैं।

विलोम शब्दों की रचना प्रायः उपसर्ग और प्रत्यय की सहायता से होती है। जैसे—पुराना-नया, रुचि-अरुचि, आय-व्यय, आकर्षण-विकर्षण, उत्थान-पतन आदि।

मूल शब्द	विलोम शब्द
अनुराग	विराग
अपकार	उपकार
अतिवृष्टि	अनावृष्टि
आयात	निर्यात
आदान	प्रदान
आशा	निराशा
आदि	अन्त
आरंभ	अंत
आय	व्यय
आलसी	परिश्रमी
इच्छा	अनिच्छा
उपकार	अपकार
दुर्गन्ध	सुगन्ध
द्रुत	मन्द
दुर्जन	सज्जन
दिवस	निशि
दाता	याचक
उचित	अनुचित
उत्थान	पतन
उदय	अस्त
अंधकार	प्रकाश
अपना	पराया
अनुकूल	प्रतिकूल
अम्ल	मधुर
अग्रज	अनुज

मूल शब्द	विलोम शब्द
घृणा	प्रेम
जय	पराजय
जड़	चेतन
ज्ञान	अज्ञान
प्राचीन	अर्वाचीन
आदि	अनादि
आदर	निरादर
आकाश	पाताल
ईश	अनीश
न्याय	अन्याय
निरर्थक	सार्थक
नया	पुराना
पाप	पुण्य
पक्ष	विपक्ष
बुराई	भलाई
भला	बुरा
भूत	भविष्य
मंगल	अमंगल
यश	अपयश
राग	विराग
लाभ	हानि
विनीत	उद्दण्ड
विरोध	समर्थन
द्वैत	अद्वैत
धर्म	अधर्म

मूल शब्द	विलोम शब्द
धनी	निर्धन
निद्रा	जागरण
निराकार	साकार
निर्गुण	सगुण
नूतन	पुरातन
प्रत्यक्ष	परोक्ष
कनिष्ठ	ज्येष्ठ
कटु	मधुर
कल्याण	अकल्याण
उत्कृष्ट	अपकृष्ट, निकृष्ट
उत्कर्ष	अपकर्ष
उन्नति	अवनति
उत्तीर्ण	अनुत्तीर्ण
उष्ण	शीतल
ऐश्वर्य	अनैश्वर्य
ऐक्य	अनैक्य
गुरु	शिष्य
चर	अचर
ज्येष्ठ	कनिष्ठ
जीवन	मरण
जन्म	मृत्यु
ज्ञात	अज्ञात
दिन	रात
देव	दनुज, दानव

मूल शब्द	विलोम शब्द
कोमल	कठोर
क्रय	विक्रय
कृतज्ञ	कृतघ्न
गुण	अवगुण
उद्दण्ड	सरल
एक	अनेक
एकार्थक	अनेकार्थक
सुख	दुःख
सम्पत्ति	विपत्ति
सपूत	कपूत
कीर्ति	अपकीर्ति
गुरु	लघु
गर्मी	सर्दी
बद्ध	मुक्त
मान	अपमान
योगी	भोगी
विरोध	समर्थन
विष	अमृत
विद्या	अविद्या
शत्रु	मित्र
शांति	अशांति
शुभ	अशुभ
स्वतंत्र	परतंत्र
स्थावर	जंगम
स्तुति	निंदा

अभ्यास प्रश्न

1. 'शाश्वत' का विलोम शब्द कौन-सा है?
   A. निषेध B. जागरण
   C. नश्वर D. विशुद्ध
2. 'आधुनिक' का विलोम शब्द है:
   A. वर्तमान B. प्राचीन
   C. निर्वाचित D. समीचीन
3. 'अल्पज्ञ' का विलोम शब्द है:
   A. कृतज्ञ B. अभिज्ञ
   C. सर्वज्ञ D. अवज्ञ
4. 'अथ' का विलोम शब्द है:
   A. इति B. पूर्व
   C. अंत D. अनन्त
5. 'अंतरंग' का विलोम शब्द है:
   A. अनुरंग B. विरंग
   C. अतिरंग D. बहिरंग
6. 'मधुर' का विलोम शब्द है:
   A. कूट B. कटु
   C. लवण D. ललित
7. 'अवनति' का विलोम शब्द है:
   A. प्रजाति B. उन्नति
   C. संगति D. सहमति
8. 'निशीथ' का विलोम शब्द है:
   A. दिन B. रात
   C. मध्याह्न D. सांझ
9. 'भीषण' का विलोम क्या है?
   A. दूषण B. भयानक
   C. शांत D. सौम्य
10. 'भोगी' का विलोम क्या है?
    A. त्यागी B. जोगी
    C. योगी D. कामी
11. 'मृसण' का विलोम क्या है?
    A. कोमल B. रूक्ष
    C. मधुर D. मोक्ष
12. 'वाह' का विलोम क्या है?
    A. ओह B. कह
    C. हाय D. इनमें से कोई नहीं
13. 'श्याम' किसका विलोम है?
    A. श्वेत का B. पीले का C. लाल का D. नदी का
14. 'ऐच्छिक' का विलोम है?
    A. करणीय B. अनिवार्य C. शैक्षिक D. आवश्यक
15. इनमें से 'सदाचार' शब्द का विलोम शब्द पहचानिए।
    A. अनाचार B. स्वेच्छाचार
    C. अत्याचार D. दुराचार

निर्देश (प्र.सं. 16 से 20 तक): *रिक्त स्थान के लिए रेखांकित शब्द का उचित विलोम शब्द चयन कीजिए।*

16. सम्पन्न व्यक्ति .... की व्यथा नहीं जान सकता।
    A. आसन्न B. निष्पन्न
    C. विपन्न D. विषण्ण
17. सभी निरक्षर .... बनें।
    A. साक्षर B. पढ़े-लिखे
    C. चतुर D. होशियार
18. जो सबको ठीक लगे वह अर्थ है, जो एक लगे वह .... है।
    A. सार्थ B. अवदर्थ
    C. अनर्थ D. व्यर्थ
19. पक्ष और .... दोनों ने ध्वनिमत से बिल पारित किया।
    A. विरोधी B. विपक्ष
    C. शत्रु D. विपक्षी
20. दुराचार से व्यक्ति का .... नष्ट हो जाता है।
    A. यश B. विचार
    C. फल D. सदाचार

उत्तरमाला

1	2	3	4	5	6	7	8	9	10
C	B	C	A	D	B	B	C	D	C
11	**12**	**13**	**14**	**15**	**16**	**17**	**18**	**19**	**20**
B	C	A	B	D	C	A	C	B	D

❊ ❊ ❊ ❊ ❊

पर्यायवाची शब्द

किसी शब्द के समान अर्थ के लिए जिन शब्दों को प्रयोग में लाया जाता है, उन्हें **पर्यायवाची शब्द** कहा जाता है। आशय यह है कि पर्याय का अभिप्राय 'बदले में आने वाला' से लिया गया है। पर्यायवाची शब्द को 'प्रतिशब्द' भी कहते हैं।

1. **अग्नि**—अनल, पावक, कृशानु, वहिन, हुताशन, धूमकेतु, वैश्वानर।
2. **अनोखा**—अद्विtीय, अद्भुत, अनूठा, अनुपम, विचित्र, विलक्षण, निराला।
3. **अमृत**—पीयूष, सुधा, अमी।
4. **आकाश**-नभ, गगन, व्योम, अम्बर।
5. **आंख**—नेत्र, चक्षु, लोचन, दृग, नयन, अक्षि, अबंक।
6. **इच्छा**—आकांक्षा, स्पृहा, मनोरथ,चाह, कामना, अभिलाषा, वांछा।
7. **इन्द्र**—सुरपति, शचिपति, मधवा, पुरंदर, बासव, शक्र, पुरुहूत।
8. **ईश्वर**—भगवान, प्रभु, परमेश्वर, परमात्मा, जगदीश, विश्वम्भर, हरि।
9. **कपड़ा**—वस्त्र, पट, चीर, वसन, अम्बर, दुकूल, परिधान।
10. **कमल**—पंकज, सरोज, जलज, पद्म, अरविंद, राजीव, तामरस, नलिन, नीरज, अब्ज, कंज, उत्पल।
11. **कामदेव**—अनंग, कंदर्प, पंचशर, मकरध्वज, मदन, मन्मथ, मार, रतिपति, स्मर, मनोज, शम्बरारि।
12. **किनारा**—तट, तीर, कूल।
13. **किरण**—अंशु, मरीचि, रश्मि, मयूख।
14. **केश**—कच, चिकुर, कुंतल, बाल, अलक।
15. **गणेश**—लम्बोदर, एकदन्त, गजवदन, विनायक, गणपति, गजानन।
16. **गंगा**—भागीरथी, जाह्नवी, सुरसरि, देवपगा, त्रिपथगा।
17. **घर**—गेह, निकेतन, सदन, भवन, गृह, धाम।
18. **घोड़ा**—तुरंग, घोटक, वाजि, हय, अश्व।
19. **चन्द्रमा**—शशि, विधु, निशाकर, इन्दु, मयंक, सुधाकर, उडपति, शशांक, सुधांशु, सोम, मृगांक, हिमकर, रजनीश, क्षपाकर।
20. **जल**—पानी, सलिल, उदक, वारि, नीर, अम्बु, तोय, पय।
21. **तलवार**—असि, करवाल, कृपाण, खड्ग।
22. **तालाब**—सर, सरोवर, तड़ाग, पुष्कर।
23. **दिन**—दिवस, वासर, दिवा, अहन्।
24. **दु:ख**—कष्ट, क्लेश, पीड़ा, विषाद, सन्ताप, व्यथा, वेदना, यातना, यन्त्रणा, व्याधि।
25. **देवता**—सुर, देव, विबुध, गोवणि, अमर।
26. **देह**—बपु, शरीर, तनु, काया, कलेवर, गात, विग्रह।
27. **धन**—द्रव्य, अर्थ, वित्त, सम्पत्ति, सम्पदा।
28. **नदी**—सरिता, तटिनी, सरि, आपत्रा, तरंगिणी, निर्सरिणी, धुनी।
29. **नौकर**—सेवक, अनुचर, किंकर, परिचारक, चाकर, भृत्य।
30. **पक्षी**—खग, नभग, द्विज, विहंग, परवेरु, गगनचर, अण्डज, पतंग।
31. **पति**—भर्ता, स्वामी, भरतार, कन्त, नाथ, वर।
32. **पत्नी**—भार्या, दारा, गृहिणी, वधू, कलत्र, अर्द्धांगिनी, कान्ता।
33. **पहाड़**—गिरि, अद्रि, शैल, कुधर, पर्वत, भूधर, महीधर, नग।
34. **पार्वती**—गौरी, उमा, भवानी, गिरिजा, शिवा, अम्बिका, रुद्राणी।
35. **पुत्र**—तनय, सुत, आत्मज, नन्दन, पूता, बेटा, सुवन।
36. **पुत्री**—तनया, सुता, आत्मजा, दुहिता, नन्दिनी, बेटी, तनुजा।
37. **पृथ्वी**—धरा, धरती, अवनि, रसा, वसुधा, भू, मही, मेदिनी, वसुन्धरा, अचला, क्षिति, पुहुमी, जगती, क्षोणि।
38. **पेड़**—तरु, विटप, पादप, वृक्ष, द्रुम, रुख।
39. **प्रकाश**—आलोक, द्युति, ज्योति, प्रभा, उद्योत, दीप्ति।
40. **प्रेम**—राग, अनुराग, प्यार, प्रीति, हित।
41. **फूल**—कुसुम, प्रसून, सुमन, पुष्प, पुहुप।
42. **बसन्त**—माधव, मधु, ऋतुराज, कुसुमाकर।
43. **वाण**—नाराच, शर, शिलीमुख, शायक, तीर, विशिख।
44. **बादल**—मेघ, बलाहक, वारिद, जलद, कन्द, पयोद, घन, पयोधर।
45. **बिजली**—चपला, चंचला, तड़ित, विद्युत, दामिनी।
46. **बुद्धि**—मेधा, मति, प्रज्ञा, मनीषा।
47. **बैर**—द्वेष, वैमनस्य, शत्रुता, विरोध।
48. **ब्रह्मा**—अज, पितामह, स्वयंभू, चतुरानन, विरंचि, विधि, विधाता।
49. **ब्राह्मण**—द्विज, विप्र, भूसूर, भूदेव।
50. **भौंरा**—मधुकर, भृंग, भ्रमर, अलि, मधुप, षट्पद, मिलिन्द, चंचरीक, शिलीमुख।
51. **मछली**—मत्स्य, झख, मीन।
52. **मनुष्य**—नर, मानव, मनुज, जन, मानुष।
53. **महादेव**—उमापति, गंगाधर, चन्द्रशेखर, शंकर, शिव, शम्भू, त्रिपुरारि, त्रिलोचन, नीलकण्ठ, गिरिजापति, धूर्जटि।
54. **मयूर**—केकी, शिखी, कलापी, सारंग।
55. **माता**—जननी, अम्बा, मां, जन्मदात्री।
56. **मूर्ख**—अज्ञानी, वालिश, मूढ़, अज्ञ।
57. **यमुना**—रवितनया, अर्कजा, कालिंदी, तरणिजा, कृष्णा।
58. **युद्ध**—रण, समर, संग्राम, लड़ाई, विग्रह।
59. **राजा**—नरेश, महीप, भूपति, भूप, नृप, भूपाल, महीश।
60. **रात**—निशा, रजनी, रात्रि, विभावरी, शर्वरी, क्षपा, यामिनी, तमी, क्षणदा।
61. **राक्षस**—निशाचर, मनुजाद, यातुधान, रजनीचर, दानव, दनुज, असुर।
62. **लक्ष्मी**—इन्दिरा, कमला, कमलासना, पद्मा, रमा, श्री, सिन्धुसुता।

63. **वन**—अरण्य, अटवी, विपिन, जंगल, कानन।

64. **विद्वान**—कोविद, पण्डित, प्राज्ञ, विदुष।

65. **विष्णु**—चतुर्भज, गोविन्द, गरुड़ध्वज, चक्रपाणि, दामोदर, नारायण, हरी, मुरारी, रमेश, केशव, माधव।

66. **शत्रु**—अरि, रिपु, बैरी, आराति, द्वेषी।

67. **समुद्र**—सिन्धु, सागर, उदधि, नदीश, रत्नाकर, पयोधि, वारीश, जलधि, अब्धि, अम्बुधि।

68. **सरस्वती**—गिरा, ब्रह्माणी, भारती, वाणी, शारदा, वीणापाणि, विमला।

69. **सांप**—सर्प, व्याल, भुजंग, उरग, नाग, अहि, पन्नगफणी, विषधर।

70. **सिंह**—केसरी, मृगपति, नाहर, केहरी, पंचानन, शार्दूल, हरि, मृगारि, नखायुध, गजारि।

71. **सुन्दरता**—रमणीयता, शोभा, कमनीयता, चारुता, रूचिरता, कांति, छवि, सौन्दर्य, श्री, रम्यता, मंजुला, घटा, सुषमा।

72. **सूर्य**—रवि, अर्क, दिनकर, तमारि, मार्तण्ड, भास्कर, भानु, आदित्य, पूषण, पतंग, अंशुमाली।

73. **सोना**—स्वर्ण, जातरूप, कंचन, कनक, हाटक, हेम, चामीकर, तामरस, हिरण्य, कुन्दन, कलघौत।

74. **स्वामी**—ईश, पति, प्रभु, नाथ, सांई।

75. **स्त्री**—नारी, अंगना, वनिता, भामिनी, कामिनी, रमणी, योषिता, ललना, अबला।

76. **स्वर्ग**—बैकुण्ठ, नाक, सुरलोक, परलोक।

77. **हवा**—अनिल, मारुत, वायु, समीर, प्रभंजन, वात, पवन।

78. **हाथी**—करी, गज, कुंजर, द्विरद, मतंग, दन्ती, वितुंड, कुम्भी, सिंधुर, हस्ती, गयंद।

79. **सिर**—मस्तिष्क, माथा, शिर, मुण्ड, मौलि, शीश।

80. **सरस्वती**—शारदा, वाणी, गिरा, भारती, वीणापाणि, ब्राह्मी।

81. **भौंह**—भ्रू, भृकुटी, तन्द्रिका, प्रतीला, भों, भंव।

82. **जगदीश**—भगवान, परमात्मा, परमेश्वर, प्रभु।

83. **जग**—संसार, भव, जगत, विश्व, लोक।

84. **तम**—अन्धकार, तमस, अन्धेरा, तिमिर।

85. **तरु**—पेड़, विटप, पादप, द्रुम, वृक्ष।

86. **आम**—रसाल, आम्र।

87. **अनादर**—अपमान, निरादर, तिरस्कार, अवहेलना, अवज्ञा।

88. **कल्पवृक्ष**—सुरतरु, पारिजात, कल्पतरु, कल्पद्रुम, मन्दार, देववृक्ष।

89. **खल**—अधम, पामर, नीच, दुष्ट, दुर्जन, कुटिल, धूर्त।

90. **गाय**—गो, धेनु, सुरभि, गवय।

91. **जीभ**—रसना, जिह्वा, रसज्ञा, रसिका।

92. **झंडी**—ध्वजा, पताका, वैजयन्ती।

93. **ढाक**—पलास, टेसू, केसू, किंशुक, सुवर्णी।

94. **दांत**—दशन, रदन, दन्त, मुखक्षुर।

95. **धन**—वित्त, सम्पत्ति, अर्थ, द्रव्य, सम्पदा, दौलत।

96. **नाव**—तरी, पोत, जलयान, नौका, नौ, तरिणी।

97. **पत्थर**—पाषाण, शिला, उपल, प्रस्तर, पाहन।

98. **बाग**—आराम, उद्यान, उपवन, वाटिका, बगीचा।

99. **ब्राह्मण**—विप्र, भूदेव, भूमिसुर, द्विज, महीदेव, वेदपाठी।

100. **चतुरानन**—ब्रह्मा, विरचि, स्वयंभू, विधि।

अभ्यास प्रश्न

1. 'मेघ' का पर्यायवाची है:
   A. नीरद B. महीधर
   C. धीर D. चारु

2. इनमें से 'बैल' किसका पर्यायवाची है?
   A. घन B. तिमिर
   C. अश्म D. आतंक

3. 'सेना' का पर्यायवाची है:
   A. घटक B. कटक
   C. दक्षक D. तारक

4. 'विवाह' का पर्यायवाची है:
   A. परिणत B. परिणति
   C. परिणय D. परिणाम

5. 'पुष्प' का पर्यायवाची है:
   A. रेखा B. माला
   C. महक D. सुमन

6. नीचे दिए गए शब्द का पर्यायवाची शब्द कौन-सा नहीं है?
   दिन
   A. वासर B. नग
   C. दिवस D. दिवा

7. 'खग' शब्द का पर्यायवाची शब्द चयन कीजिए।
   A. पशु B. कबूतर
   C. पक्षी D. तोता

8. निम्नलिखित में से कौन-सा शब्द 'नयन' का पर्यायवाची नहीं है?
   A. चक्षु B. आँख
   C. नेत्र D. ओष्ठ

9. 'सत्य' का पर्यायवाची शब्द क्या है?
A. सच B. माया
C. झूठ D. दोष

10. 'माता' का पर्यायवाची शब्द है:
A. बुआ B. बहन
C. जननी D. दादी

11. 'अचल' का पर्यायवाची है:
A. स्थिर B. जड़
C. गतिहीन D. जंगम

12. 'गंगा' का पर्यायवाची शब्द है:
A. सौदामिनी B. भागीरथी
C. स्रोतास्विनी D. कालिन्दी

13. 'सरोज' का पर्यायवाची शब्द है:
A. शिरीष B. गुलाब
C. अरविन्द D. कुमुद

14. 'भ्रमर' का पर्यायवाची शब्द बताइए:
A. पंचशर B. मधुकर
C. निशाकर D. सहचर

15. 'समुद्र' का पर्यायवाची शब्द बताइए:
A. जलधि B. जलाशय
C. जलद D. वारिद

16. 'अमृत' का पर्यायवाची है:
A. नश्वर B. आशु
C. सुधा D. आयास

17. 'धन' शब्द का पर्यायवाची है:
A. तरी B. सम्पत्ति
C. हाटक D. अब्धि

18. निम्न में से 'आँख' शब्द का पर्यायवाची कौन-सा है?
A. अतन B. देवारि
C. शुभा D. लोचन

19. 'कोशिश' का पर्यायवाची शब्द है:
A. मजबूरी B. प्रयास
C. लगातार D. कुछ करना

20. 'जीभ' का पर्यायवाची शब्द है:
A. जीव B. ध्वनि
C. रसना D. वचन

उत्तरमाला

1	2	3	4	5	6	7	8	9	10
A	C	B	C	D	B	C	D	A	C
11	**12**	**13**	**14**	**15**	**16**	**17**	**18**	**19**	**20**
A	B	C	B	A	C	B	D	B	C

❄ ❄ ❄ ❄ ❄

तुकांत और अतुकांत शब्द

तुकांत शब्द

वे शब्द जिनके अंत में आने वाले वर्ण या ध्वनि समान होते हैं, उन्हें 'तुकांत शब्द' कहते हैं। ये सुनने में समान लगते हैं। इनका प्रयोग कविताओं, गीतों और नारों को आकर्षक और यादगार बनाने के लिए किया जाता है। जैसे—आकाश-प्रकाश, गाड़ी-साड़ी, जाना-खाना आदि।

उदाहरण : 'छोटी-सी हम-झोली,
बोल रही है बोली।'

कुछ तुकांत शब्द इस प्रकार हैं :

सीता
धन

शब्द	तुकांत	शब्द	तुकांत
नट	खट	जब	तब
रवि	कवि	जान	मान
फूल	धूल	हाल	चाल

अतुकांत शब्द

वे शब्द या पंक्तियाँ जिनके अंत में समान ध्वनि का अभाव होता है, उन्हें 'अतुकांत शब्द' कहते हैं। इसमें तुकबंदी नहीं होती। यह शैली छंदमुक्त कविता के अंतर्गत आती है, जिसमें तुकबंदी की बाध्यता नहीं होती। जैसे—आसमान-पंछी, घर-पुस्तक, सूरज-धूप आदि।

उदाहरण : ''आज का दिन बहुत,
थका देने वाला था,
लेकिन रात सुकून की होगी।''

अभ्यास प्रश्न

1. 'भाव' शब्द का तुकांत शब्द कौन-सा है?
A. ताव B. नाव
C. बहाव D. ये सभी

2. 'पानी' शब्द से मिलता-जुलता (तुकांत) शब्द कौन-सा है?
A. खाना B. कहानी
C. नदी D. सागर

3. 'नीड़ा' शब्द का सही तुकांत शब्द चुनिए।
A. भीड़ B. पेड़
C. कीड़ा D. इनमें से कोई नहीं

4. इनमें से कौन-सा शब्द 'लाल' का तुकांत शब्द है?
A. लाल B. बाल
C. गोपाल D. B और C दोनों

5. अतुकांत कविता क्या है?
A. जिसमें तुकबंदी होती है
B. जिसमें तुकंबदी का अभाव होता है
C. जिसमें तुकांत शब्द अंत में आते हैं
D. इनमें से कोई नहीं

6. 'सूरज' शब्द का तुकांत शब्द क्या होगा?
A. धूप B. दूरज
C. सवेरा D. चमक

7. निम्नलिखित में से कौन-सी तुकांत जोड़ी नहीं है?
A. हवा-दवा B. घर-दर
C. आम-इमली D. पानी-बानी

8. 'गायक' शब्द का सबसे उपयुक्त तुकांत शब्द है?
A. नायक B. गायिका
C. भावुक D. नाविक

9. निम्न में से कौन-से शब्द अतुकांत हैं?
A. बात-रात B. खेल-मेल
C. नदी-पहाड़ D. दिल-मिल

10. 'किताब' का अतुकांत शब्द चुनिए।
A. हिसाब B. जवाब
C. गुलाब D. कुर्सी

11. तुकांत शब्दों की विशेषता क्या होती है?
A. अर्थ समान होता है।
B. वर्तनी समान होती है।
C. अंत में ध्वनि समान होती है।
D. शब्द छोटे होते हैं।

12. 'गाना' का अतुकांत शब्द चुनिए।
A. आना B. जाना
C. खाना D. पानी

13. निम्न में से कौन-सा युग्म अतुकांत है?
A. राम-नाम B. बात-रात
C. खेल-मेल D. घर-सड़क

14. अतुकांत शब्दों का प्रयोग मुख्यतः कहाँ होता है?
A. छंदबद्ध कविता में
B. अतुकांत कविता में
C. केवल गद्य में
D. मुहावरों में

15. 'रात' का तुकांत शब्द कौन-सा है?
A. दिन B. सूरज
C. बात D. समय

उत्तरमाला

1	2	3	4	5	6	7	8	9	10
D	B	C	D	B	B	C	A	C	D
11	**12**	**13**	**14**	**15**					
C	D	D	B	C					

❄ ❄ ❄ ❄ ❄

9 विराम चिह्न

'विराम' का अर्थ होता है–ठहरना या रुकना। लेखन को प्रभावी रूप देने के लिए लेखक द्वारा कई प्रकार के विराम चिह्नों का प्रयोग किया जाता है जो कि लेखन में भावों की अभिव्यक्ति, वाक्य का अर्थ स्पष्ट करने, उतार-चढ़ाव और ठहराव दर्शाने के लिए आवश्यक होते हैं। ऐसे ही विशेष चिह्नों को विराम चिह्न कहा जाता है।

विराम चिह्न का महत्व

विराम चिह्न एक वाक्य को दूसरे से अलग करते हैं। एक वाक्य के भीतर भी एक कोटि के कई शब्दों या वाक्यांशों या उपवाक्यों को वह अलग करता है। विराम चिह्नों के प्रयोग से भाषा में स्पष्टता आती है और भाव को समझने में सुविधा होती है।

विराम चिह्न के अभाव में वाक्य का ठीक अर्थ समझना असम्भव हो जाता है। जैसे–'उसे रोको मत जाने दो' इस वाक्य के दो सर्वथा विपरीत अर्थ हो सकते हैं।

1. उसे रोको, मत जाने दो। (यह वाक्य निषेधात्मक है)
2. उसे रोको मत, जाने दो। (यह वाक्य असार्थक है)

विराम चिह्न से ही ज्ञात हो सकता है कि वाक्य का वास्तविक अर्थ क्या है।

विराम चिह्न के प्रकार

हिन्दी में प्रचलित प्रमुख विराम चिह्न निम्न हैं :

विराम चिह्नों के नाम	चिह्न	वाक्य में प्रयोग
अल्प विराम	,	मोहन, सोहन और अनिल आएंगे
अर्द्धविराम	;	मैंने उससे कहा तो था; वो आया नहीं
पूर्ण विराम	।	'संयुक्त राष्ट्र संघ' एक श्रेष्ठतम विश्वसनीय संस्था है।
प्रश्न सूचक चिह्न	?	क्या वो आ गए?
विस्मय या सम्बोधन सूचक	!	वाह! क्या सौंदर्य है
उद्धरण चिह्न	' '	''कमजोर किसी को माफ नहीं कर सकते, माफ करना मजबूत लोगों की निशानी है'' –महात्मा गांधी
निर्देशन चिह्न	–	निम्नलिखित प्रश्नों का उत्तर दीजिए–
विवरण चिह्न	:-	पार्सल में निम्नलिखित वस्तुएं हैं :-
कोष्ठक चिह्न	( )	ग्लोबल वार्मिंग (वैश्विक ताप) मानव जीवन के लिए हानिकारक है।
लाघव चिह्न	॰	एम॰ए॰ = मास्टर ऑफ आर्ट्स
योजक चिह्न	-	'हम-तुम' साथ-साथ चलेंगे
उपविराम या कोलन	:	हिन्दी निबंध : एक श्रेष्ठ पुस्तक

अभ्यास प्रश्न

1. भाषा में उलझाव न आने देने में सहायक हैं :
A. अर्द्धविराम B. मात्राएँ
C. ध्वनि D. विराम चिह्न

2. ' , ' यह कहलाता है :
A. अर्द्धविराम B. अल्पविराम
C. शुद्ध विराम D. पूर्ण विराम

3. '।' यह कहलाता है :
A. अर्द्धविराम
B. अल्पविराम
C. उपपद
D. पूर्ण विराम

4. '?' यह कहलाता है :
A. अल्पविराम
B. प्रश्न चिह्न
C. पूर्ण विराम
D. अर्द्धविराम

5. वाक्य को बोलने या पढ़ने में थोड़ी देर का ठहराव कहलाता है :
A. अल्पविराम
B. उपपद
C. पूर्ण विराम
D. अर्द्धविराम

6. ';' यह कहलाता है :
A. अर्द्धविराम
B. अल्पविराम
C. उपपद
D. पूर्ण विराम

7. वाक्य में अल्प विराम से अधिक और पूर्णविराम से कम ठहराव आने पर लगता है :
A. अर्द्धविराम
B. उपविराम
C. योजक चिह्न
D. पूर्ण विराम

8. जहाँ प्रमुख वाक्य और अन्य वाक्य खंडों का कोई संबंध न हो, वहाँ कौन-सा विराम चिह्न लगता है?
A. पूर्ण विराम
B. उपविराम
C. अल्पविराम
D. अर्द्धविराम

9. '!' यह विराम चिह्न कहलाता है :
A. अर्द्धविराम
B. अल्पविराम
C. विस्मयादि सूचक
D. पूर्ण विराम

10. ':' यह विराम चिह्न कहलाता है :
A. उपविराम
B. अल्पविराम
C. विस्मयादि सूचक
D. पूर्ण विराम

11. '।' यह वाक्य की समाप्ति का बोधक चिह्न होता है :
A. उपविराम
B. अल्पविराम
C. विस्मयादि सूचक
D. पूर्ण विराम

12. निम्न में से किसे 'संक्षिप्त चिह्न' भी कहते हैं?
A. निर्देशन
B. अल्पविराम
C. लाघव
D. उद्धरण

13. पूर्ण अर्थ रखने वाले प्रश्नवाचक वाक्यों के अंत में यह लगता है :
A. ,
B. ।
C. :
D. ?

14. निम्न में से किसे 'सामासिक चिह्न' भी कहते हैं?
A. संयोजक चिह्न
B. पूर्णविराम चिह्न
C. अल्पविराम चिह्न
D. समानार्थक चिह्न

15. आश्चर्य, घृणा, शोक, हर्ष, प्रसन्नता, उत्साह आदि भावों की अभिव्यक्ति करने वाले वाक्यों में विस्मयादि बोधक अव्ययों के बाद यह चिह्न लगता है :
A. !
B. ।
C. ,
D. ?

16. अरे .... बदमाश जेल की चार-दीवारी फाँद गये।
रिक्त स्थान में यह विराम चिह्न आएगा :
A. ,
B. ।
C. !
D. ?

17. निम्न में से योजक चिह्न है :
A. !
B. –
C. ?
D. /

18. उद्धरण चिह्न है :
A. " "
B. ।
C. :
D. !

19. इनमें से कौन-सा विराम चिह्न है जो हिन्दी में अंग्रेजी भाषा से नहीं लिया गया है?
A. ?
B. ।
C. .
D. :

20. 'अहा!' विस्मयादि बोधक विभक्ति में कौन-सा भाव है?
A. शोक
B. घृणा
C. हर्ष
D. आश्चर्य

उत्तरमाला

1	2	3	4	5	6	7	8	9	10
D	B	D	B	A	A	A	D	C	A
11	12	13	14	15	16	17	18	19	20
D	C	D	A	A	C	B	A	B	C

❄ ❄ ❄ ❄ ❄

10 शुद्ध वर्तनी

वर्तनी के अंतर्गत शब्द ध्वनियों को जिस क्रम से और जिस रूप में उच्चारित किया जाता है उन्हें उसी क्रम से और उसी रूप में लिखा भी जाता है। अतः शुद्ध वर्तनी के लिए शुद्ध उच्चारण करना आवश्यक है। जैसे—यदि हम 'अक्षर' का उच्चारण 'अच्छर' करेंगे तो 'अक्षर' की वर्तनी शुद्ध नहीं लिख सकते।

कुछ ऐसी अशुद्धियाँ दी जा रही हैं जो प्रायः हो जाती है :

अशुद्ध	शुद्ध	अशुद्ध	शुद्ध
अगामी	आगामी	गृहणी	गृहिणी
अतिथी	अतिथि	शाबास	शाबाश
आधीन	अधीन	प्रशन	प्रश्न
अधार	आधार	गुरू	गुरु
ईकाई	इकाई	पती	पति
एरावत	ऐरावत	धोका	धोखा
उर्पयुक्त	उपर्युक्त	नर्क	नरक
दिवार	दीवार	पत्नि	पत्नी
जबाब	जवाब	नीती	नीति

अशुद्ध	शुद्ध	अशुद्ध	शुद्ध
उपर	ऊपर	कोसिस	कोशिश
वापिस	वापस	पूज्यनीय	पूजनीय
श्रीमति	श्रीमती	मूमर्ष	मुमूर्ष
दवाईयाँ	दवाइयाँ	क्षिती	क्षिति
समाजिक	सामाजिक	त्यौहार	त्योहार
सप्ताहिक	साप्ताहिक	गितांजली	गीतांजलि
कालीदास	कालिदास	त्रिपुरारी	त्रिपुरारि
इसलीए	इसलिए	प्रतिनिधी	प्रतिनिधि
नमश्कार	नमस्कार	रात्री	रात्रि
दिपावली	दीपावली	मूर्ती	मूर्ति
मँहगाई	महँगाई	जोत्सना	ज्योत्स्ना
बिमारी	बीमारी	उपलक्ष	उपलक्ष्य
प्रतिएक	प्रत्येक	व्यंग	व्यंग्य
स्वास्थ	स्वास्थ्य	सामर्थ	सामर्थ्य

अभ्यास प्रश्न

निर्देश (प्र.सं. 1 से 25 तक): *निम्नलिखित प्रश्नों में एक ही शब्द की चार अलग-अलग वर्तनियाँ दी गई हैं। इनमें से केवल एक वर्तनी सही है। उस विकल्प का चयन कीजिए।*

1. A. इकलौता B. एकलोता
C. ईकलोता D. ऐकलोता

2. A. संतुष्ट B. शंतुष्ट
C. शंतुशत D. स्न्तुष्ट

3. A. अतीथी B. अतिथि
C. आतिथी D. अथिति

4. A. आर्शीवाद B. आशिर्वाद
C. आर्शिवाद D. आशीर्वाद

5. A. समाजिक B. समाजीक
C. सामाजिक D. समजीक

6. A. संश्लेषण B. शंस्लेषण
C. षंश्लेसण D. संष्लेशण

7. A. वनवाश B. वनबास
C. बनवास D. वनवास

8. A. विशेस B. विशेष
C. विसेश D. विषेश

9. A. बाहिष्कार B. बइष्कार
C. बहिष्कार D. बहीष्कार

10. A. आकर्षक B. आक्रषक
C. अकार्षक D. आकर्शक

11. A. निरकार B. निर्कार
C. निराकार D. नीराकार

12. A. मोखिक B. मौखिक
C. मौकिख D. मौखीक

13. A. प्रतिवर्ष B. परतीवर्ष
C. प्रतिवर्श D. प्रतिबर्ष

14. A. अंर्तगत B. अंतरगंत
C. अर्न्तगत D. अन्तरगत

15. A. क्रष्ण B. कृषण
C. कृश्ण D. कृष्ण

16. A. शोणित B. शोनित
C. सोणित D. शोणीत

17. A. अधम्र B. अर्धम
C. अधर्म D. अधरम

18. A. अनूक्रम B. अनुक्रम
C. अनुकर्म D. अनुकृम

19. A. क्रम B. कृम
C. कर्मृ D. कमृ

20. A. तटस्त B. तटस्थ
C. तटश्थ D. तटष्थ

21. A. अम्रत B. अर्मत
C. अमृर्त D. अमृत

22. A. फुर्तला B. फुर्तिला
C. फुर्तीला D. फुंतीला

23. A. र्निजीव B. निर्जीव
C. निरजीव D. निज्रीव

24. A. परिकर्मा B. परिक्रमा
C. परिकृमा D. प्रिक्रमा

25. A. राशी B. राषि
C. राशि D. रासि

निर्देश (प्र.सं. 26 से 30 तक): *निम्नलिखित प्रश्नों में दिए गए विकल्पों में से अशुद्ध शब्द का चयन कीजिए।*

26. A. कौतूहल B. अनधिकार
C. निरपेक्ष D. पौराणीक

27. A. एकतारा B. जिजीविषा
C. कार्यकारणी D. अभ्यंतर

28. A. अनंग B. व्यंग
C. हास्य D. परिहास

29. A. नीती B. नदियाँ
C. कविता D. जीवित

30. A. आचार्य B. अवगुण
C. इष्ट D. उद्घोस

निर्देश (प्र.सं. 31 से 35 तक): *निम्नलिखित प्रश्नों में दिए गए विकल्पों में शुद्ध शब्द का चयन कीजिए।*

31. A. कृप्या B. चिह्न
C. आर्शीवाद D. उज्जवल

32. A. कोश्ठ B. परिशद
C. क्षुधा D. पाठसाला

33. A. प्रतिभूती B. कवयित्री
C. पड़ौसी D. बिमार

34. A. प्रसंशा B. परिस्थिती
C. प्रदर्शनी D. भगिरथी

35. A. आविष्कार B. निसब्द
C. जमाता D. देवार्षि

उत्तरमाला

1	2	3	4	5	6	7	8	9	10
A	A	B	D	C	A	D	B	C	A
11	12	13	14	15	16	17	18	19	20
C	B	A	B	D	A	C	B	A	B
21	22	23	24	25	26	27	28	29	30
D	C	B	B	C	D	C	B	A	D
31	32	33	34	35					
B	C	B	C	A					

❄ ❄ ❄ ❄ ❄

11 वाक्यांश के लिए एक शब्द

वाक्यांश के स्थान पर एक सार्थक शब्द का प्रयोग कथन को अत्यंत प्रभावशाली और रोचक बना देता है। ऐसे शब्दों के प्रयोग से न केवल विचारों को संक्षेप में व्यक्त किया जा सकता है, बल्कि समय और स्थान की भी बचत होती है। वाक्यांश के स्थान पर एक शब्द का निर्माण समास बनाकर अथवा उपसर्ग या प्रत्यय जोड़कर किया जाता है।

क्र.सं.	वाक्यांश	एक शब्द
1.	जो न जाना जा सके	अज्ञेय
2.	जिसके माँ-बाप न हो	अनाथ
3.	जो भेदा या तोड़ा न जा सके	अभेद्य
4.	अण्डे से जन्म लेने वाला	अण्डज
5.	अच्छे चरित्र वाला	सच्चरित्र
6.	आलोचना करने वाला	आलोचक
7.	आकाश में उड़ने वाला	नभचर
8.	आशा से अधिक	आशातीत
9.	अभिनय करने वाला पुरुष	अभिनेता
10.	अच्छा-बुरा समझने की शक्ति का अभाव	अविवेक
11.	अनुकरण करने योग्य	अनुकरणीय
12.	आयोजन करने वाला व्यक्ति	आयोजक
13.	अनुचित या बुरा आचरण करने वाला	दुराचारी
14.	अभी-अभी जन्म लेने वाला	नवजात
15.	जो दान देता हो	दानी
16.	जिसको भय न हो	निर्भय
17.	अच्छा लिखने वाला	सुलेखक
18.	अच्छा बोलने वाला	सुवक्ता
19.	जिसमें दया हो	दयालु
20.	जो प्रशंसा के योग्य हो	प्रशंसनीय
21.	जो जल में रहता हो	जलचर
22.	जो ईश्वर में विश्वास रखता हो	आस्तिक
23.	जिसकी तुलना न हो	अतुलनीय
24.	जो कुछ जानने की इच्छा रखता हो	जिज्ञासु

क्र.सं.	वाक्यांश	एक शब्द
25.	साथ में पढ़ने वाला	सहपाठी
26.	किसी का मजाक उड़ाना	उपहास
27.	कम खर्च करने वाला व्यक्ति	मितव्ययी
28.	किसी मत का समर्थन करने वाला	अनुमोदन
29.	किसी बात पर जोर देना	आग्रह
30.	जिस बच्चे को गोद लिया गया हो	दत्तक पुत्र
31.	जो कभी हो ही नहीं सकता	असम्भव
32.	जो मुँह से कहा न जा सके	अकथनीय
33.	भलाई चाहने वाला	हितैषी
34.	दूसरों की बातों में दखल देना	हस्तक्षेप
35.	जो सब जगह व्याप्त हो	सर्वव्यापक
36.	जिसके आने की तिथि न हो	अतिथि
37.	जो चित्र बनाता हो	चित्रकार
38.	हमेशा सत्य बोलने वाला	सत्यवादी
39.	जो दिखाई न दे	अदृश्य
40.	जिसके समान दूसरा न हो	अनुपम
41.	जिसमें धैर्य न हो	अधीर
42.	दूर की सोचने वाला	दूरदर्शी
43.	जो दूसरों पर अत्याचार करे	अत्याचारी
44.	जो कभी नष्ट न हो	अनश्वर
45.	जिस भूमि पर कुछ उग न सके	असर
46.	जो हाथ से लिखा हुआ हो	हस्तलिखित
47.	धर्म को जानने वाला	धर्मज्ञ
48.	शरण में आया हुआ	शरणागत
49.	जिसे पराजित न किया जा सके	अपराजेय
50.	जो किसी का पक्ष न ले	तटस्थ
51.	जो बड़ा भाई हो	अग्रज
52.	जहाँ पहुँचना आसान हो	सुगम
53.	स्वयं सेवा करने वाला	स्वयं सेवक

अभ्यास प्रश्न

निर्देश (प्र.सं. 1 से 35 तक): *निम्नलिखित प्रश्नों में दिए गए वाक्यांश के लिए नीचे दिए गए विकल्पों में से उचित शब्द का चयन कीजिए।*

1. जो जीता न जा सके:
A. अलौकिक B. अजेय
C. अभेद्य D. अनुकरणीय

2. जो पहले कभी नहीं हुआ:
A. अजर B. भूतपूर्व
C. अकथनीय D. अभूतपूर्व

3. जिसका पता न हो:
A. अज्ञात B. अजात
C. अजित D. अविस्मरणीय

4. जिसका विभाजन न किया जा सके:
A. विभाजित B. अनंत
C. अविभाज्य D. अनभिज्ञ

5. दूसरों की बातों में दखल देना:
A. अत्याचार B. हस्तक्षेप
C. अकिंचन D. हितैषी

6. जहाँ पहुँचा न जा सके:
A. उपकृत B. निराकार
C. अक्षम्य D. अगम्य

7. जो प्रशंसा के योग्य हो:
A. अप्रशंसक B. अप्रत्याशित
C. प्रशासक D. प्रशंसनीय

8. जो करने योग्य न हो:
A. अकरणीय B. सुकरणीय
C. करणीय D. विकरणीय

9. जो सबको समान दृष्टि से देखता हो:
A. सज्जन B. संन्यासी
C. समदर्शी D. परोपकारी

10. परीक्षा देने वाला:
A. परीक्षक B. विद्यार्थी
C. परीक्षार्थी D. शिक्षार्थी

11. जो कहने योग्य न हो:
A. अकथनीय B. अयोग्य
C. अवगुण D. अमावनात्मक

12. जो सहन न कर सके:
A. असहनीय B. असामाजिक
C. असहिष्णु D. असहाय

13. उच्चकुल में जन्म लेने वाला:
A. कुलीन B. धनी
C. रईस D. कुलिश

14. जो इन्द्रियों से परे हो:
A. इन्द्रहीन B. अगोचर
C. गोचर D. इष्टहीन

15. जिसे किसी बात का पता न हो:
A. अज्ञानी B. अल्पज्ञ
C. अनभिज्ञ D. मूर्ख

16. जिसके आर-पार देखा जा सके:
A. अतलदर्शी B. सूक्ष्मदर्शी
C. पारदर्शी D. दूरदर्शी

17. जो आँखों के सामने न हो:
A. प्रत्यक्ष B. परोक्ष
C. दूरस्थ D. अप्रत्यक्ष

18. जंगल में लगने वाली आग:
A. जठरानल B. दावानल
C. कामानल D. बड़वानल

19. जिसके पास कुछ भी न हो:
A. अज्ञ B. अकिंचन
C. गरीब D. दीन

20. थोड़ा जानने वाला:
A. अलण्या B. अल्पज्ञा
C. अल्पज्ञ D. अल्प बुद्धि

21. किसी कथा के अन्तर्गत आने वाली कोई अन्य कथा:
A. दृष्टांत B. अन्तर्कथा
C. अंतःकथा D. अंतर्दृष्टांत

22. फाल्गुन की पूर्णिमा को होने वाला हिंदुओं का प्रसिद्ध त्योहार:
A. गुरु पूर्णिमा B. वसंतोत्सव
C. दीपावली D. होली

23. यज्ञ में आहुति देने वाला:
A. पुरोहित B. हवि
C. होता D. समिधा

24. काम से जी चुराने वालाः
A. कामचोर B. बेकार
C. आलसी D. निकम्मा

25. किसी बात को करने का निश्चयः
A. विकल्प B. संकल्प
C. कल्प D. अत्यल्प

26. जिस बीमारी का ठीक होना सम्भव न होः
A. असाध्य B. विकट
C. भयानक D. घातक

27. जिस पर विजय प्राप्त कर ली गई होः
A. आक्रान्त B. अजेय
C. विजित D. पराजित

28. सूर्य के उदय होने का स्थानः
A. उदयाचल B. सूर्योदय
C. प्रभात स्थान D. गंधमादन

29. जो कहा न जा सकेः
A. अकथित B. अकथनीय
C. अकथ्य D. नामुमकिन

30. जिसे बहुत बातें करनी आती होः
A. वाचाल B. गम्भीर
C. समालोचक D. मुनि

31. जो स्त्री के वशीभूत होः
A. स्त्रीदास B. गुलाम
C. स्त्रैण D. प्रेमी

32. जिसे पढ़ना-लिखना आता होः
A. अल्पज्ञानी B. शिक्षित
C. बुद्धिजीवी D. साक्षर

33. जो अपने कर्तव्य को न जानता होः
A. अनजान B. अज्ञानी
C. किंकर्त्तव्यविमूढ़ D. कर्त्तव्यहीन

34. जो कानून के अनुकूल न होः
A. अवैध B. जघन्य
C. अवध्य D. आवेग

35. कामना पूरी होने का विश्वासः
A. प्रत्याशा B. दुराशा
C. विभावना D. सम्भावना

उत्तरमाला

1	2	3	4	5	6	7	8	9	10
B	D	A	C	B	D	D	A	C	C
11	**12**	**13**	**14**	**15**	**16**	**17**	**18**	**19**	**20**
A	A	A	B	C	C	B	B	B	C
21	**22**	**23**	**24**	**25**	**26**	**27**	**28**	**29**	**30**
B	D	C	A	B	A	C	A	B	A.
31	**32**	**33**	**34**	**35**					
C	D	A	A	A					

❋ ❋ ❋ ❋ ❋

12 संधि

संधि का अर्थ होता है, दो वर्णों का मेल। जब दो स्वर या व्यंजन मिलकर तीसरे अक्षर (स्वर या व्यंजन) में बदल जाते हैं, तब इस रूप परिवर्तन को संधि कहते हैं। संधि के तीन प्रमुख भेद हैं : 1. स्वर संधि, 2. व्यंजन संधि, 3. विसर्ग संधि

स्वर संधि

दो स्वरों के मेल से जो विकार उत्पन्न होता है, उसे स्वर संधि कहते हैं। स्वर संधि के पांच भेद होते हैं :

(*i*) **दीर्घ संधि :** जब दो समान स्वर चाहे वे दीर्घ हों या ह्रस्व, आमने-सामने आते हैं तो दोनों मिलकर दीर्घ हो जाते हैं, अर्थात् अ, इ, उ, ऋ या दीर्घ आ, ई, ऊ परस्पर मिलकर एक हो जाते हैं, तो उसे दीर्घ स्वर संधि कहते हैं जैसे–

- अ + अ = आ (नर + अधम = नराधम)
- अ + आ = आ (कार्य + आलय = कार्यालय)
- आ + अ = आ (विद्या + अर्थी = विद्यार्थी)
- आ + आ = आ (महा + आशय = महाशय)
- इ + इ = ई (मुनि + इन्द्र = मुनीन्द्र)
- इ + ई = ई (कपि + ईश = कपीश)
- ई + इ = ई (मही + इन्द्र = महीन्द्र)
- ई + ई = ई (नदी + ईश = नदीश)
- उ + उ = ऊ (साधु + उवाच = साधूवाच)
- उ + ऊ = ऊ (लघु + ऊर्मि = लघूर्मि)
- ऊ + उ = ऊ (वधू + उत्सव = वधूत्सव)
- ऊ + ऊ = ऊ (भू + ऊर्ध्व = भूर्ध्व)

(*ii*) **गुण संधि :** गुण संधि में 'अ' अथवा 'आ' के बाद यदि 'इ' अथवा 'ई' हो तो दोनों मिलकर 'ए' बन जाता है। यदि 'अ' अथवा 'आ' के बाद 'उ' अथवा 'ऊ' हो तो दोनों मिलकर 'ओ' बन जाता है। यदि 'अ' अथवा 'आ' के बाद 'ऋ' हो, तो दोनों मिलकर 'अर' बन जाता है तब गुण संधि होती है। जैसे–

- अ + इ = ए (नर + इन्द्र = नरेन्द्र)
- आ + इ = ए (महा + इन्द्र = महेन्द्र)
- अ + ई = ए (सुर + ईश = सुरेश)
- आ + ई = ए (राका + ईश = राकेश)
- अ + उ = ओ (नर + उत्तम = नरोत्तम)
- आ + उ = ओ (महा + उदर = महोदर)
- अ + ऊ = ओ (नव + ऊढ़ा = नवोढ़ा)
- आ + ऊ = ओ (गंगा + ऊर्मि = गंगोर्मि)
- अ + ऋ = अर् (देव + ऋषि = देवर्षि)
- आ + ऋ = अर् (महा + ऋषि = महर्षि)

(*iii*) **यण संधि :** 'इ', 'ई' के बाद विजातीय स्वर आने पर वह 'य' में 'उ', 'ऊ' के बाद विजातीय स्वर आने पर 'व' और 'ऋ' के बाद विजातीय स्वर आने पर 'र' में बदल जाता है तब यण संधि होती है। जैसे–

- इ + आ = या (अति + आनन्द = अत्यानन्द)
- इ + ए = ये (प्रति + एक = प्रत्येक)
- इ + उ = यु (प्रति + उत्तर = प्रत्युत्तर)
- उ + अ = व (अनु + अय = अन्वय)
- उ + आ = वा (सु + आगत = स्वागत)
- ऋ + आ = रा (मातृ + आदेश = मात्रादेश)

(*iv*) **वृद्धि संधि :** जब 'अ' अथवा 'आ' के बाद 'ए' अथवा 'ऐ' स्वर आए तो वहाँ 'ऐ' 'अ' अथवा 'आ' के बाद 'ओ' अथवा 'औ' आए तो वहाँ 'औ' हो जाता है, तब वृद्धि संधि कहलाती है। जैसे–

- अ + ए = ऐ (एक + एक = एकैक)
- आ + ए = ऐ (तथा + एव = तथैव)
- अ + ऐ = ऐ (नर + ऐश्वर्य = नरैश्वर्य)
- आ + औ = औ (महा + ओज = महौज)
- अ + औ = औ (परम + औषधम = परमौषधम)
- आ + ऐ = ऐ (महा + ऐश्वर्य = महैश्वर्य)
- आ + औ = औ (महा + औषध = महौषध)

(*v*) **अयादि संधि :** जब 'ए', 'ऐ', 'ओ', 'औ' के पश्चात् कोई विजातीय स्वर आए, तो ये क्रमशः अय, आय, अव और आव में परिवर्तित हो जाते हैं। जैसे–

- ए + अ = अय (ने + अन = नयन)
- ऐ + अ = आय (नै + अक = नायक)
- ओ + अ = अव (पो + अन = पवन)
- ओ + इ = अव (पो + इत्र = पवित्र)

- औ + अ = आव (सौ + अन = सावन)
- औ + उ = आव (भौ + उक = भावुक)

व्यंजन संधि

किसी व्यंजन के पश्चात् जब कोई व्यंजन अथवा स्वर आए तो व्यंजन + व्यंजन अथवा व्यंजन + स्वर के मेल से उत्पन्न विकार को व्यंजन संधि कहते हैं। जैसे–

- दिक् + अम्बर = दिगम्बर
- सत् + गुरू = सद्गुरू
- जगत् + ईश = जगदीश
- दिक् + अन्त = दिगन्त
- तत् + लीन = तल्लीन
- सम + गम = संगम
- उत् + नति = उन्नति

विसर्ग संधि

जब विसर्ग के साथ किसी स्वर अथवा व्यंजन का मेल होता है, तब उससे उत्पन्न होने वाले विकार को विसर्ग संधि कहते हैं। जैसे–

- निः + चल = निश्चल
- धनुः + टंकार = धनुषटंकार
- प्रातः + काल = प्रातःकाल
- पुरः + हित = पुरोहित
- मनः + भाव = मनोभाव
- निः + विकार = निर्विकार

अभ्यास प्रश्न

निर्देश (प्र.सं. 1 से 15 तक) : *निम्नलिखित प्रश्नों में दिए गए शब्दों में प्रयुक्त संधि का चयन कीजिए।*

1. नायक
A. दीर्घ संधि B. वृद्धि संधि
C. अयादि संधि D. गुण संधि

2. मतैक्य
A. दीर्घ संधि B. वृद्धि संधि
C. गुण संधि D. इनमें से कोई नहीं

3. नाविक
A. अयादि संधि B. वृद्धि संधि
C. गुण संधि D. इनमें से कोई नहीं

4. तथैव
A. दीर्घ संधि B. गुण संधि
C. वृद्धि संधि D. अयादि संधि

5. स्वागत
A. यण संधि B. गुण संधि
C. अयादि संधि D. वृद्धि संधि

6. अत्यावश्यक
A. अयादि संधि B. वृद्धि संधि
C. यण संधि D. गुण संधि

7. महेश
A. यण संधि B. गुण संधि
C. वृद्धि संधि D. दीर्घ संधि

8. महोत्सव
A. दीर्घ संधि B. यण संधि
C. गुण संधि D. वृद्धि संधि

9. सदुपाय
A. स्वर संधि B. व्यंजन संधि
C. विसर्ग संधि D. हलन्त संधि

10. भरण
A. व्यंजन संधि B. स्वर संधि
C. विसर्ग संधि D. इनमें से कोई नहीं

11. अतएव
A. स्वर संधि B. व्यंजन संधि
C. विसर्ग संधि D. इनमें से कोई नहीं

12. दुर्गम
A. स्वर संधि B. व्यंजन संधि
C. विसर्ग संधि D. इनमें से कोई नहीं

13. अधोगति
A. व्यंजन संधि B. स्वर संधि
C. विसर्ग संधि D. हलन्त संधि

14. बहिर्मुख
A. व्यंजन संधि B. स्वर संधि
C. विसर्ग संधि D. इनमें से कोई नहीं

15. रामावतार
A. स्वर संधि B. व्यंजन संधि
C. विसर्ग संधि D. इनमें से कोई नहीं

निर्देश (प्र.सं. 16 से 30 तक) : *निम्नलिखित प्रश्नों में दिये गये शब्द का सही संधि विच्छेद बताइए।*

16. गीतांजलि
A. गी + तांजलि B. गीत + आंजलि
C. गीत + अंजलि D. गीता + अंजलि

17. प्रत्येक
A. प्रत्य + एक B. प्रति + एक
C. प्रती + एक D. प्रत्य + इक

18. महीश
A. मही + श B. महि + इश
C. महि + ईश D. मही + ईश

19. सप्तर्षि
A. सप्त + ऋषि B. सप्त्र + षि
C. सप्त + रिषि D. सप्त + अर्षि

20. नयन
A. नय + न B. न + यन
C. ने + अन D. ने + यन

21. महर्षि
A. महा + अर्षि B. महा + ऋषि
C. महा + रिषि D. महा + रिशि

22. महौषध
A. महा + ओषध B. मह + औषध
C. महा + उषध D. महा + औषध

23. सच्चरित्र
A. सत् + चरित्र B. सत + चरित्र
C. सत्य + चरित्र D. सच्चा + चरित्र

24. निराधार
A. निरा + आधार B. निः + आधार
C. नि + आधार D. निर् + आधार

25. परमेश्वर
A. परम + ईश्वर B. पर + ममेश्वर
C. प + रमेश्वर D. परमो + ईश्वर

26. सज्जन
A. सज् + जन B. सद् + जन
C. सत् + जन D. स + ज + जन

27. यशोदा
A. यशो + दा B. यश + अदा
C. यशु + यदा D. यशः + दा

28. मनोयोग
A. मनोः + योग B. मनः + योग
C. मनः + आयोग D. इनमें से कोई नहीं

29. दशानन
A. दश् + आनन B. दस + आनन
C. दशान् + आनन D. दश + आनन

30. स्वागत
A. सु + आगत B. स्व + गत
C. स्वा + आगत D. स्वा + गत

31. निम्नलिखित शब्द के लिए सही संधि-विच्छेद का चयन कीजिए।
गिरीन्द्र
A. गिर + ईंद्र B. गिरि + ईंद्र
C. गिरी + इंद्र D. गिरि + इंद्र

32. निम्नलिखित में से किस शब्द की संधि सही है?
A. स्त्री + उचित = स्त्रीयोचित
B. नदी + आर्पण = नद्यार्पण
C. एक + एक = एकेक
D. पितृ + अनुमति = पित्रनुमति

33. निम्नलिखित में से किस शब्द की संधि सही नहीं है?
A. अधि + आदेश = अध्यादेश
B. अभि + आगत = अभ्यागत
C. अधि + अधीन = अध्याधीन
D. अभि + अर्थी = अभ्यर्थी

34. निम्नलिखित में से बेमेल को चुनिएः

	शब्द		संधि
A.	मूल्यांकन	–	दीर्घ
B.	परमेश्वर	–	गुण
C.	भावुक	–	विसर्ग
D.	जगन्नाथ	–	व्यंजन

35. निम्नलिखित में से बेमेल को चुनिएः

	शब्द		संधि
A.	उज्जवल	–	व्यंजन
B.	मेल	–	अयादि
C.	दुष्कर	–	विसर्ग
D.	अन्वय	–	गुण

उत्तरमाला

1	2	3	4	5	6	7	8	9	10
C	B	A	C	A	C	B	C	B	A
11	**12**	**13**	**14**	**15**	**16**	**17**	**18**	**19**	**20**
C	C	C	C	A	C	B	D	A	C
21	**22**	**23**	**24**	**25**	**26**	**27**	**28**	**29**	**30**
B	D	A	B	A	C	D	B	D	A
31	**32**	**33**	**34**	**35**					
D	D	C	C	D					

❄ ❄ ❄ ❄ ❄

13 काल

समय, क्रिया के जिस रूप से उसके होने के समय का बोध होता है, उसे **काल** कहते हैं अथवा जिस समय जो क्रिया सम्पन्न होती है, वही उसका 'काल' कहा जाता है। इस प्रकार क्रिया के जिस रूप से क्रिया के होने का समय ज्ञात होता है, उसे ही 'काल' कहते हैं।

काल के तीन भेद होते हैं:

1. वर्तमान काल 2. भूतकाल 3. भविष्यत् काल

वर्तमान काल

क्रिया के जिस रूप से कार्य के वर्तमान समय में सम्पन्न होने का बोध हो, उसे 'वर्तमान काल' कहते हैं। जैसे–वह पढ़ता है।

मोहन पुस्तक पढ़ रहा है।

वर्तमान काल के चार भेद होते हैं–

(क) **सामान्य वर्तमान :** क्रिया का वह रूप जिससे क्रिया का वर्तमान में होना पाया जाए, 'सामान्य वर्तमान' कहलाता है। जैसे– • मोहन जाता है। • राम पढ़ता है। • गीता देखती है।

(ख) **तात्कालिक/अपूर्ण वर्तमान :** क्रिया के जिस रूप से कार्य के होने या करने की निरन्तरता का बोध हो, उसे अपूर्ण वर्तमान कहते हैं। इसे 'तात्कालिक वर्तमान' भी कहते हैं।
जैसे–• मैं पत्र लिख रहा हूँ। • सुरेश गाना गा रहा है।

(ग) **पूर्ण वर्तमान :** क्रिया के जिस रूप से कार्य के वर्तमान में पूर्ण होने की जानकारी प्राप्त होती हो, उसे 'पूर्ण वर्तमान' कहते हैं। जैसे–• राम गया है। • रमेश ने रोटी खायी है।

(घ) **संभाव्य वर्तमान :** इस काल में कार्य के पूर्ण होने की संभावना रहती है। जैसे–• राम खाया हो। • वह सोया हो।

भूतकाल

क्रिया के जिस रूप से कार्य के बीते हुए समय (अतीत) में सम्पन्न (पूर्ण) होने का बोध हो, उसे **भूतकाल** कहते हैं। जैसे–• राम खा चुका था। • गीता सो गई थी।

भूतकाल के छः भेद होते हैं–

(क) **सामान्य भूत :** क्रिया के जिस रूप से कार्य के बीते हुए समय में सम्पन्न होने का बोध हो, किन्तु ठीक समय का बोध न हो, तो उसे सामान्य भूत कहते हैं। जैसे–• राम ने पत्र लिखा। • मोहन गया।

(ख) **आसन्न भूत :** क्रिया के जिस रूप से यह ज्ञात हो कि क्रिया अभी-अभी पूर्ण या समाप्त हुई है, उसे 'आसन्न भूत' कहते हैं। जैसे–• राम पत्र लिख चुका है। • वह अभी आया था।

(ग) **पूर्ण भूत :** क्रिया के जिस रूप से यह स्पष्ट ज्ञात हो कि कार्य को समाप्त हुए बहुत समय बीत चुका है, उसे 'पूर्ण भूत' कहते हैं। जैसे–• राम ने रावण को मारा था। • आशा ने गीत गाया था।

(घ) **अपूर्ण भूत :** क्रिया के जिस रूप से कार्य का बीते समय में होने का बोध हो किन्तु उसकी समाप्ति अर्थात् पूर्ण होने की जानकारी न प्राप्त हो, उसे 'अपूर्ण भूत' कहते हैं। जैसे– • रमेश पुस्तक पढ़ रहा था। • सुरेश खाना खा रहा था।

(च) **संदिग्ध भूत :** संदिग्ध भूत में इस बात का सन्देह बना रहता है कि कार्य समाप्त हुआ या नहीं। जैसे–• तुमने लिखा होगा। • उसने चुराया होगा।

(छ) **हेतुहेतुमद् भूत :** इस काल में यह पता चलता है कि यद्यपि क्रिया का समापन भूतकाल में होना था परन्तु किसी कारणवश नहीं हो सका। दूसरे शब्दों में हम कह सकते हैं कि इस काल में कार्य के होने की शर्त लगी रहती है अर्थात् एक क्रिया की सिद्धि में दूसरी क्रिया शर्त बनकर प्रयुक्त होती है। जैसे–• यदि तुम पढ़ते तो परीक्षा पास करते। • यदि वर्षा होती तो पैदावार अच्छी होती।

भविष्यत् काल

क्रिया के जिस रूप से यह पता चले कि कार्य आने वाले समय (भविष्य) में होने वाला है, उसे **भविष्यत काल** कहते हैं। जैसे–• वह नौकरी करेगा। • रमेश व्यापार करेगा।

भविष्यत् काल के तीन भेद होते हैं–

(क) **सामान्य भविष्यत् :** इस काल की क्रिया से यह पता चलता है कि कार्य स्वाभाविक रीति से भविष्य में पूरा होगा। जैसे– • मैं लिखूँगा। • वह गाँव जाएगा।

(ख) **संभाव्य भविष्यत् :** इस काल की क्रिया से भविष्यत् काल में कार्य होने की संभावना का बोध होता है। जैसे–• संभव है, वह पत्र लिखे। • संभवतः वह कल आए।

(ग) **हेतुहेतुमद् भविष्यत् :** इस काल की क्रिया से यह प्रकट होता है कि भविष्य में एक क्रिया का होना दूसरी क्रिया पर निर्भर करता है। जैसे–• अध्यापक आएं तो पढ़ाएं। • विद्यार्थी पढ़े तो परीक्षा उत्तीर्ण करे।

अभ्यास प्रश्न

1. 'श्याम दौड़ रहा है'–में कौन-सा काल है?
A. वर्तमान काल B. भूतकाल
C. भविष्यत् काल D. इनमें से कोई नहीं

2. 'बच्चा गया' इस वाक्य में प्रयुक्त काल पहचानिए।
A. पूर्ण भूतकाल B. सामान्य वर्तमान काल
C. सामान्य भूतकाल D. भविष्यत् काल

3. कौन-सा वाक्य आसन्न भूतकाल में है?
A. तू आता तो मैं जाता। B. मोहन आया, सीता गई।
C. वह आया था। D. मैंने आम खाया है।

4. 'हेमंत पत्र लिख रहा है।' काल पहचानिए।
A. अपूर्ण भूतकाल B. भविष्यत् काल
C. वर्तमान काल D. भूतकाल

5. 'मैं लखनऊ जा रहा हूँ।' वाक्य किस काल का है?
A. आसन्न भूतकाल B. सामान्य वर्तमान काल
C. भविष्य काल D. अपूर्ण वर्तमान काल

6. 'मैं आता।' काल पहचानिए।
A. सामान्य भूतकाल B. संदिग्ध भूतकाल
C. हेतुहेतुमद् भूतकाल D. आसन्न भूतकाल

7. 'वह खाना खा रही है।' वाक्य में प्रयुक्त काल पहचानिए।
A. अपूर्ण वर्तमान काल B. आसन्न भूतकाल
C. सामान्य वर्तमान काल D. पूर्ण वर्तमान काल

8. काल कितने होते हैं?
A. तीन B. चार
C. पाँच D. छह

9. 'पिताजी अखबार पढ़ रहे हैं।' इसमें प्रयुक्त काल पहचानिए।
A. भूतकाल B. वर्तमान काल
C. भविष्यत् काल D. पूर्ण भूतकाल

10. 'कुली ने सामान उठाया।' काल पहचानिए।
A. सामान्य भूतकाल B. आसन्न भूतकाल
C. पूर्ण भूतकाल D. अपूर्ण भूतकाल

11. 'राम ने रावण को तीर से मारा।' काल पहचानिए।
A. वर्तमान काल B. भविष्यत् काल
C. भूतकाल D. पूर्ण भूतकाल

12. 'हम कल ताजमहल घूमने जाएंगे।' काल पहचानिए।
A. भूतकाल B. वर्तमान काल
C. भविष्यत् काल D. पूर्ण भूतकाल

13. 'यदि रुपये होते तो मैं कम्प्यूटर खरीद लेती।' इसमें प्रयुक्त काल पहचानिए।
A. सामान्य भूतकाल B. आसन्न भूतकाल
C. संदिग्ध भूतकाल D. हेतुहेतुमद् भूतकाल

14. 'मैं खाना खाऊँगी।' इसमें प्रयुक्त काल पहचानिए।
A. सामान्य भविष्यत् काल B. संभाव्य भविष्यत् काल
C. संदिग्ध भविष्यत् काल D. इनमें से कोई नहीं

15. 'माली घास काटता है।' इसमें प्रयुक्त काल पहचानिए।
A. अपूर्ण वर्तमान काल
B. सामान्य वर्तमान काल
C. संदिग्ध वर्तमान काल
D. पूर्ण वर्तमान काल

उत्तरमाला

1	2	3	4	5	6	7	8	9	10
A	C	D	C	D	C	A	A	B	A
11	**12**	**13**	**14**	**15**					
C	C	D	A	B					

❄ ❄ ❄ ❄ ❄

14 वाक्य रचना/वाक्य विचार

वाक्य

सार्थक शब्दों का ऐसा समूह जो किसी विचार को पूर्ण करे या व्यक्त करे, उसे वाक्य कहते हैं। जैसे–मोहन अच्छा लिखता है।

वाक्य के अंग

1. **उद्देश्यः** वाक्य में जिस व्यक्ति या वस्तु के विषय में कुछ कहा जाता है, उसे उद्देश्य कहते हैं।

   नोटः कर्ता को ही उद्देश्य कहते हैं। **जैसे**–राम ध्यान से पढ़ता है। वाक्य में 'राम' शब्द उद्देश्य है।

2. **विधेयः** उद्देश्य के विषय में जो कुछ कहा जाता है, उसे विधेय कहते हैं।

दूसरे शब्दों में, कर्ता के अलावा जो भी बात वाक्य में कही जाए, उसे विधेय कहते हैं। जैसे–मोहन धीरे-धीरे चलता है। वाक्य में 'धीरे-धीरे चलता है'–विधेय है।

वाक्य के भेद

1. **रचना के आधार पर वाक्य भेद :** रचना के आधार पर वाक्य के तीन भेद होते हैं–

   (i) **सरल या साधारण वाक्यः** जिन वाक्यों में एक उद्देश्य और एक ही विधेय होता है, उन्हें सरल या साधारण वाक्य कहते हैं। जैसे–• मुकेश पढ़ता है। • स्वाती खाना खा रही है।

   उपर्युक्त वाक्यों में कर्ता एक-एक है और क्रिया भी एक-एक है। अतः ये सभी सरल या साधारण वाक्य है।

   (ii) **संयुक्त वाक्य :** जिन वाक्यों में दो या दो से अधिक सरल वाक्य समुच्चयबोधक शब्दों से जुड़े हों, उन्हें संयुक्त वाक्य कहते हैं। जैसे–• वह सुबह गया और शाम को लौट आया। • मोर नाच रहा है परंतु मोरनी चुपचाप बैठी है।

   उपर्युक्त वाक्यों में दो-दो सरल उपवाक्य हैं। इनको 'और', 'परंतु' अर्थात् समुच्चयबोधक से जोड़े हुए हैं, अतः ये संयुक्त वाक्य हैं।

   (iii) **मिश्र या मिश्रित वाक्यः** जिन वाक्यों में एक मुख्य या प्रधान वाक्य हो और अन्य आश्रित उपवाक्य हों, उन्हें मिश्रित वाक्य कहते हैं। इनमें एक मुख्य उद्देश्य के अलावा एक से अधिक समापिका क्रियाएं होती हैं। जैसे–• जो कल घर आया था, वह बाहर खड़ा है। • राधा विद्यालय नहीं जा सकी, क्योंकि वह बीमार है।

   उपर्युक्त पहले वाक्य में 'जो कल घर आया था' और दूसरे वाक्य में 'राधा विद्यालय नहीं जा सकी', प्रधान उपवाक्य है, जो क्रमशः 'वह बाहर खड़ा है' तथा 'क्योंकि वह बीमार है', आश्रित उपवाक्यों से जुड़े हैं। अतः ये मिश्र वाक्य हैं।

2. **अर्थ के आधार पर वाक्य भेद :** अर्थ के आधार पर आठ प्रकार के वाक्य होते हैं–

   (i) **विधिवाचक वाक्यः** जिससे किसी बात के होने का बोध हो, वह विधिवाचक वाक्य कहलाता है। जैसे–• राजेश व्यायाम कर रहा है। • सविता अपना कार्य कर रही है।

   (ii) **निषेधवाचक वाक्यः** जिन वाक्यों से कार्य न होने का बोध हो, वह निषेधात्मक वाक्य कहलाता है। जैसे–• उसने खाना नहीं खाया। • कक्षा में शोर मत मचाओ।

   (iii) **प्रश्नवाचक वाक्यः** वह वाक्य जिसके द्वारा किसी प्रकार के प्रश्न किये जाने का बोध हो, उसे प्रश्नवाचक वाक्य कहते हैं। जैसे–• तुम क्या खा रहे हो? • तुम क्या पढ़ रहे हो?

   (iv) **आज्ञावाचक वाक्यः** जिन वाक्यों से आज्ञा, अनुमति, प्रार्थना आदि का बोध होता है, वह आज्ञावाचक वाक्य कहलाता है। जैसे–• कृपया बैठ जाइए। • सदा सत्य बोलो।

   (v) **विस्मयादिवाचक वाक्यः** जिन वाक्यों के द्वारा विस्मय, हर्ष, शोक, घृणा, प्रशंसा आदि के भाव प्रकट किए जाते हैं, वह विस्मयादिवाचक वाक्य कहलाता है। जैसे–• वाह! कया दृश्य है। • ओह! कितनी ठंडी रात है।

   (vi) **इच्छावाचक वाक्यः** जिस वाक्य से दूसरों के लिए आशीर्वाद, कामना, इच्छा आदि का बोध हो, उसे इच्छावाचक वाक्य कहते हैं। जैसे–• भगवान तुम्हें दीर्घायु प्रदान करें। • नववर्ष मंगलमय हो।

   (vii) **संकेतवाचक वाक्यः** जिन वाक्यों में किसी संकेत या शर्त का बोध हो, उन्हें संकेतवाचक वाक्य कहते हैं। जैसे–• राम का मकान उधर है। • यदि वर्षा होती तो फसल अच्छी होती।

   (viii) **संदेहवाचक वाक्यः** जिन वाक्यों में किसी कार्य के होने के बारे में संदेह या संभावना प्रकट की जाती है, उन्हें संदेहवाचक वाक्य कहते हैं। जैसे–• पता नहीं श्याम आएगा या नहीं (संदेह) • आज पिताजी आ सकते हैं (संभावना)

अभ्यास प्रश्न

1. "अब इस दर्पण में देखकर बताओ कि तुम क्या देखते हो।" यह वाक्य हैः
A. विधिवाचक वाक्य B. सरल वाक्य
C. संयुक्त वाक्य D. मिश्र वाक्य

2. "राम आया, भाई से मिला और तुरंत लौट गया।" यह वाक्य हैः
A. सरल वाक्य B. मिश्र वाक्य
C. संयुक्त वाक्य D. संदेहवाचक वाक्य

3. "उसने परिश्रम तो बहुत किया, किंतु सफलता नहीं मिली।" यह वाक्य हैः
A. मिश्रित वाक्य B. सरल वाक्य
C. संयुक्त वाक्य D. अर्द्ध वाक्य

4. "पानी न बरसता हो धान सूख जाता।" किस प्रकार का वाक्य है?
A. इच्छावाचक वाक्य B. संदेहवाचक वाक्य
C. संकेतवाचक वाक्य D. आज्ञावाचक वाक्य

5. "मैं आज स्कूल नहीं जाऊँगा।" यह किस प्रकार का वाक्य है?
A. निषेधवाचक वाक्य B. संकेतवाचक वाक्य
C. विधिवाचक वाक्य D. प्रश्नवाचक वाक्य

6. "मजदूर मेहनत करता है, किन्तु उसके लाभ से वंचित रहता है।" यह किस प्रकार का वाक्य है?
A. सरल वाक्य B. मिश्र वाक्य
C. संयुक्त वाक्य D. इनमें से कोई नहीं

7. "व्यवहार में वह बिल्कुल वैसा ही है जैसे उसके पिताजी।" यह वाक्य हैः
A. मिश्र वाक्य B. सरल वाक्य
C. संयुक्त वाक्य D. इनमें से कोई नहीं

8. "जब तक वह रेलवे स्टेशन पहुँचा तब तक उसके दादा जा चुके थे।" यह वाक्य किस प्रकार का वाक्य है?
A. सरल वाक्य B. मिश्रित वाक्य
C. संयुक्त वाक्य D. इनमें से कोई नहीं

9. "राम पढ़ता है।" यह वाक्य किस प्रकार का वाक्य है?
A. सरल वाक्य B. संयुक्त वाक्य
C. मिश्रित वाक्य D. इनमें से कोई नहीं

10. "यदि सही दिशा में परिश्रम करोगे तो अवश्य सफल हो जाओगे।" यह वाक्य हैः
A. सरल वाक्य B. मिश्रित वाक्य
C. संयुक्त वाक्य D. इनमें से कोई नहीं

11. "ईश्वर तुम्हें सफलता दें।" यह वाक्य हैः
A. प्रश्नवाचक वाक्य B. विस्मयवाचक वाक्य
C. निषेधवाचक वाक्य D. इच्छावाचक वाक्य

12. "संतोष से बढ़कर सुख नहीं।" यह वाक्य किस प्रकार का वाक्य है?
A. मिश्र वाक्य B. सरल वाक्य
C. संयुक्त वाक्य D. इनमें से कोई नहीं

13. "आज बहुत पानी गिरा।" यह वाक्य हैः
A. सरल वाक्य B. संयुक्त वाक्य
C. मिश्र वाक्य D. उपवाक्य

14. "तुलसीदास ने कहा है कि विनाशकाल में मनुष्य की बुद्धि भ्रष्ट हो जाती है।" यह वाक्य हैः
A. साधारण वाक्य B. संयुक्त वाक्य
C. मिश्र वाक्य D. इनमें से कोई नहीं

15. निम्न में से सरल वाक्य का चयन कीजिएः
A. उसने कहा कि कार्यालय बंद हो गया।
B. सुबह हुई और वह आ गया।
C. राहुल धीरे-धीरे लिखता है।
D. जो बड़े हैं, उन्हें सम्मान दो।

उत्तरमाला

1	2	3	4	5	6	7	8	9	10
D	C	C	C	A	C	A	B	A	B
11	12	13	14	15					
D	B	A	C	C					

❄ ❄ ❄ ❄ ❄

15 वाच्य

क्रिया के जिस रूप से यह ज्ञात हो कि उसके प्रयोग का आधार कर्ता, कर्म या भाव है, उसे वाच्य कहते हैं।

वाच्य तीन प्रकार के होते हैं:

1. कर्तृवाच्य 2. कर्मवाच्य 3. भाववाच्य

1. कर्तृवाच्य

क्रिया के जिस रूप में कर्ता प्रधान हो, उसे कर्तृवाच्य कहते हैं। इसमें लिंग एवं वचन प्रायः कर्ता के अनुसार होते हैं।

जैसे—सौरभ सेब खाता है।

सौरभ	सेब खाता है।
कर्ता (एकवचन, पुल्लिंग)	क्रिया (एकवचन, पुल्लिंग)

लड़के सेब खाते हैं।

लड़के	सेब खाते हैं।
कर्ता (बहुवचन, पुल्लिंग)	क्रिया (बहुवचन, पुल्लिंग)

2. कर्मवाच्य

क्रिया के जिस रूप में कर्म प्रधान हो, उसे कर्मवाच्य कहते हैं या जहाँ क्रिया का संबंध सीधा कर्म से हो तथा क्रिया का लिंग तथा वचन कर्म के अनुसार हो, उसे कर्म वाच्य कहते हैं।

जैसे—

- रीना ने दूध पीया।
- शिखा ने पत्र लिखा।

पहले वाक्य में रीना (कर्ता) स्त्रीलिंग है परन्तु 'पीया' क्रिया का एकवचन, पुल्लिंग रूप 'दूध' (कर्म) के अनुसार आया है।

दूसरे वाक्य में शिखा (कर्ता) स्त्रीलिंग है परन्तु 'लिखा' क्रिया का एकवचन, पुल्लिंग रूप 'पत्र' (कर्म) के अनुसार आया है।

3. भाववाच्य

क्रिया के जिस रूप में न तो कर्ता की प्रधानता हो, न कर्म की, बल्कि क्रिया का भाव ही प्रधान हो, वहाँ भाववाच्य होता है। इसमें मुख्यतः अकर्मक क्रिया का ही प्रयोग होता है।

जैसे—

- सोमेश से टहला भी नहीं जाता।
- राकेश से उठा नहीं जाता।

उपर्युक्त वाक्यों में कर्ता या कर्म प्रधान न होकर भाव मुख्य हैं, अतः इनकी क्रियाएं भाववाच्य का उदाहरण हैं।

अभ्यास प्रश्न

1. इनमें से भाववाच्य वाला वाक्य कौन-सा है?
A. रक्षा दौड़ नहीं सकती।
B. हिमेश से दौड़ा नहीं जाता।
C. रमेश खाना खा सकता है।
D. मालती खाना खाती है।

2. 'स्त्री कपड़ा सीती है।' यह वाक्य .... वाच्य में है।
A. कर्म B. भाव
C. कर्तृ D. इनमें से कोई नहीं

3. 'पुस्तक पढ़ी जाती है।' वाक्य में कौन-सा वाच्य है?
A. कर्तृवाच्य B. कर्मवाच्य
C. भाववाच्य D. क्रिया वाच्य

4. 'मोहन चित्र बनाता है।' इसमें कौन-सा वाच्य है?
A. कर्तृवाच्य B. कर्मवाच्य
C. भाववाच्य D. उपरोक्त सभी

5. 'मजदूरों से पत्थर नहीं तोड़े जा रहे।' इसमें वाच्य है।
A. कर्मवाच्य B. कर्तृवाच्य
C. भाववाच्य D. इनमें से कोई नहीं

6. 'रोगी को दवा दी गई।' यह किस वाच्य का उदाहरण है?
A. कर्तृवाच्य
B. भाववाच्य
C. कर्मवाच्य
D. इनमें से कोई नहीं

7. जिस वाक्य में वाच्य बिंदु 'कर्ता' है, उसे कहते हैं:
A. कर्मवाच्य वाक्य　　B. भाववाच्य वाक्य
C. कर्तृवाच्य वाक्य　　D. इनमें से कोई नहीं

8. 'वह तख्त पर सोता है।' में कौन-सा वाच्य है?
A. कर्मवाच्य　　B. कर्तृवाच्य
C. भाववाच्य　　D. इनमें से कोई नहीं

9. 'अब तो गलती हो गयी।' इसमें कौन-सा वाच्य होगा?
A. कर्तृवाच्य　　B. भाववाच्य
C. कर्मवाच्य　　D. क्रिया विशेषण

10. 'सिपाही ने चोर को पकड़ा।' यह किस वाच्य का उदाहरण है?
A. कर्तृवाच्य　　B. कर्मवाच्य
C. भाववाच्य　　D. इनमें से कोई नहीं

11. 'नेहा से उठा नहीं जाता।' वाक्य में कौन-सा वाच्य है?
A. कर्तृवाच्य　　B. कर्मवाच्य
C. भाववाच्य　　D. इनमें से कोई नहीं

12. 'मीना दौड़ रही है।' वाक्य में कौन-सा वाच्य है?
A. कर्तृवाच्य　　B. कर्मवाच्य
C. भाववाच्य　　D. इनमें से कोई नहीं

13. जिस वाक्य में क्रिया का मुख्य संबंध भाव से हो, उसे कहते हैं?
A. कर्तृवाच्य　　B. भाववाच्य
C. कर्मवाच्य　　D. ये सभी

14. 'मुझसे गाया नहीं जाता।' वाक्य में कौन-सा वाच्य है?
A. कर्तृवाच्य　　B. कर्मवाच्य
C. भाववाच्य　　D. इनमें से कोई नहीं

15. 'मुझसे यह काम नहीं हो सकता।' में कौन-सा वाच्य है?
A. कर्तृवाच्य　　B. कर्मवाच्य
C. भाववाच्य　　D. इनमें से कोई नहीं

16. 'अबीर के द्वारा पत्र लिखा गया।' यह उदाहरण किस वाच्य का है?
A. कर्मवाच्य　　B. कर्तृवाच्य
C. भाववाच्य　　D. इनमें से कोई नहीं

17. 'गीता ने सहेलियों को बुलाया।' में कौन-सा वाच्य है?
A. कर्तृवाच्य　　B. कर्मवाच्य
C. भाववाच्य　　D. इनमें से कोई नहीं

18. 'अध्यापक ने कक्षा में गणित की परीक्षा ली।' वाक्य में कौन-सा वाच्य है?
A. भाववाच्य　　B. कर्मवाच्य
C. कर्तृवाच्य　　D. इनमें से कोई नहीं

19. 'वह लड़ाई में मारा गया।' वाक्य में प्रयुक्त वाच्य है।
A. कर्तृवाच्य　　B. कर्मवाच्य
C. भाववाच्य　　D. इनमें से कोई नहीं

20. 'विमला से दिन में सोया नहीं जाता।' यह वाक्य .... वाच्य में है।
A. कर्म　　B. कर्तृ
C. भाव　　D. कर्तृ और कर्म दोनों

21. निम्नलिखित वाक्यों में से कर्तृवाच्य वाक्य नहीं है?
A. वह पत्र लिखता है।　　B. सीता पुस्तक पढ़ती है।
C. राधा सितार बजाती है।　　D. पुस्तक पढ़ी जाती है।

22. निम्नलिखित में से कौन-सा वाक्य कर्मवाच्य का उदाहरण है?
A. मैं नहीं पढ़ता।　　B. मुझसे पत्र पढ़ा नहीं जाता।
C. उमेश नहाया।　　D. इनमें से कोई नहीं

23. निम्न में से भाववाच्य वाक्य का चयन कीजिए:
A. मेरे द्वारा पुस्तक पढ़ी गई।　　B. यहाँ बैठा नहीं जाता।
C. रेखा कपड़ा धोती है।　　D. कपड़ा सिला जाता है।

24. 'बालिका नृत्य कर रही है।' वाक्य का कर्मवाच्य है:
A. बालिका नृत्य करती है।
B. बालिका नृत्य कर चुकी है।
C. बालिका नृत्य करेगी।
D. बालिका द्वारा नृत्य किया जा रहा है।

25. 'उसने भोजन कर लिया।' वाक्य को कर्मवाच्य में बदलिए।
A. उसके द्वारा भोजन कर लिया गया।
B. क्या उसने भोजन कर लिया।
C. उसके द्वारा भोजन नहीं किया जा सका।
D. उसके द्वारा भोजन लिया गया।

उत्तरमाला

1	2	3	4	5	6	7	8	9	10
B	C	B	A	A	C	C	B	C	A
11	**12**	**13**	**14**	**15**	**16**	**17**	**18**	**19**	**20**
C	A	B	C	B	A	C	C	B	C
21	**22**	**23**	**24**	**25**					
D	B	B	D	A					

❊ ❊ ❊ ❊ ❊

16 मुहावरे एवं लोकोक्तियाँ

मुहावरा

मुहावरे हिन्दी भाषा का एक महत्वपूर्ण हिस्सा हैं, जो वाक्यांशों या वाक्यों के रूप में उपयोग होते हैं और जिनका अर्थ उनके शाब्दिक अर्थ से भिन्न होता है। वे भाषा को अधिक प्रभावशाली, आकर्षक और जीवंत बनाते हैं।

उदाहरणः राम राजा दशरथ की आँखों के तारे थे।

उपर्युक्त वाक्य में 'आँखों के तारे' ऐसा शब्द समूह है जो वाक्य में कुछ विशेष अर्थ प्रकट कर रहा है। इसका सामान्य अर्थ वाक्य में कोई महत्व नहीं रखता।

लोकोक्ति

लोकोक्ति शब्द लोक तथा उक्ति दो शब्दों के मेल से बना है। इसका अर्थ होता है कोई ऐसा पूर्ण या अपूर्ण वाक्य जिसमें कोई अनुभव, सारकथन अथवा कोई कथा छिपी होती है। जैसे–'का बरखा जब कृषि सुखाने' इसका अर्थ है कि यदि कोई काम समय पर नहीं हुआ तो असमय में उसके होने का कोई महत्व नहीं रह जाता।

लोकोक्तियों तथा मुहावरों का महत्व

भावों की अभिव्यक्ति के लिए जो भाषा हम प्रयोग करते हैं, उसमें यदि मुहावरों तथा लोकोक्तियों का मिश्रण हो जाता है तो वह कहीं अधिक प्रभावशाली, रोचक तथा ग्राह्य बन जाती है। इनके प्रयोग से आशय स्पष्ट हो जाता है तथा मन्तव्य को संक्षेप में प्रकट करने के लिए कथन सशक्त बन जाता है। यही कारण है कि प्रायः हर भाषा में लोकोक्तियों तथा मुहावरों का प्रयोग मिलता है।

क्र.सं.	मुहावरा	अर्थ
1.	**अक्ल के घोड़े दौड़ाना**	किसी बात का हल ढूंढना
2.	**आँखें खुलना**	होश आना
3.	**आपाधापी करना**	अपनी चिन्ता करना
4.	**आपे से बाहर होना**	गुस्से में सुध-बुध खो देना
5.	**आँखों में धूल झोंकना**	धोखा देना
6.	**आँखें दिखाना**	डराना
7.	**आँखें चुराना**	नजर बचाना
8.	**आँखों में खून उतर आना**	अधिक क्रोध करना
9.	**आँख मारना**	इशारा करना
10.	**आँखें फेर लेना**	बदल जाना
11.	**आँखें बिछाना**	प्रेम से स्वागत करना
12.	**आँखों के आगे अंधेरा छा जाना**	निराश हो जाना
13.	**आँखें चार होना**	दोनों का एक दूसरे को देखना
14.	**आँखें पथरा जाना**	बाट देखते-देखते थक जाना
15.	**आँखों का तारा**	अत्यन्त प्यारा
16.	**आँख लगना**	नींद आना
17.	**आँच न आने देना**	हानि न होने देना
18.	**आस्तीन का सांप**	कपटी मित्र
19.	**आसमान पर थूकना**	निर्दोष पर दोष लगाना
20.	**आग में घी डालना**	क्रोध को और बढ़ाना
21.	**आंचल पसारना**	किसी के आगे हाथ फैलाना
22.	**आगे पीछे फिरना**	खुशामद करना
23.	**आटे दाल का भाव मालूम करना**	कष्ट का अनुभव होना
24.	**अपने हाथों अपनी कब्र खोदना**	अपना नाश स्वयं करना
25.	**अरमान निकालना**	इच्छा पूरी करना
26.	**आँसू पीकर रह जाना**	मन ही मन दुःखी होना
27.	**आकाश के तारे तोड़ना**	बहुत कठिन काम करना
28.	**आकाश चूमना**	ऊंचा होना
29.	**आंधी के आम**	बहुत सस्ती वस्तु
30.	**आटा गीला होना**	संकट में पड़ना
31.	**आटा के साथ घुन पिसना**	दोषी के साथ निर्दोष पर भी संकट आना

क्र.सं.	मुहावरा	अर्थ
32.	आसमान सिर पर टूट पड़ना	विपत्ति पड़ना
33.	ईंट से ईंट बजाना	किसी को ध्वस्त करना
34.	आधा तीतर आधा बटेर	एक विचार का न होना
35.	ईंद का चांद होना	बहुत दिनों के बाद मिलना
36.	ईंट का जवाब पत्थर से देना	शत्रु का मुकाबला दृढ़ता से करना
37.	उधार खाए बैठना	ताक में रहना
38.	उलटी गंगा बहाना	प्रतिकूल बातें करना
39.	उंगली उठाना	निंदा करना
40.	उंगली पर नचाना	अपनी इच्छानुसार कार्य करवाना
41.	उगल देना	भेद प्रकट कर देना
42.	उठ जाना	मर जाना
43.	उड़ती चिड़िया को पहचानना	किसी की असलियत जान लेना
44.	उधेड़ बुन	सोच विचार
45.	उल्लू बनाना	मूर्ख बनाना
46.	उन्नीस-बीस का अन्तर	थोड़ा-बहुत फर्क
47.	एक आँख से देखना	एक समान समझना
48.	एक और एक ग्यारह	एक और एक में शक्ति
49.	एक लकड़ी से हांकना	सबके साथ एक जैसा व्यवहार
50.	एड़ी चोटी का जोर लगाना	पूरा प्रयत्न करना
51.	इधर कुआँ उधर खाई	दोनों तरफ संकट
52.	ऊँट के मुंह में जीरा	अधिक चाहने वाले को बहुत कम देना
53.	ओखली में सिर देना	जान-बूझकर आपत्ति मोल लेना
54.	होठ तक न हिलाना	आवाज तक न निकालना
55.	कंचन बरसना	बहुत लाभ होना
56.	कठपुतली बनना	दूसरे के इशारों पर चलना
57.	कफन सिर पर बांधना	मरने की परवाह न करना
58.	कमर कसना	तैयार होना
59.	कमर टूटना	सहायक न रहना
60.	कचूमर निकालना	खूब पीटना
61.	कलम तोड़ना	बहुत अच्छा लिखना
62.	कलेजा थाम कर रह जाना	बेसब्री से सहन करना
63.	कलेजा मुंह को आना	अत्यन्त दुःखी होना
64.	कलेजे पर सांप लोटना	ईर्ष्या से जलना

क्र.सं.	मुहावरा	अर्थ
65.	कच्चा चिट्ठा खोलना	रहस्य बताना
66.	कच्ची गोली न खेलना	अनुभवी होना
67.	जले पर नमक छिड़कना	दुःखी को और दुःखी करना
68.	कदम चूमना	बहुत आदर करना
69.	कन्नी काटना	बचकर निकलना
70.	करम फूटना	भाग्य खराब होना
71.	कलई खुलना	पोल खुलना
72.	कलेजा ठण्डा करना	संतुष्ट करना
73.	कसौटी पर कसना	परीक्षा करना
74.	कागजी घोड़े दौड़ाना	केवल बहुत लिखा-पढ़ी करना
75.	कान कतरना	बढ़-चढ़कर काम करना
76.	कान पर जूं न रेंगना	तनिक भी ध्यान न देना
77.	कान भरना	चुगली करना
78.	कान का कच्चा	हरेक की बात को मान लेने वाला
79.	कान खड़े होना	आश्चर्य से सुनने की उत्सुकता
80.	कान खोलना	सावधान करना
81.	कमर सीधी करना	थकान मिटाना
82.	कलेजा छलनी होना	सख्त बातों से दुःख पहुंचना
83.	कान खाना	शोर मचाना
84.	कानाफूसी करना	चुपके-चुपके बात करना
85.	काफूर होना	दूर करना, भाग जाना
86.	काम आना	युद्ध में मारा जाना
87.	काला अक्षर भैंस बराबर	बिल्कुल अनपढ़ होना
88.	काँटे बिछाना	रुकावट पैदा करना
89.	किस खेत की मूली	तुच्छ
90.	काया पलट होना	बहुत परिवर्तन होना
91.	कफन बांधकर चलना	मौत से न घबराना
92.	किताबी कीड़ा	सदा पढ़ने में लगा रहने वाला
93.	कलेजा ठंडा होना	संतोष होना
94.	कुआँ खोदना	हानि पहुंचाने की कोशिश करना
95.	कुछ कसर न उठा रखना	कुछ कसर न छोड़ना
96.	कुछ पल का मेहमान	मृत्यु के अचानक समीप होना
97.	कुत्ते की मौत मरना	बहुत दुःख उठाकर मरना
98.	कोल्हू का बैल	बहुत अधिक मेहनती
99.	काला नाग	अत्यन्त कुटिल
100.	कौड़ी-कौड़ी का मोहताज होना	अत्यन्त दरिद्र होना

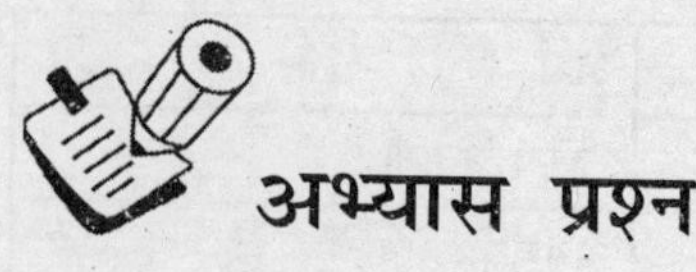

अभ्यास प्रश्न

निर्देश (प्र.सं. 1 से 13 तक): *निम्नलिखित प्रश्नों में चार विकल्प दिए गए हैं। दिए गए मुहावरे का सही अर्थ व्यक्त करने वाले विकल्प का चयन कीजिए।*

1. आँखें बिछाना
A. बहुत इंतजार करना
B. बहुत आदर करना
C. बहुत परेशान करना
D. बहुत नींद आना

2. अक्ल पर पत्थर पड़ना
A. मूर्ख बन जाना
B. बुद्धि समाप्त हो जाना
C. सोचने-विचारने की क्षमता न रहना
D. बड़ी चोट लग जाना

3. आँख में धूल झोंकना
A. कमजोर करना
B. धोखा देना
C. झूठ बोलना
D. भाग जाना

4. आग बबूला होना
A. क्रोधित होना
B. परेशान होना
C. दुःखी होना
D. खुश होना

5. इधर की दुनिया उधर करना
A. जिद पर अड़े रहना
B. असम्भव को सम्भव करना
C. दहेज कम करना
D. धनी व्यक्ति का निर्धन होना

6. ठन-ठन गोपाल
A. बना ठना नवयुवक
B. खोखला
C. धनवान
D. शक्तिशाली

7. अंग-अंग ढीला होना
A. परेशान होना
B. शिथिल गात होना
C. पिटाई होना
D. बीमार होना

8. अँधे के हाथ बटेर लगना
A. किसी वस्तु का अनायास मिलना
B. अपात्र को बहुत बड़ी सफलता मिलना
C. अप्राप्य को प्राप्त करना
D. मुसीबत पर मुसीबत आना

9. घी का लड्डू टेढ़ा भी भला
A. गुणी व्यक्ति की आलोचना
B. उपयोगी वस्तु का रूप-रंग नहीं देखा जाता
C. घी का लड्डू स्वादिष्ट होता है
D. घी का लड्डू महंगा होता है

10. कोढ़ में खाज
A. परवाह नहीं करना
B. बराबर समझना
C. एक दुःख पर दूसरा दुःख होना
D. निपट मूर्ख

11. नाक का बाल होना
A. बहुत कष्ट झेलना
B. किसी का प्रिय व्यक्ति होना
C. अपमान होना
D. अनुभवी होना

12. ओखली में सिर देना
A. सोच-समझकर कार्य करना
B. जानबूझ कर मुसीबत मोल लेना
C. बिना सोचे समझे कार्य करना
D. अनजाने गड्ढे में गिरना

13. घोड़े बेच कर सोना
A. दुःखी होकर सोना
B. अकेले सोना
C. खुश होकर सोना
D. निश्चिंत होकर सोना

14. 'इस विद्यालय में दाखिला मिलना <u>टेढ़ी खीर</u> है।' रेखांकित मुहावरे का सही अर्थ है:
A. असंभव कार्य होना
B. प्रयत्नशील होना
C. कठिन कार्य होना
D. आसान कार्य होना

15. निम्नलिखित में से किस वाक्य में 'कमर टूटना' मुहावरे का सही प्रयोग हुआ है?
A. बढ़ती महँगाई ने गरीब इंसान की कमर तोड़ दी है।
B. पुलिस ने मार-मार कर कैदी की कमर तोड़ दी।
C. सड़क दुर्घटना में एक यात्री की कमर टूट गई।
D. राम ने मेरी कमर ही तोड़ दी।

निर्देश (प्र.सं. 16 से 25 तक): *निम्नलिखित प्रश्नों में चार विकल्प दिए गए हैं। दी गई लोकोक्ति का सही अर्थ व्यक्त करने वाले विकल्प का चयन कीजिए।*

16. अन्धा बाँटे रेवड़ी फिर-फिर अपनों को देय
A. उच्च पद पाकर अपने ही लोगों को लाभान्वित करना
B. न्याय की अवहेलना करके स्वजनों को लाभान्वित करना
C. अन्धा आदमी स्वजनों का ख्याल रखता है
D. स्वार्थी व्यक्ति पक्षपात करता है

17. अकल बड़ी कि भैंस
 A. शारीरिक बल की अपेक्षा बौद्धिक बल श्रेष्ठ होता है
 B. अक्ल अमूर्त और भैंस मूर्त रूप हैं
 C. भैंस शारीरिक दृष्टि से बड़ी होती है
 D. भैंस बुद्धिमान होती है

18. होनहार विरवान के होत चीकने पात
 A. चिकने पत्तों वाला पौधा सुन्दर लगता है
 B. बागवानी का शौक अच्छी बात है
 C. होनहार बालक के लक्षण बचपन में ही प्रकट होने लगते हैं
 D. चिकने पत्तों से पता लगता है कि यह पौधा वृक्ष बन जाएगा

19. सच्चे का बोलबाला, झूठे का मुँह काला
 A. झूठ बोलना पाप है
 B. झूठ बोलने वाला अपमानित होता है
 C. असत्य बोलने वालों पर व्यंग्य
 D. सत्य की सर्वत्र विजय होती है

20. शेर भूखा रह जाए, पर घास नहीं खाता
 A. श्रेष्ठ व्यक्ति संकट में भी मर्यादा नहीं तोड़ता है
 B. शेर केवल मांसाहारी होता है
 C. शेर स्वयं शिकार होता है
 D. स्वावलम्बी व्यक्ति किसी का सहारा नहीं लेता है

21. हथेली पर सरसों नहीं जमती
 A. सरसों के लिए जमीन चाहिए हथेली नहीं
 B. हर काम में मनमानी नहीं चल सकती
 C. काम के लिए समय चाहिए, जब चाहो, तभी काम नहीं हो सकता
 D. सफलता समय पर आती है

22. आग लगे पर पानी कहाँ
 A. कलह में कभी सुख नहीं होता
 B. मुसीबत आने पर सहज नहीं टलती
 C. वक्त पर अभीष्ट वस्तु नहीं मिलती
 D. इनमें से कोई नहीं

23. घर में नहीं दाने, अम्मा चली भुनाने
 A. झूठा आडम्बर
 B. अधिक दिखावा करना
 C. डीगें हाँकना
 D. मुश्किल से गुजारा करना

24. ऊँची दुकान फीका पकवान
 A. ऊँचे पर बनी दुकान के पकवान मीठे नहीं होते
 B. ऊँची दुकान महँगी होती है
 C. दिखावटी वस्तु में गुणवत्ता कम होती है
 D. दिखावट में आकर्षण अधिक रहता है

25. न ऊधो का लेन, न माधो का देन
 A. दूसरे के झंझट में दखल देना
 B. किसी झंझट में न पड़ना
 C. किसी से उधार न लेना
 D. नगद लेन-देन करना

उत्तरमाला

1	2	3	4	5	6	7	8	9	10
B	C	B	A	B	B	B	A	B	C
11	**12**	**13**	**14**	**15**	**16**	**17**	**18**	**19**	**20**
B	B	D	C	A	D	A	C	D	A
21	**22**	**23**	**24**	**25**					
C	C	A	C	B					

❄ ❄ ❄ ❄ ❄

17 समास

समास वह शब्द-रचना है जिसमें अर्थ की दृष्टि से परस्पर स्वतंत्र संबंध रखने वाले दो अथवा दो से अधिक शब्दों के बीच की विभक्ति हटाकर जब उन्हें मिलाकर एक शब्द बनाया जाता है, तो उसे समास कहते हैं अर्थात् समास में शब्दों का परस्पर मेल होने से नवीन सार्थक शब्द की रचना होती है। परस्पर मिले शब्दों के समस्त पद अर्थात् समास किया हुआ या सामासिक शब्द कहते हैं, जैसे—यथाशक्ति, आजन्म, विद्यालय आदि।

कुल मिलाकर हिन्दी में समास के छः भेद माने जाते हैं :

- **अव्ययीभाव समास :** जिस सामासिक शब्द में प्रथम पद प्रधान और पूरा पद अव्यय होता है, उसे अव्ययीभाव समास कहते हैं, जैसे—
  प्रतिदिन – दिन-दिन   आमरण – मरण तक
  निरोग – रोग रहित   यथाशक्ति – शक्ति के अनुसार
- **तत्पुरुष समास :** जिस सामासिक शब्द में दूसरे पद की प्रधानता होती है तथा विभक्ति चिह्न लुप्त हो जाता है, उसे तत्पुरुष समास कहते हैं, जैसे—
  रचनाकार – रचना को करने वाला
  शोकाकुल – शोक से आकुल
  देशभक्ति – देश के लिए भक्ति
- **कर्मधारय समास :** जिस सामासिक शब्द में उत्तर पद प्रधान होता है, उसे कर्मधारय समास कहते हैं। इसमें पूर्व पद विशेषण और उत्तर पद विशेष्य होता है, जैसे—
  पीताम्बर – पीले हैं जो वस्त्र
  नीलकमल – नीला है जो कमल
  दीर्घायु – दीर्घ है जिसकी आयु
  सज्जन – सत् है जो जन
- **द्विगु समास :** जिस सामासिक शब्द में प्रथम पद संख्यावाची और अंतिम पद संज्ञा हो, उसे द्विगु समास कहते हैं, जैसे—
  तिरंगा – तीन रंगों वाला
  सप्तर्षि – सात ऋषियों का समूह
  नवरत्न – नौ रत्नों का समूह
  त्रिदेव – तीन देवताओं का समूह
- **द्वन्द्व समास :** जिस सामासिक शब्द के दोनों पद प्रधान हों, दोनों पद संज्ञाएँ अथवा विशेषण हों, उसे द्वन्द्व समास कहते हैं, जैसे—
  राजा-रंक – राजा और रंक;   अन्न-जल – अन्न और जल;
  पच्चीस – पाँच और बीस
- **बहुव्रीहि समास :** जिस सामासिक पद में कोई भी शब्द प्रधान नहीं होता बल्कि दोनों शब्द मिलकर एक नया अर्थ प्रकट करते हैं, जैसे—
  नीलकण्ठ – नीला है कण्ठ जिसका अर्थात् शिव
  लम्बोदर – लम्बा है उदर जिसका अर्थात् गणेश
  त्रिलोचन – तीन लोचन हैं जिनके अर्थात् शिव

समास विग्रह

समास के उन सभी शब्दों, कारक चिह्नों को पुनः ले आना जिनका लोप कर समास बनाया गया हो 'समास-विग्रह' कहलाता है, जैसे—कमल के समान चरण (चरणकमल)।

समास विग्रह में निम्नलिखित बातों को ध्यान में रखना आवश्यक है :

- समास में विद्यमान शब्दों एवं लुप्त हुए शब्दों को इस प्रकार प्रस्तुत करना कि समास का वास्तविक अर्थ स्पष्ट हो सके।
- समास-विग्रह में यथासम्भव समास के मूल शब्दों का ही प्रयोग करना चाहिए, उनके समानार्थक शब्दों का नहीं, जैसे—'चरणकमल' का विग्रह 'कमल के समान पैर' या 'पंकज के समान चरण' नहीं किया जाना चाहिए।

अभ्यास प्रश्न

निर्देश (प्र.सं. 1 से 20 तक): *निम्नलिखित प्रश्नों में दिए गए शब्दों का सही समास बताने वाले विकल्प का चयन कीजिए।*

1. चन्द्रशेखर
A. तत्पुरुष   B. कर्मधारय
C. बहुव्रीहि   D. द्विगु

2. रात-दिन
A. द्वन्द्व   B. द्विगु
C. कर्मधारय   D. अव्ययी भाव

3. यथाशक्ति
A. द्विगु   B. बहुव्रीहि
C. कर्मधारय   D. अव्ययीभाव

4. हस्तलिखित
A. कर्मधारय B. तत्पुरुष
C. बहुव्रीहि D. द्वन्द्व

5. त्रिनेत्र
A. तत्पुरुष B. बहुव्रीहि
C. द्विगु D. द्वन्द्व

6. आनन्दमग्न
A. द्विगु B. तत्पुरुष
C. बहुव्रीहि D. कर्मधारय

7. आजन्म
A. तत्पुरुष B. द्वन्द्व
C. अव्ययीभाव D. कर्मधारय

8. नीलकमल
A. बहुव्रीहि B. तत्पुरुष
C. कर्मधारय D. द्विगु

9. दशानन
A. द्विगु B. बहुव्रीहि
C. कर्मधारय D. द्वन्द्व

10. प्रतिमान
A. कर्मधारय B. अव्ययीभाव
C. बहुव्रीहि D. तत्पुरुष

11. लोकप्रिय
A. तत्पुरुष B. अव्ययीभाव
C. कर्मधारय D. बहुव्रीहि

12. वीणापाणि
A. बहुव्रीहि B. द्विगु
C. तत्पुरुष D. कर्मधारय

13. नवग्रह
A. द्विगु B. तत्पुरुष
C. द्वन्द्व D. कर्मधारय

14. देशान्तर
A. कर्मधारय B. द्विगु
C. द्वन्द्व D. बहुव्रीहि

15. वनवास
A. द्विगु B. तत्पुरुष
C. अव्ययीभाव D. कर्मधारय

16. नीति-निपुण
A. तत्पुरुष B. बहुव्रीहि C. द्वन्द्व D. द्विगु

17. पंचवटी
A. द्विगु B. बहुव्रीहि C. तत्पुरुष D. कर्मधारय

18. पीताम्बर
A. बहुव्रीहि B. द्वन्द्व C. द्विगु D. कर्मधारय

19. चतुरानन
A. कर्मधारय B. बहुव्रीहि
C. द्वन्द्व D. तत्पुरुष

20. दुअन्नी
A. तत्पुरुष B. बहुव्रीहि C. द्विगु D. द्वन्द्व

21. 'मैं रामचन्द्र जी के चरणकमल की वन्दना करती हूँ।' रेखांकित शब्द किस समास का उदाहरण है?
A. द्विगु B. कर्मधारय
C. द्वन्द्व D. अव्ययीभाव

22. 'गंगातट पर कुछ लोग भजन कर रहे थे।' रेखांकित शब्द में कौन-सा समास है?
A. द्वन्द्व B. कर्मधारय
C. तत्पुरुष D. अव्ययीभाव

23. निम्न में से कौन-सा समास-विग्रह सही नहीं है?
A. पंचानन – पाँच है जिसके आनन (शिव)
B. दाल-रोटी – दाल और रोटी
C. सुलोचना – सुन्दर है लोचन जिसके
D. पुस्तकालय – पुस्तक और आलय

24. इनमें से कौन-सा 'मालगोदाम' शब्द के समास विग्रह का सही रूप है?
A. माल से गोदाम B. माल के लिए गोदाम
C. माल और गोदाम D. माल बनाने के लिए गोदाम

25. 'नीति-निपुण' शब्द का सही समास विग्रह है :
A. नीति से निपुण B. नीति का निपुण
C. नीति में निपुण D. नीति के लिए निपुण

उत्तरमाला

1	2	3	4	5	6	7	8	9	10
C	A	D	B	C	B	C	C	B	B
11	**12**	**13**	**14**	**15**	**16**	**17**	**18**	**19**	**20**
A	A	A	A	B	A	A	D	B	C
21	**22**	**23**	**24**	**25**					
B	C	D	B	C					

❊ ❊ ❊ ❊ ❊

18 अलंकार

काव्य की शोभा बढ़ाने वाले शब्दों को अलंकार कहते हैं। जिस प्रकार नारी के सौन्दर्यवर्द्धन के लिए अनेक आभूषण होते हैं, उसी प्रकार भाषा के सौन्दर्य के उपकरणों को अलंकार कहते हैं।

शब्द और अर्थ के विशेष प्रयोग के कारण काव्य की भाषा में जो लालित्य या सौन्दर्य आ जाता है, उसे अलंकार कहते हैं।

अलंकार के भेद–इनके तीन भेद होते हैं।

1. शब्दालंकार 2. अर्थालंकार 3. उभयालंकार

1. शब्दालंकार

जहाँ वर्णों की पुनरावृत्ति अथवा समान शब्दों के एक से अधिक बार प्रयोग से भाषा में लालित्य उत्पन्न हो, वहाँ शब्दालंकार होता है।

शब्दालंकार के भेद–शब्दालंकार के तीन भेद होते हैं– *(i)* अनुप्रास *(ii)* यमक *(iii)* श्लेष

(i) अनुप्रास अलंकार

अनुप्रास शब्द अनु (बार-बार) और प्रास (चमत्कारित ढंग से रचना) दो शब्दों के मेल से बना है, अर्थात् जहाँ समान वर्णों की चमत्कारित ढंग से पुनरावृत्ति एक या अनेक बार हो भले ही स्वरों में वैषम्य हो, वहाँ अनुप्रास अलंकार होता है।

उदाहरण– 'सम ससुर गुरु सुजन सुहाई।
सुठि सुन्दर सुशील सुखदाई।।'

अनुप्रास अलंकार के भेद–अनुप्रास अलंकार के तीन भेद होते हैं।

(अ) छेकानुप्रास– जहाँ एक या अनेक वर्णों की आवृत्ति केवल दो बार होती है उसे छेकानुप्रास कहते हैं, जैसे–
"राधा के घर बैन सुनि, चीनी चकित सुभाय।
दास दुखी मिशरी मुरी, सुधा रही सकुचाय।"
इसमें च, द, म और स की आवृत्ति भाव दो बार हुई है। अतः यहाँ छेकानुप्रास है।

(ब) वृत्यानुप्रास–जहाँ एक या अनेक वर्णों की आवृत्ति बार-बार हो वहाँ वृत्यानुप्रास होता है, जैसे–
"तरनि-तनूजा तट तमाल तरुवर बहु छाये।"
यहाँ 'त' शब्द की आवृत्ति बार-बार होने से वृत्यानुप्रास हुआ।

(स) लाटानुप्रास–जहाँ शब्दों या वर्णों की आवृत्ति बार-बार हो तथा प्रत्येक स्थान पर अर्थ भी वही रहे पर अन्वय करने पर भिन्नता आ जाय वहाँ लाटानुप्रास होता है, जैसे–
"लाली मेरे लाल की जित देखो तित लाल।"
"लाली देखन मैं चली मैं भी हो गयी लाल।"
यहाँ पर दोनों स्थानों में 'लाल' और 'लाली' शब्द देखने से एक ही प्रतीत होते हैं पर दोनों में अन्वय करने पर भिन्नता आ जाती है।

(ii) यमक अलंकार

जहाँ एक ही शब्द अधिक बार प्रयुक्त हो लेकिन अर्थ हर बार भिन्न हो, वहाँ यमक अलंकार होता है।

उदाहरण– कनक-कनक तें सौगुनी, मादकता अधिकाय।
वा खाये बौराय नर, वा पाये बौराय।।

यहाँ कनक शब्द की दो बार आवृत्ति हुई है जिसमें एक कनक का अर्थ धतूरा, और दूसरे का स्वर्ण है।

(iii) श्लेष अलंकार

जहाँ पर एक शब्द के दो अर्थ होते हैं, श्लेष अलंकार होता है।

उदाहरण– चिर जीवो जोरी जुरै, क्यों न सनेह गम्भीर
को घटि ये वृषभानुजा, 'व हलधर के वीर।।

यहाँ 'वृषभानुजा' और हलधर के दो-दो अर्थ हैं 'वृषभानुजा' शब्द का एक अर्थ है-वृषभानु की पुत्री राधिका और दूसरा अर्थ है–वृषभ की अनुजा अर्थात् बैल की बहन (गाय)। इसी प्रकार 'हलधर' के दो अर्थ हैं–एक हलधर अर्थात् श्री कृष्ण के भाई बलराम और दूसरा हलधर-हल को धारण करने वाला अर्थात् बैल। इन दोनों शब्दों के अर्थों से दोहे के अलग-अलग दो अर्थ निकलते हैं। अतः यह श्लेष अलंकार है।

2. अर्थालंकार

जहाँ शब्द के आन्तरिक अर्थ से भाषा या वाणी का सौन्दर्य बढ़े, वहाँ अर्थालंकार होता है। अर्थालंकार के भेद–अर्थालंकार के 9 भेद होते हैं।

(i) उपमालंकार

जहाँ दो वस्तुओं में अन्तर रहते हुए भी आकृति एवं गुण की समता दिखाई जाय वहाँ उपमालंकार होता है।

उपमा के चार अंग हैं–

(क) उपमेय–जिस वस्तु का वर्णन किया जाता है उसे उपमेय कहते हैं।

(ख) उपमान–जिस वस्तु से समता की जाती है उसे उपमान कहते हैं।

(ग) साधारण धर्म–जिस विशेषता के कारण उपमेय और उपमान की समानता दिखाई जाती है उसे साधारण धर्म कहते हैं।

(घ) **वाचक**–जिस शब्द से उपमेय और उपमान की समता सूचित की जाती है, उसे वाचक कहते हैं।

वाचक शब्द ये हैं–

सो, से, सी, इव, तूल, लौ, सम, सदृश, समान।
ज्यों, जैसे, इयि, सरिस, जिमि, उपमा वाचक जान।।

उपमा का उदाहरण– ''दादुर धुनि चहुँदिशा सुहाई।
वेद पढ़त जनु वटु समुदाई।।''

इसमें 'दादुर' उपमेय, 'वटु' उपमान, 'धुनि' साधारण धर्म और 'जनु' वाचक है।

उपमा के दो भेद होते हैं–

(अ) **पूर्णोपमा**–इसमें उपमा के सभी अंग जैसे– उपमेय, उपमान, साधारण धर्म एवं वाचक उपस्थित होते हैं, अतः यह पूर्णोपमा कहलाती है, यथा–

''सागर-सा गम्भीर हृदय हो,
गिरि-सा ऊँचा हो जिसका मन।''

इसमें सागर तथा गिरि उपमान, मन और हृदय उपमेय, सा वाचक, गम्भीर एवं ऊँचा साधारण धर्म हैं।

(ब) **लुप्तोपमा**–जहाँ उपमा के चारों अंगों में से किसी एक, दो या तीनों का लोप हो वहाँ लुप्तोपमा होती है।

"कल्पना-सी अतिशय कोमल।"

इसमें उपमेय लुप्त है। इसमें कल्पलता उपमान है, 'अतिशय कोमल' साधारण धर्म।

(*ii*) रूपक अलंकार

जहाँ उपमेय पर उपमान का आरोप किया जाय वहाँ रूपक अलंकार होता है अर्थात् उपमेय और उपमान में कोई अन्तर न दिखाई पड़े।

उदाहरण– उदित उदय गिरि मंच पर रघुबर बाल पतंग।
बिकसे सन्त सरोज सब हरषे लोचन भृंग।।

यहाँ 'मंच' में उदय गिरि पर्वत का, 'रघुबर' में मोर के शिशु-सूर्य का, 'सन्त' में सरोज का तथा 'लोचन' में भृंग का अर्थात् भ्रमर का आरोप किया गया है।

रूपक अलंकार के तीन भेद होते हैं–

1. **सम रूपक**–इसमें उपमेय एवं उपमान में समानता दिखाई जाती है। कोई भी एक दूसरे की अपेक्षा कम या अधिक नहीं होता है–तब सम, अभेद या तद्रूप रूपक होता है। जैसे–मुख चंद्र है।

   (अ) **सांग रूपक**–इसमें रूपक के सभी अंग उपस्थित रहकर उपमान का उपमेय पर आरोप प्रकट करते हैं।

   (ब) **निरंग रूपक**–इसमें उपमेय पर उपमान के प्रधान गुण का आरोप होता है।

   (स) **परंपरित रूपक**–इसमें दो रूपक होते हैं अर्थात् रूपक अपने स्पष्टीकरण के लिए अप्रधान रूपक पर आश्रित होता है।

   उदाहरण– "टूक-टूक हवै है मन मुकुट हमारे, हाथ।
   चूकिहू कठोर बैन-पाहन चलाओ ना।
   एक मनमोहन तो हिय बसि के उजारयौं हमें
   हिय में अनेक मनमोहन बसाओ ना।।"

   इनमें मन पर मुकुट का एवं बैन पर पाहन का आरोप किया गया है।

2. **अधिक रूपक**–जहाँ उपमेय में उपमान की तुलना में कुछ अधिकता दिखाई जाती है, तब वहाँ अधिक रूपक होता है। जैसे– मुख निष्कलंक चंद्रमा है।

3. **न्यून रूपक**–जब उपमान की तुलना में उपमेय को न्यून दिखाया जाता है, तब उसे न्यून रूपक कहते हैं। जैसे–मुख घर को प्रकाशित करने वाला चंद्रमा है।

(*iii*) उत्प्रेक्षा अलंकार

जब उपमेय में उपमान से भिन्नता जानते हुए भी उसमें उपमान की संभावना की जाती है, तब उत्प्रेक्षा अलंकार होता है। इस अलंकार के वाचक शब्द मनु, मानो, इव, जनु, जानो, आदि होते हैं।

उदाहरण– "लता-भवन ते प्रगट में तेहि अवसर दोऊ भाई।
निकसे जनु जुग विमल विधु जलद पटल बिलगाई।"

इसमें लता भवन से निकलते हुए दोनों भाई अर्थात् राम एवं लक्ष्मण को बादलों से निकलते हुए दो चन्द्रमा बताया गया है। यहाँ भिन्नता से अभिन्नता दिखाई गई है अतः उत्प्रेक्षा है।

उत्प्रेक्षा अलंकार के तीन भेद होते हैं–

(अ) **वस्तुप्रेक्षा**–जहाँ प्रस्तुत में अप्रस्तुत की सम्भावना प्रकट की जाय उसे वस्तुप्रेक्षा कहते हैं।

उदाहरण– "सखि सोहत गोपाल के, उर गुज्जन की माल।
बाहर लसत मनो पिये, दावानल की ज्वाल।"

(ब) **हेतुत्प्रेक्षा**–जहाँ अहेतु में हेतु की सम्भावना की जाती है। अर्थात् जहाँ वास्तविक कारण को छोड़कर अन्य हेतु को मान लिया जाता है।

(स) **फलोत्प्रेक्षा**–इनमें वास्तविक फल के न होने पर भी उसी को फल मान लिया जाता है।

उदाहरण– "खंजरी नहिं लखि परत कुछ रिन साँची बात।
बाल दृगन सम हीन को करन मनो तप जात।।"

(*iv*) अपहनुति अलंकार

अपहनुति का अर्थ ही होता है 'छिपना', अतः इस अलंकार में उपमेय को छिपाकर उपमान को स्थापित किया जाता है। अर्थात् इसमें सत्य को छिपाकर असत्य को सत्य बना दिया जाता है।

उदाहरण– "उड़न पराग न चित्त उड़ावत।
भ्रमर भ्रमत नहीं जीव भ्रमावत।।"

अपहनुति अलंकार के भेद–इस अलंकार के छः भेद होते हैं : 1. शुद्ध, 2. हेतु, 3. पर्यस्त, 4. भ्रान्त, 5. धेय, 6. केतव

(*v*) सन्देह अलंकार

जहाँ दो वस्तुओं में समता होने के कारण दोनों के एक ही होने का सन्देह हो जाता है, पर निश्चय नहीं हो पाता, सन्देह अलंकार कहते हैं, अर्थात् उपमेय का उपमान के रूप में वर्णन किया जाता है।

उदाहरण– "सारी बीच नारी है कि नारी बीच सारी है,
कि सारी ही की नारी है कि नारी ही कि सारी है।"

इसमें चीर हरण के समय बढ़ती हुई द्रोपदी की साड़ी को देखकर नारी में सारी एवं सारी में नारी का सन्देह होता है। सन्देह और भ्रान्तिमान, अलंकार में यही अन्तर होता है कि सन्देह अलंकार में निश्चय नहीं होता, मात्र संशय ही रहता है परन्तु भ्रान्तिमान अलंकार में निश्चय रहता है।

(*vi*) भ्रान्तिमान अलंकार

जहाँ उपमान एवं उपमेय दोनों को एक साथ देखने पर उपमान का निश्चयात्मक भ्रम हो जाए अर्थात् जहाँ एक वस्तु को देखने पर दूसरी वस्तु का भ्रम हो जाए, वहाँ भ्रान्तिमान अलंकार होता है।

उदाहरण– "पाँव महावर दैन को नाइनि बैठी आय।
फिरि-फिरि जानि महावरी एँड़ी मोड़ती जाय।

इसमें नायिका की लाल एँड़ियों को देखकर नाइन महावर समझ कर रगड़ती जाती है।

एक अन्य उदाहरण–

"नाक का मोती अधर की कांति से
बीज दाड़िम का समझ कर भ्रान्ति से।
देखकर सहसा हुआ शुक मौन है
सोचता है, अन्य शुक यह कौन है?

इसमें नायिका की नुकीली नाक को देखकर तोता नाक में पहने मोती को अनार का दाना समझता है।

(*vii*) दृष्टांत अलंकार

जहाँ दो वाक्यों में बिम्ब-प्रतिबिम्ब का भाव हो अर्थात् जहाँ दो वाक्यों के गुण तो अलग-अलग हों परन्तु प्रथम वाक्य को स्पष्ट करने के लिए दूसरे वाक्य का प्रयोग होता है। उसे दृष्टांत अलंकार कहते हैं।

उदाहरण– "बड़े न छूजै गुननु, विरद बड़ाई पाइ।
कहत धतूरे सौ कनक, गहनों गदयों न जाई"

यहाँ पर गुणों से बना होना एक बात और 'गहने गढ़ना 'दूसरी बात है। फिर भी 'बिना गुणों के बड़ा होना 'तथा धतूरे से गहना गढ़ना दोनों धर्म समान ज्ञात होते हैं और पुनः प्रथम कथन का स्पष्टीकरण द्वितीय से किया गया है। अतः यहाँ दृष्टांत अलंकार है।

(*viii*) व्याजस्तुति अलंकार

इसमें किसी की व्यंग रूप में स्तुति की जाती है, अर्थात् जो इस स्तुति के योग्य नहीं है उसकी भी स्तुति की जाती है मात्र दिखाने के लिए पर वास्तव में यह स्तुति नहीं होती– यह एक प्रकार का व्यंग्य होता है।

उदाहरण–

"ऊधौ भलो कियो तुम आयो,
पर निर्गुण भक्ति की यह गठरी क्यों लायो।"

इसमें ब्रज-गोपियाँ ऊधो को आया देखकर चिढ़ जाती हैं कि ये क्यों चले आये और श्याम को क्यों नहीं लाये। घर पर आये मेहमान का स्पष्ट शब्दों में अनादर नहीं करके व्याज स्तुति द्वारा प्रशंसा करती हैं (वे कहती हैं कि ऊधो अच्छा हुआ कि तुम आ गये लेकिन निर्गुण भक्ति की गठरी क्यों उपहार स्वरूप हमारे लिए लाये हो? हमें यह गठरी नहीं चाहिए।

(*ix*) अर्थान्तरन्यास अलंकार

जहाँ सामान्य कथन का किसी भी विशेष कथन द्वारा समर्थन किया जाता है, वहाँ अर्थान्तरन्यास अलंकार होता है।

उदाहरण–

लोकन के अपवाद को डर करिए दिन-रैन।
रघुपति सीता परिहरी सुनत रजक कर बैन।।

इस उदाहरण में सामान्य कथन तो यह है कि लोक अपवाद से डरना चाहिए और विशेष कथन द्वारा समर्थन किया है कि राम ने भी धोबी की निंदा सुनकर सीता का परित्याग कर दिया था।

3. उभयालंकार

जहाँ शब्द में भी अलंकार हो और अर्थ में भी अलंकार हो वहाँ उभयालंकार की स्थिति होती है। उभयालंकार कोई अलंकार नहीं है। यह एक स्थिति है जिसमें शब्द और अर्थ दोनों में चमत्कार दिखते हैं। उभयालंकार का मतलब ही है– दोनों अलंकार यानी शब्द में भी अलंकार (शब्दालंकार) और अर्थ में भी अलंकार (अर्थालंकार)। वस्तुतः विद्यार्थी शब्दालंकार और अर्थालंकार ही पढ़ते हैं। काव्य शास्त्रवेत्ताओं ने उभयालंकार को अलंकार के भेदों में जोड़ कर तीन भेद कर डाले हैं। वस्तुतः अलंकार के दो ही भेद हैं– शब्दालंकार और अर्थालंकार। उभय (दोनों) + अलंकार = उभयालंकार। श्रेष्ठ कवियों की रचनाओं में उभयालंकार प्राप्त होते हैं।

जैसे–"कजरारी अंखियन में कजरारी न लखाय।"

यहाँ 'कजरारी' शब्द के दोहराव से शब्दालंकार और अर्थ की सुंदरता से अर्थालंकार दोनों मौजूद हैं।

अभ्यास प्रश्न

1. "माला फेरत जुग भया, फिरा न मन का फेर।
कर का मनका डारि दे, मन का मनका फेर।।"
उपर्युक्त दोहे में कौन-सा अलंकार है?
A. रूपक
B. यमक
C. उपमा
D. अनुप्रास

2. "पापी मनुज भी आज मुख से, राम नाम निकालते" इस काव्य पंक्ति में अलंकार है :
A. विभावना B. विरोधाभास
C. दृष्टांत D. अनुमान

3. "तीन बेर खाती थी वे तीन बेर खाती हैं" में प्रयुक्त अलंकार है :
A. यमक B. अनुप्रास
C. श्लेष D. अन्योक्ति

4. ''अम्बर-पनघट में डुबो रही, तारा-घट ऊषा-नागरी'', में कौन-सा अलंकार है?
A. उपमा B. रूपक
C. श्लेष D. अनुप्रास

5. ''काली घटा का घमंड घटा।''
उपर्युक्त पंक्ति में कौन-सा अलंकार है?
A. यमक B. उत्प्रेक्षा
C. उपमा D. रूपक

6. ''सजल नीरद सी कलाकांति थी''
पंक्ति के रेखांकित अंश में अलंकार है :
A. उत्प्रेक्षा B. उपमा
C. रूपक D. यमक

7. ''संतो भाई आई ज्ञान की आंधी रे''—पंक्ति में कौन-सा अलंकार है?
A. रूपक B. अतिश्योक्ति
C. उपमा D. अन्योक्ति

8. ''बीती विभावरी जाग री, अंबर पनघट में डुबो रही,
तारा-घट उषा नागरी।''
इस पंक्ति में कौन-सा अलंकार है?
A. उत्प्रेक्षा B. उपमा
C. रूपक D. यमक

9. ''बिन घनश्याम धाम-धाम ब्रज मण्डल में, ऊधौ नित बसति बहार बरसा की है।'' इस पंक्ति में कौन-सा अलंकार है?
A. रूपक B. यमक
C. उपमा D. श्लेष

10. ''रहिमन पानी राखिए, बिन पानी सब सून।
पानी गए न ऊबरे, मोती मानस चून।।''
उपर्युक्त दोहे में कौन-सा अलंकार है?
A. श्लेष B. उत्प्रेक्षा
C. रूपक D. यमक

11. ''सारी बीच नारी है कि नारी बीच सारी है।
सारी ही की नारी है कि नारी की ही सारी है।।''
यहाँ कौन-सा अलंकार है?
A. अन्योक्ति B. उपमा
C. सन्देह D. विरोधाभास

12. ''देखि सुदामा की दीन दशा, करुणा करिके करुणानिधि रोए।''
इस पंक्ति में कौन-सा अलंकार है?
A. उपमा B. अतिश्योक्ति
C. यमक D. अनुप्रास

13. जहाँ उपमा अलंकार का सौन्दर्य अर्थ में निहित हो, वह कौन-सा अलंकार कहलाता है?
A. शब्दालंकार B. उभयालंकार
C. अर्थालंकार D. इनमें से कोई नहीं

14. जहाँ एक ही वर्ण (अक्षर) की बार-बार आवृत्ति होती है, वहाँ अलंकार होगा :
A. अनुप्रास B. यमक
C. श्लेष D. उपमा

15. जहाँ उपमेय में अनेक उपमानों की शंका होती है, वहाँ कौन-सा अलंकार होता है?
A. यमक B. श्लेष
C. सन्देह D. भ्रांतिमान

16. ''भारत के सम भारत है'' में कौन-सा अलंकार है?
A. रूपक B. यमक
C. उपमा D. अनन्वय

17. ''पूत कपूत तो क्यों धन संचय,
पूत सपूत तो क्यों धन संचय।''
इस पंक्ति में कौन-सा अलंकार है?
A. लाटानुप्रास B. छेकानुप्रास
C. वृत्यानुप्रास D. अन्त्यानुप्रास

18. ''रहिमन पुतरी स्याम, मनहुँ जलज मधुकर लसै।'' इस पंक्ति में कौन-सा अलंकार है?
A. रूपक B. उत्प्रेक्षा
C. यमक D. उपमा

19. ''नर हो, न निराश करो मन को'' में कौन-सा अलंकार है?
A. यमक B. श्लेष
C. अनुप्रास D. उपमा

20. जहाँ उपमेय में उपमान की कल्पना की गई हो, वहाँ निम्नलिखित में से कौन-सा अलंकार होगा?
A. उपमा B. रूपक
C. यमक D. उत्प्रेक्षा

उत्तरमाला

1	2	3	4	5	6	7	8	9	10
B	B	A	B	A	B	A	C	D	A
11	**12**	**13**	**14**	**15**	**16**	**17**	**18**	**19**	**20**
C	B	C	A	C	D	A	B	C	D

❋ ❋ ❋ ❋ ❋

19 रचनाएँ एवं रचयिता

भारतीय हिंदी साहित्य अत्यंत समृद्ध और विविधतापूर्ण है। इसमें कवियों और लेखकों ने अपनी रचनाओं के माध्यम से समाज, संस्कृति, प्रकृति, प्रेम, भक्ति, राष्ट्रभक्ति तथा जीवन के विविध पक्षों को अभिव्यक्त किया है।

काव्य और गद्य साहित्य दोनों ही मानव जीवन के अनुभवों, भावनाओं और विचारों को सुंदर भाषा और शैली में प्रस्तुत करते हैं।

कवियों की रचनाएँ जहाँ भावनात्मक, लयात्मक और कल्पनाशील होती हैं, वहीं लेखकों की रचनाएँ विचारप्रधान, विश्लेषणात्मक तथा सामाजिक यथार्थ को उजागर करने वाली होती हैं।

कवियों और लेखकों की रचनाएँ

क्र.सं.	कवि/लेखक	काल	प्रमुख रचनाएँ
1.	कबीरदास	भक्तिकाल	साखी, सबद, रमैनी
2.	तुलसीदास	भक्तिकाल	रामचरितमानस, विनय पत्रिका, कवितावली
3.	सूरदास	भक्तिकाल	सूरसागर, सूरसारावली
4.	रहीम	भक्तिकाल	रहीम दोहावली
5.	मीराबाई	भक्तिकाल	मीरा पदावली
6.	रसखान	भक्तिकाल	प्रेमवाटिका
7.	भूषण	रीतिकाल	शिवराज भूषण
8.	देव	रीतिकाल	भावविलास
9.	बिहारी	रीतिकाल	बिहारी सतसई
10.	महादेवी वर्मा	छायावाद	यामा, नीरजा, सांध्यगीत
11.	जयशंकर प्रसाद	छायावाद	कामायनी, आंसू, लहर
12.	सूर्यकांत त्रिपाठी 'निराला'	छायावाद	सरोज स्मृति, अनामिका
13.	सुमित्रानंदन पंत	छायावाद	पल्लव, गुंजन
14.	हरिवंश राय बच्चन	आधुनिक	मधुशाला, मधुबाला, मधुकलश
15.	प्रेमचंद	आधुनिक	गोदान, गबन, निर्मला
16.	अज्ञेय	आधुनिक	शेखर : एक जीवनी, नदी के द्वीप
17.	जयशंकर प्रसाद	नाटक	स्कंदगुप्त, चंद्रगुप्त, ध्रुवस्वामिनी
18.	रामधारी सिंह दिनकर	आधुनिक	रश्मिरथी, कुरुक्षेत्र
19.	मैथिलीशरण गुप्त	आधुनिक	भारत-भारती, साकेत
20.	माखनलाल चतुर्वेदी	आधुनिक	पुष्प की अभिलाषा
21.	सुभद्रा कुमारी चौहान	आधुनिक	झाँसी की रानी
22.	नागार्जुन	आधुनिक	युगधारा, बादल को घिरते देखा है
23.	भवानी प्रसाद मिश्र	आधुनिक	गीत फरोश
24.	धर्मवीर भारती	आधुनिक	गुनाहों का देवता
25.	फणीश्वर नाथ रेणु	आधुनिक	मैला आँचल
26.	भीष्म साहनी	आधुनिक	तमस
27.	निर्मल वर्मा	आधुनिक	लाल टीन की छत
28.	मोहन राकेश	आधुनिक	आषाढ़ का एक दिन
29.	राजेंद्र यादव	आधुनिक	सारा आकाश
30.	अमृतलाल नागर	आधुनिक	बूंद और समुद्र
31.	हजारी प्रसाद द्विवेदी	आधुनिक	बाणभट्ट की आत्मकथा
32.	शिवानी	आधुनिक	कृष्णकली

अभ्यास प्रश्न

1. 'कनुप्रिया' के रचनाकार कौन हैं?
A. रांगेय राघव B. भगवतीचरण वर्मा
C. नागार्जुन D. धर्मवीर भारती

2. 'तुलसीदास के रचनाकार हैं :
A. केशवदास B. सूर्यकान्त त्रिपाठी 'निराला'
C. डॉ. रामविलास शर्मा D. महादेवी वर्मा

3. 'अन्या से अनन्या' आत्मकथा किसकी है?
A. प्रभा खेतान B. सुषमा बेदी
C. उषा प्रियंवदा D. मन्नू भंडारी

4. 'वैदेही वनवास' किसकी रचना है?
A. मैथिलीशरण गुप्त
B. अयोध्यासिंह उपाध्याय 'हरिऔध'
C. रामधारी सिंह 'दिनकर'
D. श्रीधर 'पाठक'

5. भारतेन्दु युग में निकलने वाली पत्रिका-युग्म है :
A. कविवचन सुधा–हिंदी प्रदीप
B. सरस्वती–माधुरी
C. कल्पना–ज्ञानोदय
D. नवनीत–कादम्बिनी

6. 'वीरों का कैसा हो वसंत' कविता किसने लिखी है?
A. सुमित्रा कुमारी चौहान B. सुभद्रा कुमारी चौहान
C. माखनलाल चतुर्वेदी D. रामधारी सिंह 'दिनकर'

7. 'कवितावली' के रचनाकार हैं :
A. सूरदास B. जायसी
C. तुलसीदास D. घनानंद

8. 'भूषण' किस काल के कवि हैं?
A. वीरगाथा काल B. भक्तिकाल
C. रीतिकाल D. आदिकाल

9. 'मृगावती' किसकी रचना है?
A. कुतुबन B. उसमान
C. मंझन D. जायसी

10. 'आचरण की सभ्यता' किसका निबंध है?
A. महावीर प्रसाद द्विवेदी B. सरदार पूर्ण सिंह
C. रामचन्द्र शुक्ल D. पद्म सिंह

11. 'आनंद कादम्बिनी' के संपादक कौन थे?
A. बाबू महादेव सेठ B. चन्द्रधर शर्मा 'गुलेरी'
C. बद्रीनाथ चौधरी D. अम्बिका प्रसाद व्यास

12. आदिकाल के लिए 'वीरगाथा काल' नाम किसने प्रस्तावित किया?
A. डॉ. राम कुमार वर्मा B. महापंडित राहुल सांकृत्यायन
C. आचार्य रामचन्द्र शुक्ल D. आचार्य हजारीप्रसाद द्विवेदी

13. लेखक और उसकी रचना का कौन-सा जोड़ा गलत है?
A. स्कन्दगुप्त – लक्ष्मीनारायण मिश्र
B. संस्कृति के चार अध्याय – रामधारी सिंह 'दिनकर'
C. रसज्ञ-रंजन – आचार्य महावीर प्रसाद द्विवेदी
D. अशोक के फूल – आचार्य हजारी प्रसाद द्विवेदी

14. कवि और उनकी रचना का कौन-सा जोड़ा सही नहीं है?
A. परिमल – सूर्यकांत त्रिपाठी 'निराला'
B. शिवराज भूषण – भूषण
C. शब्द रसायन – देव
D. उद्धव शतक – भारतेन्दु हरिश्चंद्र

15. लेखक और उसकी कृति के युग्म में कौन-सा युग्म गलत है?
A. आर्यों का आदि देश – डॉ. सम्पूर्णानंद
B. वोल्गा से गंगा – राहुल सांकृत्यायन
C. सूरज का सातवाँ घोड़ा – धर्मवीर भारती
D. दर्शन दिग्दर्शन – रामचंद्र शुक्ल

16. 'पृथ्वीराज रासो' हिन्दी साहित्य के किस काल में लिखा गया?
A. आदिकाल B. भक्तिकाल
C. रीतिकाल D. आधुनिककाल

17. 'हिमतरंगिनी' किसका काव्य संग्रह है?
A. दिनकर B. रामकुमार वर्मा
C. माखनलाल चतुर्वेदी D. भगवतीचरण वर्मा

18. 'सूरसागर' के रचयिता कौन हैं?
A. विद्यापति B. जयदेव
C. तुलसीदास D. सूरदास

19. 'लोकायतन' महाकाव्य के रचयिता कौन हैं?
A. जयशंकर प्रसाद B. सुमित्रानंदन पंत
C. सूर्यकांत त्रिपाठी 'निराला' D. धूमिल

20. 'आषाढ़ का एक दिन' के रचनाकार कौन हैं?
A. जगदीश चन्द्र माथुर B. मोहन राकेश
C. नरेश मेहता D. धर्मवीर भारती

21. 'बीसलदेव रासो' के रचनाकार कौन हैं?
A. नरपति नाल्ह B. चंदबरदाई
C. धनपाल D. जयानक

22. 'नदी के द्वीप' किसकी रचना है?
A. मैथिलीशरण गुप्त B. सूर्यकांत त्रिपाठी 'निराला'
C. नागार्जुन D. अज्ञेय

23. 'चाँद का मुँह टेढ़ा है' के लेखक हैं :
A. यशपाल B. गजानन माधव मुक्तिबोध
C. अमृतराय D. नागार्जुन

24. डॉ. नगेन्द्र ने किस युग को 'स्थूल के प्रति सूक्ष्म का विद्रोह' कहा है?
A. भारतेन्दु युग B. रीतिकाल
C. छायावाद D. भक्तिकाल

25. 'वरदान' उपन्यास के लेखक कौन हैं?
A. प्रेमचंद B. भीष्म साहनी
C. कमलेश्वर D. यशपाल

26. 'कल्पलता' किसके निबंधों का संग्रह है?
A. कन्हैयालाल मिश्र 'प्रभाकर'
B. हजारी प्रसाद द्विवेदी
C. कुबेरनाथ राय
D. सरदार पूर्ण सिंह

27. 'प्रकृति के सुकुमार कवि' कहे जाते हैं :
A. सूर्यकांत त्रिपाठी 'निराला' B. सुमित्रानंदन पंत
C. जयशंकर प्रसाद D. कबीर

28. 'युगे-युगे क्रांति' के रचनाकार कौन हैं?
A. विष्णु प्रभाकर B. जैनेन्द्र
C. बालकृष्ण भट्ट D. शरद जोशी

29. 'गुड़िया भीतर गुड़िया' के रचनाकार कौन हैं?
A. कृष्णा सोबती B. मैत्रेयी पुष्पा
C. प्रभा खेतान D. उषा प्रियंवदा

30. 'प्रभु जी तुम चंदन हम पानी' पंक्ति किस कवि की है?
A. कबीरदास B. रैदास
C. हरिदास निरंजनी D. दादू दयाल

उत्तरमाला

1	2	3	4	5	6	7	8	9	10
D	B	A	B	A	B	C	C	A	B
11	12	13	14	15	16	17	18	19	20
C	C	A	D	D	A	C	D	B	B
21	22	23	24	25	26	27	28	29	30
A	D	B	C	A	B	B	A	B	B

❄ ❄ ❄ ❄ ❄

SECTION-B

भाषा विकास का शिक्षा शास्त्र

भाषा, भाव, विचार तथा अनुभवों को अभिव्यक्त करने का सर्वोत्तम साधन है। भावों का प्रकाशन व्यक्ति कई प्रकार से करता है, जैसे—अंग संचालन द्वारा, वस्तु अथवा चित्र दिखाकर, विभिन्न क्रियाकलापों के माध्यम से और भाषा व्यवहार द्वारा। परन्तु केवल अंग संचालन और विभिन्न क्रियाओं द्वारा भावों की अभिव्यक्ति में वैसी पूर्णता नहीं होती जैसी ध्वनि संकेतों द्वारा होती है।

भाषा व्यवहार के माध्यम से व्यक्ति अपने भावों तथा विचारों की अभिव्यक्ति दो रूपों में करता है—बोलकर और लिखकर। मौखिक तथा लिखित रूप में विचारों को प्रकट करने के लिए भाषा का सहारा लिया जाता है। भाषा ध्वनि प्रतीकों से निर्मित होती है। अतः भाषा को सार्थक ध्वनि प्रतीकों की व्यवस्था कहा जाता है जिसके द्वारा किसी समाज के लोग आपस में अपने भावों तथा विचारों का आदान-प्रदान बोलकर या लिखकर करते हैं।

भाषा की निम्नलिखित विशेषताएँ होती हैं:

1. भाषा संप्रेषण अर्थात् अभिव्यक्ति और बोधन का सर्वश्रेष्ठ साधन है, जो मूलतः सामाजिक और पारंपरिक होती है।
2. भाषा एक अर्जित सामाजिक निधि है, अर्थात् प्रत्येक व्यक्ति को इसे सीखना होता है और यह समाज में रहकर ही संभव होता है। कोई व्यक्ति इसे जन्म से ही प्राप्त नहीं कर लेता है। वह जिस समाज में रहता है, उस समाज की भाषा वह सीख लेता है। भाषा का यह अर्जन उसी प्रकार होता है जैसे बालक अन्य सामाजिक आचरण या क्रियाकलापों को सीखता है।
3. भाषा विविध रूपी होती है। जहाँ एक ओर भाषा के अनेक रूप उसके बोलने वाले समाज के वर्ग तथा स्तर-भेद के अनुसार होते हैं, वहीं, उस समाज के इतिहास और भूगोल (भौगोलिक वितरण) के अनुसार भी भाषा के अनेक रूप होते हैं। इस प्रकार सामाजिक वर्ग-भेद के अनुसार विभिन्न जातियों या सामाजिक वर्गों की विभिन्न बोलियाँ होती हैं और वर्ग में स्तर-भेद के अनुसार उच्च, मध्य और निम्न वर्ग की बोलियाँ होती हैं। इन सभी भौगोलिक, सामाजिक आदि बोलियों में मानक बोली भी एक होती है, जिसे उच्च स्तर पर शिक्षा, साहित्य, राजकाज, जनसंचार, पत्रकारिता आदि के क्षेत्र में प्रयुक्त किया जाता है।

शिक्षण, अधिगम एवं अधिग्रहण

शिक्षण का उद्देश्य है— छात्रों में समाजोपयोगी व्यावहारिक बदलाव लाना। छात्रों को उनकी सामाजिक मान्यताओं एवं आवश्यकताओं के अनुरूप बदलना। उन्हें एक सामाजिक प्राणी बनाना। ये सभी चीजें तभी संभव हैं जब शिक्षण प्रभावी हो। शिक्षण का प्रभावी होना, शिक्षण के तरीके पर निर्भर है। शिक्षण के प्रभावी होने में शिक्षण के सिद्धान्तों की महत्त्वपूर्ण भूमिका होती है।

शिक्षण के तीन महत्त्वपूर्ण आयाम हैं—शिक्षक, छात्र एवं विषय। इन तीनों में से किसी एक की अनुपस्थिति से शिक्षण नहीं हो सकता है। शिक्षण में शिक्षक का एक अहम रोल है। किसी भी व्यक्ति में शिक्षक के गुण जन्मजात होते हैं। शोध एवं प्रशिक्षण उसके इन गुणों को परिवर्द्धित करते हैं। शोध एवं प्रशिक्षण एक अच्छे शिक्षक को और अच्छा या बेहतर तथा एक बेहतर शिक्षक को सर्वश्रेष्ठ बनाते हैं। शिक्षा किसी भी व्यक्ति के अन्दर मौजूद अच्छाई एवं ज्ञान को जागृत करने का माध्यम माना जा सकता है। शिक्षण के उद्देश्य को पूरा करने के लिए शिक्षक को समय के साथ विकसित हुए विभिन्न तरीकों का प्रयोग करना चाहिये। छात्रों में सोचने, विचार करने एवं विश्लेषण करने की आदत को बढ़ावा देना चाहिये। छात्रों के प्रश्न करने पर उन्हें यथोचित समाधान देना चाहिए और उनके प्रश्न पूछने की आदत को बढ़ावा देना चाहिये। सोचने, विचारने, विश्लेषण करने का प्रारंभ कौतुहल के साथ होता है। अतः शिक्षक को छात्रों में कौतुहल जागृत करना होगा। किसी भी विषय का शिक्षण प्रारंभ करते समय उस विषय में छात्रों की उत्सुकता को जगाना चाहिये तभी छात्र पूर्णरूप से उस विषय में अपनी सहभागिता प्रकट करते हैं। बिना छात्रों की सहभागिता के शिक्षण पूर्ण नहीं हो सकता है।

शिक्षा उन सभी प्रक्रियाओं का सम्मिलित रूप है जिनके द्वारा किसी भी व्यक्ति में सामाजिक व्यवहार विकसित किया जाता है ताकि वह समाज का एक अंग बन सके और समाज के विकास में योगदान दे सके। प्रत्येक व्यक्ति में गुण एवं क्षमताएं जन्म से ही होती हैं यद्यपि इनका पोषण एवं विकास अलग-अलग तरीकों से किया जा सकता है। हर व्यक्ति अपने-आप में अन्य लोगों से अलग होता है। अतः शिक्षण में हर व्यक्ति के लिये अलग-अलग तकनीकों एवं तरीकों को अपनाना पड़ सकता है जबकि कुछ मूल बातें सबके लिये समान होती हैं।

अधिगम एक प्रक्रिया है जो सतत चलती है। यह एक जटिल सामाजिक, सांस्कृतिक एवं आचार सम्बन्धी प्रक्रिया है जिसे एक सामाजिक

एवं सांस्कृतिक प्रकरण हेतु तैयार एवं विकसित किया जाता है। यह सामाजिक व्यवस्था, सांस्कृतिक वातावरण, सामाजिक एवं मानवीय मूल्यों, आचार-विचार अर्थात् तत्कालीन सामाजिक संगठन से सीधे सम्बन्धित है। सामाजिक संगठन में हमेशा बदलाव होता रहता है। अतः शिक्षा की व्यवस्था एवं परिभाषा भी समय स्थान एवं समाज के अनुसार परिवर्तित होती रहती है।

शिक्षा की परिभाषा

अलग-अलग विचारकों ने शिक्षण एवं शिक्षा को अलग-अलग तरह से परिभाषित किया है।

- **मैरिसन :** शिक्षण एक ऐसी अनुशासित सामाजिक प्रक्रिया है जिसमें शिक्षक अपने से कम अनुभवी लोगों के व्यवहार को प्रभावित करता है और उन्हें समाजोपयोगी बनाने में सहायक होता है।
- **ब्रुबेकर :** शिक्षण में छात्र मुख्य भूमिका का निर्वहन करते हैं और शिक्षक सीखने योग्य स्थितियाँ बनाता है।
- **स्मिथ :** शिक्षण एक ऐसा व्यवस्थित प्रक्रम है जिसमें छात्र विभिन्न क्रियाकलापों द्वारा कुछ सीखता है।

इनके अतिरिक्त विभिन्न शिक्षाशास्त्रियों ने शिक्षण एवं शिक्षा को अलग-अलग तरह से परिभाषित किया है। सभी परिभाषाओं का विश्लेषण करने पर हम पाते हैं कि कोई भी परिभाषा शिक्षण को पूर्णतः परिभाषित करने में असमर्थ है। कोई भी परिभाषा तब सम्पूर्ण मानी जाती है जब वह बताये कि :

1. परिभाषित शब्द या शब्द समूह प्रक्रिया है अथवा उत्पादन
2. परिभाषित शब्द या शब्द समूह के संगठनात्मक कारक क्या हैं?
3. परिभाषित शब्द या शब्द समूह के मूल उद्देश्य क्या हैं?
4. और इन तीनों के साथ इसके संगठन जन्य और संरचनात्मक कारकों की भी चर्चा होनी चाहिये।

इन सभी बिन्दुओं को सम्मिलित करते हुए शिक्षण को परिभाषित करना बहुत कठिन है, जो सर्वमान्य हो। फिर भी कार्यकारी रूप में शिक्षण को निम्नलिखित रूप में परिभाषित कर सकते हैं–"शिक्षण एक ऐसा त्रिध्रुवीय प्रक्रम है जिसमें छात्र, शिक्षक एवं समाज तीनों ध्रुवों का निर्माण करते हैं और शिक्षक छात्रों में समाजोपयोगी बदलाव लाता है।" शिक्षण एक आधारभूत संकल्पना नहीं है क्योंकि यह सामाजिक एवं मानवीय कारकों से प्रभावित होता है जो स्वयं में परिवर्तनशील है। शिक्षण में कला एवं विज्ञान दोनों समाहित हैं। यह एक ऐसा पेशेवर कार्य है जिसमें शिक्षक एवं छात्र दोनों शामिल होते हैं, जिसका उद्देश्य छात्रों में समाजोपयोगी बदलाव लाना होता है। शिक्षण का मूल्यांकन शिक्षण की कमियों को दूर करने के लिये और इसमें सुधार के लिये आवश्यक है।

शिक्षण में सम्प्रेषण बहुत महत्त्वपूर्ण होता है। यह एक ऐसी पारस्परिक क्रिया है जिसे किसी प्रयोजन या उद्देश्य के साथ किया जाता है। शिक्षण के कई रूप एवं स्वरूप हो सकते हैं। औपचारिक, अनौपचारिक, दैशिक, अनुदैशिक, रचनात्मक, conditional, indoctrination, remedial इत्यादि। शिक्षण एक व्यापक शब्द है। Condition, प्रशिक्षण, निर्देशन जैसे शब्द शिक्षण के एक भाग को व्यक्त करते हैं। ये शब्द शिक्षण के पर्यायवाची नहीं हैं। शिक्षण का उद्देश्य छात्रों के व्यवहार को समाजोपयोगी बनाना है और ये सभी जैसे प्रशिक्षण इत्यादि उसके आचरण एवं व्यवहार को उपयोगी बनाने में सहायक होते हैं। निर्देशन या Indoctrination ज्ञानार्जन एवं विश्वास निर्माण के कारक हैं। प्रशिक्षण एवं शिक्षण के बीच के अन्तर को हम उनके द्वारा उत्पादित बुद्धिमतापूर्ण व्यवहार में आने वाले अन्तर के रूप में देख सकते हैं। Instruction और Indoctrination, Conditioning और Training की अपेक्षा ऊँचे बौद्धिक स्तर पर कार्य करता है जहाँ हम किसी भी व्यक्ति में विश्वास एवं विचारों का निर्माण करते हैं।

विश्लेषण के आधार पर हम शिक्षण को पूर्ण परिभाषित संभागों में विभाजित कर सकते हैं। शिक्षण एक अन्योन्यक्रिया है अतः यह केवल शिक्षण क्षमता पर ही निर्भर नहीं है। हां, शिक्षण क्षमता, शिक्षण का एक महत्त्वपूर्ण उपबन्ध है। शिक्षक केवल एक क्षमतावान उद्यमी नहीं है बल्कि उसमें उत्कृष्ट स्तर पर कार्य करने की क्षमता, उपयुक्त निर्णय लेने की क्षमता एवं व्यवहार में आवश्यक परिवर्तन लाने के लिये आवश्यक प्रभाव डालने की भी क्षमता होनी चाहिये।

शिक्षण एवं शिक्षण विधियों में समयानुकूल परिवर्तन कर हम इसे और प्रभावी बना सकते हैं। इसके लिये नये शिक्षण सामग्रियों एवं प्रविधियों का भी प्रयोग किया जा सकता है। शिक्षा मनुष्य को समाजोपयोगी बनाने का साधन है। यह सभी उम्र के लोगों में सृजनात्मक क्षमता बढ़ाने में उपयोगी है। मानवीय जीवन के दो पक्ष हैं–जैविक एवं सामाजिक। सामाजिक पक्ष का संरक्षण एवं संप्रेषण शिक्षा के द्वारा किया जाता है। यह एक त्रिकोणीय व्यवस्था है जिसके तीनों मूल बिन्दुओं के रूप में शिक्षक छात्र एवं समाज होते हैं। छात्र एक Dependent Variable है जबकि शिक्षक Independent Variable. सामाजिक वातावरण इन दोनों को सम्बन्धित कर इन्हें दिशा प्रदान करता है। शिक्षण एक सामाजिक आवश्यकता है।

यह व्यक्ति को सामाजिक बनाता है। किसी भी व्यक्ति के सामाजिक स्वीकार्यता एवं समायोजन में सहायक होता है। शिक्षक इस पूरी प्रक्रिया में सबसे महत्त्वपूर्ण भूमिका का निर्वहन करता है। शिक्षा राष्ट्र के विकास में सबसे महत्त्वपूर्ण कारक है। शिक्षक को पाठ्यचर्या के अनुरूप चलना पड़ता है। लेकिन उसका कार्य इससे अधिक होता है। उसे बौद्धिक एवं सामाजिक नेतृत्व देना होता है। शिक्षक, शिक्षा के सम्पूर्ण प्रक्रिया के केन्द्र में होता है।

शिक्षक के कुछ विशेष गुण हैं–

1. अच्छा स्वास्थ्य क्योंकि स्वस्थ तन में ही स्वस्थ मन होता है।
2. कार्य के प्रति उत्सुकता एवं उत्साह
3. अपने ज्ञान का लगातार परिमार्जन एवं परिवर्द्धन
4. धैर्य एवं सहनशीलता

5. प्यार एवं दया की भावना ताकि वह कक्षा में शिक्षा के लायक वातावरण बना सके।
6. समानता की भावना अर्थात् सभी छात्र उसके लिये एक समान हों।
7. पूर्वाग्रह मुक्त होना
8. Well Dressed होना
9. साफ एवं मधुर आवाज
10. आत्मविश्वास एवं मजबूत इच्छाशक्ति
11. ईमानदारी
12. सामाजिक अनुभव
13. कोई गलत आदत नहीं होनी चाहिए।
14. अपने पेशे के प्रति रुचि, Devotion होना चाहिये।
15. अपने विषय का विशेषज्ञ होना चाहिये। अपना ज्ञान बढ़ाने के लिए उसे हमेशा एक विचारक, विश्लेषक एवं Voracious Reader होना चाहिये।
16. शिक्षण के विभिन्न तरीकों का प्रशिक्षण जैसे पाठ की तैयारी, योजना, उसका कक्षा में संप्रेक्षण, प्रयोगशाला व्यवस्था आदि का प्रशिक्षण प्राप्त होना चाहिये।
17. उसे बाल मनोविज्ञान एवं सीखने की प्रक्रिया का प्रायोगिक अनुभव हो।
18. अच्छा शोधकर्त्ता होना चाहिये।
19. छात्रों पर नियंत्रण होना चाहिये ताकि छात्र उसकी बात मानें एवं कक्षा में शान्ति व्यवस्था बनी रहे।
20. शिक्षक को सामाजिक एवं व्यक्तिगत आवश्यकताओं की पूर्ण जानकारी होनी चाहिये जिसके लिये वह शिक्षण कार्य कर रहा होता है। अर्थात् उसे छात्रों की समस्याओं एवं उनके समाधान के तरीकों की जानकारी होनी चाहिये।
21. हर छात्र को कार्य करने के लिए पर्याप्त अवसर प्रदान करे। वह यह न सोचे कि उसे हर प्रश्न का उत्तर ज्ञात है। जब भी उसे किसी प्रश्न का उत्तर ज्ञात न हो तो वह छात्र से समय लेकर यथाशीघ्र एवं यथासंभव उस प्रश्न का उत्तर उपलब्ध कराये। कभी भी छात्रों को गलत सूचना न दे। साथ ही वह छात्रों को प्रश्न पूछने एवं उत्तर खोजने के लिये प्रोत्साहित करे।
22. छात्रों को नये विषयों एवं क्षेत्रों की जानकारी दे एवं उनके विषय में जानने के लिये प्रोत्साहित करे।
23. शिक्षकों को Idealist in Method एवं Pragmatic in Approach होना चाहिये।
24. अगर छात्र कभी भी शिक्षक का ध्यान उसकी किसी गलती की तरफ दिलाता है तो उसे हतोत्साहित न करे।
25. छात्रों में सीखने के प्रति उत्साह जगाए और सीखने की प्रक्रिया के प्रति रुचि जागृत करे।
26. शिक्षक को यह पूर्णतः सुनिश्चित करना होगा कि छात्रों ने पाठ को पूरी तरह समझ लिया है। कमजोर छात्रों पर ज्यादा ध्यान देना चाहिए।
27. शिक्षक को Extra Curricular Activity जैसे नाटक, सैर, खेलकूद इत्यादि को भी आयोजित करना चाहिये। साथ ही छात्रों को इनमें भाग लेने के लिये प्रोत्साहित करना चाहिये।
28. शिक्षक को co-curricular activities जैसे वाद-विवाद प्रतियोगिता, निबन्ध लेखन, क्विज, सेमिनार इत्यादि का भी आयोजन करना चाहिये जो छात्रों की समझ को विकसित करते हैं।
29. शिक्षक को Grading, Marking इत्यादि में कभी भी पक्षपात नहीं करना चाहिये।

शिक्षण के पाँच पायदान

शिक्षण के पाँच महत्त्वपूर्ण पायदान हैं–

1. **तैयारी :** यह शिक्षण का आरंभिक पायदान है। किसी भी विषय को समझने के लिये शिक्षक एवं छात्र दोनों की तैयारी महत्त्वपूर्ण है। सबसे पहले नये पाठ या विषयवस्तु को Introduce करना चाहिये। इसके लिये कई ढंग अपनाये जा सकते हैं। शिक्षक पिछले पाठ से प्रश्न पूछ कर उसे नये पाठ से सम्बन्धित कर सकता है। वह कुछ Relevant Topics की चर्चा भी कर सकता है। किसी कहानी का प्रयोग भी पाठ की प्रस्तुति के लिये किया जा सकता है। लेकिन यह पाठ्य परिचय हमेशा संक्षेप में होना चाहिये और इससे छात्रों में नये पाठ के प्रति अभिरुचि जागृत होनी चाहिए।
2. **प्रस्तुतीकरण :** यहाँ से वास्तविक पाठ प्रारंभ होता है। शिक्षक को यहाँ अपने पाठ से सम्बन्धित लक्ष्य को बताना चाहिये। छात्रों को यह जानकारी होनी चाहिये कि वे क्या सीखने जा रहे हैं। उन्हें नई चीज को सीखने के लिये तैयार होना चाहिए। शिक्षक का विषय के मूल या लक्ष्य को बताना छात्रों को तैयार होने में मदद करता है। तथ्यों को शिक्षक व्यवस्थित करता है। वह छात्रों को प्रस्तुत किये गये तथ्यों को observe, compare and contrast करने के लिए उत्साहित करता है। आवश्यक तथ्यों को Black Board पर लिखा जाता है। प्रस्तुतीकरण में छात्रों की मानसिकता भी महत्त्वपूर्ण भूमिका निभाती है।

   प्रस्तुति में विषय या पाठ से चुने गये क्षेत्र भी महत्त्वपूर्ण होते हैं। शिक्षक के लिये यह आवश्यक नहीं है कि वह पाठ्यक्रम में दिये गये सभी क्षेत्रों को एक साथ ले, वह कुछ भागों को छात्रों की स्वयं शिक्षा के लिये भी छोड़ सकता है। उसे विषय को इस तरह प्रस्तुत करना होता है कि सभी छात्र आसानी से उसे समझ सकें।

3. **तुलना** : यह सीखने-सिखाने की प्रक्रिया का तीसरा पायदान है। इसमें किसी भी विषय के विषय-वस्तु पर दो तरह के विचारों को रखा जाता है एवं छात्र से उन दोनों का विश्लेषण कर उनकी तुलना के लिये कहा जाता है। इससे छात्र की विषय के प्रति जागरूकता एवं समझ दोनों बढ़ती है। फिर उनके द्वारा विश्लेषित तथ्यों की व्याख्या की जाती है।

4. **सामान्यीकरण** : दिये गये तथ्यों के निरीक्षण, तुलनात्मक अध्ययन एवं उन पर विचार के द्वारा अलग-अलग निष्कर्ष निकाले जाते हैं। उन्हें एक निश्चित तरीके से व्यवस्थित कर एक सार्वभौमिक सत्य की स्थापना की जाती है। गणित का कोई भी प्रमेय, विज्ञान का कोई भी नियम या व्याकरण में कोई परिभाषा, पाठ का सामान्यीकरण कहलाता है। इसमें सबसे महत्त्वपूर्ण होता है कि छात्र बताये गये नियमों या सिद्धान्तों को समझ ले।

5. **उपयोग** : यह सीखने-सिखाने की प्रक्रिया का अंतिम पायदान है। इसमें सामान्यीकृत किये गये बिन्दुओं के प्रयोग के विषय में बताया जाता है। उपयोग के बिना ज्ञान अधूरा या अपूर्ण होता है। ज्ञान का कोई महत्त्व नहीं होता अगर उससे आगे कोई अन्य खोज न हो या नई परिस्थितियों में वह अनुपयोगी हो जाये। अतः ज्ञान के आगे अन्य खोजों में प्रयोग एवं नई परिस्थितियों में उसका उपयोग ही सीखने की प्रक्रिया को अर्थपूर्ण, वास्तविक एवं स्थायी बनाता है। छात्रों ने कितना सीखा है इसके लिये हम विभिन्न तरह की प्रश्नावलियों का प्रयोग कर सकते हैं।

भाषा अध्यापन के सिद्धान्त

शिक्षण एक जटिल सामाजिक प्रक्रिया है और शिक्षक इसमें महत्त्वपूर्ण भूमिका का निर्वहन करते हैं। शिक्षण कुछ सिद्धान्तों पर आधारित होता है—

1. विषय का प्रभावी प्रस्तुतीकरण। व्याख्या स्पष्ट होनी चाहिये। छात्रों में कौतुहल एवं जिज्ञासा जागृत करनी चाहिये ताकि वे विषय में रुचि लें।
2. छात्रों की समस्याओं का समाधान करना चाहिये और उन्होंने पाठ को ठीक से समझा है कि नहीं इसके लिये उपयुक्त प्रश्न पूछने चाहिए।
3. विषय वस्तु को तर्क संगत ढंग से Organise एवं Arrange करना चाहिये।
4. शिक्षण लोकतंत्र के सिद्धान्तों पर होना चाहिये अर्थात् इसमें शिक्षक एवं छात्रों के बीच close interaction होना चाहिये ताकि वे अपने संदेह, विचार एवं धारणा को व्यक्त कर सकें।
5. एक Resourceful शिक्षक जिसमें शिक्षण अभिरुचि एवं शिक्षण के प्रति विशुद्ध लगाव हो, अपने छात्रों के प्रति लाभदायक होता है।
6. शिक्षण छात्रों में रुचि एवं कौतुहल जगाने वाला होना चाहिये यह छात्रों को प्रेरित करने वाला होना चाहिये। इसके लिये Innovative Teaching Methods एवं दूसरे तकनीकों का प्रयोग किया जा सकता है।
7. सीखने के लिये मनोवैज्ञानिक एवं भौतिक वातावरण होना चाहिये।
8. संप्रेषण क्षमताएं शिक्षण के लिये निर्णायक होती हैं। इसमें वाचन क्षमता के अतिरिक्त वाचिक मुद्रायें जैसे gesture, expression इत्यादि भी महत्त्वपूर्ण होते हैं।
9. छात्र एवं शिक्षक के बीच सम्बन्ध मधुर होने चाहिये एवं एक विश्वास होना चाहिये।
10. आधुनिक तकनीकों, तरीकों एवं उपकरणों का प्रयोग भी होना चाहिये क्योंकि ये छात्र में सीखने की उत्सुकता पैदा करते हैं।
11. कक्षा में सीखने योग्य वातावरण बनाने के लिए छात्रों की आवश्यकताओं को ध्यान में रखना आवश्यक है।
12. अच्छे व्यवहार एवं प्रदर्शन के लिये ईनाम देने चाहिये एवं दुर्व्यवहार के लिए दंड। सामान्यतः दण्ड देने से बचना चाहिये।

श्रवण की भूमिका

बालक की अधिकांश भावी शिक्षा उसकी श्रवण शक्ति पर ही अवलम्बित होती है। जनधारणा तो यहाँ तक है कि वीर अभिमन्यु ने चक्रव्यूह भंग करने की शिक्षा अपनी माता के गर्भ में उस समय सीख ली थी जब अर्जुन सुभद्रा को व्यूह-भंग करने की विधि सुना रहे थे।

वैदिककालीन और उत्तर वैदिककालीन जितना भी साहित्य था वह सुनकर ही याद किया जाता था। यही कारण है कि वेद को श्रुति भी कहा जाता है। ऋषि-मुनि विभिन्न वैदिक शाखाएँ अपने ज्ञान को वंश परम्परा में सुनकर ही स्मरण रखते थे। यही शाखाएँ तत्कालीन पुस्तकें और उन शाखाओं के बहुसंख्यक शिष्य ही उन पुस्तकों के बोलते पृष्ठ थे।

श्रेष्ठ श्रोता श्रेष्ठ बुद्धि वाला भी होता है। बालक में अच्छे श्रोता के लक्षणों का विकास प्रयत्न पूर्वक करके उसके ज्ञान में असाधारण वृद्धि की जा सकती है।

अच्छा वक्ता होने के लिए अच्छा श्रोता होना आवश्यक है। श्रवण चिंतन-मनन करने एवं अपना मंतव्य स्थिर करने का श्रेष्ठ साधन है। चिंतन-मनन से वाणी में प्रखरता आती है और अभिव्यक्ति में तीक्ष्णता।

श्रवण की शिक्षा के महत्त्व को देखते हुए प्राथमिक, माध्यमिक, उच्चतर-माध्यमिक तथा विश्वविद्यालय के स्तर पर भी इसकी परीक्षा का प्रावधान किया जाता है।

प्राथमिक स्तर पर यह भाषाकला शिक्षण के रूप में, बड़ी कक्षाओं तथा विश्वविद्यालयों में इसे भाषणमाला (Speech Courses) के रूप में तथा उद्योग के क्षेत्र में इसे संपर्क और प्रबंध पाठ्यक्रम के रूप में स्थान दिया जाता है।

मौखिक अभिव्यक्ति (बोलने) की भूमिका

शिक्षा के क्षेत्र में बोलचाल की शिक्षा या मौखिक अभिव्यक्ति का ऐतिहासिक महत्त्व है। वैदिक युग का समग्र ज्ञान मौखिक रूप से ही गुरु-शिष्यों में चलता रहा।

बौद्ध तथा जैन काल में भी शिक्षा का मुख्य माध्यम बोलचाल ही रहा। मिस्र, यूनान तथा इंग्लैंड आदि के शिक्षा शास्त्र के इतिहास के अवलोकन से ज्ञात होता है कि इन देशों में भी मौखिक अभिव्यक्ति का शिक्षा में प्रमुख स्थान था।

ब्रिटिश शासन काल में शिक्षा के क्षेत्र में बोलचाल की शिक्षा का ह्रास हुआ क्योंकि उनको क्लर्कों की आवश्यकता थी, स्वतंत्र रूप से विचार अभिव्यक्त करने वालों की नहीं।

भारत के स्वतंत्र होने के बाद प्रजातांत्रिक प्रणाली में बोलचाल की शिक्षा के महत्त्व को पुनः स्थापित किया गया। कुशल वक्ताओं द्वारा ही प्रजा के हितों की रक्षा संभव है।

भाषा शिक्षण के प्रायः सभी स्तरों पर बोलचाल की शिक्षा का महत्त्व है। आरंभिक कक्षाओं में तो बोलचाल की शिक्षा की और भी अधिक आवश्यकता होती है। आरंभिक कक्षा में बालक सामाजिक, आर्थिक, धार्मिक तथा बौद्धिक दृष्टि से भिन्न-भिन्न परिवारों से आते हैं। वे भिन्न-भिन्न प्रकार की बोलियाँ बोलते हैं। पर उन्हें अध्ययन में एक मानक भाषा की आवश्यकता होती है। स्वभावतः पठन से पहले मौखिक अभिव्यक्ति पर बल देना आवश्यक है।

बोलचाल में पटुता, मधुरता एवं प्रभावोत्पादकता कई रोजगारों के लिए आवश्यक होती है। ऐसे क्षेत्र में उन्नति के लिए स्पष्टता एवं व्यावहारिकता आवश्यक होती है।

भाषा का कार्य एवं महत्त्व : बच्चों के लिए एक साधन के रूप में भाषा

भाषा व्यक्ति, समाज, राष्ट्र तथा अन्तर्राष्ट्रीय विकास के लिए संजीवनी है। इस प्रकाश-स्रोत के अभाव में सर्वत्र अज्ञान और अंधकार है। सद्-असद्, करणीय-अकरणीय, गमनीय-अगमनीय का बोध भाषा ही कराती है।

1. भाषा व्यक्ति और उसके व्यक्तित्व के विकास का महत्त्वपूर्ण आधार है। व्यक्ति अपने अन्तस् को भाषा के माध्यम से अभिव्यक्त करता है। इसी अभिव्यक्ति के साथ उसके अन्दर छिपी अनंत शक्ति अभिव्यक्त होती है। जिसकी अभिव्यक्ति जितनी स्पष्ट होगी उसके व्यक्तित्व का विकास भी उतना प्रभावशाली ढंग से होगा।

   भाषा के माध्यम से ही व्यक्ति बाह्य जगत का ज्ञान प्राप्त करता है। मूक और बधिर व्यक्ति के व्यक्तित्व का पूर्ण विकास इसलिए संभव नहीं हो पाता कि वह भाषा-सी अलौकिक देन से वंचित रह जाता है।

2. भाषा के माध्यम से समाज के दैनिक व्यापार सम्पन्न होते हैं, संस्कृति भी अनुजीवित रहती है। जीव-जगत, आत्मा-परमात्मा, लोक-परलोक, प्रकृति-पुरुष आदि के विषय में निर्धारित धारणाएँ आज भी भाषा के माध्यम से हमारे पास संचित हैं।

   विभिन्न जातियों, धर्मों, क्षेत्रों के लोगों के बीच में एकता का आधार भी भाषा ही है।

3. राष्ट्र के विस्तृत भू-भाग के शासन का संचालन भाषा के माध्यम से होता है। राष्ट्रों के बीच विचार-विनिमय, व्यापार, सांस्कृतिक आदान-प्रदान का साधन भी कोई न कोई भाषा ही होती है। यदि भाषाएँ न होतीं तो विभिन्न राष्ट्रों के महापुरुषों की विचारधारा राष्ट्र विशेष तक सीमित होकर रह जाती।

4. प्रत्येक भाषा में साहित्यिक और कलागत विविधताएँ होती हैं। गद्य तथा पद्य साहित्य के महत्त्वपूर्ण अंग हैं। इसी प्रकार कहानी, निबन्ध, जीवनी, आत्मकथा, संस्मरण, पत्र लेखन, नाटक, उपन्यास आदि साहित्य की कुछ महत्त्वपूर्ण विधाएँ हैं। भाषा शिक्षण के माध्यम से इन विधाओं का परिचय विद्यार्थियों को दिया जाता है।

   इसी प्रकार छन्द और अलंकार भाषा के कलापक्ष को निखारते हैं। ये भाषा में एक नए रक्त का संचार करते हैं। भाषा शिक्षण इन महत्त्वपूर्ण अवयवों की ओर विद्यार्थी का ध्यान आकर्षित करता है। सुनने और पढ़ने के विविध अवसरों से इस पक्ष की सराहना करने तथा बोलने और लिखने के माध्यम से इनका प्रयोग करने के अवसर मिलते हैं।

5. जीविका उपार्जन मानव की आधारभूत आवश्यकताओं में से है। साधारण श्रमिक से लेकर उच्च पदों तक की सफलता के लिए भाषा कौशल की आवश्यकता है। तकनीकी युग में साधारण श्रमिक को देश-विदेश के कितने शब्द दैनिक व्यवहार में लाने पड़ते हैं। भाषा की कुशलता उसे अपने व्यवसाय की आधारभूत शब्दावली को समझने में सहायक होती है। कार्यालयों में काम-काज करने वाले बाबुओं को टाइप, अशुलिपि, टिप्पण आदि में भाषा का कुशल प्रयोग ही सहायक होता है। अध्यापन व्यवसाय में भाषा की निपुणता ही विद्यार्थियों के व्यक्तित्व को प्रभावित करती है। जीवन का कोई भी ऐसा कार्यक्षेत्र नहीं जहाँ भाषा जीविका-उपार्जन में सहायक न होती हो।

विचारों के संप्रेषण के लिए भाषा के अध्ययन में व्याकरण की भूमिका

1. उच्चारण की शुद्धता के लिए व्याकरण का अध्ययन आवश्यक है। अतः अन्य शास्त्र न पढ़ने पर उतनी हानि नहीं होती जितनी व्याकरण न पढ़ने से। उच्चारण भेद के कारण अर्थ का अनर्थ हो जाता है।

2. व्याकरण से भाषा की रचना, शब्दों की व्युत्पत्ति, शब्दों का शुद्ध प्रयोग आदि के विषय में जानकारी प्राप्त होती है।
3. किसी भाषा के पूर्ण ज्ञान के लिए व्याकरण का ज्ञान होना परम आवश्यक है।
4. व्याकरण भाषा के नियमों का पता लगाकर इसके सिद्धांतों को स्थिर करता है।
5. तुलनात्मक विधि से अन्य भाषा सीखने में व्याकरण के अध्यापन से मदद मिलती है।

कक्षा में भाषा अध्यापन की चुनौतियाँ

विविधता वाले क्लास में शिक्षण की चुनौतियाँ

कक्षा में विभिन्न पृष्ठभूमि वाले छात्र होते हैं। इनकी मातृभाषा एवं ज्ञान का स्तर भिन्न-भिन्न होता है। इनके उच्चारण एवं बोलचाल में इनकी मातृभाषा का प्रभाव अधिक होता है। अध्यापन आरंभ करने से पहले अध्यापक को छात्रों के पूर्व ज्ञान का पता होना चाहिए। ऐसा न होने पर छात्र एवं अध्यापक के बीच दूरी बनी रहती है। बच्चों के पूर्व ज्ञान का पता लगने पर पाठ का आरंभ उसी से संबंधित करके होना चाहिए। इससे बच्चों को यह अनुभूति होती है कि जो ज्ञान वे प्राप्त करेंगे उसका संबंध पिछले ज्ञान से है। जहाँ तक संभव हो अध्यापक को मानक भाषा का प्रयोग करना चाहिए।

बच्चों में वैयक्तिक भिन्नता प्रकृति प्रदत्त होती है। कोई बच्चा भावुक होता है तो कोई कम संवेदनशील। किसी का हृदय पक्ष प्रबल होता है तो किसी का बुद्धि पक्ष। ज्ञान की ग्रहणशील शक्ति भी सबमें समान नहीं होती। अध्यापक को सभी की प्रकृति को उदारता से स्वीकार करना चाहिए और सभी को सम्मान देना चाहिए।

क्लास में तीव्र बुद्धि छात्र अक्सर बाजी मार ले जाते हैं। वे शिक्षक का अधिकांश समय अपने लिए अर्जित कर लेते हैं। ऐसे में क्लास में उनका एकाधिकार स्थापित हो जाता है। शिक्षक को चाहिए कि वह क्लास में ऐसा माहौल बनाए जिसमें सभी छात्र निर्भीक होकर प्रश्न पूछ सकें एवं अपनी शंका का निवारण कर सकें।

ऐसे क्लास में अध्यापक को शिक्षण की विभिन्न युक्तियों का प्रयोग करना चाहिए। जैसे– स्लाइड, मानचित्र, ग्राफ, तस्वीर, वीडियो आदि। ये अलग-अलग पृष्ठभूमि के छात्रों को संतोषप्रद निदान प्रस्तुत करते हैं।

भाषागत कठिनाइयाँ एवं दोष

1. **संयुक्त वर्ण का लेखन :** संयुक्त वर्ण देवनागरी लिपि की विशेषता है। इनकी आवश्यकता शुद्ध उच्चारण के लिए अनुभव की गई। नीचे संयुक्त वर्णों की एक सूची दी जा रही है–

क् + क = क्क – पक्का
क् + म = क्म – रुक्मणी
क् + र = क्र – क्रम
क् + ष = क्ष – क्षमा
क् + त = क्त – भक्त
क् + ल = क्ल – क्लेश
क् + श = क्श – नक्शा

2. **इ की मात्रा का प्रयोग :** अर्धव्यंजन के कुछ उदाहरण ऐसे हैं जिनके साथ ह्रस्व "इ" की मात्रा का योग विशेष प्रकार से होता है। "इ" की मात्रा एक नहीं बल्कि दो व्यंजन पीछे चली जाती है। जैसे–

1. पण्डित	4. चिट्ठियाँ
2. मस्जिद	5. पश्चिम
3. अग्नि	

3. **पंचम–अक्षर का प्रयोग :** ङ, ञ, ण, न, म क्रमशः कवर्ग, चवर्ग, टवर्ग, तवर्ग तथा पवर्ग के पंचम अक्षर हैं। जिस समय ये व्यंजन स्वर विहीन होते हैं तो इनको विकल्प से अनुस्वार या वर्ण पर बिन्दी के रूप में लिखा जाता है। लेखन और प्रकाशन सुविधा के लिए विकल्प से अनुस्वार को प्रोत्साहन देना अच्छा है लेकिन भाषा के सीखने वाले को पंचम अक्षर नियम का ज्ञान अवश्य होना चाहिए।

नियम अनुसार प्रत्येक वर्ग के किसी वर्ण से पहले यदि स्वर विहीन पंचम वर्ण आए तो सवर्गी अर्थात् उसी वर्ग का पंचम वर्ण लगेगा अन्य का नहीं। नीचे इस बात को शुद्ध और अशुद्ध शब्दों के उदाहरण देकर स्पष्ट किया गया है–

	शुद्ध	अशुद्ध
अङ्ग/	अङ्ग/अंग	अण्ग
शङ्ख/	शङ्ख/शंख	शञ्ख
पञ्जा/	पंजा	पन्जा
पञ्छी/	पंछी	पन्छी
झण्डा/	झंडा	झन्डा
ठण्डा/	ठंडा	ठन्डा
आनन्द/	आनंद	आन्नद
कम्पन/	कंपन	कम्पन

4. **र के योग संबंधी अशुद्धियाँ :** ट ड न ह आदि ध्वनियों में र का योग वर्ण के नीचे होता है। जैसे–ट्रंक। ड्रामा। द्रष्टा। ह्रास आदि। क, ग, फ, स आदि वर्णों में इसका योग खड़ी पाई के साथ होता है। जैसे–

ग्राम	पात्र
क्रम	फ्राक

5. **र और ऋ में भ्रम :** ऋ की मात्रा प्रायः अक्षर के नीचे लगाई जाती है, जबकि र की मात्रा अक्षर से संयुक्त होती है।

- "ऋ" मात्रा वाले शब्द–

  गृह। पृथक। वृथा। शृंगार। सृष्टि। वृद्धि।

- "र्" युक्त शब्द–

  ह्रास। ग्रह। स्रष्टा। ब्रज।

6. **रेफ (र्) का प्रयोग :** 'र्' से बनने वाले शब्दों के पठन और लेखन दोनों में भूल हो जाती है। र् जिस वर्ण के साथ जोड़ा जाता है उससे पहले बोला जाता है। जैसे–मर्मज्ञ। ऐसे कुछ शब्द नीचे दिए जा रहे हैं।

मूर्ख	मार्ग	दीर्घ
अर्जुन	निर्झर	कर्ण
दर्द	निर्धन	दर्पण, आदि।

यदि किसी शब्द में र् के बाद दो या दो से अधिक अर्ध वर्ण हों तो र् का योग पूर्ण वर्ण पर ही होता है, जैसे–वर्त्स्य। यहाँ र् त् से पूर्व उच्चरित होता है।

7. **कहीं-कहीं अनुस्वार और अनुनासिक में भी भ्रम होता है।** यथा–

शुद्ध	अशुद्ध
चाँद	चांद
दाँत	दांत
हँसना	हंसना

8. **प्रत्यय प्रयोग :** कुछ प्रत्ययों के योग से मूल शब्द में परिवर्तन आ जाता है। उदाहरण के लिए "इक" प्रत्यय के योग में पूर्व स्वर की वृद्धि होती है–

मंगल	मांगलिक
समाज	सामाजिक
इतिहास	ऐतिहासिक
भूगोल	भौगोलिक
एक	ऐकिक
उद्योग	औद्योगिक

9. **वचन परिवर्तन :** एकवचन को बहुवचन बनाते समय अंत की दीर्घ ई तथा ऊ ह्रस्व हो जाते हैं। यथा :–

एकवचन	बहुवचन
नदी	नदियाँ
बिन्दी	बिन्दियाँ
भालू	भालुओं
हिन्दू	हिन्दुओं

10. **लिंग परिवर्तन सम्बन्धी :**

(क) लिंग परिवर्तन के समय "इन" प्रत्यय जुड़ने पर जो स्त्रीलिंग रूप बनाया जाता है उससे अंत की दीर्घ "ई" बहुधा ह्रस्व हो जाती है। जैसे–

धोबी	धोबिन
स्वामी	स्वामिन

(ख) हिन्दी में स्त्रीलिंग के रूप कुछ स्थितियों में स्वतंत्र होते हैं, "ई" प्रत्यय लगा कर नहीं। यथा:–

सम्राट	साम्राज्ञी
कवि	कवयित्री

11. **संधि :** दो शब्दों में संधि करते समय भी उनमें आने वाले परिवर्तन के प्रति सावधान रहने की आवश्यकता होती है। नीचे इसी प्रकार के कुछ उदाहरण दिए गए हैं :–

सत् + गति = सदगति

निर् + अपराध = निरपराध

जन्म + अष्टमी = जन्माष्टमी

महत् + त्व = महत्त्व

निः + रोग = नीरोग

निः + काम = निष्काम

12. **समास :** दो शब्दों का सामासिक रूप बनने पर उनमें परिवर्तन हो जाता है। प्रथम शब्द के अंत की दीर्घ "ई" ह्रस्व "इ" में परिवर्तन हो जाती है। यथा–

मंत्री + मंडल = मंत्रिमंडल

खेती + हर = खेतिहर

13. **विभक्ति चिह्न :** हिंदी में विभक्ति चिह्नों के प्रयोग में एकरूपता नहीं है। कभी ये शब्द के साथ लिखे जाते हैं तो कभी उससे अलग। हिंदी के विभक्ति-चिह्न सभी प्रकार के संज्ञा शब्दों में प्रातिपदिक से पृथक् लिखने चाहिए, जैसे– राम ने, रावण को, सीता से आदि। सर्वनाम शब्दों में ये चिह्न प्रातिपदिक के साथ मिलाकर लिखे जाने चाहिए, जैसे–मैंने, उसको, इसकी, उसपर।

सर्वनामों के साथ यदि दो विभक्ति चिह्न हों तो उनमें से पहला सर्वनाम के साथ एवं दूसरा पृथक लिखा जाना चाहिए, जैसे–

उसके लिए

उसपर से

इसमें से

14. **क्रियापद :** संयुक्त क्रियाओं में सभी अंगभूत क्रियाएँ पृथक्-पृथक् लिखी जानी चाहिए, एक साथ नहीं, जैसे–

खाया करता है।

कर सकता है।

जा सकता है।

चलता रहेगा।

मिला करता था।

हंसा करता था।

बढ़ रहा होगा, आदि।

15. अव्यय : सम्मान सूचक अव्यय जी और श्री के प्रयोग में द्विरूपता मिलती है, कभी तो ये शब्द के साथ मिलाकर लिखे जाते हैं तो कभी शब्द से अलग, जैसे–

गांधीजी – गांधी जी

श्रीराम – श्री राम

ये शब्द अव्यय के साथ मिलाकर ही लिखे जाने चाहिए।

समस्त पदों में प्रति, मात्र, यथा आदि जैसे अव्यय शब्द के साथ ही लिखने चाहिए, जैसे–

प्रतिदिन

मानवमात्र

यथाशक्ति, आदि

न कि इस रूप में –

प्रति-दिन

मानव मात्र

यथा शक्ति।

16. श्रुति मूलक 'य' एवं 'व' का प्रयोग : हिंदी में स्वर ध्वनियों के विकल्प में श्रुति मूलक 'य' एवं 'व' का प्रयोग किया जाता है। ऐसे में स्वर ध्वनियों के प्रयोग को ही जारी रखना चाहिए। जैसे–

शुद्ध	–	**अशुद्ध**
गए	–	गये (य-श्रुति)
नई	–	नयी (य-श्रुति)
हुआ	–	हुवा (व-श्रुति)

पर जिन शब्दों के मूल में 'य' ध्वनि है, उसके स्थान पर स्वर का प्रयोग उचित नहीं है, जैसे–

शुद्ध	–	**अशुद्ध**
अव्ययी भाव	–	अव्यई भाव (स्वर)
दायित्व	–	दाइत्व (स्वर)

17. विदेशी ध्वनियाँ : अंग्रेजी एवं अरबी-फारसी के वे शब्द जो हिंदी के अंग बन चुके हैं और जिन विदेशी ध्वनियों का हिंदी ध्वनियों में रूपांतरण हो चुका है, वे हिंदी रूप में ही स्वीकार किए जा सकते हैं, जैसे–

हिंदी	**अरबी-फारसी**
कलम	क़लम
जिद	ज़िद
किला	क़िला

परंतु जहाँ उसका शुद्ध विदेशी रूप में प्रयोग अभीष्ट हो अथवा उच्चारणगत भेद बताना आवश्यक हो, वहां हिंदी में प्रयुक्त शब्द के नीचे नुक्ते लगाए जा सकते हैं। जैसे–

हिंदी	**अरबी-फारसी**
गजल	ग़जल
फनकार	फ़नकार
जिस्म	ज़िस्म

शारीरिक-मानसिक विकार (Disorder)

विद्यालयों में ऐसे बच्चे भी प्रवेश पाते हैं जो शारीरिक एवं मानसिक रूप से बाधित होते हैं। शारीरिक रूप से बाधित बच्चों में प्रायः तीन प्रकार की असमर्थताएं पाई जाती हैं–दृष्टि संबंधी, श्रवण संबंधी एवं वाक् संबंधी। ऐसे बच्चों को सुनना, बोलना, पढ़ना तथा लिखना सीखने संबंधी विशेष आवश्यकताएँ होती हैं।

बुद्धि की मंदता एवं शारीरिक दोष वर्तनी की अशुद्धियों के कारण बनते हैं। यदि कोई बालक मंदबुद्धि है तो उसे मारपीट कर या डरा-धमका कर हतोत्साहित नहीं करना चाहिए। उसकी मानसिक सीमाओं को देखकर सहानुभूति का व्यवहार करना चाहिए।

बच्चों के शारीरिक दोष का पता चलने पर अभिभावकों की सहायता से उन बच्चों का उपचार कराना चाहिए। पढ़ाई-लिखाई से पहले उत्तम स्वास्थ्य आवश्यक है।

भाषा कौशल

श्रवण (Listening)

भाषायी कौशलों में श्रवण एक महत्त्वपूर्ण कौशल है। शिशु के जन्म से ही इस कौशल के सीखने का क्रम आरंभ हो जाता है।

सुनना एक प्रकृति प्रदत्त शक्ति है। इसका लाभ वही उठा सकते हैं जिनकी श्रवणेन्द्रिय ठीक हो। इसमें विकार होने से श्रवण दोष उत्पन्न हो जाते हैं।

सामान्यतः श्रवण का अर्थ किसी ध्वनि, बातचीत, वाद्य-संगीत आदि के सुनने से लिया जाता है। किन्तु यह सुनने का बहुत सीमित अर्थ है। भाषा शिक्षण के संदर्भ में "श्रवण" का अर्थ सुनकर भाव-अधिगम या भावग्रहण करना है।

श्रवण में किसी कथन को ध्यानपूर्वक सुनने, सुनी हुई बात पर चिन्तन-मनन करने, अपना मंतव्य स्थिर करने और तदनुसार आचरण या व्यवहार करने जैसी जटिल प्रक्रियाएँ सम्मिलित हैं।

श्रवण कौशल के विकास के अवसर

विद्यार्थियों को मोटे तौर पर निम्नलिखित स्थितियों में सार्थक श्रवण के अवसर प्राप्त होते हैं:

(1) कक्षा शिक्षण के दौरान

(2) सहशैक्षिक क्रियाओं के दौरान

(3) कक्षेतर कार्यकलापों के दौरान

(1) कक्षा शिक्षण के दौरान

कक्षा शिक्षण के दौरान विद्यार्थियों को बालगीत, कविता, कहानी आदि के माध्यम से श्रवण कौशल के विकास के अवसर उपलब्ध कराए जाते हैं।

(2) सहशैक्षिक क्रियाओं के दौरान

सहशैक्षिक क्रियाओं द्वारा भी श्रवण शक्ति का विकास कराया जा सकता है। उदाहरण के लिए जिस एकांकी को विद्यार्थियों ने कक्षा में पढ़ा है उसका कक्षाभिनय कराया जा सकता है। इससे विद्यार्थियों को श्रवण लाभ होगा और साथ ही साथ मनोरंजन भी। ऐसे श्रवण बाधित विद्यार्थी जिन्हें कुछ कम या ऊँचा सुनाई देता है, उन्हें इन कार्यक्रमों में विशेषरूप से सम्मिलित कर लाभान्वित किया जा सकता है।

सहशैक्षिक कार्यक्रमों के आयोजन से विद्यार्थी उत्तरोत्तर लाभान्वित हो सकते हैं:

1. समाचार वाचन
2. कविता वाचन प्रतियोगिता
3. कहानी प्रतियोगिता
4. वाद विवाद प्रतियोगिता
5. आशुभाषण प्रतियोगिता

(3) कक्षेतर कार्यकलापों के दौरान

कक्षेतर कार्यकलापों द्वारा भी श्रवण कौशल का विकास कराया जा सकता है, जैसे–

1. **आकाशवाणी कार्यक्रम द्वारा :** अनेक राज्यों में आकाशवाणी से विद्यार्थियों के लिए कार्यक्रमों का प्रसारण होता है। कक्षा के अनुसार इन कार्यक्रमों का लाभ विद्यार्थी उठा सकते हैं। शिक्षण अभ्यास के दौरान अध्यापन को आकाशवाणी के कार्यक्रम के अनुसार आयोजित किया जा सकता है।
2. **दूरदर्शन द्वारा :** दूरदर्शन के कुछ उपयोगी कार्यक्रमों को देखकर सुनने के लिए विद्यार्थियों को प्रोत्साहित किया जाना चाहिए।
3. **वृत्त चल-चित्रों द्वारा :** वृत्त चल-चित्रों को दिखाकर सुनने के अवसर देना भी विद्यार्थियों के लिए लाभदायक हो सकता है।
4. **टेप-रिकार्ड द्वारा :** उपयोगी कार्यक्रमों को टेप-रिकार्डर पर रिकार्ड करके विद्यार्थियों को सुनाना।
5. **साप्ताहिक छात्र सभाओं द्वारा :** विद्यार्थियों को इन सभाओं में सम्मिलित होने को प्रेरित करना चाहिए।

मौखिक अभिव्यक्ति (Speaking)

अपने भावों और विचारों को प्रभावी ढंग से सार्थक शब्दों में बोलकर व्यक्त करने को 'मौखिक अभिव्यक्ति' कहते हैं। इसमें वक्ता तथा श्रोता दोनों का होना आवश्यक होता है। प्राथमिक तथा उच्च प्राथमिक कक्षा में पहुँचते-पहुँचते बालकों में मौखिक अभिव्यक्ति संबंधी योग्यता का उचित विकास होने से उनके व्यवहार में कुछ परिवर्तन आ जाते हैं। मौखिक अभिव्यक्ति को प्रभावी बनाने के लिए निम्नांकित पक्षों पर ध्यान देना आवश्यक होता है–

1. **शुद्ध उच्चारण :** शुद्ध उच्चारण शिक्षित व्यक्ति का लक्षण है। वक्ता के शुद्ध उच्चारण का श्रोता पर गहरा प्रभाव पड़ता है। श-स, न-ण, छ-क्ष, व-ब, त्र, द्य, प्र, आदि ऐसी ध्वनियाँ या व्यंजन गुच्छ हैं जिनका अशुद्ध उच्चारण उपहास का कारण बनता है। उच्चारण के समय एक-एक वर्ण या शब्द स्पष्ट रूप से व्यक्त होना चाहिए।
2. **उचित गति, बलाघात तथा अनुतान :** बोलने की गति तेज, मन्द या सामान्य होती है। यदि वक्ता तेज गति से भावाभिव्यक्ति करता है तो श्रोता को भाव ग्रहण करने में कठिनाई होती है। बहुत धीमे बोलने से भी विचारों का तारतम्य टूट जाता है। अतः भावाभिव्यक्ति की गति सामान्य होनी चाहिए।
   अपने किसी कथ्य को प्रमुखता देने के लिए वक्ता एक वाक्य में किसी अक्षर/शब्द पर बल देता है ताकि श्रोता को भाव विशेष की गंभीरता या विशेषता का पता लग जाए।
3. **उचित हाव-भाव :** श्रोता पर वक्ता के उचित हाव-भाव या अंग संचालन का भी प्रभाव पड़ता है। हाव-भाव या अंग संचालन से अभिप्राय है गर्दन घुमा कर दाएँ और बाएँ बैठे श्रोताओं को निहारना ताकि वे वक्ता से निकटता का संबंध अनुभव कर सकें, मुखाकृति पर भावानुकूल हर्ष, उत्साह, करुणा, क्रोध आदि भाव लाना, हाथ की मुद्राओं द्वारा अपनी बात को प्रभावोत्पादक बनाना। अंग संचालन के समय यह ध्यान रहे कि उसमें किसी प्रकार का बनावटीपन न आए। इसी प्रकार हाव-भाव उचित सीमा तक रहने चाहिए।
4. **निस्संकोच भावाभिव्यक्ति :** आरम्भ से ही बच्चों को बिना झिझके बोलने के लिए प्रोत्साहित करना चाहिए। यदि किसी कारणवश वे अपनी बात प्रकट करने में झिझकते हैं तो उस कारण का पता लगाकर उसे दूर करने का प्रयास करना चाहिए। कक्षा में विद्यार्थियों को समय-समय पर बोलने के लिए प्रेरित करते रहना चाहिए।
5. **विचारों में क्रमबद्धता :** शुद्ध उच्चारण के साथ अपने भावों व विचारों को सुव्यवस्थित तथा क्रमबद्ध रूप में प्रकट करना मौखिक अभिव्यक्ति को प्रभावी बनाता है।

मौखिक अभिव्यक्ति के रूप

मौखिक अभिव्यक्ति के मोटे-तौर पर दो रूप हैं–अनौपचारिक तथा औपचारिक। घर-परिवार, हाट-बाजार, यात्राकाल तथा खेल-कूद आदि स्थानों पर व्यक्तियों के बीच जो बातचीत होती है वह अनौपचारिक वार्ता कहलाती है। अनौपचारिक अभिव्यक्ति की शब्दावली, वाक्य विन्यास तथा विषय बहुत अधिक व्यवस्थित नहीं होते। औपचारिक अभिव्यक्ति

का विषय सीमाबद्ध होता है। विचारों में श्रृंखलाबद्ध व्यवस्था होती है तथा शब्दावली और वाक्य विन्यास में शुद्धता पर ध्यान रखा जाता है।

औपचारिक मौखिक अभिव्यक्ति को दो उप भागों में बांटा जा सकता है—साहित्यिक तथा व्यावहारिक।

साहित्यिक मौखिक अभिव्यक्ति से अभिप्राय है—साहित्यिक विधाओं के रूप में अपने विचारों को श्रोताओं के सामने प्रस्तुत करना, जैसे—कहानी, नाटक, कविता-पाठ, भाषण, वाद-विवाद आदि।

हम समाज में अनेक व्यक्तियों से मिलते हैं, उनका स्वागत करते हैं, उनके प्रति धन्यवाद ज्ञापन करते हैं तथा परिचय अथवा विदाई के समय शिष्टाचार के कुछ शब्दों का प्रयोग करते हैं। यह औपचारिक मौखिक अभिव्यक्ति का व्यावहारिक पक्ष है।

मौखिक अभिव्यक्ति का विकास

अनौपचारिक रूप में बातचीत करने से भी बालक विचारों को प्रकट करना सीखता है। विभिन्न स्थितियों—खेलकूद के मैदान में, रेलवे स्टेशन पर, मेले में, प्रदर्शनी में वह बातचीत में भाग लेता है और अभिव्यक्ति की नई-नई शब्दावली सीखता है।

प्रौद्योगिकी के इस युग में मौखिक अभिव्यक्ति को विकसित करने के लिए ध्वनि यंत्रों की सहायता भी ली जाती है।

बाल सभा के समय माइक्रोफोन पर बुलवाने का अभ्यास करवाना चाहिए। आजकल कहानियों तथा कविताओं को कैसेट रूप में प्रस्तुत करने का प्रचलन हो गया है। सुनी हुई कहानी या कविता को टेपरिकार्डर पर टेप करवाया जा सकता है।

विद्यार्थी आदर्श वाचन भी सुन सकते हैं और अपना वाचन भी। इस प्रकार अपने पठन का आदर्श वाचन से मिलान कर अपनी कमियों का पता लगा सकते हैं और अपने वाचन में स्वयं सुधार कर सकते हैं।

पठन (Reading)

पठन भाषा के चार कौशलों (सुनना, बोलना, पढ़ना, लिखना) में से एक कौशल है किन्तु पठन-योग्यता पर ही बहुत कुछ अन्य कौशलों (सुनकर समझना, बोलना, लिखना) का उत्तरोत्तर विकास संभव है। हम जितना ही अधिक पढ़ते हैं उतना ही अधिक समझने की शक्ति बढ़ती है। परिणामतः उतना ही अच्छा बोल और लिख सकते हैं।

पठन भाषा-ज्ञान का ही नहीं, अपितु समस्त विषयों के ज्ञानार्जन का मुख्य साधन है। इस कारण उसका अर्थ व्यापक हो गया है और वह शिक्षा का पर्याप्य बन गया है।

पठन के प्रकार

पठन के दो प्रकार हैं—सस्वर और मौन। सस्वर पठन में शब्दों का उच्चारण, वाक्यों का सार्थक शब्द समूहों में विभाजन, अनुतान, विराम चिह्न, प्रवाह आदि महत्त्वपूर्ण हैं क्योंकि वह मौखिक अभिव्यक्ति के बहुत निकट है। मौन पठन में स्वरहीनता, पठन गति, तथा अर्थग्रहण पर विशेष ध्यान दिया जाता है।

सस्वर

सस्वर पठन एक कौशल है। सस्वर पठन दूसरों के लिए किया जाता है, अतएव यह औपचारिक है। इसके अंतर्गत निम्न बातों पर ध्यान दिया जाता है—

- शब्दों का शुद्ध उच्चारण
- शुद्ध बलाघात
- अनुतान, वाक्यों का सार्थक पदबंधों में विभाजन
- विराम चिह्नों का प्रयोग
- सामग्री की प्रकृति के अनुकूल भावपूर्ण वाचन, आदि।

मौन पठन

मौन पठन में अर्थग्रहण पर बल होता है। इसीलिए यह ज्ञानार्जन का मुख्य आधार है।

मौन पठन विभिन्न संदर्भों में अपने लिए ही किया जाता है। अतएव यह अनौपचारिक है। इसके अन्तर्गत सभी प्रकार की शैक्षिक, कार्यालयी, व्यावसायिक, अनौपचारिक सामग्री का पठन सम्मिलित है। मौन पठन में पठन की गति तीव्र होती है।

लेखन (Writing)

लेखन एक कला है जो दो चरणों में विकसित होती है। पहला चरण भाषा की ध्वनियों को लिपिबद्ध करके उनको शुद्ध, सुपाठ्य एवं सुंदर रूप में प्रस्तुत करने की कुशलता से संबंधित है तो दूसरे चरण में लिपि-प्रतीकों के माध्यम से अपने भावों/विचारों की सुस्पष्ट, अर्थपूर्ण एवं प्रभावी अभिव्यक्ति की योग्यता सन्निहित है।

लेखन के प्रकार

सामान्यतया यह अभ्यास तीन प्रकार का होता है : सुलेख, अनुलेख और श्रुतलेख।

1. **सुलेख :** सुन्दर लेख को सुलेख कहते हैं। यह लेखन का प्रथम और आवश्यक गुण है। सुलेख लिखते समय वर्ण के विभिन्न अवयवों की बनावट, उनकी स्पष्टता तथा सुडौलता, वर्णों में स्वर-मात्राओं का उचित योग, वर्ण से वर्ण और शब्द से शब्द के बीच की उचित दूरी, सीधी शिरारेखा आदि बिन्दुओं पर भी विशेष ध्यान दिया जाता है।
2. **अनुलेख :** अनुलेख से अभिप्राय है पुस्तक की सामग्री को ज्यों का त्यों देखकर लेख लिखना। अनुलेख का मुख्य उद्देश्य है—शुद्ध वर्तनी सहित लेख का अभ्यास कराना।
3. **श्रुतलेख :** सुनकर लिखे गए लेख को श्रुतलेख कहते हैं। इसका उद्देश्य वक्ता द्वारा उच्चरित ध्वनियों को कान लगाकर सुनना तथा तदनुरूप उचित गति स्पष्टता एवं शुद्धता से लिखने का अभ्यास करना है।

   श्रुतलेख सूक्ष्म ध्वनि भेद वाले वर्णों तथा ड-ढ, ढ-ढ़, ड-ड़ आदि का लेखन अथवा ह्रस्व-दीर्घ मात्रा के श्रवण अभ्यास के लिए देना अधिक उपयुक्त रहता है।

भाषा बोध एवं प्रवीणता का मूल्यांकन

मूल्यांकन विद्यार्थी के ज्ञानात्मक, भावात्मक तथा मनोप्रेरित (साइकोजेनिक) क्षेत्र को परखने के लिए निरन्तर चलती रहने वाली वह प्रक्रिया है जिसमें मानक तथा अमानक परीक्षा-साधनों का प्रयोग करते हुए निदानात्मक तथा उपचारात्मक पद्धति अपनाकर विद्यार्थी के गुण-दोषों का वर्णन किया जाता है। इस पद्धति के अनुसार विद्यार्थी के भावी चलन के बारें में भविष्यवाणी की जा सकती है।

मूल्यांकन का क्षेत्र परीक्षा से विस्तृत है। परीक्षा या मापन केवल यह बता सकता है कि किसी विशेष समय में परीक्षार्थी की बौद्धिक क्षमता की स्थिति क्या है। मूल्यांकन में परीक्षार्थी की स्थिति विशेष के अतिरिक्त उस स्थिति का कारण और उसके सुधारने के उपायों पर भी विचार किया जाता है।

मूल्यांकन उद्देश्य आधारित होता है। मूल्यांकन के लिए ऐसी विधियों का प्रयोग किया जाता है जिसका हर बिन्दु किसी न किसी उद्देश्य की जाँच करता है। भाषा के मूल्यांकन के लिए भी इस प्रकार की विधियों का प्रयोग किया जा सकता है।

मूल्यांकन उद्देश्य प्रेरित होता है। भाषा के विभिन्न कौशलों— सुनना-बोलना, लिखना-पढ़ना—के मूल्यांकन के समय भी इन बातों का ध्यान रखना चाहिए।

सुनने की योग्यता का मूल्यांकन

सुनने की योग्यता के मूल्यांकन के लिए निम्नलिखित श्रुतसामग्री का प्रयोग किया जा सकता है:—

1. सस्वर वाचन
2. वार्तालाप
3. वाद-विवाद
4. कविता
5. कहानी
6. आकाशवाणी तथा दूरदर्शन से प्रसारित कार्यक्रम
7. टेप पर रिकार्ड की गई सामग्री

सुनने की योग्यता के मूल्यांकन के समय बालक में हुए निम्नलिखित परिवर्तनों की ओर ध्यान देना चाहिए—

1. वह सुनने के शिष्टाचार का कितना पालन करता है?
2. वह कितनी तन्मयता से सुनता है?
3. वह कितने मनोयोगपूर्वक सुनता है?
4. क्या वह बलाघात व अनुतान के उतार-चढ़ाव के अनुसार अर्थ ग्रहण कर पाता है?
5. वह श्रुत सामग्री के विषय, महत्त्वपूर्ण विचारों, भावों तथा तथ्यों को कितना समझता है?
6. वह श्रुत सामग्री के केन्द्रीय भावों को कितना ग्रहण कर पाता है?
7. वह भाषा एवं शैली की दृष्टि से साहित्यिक अंशों की व्यापक तुलना कर पाता है या नहीं।
8. वह श्रुत सामग्री के सुन्दर स्थलों को पहचान कर पाता है या नहीं।

सुनकर अर्थ ग्रहण करने की योग्यता का मूल्यांकन हमारे विद्यालयों में नहीं के समान है। यही कारण है कि बालसभा, विद्यालय के उत्सव, पास-पड़ोस के उत्सव, राजनीतिक भाषणों आदि का श्रोताओं पर वांछित प्रभाव नहीं पड़ पा रहा है। विद्यालयों का दायित्व है कि वे भाषा के इन महत्त्वपूर्ण गुणों की ओर विद्यार्थियों का ध्यान आकृष्ट कराएँ।

मौखिक अभिव्यक्ति की योग्यता का मूल्यांकन

मौखिक अभिव्यक्ति का मूल्यांकन करते समय विद्यार्थी के निम्नलिखित गुणों का मूल्यांकन होना चाहिए:—

1. सुश्रव्य वाणी में बोलना।
2. शुद्ध उच्चारण, उचित बलाघात और अनुतान के उतार चढ़ाव के अनुसार बोलना।
3. उचित विराम या उचित प्रवाह के साथ बोलना।
4. व्याकरण सम्मत भाषा का प्रयोग करना।
5. क्रमबद्धता, सुसम्बद्धता बनाए रखना।
6. प्रसंगानुकूल उचित शब्दों, मुहावरों और सूक्तियों का प्रयोग करना।
7. भावानुकूलन ढंग से विचारों को प्रकट करना।
8. विचारों को अपनी भाषा में व्यक्त करना।
9. विषय की एकता बनाए रखना।
10. प्रसंगानुसार उचित गति के साथ बोलना।

मौखिक अभिव्यक्ति का मूल्यांकन प्राथमिक कक्षा से उच्च कक्षाओं तक निरन्तर चलता रहना चाहिए। इससे विद्यार्थियों को साक्षात्कार के समय सफलता प्राप्त करने में सहायता मिलेगी।

पढ़कर अर्थग्रहण करने की योग्यता का मूल्यांकन

आज विद्यालयों में पढ़कर अर्थ ग्रहण करने की शक्ति के मूल्यांकन पर ही अधिक बल दिया जाता है। हमारी परीक्षा प्रणाली इसके लिए अनेक अवसर प्रदान करती है। इस योग्यता के मूल्यांकन के लिए विद्यार्थी के निम्नलिखित पक्षों की ओर विशेष ध्यान रखना चाहिए—

1. मनोयोगपूर्वक पढ़ पाने की क्षमता।
2. ग्रहणशीलता की स्थिति बनाए रखना।
3. भावानुरूप सस्वर वाचन करना।
4. शुद्ध उच्चारण, बलाघात व अनुतान के उतार-चढ़ाव।

5. शब्दों, मुहावरों तथा उक्तियों का प्रसंगानुकूल भाव ग्रहण।
6. छन्द, अलंकार, प्रस्तुत-अप्रस्तुत तथा मूर्त-अमूर्त विधानों को पहचान पाना।
7. भावपक्ष की दृष्टि से सुन्दर स्थलों की पहचान कर पाना।
8. महत्त्वपूर्ण विचारों, भावों, तथ्यों का चयन करना।
9. पठित सामग्री का सारांश तथा केन्द्रीय भाव ग्रहण कर पाने की क्षमता।
10. लेखक के मनोभावों को समझ पाना।

पठित सामग्री की अर्थग्रहण कुशलता के मूल्यांकन के लिए मौखिक तथा लिखित दोनों प्रकार की परीक्षाओं का प्रयोग किया जा सकता है।

लिखित अभिव्यक्ति की योग्यता का मूल्यांकन

लिखित अभिव्यक्ति का हमारी परीक्षा पद्धति में महत्त्वपूर्ण स्थान है। फिर भी अधिकांश विद्यार्थियों की लेखन अभिव्यक्ति संतोषजनक नहीं है। इस असंतोषजनक स्थिति का प्रमुख कारण यह है कि हमारे मूल्यांकन के मापदण्ड बहुधा दोषपूर्ण होते हैं। जिन पक्षों का मूल्यांकन होना चाहिए वे उपेक्षित रह जाते हैं। मूल्यांकनकर्ता लिखित अभिव्यक्ति के मुख्य उद्देश्यों को सम्मुख रख कर प्रश्न पत्र का निर्माण नहीं करते तथा परीक्षक भी इनके प्रति उदासीन भाव से कार्य लेते हैं।

विद्यार्थी की लिखित अभिव्यक्ति का मूल्यांकन करते समय निम्नलिखित उद्देश्यों को ध्यान में रखना चाहिए:—

1. शुद्ध वर्तनी का प्रयोग।
2. विराम चिह्नों का सही प्रयोग।
3. व्याकरण सम्मत भाषा का प्रयोग।
4. प्रसंगानुकूल उचित शब्दों, मुहावरों, लोकोक्तियों का प्रयोग।
5. विषय तथा अभिव्यक्ति के अनुकूल शैली का प्रयोग।
6. यथोचित अनुच्छेदों का निर्माण।
7. क्रमबद्धता बनाए रखना।
8. उचित गति से लिखने की क्षमता।
9. लेखन में मौलिक शैली का प्रयोग।

लिखित अभिव्यक्ति के मूल्यांकन के लिए अनुच्छेद लेखन, निबंध लेखन, कहानी लेखन, पत्र लेखन, सारांश लेखन आदि विधियाँ अपनाई जा सकती हैं।

शिक्षण-अधिगम सामग्री

शिक्षण प्रक्रिया को सुचारू रूप से संपन्न करने के लिए अनेक प्रकार की सामग्री की आवश्यकता होती है। मोटे तौर पर शिक्षण में प्रयुक्त सामग्री को दो वर्गों में रखा जा सकता है। पहले वर्ग में वह सामग्री आती है, जिसका शिक्षक तथा शिक्षार्थी दोनों ही नियमित रूप से प्रयोग करते हैं, जैसे—पाठ्यपुस्तक, पूरक पुस्तक तथा अभ्यास-पुस्तिका (विशेषतः प्राथमिक स्तर पर)। वस्तुतः इस प्रकार की सामग्री शिक्षण प्रक्रिया का अभिन्न अंग है, क्योंकि शिक्षक तथा शिक्षार्थी दोनों को ही इसके प्रयोग की आवश्यकता होती है।

दूसरे वर्ग में वह सामग्री आती है जो कक्षा में प्रस्तुत विषयवस्तु को विद्यार्थियों के लिए सुस्पष्ट, सुबोध, सुग्राह्य एवं सजीव बनाने में शिक्षक की सहायता करती है। इसके अंतर्गत श्यामपट्ट, चार्ट, चित्र, मॉडल जैसे—पारंपरिक उपकरण तथा स्लाइड, पारदर्शी चित्र, टेप (कैसेट) जैसे आधुनिक उपकरण और रेडियो, दूरदर्शन, चलचित्र जैसे जनसंचार माध्यम आते हैं।

पाठ्यपुस्तक

शिक्षण प्रक्रिया में पाठ्यपुस्तक का अपना एक विशिष्ट स्थान है। वास्तव में यह संपूर्ण शिक्षण प्रक्रिया की आधारशिला है। यह एक ओर अध्यापक का शिक्षण-विषय के पाठ्यक्रम की सीमा के संदर्भ में मार्गदर्शन करती है तो दूसरी ओर विद्यार्थी के सम्मुख लक्ष्य का स्वरूप स्पष्ट करती है।

जब हम मातृभाषा का अध्ययन करते हैं तो पाठ्यपुस्तक का महत्त्व और भी बढ़ जाता है, क्योंकि मातृभाषा का विषय क्षेत्र अत्यंत व्यापक और बहुमुखी होने के कारण उसकी पाठ्यपुस्तक की सामग्री व्यापक एवं विविधतापूर्ण होती है। इतना ही नहीं, मातृभाषा की पाठ्यपुस्तक में समाहित सामग्री में वैचारिक तथा भाषिक दोनों पक्षों का ध्यान भी रखना होता है और साथ में विविध साहित्यिक रूपों एवं विधाओं का समावेश भी करना होता है।

किसी भी पाठ्यपुस्तक के दो पक्ष होते हैं :

1. भाव पक्ष, तथा
2. कला पक्ष

1. भाव पक्ष

पाठ्यपुस्तक इस उद्देश्य से तैयार की जाती है कि उसके अध्ययन से विद्यार्थियों में अपेक्षित योग्यताओं का विकास हो सके। ये योग्यताएँ शिक्षण उद्देश्य कहलाती हैं। इन शिक्षण उद्देश्यों के अन्तर्गत विभिन्न प्रकार की विषयवस्तु का ज्ञान, भाषाई कौशल और सद्प्रवृत्तियाँ आती हैं। पाठ्य-सामग्री के भाव पक्ष के संदर्भ में उस विषय के शिक्षण उद्देश्यों का अत्यंत महत्त्व है। इस संबंध में निम्नलिखित तीन बातों को ध्यान में रखा जाता है :

(*i*) भावों का चयन।

(*ii*) भावों का क्रमिक स्तरीकरण।

(*iii*) भावों का प्रस्तुतीकरण।

2. कला पक्ष

पाठ्य-सामग्री के कला पक्ष के अंतर्गत उसके बाहरी और आंतरिक दोनों रूप आते हैं। बाहरी रूप के अंतर्गत पुस्तक का आकार तथा उसकी मोटाई ऐसी होनी चाहिए जिससे उस आयु वर्ग के बच्चों को उसे एक स्थान से दूसरे स्थान तक ले जाने में सुविधा हो और पुस्तक को हाथ में उठाकर पढ़ने में भी असुविधा न हो।

पुस्तक की छपाई, शुद्ध वर्तनी एवं चित्र रूप पक्ष के अंतर्गत ही आते हैं। छोटे बालकों के लिए टाइप का आकार बड़ा होना चाहिए। बढ़ती हुई कक्षाओं में यह आकार छोटा होता जाता है।

पुस्तक की वर्तनी के संबंध में सबसे प्रमुख बात यह है कि शब्दों की वर्तनी शुद्ध हो। दूसरी बात भिन्न रूपों वाले— अ, फ, क्ष, झ आदि जैसे अक्षरों का मानक रूप ही पूरी पुस्तक में प्रयुक्त हो। चाहिए, जाए, लाए जैसे शब्दों को पुस्तक में एक ही रूप में प्रस्तुत किया जाना चाहिए।

पाठ्य सामग्री में चित्र बहुत महत्त्वपूर्ण होते हैं। पाठ्य-सामग्री में केवल वे चित्र दिए जाने चाहिएँ जो उनका अंग बन सकें और उसके पूरक हों। इनमें से कुछ चित्र काल्पनिक होते हैं और कुछ तथ्यात्मक। छोटी कक्षाओं की शिक्षण सामग्री में फोटो तथा तस्वीर वाले चित्र अधिक उपयोगी होते हैं और बड़ी कक्षाओं की सामग्री में कार्टूनों तथा रेखा वाले और तथ्यात्मक फोटो आवश्यक और उपयोगी हैं। चित्रों का स्थान भी इसी आधार पर निर्धारित किया जाता है जिससे उनका लिखित सामग्री के साथ तादात्म्य स्थापित हो सके। यदि किसी चित्र को बार-बार देखने की आवश्यकता हो तो वह सामग्री के बीच में देना चाहिए। यदि कोई चित्र सामग्री की पृष्ठभूमि के रूप में कार्य करता हो तो उसे पूरे पृष्ठ पर फैलाना चाहिए। यदि लिखित सामग्री को पढ़ने की प्रेरणा देना चित्र का उद्देश्य हो तो वह सामग्री के प्रारंभ में दिया जा सकता है। चित्रों के रंग भी बहुत महत्त्वपूर्ण होते हैं।

चित्र

भाषा के कठिन एवं गहन स्थलों को स्पष्ट करने में चित्रों तथा चित्र-शृंखलाओं की उपयोगिता सर्वमान्य है। चित्रों से अभिव्यक्ति में विस्तार एवं गहनता आती है। चित्र शब्दों और कहानियों का प्रतिनिधित्व करते हैं। क्रियाशील चित्र-शृंखला रचना और कहानी शिक्षण का श्रेष्ठ साधन है। शब्दों और चित्रों का समन्वय भाषा शिक्षण की प्रक्रिया को जीवंत बना देता है।

रेखाचित्र

इसके अंतर्गत चार्टों, पोस्टरों, कार्टूनों, हास्य-व्यंग्य चित्रों, मानचित्रों आदि का समावेश होता है। फ्लैनलग्राफ पर क्रमबद्ध रूप में व्याकरण के लिंग, वचन, कारक, क्रिया, विशेषण आदि के भेदों को चार्ट के रूप में प्रदर्शित किया जा सकता है। मानचित्रों के प्रयोग से प्रदेशों का भाषावार वर्गीकरण दिखाया जा सकता है। पोस्टर, कार्टून और हास्य-व्यंग्य चित्र किसी व्यक्ति, विचार एवं स्थिति के चित्र होते हैं जिनका जनसमूह पर गहरा प्रभाव पड़ता है। इनसे उपहासात्मक किंतु विचारपरक हास्य-व्यंग्य एवं अतिश्योक्तिपूर्ण स्थलों के गूढ़ भावों का स्पष्टीकरण होता है। ये विचारों को क्रमबद्ध तथा गतिमय रूप में प्रस्तुत करते हैं।

फ्लैश कार्ड

ये शिक्षण के प्रभावशाली दृश्य उपकरण हैं। ये चित्रात्मक और लिखित दोनों प्रकार के हों सकते हैं।

वर्णमाला-शिक्षण में फ्लैश कार्डों का विशेष महत्त्व है। एक वर्ण को सिखाने के लिए फ्लैश कार्ड पर अनेक शब्द दिए जाते हैं जो उस वर्ण से आरंभ होते हैं।

इनमें शब्दों के साथ उनके चित्र भी दिए जाते हैं। आरंभिक कक्षाओं में शब्दों और वाक्यों के चित्र सहित फ्लैश कार्ड अधिक उपयोगी सिद्ध होते हैं। इनसे किसी एक वस्तु, घटना या तथ्य की झलक एक दृष्टि में प्रस्तुत की जा सकती है।

ग्रामोफोन और लिंग्वाफोन

इनके रिकार्डों द्वारा उच्चारण के विभिन्न अभ्यासों के अंतर्गत बलाघात, सुर, विवृत्ति और अनुतान का सहज रूप में अभ्यास कराया जा सकता है। इनमें महापुरुषों के भाषणों, उत्कृष्ट कवियों की कविताओं और नाटकीय संवाद को सुना जा सकता है। उच्चारण, सस्वर पाठ और भाषण कला की प्रवीणता प्राप्त करने में इनका प्रयोग विशेष उपयोगी है।

टेप

उत्कृष्ट वक्ता के भाषणों, गीतों, नाटकीय कथनोपकथन, कविताओं और भाषा कौशलों विशेषतः उच्चारण और वाचन पाठों का अंकन करके ''प्लेबैक उपकरण'' (रिकार्ड प्लेयर) द्वारा जब चाहे, तब सुना और सुनाया जा सकता है।

रेडियो

शिक्षण का एक अत्यंत उपयोगी एवं सुलभ साधन है। समाचार, नाटक, भजन, गीत, संगीत, कहानियों, कविताओं, संवादों आदि की आकर्षक एवं प्रभावशाली प्रस्तुति से विद्यार्थी मनोरंजनात्मक ढंग से शुद्ध उच्चारण एवं आत्मप्रकाशन की क्षमता विकसित कर सकते हैं।

दूरदर्शन और चलचित्र

दूरदर्शन और चलचित्रों के कार्यक्रम देश-विदेश की घटनाओं, कार्यकलापों और दृश्यों को सजीव एवं यथार्थ रूप में प्रस्तुत करते हैं। दूरदर्शन आधुनिक युग की सबसे बड़ी देन है। इसके कार्यक्रम हमारी सामाजिक संस्कृति की झलक प्रदर्शित करते हैं। इनसे राष्ट्र के नागरिकों और विद्यार्थियों में एकता और सद्भावना उत्पन्न होती है और वे राष्ट्र की मुख्य धारा में समाहित होने की प्रेरणा ग्रहण करते हैं।

इनके माध्यम से जन शिक्षा का आसानी से प्रचार-प्रसार और विस्तार किया जा सकता है। ये जीवन के सभी पक्षों से संबंधित कार्यक्रमों का प्रसारण करते हैं। इनके द्वारा समाज की मान्यताओं, जीवन मूल्यों, सांस्कृतिक परंपराओं आदि की जानकारी विद्यार्थियों को प्राप्त होती है। इसके अतिरिक्त भाषाई पाठों का प्रसारण भी दूरदर्शन पर होता है जिससे विद्यार्थी सरल एवं रोचक वातावरण में पाठ की विषयवस्तु को अनायास ही सीख लेते हैं। इन कार्यक्रमों से शिक्षकों और छात्राध्यापकों को कक्षा शिक्षण में प्रयुक्त होने वाली विधियों, तकनीकों और उपागमों का भी व्यावहारिक ज्ञान प्राप्त होता है।

उपचारात्मक शिक्षण

विशेष आवश्यकता वाले बच्चों की कठिनाइयों की पहचान कर उन कठिनाइयों को दूर करते हुए शिक्षण कार्य करना उपचारात्मक शिक्षण कहलाता है। अध्यापक छात्रों के दोषों में यथासंभव सुधार लाने तथा उसकी भाषा संबंधी कठिनाइयों को दूर करने के लिए निम्नलिखित उपचारात्मक सहायता कर सकते हैं :

1. ऊँचा सुनने/कम सुनने तथा मानसिक रूप से बाधित बच्चों को कक्षा में अगली पंक्ति में बैठाने की व्यवस्था करनी चाहिए ताकि वे अध्यापक के चेहरे के हाव-भाव को ध्यान से देख सकें तथा उसके द्वारा कही गई बात को अच्छी तरह समझ सकें।
2. पढ़ाते समय शब्दों को ऊँची और स्पष्ट आवाज में तथा उचित गति से बोलना चाहिए।
3. श्रवण शक्ति तथा स्मरण शक्ति की कमी को पूरा करने के लिए अधिकाधिक दृश्य संकेतों तथा दृश्य सामग्री जैसे–चार्ट, चित्र, मॉडल आदि का प्रयोग करना उचित होता है। मनोरंजक कार्यकलापों का आयोजन करके ऐसे विद्यार्थियों को कक्षा में अतिरिक्त श्रवण के अवसर प्रदान किए जा सकते हैं। जैसे–चित्र कार्डों को दिखाकर छोटी-छोटी कहानियाँ तथा बालगीत अभिनयपूर्ण ढंग से सुनाना और घटनाओं का वर्णन करना आदि।
4. कठिन शब्दों या वाक्यांशों के अर्थ को स्पष्ट करने के लिए उसे बालक के अनुभव या ठोस वस्तु या परिस्थिति से जोड़कर।
5. श्रवण कौशल के विकास के लिए लघु प्रश्न पूछने की पद्धति अपनानी चाहिए।
6. संवेगात्मक तथा सूक्ष्म संकल्पनाओं को समझाने के लिए कक्षा में क्रियात्मक परिस्थितियाँ निर्मित करना, जैसे–प्रसन्नता, नाराजगी, घृणा, आशा, निराशा आदि भावों की अभिव्यक्ति को नाटकीय स्थिति में ढालकर व्यक्त करना।

मौखिक अभिव्यक्ति संबंधी दोषों तथा उनके कारणों का पता लगा लेने के पश्चात् अध्यापक उन्हें सुधारने के लिए निम्नलिखित उपचारात्मक उपाय कर सकते हैं :

1. तुतलाने वाले बच्चों को ध्वनियों का निरंतर उच्चारण अभ्यास कराना चाहिए।
2. हकलाने तथा मानसिक रूप से बाधित बच्चों को यथासंभव बोलने तथा सस्वर पठन का अतिरिक्त अवसर देना चाहिए। उनका मनोबल ऊँचा करने के लिए उन पर व्यक्तिगत रूप से ध्यान देना चाहिए। उनके साथ प्रेम एवं सहानुभूति का व्यवहार करना चाहिए।
3. अन्य बच्चों को उनके साथ घुलने-मिलने के लिए प्रोत्साहित करना चाहिए।
4. कक्षा में उनके प्रति उदारतापूर्ण दृष्टिकोण अपनाना चाहिए।
5. कठिन ध्वनियों का शुद्ध उच्चारण सिखाने के लिए टेप-रिकार्डर, ग्रामोफोन, रेडियो, टेलीविजन आदि दृश्य-श्रव्य साधनों का प्रयोग करना चाहिए।

पठन कौशल संबंधी दोषों को दूर करने के लिए निम्न प्रयास किए जाने चाहिए।

- इन बच्चों को अभ्यास और आवृत्ति की आवश्यकता सामान्य बच्चों से अधिक होती है। अतः इन्हें वर्णो एवं मात्रा चिह्नों का बार-बार अभ्यास कराना चाहिए।
- जिन वर्णों या शब्दों की पढ़ने की अशुद्धियाँ वे अक्सर करते हैं उनकी सूची बनाकर उन वर्णों की मूर्त या ठोस वस्तुओं के माध्यम से पढ़ना सिखाएँ, जैसे–वर्ण विशेष की आकृति, चित्र, फ्लैश कार्ड दिखाकर उसे पढ़ने का अभ्यास कराना।
- सही सस्वर वाचन करने पर इन बच्चों की तुरन्त प्रशंसा करें।

लेखन संबंधी दोष को दूर करने के लिए निम्न उपाय किए जाने चाहिए–

1. 5 वर्ष से अधिक आयु का बच्चा शारीरिक और मानसिक रूप से लिखना सीखने के योग्य हो जाता है। इस अवस्था से पूर्व लिखना सीखने का अभ्यास नहीं कराना चाहिए।
2. व्यक्तिगत स्तर पर अशुद्धि संशोधन के बिना लेखन दोषों का निराकरण कठिन होता है। प्राथमिक स्तर पर तो इस ओर विशेष ध्यान देने की आवश्यकता है।
3. विद्यार्थी जिन शब्दों को अशुद्ध लिखता है बहुत संभव है उसका कारण अशुद्ध उच्चारण हो।

   यथा–श-ष-स, प्र-पर, छ-क्ष, त्र-तर आदि का उच्चारण अशुद्ध होने से लेखन में भी दोष आ सकता है। अतः इन ध्वनियों से युक्त शब्दों के शुद्ध उच्चारण और लेखन का अभ्यास कराया जाना चाहिए।
4. शब्दों के शुद्ध उच्चारण को सुनने, उचित गति से लिखने तथा अशुद्धियों की जाँच के लिए श्रुतलेख श्रेष्ठ साधन है। इसका अभ्यास छात्रों को नियमित रूप से कराया जाना चाहिए।
5. हर बच्चे की अपनी शारीरिक और मानसिक सीमा होती है। प्रत्येक बालक के प्रति स्नेह और सम्मान का बर्ताव किया जाए और उसे उचित विधि से लेखन के प्रति प्रोत्साहित किया जाए। विशेष आवश्यकता वाले विद्यार्थियों को लेखन सिखाने के लिए और भी सावधानी बरतनी चाहिए।

❈ ❈ ❈ ❈ ❈

अभ्यास प्रश्न

1. अध्यापक को कक्षा में अपनी आवाज को रखना चाहिये :
A. पर्याप्त ऊंची B. धीमी
C. मध्यम D. कभी धीमी कभी तेज

2. यदि कुछ विद्यार्थी परीक्षा में फेल हो जाते हैं तो यह गलती है :
A. अध्यापकों की B. प्रधानाध्यापक की
C. स्वयं छात्रों की D. पाठ्यपुस्तकों की

3. वह अध्यापक जो अपने छात्रों का ध्यान आकर्षित करने में सफल न हो रहा हो तो उसे चाहिये कि :
A. वह अपनी शिक्षण विधि का मूल्यांकन करके उसमें सुधार लाये
B. वह अपने पद से त्यागपत्र दे दे
C. वह अपने शिष्यों में गलती ढूंढे
D. वह डिक्टेशन देना आरम्भ कर दे

4. यदि पीछे बैठने वाले सदैव बातचीत में ही व्यस्त हों तो अध्यापक को चाहिये कि वह :
A. उन्हें जो कुछ वे कर रहे हैं करने दे
B. उन्हें दन्ड दे
C. उन्हें आगे बिठाये और उन पर नजर रखे
D. उपरोक्त कोई नहीं

5. अध्यापक को :
A. अध्यापन आरम्भ करने से पूर्व पाठ का परिचय कराना चाहिये
B. अपनी भाषा में दक्ष होना चाहिये
C. अपने विषय में निपुण होना चाहिये
D. उपरोक्त सभी

6. यदि अध्यापक छात्र के प्रश्न का उत्तर देने में असमर्थ हो तो उसे चाहिये कि वह :
A. कहे कि वह जानकारी प्राप्त करने के बाद उत्तर देगा
B. शिष्यों को डांटे-फटकारे
C. कहे कि प्रश्न ही गलत है
D. उपरोक्त कोई नहीं

7. निम्न शिक्षण-प्रक्रियाओं को क्रम में लिखो :
(*i*) वर्तमान ज्ञान को पिछले ज्ञान से सम्बद्ध करना
(*ii*) मूल्यांकन
(*iii*) पुनर्शिक्षण
(*iv*) उद्देश्यों की संरचना
(*v*) सामग्री को प्रस्तुत करना
A. (*i*), (*ii*), (*iii*), (*iv*), (*v*)
B. (*ii*), (*i*), (*iii*), (*iv*), (*v*)
C. (*v*), (*iv*), (*iii*), (*i*), (*ii*)
D. (*iv*), (*i*), (*v*), (*ii*), (*iii*)

8. दूरदर्शन सामग्री का प्रयोग :
A. ध्यान केन्द्रण तथा ज्ञान को बढ़ाता है
B. अध्यापक के बोझ को कम करता है
C. स्मरणशक्ति में वृद्धि करता है
D. उपरोक्त सभी

9. यदि छात्र आपकी बात नहीं समझ पा रहे हैं तो :
A. आपको उन्हें संकेत (prompt) देना चाहिये
B. सामग्री को सरल बनाना चाहिये
C. उदाहरण देकर समझाना चाहिये
D. उपरोक्त सभी

10. सूक्ष्म शिक्षण लाभदायक है :
A. प्राथमिक कक्षा के छात्रों के लिए
B. जूनियर कक्षा के छात्रों के लिए
C. 10 + 2 कक्षा के छात्रों के लिए
D. उच्च तथा प्राथमिक दोनों कक्षाओं के छात्रों के लिए

11. यदि छात्र आप पर फब्तियां कसते हैं तो आप :
A. उन्हें दंड देंगे
B. उन्हें कॉलेज से निकाल देंगे
C. उनकी परीक्षा-पुस्तिकाओं का मूल्यांकन करते समय आप उनसे बदला लेंगे
D. उनकी परीक्षा-पुस्तिकाओं का मूल्यांकन के समय भी आप गैर-जानिबदार रहेंगे

12. शिक्षण में छात्रों की सर्वाधिक भागीदारी सम्भव है :
A. व्याख्यान विधि द्वारा B. चर्चा विधि द्वारा
C. पुस्तक विधि द्वारा D. ऑडियो-विजुअल एड द्वारा

13. नये आये अध्यापक की सफलता के लिए निम्न में से कौन-सा घटक सर्वाधिक महत्त्वपूर्ण है?
A. विद्वता
B. संप्रेषण योग्यता

C. अध्यापक का व्यक्तित्व तथा उसकी छात्रों तथा कक्षा से मेल खाने की अभिक्षमता
D. संगठनात्मक योग्यता

14. निम्न सभी एक प्रभावशाली शिक्षक की विशेषताएं हैं केवल एक को छोड़कर :
A. स्टैन्डर्ड को बनाये रखने पर जोर देना
B. लक्ष्यों के स्पष्टीकरण हेतु सामूहिक चर्चा पर बल देना
C. समस्या उत्पन्न करने वाली परिस्थितियों के तुरन्त नियन्त्रण पर जोर देना
D. कक्षा के छात्रों के साथ विभेदात्मक व्यवहार करना

15. एक प्रभावशाली शिक्षण का तात्पर्य नहीं है :
A. अध्यापक उत्साहपूर्वक पढ़ाता है
B. अध्यापक अपने छात्रों में गलती ढूंढता है
C. अध्यापक शिक्षण पर अधिक तथा कक्षा-नियन्त्रण पर कम जोर देता है
D. अध्यापक की रुचि विषय-सामग्री को छात्रों को समझाने में है न कि पाठ्यक्रम पूरा करने में

16. शिक्षा की के. जी. प्रथा का तात्पर्य है बच्चों का उद्यान। इसका जन्मदाता है :
A. डेवी B. फ्रूबेल
C. प्लेटो D. स्पेन्सर

17. प्रजातान्त्रिक समाज वह है, जो :
A. स्वतन्त्रता, समानता, बन्धुत्व तथा न्याय के सिद्धान्तों का पालन करता है
B. सूझ-बूझ रखने वाले व्यक्तियों का तिरस्कार नहीं करता है
C. समान शिक्षा के अवसर में विश्वास रखता है
D. उपरोक्त सभी

18. एक प्रभावशाली अध्यापक पालन करता है :
A. प्रजातान्त्रिक समाज के नियमों का
B. स्वतन्त्र समाज के नियमों का
C. तानाशाही समाज के नियमों का
D. परिस्थितियों के अनुसार सभी का

19. सहायक शिक्षण सामग्री के रूप में टी. वी., रेडियो से उत्तम है क्योंकि :
A. यह मंहगा है
B. इसमें दो इन्द्रियां—सुनना तथा देखना दोनों साथ-साथ प्रयोग होती हैं। जिसके फलस्वरूप लड़कों को अधिक आसानी से समझ में आता है
C. यह छात्रों द्वारा आमतौर पर पसन्द किया जाता है
D. उपरोक्त सभी

20. सबसे बड़ा उत्तरदायित्व जो स्कूल में काम करने वालों पर आता है वह यह है कि :
A. वे बच्चों तथा समाज दोनों की आवश्यकताओं में सामन्जस्य स्थापित करते हैं जिससे दोनों को लाभ होता है
B. वे बच्चों को नौकरी पाने के योग्य बनाते हैं
C. वे स्कूल के कार्यक्रमों को बच्चे की आवश्यकता तथा रुचि के अनुसार तैयार करते हैं
D. A तथा C दोनों

21. सबसे उत्तम शिक्षा कार्यक्रम वह है जो कि :
A. बच्चों की आवश्यकतानुसार हो
B. बच्चों की योग्यतानुसार हो
C. बच्चों की रुचि के अनुसार हो
D. उपरोक्त सभी

22. लेक्चर देते समय यदि कक्षा में कुछ व्यवधान (शोर) हो रहा हो तो अध्यापक को चाहिये कि वह :
A. थोड़ी देर चुप रहे फिर पढ़ाना आरम्भ करे
B. कक्षा में जो कुछ हो रहा है उसकी कोई चिन्ता न करे
C. शोर शराबा करने वाले लड़कों को दंड दे
D. उपरोक्त सभी

23. Learning (सीखना) का सबसे समुचित अर्थ है :
A. ज्ञान देना
B. व्यवहार में परिवर्तन
C. व्यक्तिगत रूप से माहौल में ढलना
D. हुनर की प्राप्ति

24. अन्तिम विश्लेषण में शिक्षण को विशेष रूप से समझना चाहिये :
A. प्रश्न पूछने तथा ज्ञान के मूल्यांकन की प्रक्रिया
B. विद्यार्थियों की गतिविधियों को निर्दिष्ट करना
C. विद्यार्थियों के वाचन का श्रवण
D. उपरोक्त सभी

25. अध्यापक के कार्य हैं :
A. बच्चे का मार्गदर्शन करना, प्रगति में उनकी सहायता करना तथा मूल्यांकन
B. घर का काम चेक करना, उनका मार्गदर्शन करना तथा आगे का काम देना
C. उपरोक्त दोनों
D. कोई नहीं

26. कक्षा में अध्यापक है :
A. समूह का अध्यक्ष
B. समूह का निर्देशक
C. समूह का नेता तथा मार्गदर्शक
D. उपरोक्त सभी

27. अध्यापक का प्राथमिक उत्तरदायित्व निहित है :
A. शैक्षिक अनुभवों को सुनियोजित करने में
B. नीतियों को लागू करने में
C. छात्रों का रिकार्ड रखने में
D. उपरोक्त सभी

28. अपने विद्यार्थियों से गहरा तालमेल बनाने के लिए आपको :
A. उनका मार्गदर्शन करना चाहिये
B. उनके साथ खुलेपन का व्यवहार करना चाहिये
C. संप्रेषण में सक्षम होना चाहिये
D. उपरोक्त सभी

29. मौखिक मार्गदर्शन सबसे कम प्रभावशाली है :
A. अभिवृत्ति के शिक्षण में
B. अवधारणा तथा तथ्य के शिक्षण में
C. परस्पर सम्बन्ध के शिक्षण में
D. हुनर (skills) के शिक्षण में

30. अध्यापन आरम्भ करने से पूर्व शिक्षक को चाहिये कि :
A. वह अपने विद्यार्थियों के वर्तमान तथा भूत के विषय में जाने
B. वह विद्यार्थियों के मस्तिष्क पर काम कर रहे वातावरण के विचलनों से भिज्ञ हो
C. वह अपने विद्यार्थियों की जिज्ञासा को उजागर करने में सक्षम हो
D. उपरोक्त सभी

31. किसी स्कूल/कॉलेज में शिक्षा की गुणवत्ता को मापा जा सकता है :
A. उपलब्ध बुनियादी सुविधाओं द्वारा
B. उपलब्ध जनशक्ति, अध्यापक तथा प्रधानाचार्य के माध्यम से
C. छात्रों की शैक्षिक प्रगति के माध्यम से
D. उपरोक्त सभी द्वारा

32. यूनेस्को (UNESCO) प्रकाशन की व्याख्या के अनुसार अध्यापक के अन्दर कौन-सा व्यावसायिक गुण होना चाहिये?
A. अपने विषय में दक्षता तथा शिक्षण में निपुणता
B. शिक्षण-पद्धति में प्रतिक्षण नयापन
C. व्यवसाय के प्रति न्याय व ईमानदारी
D. उपरोक्त सभी

33. शिक्षण का पहला चरण है :
A. पहले से योजना बनाना
B. पाठ्यसामग्री को सुसंगठित करना
C. विद्यार्थियों की बैकग्राउन्ड को जानना
D. कोई नहीं

34. यदि कोई छात्र कक्षा में बेहोश हो जाता है तो आप सबसे पहले क्या करेंगे?
A. प्रधानाचार्य के कार्यालय की ओर दौड़ेंगे तथा सहायता के लिए कहेंगे
B. बच्चे के माता-पिता को टेलीफोन करेंगे तथा उनकी प्रतीक्षा करेंगे
C. उसे प्रथम सहायता चिकित्सा देंगे तथा किसी निकट के डॉक्टर से सम्पर्क करेंगे
D. उस लड़के को घर भेजने का प्रबन्ध करेंगे

35. यदि सामान्य लड़कों के साथ आपको किसी नेत्रहीन को पढ़ाने का अवसर मिले तो आपका व्यवहार कैसा होगा?
A. आप सहानुभूति से उसकी देख-रेख करेंगे
B. आप उस पर कोई अतिरिक्त ध्यान नहीं देंगे क्योंकि इससे शेष छात्रों की क्षति होगी
C. आप उसको आगे की सीट पर बिठायेंगे और अपने अध्यापन को उसकी क्षमतानुसार इस प्रकार सुनियोजित करेंगे कि उससे अन्य छात्रों को क्षति न हो
D. उपरोक्त कोई नहीं

36. एक नया अध्यापक, जिसके साथ कक्षा में कुछ बच्चे गलत ढंग से व्यवहार करते हैं, वह उनसे निपटेगा :
A. दण्डात्मक तरीकों को अपना कर
B. अपने अन्दर सुधार लाकर और उसे छात्रों के सामने अच्छे अन्दाज से पेश करके
C. प्रधानाचार्य से सलाह के बाद अपनी कक्षा को बदल कर
D. उन्हें स्कूल से निकाल देने की धमकी देकर

37. यदि कोई लड़का पीछे बैठता है और श्यामपट्ट को ठीक से नहीं देख पाता है, परिणामस्वरूप वह बार-बार खड़ा होकर देखता है और बैठ जाता है। इस केस के सम्बन्ध में आप क्या निष्कर्ष निकालेंगे?
A. अपने सहपाठियों की तुलना में वह छात्र नाटा है
B. श्यामपट्ट पर रोशनी की चमक पड़ रही है
C. बच्चा दूरदृष्टि दोष रखता है
D. A और C दोनों

38. बच्चे की श्रवण-क्षमता में विकार हो सकता है यदि :
A. वह असामान्य रूप से बहुत जोर से बोलता है
B. बातचीत के दौरान वह वक्ता के निकट आ जाता है
C. वह अध्यापक से आमतौर पर फिर से कहिये, फिर से कहिये, कहता रहता है
D. उपरोक्त सभी

39. यदि कोई छात्रा आपसे अपनी डाक आपके पते पर मंगाने के लिए कहती है तो :
A. आप उसे इसकी अनुमति नहीं देंगे क्योंकि यह आपके सिद्धान्तों के विरुद्ध है
B. आप उसे अपना पता नहीं देंगे कि कहीं यह आप के विरुद्ध कोई चाल न हो
C. आप उसे इसकी अनुमति दे देंगे क्योंकि एक अध्यापक के नाते आपको ऐसा करना चाहिये
D. आप उसे व्यक्तिगत लगाव के कारण इसकी अनुमति दे देंगे

40. यदि कोई उच्च जाति का अध्यापक किसी नीची जाति के छात्र के साथ भेदभाव करता है तो उसका व्यवहार :
A. उसके अपने धर्मानुसार सही है
B. राष्ट्रीय सोच तथा समय की जरूरत के विरुद्ध है
C. संवैधानिक प्रावधानों के विरुद्ध नहीं है
D. यूनेस्को (UNESCO) के अध्यापकों के व्यवसायवाद के नियमों के विरुद्ध नहीं है

41. पद्य पाठ का सर्वाधिक महत्त्वपूर्ण सोपान है :
A. प्रस्तावना B. भाव विश्लेषण
C. समभावी कविता D. आदर्श प्रस्तावना

42. 'कलेजा मुंह को आना' मुहावरे का सही अर्थ है :
A. बहुत दुखी होना B. क्रोध करना
C. धोखा खाना D. मूर्ख बनना

43. आकाश का विलोम है :
A. धरती B. पाताल
C. गगन D. नभ

44. निम्न में से कौन एक भिन्न है?
A. अहं B. दर्प
C. अहंकार D. निराला

45. सहिष्णुता शब्द है :
A. विशेषण B. अव्यय
C. भाववाचक संज्ञा D. सर्वनाम

46. उल्लास का समानार्थक शब्द है :
A. उत्साह B. दुःख
C. प्रसन्नता D. ताजगी

47. सज्जन शब्द का संधि विच्छेद है :
A. सज् + जन B. सः + जन
C. सत् + जन D. सा + जन

48. पर्यावरण का शब्दार्थ है :
A. जलमंडल B. स्थलमंडल
C. वायुमंडल D. वातावरण

49. निम्नलिखित में से रचनात्मक शिक्षण की विधि नहीं है :
A. कक्षा नियम विधि
B. आदर्श अभिनय विधि
C. व्याख्या विधि
D. भाषा-संसर्ग विधि

50. समवाय विधि प्रयुक्त होती है :
A. निबंध शिक्षण में B. कहानी शिक्षण में
C. कविता शिक्षण में D. उपरोक्त सभी में

51. निम्न में कौन दृश्य-श्रव्य उपकरण है :
A. दूरदर्शन B. टेलीफोन
C. ग्रामोफोन D. रेडियो

52. बालकों के शब्दकोष होने चाहिए :
A. भाषात्मक B. काव्यात्मक
C. चित्रात्मक D. मनोविश्लेषणात्मक

53. सक्षम शब्द का समानार्थक है :
A. समर्थ B. शक्तिशाली
C. कायर D. निर्माता

54. विहंगम दृष्टि का अभिप्राय है :
A. एक झलक B. गहन दृष्टि
C. गहन चिंतन D. इनमें से कोई नहीं

55. विधाता की अनुपम रचना है :
A. मानव B. समुद्र
C. वन D. पृथ्वी

56. नीरस का संधि विच्छेद है :
A. नी + रस B. नि + रस
C. निः + रस D. नीः + रस

57. अक्षर बोध प्रणाली से छात्रों का :
A. उच्चारण शुद्ध होता है
B. वाक्यों का क्रमबद्ध ज्ञान होता है
C. विवरण दोष नहीं आ पाता है
D. उपरोक्त सभी

58. नैदानिक परीक्षण का उद्देश्य है :
A. छात्र की कमजोरियों का पता लगाना
B. छात्र में सद्वृत्तियों का विकास करना
C. छात्र की अभिव्यक्ति में सुधार लाना
D. छात्र की भाषा संबंधी क्षमता का मूल्यांकन करना

59. निर्देशित स्वाध्याय प्रणाली का सोपान है :
A. नियोजन B. क्रियान्वयन
C. उपरोक्त दोनों D. कोई भी नहीं

60. पेडागॉजी कहलाता है :
A. शिक्षण विज्ञान
B. सीखने की कला
C. शिक्षण-अधिगम विज्ञान व कला दोनों
D. संप्रेषण विज्ञान

61. निम्नलिखित में से कौन-सा वैकल्पिक पाठशाला का अर्थ नहीं है?
A. चरवाहा विद्यालय
B. विद्यालय से बाहर रहे बच्चों की शिक्षा
C. आसपास/पड़ोस के बच्चों की शिक्षा उनके पड़ोस में
D. निर्माण कार्य के पास बच्चों की शिक्षा

62. निम्नलिखित में से कौन-सी बात कौशल सीखने की एक प्रावस्था नहीं हो सकती है?
A. संविधि B. भेद बोध
C. अभ्यास D. कल्पना

63. शिक्षण कार्य के लिए निम्नलिखित में से कौन सबसे अधिक निर्णायक है?
A. अधिगम को प्रभावी बनाना
B. ज्ञान देना
C. कक्षा का संप्रबंधन
D. छात्रों के साथ संप्रेषण

64. गरीबों की मदद करना एक कर्त्तव्य है, क्योंकि :
A. हम गरीब हैं
B. हम अमीर हैं
C. हम उस समाज से संबंध रखते हैं
D. हम उनकी अच्छाई चाहते हैं

65. 'हमें दूसरे के ओहदों का हमेशा ध्यान रखना चाहिए।' यह एक है :
A. साधारण वाक्य
B. जटिल वाक्य
C. मिश्रित वाक्य
D. मुहावरा

66. वर्ण को कहते हैं :
A. मौलिक ध्वनि
B. लघुत्तम अक्षर
C. मूल ध्वनियां
D. वृहत्तम अक्षर

67. नीलकंठ शब्द किस वर्ग का है?
A. रूढ़ि
B. योगरूढ़
C. यौगिक
D. इनमें से कोई नहीं

68. बुढ़ापा क्या है :
A. भाववाचक संज्ञा
B. व्यक्तिवाचक संज्ञा
C. क्रिया विशेषण
D. जाति वाचक संज्ञा

69. प्रत्यय कहाँ जोड़े जाते हैं?
A. शब्द के आरंभ में
B. शब्द के अंत में
C. शब्द के बीच में
D. शब्द के उस भाग में जहां उपयुक्त लगे

70. नमस्ते में कौन-सी संधि है?
A. व्यंजन संधि
B. स्वर संधि
C. विसर्ग संधि
D. इनमें से कोई नहीं

71. संचय का संधि विग्रह है :
A. सत् + चय
B. सम् + चय
C. सं + चय
D. सः + चय

72. जन्मांध में कौन सा समास है?
A. तत्पुरुष
B. द्वन्द्व
C. बहुव्रीहि
D. अव्ययीभाव

73. अकथ का विपरीतार्थक शब्द होगा :
A. कथनीय
B. मान्य
C. कथ्य
D. चिंतनीय

74. अक्ल का दुश्मन का क्या तात्पर्य है?
A. बेवकूफ
B. महामूर्ख
C. पागल
D. बुद्धिहीन

75. हमारी परीक्षा प्रणाली में सुधार का सर्वोत्तम तरीका होगा :
A. आंतरिक मूल्यांकन
B. बाह्य मूल्यांकन
C. उपरोक्त दोनों
D. इनमें से कोई भी नहीं

76. वर्तमान नर्सरी विद्यालयों में प्रवेश विवाद के मूल में है :
A. कोर्ट का फैसला
B. गांगुली कमेटी रिपोर्ट
C. नई शिक्षा नीति
D. कोठारी कमीशन

77. भाषा शिक्षण की किस विधि का प्रयोग लाभकर होता है?
A. प्रश्नोतर विधि
B. खेल विधि
C. डाल्टन विधि
D. इनमें से कोई नहीं

78. कविता किसका विषय है?
A. अनुभूति का
B. विधा का
C. रस का
D. आनन्द का

79. सम्प्रेषण की कुशलता बढ़ती है :
A. अंतःक्रिया से
B. अनुभव से
C. धन से
D. प्रशिक्षण से

80. रूपरेखा शिक्षण विधि का संबंध है :
A. गद्य शिक्षण से
B. कहानी शिक्षण से
C. व्याकरण शिक्षण से
D. रचना शिक्षण से

81. जीवन में सफल होने के लिए छात्रों को क्या करने के लिए प्रोत्साहित करना चाहिए?
A. चयनित अध्ययन
B. आकस्मिक अध्ययन
C. गहन अध्ययन
D. कण्ठस्थीकरण करके सीखना

82. बुनियादी शिक्षा का विचार निम्न में से किसने दिया?
A. डॉ. जाकिर हुसैन
B. डॉ. राजेन्द्र प्रसाद
C. महात्मा गांधी
D. रवीन्द्रनाथ टैगोर

83. बालिकाओं की शिक्षा को प्राथमिकता देनी चाहिए, क्योंकि :
A. लड़कियाँ लड़कों की अपेक्षा अधिक होशियार होती हैं
B. लड़कियाँ संख्या में लड़कों से कम हैं
C. भूतकाल में लड़कों की तुलना में लड़कियों के साथ भेदभाव किया गया है
D. केवल लड़कियां ही सामाजिक परिवर्तन का नेतृत्व करने में सक्षम हैं

84. सम्मिलित (Inclusive) शिक्षा की सफलता निर्भर करती है :
A. समुदाय के सहारे पर
B. शिक्षण-अधिगम सामग्रियों की उच्च्व कोटि की गुणवत्ता पर
C. पाठ्य-पुस्तकों की उत्कृष्टता पर
D. अध्यापकों में अभिवृत्यात्मक परिवर्तन पर

85. पाठ्य-सहगामी क्रियाओं का आयोजन करना किसका दायित्व होना चाहिए?
A. प्रधानाध्यापक का
B. इस कार्य के लिए नियुक्त अध्यापक का
C. उन अध्यापकों का जो इसमें रुचि रखते हैं
D. सभी अध्यापकों का

86. छात्रों के अनुतीर्ण रहने पर समझना चाहिए कि :
A. व्यवस्था ही असफल हो गई है
B. अध्यापक की असफलता है
C. पाठ्य-पुस्तकों की असफलता है
D. व्यक्तिगत छात्र की असफलता है

87. छात्रों का सामयिक परीक्षण होना चाहिए ताकि :
A. छात्रों की प्रगति उनके अभिभावकों को सूचित की जा सके
B. नियमानुसार निर्धारित अभ्यास करवाया जा सके
C. छात्रों को अंतिम परीक्षाओं के लिए प्रशिक्षित किया जा सके
D. परिणामों से प्राप्त प्रतिपुष्टि के आधार पर सुधारात्मक उपाय अपनाए जा सकें

88. गृहकार्य जांचने का सबसे अच्छा उपाय है :
A. प्रबुद्ध छात्रों द्वारा इसे संपन्न करा देना
B. कक्षा में सामूहिक रूप से उत्तरों की जांच करा देना
C. नमूने के आधार पर इन्हें जांच डालना
D. नियमित रूप से स्वयं अध्यापक/अध्यापिका द्वारा उनकी जांच करना

89. कण्ठ का विशेषण है :
A. कण्ठी
B. काठी
C. कण्ठक
D. कण्ठ्य

90. निम्न में कौन सी वर्तनी शुद्ध है?
A. श्रीहरी
B. पूजनीय
C. मनः कामना
D. कवित्री

91. इनमें कौन-सा वाक्य अशुद्ध है?
A. मैंने थोड़ी देर बाद जाना है
B. आप सपरिवार आमंत्रित हैं
C. कृपया हमारे घर आइए
D. आप जब भी आएं, मुझसे मिलें

92. अभिमुख होने के अर्थ में किस मुहावरे का प्रयोग है?
A. छत्तीस का आंकड़ा होना
B. एक और एक ग्यारह होना
C. निन्यानवे का चक्कर
D. तिरेसठ की तरह होना

93. 'बतरस लालच लाल की :
मुरली धरी लुकाई
सौंह करैं, भौंहनि हँसै
देन कहैं नट जाँइ।'
यहां नट शब्द का क्या अर्थ है?
A. नाटक करना
B. छिप जाना
C. मना करना
D. झगड़ा करना

94. 'कमर टूट जाना' का अर्थ है :
A. कमर की हड्डी टूटना
B. घबरा जाना
C. असफल होना
D. शक्ति या साहस न रहना

95. हमारे जीवन का उद्देश्य है कि दूसरों की सहायता करें। यह किस प्रकार का वाक्य है?
A. संयुक्त
B. सरल
C. साधारण
D. मिश्र

96. 'लाली मेरे लाल की ....' यहां लाल से क्या अभिप्राय है?
A. बेटा
B. कीमती पत्थर
C. ईश्वर
D. मनुष्य

97. नीरव में कौन-सी संधि है?
A. स्वर संधि
B. व्यंजन संधि
C. विसर्ग संधि
D. दीर्घ संधि

98. मधुकर का समानार्थक शब्द क्या है?
A. शहद
B. भ्रमर
C. रीछ
D. रोटी

99. हथेली पर सरसों जमाना का क्या अर्थ है?
A. जादू दिखाना
B. काम झटपट कर लेना
C. अच्छी खेती करना
D. असंभव कार्य कर लेना

100. विकलांग बच्चों के साथ किस प्रकार का व्यवहार किया जाना चाहिए?
A. उन्हें सामान्य विद्यालयों एवं सामान्य बच्चों से दूर रखा जाए
B. सामान्य बच्चों की तरह उन्हें भी अवसर दिए जाएं
C. उन्हें एक जिम्मेदारी समझ कर दया की भावना से उनकी सहायता की जाए
D. विशेष सुविधाएं प्रदान कर उन्हें सामान्य विद्यालयों में समाकलित की जाए

101. 'सीता हँसती है' वाक्य में कौन-सी क्रिया है?
A. अकर्मक
B. द्विकर्मक
C. विकर्मक
D. सकर्मक

102. 'राम से बैठा नहीं गया' यहां कौन सा वाच्य है?
A. भाव वाच्य
B. कर्मवाच्य
C. कर्तृवाच्य
D. मिश्रवाच्य

103. तत्पुरुष समास में कौन-सा पद प्रधान होता है?
A. पूर्व पद
B. अन्य पद
C. उभय पद
D. उत्तर पद

104. ब्रजभाषा का विकास किस भाषा से हुआ?
A. अर्धमागधी
B. शौरसेनी
C. पालि
D. पैशाची

105. विकलांग बच्चों के संदर्भ में प्रारंभिक शिक्षा के सार्वभौमिकरण के लिए कौन सी अधिकतम आयु निर्धारित की गई है?
A. 11 वर्ष
B. 14 वर्ष
C. 16 वर्ष
D. 18 वर्ष

106. विकलांग बच्चों की समेकित शिक्षा का निहितार्थ है :
A. कुछ शिक्षा सामान्य विद्यालयों में हो और कुछ विशेष विद्यालयों में हो
B. ऐसे बच्चों को केवल विशेष अध्यापक ही पढ़ाएँ
C. सामान्य बच्चों के साथ ही उनकी पढ़ाई का प्रावधान हो
D. विकलांगता के अनुरूप विशेष विद्यालयों में दाखिला

107. देवनागरी लिपि किस भाषा की लिपि है?
A. तमिल
B. पंजाबी
C. हिन्दी
D. उर्दू

108. हिंदी का सबसे बड़ा गुण यह है कि :
A. इसमें वैज्ञानिक आविष्कारों को स्वीकार करने की क्षमता है
B. इसने अपने को दूसरी भाषाओं के संपर्क से अलग रखा है
C. इसने संस्कृत के साथ अन्य भाषाओं के शब्दों को भी अपनाया है
D. यह भारत की सबसे समृद्ध भाषा है

109. हिंदी राष्ट्रभाषा इसलिए रही क्योंकि :
A. गांधीजी इसके पक्षपाती थे
B. यह अंतरप्रांतीय भाषा थी
C. यह सार्वजनिक व्यापार की भाषा थी
D. यह देश में उत्तर से दक्षिण और पूरब से पश्चिम तक परस्पर बातचीत और विचार-विनिमय के लिए प्रयोग में लाई जाती थी

110. राष्ट्र भाषा में :
A. हिंदू संस्कृति के गुण होने चाहिए
B. राजभाषा के गुण होने चाहिए
C. सामासिक संस्कृति के गुण होने चाहिए
D. शुद्ध भाषा के गुण होने चाहिए

111. हिंदी के उदात्त साहित्य का मूल है :
A. रस
B. कामुकता
C. कलुषित आक्रोश
D. दुखान्त परिणति

112. प्रासंगिक शब्द का सही अर्थ चुनकर बताएं :
A. तराजू की डंडी से संबंधित
B. दरबान
C. मामले से जुड़ा हुआ
D. साथ निभाने वाला

113. उद्देश्य निष्ठ मूल्यांकन की विशेषताएँ हैं :
A. वस्तुनिष्ठता और विभेदकारी
B. व्यापकता और व्यावहारिकता
C. विश्वसनीयता और वैधता
D. उपरोक्त सभी

114. देवनागरी लिपि अन्य लिपियों की तुलना में कहीं अधिक :
A. ध्वन्यात्मक है
B. कलात्मक है
C. वैज्ञानिक है
D. उपरोक्त सभी

115. वाद-विवाद प्रतियोगिता में आपको निर्णायक बनाए जाने पर आप :
A. साथी निर्णायक के निर्णय के अनुरूप निर्णय करेंगे
B. प्रभावी वक्ता को प्रमुखता देंगे
C. अपने विद्यालय के छात्र को प्रमुखता देंगे
D. छात्र नेता को प्रमुखता देंगे

116. आप कक्षा में धीरे-धीरे सीखने वाले छात्र के लिए क्या करेंगे?
A. अन्य छात्रों की अपेक्षा अधिक गृह कार्य देंगे
B. उसको पारितोषिक प्राप्त करने को प्रोत्साहित करेंगे
C. उसका व्यक्तित्व शिक्षण करेंगे
D. उसका कारण जानकर उपचारात्मक विधि अपनाएंगे

117. एक अच्छे अध्यापक के लिए संतोष की वस्तु है :
A. उच्च पद
B. धन
C. आदर-सम्मान
D. जन समर्थन

118. कक्षा में शिक्षक को अधिकाधिक प्रश्न पूछने चाहिए, क्योंकि इससे :
A. प्रधानाचार्य प्रसन्न होते हैं
B. कक्षा का अनुशासन बनता है
C. छात्रों को अभिव्यक्ति का अवसर मिलता है
D. शिक्षक को अभिव्यक्ति का अवसर मिलता है

119. अपेक्षा का विपरीत शब्द है :
A. अनादर
B. आदर
C. सत्कार
D. उपेक्षा

120. अंधाधुंध शब्द का अर्थ है :
A. तीव्र गति से
B. धीमी गति से
C. विवेक रहित
D. विवेक सहित

121. एक बच्चा बिना औपचारिक शिक्षा के, परिवार और परिवेश से भाषा सीख लेता है, जबकि विद्यालय में वह व्याकरण के नियम सीखता है। यह उदाहरण किस सिद्धांत को दर्शाता है?
A. केवल अधिगम
B. केवल अर्जन
C. अर्जन और अधिगम का अंतर
D. भाषा अनुकरण सिद्धांत

122. निम्नलिखित में से कौन-सा कथन 'अर्जन' की विशेषता को सबसे सटीक रूप से दर्शाता है?
A. यह औपचारिक कक्षा में होता है
B. इसमें व्याकरणिक नियमों का सचेत ज्ञान शामिल होता है
C. यह प्राकृतिक और अवचेतन प्रक्रिया है
D. यह केवल लिखित भाषा तक सीमित है

123. एक शिक्षक भाषा शिक्षण में केवल व्याकरण नियमों पर जोर देता है और संवादात्मक अभ्यास को नजरअंदाज करता है। यह किस प्रकार की प्रक्रिया को अधिक बढ़ावा देता है?
A. अर्जन
B. अधिगम
C. दोनों समान रूप से
D. कोई नहीं

124. 'अर्जन-अधिगम परिकल्पना' किससे संबंधित है?
A. जीन पियाजे B. नोम चॉम्स्की
C. स्टीफन क्रैशन D. वाइगोत्स्की

125. एक विद्यार्थी व्याकरण के नियम जानता है, लेकिन बोलते समय सही प्रयोग नहीं कर पाता। यह स्थिति क्या दर्शाती है?
A. अर्जन की कमी B. अधिगम की कमी
C. दोनों की कमी D. कोई समस्या नहीं

126. एक शिक्षक भाषा कक्षा में विद्यार्थियों को वास्तविक जीवन की स्थितियों (जैसे बाजार, बातचीत) में भाषा प्रयोग करने के अवसर देता है। यह किस सिद्धांत पर आधारित है?
A. संरचनात्मक दृष्टिकोण B. संप्रेषणात्मक दृष्टिकोण
C. व्याकरण-अनुवाद विधि D. श्रवण-दृष्टि विधि

127. भाषा शिक्षण में 'सरल से कठिन' और 'ज्ञात से अज्ञात' का सिद्धांत किससे संबंधित है?
A. मनोवैज्ञानिक सिद्धांत B. भाषावैज्ञानिक सिद्धांत
C. सामाजिक सिद्धांत D. व्याकरणिक सिद्धांत

128. एक शिक्षक पहले भाषा के नियम सिखाता है और फिर उदाहरण देता है। यह किस सिद्धांत का उदाहरण है?
A. आगमन विधि B. निगमन विधि
C. संप्रेषणात्मक विधि D. प्रत्यक्ष विधि

129. 'भाषा को एक सामाजिक व्यवहार के रूप में सिखाया जाना चाहिए'—यह विचार किस सिद्धांत से संबंधित है?
A. संरचनात्मक सिद्धांत
B. व्यवहारवादी सिद्धांत
C. सामाजिक-सांस्कृतिक सिद्धांत
D. औपचारिक सिद्धांत

130. एक भाषा शिक्षक विद्यार्थियों को अधिक से अधिक सुनने और बोलने के अवसर देता है तथा मातृभाषा का प्रयोग कम करता है। यह किस सिद्धांत को दर्शाता है?
A. व्याकरण-अनुवाद विधि B. प्रत्यक्ष विधि
C. द्विभाषिक विधि D. संरचनात्मक विधि

131. एक बच्चा अपने अनुभवों को साझा करने, प्रश्न पूछने और अपनी आवश्यकताएँ व्यक्त करने के लिए भाषा का उपयोग करता है। यह भाषा के किस कार्य को दर्शाता है?
A. केवल सूचना देना B. संप्रेषणात्मक कार्य
C. सौंदर्यात्मक कार्य D. संरचनात्मक कार्य

132. भाषा सीखने में 'सुनना' क्यों महत्वपूर्ण माना जाता है?
A. यह केवल परीक्षा के लिए उपयोगी है
B. यह पढ़ने का आधार है
C. यह बोलने की क्षमता का आधार बनता है
D. इसका कोई विशेष महत्व नहीं

133. एक शिक्षक कक्षा में बच्चों को कहानी सुनाता है और उनसे अपने शब्दों में उसे दोहराने को कहता है। यह गतिविधि किस सिद्धांत को दर्शाती है?
A. रटने का सिद्धांत B. निष्क्रिय अधिगम
C. सक्रिय भाषा प्रयोग D. व्याकरणिक अधिगम

134. 'बालक भाषा का उपयोग एक उपकरण के रूप में अपने विचारों को व्यवस्थित करने और समस्या समाधान के लिए करता है।' यह विचार किससे संबंधित है?
A. व्यवहारवादी सिद्धांत
B. संरचनात्मक सिद्धांत
C. संज्ञानात्मक/सामाजिक-सांस्कृतिक सिद्धांत
D. व्याकरण-अनुवाद विधि

135. एक बालक खेल के दौरान अपने साथियों को निर्देश देता है, नियम समझाता है और बातचीत करता है। यह भाषा के किस उपयोग को दर्शाता है?
A. केवल औपचारिक उपयोग
B. सामाजिक अंतःक्रिया का माध्यम
C. व्याकरणिक शुद्धता
D. निष्क्रिय अधिगम

136. एक विद्यार्थी बिना व्याकरणिक शुद्धता के भी अपने विचार प्रभावी रूप से व्यक्त कर लेता है। यह किस दृष्टिकोण का समर्थन करता है?
A. व्याकरण सर्वोपरि है
B. संप्रेषण व्याकरण से अधिक महत्वपूर्ण है
C. केवल लिखित भाषा महत्वपूर्ण है
D. भाषा केवल नियमों का समूह है

137. भाषा अधिगम में व्याकरण की भूमिका को 'सहायक, न कि प्रमुख' किसने माना?
A. जीन पियाजे B. नोम चॉम्स्की
C. स्टीफन क्रैशन D. बी. एफ. स्किनर

138. एक शिक्षक कक्षा में पहले भाषा का प्रयोग करवाता है और बाद में त्रुटियों को सुधारता है। यह किस दृष्टिकोण को दर्शाता है?
A. व्याकरण-अनुवाद विधि B. संप्रेषणात्मक दृष्टिकोण
C. संरचनात्मक दृष्टिकोण D. रटने की विधि

139. 'व्याकरण भाषा की संरचना को समझने का माध्यम है, लेकिन इसका अत्यधिक जोर संप्रेषण में बाधा बन सकता है।' यह कथन किस प्रकार के संतुलन को दर्शाता है?
A. केवल शुद्धता
B. केवल प्रवाह
C. शुद्धता और प्रवाह का संतुलन
D. किसी का भी महत्व नहीं

140. एक बालक बोलते समय व्याकरणिक नियमों के बारे में नहीं सोचता, फिर भी सही वाक्य बना लेता है। यह क्या दर्शाता है?
A. औपचारिक अधिगम B. व्याकरण-अनुवाद विधि
C. भाषा अर्जन D. नियम आधारित अधिगम

141. एक कक्षा में विभिन्न भाषाई पृष्ठभूमि के बच्चे हैं। शिक्षक को भाषा शिक्षण में सबसे बड़ी चुनौती क्या होगी?
A. केवल पाठ्यपुस्तक पूरा करना
B. सभी बच्चों को एक ही तरीके से पढ़ाना
C. बच्चों की विविध भाषाई आवश्यकताओं के अनुसार रणनीति बनाना
D. केवल व्याकरण सिखाना

142. एक बालक बार-बार 'मैं गया था' की जगह 'मैं गई था' बोलता है। यह किस प्रकार की त्रुटि है?
A. वर्तनी त्रुटि B. लिंग संबंधी त्रुटि
C. उच्चारण त्रुटि D. अर्थ संबंधी त्रुटि

143. भाषा अधिगम में त्रुटियों को किस रूप में देखा जाना चाहिए?
A. केवल कमजोरी के रूप में
B. दंड देने योग्य गलती
C. सीखने की प्रक्रिया का स्वाभाविक भाग
D. अनदेखा करने योग्य

144. एक बालक को ध्वनियों के उच्चारण में लगातार कठिनाई होती है, जैसे 'क' को 'त' बोलना। यह किस प्रकार की समस्या है?
A. सामान्य त्रुटि B. भाषाई विविधता
C. भाषाई विकार D. व्याकरणिक त्रुटि

145. एक शिक्षक विविध कक्षा में भाषा सिखाते समय समूह कार्य, चित्र, और गतिविधि-आधारित शिक्षण का प्रयोग करता है। यह किस चुनौती का समाधान है?
A. केवल परीक्षा की तैयारी
B. भाषाई विविधता को अनदेखा करना
C. भिन्न शिक्षार्थियों की आवश्यकताओं को पूरा करना
D. केवल व्याकरण सिखाना

146. एक शिक्षक पहले विद्यार्थियों को कहानी सुनाता है, फिर उनसे उस पर चर्चा कराता है और अंत में लिखने को कहता है। यह किस सिद्धांत को दर्शाता है?
A. केवल लेखन कौशल B. कौशलों का पृथक्करण
C. समेकित भाषा कौशल D. व्याकरण आधारित शिक्षण

147. भाषा अधिगम में 'सुनना' को सबसे पहले क्यों विकसित किया जाता है?
A. यह सबसे कठिन कौशल है
B. यह पढ़ने का विकल्प है
C. यह अन्य कौशलों (विशेषकर बोलना) का आधार है
D. इसका कोई विशेष महत्व नहीं

148. एक विद्यार्थी पाठ को पढ़ तो लेता है, लेकिन उसका अर्थ नहीं समझ पाता। यह किस कौशल की कमी को दर्शाता है?
A. यांत्रिक पठन B. समझ आधारित पठन
C. लेखन कौशल D. बोलने का कौशल

149. एक शिक्षक विद्यार्थियों को स्वतंत्र रूप से अपने विचार लिखने के लिए प्रेरित करता है, भले ही उसमें कुछ त्रुटियाँ हों। यह किस दृष्टिकोण को दर्शाता है?
A. शुद्धता-आधारित दृष्टिकोण
B. रटने की विधि
C. सृजनात्मक लेखन
D. व्याकरण-अनुवाद विधि

150. भाषा कौशलों के विकास में सामाजिक अंतःक्रिया की भूमिका को किसने प्रमुखता दी?
A. बी. एफ. स्किनर B. लेव वाइगोत्स्की
C. जीन पियाजे D. नोम चॉम्स्की

151. एक शिक्षक विद्यार्थियों की 'सुनने की समझ' का मूल्यांकन करना चाहता है। निम्नलिखित में से सबसे उपयुक्त विधि कौन-सी है?
A. व्याकरण के नियम लिखवाना
B. कहानी सुनाकर प्रश्न पूछना
C. निबंध लिखवाना
D. शब्दार्थ याद कराना

152. 'प्रवीणता' का सही अर्थ क्या है?
A. केवल व्याकरण का ज्ञान
B. भाषा का वास्तविक जीवन में प्रभावी उपयोग
C. केवल लिखने की क्षमता
D. शब्दों का रटना

153. एक विद्यार्थी शुद्ध वाक्य बना लेता है, लेकिन अपने विचार स्पष्ट रूप से व्यक्त नहीं कर पाता। यह किस बात को दर्शाता है?
A. उच्च प्रवीणता B. केवल व्याकरणिक दक्षता
C. उच्च बोधगम्यता D. पूर्ण भाषा कौशल

154. पढ़ने की बोधगम्यता का सही मूल्यांकन किससे होगा?
A. पाठ का मौखिक वाचन
B. शब्दों की गिनती
C. पाठ पर आधारित प्रश्नों के उत्तर
D. व्याकरण के नियम

155. एक शिक्षक विद्यार्थियों के बोलने के कौशल का मूल्यांकन करते समय प्रवाह, उच्चारण और विचार अभिव्यक्ति को ध्यान में रखता है। यह किस प्रकार का मूल्यांकन है?
A. केवल लिखित मूल्यांकन B. समग्र मूल्यांकन
C. वस्तुनिष्ठ परीक्षण D. रटने पर आधारित मूल्यांकन

156. एक शिक्षक केवल पाठ्यपुस्तक पर निर्भर रहने के बजाय वीडियो, चित्र और ऑडियो का उपयोग करता है। यह किस सिद्धांत को दर्शाता है?
A. एकमात्र संसाधन आधारित शिक्षण
B. बहु-संसाधन शिक्षण
C. रटने की विधि
D. केवल व्याकरण शिक्षण

157. पाठ्यपुस्तक की सबसे महत्वपूर्ण भूमिका क्या है?
A. केवल परीक्षा की तैयारी
B. शिक्षक का विकल्प
C. अधिगम के लिए संरचित मार्गदर्शन प्रदान करना
D. केवल व्याकरण सिखाना

158. एक बहुभाषी कक्षा में शिक्षक बच्चों की मातृभाषा का उपयोग सीखने में सहायक के रूप में करता है। यह किस दृष्टिकोण को दर्शाता है?
A. एकभाषिक दृष्टिकोण
B. बहुभाषिक/समावेशी दृष्टिकोण
C. व्याकरण-अनुवाद विधि
D. केवल लक्ष्य भाषा दृष्टिकोण

159. मल्टीमीडिया सामग्री का उपयोग भाषा अधिगम में क्यों प्रभावी है?
A. यह केवल मनोरंजन के लिए है
B. यह सभी कौशलों को एक साथ विकसित करता है
C. यह केवल पढ़ने में मदद करता है
D. इसका कोई शैक्षिक महत्व नहीं

160. एक शिक्षक कक्षा में स्थानीय कहानियाँ, लोकभाषा और विद्यार्थियों के अनुभवों को शिक्षण सामग्री के रूप में उपयोग करता है। यह किस प्रकार के संसाधन का उदाहरण है?
A. केवल पाठ्यपुस्तक आधारित
B. कृत्रिम संसाधन
C. बहुभाषी एवं संदर्भ-आधारित संसाधन
D. व्याकरण आधारित सामग्री

उत्तरमाला

1	2	3	4	5	6	7	8	9	10
A	C	A	C	D	A	D	A	C	D
11	12	13	14	15	16	17	18	19	20
D	B	C	C	B	B	D	A	B	D
21	22	23	24	25	26	27	28	29	30
D	A	B	B	A	C	A	D	D	D
31	32	33	34	35	36	37	38	39	40
D	D	A	C	C	B	D	D	A	B
41	42	43	44	45	46	47	48	49	50
B	A	B	D	C	A	C	D	D	A
51	52	53	54	55	56	57	58	59	60
A	C	A	A	A	C	A	A	C	C
61	62	63	64	65	66	67	68	69	70
A	A	A	C	A	C	B	A	B	C
71	72	73	74	75	76	77	78	79	80
B	A	A	D	C	B	B	A	D	D
81	82	83	84	85	86	87	88	89	90
C	C	C	A	D	A	D	D	D	B
91	92	93	94	95	96	97	98	99	100
A	D	C	D	A	A	C	B	D	B
101	102	103	104	105	106	107	108	109	110
A	C	D	B	D	D	C	C	D	C
111	112	113	114	115	116	117	118	119	120
A	C	D	D	B	D	C	C	D	C
121	122	123	124	125	126	127	128	129	130
C	C	B	C	A	B	A	B	C	B
131	132	133	134	135	136	137	138	139	140
B	C	C		B	B	C	B	C	C
141	142	143	144	145	146	147	148	149	150
C	B	C	C	C	C	C	B	C	B
151	152	153	154	155	156	157	158	159	160
B	B	B	C	B	B	C	B	B	C

❄ ❄ ❄ ❄ ❄